Core Reference

Microsoft

3
Third Edition

PROGRAMMING MICROSOFT
WINDOWS CE
.NET

Microsoft®
.net™

Douglas Boling

PUBLISHED BY
Microsoft Press
A Division of Microsoft Corporation
One Microsoft Way
Redmond, Washington 98052-6399

Library of Congress Cataloging-in-Publication Data
Boling, Douglas McConnaughey, 1960-
    Programming Microsoft Windows CE .NET / Douglas Boling.--3rd ed.
        p. cm.
    Includes index.
    ISBN 0-7356-1884-4
    1. Microsoft Windows (Computer file)   2. Operating systems (Computers)   3. Microsoft .NET.   I. Title.

    QA76.76.O63B625   2003
    005.4'469--dc21   2003042205

Printed and bound in the United States of America.

3 4 5 6 7 8 9   QWT   8 7 6

Distributed in Canada by H.B. Fenn and Company Ltd.

A CIP catalogue record for this book is available from the British Library.

Microsoft Press books are available through booksellers and distributors worldwide. For further information about international editions, contact your local Microsoft Corporation office or contact Microsoft Press International directly at fax (425) 936-7329. Visit our Web site at www.microsoft.com/mspress. Send comments to *mspinput@microsoft.com*.

Acquisitions Editor: Anne Hamilton   **Interior Artist:** Michael Kloepfer
Project Editor: Kathleen Atkins   **Proofreader:** nSight, Inc.
Technical Editor: Jim Fuchs   **Indexer:** Julie Hatley
Interior Graphic Designer: James D. Kramer   **Cover Designer:** Methodologie, Inc.
Principal Compositor: Dan Latimer

Body Part No. X09-39008

To Nancy Jane

Contents at a Glance

Table of Contents

Part II   Windows CE Programming

7   Memory Management   357

8   Files and the Registry   385

Acknowledgments

Books are produced by diverse teams of talented people. My name appears on the cover, but countless others were involved in this book's creation. The teams of people who worked on this edition all pushed themselves to the max to complete this revision.

First, there's the talented team at Microsoft Press. Kathleen Atkins, the project leader and editor of all three editions of this book, took my gnarled syntax and confused text and made it readable. The technical editor for this edition, as well as the first edition of the book, was Jim Fuchs. Jim provided a great sanity check for me as well as providing a huge amount of help in getting the CD organized and produced. Shawn Peck performed the copyediting duties, keeping the text within the rules of the English language. Dan Latimer performed the desktop publishing duties, and Michael Kloepfer produced the illustrations. Thanks to Julie Hatley for the index. Anne Hamilton, who was the acquisitions editor for both the second and third editions of the book, deserves credit for getting these revisions released. Thanks, Anne, for all your efforts in keeping this book up-to-date.

Thanks also to the various Microsoft development and marketing teams. Over the years, they have tolerated my endless questions. Thanks to Mike Thomson, Michael Malueg, and Andrew Pearson for answering questions and reviewing chapters. Ori Amiga on the Pocket PC team provided all manner of priceless assistance: answering questions, getting new builds, and even providing hardware. Thanks also to Dominique Fortier, who provided great assistance on the Pocket PC, Bluetooth, and OBEX content in this edition. I had great support from the Compact Framework team from Craig Neable, Mark Gilbert, and Kei Amos. A special thank-you goes to Jeana Jorgensen, who, across a variety of jobs at Microsoft, has always tolerated my cries for help no matter the hour or relevance to her job. Thanks to all of you. Your help made this book so much better than it would have been without you.

I also need to acknowledge Tatia Meghdadi, John Doub, and the team at Socket Communication, who provided Bluetooth hardware and software for testing.

A special thanks goes to my agent, Claudette Moore, and the team at Moore Literary Agency. Claudette handled all the business details, freeing me to deal with the fun stuff.

This edition of *Programming Windows CE* builds on the foundation of the two earlier editions, so what you read is based on work from a much larger team. In addition to the people already mentioned, other folks from Microsoft Press have helped immensely in the editing and production of the earlier editions of the book. They include Brian Johnson, Julie Xiao, Rebecca McKay, Rob Nance, Cheryl Penner, Elizabeth Hansford, and Michael Victor.

My personal support team is headed by my wife, Nancy. Thanks, Nancy, for the support, help, and love. The personal support team also includes our boys, Andy, Sam, and Jake. They make sure I always remember what is important in life. I also must acknowledge my parents, Ronald and Jane Boling. They are my role models.

Introduction

I've been working with Microsoft Windows CE for almost as long as it's been in existence. A Windows programmer for many years, I'm amazed by the number of different, typically quite small, systems to which I can apply my Windows programming experience. These Windows CE systems run the gamut from PC-like mini-laptops to cellular phones to embedded devices buried deep in some large piece of industrial equipment. The use of the Win32 API in Windows CE enables tens of thousands of Windows programmers to write applications for an entirely new class of systems. The subtle differences, however, make writing Windows CE code somewhat different from writing for the desktop versions of Windows. It's those differences that I'll address in this book.

Just What Is Windows CE?

Windows CE is the smallest and arguably the most interesting of the Microsoft Windows operating systems. Windows CE was designed from the ground up to be a small ROM-based operating system with a Win32 subset API. Windows CE extends the Windows API into the markets and machines that can't support the larger footprints of the Windows XP kernel.

The now-defunct Windows 95/98/Me line was a great operating system for users who needed backward compatibility with MS-DOS and Windows 2.*x* and 3.*x* programs. Although it had shortcomings, Windows Me succeeded amazingly well at this difficult task. The Windows NT/2000/XP line, on the other hand, is written for the enterprise. It sacrifices compatibility and size to achieve its high level of reliability and robustness. Windows XP Home Edition is a version of Windows XP built for the home user that does strive for compatibility, but this is secondary to its primary goal of stability.

Windows CE isn't backward compatible with MS-DOS or Windows. Nor is it an all-powerful operating system designed for enterprise computing. Instead, Windows CE is a lightweight, multithreaded operating system with an optional graphical user interface. Its strength lies in its small size, its Win32 subset API, and its multiplatform support.

Windows CE also forms the foundation for the initial version of the .NET Compact Framework, a version of the .NET runtime for mobile and embedded devices. The Compact Framework provides the same powerful .NET runtime environment with a smaller class library so that it fits in small battery-powered devices.

A Little Windows CE History

To understand the history of Windows CE, you need to understand the differences between the operating system and the products that use it. The operating system is developed by a core group of programmers inside Microsoft. Their product is the operating system itself. Other groups, who develop devices such as the Pocket PC, use the newest version of the operating system that's available at the time their product is to be released. This dichotomy has created some confusion about how Windows CE has evolved. Let's examine the history of each, the devices and the operating system itself.

The Devices

The first products designed for Windows CE were handheld "organizer" devices with 480-by-240 or 640-by-240 screens and chiclet keyboards. These devices, dubbed Handheld PCs, were first introduced in late 1996. Fall Comdex 97 saw the release of a dramatically upgraded version of the operating system, Windows CE 2.0, with newer hardware in a familiar form—this time the box came with a 640-by-240 landscape screen, sometimes in color, and a somewhat larger keyboard.

In January 1998 at the Consumer Electronics Show, Microsoft announced two new platforms, the Palm-size PC and the Auto PC. The Palm-size PC was aimed directly at the pen-based organizer market dominated by Palm OS–based systems. The Palm-size PC featured a portrait mode and a 240-by-320 screen, and it used stylus-based input. Unfortunately for Windows CE fans, the public reception of the original Palm-size PC was less than enthusiastic.

Later that year, a new class of mini-laptop–style Windows CE machines with touch-typable keyboards and VGA or Super VGA screens made their appearance. These machines, called H/PC Professionals, provided 10 hours of battery life combined with improved versions of Microsoft's Pocket Office applications. Many of these machines had built-in modems, and some even diverged from the then-standard touch screen, sporting track pads or IBM's TrackPoint devices.

In April 2000, Microsoft introduced the Pocket PC, a greatly enhanced version of the old Palm-size PC. The original Pocket PC used a prerelease of the more full-featured Windows CE 3.0 operating system under the covers. The user interface of the Pocket PC was also different, with a cleaner, 2D, look and a revised home page, the Today screen. The most important feature of the Pocket PC, however, was the greatly improved performance of Windows CE. Much work had been done to tune Windows CE for better performance. That improvement, coupled with faster CPUs, allowed the system to run with the zip expected from a pocket organizer. With the Pocket PC, the inevitability of Moore's Law enabled Windows CE devices to cross over the line: the hardware at this point was now capable of providing the computing power that Windows CE required.

The Handheld PC was updated in 2000 to use Windows CE 3.0. Although these systems (now called the Handheld PC 2000) haven't been a consumer success, they have found a home in the industrial market, where their relative low cost, large screens, and great battery life satisfy a unique niche market.

The Pocket PC was updated in late 2001 with a release named Pocket PC 2002. This release was based on the final released version of Windows CE 3.0 and contained some user interface improvements. An exciting development was the addition of the Pocket PC Phone Edition, which integrated cellular phone support into a Pocket PC device. These devices combined the functionality of a Pocket PC with the connectivity of a cellular phone, enabling a new generation of mobile but always connected software.

Another group within Microsoft released the Smart Display, a Windows CE .NET 4.1–based system that integrated a tablet form factor device with wireless networking and a base connected to a PC. When the Smart Display is in its base, it's a second monitor; when removed, it becomes a mobile display for the PC.

In the spring of 2003, the Pocket PC team released an update of the Pocket PC called the Pocket PC 2003. This system, while not providing much of a change to the user interface, did provide a huge increase in stability and performance because it was based on Windows CE .NET 4.2. The Pocket PC 2003 also added integrated Bluetooth support for those OEMs that chose to include it.

Microsoft has also been working with OEMs to produce cellular phones based on Windows CE. A smattering of these phones, called Smartphones, were released in late 2002 and were initially based on Windows CE 3.0. An upgrade in 2003 moved the Smartphone to Windows CE 4.2 and increased the feature set of the device to include the .NET runtime.

New devices are being introduced all the time. An example are the Media to Go devices, which are mobile video players using a hard disk for storage. The power of the Windows CE operating system enables applications that are beyond the capability of systems with simpler operating systems to run on these devices.

The Operating System

Although these consumer-oriented products made the news, more important development work was going on in the operating system itself. The Windows CE operating system has evolved from the days of 1.0, when it was a simple organizer operating system with high hopes. Starting with Windows CE 2.0 and continuing to this day, Microsoft has released embedded versions of Windows CE that developers can use on their custom hardware. Although consumer platforms such as the Pocket PC get most of the publicity, the improvements to the base operating system are what enable devices such as the Pocket PC and the Smartphone.

Windows CE 2.0 was released with the introduction of the Handheld PC 2.0 at Fall Comdex 1997. Windows CE 2.0 added networking support, including Windows standard network functions, a Network Driver Interface Specification (NDIS) miniport driver model, and a generic NE2000 network card driver. Added COM support allowed scripting, although the support was limited to in-proc servers. A display driver model was also introduced that allowed for pixel depths other than the original 2-bits-per-pixel displays of Windows CE 1.0. Windows CE 2.0 was also the first version of the operating system to be released separately from a product such as the H/PC. Developers could purchase the Windows CE Embedded Toolkit (ETK), which allowed them to customize Windows CE to unique hardware platforms. Developers who used the ETK, however, soon found that the goal of the product exceeded its functionality.

With the release of the original Palm-size PC in early 1998, Windows CE was improved yet again. Although Windows CE 2.01 wasn't released in an ETK form, it was notable for its effort to reduce the size of the operating system and applications. In Windows CE 2.01, the C runtime library, which includes functions such as *strcpy* to copy strings, was moved from a statically linked library attached to each EXE and DLL into the operating system itself. This change dramatically reduced the size of both the operating system and the applications themselves.

In August 1998, Microsoft introduced the H/PC Professional with a new version of the operating system, 2.11. Windows CE 2.11 was a service pack update to Windows CE 2.1, which was never formally released. Later in the year, Windows CE 2.11 was released to the embedded community as Microsoft Windows CE Platform Builder version 2.11. This release included support for an improved object store that allowed files in the object store to be larger than 4 MB. This release also added support for a console and a Windows CE version of CMD.exe, the classic MS-DOS–style command shell. Windows CE 2.11 also included Fast IR to support IrDA's 4-MB infrared standard, as well as some specialized functions for IP multicast. An initial hint of security was introduced in Windows CE 2.11: a device could now examine and reject the loading of unrecognized modules.

Windows CE 2.12 was also a service pack release to the 2.1, or Birch, release of Windows CE. The big news in this release was a greatly enhanced set of Platform Builder tools that included a graphical front end. The operating system was tweaked with a new notification interface that combined the disparate notification functions. The notification user interface was exposed in the Platform Builder to allow embedded developers to customize the notification dialog boxes. A version of Microsoft's PC-based Internet Explorer 4.0 was also ported to Windows CE as the Genie, or Generic IE control. This HTML browser control complements the simpler but smaller Pocket Internet Explorer. Microsoft Message Queue support was added as well. The "go/no go" security of Windows CE 2.11 was enhanced to include a "go, but don't trust" option. Untrusted modules can run—but not call—a set of critical functions, nor can they modify parts of the registry.

The long-awaited Windows CE 3.0 was finally released in mid-2000. This release followed the April release of the Pocket PC, which used a slightly earlier internal build of Windows CE 3.0. The big news for Windows CE 3.0 was its kernel, which was optimized for better real-time support. The enhanced kernel support includes 256 thread priorities (up from 8 in earlier versions of Windows CE), an adjustable thread quantum, nested interrupt service routines, and reduced latencies within the kernel.

The improvements in Windows CE 3.0 didn't stop at the kernel. A new COM component was added to complement the in-proc COM support available since Windows CE 2.0. This new component included full COM out-of-proc and DCOM support. The object store was also improved to support up to 256 MB of RAM. File size limits within the object store were increased to 32 MB per file. An Add-On Pack for the Platform Builder 3.0 added even more features, including improved multimedia support though a media player control; improved networking support (and XML support) with PPTP, ICS, and remote desktop display support; and a formal introduction of the DirectX API.

The next release of Windows CE involved more than just new features; the name of the product was also changed. Windows CE .NET 4.0, released in early 2001, changed the way virtual memory was organized, effectively doubling the virtual memory space per application. Windows CE .NET 4.0 also added a new driver loading model, services support, a new file-based registry option, Bluetooth, 802.11, and 1394 support. Ironically, while .NET was added to the name, Windows CE .NET 4.0 didn't support the .NET Compact Framework.

Late in 2001, Windows CE 4.1 was a follow-on to Windows CE 4.0, adding IP v6, Winsock 2, a bunch of new supporting applets, and an example Power Manager. Windows CE 4.1 also supports the .NET Compact Framework. The final bits of the .NET runtime were released as a quick fix engineering (QFE) package after the operating system shipped.

The second quarter of 2003 saw the release of Windows CE .NET 4.2. This update provided cool new features for OEMs wanting to support Pocket PC applications on embedded systems. The Pocket PC–specific APIs that support menu bars, the soft input panel (SIP), and other shell features were moved to the base operating system. The Explorer shell was rewritten to support namespace extensions. The performance of the kernel was improved by directly supporting hardware paging tables on some CPUs.

Because Windows CE is a work in progress, the next version of Windows CE is being developed. I'll be updating my Web site, *www.bolingconsulting.com*, with information about this release as it becomes available.

Why You Should Read This Book

Programming Microsoft Windows CE is written for anyone who will be writing applications for Windows CE or the .NET Compact Framework. Embedded systems programmers using Windows CE for a specific application, Windows programmers interested in writing or porting an existing Windows application, and even developers of managed code can use the information in this book to make their tasks easier.

The embedded systems programmer, who might not be as familiar with the Win32 API as the Windows programmer, can read the first section of the book to become familiar with Windows programming. Although this section isn't the comprehensive tutorial that can be found in books such as *Programming Windows*, by Charles Petzold, it does provide a base that will carry the reader through the other chapters in the book. It can also help the embedded systems programmer develop fairly complex and quite useful Windows CE programs.

The experienced Windows programmer can use the book to learn about the differences among the Win32 APIs used by Windows CE and Windows XP. The differences between Windows CE and Windows XP are significant. The small footprint of Windows CE means that many of the overlapping APIs in the Win32 model aren't supported. Some sections of the Win32 API aren't supported at all. On the other hand, because of its unique setting, Windows CE extends the Win32 API in a number of areas that are covered in this text.

This book is also useful for the developer using the .NET Compact Framework. The Compact Framework currently has gaps in its functionality: it requires managed applications to make calls to the operating system to perform certain tasks. The book is a great guide to what's available in the operating system. A chapter in this book discusses the unique nature of developing managed code on Windows CE–based devices.

The method used by *Programming Windows CE* is to teach by example. I wrote numerous Windows CE example programs specifically for this book. The source for each of these examples is printed in the text. Both the source and the final compiled programs for a number of the processors supported by Windows CE are also provided on the accompanying CD.

The examples in this book are all written directly to the API, the so-called "Petzold" method of programming. Since the goal of this book is to teach you how to write programs for Windows CE, the examples avoid using a class library such as MFC, which obfuscates the unique nature of writing applications for Windows CE. Some people would say that the availability of MFC on Windows CE eliminates the need for direct knowledge of the Windows CE API. I believe the opposite is true. Knowledge of the Windows CE API enables more efficient use of MFC. I also believe that truly knowing the operating system also dramatically simplifies the debugging of applications.

What's New in the Third Edition

The third edition of this book is a major revision that adds significant new text about a variety of subjects from the Smartphone to Bluetooth. The book has been updated to cover the new features of Windows CE .NET 4.2. New chapters have also been added to cover the Smartphone and the .NET Compact Framework. A number of chapters have been significantly expanded to cover topics such as OBEX, Bluetooth, and services. Other chapters have been reorganized to better present the topics.

A chapter has been added covering the Smartphone and the communication features of the Pocket PC Phone Edition. This chapter covers how to write applications for the Smartphone 2003 device. Also covered is how to write applications that work with the connection manager and send and receive messages through the Short Message Service (SMS) system on both the Smartphone and the Pocket PC Phone Edition.

There is a new chapter on the .NET Compact Framework. This chapter covers how to write managed applications on Windows CE. After an introduction to managed applications, the chapter concentrates on Windows Forms applications, the unique classes of the .NET Compact Framework. A significant portion of the chapter covers how to call from managed code to unmanaged or native code since there are times when the managed class library doesn't provide the functionality necessary for the application.

The device-to-device communication chapter contains coverage on Bluetooth and OBEX. Bluetooth is a wireless communication standard that frankly isn't well explained in many texts. This chapter explains Bluetooth and provides a simple, straightforward example of its use. It also contains a section on OBEX, the Object Exchange standard that's used by both Bluetooth and Infrared Data Association (IrDA). Another example in the chapter uses OBEX to send files to other devices over either Bluetooth or IrDA.

The Pocket PC chapters have been updated to cover the new features of the Pocket PC 2003 devices. The menu bar example from the Pocket PC chapter in the second edition of this book has been moved to the common controls chapter, reflecting the move of the Pocket PC API to the general operating system features in the latest version of Windows CE.

The drivers and services chapter has been updated to cover Windows CE services. Windows CE services were introduced in Windows CE .NET 4.0. Services provide a way to have code running in the background without the overhead of a separate process for the service. The operating system also provides a *super service* that can monitor IP ports and notify a service when a client connects to that port. A simple Windows CE service example is provided in the chapter, demonstrating how to write a service and use the features of the super service.

For those owners of the first edition of this book, this edition contains all the new features of the second edition as well. Those updates included extensive coverage of the Pocket PC and Windows CE device drivers. Also, the new memory management and threading features that have been implemented since the first edition was published make this edition a significant update.

.NET Compact Framework

A developer would have had to be on a desert island somewhere not to have heard of Microsoft's .NET initiative. This initiative consists of a run-time environment that isolates code from the hardware while at the same time providing a type-safe runtime for increased security. A smaller version of this runtime has been written for embedded and battery powered devices. The initial version of the .NET Compact Framework runs on top of Windows CE on the Pocket PC and on embedded systems based on Windows CE .NET 4.1 and later.

The unique requirements of embedded devices will make it a challenge to write applications using only managed code. Embedded applications and some mobile applications require the application to be tightly integrated with the device. Because one of the features of the runtime is to isolate the hardware from the application, an embedded managed application sometimes needs to break the bounds of the runtime and directly access some operating system functions.

As previously mentioned, the Compact Framework chapter spends a significant amount of time discussing how managed applications can access the operating system. This discussion includes the techniques for marshaling parameters across the managed/native code boundary—a task that's somewhat more difficult in the Compact Framework than on the desktop.

What About MFC?

I used to have a stock answer for people who asked me whether they should use MFC to build Windows CE applications: Don't do it! The old Windows CE systems with their slow CPUs were hard-pressed to run complex, full-featured MFC applications. These days, I'm a little less dogmatic. The newest Windows CE platforms are now fast enough to allow MFC-based applications to run with reasonable performance. The MFC runtime library is included in ROM on these devices, so the footprint of the application is simply the code, not the code plus the MFC runtime.

But just as speed and the runtime have been added to the platforms, the sun is setting on MFC. Microsoft no longer pushes development of MFC applications. Instead, the .NET environment is the development target of choice. So should you develop in MFC? I say no, not for new projects. For old ones, there still is a place for MFC simply so that the projects don't have to be ported to other tools.

Windows CE Development Tools

This book is written with the assumption that the reader knows C and is at least familiar with Microsoft Windows. All native code development was done with Microsoft eMbedded Visual C++ under Windows XP. To compile the example programs in this book, you need Microsoft eMbedded Visual C++ 4.0, which is conveniently supplied on the companion CD. You also need the appropriate platform SDKs for the Windows CE device you're targeting.

Each example already has a predefined project set up, but you can also choose to create the projects from scratch. For almost all the examples, simply create a generic WCE Application project. For the examples that require access to functions unique to the Pocket PC, special code links to those functions, even though the project settings don't specifically define a Pocket PC application.

For developers who want to build applications that run on the Pocket PC 2000 and 2002, you need to use Embedded Visual C++ 3.0. Unfortunately, there isn't enough room on the companion CD for both eVC 3 and eVC 4, but eVC 3 is available as a download from the Microsoft Web site. You'll also need the appropriate SDKs for those older Pocket PC systems. Many of the examples in the book can be compiled for the older Pocket PC devices. Some examples, however, such as the Bluetooth, OBEX, and services examples, use features that aren't available on the older systems.

.NET Compact Framework applications are developed with Visual Studio .NET 2003. This tool isn't provided on the CD because it's huge and, unfortunately for us programmers, not free. Still, this tool is an incredibly productive development environment. For those interested in developing managed code, the pain of the cost of upgrading is mitigated by the increase in developer productivity. You'll need Visual Studio .NET 2003 to compile the examples in the Compact Framework chapter. This tool provides the necessary runtimes for all Pocket PC devices as well as embedded versions of Windows CE based on version 4.1 or later.

Target Systems

You don't need to have a Windows CE target device to experience the sample programs provided by this book. The various platform SDKs come with a Windows CE emulator that lets you perform basic testing of a Windows CE program under Windows XP. This emulator comes in handy when you don't have an actual device handy. The emulator runs a version of Windows CE inside a PC emulator which results in an actual Windows CE operating system runtime executing on the PC.

You should consider a number of factors when deciding which Windows CE hardware to use for testing. First, if the application is to be a commercial product, you should buy at least one system for each type of target CPU. You need to test against all the target CPUs because, although the source code will probably be identical, the resulting executable will be different in size and so will the memory allocation footprint for each target CPU.

What's on the CD

The companion CD contains the source code for all the examples in the book. I've also provided project files for Microsoft eMbedded Visual C++ so that you can open preconfigured projects. All the examples have been designed to compile for systems based on Windows CE 4.2, Pocket PC 2003, and Smartphone 2003.

In addition to the examples, the CD also includes a free copy of Microsoft eMbedded Visual C++ 4.0. This is the same full-featured eMbedded Visual C++ product that you can download from Microsoft's Web site or pay to have sent to you on CD. Consider these tools the prize in the Cracker Jack box. Also included is the platform SDK for the Pocket PC 2003.

The companion CD contains a StartCD program that provides you with a graphical interface from which you can access the contents of the CD. This program will autorun when the CD is inserted into your CD-ROM drive if you have that feature enabled in Windows. If you don't have autorun enabled, just navigate to the root directory of the CD and run StartCD.exe from Windows Explorer. The file Readme.txt, available from the StartCD program or in the root directory of the CD, will give you additional information about the contents of the CD, system requirements for the included tools and SDK, and information about support options for the included products.

The following are the system requirements for installing and running Microsoft eMbedded Visual C++. Please note that to run the eMbedded Visual C++, you'll need to be using Windows 2000, Windows XP, or Windows Server 2003.

- PC with Pentium processor; Pentium 150 MHz or higher processor recommended

- Microsoft Windows XP, Windows 2000 Service Pack 2 (or later) or Windows Server 2003

- 32 MB of RAM (48 MB recommended)

- Hard disk space required: minimum installation: about 360 MB; complete installation: about 720 MB

- CD-ROM drive compatible with multimedia PC specification

- VGA or higher-resolution monitor required; Super VGA recommended

- Microsoft Mouse or compatible pointing device

Other Sources

Although I have attempted to make *Programming Microsoft Windows CE* a one-stop shop for Windows CE programming, no one book can cover everything. To learn more about Windows programming in general, I suggest the classic text *Programming Windows* (Microsoft Press, 1998) by Charles Petzold. This is, by far, the best book for learning Windows programming. Charles presents examples that show how to tackle difficult but common Windows problems. To learn more about the Win32 kernel API, I suggest Jeff Richter's *Programming Applications for Microsoft Windows* (Microsoft Press, 1999). Jeff covers the techniques of process, thread, and memory management down to the most minute detail. For learning more about MFC programming, there's no better text than Jeff Prosise's *Programming Windows with MFC* (Microsoft Press, 1999). This book is the "Petzold" of MFC programming and simply a required read for MFC programmers.

To learn more about .NET programming, I recommend *Programming Windows with C#* (Microsoft Press, 2002), by Charles Petzold. Charles has applied his amazing skills to the Windows Forms part of the .NET Framework. This is a great book to come up to speed on the client side of .NET programming.

Support

Every effort has been made to ensure the accuracy of this book and the contents of the sample files on the CD-ROM. Microsoft Press provides corrections and additional content for its books through the World Wide Web at this location:

http:/www.microsoft.com/mspress/support/

If you have problems, comments, or ideas regarding this book or the CD-ROM, please send them to Microsoft Press.

Send e-mail to

mspinput@microsoft.com

Or send postal mail to

Microsoft Press

Attn: *Programming Microsoft Windows CE*, Third Edition, Editor

One Microsoft Way

Redmond, WA 98052-6399

Please note that product support is not offered through these mail addresses. For further information regarding Microsoft software support options, please go to *http://support.microsoft.com/directory/* or call Microsoft Support Network Sales at (800) 936-3500.

Visit the Microsoft Press Web Site

You are also invited to visit the Microsoft Press World Wide Web site at the following location:

http://www.microsoft.com/mspress/

You'll find descriptions for the complete line of Microsoft Press books, information about ordering titles, notice of special features and events, additional content for Microsoft Press books, and much more.

You can also find out the latest in Microsoft Windows CE .NET software developments and news from Microsoft Corporation by visiting the following Web site:

http://www.microsoft.com/windows/embedded/ce.net/

Updates and Feedback

No book about Windows CE can be completely current for any length of time. I maintain a Web page, *http://www.bolingconsulting.com/cebook.htm*, where I'll keep a list of errata, along with updates describing any features found in sub sequent versions of Windows CE. Check out this page to see information on new versions of Windows CE as they're released.

Although I have striven to make the information in this book as accurate as possible, you'll undoubtedly find errors. If you find a problem with the text or just have ideas about how to make the next version of the book better, please drop me a note at *CEBook@bolingconsulting.com*. I can't promise you that I'll answer all your notes, but I will read every one.

Doug Boling
Tahoe City, California
April 2003

Part I

Windows Programming Basics

1

Hello Windows CE

Since the classic *The C Programming Language*, programming books traditionally start with a "hello, world" program. It's a logical place to begin. Every program has a basic underlying structure that, when not obscured by some complex task it was designed to perform, can be analyzed to reveal the foundation shared by all programs running on its operating system.

In this programming book, the "hello, world" chapter covers the details of setting up and using the programming environment. The environment for developing Microsoft Windows CE applications is somewhat different from that for developing standard Microsoft Windows applications because Windows CE programs are written on PCs running Microsoft Windows XP and debugged mainly on separate Windows CE–based target devices.

While experienced Windows programmers might be tempted to skip this chapter and move on to meatier subjects, I suggest that they—you—at least skim the chapter to note the differences between a standard Windows program and a Windows CE program. A number of subtle and significant differences in both the development process and the basic program skeleton for Windows CE applications are covered in this first chapter.

What Is Different About Windows CE

Windows CE has a number of unique characteristics that make it different from other Windows platforms. First of all, the systems running Windows CE are most likely not using an Intel x86–compatible microprocessor. Instead, Windows CE runs on 4 different CPU families, SHx, MIPS, ARM, and x86. Fortunately, the development environment isolates the programmer from almost all of the differences among the various CPUs.

Nor can a Windows CE program be assured of a screen or a keyboard. Pocket PC devices have a 240-by-320-pixel portrait-style screen, while other systems might have screens with more traditional landscape orientations in 480-by-240, 640-by-240, or 640-by-480-pixel resolution. An embedded device might not have a display at all. The target devices might not support color. And, instead of a mouse, most Windows CE devices have a touch screen. On a touch-screen device, left mouse button clicks are achieved by means of a tap on the screen, but no obvious method exists for delivering right mouse button clicks. To give you some method of delivering a right click, the Windows CE convention is to hold down the Alt key while tapping. It's up to the Windows CE application to interpret this sequence as a right mouse click.

Fewer Resources in Windows CE Devices

The resources of the target devices vary radically across systems that run Windows CE. When writing a standard Windows program, the programmer can make a number of assumptions about the target device, almost always an IBM-compatible PC. The target device will have a hard disk for mass storage and a virtual memory system that uses the hard disk as a swap device to emulate an almost unlimited amount of (virtual) RAM. The programmer knows that the user has a keyboard, a two-button mouse, and a monitor that these days almost assuredly supports 256 colors and a screen resolution of at least 800 by 600 pixels.

Windows CE programs run on devices that almost never have hard disks for mass storage. The absence of a hard disk means more than just not having a place to store large files. Without a hard disk, virtual RAM can't be created by swapping data to the disk. So Windows CE programs are almost always run in a low-memory environment. Memory allocations can, and often do, fail because of the lack of resources. Windows CE might terminate a program automatically when free memory reaches a critically low level. This RAM limitation has a surprisingly large impact on Windows CE programs and is one of the main challenges involved in porting existing Windows applications to Windows CE.

Unicode

One characteristic that a programmer can count on when writing Windows CE applications is Unicode. Unicode is a standard for representing a character as a 16-bit value as opposed to the ASCII standard of encoding a character into a single 8-bit value. Unicode allows for fairly simple porting of programs to different international markets because all the world's known characters can be represented in one of the 65,536 available Unicode values. Dealing with Unicode is relatively painless as long as you avoid the dual assumptions made by most programmers that strings are represented in ASCII and that characters are stored in single bytes.

A consequence of a program using Unicode is that with each character taking up two bytes instead of one, strings are now twice as long. A programmer must be careful making assumptions about buffer length and string length. No longer should you assume that a 260-byte buffer can hold 259 characters and a terminating zero. Instead of the standard *char* data type, you should use the *TCHAR* data type. *TCHAR* is defined to be *char* for Microsoft Windows 95 and Microsoft Windows 98 development and unsigned short for Unicode-enabled applications for Microsoft Windows 2000, Windows XP, and Windows CE development. These types of definitions allow source-level compatibility across ASCII- and Unicode-based operating systems.

New Controls

Windows CE includes a number of new Windows controls designed for specific environments. New controls include the command bar and menu bar controls that provide menu- and toolbar-like functions all on one space-saving line, critical on the smaller screens of Windows CE devices. Other controls have been enhanced for Windows CE. A version of the edit control in Windows CE can be set to automatically capitalize the first letter of a word, great for the keyboardless design of a PDA. Windows CE also supports most of the controls available on desktop versions of Windows. Some of these controls are even more at home on Windows CE devices than on the desktop. For example, the date and time picker control and calendar control assist calendar and organizer applications suitable for handheld devices, such as the Handheld PC (H/PC) and the Pocket PC. Other standard Windows controls have reduced function, reflecting the compact nature of Windows CE hardware-specific OS configurations.

Componentization

Another aspect of Windows CE programming to be aware of is that Windows CE can be broken up and reconfigured by Microsoft or by OEMs so that it can be better adapted to a target market or device. Windows programmers usually just check the version of Windows to see whether it is from the Microsoft Windows 95, 98, or Me line or Windows 2000, XP line; by knowing the version they can determine what API functions are available to them. Windows CE, however, can be configured in countless ways.

By far, the most popular configuration of Windows CE today is the Pocket PC. Microsoft defines the specific set of Windows CE components that are present in all Pocket PC–branded devices. However, some OEMs produce PDA devices that use Windows CE but are not branded as Pocket PCs. These devices have a subtly different API from that of the Pocket PC devices. If you are unaware of this, you can easily write a program that works on one platform but not on another. In embedded platforms, the OEM decides the components to include and can create a Software Development Kit (an SDK) specialized for its specific platform. If the OEM is interested in third-party development, it can make available a customized SDK for its device. New platforms are continually being released, with much in common but also with many differences among them. Programmers need to understand the target platform and to have their programs check what functions are available on that particular platform before trying to use a set of functions that might not be supported on that device.

Win32 Subset

Finally, because Windows CE is so much smaller than Windows XP, it simply can't support all the function calls that its larger cousins do. While you'd expect an operating system that didn't support printing, such as Windows CE on the original models, not to have any calls to printing functions, Windows CE also removes some redundant functions supported by its larger cousins. If Windows CE doesn't support your favorite function, a different function or set of functions will probably work just as well. Sometimes Windows CE programming seems to consist mainly of figuring out ways to implement a feature using the sparse API of Windows CE. If thousands of functions can be called sparse.

It's Still Windows Programming

While differences between Windows CE and the other versions of Windows do exist, they shouldn't be overstated. Programming a Windows CE application is programming a Windows application. It has the same message loop, the same windows, and for the most part, the same resources and the same controls. The differences don't hide the similarities. One of the key similarities is the tradition of Hungarian notation.

Hungarian Notation

A tradition, and a good one, of almost all Windows programs since Charles Petzold wrote *Programming Microsoft Windows* is Hungarian notation. This programming style, developed years ago by Charles Simonyi at Microsoft, prefixes all variables in the program usually with one or two letters indicating the variable type. For example, a string array named *Name* would instead be named *szName*, with the *sz* prefix indicating that the variable type is a zero-terminated string. The value of Hungarian notation is the dramatic improvement in readability of the source code. Another programmer, or you after not looking at a piece of code for a while, won't have to look repeatedly at a variable's declaration to determine its type. Table 1-1 shows typical Hungarian prefixes for variables.

Table 1-1   Hungarian Prefixes for Variables

Variable Type	Hungarian Prefix
Integer	*i* or *n*
Word (16-bit)	*w* or *s*
Double word (32-bit unsigned)	*Dw*
Long (32-bit signed)	*L*
Char	*C*
String	*Sz*
Pointer	*P*
Long pointer	*lp*
Handle	*h*
Window handle	*hwnd*
Struct size	*cb*

You can see a few vestiges of the early days of Windows. The *lp*, or long pointer, designation refers to the days when, in the Intel 16-bit programming model, pointers were either short (a 16-bit offset) or long (a segment plus an offset). Other prefixes are formed from the abbreviation of the type. For example, a handle to a brush is typically specified as *hbr*. Prefixes can be combined, as in *lpsz*, which designates a long pointer to a zero-terminated string. Most of the structures defined in the Windows API use Hungarian notation in their field names. I use this notation as well throughout this book, and I encourage you to use this notation in your programs.

Your First Windows CE Application

Enough talk; let's look at your first Windows CE program. Listing 1-1 shows Hello1, a simple Hello World application written for Windows CE.

Hello1.cpp

```
//======================================================================
// Hello1 - A simple application for Windows CE
//
// Written for the book Programming Windows CE
// Copyright (C) 2003 Douglas Boling
//======================================================================
#include "windows.h"


//
// Program entry point
//
int WINAPI WinMain (HINSTANCE hInstance, HINSTANCE hPrevInstance,
                    LPWSTR lpCmdLine, int nCmdShow) {

    printf ("Hello World\n");
    return 0;
}
```

Listing 1-1   Hello1, A simple Windows application

As you can see, aside from the entry point of the program, the code looks fairly similar to the classic Kernighan and Ritchie version. Starting from just below the comments, we have the line

```
#include "windows.h"
```

which is the root of a vast array of include files that define the Windows CE API, as well as the structures and constants they use.

The entry point of the program is the biggest difference between this program and a standard C program. Instead of the C standard

```
int main (char **argv, int argc)
```

the Windows CE build environment expects the standard Windows entry point,[1] as in

```
int WINAPI WinMain (HINSTANCE hInstance, HINSTANCE hPrevInstance,
                    LPWSTR lpCmdLine, int nCmdShow);
```

Windows CE differs in some ways from the desktop versions of Windows. The first of the four parameters passed, *hInstance*, identifies the specific instance of the program to other applications and to Windows API functions that need to identify the EXE. The *hPrevInstance* parameter is left over from the

---

1. While it is technically possible to change the entry point prototype to match the C standard entry point, it typically isn't worth the trouble.

old Win16 API (Windows 3.1 and earlier). In all Win32 operating systems, including Windows CE, *hPrevInstance* is always 0 and can be ignored.

The *lpCmdLine* parameter points to a Unicode string that contains the text of the command line. Applications launched from Microsoft Windows Explorer usually have no command-line parameters. But in some instances, such as when the system automatically launches a program, the system includes a command-line parameter to indicate why the program was started. The *lpCmdLine* parameter provides us with one of the first instances in which Windows CE differs from Windows XP. Under Windows CE, the command-line string is a Unicode string. In all other versions of Windows, the string is always ASCII.

The final parameter, *nCmdShow*, specifies the initial state of the program's main window. It is passed by the parent application, usually Explorer, and is a recommendation of how the application should configure its main window. This parameter might specify that the window be initially displayed as an icon (*SW_SHOWMINIMIZE*), maximized (*SW_SHOWMAXIMIZED*) to cover the entire desktop, or normal (*SW_RESTORE*), indicating that the window is placed on the screen in the standard resizeable state. Other values specify that the initial state of the window should be invisible to the user or that the window should be visible but incapable of becoming the active window. Under Windows CE, the values for this parameter are limited to only three allowable states: normal (*SW_SHOW*), hidden (*SW_HIDE*), and show without activate (*SW_SHOWNOACTIVATE*). Unless an application needs to force its window to a predefined state, this parameter is simply passed without modification to the *ShowWindow* function after the program's main window has been created.

The next line is the only functioning line of the application.

```
printf ("Hello World\n");
```

Windows CE supports most of the standard C library, including *printf*, *getchar*, and so forth. An interesting aspect of this line is that unlike almost everywhere else in Windows CE, the string is not Unicode but ANSI. There is a logical reason for this. For the C standard library to be compliant with the ANSI standard, *printf* and the other string library functions such as *strcpy* use ANSI strings. Of course, Windows CE supports the Unicode versions of the standard functions such as *wprintf*, *getwchar*, and *wcscpy*.

Finally the program ends with

```
return 0;
```

The value passed in the return line is available to other processes that use the Win32 API *GetExitCodeProcess*.

Building Your First Application

To create Hello1 from scratch on your system, start Microsoft eMbedded Visual C++ and create a new project by selecting the New command on the File menu. The first change from standard Win32 programming becomes evident when you see the new project dialog box. You'll have the opportunity to select from a number of platforms, as shown in Figure 1-1. For non-MFC or ATL projects, the chief decision is to choose between WCE Pocket PC Application (to build code for a Pocket PC) and WCE Application (for all other Windows CE systems). You'll also pick the allowable target CPUs. For example, selecting Win32 (WCE MIPII) enables compiling to a Windows CE platform with a MIPS CPU. No matter what target device you have, be sure to check the WCE emulator target. This allows you to run the sample program in the emulator under Windows XP.

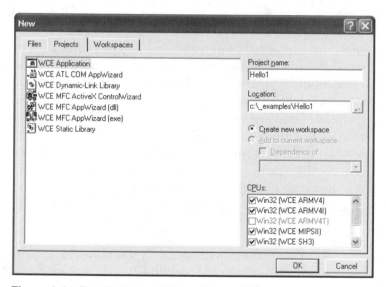

Figure 1-1   The Platforms list box allows eMbedded Visual C++ to target different Windows CE platforms

eMbedded Visual C++ will next ask you whether you want to create an empty project, a simple program, or a Hello World application. For all the examples in this book, pick Empty Project. This choice prevents the code wizards from adding any extra code to the examples. Create new files for Hello1.cpp from the File menu by clicking New.

After you have created the proper source files for Hello1 or copied them from the CD, select the target Win32 (WCE x86em) Debug and then build the program. This step compiles the source and, assuming you have no compilation errors, automatically launches the emulator and inserts the EXE into the emulator file system; you can then launch Hello1. If you're running Windows 98 or

Windows Me, the system displays an error message because the emulator runs only under Windows 2000 or Windows XP.

If you have a Windows CE system available, such as a Pocket PC (PPC), attach the PPC to the PC the same way you would to sync the contents of the PPC with the PC. Open Microsoft ActiveSync, and establish a connection between the PPC and the PC. While it's not strictly necessary to have the Active-Sync connection to your Windows CE device running (eMbedded Visual C++ is supposed to make this connection automatically), I've found that having it running makes for a more stable connection between the development environment and the Windows CE system.

Once the link between the PC and the Windows CE device is up and running, switch back to eMbedded Visual C++, select the compile target appropriate for the target device (for example, Win32 [WCE ARM] Debug for an iPaq Pocket PC), and rebuild. As in the case of building for the emulator, if there are no errors, eMbedded Visual C++ automatically downloads the compiled program to the remote device. The program is placed either in the root directory of the object store or, in the case of the Pocket PC, in the \windows\start menu directory.

Running the Program

To run Hello1 on an embedded Windows CE deviceH/PC, simply click on the My ComputerHandheld PC icon to bring up the files in the root directory. At that point, a double-tap on the application's icon launches the program.

To run the program on a Pocket PC, simply select the program from the Start menu on the device. The program appears there because eMbedded Visual C++ downloads the application to be the \windows\start menu directory. This way, a downloaded application is automatically visible on the Start menu.

What's Wrong?

If you start Hello1 by clicking on the icon or by selecting the program on the start menu of a Pocket PC, nothing seems to happen. On a Handheld PC, the program appears to make the screen flash. This is because the program starts, writes to the console, and terminates. Unless you start the program from an already created console, Windows CE creates the console window when Hello1 executes the *printf* statement and closes the console automatically when Hello1 terminates.

On a Pocket PC, the application runs, but the Pocket PC doesn't come with support to display the console functions such as the output from *printf*. It's possible to add console support to a Pocket PC by adding a driver, console.dll, to the Windows directory of the Pocket PC. That driver must be written to take input from the driver interface, create a window on the screen, and print out the strings. The console driver available on Handheld PCs and in embedded versions of Windows CE does this.

Hello2

Now that we have the basics down, it's time to upgrade Hello1 to something you can at least see. Because many Windows CE systems don't have the console driver, Hello2 creates a message box with the "Hello CE" text instead of using *printf.* Hello2 is shown in Listing 1-2.

Hello2.cpp

```cpp
//======================================================================
// Hello2 - A simple application for Windows CE
//
// Written for the book Programming Windows CE
// Copyright (C) 2003 Douglas Boling
//======================================================================
#include "windows.h"


//
// Program entry point
//
int WINAPI WinMain (HINSTANCE hInstance, HINSTANCE hPrevInstance,
                    LPWSTR lpCmdLine, int nCmdShow) {

    MessageBox (NULL, TEXT ("Hello World"), TEXT ("Hello2"), MB_OK);
    return 0;
}
```

Listing 1-2   Hello2, a simple Windows application using the *Message-Box* function

When you compile and run Hello2, you should see a small window like the one shown in Figure 1-2.

Figure 1-2   Hello2 running on a Windows CE desktop

The *MessageBox* function that replaces *printf* provides two features for Hello2. First and most obvious, it creates a window and places the "Hello World" text in the window. The second feature is that the *MessageBox* function doesn't return until the user closes the message box window. This feature allows Hello2 to keep running until the user dismisses the window.

The *MessageBox* function is prototyped as

```
int MessageBox (HWND hWnd, LPCTSTR lpText, LPCTSTR lpCaption, UINT uType);
```

The first parameter of *MessageBox* is the handle to the top-level window that will be the parent of the message box when it is displayed. For now, we can leave this parameter *NULL* because Hello2 doesn't have any other windows. The second parameter is the text that appears in the window. Notice that the string passed is couched in the *TEXT* macro, ensuring that it will be compiled as Unicode. The third parameter, *lpCaption*, is the text that will appear in the title bar of the window. The last parameter, *uType*, is a series of flags that specify how the message box appears on the screen. The flags specify the number and type of buttons on the message box; the icon, if any, on the message box; and the settings of style flags for the message box window.

The flags listed in Table 1-2 are valid under Windows CE.

Table 1-2   Default Flags

Flags	Button or Icon
For Buttons:	
MB_OK	OK
MB_OKCANCEL	OK and Cancel
MB_RETRYCANCEL	Retry and Cancel
MB_YESNO	Yes and No
MB_YESNOCANCEL	Yes, No, and Cancel
MB_ABORTRETRYIGNORE	Abort, Retry, and Ignore
For Icons:	
MB_ICONEXCLAMATION, MB_ICONWARNING	Exclamation point
MB_ICONINFORMATION, MB_ICONASTERISK	Lower case *i* within a circle
MB_ICONQUESTION	Question mark
MB_YESNO	Yes and No
MB_ICONSTOP, MB_ICONERROR, MB_ICONHAND	Stop sign
MB_DEFBUTTON1	First button
MB_DEFBUTTON2	Second button
MB_DEFBUTTON3	Third button

(continued)

Table 1-2   Default Flags   *(continued)*

Flags	Button or Icon
For Window Styles:	
MB_SETFOREGROUND	Bring the message box to the foreground.
MB_TOPMOST	Make the message box the top-most window.

The return value from *MessageBox* indicates the button pressed by the user. The return values are as follows:

IDOK	OK button pressed
IDYES	Yes button pressed
IDNO	No button pressed
IDCANCEL	Cancel button pressed or Esc key pressed
IDABORT	Abort button pressed
IDRETRY	Retry button pressed
IDIGNORE	Ignore button pressed

MessageBox is a handy function to have an application display a simple but informative dialog box.

One gotcha to look out for here: If you're debugging and recompiling the program, it can't be downloaded again if an earlier version of the program is still running on the target system. That is, make sure Hello2 isn't running on the remote system when you start a new build in eMbedded Visual C++, or the autodownload part of the compile process will fail. If this happens, close the application and choose the Update Remote File menu command in eMbedded Visual C++ to download the newly compiled file.

Hello2 displays a simple window, but that window is only as configurable as the *MessageBox* function allows. How about showing a window that is completely configurable by the application? Before we can do that, a quick review of how a Windows application really works is in order.

Anatomy of a Windows-Based Application

Windows-based programming is far different from MS-DOS–based or Unix-based programming. An MS-DOS or Unix program uses *getc-* and *putc*-style functions to read characters from the keyboard and write them to the screen whenever the program needs to do so. This is the classic "pull" style used by MS-DOS and Unix programs, which are procedural. A Windows program, on the other hand, uses a "push" model, in which the program must be written to react to notifications from the operating system that a key has been pressed or a command has been received to repaint the screen.

Windows applications don't ask for input from the operating system; the operating system notifies the application that input has occurred. The operating system achieves these notifications by sending *messages* to an application window. All windows are specific instances of a *window class*. Before we go any further, let's be sure we understand these terms.

The Window Class

A window is a region on the screen, rectangular in all but the most contrived of cases, that has a few basic parameters, such as position—*x*, *y*, and *z* (a window is over or under other windows on the screen)—visibility, and hierarchy—the window fits into a parent/child window relationship on the system *desktop*, which also happens to be a window.

Every window created is a specific instance of a window class. A window class is a template that defines a number of attributes common to all the windows of that class. In other words, windows of the same class have the same attributes. The most important of the shared attributes is the *window procedure*.

The Window Procedure

The behavior of all windows belonging to a class is defined by the code in its window procedure for that class. The window procedure handles all notifications and requests sent to the window. These notifications are sent either by the operating system, indicating that an event has occurred to which the window must respond, or by other windows querying the window for information.

These notifications are sent in the form of messages. A message is nothing more than a call being made to a window procedure, with a parameter indicating the nature of the notification or request. Messages are sent for events such as a window being moved or resized or to indicate a key press. The values used to indicate messages are defined by Windows. Applications use predefined constants, such as *WM_CREATE* and *WM_MOVE*, when referring to messages. Since hundreds of messages can be sent, Windows conveniently provides a default processing function to which a message can be passed when no special processing is necessary by the window class for that message.

The Life of a Message

Stepping back for a moment, let's look at how Windows coordinates all of the messages going to all of the windows in a system. Windows monitors all the sources of input to the system, such as the keyboard, mouse, touch screen, and any other hardware that could produce an event that might interest a window. As an event occurs, a message is composed and directed to a specific window. Instead of Windows directly calling the window procedure, the system imposes an intermediate step. The message is placed in a message queue for the application that owns the window. When the application is prepared to receive the message, it pulls it out of the queue and tells Windows to dispatch that message to the proper window in the application.

If it seems to you that a number of indirections are involved in that process, you're right. Let's break it down.

1.   An event occurs, so a message is composed by Windows and placed in a message queue for the application that owns the destination window. In Windows CE, as in Windows XP, each application has its own unique message queue.[1] (This is a break from Windows 3.1 and earlier versions of Windows, where there was only one, systemwide, message queue.) Events can occur, and therefore messages can be composed, faster than an application can process them. The queue allows an application to process messages at its own rate, although the application had better be responsive or the user will see a jerkiness in the application. The message queue also allows Windows to set a notification in motion and continue with other tasks without having to be limited by the responsiveness of the application to which the message is being sent.

---

1.   Technically, each thread in a Windows CE application can have a message queue. I'll talk about threads later in the book.

2. The application removes the message from its message queue and calls Windows back to dispatch the message. While it may seem strange that the application gets a message from the queue and then simply calls Windows back to process the message, there's a method to this madness. Having the application pull the message from the queue allows it to preprocess the message before it asks Windows to dispatch the message to the appropriate window. In a number of cases, the application might call different functions in Windows to process specific kinds of messages.

3. Windows dispatches the message; that is, it calls the appropriate window procedure. Instead of having the application directly call the window procedure, another level of indirection occurs, allowing Windows to coordinate the call to the window procedure with other events in the system. The message doesn't stand in another queue at this point, but Windows might need to make some preparations before calling the window procedure. In any case, the scheme relieves the application of the obligation to determine the proper destination window—Windows does this instead.

4. The window procedure processes the message. All window procedures have the same calling parameters: the handle of the specific window instance being called, the message, and two generic parameters that contain data specific to each message type. The window handle differentiates each instance of a window for the window procedure. The message parameter, of course, indicates the event that the window must react to. The two generic parameters contain data specific to the message being sent. For example, in a *WM_MOVE* message indicating that the window is about to be moved, one of the generic parameters points to a structure containing the new coordinates of the window.

Hello3

Enough review. It's time to jump into a full-fledged Windows application, Hello3. While the entire program files for this and all examples in the book are available in the companion CD-ROM, I suggest that, as in the earlier example, you avoid simply loading the project file from the CD and instead type in the entire example by hand. By performing this somewhat tedious task, you'll see the differences in the development process as well as the subtle program

differences between standard Win32 programs and Windows CE programs.
Listing 1-3 contains the complete source code for Hello3.

Hello3.cpp
```
//======================================================================
// Hello3 - A simple application for Windows CE
//
// Written for the book Programming Windows CE
// Copyright (C) 2003 Douglas Boling
//======================================================================
#include <windows.h>                        // For all that Windows stuff

LRESULT CALLBACK MainWndProc (HWND, UINT, WPARAM, LPARAM);


//======================================================================
// Program entry point
//
int WINAPI WinMain (HINSTANCE hInstance, HINSTANCE hPrevInstance,
                    LPWSTR lpCmdLine, int nCmdShow) {
    WNDCLASS wc;
    HWND hWnd;
    MSG msg;

    // Register application main window class.
    wc.style = 0;                           // Window style
    wc.lpfnWndProc = MainWndProc;           // Callback function
    wc.cbClsExtra = 0;                      // Extra class data
    wc.cbWndExtra = 0;                      // Extra window data
    wc.hInstance = hInstance;               // Owner handle
    wc.hIcon = NULL,                        // Application icon
    wc.hCursor = LoadCursor (NULL, IDC_ARROW);// Default cursor
    wc.hbrBackground = (HBRUSH) GetStockObject (WHITE_BRUSH);
    wc.lpszMenuName =  NULL;                // Menu name
    wc.lpszClassName = TEXT("MyClass");     // Window class name

    if (RegisterClass (&wc) == 0) return -1;

    // Create main window.
    hWnd = CreateWindowEx(WS_EX_NODRAG,     // Ex style flags
                    TEXT("MyClass"),        // Window class
                    TEXT("Hello"),          // Window title
                    // Style flags
                    WS_VISIBLE | WS_CAPTION | WS_SYSMENU,
                    CW_USEDEFAULT,          // x position
                    CW_USEDEFAULT,          // y position
                    CW_USEDEFAULT,          // Initial width
```

Listing 1-3   The Hello3 program

```
                              CW_USEDEFAULT,      // Initial height
                              NULL,               // Parent
                              NULL,               // Menu, must be null
                              hInstance,          // Application instance
                              NULL);              // Pointer to create
                                                  // parameters
    if (!IsWindow (hWnd)) return -2;  // Fail code if not created.

    // Standard show and update calls
    ShowWindow (hWnd, nCmdShow);
    UpdateWindow (hWnd);

    // Application message loop
    while (GetMessage (&msg, NULL, 0, 0)) {
        TranslateMessage (&msg);
        DispatchMessage (&msg);
    }
    // Instance cleanup
    return msg.wParam;
}
//======================================================================
// MainWndProc - Callback function for application window
//
LRESULT CALLBACK MainWndProc (HWND hWnd, UINT wMsg, WPARAM wParam,
                              LPARAM lParam) {
    PAINTSTRUCT ps;
    RECT rect;
    HDC hdc;

    switch (wMsg) {
    case WM_PAINT:
        // Get the size of the client rectangle
        GetClientRect (hWnd, &rect);

        hdc = BeginPaint (hWnd, &ps);
        DrawText (hdc, TEXT ("Hello Windows CE!"), -1, &rect,
                  DT_CENTER | DT_VCENTER | DT_SINGLELINE);

        EndPaint (hWnd, &ps);
        return 0;

    case WM_DESTROY:
        PostQuitMessage (0);
        break;
    }
    return DefWindowProc (hWnd, wMsg, wParam, lParam);
}
```

Hello3 shows all aspects of a Windows program, from registering the window class to the creation of the window to the window procedure. Hello3 has the same entry point, *WinMain*, as the first two examples; but because it creates its own window, it must register a window class for the main window, create the window, and provide a message loop to process the messages for the window.

Registering the Window Class

In *WinMain*, Hello3 registers the window class for the main window. Registering a window class is simply a matter of filling out a rather extensive structure describing the class and calling the *RegisterClass* function. *RegisterClass* and the *WNDCLASS* structure are defined as follows:

```
ATOM RegisterClass (const WNDCLASS *lpWndClass);

typedef struct _WNDCLASS {
    UINT style;
    WNDPROC lpfnWndProc;
    int cbClsExtra;
    int cbWndExtra;
    HANDLE hInstance;
    HICON hIcon;
    HCURSOR hCursor;
    HBRUSH hbrBackground;
    LPCTSTR lpszMenuName;
    LPCTSTR lpszClassName;
} WNDCLASS;
```

The parameters assigned to the fields of the *WNDCLASS* structure define how all instances of the main window for Hello3 will behave. The initial field, *style*, sets the class style for the window. In Windows CE, the class styles are limited to the following:

- ***CS_GLOBALCLASS*** indicates that the class is global. This flag is provided only for compatibility because all window classes in Windows CE are process global.

- ***CS_HREDRAW*** tells the system to force a repaint of the window if the window is sized horizontally.

- ***CS_VREDRAW*** tells the system to force a repaint of the window if the window is sized vertically.

- ***CS_NOCLOSE*** disables the Close button if one is present on the title bar.

- ***CS_PARENTDC*** causes a window to use its parent's device context.

- ***CS_DBLCLKS*** enables notification of double-clicks (double-taps under Windows CE) to be passed to the parent window.

The *lpfnWndProc* field should be loaded with the address of the window's window procedure. Because this field is typed as a pointer to a window procedure, the declaration to the procedure must be defined in the source code before the field is set. Otherwise, the compiler's type checker will flag this line with a warning.

The *cbClsExtra* field allows the programmer to add extra space in the class structure to store class-specific data known only to the application. The *cbWndExtra* field is much handier. This field adds space to the Windows internal structure responsible for maintaining the state of each instance of a window. Instead of storing large amounts of data in the window structure itself, an application should store a pointer to an application-specific structure that contains the data unique to each instance of the window. Under Windows CE, both the *cbClsExtra* and *cbWndExtra* fields must be multiples of 4 bytes.

The *hInstance* field must be filled with the program's instance handle, which specifies the owning process of the window. The *hIcon* field is set to the handle of the window's default icon. The *hIcon* field isn't supported under Windows CE and should be set to *NULL*. (In Windows CE, the icon for the class is set after the first window of this class is created. For Hello3, however, no icon is supplied, and unlike other versions of Windows, Windows CE doesn't have any predefined icons that can be loaded.)

Unless the application being developed is designed for a Windows CE system with a mouse, the next field, *hCursor*, must be set to *NULL*. Fortunately, the function call *LoadCursor (IDC_ARROW)* returns *NULL* if the system doesn't support cursors.

The *hbrBackground* field specifies how Windows CE draws the background of the window. Windows uses the *brush*, a small predefined array of pixels, specified in this field to draw the background of the window. Windows CE provides a number of predefined brushes that you can load using the *GetStockObject* function. If the *hbrBackground* field is *NULL*, the window must handle the *WM_ERASEBKGND* message sent to the window telling it to redraw the background of the window.

The *lpszMenuName* field must be set to *NULL* because Windows CE doesn't support windows directly having a menu. In Windows CE, menus are provided by command bar, command band, or menu bar controls that the main window can create.

Finally the *lpszClassName* parameter is set to a programmer-defined string that identifies the class name to Windows. Hello3 uses the string "MyClass".

After the entire *WNDCLASS* structure has been filled out, the *RegisterClass* function is called with a pointer to the *WNDCLASS* structure as its only parameter. If the function is successful, a value identifying the window class is returned. If the function fails, the function returns 0.

Creating the Window

Once the window class has been registered successfully, the main window can be created. All Windows programmers learn early in their Windows programming lives the *CreateWindow* and *CreateWindowEx* function calls. The prototype for *CreateWindowEx* is as follows:

```
HWND CreateWindowEx (DWORD dwExStyle, LPCTSTR lpClassName,
                     LPCTSTR lpWindowName, DWORD dwStyle,
                     int x, int y, int nWidth, int nHeight,
                     HWND hWndParent, HMENU hMenu,
                     HINSTANCE hInstance, LPVOID lpParam);
```

Although the number of parameters looks daunting, the parameters are fairly logical once you learn them. The first parameter is the extended style flags. The extended style flags supported by Windows CE are as follows:

- **WS_EX_TOPMOST**   Window is topmost.

- **WS_EX_WINDOWEDGE**   Window has a raised edge.

- **WS_EX_CLIENTEDGE**   Window has a sunken edge.

- **WS_EX_STATICEDGE**   3D look for static windows.

- **WS_EX_OVERLAPPEDWINDOW**   Combines *WS_EX_WINDOWEDGE* and *WS_EX_CLIENTEDGE*.

- **WS_EX_CAPTIONOKBUTTON**   Window has an OK button on caption.

- **WS_EX_CONTEXTHELP**   Window has help button on caption.

- **WS_EX_NOACTIVATE**   Window is not activated when clicked.

- **WS_EX_NOANIMATION**   Top-level window will not have exploding rectangles when created nor have a button on the taskbar.

- **WS_EX_NODRAG**   Prevents window from being moved.

The *dwExStyle* parameter is the only difference between *CreateWindowEx* and *CreateWindow*. In fact, if you look at the declaration of *CreateWindow* in the Windows CE header files, it's simply a call to *CreateWindowEx* with the *dwExStyle* parameter set to 0.

The second parameter is the name of the window class of which our window will be an instance. In the case of Hello3, the class name is *MyClass*, which matches the name of the class registered in *RegisterClass*.

The next field is referred to as the *window text*. In other versions of Windows, this is the text that would appear on the title bar of a standard window. On

H/PCs, main windows rarely have title bars; this text is used only on the taskbar button for the window. On the Pocket PC, however, this text is shown on the navigation bar at the top of the display. The text is couched in a *TEXT* macro, which ensures that the string will be converted to Unicode under Windows CE.

The style flags specify the initial styles for the window. The style flags are used both for general styles that are relevant to all windows in the system and for class-specific styles, such as those that specify the style of a button or a list box. In this case, all we need to specify is that the window be created initially visible with the *WS_VISIBLE* flag. Experienced Win32 programmers should refer to the documentation for *CreateWindow* because a number of window style flags aren't supported under Windows CE.

The next four fields specify the initial position and size of the window. Since most applications under Windows CE are full-screen windows, the size and position fields are set to default values, which are indicated by the CW_USEDEFAULT flag in each of the fields. The default value settings create a window that is sized to fit the entire screen under the current versions of Windows CE. Be careful not to assume any particular screen size for a Windows CE device because different implementations have different screen sizes.

The next field is set to the handle of the parent window. Because this is the top-level window, the parent window field is set to *NULL*. The menu field is also set to *NULL* because Windows CE does not support menus on top-level windows.

The *hInstance* parameter is the same instance handle that was passed to the program. Creation of windows is one case in which that instance handle, saved at the start of the routine, comes in handy. The final parameter is a pointer that can be used to pass data from the *CreateWindow* call to the window procedure during the *WM_CREATE* message. In this example, no additional data needs to be passed, so the parameter is set to *NULL*.

If successful, the *CreateWindow* call returns the handle to the window just created, or it returns 0 if an error occurred during the function. That window handle is then used in the two statements (*ShowWindow* and *UpdateWindow*) just after the error-checking *if* statement. The *ShowWindow* function modifies the state of the window to conform with the state given in the *nCmdShow* parameter passed to *WinMain*. The *UpdateWindow* function forces Windows to send a *WM_PAINT* message to the window that has just been created.

The Message Loop

After the main window has been created, *WinMain* enters the message loop, which is the heart of every Windows application. Hello3's message loop is shown at the top of the next page.

```
while (GetMessage (&msg, NULL, 0, 0)) {
    TranslateMessage (&msg);
    DispatchMessage (&msg);
}
```

The loop is simple: *GetMessage* is called to get the next message in the application's message queue. If no message is available, the call waits, blocking that application's thread until a message is available. When a message is available, the call returns with the message data contained in a *MSG* structure. The *MSG* structure itself contains fields that identify the message, provide any message-specific parameters, and identify the last point on the screen touched by the pen before the message was sent. This location information is different from the standard Win32 message point data in that in Windows XP the point returned is the current mouse position instead of the last point clicked (or tapped, as in Windows CE).

The *TranslateMessage* function translates appropriate keyboard messages into a character message. (I'll talk about others of these filter messages, such as *IsDialogMsg*, later.) The *DispatchMessage* function then tells Windows to forward the message to the appropriate window in the application.

This *GetMessage*, *TranslateMessage*, *DispatchMessage* loop continues until *GetMessage* receives a *WM_QUIT* message, which, unlike all other messages, causes *GetMessage* to return 0. As can be seen from the *while* clause, the return value 0 by *GetMessage* causes the loop to terminate.

After the message loop terminates, the program can do little else but clean up and exit. In the case of Hello3, the program simply returns from *WinMain*. The value returned by *WinMain* becomes the return code of the program. Traditionally, the return value is the value in the *wParam* parameter of the last message (*WM_QUIT*). The *wParam* value of *WM_QUIT* is set when that message is sent in response to a *PostQuitMessage* call made by the application.

The Window Procedure

The messages sent or posted to the Hello3 main window are sent to the procedure *MainWndProc*. *MainWndProc*, like all window procedures, is prototyped as follows:

```
LRESULT CALLBACK MainWndProc (HWND hWnd, UINT wMsg, WPARAM wParam,
                             LPARAM lParam);
```

The *LRESULT* return type is actually just a long (a *long* is a 32-bit value under Windows) but is typed this way to provide a level of indirection between the source code and the machine. While you can easily look into the include files to determine the real type of variables that are used in Windows programming, this can cause problems when you're attempting to move your code across platforms. Although it can be useful to know the size of a variable type for memory use calculations, there is no good reason to use (and plenty of reasons not to use) the type definitions provided by windows.h.

The *CALLBACK* type definition specifies that this function is an external entry point into the EXE, necessary because Windows calls this procedure directly. On the desktop, *CALLBACK* indicates that the parameters will be put in a Pascal-like right-to-left push onto the program stack, which is the reverse of the standard C-language method. The reason for using the Pascal language stack frame for external entry points goes back to the very earliest days of Windows development. The use of a fixed-size, Pascal stack frame meant that the called procedure cleaned up the stack instead of leaving it for the caller to do. This reduced the code size of Windows and its bundled accessory programs sufficiently so that the early Microsoft developers thought it was a good move. Windows CE applications use a C stack frame for all functions, regardless of whether they are externally callable.

The first of the parameters passed to the window procedure is the window handle, which is useful when you need to define the specific instance of the window. The *wMsg* parameter indicates the message being sent to the window. This isn't the *MSG* structure used in the message loop in *WinMain*, but a simple, unsigned integer containing the message value. The remaining two parameters, *wParam* and *lParam*, are used to pass message-specific data to the window procedure. The names *wParam* and *lParam* come to us from the Win16 days, when *wParam* was a 16-bit value and *lParam* was a 32-bit value. In Windows CE, as in other Win32 operating systems, both the *wParam* and *lParam* parameters are 32 bits wide.

Hello3 has a traditional window procedure that consists of a switch statement that parses the *wMsg* message ID parameter. The switch statement for Hello3 contains two case statements, one to parse the *WM_PAINT* message and one for the *WM_DESTROY* message. This is about as simple as a window procedure can get.

WM_PAINT

Painting the window, and therefore processing the *WM_PAINT* message, is one of the critical functions of any Windows program. As a program processes the *WM_PAINT* message, the look of the window is achieved. Aside from painting the default background with the brush you specified when you registered the window class, Windows provides no help for processing this message. The lines of Hello3 that process the *WM_PAINT* messages are shown below here:

```
case WM_PAINT:
    // Get the size of the client rectangle
    GetClientRect (hWnd, &rect);

    hdc = BeginPaint (hWnd, &ps);
    DrawText (hdc, TEXT ("Hello Windows CE!"), -1, &rect,
              DT_CENTER | DT_VCENTER | DT_SINGLELINE);

    EndPaint (hWnd, &ps);
    return 0;
```

Before the window can be drawn, the routine must determine its size. In a Windows program, a standard window is divided into two areas, the nonclient area and the client area. A window's title bar and its sizing border commonly make up the nonclient area of a window, and Windows is responsible for drawing it. The client area is the interior part of the window, and the application is responsible for drawing that. An application determines the size and location of the client area by calling the *GetClientRect* function. The function returns a *RECT* structure that contains left, top, right, and bottom elements that delineate the boundaries of the client rectangle. The advantage of the client vs. nonclient area concept is that an application doesn't have to account for drawing such standard elements of a window as the title bar.

Other versions of Windows supply a series of *WM_NCxxx* messages that enable your applications to take over the drawing of the nonclient area. In Windows CE, windows seldom have title bars. Because there's so little nonclient area, the Windows CE team decided not to send the nonclient messages to the window procedure.

All drawing performed in a *WM_PAINT* message must be enclosed by two functions, *BeginPaint* and *EndPaint*. The *BeginPaint* function returns an *HDC*, or handle to a device context. A *device context* is a logical representation of a physical display device such as a video screen or a printer. Windows programs never modify the display hardware directly. Instead, Windows isolates the program from the specifics of the hardware with, among other tools, device contexts.

BeginPaint also fills in a *PAINTSTRUCT* structure that contains a number of useful parameters:

```
typedef struct tagPAINTSTRUCT {
    HDC  hdc;
    BOOL fErase;
    RECT rcPaint;
    BOOL fRestore;
    BOOL fIncUpdate;
    BYTE rgbReserved[32];
} PAINTSTRUCT;
```

The *hdc* field is the same handle that's returned by the *BeginPaint* function. The *fErase* field indicates whether the window procedure needs to redraw the background of the window. The *rcPaint* field is a *RECT* structure that defines the client area that needs repainting. Hello3 ignores this field and assumes that the entire client window needs repainting for every *WM_PAINT* message, but this field is quite handy when performance is an issue because only part of the window might need repainting. Windows actually prevents repainting outside the *rcPaint* rectangle, even when a program attempts to do so. The other fields in the structure, *fRestore*, *fIncUpdate*, and *rgbReserved*, are used internally by Windows and can be ignored by the application.

The only painting that takes place in Hello3 occurs in one line of text in the window. To do the painting, Hello3 calls the *DrawText* function. I cover the details of *DrawText* in Chapter 2, but if you look at the function it's probably obvious to you that this call draws the string "Hello Windows CE" on the window. After *DrawText* returns, *EndPaint* is called to inform Windows that the program has completed its update of the window.

Calling *EndPaint* also validates any area of the window you didn't paint. Windows keeps a list of areas of a window that are *invalid* (areas that need to be redrawn) and *valid* (areas that are up-to-date). By calling the *BeginPaint* and *EndPaint* pair, you tell Windows that you've taken care of any invalid areas in your window, whether or not you've actually drawn anything in the window. In fact, you must call *BeginPaint* and *EndPaint*, or validate the invalid areas of the window by other means, or Windows will simply continue to send *WM_PAINT* messages to the window until those invalid areas are validated.

WM_DESTROY

The other message processed by Hello3 is the *WM_DESTROY* message. The *WM_DESTROY* message is sent when a window is about to be destroyed. Because this window is the main window of the application, the application should terminate when the window is destroyed. To make this happen, the code processing the *WM_DESTROY* message calls *PostQuitMessage*. This function places a *WM_QUIT* message in the message queue. The one parameter of this function is the return code value that will be passed back to the application in the *wParam* parameter of the *WM_QUIT* message.

As I've mentioned, when the message loop sees a *WM_QUIT* message, it exits the loop. The *WinMain* function then calls *TermInstance*, which, in the case of Hello3, does nothing but return. *WinMain* then returns, terminating the program.

Hello3 is the classic Windows program. This programming style is sometimes call the Petzold method of Windows programming in homage to the ultimate guru of Windows programming, Charles Petzold. Charles's book *Programming Microsoft Windows* is currently in its fifth edition and is still the best book for learning Windows programming.

I prefer a somewhat different layout of my Windows programs. In a sense, it's simply a method of componentizing the function of a Windows program which, for me, makes it much easier to copy parts of one program to another. In the final example of this chapter, I introduce this programming style along with a few extra features that are necessary for Windows CE applications.

HelloCE

One criticism of the typical SDK style of Windows programming has always been the huge *switch* statement in the window procedure. The *switch* statement parses the message to the window procedure so that each message can be handled independently. This standard structure has the one great advantage of enforcing a similar structure across almost all Windows applications, making it much easier for one programmer to understand the workings of another programmer's code. The disadvantage is that all the variables for the entire window procedure typically appear jumbled at the top of the procedure.

Over the years, I've developed a different style for my Windows programs. The idea is to break up the *WinMain* and *WinProc* procedures into manageable units that can be easily understood and easily transferred to other Windows programs. *WinMain* is broken up into procedures that perform application initialization, instance initialization, and instance termination. Also in *WinMain* is the ubiquitous message loop that's the core of all Windows programs.

I break the window procedure into individual procedures, with each handling a specific message. What remains of the window procedure itself is a fragment of code that simply looks up the message that's being passed to see whether a procedure has been written to handle that message. If so, that procedure is called. If not, the message is passed to the default window procedure.

This structure divides the handling of messages into individual blocks that can be more easily understood. Also, with greater isolation of one message-handling code fragment from another, you can more easily transfer the code that handles a specific message from one program to the next. I first saw this structure described a number of years ago by Ray Duncan in one of his old "Power Programming" columns in *PC Magazine*. Ray is one of the legends in the field of MS-DOS and OS/2 programming. I've since modified the design a bit to fit my needs, but Ray should get the credit for this program structure.

The Code

The source code for HelloCE is shown in Listing 1-4.

```
HelloCE.h
//======================================================================
// Header file
//
// Written for the book Programming Windows CE
// Copyright (C) 2003 Douglas Boling
//======================================================================
// Returns number of elements
#define dim(x) (sizeof(x) / sizeof(x[0]))


//----------------------------------------------------------------------
// Generic defines and data types
//
struct decodeUINT {                              // Structure associates
    UINT Code;                                   // messages
                                                 // with a function.
    LRESULT (*Fxn)(HWND, UINT, WPARAM, LPARAM);
};
struct decodeCMD {                               // Structure associates
    UINT Code;                                   // menu IDs with a
    LRESULT (*Fxn)(HWND, WORD, HWND, WORD);      // function
};


//----------------------------------------------------------------------
// Function prototypes
//
HWND InitInstance (HINSTANCE, LPWSTR, int);
int TermInstance (HINSTANCE, int);

// Window procedures
LRESULT CALLBACK MainWndProc (HWND, UINT, WPARAM, LPARAM);

// Message handlers
LRESULT DoPaintMain (HWND, UINT, WPARAM, LPARAM);
LRESULT DoDestroyMain (HWND, UINT, WPARAM, LPARAM);
```

Listing 1-4   The HelloCE program   *(continued)*

Listing 1-4   *(continued)*

HelloCE.cpp

```cpp
//======================================================================
// HelloCE - A simple application for Windows CE
//
// Written for the book Programming Windows CE
// Copyright (C) 2003 Douglas Boling
//======================================================================
#include <windows.h>                    // For all that Windows stuff
#include "helloce.h"                    // Program-specific stuff


//----------------------------------------------------------------------
// Global data
//
const TCHAR szAppName[] = TEXT("HelloCE");
HINSTANCE hInst;                        // Program instance handle

// Message dispatch table for MainWindowProc
const struct decodeUINT MainMessages[] = {
    WM_PAINT, DoPaintMain,
    WM_DESTROY, DoDestroyMain,
};


//======================================================================
// Program entry point
//
int WINAPI WinMain (HINSTANCE hInstance, HINSTANCE hPrevInstance,
                    LPWSTR lpCmdLine, int nCmdShow) {
    MSG msg;
    int rc = 0;
    HWND hwndMain;

    // Initialize this instance.
    hwndMain = InitInstance (hInstance, lpCmdLine, nCmdShow);
    if (hwndMain == 0) return 0x10;

    // Application message loop
    while (GetMessage (&msg, NULL, 0, 0)) {
        TranslateMessage (&msg);
        DispatchMessage (&msg);
    }
    // Instance cleanup
    return TermInstance (hInstance, msg.wParam);
}
```

```
//----------------------------------------------------------------------
// InitInstance - Instance initialization
//
HWND InitInstance (HINSTANCE hInstance, LPWSTR lpCmdLine, int nCmdShow) {
    WNDCLASS wc;
    HWND hWnd;

    // Save program instance handle in global variable.
    hInst = hInstance;

#if defined(WIN32_PLATFORM_PSPC)
    // If Pocket PC, only allow one instance of the application
    hWnd = FindWindow (szAppName, NULL);
    if (hWnd) {
        SetForegroundWindow ((HWND)(((DWORD)hWnd) | 0x01));
        return 0;
    }
#endif

    // Register application main window class.
    wc.style = 0;                                   // Window style
    wc.lpfnWndProc = MainWndProc;                   // Callback function
    wc.cbClsExtra = 0;                              // Extra class data
    wc.cbWndExtra = 0;                              // Extra window data
    wc.hInstance = hInstance;                       // Owner handle
    wc.hIcon = NULL,                                // Application icon
    wc.hCursor = LoadCursor (NULL, IDC_ARROW);// Default cursor
    wc.hbrBackground = (HBRUSH) GetStockObject (WHITE_BRUSH);
    wc.lpszMenuName = NULL;                         // Menu name
    wc.lpszClassName = szAppName;                   // Window class name

    if (RegisterClass (&wc) == 0) return 0;

    // Create main window.
    hWnd = CreateWindow (szAppName,                 // Window class
                        TEXT("HelloCE"),      // Window title
                        // Style flags
                        WS_VISIBLE | WS_CAPTION | WS_SYSMENU,
                        CW_USEDEFAULT,        // x position
                        CW_USEDEFAULT,        // y position
                        CW_USEDEFAULT,        // Initial width
                        CW_USEDEFAULT,        // Initial height
                        NULL,                 // Parent
                        NULL,                 // Menu, must be null
                        hInstance,            // Application instance
```

(continued)

Listing 1-4   *(continued)*

```
                    NULL);                    // Pointer to create
                                              // parameters
    if (!IsWindow (hWnd)) return 0;  // Fail code if not created.

    // Standard show and update calls
    ShowWindow (hWnd, nCmdShow);
    UpdateWindow (hWnd);
    return hWnd;
}
//-----------------------------------------------------------------------
// TermInstance - Program cleanup
//
int TermInstance (HINSTANCE hInstance, int nDefRC) {
    return nDefRC;
}
//=======================================================================
// Message handling procedures for main window
//
//-----------------------------------------------------------------------
// MainWndProc - Callback function for application window
//
LRESULT CALLBACK MainWndProc (HWND hWnd, UINT wMsg, WPARAM wParam,
                              LPARAM lParam) {
    INT i;
    //
    // Search message list to see if we need to handle this
    // message.  If in list, call procedure.
    //
    for (i = 0; i < dim(MainMessages); i++) {
        if (wMsg == MainMessages[i].Code)
            return (*MainMessages[i].Fxn)(hWnd, wMsg, wParam, lParam);
    }
    return DefWindowProc (hWnd, wMsg, wParam, lParam);
}
//-----------------------------------------------------------------------
// DoPaintMain - Process WM_PAINT message for window.
//
LRESULT DoPaintMain (HWND hWnd, UINT wMsg, WPARAM wParam,
                     LPARAM lParam) {
    PAINTSTRUCT ps;
    RECT rect;
    HDC hdc;

    // Get the size of the client rectangle
    GetClientRect (hWnd, &rect);
```

```
    hdc = BeginPaint (hWnd, &ps);
    DrawText (hdc, TEXT ("Hello Windows CE!"), -1, &rect,
              DT_CENTER | DT_VCENTER | DT_SINGLELINE);

    EndPaint (hWnd, &ps);
    return 0;
}
//-------------------------------------------------------------
// DoDestroyMain - Process WM_DESTROY message for window.
//
LRESULT DoDestroyMain (HWND hWnd, UINT wMsg, WPARAM wParam,
                       LPARAM lParam) {
    PostQuitMessage (0);
    return 0;
}
```

If you look over the source code for HelloCE, you'll see the standard boilerplate for all programs in this book. A few variables defined globally follow the defines and includes. I know plenty of good arguments why no global variables should appear in a program, but I use them as a convenience that shortens and clarifies the example programs in the book. Each program defines an *szAppName* Unicode string to be used in various places in that program. I also use the *hInst* variable a number of places, and I'll mention it when I cover the *InitInstance* procedure. The final global structure is a list of messages along with associated procedures to process the messages. This structure is used by the window procedure to associate messages with the procedure that handles them.

In HelloCE, *WinMain* has two basic functions: it calls *InitInstance* (where the application initialization code is kept), processes the message in the message loop, and calls *TerminateInstance* when the message loop exits. In this program template, *WinMain* becomes a boilerplate routine that almost never changes. In general, the only changes that are made to *WinMain* concern modification of the processing of the message loop to process for keyboard accelerators, watch for modeless dialog box messages or other tasks.

InitInstance

The main task of *InitInstance* is to register the main window's window class, create the application's main window, and display it in the form specified in the *nCmdShow* parameter passed to *WinMain*. There is also some conditionally compiled code that, if compiled for a Pocket PC, prevents more than one instance of the program from running at any one time.

The first task performed by *InitInstance* is to save the program's instance handle *hInstance* in a global variable named *hInst*. The instance handle for a program is useful at a number of points in a Windows application. I save the value here because the instance handle is known, and this is a convenient place in the program to store it.

When running on a Pocket PC, HelloCE uses *FindWindow* to see whether another copy of itself is currently running. This function searches the top-level windows in the system looking for ones that match the class name or the window title or both. If a match is found, the window is brought to the foreground with *SetForegroundWindow*. The routine then exits with a zero return code, which causes *WinMain* to exit, terminating the application. I'll spend more time talking about the Pocket PC–specific code in Chapter 17.

These Pocket PC–specific lines are enclosed in *#if* and *#endif* lines. These lines tell the compiler to include them only if the condition of the *#if* statement is true—in this case, if the constant *WIN32_PLATFORM_PSPC* is defined. This constant is defined in the Project Settings for the project. A quick look at the C/C++ tab of the Project Settings dialog box shows an entry field for Preprocessor Definitions. In this field, one of the definitions is *$(CePlatform)*, which is a placeholder for a registry value. Deep in the registry, under the key *[HKEY_LOCAL_MACHINE]\Software\Microsoft\Windows CE Tools\Platform Manager*, you can find series of registry keys, one for each target platform installed in eMbedded Visual C++. The CePlatform value is defined differently depending on the target project. For Pocket PC and old Palm-size PC projects, CePlatform is defined as *WIN32_PLATFORM_PSPC*.

The registering of the window class and the creation of the main window are quite similar to those in the Hello3 example. The only difference is the use of the global string *szAppName* as the class name of the main window class. Each time I use this template, I change the *szAppName* string to match the program name. This keeps the window class names somewhat unique for the different applications, enabling the *FindWindow* code in HelloCE to work.

That completes the *InitInstance* function. At this point, the application's main window has been created and updated. So even before we have entered the message loop, messages have been sent to the main window's window procedure. It's about time to look at this part of the program.

MainWndProc

You spend most of your programming time with the window procedure when you're writing a Windows program. The window procedure is the core of the program, the place where the actions of the program's windows create the personality of the program.

It's in the window procedure that my programming style differs significantly from most Windows programs written without the help of a class library such as MFC. For almost all of my programs, the window procedure is identical to the one previously shown in HelloCE. Before continuing, I repeat: this program structure isn't specific to Windows CE. I use this style for all my Windows applications, whether they are for Windows 3.1, Windows Me, Windows XP, or Windows CE.

This style reduces the window procedure to a simple table lookup function. The idea is to scan the *MainMessages* table defined early in the C file for the message value in one of the entries. If the message is found, the associated procedure is then called, passing the original parameters to the procedure processing the message. If no match is found for the message, the *DefWindowProc* function is called. *DefWindowProc* is a Windows function that provides a default action for all messages in the system, which frees a Windows program from having to process every message being passed to a window.

The message table associates message values with a procedure to process it. The table is listed below:

```
// Message dispatch table for MainWindowProc
const struct decodeUINT MainMessages[] = {
    WM_PAINT, DoPaintMain,
    WM_DESTROY, DoDestroyMain,
};
```

The table is defined as a constant, not just as good programming practice but also because it's helpful for memory conservation. Since Windows CE programs can be executed in place in ROM, data that doesn't change should be marked constant. This allows the Windows CE program loader to leave such constant data in ROM instead of loading a copy into RAM, thus saving precious RAM.

The table itself is an array of a simple two-element structure. The first entry is the message value, followed by a pointer to the function that processes the message. While the functions could be named anything, I'm using a consistent structure throughout the book to help you keep track of them. The names are composed of a *Do* prefix (as a bow to object-oriented practice), followed by the message name and a suffix indicating the window class associated with the table. So *DoPaintMain* is the name of the function that processes *WM_PAINT* messages for the main window of the program.

DoPaintMain and DoDestroyMain

The two message processing routines in HelloCE are *DoPaintMain* and *DoDestroyMain*. They mimic the function of the case clauses in Hello3. The advantage of the separate routines is that the code and their local variables are isolated to the routine. In Hello3's window procedure, the local variables specific to the paint code are bundled at the top of the routine. The encapsulation of the code makes it easy to cut and paste the code into the next application you write.

Running HelloCE

After you've entered the program into eMbedded Visual C++ and built it, you can execute it remotely from inside Visual C++ by selecting Execute HelloCE.exe from the Build menu or by pressing Ctrl-F5. The program displays the Hello Windows CE text in the middle of an empty window, as shown in Figure 1-3. Figure 1-4 shows HelloCE running on a Pocket PC. Tapping on the Close button on the title bar causes Windows CE to send a *WM_CLOSE* message to the window. Although HelloCE doesn't explicitly process the *WM_CLOSE* message, the *DefWindowProc* procedure enables default processing by destroying the main window. As the window is being destroyed, a *WM_DESTROY* message is sent, which causes *PostQuitMessage* to be called.

Figure 1-3   The HelloCE window on an embedded Windows CE system

As I said, HelloCE is a very basic Windows CE program, but it gives you a skeleton application on which you can build. If you look at the file HelloCE.exe using Explorer, you'll see that the program is represented by a generic icon. When HelloCE is running, the button on the taskbar in Figure 1-3 representing HelloCE has no icon displayed next to the text. Adding a custom icon to a program and how the *DrawText* function works are a couple of the topics I'll address in the next few chapters.

Figure 1-4   The HelloCE window on a Pocket PC

Figure 1-4 shows a problem that HelloCE has running on a Pocket PC. The HelloCE window extends to the bottom of the screen. Depending on how you switch between applications, the button to display the SIP may appear over the top of the HelloCE window. Applications designed specifically for the Pocket PC will create a menu bar at the bottom of the screen that among other things contains the button necessary to display the soft keyboard. It must also resize its window manually to avoid covering, or being covered, by the menu bar. We'll see later in the book how to design an application specifically for the Pocket PC user interface. Rest assured that the lessons covering Windows CE in the early parts of the book apply as much to Pocket PC devices as to other Windows CE systems.

2

Drawing on the Screen

In Chapter 1, the example program HelloCE had one task: to display a line of text on the screen. Displaying that line took only one call to *DrawText*, with Windows CE taking care of such details as the font and its color, the positioning of the line of text inside the window, and so forth. Given the power of a graphical user interface (GUI), however, an application can do much more than simply print a line of text on the screen. It can craft the look of the display down to the most minute of details.

Over the life of the Microsoft Windows operating system, the number of functions available for crafting these displays has expanded dramatically. With each successive version of Windows, functions have been added that extend the tools available to the programmer. As functions were added, the old ones remained so that even if a function had been superseded by a new function, old programs would continue to run on the newer versions of Windows. The approach in which function after function is piled on while the old functions are retained for backward compatibility was discontinued with the initial version of Windows CE. Because of the requirement to produce a smaller version of Windows, the CE team took a hard look at the Win32 API and replicated only the functions absolutely required by applications written for the Windows CE target market.

One of the areas of the Win32 API hardest hit by this reduction was graphical functions. It's not that you now lack the functions to do the job—it's just that the high degree of redundancy in the Win32 API led to some major pruning of the graphical functions. An added challenge for the programmer is that different Windows CE platforms have subtly different sets of supported APIs. One of the ways in which Windows CE graphics support differs from that of its desktop cousins is that Windows CE doesn't support the different mapping modes available under other implementations of Windows. Instead, the Windows CE device contexts are always set to the *MM_TEXT* mapping mode. Coordinate transformations are also not supported under Windows CE. While these features can be quite useful for some types of applications, such as desktop publishing, their necessity in the Windows CE environment of small portable devices isn't as clear. So when you're reading about the functions and techniques used in this chapter, remember that some might not be supported on all platforms. So that a program can determine what functions are supported, Windows has always had the *GetDeviceCaps* function, which returns the capabilities of the current graphic device. Throughout this chapter, I'll refer to *GetDevice-Caps* when determining what functions are supported on a given device.

This chapter, like the other chapters in Part I of this book, reviews the drawing features supported by Windows CE. One of the most important facts to remember is that while Windows CE doesn't support the full Win32 graphics API, its rapid evolution has resulted in it supporting some of the newest functions in Win32—some so new that you might not be familiar with them. This chapter shows you the functions you can use and how to work around the areas where certain functions aren't supported under Windows CE.

Painting Basics

Historically, Windows has been subdivided into three main components: the kernel, which handles the process and memory management; User, which handles the windowing interface and controls; and the Graphics Device Interface, or GDI, which performs the low-level drawing. In Windows CE, User and GDI are combined into the Graphics Windowing and Event handler, or GWE. At times, you might hear a Windows CE programmer talk about the GWE. The GWE is nothing really new—just a different packaging of standard Windows parts. In this book, I usually refer to the graphics portion of the GWE under its old name, GDI, to be consistent with standard Windows programming terminology.

But whether you're programming for Windows CE, Windows 2000, or Windows XP, there's more to drawing than simply handling the *WM_PAINT* message. It's helpful to understand just when and why a *WM_PAINT* message is sent to a window.

Valid and Invalid Regions

When for some reason an area of a window is exposed to the user, that area, or *region*, as it's referred to in Windows, is marked invalid. When no other messages are waiting in an application's message queue and the application's window contains an invalid region, Windows sends a *WM_PAINT* message to the window. As mentioned in Chapter 1, any drawing performed in response to a *WM_PAINT* message is couched in calls to *BeginPaint* and *EndPaint*. *BeginPaint* actually performs a number of actions. It marks the invalid region as valid, and it computes the *clipping* region. The clipping region is the area to which the painting action will be limited. *BeginPaint* then sends a *WM_ERASEBACKGROUND* message, if needed, to redraw the background, and it hides the caret—the text entry cursor—if it's displayed. Finally *BeginPaint* retrieves the handle to the display device context so that it can be used by the application. The *EndPaint* function releases the device context and redisplays the caret if necessary. If no other action is performed by a *WM_PAINT* procedure, you must at least call *BeginPaint* and *EndPaint* if only to mark the invalid region as valid.

Alternatively, you can call to *ValidateRect* to blindly validate the region. But no drawing can take place in that case because an application must have a handle to the device context before it can draw anything in the window.

Often an application needs to force a repaint of its window. An application should never post or send a *WM_PAINT* message to itself or to another window. Instead, you use the following function:

```
BOOL InvalidateRect (HWND hWnd, const RECT *lpRect, BOOL bErase);
```

Notice that *InvalidateRect* doesn't require a handle to the window's device context, only to the window handle itself. The *lpRect* parameter is the area of the window to be invalidated. This value can be *NULL* if the entire window is to be invalidated. The *bErase* parameter indicates whether the background of the window should be redrawn during the *BeginPaint* call as mentioned above. Note that unlike other versions of Windows, Windows CE requires that the *hWnd* parameter be a valid window handle.

Device Contexts

A *device context*, often referred to simply as a DC, is a tool that Windows uses to manage access to the display and printer, although for the purposes of this chapter I'll be talking only about the display. Also, unless otherwise mentioned, the explanation that follows applies to Windows in general and isn't specific to Windows CE.

Windows applications never write directly to the screen. Instead, they request a handle to a display device context for the appropriate window and then, using the handle, draw to the device context. Windows then arbitrates and manages getting the pixels from the DC to the screen.

BeginPaint, which should be called only in a *WM_PAINT* message, returns a handle to the display DC for the window. An application usually performs its drawing to the screen during the *WM_PAINT* messages. Windows treats painting as a low-priority task, which is appropriate since having painting at a higher priority would result in a flood of paint messages for every little change to the display. Allowing an application to complete all its pending business by processing all waiting messages results in all the invalid regions being painted efficiently at once. Users don't notice the minor delays caused by the low priority of the *WM_PAINT* messages.

Of course, there are times when painting must be immediate. An example of such a time might be when a word processor needs to display a character immediately after its key is pressed. To draw outside a *WM_PAINT* message, the handle to the DC can be obtained using this:

```
HDC GetDC (HWND hWnd);
```

GetDC returns a handle to the DC for the client portion of the window. Drawing can then be performed anywhere within the client area of the window because this process isn't like processing inside a *WM_PAINT* message; there's no clipping to restrict you from drawing in an invalid region.

Windows CE supports another function that can be used to receive the DC. It is

```
HDC GetDCEx (HWND hWnd, HRGN hrgnClip, DWORD flags);
```

GetDCEx allows you to have more control over the device context returned. The new parameter, *hrgnClip*, lets you define the clipping region, which limits drawing to that region of the DC. The *flags* parameter lets you specify how the DC acts as you draw on it. Note that Windows CE doesn't support the following flags: *DCX_PARENTCLIP*, *DCX_NORESETATTRS*, *DCX_LOCKWINDOWUPDATE*, and *DCX_VALIDATE*.

After the drawing has been completed, a call must be made to release the device context:

```
int ReleaseDC (HWND hWnd, HDC hDC);
```

Device contexts are a shared resource, and therefore an application must not hold the DC for any longer than necessary.

While *GetDC* is used to draw inside the client area, sometimes an application needs access to the nonclient areas of a window, such as the title bar. To retrieve a DC for the entire window, make the following call:

```
HDC GetWindowDC (HWND hWnd);
```

As before, the matching call after the drawing has been completed for *GetWindowDC* is *ReleaseDC*.

The DC functions under Windows CE are identical to the device context functions under Windows XP. This should be expected because DCs are the core of the Windows drawing philosophy. Changes to this area of the API would result in major incompatibilities between Windows CE applications and their desktop counterparts.

Writing Text

In Chapter 1, the HelloCE example displayed a line of text using a call to *Draw-Text*. That line from the example is shown here:

```
DrawText (hdc, TEXT ("Hello Windows CE!"), -1, &rect,
        DT_CENTER | DT_VCENTER | DT_SINGLELINE);
```

DrawText is a fairly high-level function that allows a program to display text while having Windows deal with most of the details. The first few parameters of *DrawText* are almost self-explanatory. The handle of the device context being used is passed, along with the text to display couched in a *TEXT* macro, which declares the string as a Unicode string necessary for Windows CE. The third parameter is the number of characters to print, or as is the case here, a −1 indicating that the string being passed is null terminated and Windows should compute the length.

The fourth parameter is a pointer to a rect structure that specifies the formatting rectangle for the text. *DrawText* uses this rectangle as a basis for formatting the text to be printed. How the text is formatted depends on the function's last parameter, the formatting flags. These flags specify how the text is to be placed within the formatting rectangle, or in the case of the *DT_CALCRECT* flag, the flags have *DrawText* compute the dimensions of the text that is to be printed. *DrawText* even formats multiple lines with line breaks automatically computed. In the case of HelloCE, the flags specify that the text should be centered horizontally (*DT_CENTER*), and centered vertically (*DT_VCENTER*). The *DT_VCENTER* flag works only on single lines of text, so the final parameter, *DT_SINGLELINE*, specifies that the text shouldn't be flowed across multiple lines if the rectangle isn't wide enough to display the entire string.

Another way to draw text is by employing the following function:

```
BOOL ExtTextOut (HDC hdc, int X, int Y, UINT fuOptions,
                const RECT *lprc, LPCTSTR lpString,
                UINT cbCount, const int *lpDx);
```

The *ExtTextOut* function has a few advantages over *DrawText*. First, *ExtTextOut* tends to be faster for drawing single lines of text. Second, the text isn't formatted inside a rectangle; instead, *x* and *y* starting coordinates are passed, specifying where the text will be drawn. Generally, the point defined by the coordinates is the upper left corner of the rectangle, but this can be changed with the text alignment settings of the DC. The *rect* parameter that's passed is used as a clipping rectangle or, if the background mode is opaque, the area where the background color is drawn. This rectangle parameter can be *NULL* if you don't want any clipping or opaquing. The next two parameters are the text and the character count. The last parameter, *ExtTextOut*, allows an application to specify the horizontal distance between adjacent character cells.

Windows CE differs from other versions of Windows in having only these two text drawing functions for displaying text. You can emulate most of what you can do with the text functions typically used in other versions of Windows, such as *TextOut* and *TabbedTextOut*, by using either *DrawText* or *ExtTextOut*. This is one of the areas in which Windows CE has broken with earlier versions of Windows, sacrificing backward compatibility to achieve a smaller operating system.

Device Context Attributes

What I haven't mentioned yet about HelloCE's use of *DrawText* is the large number of assumptions the program makes about the DC configuration when displaying the text. Drawing in a Windows device context takes a large number of parameters, such as foreground and background color and how the text should be drawn over the background as well as the font of the text. Instead of specifying all these parameters for each drawing call, the device context keeps track of the current settings, referred to as *attributes*, and uses them as appropriate for each call to draw to the device context.

Foreground and Background Colors

The most obvious of the text attributes are the foreground and background color. Two functions, *SetTextColor* and *GetTextColor*, allow a program to set and retrieve the current color. These functions work well with both gray-scale screens and the color screens supported by Windows CE devices.

To determine how many colors a device supports, use *GetDeviceCaps* as mentioned previously. The prototype for this function is the following:

```
int GetDeviceCaps (HDC hdc, int nIndex);
```

You need the handle to the DC being queried because different DCs have different capabilities. For example, a printer DC differs from a display DC. The second parameter indicates the capability being queried. In the case of returning the colors available on the device, the *NUMCOLORS* value returns the number of colors as long as the device supports 256 colors or fewer. Beyond that, the returned value for *NUMCOLORS* is −1 and the colors can be returned using the *BITSPIXEL* value, which returns the number of bits used to represent each pixel. This value can be converted to the number of colors by raising 2 to the power of the *BITSPIXEL* returned value, as in the following code sample:

```
nNumColors = GetDeviceCaps (hdc, NUMCOLORS);
if (nNumColors == -1)
    nNumColors = 1 << GetDeviceCaps (hdc, BITSPIXEL);
```

Text Alignment

When displaying text with *ExtTextOut*, the system uses the text alignment of the DC to determine where to draw the text. The text can be aligned both horizontally and vertically, using this function:

```
UINT WINAPI SetTextAlign (HDC hdc, INT fmode);
```

The alignment flags passed to *fmode* are as follows:

- **TA_LEFT** The left edge of the text is aligned with the reference point.

- **TA_RIGHT** The right edge of the text is aligned with the reference point.

- **TA_TOP** The top edge of the text is aligned with the reference point.

- **TA_CENTER** The text is centered horizontally with the reference point.

- **TA_BOTTOM** The bottom edge of the text is aligned with the reference point.

- **TA_BASELINE** The base line of the text is aligned with the reference point.

- **TA_NOUPDATECP** The current point of the DC is not updated after the *ExtTextOut* call.

- **TA_UPDATECP** The current point of the DC is updated after the *ExtTextOut* call.

The reference point in the description refers to the *x* and *y* coordinates passed to the *ExtTextOut* function. For each call to *SetTextAlign*, a flag for vertical alignment and a flag for horizontal alignment can be combined.

Because it might be difficult to visualize what each of these flags does, Figure 2-1 shows the results of each flag. In the figure, the *X* is the reference point.

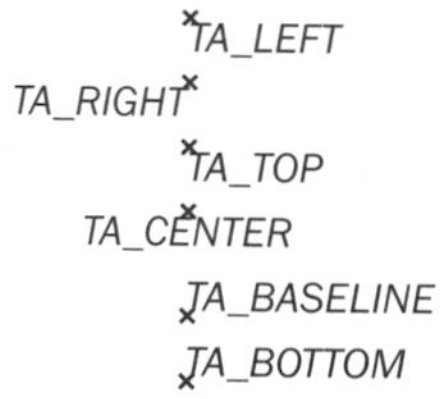

```
        ˣTA_LEFT
TA_RIGHTˣ
         ˣTA_TOP
TA_CЕNTER
         ₓTA_BASELINE
         ₓTA_BOTTOM
```

Figure 2-1 The relationship between the current drawing point and the text alignment flags

Drawing Mode

Another attribute that affects text output is the background mode. When letters are drawn on the device context, the system draws the letters themselves in the foreground color. The space between the letters is another matter. If the background mode is set to opaque, the space is drawn with the current background color. But if the background mode is set to transparent, the space between the letters is left in whatever state it was in before the text was drawn. While this might not seem like a big difference, imagine a window background filled with a drawing or graph. If text is written over the top of the graph and the background mode is set to opaque, the area around the text will be filled, and the background color will overwrite the graph. If the background mode is transparent, the text will appear as if it had been placed on the graph, and the graph will show through between the letters of the text.

The TextDemo Example Program

The TextDemo program, shown in Listing 2-1, demonstrates the relationships among the text color, the background color, and the background mode.

```
TextDemo.h
//======================================================================
// Header file
//
// Written for the book Programming Windows CE
// Copyright (C) 2003 Douglas Boling

//======================================================================
// Returns number of elements
#define dim(x) (sizeof(x) / sizeof(x[0]))


//----------------------------------------------------------------------
```

Listing 2-1 The TextDemo program

```
// Generic defines and data types
//
struct decodeUINT {                         // Structure associates
    UINT Code;                              // messages
                                            // with a function.
    LRESULT (*Fxn)(HWND, UINT, WPARAM, LPARAM);
};
struct decodeCMD {                          // Structure associates
    UINT Code;                              // menu IDs with a
    LRESULT (*Fxn)(HWND, WORD, HWND, WORD); // function.
};


//-----------------------------------------------------------------
// Function prototypes
//
HWND InitInstance (HINSTANCE, LPWSTR, int);
int TermInstance (HINSTANCE, int);

// Window procedures
LRESULT CALLBACK MainWndProc (HWND, UINT, WPARAM, LPARAM);

// Message handlers
LRESULT DoPaintMain (HWND, UINT, WPARAM, LPARAM);
LRESULT DoDestroyMain (HWND, UINT, WPARAM, LPARAM);
```

TextDemo.cpp

```
//=================================================================
// TextDemo - Text output demo
//
// Written for the book Programming Windows CE
// Copyright (C) 2003 Douglas Boling
//=================================================================
#include <windows.h>                        // For all that Windows stuff
#include "TextDemo.h"                        // Program-specific stuff


//-----------------------------------------------------------------
// Global data
//
const TCHAR szAppName[] = TEXT ("TextDemo");
HINSTANCE hInst;                            // Program instance handle

// Message dispatch table for MainWindowProc
const struct decodeUINT MainMessages[] = {
    WM_PAINT, DoPaintMain,
    WM_DESTROY, DoDestroyMain,
};
```

(continued)

Listing 2-1   *(continued)*

```c
//========================================================================
// Program Entry Point
//
int WINAPI WinMain (HINSTANCE hInstance, HINSTANCE hPrevInstance,
                    LPWSTR lpCmdLine, int nCmdShow) {
    MSG msg;
    int rc = 0;
    HWND hwndMain;

    // Initialize this instance.
    hwndMain = InitInstance (hInstance, lpCmdLine, nCmdShow);
    if (hwndMain == 0)
        return 0x10;

     // Application message loop
    while (GetMessage (&msg, NULL, 0, 0)) {
        TranslateMessage (&msg);
        DispatchMessage (&msg);
    }
    // Instance cleanup
    return TermInstance (hInstance, msg.wParam);
}
//------------------------------------------------------------------------
// InitInstance - Instance initialization
//
HWND InitInstance (HINSTANCE hInstance, LPWSTR lpCmdLine, int nCmdShow){
    WNDCLASS wc;
    HWND hWnd;

    hInst = hInstance;    // Save handle in global variable.

#if defined(WIN32_PLATFORM_PSPC)
    // If Pocket PC, allow only one instance of the application.
    hWnd = FindWindow (szAppName, NULL);
    if (hWnd) {
        SetForegroundWindow ((HWND)(((DWORD)hWnd) | 0x01));
        return 0;
    }
#endif
    // Register application main window class.
    wc.style = 0;                             // Window style
    wc.lpfnWndProc = MainWndProc;             // Callback function
    wc.cbClsExtra = 0;                        // Extra class data
    wc.cbWndExtra = 0;                        // Extra window data
    wc.hInstance = hInstance;                 // Owner handle
    wc.hIcon = NULL,                          // Application icon
```

```
    wc.hCursor = LoadCursor (NULL, IDC_ARROW);// Default cursor
    wc.hbrBackground = (HBRUSH) GetStockObject (WHITE_BRUSH);
    wc.lpszMenuName =  NULL;                   // Menu name
    wc.lpszClassName = szAppName;              // Window class name

    if (RegisterClass (&wc) == 0) return 0;

    // Create main window.
    hWnd = CreateWindowEx (WS_EX_NODRAG,       // Ex Style flags
                    szAppName,                 // Window class
                    TEXT("TextDemo"),          // Window title
                    // Style flags
                    WS_VISIBLE | WS_CAPTION | WS_SYSMENU,
                    CW_USEDEFAULT,             // x position
                    CW_USEDEFAULT,             // y position
                    CW_USEDEFAULT,             // Initial width
                    CW_USEDEFAULT,             // Initial height
                    NULL,                      // Parent
                    NULL,                      // Menu, must be null
                    hInstance,                 // Application instance
                    NULL);                     // Pointer to create
                                               // Parameters
    // Return fail code if window not created.
    if ((!hWnd) || (!IsWindow (hWnd))) return 0;

    // Standard show and update calls
    ShowWindow (hWnd, nCmdShow);
    UpdateWindow (hWnd);
    return hWnd;
}
//----------------------------------------------------------------------
// TermInstance - Program cleanup
//
int TermInstance (HINSTANCE hInstance, int nDefRC) {
    return nDefRC;
}
//======================================================================
// Message handling procedures for MainWindow
//
//----------------------------------------------------------------------
// MainWndProc - Callback function for application window
//
LRESULT CALLBACK MainWndProc (HWND hWnd, UINT wMsg, WPARAM wParam,
                        LPARAM lParam) {
    INT i;
    //
    // Search message list to see if we need to handle this
```

(continued)

Listing 2-1   *(continued)*

```
    // message.  If in list, call procedure.
    //
    for (i = 0; i < dim(MainMessages); i++) {
        if (wMsg == MainMessages[i].Code)
            return (*MainMessages[i].Fxn)(hWnd, wMsg, wParam, lParam);
    }
    return DefWindowProc (hWnd, wMsg, wParam, lParam);
}
//----------------------------------------------------------------------
// DoPaintMain - Process WM_PAINT message for window.
//
LRESULT DoPaintMain (HWND hWnd, UINT wMsg, WPARAM wParam,
                     LPARAM lParam) {
    PAINTSTRUCT ps;
    RECT rect, rectCli;
    HBRUSH hbrOld;
    HDC hdc;
    INT i, cy;
    DWORD dwColorTable[] = {0x00000000, 0x00808080,
                            0x00cccccc, 0x00ffffff};

    GetClientRect (hWnd, &rectCli);

    hdc = BeginPaint (hWnd, &ps);

    // Get the height and length of the string.
    DrawText (hdc, TEXT ("Hello Windows CE"), -1, &rect,
              DT_CALCRECT | DT_CENTER | DT_SINGLELINE);

    cy = rect.bottom - rect.top + 5;

    // Draw black rectangle on right half of window.
    hbrOld = (HBRUSH)SelectObject (hdc, GetStockObject (BLACK_BRUSH));
    Rectangle (hdc, rectCli.left + (rectCli.right - rectCli.left) / 2,
               rectCli.top, rectCli.right, rectCli.bottom);
    SelectObject (hdc, hbrOld);

    rectCli.bottom = rectCli.top + cy;
    SetBkMode (hdc, TRANSPARENT);
    for (i = 0; i < 4; i++) {
        SetTextColor (hdc, dwColorTable[i]);
        SetBkColor (hdc, dwColorTable[3-i]);

        DrawText (hdc, TEXT ("Hello Windows CE"), -1, &rectCli,
                  DT_CENTER | DT_SINGLELINE);
```

```
        rectCli.top += cy;
        rectCli.bottom += cy;
    }

    SetBkMode (hdc, OPAQUE);
    for (i = 0; i < 4; i++) {
        SetTextColor (hdc, dwColorTable[i]);
        SetBkColor (hdc, dwColorTable[3-i]);

        DrawText (hdc, TEXT ("Hello Windows CE"), -1, &rectCli,
                  DT_CENTER | DT_SINGLELINE);
        rectCli.top += cy;
        rectCli.bottom += cy;
    }
    EndPaint (hWnd, &ps);
    return 0;
}
//----------------------------------------------------------------
// DoDestroyMain - Process WM_DESTROY message for window.
//
LRESULT DoDestroyMain (HWND hWnd, UINT wMsg, WPARAM wParam,
                       LPARAM lParam) {
    PostQuitMessage (0);
    return 0;
}
```

The meat of TextDemo is in the *OnPaintMain* function. The first call to *DrawText* doesn't draw anything in the device context. Instead, the *DT_CALCRECT* flag instructs Windows to store the dimensions of the rectangle for the text string in *rect*. This information is used to compute the height of the string, which is stored in *cy*. Next, a black rectangle is drawn on the right side of the window. I'll talk about how a rectangle is drawn later in the chapter; it's used in this program to produce two different backgrounds before the text is written. The function then prints out the same string using different foreground and background colors and both the transparent and opaque drawing modes. The result of this combination is shown in Figure 2-2.

The first four lines are drawn using the transparent mode. The second four are drawn using the opaque mode. The text color is set from black to white so that each line drawn uses a different color, while at the same time the background color is set from white to black. In transparent mode, the background color is irrelevant because it isn't used; but in opaque mode, the background color is readily apparent on each line.

Figure 2-2   TextDemo shows how the text color, background color, and background mode relate.

Fonts

If the ability to set the foreground and background colors were all the flexibility that Windows provided, we might as well be back in the days of MS-DOS and character attributes. Arguably, the most dramatic change from MS-DOS is Windows' ability to change the font used to display text. All Windows operating systems are built around the concept of *WYSIWYG*—what you see is what you get—and changeable fonts are a major tool used to achieve that goal.

Two types of fonts appear in all Windows operating systems—*raster* and *TrueType*. Raster fonts are stored as bitmaps, small pixel-by-pixel images, one for each character in the font. Raster fonts are easy to store and use but have one major problem: they don't scale well. Just as a small picture looks grainy when blown up to a much larger size, raster fonts begin to look blocky as they are scaled to larger and larger font sizes.

TrueType fonts solve the scaling problem. Instead of being stored as images, each TrueType character is stored as a description of how to draw the character. The font engine, which is the part of Windows that draws characters on the screen, then takes the description and draws it on the screen in any size needed. A Windows CE system can support either TrueType or raster fonts, but not both. Fortunately, the programming interface is the same for both raster and TrueType fonts, relieving Windows developers from worrying about the font technology in all but the most exacting of applications.

The font functions under Windows CE closely track the same functions under other versions of Windows. Let's look at the functions used in the life of a font, from creation through selection in a DC and finally to deletion of the font. How to query the current font as well as enumerate the available fonts is also covered in the following sections.

Creating a Font

Before an application is able to use a font other than the default font, the font must be created and then selected into the device context. Any text drawn in a DC after the new font has been selected into the DC will then use the new font

Creating a font in Windows CE can be accomplished this way:

```
HFONT CreateFontIndirect (const LOGFONT *lplf);
```

This function is passed a pointer to a *LOGFONT* structure that must be filled with the description of the font you want.

```
typedef struct tagLOGFONT {
    LONG lfHeight;
    LONG lfWidth;
    LONG lfEscapement;
    LONG lfOrientation;
    LONG lfWeight;
    BYTE lfItalic;
    BYTE lfUnderline;
    BYTE lfStrikeOut;
    BYTE lfCharSet;
    BYTE lfOutPrecision;
    BYTE lfClipPrecision;
    BYTE lfQuality;
    BYTE lfPitchAndFamily;
    TCHAR lfFaceName[LF_FACESIZE];
} LOGFONT;
```

The *lfHeight* field specifies the height of the font in device units. If this field is 0, the font manager returns the default font size for the font family requested. For most applications, however, you want to create a font of a particular point size. The following equation can be used to convert point size to the *lfHeight* field:

lfHeight = –1 * (PointSize * GetDeviceCaps (hdc, LOGPIXELSY) / 72);

Here *GetDeviceCaps* is passed a *LOGPIXELSY* field instructing it to return the number of logical pixels per inch in the vertical direction. The 72 is the number of *points* (a typesetting unit of measure) per inch.

The *lfWidth* field specifies the average character width. Since the height of a font is more important than its width, most programs set this value to 0. This tells the font manager to compute the proper width based on the height of the font. The *lfEscapement* and *lfOrientation* fields specify the angle in tenths of degrees of the base line of the text and the x-axis. The *lfWeight* field specifies the boldness of the font from 0 through 1000, with 400 being a normal font and 700 being bold. The next three fields specify whether the font is to be italic, underline, or strikeout.

The *lpCharSet* field specifies the character set you have chosen. This field is more important in international releases of software, where it can be used to request a specific language's character set. The *lfOutPrecision* field can be used to specify how closely Windows matches your requested font. Among a number of flags available, an *OUT_TT_ONLY_PRECIS* flag specifies that the font created must be a TrueType font. The *lfClipPrecision* field specifies how Windows should clip characters that are partially outside the region being displayed.

The *lfQuality* field is set to one of the following:

- **DEFAULT_QUALITY**   Default system quality.

- **DRAFT_QUALITY**   Sacrifice quality for speed.

- **CLEARTYPE_QUALITY**   Render text using ClearType technology.

- **CLEARTYPE_COMPAT_QUALITY**   Render text using ClearType. Use the same spacing as non-ClearType font.

ClearType is a text display technology that provides a sharper look for fonts using the ability to address the individual red, green, and blue LEDs that make up a pixel on a color LCD display. Depending on the system, ClearType might not be supported or it might be enabled for all fonts in the system. For systems that support ClearType but don't enabled it globally, using the *CLEARTYPE_QUALITY* or *CLEARTYPE_COMPAT_QUALITY* flags will create a font that will be rendered using ClearType. Because ClearType doesn't improve the look of all fonts, you should test to see whether applying ClearType improves the rendering of your chosen font.

The *lfPitchAndFamily* field specifies the family of the font you want. This field is handy when you're requesting a family such as Swiss, which features proportional fonts without serifs, or a family such as Roman, which features proportional fonts with serifs, but you don't have a specific font in mind. You can also use this field to specify simply a proportional or a monospaced font and allow Windows to determine which font matches the other specified characteristics passed into the *LOGFONT* structure. Finally, the *lfFaceName* field can be used to specify the typeface name of a specific font.

When *CreateFontIndirect* is called with a filled *LOGFONT* structure, Windows creates a logical font that best matches the characteristics provided. To use the font, however, the final step of selecting the font into a device context must be made.

Selecting a Font into a Device Context

You select a font into a DC by using the following function:

```
HGDIOBJ SelectObject (HDC hdc, HGDIOBJ hgdiobj);
```

This function is used for more than just setting the default font; you use this function to select other GDI objects, as we shall soon see. The function returns the previously selected object (in our case, the previously selected font), which should be saved so that it can be selected back into the DC when we're finished with the new font. The line of code looks like the following:

```
hOldFont = (HFONT)SelectObject (hdc, hFont);
```

When the logical font is selected, the system determines the closest match to the logical font from the fonts available in the system. For devices without TrueType fonts, this match could be a fair amount off from the specified parameters. Because of this, never assume that just because you've requested a particular font, the font returned exactly matches the one you requested. For example, the height of the font you asked for might not be the height of the font that's selected into the device context.

Querying a Font's Characteristics

To determine the characteristics of the font that is selected into a device context, a call to

```
BOOL GetTextMetrics (HDC hdc, LPTEXTMETRIC lptm);
```

returns the characteristics of that font. A *TEXTMETRIC* structure is returned with the information and is defined as

```
typedef struct tagTEXTMETRIC {
    LONG tmHeight;
    LONG tmAscent;
    LONG tmDescent;
    LONG tmInternalLeading;
    LONG tmExternalLeading;
    LONG tmAveCharWidth;
    LONG tmMaxCharWidth;
    LONG tmWeight;
    LONG tmOverhang;
    LONG tmDigitizedAspectX;
    LONG tmDigitizedAspectY;
    char tmFirstChar;
    char tmLastChar;
    char tmDefaultChar;
    char tmBreakChar;
    BYTE tmItalic;
    BYTE tmUnderlined;
    BYTE tmStruckOut;
    BYTE tmPitchAndFamily;
    BYTE tmCharSet;
} TEXTMETRIC;
```

The *TEXTMETRIC* structure contains a number of the fields we saw in the *LOGFONT* structure, but this time the values listed in *TEXTMETRIC* are the values of the font that's selected into the device context. Figure 2-3 shows the relationship of some of the fields to actual characters.

Aside from determining whether you really got the font you wanted, the *GetTextmetrics* call has another valuable purpose—determining the height of the font. Recall that in TextDemo, the height of the line was computed using a call to *DrawText*. While that method is convenient, it tends to be slow. You can use the *TEXTMETRIC* data to compute this height in a much more straightforward manner. By adding the *tmHeight* field, which is the height of the characters, to the *tmExternalLeading* field, which is the distance between the bottom pixel of one row and the top pixel of the next row of characters, you can determine the vertical distance between the baselines of two lines of text.

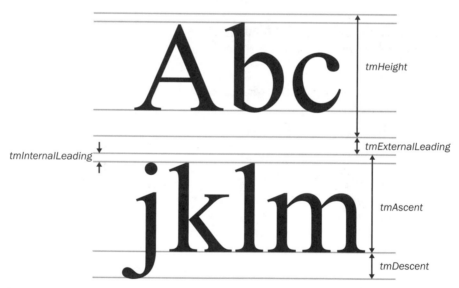

Figure 2-3   Fields from the *TEXTMETRIC* structure and how they relate to a font

Although *GetTextMetrics* is great for determining the height of a font, it provides only the average and maximum widths of a font. If more detail is needed for a TrueType font, the function

```
BOOL GetCharABCWidths (HDC hdc, UINT uFirstChar, UINT uLastChar,
                       LPABC lpabc);
```

can be used. *GetCharABCWidths* returns the "ABC" widths of a series of characters delineated by the *uFirstChar* and *uLastChar* parameters. The font examined is the font currently selected in the device context specified by the *hdc* parameter. The ABC structure is defined as follows:

```
typedef struct _ABC {
    int     abcA;
    UINT    abcB;
    int     abcC;
} ABC;
```

The *abcA* field is the distance to add to the current position before drawing the character, or *glyph*. The *abcB* field is the width of the glyph, while the *abcC* field is the distance to add to the current position after drawing the glyph. Both *abcA* and *abcC* can be negative to indicate underhangs and overhangs.

To examine the widths of bitmap fonts, *GetCharWidth32* can be used. It returns an array of character widths for each character in a range of characters.

Destroying a Font

Like other GDI resources, fonts must be destroyed after the program has finished using them. Failure to delete fonts before terminating a program causes what's known as a *resource leak*—an orphaned graphic resource that's taking up valuable memory but that's no longer owned by an application.

To destroy a font, first deselect it from any device contexts it has been selected into. You do this by calling *SelectObject*; the font passed is the font that was returned by the original *SelectObject* call made to select the font. After the font has been deselected, a call to

```
BOOL DeleteObject (HGDIOBJ hObject);
```

(with *hObject* containing the font handle) deletes the font from the system.

As you can see from this process, font management is no small matter in Windows. The many parameters of the *LOGFONT* structure might look daunting, but they give an application tremendous power to specify a font exactly.

One problem when dealing with fonts is determining just what types of fonts are available on a specific device. Windows CE devices come with a set of standard fonts, but a specific system might have been loaded with additional fonts by either the manufacturer or the user. Fortunately, Windows provides a method for enumerating all the available fonts in a system.

Enumerating Fonts

To determine what fonts are available on a system, Windows provides this function:

```
int EnumFontFamilies (HDC hdc, LPCTSTR lpszFamily,
                    FONTENUMPROC lpEnumFontFamProc, LPARAM lParam);
```

This function lets you list all the font families as well as each font within a family. The first parameter is the obligatory handle to the device context. The second parameter is a string to the name of the family to enumerate. If this parameter is null, the function enumerates each of the available families.

The third parameter is something different—a pointer to a function provided by the application. The function is a callback function that Windows calls once for each font being enumerated. The final parameter, *lParam*, is a generic parameter that can be used by the application. This value is passed unmodified to the application's callback procedure.

While the name of the callback function can be anything, the prototype of the callback must match the declaration:

```
int CALLBACK EnumFontFamProc (LOGFONT *lpelf, TEXTMETRIC *lpntm,
                              DWORD FontType, LPARAM lParam);
```

The first parameter passed back to the callback function is a pointer to a *LOGFONT* structure describing the font being enumerated. The second parameter, a pointer to a textmetric structure, further describes the font. The font type parameter indicates whether the font is a raster or TrueType font.

The FontList Example Program

The FontList program, shown in Listing 2-2, uses the *EnumFontFamilies* function in two ways to enumerate all fonts in the system.

```
FontList.h
//======================================================================
// Header file
//
// Written for the book Programming Windows CE
// Copyright (C) 2003 Douglas Boling
//======================================================================
// Returns number of elements
#define dim(x) (sizeof(x) / sizeof(x[0]))
//----------------------------------------------------------------------
// Generic defines and data types
//
struct decodeUINT {                                 // Structure associates
    UINT Code;                                      // messages
                                                    // with a function.
    LRESULT (*Fxn)(HWND, UINT, WPARAM, LPARAM);
};
struct decodeCMD {                                  // Structure associates
    UINT Code;                                      // menu IDs with a
    LRESULT (*Fxn)(HWND, WORD, HWND, WORD);         // function.
};
```

Listing 2-2   The FontList program enumerates all fonts in the system.

```
//-----------------------------------------------------------------
// Program-specific structures
//
#define FAMILYMAX   24
typedef struct {
    int nNumFonts;
    TCHAR szFontFamily[LF_FACESIZE];
} FONTFAMSTRUCT;
typedef FONTFAMSTRUCT *PFONTFAMSTRUCT;

typedef struct {
    INT yCurrent;
    HDC hdc;
} PAINTFONTINFO;
typedef PAINTFONTINFO *PPAINTFONTINFO;


//-----------------------------------------------------------------
// Function prototypes
//
HWND InitInstance (HINSTANCE, LPWSTR, int);
int TermInstance (HINSTANCE, int);

// Window procedures
LRESULT CALLBACK MainWndProc (HWND, UINT, WPARAM, LPARAM);

// Message handlers
LRESULT DoCreateMain (HWND, UINT, WPARAM, LPARAM);
LRESULT DoPaintMain (HWND, UINT, WPARAM, LPARAM);
LRESULT DoDestroyMain (HWND, UINT, WPARAM, LPARAM);
```

FontList.cpp

```
//=================================================================
// FontList - Lists the available fonts in the system
//
// Written for the book Programming Windows CE
// Copyright (C) 2003 Douglas Boling
//=================================================================
#include <windows.h>                   // For all that Windows stuff
#include "FontList.h"                  // Program-specific stuff


//-----------------------------------------------------------------
// Global data
//
const TCHAR szAppName[] = TEXT ("FontList");
HINSTANCE hInst;                       // Program instance handle
```

(continued)

Listing 2-2   *(continued)*

```
FONTFAMSTRUCT ffs[FAMILYMAX];
INT sFamilyCnt = 0;

// Message dispatch table for MainWindowProc
const struct decodeUINT MainMessages[] = {
    WM_CREATE, DoCreateMain,
    WM_PAINT, DoPaintMain,
    WM_DESTROY, DoDestroyMain,
};


//======================================================================
// Program entry point
//
int WINAPI WinMain (HINSTANCE hInstance, HINSTANCE hPrevInstance,
                    LPWSTR lpCmdLine, int nCmdShow) {
    MSG msg;
    int rc = 0;
    HWND hwndMain;

    // Initialize this instance.
    hwndMain = InitInstance (hInstance, lpCmdLine, nCmdShow);
    if (hwndMain == 0)
        return 0x10;
    // Application message loop
    while (GetMessage (&msg, NULL, 0, 0)) {
        TranslateMessage (&msg);
        DispatchMessage (&msg);
    }
    // Instance cleanup
    return TermInstance (hInstance, msg.wParam);
}
//----------------------------------------------------------------------
// InitInstance - Instance initialization
//
HWND InitInstance (HINSTANCE hInstance, LPWSTR lpCmdLine, int nCmdShow) {
    WNDCLASS wc;
    HWND hWnd;

    // Save program instance handle in global variable.
    hInst = hInstance;

#if defined(WIN32_PLATFORM_PSPC)
    // If Pocket PC, allow only one instance of the application.
    hWnd = FindWindow (szAppName, NULL);
    if (hWnd) {
        SetForegroundWindow ((HWND)(((DWORD)hWnd) | 0x01));
        return 0;
    }
```

```
#endif
    // Register application main window class.
    wc.style = 0;                               // Window style
    wc.lpfnWndProc = MainWndProc;               // Callback function
    wc.cbClsExtra = 0;                          // Extra class data
    wc.cbWndExtra = 0;                          // Extra window data
    wc.hInstance = hInstance;                   // Owner handle
    wc.hIcon = NULL,                            // Application icon
    wc.hCursor = LoadCursor (NULL, IDC_ARROW);// Default cursor
    wc.hbrBackground = (HBRUSH) GetStockObject(WHITE_BRUSH);
    wc.lpszMenuName =  NULL;                    // Menu name
    wc.lpszClassName = szAppName;               // Window class name

    if (RegisterClass (&wc) == 0) return 0;


    // Create main window.
    hWnd = CreateWindowEx (WS_EX_NODRAG,        // Ex style flags
                    szAppName,                  // Window class
                    TEXT("Font Listing"),// Window title
                    // Style flags
                    WS_VISIBLE | WS_CAPTION | WS_SYSMENU,
                    CW_USEDEFAULT,              // x position
                    CW_USEDEFAULT,              // y position
                    CW_USEDEFAULT,              // Initial width
                    CW_USEDEFAULT,              // Initial height
                    NULL,                       // Parent
                    NULL,                       // Menu, must be null
                    hInstance,                  // Application instance
                    NULL);                      // Pointer to create
                                                // parameters
    // Return fail code if window not created.
    if (!IsWindow (hWnd)) return 0;


    // Standard show and update calls
    ShowWindow (hWnd, nCmdShow);
    UpdateWindow (hWnd);
    return hWnd;
}
//-------------------------------------------------------------------
// TermInstance - Program cleanup
//
int TermInstance (HINSTANCE hInstance, int nDefRC) {
    return nDefRC;
}
//===================================================================
// Font callback functions
//
//-------------------------------------------------------------------
```

(continued)

Listing 2-2   *(continued)*

```
// FontFamilyCallback - Callback function that enumerates the font
// families
//
int CALLBACK FontFamilyCallback (CONST LOGFONT *lplf,
                                 CONST TEXTMETRIC *lpntm,
                                 DWORD nFontType, LPARAM lParam) {
    int rc = 1;

    // Stop enumeration if array filled.
    if (sFamilyCnt >= FAMILYMAX)
        return 0;
    // Copy face name of font.
    lstrcpy (ffs[sFamilyCnt++].szFontFamily, lplf->lfFaceName);
    return rc;
}
//---------------------------------------------------------------------
// EnumSingleFontFamily - Callback function that enumerates fonts
//
int CALLBACK EnumSingleFontFamily (CONST LOGFONT *lplf,
                                   CONST TEXTMETRIC *lpntm,
                                   DWORD nFontType, LPARAM lParam) {
    PFONTFAMSTRUCT pffs;

    pffs = (PFONTFAMSTRUCT) lParam;
    pffs->nNumFonts++;     // Increment count of fonts in family
    return 1;
}

//---------------------------------------------------------------------
// PaintSingleFontFamily - Callback function that draws a font
//
int CALLBACK PaintSingleFontFamily (CONST LOGFONT *lplf,
                                    CONST TEXTMETRIC *lpntm,
                                    DWORD nFontType, LPARAM lParam) {
    PPAINTFONTINFO ppfi;
    TCHAR szOut[256];
    INT nFontHeight, nPointSize;
    HFONT hFont, hOldFont;

    ppfi = (PPAINTFONTINFO) lParam;  // Translate lParam into struct
                                     // pointer.

    // Create the font from the LOGFONT structure passed.
    hFont = CreateFontIndirect (lplf);

    // Select the font into the device context.
    hOldFont = (HFONT)SelectObject (ppfi->hdc, hFont);
```

```
    // Compute font size.
    nPointSize = (lplf->lfHeight * 72) /
                GetDeviceCaps(ppfi->hdc,LOGPIXELSY);


    // Format string and paint on display.
    wsprintf (szOut, TEXT ("%s    Point:%d"), lplf->lfFaceName,
            nPointSize);
    ExtTextOut (ppfi->hdc, 25, ppfi->yCurrent, 0, NULL,
            szOut, lstrlen (szOut), NULL);


    // Compute the height of the default font.
    nFontHeight = lpntm->tmHeight + lpntm->tmExternalLeading;
    // Update new draw point.
    ppfi->yCurrent += nFontHeight;
    // Deselect font and delete.
    SelectObject (ppfi->hdc, hOldFont);
    DeleteObject (hFont);
    return 1;
}
//===================================================================
// Message handling procedures for MainWindow
//
//-------------------------------------------------------------------
// MainWndProc   Callback function for application window
//
LRESULT CALLBACK MainWndProc (HWND hWnd, UINT wMsg, WPARAM wParam,
                            LPARAM lParam) {
    INT i;
    //
    // Search message list to see if we need to handle this
    // message.  If in list, call procedure.
    //
    for (i = 0; i < dim(MainMessages); i++) {
        if (wMsg == MainMessages[i].Code)
            return (*MainMessages[i].Fxn)(hWnd, wMsg, wParam, lParam);
    }
    return DefWindowProc (hWnd, wMsg, wParam, lParam);
}
//-------------------------------------------------------------------
// DoCreateMain - Process WM_CREATE message for window.
//
LRESULT DoCreateMain (HWND hWnd, UINT wMsg, WPARAM wParam,
                    LPARAM lParam) {
    HDC hdc;
    INT i, rc;

    //Enumerate the available fonts.
    hdc = GetDC (hWnd);
```

(continued)

Listing 2-2 *(continued)*

```
    rc = EnumFontFamilies ((HDC)hdc, (LPTSTR)NULL,
        FontFamilyCallback, 0);

    for (i = 0; i < sFamilyCnt; i++) {
        ffs[i].nNumFonts = 0;
        rc = EnumFontFamilies ((HDC)hdc, ffs[i].szFontFamily,
                               EnumSingleFontFamily,
                               (LPARAM)(PFONTFAMSTRUCT)&ffs[i]);
    }
    ReleaseDC (hWnd, hdc);
    return 0;
}
//-----------------------------------------------------------------
// DoPaintMain - Process WM_PAINT message for window.
//
LRESULT DoPaintMain (HWND hWnd, UINT wMsg, WPARAM wParam,
                     LPARAM lParam) {
    PAINTSTRUCT ps;
    RECT rect;
    HDC hdc;
    TEXTMETRIC tm;
    INT nFontHeight, i;
    TCHAR szOut[256];
    PAINTFONTINFO pfi;

    GetClientRect (hWnd, &rect);

    hdc = BeginPaint (hWnd, &ps);

    // Get the height of the default font.
    GetTextMetrics (hdc, &tm);
    nFontHeight = tm.tmHeight + tm.tmExternalLeading;

    // Initialize struct that is passed to enumerate function.
    pfi.yCurrent = rect.top;
    pfi.hdc = hdc;
    for (i = 0; i < sFamilyCnt; i++) {

        // Format output string, and paint font family name.
        wsprintf (szOut, TEXT("Family: %s    "),
                  ffs[i].szFontFamily);
        ExtTextOut (hdc, 5, pfi.yCurrent, 0, NULL,
                    szOut, lstrlen (szOut), NULL);
        pfi.yCurrent += nFontHeight;

        // Enumerate each family to draw a sample of that font.
        EnumFontFamilies ((HDC)hdc, ffs[i].szFontFamily,
```

```
                            PaintSingleFontFamily,
                            (LPARAM)&pfi);
    }
    EndPaint (hWnd, &ps);
    return 0;
}
//------------------------------------------------------------------
// DoDestroyMain - Process WM_DESTROY message for window.
//
LRESULT DoDestroyMain (HWND hWnd, UINT wMsg, WPARAM wParam,
                       LPARAM lParam) {
    PostQuitMessage (0);
    return 0;
}
```

Enumerating the different fonts begins when the application is processing the *WM_CREATE* message in *OnCreateMain*. Here *EnumFontFamilies* is called with the *FontFamily* field set to *NULL* so that each family will be enumerated. The callback function is *FontFamilyCallback*, where the name of the font family is copied into an array of strings.

The remainder of the work is performed during the processing of the *WM_PAINT* message. The *OnPaintMain* function begins with the standard litany of getting the size of the client area and calling *BeginPaint*, which returns the handle to the device context of the window. *GetTextMetrics* is then called to compute the row height of the default font. A loop is then entered in which *EnumerateFontFamilies* is called for each family name that had been stored during the enumeration process in *OnCreateMain*. The callback process for this callback sequence is somewhat more complex than the code we've seen so far.

The *PaintSingleFontFamily* callback procedure, used in the enumeration of the individual fonts, employs the *lParam* parameter to retrieve a pointer to a *PAINTFONTINFO* structure defined in FontList.h. This structure contains the current vertical drawing position as well as the handle to the device context. By using the *lParam* pointer, FontList avoids having to declare global variables to communicate with the callback procedure.

The callback procedure next creates the font using the pointer to *LOGFONT* that was passed to the callback procedure. The new font is then selected into the device context, while the handle to the previously selected font is retained in *hOldFont*. The point size of the enumerated font is computed using the inverse of the equation mentioned earlier in the chapter. The callback procedure then produces a line of text showing the name of the font family along with the point size of this particular font. Instead of using *DrawText*, the callback uses *ExtTextOut* to draw the string.

After displaying the text, the function computes the height of the line of text just drawn using the combination of *tmHeight* and *tmExternalLeading* that was provided in the passed *TEXTMETRIC* structure. The new font is then deselected using a second call to *SelectObject*, this time passing the handle to the font that was the original selected font. The new font is then deleted using *DeleteObject*. Finally, the callback function returns a nonzero value to indicate to Windows that it is okay to make another call to the *enumerate* callback.

Figure 2-4 shows the Font Listing window. Notice that the font names are displayed in that font and that each font has a specific set of available sizes.

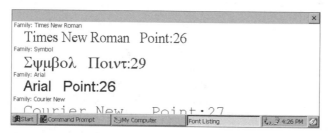

Figure 2-4   The Font Listing window shows some of the available fonts for a Handheld PC.

Unfinished Business

If you look closely at Figure 2-4, you'll notice a problem with the display. The list of fonts just runs off the bottom edge of the Font Listing window. The solution for this problem is to add a scroll bar to the window. Since I'll provide a complete explanation of window controls, including scroll bars, in Chapter 4, I'll hold off describing how to properly implement the solution until then.

Bitmaps

Bitmaps are graphical objects that can be used to create, draw, manipulate, and retrieve images in a device context. Bitmaps are everywhere within Windows, from the little Windows logo on the Start button to the Close button on the title bar. Think of a bitmap as a picture composed of an array of pixels that can be painted onto the screen. Like any picture, a bitmap has height and width. It also has a method for determining what color or colors it uses. Finally, a bitmap has an array of bits that describe each pixel in the bitmap.

Historically, bitmaps under Windows have been divided into two types; *device-dependent bitmaps* (DDBs) and *device-independent bitmaps* (DIBs). DDBs are bitmaps that are tied to the characteristics of a specific DC and can't easily be rendered on DCs with different characteristics. DIBs, on the other hand, are independent of any device and therefore must carry around enough information so that they can be rendered accurately on any device.

Windows CE contains many of the bitmap functions available in other versions of Windows. The differences include a new four-color bitmap format not supported anywhere but on Windows CE and a different method for manipulating DIBs.

Device-Dependent Bitmaps

A device-dependent bitmap can be created with this function:

```
HBITMAP CreateBitmap (int nWidth, int nHeight, UINT cPlanes,
                 UINT cBitsPerPel, CONST VOID *lpvBits);
```

The *nWidth* and *nHeight* parameters indicate the dimensions of the bitmap. The *cPlanes* parameter is a historical artifact from the days when display hardware implemented each color within a pixel in a different hardware plane. For Windows CE, this parameter must be set to 1. The *cBitspPerPel* parameter indicates the number of bits used to describe each pixel. The number of colors is 2 to the power of the *cBitspPerPel* parameter. Under Windows CE, the allowable values are 1, 2, 4, 8, 16, and 24. As I said, the four-color bitmap is unique to Windows CE and isn't supported under other Windows platforms.

The final parameter is a pointer to the bits of the bitmap. Under Windows CE, the bits are always arranged in a packed pixel format; that is, each pixel is stored as a series of bits within a byte, with the next pixel starting immediately after the first. The first pixel in the array of bits is the pixel located in the upper left corner of the bitmap. The bits continue across the top row of the bitmap, then across the second row, and so on. Each row of the bitmap must be double-word (4-byte) aligned. If any pad bytes are required at the end of a row to align the start of the next row, they should be set to 0. Figure 2-5 illustrates this scheme, showing a 126-by-64-pixel bitmap with 8 bits per pixel.

The function

```
HBITMAP CreateCompatibleBitmap (HDC hdc, int nWidth, int nHeight);
```

creates a bitmap whose format is compatible with the device context passed to the function. So if the device context is a four-color DC, the resulting bitmap is a four-color bitmap as well. This function comes in handy when you're manipulating images on the screen because it makes it easy to produce a blank bitmap that's directly color compatible with the screen.

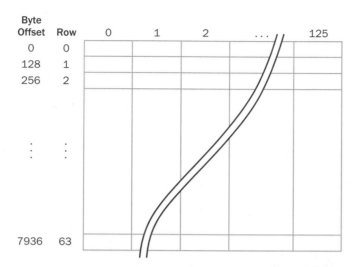

Figure 2-5   Layout of bytes within a bitmap

Device-Independent Bitmaps

The fundamental difference between DIBs and their device-dependent cousins is that the image stored in a DIB comes with its own color information. Almost every bitmap file since Windows 3.0, which used the files with the BMP extension, contains information that can be directly matched with the information needed to create a DIB in Windows.

In the early days of Windows, it was a rite of passage for a programmer to write a routine that manually read a DIB file and converted the data to a bitmap. These days, the same arduous task can be accomplished with the following function, unique to Windows CE:

```
HBITMAP SHLoadDIBitmap (LPCTSTR szFileName);
```

It loads a bitmap directly from a bitmap file and provides a handle to the bitmap. In Windows XP the same process can be accomplished with *LoadImage* using the *LR_LOADFROMFILE* flag, but this flag isn't supported under the Windows CE implementation of *LoadImage*.

DIB Sections

While Windows CE makes it easy to load a bitmap file, sometimes you must read what is on the screen, manipulate it, and redraw the image back to the screen. This is another case in which DIBs are better than DDBs. While the bits of a device-dependent bitmap are obtainable, the format of the buffer is directly dependent on the screen format. By using a DIB, or more precisely, something called a DIB section, your program can read the bitmap into a buffer that has a predefined format without worrying about the format of the display device.

While Windows has a number of DIB creation functions that have been added over the years since Windows 3.0, Windows CE carries over only a handful of DIB functions from Windows XP. Here is the first of these functions:

```
HBITMAP CreateDIBSection (HDC hdc, const BITMAPINFO *pbmi,
                          UINT iUsage, void *ppvBits,
                          HANDLE hSection, DWORD dwOffset);
```

Because they're a rather late addition to the Win32 API, DIB sections might be new to Windows programmers. DIB sections were invented to improve the performance of applications on Windows NT that directly manipulated bitmaps. In short, a DIB section allows a programmer to select a DIB in a device context while still maintaining direct access to the bits that compose the bitmap. To achieve this, a DIB section associates a memory DC with a buffer that also contains the bits of that DC. Because the image is mapped to a DC, other graphics calls can be made to modify the image. At the same time, the raw bits of the DC, in DIB format, are available for direct manipulation. While the improved performance is all well and good on Windows NT, the relevance to the Windows CE programmer is the ease with which an application can work with bitmaps and manipulate their contents.

This call's parameters lead with the pointer to a *BITMAPINFO* structure. The structure describes the layout and color composition of a device-independent bitmap and is a combination of a *BITMAPINFOHEADER* structure and an array of *RGBQUAD* values that represent the palette of colors used by the bitmap.

The *BITMAPINFOHEADER* structure is defined as the following:

```
typedef struct tagBITMAPINFOHEADER{
    DWORD biSize;
    LONG biWidth;
    LONG biHeight;
    WORD biPlanes;
    WORD biBitCount;
    DWORD biCompression;
    DWORD biSizeImage;
    LONG biXPelsPerMeter;
    LONG biYPelsPerMeter;
    DWORD biClrUsed;
    DWORD biClrImportant;
} BITMAPINFOHEADER;
```

As you can see, this structure contains much more information than just the parameters passed to *CreateBitmap*. The first field is the size of the structure and must be filled in by the calling program to differentiate this structure from the similar *BITMAPCOREINFOHEADER* structure that's a holdover from the OS/2 presentation manager. The *biWidth*, *biHeight*, *biPlanes*, and *biBitCount* fields are similar to their like-named parameters to the *CreateBitmap* call—with one exception. The sign of the *biHeight* field specifies the organization of the bit array. If *biHeight* is negative, the bit array is organized in a top-down format, as is *CreateBitmap*. If *biHeight* is positive, the array is organized in a bottom-up format, in which the bottom row of the bitmap is defined by the first bits in the array. As with the *CreateBitmap* call, the *biPlanes* field must be set to 1.

The *biCompression* field specifies the compression method used in the bit array. Under Windows CE, the allowable flags for this field are *BI_RGB*, indicating that the buffer isn't compressed, and *BI_BITFIELDS*, indicating that the pixel format is specified in the first three entries in the color table. The *biSizeImage* parameter is used to indicate the size of the bit array; when used with *BI_RGB*, however, the *biSizeImage* field can be set to 0, which means that the array size is computed using the dimensions and bits per pixel information provided in the *BITMAPINFOHEADER* structure.

The *biXPelsPerMeter* and *biYPelsPerMeter* fields provide information to accurately scale the image. For *CreateDIBSection*, however, these parameters can be set to 0. The *biClrUsed* parameter specifies the number of colors in the palette that are actually used. In a 256-color image, the palette will have 256 entries, but the bitmap itself might need only 100 or so distinct colors. This field helps the palette manager, the part of Windows that manages color matching, to match the colors in the system palette with the colors required by the bitmap. The *biClrImportant* field further defines the colors that are *really* required as opposed to those that are used. For most color bitmaps, these two fields are set to 0, indicating that all colors are used and that all colors are important.

As I mentioned above, an array of *RGBQUAD* structures immediately follows the *BITMAPINFOHEADER* structure. The *RGBQUAD* structure is defined as follows:

```
typedef struct tagRGBQUAD { /* rgbq */
    BYTE rgbBlue;
    BYTE rgbGreen;
    BYTE rgbRed;
    BYTE rgbReserved;
} RGBQUAD;
```

This structure allows for 256 shades of red, green, and blue. While almost any shade of color can be created using this structure, the color that's actually rendered on the device will, of course, be limited by what the device can display.

The array of *RGBQUAD* structures, taken as a whole, describe the palette of the DIB. The palette is the list of colors in the bitmap. If a bitmap has a palette, each entry in the bitmap array contains not colors, but an index into the palette that contains the color for that pixel. While redundant on a monochrome bitmap, the palette is quite important when rendering color bitmaps on color devices. For example, a 256-color bitmap has one byte for each pixel, but that byte points to a 24-bit value that represents equal parts red, green, and blue colors. So while a 256-color bitmap can contain only 256 distinct colors, each of those colors can be one of 16 million colors rendered using the 24-bit palette entry. For convenience in a 32-bit world, each palette entry, while containing only 24 bits of color information, is padded out to a 32-bit-wide entry—hence the name of the data type: *RGBQUAD*.

Of the remaining four *CreateDIBSection* parameters, only two are used under Windows CE. The *iUsage* parameter indicates how the colors in the palette are represented. If the parameter is *DIB_RGB_COLORS*, the bits in the bitmap contain the full RGB color information for each pixel. If the parameter is *DIB_PAL_COLORS*, the bitmap pixels contain indexes into the palette currently selected in the DC. The *ppvBits* parameter is a pointer to a variable that receives the pointer to the bitmap bits that compose the bitmap image. The final two parameters, *hSection* and *dwOffset*, aren't supported under Windows CE and must be set to 0. In other versions of Windows, they allow the bitmap bits to be specified by a memory-mapped file. While Windows CE does support memory-mapped files, they aren't supported by *CreateDIBSection*.

Two functions exist to manage the palette of the DIB, as follows:

```
UINT GetDIBColorTable (HDC hdc, UINT uStartIndex,
                       UINT cEntries, RGBQUAD *pColors);
```

and

```
UINT SetDIBColorTable (HDC hdc, UINT uStartIndex,
                       UINT cEntries, RGBQUAD *pColors);
```

For both of these functions, *uStartIndex* indicates the first entry into the palette array to set or query. The *cEntries* parameter indicates how many palette entries to change. The pointer to the *RGBQUAD* array is the array of colors either being set, for *SetDIBColorTable*, or queried, for *GetDIBColorTable*.

Drawing Bitmaps

Creating and loading bitmaps is all well and good, but there's not much point to it unless the bitmaps you create can be rendered on the screen. Drawing a bitmap isn't as straightforward as you might think. Before a bitmap can be drawn in a screen DC, it must be selected into a DC and then copied over to the screen device context. While this process sounds convoluted, there is rhyme to this reason.

The process of selecting a bitmap into a device context is similar to selecting a logical font into a device context; it converts the ideal to the actual. Just as Windows finds the best possible match to a requested font, the bitmap selection process must match the available colors of the device to the colors requested by a bitmap. Only after this is done can the bitmap be rendered on the screen. To help with this intermediate step, Windows provides a shadow type of DC, a *memory device context*.

To create a memory device context, use this function:

```
HDC CreateCompatibleDC (HDC hdc);
```

This function creates a memory DC that's compatible with the current screen DC. Once created, the source bitmap is selected into this memory DC using the same *SelectObject* function you used to select a logical font. Finally, the bitmap is copied from the memory DC to the screen DC using one of the bit functions, *BitBlt* or *StretchBlt*.

The workhorse of bitmap functions is the following:

```
BOOL BitBlt (HDC hdcDest, int nXDest, int nYDest, int nWidth,
             int nHeight, HDC hdcSrc, int nXSrc,  int nYSrc,
             DWORD dwRop);
```

Fundamentally, the *BitBlt* function, pronounced *bit blit*, is just a fancy *memcopy* function, but since it operates on device contexts, not memory, it's something far more special. The first parameter is a handle to the destination device context—the DC to which the bitmap is to be copied. The next four parameters specify the location and size of the destination rectangle where the bitmap is to end up. The next three parameters specify the handle to the source device context and the location within that DC of the upper left corner of the source image.

The final parameter, *dwRop*, specifies how the image is to be copied from the source to the destination device contexts. The ROP code defines how the source bitmap and the current destination are combined to produce the final image. The ROP code for a simple copy of the source image is *SRCCOPY*. The ROP code for combining the source image with the current destination is *SRC-PAINT*. Copying a logically inverted image, essentially a negative of the source image, is accomplished using *SRCINVERT*. Some ROP codes also combine the currently selected brush into the equation to compute the resulting image. A large number of ROP codes are available, too many for me to cover here. For a complete list, check out the Windows CE programming documentation.

The following code fragment sums up how to paint a bitmap:

```
// Create a DC that matches the device.
hdcMem = CreateCompatibleDC (hdc);

// Select the bitmap into the compatible device context.
hOldSel = SelectObject (hdcMem, hBitmap);

// Get the bitmap dimensions from the bitmap.
GetObject (hBitmap, sizeof (BITMAP), &bmp);

// Copy the bitmap image from the memory DC to the screen DC.
BitBlt (hdc, rect.left, rect.top, bmp.bmWidth, bmp.bmHeight,
        hdcMem, 0, 0, SRCCOPY);

// Restore original bitmap selection and destroy the memory DC.
SelectObject (hdcMem, hOldSel);
DeleteDC (hdcMem);
```

The memory device context is created, and the bitmap to be painted is selected into that DC. Since you might not have stored the dimensions of the bitmap to be painted, the routine makes a call to *GetObject*. *GetObject* returns information about a graphics object, in this case, a bitmap. Information about fonts and other graphic objects can be queried using this useful function. Next, *BitBlt* is used to copy the bitmap into the screen DC. To clean up, the bitmap is deselected from the memory device context and the memory DC is deleted using *DeleteDC*. Don't confuse *DeleteDC* with *ReleaseDC*, which is used to free a display DC. *DeleteDC* should be paired only with *CreateCompatibleDC*, and *ReleaseDC* should be paired only with *GetDC* or *GetWindowDC*.

Instead of merely copying the bitmap, stretch or shrink it using this function:

```
BOOL StretchBlt (HDC hdcDest, int nXOriginDest, int nYOriginDest,
                 int nWidthDest, int nHeightDest, HDC hdcSrc,
                 int nXOriginSrc, int nYOriginSrc, int nWidthSrc,
                 int nHeightSrc, DWORD dwRop);
```

The parameters in *StretchBlt* are the same as those used in *BitBlt*, with the exception that now the width and height of the source image can be specified. Here again, the ROP codes specify how the source and destination are combined to produce the final image.

Windows CE also has another bitmap function. It is

```
BOOL TransparentImage (HDC hdcDest, LONG DstX, LONG DstY, LONG DstCx,
                       LONG DstCy, HANDLE hSrc, LONG SrcX, LONG SrcY,
                       LONG SrcCx, LONG SrcCy, COLORREF TransparentColor);
```

This function is similar to *StretchBlt*, with two very important exceptions. First, you can specify a color in the bitmap to be the transparent color. When the bitmap is copied to the destination, the pixels in the bitmap that are the transparent color are not copied. The second difference is that the *hSrc* parameter can be either a device context or a handle to a bitmap, which allows you to bypass the requirement to select the source image into a device context before rendering it on the screen. *TransparentImage* is essentially the same function as Windows 2000's *TransparentBlt* function with the exception that *TransparentBlt* can't directly use a bitmap as the source.

As in other versions of Windows, Windows CE supports two other blit functions: *PatBlt* and *MaskBlt*. The *PatBlt* function combines the currently selected brush with the current image in the destination DC to produce the resulting image. I cover brushes later in this chapter. The *MaskBlt* function is similar to *BitBlt* but encompasses a masking image that provides the ability to draw only a portion of the source image onto the destination DC.

Lines and Shapes

One of the areas in which Windows CE provides substantially less functionality than other versions of Windows is in the primitive line-drawing and shape-drawing functions. Gone are the *Chord*, *Arc*, and *Pie* functions that created complex circular shapes. Gone too are most of the functions using the concept of *current point*. Other than *MoveToEx*, *LineTo*, and *GetCurrentPositionEx*, none of the GDI functions dealing with current point are supported in Windows CE. So drawing a series of connected lines and curves using calls to *ArcTo*, *PolyBezierTo*, and so forth is no longer possible. But even with the loss of a number of graphic functions, Windows CE still provides the essential functions necessary to draw lines and shapes.

Lines

Drawing one or more lines is as simple as a call to

```
BOOL Polyline (HDC hdc, const POINT *lppt, int cPoints);
```

The second parameter is a pointer to an array of *POINT* structures that are defined as the following:

```
typedef struct tagPOINT {
    LONG x;
    LONG y;
} POINT;
```

Each *x* and *y* combination describes a pixel from the upper left corner of the screen. The third parameter is the number of point structures in the array. So to draw a line from (0, 0) to (50, 100), the code would look like this:

```
POINTS pts[2];

pts[0].x = 0;
pts[0].y = 0;
pts[1].x = 50;
pts[1].y = 100;
PolyLine (hdc, &pts, 2);
```

Another way to draw the same line would be to use the *MoveToEx* and *LineTo* functions. They are prototyped as follows:

```
BOOL WINAPI MoveToEx (HDC hdc, int X, int Y, LPPOINT lpPoint);
BOOL WINAPI LineTo (HDC hdc, int X, int Y);
```

To use the functions to draw a line, first call *MoveToEx* to move the current point to the starting coordinates of the line, and then call *LineTo*, passing the ending coordinates. The calls to draw the same line as before using these functions would be as follows:

```
MoveToEx (hdc, 0, 0, NULL);
LineTo (hdc, 50, 100);
```

To query the current point, call the following function:

```
WINGDIAPI BOOL WINAPI GetCurrentPositionEx (HDC hdc, LPPOINT pPoint);
```

Just as in the early text examples, these code fragments make a number of assumptions about the default state of the device context. For example, just what does the line drawn between (0, 0) and (50, 100) look like? What is its width and its color, and is it a solid line? All versions of Windows, including Windows CE, allow these parameters to be specified.

Pens

The tool for specifying the appearance of lines and the outline of shapes is called, appropriately enough, a *pen*. A pen is another GDI object and, like the others described in this chapter, is created, selected into a device context, used, deselected, and then destroyed. Among other stock GDI objects, stock pens can be retrieved using the following code:

```
HGDIOBJ GetStockObject (int fnObject);
```

All versions of Windows provide three stock pens, each 1 pixel wide. The stock pens come in 3 colors: white, black, and null. When you use *GetStockObject*, the call to retrieve one of those pens employs the parameters *WHITE_PEN*,

BLACK_PEN, and *NULL_PEN* respectively. Unlike standard graphic objects created by applications, stock objects should never be deleted by the application. Instead, the application should simply deselect the pen from the device context when it's no longer needed.

To create a custom pen under Windows, two functions are available. The first is this:

```
HPEN CreatePen (int fnPenStyle, int nWidth, COLORREF crColor);
```

The *fnPenStyle* parameter specifies the appearance of the line to be drawn. For example, the *PS_DASH* flag can be used to create a dashed line. Windows CE supports only *PS_SOLID*, *PS_DASH*, and *PS_NULL* style flags. The *nWidth* parameter specifies the width of the pen. Finally, the *crColor* parameter specifies the color of the pen. The *crColor* parameter is typed as *COLORREF*, which can be constructed using the *RGB* macro. The *RGB* macro is as follows:

```
COLORREF RGB (BYTE bRed, BYTE bGreen, BYTE bBlue);
```

So to create a solid red pen, the code would look like this:

```
hPen = CreatePen (PS_SOLID, 1, RGB (0xff, 0, 0));
```

The other pen creation function is the following:

```
HPEN CreatePenIndirect (const LOGPEN *lplgpn);
```

where the logical pen structure *LOGPEN* is defined as

```
typedef struct tagLOGPEN {
    UINT lopnStyle;
    POINT lopnWidth;
    COLORREF lopnColor;
} LOGPEN;
```

CreatePenIndirect provides the same parameters to Windows, in a different form. To create the same 1-pixel-wide red pen with *CreatePenIndirect*, the code would look like this:

```
LOGPEN lp;
HPEN hPen;
lp.lopnStyle = PS_SOLID;
lp.lopnWidth.x = 1;
lp.lopnWidth.y = 1;
lp.lopnColor = RGB (0xff, 0, 0);

hPen = CreatePenIndirect (&lp);
```

Windows CE devices don't support complex pens such as wide (more than one pixel wide) dashed lines. To determine what's supported, our old friend *GetDeviceCaps* comes into play, taking *LINECAPS* as the second parameter. Refer to the Windows CE documentation for the different flags returned by this call.

Shapes

Lines are useful but Windows also provides functions to draw shapes, both filled and unfilled. Here Windows CE does a good job supporting most of the functions familiar to Windows programmers. The *Rectangle*, *RoundRect*, *Ellipse*, and *Polygon* functions are all supported.

Brushes

Before I can talk about shapes such as rectangles and ellipses, I need to describe another GDI object that I've mentioned only briefly before now, called a *brush*. A brush is a bitmap, typically 8 by 8 pixels, used to fill shapes. It's also used by Windows to fill the background of a client window. Windows CE provides a number of stock brushes and also the ability to create a brush from an application-defined pattern. A number of stock brushes, each a solid color, can be retrieved using *GetStockObject*. Among the brushes available is one for each of the grays of a four-color grayscale display: white, light gray, dark gray, and black.

To create solid color brushes, the function to call is the following:

```
HBRUSH CreateSolidBrush (COLORREF crColor);
```

The *crColor* parameter specifies the color of the brush. The color is specified using the *RGB* macro.

To create custom pattern brushes, Windows CE supports the Win32 function:

```
HBRUSH CreateDIBPatternBrushPt (const void *lpPackedDIB,
                                UINT iUsage);
```

The first parameter to this function is a pointer to a DIB in *packed* format. This means that the pointer points to a buffer that contains a *BITMAPINFO* structure immediately followed by the bits in the bitmap. Remember that a *BITMAPINFO* structure is actually a *BITMAPINFOHEADER* structure followed by a palette in *RGBQUAD* format, so the buffer contains everything necessary to create a DIB—that is, bitmap information, a palette, and the bits to the bitmap. If the second parameter is set to *DIB_RGB_COLORS*, the palette specified contains *RGBQUAD* values in each entry. For 8-bits-per-pixel bitmaps, the complementary flag *DIB_PAL_COLORS* can be specified, but Windows CE ignores the bitmap's color table.

The *CreateDIBPatternBrushPt* function is more important under Windows CE because the hatched brushes, supplied under other versions of Windows by the *CreateHatchBrush* function, aren't supported under Windows CE. Hatched brushes are brushes composed of any combination of horizontal, vertical, or diagonal lines. Ironically, they're particularly useful with grayscale displays because you can use them to accentuate different areas of a chart with different hatch patterns. You can reproduce these brushes, however, by using *Create-DIBPatternBrushPt* and the proper bitmap patterns. The Shapes code example, later in the chapter, demonstrates a method for creating hatched brushes under Windows CE.

By default, the brush origin will be in the upper left corner of the window. This isn't always what you want. Take, for example, a bar graph where the bar filled with a hatched brush fills a rectangle from (100, 100) to (125, 220). Since this rectangle isn't divisible by 8 (brushes typically being 8 by 8 pixels square), the upper left corner of the bar will be filled with a partial brush that might not look pleasing to the eye.

To avoid this situation, you can move the origin of the brush so that each shape can be drawn with the brush aligned correctly in the corner of the shape to be filled. The function available for this remedy is the following:

```
BOOL SetBrushOrgEx (HDC hdc, int nXOrg, int nYOrg, LPPOINT lppt);
```

The *nXOrg* and *nYOrg* parameters allow the origin to be set between 0 and 7 so that you can position the origin anywhere in the 8-by-8 space of the brush. The *lppt* parameter is filled with the previous origin of the brush so that you can restore the previous origin if necessary.

Rectangles

The rectangle function draws either a filled or a hollow rectangle; the function is defined as the following:

```
BOOL Rectangle (HDC hdc, int nLeftRect, int nTopRect,
                int nRightRect, int nBottomRect);
```

The function uses the currently selected pen to draw the outline of the rectangle and the current brush to fill the interior. To draw a hollow rectangle, select the null brush into the device context before calling *Rectangle*.

The actual pixels drawn for the border are important to understand. Say we're drawing a 5-by-7 rectangle at 0, 0. The function call would look like this:

```
Rectangle (0, 0, 5, 7);
```

Assuming that the selected pen was 1 pixel wide, the resulting rectangle would look like the one shown in Figure 2-6.

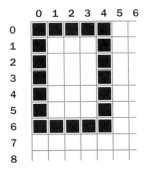

Figure 2-6   Magnified view of a rectangle drawn with the *Rectangle*
function

Notice how the right edge of the rectangle is actually drawn in column 4 and that the bottom edge is drawn in row 6. This is standard Windows practice. The rectangle is drawn inside the right and bottom boundary specified for the *Rectangle* function. If the selected pen is wider than one pixel, the right and bottom edges are drawn with the pen centered on the bounding rectangle. (Other versions of Windows support the *PS_INSIDEFRAME* pen style that forces the rectangle to be drawn inside the frame regardless of the pen width.)

Circles and Ellipses

Circles and ellipses can be drawn with this function:

```
BOOL Ellipse (HDC hdc, int nLeftRect, int nTopRect,
              int nRightRect, int nBottomRect);
```

The ellipse is drawn using the rectangle passed as a bounding rectangle, as shown in Figure 2-7. As with the *Rectangle* function, while the interior of the ellipse is filled with the current brush, the outline is drawn with the current pen.

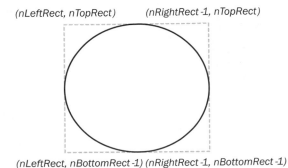

Figure 2-7   The ellipse is drawn within the bounding rectangle passed to
the *Ellipse* function.

Round Rectangles

The *RoundRect* function

```
BOOL RoundRect (HDC hdc, int nLeftRect, int nTopRect,
                int nRightRect, int nBottomRect,
                int nWidth, int nHeight);
```

draws a rectangle with rounded corners. The roundedness of the corners is defined by the last two parameters that specify the width and height of the ellipse used to round the corners, as shown in Figure 2-8. Specifying the ellipse height and width enables your program to draw identically symmetrical rounded corners. Shortening the ellipse height flattens out the sides of the rectangle, while shortening the width of the ellipse flattens the top and bottom of the rectangle.

(nLeftRect, nTopRect)

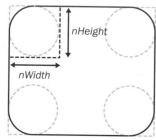

(nRightRect, nBottomRect)

Figure 2-8   The height and width of the ellipse define the round corners of the rectangle drawn by *RoundRect*.

Polygons

Finally, the *Polygon* function

```
BOOL Polygon (HDC hdc, const POINT *lpPoints, int nCount);
```

draws a many-sided shape. The second parameter is a pointer to an array of point structures defining the points that delineate the polygon. The resulting shape has one more side than the number of points because the function automatically completes the last line of the polygon by connecting the last point with the first.

Fill Functions

The preceding functions use a combination of a brush and a pen to draw shapes in the device context. Functions are available to fill areas without dealing with the pen that would normally outline the shape. The first of these functions is as follows:

```
int FillRect (HDC hDC, CONST RECT* lprc, HBRUSH hbr);
```

The parameters of *FillRect* are the handle to the device context, the rectangle to fill, and the brush to fill the rectangle. *FillRect* is a quick and convenient way to paint a solid color or pattern in a rectangular area.

While *FillRect* is convenient, *GradientFill* is cool. *GradientFill* fills a rectangular area that starts on one side with one color and then has a smooth transition to another color on the other side. Figure 2-9 shows a window in which the client area is painted with *GradientFill*. The black-and-white illustration doesn't do the image justice, but even in this figure it's easy to see the smooth nature of the transition.

Figure 2-9   A window painted with the *GradientFill* function.

The prototype of *GradientFill* looks like this:

```
BOOL GradientFill (HDC hdc, PTRIVERTEX pVertex, ULONG dwNumVertex,
                   PVOID pMesh, ULONG dwNumMesh, ULONG dwMode);
```

The first parameter is the obligatory handle to the device context. The *pVertex* parameter points to an array of *TRIVERTEX* structures, while the *dwNumVertex* parameter contains the number of entries in the *TRIVERTEX* array. The *TRIVERTEX* structure is defined as follows:

```
struct _TRIVERTEX {
    LONG       x;
    Long       y;
    COLOR16    Red;
    COLOR16    Green;
    COLOR16    Blue;
    COLOR16    Alpha;s
} TRIVERTEX;
```

The fields of the *TRIVERTEX* structure describe a point in the device context and an RGB color. The points should describe the upper left and lower right corners of the rectangle being filled. The *pMesh* parameter of *GradientFill* points to a *GRADIENT_RECT* structure defined as follows:

```
struct _GRADIENT_RECT
{
    ULONG UpperLeft;
    ULONG LowerRight;
} GRADIENT_RECT;
```

The *GRADIENT_RECT* structure simply specifies which of the entries in the *TRIVERTEX* structure delineates the upper left and lower right corners. Finally, the *dwNumMesh* parameter of *GradientFill* contains the number of *GRADIENT_RECT* structures, while the *dwMode* structure contains a flag indicating whether the fill should be left to right (*GRADIENT_FILL_RECT_H*) or top to bottom (*GRADIENT_FILL_RECT_V*). The *GradientFill* function is more complex than is apparent because on the desktop, it can also perform a triangular fill that isn't supported by Windows CE. Here's the code fragment that created the window in Figure 2-9:

```
TRIVERTEX vert[2];
GRADIENT_RECT gRect;

vert [0] .x        =   prect->left;
vert [0] .y        =   prect->top;
vert [0] .Red      =   0x0000;
vert [0] .Green    =   0x0000;
vert [0] .Blue     =   0xff00;
vert [0] .Alpha    =   0x0000;

vert [1] .x        =   prect->right;
vert [1] .y        =   prect->bottom;
vert [1] .Red      =   0x0000;
vert [1] .Green    =   0xff00;
vert [1] .Blue     =   0x0000;
vert [1] .Alpha    =   0x0000;

gRect.UpperLeft = 0;
gRect.LowerRight = 1;

GradientFill(hdc,vert,2,&gRect,1,GRADIENT_FILL_RECT_H);
```

The Shapes Example Program

The Shapes program, shown in Listing 2-3, demonstrates a number of these functions. In Shapes, four figures are drawn, each filled with a different brush.

Shapes.h

```
//======================================================================
// Header file
//
// Written for the book Programming Windows CE
// Copyright (C) 2003 Douglas Boling
//======================================================================
// Returns number of elements
#define dim(x) (sizeof(x) / sizeof(x[0]))


//----------------------------------------------------------------------
// Generic defines and data types
//
struct decodeUINT {                                   // Structure associates
    UINT Code;                                        // messages
                                                      // with a function.
    LRESULT (*Fxn)(HWND, UINT, WPARAM, LPARAM);
};
struct decodeCMD {                                    // Structure associates
    UINT Code;                                        // menu IDs with a
    LRESULT (*Fxn)(HWND, WORD, HWND, WORD);           // function.
};


//----------------------------------------------------------------------
// Defines used by MyCreateHatchBrush
//
typedef struct {
    BITMAPINFOHEADER bmi;
    COLORREF dwPal[2];
    BYTE bBits[64];
} BRUSHBMP;

#define HS_HORIZONTAL       0        /* ----- */
#define HS_VERTICAL         1        /* ||||| */
#define HS_FDIAGONAL        2        /* \\\\\ */
#define HS_BDIAGONAL        3        /* ///// */
#define HS_CROSS            4        /* +++++ */
#define HS_DIAGCROSS        5        /* xxxxx */


//----------------------------------------------------------------------
// Function prototypes
//
HWND InitInstance (HINSTANCE, LPWSTR, int);
int TermInstance (HINSTANCE, int);

// Window procedures
LRESULT CALLBACK MainWndProc (HWND, UINT, WPARAM, LPARAM);
```

Listing 2-3   The Shapes program   *(continued)*

Listing 2-3   *(continued)*

```
// Message handlers
LRESULT DoPaintMain (HWND, UINT, WPARAM, LPARAM);
LRESULT DoDestroyMain (HWND, UINT, WPARAM, LPARAM);
```

Shapes.cpp

```
//======================================================================
// Shapes- Brush and shapes demo for Windows CE
//
// Written for the book Programming Windows CE
// Copyright (C) 2003 Douglas Boling
//======================================================================
#include <windows.h>                    // For all that Windows stuff
#include "shapes.h"                     // Program-specific stuff


//----------------------------------------------------------------
// Global data
//
const TCHAR szAppName[] = TEXT ("Shapes");
HINSTANCE hInst;                        // Program instance handle

// Message dispatch table for MainWindowProc
const struct decodeUINT MainMessages[] = {
    WM_PAINT, DoPaintMain,
    WM_DESTROY, DoDestroyMain,
};


//======================================================================
//
// Program entry point
//
int WINAPI WinMain (HINSTANCE hInstance, HINSTANCE hPrevInstance,
                    LPWSTR lpCmdLine, int nCmdShow) {
    MSG msg;
    HWND hwndMain;

    // Initialize this instance.
    hwndMain = InitInstance(hInstance, lpCmdLine, nCmdShow);
    if (hwndMain == 0)
        return 0x10;

    // Application message loop
    while (GetMessage (&msg, NULL, 0, 0)) {
        TranslateMessage (&msg);
        DispatchMessage (&msg);
    }
    // Instance cleanup
    return TermInstance (hInstance, msg.wParam);
```

```
}
//------------------------------------------------------------------
// InitInstance - Instance initialization
//
HWND InitInstance (HINSTANCE hInstance, LPWSTR lpCmdLine, int nCmdShow){
    WNDCLASS wc;
    HWND hWnd;

    // Save program instance handle in global variable.
    hInst = hInstance;

#if defined(WIN32_PLATFORM_PSPC)
    // If Pocket PC, allow only one instance of the application.
    hWnd = FindWindow (szAppName, NULL);
    if (hWnd) {
        SetForegroundWindow ((HWND)(((DWORD)hWnd) | 0x01));
        return 0;
    }
#endif
    // Register application main window class.
    wc.style = 0;                                  // Window style
    wc.lpfnWndProc = MainWndProc;                  // Callback function
    wc.cbClsExtra = 0;                             // Extra class data
    wc.cbWndExtra = 0;                             // Extra window data
    wc.hInstance = hInstance;                      // Owner handle
    wc.hIcon = NULL,                               // Application icon
    wc.hCursor = LoadCursor (NULL, IDC_ARROW);// Default cursor
    wc.hbrBackground = (HBRUSH) GetStockObject (WHITE_BRUSH);
    wc.lpszMenuName =  NULL;                       // Menu name
    wc.lpszClassName = szAppName;                  // Window class name

    if (RegisterClass (&wc) == 0) return 0;
    // Create main window.
    hWnd = CreateWindowEx (WS_EX_NODRAG,           // Ex Style
                           szAppName,              // Window class
                           TEXT("Shapes"),         // Window title
                           WS_VISIBLE,             // Style flags
                           CW_USEDEFAULT,          // x position
                           CW_USEDEFAULT,          // y position
                           CW_USEDEFAULT,          // Initial width
                           CW_USEDEFAULT,          // Initial height
                           NULL,                   // Parent
                           NULL,                   // Menu, must be null
                           hInstance,              // Application instance
                           NULL);                  // Pointer to create
                                                   // parameters
    // Return fail code if window not created.
    if (!IsWindow (hWnd)) return 0;
```

(continued)

Listing 2-3 *(continued)*

```c
    // Standard show and update calls
    ShowWindow (hWnd, nCmdShow);
    UpdateWindow (hWnd);
    return hWnd;
}
//-----------------------------------------------------------------------
// TermInstance - Program cleanup
//
int TermInstance (HINSTANCE hInstance, int nDefRC) {

    return nDefRC;
}
//=======================================================================
// Message handling procedures for MainWindow
//


//-----------------------------------------------------------------------
// MainWndProc - Callback function for application window
//
LRESULT CALLBACK MainWndProc (HWND hWnd, UINT wMsg, WPARAM wParam,
                             LPARAM lParam) {
    INT i;
    //
    // Search message list to see if we need to handle this
    // message. If in list, call procedure.
    //
    for (i = 0; i < dim(MainMessages); i++) {
        if (wMsg == MainMessages[i].Code)
            return (*MainMessages[i].Fxn)(hWnd, wMsg, wParam, lParam);
    }
    return DefWindowProc (hWnd, wMsg, wParam, lParam);
}
//-----------------------------------------------------------------------
// MyCreateHatchBrush - Creates hatched brushes
//
HBRUSH MyCreateHatchBrush (INT fnStyle, COLORREF clrref) {
    BRUSHBMP brbmp;
    BYTE *pBytes;
    int i;
    DWORD dwBits[6][2] = {
        {0x000000ff,0x00000000}, {0x10101010,0x10101010},
        {0x01020408,0x10204080}, {0x80402010,0x08040201},
        {0x101010ff,0x10101010}, {0x81422418,0x18244281},
    };

    if ((fnStyle < 0) || (fnStyle > dim(dwBits)))
        return 0;
    memset (&brbmp, 0, sizeof (brbmp));
```

```
    brbmp.bmi.biSize = sizeof (BITMAPINFOHEADER);
    brbmp.bmi.biWidth = 8;
    brbmp.bmi.biHeight = 8;
    brbmp.bmi.biPlanes = 1;
    brbmp.bmi.biBitCount = 1;
    brbmp.bmi.biClrUsed = 2;
    brbmp.bmi.biClrImportant = 2;

    // Initialize the palette of the bitmap.
    brbmp.dwPal[0] = PALETTERGB(0xff,0xff,0xff);
    brbmp.dwPal[1] = PALETTERGB((BYTE)((clrref >> 16) & 0xff),
                                (BYTE)((clrref >> 8) & 0xff),
                                (BYTE)(clrref & 0xff));

    // Write the hatch data to the bitmap.
    pBytes = (BYTE *)&dwBits[fnStyle];
    for (i = 0; i < 8; i++)
        brbmp.bBits[i*4] = *pBytes++;

    // Return the handle of the brush created.
    return CreateDIBPatternBrushPt (&brbmp, DIB_RGB_COLORS);
}
//----------------------------------------------------------------
// DoPaintMain - Process WM_PAINT message for window.
//
LRESULT DoPaintMain (HWND hWnd, UINT wMsg, WPARAM wParam,
                     LPARAM lParam) {
    PAINTSTRUCT ps;
    RECT rect;
    HDC hdc;
    POINT ptArray[6];
    HBRUSH hBr, hOldBr;
    TCHAR szText[128];

    GetClientRect (hWnd, &rect);
    hdc = BeginPaint (hWnd, &ps);

    // Draw ellipse.
    hBr = (HBRUSH) GetStockObject (DKGRAY_BRUSH);
    hOldBr = (HBRUSH) SelectObject (hdc, hBr);
    Ellipse (hdc, 10, 50, 90, 130);
    SelectObject (hdc, hOldBr);

    // Draw round rectangle.
    hBr = (HBRUSH) GetStockObject (LTGRAY_BRUSH);
    hOldBr = (HBRUSH) SelectObject (hdc, hBr);
    RoundRect (hdc, 95, 50, 150, 130, 30, 30);
    SelectObject (hdc, hOldBr);
```

(continued)

Listing 2-3 *(continued)*

```
    // Draw hexagon using Polygon.
    hBr = (HBRUSH) GetStockObject (WHITE_BRUSH);
    hOldBr = (HBRUSH) SelectObject (hdc, hBr);
    ptArray[0].x = 192;
    ptArray[0].y = 50;
    ptArray[1].x = 155;
    ptArray[1].y = 75;
    ptArray[2].x = 155;
    ptArray[2].y = 105;
    ptArray[3].x = 192;
    ptArray[3].y = 130;
    ptArray[4].x = 230;
    ptArray[4].y = 105;
    ptArray[5].x = 230;
    ptArray[5].y = 75;

    Polygon (hdc, ptArray, 6);
    SelectObject (hdc, hOldBr);

    hBr = (HBRUSH) MyCreateHatchBrush (HS_DIAGCROSS, RGB (0, 0, 0));
    hOldBr = (HBRUSH) SelectObject (hdc, hBr);
    Rectangle (hdc, 10, 145, 225, 210);
    SelectObject (hdc, hOldBr);
    DeleteObject (hBr);

    SetBkMode (hdc, OPAQUE);
    lstrcpy (szText, TEXT ("Opaque background"));
    ExtTextOut (hdc, 20, 160, 0, NULL,
                szText, lstrlen (szText), NULL);

    SetBkMode (hdc, TRANSPARENT);
    lstrcpy (szText, TEXT ("Transparent background"));
    ExtTextOut (hdc, 20, 185, 0, NULL,
                szText, lstrlen (szText), NULL);

    EndPaint (hWnd, &ps);
    return 0;
}
//-------------------------------------------------------------------------
// DoDestroyMain - Process WM_DESTROY message for window
//
LRESULT DoDestroyMain (HWND hWnd, UINT wMsg, WPARAM wParam,
                       LPARAM lParam) {
    PostQuitMessage (0);
    return 0;
}
```

In Shapes, *OnPaintMain* draws the four figures using the different functions discussed earlier. For each of the shapes, a different brush is created, selected into the device context, and, after the shape has been drawn, deselected from the DC. The first three shapes are filled with solid grayscale shades. These solid brushes are loaded with the *GetStockObject* function. The final shape is filled with a brush created with the *CreateDIBPatternBrushPt*. The creation of this brush is segregated into a function called *MyCreateHatchBrush* that mimics the *CreateHatchBrush* function not available under Windows CE. To create the hatched brushes, a black-and-white bitmap is built by filling in a bitmap structure and setting the bits to form the hatch patterns. The bitmap itself is the 8-by-8 bitmap specified by *CreateDIBPatternBrushPt*. Since the bitmap is monochrome, its total size, including the palette and header, is only around 100 bytes. Notice, however, that since each scan line of a bitmap must be double-word aligned, the last three bytes of each one-byte scan line are left unused.

Finally the program completes the painting by writing two lines of text into the lower rectangle. The text further demonstrates the difference between the opaque and transparent drawing modes of the system. In this case, the opaque mode of drawing the text might be a better match for the situation because the hatched lines tend to obscure letters drawn in transparent mode. A view of the Shapes window is shown in Figure 2-10.

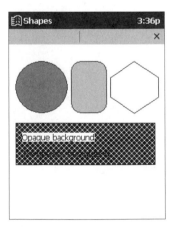

Figure 2-10   The Shapes example demonstrates drawing different filled shapes.

To keep things simple, the Shapes example assumes that it's running on at least a 240-pixel-wide display. This allows Shapes to work equally well on a Handheld PC and a Pocket PC. I have barely scratched the surface of the abilities of the Windows CE GDI portion of GWE. The goal of this chapter wasn't to provide total presentation of all aspects of GDI programming. Instead, I wanted to demonstrate the methods available for basic drawing and text support under Windows CE. In other chapters in the book, I extend some of the techniques touched on in this chapter. I talk about these new techniques and newly introduced functions at the point, generally, where I demonstrate how to use them in code. To further your knowledge, I recommend *Programming Windows*, 5th edition, by Charles Petzold (Microsoft Press, 1998), as the best source for learning about the Windows GDI.

Now that we've looked at output, it's time to turn our attention to the input side of the system—the keyboard and the touch panel.

3

Input: Keyboard, Mouse, and Touch Screen

Traditionally, Microsoft Windows platforms have allowed users two methods of input: the keyboard and the mouse. Windows CE continues this tradition but on most systems replaces the mouse with a stylus and touch screen. Programmatically, the change is minor because the messages from the stylus are mapped to the mouse messages used in other versions of Windows. A more subtle but also more important change from versions of Windows that run on PCs is that a system running Windows CE might have either a tiny keyboard or no keyboard at all. This arrangement makes the stylus input that much more important for Windows CE systems.

The Keyboard

While keyboards play a lesser role in Windows CE, they're still the best means of entering large volumes of information. Even on systems without a physical keyboard such as the Pocket PC, *soft* keyboards—controls that simulate keyboards on a touch screen—will most likely be available to the user. Given this, proper handling of keyboard input is critical to all but the most specialized of Windows CE applications. While I'll talk at length about soft keyboards later in the book, one point should be made here. To the application, input from a soft keyboard is no different from input from a traditional "hard" keyboard.

Input Focus

Under Windows operating systems, only one window at a time has the input focus. The focus window receives all keyboard input until it loses focus to another window. The system assigns the keyboard focus using a number of rules, but most often the focus window is the current active window. The active window, you'll recall, is the top-level window, the one with which the user is currently interacting. With rare exceptions, the active window also sits at the top of the Z-order; that is, it's drawn on top of all other windows in the system. In the Explorer, the user can change the active window by pressing Alt-Esc to switch between programs or by tapping on another top-level window's button on the task bar. The focus window is either the active window or one of its child windows.

Under Windows, a program can determine which window has the input focus by calling

```
HWND GetFocus (void);
```

The focus can be changed to another window by calling

```
HWND SetFocus (HWND hWnd);
```

Under Windows CE, the target window of *SetFocus* is limited. The window being given the focus by *SetFocus* must have been created by the thread calling *SetFocus*. An exception to this rule occurs if the window losing focus is related to the window gaining focus by a parent/child or sibling relationship; in this case, the focus can be changed even if the windows were created by different threads.

When a window loses focus, Windows sends a *WM_KILLFOCUS* message to that window informing it of its new state. The *wParam* parameter contains the handle of the window that will be gaining the focus. The window gaining focus receives a *WM_SETFOCUS* message. The *wParam* parameter of the *WM_SETFOCUS* message contains the handle of the window losing focus.

Now for a bit of motherhood. Programs shouldn't change the focus window without some input from the user. Otherwise, the user can easily become confused. A proper use of *SetFocus* is to set the input focus to a child window (more than likely a control) contained in the active window. In this case, a window would respond to the *WM_SETFOCUS* message by calling *SetFocus* with the handle of a child window contained in the window to which the program wants to direct keyboard messages.

Keyboard Messages

Windows CE practices the same keyboard message processing as its larger desktop relations with a few small exceptions, which I cover shortly. When a key is pressed, Windows sends a series of messages to the focus window, typically beginning with a *WM_KEYDOWN* message. If the key pressed represents a character such as a letter or number, Windows follows the *WM_KEYDOWN* with a *WM_CHAR* message. (Some keys, such as function keys and cursor keys, don't represent characters, so *WM_CHAR* messages aren't sent in response to those keys. For those keys, a program must interpret the *WM_KEYDOWN* message to know when the keys are pressed.) When the key is released, Windows sends a *WM_KEYUP* message. If a key is held down long enough for the auto-repeat feature to kick in, multiple *WM_KEYDOWN* and *WM_CHAR* messages are sent for each auto-repeat until the key is released when the final *WM_KEYUP* message is sent. I used the word *typically* to qualify this process because if the Alt key is being held when another key is pressed, the messages I've just described are replaced by *WM_SYSKEYDOWN*, *WM_SYSCHAR*, and *WM_SYSKEYUP* messages.

For all of these messages, the generic parameters *wParam* and *lParam* are used in mostly the same manner. For *WM_KEYxx* and *WM_SYSKEYxx* messages, the *wParam* value contains the virtual key value, indicating the key being pressed. All versions of Windows provide a level of indirection between the keyboard hardware and applications by translating the scan codes returned by the keyboard into virtual key values. You see a list of the *VK_xx* values and their associated keys in Table 3-1. While the table of virtual keys is extensive, not all keys listed in the table are present on Windows CE devices. For example, function keys, a mainstay on PC keyboards and listed in the virtual key table, aren't present on most Windows CE keyboards. In fact, a number of keys on a PC keyboard are left off the space-constrained Windows CE keyboards. A short list of the keys not typically used on Windows CE devices is presented in Figure 3-1. This list is meant to inform you that these keys might not exist, not to indicate that the keys *never* exist on Windows CE keyboards.

Table 3-1   Virtual Keys

Constant	Value	Keyboard Equivalent
VK_LBUTTON	01	Stylus tap
VK_RBUTTON	02	Mouse right button[*]
VK_CANCEL	03	Control-break processing
VK_RBUTTON	04	Mouse middle button[*]
--	05–07	Undefined
VK_BACK	08	Backspace key
VK_TAB	09	Tab key

(continued)

Table 3-1 **Virtual Keys** *(continued)*

Constant	Value	Keyboard Equivalent
--	0A–0B	Undefined
VK_CLEAR	0C	Clear key
Constant	Value	Keyboard Equivalent
VK_RETURN	0D	Enter key
--	0E–0F	Undefined
VK_SHIFT	10	Shift key
VK_CONTROL	11	Ctrl key
VK_MENU	12	Alt key
VK_CAPITAL	14	Caps Lock key
--	15–19	Reserved for Kanji systems
--	1A	Undefined
VK_ESCAPE	1B	Escape key
--	1C–1F	Reserved for Kanji systems
VK_SPACE	20	Spacebar
VK_PRIOR	21	Page Up key
VK_NEXT	22	Page Down key
VK_END	23	End key
VK_HOME	24	Home key
VK_LEFT	25	Left Arrow key
VK_UP	26	Up Arrow key
VK_RIGHT	27	Right Arrow key
VK_DOWN	28	Down Arrow key
VK_SELECT	29	Select key
--	2A	Original equipment manufacturer (OEM)–specific
VK_EXECUTE	2B	Execute key
VK_SNAPSHOT	2C	Print Screen key for Windows 3.0 and later
VK_INSERT	2D	Insert[‡]
VK_DELETE	2E	Delete[†]
VK_HELP	2F	Help key
VK_0–VK_9	30–39	0–9 keys
--	3A–40	Undefined

Table 3-1   Virtual Keys   *(continued)*

Constant	Value	Keyboard Equivalent
VK_A–VK_Z	41–5A	A through Z keys
VK_LWIN	5B	Windows key
VK_RWIN	5C	Windows key[‡]
VK_APPS	5D	
--	5E–5F	Undefined
VK_NUMPAD0–9	60–69	Numeric keypad 0–9 keys
VK_MULTIPLY	6A	Numeric keypad Asterisk (*) key
VK_ADD	6B	Numeric keypad Plus sign (+) key
VK_SEPARATOR	6C	Separator key
VK_SUBTRACT	6D	Numeric keypad Minus sign (-) key
VK_DECIMAL	6E	Numeric keypad Period (.) key
VK_DIVIDE	6F	Numeric keypad Slash mark (/) key
VK_F1–VK_F24	70–87	F1–F24[‡]
--	88–8F	Unassigned
VK_NUMLOCK	90	Num Lock[‡]
VK_SCROLL	91	Scroll Lock[‡]
--	92–9F	Unassigned
VK_LSHIFT	A0	Left Shift[\]
VK_RSHIFT	A1	Right Shift[\]
VK_LCONTROL	A2	Left Control[\]
VK_RCONTROL	A3	Right Control[\]
VK_LMENU	A4	Left Alt[\]
VK_RMENU	A5	Right Alt[\]
--	A6–B9	Unassigned
VK_SEMICOLON	BA	; key
VK_EQUAL	BB	= key
VK_COMMA	BC	, key
VK_HYPHEN	BD	- key
VK_PERIOD	BE	. key
VK_SLASH	BF	/ key
VK_BACKQUOTE	C0	` key

(continued)

Table 3-1 **Virtual Keys** *(continued)*

Constant	Value	Keyboard Equivalent
--	C1–DA	Unassigned§
VK_LBRACKET	DB	[key
VK_BACKSLASH	DC	\ key
VK_RBRACKET	DD	] key
VK_APOSTROPHE	DE	' key
VK_OFF	DF	Power button
--	E5	Unassigned
--	E6	OEM-specific
--	E7–E8	Unassigned
--	E9–F5	OEM-specific
VK_ATTN	F6	
VK_CRSEL	F7	
VK_EXSEL	F8	
VK_EREOF	F9	
VK_PLAY	FA	
VK_ZOOM	FB	
VK_NONAME	FC	
VK_PA1	FD	
VK_OEM_CLEAR	FE	

* Mouse right and middle buttons are defined but are relevant only on a Windows CE system equipped with a mouse.

† On some Windows CE systems, Delete is simulated with Shift-Backspace

‡ Many Windows CE Systems don't have this key

\ These constants can be used only with *GetKeyState* and *GetAsyncKeyState*.

§ These codes are used by the application launch keys on systems that have them.

For the *WM_CHAR* and *WM_SYSCHAR* messages, the *wParam* value contains the Unicode character represented by the key. Most often an application can simply look for *WM_CHAR* messages and ignore *WM_KEYDOWN* and *WM_KEYUP*. The *WM_CHAR* message allows for a second level of abstraction so that the application doesn't have to worry about the up or down state of the keys and can concentrate on the characters being entered by means of the keyboard.

The *lParam* value of any of these keyboard messages contains further information about the pressed key. The format of the *lParam* parameter is shown in Figure 3-2.

Insert
Delete (Many Windows CE keyboards use Shift-Backspace for this function.)
Num Lock
Pause
Print Screen
Scroll Lock
Function Keys
Windows Context Menu key

Figure 3-1   Keys on a PC keyboard that are rarely on a Windows CE keyboard

The low word, bits 0 through 15, contains the repeat count of the key. Sometimes keys on a Windows CE device can be pressed faster than Windows CE can send messages to the focus application. In these cases, the repeat count contains the number of times the key has been pressed. Bit 29 contains the context flag. If the Alt key was being held down when the key was pressed, this bit will be set. Bit 30 contains the previous key state. If the key was previously down, this bit is set; otherwise, it's 0. Bit 30 can be used to determine whether the key message is the result of an auto-repeat sequence. Bit 31 indicates the transition state. If the key is in transition from down to up, Bit 31 is set. Bits 16 through 28 are used to indicate the key scan code. In many cases, Windows CE doesn't support this field. However, on some of the newer Windows CE platforms where scan codes are necessary, this field does contain the scan code. You shouldn't plan on the scan code field being available unless you know it's supported on your specific platform.

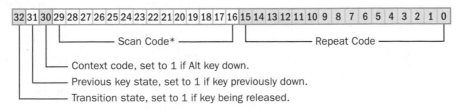

Many Windows CE devices don't support this field.

Figure 3-2   The layout of the *lParam* value for key messages

One additional keyboard message, *WM_DEADCHAR*, can sometimes come into play. You send it when the pressed key represents a dead character, such as an umlaut, that you want to combine with a character to create a different character. In this case, the *WM_DEADCHAR* message can be used to prevent the text entry point (the caret) from advancing to the next space until the second key is pressed so that you can complete the combined character.

The *WM_DEADCHAR* message has always been present under Windows, but under Windows CE it takes on a somewhat larger role. With the internationalization of small consumer devices that run Windows CE, programmers should plan for, and if necessary use, the *WM_DEADCHAR* message that is so often necessary in foreign language systems.

Keyboard Functions

You'll find useful a few other keyboard state–determining functions for Windows applications. Among the keyboard functions, two are closely related but often confused: *GetKeyState* and *GetAsyncKeyState*.

GetKeyState, prototyped as

```
SHORT GetKeyState (int nVirtKey);
```

returns the up/down state of the shift keys, Ctrl, Alt, and Shift, and indicates whether any of these keys is in a toggled state. If the keyboard has two keys with the same function—for example, two Shift keys, one on each side of the keyboard—this function can also be used to differentiate which of them is being pressed. (Most keyboards have left and right Shift keys, and some include left and right Ctrl and Alt keys.)

You pass to the function the virtual key code for the key being queried. If the high bit of the return value is set, the key is down. If the least significant bit of the return value is set, the key is in a toggled state; that is, it has been pressed an odd number of times since the system was started. The state returned is the state at the time the most recent message was read from the message queue, which isn't necessarily the real-time state of the key. An interesting aside: notice that the virtual key label for the Alt key is *VK_MENU*, which relates to the windows convention that the Alt-Shift key combination works in concert with other keys to access various menus from the keyboard.

Note that the *GetKeyState* function is limited under Windows CE to querying the state of the shift keys. Under other versions of Windows, *GetKeyState* can determine the state of every key on the keyboard.

To determine the real-time state of a key, use

```
SHORT GetAsyncKeyState (int vKey);
```

As with *GetKeyState*, you pass to this function the virtual key code for the key being queried. The *GetAsyncKeyState* function returns a value subtly different from the one returned by *GetKeyState*. As with the *GetKeyState* function, the high bit of the return value is set while the key is being pressed. However, the least significant bit is then set if the key was pressed after a previous call to *GetAsyncKeyState*. Like *GetKeyState*, the *GetAsyncKeyState* function can distinguish the left and right Shift, Ctrl, and Alt keys. In addition, by passing the *VK_LBUTTON* virtual key value, *GetAsyncKeyState* determines whether the stylus is currently touching the screen.

An application can simulate a keystroke using the *keybd_event* function:

```
VOID keybd_event (BYTE bVk, BYTE bScan, DWORD dwFlags,
                    DWORD dwExtraInfo);
```

The first parameter is the virtual key code of the key to simulate. The *bScan* code should be set to *NULL* under Windows CE. The *dwFlags* parameter can have two possible flags: *KEYEVENTF_KEYUP* indicates that the call is to emulate a key up event, while *KEYEVENTF_SILENT* indicates that the simulated key press won't cause the standard keyboard click that you normally hear when you press a key. So to fully simulate a key press, *keybd_event* should be called twice, once without *KEYEVENTF_KEYUP* to simulate a key down, and then once again, this time *with KEYEVENTF_KEYUP* to simulate the key release. When simulating a shift key, specify the specific left or right VK code, as in *VK_LSHIFT* or *VF_RCONTROL*.

A function unique to Windows CE is

```
BOOL PostKeybdMessage (HWND hwnd, UINT VKey,
                        KEY_STATE_FLAGS KeyStateFlags,
                        UINT cCharacters, UINT *pShiftStateBuffer,
                        UINT *pCharacterBuffer );
```

This function sends a series of keys to the specified window. The *hwnd* parameter is the target window. This window must be owned by the calling thread. The *VKey* parameter should be zero. *KeyStateFlags* specifies the key state for all the keys being sent. The *cCharacters* parameter specifies the number of keys being sent. The *pShiftStateBuffer* parameter points to an array that contains a shift state for each key sent, while *pCharacterBuffer* points to the VK codes of the keys being sent. Unlike *keybd_event*, this function doesn't change the global state of the keyboard.

One final keyboard function, *MapVirtualKey*, translates virtual key codes to characters. *MapVirtualKey* in Windows CE doesn't translate keyboard scan codes to and from virtual key codes, although it does so in other versions of Windows. The prototype of the function is the top of the following page.

```
UINT MapVirtualKey (UINT uCode, UINT uMapType);
```

Under Windows CE, the first parameter is the virtual key code to be translated, while the second parameter, *uMapType*, indicates how the key code is translated. *MapVirtualKey* is dependent on the keyboard device driver implementing a supporting function. Many OEMs don't implement this supporting function, so on their systems, *MapVirtualKey* fails.

Testing for the Keyboard

To determine whether a keyboard is even present in the system, you can call

```
DWORD GetKeyboardStatus (VOID);
```

This function returns the *KBDI_KEYBOARD_PRESENT* flag if a hardware keyboard is present in the system. This function also returns a *KBDI_KEYBOARD_ENABLED* flag if the keyboard is enabled. To disable the keyboard, a call can be made to

```
BOOL EnableHardwareKeyboard (BOOL bEnable);
```

with the *bEnable* flag set to *FALSE*. You might want to disable the keyboard in a system for which the keyboard folds around behind the screen; in such a system, a user could accidentally hit keys while using the stylus.

The KeyTrac Example Program

The following example program, KeyTrac, displays the sequence of keyboard messages. Programmatically, KeyTrac isn't much of a departure from the earlier programs in the book. The difference is that the keyboard messages I've been describing are all trapped and recorded in an array that's then displayed during the *WM_PAINT* message. For each keyboard message, the message name is recorded along with the *wParam* and *lParam* values and a set of flags indicating the state of the shift keys. The key messages are recorded in an array because these messages can occur faster than the redraw can occur. Figure 3-3 shows the KeyTrac window after a few keys have been pressed.

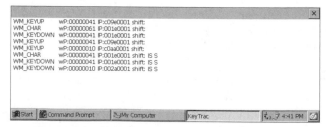

Figure 3-3 The KeyTrac window after a Shift-A key combination followed by a lowercase *a* key press

The best way to learn about the sequence of the keyboard messages is to run KeyTrac, press a few keys, and watch the messages scroll down the screen. Pressing a character key such as the *a* results in three messages: *WM_KEYDOWN*, *WM_CHAR*, and *WM_KEYUP*. Holding down the Shift key while pressing the *a* and then releasing the Shift key produces a key-down message for the Shift key followed by the three messages for the *a* key followed by a key-up message for the Shift key. Because the Shift key itself isn't a character key, no *WM_CHAR* message is sent in response to it. However, the *WM_CHAR* message for the *a* key now contains a *0x41* in the *wParam* value, indicating that an uppercase *A* was entered instead of a lowercase *a*.

Listing 3-1 shows the source code for the KeyTrac program.

KeyTrac.h
```
//======================================================================
// Header file
//
// Written for the book Programming Windows CE
// Copyright (C) 2003 Douglas Boling
//======================================================================
// Returns number of elements
#define dim(x) (sizeof(x) / sizeof(x[0]))


//----------------------------------------------------------------------
// Generic defines and data types
//
struct decodeUINT {                             // Structure associates
    UINT Code;                                  // messages
                                                // with a function.
    LRESULT (*Fxn)(HWND, UINT, WPARAM, LPARAM);
};
struct decodeCMD {                              // Structure associates
    UINT Code;                                  // menu IDs with a
    LRESULT (*Fxn)(HWND, WORD, HWND, WORD);     // function.
};


//----------------------------------------------------------------------
// Program-specific defines and structures
//
typedef struct {
    UINT wKeyMsg;
    INT wParam;
    INT lParam;
    LPCTSTR pszMsgTxt;
    TCHAR szShift[20];
} MYKEYARRAY, *PMYKEYARRAY;
```

Listing 3-1   The KeyTrac program   *(continued)*

Listing 3-1 *(continued)*

```
// Structure to associate messages with text name of message
typedef struct {
    UINT wMsg;
    LPCTSTR pName;
} KEYNAMESTRUCT;

//------------------------------------------------------------------
// Function prototypes
//
HWND InitInstance (HINSTANCE, LPWSTR, int);
int TermInstance (HINSTANCE, int);

// Window procedures
LRESULT CALLBACK MainWndProc (HWND, UINT, WPARAM, LPARAM);
// Message handlers
LRESULT DoCreateMain (HWND, UINT, WPARAM, LPARAM);
LRESULT DoPaintMain (HWND, UINT, WPARAM, LPARAM);
LRESULT DoKeysMain (HWND, UINT, WPARAM, LPARAM);
LRESULT DoDestroyMain (HWND, UINT, WPARAM, LPARAM);
```

KeyTrac.cpp

```
//======================================================================
// KeyTrac - displays keyboard messages
//
// Written for the book Programming Windows CE
// Copyright (C) 2003 Douglas Boling
//======================================================================
#include <windows.h>                 // For all that Windows stuff
#include <commctrl.h>                // Command bar includes
#include "keytrac.h"                 // Program-specific stuff

// The include and lib files for the Pocket PC are conditionally
// included so that this example can share the same project file.  This
// is necessary since this example must have a menu bar on the Pocket
// PC to have a SIP button.
#if defined(WIN32_PLATFORM_PSPC)
#include <aygshell.h>                // Add Pocket PC includes.
#pragma comment( lib, "aygshell" )   // Link Pocket PC lib for menu bar.
#endif

//------------------------------------------------------------------
// Global data
//
const TCHAR szAppName[] = TEXT ("KeyTrac");
HINSTANCE hInst;                     // Program instance handle
```

```
// Program-specific global data
MYKEYARRAY ka[16];
int nKeyCnt = 0;
int nFontHeight;

// Array associates key messages with text tags
KEYNAMESTRUCT knArray[] = {{WM_KEYDOWN,     TEXT ("WM_KEYDOWN")},
                           {WM_KEYUP,       TEXT ("WM_KEYUP")},
                           {WM_CHAR,        TEXT ("WM_CHAR")},
                           {WM_SYSCHAR,     TEXT ("WM_SYSCHAR")},
                           {WM_SYSKEYUP,    TEXT ("WM_SYSKEYUP")},
                           {WM_SYSKEYDOWN,  TEXT ("WM_SYSKEYDOWN")},
                           {WM_DEADCHAR,    TEXT ("WM_DEADCHAR")},
                           {WM_SYSDEADCHAR, TEXT ("WM_SYSDEADCHAR")}};
// Message dispatch table for MainWindowProc
const struct decodeUINT MainMessages[] = {
    WM_CREATE, DoCreateMain,
    WM_PAINT, DoPaintMain,
    WM_KEYUP, DoKeysMain,
    WM_KEYDOWN, DoKeysMain,
    WM_CHAR, DoKeysMain,
    WM_DEADCHAR, DoKeysMain,
    WM_SYSCHAR, DoKeysMain,
    WM_SYSDEADCHAR, DoKeysMain,
    WM_SYSKEYDOWN, DoKeysMain,
    WM_SYSKEYUP, DoKeysMain,
    WM_DESTROY, DoDestroyMain,
};


//=====================================================================
// Program entry point
//
 int WINAPI WinMain (HINSTANCE hInstance, HINSTANCE hPrevInstance,
                     LPWSTR lpCmdLine, int nCmdShow) {
    MSG msg;
    int rc = 0;
    HWND hwndMain;

    // Initialize this instance.
    hwndMain = InitInstance (hInstance, lpCmdLine, nCmdShow);
    if (hwndMain == 0)
        return 0x10;

    // Application message loop
    while (GetMessage (&msg, NULL, 0, 0)) {
        TranslateMessage (&msg);
        DispatchMessage (&msg);
    }
```

(continued)

Listing 3-1   *(continued)*

```
    // Instance cleanup
    return TermInstance (hInstance, msg.wParam);
}
//----------------------------------------------------------------
// InitInstance - Instance initialization
//
HWND InitInstance (HINSTANCE hInstance, LPWSTR lpCmdLine, int nCmdShow) {
    WNDCLASS wc;
    HWND hWnd;

#if defined(WIN32_PLATFORM_PSPC)
    // If Pocket PC, allow only one instance of the application
    hWnd = FindWindow (szAppName, NULL);
    if (hWnd) {
        SetForegroundWindow ((HWND)(((DWORD)hWnd) | 0x01));
        return 0;
    }
#endif
    hInst = hInstance;  // Save program instance handle

    // Register application main window class.
    wc.style = 0;                                  // Window style
    wc.lpfnWndProc = MainWndProc;                  // Callback function
    wc.cbClsExtra = 0;                             // Extra class data
    wc.cbWndExtra = 0;                             // Extra window data
    wc.hInstance = hInstance;                      // Owner handle
    wc.hIcon = NULL,                               // Application icon
    wc.hCursor = LoadCursor (NULL, IDC_ARROW);// Default cursor
    wc.hbrBackground = (HBRUSH) GetStockObject (WHITE_BRUSH);
    wc.lpszMenuName =  NULL;                       // Menu name
    wc.lpszClassName = szAppName;                  // Window class name

    if (RegisterClass(&wc) == 0) return 0;

    // Create main window.
    hWnd = CreateWindowEx (WS_EX_NODRAG, szAppName, TEXT ("KeyTrac"),
                           WS_VISIBLE | WS_CAPTION | WS_SYSMENU,
                           CW_USEDEFAULT, CW_USEDEFAULT,
                           CW_USEDEFAULT, CW_USEDEFAULT,
                           NULL, NULL, hInstance, NULL);

    // Fail if window not created
    if (!IsWindow (hWnd)) return 0;

    // Standard show and update calls
    ShowWindow (hWnd, nCmdShow);
```

```
        UpdateWindow (hWnd);
        return hWnd;
}
//------------------------------------------------------------------------
// TermInstance - Program cleanup
//
int TermInstance (HINSTANCE hInstance, int nDefRC) {
        return nDefRC;
}
//========================================================================
// Message handling procedures for MainWindow
//
//------------------------------------------------------------------------
// MainWndProc - Callback function for application window
//
LRESULT CALLBACK MainWndProc (HWND hWnd, UINT wMsg, WPARAM wParam,
                             LPARAM lParam) {
    INT i;
    //
    // Search message list to see if we need to handle this
    // message. If in list, call procedure.
    //
    for (i = 0; i < dim(MainMessages); i++) {
        if (wMsg == MainMessages[i].Code)
            return (*MainMessages[i].Fxn)(hWnd, wMsg, wParam, lParam);
    }
    return DefWindowProc (hWnd, wMsg, wParam, lParam);
}
//------------------------------------------------------------------------
// DoCreateMain - Process WM_CREATE message for window.
//
LRESULT DoCreateMain (HWND hWnd, UINT wMsg, WPARAM wParam,
                     LPARAM lParam) {
    HDC hdc;
    TEXTMETRIC tm;

#if defined(WIN32_PLATFORM_PSPC) && (_WIN32_WCE >= 300)
    SHMENUBARINFO mbi;                          // For Pocket PC, create
    memset(&mbi, 0, sizeof(SHMENUBARINFO)); // menu bar so that we
    mbi.cbSize = sizeof(SHMENUBARINFO);     // have a sip button
    mbi.hwndParent = hWnd;
    mbi.dwFlags = SHCMBF_EMPTYBAR;              // No menu
    SHCreateMenuBar(&mbi);
#endif

    // Get the height of the default font.
    hdc = GetDC (hWnd);
```

(continued)

Listing 3-1   *(continued)*

```
    GetTextMetrics (hdc, &tm);
    nFontHeight = tm.tmHeight + tm.tmExternalLeading;
    ReleaseDC (hWnd, hdc);
    return 0;
}
//-----------------------------------------------------------------
// DoPaintMain - Process WM_PAINT message for window.
//
LRESULT DoPaintMain (HWND hWnd, UINT wMsg, WPARAM wParam,
                     LPARAM lParam) {
    PAINTSTRUCT ps;
    RECT rect, rectOut;
    TCHAR szOut[256];
    HDC hdc;
    INT i, j;
    LPCTSTR pKeyText;

    GetClientRect (hWnd, &rect);

    // Create a drawing rectangle for the top line of the window.
    rectOut = rect;
    rectOut.bottom = rectOut.top + nFontHeight;

    hdc = BeginPaint (hWnd, &ps);

    if (nKeyCnt) {
        for (i = 0; i < nKeyCnt; i++) {
            // Create string containing wParam, lParam, and shift data.
            wsprintf (szOut, TEXT ("wP:%08x lP:%08x shift: %s"),
                      ka[i].wParam, ka[i].lParam, ka[i].szShift);

            // Look up name of key message.
            for (j = 0; j < dim (knArray); j++)
                if (knArray[j].wMsg == ka[i].wKeyMsg)
                    break;
            // See if we found the message.
            if (j < dim (knArray))
                pKeyText = knArray[j].pName;
            else
                pKeyText = TEXT ("Unknown");
            // Scroll the window one line.
            ScrollDC (hdc, 0, nFontHeight, &rect, &rect, NULL, NULL);

            // See if wide or narrow screen.
            if (GetSystemMetrics (SM_CXSCREEN) < 480) {
```

```
                           // If Pocket PC, display info on 2 lines
                           ExtTextOut (hdc, 10, rect.top, ETO_OPAQUE, &rectOut,
                                       szOut, lstrlen (szOut), NULL);


                           // Scroll the window another line.
                           ScrollDC(hdc, 0, nFontHeight, &rect, &rect, NULL, NULL);
                           ExtTextOut (hdc, 5, rect.top, ETO_OPAQUE, &rectOut,
                                       pKeyText, lstrlen (pKeyText), NULL);
                   } else {
                           // Wide screen, print all on one line.
                           ExtTextOut (hdc, 5, rect.top, ETO_OPAQUE, &rectOut,
                                       pKeyText, lstrlen (pKeyText), NULL);
                           ExtTextOut (hdc, 100, rect.top, 0, NULL,
                                       szOut, lstrlen (szOut), NULL);

                   }
           }
           nKeyCnt = 0;
   }
   EndPaint (hWnd, &ps);
   return 0;
}
//----------------------------------------------------------------------
// DoKeysMain - Process all keyboard messages for window.
//
LRESULT DoKeysMain (HWND hWnd, UINT wMsg, WPARAM wParam,
                    LPARAM lParam) {

   if (nKeyCnt >= 16) return 0;

   ka[nKeyCnt].wKeyMsg = wMsg;
   ka[nKeyCnt].wParam = wParam;
   ka[nKeyCnt].lParam = lParam;

   // Capture the state of the shift flags.
   ka[nKeyCnt].szShift[0] = TEXT ('\0');
   if (GetKeyState (VK_LMENU))
       lstrcat (ka[nKeyCnt].szShift, TEXT ("lA "));
   if (GetKeyState (VK_RMENU))
       lstrcat (ka[nKeyCnt].szShift, TEXT ("rA "));
   if (GetKeyState (VK_MENU))
       lstrcat (ka[nKeyCnt].szShift, TEXT ("A "));
   if (GetKeyState (VK_LCONTROL))
       lstrcat (ka[nKeyCnt].szShift, TEXT ("lC "));
   if (GetKeyState (VK_RCONTROL))
       lstrcat (ka[nKeyCnt].szShift, TEXT ("rC "));
   if (GetKeyState (VK_CONTROL))
       lstrcat (ka[nKeyCnt].szShift, TEXT ("C "));
```

(continued)

Listing 3-1   *(continued)*

```
    if (GetKeyState (VK_LSHIFT))
        lstrcat (ka[nKeyCnt].szShift, TEXT ("lS "));
    if (GetKeyState (VK_RSHIFT))
        lstrcat (ka[nKeyCnt].szShift, TEXT ("rS "));
    if (GetKeyState (VK_SHIFT))
        lstrcat (ka[nKeyCnt].szShift, TEXT ("S "));

    nKeyCnt++;
    InvalidateRect (hWnd, NULL, FALSE);
    return 0;
}
//-------------------------------------------------------------------
// DoDestroyMain - Process WM_DESTROY message for window.
//
LRESULT DoDestroyMain (HWND hWnd, UINT wMsg, WPARAM wParam,
                       LPARAM lParam) {
    PostQuitMessage (0);
    return 0;
}
```

Here are a few more characteristics of KeyTrac to notice. After each key-board message is recorded, an *InvalidateRect* function is called to force a redraw of the window and therefore also a *WM_PAINT* message. As I men-tioned in Chapter 2, a program should never attempt to send or post a *WM_PAINT* message to a window because Windows needs to perform some setup before it calls a window with a *WM_PAINT* message.

Another device context function used in KeyTrac is

```
BOOL ScrollDC (HDC hDC, int dx, int dy, const RECT *lprcScroll,
        const RECT *lprcClip, HRGN hrgnUpdate,
        LPRECT lprcUpdate);
```

which scrolls an area of the device context either horizontally or vertically, but under Windows CE, not both directions at the same time. The three rectangle parameters define the area to be scrolled, the area within the scrolling area to be clipped, and the area to be painted after the scrolling ends. Alternatively, a handle to a region can be passed to *ScrollDC*. That region is defined by *ScrollDC* to encompass the region that needs painting after the scroll.

Finally, if the KeyTrac window is covered up for any reason and then reexposed, the message information on the display is lost. This behavior occurs because a device context doesn't store the bit information of the display. The application is responsible for saving any information necessary to completely restore the client area of the screen. Since KeyTrac doesn't save this informa-tion, it's lost when the window is covered up.

The Mouse and the Touch Screen

Unlike desktop PCs, Windows CE devices don't always have a mouse. Instead, many Windows CE devices have a touch screen and stylus combination. For Windows CE systems that do have a mouse, the programming interface is identical to the desktop.

Mouse Messages

Whenever the mouse cursor moves across the display, the topmost window at that point receives a *WM_MOUSEMOVE* message. If the user clicks the left or right mouse button, the window receives a *WM_LBUTTONDOWN* or *LB_RBUTTONDOWN* message. When the user releases the button, the window receives a *WM_LBUTTONUP* or *WM_RBUTTONUP* message. If the user presses and releases the mouse wheel, the window receives a *WM_MBUTTONDOWN* followed by a *WM_MBUTTONUP* message.

For all of these messages, the *wParam* and *lParam* parameters are loaded with the same values. The *wParam* parameter contains a set of bit flags indicating whether the Ctrl or Shift keys on the keyboard are currently held down. As in other versions of Windows, the Alt key state isn't provided in these messages. To get the state of the Alt key when the message was sent, use the *GetKeyState* function.

The *lParam* parameter contains two 16-bit values that indicate the position on the screen of the tap. The low-order 16 bits contain the *x* (horizontal) location relative to the upper left corner of the client area of the window, while the high-order 16 bits contain the *y* (vertical) position.

If the user *double-taps*, that is, taps twice on the screen at the same location and within a predefined time, Windows sends a *WM_LBUTTONDBLCLK* message to the double-tapped window, but only if that window's class was registered with the CS_DBLCLKS style. The class style is set when the window class is registered with *RegisterClass*.

You can differentiate between a tap and a double-tap by comparing the messages sent to the window. When a double-tap occurs, a window first receives the *WM_LBUTTONDOWN* and *WM_LBUTTONUP* messages from the original tap. Then a *WM_LBUTTONDBLCLK* is sent followed by another *WM_LBUTTONUP*. The trick is to refrain from acting on a *WM_LBUTTONDOWN* message in any way that precludes action on a subsequent *WM_LBUTTONDBLCLK*. This is usually not a problem because taps usually select an object, while double-tapping launches the default action for the object.

If the user rolls the mouse wheel, the window receives *WM_MOUSEWHEEL* messages. For this message, the contents of *lParam* is the same as the other mouse messages, the horizontal and vertical location of the mouse cursor. The low word of the *wParam* parameter contains the same bit flags indicating the the keys currently held down. The high work of *wParam* contains the distance the wheel was rotated expressed in multiples of a constant *WHEEL_DELTA*. If the value is positive, the rotation is away from the user. A negative value indicates the wheel was rotated back toward the user.

Working with the Touch Screen

The touch screen and stylus combination is relatively new to Windows platforms, but fortunately, its integration into Windows CE applications is relatively painless. The best way to deal with the stylus is to treat it as a single-button mouse. The stylus creates the same mouse messages that are provided by the mouse in other versions of Windows and by Windows CE systems that use a mouse. The differences that do appear between a mouse and a stylus are due to the different physical realities of the two input devices.

Unlike a mouse, a stylus doesn't have a cursor to indicate its current position. Therefore, a stylus can't *hover* over a point on the screen in the way that the mouse cursor does. A cursor hovers when a user moves it over a window without pressing a mouse button. This concept can't be applied to programming for a stylus because the touch screen can't detect the position of the stylus when it isn't in contact with the screen.

Another consequence of the difference between a stylus and a mouse is that without a mouse cursor, an application can't provide feedback to the user by means of changes in appearance of a hovering cursor. Touch screen–based Windows CE systems do support setting the cursor for one classic Windows method of user feedback. The busy hourglass cursor, indicating that the user must wait for the system to complete processing, is supported under Windows CE so that applications can display the busy hourglass in the same manner as applications running under other versions of Windows, using the *SetCursor* function.

Stylus Messages

When the user presses the stylus on the screen, the topmost window under that point receives the input focus if it didn't have it before and then receives a *WM_LBUTTONDOWN* message. When the user lifts the stylus, the window receives a *WM_LBUTTONUP* message. Moving the stylus within the same window while it's down causes *WM_MOUSEMOVE* messages to be sent to the window.

Inking

A typical application for a handheld device is capturing the user's writing on the screen and storing the result as *ink*. This process isn't handwriting recognition—simply ink storage. At first pass, the best way to accomplish this would be to store the stylus points passed in each *WM_MOUSEMOVE* message. The problem is that sometimes small CE-type devices can't send these messages fast enough to achieve a satisfactory resolution. Under Windows CE, a function call has been added to assist programmers in tracking the stylus.

```
BOOL GetMouseMovePoints (PPOINT pptBuf, UINT nBufPoints,
                         UINT *pnPointsRetrieved);
```

GetMouseMovePoints returns a number of stylus points that didn't result in *WM_MOUSEMOVE* messages. The function is passed an array of points, the size of the array (in points), and a pointer to an integer that will receive the number of points passed back to the application. Once received, these additional points can be used to fill in the blanks between the last *WM_MOUSEMOVE* message and the current one.

GetMouseMovePoints does throw one curve at you. It returns points in the resolution of the touch panel, not the screen. This touch panel resolution is generally set at four times the screen resolution, so you need to divide the coordinates returned by *GetMouseMovePoints* by 4 to convert them to screen coordinates. The extra resolution helps programs such as handwriting recognizers.

A short example program, PenTrac, illustrates the difference that *GetMouseMovePoints* can make. Figure 3-4 shows the PenTrac window. Notice the two lines of dots across the window. The top line was drawn using points from *WM_MOUSEMOVE* only. The second line included points that were queried with *GetMouseMovePoints*. The black dots were queried from *WM_MOUSEMOVE*, while the red (lighter) dots were locations queried with *GetMouseMovePoints*.

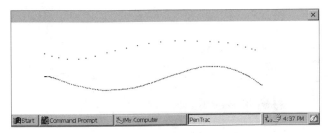

Figure 3-4   The PenTrac window showing two lines drawn

The source code for PenTrac is shown in Listing 3-2. The program places a dot on the screen for each *WM_MOUSEMOVE* or *WM_LBUTTONDOWN* message it receives. If the Shift key is held down during the mouse move messages, PenTrac also calls *GetMouseMovePoints* and marks those points in the window in red to distinguish them from the points returned by the mouse messages alone.

PenTrac cheats a little to enhance the effect of *GetMouseMovePoints*. The *DoMouseMain* routine, which handles *WM_MOUSEMOVE* and *WM_LBUTTONDOWN* messages, calls the function *sleep* to kill a few milliseconds. This delay simulates a slow-responding application that might not have time to process every mouse move message in a timely manner.

```
PenTrac.h
//======================================================================
// Header file
//
// Written for the book Programming Windows CE
// Copyright (C) 2003 Douglas Boling
//======================================================================
// Returns number of elements.
#define dim(x) (sizeof(x) / sizeof(x[0]))

//----------------------------------------------------------------------
// Generic defines and data types
//
struct decodeUINT {                             // Structure associates
    UINT Code;                                  // messages
                                                // with a function.
    LRESULT (*Fxn)(HWND, UINT, WPARAM, LPARAM);
};
struct decodeCMD {                              // Structure associates
    UINT Code;                                  // menu IDs with a
    LRESULT (*Fxn)(HWND, WORD, HWND, WORD);     // function.
};

//----------------------------------------------------------------------
// Function prototypes
//
HWND InitInstance (HINSTANCE, LPWSTR, int);
int TermInstance (HINSTANCE, int);

// Window procedures
LRESULT CALLBACK MainWndProc (HWND, UINT, WPARAM, LPARAM);

// Message handlers
LRESULT DoPaintMain (HWND, UINT, WPARAM, LPARAM);
LRESULT DoMouseMain (HWND, UINT, WPARAM, LPARAM);
LRESULT DoDestroyMain (HWND, UINT, WPARAM, LPARAM);
```

Listing 3-2 The PenTrac program

PenTrac.cpp

```
//======================================================================
// PenTrac - Tracks stylus movement
//
// Written for the book Programming Windows CE
// Copyright (C) 2003 Douglas Boling
//======================================================================
#include <windows.h>                    // For all that Windows stuff
#include "pentrac.h"                    // Program-specific stuff


//----------------------------------------------------------------------
// Global data
//
const TCHAR szAppName[] = TEXT ("PenTrac");
HINSTANCE hInst;                        // Program instance handle

// Message dispatch table for MainWindowProc
const struct decodeUINT MainMessages[] = {
    WM_LBUTTONDOWN, DoMouseMain,
    WM_MOUSEMOVE, DoMouseMain,
    WM_DESTROY, DoDestroyMain,
};


//======================================================================
// Program entry point
//
int WINAPI WinMain (HINSTANCE hInstance, HINSTANCE hPrevInstance,
                    LPWSTR lpCmdLine, int nCmdShow) {
    MSG msg;
    int rc = 0;
    HWND hwndMain;

    // Initialize this instance.
    hwndMain = InitInstance (hInstance, lpCmdLine, nCmdShow);
    if (hwndMain == 0)
        return 0x10;

    // Application message loop
    while (GetMessage (&msg, NULL, 0, 0)) {
        TranslateMessage (&msg);
        DispatchMessage (&msg);
    }
    // Instance cleanup
    return TermInstance (hInstance, msg.wParam);
}
```

(continued)

Listing 3-2   *(continued)*

```
//-------------------------------------------------------------------------
// InitApp - Application initialization
//
HWND InitInstance (HINSTANCE hInstance, LPWSTR lpCmdLine, int nCmdShow) {
    WNDCLASS wc;
    HWND hWnd;

#if defined(WIN32_PLATFORM_PSPC)
    // If Pocket PC, allow only one instance of the application
    hWnd = FindWindow (szAppName, NULL);
    if (hWnd) {
        SetForegroundWindow ((HWND)(((DWORD)hWnd) | 0x01));
        return 0;
    }
#endif
    // Save program instance handle in global variable.
    hInst = hInstance;

    // Register application main window class.
    wc.style = 0;                                // Window style
    wc.lpfnWndProc = MainWndProc;                // Callback function
    wc.cbClsExtra = 0;                           // Extra class data
    wc.cbWndExtra = 0;                           // Extra window data
    wc.hInstance = hInstance;                    // Owner handle
    wc.hIcon = NULL,                             // Application icon
    wc.hCursor = LoadCursor (NULL, IDC_ARROW);// Default cursor
    wc.hbrBackground = (HBRUSH) GetStockObject (WHITE_BRUSH);
    wc.lpszMenuName =  NULL;                     // Menu name
    wc.lpszClassName = szAppName;                // Window class name

    if (RegisterClass (&wc) == 0) return 0;

    // Create main window.
    hWnd = CreateWindowEx (WS_EX_NODRAG, szAppName, TEXT ("PenTrac"),
                       WS_VISIBLE | WS_CAPTION | WS_SYSMENU,
                       CW_USEDEFAULT, CW_USEDEFAULT, CW_USEDEFAULT,
                       CW_USEDEFAULT, NULL, NULL, hInstance, NULL);
    // Return fail code if window not created.
    if (!IsWindow (hWnd)) return 0;

    // Standard show and update calls
    ShowWindow (hWnd, nCmdShow);
    UpdateWindow (hWnd);
    return hWnd;
}
//-------------------------------------------------------------------------
// TermInstance - Program cleanup
```

```
//
int TermInstance (HINSTANCE hInstance, int nDefRC) {
    return nDefRC;
}
//=============================================================================
// Message handling procedures for MainWindow
//


//----------------------------------------------------------------------------
// MainWndProc - Callback function for application window
//
LRESULT CALLBACK MainWndProc (HWND hWnd, UINT wMsg, WPARAM wParam,
                             LPARAM lParam) {
    INT i;
    //
    // Search message list to see if we need to handle this
    // message.  If in list, call procedure.
    //
    for (i = 0; i < dim(MainMessages); i++) {
        if (wMsg == MainMessages[i].Code)
            return (*MainMessages[i].Fxn)(hWnd, wMsg, wParam, lParam);
    }
    return DefWindowProc (hWnd, wMsg, wParam, lParam);
}
//----------------------------------------------------------------------------
// DoMouseMain - Process WM_LBUTTONDOWN and WM_MOUSEMOVE messages
// for window.
//
LRESULT DoMouseMain (HWND hWnd, UINT wMsg, WPARAM wParam,
                     LPARAM lParam) {
    POINT pt[64];
    POINT ptM;
    UINT i, uPoints = 0;
    HDC hdc;

    ptM.x = LOWORD (lParam);
    ptM.y = HIWORD (lParam);
    hdc = GetDC (hWnd);
    // If shift and mouse move, see if any lost points.
    if (wMsg == WM_MOUSEMOVE) {
        if (wParam & MK_SHIFT)
            GetMouseMovePoints (pt, 64, &uPoints);

        for (i = 0; i < uPoints; i++) {
            pt[i].x /= 4;  // Convert move pts to screen coords
            pt[i].y /= 4;
            // Covert screen coordinates to window coordinates
```

(continued)

Listing 3-2 *(continued)*

```
            MapWindowPoints (HWND_DESKTOP, hWnd, &pt[i], 1);
            SetPixel (hdc, pt[i].x,   pt[i].y, RGB (255, 0, 0));
            SetPixel (hdc, pt[i].x+1, pt[i].y, RGB (255, 0, 0));
            SetPixel (hdc, pt[i].x,   pt[i].y+1, RGB (255, 0, 0));
            SetPixel (hdc, pt[i].x+1, pt[i].y+1, RGB (255, 0, 0));
        }
    }
    // The original point is drawn last in case one of the points
    // returned by GetMouseMovePoints overlaps it.
    SetPixel (hdc, ptM.x, ptM.y, RGB (0, 0, 0));
    SetPixel (hdc, ptM.x+1, ptM.y, RGB (0, 0, 0));
    SetPixel (hdc, ptM.x, ptM.y+1, RGB (0, 0, 0));
    SetPixel (hdc, ptM.x+1, ptM.y+1, RGB (0, 0, 0));
    ReleaseDC (hWnd, hdc);

    // Kill time to make believe we are busy.
    Sleep(25);
    return 0;
}
//--------------------------------------------------------------------
// DoDestroyMain - Process WM_DESTROY message for window.
//
LRESULT DoDestroyMain (HWND hWnd, UINT wMsg, WPARAM wParam,
                       LPARAM lParam) {
    PostQuitMessage (0);
    return 0;
}
```

Input Focus and Mouse Messages

Here are some subtleties to note about circumstances that rule how and when mouse messages initiated by stylus input are sent to different windows. As I mentioned previously, the input focus of the system changes when the stylus is pressed against a window. However, dragging the stylus from one window to the next won't cause the new window to receive the input focus. The down tap sets the focus, not the process of dragging the stylus across a window. When the stylus is dragged outside the window, that window stops receiving *WM_MOUSEMOVE* messages but retains input focus. Because the tip of the stylus is still down, no other window will receive the *WM_MOUSEMOVE* messages. This is akin to using a mouse and dragging the mouse outside a window with a button held down.

To continue to receive mouse messages even if the stylus moves off its window, an application can call

```
HWND SetCapture (HWND hWnd);
```

passing the handle of the window to receive the mouse messages. The function returns the handle of the window that previously had captured the mouse or

NULL if the mouse wasn't previously captured. To stop receiving the mouse messages initiated by stylus input, the window calls

```
BOOL ReleaseCapture (void);
```

Only one window can capture the stylus input at any one time. To determine whether the stylus has been captured, an application can call

```
HWND GetCapture (void);
```

which returns the handle of the window that has captured the stylus input or 0 if no window has captured the stylus input—although please note one caveat. *The window that has captured the stylus must be in the same thread context as the window calling the function.* This limitation means that if the stylus has been captured by a window in another application, *GetCapture* still returns 0.

If a window has captured the stylus input and another window calls *Get-Capture*, the window that had originally captured the stylus receives a *WM_CAPTURECHANGED* message. The *lParam* parameter of the message contains the handle of the window that has gained the capture. You shouldn't attempt to take back the capture by calling *GetCapture* in response to this message. In general, since the stylus is a shared resource, applications should be wary of capturing the stylus for any length of time and should be able to handle gracefully any loss of capture.

Another interesting tidbit: Just because a window has captured the mouse, that doesn't prevent a tap on another window from gaining the input focus for that window. You can use other methods for preventing the change of input focus, but in almost all cases, it's better to let the user, not the applications, decide which top-level window should have the input focus.

Right-Button Clicks

When you click the right mouse button on an object in Windows systems, the action typically calls up a context menu, which is a stand-alone menu displaying a set of choices for what you can do with that particular object. On a system with a mouse, Windows sends *WM_RBUTTONDOWN* and *WM_RBUTTONUP* messages indicating a right-button click. When you use a stylus, you don't have a right button. The Windows CE guidelines, however, allow you to simulate a right-button click using a stylus. The guidelines specify that if a user holds down the Alt key while tapping the screen with the stylus, a program should act as if a right mouse button were being clicked and display any appropriate context menu. There's no *MK_ALT* flag in the *wParam* value of *WM_LBUTTONDOWN*, so the best way to determine whether the Alt key is pressed is to use *GetKeyState* with *VK_MENU* as the parameter and test for the most significant bit of the return value to be set. *GetKeyState* is more appropriate in this case because the value returned will be the state of the key at the time the mouse message was pulled from the message queue.

On systems without a keyboard, the tap-and-hold gesture is used to simulate a right mouse click. The function *SHRecognizeGesture* can be used on Pocket PCs and, with the proper shell componets, embedded Windows CE systems to detect a tap and hold. The function is prototyped as

```
WINSHELLAPI DWORD SHRecognizeGesture(SHRGINFO *shrg);
```

The only parameter is the address of a *SHRGINFO* structure defined as

```
typedef struct tagSHRGI {
    DWORD cbSize;
    HWND hwndClient;
    POINT ptDown;
    DWORD dwFlags;
} SHRGINFO, *PSHRGINFO;
```

The *cbSize* field must be filled with the size of the structure. The *hwndClient* field should be set to the handle of the window that is calling the function. The *ptDown* field is a structure that should be filled with the point where the gesture is being recognized. The *dwFlags* field can contain a number of flags. The *SHRG_RETURNCMD* flag causes the function to return *GN_CONTEXTMENU* if the user properly gestures with a tap and hold or zero otherwise. The *SHRG_NOTIFYPARENT* flag causes a *WM_NOTIFY* message to be sent to the parent window if the gesture is properly recognized. Finally, the *SHRG_LONGDELAY* flag requires the user to hold the tap for a longer period of time before the gesture is recognized.

The TicTac1 Example Program

To demonstrate stylus programming, I have written a trivial tic-tac-toe game. The TicTac1 window is shown in Figure 3-5. The source code for the program is shown in Listing 3-3. This program doesn't allow you to play the game against the computer, nor does it determine the end of the game—it simply draws the board and keeps track of the X's and O's. Nevertheless, it demonstrates basic stylus interaction.

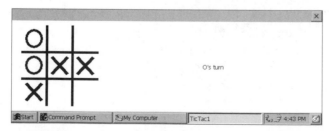

Figure 3-5   The TicTac1 window

TicTac1.h

```
//=========================================================================
// Header file
//
// Written for the book Programming Windows CE
// Copyright (C) 2003 Douglas Boling
//=========================================================================
// Returns number of elements
#define dim(x) (sizeof(x) / sizeof(x[0]))
//-------------------------------------------------------------------------
// Generic defines and data types
//
struct decodeUINT {                             // Structure associates
    UINT Code;                                  // messages
                                                // with a function.
    LRESULT (*Fxn)(HWND, UINT, WPARAM, LPARAM);
};
struct decodeCMD {                              // Structure associates
    UINT Code;                                  // menu IDs with a
    LRESULT (*Fxn)(HWND, WORD, HWND, WORD);     // function.
};


//-------------------------------------------------------------------------
// Function prototypes
//
HWND InitInstance (HINSTANCE, LPWSTR, int);
int TermInstance (HINSTANCE, int);


// Window procedures
LRESULT CALLBACK MainWndProc (HWND, UINT, WPARAM, LPARAM);


// Message handlers
 LRESULT DoSizeMain (HWND, UINT, WPARAM, LPARAM);
LRESULT DoPaintMain (HWND, UINT, WPARAM, LPARAM);
LRESULT DoLButtonDownMain (HWND, UINT, WPARAM, LPARAM);
LRESULT DoLButtonUpMain (HWND, UINT, WPARAM, LPARAM);
LRESULT DoDestroyMain (HWND, UINT, WPARAM, LPARAM);


// Game function prototypes
void DrawXO (HDC hdc, HPEN hPen, RECT *prect, INT nCell, INT nType);
void DrawBoard (HDC hdc, RECT *prect);
```

Listing 3-3   The TicTac1 program   *(continued)*

Listing 3-3 *(continued)*

TicTac1.cpp

```cpp
//======================================================================
// TicTac1 - Simple tic-tac-toe game
//
// Written for the book Programming Windows CE
// Copyright (C) 2003 Douglas Boling
//
//======================================================================
#include <windows.h>                    // For all that Windows stuff
#include <commctrl.h>                   // Command bar includes
#include "tictac1.h"                    // Program-specific stuff


//----------------------------------------------------------------------
// Global data
//
const TCHAR szAppName[] = TEXT ("TicTac1");
HINSTANCE hInst;                        // Program instance handle

// State data for game
RECT rectBoard = {0, 0, 0, 0};          // Used to place game board.
RECT rectPrompt;                        // Used to place prompt.
BYTE bBoard[9];                         // Keeps track of X's and O's.
BYTE bTurn = 0;                         // Keeps track of the turn.

// Message dispatch table for MainWindowProc
const struct decodeUINT MainMessages[] = {
    WM_SIZE, DoSizeMain,
    WM_PAINT, DoPaintMain,
    WM_LBUTTONUP, DoLButtonUpMain,
    WM_DESTROY, DoDestroyMain,
};


//======================================================================
//
// Program entry point
//
int WINAPI WinMain (HINSTANCE hInstance, HINSTANCE hPrevInstance,
                    LPWSTR lpCmdLine, int nCmdShow) {
    MSG msg;
    HWND hwndMain;

    // Initialize this instance.
    hwndMain = InitInstance (hInstance, lpCmdLine, nCmdShow);
    if (hwndMain == 0)
        return 0x10;
    // Application message loop
    while (GetMessage (&msg, NULL, 0, 0)) {
```

```
        TranslateMessage (&msg);
        DispatchMessage (&msg);
    }
    // Instance cleanup
    return TermInstance (hInstance, msg.wParam);
}
//-------------------------------------------------------------------------
// InitInstance - Instance initialization
//
HWND InitInstance (HINSTANCE hInstance, LPWSTR lpCmdLine, int nCmdShow) {
    WNDCLASS wc;
    HWND hWnd;

    // Save program instance handle in global variable.
    hInst = hInstance;

#if defined(WIN32_PLATFORM_PSPC)
    // If Pocket PC, allow only one instance of the application.
    hWnd = FindWindow (szAppName, NULL);
    if (hWnd) {
        SetForegroundWindow ((HWND)(((DWORD)hWnd) | 0x01));
        return 0;
    }
#endif
    // Register application main window class.
    wc.style = 0;                                // Window style
    wc.lpfnWndProc = MainWndProc;                // Callback function
    wc.cbClsExtra = 0;                           // Extra class data
    wc.cbWndExtra = 0;                           // Extra window data
    wc.hInstance = hInstance;                    // Owner handle
    wc.hIcon = NULL,                             // Application icon
    wc.hCursor = LoadCursor (NULL, IDC_ARROW);// Default cursor
    wc.hbrBackground = (HBRUSH) GetStockObject (WHITE_BRUSH);
    wc.lpszMenuName =  NULL;                     // Menu name
    wc.lpszClassName = szAppName;                // Window class name

    if (RegisterClass (&wc) == 0) return 0;

    // Create main window.
    hWnd = CreateWindowEx (WS_EX_NODRAG, szAppName, TEXT ("TicTac1"),
                      WS_VISIBLE | WS_CAPTION | WS_SYSMENU,
                      CW_USEDEFAULT, CW_USEDEFAULT,
                      CW_USEDEFAULT, CW_USEDEFAULT,
                      NULL, NULL, hInstance, NULL);
    // Return fail code if window not created.
    if (!IsWindow (hWnd)) return 0;
```

(continued)

Listing 3-2 *(continued)*

```
    // Standard show and update calls
    ShowWindow (hWnd, nCmdShow);
    UpdateWindow (hWnd);
    return hWnd;
}
//-----------------------------------------------------------------------
// TermInstance - Program cleanup
//
 int TermInstance (HINSTANCE hInstance, int nDefRC) {

    return nDefRC;
}
//=======================================================================
// Message handling procedures for MainWindow
//
//-----------------------------------------------------------------------
// MainWndProc - Callback function for application window
//
LRESULT CALLBACK MainWndProc (HWND hWnd, UINT wMsg, WPARAM wParam,
                             LPARAM lParam) {
    INT i;
    //
    // Search message list to see if we need to handle this
    // message. If in list, call procedure.
    //
    for (i = 0; i < dim(MainMessages); i++) {
        if (wMsg == MainMessages[i].Code)
            return (*MainMessages[i].Fxn)(hWnd, wMsg, wParam, lParam);
    }
    return DefWindowProc(hWnd, wMsg, wParam, lParam);
}
//-----------------------------------------------------------------------
// DoSizeMain - Process WM_SIZE message for window.
//
LRESULT DoSizeMain (HWND hWnd, UINT wMsg, WPARAM wParam,
                   LPARAM lParam) {
    RECT rect;
    INT i;
    // Adjust the size of the client rect to take into account
    // the command bar height.
    GetClientRect (hWnd, &rect);

    // Initialize the board rectangle if not yet initialized.
    if (rectBoard.right == 0) {

        // Initialize the board.
        for (i = 0; i < dim(bBoard); i++)
            bBoard[i] = 0;
    }
```

```
      // Define the playing board rect.
      rectBoard = rect;
      rectPrompt = rect;
      // Layout depends on portrait or landscape screen.
      if (rect.right - rect.left > rect.bottom - rect.top) {
          rectBoard.left += 20;
          rectBoard.top += 10;
          rectBoard.bottom -= 10;
          rectBoard.right = rectBoard.bottom - rectBoard.top + 10;

          rectPrompt.left = rectBoard.right + 10;

      } else {
          rectBoard.left += 20;
          rectBoard.right -= 20;
          rectBoard.top += 10;
          rectBoard.bottom = rectBoard.right - rectBoard.left + 10;

          rectPrompt.top = rectBoard.bottom + 10;
      }
      return 0;
}


//-----------------------------------------------------------------------
// DoPaintMain - Process WM_PAINT message for window.
//
LRESULT DoPaintMain (HWND hWnd, UINT wMsg, WPARAM wParam,
                     LPARAM lParam) {
    PAINTSTRUCT ps;
    RECT rect;
    HFONT hFont, hOldFont;
    HDC hdc;

    GetClientRect (hWnd, &rect);

    hdc = BeginPaint (hWnd, &ps);

    // Draw the board.
    DrawBoard (hdc, &rectBoard);

    // Write the prompt to the screen.
    hFont = (HFONT)GetStockObject (SYSTEM_FONT);
    hOldFont = (HFONT)SelectObject (hdc, hFont);
    if (bTurn == 0)
        DrawText (hdc, TEXT (" X's turn"), -1, &rectPrompt,
                  DT_CENTER | DT_VCENTER | DT_SINGLELINE);
    else
        DrawText (hdc, TEXT (" O's turn"), -1, &rectPrompt,
                  DT_CENTER | DT_VCENTER | DT_SINGLELINE);
```

(continued)

Listing 3-3 *(continued)*

```
    SelectObject (hdc, hOldFont);
    EndPaint (hWnd, &ps);
    return 0;
}
//-----------------------------------------------------------------------
// DoLButtonUpMain - Process WM_LBUTTONUP message for window.
//
LRESULT DoLButtonUpMain (HWND hWnd, UINT wMsg, WPARAM wParam,
                         LPARAM lParam) {
    POINT pt;
    INT cx, cy, nCell = 0;

    pt.x = LOWORD (lParam);
    pt.y = HIWORD (lParam);
    // See if pen on board.  If so, determine which cell.
    if (PtInRect (&rectBoard, pt)){
        // Normalize point to upper left corner of board.
        pt.x -= rectBoard.left;
        pt.y -= rectBoard.top;

        // Compute size of each cell.
        cx = (rectBoard.right - rectBoard.left)/3;
        cy = (rectBoard.bottom - rectBoard.top)/3;

        // Find column.
        nCell = (pt.x / cx);
        // Find row.
        nCell += (pt.y / cy) * 3;

        // If cell empty, fill it with mark.
        if (bBoard[nCell] == 0) {
            if (bTurn) {
                bBoard[nCell] = 2;
                bTurn = 0;
            } else {
                bBoard[nCell] = 1;
                bTurn = 1;
            }
            InvalidateRect (hWnd, NULL, FALSE);
        } else {
            // Inform the user of the filled cell.
            MessageBeep (0);
            return 0;
        }
    }
    return 0;
}
```

```
//------------------------------------------------------------------
// DoDestroyMain - Process WM_DESTROY message for window.
//
LRESULT DoDestroyMain (HWND hWnd, UINT wMsg, WPARAM wParam,
                       LPARAM lParam) {
    PostQuitMessage (0);
    return 0;
}
//==================================================================
// Game-specific routines
//
//------------------------------------------------------------------
// DrawXO - Draw a single X or O in a square.
//
void DrawXO (HDC hdc, HPEN hPen, RECT *prect, INT nCell, INT nType) {
    POINT pt[2];
    INT cx, cy;
    RECT rect;

    cx = (prect->right - prect->left)/3;
    cy = (prect->bottom - prect->top)/3;

    // Compute the dimensions of the target cell.
    rect.left = (cx * (nCell % 3) + prect->left) + 10;
    rect.right = rect.right =  rect.left + cx - 20;
    rect.top = cy * (nCell / 3) + prect->top + 10;
    rect.bottom = rect.top + cy - 20;

    // Draw an X ?
    if (nType == 1) {
        pt[0].x = rect.left;
        pt[0].y = rect.top;
        pt[1].x = rect.right;
        pt[1].y = rect.bottom;
        Polyline (hdc, pt, 2);

        pt[0].x = rect.right;
        pt[1].x = rect.left;
        Polyline (hdc, pt, 2);
    // How about an O ?
    } else if (nType == 2) {
        Ellipse (hdc, rect.left, rect.top, rect.right, rect.bottom);
    }
    return;
}
//------------------------------------------------------------------
// DrawBoard - Draw the tic-tac-toe board.
//   VK_MENU
```

(continued)

Listing 3-3   *(continued)*

```c
void DrawBoard (HDC hdc, RECT *prect) {
    HPEN hPen, hOldPen;
    POINT pt[2];
    LOGPEN lp;
    INT i, cx, cy;

    // Create a nice thick pen.
    lp.lopnStyle = PS_SOLID;
    lp.lopnWidth.x = 5;
    lp.lopnWidth.y = 5;
    lp.lopnColor = RGB (0, 0, 0);
    hPen = CreatePenIndirect (&lp);

    hOldPen = (HPEN)SelectObject (hdc, hPen);

    cx = (prect->right - prect->left)/3;
    cy = (prect->bottom - prect->top)/3;

    // Draw lines down.
    pt[0].x = cx + prect->left;
    pt[1].x = cx + prect->left;
    pt[0].y = prect->top;
    pt[1].y = prect->bottom;
    Polyline (hdc, pt, 2);
    pt[0].x += cx;
    pt[1].x += cx;
    Polyline (hdc, pt, 2);

    // Draw lines across.
    pt[0].x = prect->left;
    pt[1].x = prect->right;
    pt[0].y = cy + prect->top;
    pt[1].y = cy + prect->top;
    Polyline (hdc, pt, 2);

    pt[0].y += cy;
    pt[1].y += cy;
    Polyline (hdc, pt, 2);

    // Fill in X's and O's.
    for (i = 0; i < dim (bBoard); i++)
        DrawXO (hdc, hPen, &rectBoard, i, bBoard[i]);

    SelectObject (hdc, hOldPen);
    DeleteObject (hPen);
    return;
}
```

The action in TicTac1 is centered around three routines: *DrawBoard*, *DrawXO*, and *DoLButtonUpMain*. The first two perform the tasks of drawing the playing board. The routine that determines the location of a tap on the board (and therefore is more relevant to our current train of thought) is *DoLButtonUpMain*. As the name suggests, this routine is called in response to a *WM_LBUTTONUP* message. The first action to take is to call

```
BOOL PtInRect (const RECT *lprc, POINT pt);
```

which determines whether the tap is even on the game board. The program knows the location of the tap because it's passed in the *lParam* value of the message. The board rectangle is computed when the program starts in *DoSizeMain*. Once the tap is localized to the board, the program determines the location of the relevant cell within the playing board by dividing the coordinates of the tap point within the board by the number of cells across and down.

I mentioned that the board rectangle was computed during the *DoSizeMain* routine, which is called in response to a *WM_SIZE* message. While it might seem strange that Windows CE supports the *WM_SIZE* message common to other versions of Windows, it needs to support this message because a window is sized frequently: first right after it's created and then each time it's minimized and restored. You might think that another possibility for determining the size of the window would be during the *WM_CREATE* message. The *lParam* parameter points to a *CREATESTRUCT* structure that contains, among other things, the initial size and position of the window. The problem with using those numbers is that the size obtained is the total size of the window, not the size of the client area, which is what we need. Under Windows CE, most windows have no title bar and no border, but some have both and many have scroll bars, so using these values can cause trouble. So now, with the TicTac1 example, we have a simple program that uses the stylus effectively but isn't complete. To restart the game, we must exit and restart TicTac1. We can't take back a move or have O start first. We need a method for sending these commands to the program. Sure, using keys would work. Another solution would be to create hot spots on the screen that when tapped, provided the input necessary. Clearly this example needs some extra pieces to make it complete. I've taken the discussion of Windows as far as I can without a more complete discussion of the basic component of the operating system, the windows themselves. It's time to take a closer look at windows, child windows, and controls.

4

Windows, Controls, and Menus

Understanding how windows work and relate to each other is the key to understanding the user interface of the Microsoft Windows operating system, whether it be Microsoft Windows XP or Microsoft Windows CE. Everything you see on a Windows display is a window. The desktop is a window, the taskbar is a window, even the Start button on the taskbar is a window. Windows are related to one another according to one relationship model or another; they may be in *parent/child*, *sibling*, or *owner/owned* relationships. Windows supports a number of predefined window classes, called *controls*. These controls simplify the work of programmers by providing a range of predefined user interface elements as simple as a button or as complex as a multiline text editor. Windows CE supports the same standard set of built-in controls as the other versions of Windows. These built-in controls shouldn't be confused with the complex controls provided by the common control library. I'll talk about those controls in the next chapter.

Child Windows

Each window is connected via a parent/child relationship scheme. Applications create a main window with no parent, called a *top-level window*. That window might (or might not) contain windows, called *child* windows. A child window is clipped to its parent. That is, no part of a child window is visible beyond the edge of its parent. Child windows are automatically destroyed when their parent windows are destroyed. Also, when a parent window moves, its child windows move with it.

129

Child windows are programmatically identical to top-level windows. You use the *CreateWindow* or *CreateWindowEx* function to create them, each has a window procedure that handles the same messages as its top-level window, and each can, in turn, contain its own child windows. To create a child window, use the *WS_CHILD* window style in the *dwStyle* parameter of *CreateWindow* or *CreateWindowEx*. In addition, the *hMenu* parameter, unused in top-level Windows CE windows, passes an ID value that you can use to reference the window.

Under Windows CE, there's one other major difference between top-level windows and child windows. The Windows CE shell sends *WM_HIBERNATE* messages only to top-level windows that have the *WS_OVERLAPPED* and *WS_VISIBLE* styles. (Window visibility in this case has nothing to do with what a user sees. A window can be "visible" to the system and still not be seen by the user if other windows are above it in the Z-order.) This means that child windows and most dialog boxes aren't sent *WM_HIBERNATE* messages. Top-level windows must either manually send a *WM_HIBERNATE* message to their child windows as necessary or perform all the necessary tasks themselves to reduce the application's memory footprint. On Windows CE systems that use the standard "Explorer shell," which supports application buttons on the taskbar, the rules for determining the target of *WM_HIBERNATE* messages are also used to determine what windows get buttons on the taskbar.

In addition to the parent/child relationship, windows also have an owner/owned relationship. Owned windows aren't clipped to their owners. However, they always appear "above" (in Z-order) the window that owns them. If the owner window is minimized, all windows it owns are hidden. Likewise, if a window is destroyed, all windows it owns are destroyed.

Window Management Functions

Given the windows-centric nature of Windows, it's not surprising that you can choose from a number of functions that enable a window to interrogate its environment so that it might determine its location in the window family tree. To find its parent, a window can call

```
HWND GetParent (HWND hWnd);
```

This function is passed a window handle and returns the handle of the calling window's parent window. If the window has no parent, the function returns *NULL*.

Enumerating Windows

GetWindow, prototyped as

```
HWND GetWindow (HWND hWnd, UINT uCmd);
```

is an omnibus function that allows a window to query its children, owner, and siblings. The first parameter is the window's handle, while the second is a constant that indicates the requested relationship. The *GW_CHILD* constant returns a handle to the first child window of a window. *GetWindow* returns windows in Z-order, so the first window in this case is the child window highest in the Z-order. If the window has no child windows, this function returns *NULL*. The two constants, *GW_HWNDFIRST* and *GW_HWNDLAST*, return the first and last windows in the Z-order. If the window handle passed is a top-level window, these constants return the first and last topmost windows in the Z-order. If the window passed is a child window, the *GetWindow* function returns the first and last sibling window. The *GW_HWNDNEXT* and *GW_HWNDPREV* constants return the next lower and next higher windows in the Z-order. These constants allow a window to iterate through all the sibling windows by getting the next window, then using that window handle with another call to *GetWindow* to get the next, and so on. Finally, the *GW_OWNER* constant returns the handle of the owner of a window.

Another way to iterate through a series of windows is

```
BOOL EnumWindows (WNDENUMPROC lpEnumFunc, LPARAM lParam);
```

This function calls the callback function pointed to by *lpEnumFunc* once for each top-level window on the desktop, passing the handle of each window in turn. The *lParam* value is an application-defined value, which is also passed to the enumeration function. This function is better than iterating through a *GetWindow* loop to find the top-level windows because it always returns valid window handles; it's possible that a *GetWindow* iteration loop will get a window handle whose window is destroyed before the next call to *GetWindow* can occur. However, since *EnumWindows* works only with top-level windows, *GetWindow* still has a place when a program is iterating through a series of child windows.

Finding a Window

To get the handle of a specific window, use the function

```
HWND FindWindow (LPCTSTR lpClassName, LPCTSTR lpWindowName);
```

This function can find a window either by means of its window class name or by means of a window's title text. This function is handy when an application is just starting up; it can determine whether another copy of the application is already running. All an application has to do is call *FindWindow* with the name of the window class for the main window of the application. Because an application almost always has a main window while it's running, a *NULL* returned by *FindWindow* indicates that the function can't locate another window with the specified window class—therefore, it's almost certain that another copy of the application isn't running.

You can find the handle to the desktop window by using the function

```
HWND GetDesktopWindow (void);
```

Editing the Window Structure Values

The pair of functions

```
LONG GetWindowLong (HWND hWnd, int nIndex);
```

and

```
LONG SetWindowLong (HWND hWnd, int nIndex, LONG dwNewLong);
```

allow an application to edit data in the window structure for a window. Remember that the *WNDCLASS* structure passed to the *RegisterClass* function has a field, *cbWndExtra*, that controls the number of extra bytes that are to be allocated after the structure. If you allocated extra space in the window structure when the window class was registered, you can access those bytes using the *GetWindowLong* and *SetWindowLong* functions. Under Windows CE, the data must be allocated and referenced in 4-byte (integer sized and aligned) blocks. So if a window class was registered with 12 in the *cbWndExtra* field, an application can access those bytes by calling *GetWindowLong* or *SetWindowLong* with the window handle and by setting the values 0, 4, and 8 in the *nIndex* parameter.

GetWindowLong and *SetWindowLong* support a set of predefined index values that allow an application access to some of the basic parameters of a window. Here is a list of the supported values for Windows CE.

- ***GWL_STYLE*** The style flags for the window

- ***GWL_EXSTYLE*** The extended style flags for the window

- ***GWL_WNDPROC*** The pointer to the window procedure for the window

- ***GWL_ID*** The ID value for the window

- ***GWL_USERDATA*** An application-usable 32-bit value

Dialog box windows support the following additional values:

- **DWL_DLGPROC**   The pointer to the dialog procedure for the window

- **DWL_MSGRESULT**   The value returned when the dialog box function returns

- **DWL_USER**   An application-usable 32-bit value

Windows CE doesn't support the *GWL_HINSTANCE* and *GWL_HWNDPARENT* values supported by Windows 2000 and Windows XP.

Changing the Style Flags

Editing the window structure can be useful in a number of ways. The style bits of a window can be changed after the window has been created to change its default actions and look. For example, the title bar of a window can be shown or hidden by toggling the *WS_CAPTION* style bit. After changing any style flag that modifies the look of the window, it's customary to force the system to redraw the nonclient area of the window with a call to *SetWindowPos*.

SetWindowPos is one of those functions used all the time in Windows. It allows the application to move, size, change the Z-order of, and as in this case, redraw the nonclient area of the window. Its prototype is

```
BOOL SetWindowPos (HWND hWnd, HWND hWndInsertAfter, int X, int Y,
                   int cx, int cy, UINT uFlags);
```

The first parameter is the handle of the window that will be changed. The *hWndInsertAfter* parameter optionally allows the function to set the Z-order of the window. This parameter can be either a window handle or one of four flags that position the window either at the top or the bottom of the Z-order. The flags are shown here:

- **HWND_BOTTOM**   The window underneath all windows on the desktop

- **HWND_TOP**   The window on top of all windows

- **HWND_TOPMOST**   The window to always be placed on top of other windows, even when the window is deactivated

- **HWND_NOTTOPMOST**   The window on top of all other nontopmost windows but not marked as a topmost window so that it will be covered when another window is activated

The *X*, *Y*, *cx*, and *cy* parameters optionally specify the position and size of the window. The flags parameter contains one or more flags that describe the task to accomplish. The flags are as follows:

- **SWP_NOMOVE**   Don't move the window.

- **SWP_NOSIZE**   Don't resize the window.

- **SWP_NOZORDER**   Don't set the window's Z-order.

- **SWP_NOACTIVATE**   If the Z-order is set, don't activate the window.

- **SWP_DRAWFRAME**   Redraw the nonclient area.

- **SWP_FRAMECHANGED**   Recalculate the nonclient area, and then redraw.

Two other flags, *SWP_SHOWWINDOW* and *SWP_HIDEWINDOW*, show and hide the window, but it's easier to call the *ShowWindow* function to show or hide a window. To use *SetWindowPos* to force the frame to be redrawn after the style bits are changed, the call would be

```
SetWindowPos (hWnd, 0, 0, 0, 0, 0,
              SWP_NOMOVE | SWP_NOSIZE | SWP_NOZORDER | SWP_FRAMECHANGED);
```

Subclassing a Window

Another use of *SetWindowLong* is to subclass a window. Subclassing a window allows an application to essentially derive an instance of a new window class from a preexisting window class. The classic use for subclassing is to modify the behavior of a window control, such as an edit control.

The process of subclassing is actually quite simple. A window procedure is created that provides only the new functionality required of the subclassed window. A window is then creating using the base window class. *GetWindowLong* is called to get and save the pointer to the original window procedure for the window. *SetWindowLong* is then called to set the window procedure for this instance of the window to the new window procedure. The new window procedure then receives the message sent to the window. Any messages not acted upon by the new window procedure are passed on to the old window procedure with the function *CallWindowProc*. The following code shows a window being created and then subclassed. The subclass procedure then intercepts the *WM_LBUTTONDOWN* message and beeps the speaker when the window receives that message.

```
// Prototype of subclass procedure
LRESULT CALLBACK SCWndProc(HWND hWnd, UINT wMsg, WPARAM wParam,
```

```
                        LPARAM lParam);

// Variable that holds the pointer to the original WndProc
WNDPROC lpfnOldProc = 0;
//
// Routine that subclasses the requested window.
//
BOOL SubClassThisWnd (HWND hwndSC) {

    if (lpfnOldProc == 0) {
        // Get and save the pointer to the original window procedure
        lpfnOldProc = (WNDPROC)GetWindowLong (hwndSC, GWL_WNDPROC);

        // Point to new window procedure
        return SetWindowLong (hwndSC, GWL_WNDPROC, (DWORD)SCWndProc);
    }
    return FALSE;
}
//
// Subclass procedure
//
LRESULT CALLBACK SCWndProc(HWND hWnd, UINT wMsg, WPARAM wParam,
                           LPARAM lParam) {
    switch (wMsg) {

    case WM_LBUTTONDOWN:
        MessageBeep(0);
        break;
    }
    return CallWindowProc (lpfnOldProc, hWnd, wMsg, wParam, lParam);
}
```

To un-subclass the window, the program simply calls *SetWindowLong* to set the *WndProc* pointer back to the original window procedure.

Windows Controls

Were it not for the Windows Control library, programming Windows applications would be a slow and arduous process. In addition, every application would have its own look and feel. This would force the user to learn a new way of working with each new application. Fortunately, this scenario is avoided with an assortment of controls that the operating system provides. In short, controls are simply predefined window classes. Each has a custom window procedure supplied by Windows that gives each of these controls a tightly defined user and programming interface.

Since a control is just another window, it can be created with a call to *CreateWindow* or *CreateWindowEx*. Controls notify the parent window of events via *WM_COMMAND* messages encoding events and the ID and window handle of the control encoded in the parameters of the message.

Like all messages, *WM_COMMAND* contains two generic parameters, *wParam* and *lParam*. For a *WM_COMMAND* message, the high word of *wParam* contains the notification code, the reason for the *WM_COMMAND* message being sent. The low word of *wParam* contains the ID value of the control that sent the message. The ID is a word that's typically defined when the control is created and, to be useful, should be unique among all the sibling windows of the control. The *lParam* value contains the handle of the child window that sent the control. In general, it's easier to track the source of a *WM_COMMAND* message though the control ID rather than the window handle of the control, but both are available in the message. The following code is typical of the first few lines of a *WM_COMMAND* handler:

```
case WM_COMMAND:
    WORD idItem, wNotifyCode;
    HWND hwndCtl;

    // Parse the parameters.
    idItem = (WORD) LOWORD (wParam);
    wNotifyCode = (WORD) HIWORD(wParam);
    hwndCtl = (HWND) lParam;
```

From this point, the *WM_COMMAND* handler typically uses the ID of the control and then uses the notification code to determine why the *WM_COMMAND* message was sent.

Controls can also be configured and manipulated using predefined messages sent to the control. Among other things, applications can set the state of buttons, add items to or delete items from list boxes, and set the selection of text in edit boxes, all by sending messages to the controls. Controls are typically indentified by their ID, but many Windows functions require the handle of the control. The *GetDlgItem* function provides a simple conversion. The function is prototyped as

```
HWND GetDlgItem (HWND hDlg, int nIDDlgItem);
```

The two parameters are the handle of the parent window of the control and the ID value for the control. Although the name implies that the function can be used only in dialog boxes, something I'll talk about in Chapter 6, it works quite fine for a control in any window.

Another convenient function to send a message to a control is *SendDlg-ItemMessage*. This function sends a message to a child window with a specific ID. The prototype of the message is shown here:

```
LONG SendDlgItemMessage (HWND hParent, int nIDChild, UINT Msg,
                         WPARAM wParam, LPARAM lParam);
```

The parameters are similar to those for *SendMessage*. In fact, the following code is functionally identical to that of *SendDlgItemMessage*:

```
LONG SendMessage (GetDlgItem (hParent, nIDChild), Msg, wParam, lParam);
```

The only difference is the convenience of not having to embed the *GetDlgItem* call within *SendMessage*.

There are six predefined window control classes. They are

- **Button**   A wide variety of buttons

- **Edit**   A window that can be used to enter or display text

- **List**   A window that contains a list of strings

- **Combo**   A combination edit box and list box

- **Static**   A window that displays text or graphics that a user can't change

- **Scroll bar**   A scroll bar not attached to a specific window

Each of these controls has a wide range of function, far too much for me to cover completely in this chapter. But I'll quickly review these controls, mentioning at least the highlights. Afterward, I'll show you an example program, CtlView, to demonstrate these controls and their interactions with their parent windows.

Button Controls

Button controls enable several forms of input to the program. Buttons come in many styles, including push buttons, check boxes, and radio buttons. Each style is designed for a specific use—for example, push buttons are designed for receiving momentary input, check boxes are designed for on/off input, and radio buttons allow a user to select one of a number of choices.

Push Buttons

In general, push buttons are used to invoke some action. When a user presses a push button using a stylus, the button sends a *WM_COMMAND* message with a *BN_CLICKED* (for button notification clicked) notify code in the high word of the *wParam* parameter.

Check Boxes

Check boxes display a square box and a label that asks the user to specify a choice. A check box retains its state, either checked or unchecked, until the user clicks it again or the program forces the button to change state. In addition to the standard *BS_CHECKBOX* style, check boxes can come in a three-state style, *BS_3STATE*, that allows the button to be disabled and shown grayed out. Two additional styles, *BS_AUTOCHECKBOX* and *BS_AUTO3STATE*, automatically update the state and look of the control to reflect the checked, the unchecked, and, in the case of the three-state check box, the disabled state.

As with push buttons, check boxes send a *BN_CLICKED* notification when the button is clicked. Unless the check box has one of the automatic styles, it's the responsibility of the application to manually change the state of the button. This can be done by sending a *BM_SETCHECK* message to the button with the *wParam* set to 0 to uncheck the button or 1 to check the button. The three-state check boxes have a third, disabled, state that can be set by means of the *BM_SETCHECK* message with the *wParam* value set to 2. An application can determine the current state using the *BM_GETCHECK* message.

Radio Buttons

Radio buttons allow a user to select from a number of choices. Radio buttons are grouped in a set, with only one of the set ever being checked at a time. If it's using the standard *BS_RADIOBUTTON* style, the application is responsible for checking and unchecking the radio buttons so that only one is checked at a time. However, like check boxes, radio buttons have an alternative style, *BS_AUTORADIOBUTTON*, that automatically maintains the group of buttons so that only one is checked.

Group Boxes

Strangely, the group box is also a type of button. A group box appears to the user as a hollow box with an integrated text label surrounding a set of controls that are naturally grouped together. Group boxes are merely an organizational device and have no programming interface other than the text of the box, which is specified in the window title text upon creation of the group box. Group boxes should be created after the controls within the box are created. This ensures that the group box will be "beneath" the controls it contains in the window Z-order.

You should also be careful when using group boxes on Windows CE devices. The problem isn't with the group box itself, but with the small size of the Windows CE screen. Group boxes take up valuable screen real estate that can be better used by functional controls. This is especially the case on the Pocket PC with its very small screen. In many cases, a line drawn between sets of controls can visually group the controls as well as a group box can.

Customizing the Appearance of a Button

You can further customize the appearance of the buttons described so far by using a number of additional styles. The styles, *BS_RIGHT*, *BS_LEFT*, *BS_BOTTOM*, and *BS_TOP*, allow you to position the button text in a place other than the default center of the button. The *BS_MULTILINE* style allows you to specify more than one line of text in the button. The text is flowed to fit within the button. The newline character (\n) in the button text can be used to specifically define where line breaks occur. Windows CE doesn't support the *BS_ICON* and *BS_BITMAP* button styles supported by other versions of Windows.

Owner-Draw Buttons

You can totally control the look of a button by specifying the *BS_OWNERDRAW* style. When a button is specified as owner-draw, its owner window is entirely responsible for drawing the button for all the states in which it might occur. When a window contains an owner-draw button, it's sent a *WM_DRAWITEM* message to inform it that a button needs to be drawn. For this message, the *wParam* parameter contains the ID value for the button and the *lParam* parameter points to a *DRAWITEMSTRUCT* structure defined as

```
typedef struct tagDRAWITEMSTRUCT {
    UINT   CtlType;
    UINT   CtlID;
    UINT   itemID;
    UINT   itemAction;
    UINT   itemState;
    HWND   hwndItem;
    HDC    hDC;
    RECT   rcItem;
    DWORD  itemData;
} DRAWITEMSTRUCT;
```

The *CtlType* field is set to *ODT_BUTTON*, while the *CtlID* field, like the *wParam* parameter, contains the button's ID value. The *itemAction* field contains flags that indicate what needs to be drawn and why. The most significant of these fields is *itemState*, which contains the state (selected, disabled, and so forth) of the button. The *hDC* field contains the device context handle for the button window, while the *rcItem* RECT contains the dimensions of the button. The *itemData* field is *NULL* for owner-draw buttons.

As you might expect, the *WM_DRAWITEM* handler contains a number of GDI calls to draw lines, rectangles, and whatever else is needed to render the button. An important aspect of drawing a button is matching the standard colors of the other windows in the system. Since these colors can change, they shouldn't be hard coded. You can query to find out which are the proper colors by using the function

```
DWORD GetSysColor (int nIndex);
```

This function returns an RGB color value for the colors defined for different aspects of windows and controls in the system. Among a number of predefined index values passed in the index parameter, an index of *COLOR_BTNFACE* returns the proper color for the face of a button, while *COLOR_BTNSHADOW* returns the dark color for creating the three-dimensional look of a button.

The Edit Control

The edit control is a window that allows the user to enter and edit text. As you might imagine, the edit control is one of the handiest controls in the Windows control pantheon. The edit control is equipped with full editing capability, including cut, copy, and paste interaction with the system clipboard, all without assistance from the application. Edit controls display a single line or, when the *ES_MULTILINE* style is specified, multiple lines of text. The Notepad accessory, provided with the desktop versions of Windows, is simply a top-level window that contains a multiline edit control.

The edit control has a few other features that should be mentioned. An edit control with the *ES_PASSWORD* style displays an asterisk (*) character by default in the control for each character typed; the control saves the real character. The *ES_READONLY* style protects the text contained in the control so that it can be read, or copied into the clipboard, but not modified. The *ES_LOWERCASE* and *ES_UPPERCASE* styles force characters entered into the control to be changed to the specified case.

You can add text to an edit control by using the *WM_SETTEXT* message and retrieve text by using the *WM_GETTEXT* message. Selection can be controlled using the *EM_SETSEL* message. This message specifies the starting and ending characters in the selected area. Other messages allow the position of the caret (the marker that indicates the current entry point in an edit field) to be queried and set. Multiline edit controls contain a number of additional messages to control scrolling as well as to access characters by line and column position.

The List Box Control

The list box control displays a list of text items so that the user might select one or more of the items within the list. The list box stores the text, optionally sorts the items, and manages the display of the items, including scrolling. List boxes can be configured to allow selection of a single item or multiple items or to prevent any selection at all.

You can add an item to a list box by sending an *LB_ADDSTRING* or *LB_INSERTSTRING* message to the control, passing a pointer to the string to add the *lParam* parameter. The *LB_ADDSTRING* message places the newly added string at the end of the list of items, while *LB_INSERTSTRING* can place the string anywhere within the list of items in the list box. The list box can be searched for a particular item using the *LB_FIND* message.

Selection status can be queried using *LB_GETCURSEL* for single selection list boxes. For multiple selection list boxes, *LB_GETSELCOUNT* and *LB_GETSELITEMS* can be used to retrieve the items currently selected. Items in the list box can be selected programmatically using the *LB_SETCURSEL* and *LB_SETSEL* messages.

Windows CE supports most of the list box functionality available in other versions of Windows with the exception of owner-draw list boxes, as well as the *LB_DIR* family of messages. A new style, *LBS_EX_CONSTSTRINGDATA*, is supported under Windows CE. A list box with this style doesn't store strings passed to it. Instead, the pointer to the string is stored, and the application is responsible for maintaining the string. For large arrays of strings that might be loaded from a resource, this procedure can save RAM because the list box won't maintain a separate copy of the list of strings.

The Combo Box Control

The combo box is (as the name implies) a combination of controls—in this case, a single-line edit control and a list box. The combo box is a space-efficient control for selecting one item from a list of many or for providing an edit field with a list of predefined suggested entries. Under Windows CE, the combo box comes in two styles: drop-down and drop-down list. (Simple combo boxes aren't supported.) The drop-down style combo box contains an edit field with a button at the right end. Clicking on the button displays a list box that might contain more selections. Clicking on one of the selections fills the edit field of the combo box with the selection. The drop-down list style replaces the edit box with a static text control. This allows the user to select from an item in the list but prevents the user from entering an item that's not in the list.

Because the combo box combines the edit and list controls, a list of the messages used to control the combo box strongly resembles a merged list of the messages for the two base controls. *CB_ADDSTRING*, *CB_INSERTSTRING*, and *CB_FINDSTRING* act like their list box cousins. Likewise, the *CB_SETEDITSELECT* and *CB_GETEDITSELECT* messages set and query the selected characters in the edit box of a drop-down or a drop-down list combo box. To control the drop-down state of a drop-down or drop-down list combo box, the messages *CB_SHOWDROPDOWN* and *CB_GETDROPPEDSTATE* can be used.

As in the case of the list box, Windows CE doesn't support owner-draw combo boxes. However, the combo box supports the *CBS_EX_CONSTSTRINGDATA* extended style, which instructs the combo box to store a pointer to the string for an item instead of the string itself. As with the list box *LBS_EX_CONSTSTRINGDATA* style, this procedure can save RAM if an application has a large array of strings stored in ROM because the combo box won't maintain a separate copy of the list of strings.

Static Controls

Static controls are windows that display text, icons, or bitmaps not intended for user interaction. You can use static text controls to label other controls in a window. What a static control displays is defined by the text and the style for the control. Under Windows CE, static controls support the following styles:

- **SS_LEFT**   Displays a line of left-aligned text. The text is wrapped if necessary, to fit inside the control.

- **SS_CENTER**   Displays a line of text centered in the control. The text is wrapped if necessary, to fit inside the control.

- **SS_RIGHT**   Displays a line of text aligned with the right side of the control. The text is wrapped if necessary, to fit inside the control.

- **SS_LEFTNOWORDWRAP**   Displays a line of left-aligned text. The text isn't wrapped to multiple lines. Any text extending beyond the right side of the control is clipped.

- **SS_BITMAP**   Displays a bitmap. Window text for the control specifies the name of the resource containing the bitmap.

- **SS_ICON**   Displays an icon. Window text for the control specifies the name of the resource containing the icon.

Static controls with the *SS_NOTIFY* style send a *WM_COMMAND* message when the control is clicked, enabled, or disabled, although the Windows CE version of the static control doesn't send a notification when it's double-clicked. The *SS_CENTERIMAGE* style, used in combination with the *SS_BITMAP* or *SS_ICON* style, centers the image within the control. The *SS_NOPREFIX* style can be used in combination with the text styles. It prevents the ampersand (&) character from being interpreted as indicating that the next character is an accelerator character.

Windows CE doesn't support static controls that display filled or hollow rectangles such as those drawn with the *SS_WHITEFRAME* or *SS_BLACKRECT* style. Also, Windows CE doesn't support owner-draw static controls.

The Scroll Bar Control

The scroll bar control is a somewhat different beast from the other controls. Scroll bars are typically seen attached to the sides of windows to control the data being viewed in the window. Indeed, other window controls, such as the edit box and the list box, use the scroll bar control internally. Because of this tight relationship to the parent window, the interface of a scroll bar is different from that of the other controls.

Instead of using *WM_COMMAND* messages to report actions, scroll bars use *WM_VSCROLL* and *WM_HSCROLL* messages. *WM_VSCROLL* messages are sent by vertically oriented scroll bars, whereas *WM_HSCROLL* messages are sent by horizontally oriented scroll bars. In addition, instead of something like a *SB_SETPOSITION* message being sent to a scroll bar to set its position, there are dedicated functions to do this. Let's look at this unique interface.

Scroll Bar Messages

A *WM_VSCROLL* message is sent to the owner of a vertical scroll bar any time the user taps on the scroll bar to change its position. A complementary message, *WM_HSCROLL*, is identical to *WM_VSCROLL* but is sent when the user taps on a horizontal scroll bar. For both these messages, the *wParam* and *lParam* assignments are the same. The low word of the *wParam* parameter contains a code indicating why the message was sent. Figure 4-1 shows a diagram of horizontal and vertical scroll bars and how tapping on different parts of the scroll bars results in different messages. The high word of *wParam* is the position of the thumb, but this value is valid only while you're processing the *SB_THUMBPOSITION* and *SB_THUMBTRACK* codes, which I'll explain shortly. If the scroll bar sending the message is a stand-alone control and not attached to a window, the *lParam* parameter contains the window handle of the scroll bar.

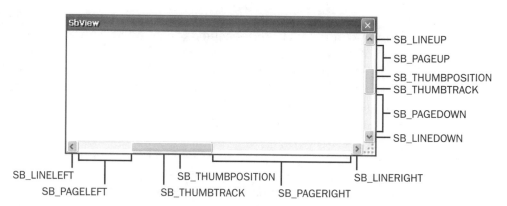

Figure 4-1   Scroll bars and their hot spots

The scroll bar message codes sent by the scroll bar allow the program to react to all the different user actions allowable by a scroll bar. The response required by each code is listed in the following table, Table 4-1.

The *SB_LINExxx* and *SB_PAGExxx* codes are pretty straightforward. You move the scroll position either a line or a page at a time. The *SB_THUMBPOSITION* and *SB_THUMBTRACK* codes can be processed in one of two ways. When the user drags the scroll bar thumb, the scroll bar sends *SB_THUMBTRACK* code so that a program can interactively track the dragging of the thumb. If your application is fast enough, you can simply process the *SB_THUMBTRACK* code and interactively update the display. If you field the *SB_THUMBTRACK* code, however, your application must be quick enough to redraw the display so that the thumb can be dragged without hesitation or jumping of the scroll bar. This is especially a problem on the slower devices that run Windows CE.

Table 4-1   Scroll Codes

Codes	Response
For *WM_VSCROLL*	
SB_LINEUP	Program should scroll the screen up one line.
SB_LINEDOWN	Program should scroll the screen down one line.
SB_PAGEUP	Program should scroll the screen up one screen's worth of data.
SB_PAGEDOWN	Program should scroll the screen down one screen's worth of data.

Table 4-1 **Scroll Codes**   *(continued)*

Codes	Response
For *WM HSCROLL*	
SB_LINELEFT	Program should scroll the screen left one character.
SB_LINERIGHT	Program should scroll the screen right one character.
SB_PAGELEFT	Program should scroll the screen left one screen's worth of data.
SB_PAGERIGHT	Program should scroll the screen right one screen's worth of data.
For both *WM_VSCROLL* and *WM_HSCROLL*	
SB_THUMBTRACK	Programs with enough speed to keep up should update the display with the new scroll position.
SB_THUMBPOSITION	Programs that can't update the display fast enough to keep up with the *SB_THUMBTRACK* message should update the display with the new scroll position.
SB_ENDSCROLL	This code indicates that the scroll bar has completed the scroll event. No action is required by the program.
SB_TOP	Program should set the display to the top or left end of the data.
SB_BOTTOM	Program should set the display to the bottom or right end of the data.

If your application (or the system it's running on) is too slow to quickly update the display for every *SB_THUMBTRACK* code, you can ignore the *SB_THUMBTRACK* and wait for the *SB_THUMBPOSITION* code that's sent when the user drops the scroll bar thumb. Then you have to update the display only once, after the user has finished moving the scroll bar thumb.

Configuring a Scroll Bar

To use a scroll bar, an application should first set the minimum and maximum values—the range of the scroll bar, along with the initial position. Windows CE scroll bars, like their desktop cousins, support proportional thumb sizes, which provide feedback to the user about the size of the current visible page compared with the entire scroll range. To set all these parameters, Windows CE applications should use the *SetScrollInfo* function, prototyped as

```
int SetScrollInfo (HWND hwnd, int fnBar, LPSCROLLINFO lpsi, BOOL fRedraw);
```

The first parameter is either the handle of the window that contains the scroll bar or the window handle of the scroll bar itself. The second parameter, *fnBar*, is a flag that determines the use of the window handle. The scroll bar flag can be one of three values: *SB_HORZ* for a window's standard horizontal scroll bar, *SB_VERT* for a window's standard vertical scroll bar, or *SB_CTL* if the scroll bar being set is a stand-alone control. Unless the scroll bar is a control, the window handle is the handle of the window containing the scroll bar. With *SB_CTL*, however, the handle is the window handle of the scroll bar control itself. The last parameter is *fRedraw*, a Boolean value that indicates whether the scroll bar should be redrawn after the call has been completed.

The third parameter is a pointer to a *SCROLLINFO* structure, which is defined as

```
typedef struct tagSCROLLINFO {
    UINT cbSize;
    UINT fMask;
    int    nMin;
    int    nMax;
    UINT nPage;
    int    nPos;
    int    nTrackPos;
} SCROLLINFO;
```

This structure allows you to completely specify the scroll bar parameters. The *cbSize* field must be set to the size of the *SCROLLINFO* structure. The *fMask* field contains flags indicating what other fields in the structure contain valid data. The *nMin* and *nMax* fields can contain the minimum and maximum scroll values the scroll bar can report. Windows looks at the values in these fields if the *fMask* parameter contains the *SIF_RANGE* flag. Likewise, the *nPos* field sets the position of the scroll bar within its predefined range if the *fMask* field contains the *SIF_POS* flag.

The *nPage* field allows a program to define the size of the currently viewable area of the screen in relation to the entire scrollable area. This allows a user to have a feel for how much of the entire scrolling range is currently visible. This field is used only if the *fMask* field contains the *SIF_PAGE* flag. The last member of the *SCROLLINFO* structure, *nTrackPos*, isn't used by the *SetScrollInfo* call and is ignored.

The *fMask* field can contain one last flag. Passing an *SIF_DISABLENOSCROLL* flag causes the scroll bar to be disabled but still visible. This is handy when the entire scrolling range is visible within the viewable area and no scrolling is necessary. Disabling the scroll bar in this case is often preferable to simply removing the scroll bar completely.

Those with a sharp eye for detail will notice a problem with the width of the fields in the *SCROLLINFO* structure. The *nMin*, *nMax*, and *nPos* fields are integers and therefore, in the world of Windows CE, are 32 bits wide. On the other hand, the *WM_HSCROLL* and *WM_VSCROLL* messages can return only a 16-bit position in the high word of the *wParam* parameter. If you're using scroll ranges greater than 65,535, use this function:

```
BOOL GetScrollInfo (HWND hwnd, int fnBar, LPSCROLLINFO lpsi);
```

As with *SetScrollInfo*, the flags in the *fnBar* field indicate the window handle that should be passed to the function. The *SCROLLINFO* structure is identical to the one used in *SetScrollInfo*; however, before it can be passed to *GetScrollInfo*, it must be initialized with the size of the structure in *cbSize*. An application must also indicate what data it wants the function to return by setting the appropriate flags in the *fMask* field. The flags used in *fMask* are the same as the ones used in *SetScrollInfo*, with a couple of additions. Now an *SIF_TRACKPOS* flag can be passed to have the scroll bar return its current thumb position. When called during a *WM_xSCROLL* message, the *nTrackPos* field contains the real time position, while the *nPos* field contains the scroll bar position at the start of the drag of the thumb.

The scroll bar is an unusual control in that it can be added easily to windows simply by specifying a window style flag. It's also unusual in that the control is placed outside the client area of the window. The reason for this assistance is that scroll bars are commonly needed by applications, so the Windows developers made it easy to attach scroll bars to windows. Now let's look at the other basic Windows controls.

The CtlView Example Program

The CtlView example program, shown in Listing 4-1, demonstrates all the controls I've just described. The example makes use of several application-defined child windows that contain various controls. You switch between the different child windows by clicking on one of five radio buttons displayed across the top of the main window. As each of the controls reports a notification through a *WM_COMMAND* message, that notification is displayed in a list box on the right side of the window. CtlView is handy for observing just what messages a control sends to its parent window and when they're sent. CtlView is designed to use different control layouts depending on the width of the screen. This means that even on the Pocket PC's narrow screen, all the controls are visible.

CtlView.h

```
//======================================================================
// Header file
//
// Written for the book Programming Windows CE
// Copyright (C) 2003 Douglas Boling
//======================================================================
// Returns number of elements
#define dim(x) (sizeof(x) / sizeof(x[0]))
//----------------------------------------------------------------------
// Generic defines and data types
//
struct decodeUINT {                          // Structure associates
    UINT Code;                               // messages
                                             // with a function.
    LRESULT (*Fxn)(HWND, UINT, WPARAM, LPARAM);
};
struct decodeCMD {                           // Structure associates
    UINT Code;                               // menu IDs with a
    LRESULT (*Fxn)(HWND, WORD, HWND, WORD);  // function.
};


//----------------------------------------------------------------------
// Generic defines used by application
#define  IDI_BTNICON        20               // Icon used on button

#define  ID_ICON            1                // Icon ID
#define  IDC_CMDBAR         2                // Command bar ID
#define  IDC_RPTLIST        3                // Report window ID

// Client window IDs go from 5 through 9.
#define  IDC_WNDSEL         5                // Starting client
                                             // window IDs

// Radio button IDs go from 10 through 14.
#define  IDC_RADIOBTNS      10               // Starting ID of
                                             // radio buttons

// Button window defines
#define  IDC_PUSHBTN    100
#define  IDC_CHKBOX     101
#define  IDC_ACHKBOX    102
#define  IDC_A3STBOX    103
#define  IDC_RADIO1     104
#define  IDC_RADIO2     105
#define  IDC_OWNRDRAW   106
// Edit window defines
```

Listing 4-1 The CtlView program

```
#define   IDC_SINGLELINE 100
#define   IDC_MULTILINE  101
#define   IDC_PASSBOX    102


// List box window defines
#define   IDC_COMBOBOX   100
#define   IDC_SNGLELIST  101
#define   IDC_MULTILIST  102

// Static control window defines
#define   IDC_LEFTTEXT   100
#define   IDC_RIGHTTEXT  101
#define   IDC_CENTERTEXT 102
#define   IDC_ICONCTL    103
#define   IDC_BITMAPCTL  104
// Scroll bar window defines
#define   IDC_LRSCROLL   100
#define   IDC_UDSCROLL   101


// User-defined message to add a line to the window
#define MYMSG_ADDLINE   (WM_USER + 10)

typedef struct {
    TCHAR *szClass;
    int   nID;
    TCHAR *szTitle;
    int   x;
    int   y;
    int   cx;
    int   cy;
    DWORD lStyle;
} CTLWNDSTRUCT, *PCTLWNDSTRUCT;

typedef struct {
    WORD wMsg;
    int nID;
    WPARAM wParam;
    LPARAM lParam;
} CTLMSG, * PCTLMSG;

typedef struct {
    TCHAR *pszLabel;
    WORD wNotification;
} NOTELABELS, *PNOTELABELS;
//----------------------------------------------------------------------
// Function prototypes
//
```

(continued)

Listing 4-1   *(continued)*

```
HWND InitInstance (HINSTANCE, LPWSTR, int);
int TermInstance (HINSTANCE, int);

// Window procedures
LRESULT CALLBACK FrameWndProc (HWND, UINT, WPARAM, LPARAM);
LRESULT CALLBACK ClientWndProc (HWND, UINT, WPARAM, LPARAM);

// Message handlers
LRESULT DoCreateFrame (HWND, UINT, WPARAM, LPARAM);
LRESULT DoSizeFrame (HWND, UINT, WPARAM, LPARAM);
LRESULT DoCommandFrame (HWND, UINT, WPARAM, LPARAM);
LRESULT DoAddLineFrame (HWND, UINT, WPARAM, LPARAM);
LRESULT DoDestroyFrame (HWND, UINT, WPARAM, LPARAM);

//-------------------------------------------------------------------
// Window prototypes and defines for BtnWnd
//
#define BTNWND      TEXT ("ButtonWnd")
int InitBtnWnd (HINSTANCE);

// Window procedures
LRESULT CALLBACK BtnWndProc (HWND, UINT, WPARAM, LPARAM);

LRESULT DoCreateBtnWnd (HWND, UINT, WPARAM, LPARAM);
LRESULT DoCtlColorBtnWnd (HWND, UINT, WPARAM, LPARAM);
LRESULT DoCommandBtnWnd (HWND, UINT, WPARAM, LPARAM);
LRESULT DoDrawItemBtnWnd (HWND, UINT, WPARAM, LPARAM);
LRESULT DoMeasureItemBtnWnd (HWND, UINT, WPARAM, LPARAM);

//-------------------------------------------------------------------
// Window prototypes and defines for EditWnd
//
#define EDITWND     TEXT ("EditWnd")
int InitEditWnd (HINSTANCE);

// Window procedures
LRESULT CALLBACK EditWndProc (HWND, UINT, WPARAM, LPARAM);

LRESULT DoCreateEditWnd (HWND, UINT, WPARAM, LPARAM);
LRESULT DoCommandEditWnd (HWND, UINT, WPARAM, LPARAM);
LRESULT DoDrawItemEditWnd (HWND, UINT, WPARAM, LPARAM);
LRESULT DoMeasureItemEditWnd (HWND, UINT, WPARAM, LPARAM);
//-------------------------------------------------------------------
// Window prototypes and defines for ListWnd
//
#define LISTWND     TEXT ("ListWnd")
int InitListWnd (HINSTANCE);
```

```
// Window procedures
LRESULT CALLBACK ListWndProc (HWND, UINT, WPARAM, LPARAM);


LRESULT DoCreateListWnd (HWND, UINT, WPARAM, LPARAM);
LRESULT DoCommandListWnd (HWND, UINT, WPARAM, LPARAM);
LRESULT DoDrawItemListWnd (HWND, UINT, WPARAM, LPARAM);
LRESULT DoMeasureItemListWnd (HWND, UINT, WPARAM, LPARAM);


//-------------------------------------------------------------------
// Window prototypes and defines for StatWnd
//
#define STATWND    TEXT ("StaticWnd")
int InitStatWnd (HINSTANCE);

// Window procedures
LRESULT CALLBACK StatWndProc (HWND, UINT, WPARAM, LPARAM);


LRESULT DoCreateStatWnd (HWND, UINT, WPARAM, LPARAM);
LRESULT DoCommandStatWnd (HWND, UINT, WPARAM, LPARAM);
LRESULT DoDrawItemStatWnd (HWND, UINT, WPARAM, LPARAM);
LRESULT DoMeasureItemStatWnd (HWND, UINT, WPARAM, LPARAM);


//-------------------------------------------------------------------
// Window prototypes and defines ScrollWnd
//
#define SCROLLWND    TEXT ("ScrollWnd")
int InitScrollWnd (HINSTANCE);

// Window procedures
LRESULT CALLBACK ScrollWndProc (HWND, UINT, WPARAM, LPARAM);


LRESULT DoCreateScrollWnd (HWND, UINT, WPARAM, LPARAM);
LRESULT DoVScrollScrollWnd (HWND, UINT, WPARAM, LPARAM);
LRESULT DoHScrollScrollWnd (HWND, UINT, WPARAM, LPARAM);
```

CtlView.cpp

```
//===================================================================
// CtlView - Lists the available fonts in the system.
//
// Written for the book Programming Windows CE
// Copyright (C) 2003 Douglas Boling
//===================================================================
#include <windows.h>              // For all that Windows stuff
#include <commctrl.h>             // Command bar includes
#include "CtlView.h"              // Program-specific stuff
```

(continued)

Listing 4-1   *(continued)*

```
//------------------------------------------------------------------------
// Global data
//
const TCHAR szAppName[] = TEXT ("CtlView");
HINSTANCE hInst;                          // Program instance handle

// Message dispatch table for FrameWindowProc
const struct decodeUINT FrameMessages[] = {
    WM_CREATE, DoCreateFrame,
    WM_SIZE, DoSizeFrame,
    WM_COMMAND, DoCommandFrame,
    MYMSG_ADDLINE, DoAddLineFrame,
    WM_DESTROY, DoDestroyFrame,
};

typedef struct {
    TCHAR *szTitle;
    int   nID;
    TCHAR *szCtlWnds;
    HWND  hWndClient;
} RBTNDATA;

// Text for main window radio buttons
TCHAR *szBtnTitle[] = {TEXT ("Buttons"), TEXT ("Edit"), TEXT ("List"),
                       TEXT ("Static"), TEXT ("Scroll")};
// Class names for child windows containing controls
TCHAR *szCtlWnds[] = {BTNWND, EDITWND, LISTWND, STATWND, SCROLLWND};

int nWndSel = 0;

//========================================================================
// Program entry point
//
int WINAPI WinMain (HINSTANCE hInstance, HINSTANCE hPrevInstance,
                    LPWSTR lpCmdLine, int nCmdShow) {
    MSG msg;
    int rc = 0;
    HWND hwndFrame;

    // Initialize application.
    hwndFrame = InitInstance (hInstance, lpCmdLine, nCmdShow);
    if (hwndFrame == 0)
        return 0x10;

    // Application message loop
    while (GetMessage (&msg, NULL, 0, 0)) {
        TranslateMessage (&msg);
```

```
            DispatchMessage (&msg);
    }
    // Instance cleanup
    return TermInstance (hInstance, msg.wParam);
}
//---------------------------------------------------------------------
// InitInstance - Instance initialization
//
HWND InitInstance (HINSTANCE hInstance, LPWSTR lpCmdLine, int nCmdShow) {
    WNDCLASS wc;
    HWND hWnd;

    // Save program instance handle in global variable.
    hInst = hInstance;

#if defined(WIN32_PLATFORM_PSPC)
    // If Pocket PC, allow only one instance of the application
    hWnd = FindWindow (szAppName, NULL);
    if (hWnd) {
        SetForegroundWindow ((HWND)(((DWORD)hWnd) | 0x01));
        return 0;
    }
#endif
    // Register application frame window class.
    wc.style = 0;                                // Window style
    wc.lpfnWndProc = FrameWndProc;               // Callback function
    wc.cbClsExtra = 0;                           // Extra class data
    wc.cbWndExtra = 0;                           // Extra window data
    wc.hInstance = hInstance;                    // Owner handle
    wc.hIcon = NULL,                             // Application icon
    wc.hCursor = LoadCursor (NULL, IDC_ARROW);// Default cursor
    wc.hbrBackground = (HBRUSH) GetSysColorBrush (COLOR_STATIC);
    wc.lpszMenuName =  NULL;                     // Menu name
    wc.lpszClassName = szAppName;                // Window class name

    if (RegisterClass (&wc) == 0) return 0;

    // Initialize client window classes
    if (InitBtnWnd (hInstance) != 0) return 0;
    if (InitEditWnd (hInstance) != 0) return 0;
    if (InitListWnd (hInstance) != 0) return 0;
    if (InitStatWnd (hInstance) != 0) return 0;
    if (InitScrollWnd (hInstance) != 0) return 0;

    // Create frame window.
    hWnd = CreateWindowEx (WS_EX_NODRAG, szAppName, TEXT ("Control View"),
                        WS_VISIBLE | WS_CAPTION | WS_SYSMENU,
```

(continued)

Listing 4-1   *(continued)*

```
                          CW_USEDEFAULT, CW_USEDEFAULT, CW_USEDEFAULT,
                          CW_USEDEFAULT, NULL, NULL, hInstance, NULL);
    // Return fail code if window not created.
    if (!IsWindow (hWnd)) return 0;

    // Standard show and update calls
    ShowWindow (hWnd, nCmdShow);
    UpdateWindow (hWnd);

    return hWnd;
}
//---------------------------------------------------------------------------
// TermInstance - Program cleanup
//
int TermInstance (HINSTANCE hInstance, int nDefRC) {

    return nDefRC;
}
//===========================================================================
// Message handling procedures for FrameWindow
//
//---------------------------------------------------------------------------
// FrameWndProc - Callback function for application window
//
LRESULT CALLBACK FrameWndProc (HWND hWnd, UINT wMsg, WPARAM wParam,
                               LPARAM lParam) {
    int i;
    //
    // Search message list to see if we need to handle this
    // message.  If in list, call procedure.
    //
    for (i = 0; i < dim(FrameMessages); i++) {
        if (wMsg == FrameMessages[i].Code)
            return (*FrameMessages[i].Fxn)(hWnd, wMsg, wParam, lParam);
    }
    return DefWindowProc (hWnd, wMsg, wParam, lParam);
}
//---------------------------------------------------------------------------
// DoCreateFrame - Process WM_CREATE message for window.
//
LRESULT DoCreateFrame (HWND hWnd, UINT wMsg, WPARAM wParam,
                       LPARAM lParam) {
    HWND hwndChild;
    INT i;

    // Set currently viewed window
    nWndSel = 0;
```

```
// Create the radio buttons.
for (i = 0; i < dim(szBtnTitle); i++) {
    hwndChild = CreateWindow (TEXT ("BUTTON"),
                             szBtnTitle[i], BS_AUTORADIOBUTTON |
                             WS_VISIBLE | WS_CHILD, 0,
                             0, 80, 20, hWnd,
                             (HMENU)(IDC_RADIOBTNS+i), hInst, NULL);

    // Destroy frame if window not created.
    if (!IsWindow (hwndChild)) {
        DestroyWindow (hWnd);
        break;
    }
}
// Create report window.  Size it so that it fits either on the right
// or below the control windows, depending on the size of the screen.
hwndChild = CreateWindowEx (WS_EX_CLIENTEDGE, TEXT ("listbox"),
                     TEXT (""), WS_VISIBLE | WS_CHILD | WS_VSCROLL |
                     LBS_USETABSTOPS | LBS_NOINTEGRALHEIGHT, 0, 0,
                     100, 100,hWnd, (HMENU)IDC_RPTLIST, hInst, NULL);

// Destroy frame if window not created.
if (!IsWindow (hwndChild)) {
    DestroyWindow (hWnd);
    return 0;
}
// Initialize tab stops for display list box.
i = 24;
SendMessage (hwndChild, LB_SETTABSTOPS, 1, (LPARAM)&i);

// Create the child windows.  Size them so that they fit under
// the command bar and fill the left side of the child area.
for (i = 0; i < dim(szCtlWnds); i++) {
    hwndChild = CreateWindowEx (WS_EX_CLIENTEDGE, szCtlWnds[i],
                         TEXT (""), WS_CHILD, 0, 0, 200, 200, hWnd,
                         (HMENU)(IDC_WNDSEL+i), hInst, NULL);

    // Destroy frame if client window not created.
    if (!IsWindow (hwndChild)) {
        DestroyWindow (hWnd);
        return 0;
    }
}
// Check one of the auto radio buttons.
SendDlgItemMessage (hWnd, IDC_RADIOBTNS+nWndSel, BM_SETCHECK, 1, 0);
hwndChild = GetDlgItem (hWnd, IDC_WNDSEL+nWndSel);
ShowWindow (hwndChild, SW_SHOW);
```

(continued)

Listing 4-1   *(continued)*

```
    return 0;
}
//----------------------------------------------------------------------
// DoSizeFrame - Process WM_SIZE message for window.
//
LRESULT DoSizeFrame (HWND hWnd, UINT wMsg, WPARAM wParam,
                     LPARAM lParam) {
    int nWidth, nHeight;
    int i, x, y, cx, cy;
    BOOL bWide = TRUE;
    RECT rect;
    GetWindowRect (hWnd, &rect);
    GetClientRect (hWnd, &rect);
    // These arrays are used to adjust between wide and narrow screens.
    POINT ptRBtnsN[] = {{5,0}, {90,0}, {180,0}, {5,20}, {90,20}};
    POINT ptRBtnsW[] = {{5,0}, {90,0}, {180,0}, {270,0}, {360,0}};
    LPPOINT pptRbtns = ptRBtnsW;

    nWidth = LOWORD (lParam);
    nHeight = HIWORD (lParam);

    // Use different layouts for narrow (Pocket PC) screens.
    if (GetSystemMetrics (SM_CXSCREEN) < 480) {
        pptRbtns = ptRBtnsN;
        bWide = FALSE;
    }
    // Move the radio buttons.
    for (i = 0; i < dim(szBtnTitle); i++)
        SetWindowPos (GetDlgItem (hWnd, IDC_RADIOBTNS+i), 0,
                      pptRbtns[i].x, pptRbtns[i].y,
                      0, 0, SWP_NOSIZE | SWP_NOZORDER);

    // Size report window so that it fits either on the right or
    // below the control windows, depending on the size of the screen.
    x =  bWide ? nWidth/2 : 0;
    y =  bWide ? 20 : (nHeight)/2 + 40;
    cx = bWide ? nWidth/2 : nWidth;
    cy = nHeight - y;

    SetWindowPos (GetDlgItem (hWnd, IDC_RPTLIST), 0, x, y, cx, cy,
                  SWP_NOZORDER);

    // Size the child windows so that they fit under
    // the command bar and fill the left side of the child area.
    x =  0;
    y =  bWide ? 20 : 40;
```

```
    cx = bWide ? nWidth/2 : nWidth;
    cy = bWide ? nHeight : (nHeight)/2+40;

    for (i = 0; i < dim(szCtlWnds); i++)
        SetWindowPos (GetDlgItem (hWnd, IDC_WNDSEL+i), 0, x, y, cx, cy,
                      SWP_NOZORDER);
    return 0;
}
//-------------------------------------------------------------------------
// DoCommandFrame - Process WM_COMMAND message for window.
//
LRESULT DoCommandFrame (HWND hWnd, UINT wMsg, WPARAM wParam,
                        LPARAM lParam) {

    HWND hwndTemp;
    int nBtn;
    // Don't look at list box messages.
    if (LOWORD (wParam) == IDC_RPTLIST)
        return 0;
    nBtn = LOWORD (wParam) - IDC_RADIOBTNS;
    if (nWndSel != nBtn) {

        // Hide the currently visible window.
        hwndTemp = GetDlgItem (hWnd, IDC_WNDSEL+nWndSel);
        ShowWindow (hwndTemp, SW_HIDE);

        // Save the current selection.
        nWndSel = nBtn;
        // Show the window selected via the radio button.
        hwndTemp = GetDlgItem (hWnd, IDC_WNDSEL+nWndSel);
        ShowWindow (hwndTemp, SW_SHOW);
    }
    return 0;
}
//-------------------------------------------------------------------------
// DoAddLineFrame - Process MYMSG_ADDLINE message for window.
//
LRESULT DoAddLineFrame (HWND hWnd, UINT wMsg, WPARAM wParam,
                        LPARAM lParam) {
    TCHAR szOut[128];
    int i;

    if (LOWORD (wParam) == 0xffff)
        wsprintf (szOut, TEXT ("      \t %s"), (LPTSTR)lParam);
    else
        wsprintf (szOut, TEXT ("id:%3d \t %s"), LOWORD (wParam),
                  (LPTSTR)lParam);
```

(continued)

Listing 4-1 *(continued)*

```
    i = SendDlgItemMessage (hWnd, IDC_RPTLIST, LB_ADDSTRING, 0,
                            (LPARAM)(LPCTSTR)szOut);

    if (i != LB_ERR)
        SendDlgItemMessage (hWnd, IDC_RPTLIST, LB_SETTOPINDEX, i,
                            (LPARAM)(LPCTSTR)szOut);
    return 0;
}
//-----------------------------------------------------------------------
// DoDestroyFrame - Process WM_DESTROY message for window.
//
LRESULT DoDestroyFrame (HWND hWnd, UINT wMsg, WPARAM wParam,
                        LPARAM lParam) {
    PostQuitMessage (0);
    return 0;
}
```

BtnWnd.cpp

```
//=======================================================================
// BtnWnd - Button window code
//
// Written for the book Programming Windows CE
// Copyright (C) 2003 Douglas Boling
//=======================================================================
#include <windows.h>                    // For all that Windows stuff
#include "Ctlview.h"                    // Program-specific stuff

extern HINSTANCE hInst;

LRESULT DrawButton (HWND hWnd, LPDRAWITEMSTRUCT pdi);
//-----------------------------------------------------------------------
// Global data
//

// Message dispatch table for BtnWndWindowProc
const struct decodeUINT BtnWndMessages[] = {
    WM_CREATE, DoCreateBtnWnd,
    WM_CTLCOLORSTATIC, DoCtlColorBtnWnd,
    WM_COMMAND, DoCommandBtnWnd,
    WM_DRAWITEM, DoDrawItemBtnWnd,
};

// Structure defining the controls in the window
CTLWNDSTRUCT  Btns [] = {
    {TEXT ("BUTTON"), IDC_PUSHBTN, TEXT ("Button"),
     10,  10, 120,  23, BS_PUSHBUTTON | BS_NOTIFY},
```

```
    {TEXT ("BUTTON"), IDC_CHKBOX, TEXT ("Check box"),
     10,  35, 120,  23, BS_CHECKBOX},
    {TEXT ("BUTTON"), IDC_ACHKBOX, TEXT ("Auto check box"),
     10,  60, 110,  23, BS_AUTOCHECKBOX},
    {TEXT ("BUTTON"), IDC_A3STBOX, TEXT ("Multiline auto 3-state box"),
    140,  60,  90,  52, BS_AUTO3STATE | BS_MULTILINE},
    {TEXT ("BUTTON"), IDC_RADIO1, TEXT ("Auto radio button 1"),
     10,  85, 120,  23, BS_AUTORADIOBUTTON},
    {TEXT ("BUTTON"), IDC_RADIO2, TEXT ("Auto radio button 2"),
     10, 110, 120,  23, BS_AUTORADIOBUTTON},
    {TEXT ("BUTTON"), IDC_OWNRDRAW, TEXT ("OwnerDraw"),
    150,  10,  44,  44, BS_PUSHBUTTON | BS_OWNERDRAW},
};
// Structure labeling the button control WM_COMMAND notifications
NOTELABELS nlBtn[] = {{TEXT ("BN_CLICKED "),       0},
                      {TEXT ("BN_PAINT    "),      1},
                      {TEXT ("BN_HILITE   "),      2},
                      {TEXT ("BN_UNHILITE"),       3},
                      {TEXT ("BN_DISABLE "),       4},
                      {TEXT ("BN_DOUBLECLICKED"), 5},
                      {TEXT ("BN_SETFOCUS "),      6},
                      {TEXT ("BN_KILLFOCUS"),      7}
};
// Handle for icon used in owner-draw icon
HICON hIcon = 0;
//-------------------------------------------------------------------------
// InitBtnWnd - BtnWnd window initialization
//
int InitBtnWnd (HINSTANCE hInstance) {
    WNDCLASS wc;

    // Register application BtnWnd window class.
    wc.style = 0;                                // Window style
    wc.lpfnWndProc = BtnWndProc;                 // Callback function
    wc.cbClsExtra = 0;                           // Extra class data
    wc.cbWndExtra = 0;                           // Extra window data
    wc.hInstance = hInstance;                    // Owner handle
    wc.hIcon = NULL,                             // Application icon
    wc.hCursor = LoadCursor (NULL, IDC_ARROW);// Default cursor
    wc.hbrBackground = (HBRUSH) GetStockObject (WHITE_BRUSH);
    wc.lpszMenuName =  NULL;                     // Menu name
    wc.lpszClassName = BTNWND;                   // Window class name

    if (RegisterClass (&wc) == 0) return 1;

    return 0;
}
```

(continued)

Listing 4-1   *(continued)*

```
//=========================================================================
// Message handling procedures for BtnWindow
//-------------------------------------------------------------------------
// BtnWndWndProc - Callback function for application window
//
LRESULT CALLBACK BtnWndProc (HWND hWnd, UINT wMsg, WPARAM wParam,
                            LPARAM lParam) {
    int i;
    //
    // Search message list to see if we need to handle this
    // message.  If in list, call procedure.
    //
    for (i = 0; i < dim(BtnWndMessages); i++) {
        if (wMsg == BtnWndMessages[i].Code)
            return (*BtnWndMessages[i].Fxn)(hWnd, wMsg, wParam, lParam);
    }
    return DefWindowProc (hWnd, wMsg, wParam, lParam);
}
//-------------------------------------------------------------------------
// DoCreateBtnWnd - Process WM_CREATE message for window.
//
LRESULT DoCreateBtnWnd (HWND hWnd, UINT wMsg, WPARAM wParam,
                       LPARAM lParam) {
    int i;

    for (i = 0; i < dim(Btns); i++) {

        CreateWindow (Btns[i].szClass, Btns[i].szTitle,
                      Btns[i].lStyle | WS_VISIBLE | WS_CHILD,
                      Btns[i].x, Btns[i].y, Btns[i].cx, Btns[i].cy,
                      hWnd, (HMENU) Btns[i].nID, hInst, NULL);
    }
    hIcon = LoadIcon (hInst, TEXT ("TEXTICON"));

    // We need to set the initial state of the radio buttons.
    CheckRadioButton (hWnd, IDC_RADIO1, IDC_RADIO2, IDC_RADIO1);
    return 0;
}
//-------------------------------------------------------------------------
// DoCtlColorBtnWnd - process WM_CTLCOLORxx messages for window.
//
LRESULT DoCtlColorBtnWnd (HWND hWnd, UINT wMsg, WPARAM wParam,
                         LPARAM lParam) {
    return (LRESULT)GetStockObject (WHITE_BRUSH);
}
```

```
//-------------------------------------------------------------------
// DoCommandBtnWnd - Process WM_COMMAND message for window.
//
LRESULT DoCommandBtnWnd (HWND hWnd, UINT wMsg, WPARAM wParam,
                            LPARAM lParam) {
    TCHAR szOut[128];
    int i;
    // Since the Check Box button is not an auto check box, it
    // must be set manually.
    if ((LOWORD (wParam) == IDC_CHKBOX) &&
        (HIWORD (wParam) == BN_CLICKED)) {
        // Get the current state, complement, and set.
        i = SendDlgItemMessage (hWnd, IDC_CHKBOX, BM_GETCHECK, 0, 0);
        if (i == 0)
            SendDlgItemMessage (hWnd, IDC_CHKBOX, BM_SETCHECK, 1, 0);
        else
            SendDlgItemMessage (hWnd, IDC_CHKBOX, BM_SETCHECK, 0, 0);
    }

    // Report WM_COMMAND messages to main window.
    for (i = 0; i < dim(nlBtn); i++) {
        if (HIWORD (wParam) == nlBtn[i].wNotification) {
            lstrcpy (szOut, nlBtn[i].pszLabel);
            break;
        }
    }
    if (i == dim(nlBtn))
        wsprintf (szOut, TEXT ("notification: %x"), HIWORD (wParam));

    SendMessage (GetParent (hWnd), MYMSG_ADDLINE, wParam,
                (LPARAM)szOut);
    return 0;
}
//-------------------------------------------------------------------
// DoDrawItemBtnWnd - Process WM_DRAWITEM message for window.
//
LRESULT DoDrawItemBtnWnd (HWND hWnd, UINT wMsg, WPARAM wParam,
                            LPARAM lParam) {

    return DrawButton (hWnd, (LPDRAWITEMSTRUCT)lParam);
}


//-------------------------------------------------------------------
// DrawButton - Draws an owner-draw button
//
LRESULT DrawButton (HWND hWnd, LPDRAWITEMSTRUCT pdi) {
```

(continued)

Listing 4-1   *(continued)*

```
HPEN hPenShadow, hPenLight, hPenDkShadow, hRedPen, hOldPen;

HBRUSH hBr, hOldBr;
LOGPEN lpen;
TCHAR szOut[128];
POINT ptOut[3], ptIn[3];
// Reflect the messages to the report window.
wsprintf (szOut, TEXT ("WM_DRAWITEM Act:%x  State:%x"),
          pdi->itemAction, pdi->itemState);
SendMessage (GetParent (hWnd), MYMSG_ADDLINE, pdi->CtlID,
            (LPARAM)szOut);

// Create pens for drawing.
lpen.lopnStyle = PS_SOLID;
lpen.lopnWidth.x = 3;
lpen.lopnWidth.y = 3;
lpen.lopnColor = GetSysColor (COLOR_3DSHADOW);
hPenShadow = CreatePenIndirect (&lpen);

lpen.lopnColor = RGB (255, 0, 0);
hRedPen = CreatePenIndirect (&lpen);

lpen.lopnWidth.x = 1;
lpen.lopnWidth.y = 1;
lpen.lopnColor = GetSysColor (COLOR_3DLIGHT);
hPenLight = CreatePenIndirect (&lpen);

lpen.lopnColor = GetSysColor (COLOR_3DDKSHADOW);
hPenDkShadow = CreatePenIndirect (&lpen);

// Create a brush for the face of the button.
hBr = CreateSolidBrush (GetSysColor (COLOR_3DFACE));

// Draw a rectangle with a thick outside border to start the
// frame drawing.
hOldPen = (HPEN_SelectObject (pdi->hDC, hPenShadow);
hOldBr = (HBRUSH)SelectObject (pdi->hDC, hBr);
Rectangle (pdi->hDC, pdi->rcItem.left, pdi->rcItem.top,
           pdi->rcItem.right, pdi->rcItem.bottom);

// Draw the upper left inside line.
ptIn[0].x = pdi->rcItem.left + 1;
ptIn[0].y = pdi->rcItem.bottom - 2;
ptIn[1].x = pdi->rcItem.left + 1;
ptIn[1].y = pdi->rcItem.top + 1;
ptIn[2].x = pdi->rcItem.right - 2;
ptIn[2].y = pdi->rcItem.top + 1;
```

```
// Select a pen to draw shadow or light side of button.
if (pdi->itemState & ODS_SELECTED) {
    SelectObject (pdi->hDC, hPenDkShadow);
} else {
    SelectObject (pdi->hDC, hPenLight);
}
Polyline (pdi->hDC, ptIn, 3);
// If selected, also draw a bright line inside the lower
// right corner.
if (pdi->itemState & ODS_SELECTED) {
    SelectObject (pdi->hDC, hPenLight);
    ptIn[1].x = pdi->rcItem.right - 2;
    ptIn[1].y = pdi->rcItem.bottom - 2;
    Polyline (pdi->hDC, ptIn, 3);
}

// Now draw the black outside line on either the upper left or lower
// right corner.
ptOut[0].x = pdi->rcItem.left;
ptOut[0].y = pdi->rcItem.bottom - 1;
ptOut[2].x = pdi->rcItem.right - 1;
ptOut[2].y = pdi->rcItem.top;

SelectObject (pdi->hDC, hPenDkShadow);
if (pdi->itemState & ODS_SELECTED) {
    ptOut[1].x = pdi->rcItem.left;
    ptOut[1].y = pdi->rcItem.top;
} else {
    ptOut[1].x = pdi->rcItem.right - 1;
    ptOut[1].y = pdi->rcItem.bottom - 1;
}
Polyline (pdi->hDC, ptOut, 3);

// Draw the triangle.
ptOut[0].x = (pdi->rcItem.right - pdi->rcItem.left)/2;
ptOut[0].y = pdi->rcItem.top + 4;
ptOut[1].x = pdi->rcItem.left + 3;
ptOut[1].y = pdi->rcItem.bottom - 6;
ptOut[2].x = pdi->rcItem.right - 6;
ptOut[2].y = pdi->rcItem.bottom - 6;
SelectObject (pdi->hDC, hRedPen);
Polygon (pdi->hDC, ptOut, 3);

// If button has the focus, draw the dotted rect inside the button.
if (pdi->itemState & ODS_FOCUS) {
    pdi->rcItem.left += 3;
    pdi->rcItem.top += 3;
```

(continued)

Listing 4-1   *(continued)*

```
        pdi->rcItem.right -= 4;
        pdi->rcItem.bottom -= 4;
        DrawFocusRect (pdi->hDC, &pdi->rcItem);
    }
    // Clean up. First select the original brush and pen into the DC.
    SelectObject (pdi->hDC, hOldBr);
    SelectObject (pdi->hDC, hOldPen);

    // Now delete the brushes and pens created.
    DeleteObject (hBr);
    DeleteObject (hPenShadow);
    DeleteObject (hPenDkShadow);
    DeleteObject (hPenLight);
    return 0;
}
```

EditWnd.cpp

```
//======================================================================
// EditWnd - Edit control window code
//
// Written for the book Programming Windows CE
// Copyright (C) 2003 Douglas Boling
//======================================================================
#include <windows.h>                    // For all that Windows stuff
#include "Ctlview.h"                    // Program-specific stuff

extern HINSTANCE hInst;
//----------------------------------------------------------------------
// Global data
//
// Message dispatch table for EditWndWindowProc
const struct decodeUINT EditWndMessages[] = {
    WM_CREATE, DoCreateEditWnd,
    WM_COMMAND, DoCommandEditWnd,
};

// Structure defining the controls in the window
CTLWNDSTRUCT  Edits[] = {
    {TEXT ("edit"), IDC_SINGLELINE, TEXT ("Single line edit control"),
     10,  10, 180,  23, ES_AUTOHSCROLL},

    {TEXT ("edit"), IDC_MULTILINE, TEXT ("Multiline edit control"),
     10,  35, 180,  70, ES_MULTILINE | ES_AUTOVSCROLL},
```

```
    {TEXT ("edit"), IDC_PASSBOX, TEXT (""),
     10, 107, 180,  23, ES_PASSWORD},
};
// Structure labeling the edit control WM_COMMAND notifications
NOTELABELS nlEdit[] = {{TEXT ("EN_SETFOCUS "), 0x0100},
                       {TEXT ("EN_KILLFOCUS"), 0x0200},
                       {TEXT ("EN_CHANGE   "), 0x0300},
                       {TEXT ("EN_UPDATE   "), 0x0400},
                       {TEXT ("EN_ERRSPACE "), 0x0500},
                       {TEXT ("EN_MAXTEXT  "), 0x0501},
                       {TEXT ("EN_HSCROLL  "), 0x0601},
                       {TEXT ("EN_VSCROLL  "), 0x0602},
};
//----------------------------------------------------------------------
// InitEditWnd - EditWnd window initialization
//
int InitEditWnd (HINSTANCE hInstance) {
    WNDCLASS wc;

    // Register application EditWnd window class.
    wc.style = 0;                               // Window style
    wc.lpfnWndProc = EditWndProc;               // Callback function
    wc.cbClsExtra = 0;                          // Extra class data
    wc.cbWndExtra = 0;                          // Extra window data
    wc.hInstance = hInstance;                   // Owner handle
    wc.hIcon = NULL,                            // Application icon
    wc.hCursor = LoadCursor (NULL, IDC_ARROW);// Default cursor
    wc.hbrBackground = (HBRUSH) GetStockObject (WHITE_BRUSH);
    wc.lpszMenuName =  NULL;                    // Menu name
    wc.lpszClassName = EDITWND;                 // Window class name

    if (RegisterClass (&wc) == 0) return 1;

    return 0;
}
//======================================================================
// Message handling procedures for EditWindow
//----------------------------------------------------------------------
// EditWndWndProc - Callback function for application window
//
LRESULT CALLBACK EditWndProc (HWND hWnd, UINT wMsg, WPARAM wParam,
                              LPARAM lParam) {
    int i;
    //
    // Search message list to see if we need to handle this
```

(continued)

Listing 4-1   *(continued)*

```
    // message.  If in list, call procedure.
    //
    for (i = 0; i < dim(EditWndMessages); i++) {
        if (wMsg == EditWndMessages[i].Code)
            return (*EditWndMessages[i].Fxn)(hWnd, wMsg, wParam, lParam);
    }
    return DefWindowProc (hWnd, wMsg, wParam, lParam);
}
//-------------------------------------------------------------------------
// DoCreateEditWnd - Process WM_CREATE message for window.
//
LRESULT DoCreateEditWnd (HWND hWnd, UINT wMsg, WPARAM wParam,
                         LPARAM lParam) {
    int i;

    for (i = 0; i < dim(Edits); i++) {

        CreateWindow (Edits[i].szClass, Edits[i].szTitle,
                      Edits[i].lStyle | WS_VISIBLE | WS_CHILD | WS_BORDER,
                      Edits[i].x, Edits[i].y, Edits[i].cx, Edits[i].cy,
                      hWnd, (HMENU) Edits[i].nID, hInst, NULL);
    }
    return 0;
}
//-------------------------------------------------------------------------
// DoCommandEditWnd - Process WM_COMMAND message for window.
//
LRESULT DoCommandEditWnd (HWND hWnd, UINT wMsg, WPARAM wParam,
                          LPARAM lParam) {
    TCHAR szOut[128];
    int i;

    for (i = 0; i < dim(nlEdit); i++) {
        if (HIWORD (wParam) == nlEdit[i].wNotification) {
            lstrcpy (szOut, nlEdit[i].pszLabel);
            break;
        }
    }

    if (i == dim(nlEdit))
        wsprintf (szOut, TEXT ("notification: %x"), HIWORD (wParam));

    SendMessage (GetParent (hWnd), MYMSG_ADDLINE, wParam,
                 (LPARAM)szOut);
    return 0;
}
```

ListWnd.cpp

```
//======================================================================
// ListWnd - List box control window code
//
// Written for the book Programming Windows CE
// Copyright (C) 2003 Douglas Boling
//======================================================================
#include <windows.h>                      // For all that Windows stuff
#include "Ctlview.h"                      // Program-specific stuff

extern HINSTANCE hInst;
//----------------------------------------------------------------------
// Global data
//
// Message dispatch table for ListWndWindowProc
const struct decodeUINT ListWndMessages[] = {
    WM_CREATE, DoCreateListWnd,
    WM_COMMAND, DoCommandListWnd,
};

// Structure defining the controls in the window
CTLWNDSTRUCT  Lists[] = {
    {TEXT ("combobox"), IDC_COMBOBOX, TEXT (""), 10,  10, 205, 100,
     WS_VSCROLL},

    {TEXT ("Listbox"), IDC_SNGLELIST, TEXT (""),  10,  35, 100, 90,
     WS_VSCROLL | LBS_NOTIFY},

    {TEXT ("Listbox"), IDC_MULTILIST, TEXT (""), 115,  35, 100, 90,
     WS_VSCROLL | LBS_EXTENDEDSEL | LBS_NOTIFY}
};
// Structure labeling the list box control WM_COMMAND notifications
NOTELABELS nlList[] = {{TEXT ("LBN_ERRSPACE "), (-2)},
                       {TEXT ("LBN_SELCHANGE"), 1},
                       {TEXT ("LBN_DBLCLK   "), 2},
                       {TEXT ("LBN_SELCANCEL"), 3},
                       {TEXT ("LBN_SETFOCUS "), 4},
                       {TEXT ("LBN_KILLFOCUS"), 5},
};
// Structure labeling the combo box control WM_COMMAND notifications
NOTELABELS nlCombo[] = {{TEXT ("CBN_ERRSPACE      "), (-1)},
                        {TEXT ("CBN_SELCHANGE    "), 1},
                        {TEXT ("CBN_DBLCLK       "), 2},
                        {TEXT ("CBN_SETFOCUS     "), 3},
                        {TEXT ("CBN_KILLFOCUS    "), 4},
                        {TEXT ("CBN_EDITCHANGE   "), 5},
```

(continued)

Listing 4-1 *(continued)*

```
                              {TEXT ("CBN_EDITUPDATE  "), 6},
                              {TEXT ("CBN_DROPDOWN    "), 7},
                              {TEXT ("CBN_CLOSEUP     "), 8},
                              {TEXT ("CBN_SELENDOK    "), 9},
                              {TEXT ("CBN_SELENDCANCEL"), 10},
};
//-------------------------------------------------------------------------
// InitListWnd - ListWnd window initialization
//
int InitListWnd (HINSTANCE hInstance) {
    WNDCLASS wc;

    // Register application ListWnd window class.
    wc.style = 0;                               // Window style
    wc.lpfnWndProc = ListWndProc;               // Callback function
    wc.cbClsExtra = 0;                          // Extra class data
    wc.cbWndExtra = 0;                          // Extra window data
    wc.hInstance = hInstance;                   // Owner handle
    wc.hIcon = NULL,                            // Application icon
    wc.hCursor = LoadCursor (NULL, IDC_ARROW);  // Default cursor
    wc.hbrBackground = (HBRUSH) GetStockObject (WHITE_BRUSH);
    wc.lpszMenuName =  NULL;                    // Menu name
    wc.lpszClassName = LISTWND;                 // Window class name

    if (RegisterClass (&wc) == 0) return 1;

    return 0;
}
//=========================================================================
// Message handling procedures for ListWindow
//-------------------------------------------------------------------------
// ListWndProc - Callback function for application window
//
LRESULT CALLBACK ListWndProc (HWND hWnd, UINT wMsg, WPARAM wParam,
                              LPARAM lParam) {
    int i;
    //
    // Search message list to see if we need to handle this
    // message.  If in list, call procedure.
    //
    for (i = 0; i < dim(ListWndMessages); i++) {
        if (wMsg == ListWndMessages[i].Code)
            return (*ListWndMessages[i].Fxn)(hWnd, wMsg, wParam, lParam);
    }
    return DefWindowProc (hWnd, wMsg, wParam, lParam);
}
```

```
//-------------------------------------------------------------------
// DoCreateListWnd - Process WM_CREATE message for window.
//
LRESULT DoCreateListWnd (HWND hWnd, UINT wMsg, WPARAM wParam,
                         LPARAM lParam) {
    int i;
    TCHAR szOut[64];
    for (i = 0; i < dim(Lists); i++) {

        CreateWindow (Lists[i].szClass, Lists[i].szTitle,
                      Lists[i].lStyle | WS_VISIBLE | WS_CHILD | WS_BORDER,
                      Lists[i].x, Lists[i].y, Lists[i].cx, Lists[i].cy,
                      hWnd, (HMENU) Lists[i].nID, hInst, NULL);
    }
    for (i = 0; i < 20; i++) {
        wsprintf (szOut, TEXT ("Item %d"), i);
        SendDlgItemMessage (hWnd, IDC_SNGLELIST, LB_ADDSTRING, 0,
                            (LPARAM)szOut);

        SendDlgItemMessage (hWnd, IDC_MULTILIST, LB_ADDSTRING, 0,
                            (LPARAM)szOut);

        SendDlgItemMessage (hWnd, IDC_COMBOBOX, CB_ADDSTRING, 0,
                            (LPARAM)szOut);
    }
    // Set initial selection.
    SendDlgItemMessage (hWnd, IDC_COMBOBOX, CB_SETCURSEL, 0, 0);
    return 0;
}
//-------------------------------------------------------------------
// DoCommandListWnd - Process WM_COMMAND message for window.
//
LRESULT DoCommandListWnd (HWND hWnd, UINT wMsg, WPARAM wParam,
                          LPARAM lParam) {
    TCHAR szOut[128];
    int i;

    if (LOWORD (wParam) == IDC_COMBOBOX) {
        for (i = 0; i < dim(nlCombo); i++) {
            if (HIWORD (wParam) == nlCombo[i].wNotification) {
                lstrcpy (szOut, nlCombo[i].pszLabel);
                break;
            }
        }
        if (i == dim(nlList))
            wsprintf (szOut, TEXT ("notification: %x"), HIWORD (wParam));
```

(continued)

Listing 4-1 *(continued)*

```
    } else {
        for (i = 0; i < dim(nlList); i++) {
            if (HIWORD (wParam) == nlList[i].wNotification) {
                lstrcpy (szOut, nlList[i].pszLabel);
                break;
            }
        }
        if (i == dim(nlList))
            wsprintf (szOut, TEXT ("notification: %x"), HIWORD (wParam));
    }
    SendMessage (GetParent (hWnd), MYMSG_ADDLINE, wParam,
                 (LPARAM)szOut);
    return 0;
}
```

StatWnd.cpp

```
//======================================================================
// StatWnd - Static control window code
//
// Written for the book Programming Windows CE
// Copyright (C) 2003 Douglas Boling
//======================================================================
#include <windows.h>                    // For all that Windows stuff
#include "Ctlview.h"                    // Program-specific stuff

extern HINSTANCE hInst;
//----------------------------------------------------------------------
// Global data
//
// Message dispatch table for StatWndWindowProc
const struct decodeUINT StatWndMessages[] = {
    WM_CREATE, DoCreateStatWnd,
    WM_COMMAND, DoCommandStatWnd,
};

// Structure defining the controls in the window
CTLWNDSTRUCT  Stats [] = {
    {TEXT ("static"), IDC_LEFTTEXT, TEXT ("Left text"),
     10,  10, 120,  23, SS_LEFT | SS_NOTIFY},

    {TEXT ("static"), IDC_RIGHTTEXT, TEXT ("Right text"),
     10,  35, 120,  23, SS_RIGHT},

    {TEXT ("static"), IDC_CENTERTEXT, TEXT ("Center text"),
     10,  60, 120,  23, SS_CENTER | WS_BORDER},
};
```

```
// Structure labeling the static control WM_COMMAND notifications
NOTELABELS nlStatic[] = {{TEXT ("STN_CLICKED"), 0},
                         {TEXT ("STN_ENABLE "), 2},
                         {TEXT ("STN_DISABLE"), 3},
};
//----------------------------------------------------------------------
// InitStatWnd - StatWnd window initialization
//
int InitStatWnd (HINSTANCE hInstance) {
    WNDCLASS wc;

    // Register application StatWnd window class.
    wc.style = 0;                                  // Window style
    wc.lpfnWndProc = StatWndProc;                  // Callback function
    wc.cbClsExtra = 0;                             // Extra class data
    wc.cbWndExtra = 0;                             // Extra window data
    wc.hInstance = hInstance;                      // Owner handle
    wc.hIcon = NULL,                               // Application icon
    wc.hCursor = LoadCursor (NULL, IDC_ARROW);// Default cursor
    wc.hbrBackground = (HBRUSH) GetStockObject (WHITE_BRUSH);
    wc.lpszMenuName =  NULL;                        // Menu name
    wc.lpszClassName = STATWND;                     // Window class name

    if (RegisterClass (&wc) == 0) return 1;

    return 0;
}
//======================================================================
// Message handling procedures for StatWindow
//----------------------------------------------------------------------
// StatWndProc - Callback function for application window
//
LRESULT CALLBACK StatWndProc (HWND hWnd, UINT wMsg, WPARAM wParam,
                              LPARAM lParam) {
    int i;
    //
    // Search message list to see if we need to handle this
    // message.  If in list, call procedure.
    //
    for (i = 0; i < dim(StatWndMessages); i++) {
        if (wMsg == StatWndMessages[i].Code)
            return (*StatWndMessages[i].Fxn)(hWnd, wMsg, wParam, lParam);
    }
    return DefWindowProc (hWnd, wMsg, wParam, lParam);
}
```

(continued)

Listing 4-1 *(continued)*

```
//-----------------------------------------------------------------
// DoCreateStatWnd - Process WM_CREATE message for window.
//
LRESULT DoCreateStatWnd (HWND hWnd, UINT wMsg, WPARAM wParam,
                         LPARAM lParam) {
    int i;

    for (i = 0; i < dim(Stats); i++) {

        CreateWindow (Stats[i].szClass, Stats[i].szTitle,
                      Stats[i].lStyle | WS_VISIBLE | WS_CHILD,
                      Stats[i].x, Stats[i].y, Stats[i].cx, Stats[i].cy,
                      hWnd, (HMENU) Stats[i].nID, hInst, NULL);
    }
    return 0;
}
//-----------------------------------------------------------------
// DoCommandStatWnd - Process WM_COMMAND message for window.
//
LRESULT DoCommandStatWnd (HWND hWnd, UINT wMsg, WPARAM wParam,
                          LPARAM lParam) {
    TCHAR szOut[128];
    int i;

    for (i = 0; i < dim(nlStatic); i++) {
        if (HIWORD (wParam) == nlStatic[i].wNotification) {
            lstrcpy (szOut, nlStatic[i].pszLabel);
            break;
        }
    }
    if (i == dim(nlStatic))
        wsprintf (szOut, TEXT ("notification: %x"), HIWORD (wParam));

    SendMessage (GetParent (hWnd), MYMSG_ADDLINE, wParam,
                 (LPARAM)szOut);
    return 0;
}
```

ScrollWnd.cpp

```
//=================================================================
// ScrollWnd - Scroll bar control window code
//
// Written for the book Programming Windows CE
// Copyright (C) 2001 Douglas Boling
//=================================================================
```

```
#include <windows.h>                    // For all that Windows stuff
#include "Ctlview.h"                     // Program-specific stuff

extern HINSTANCE hInst;
//-------------------------------------------------------------------------
// Global data
//
// Message dispatch table for ScrollWndWindowProc
const struct decodeUINT ScrollWndMessages[] = {
    WM_CREATE, DoCreateScrollWnd,
    WM_HSCROLL, DoVScrollScrollWnd,
    WM_VSCROLL, DoVScrollScrollWnd,
};

// Structure defining the controls in the window
CTLWNDSTRUCT  Scrolls [] = {
    {TEXT ("Scrollbar"), IDC_LRSCROLL, TEXT (""),
     10,  10, 150,  23, SBS_HORZ},

    {TEXT ("Scrollbar"), IDC_UDSCROLL, TEXT (""),
     180,  10,  23, 120, SBS_VERT},
};

// Structure labeling the scroll bar control scroll codes for WM_VSCROLL
NOTELABELS nlVScroll[] = {{TEXT ("SB_LINEUP        "), 0},
                          {TEXT ("SB_LINEDOWN      "), 1},
                          {TEXT ("SB_PAGEUP        "), 2},
                          {TEXT ("SB_PAGEDOWN      "), 3},
                          {TEXT ("SB_THUMBPOSITION"), 4},
                          {TEXT ("SB_THUMBTRACK    "), 5},
                          {TEXT ("SB_TOP           "), 6},
                          {TEXT ("SB_BOTTOM        "), 7},
                          {TEXT ("SB_ENDSCROLL     "), 8},

};
// Structure labeling the scroll bar control scroll codes for WM_HSCROLL
NOTELABELS nlHScroll[] = {{TEXT ("SB_LINELEFT      "), 0},
                          {TEXT ("SB_LINERIGHT     "), 1},
                          {TEXT ("SB_PAGELEFT      "), 2},
                          {TEXT ("SB_PAGERIGHT     "), 3},
                          {TEXT ("SB_THUMBPOSITION"), 4},
                          {TEXT ("SB_THUMBTRACK    "), 5},
                          {TEXT ("SB_LEFT          "), 6},
                          {TEXT ("SB_RIGHT         "), 7},
                          {TEXT ("SB_ENDSCROLL     "), 8},

};
```

(continued)

Listing 4-1   *(continued)*

```
//-----------------------------------------------------------------------
// InitScrollWnd - ScrollWnd window initialization
//
int InitScrollWnd (HINSTANCE hInstance) {
    WNDCLASS wc;

    // Register application ScrollWnd window class.
    wc.style = 0;                                   // Window style
    wc.lpfnWndProc = ScrollWndProc;                 // Callback function
    wc.cbClsExtra = 0;                              // Extra class data
    wc.cbWndExtra = 0;                              // Extra window data
    wc.hInstance = hInstance;                       // Owner handle
    wc.hIcon = NULL,                                // Application icon
    wc.hCursor = LoadCursor (NULL, IDC_ARROW);// Default cursor
    wc.hbrBackground = (HBRUSH) GetStockObject (WHITE_BRUSH);
    wc.lpszMenuName =  NULL;                        // Menu name
    wc.lpszClassName = SCROLLWND;                   // Window class name

    if (RegisterClass (&wc) == 0) return 1;

    return 0;
}
//=======================================================================
// Message handling procedures for ScrollWindow
//-----------------------------------------------------------------------
// ScrollWndProc - Callback function for application window
//
LRESULT CALLBACK ScrollWndProc (HWND hWnd, UINT wMsg, WPARAM wParam,
                                LPARAM lParam) {
    int i;
    //
    // Search message list to see if we need to handle this
    // message.  If in list, call procedure.
    //
    for (i = 0; i < dim(ScrollWndMessages); i++) {
        if (wMsg == ScrollWndMessages[i].Code)
            return (*ScrollWndMessages[i].Fxn)(hWnd, wMsg, wParam, lParam);
    }
    return DefWindowProc (hWnd, wMsg, wParam, lParam);
}
//-----------------------------------------------------------------------
// DoCreateScrollWnd - Process WM_CREATE message for window.
//
LRESULT DoCreateScrollWnd (HWND hWnd, UINT wMsg, WPARAM wParam,
                           LPARAM lParam) {
    int i;
```

```
    for (i = 0; i < dim(Scrolls); i++) {
        CreateWindow (Scrolls[i].szClass, Scrolls[i].szTitle,
                      Scrolls[i].lStyle | WS_VISIBLE | WS_CHILD,
                      Scrolls[i].x, Scrolls[i].y, Scrolls[i].cx,
                      Scrolls[i].cy,
                      hWnd, (HMENU) Scrolls[i].nID, hInst, NULL);
    }
    return 0;
}
//------------------------------------------------------------------------
// DoVScrollScrollWnd - Process WM_VSCROLL message for window.
//
LRESULT DoVScrollScrollWnd (HWND hWnd, UINT wMsg, WPARAM wParam,
                            LPARAM lParam) {
    TCHAR szOut[128];
    SCROLLINFO si;
    int i, sPos;

    // Update the report window.
    if (GetDlgItem (hWnd, 101) == (HWND)lParam) {

        for (i = 0; i < dim(nlVScroll); i++) {
            if (LOWORD (wParam) == nlVScroll[i].wNotification) {
                lstrcpy (szOut, nlVScroll[i].pszLabel);
                break;
            }
        }
        if (i == dim(nlVScroll))
            wsprintf (szOut, TEXT ("notification: %x"), HIWORD (wParam));
    } else {
        for (i = 0; i < dim(nlHScroll); i++) {
            if (LOWORD (wParam) == nlHScroll[i].wNotification) {
                lstrcpy (szOut, nlHScroll[i].pszLabel);
                break;
            }
        }
        if (i == dim(nlHScroll))
            wsprintf (szOut, TEXT ("notification: %x"), HIWORD (wParam));
    }
    SendMessage (GetParent (hWnd), MYMSG_ADDLINE, -1, (LPARAM)szOut);

    // Get scroll bar position.
    si.cbSize = sizeof (si);
    si.fMask = SIF_POS;
    GetScrollInfo ((HWND)lParam, SB_CTL, &si);
    sPos = si.nPos;
```

(continued)

Listing 4-1 *(continued)*

```
// Act on the scroll code.
switch (LOWORD (wParam)) {
case SB_LINEUP:        // Also SB_LINELEFT
    sPos -= 2;
    break;
case SB_LINEDOWN:      // Also SB_LINERIGHT
    sPos += 2;
    break;

case SB_PAGEUP:        // Also SB_PAGELEFT
    sPos -= 10;
    break;

case SB_PAGEDOWN:      // Also SB_PAGERIGHT
    sPos += 10;
    break;

case SB_THUMBPOSITION:
    sPos = HIWORD (wParam);
    break;
}
// Check range.
if (sPos < 0)
    sPos = 0;
if (sPos > 100)
    sPos = 100;

// Update scroll bar position.
si.cbSize = sizeof (si);
si.nPos = sPos;
si.fMask = SIF_POS;
SetScrollInfo ((HWND)lParam, SB_CTL, &si, TRUE);
return 0;
}
```

When the CtlView program starts, the *WM_CREATE* handler of the main window, *DoCreateFrame*, creates a row of radio buttons across the top of the window, a list box for message reporting, and five different child windows. (The five child windows are all created without the *WS_VISIBLE* style, so they're initially hidden.) Each of the child windows in turn creates a number of controls. Before returning from *DoCreateFrame*, CtlView checks one of the auto radio buttons and makes the BtnWnd child window (the window that contains the example button controls) visible using *ShowWindow*.

The *WM_SIZE* handler of the main window, *DoSizeMain*, positions each of the child windows in the frame window. This needs to be done here because the window size parameters in *WM_CREATE* don't take into account the size of the caption bar.

As each of the controls on the child windows is tapped, clicked, or selected, the control sends *WM_COMMAND* messages to its parent window. That window in turn sends the information from the *WM_COMMAND* message to its parent, the frame window, using the application-defined message *MYMSG_ADDLINE*. There the notification data is formatted and displayed in the list box on the right side, or below on the Pocket PC, of the frame window.

The other function of the frame window is to switch between the different child windows. The application accomplishes this by displaying only the child window that matches the selection of the radio buttons across the top of the frame window. The processing for this is done in the *WM_COMMAND* handler, *DoCommandFrame* in CtlView.cpp.

The best way to discover how and when these controls send notifications is to run the example program and use each of the controls. Figure 4-2 shows the Control View window with the button controls displayed. As each of the buttons is clicked, a *BN_CLICKED* notification is sent to the parent window of the control. The parent window simply labels the notification and forwards it to the display list box. Because the Check Box button isn't an auto check box, Ctl-View must manually change the state of the check box when a user clicks it. The other check boxes and radio buttons, however, do automatically change state because they were created with the *BS_AUTOCHECKBOX*, *BS_AUTO3STATE*, and *BS_AUTORADIOBUTTON* styles. The square button with the exclamation mark inside a triangular icon is an owner-draw button.

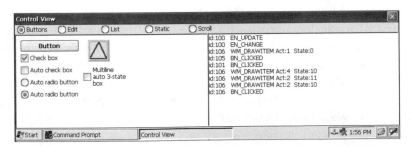

Figure 4-2   The Control View window with the button child window displayed in the left pane

The source code for each child window is contained in a separate file. The source for the window containing the button controls is contained in BtnWnd.cpp. The file contains an initialization routine (*InitBtnWnd*) that registers the window and a window procedure (*BtnWndProc*) for the window itself. The button controls themselves are created during the *WM_CREATE* message using *CreateWindow*. The position, style, and other aspects of each control are contained in an array of structures named *Btns*. The *DoCreateBtnWnd* function cycles through each of the entries in the array, calling *CreateWindow* for each one. Each child window in CtlView uses a similar process to create its controls.

To support the owner-draw button, *BtnWndProc* must handle the *WM_DRAWITEM* message. The *WM_DRAWITEM* message is sent when the button needs to be drawn because it has changed state, gained or lost the focus, or been uncovered. Although the *DrawButton* function (called each time a *WM_DRAWITEM* message is received) expends a great deal of effort to make the button look like a standard button, there's no reason a button can't have any look you want.

The other window procedures provide only basic support for their controls. The *WM_COMMAND* handlers simply reflect the notifications back to the main window. The ScrollWnd child window procedure, *ScrollWndProc*, handles *WM_VSCROLL* and *WM_HSCROLL* messages because that's how scroll bar controls communicate with their parent windows.

Controls and Colors

Finally, a word about colors. In CtlView, the frame window class is registered in a subtly different way from the way I've registered it in previous programs. In the CtlView example, I set the background brush for the frame window using the line

```
wc.hbrBackground = (HBRUSH)GetSysColorBrush (COLOR_STATIC);
```

This sets the background color of the frame window to the same background color I used to draw the radio buttons. The function *GetSysColorBrush* returns a brush that matches the color used by the system to draw various objects in the system. In this case, the constant *COLOR_STATIC* is passed to *GetSysColorBrush*, which then returns the background color Windows uses when drawing static text and the text for check box and radio buttons. This makes the frame window background match the static text background.

In the window that contains the button controls, the check box and radio button background is changed to match the white background of the button window, by fielding the *WM_CTLCOLORSTATIC* message. This message is sent to the parent of a static control or a button control when the button is a check box or radio button to ask the parent which colors to use when drawing the control. In CtlView, the button window returns the handle to a white brush so that the control background matches the white background of the window. You modify the color of a push button by fielding the *WM_CTLCOLORBUTTON* message. Other controls send different *WM_CTLCOLORxxx* messages so that the colors used to draw them can be modified by the parent window. Another example of the use of the *WM_CTLCOLORSTATIC* message can be seen in the PowerBar example in Chapter 18.

Menus

Menus are a mainstay of Windows input. Although each application might have a different keyboard and stylus interface, almost all have sets of menus that are organized in a structure familiar to the Windows user.

Windows CE programs use menus a little differently from other Windows programs, the most obvious difference being that in Windows CE, menus aren't part of the standard top-level window. Instead, menus are attached to a command bar or menu bar control that has been created for the window. Other than this change, the functions of the menu and the way menu selections are processed by the application match the other versions of Windows, for the most part. Because of this general similarity, I give you only a basic introduction to Windows menu management in this section.

Creating a menu is as simple as calling

```
HMENU CreateMenu (void);
```

The function returns a handle to an empty menu. To add an item to a menu, two calls can be used. The first

```
BOOL AppendMenu (HMENU hMenu, UINT fuFlags, UINT idNewItem,
                 LPCTSTR lpszNewItem);
```

appends a single item to the end of a menu. The *fuFlags* parameter is set with a series of flags indicating the initial condition of the item. For example, the item might be initially disabled (thanks to the *MF_GRAYED* flag) or have a check mark next to it (courtesy of the *MF_CHECKED* flag). Almost all calls specify the *MF_STRING* flag, indicating that the *lpszNewItem* parameter contains a string that will be the text for the item. The *idNewItem* parameter contains an ID value that will be used to identify the item when it's selected by the user or to indicate that the state of the menu item needs to be changed.

Another call that can be used to add a menu item is this one:

```
BOOL InsertMenu (HMENU hMenu, UINT uPosition, UINT uFlags,
                 UINT uIDNewItem, LPCTSTR lpNewItem);
```

This call is similar to *AppendMenu*, with the added flexibility that the item can be inserted anywhere within a menu structure. For this call, the *uFlags* parameter can be passed one of two additional flags: *MF_BYCOMMAND* or *MF_BYPOSITION*, which specify how to locate where the menu item is to be inserted into the menu.

Menus can be nested to provide a cascading effect. To add a cascading menu, or submenu, create the menu you want to attach using

```
HMENU CreatePopupMenu (void);
```

Then use *InsertMenu*, or *AppendMenu* to construct the menu. Then insert or append the submenu to the main menu using either *InsertMenu* or *Append-Menu* with the *MF_POPUP* flag in the flags parameter. In this case, the *uIDNew-Item* parameter contains the handle to the submenu, while *lpNewItem* contains the string that will be on the menu item.

You can query and manipulate a menu item to add or remove check marks or to enable or disable it by means of a number of functions. This function,

```
BOOL EnableMenuItem (HMENU hMenu, UINT uIDEnableItem, UINT uEnable);
```

can be used to enable or disable an item. The flags used in the *uEnable* parameter are similar to the flags used with other menu functions. Under Windows CE, the flag you use to disable a menu item is *MF_GRAYED*, not *MF_DISABLED*. The function

```
DWORD CheckMenuItem (HMENU hmenu, UINT uIDCheckItem, UINT uCheck);
```

can be used to check and uncheck a menu item. Many other functions are available to query and manipulate menu items. Check the SDK documentation for more details.

The following code fragment creates a simple menu structure:

```
hMainMenu = CreateMenu ();

hMenu = CreatePopupMenu ();
AppendMenu (hMenu, MF_STRING | MF_ENABLED, 100, TEXT ("&New"));
AppendMenu (hMenu, MF_STRING | MF_ENABLED, 101, TEXT ("&Open"));
AppendMenu (hMenu, MF_STRING | MF_ENABLED, 101, TEXT ("&Save"));
AppendMenu (hMenu, MF_STRING | MF_ENABLED, 101, TEXT ("E&xit"));

AppendMenu (hMainMenu, MF_STRING | MF_ENABLED | MF_POPUP, (UINT)hMenu,
            TEXT ("&File"));

hMenu = CreatePopupMenu ();
AppendMenu (hMenu, MF_STRING | MF_ENABLED, 100, TEXT ("C&ut"));
AppendMenu (hMenu, MF_STRING | MF_ENABLED, 101, TEXT ("&Copy"));
AppendMenu (hMenu, MF_STRING | MF_ENABLED, 101, TEXT ("&Paste"));

AppendMenu (hMainMenu, MF_STRING | MF_ENABLED | MF_POPUP,
            (UINT)hMenu, TEXT ("&Edit"));

hMenu = CreatePopupMenu ();
AppendMenu (hMenu, MF_STRING | MF_ENABLED, 100, TEXT ("&About"));

AppendMenu (hMainMenu, MF_STRING | MF_ENABLED | MF_POPUP,
            (UINT)hMenu, TEXT ("&Help"));
```

Once a menu has been created, it can be displayed with the *TrackPopup-Menu* function, prototyped as

```
BOOL TrackPopupMenuEx (HMENU hmenu, UINT uFlags, int x, int y,
                       HWND hwnd, LPTPMPARAMS lptpm);
```

The first parameter is the handle of the menu. The *uFlags* parameter sets the alignment for the menu in relation to the position parameters *x* and *y*. Another flag, *TPM_RETURNCMD*, causes the function to return the ID value of the selected menu item instead of generating a *WM_COMMAND* message. The *hwnd* parameter is the handle to the window that will receive all messages relating to the menu, including the resultant *WM_COMMAND* if the user selects a menu item. The final item, *lptpm*, points to a *TPMPARAMS* structure that contains a size value and a rectangle structure. The rectangle structure defines the rectangle on the screen that the menu *shouldn't* cover. This parameter can be null if no exclusion rectangle needs to be specified.

Handling Menu Commands

When a user selects a menu item, Windows sends a *WM_COMMAND* message to the window that owns the menu. The low word of the *wParam* parameter contains the ID of the menu item that was selected. The high word of *wParam* contains the notification code. For a menu selection, this value is always 0. The *lParam* parameter is 0 for *WM_COMMAND* messages sent due to a menu selection. So to act on a menu selection, a window needs to field the *WM_COMMAND* message, decode the ID passed, and act according to the menu item that was selected.

Now that I've covered the basics of menu creation, you might wonder where all this menu creation code sits in a Windows program. The answer is, it doesn't. Instead of dynamically creating menus on the fly, most Windows programs simply load a menu template from a *resource*. To learn more about this, let's spend the remainder of this chapter looking at resources.

Resources

Resources are read-only data segments of an application or a DLL that are linked to the module after it has been compiled. The point of a resource is to give a developer a compiler-independent place for storing content data such as dialog boxes, strings, bitmaps, icons, and yes, menus. Since resources aren't compiled in a program, they can be changed without your having to recompile the application.

You create a resource by building an ASCII file—called a *resource script*—describing the resources. Your ASCII file has the extension RC. You compile this file with a resource compiler, which is provided by every maker of Windows development tools, and then you link it into the compiled executable again using the linker. These days, these steps are masked by a heavy layer of visual tools, but the fundamentals remain the same. For example, eMbedded Visual C++ creates and maintains an ASCII resource (RC) file even though few programmers directly look at the resource file text any more.

It's always a struggle for the author of a programming book to decide how to approach tools. Some lay out a very high level of instruction, talking about menu selections and describing dialog boxes for specific programming tools. Others show the reader how to build all the components of a program from the ground up, using ASCII files and command line compilers. Resources can be approached the same way: I could describe how to use the visual tools or how to create the ASCII files that are the basis for the resources. In this book, I stay primarily at the ASCII resource script level since the goal is to teach Windows CE programming, not how to use a particular set of tools. I'll show how to create and use the ASCII RC file for adding menus and the like, but later in the book in places where the resource file isn't relevant, I won't always include the RC file in the listings. The files are, of course, on the CD included with this book.

Resource Scripts

Creating a resource script is as easy as using Notepad to create a text file. The language used is simple, with C-like tendencies. Comment lines are prefixed by a double slash (//), and files can be included using a *#include* statement.

An example menu template would be the following:

```
//
// A menu template
//
ID_MENU MENU DISCARDABLE
BEGIN
    POPUP "&File"
    BEGIN
        MENUITEM "&Open...",                100
        MENUITEM "&Save...",                101
        MENUITEM SEPARATOR
        MENUITEM "E&xit",                   120
    END
    POPUP "&Help"
    BEGIN
        MENUITEM "&About",                  200
    END
END
```

The initial *ID_MENU* is the ID value for the resource. Alternatively, this ID value can be replaced by a string identifying the resource. The ID value method provides more compact code, while using a string may provide more readable code when the application loads the resource in the source file. The next word, *MENU*, identifies the type of resource. The menu starts with *POPUP*, indicating that the menu item *File* is actually a pop-up (cascade) menu attached to the main menu. Because it's a menu within a menu, it too has *BEGIN* and *END* keywords surrounding the description of the File menu. The ampersand (&) character tells Windows that the next character should be the key assignment for that menu item. The character following the ampersand is automatically underlined by Windows when the menu item is displayed, and if the user presses the Alt key along with the character, that menu item is selected. Each item in a menu is then specified by the *MENUITEM* keyword followed by the string used on the menu. The ellipsis following the *Open* and *Save* strings is a Windows UI custom indicating to the user that selecting that item displays a dialog box. The numbers following the *Open*, *Save*, *Exit*, and *About* menu items are the menu identifiers. These values identify the menu items in the *WM_COMMAND* message. It's good programming practice to replace these values with equates that are defined in a common include file so that they match the *WM_COMMAND* handler code.

Table 4-2 lists other resource types that you might find in a resource file. The *DISCARDABLE* keyword is optional and tells Windows that the resource can be discarded from memory if it's not in use. The remainder of the menu is couched in *BEGIN* and *END* keywords, although the bracket characters { and } are recognized as well.

Table 4-2   The Resource Types Allowed by the Resource Compiler[*]

Resource Type	Explanation
MENU	Defines a menu
ACCELERATORS	Defines a keyboard accelerator table
DIALOG	Defines a dialog box template
BITMAP	Includes a bitmap file as a resource
ICON	Includes an icon file as a resource
FONT	Includes a font file as a resource
RCDATA	Defines application-defined binary data block
STRINGTABLE	Defines a list of strings
VERSIONINFO	Includes file version information

[*] The SHMENUBAR resource type used by the Pocket PC is actually defined as RCDATA inside a wizard-generated include file.

Icons

Now that we're working with resource files, it's a trivial matter to modify the icon that the Windows CE shell uses to display a program. Simply create an icon with your favorite icon editor, and add to the resource file an icon statement such as

```
ID_ICON ICON "iconname.ico"
```

When Windows displays a program in Windows Explorer, it looks inside the EXE file for the first icon in the resource list and uses it to represent the program.

Having that icon represent an application's window is somewhat more of a chore. Windows CE uses a small 16-by-16-pixel icon on the taskbar to represent windows on the desktop. Under the desktop versions of Windows, the *RegisterClassEx* function can be used to associate a small icon with a window, but Windows CE doesn't support this function. Instead, the icon must be explicitly loaded and assigned to the window. The following code fragment assigns a small icon to a window.

```
hIcon = (HICON) SendMessage (hWnd, WM_GETICON, FALSE, 0);
if (hIcon == 0) {
    hIcon = LoadImage (hInst, MAKEINTRESOURCE (ID_ICON1), IMAGE_ICON,
                       16, 16, 0);
    SendMessage (hWnd, WM_SETICON, FALSE, (LPARAM)hIcon);
}
```

The first *SendMessage* call gets the currently assigned icon for the window. The *FALSE* value in *wParam* indicates that we're querying the small icon for the window. If this returns 0, indicating that no icon has been assigned, a call to *LoadImage* is made to load the icon from the application resources. The *Load-Image* function can take either a text string or an ID value to identify the resource being loaded. In this case, the *MAKEINTRESOURCE* macro is used to label an ID value to the function. The icon being loaded must be a 16-by-16 icon because under Windows CE, *LoadImage* won't resize the icon to fit the requested size. Also under Windows CE, *LoadImage* is limited to loading icons and bitmaps from resources. Windows CE provides the function *SHLoadDIBitmap* to load a bitmap from a file.

Unlike other versions of Windows, Windows CE stores window icons on a per-class basis. So if two windows in an application have the same class, they share the same window icon. A subtle caveat here—window classes are specific to a particular instance of an application. If you have two different instances of the application FOOBAR, they each have different window classes, so they may have different window icons, even though they were registered with the same class information. If the second instance of FOOBAR had two windows of the same class open, those two windows would share the same icon, independent of the window icon in the first instance of FOOBAR.

Accelerators

Another resource that can be loaded is a keyboard accelerator table. This table is used by Windows to enable developers to designate shortcut keys for specific menus or controls in your application. Specifically, accelerators provide a direct method for a key combination to result in a *WM_COMMAND* message being sent to a window. These accelerators are different from the Alt-F key combination that, for example, can be used to access a File menu. File menu key combinations are handled automatically as long as the File menu item string was defined with the && character, as in &File. The keyboard accelerators are independent of menus or any other controls, although their assignments typically mimic menu operations, as in using Ctrl-O to open a file.

Below is a short resource script that defines a couple of accelerator keys.

```
ID_ACCEL ACCELERATORS DISCARDABLE
BEGIN
    "N", IDM_NEWGAME, VIRTKEY, CONTROL
    "Z", IDM_UNDO,   VIRTKEY, CONTROL
END
```

As with the menu resource, the structure starts with an ID value. The ID value is followed by the type of resource and, again optionally, the *discardable* keyword. The entries in the table consist of the letter identifying the key, followed by the ID value of the command, *VIRTKEY*, which indicates that the letter is actually a virtual key value, followed finally by the *CONTROL* keyword, indicating that Control must be pressed with the key.

Simply having the accelerator table in the resource doesn't accomplish much. The application must load the accelerator table and, for each message it pulls from the message queue, see whether an accelerator has been entered. Fortunately, this is accomplished with a few simple modifications to the main mes sage loop of a program. Here's a modified main message loop that handles keyboard accelerators:

```
// Load accelerator table.
hAccel = LoadAccelerators (hInst, MAKEINTRESOURCE (ID_ACCEL));

// Application message loop
while (GetMessage (&msg, NULL, 0, 0)) {
    // Translate accelerators
    if (!TranslateAccelerator (hwndMain, hAccel, &msg)) {
        TranslateMessage (&msg);
        DispatchMessage (&msg);
    }
}
```

The first difference in this main message loop is the loading of the accelerator table using the *LoadAccelerators* function. Then, after each message is pulled from the message queue, a call is made to *TranslateAccelerator*. If this function translates the message, it returns *TRUE*, which skips the standard *TranslateMessage* and *DispatchMessage* loop body. If no translation was performed, the loop body executes normally.

Bitmaps

Bitmaps can also be stored as resources. Windows CE works with bitmap resources somewhat differently from other versions of Windows. With Windows CE, the call

```
HBITMAP LoadBitmap(HINSTANCE hInstance, LPCTSTR lpBitmapName);
```

loads a read-only version of the bitmap. This means that after the bitmap is selected into a device context, the image can't be modified by other drawing actions in that DC. To load a read/write version of a bitmap resource, use the *LoadImage* function.

Strings

String resources are a good method for reducing the memory footprint of an application while keeping language-specific information out of the code to be compiled. An application can call

```
int LoadString(HINSTANCE hInstance, UINT uID, LPTSTR lpBuffer,
               int nBufferMax);
```

to load a string from a resource. The ID of the string resource is *uID*, the *lpBuffer* parameter points to a buffer to receive the string, and *nBufferMax* is the size of the buffer. To conserve memory, *LoadString* has a new feature under Windows CE. If *lpBuffer* is *NULL*, *LoadString* returns a read-only pointer to the string as the return value. Simply cast the return value as a pointer and use the string as needed. The length of the string will be located in the word immediately preceding the start of the string. Note that by default the resource compiler removes terminating zeros from string resources. If you want to read string resources directly and have them be zero terminated, invoke the resource compiler with the *−r* command line switch. Although I'll be covering memory management and strategies for memory conservation in Chapter 7, one quick note here. It's not a good idea to load a number of strings from a resource into memory. This just uses memory both in the resource and in RAM. If you need a number of strings at the same time, it might be a better strategy to use the new feature of *LoadString* to return a pointer directly to the resource itself. As an alternative, you can have the strings in a read-only segment compiled with the program. You lose the advantage of a separate string table, but you reduce your memory footprint.

The DOIView Example Program

The following example, DOIView, demonstrates the use of resources, keyboard accelerators, and pop-up menus. DOIView, short for Declaration of Independence View, displays the United States Declaration of Independence in a window. The text for the program is stored as a series of string resources. DOIView formats the text to fit the application window and uses scroll bars to scroll the text.

Figure 4-3 shows the DOIView window. The keys Ctrl-H and Ctrl-E scroll the document to the start (home) and end of the document. You can also tap on the window to display a short menu that allows you to quickly scroll to the start or end of the document as well as end the program.

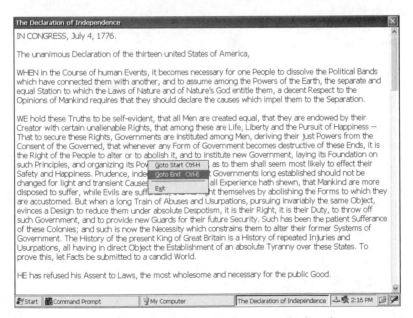

Figure 4-3   The DOI View window with the menu displayed

The source for DOIView is shown in Listing 4-2. Notice the inclusion of a third file, DOIView.rc, which contains the resource script for the program. DOIView.rc contains the menu resource, a line to include the icon for the program, and a string table that contains the text to be displayed. Since string resources are limited to 4092 characters, the text is contained in multiple strings.

DOIView.rc

```
//======================================================================
// DOIView - Resource file
//
// Written for the book Programming Windows CE
// Copyright (C) 2003 Douglas Boling
//
//======================================================================
#include "DOIView.h"


//----------------------------------------------------------------------
// Icon
//
ID_ICON ICON "DOIView.ico"


//----------------------------------------------------------------------
// Menu
//
ID_MENU MENU DISCARDABLE
BEGIN
    POPUP "&File"
    BEGIN
        MENUITEM "&Goto Start\tCtrl-H",          IDM_HOME
        MENUITEM "&Goto End\tCtrl-E",            IDM_END
        MENUITEM SEPARATOR
        MENUITEM "E&xit",                        IDM_EXIT
    END
END
//----------------------------------------------------------------------
// Accelerator table
//
ID_ACCEL ACCELERATORS DISCARDABLE
BEGIN
    "H", IDM_HOME, VIRTKEY, CONTROL
    "E", IDM_END,  VIRTKEY, CONTROL
END
//----------------------------------------------------------------------
// String table
//
STRINGTABLE DISCARDABLE
BEGIN
    IDS_DOITEXT, "IN CONGRESS, July 4, 1776.\012The unanimous \
Declaration of the thirteen united States of America,\012WHEN in the \
Course of human Events, it becomes necessary for one People to \
```

Listing 4-2   The DOIView program

```
dissolve the Political Bands which have connected them with another, \
and to assume among the Powers of the Earth, the separate and equal \
Station to which the Laws of Nature and of Nature's God entitle them, \
a decent Respect to the Opinions of Mankind requires that they should \
declare the causes which impel them to the Separation.\012\
WE hold these Truths to be self-evident, that all Men are created \
equal, that they are endowed by their Creator with certain \
unalienable Rights, that among these are Life, Liberty and the Pursuit \
of Happiness -- That to secure these Rights, Governments are \
instituted among Men, deriving their just Powers from the Consent of \
the Governed, that whenever any Form of Government becomes destructive \
of these Ends, it is the Right of the People to alter or to abolish \
it, and to institute new Government, laying its Foundation on such \
Principles, and organizing its Powers in such Form, as to them shall \
seem most likely to effect their Safety and Happiness. Prudence, \
indeed, will dictate that Governments long established should \
not be changed for light and transient Causes; and accordingly all \
Experience hath shewn, that Mankind are more disposed to suffer, while \
Evils are sufferable, than to right themselves by abolishing the Forms \
to which they are accustomed. But when a long Train of Abuses and \
Usurpations, pursuing invariably the same Object, evinces a Design to \
reduce them under absolute Despotism, it is their Right, it is their \
Duty, to throw off such Government, and to provide new Guards for \
their future Security. Such has been the patient Sufferance of these \
Colonies; and \
such is now the Necessity which constrains them to alter their \
former Systems of Government. The History of the present King of Great \
Britain is a History of repeated Injuries and Usurpations, all having \
in direct Object the Establishment of an absolute Tyranny over these \
States. To prove this, let Facts be submitted to a candid World.\012\
HE has refused his Assent to Laws, the most wholesome and \
necessary for the public Good.\012HE has forbidden his Governors to \
pass Laws of immediate and pressing Importance, unless suspended in \
their Operation till his Assent should be obtained; and when so \
suspended, he has utterly neglected to attend to them.\012\
HE has refused to pass other Laws for the Accommodation of large \
Districts of People, unless those People would relinquish the Right of \
Representation in the Legislature, a Right inestimable to them, and \
formidable to Tyrants only.\012HE has called together Legislative \
Bodies at Places unusual, uncomfortable, and distant from the \
Depository of their public Records, for the sole Purpose of fatiguing \
them into Compliance with his Measures.\012\
HE has dissolved Representative Houses repeatedly, for opposing \
with manly Firmness his Invasions on the Rights of the People.\012HE \
has refused for a long Time, after such Dissolutions, to cause others \
to be elected; whereby the Legislative Powers, incapable of the \
```

(continued)

Listing 4-2   *(continued)*

```
Annihilation, have returned to the People at large for their exercise; \
the State remaining in the mean time exposed to all the Dangers of \
Invasion from without, and the Convulsions within.\012\
HE has endeavoured to prevent the Population of these States; \
for that Purpose obstructing the Laws for Naturalization of Foreigners\
; refusing to pass others to encourage their Migrations hither, and \
raising the Conditions of new Appropriations of Lands.\012HE has \
obstructed the Administration of Justice, by refusing his Assent to \
Laws for establishing Judiciary Powers.\012HE has made Judges \
dependent on his Will alone, for the Tenure of their Offices, and the \
Amount and Payment of their Salaries.\012"

    IDS_DOITEXT1, "HE has erected a Multitude of new Offices, and sent \
hither Swarms of Officers to harrass our People, and eat out their \
Substance.\012HE has kept among us, in Times of Peace, Standing \
Armies, without the consent of our Legislatures.\012HE has affected to \
render the Military independent of and superior to the Civil Power.\012\
HE has combined with others to subject us to a Jurisdiction \
foreign to our Constitution, and unacknowledged by our Laws; giving \
his Assent to their Acts of pretended Legislation:\012FOR quartering \
large Bodies of Armed Troops among us;\012FOR protecting them, by a \
mock Trial, from Punishment for any Murders which they should commit \
on the Inhabitants of these States:\012FOR cutting off our Trade with \
all Parts of the World:\012\
FOR imposing Taxes on us without our Consent:\012FOR depriving \
us, in many Cases, of the Benefits of Trial by Jury:\012FOR \
transporting us beyond Seas to be tried for pretended Offences:\012\
FOR abolishing the free System of English Laws in a neighbouring \
Province, establishing therein an arbitrary Government, and enlarging \
its Boundaries, so as to render it at once an Example and fit \
Instrument for introducing the same absolute Rules into these \
Colonies:\012\
FOR taking away our Charters, abolishing our most valuable Laws, \
and altering fundamentally the Forms of our Governments:\012FOR \
suspending our own Legislatures, and declaring themselves invested \
with Power to legislate for us in all Cases whatsoever.\012HE has \
abdicated Government here, by declaring us out of his Protection and \
waging War against us.\012HE has plundered our Seas, ravaged our \
Coasts, burnt our Towns, and destroyed the Lives of our People.\012\
HE is, at this Time, transporting large Armies of foreign \
Mercenaries to compleat the Works of Death, Desolation, and Tyranny, \
already begun with circumstances of Cruelty and Perfidy, scarcely \
paralleled in the most barbarous Ages, and totally unworthy the Head \
of a civilized Nation.\012HE has constrained our fellow Citizens taken \
Captive on the high Seas to bear Arms against their Country, to become \
the Executioners of their Friends and Brethren, or to fall themselves \
by their Hands.\012\
```

```
HE has excited domestic Insurrections amongst us, and has \
endeavoured to bring on the Inhabitants of our Frontiers, the \
merciless Indian Savages, whose known Rule of Warfare, is an \
undistinguished Destruction, of all Ages, Sexes and Conditions.\012IN \
every stage of these Oppressions we have Petitioned for Redress in the \
most humble Terms: Our repeated Petitions have been answered only by \
repeated Injury. A Prince, whose Character is thus marked by every act \
which may define a Tyrant, is unfit to be the Ruler of a free People. \
NOR have we been wanting in Attentions to our Brittish Brethren. \
We have warned them from Time to Time of Attempts by their Legislature \
to extend an unwarrantable Jurisdiction over us. We have reminded them \
of the Circumstances of our Emigration and Settlement here. We have \
appealed to their native Justice and Magnanimity, and we have conjured \
them by the Ties of our common Kindred to disavow these Usurpations, \
which, would inevitably interrupt our Connections and Correspondence. \
They too have been deaf to the Voice of Justice and of Consanguinity. \
We must, therefore, acquiesce in the Necessity, which denounces our \
Separation, and hold them, as we hold the rest of Mankind, Enemies in \
War, in Peace, Friends.\012"

    IDS_DOITEXT2, "WE, therefore, the Representatives of the UNITED \
STATES OF AMERICA, in GENERAL CONGRESS, Assembled, appealing to the \
Supreme Judge of the World for the Rectitude of our Intentions, do, in \
the Name, and by Authority of the good People of these Colonies, \
solemnly Publish and Declare, That these United Colonies are, and of \
Right ought to be, FREE AND INDEPENDENT STATES; that they are absolved \
from all Allegiance to the British Crown, and that all political \
Connection between them and the State of Great-Britain, is and ought \
to be totally dissolved; and that as FREE AND INDEPENDENT STATES, they \
have full Power to levy War, conclude Peace, contract Alliances, \
establish Commerce, and to do all other Acts and Things which \
INDEPENDENT STATES may of right do. And for the support of this \
Declaration, with a firm Reliance on the Protection of divine \
Providence, we mutually pledge to each other our Lives, our Fortunes, \
and our sacred Honor."
END
```

DOIView.h

```
//======================================================================
// Header file
//
// Written for the book Programming Windows CE
// Copyright (C) 2003 Douglas Boling
//======================================================================
// Returns number of elements
#define dim(x) (sizeof(x) / sizeof(x[0]))
```

(continued)

Listing 4-2 *(continued)*

```
//-----------------------------------------------------------------------
// Generic defines and data types
//
struct decodeUINT {                                    // Structure associates
    UINT Code;                                         // messages
                                                       // with a function.
    LRESULT (*Fxn)(HWND, UINT, WPARAM, LPARAM);
};
struct decodeCMD {                                     // Structure associates
    UINT Code;                                         // menu IDs with a
    LRESULT (*Fxn)(HWND, WORD, HWND, WORD);            // function
};
#define    ID_MENU        10
#define    ID_ACCEL       11

#define    IDM_HOME       100
#define    IDM_END        101
#define    IDM_EXIT       102

#define    IDS_DOITEXT    1000                         // These IDs must be
#define    IDS_DOITEXT1   1001                         // consecutive
#define    IDS_DOITEXT2   1002


//-----------------------------------------------------------------------
// Function prototypes
//
LPTSTR WrapString (HDC hdc, LPTSTR pszText, int *pnLen, int nWidth,
                   BOOL *fEOL);

HWND InitInstance (HINSTANCE, LPWSTR, int);
int TermInstance (HINSTANCE, int);

// Window procedures
LRESULT CALLBACK MainWndProc (HWND, UINT, WPARAM, LPARAM);

// Message handlers
LRESULT DoCreateMain (HWND, UINT, WPARAM, LPARAM);
LRESULT DoSizeMain (HWND, UINT, WPARAM, LPARAM);
LRESULT DoCommandMain (HWND, UINT, WPARAM, LPARAM);
LRESULT DoLButtonDownMain (HWND, UINT, WPARAM, LPARAM);
LRESULT DoRButtonUpMain (HWND, UINT, WPARAM, LPARAM);
LRESULT DoVScrollMain (HWND, UINT, WPARAM, LPARAM);
LRESULT DoPaintMain (HWND, UINT, WPARAM, LPARAM);
LRESULT DoDestroyMain (HWND, UINT, WPARAM, LPARAM);
```

```
// Command functions
LPARAM DoMainCommandHome (HWND, WORD, HWND, WORD);
LPARAM DoMainCommandEnd (HWND, WORD, HWND, WORD);
LPARAM DoMainCommandExit (HWND, WORD, HWND, WORD);
```

DOIView.cpp

```
//======================================================================
// DOIView - Demonstrates window scroll bars
//
// Written for the book Programming Windows CE
// Copyright (C) 2003 Douglas Boling
//======================================================================
#include <windows.h>                  // For all that Windows stuff
#include "DOIView.h"                  // Program-specific stuff
#include <aygshell.h>                 // Extended shell API


//----------------------------------------------------------------------
// Global data
//
const TCHAR szAppName[] = TEXT("DOIView");
HINSTANCE hInst;                      // Program instance handle


#define WM_MYMSG   (WM_USER + 100)
// Message dispatch table for MainWindowProc
const struct decodeUINT MainMessages[] = {
    WM_CREATE, DoCreateMain,
    WM_SIZE, DoSizeMain,
    WM_LBUTTONDOWN, DoLButtonDownMain,
    WM_COMMAND, DoCommandMain,
    WM_VSCROLL, DoVScrollMain,
    WM_PAINT, DoPaintMain,
    WM_DESTROY, DoDestroyMain,
};

// Command Message dispatch for MainWindowProc
const struct decodeCMD MainCommandItems[] = {
    IDM_HOME, DoMainCommandHome,
    IDM_END, DoMainCommandEnd,
    IDM_EXIT, DoMainCommandExit,
};

typedef struct {
    LPTSTR pszLine;
```

(continued)

Listing 4-2   *(continued)*

```
    int nLen;
} LINEARRAY, *PLINEARRAY;

#define MAXLINES 1000
LINEARRAY laText[MAXLINES];
int nNumLines = 0;
int nFontHeight = 1;
int nLinesPerPage = 1;

LPTSTR pszDeclaration;
HFONT hFont;

int nVPos, nVMax;
BOOL fFirst = TRUE;
//======================================================================
// Program entry point
//
int WINAPI WinMain (HINSTANCE hInstance, HINSTANCE hPrevInstance,
                    LPWSTR lpCmdLine, int nCmdShow) {
    MSG msg;
    int rc = 0;
    HWND hwndMain;
    HACCEL hAccel;

    // Initialize this instance.
    hwndMain = InitInstance (hInstance, lpCmdLine, nCmdShow);
    if (hwndMain == 0) return 0x10;

    // Load accelerator table.
    hAccel = LoadAccelerators (hInst, MAKEINTRESOURCE (ID_ACCEL));

    // Application message loop
    while (GetMessage (&msg, NULL, 0, 0)) {
        // Translate accelerators
        if (!TranslateAccelerator (hwndMain, hAccel, &msg)) {
            TranslateMessage (&msg);
            DispatchMessage (&msg);
        }
    }
    // Instance cleanup
    return TermInstance (hInstance, msg.wParam);
}
//----------------------------------------------------------------------
// InitInstance - Instance initialization
//
```

```
HWND InitInstance (HINSTANCE hInstance, LPWSTR lpCmdLine, int nCmdShow) {
    WNDCLASS wc;
    HWND hWnd;
    PBYTE pRes, pBuff;
    int nStrLen = 0, i = 0;

    // Save program instance handle in global variable.
    hInst = hInstance;

#if defined(WIN32_PLATFORM_PSPC)
    // If Pocket PC, only allow one instance of the application
    hWnd = FindWindow (szAppName, NULL);
    if (hWnd) {
        SetForegroundWindow ((HWND)(((DWORD)hWnd) | 0x01));
        return 0;
    }
#endif

    // Load text from multiple string resources into one large buffer
    pBuff = (PBYTE)LocalAlloc (LPTR, 8);
    while (pRes = (PBYTE)LoadString (hInst, IDS_DOITEXT + i++, NULL, 0))
    {
        // Get the length of the string resource
        int nLen = *(PWORD)(pRes-2) * sizeof (TCHAR);
        // Resize buffer
        pBuff = (PBYTE)LocalReAlloc (pBuff, nStrLen + 8 + nLen,
                                     LMEM_MOVEABLE | LMEM_ZEROINIT);
        if (pBuff == NULL) return 0;
        // Copy resource into buffer
        memcpy (pBuff + nStrLen, pRes, nLen);
        nStrLen += nLen;
    }

    *(TCHAR *)(pBuff + nStrLen) = TEXT ('\0');
    pszDeclaration = (LPTSTR)pBuff;

    // Register application main window class.
    wc.style = 0;                               // Window style
    wc.lpfnWndProc = MainWndProc;               // Callback function
    wc.cbClsExtra = 0;                          // Extra class data
    wc.cbWndExtra = 0;                          // Extra window data
    wc.hInstance = hInstance;                   // Owner handle
    wc.hIcon = NULL,                            // Application icon
    wc.hCursor = LoadCursor (NULL, IDC_ARROW);// Default cursor
    wc.hbrBackground = (HBRUSH) GetStockObject (WHITE_BRUSH);
    wc.lpszMenuName =  NULL;                     // Menu name
```

(continued)

Listing 4-2   *(continued)*

```
        wc.lpszClassName = szAppName;                    // Window class name

        if (RegisterClass (&wc) == 0) return 0;

        // Create main window.
        hWnd = CreateWindowEx (WS_EX_NODRAG, szAppName,
                               TEXT("The Declaration of Independence"),
                               WS_VSCROLL | WS_VISIBLE | WS_CAPTION |
                               WS_SYSMENU, CW_USEDEFAULT, CW_USEDEFAULT,
                               CW_USEDEFAULT, CW_USEDEFAULT, NULL,
                               NULL, hInstance, NULL);

        if (!IsWindow (hWnd)) return 0;   // Fail code if not created.

        // Standard show and update calls
        ShowWindow (hWnd, nCmdShow);
        UpdateWindow (hWnd);
        return hWnd;
    }
    //------------------------------------------------------------------------
    // TermInstance - Program cleanup
    //
    int TermInstance (HINSTANCE hInstance, int nDefRC) {
        LocalFree (pszDeclaration);
        return nDefRC;
    }
    //========================================================================
    // Message handling procedures for main window
    //
    //------------------------------------------------------------------------
    // MainWndProc - Callback function for application window
    //
    LRESULT CALLBACK MainWndProc (HWND hWnd, UINT wMsg, WPARAM wParam,
                                  LPARAM lParam) {
        int i;
        //
        // Search message list to see if we need to handle this
        // message.  If in list, call procedure.
        //
        for (i = 0; i < dim(MainMessages); i++) {
            if (wMsg == MainMessages[i].Code)
                return (*MainMessages[i].Fxn)(hWnd, wMsg, wParam, lParam);
        }
        return DefWindowProc (hWnd, wMsg, wParam, lParam);
    }
```

```
//-------------------------------------------------------------------
// DoCreateMain - Process WM_CREATE message for window.
//
LRESULT DoCreateMain (HWND hWnd, UINT wMsg, WPARAM wParam,
                      LPARAM lParam) {
    TEXTMETRIC tm;
    HDC hdc = GetDC (hWnd);
    LOGFONT lf;
    HFONT hFontWnd;

    hFontWnd = (HFONT)GetStockObject (SYSTEM_FONT);
    GetObject (hFontWnd, sizeof (LOGFONT), &lf);

    lf.lfHeight = -12 * GetDeviceCaps(hdc, LOGPIXELSY)/ 72;
    lf.lfWeight = 0;
    hFont = CreateFontIndirect (&lf);
    SendMessage (hWnd, WM_SETFONT, (WPARAM)hFont, 0);

    // Get the height of the default font.
    hFontWnd = (HFONT)SelectObject (hdc, hFont);
    GetTextMetrics (hdc, &tm);
    nFontHeight = tm.tmHeight + tm.tmExternalLeading;
    SelectObject (hdc, hFontWnd);

    ReleaseDC (hWnd, hdc);
    return 0;
}
//-------------------------------------------------------------------
// DoSizeMain - Process WM_SIZE message for window.
//
LRESULT DoSizeMain (HWND hWnd, UINT wMsg, WPARAM wParam,
                    LPARAM lParam) {
    RECT rect;
    HDC hdc = GetDC (hWnd);
    GetClientRect (hWnd, &rect);
    int i = 0, nChars, nWidth;
    LPTSTR pszWndText = pszDeclaration;
    SCROLLINFO si;
    HFONT hFontWnd;
    BOOL fNewLine;

    hFontWnd = (HFONT)SelectObject (hdc, hFont);

    // Compute the line breaks
    nWidth = rect.right - rect.left - 10;
    while (i < MAXLINES){
```

(continued)

Listing 4-2   *(continued)*

```
        pszWndText = WrapString (hdc, pszWndText, &nChars, nWidth,
                                 &fNewLine);
        if (pszWndText == 0)
            break;
        laText[i].pszLine = pszWndText;
        laText[i].nLen = nChars;
        i++;
        if (fNewLine) {
            laText[i].nLen = 0;
            i++;
        }
        pszWndText += nChars;
    }
    nNumLines = i;
    nLinesPerPage = (rect.bottom - rect.top)/nFontHeight;

    // Compute lines per window and total lenght
    si.cbSize = sizeof (si);
    si.nMin = 0;
    si.nMax = nNumLines;
    si.nPage = nLinesPerPage;
    si.nPos = nVPos;
    si.fMask = SIF_ALL;
    SetScrollInfo (hWnd, SB_VERT, &si, TRUE);

    // Clean up
    SelectObject (hdc, hFontWnd);
    ReleaseDC (hWnd, hdc);
    InvalidateRect (hWnd, NULL, TRUE);
    return 0;
}
//----------------------------------------------------------------------
// DoCommandMain - Process WM_COMMAND message for window.
//
//
LRESULT DoCommandMain (HWND hWnd, UINT wMsg, WPARAM wParam,
                       LPARAM lParam) {
    WORD idItem, wNotifyCode;
    HWND hwndCtl;
    int  i;

    // Parse the parameters.
    idItem = (WORD) LOWORD (wParam);
    wNotifyCode = (WORD) HIWORD(wParam);
    hwndCtl = (HWND) lParam;
```

```
    // Call routine to handle control message.
    for (i = 0; i < dim(MainCommandItems); i++) {
        if (idItem == MainCommandItems[i].Code)
            return (*MainCommandItems[i].Fxn)(hWnd, idItem, hwndCtl,
                                              wNotifyCode);
    }
    return 0;
}
//-----------------------------------------------------------------------
// DoLButtonDownMain - Process WM_LBUTTONDOWN message for window.
//
LRESULT DoLButtonDownMain (HWND hWnd, UINT wMsg, WPARAM wParam,
                           LPARAM lParam) {
    HMENU hMenuMain, hMenu;
    POINT pt;
    int rc;

    // Display the menu at the point of the tap
    pt.x = LOWORD (lParam);
    pt.y = HIWORD (lParam);

    SHRGINFO sri;
    sri.cbSize = sizeof (sri);
    sri.dwFlags = 1;
    sri.hwndClient = hWnd;
    sri.ptDown = pt;

    // See if tap and hold
    rc = SHRecognizeGesture (&sri);
    if (rc == 0) return 0;

    // Display the menu at the point of the tap
    // First, convert to desktop coordinates
    MapWindowPoints (hWnd, HWND_DESKTOP, &pt, 1);
    pt.x += 5;
    hMenuMain = LoadMenu (hInst, MAKEINTRESOURCE (ID_MENU));
    hMenu = GetSubMenu (hMenuMain, 0);
    TPMPARAMS tpm;
    tpm.cbSize = sizeof (tpm);
    GetClientRect (hWnd, &tpm.rcExclude);
    TrackPopupMenuEx (hMenu, TPM_LEFTALIGN | TPM_TOPALIGN,
                      pt.x, pt.y, hWnd, &tpm);
    DestroyMenu (hMenuMain);
    DestroyMenu (hMenu);
    return 0;
}
```

(continued)

Listing 4-2   *(continued)*

```
//---------------------------------------------------------------------------
// DoVScrollMain - Process WM_VSCROLL message for window.
//
LRESULT DoVScrollMain (HWND hWnd, UINT wMsg, WPARAM wParam,
                       LPARAM lParam) {
    RECT rect;
    SCROLLINFO si;
    int sOldPos = nVPos;

    GetClientRect (hWnd, &rect);

    switch (LOWORD (wParam)) {
    case SB_LINEUP:
        nVPos -= 1;
        break;

    case SB_LINEDOWN:
        nVPos += 1;
        break;

    case SB_PAGEUP:
        nVPos -= nLinesPerPage;
        break;

    case SB_PAGEDOWN:
        nVPos += nLinesPerPage;
        break;

    case SB_THUMBTRACK:
    case SB_THUMBPOSITION:
        nVPos = HIWORD (wParam);
        break;
    }
    // Check range.
    if (nVPos < 0)
        nVPos = 0;
    if (nVPos > nNumLines-1)
        nVPos = nNumLines-1;

    // If scroll position changed, update scrollbar and
    // force redraw of window.
    if (nVPos != sOldPos) {
        si.cbSize = sizeof (si);
        si.nPos = nVPos;
        si.fMask = SIF_POS;
        SetScrollInfo (hWnd, SB_VERT, &si, TRUE);
```

```
            InvalidateRect (hWnd, NULL, TRUE);
    }
    return 0;
}
//--------------------------------------------------------------------
// DoPaintMain - Process WM_PAINT message for window.
//
LRESULT DoPaintMain (HWND hWnd, UINT wMsg, WPARAM wParam,
                     LPARAM lParam) {
    PAINTSTRUCT ps;
    HFONT hFontWnd;
    RECT rect;
    HDC hdc;
    int i, y = 5;

    hdc = BeginPaint (hWnd, &ps);

    GetClientRect (hWnd, &rect);

    hFontWnd = (HFONT)SelectObject (hdc, hFont);

    // Draw the text
    for (i = nVPos; i < nNumLines; i++) {
        if (y > rect.bottom - nFontHeight - 10)
            break;
        if (laText[i].nLen)
            ExtTextOut (hdc, 5, y, TRANSPARENT, NULL, laText[i].pszLine,
                        laText[i].nLen, NULL);
        y += nFontHeight;
    }
    SelectObject (hdc, hFontWnd);
    EndPaint (hWnd, &ps);
    return 0;
}
//--------------------------------------------------------------------
// DoDestroyMain - Process WM_DESTROY message for window.
//
LRESULT DoDestroyMain (HWND hWnd, UINT wMsg, WPARAM wParam,
                       LPARAM lParam) {
    PostQuitMessage (0);
    return 0;
}
//====================================================================
// Command handler routines
//
```

(continued)

Listing 4-2 *(continued)*

```
//-----------------------------------------------------------------
// DoMainCommandHome - Process Program Home command.
//
LPARAM DoMainCommandHome (HWND hWnd, WORD idItem, HWND hwndCtl,
                          WORD wNotifyCode) {
    SCROLLINFO si;
    if (nVPos != 0) {
        nVPos = 0;

        si.cbSize = sizeof (si);
        si.nPos = nVPos;
        si.fMask = SIF_POS;
        SetScrollInfo (hWnd, SB_VERT, &si, TRUE);

        InvalidateRect (hWnd, NULL, TRUE);
    }
    return 0;
}
//-----------------------------------------------------------------
// DoMainCommandEnd - Process End command.
//
LPARAM DoMainCommandEnd (HWND hWnd, WORD idItem, HWND hwndCtl,
                         WORD wNotifyCode) {
    SCROLLINFO si;
    int nEndPos = nNumLines - nLinesPerPage + 1;

    if (nVPos != nEndPos) {
        nVPos = nEndPos;

        si.cbSize = sizeof (si);
        si.nPos = nVPos;
        si.fMask = SIF_POS;
        SetScrollInfo (hWnd, SB_VERT, &si, TRUE);

        InvalidateRect (hWnd, NULL, TRUE);
    }
    return 0;
}
//-----------------------------------------------------------------
// DoMainCommandExit - Process Program Exit command.
//
LPARAM DoMainCommandExit (HWND hWnd, WORD idItem, HWND hwndCtl,
                          WORD wNotifyCode) {

    SendMessage (hWnd, WM_CLOSE, 0, 0);
    return 0;
}
```

```
//-----------------------------------------------------------------------
// WrapString - Determine a length that will fit with a width
//
LPTSTR WrapString (HDC hdc, LPTSTR pszText, int *pnLen, int nWidth,
                   BOOL *fEOL) {
    LPTSTR pszStr, pszStart;
    SIZE Size;

    *fEOL = FALSE;
    *pnLen = 0;

    // Skip to first non-space char
    for (; (*pszText!=TEXT('\0')) && (*pszText<=TEXT (' ')); pszText++);

    pszStart = pszText;

    if (*pszText == 0)
        return 0;

    while (1) {
        pszStr = pszText;
        // Find end of the next word
        for (; (*pszText!=TEXT('\0')) && *pszText>TEXT (' ');pszText++);

        // Get length of the string
        GetTextExtentPoint (hdc, pszStart, pszText - pszStart, &Size);

        if (Size.cx > nWidth)
            break;
        if ((*pszText == TEXT ('\0'))  || (*pszText == TEXT ('\r')) ||
            (*pszText == TEXT ('\n'))) {
            *fEOL = TRUE;
            pszStr = pszText;
            break;
        }
        // slip past space
        pszText++;
    }
    *pnLen = pszStr - pszStart;
    return pszStart;
}
```

When the program is launched, it reads the string resources into one large buffer. To reduce the memory impact, the string resources are accessed by passing a *NULL* buffer pointer to the *LoadString* function. That causes *LoadString* to return a pointer to the resource in its return value. Note that these strings aren't zero delimited in this case, so DOIView reads the word before the string to get the number of characters. Because the strings are Unicode, the string length is then multiplied by the size of *TCHAR* to get the size of the buffer needed for the string.

The main window of DOIView handles a few extra messages. The *WM_SIZE* handler reformats the text by calling *WrapString*. This routine measures the length of each line by calling *GetTextExtentPoint*. If the length is less than the width of the window, the routine then adds another word to the line and remeasures. This continues until the proper number of words is added to the line to fit within the window. The *WM_PAINT* handler draws the lines of text starting with the top line to be displayed, defined by the current scroll position.

The *WM_VSCROLL* routine handles the messages from the vertical scroll bar. When the notification is a *SB_PAGEUP* or *SB_PAGEDOWN*, the routine subtracts or adds the number of lines displayed in the window to the current scroll position. The *WM_LBUTTONDOWN* handler loads a menu from a menu resource. The menu has three commands: Home, to scroll to the top of the document; End, to scroll to the bottom; and Exit, which quits the program. DOI-View also responds to accelerator keys: Ctrl-H for Home and Ctrl-E for End.

This chapter has covered a huge amount of ground, from basic child windows to controls and on to resources and menus. My goal wasn't to teach everything there is to know about these topics. Instead, I've tried to introduce these program elements, provide a few examples, and point out the subtle differences between the way they're handled by Windows CE and the desktop versions of Windows.

Although the Windows controls are useful and quite handy, the next chapter covers the common controls. These controls are a far more powerful, and more complex, set of controls, which Windows CE also supports.

5

Common Controls and Windows CE

As Microsoft Windows matured as an operating system, it became apparent that the basic controls provided by Windows were insufficient for the sophisticated user interfaces that users demanded. Microsoft developed a series of additional controls, called common controls, for their internal applications and later made the dynamic-link library (DLL) containing the controls available to application developers. Starting with Microsoft Windows 95 and Microsoft Windows NT 3.5, the common control library was bundled with the operating system. (Although this hasn't stopped Microsoft from making interim releases of the DLL as the common control library was enhanced.) With each release of the common control DLL, new controls and new features are added to old controls. As a group, the common controls are less mature than the standard Windows controls and therefore show greater differences between implementations across the various versions of Windows. These differences aren't just between Microsoft Windows CE and other versions of Windows, but also between Windows Me, Windows 2000, and Windows XP. The functionality of the common controls in Windows CE tracks most closely with the common controls delivered with Windows 98, although not all of the Windows 98 features are supported.

It isn't the goal of this chapter to cover in depth all the common controls. That would take an entire book. Instead, I'll cover the controls and features of controls the Windows CE programmer will most often need when writing Windows CE applications. I'll start with the command bar and menu bar controls and then look at the month calendar and time and date picker controls. Finally, I'll finish up with the list view control. By the end of the chapter, you might not know every common control inside and out, but you will be able to see how the common controls work in general. And you'll have the background to look at the documentation and understand the common controls not covered.

Programming Common Controls

Because the common controls are separate from the core operating system, the DLL that contains them must be initialized before any of the common controls can be used. Under all versions of Windows, including Windows CE, you can call the function

```
void InitCommonControls (void);
```

to load the library and register many of the common control classes. This call doesn't initialize the month calendar, time picker, up/down, IP address, or other newer common controls. To initialize those controls, use the function

```
BOOL InitCommonControlsEx (LPINITCOMMONCONTROLSEX lpInitCtrls);
```

This function allows an application to load and initialize only selected common controls. This function is handy under Windows CE because loading only the necessary controls can reduce the memory impact. The only parameter to this function is a two-field structure that contains a size field and a field that contains a set of flags indicating which common controls should be registered. Table 5-1 shows the available flags and their associated controls.

Table 5-1   Flags for Selected Common Controls

Flag	Control Classes Initialized
ICC_BAR_CLASSES	Toolbar
	Status bar
	Trackbar
	Command bar
ICC_COOL_CLASSES	Rebar
ICC_DATE_CLASSES	Date and time picker
	Month calendar control
ICC_LISTVIEW_CLASSES	List view
	Header control
ICC_PROGRESS_CLASS	Progress bar control
ICC_TAB_CLASSES	Tab control
ICC_TREEVIEW_CLASSES	Tree view control

Table 5-1   Flags for Selected Common Controls   *(continued)*

Flag	Control Classes Initialized
ICC_UPDOWN_CLASS	Up-Down control
ICC_TOOLTIP_CLASSES	Tool tip control
ICC_CAPEDIT_CLASS	Cap edit control

Once the common control DLL has been initialized, these controls can be treated like any other control. But since the common controls aren't formally part of the Windows core functionality, an additional include file, CommCtrl.h, must be included.

The programming interface for the common controls is similar to that for standard Windows controls. Each of the controls has a set of custom style flags that configure the look and behavior of the control. Messages specific to each control are sent to configure and manipulate the control and cause it to perform actions. One major difference between the standard Windows controls and common controls is that notifications of events or requests for service are sent via *WM_NOTIFY* messages instead of *WM_COMMAND* messages as in the standard controls. This technique allows the notifications to contain much more information than would be allowed using *WM_COMMAND* message notifications. In addition, the technique has allowed the *WM_NOTIFY* message to be extended and adapted for each of the controls that use it.

At a minimum, the *WM_NOTIFY* message is sent with *lParam* pointing to an *NMHDR* structure defined as the following:

```
typedef struct tagNMHDR {
    HWND hwndFrom;
    UINT idFrom;
    UINT code;
} NMHDR;
```

The *hwndFrom* field contains the handle of the window that sent the notify message. For property sheets, this is the property sheet window. The *idFrom* field contains the ID of the control if a control is sending the notification. Finally, the code field contains the notification code. While this basic structure doesn't contain any more information than the *WM_COMMAND* message, it's almost always extended, with additional fields appended to it. The notification code then indicates which, if any, additional fields are appended to the notification structure.

One additional difference in programming common controls is that most of the control-specific messages that can be sent to the common controls have predefined macros that make sending the message look as if your application is calling a function. So instead of using an *LVM_INSERTITEM* message to a list view control to insert an item, as in

```
nIndex = (int) SendMessage (hwndLV, LVM_INSERTITEM, 0, (LPARAM)&lvi);
```

an application could just as easily have used the line

```
nIndex = ListView_InsertItem (hwndLV, &lvi);
```

There's no functional difference between the two lines; the advantage of these macros is clarity. The macros themselves are defined in CommCtrl.h along with the other definitions required for programming the common controls. One problem with the macros is that the compiler doesn't perform the type checking on the parameters that would normally occur if the macro were an actual function. This is also true of the *SendMessage* technique, in which the parameters must be typed as *WPARAM* and *LPARAM* types, but at least with messages the lack of type checking is obvious. All in all, though, the macro route provides better readability. One exception to this system of macros is the calls made to the command bar control and the command bands control. Those controls actually have a number of true functions in addition to a large set of macro-wrapped messages. As a rule, I'll talk about messages as messages, not as their macro equivalents. That should help differentiate a message or a macro from a true function.

The Common Controls

A prime Windows CE target niche—small personal productivity devices—has driven the requirements for the common controls in Windows CE. The frequent need for time and date references for schedule and task management applications has led to inclusion of the date and time picker control and the month calendar control. The small screens of personal productivity devices inspired the space-saving command bar. Mating the command bar with the rebar control that was created for Internet Explorer 3.0 has produced the command bands control. The command bands control provides even more room for menus, buttons, and other controls across the top of a Windows CE application.

Finally, Pocket PC developers are familiar with the menu bar. This control was added to the Windows CE common controls in Windows CE .NET 4.2. I'll cover the menu bar after I discuss the command bar and command bands controls.

The Command Bar

Briefly, a command bar control combines a menu and a toolbar. This combination is valuable because the combination of a menu and toolbar on one line saves screen real estate on space-constrained Windows CE displays. To the programmer, the command bar looks like a toolbar with a number of helper functions that make programming the command bar a breeze. In addition to the command bar functions, you can also use most toolbar messages when you're working with command bars. A window with a command bar is shown in Figure 5-1.

Figure 5-1   A window with a command bar control

Creating a Command Bar

You build a command bar in a number of steps, each defined by a particular function. The command bar is created, the menu is added, buttons are added, other controls are added, tooltips are added, and finally, the Close and Help buttons are appended to the right side of the command bar.

You begin the process of creating a command bar with a call to

```
HWND CommandBar_Create (HINSTANCE hInst, HWND hwndParent,
                    int idCmdBar);
```

The function requires the program's instance handle, the handle of the parent window, and an ID value for the control. If successful, the function returns the handle to the newly created command bar control. But a bare command bar isn't much use to the application. It takes a menu and a few buttons to jazz it up.

Command Bar Menus

You can add a menu to a command bar by calling one of two functions. The first function is this:

```
BOOL CommandBar_InsertMenubar (HWND hwndCB, HINSTANCE hInst,
                        WORD idMenu, int iButton);
```

The first two parameters of this function are the handle of the command bar and the instance handle of the application. The *idMenu* parameter is the resource ID of the menu to be loaded into the command bar. The last parameter is the index of the button to the immediate left of the menu. Because the Windows CE guidelines specify that the menu should be at the left end of the command bar, this parameter should be set to 0, which indicates that all the buttons are to the right of the menu.

A shortcoming of the *CommandBar_InsertMenubar* function is that it requires the menu to be loaded from a resource. You can't configure the menu on the fly. Of course, it would be possible to load a dummy menu and manipulate the contents of the menu with the various menu functions, but here's an easier method.

The function

```
BOOL CommandBar_InsertMenubarEx (HWND hwndCB, HINSTANCE hInst,
                                 LPTSTR pszMenu, int iButton);
```

has a set of parameters similar to *CommandBar_InsertMenubar* with the exception of the third parameter, *pszMenu*. This parameter can be either the name of a menu resource or the handle to a menu previously created by the program. If the *pszMenu* parameter is a menu handle, the *hInst* parameter must be *NULL*.

Once a menu has been loaded into a command bar, the handle to the menu can be retrieved at any time using

```
HMENU CommandBar_GetMenu (HWND hwndCB, int iButton);
```

The second parameter, *iButton*, is the index of the button to the immediate left of the menu. This mechanism provides the ability to identify more than one menu on the command bar. However, given the Windows CE design guidelines, you should see only one menu on the bar. With the menu handle, you can manipulate the structure of the menu using the many menu functions available.

If an application modifies the menu on the command bar, the application must call

```
BOOL CommandBar_DrawMenuBar (HWND hwndCB, int iButton);
```

which forces the menu on the command bar to be redrawn. Here again, the parameters are the handle to the command bar and the index of the button to the left of the menu. Under Windows CE, you must use *CommandBar_DrawMenuBar* instead of *DrawMenuBar*, which is the standard function used to redraw the menu under other versions of Windows.

Command Bar Buttons

Adding buttons to a command bar is a two-step process and is similar to adding buttons to a toolbar. First the bitmap images for the buttons must be added to the command bar. Second the buttons are added, with each of the buttons referencing one of the images in the bitmap list that was previously added.

The command bar maintains its own list of bitmaps for the buttons in an internal image list. Bitmaps can be added to this image list one at a time or as a group of images contained in a long and narrow bitmap. For example, for a bitmap to contain four 16-by-16-pixel images, the dimensions of the bitmap added to the command bar would be 64 by 16 pixels. Figure 5-2 shows this bitmap image layout.

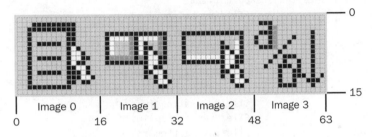

Figure 5-2   Layout of a bitmap that contains four 16-by-16-pixel images

Loading an image bitmap is accomplished using

```
int CommandBar_AddBitmap (HWND hwndCB, HINSTANCE hInst, int idBitmap,
                          int iNumImages, int iImageWidth, int iImageHeight);
```

The first two parameters are, as is usual with a command bar function, the handle to the command bar and the instance handle of the executable. The third parameter, *idBitmap*, is the resource ID of the bitmap image. The fourth parameter, *iNumImages*, should contain the number of images in the bitmap being loaded. Multiple bitmap images can be loaded into the same command bar by calling *CommandBar_AddBitmap* as many times as is needed. The last two parameters are the dimensions of the images within the bitmap; set both these parameters to 16.

Two predefined bitmaps provide a number of images that are commonly used in command bars and toolbars. You load these images by setting the *hInst* parameter in *CommandBar_AddBitmap* to *HINST_COMMCTRL* and setting the *idBitmap* parameter to either *IDB_STD_SMALL_COLOR* or *IDB_VIEW_SMALL_COLOR*. The images contained in these bitmaps are shown in Figure 5-3. The buttons on the top line contain the bitmaps from the standard bitmap, while the second-line buttons contain the bitmaps from the standard view bitmap.

Figure 5-3   Images in the two standard bitmaps provided by the common control DLL

The index values to these images are defined in CommCtrl.h, so you don't need to know the exact order in the bitmaps. The constants are

```
Constants to access the standard bitmap
STD_CUT                        Edit/Cut button image
STD_COPY                       Edit/Copy button image
STD_PASTE                      Edit/Paste button image
STD_UNDO                       Edit/Undo button image
STD_REDOW                      Edit/Redo button image
STD_DELETE                     Edit/Delete button image
STD_FILENEW                    File/New button image
STD_FILEOPEN                   File/Open button image
STD_FILESAVE                   File/Save button image
STD_PRINTPRE                   Print preview button image
STD_PROPERTIES                 Properties button image
STD_HELP                       Help button (Use Commandbar_Addadornments
                               function to add a help button to the
                               command bar.)
STD_FIND                       Find button image
STD_REPLACE                    Replace button image
STD_PRINT                      Print button image


Constants to access the standard view bitmap
VIEW_LARGEICONS                View/Large Icons button image
VIEW_SMALLICONS                View/Small Icons button image
VIEW_LIST                      View/List button image
VIEW_DETAILS                   View/Details button image
VIEW_SORTNAME                  Sort by name button image
VIEW_SORTSIZE                  Sort by size button image
VIEW_SORTDATE                  Sort by date button image
VIEW_SORTTYPE                  Sort by type button image
VIEW_PARENTFOLDER              Go to Parent folder button image
VIEW_NETCONNECT                Connect network drive button image
VIEW_NETDISCONNECT             Disconnect network drive button image
VIEW_NEWFOLDER                 Create new folder button image
```

Referencing Images

The images loaded into the command bar are referenced by their index into the list of images. For example, if the bitmap loaded contained five images, and the image to be referenced was the fourth image into the bitmap, the zero based index value would be 3.

If more than one set of bitmap images was added to the command bar using multiple calls to *CommandBar_AddBitmap*, the images' subsequent lists are referenced according to the previous count of images plus the index into that list. For example, if two calls were made to *CommandBar_AddBitmap* to add two sets of images, with the first call adding five images and the second adding four images, the third image of the second set would be referenced with the total number of images added in the first bitmap (5) plus the index into the second bitmap (2), resulting in an index value of 5 + 2 = 7.

Once the bitmaps have been loaded, the buttons can be added using one of two functions. The first function is this one:

```
BOOL CommandBar_AddButtons (HWND hwndCB, UINT uNumButtons,
                    LPTBBUTTON lpButtons);
```

CommandBar_AddButtons adds a series of buttons to the command bar at one time. The function is passed a count of buttons and a pointer to an array of *TBBUTTON* structures. Each element of the array describes one button. The *TBBUTTON* structure is defined as the following:

```
typedef struct {
    int iBitmap;
    int idCommand;
    BYTE fsState;
    BYTE fsStyle;
    DWORD dwData;
    int iString;
} TBBUTTON;
```

The *iBitmap* field specifies the bitmap image to be used by the button. This is, as I just explained, the zero-based index into the list of images. The second parameter is the command ID of the button. This ID value is sent via a *WM_COMMAND* message to the parent when a user clicks the button.

The *fsState* field specifies the initial state of the button. The allowable values in this field are the following:

- **TBSTATE_ENABLED**   The button is enabled. If this flag isn't specified, the button is disabled and is grayed.

- **TBSTATE_HIDDEN**   The button isn't visible on the command bar.

- **TBSTATE_PRESSED** This button is displayed in a depressed state.

- **TBSTATE_CHECKED** The button is initially checked. This state can be used only if the button has the *TBSTYLE_CHECKED* style.

- **TBSTATE_INDETERMINATE** The button is grayed.

One last flag is specified in the documentation, *TBSTATE_WRAP*, but it doesn't have a valid use in a command bar. This flag is used by toolbars when a toolbar wraps across more than one line.

The *fsStyle* field specifies the initial style of the button, which defines how the button acts. The button can be defined as a standard push button, a check button, a drop-down button, or a check button that resembles a radio button but allows only one button in a group to be checked. The possible flags for the *fsStyle* field are the following:

- **TBSTYLE_BUTTON** The button looks like a standard push button.

- **TBSTYLE_CHECK** The button is a check button that toggles between checked and unchecked states each time the user clicks the button.

- **TBSTYLE_GROUP** Defines the start of a group of buttons.

- **TBSTYLE_CHECKGROUP** The button is a member of a group of check buttons that act like radio buttons in that only one button in the group is checked at any one time.

- **TBSTYLE_DROPDOWN** The button is a drop-down list button.

- **TBSTYLE_AUTOSIZE** The button's size is defined by the button text.

- **TBSTYLE_SEP** Defines a separator (instead of a button) that inserts a small space between buttons.

The *dwData* field of the *TBBUTTON* structure is an application-defined value. This value can be set and queried by the application using the *TB_SETBUTTONINFO* and *TB_GETBUTTONINFO* messages. The *iString* field defines the index into the command bar string array that contains the text for the button. The *iString* field can also be filled with a pointer to a string that contains the text for the button.

The other function that adds buttons to a command bar is this one:

```
BOOL CommandBar_InsertButton (HWND hwndCB, int iButton,
                    LPTBBUTTON lpButton);
```

This function inserts one button into the command bar to the left of the button referenced by the *iButton* parameter. The parameters in this function mimic the parameters in *CommandBar_AddButtons* with the exception that the *lpButton* parameter points to a single *TBBUTTON* structure. The *iButton* parameter specifies the position on the command bar of the new button.

Working with Command Bar Buttons

When a user presses a command bar button other than a drop-down button, the command bar sends a *WM_COMMAND* message to the parent window of the command bar. So handling button clicks on the command bar is just like handling menu commands. In fact, since many of the buttons on the command bar have menu command equivalents, it's customary to use the same command IDs for the buttons and the like functioning menus, thus removing the need for any special processing for the command bar buttons.

The command bar maintains the checked and unchecked state of check and checkgroup buttons. After the buttons have been added to the command bar, their states can be queried or set using two messages, *TB_ISBUTTONCHECKED* and *TB_CHECKBUTTON*. (The *TB_* prefix in these messages indicates the close relationship between the command bar and the toolbar controls.) The *TB_ISBUTTONCHECKED* message is sent with the ID of the button to be queried passed in the *wParam* parameter this way:

```
fChecked = SendMessage (hwndCB, TB_ISBUTTONCHECKED, wID, 0);
```

where *hwndCB* is the handle to the command bar containing the button. If the return value from the *TB_ISBUTTONCHECKED* message is nonzero, the button is checked. To place a button in the checked state, send a *TB_CHECKBUTTON* message to the command bar, as in

```
SendMessage (hwndCB, TB_CHECKBUTTON, wID, TRUE);
```

To uncheck a checked button, replace the *TRUE* value in *lParam* with *FALSE*.

Disabled Buttons

Windows CE allows you to easily modify the way a command bar or toolbar button looks when the button is disabled. Command bars and toolbars maintain two image lists: the standard image list that I described previously and a disabled image list used to store bitmaps that you can employ for disabled buttons.

To use this feature, you need to create and load a second image list for disabled buttons. The easiest way to do this is to create the image list for the normal states of the buttons using the techniques I described when I talked about *CommandBar_AddBitmap*. (Image lists in toolbars are loaded with the message *TB_LOADIMAGES*.) Once that image list is complete, simply copy the original image list and modify the bitmaps of the images to create disabled counterparts to the original images. Then load the new image list back into the command bar or toolbar. A short code fragment that accomplishes this chore is shown here.

```
HBITMAP hBmp, hMask;
HIMAGELIST hilDisabled, hilEnabled;

// Load the bitmap and mask to be used in the disabled image list.
hBmp = LoadBitmap (hInst, TEXT ("DisCross"));
hMask = LoadBitmap (hInst, TEXT ("DisMask"));

// Get the standard image list and copy it.
hilEnabled = (HIMAGELIST)SendMessage (hwndCB, TB_GETIMAGELIST, 0, 0);
hilDisabled = ImageList_Duplicate (hilEnabled);

// Replace one bitmap in the disabled list.
ImageList_Replace (hilDisabled, VIEW_LIST, hBmp, hMask);

// Set the disabled image list.
SendMessage (hwndCB, TB_SETDISABLEDIMAGELIST, 0, (LPARAM) hilDisabled);
```

The code fragment first loads a bitmap and a mask bitmap that will replace one of the images in the disabled image list. You retrieve the current image list by sending a *TB_GETIMAGELIST* message to the command bar, and then you duplicate it using *ImageList_Duplicate*. One image in the image list is then replaced by the bitmap that was loaded earlier.

This example replaces only one image, but in a real-world example many images might be replaced. If all the images were replaced, it might be easier to build the disabled image list from scratch instead of copying the standard image list and replacing a few bitmaps in it. Once the new image list is created, you load it into the command bar by sending a *TB_SETDISABLEDIMAGELIST* message. The code that I just showed you works just as well for toolbars under Windows CE as it does for command bars.

Drop-Down Buttons

The drop-down list button is a more complex animal than the standard button on a command bar. The button looks to the user like a button that, when pressed, displays a list of items for the user to select from. To the programmer, a drop-down button is actually a combination of a button and a menu that is displayed when the user clicks on the button. Unfortunately, the command bar does little to support a drop-down button except to modify the button appearance to indicate that the button is a drop-down button and to send a special notification when the button is clicked by the user. It's up to the application to display the menu.

The notification of the user clicking a drop-down button is sent to the parent window of the command bar by a *WM_NOTIFY* message with the notification value *TBN_DROPDOWN*. When the parent window receives the *TBN_DROPDOWN* notification, it must create a pop-up menu immediately below the drop-down button identified in the notification. The menu is filled by the parent window with whatever selections are appropriate for the button. When one of the menu items is selected, the menu will send a *WM_COMMAND* message indicating the menu item picked, and the menu will be dismissed. The easiest way to understand how to handle a drop-down button notification is to look at the following procedure that handles a *TBN_DROPDOWN* notification.

```
LRESULT DoNotifyMain (HWND hWnd, UINT wMsg, WPARAM wParam,
                      LPARAM lParam) {
    LPNMHDR pNotifyHeader;
    LPNMTOOLBAR pNotifyToolBar;
    RECT rect;
    TPMPARAMS tpm;
    HMENU hMenu;

    // Get pointer to notify message header.
    pNotifyHeader = (LPNMHDR)lParam;

    if (pNotifyHeader->code == TBN_DROPDOWN) {

        // Get pointer to toolbar notify structure.
        pNotifyToolBar = (LPNMTOOLBAR)lParam;

        // Get the rectangle of the drop-down button.
        SendMessage (pNotifyHeader->hwndFrom, TB_GETRECT,
                    pNotifyToolBar->iItem, (LPARAM)&rect);

        // Convert rect to screen coordinates.  The rect is
        // considered here to be an array of 2 POINT structures.
        MapWindowPoints (pNotifyHeader->hwndFrom, HWND_DESKTOP,
                        (LPPOINT)&rect, 2);

        // Prevent the menu from covering the button.
        tpm.cbSize = sizeof (tpm);
        CopyRect (&tpm.rcExclude, &rect);

        // Load the menu resource to display under the button.
        hMenu = GetSubMenu (LoadMenu (hInst, TEXT ("popmenu")),0);
```

(continued)

```
            // Display the menu.  This function returns after the
            // user makes a selection or dismisses the menu.
            TrackPopupMenuEx (hMenu, TPM_LEFTALIGN | TPM_VERTICAL,
                            rect.left, rect.bottom, hWnd, &tpm);
        }
    return 0;
}
```

After the code determines that the message is a *TBN_DROPDOWN* notification, the first task of the notification handler code is to get the rectangle of the drop-down button. The rectangle is queried so that the drop-down menu can be positioned immediately below the button. To do this, the routine sends a *TB_GETRECT* message to the command bar with the ID of the drop-down button passed in *wParam* and a pointer to a rectangle structure in *lParam*.

Because the rectangle returned is in the coordinate base of the parent window, and pop-up menus are positioned in screen coordinates, the coordinates must be converted from one basis to the other. You accomplish this using the function

```
MapWindowPoints (HWND hwndFrom, HWND hwndTo,
                LPPOINT lppoints, UINT cPoints);
```

The first parameter is the handle of the window in which the coordinates are originally based. The second parameter is the handle of the window to which you want to map the coordinates. The third parameter is a pointer to an array of points to be translated; the last parameter is the number of points in the array. In the routine I just showed you, the window handles are the command bar handle and the desktop window handle, respectively.

Once the rectangle has been translated into desktop coordinates, the pop-up, or context, menu can be created. You do this by first loading the menu from the resource and then displaying the menu with a call to *TrackPopupMenuEx*. If you recall the discussion of *TrackPopupMenuEx* from the preceding chapter, the *TPMPARAMS* structure contains a rectangle that won't be covered up by the menu when it's displayed. For our purposes, this rectangle is set to the dimensions of the drop-down button so that the button won't be covered by the pop-up menu. The *fuFlags* field can contain a number of values that define the placement of the menu. For drop-down buttons, the only flag needed is *TPM_VERTICAL*. If *TPM_VERTICAL* is set, the menu leaves uncovered as much of the horizontal area of the exclude rectangle as possible. The *TrackPopupMenuEx* function doesn't return until an item on the menu has been selected or the menu has been dismissed by the user tapping on another part of the screen.

Combo Boxes on the Command Bar

Combo boxes on a command bar are much easier to implement than drop-down buttons. You add a combo box by calling

```
HWND CommandBar_InsertComboBox (HWND hwndCB, HINSTANCE hInst,
                                int iWidth, UINT dwStyle,
                                WORD idComboBox,
                                int iButton);
```

This function inserts a combo box on the command bar to the left of the button indicated by the *iButton* parameter. The width of the combo box is specified, in pixels, by the *iWidth* parameter. The *dwStyle* parameter specifies the style of the combo box. The allowable style flags are any valid Windows CE combo box style and window styles. The function automatically adds the *WS_CHILD* and *WS_VISIBLE* flags when creating the combo box. The *idComboBox* parameter is the ID for the combo box that will be used when *WM_COMMAND* messages are sent notifying the parent window of a combo box event. Experienced Windows programmers will be happy to know that *CommandBar_InsertComboBox* takes care of all the "parenting" problems that occur when a control is added to a standard Windows toolbar. That one function call is all that is needed to create a properly functioning combo box on the command bar.

Once a combo box is created, you program it on the command bar the same way you would a standalone combo box. Since the combo box is a child of the command bar, you must query the window handle of the combo box by passing the handle of the command bar to *GetDlgItem* with the ID value of the combo box, as in the following code:

```
hwndCombobox = GetDlgItem (GetDlgItem (hWnd, IDC_CMDBAR),
                           IDC_COMBO));
```

However, the *WM_COMMAND* messages from the combo box are sent directly to the parent of the command bar, so handling combo box events is identical to handling them from a combo box created as a child of the application's top-level window.

Command Bar Tooltips

Tooltips are small windows that display descriptive text that labels a command bar button when the stylus is held down over the control. The command bar implements tooltips in its own unique way.

You add tooltips to a command bar by using this function:

```
BOOL CommandBar_AddToolTips (HWND hwndCB, UINT uNumToolTips,
                             LPTSTR lpToolTips);
```

The *lpToolTips* parameter must point to an array of pointers to strings. The *uNumToolTips* parameter should be set to the number of elements in the string pointer array. The *CommandBar_AddToolTips* function doesn't copy the strings into its own storage. Instead, the location of the string array is saved. This means that the block of memory containing the string array must not be released until the command bar is destroyed.

Each string in the array becomes the tooltip text for a control or separator on the command bar, excluding the menu. The first string in the array becomes the tooltip for the first control or separator, the second string is assigned to the second control or separator, and so on. So even though combo boxes and separators don't display tooltips, they must have entries in the string array so that all the text lines up with the proper buttons.

Other Command Bar Functions

A number of other functions assist in command bar management. The *CommandBar_Height* function returns the height of the command bar and is used in all the example programs that use the command bar. Likewise, the *CommandBar_AddAdornments* function is also used whenever a command bar is used. This function, prototyped as

```
BOOL CommandBar_AddAdornments (HWND hwndCB, DWORD dwFlags,
                              DWORD dwReserved);
```

places a Close button and, if you want, a Help button and an OK button on the extreme right of the command bar. You pass a *CMDBAR_HELP* flag to the *dwFlags* parameter to add a Help button, and you pass a *CMDBAR_OK* flag to add an OK button.

The Help button is treated differently from other buttons on the command bar. When the Help button is pressed, the command bar sends a *WM_HELP* message to the owner of the command bar instead of the standard *WM_COMMAND* message. The OK button's action is more traditional. When you tap it, you send a *WM_COMMAND* message with the control ID *IDOK*. The *CommandBar_AddAdornments* function must be called after all other controls of the command bar have been added.

If your top-level window is resizeable, you must notifiy the command bar of resize during the *WM_SIZE* message by sending a *TB_AUTOSIZE* message to the command bar and then calling

```
BOOL CommandBar_AlignAdornments (HWND hwndCB);
```

The only parameter is the handle to the command bar. A command bar can be hidden by calling

```
BOOL CommandBar_Show (HWND hwndCB, BOOL fShow);
```

The *fShow* parameter is set to *TRUE* to show a command bar and *FALSE* to hide a command bar. The visibility of a command bar can be queried with this:

```
BOOL CommandBar_IsVisible (HWND hwndCB);
```

Finally, a command bar can be destroyed using this:

```
void CommandBar_Destroy (HWND hwndCB);
```

Although a command bar is automatically destroyed when its parent window is destroyed, sometimes it's more convenient to destroy a command bar manually. This is often done if a new command bar is needed for a different mode of the application. Of course, you can create multiple command bars, hiding all but one and switching between them by showing only one at a time, but this isn't good programming practice under Windows CE because all those hidden command bars take up valuable RAM that could be used elsewhere. The proper method is to destroy and create command bars on the fly. You can create a command bar fast enough so that a user shouldn't notice any delay in the application when a new command bar is created.

Design Guidelines for Command Bars

Because command bars are a major element of Windows CE applications, it's not surprising that Microsoft has a rather strong set of rules for their use. Many of these rules are similar to the design guidelines for other versions of Windows, such as the recommendations for the ordering of main menu items and the use of tooltips. Most of these guidelines are already second nature to Windows programmers.

The menu should be the leftmost item on the command bar. The order of the main menu items should be from left to right: File, Edit, View, Insert, Format, Tools, and Window. Of course, most applications have all of those menu items, but the order of the items used should follow the suggested order. For buttons, the order is from left to right: New, Open, Save, and Print for file actions; and Bold, Italic, and Underline for font style.

The CmdBar Example

The CmdBar example demonstrates the basics of command bar operation. On startup, the example creates a bar with only a menu and a close button. Selecting the different items from the view menu creates various command bars showing the capabilities of the command bar control. The source code for CmdBar is shown in Listing 5-1.

CmdBar.rc
```
//======================================================================
// Resource file
//
// Written for the book Programming Windows CE
// Copyright (C) 2003 Douglas Boling
//======================================================================
#include "windows.h"
#include "CmdBar.h"                       // Program-specific stuff
//----------------------------------------------------------------------
// Icons and bitmaps
//
ID_ICON       ICON    "cmdbar.ico"       // Program icon
DisCross      BITMAP  "cross.bmp"        // Disabled button image
DisMask       BITMAP  "mask.bmp"         // Disabled button image mask
SortDropBtn   BITMAP  "sortdrop.bmp"     // Sort drop-down button image


//----------------------------------------------------------------------
// Menu
//
ID_MENU MENU DISCARDABLE
BEGIN
    POPUP "&File"
    BEGIN
        MENUITEM "E&xit",                IDM_EXIT
    END

    POPUP "&View"
    BEGIN
        MENUITEM "&Standard",            IDM_STDBAR
        MENUITEM "&View",                IDM_VIEWBAR
        MENUITEM "&Combination",         IDM_COMBOBAR
    END
    POPUP "&Help"
    BEGIN
        MENUITEM "&About...",            IDM_ABOUT
    END
END

popmenu MENU DISCARDABLE
BEGIN
    POPUP "&Sort"
    BEGIN
        MENUITEM "&Name",                IDC_SNAME
        MENUITEM "&Type",                IDC_STYPE
        MENUITEM "&Size",                IDC_SSIZE
```

Listing 5-1   The CmdBar program

```
        MENUITEM "&Date",                        IDC_SDATE
    END
END


//-----------------------------------------------------------------
// About box dialog template
//
aboutbox DIALOG discardable 10, 10, 160, 45
STYLE  WS_POPUP | WS_VISIBLE | WS_CAPTION | WS_SYSMENU |
       DS_CENTER | DS_MODALFRAME
CAPTION "About"
BEGIN
    ICON  ID_ICON,                    -1,    5,   5,  10,  10
    LTEXT "CmdBar - Written for the book Programming Windows \
           CE Copyright 2003 Douglas Boling"
                                      -1,   40,   5, 110,  35
END
```

CmdBar.h

```
//=========================================================================
// Header file
//
// Written for the book Programming Windows CE
// Copyright (C) 2003 Douglas Boling
//=========================================================================
// Returns number of elements
#define dim(x) (sizeof(x) / sizeof(x[0]))


//-------------------------------------------------------------------------
// Generic defines and data types
//
struct decodeUINT {                         // Structure associates
    UINT Code;                              // messages
                                            // with a function.
    LRESULT (*Fxn)(HWND, UINT, WPARAM, LPARAM);
};
struct decodeCMD {                          // Structure associates
    UINT Code;                              // menu IDs with a
    LRESULT (*Fxn)(HWND, WORD, HWND, WORD); // function.
};


//-------------------------------------------------------------------------
// Generic defines used by application
#define  IDC_CMDBAR       1                 // Command band ID
#define  ID_ICON         10                 // Icon resource ID
```

(continued)

Listing 5-1   *(continued)*

```
#define  ID_MENU          11                      // Main menu resource ID
#define  IDC_COMBO         12                      // Combo box on cmd bar ID

// Menu item IDs
#define  IDM_EXIT          101             // File menu
#define  IDM_STDBAR        111             // View menu
#define  IDM_VIEWBAR       112
#define  IDM_COMBOBAR      113
#define  IDM_ABOUT         120             // Help menu
// Command bar button IDs
#define  IDC_NEW           201
#define  IDC_OPEN          202
#define  IDC_SAVE          203
#define  IDC_CUT           204
#define  IDC_COPY          205
#define  IDC_PASTE         206
#define  IDC_PROP          207

#define  IDC_LICON         301
#define  IDC_SICON         302
#define  IDC_LIST          303
#define  IDC_RPT           304
#define  IDC_SNAME         305
#define  IDC_STYPE         306
#define  IDC_SSIZE         307
#define  IDC_SDATE         308
#define  IDC_DPSORT        350

#define  STD_BMPS          (STD_PRINT+1)       // Number of bmps in
                                               // std imglist
#define  VIEW_BMPS         (VIEW_NEWFOLDER+1)  // Number of bmps in
                                               // view imglist
//------------------------------------------------------------------------
// Function prototypes
//
HWND InitInstance (HINSTANCE, LPWSTR, int);
int TermInstance (HINSTANCE, int);

// Window procedures
LRESULT CALLBACK MainWndProc (HWND, UINT, WPARAM, LPARAM);

// Message handlers
LRESULT DoCreateMain (HWND, UINT, WPARAM, LPARAM);
LRESULT DoSizeMain (HWND, UINT, WPARAM, LPARAM);
LRESULT DoCommandMain (HWND, UINT, WPARAM, LPARAM);
```

```
LRESULT DoNotifyMain (HWND, UINT, WPARAM, LPARAM);
LRESULT DoDestroyMain (HWND, UINT, WPARAM, LPARAM);


// Command functions
LPARAM DoMainCommandExit (HWND, WORD, HWND, WORD);
LPARAM DoMainCommandVStd (HWND, WORD, HWND, WORD);
LPARAM DoMainCommandVView (HWND, WORD, HWND, WORD);
LPARAM DoMainCommandVCombo (HWND, WORD, HWND, WORD);
LPARAM DoMainCommandAbout (HWND, WORD, HWND, WORD);
// Dialog procedures
BOOL CALLBACK AboutDlgProc (HWND, UINT, WPARAM, LPARAM);
```

CmdBar.cpp

```
//======================================================================
// CmdBar - Command bar demonstration
//
// Written for the book Programming Windows CE
// Copyright (C) 2003 Douglas Boling
//======================================================================
#include <windows.h>                    // For all that Windows stuff
#include <commctrl.h>                   // Command bar includes
#include "CmdBar.h"                     // Program-specific stuff
//----------------------------------------------------------------------
// Global data
//
const TCHAR szAppName[] = TEXT ("CmdBar");
HINSTANCE hInst;                        // Program instance handle

// Message dispatch table for MainWindowProc
const struct decodeUINT MainMessages[] = {
    WM_CREATE, DoCreateMain,
    WM_SIZE, DoSizeMain,
    WM_COMMAND, DoCommandMain,
    WM_NOTIFY, DoNotifyMain,
    WM_DESTROY, DoDestroyMain,
};

// Command Message dispatch for MainWindowProc
const struct decodeCMD MainCommandItems[] = {
    IDM_EXIT, DoMainCommandExit,
    IDM_STDBAR, DoMainCommandVStd,
    IDM_VIEWBAR, DoMainCommandVView,
    IDM_COMBOBAR, DoMainCommandVCombo,
    IDM_ABOUT, DoMainCommandAbout,
};
```

(continued)

Listing 5-1 *(continued)*

```
// Standard file bar button structure
const TBBUTTON tbCBStdBtns[] = {
// BitmapIndex        Command       State         Style          UserData String
   {0,                0,            0,            TBSTYLE_SEP,        0,   0},
   {STD_FILENEW,      IDC_NEW,      TBSTATE_ENABLED,
                                                  TBSTYLE_BUTTON,     0,   0},
   {STD_FILEOPEN,     IDC_OPEN,     TBSTATE_ENABLED,
                                                  TBSTYLE_BUTTON,     0,   0},
   {STD_FILESAVE,     IDC_SAVE,     TBSTATE_ENABLED,
                                                  TBSTYLE_BUTTON,     0,   0},
   {0,                0,            0,            TBSTYLE_SEP,        0,   0},
   {STD_CUT,          IDC_CUT,      TBSTATE_ENABLED,
                                                  TBSTYLE_BUTTON,     0,   0},
   {STD_COPY,         IDC_COPY,     TBSTATE_ENABLED,
                                                  TBSTYLE_BUTTON,     0,   0},
   {STD_PASTE,        IDC_PASTE,    TBSTATE_ENABLED,
                                                  TBSTYLE_BUTTON,     0,   0},
   {0,                0,            0,            TBSTYLE_SEP,        0,   0},
   {STD_PROPERTIES,   IDC_PROP,     TBSTATE_ENABLED,
       TBSTYLE_BUTTON,    0,    0}
};

// Standard view bar button structure
const TBBUTTON tbCBViewBtns[] = {
// BitmapIndex        Command       State         Style          UserData String
   {0,                0,            0,            TBSTYLE_SEP,        0,   0},
   {VIEW_LARGEICONS,  IDC_LICON,    TBSTATE_ENABLED | TBSTATE_CHECKED,
                                                  TBSTYLE_CHECKGROUP, 0,   0},
   {VIEW_SMALLICONS,  IDC_SICON,    TBSTATE_ENABLED,
                                                  TBSTYLE_CHECKGROUP, 0,   0},
   {VIEW_LIST,        IDC_LIST,     0,            TBSTYLE_CHECKGROUP, 0,   0},
   {VIEW_DETAILS,     IDC_RPT,      TBSTATE_ENABLED,
                                                  TBSTYLE_CHECKGROUP, 0,   0},
   {0,                0,            TBSTATE_ENABLED,
                                                  TBSTYLE_SEP,        0,   0},
   {VIEW_SORTNAME,    IDC_SNAME,    TBSTATE_ENABLED | TBSTATE_CHECKED,
                                                  TBSTYLE_CHECKGROUP, 0,   0},
   {VIEW_SORTTYPE,    IDC_STYPE,    TBSTATE_ENABLED,
                                                  TBSTYLE_CHECKGROUP, 0,   0},
   {VIEW_SORTSIZE,    IDC_SSIZE,    TBSTATE_ENABLED,
                                                  TBSTYLE_CHECKGROUP, 0,   0},
   {VIEW_SORTDATE,    IDC_SDATE,    TBSTATE_ENABLED,
                                                  TBSTYLE_CHECKGROUP, 0,   0},
   {0,                0,            0,            TBSTYLE_SEP,        0,   0},
};
```

```
// Tooltip string list for view bar
const TCHAR *pViewTips[] = {TEXT (""), TEXT ("Large"), TEXT ("Small"),
                            TEXT ("List"), TEXT ("Details"), TEXT (""),
                            TEXT ("Sort by Name"), TEXT ("Sort by Type"),
                            TEXT ("Sort by Size"), TEXT ("Sort by Date"),
};

// Combination standard and view bar button structure
const TBBUTTON tbCBCmboBtns[] = {
// BitmapIndex           Command       State         Style           UserData String
   {0,                   0,            0,            TBSTYLE_SEP,          0,  0},
   {STD_FILENEW,         IDC_NEW,      TBSTATE_ENABLED,
                                                     TBSTYLE_BUTTON,       0,  0},
   {STD_FILEOPEN,        IDC_OPEN,     TBSTATE_ENABLED,
                                                     TBSTYLE_BUTTON,       0,  0},
   {STD_PROPERTIES,      IDC_PROP,     TBSTATE_ENABLED,
                                                     TBSTYLE_BUTTON,       0,  0},
   {0,                   0,            0,            TBSTYLE_SEP,          0,  0},
   {STD_CUT,             IDC_CUT,      TBSTATE_ENABLED,
                                                     TBSTYLE_BUTTON,       0,  0},
   {STD_COPY,            IDC_COPY,     TBSTATE_ENABLED,
                                                     TBSTYLE_BUTTON,       0,  0},
   {STD_PASTE,           IDC_PASTE,    TBSTATE_ENABLED,
                                                     TBSTYLE_BUTTON,       0,  0},
   {0,                   0,            0,            TBSTYLE_SEP,          0,  0},
   {STD_BMPS + VIEW_LARGEICONS,
                         IDC_LICON, TBSTATE_ENABLED | TBSTATE_CHECKED,
                                                     TBSTYLE_CHECKGROUP, 0,  0},
   {STD_BMPS + VIEW_SMALLICONS,
                         IDC_SICON, TBSTATE_ENABLED,
                                                     TBSTYLE_CHECKGROUP, 0,  0},
   {STD_BMPS + VIEW_LIST,
                         IDC_LIST,  TBSTATE_ENABLED,
                                                     TBSTYLE_CHECKGROUP, 0,  0},
   {STD_BMPS + VIEW_DETAILS,
                         IDC_RPT,   TBSTATE_ENABLED,
                                                     TBSTYLE_CHECKGROUP, 0,  0},
   {0,                   0,            0,            TBSTYLE_SEP,          0,  0},
   {STD_BMPS + VIEW_BMPS,
                         IDC_DPSORT,TBSTATE_ENABLED,
                                                     TBSTYLE_DROPDOWN,   0,  0}
};

//======================================================================
// Program entry point
//
```

(continued)

Listing 5-1 *(continued)*

```
int WINAPI WinMain (HINSTANCE hInstance, HINSTANCE hPrevInstance,
                    LPWSTR lpCmdLine, int nCmdShow) {
    HWND hwndMain;
    MSG msg;
    int rc = 0;

    // Initialize application.

    hwndMain = InitInstance (hInstance, lpCmdLine, nCmdShow);
    if (hwndMain == 0) return 0x10;

    // Application message loop
    while (GetMessage (&msg, NULL, 0, 0)) {
        TranslateMessage (&msg);
        DispatchMessage (&msg);
    }
    // Instance cleanup
    return TermInstance (hInstance, msg.wParam);
}
//--------------------------------------------------------------------
// InitInstance - Instance initialization
//
HWND InitInstance (HINSTANCE hInstance, LPWSTR lpCmdLine, int nCmdShow){
    HWND hWnd;
    DWORD dwStyle = WS_VISIBLE;
    int x = CW_USEDEFAULT, y = CW_USEDEFAULT;
    int cx = CW_USEDEFAULT, cy = CW_USEDEFAULT;
    WNDCLASS wc;
    INITCOMMONCONTROLSEX icex;

#if defined(WIN32_PLATFORM_PSPC)
    // If Pocket PC, allow only one instance of the application.
    hWnd = FindWindow (szAppName, NULL);
    if (hWnd) {
        SetForegroundWindow ((HWND)(((DWORD)hWnd) | 0x01));
        return 0;
    }
#endif
    // Register application main window class.
    wc.style = 0;                              // Window style
    wc.lpfnWndProc = MainWndProc;              // Callback function
    wc.cbClsExtra = 0;                         // Extra class data
    wc.cbWndExtra = 0;                         // Extra window data
    wc.hInstance = hInstance;                  // Owner handle
    wc.hIcon = NULL,                           // Application icon
    wc.hCursor = LoadCursor (NULL, IDC_ARROW);// Default cursor
```

```
    wc.hbrBackground = (HBRUSH) GetStockObject (WHITE_BRUSH);
    wc.lpszMenuName =  NULL;                      // Menu name
    wc.lpszClassName = szAppName;                 // Window class name

    if (RegisterClass (&wc) == 0) return 0;

    // Load the command bar common control class.
    icex.dwSize = sizeof (INITCOMMONCONTROLSEX);
    icex.dwICC = ICC_BAR_CLASSES;
    InitCommonControlsEx (&icex);


#ifndef WIN32_PLATFORM_PSPC
    dwStyle |= WS_CAPTION | WS_SIZEBOX | WS_MAXIMIZEBOX | WS_MINIMIZEBOX;
    x = y = 10;
    cx = GetSystemMetrics (SM_CXSCREEN) - 30;
    cy = GetSystemMetrics (SM_CYSCREEN) - 50
#endif
    // Save program instance handle in global variable.
    hInst = hInstance;

    // Create main window.
    hWnd = CreateWindow (szAppName, TEXT ("CmdBar Demo"), dwStyle,
                         x, y, cx, cy, NULL, NULL, hInstance, NULL);
    // Return fail code if window not created.
    if (!IsWindow (hWnd)) return 0;

    // Standard show and update calls
    ShowWindow (hWnd, nCmdShow);
    UpdateWindow (hWnd);
    return hWnd;
}
//----------------------------------------------------------------------
// TermInstance - Program cleanup
//
int TermInstance (HINSTANCE hInstance, int nDefRC) {
    return nDefRC;
}
//======================================================================
// Message handling procedures for MainWindow
//----------------------------------------------------------------------
// MainWndProc - Callback function for application window
//
LRESULT CALLBACK MainWndProc (HWND hWnd, UINT wMsg, WPARAM wParam,
                              LPARAM lParam) {
    int i;
```

(continued)

Listing 5-1   *(continued)*

```
    //
    // Search message list to see if we need to handle this
    // message. If in list, call procedure.
    //
    for (i = 0; i < dim(MainMessages); i++) {
        if (wMsg == MainMessages[i].Code)
            return (*MainMessages[i].Fxn)(hWnd, wMsg, wParam, lParam);
    }
    return DefWindowProc (hWnd, wMsg, wParam, lParam);
}
//----------------------------------------------------------------------
// DoCreateMain - Process WM_CREATE message for window.
//
LRESULT DoCreateMain (HWND hWnd, UINT wMsg, WPARAM wParam,
                      LPARAM lParam) {
    HWND hwndCB;

    // Create a minimal command bar that has only a menu and an
    // exit button.
    hwndCB = CommandBar_Create (hInst, hWnd, IDC_CMDBAR);

    // Insert the menu.
    CommandBar_InsertMenubar (hwndCB, hInst, ID_MENU, 0);

    // Add exit button to command bar.
    CommandBar_AddAdornments (hwndCB, 0, 0);
    return 0;
}
//----------------------------------------------------------------------
// DoSizeMain - Process WM_SIZE message for window.
//
LRESULT DoSizeMain (HWND hWnd, UINT wMsg, WPARAM wParam,
                    LPARAM lParam) {
#ifndef WIN32_PLATFORM_PSPC
    HWND hwndCB = GetDlgItem (hWnd, IDC_CMDBAR);
    // Tell the command bar to resize itself and reposition Close button.
    SendMessage(hwndCB, TB_AUTOSIZE, 0L, 0L);
    CommandBar_AlignAdornments(hwndCB);
#endif //WIN32_PLATFORM_PSPC
    return 0;
}
//----------------------------------------------------------------------
// DoCommandMain - Process WM_COMMAND message for window.
//
LRESULT DoCommandMain (HWND hWnd, UINT wMsg, WPARAM wParam,
                       LPARAM lParam) {
```

```
      WORD idItem, wNotifyCode;
      HWND hwndCtl;
      INT  i;

      // Parse the parameters.
      idItem = (WORD) LOWORD (wParam);
      wNotifyCode = (WORD) HIWORD (wParam);
      hwndCtl = (HWND) lParam;

      // Call routine to handle control message.
      for (i = 0; i < dim(MainCommandItems); i++) {
          if (idItem == MainCommandItems[i].Code)
              return (*MainCommandItems[i].Fxn)(hWnd, idItem, hwndCtl,
                                                wNotifyCode);
      }
      return 0;
}
//----------------------------------------------------------------------
// DoNotifyMain - Process WM_NOTIFY message for window.
//
LRESULT DoNotifyMain (HWND hWnd, UINT wMsg, WPARAM wParam,
                      LPARAM lParam) {
      LPNMHDR pNotifyHeader;
      LPNMTOOLBAR pNotifyToolBar;
      RECT rect;
      TPMPARAMS tpm;
      HMENU hMenu;

      // Get pointer to notify message header.
      pNotifyHeader = (LPNMHDR)lParam;

      if (pNotifyHeader->code == TBN_DROPDOWN) {

          // Get pointer to toolbar notify structure.
          pNotifyToolBar = (LPNMTOOLBAR)lParam;

          if (pNotifyToolBar->iItem == IDC_DPSORT) {

              // Get the rectangle of the drop-down button.
              SendMessage (pNotifyHeader->hwndFrom, TB_GETRECT,
                           pNotifyToolBar->iItem, (LPARAM)&rect);

              // Convert rect to screen coordinates.  The rect is
              // considered here to be an array of 2 POINT structures.
              MapWindowPoints (pNotifyHeader->hwndFrom, HWND_DESKTOP,
                               (LPPOINT)&rect, 2);
```

(continued)

Listing 5-1   *(continued)*

```
            // Prevent the menu from covering the button.
            tpm.cbSize = sizeof (tpm);
            CopyRect (&tpm.rcExclude, &rect);

            hMenu = GetSubMenu (LoadMenu (hInst, TEXT ("popmenu")),0);
            TrackPopupMenuEx (hMenu, TPM_LEFTALIGN | TPM_VERTICAL,
                              rect.left, rect.bottom, hWnd, &tpm);
        }
    }
    return 0;
}
//-----------------------------------------------------------------------
// DoDestroyMain - Process WM_DESTROY message for window.
//
LRESULT DoDestroyMain (HWND hWnd, UINT wMsg, WPARAM wParam,
                       LPARAM lParam) {
    PostQuitMessage (0);
    return 0;
}
//=======================================================================
// Command handler routines
//-----------------------------------------------------------------------
// DoMainCommandExit - Process Program Exit command.
//
LPARAM DoMainCommandExit (HWND hWnd, WORD idItem, HWND hwndCtl,
                          WORD wNotifyCode) {

    SendMessage (hWnd, WM_CLOSE, 0, 0);
    return 0;
}
//-----------------------------------------------------------------------
// DoMainCommandViewStd - Displays a standard edit-centric command bar
//
LPARAM DoMainCommandVStd (HWND hWnd, WORD idItem, HWND hwndCtl,
                          WORD wNotifyCode) {
    HWND hwndCB;

    // If a command bar exists, kill it.
    if (hwndCB = GetDlgItem (hWnd, IDC_CMDBAR))
        CommandBar_Destroy (hwndCB);

    // Create a command bar.
    hwndCB = CommandBar_Create (hInst, hWnd, IDC_CMDBAR);
    // Insert a menu.
    CommandBar_InsertMenubar (hwndCB, hInst, ID_MENU, 0);
```

```
    // Insert buttons.
    CommandBar_AddBitmap (hwndCB, HINST_COMMCTRL, IDB_STD_SMALL_COLOR,
                          STD_BMPS, 0, 0);

    CommandBar_AddButtons (hwndCB, dim(tbCBStdBtns), tbCBStdBtns);

    // Add exit button to command bar.
    CommandBar_AddAdornments (hwndCB, 0, 0);
    return 0;
}
//-------------------------------------------------------------------------
// DoMainCommandVVView - Displays a standard edit-centric command bar
//
LPARAM DoMainCommandVVView (HWND hWnd, WORD idItem, HWND hwndCtl,
                            WORD wNotifyCode) {
    INT i;
    HWND hwndCB;
    TCHAR szTmp[64];
    HBITMAP hBmp, hMask;
    HIMAGELIST hilDisabled, hilEnabled;

    // If a command bar exists, kill it.
    if (hwndCB = GetDlgItem (hWnd, IDC_CMDBAR))
        CommandBar_Destroy (hwndCB);
    // Create a command bar.
    hwndCB = CommandBar_Create (hInst, hWnd, IDC_CMDBAR);

    // Insert a menu.
    CommandBar_InsertMenubar (hwndCB, hInst, ID_MENU, 0);

    // Insert buttons, first add a bitmap and then the buttons.
    CommandBar_AddBitmap (hwndCB, HINST_COMMCTRL, IDB_VIEW_SMALL_COLOR,
                          VIEW_BMPS, 0, 0);

    // Load bitmaps for disabled image.
    hBmp = LoadBitmap (hInst, TEXT ("DisCross"));
    hMask = LoadBitmap (hInst, TEXT ("DisMask"));

    // Get the current image list and copy.
    hilEnabled = (HIMAGELIST)SendMessage (hwndCB, TB_GETIMAGELIST, 0, 0);
    hilDisabled = ImageList_Duplicate (hilEnabled);
    // Replace a button image with the disabled image.
    ImageList_Replace (hilDisabled, VIEW_LIST, hBmp, hMask);

    // Set disabled image list.
    SendMessage (hwndCB,  TB_SETDISABLEDIMAGELIST, 0,
                 (LPARAM)hilDisabled);
```

(continued)

Listing 5-1   *(continued)*

```
    // Add buttons to the command bar.
    CommandBar_AddButtons (hwndCB, dim(tbCBViewBtns), tbCBViewBtns);

    // Add tooltips to the command bar.
    CommandBar_AddToolTips (hwndCB, dim(pViewTips), pViewTips);

    // Add a combo box between the view icons and the sort icons.
    CommandBar_InsertComboBox (hwndCB, hInst, 75,
                            CBS_DROPDOWNLIST | WS_VSCROLL,
                            IDC_COMBO, 6);
    // Fill in combo box.
    for (i = 0; i < 10; i++) {
        wsprintf (szTmp, TEXT ("Item %d"), i);
        SendDlgItemMessage (hwndCB, IDC_COMBO, CB_INSERTSTRING, -1,
                        (LPARAM)szTmp);
    }
    SendDlgItemMessage (hwndCB, IDC_COMBO, CB_SETCURSEL, 0, 0);

    // Add exit button to command bar.
    CommandBar_AddAdornments (hwndCB, 0, 0);
    return 0;
}
//----------------------------------------------------------------------
// DoMainCommandVCombo - Displays a combination of file and edit buttons
//
LPARAM DoMainCommandVCombo (HWND hWnd, WORD idItem, HWND hwndCtl,
                            WORD wNotifyCode) {
    HWND hwndCB;

    // If a command bar exists, kill it.
    if (hwndCB = GetDlgItem (hWnd, IDC_CMDBAR))
        CommandBar_Destroy (hwndCB);

    // Create a command bar.
    hwndCB = CommandBar_Create (hInst, hWnd, IDC_CMDBAR);

    // Insert a menu.
    CommandBar_InsertMenubar (hwndCB, hInst, ID_MENU, 0);
    // Add two bitmap lists plus custom bmp for drop-down button.
    CommandBar_AddBitmap (hwndCB, HINST_COMMCTRL, IDB_STD_SMALL_COLOR,
                        STD_BMPS, 0, 0);
    CommandBar_AddBitmap (hwndCB, HINST_COMMCTRL, IDB_VIEW_SMALL_COLOR,
                        VIEW_BMPS, 0, 0);
    CommandBar_AddBitmap (hwndCB, NULL,
                        (int)LoadBitmap (hInst, TEXT ("SortDropBtn")),
                        1, 0, 0);
```

```
        CommandBar_AddButtons (hwndCB, dim(tbCBCmboBtns), tbCBCmboBtns);

        // Add exit button to command bar.
        CommandBar_AddAdornments (hwndCB, 0, 0);
        return 0;
}
//-------------------------------------------------------------------------
// DoMainCommandAbout - Process the Help | About menu command.
//
LPARAM DoMainCommandAbout(HWND hWnd, WORD idItem, HWND hwndCtl,
                          WORD wNotifyCode) {

        // Use DialogBox to create modal dialog box.
        DialogBox (hInst, TEXT ("aboutbox"), hWnd, AboutDlgProc);
        return 0;
}
//=========================================================================
// About Dialog procedure
//
BOOL CALLBACK AboutDlgProc (HWND hWnd, UINT wMsg, WPARAM wParam,
                           LPARAM lParam) {

    switch (wMsg) {
        case WM_COMMAND:
            switch (LOWORD (wParam)) {
                case IDOK:
                case IDCANCEL:
                    EndDialog (hWnd, 0);
                    return TRUE;
            }
        break;
    }
    return FALSE;
}
```

Each of the three command bars created in CmdBar demonstrates different capabilities of the command bar control. The first command bar, created in the routine *DoMainCommandVStd*, creates a vanilla command bar with a menu and a set of buttons. The button structure for this command bar is defined in the array *tbCBStdBtns*, which is defined near the top of CmdBar.cpp.

The second command bar, created in the routine *DoMainCommand-VView*, contains two groups of checkgroup buttons separated by a combo box. This command bar also demonstrates the use of a separate image for a disabled button. The list view button, the third button on the bar, is disabled. The image for that button in the image list for disabled buttons is replaced with a bitmap that looks like an X.

The *DoMainCommandVCombo* routine creates the third command bar. It uses both the standard and view bitmap images as well as a custom bitmap for a drop-down button. This command bar demonstrates the technique of referencing the images in an image list that contains multiple bitmaps. The drop-down button is serviced by the *DoNotifyMain* routine, where a pop-up menu is loaded and displayed when a *TBN_DROPDOWN* notification is received.

Finally, when CmdBar is compiled for an embedded version of Windows CE, it looks a bit different because of the style flags in *CreateWindow*. The main window has a caption bar and doesn't fill the entire screen. You can size the window by dragging the edge of the window and move the window by dragging the caption bar. This program shows off the ability of a command bar to resize itself with a little help from some code in the *WM_SIZE* message handler.

Command Bands

A command bands control is a rebar control that, by default, contains a command bar in each band of the control. The rebar control is a container of controls that the user can drag around the application window. Given that command bands are nothing more than command bars in a rebar control, knowing how to program a command bar is most of the battle when learning how to program the command bands control.

Each individual band of the command bands control can have a "gripper" that can be used to drag the band to a new position. A band can be in a minimized state, showing only its gripper and, if you want, an icon; in a maximized state, covering up the other bands on the line; or restored, sharing space with the other bands on the same line. You can even move bands to a new row, creating a multiple-row command band. Figure 5-4 shows a window with a command bands control in two rows across the top of the window.

Figure 5-4   A window with a command bands control

The standard use of a command bands control is to break up the elements of a command bar—menu, buttons, and other controls—into separate bands. This allows users to rearrange these elements as they see fit. Users can also expose or overlap separate bands as needed in order to provide a larger total area for menus, buttons, and other controls.

Creating a Command Bands Control

Creating a command bands control is straightforward, if a bit more complicated than creating a command bar control. You create the control by calling

```
HWND CommandBands_Create (HINSTANCE hInst, HWND hWndParent, UINT wID,
                          DWORD dwStyles, HIMAGELIST himl);
```

The *dwStyles* parameter accepts a number of flags that define the look and operation of the command bands control. These styles match the rebar styles; the command bands control is, after all, closely related to the rebar control.

- ■ **RBS_AUTOSIZE**   Bands are automatically reformatted if the size or position of the control is changed.

- ■ **RBS_BANDBORDERS**   Each band is drawn with lines to separate adjacent bands.

Image Lists for Command Bands Controls

I touched on image lists earlier. Command bars and toolbars use image lists internally to manage the images used on buttons. Image lists can be managed in a standalone image list control. This control is basically a helper control that assists applications in managing a series of like-size images. The image list control in Windows CE is identical to the image list control under Windows 2000 and Windows Me, with the exception that the Windows CE version can't contain cursors for systems built without mouse/cursor support. For the purposes of the command bands control, the image list just needs to be created and a set of bitmaps added that will represent the individual bands when they're minimized. An example of the minimal code required for this is shown here:

```
himl = ImageList_Create (16, 16, ILC_COLOR, 2, 0);
hBmp = LoadBitmap (hInst, TEXT ("CmdBarBmps"));
ImageList_Add (himl, hBmp, NULL);
DeleteObject (hBmp);
```

The *ImageList_Create* function takes the dimensions of the images to be loaded, the format of the images (*ILC_COLOR* is the default), the number of images initially in the list, and the number to be added. The two images are then added by loading a double-wide bitmap that contains two images and calling *ImageList_Add*. After the bitmap has been loaded into the image list, it should be deleted.

- **RBS_FIXEDORDER**   Bands can be moved but always remain in the same order.

- **RBS_SMARTLABELS**   When minimized, a band is displayed with its icon. When the band is restored or maximized, its label text is displayed.

- **RBS_VARHEIGHT**   Each row in the control is vertically sized to the minimum required by the bands on that row. Without this flag, the height of every row is defined by the height of the tallest band in the control.

- **CCS_VERT**   Creates a vertical command bands control.

- **RBS_VERTICALGRIPPER**   Displays a gripper appropriate for a vertical command bar. This flag is ignored unless *CCS_VERT* is set.

Of these styles, *RBS_SMARTLABELS* and *RBS_VARHEIGHT* are the two most frequently used flags. The *RBS_SMARTLABELS* flag lets you choose an attractive appearance for the command bands control without requiring any effort from the application. The *RBS_VARHEIGHT* flag is important if you use controls in a band other than the default command bar. The *CCS_VERT* style creates a vertical command bands control, but because Windows CE doesn't support vertical menus, any band with a menu won't be displayed correctly in a vertical band. As you'll see, however, you can hide a particular band when the control is oriented vertically.

Adding Bands

You can add bands to your application by passing an array of *REBARBAND-INFO* structures that describe each band to the control. The function is

```
BOOL CommandBands_AddBands (HWND hwndCmdBands, HINSTANCE hinst,
                            UINT cBands, LPREBARBANDINFO prbbi);
```

Before you call this function, you must fill out a *REBARBANDINFO* structure for each of the bands to be added to the control. The structure is defined as

```
typedef struct tagREBARBANDINFO{
    UINT cbSize;
    UINT fMask;
    UINT fStyle;
    COLORREF clrFore;
    COLORREF clrBack;
    LPSTR lpText;
    UINT cch;
    int iImage;
```

```
    HWND hwndChild;
    UINT cxMinChild;
    UINT cyMinChild;
    UINT cyMinChild;
    UINT cx:
    HBITMAP hbmBack;
    UINT wID;
    UINT cyChild;
    UINT cyMaxChild;
    UINT cyIntegral;
    UINT cxIdeal;
    LPARAM lParam;
} REBARBANDINFO;
```

Fortunately, although this structure looks imposing, many of the fields can be ignored because there are default actions for uninitialized fields. As usual with a Windows structure, the *cbSize* field must be filled with the size of the structure as a fail-safe measure when the structure is passed to Windows. The *fMask* field is filled with a number of flags that indicate which of the remaining fields in the structure are filled with valid information. I'll describe the flags as I cover each of the fields.

The *fStyle* field must be filled with the style flags for the band if the *RBBIM_STYLE* flag is set in the *fMask* field. The allowable flags are the following:

■ ***RBBS_BREAK***   The band will start on a new line.

■ ***RBBS_FIXEDSIZE***   The band can't be sized. When this flag is specified, the gripper for the band isn't displayed.

■ ***RBBS_HIDDEN***   The band won't be visible when the command band is created.

■ ***RBBS_GRIPPERALWAYS***   The band will have a sizing grip, even if it's the only band in the command band.

■ ***RBBS_NOGRIPPER***   The band won't have a sizing grip. The band therefore can't be moved by the user.

■ ***RBBS_NOVERT***   The band won't be displayed if the command bands control is displayed vertically due to the *CCS_VERT* style.

■ ***RBBS_CHILDEDGE***   The band will be drawn with an edge at the top and bottom of the band.

■ ***RBBS_FIXEDBMP***   The background bitmap of the band doesn't move when the band is resized.

For the most part, these flags are self-explanatory. Although command bands are usually displayed across the top of a window, they can be created as vertical bands and displayed down the left side of a window. In that case, the *RBBS_NOVERT* style allows the programmer to specify which bands won't be displayed when the command band is in a vertical orientation. Bands containing menus or wide controls are candidates for this flag because they won't be displayed correctly on vertical bands.

You can fill the *clrFore* and *clrBack* fields with a color that the command band will use for the foreground and background colors when your application draws the band. These fields are used only if the *RBBIM_COLORS* flag is set in the mask field. These fields, along with the *hbmBack* field, which specifies a background bitmap for the band, are useful only if the band contains a transparent command bar. Otherwise, the command bar covers most of the area of the band, obscuring any background bitmap or special colors. I'll explain how to make a command bar transparent in the section "Configuring Individual Bands."

The *lpText* field specifies the optional text that labels the individual band. This text is displayed at the left end of the bar immediately to the right of the gripper. The *iImage* field is used to specify a bitmap that will also be displayed on the left end of the bar. The *iImage* field is filled with an index to the list of images contained in the image list control. The text and bitmap fields take added significance when paired with the *RBS_SMARTLABELS* style of the command band control. When that style is specified, the text is displayed when the band is restored or maximized and the bitmap is displayed when the band is minimized. This technique is used by the H/PC Explorer on its command band control.

The *wID* field should be set to an ID value that you use to identify the band. The band ID is important if you plan on configuring the bands after they have been created or if you think you'll be querying their state. Even if you don't plan to use band IDs in your program, it's important that each band ID be unique because the control itself uses the IDs to manage the bands. This field is checked only if the *RBBIM_ID* flag is set in the *fMask* field.

The *hwndChild* field is used if the default command bar control in a band is replaced by another control. To replace the command bar control, the new control must first be created and the window handle of the control then placed in the *hwndChild* field. The *hwndChild* field is checked only if the *RBBIM_CHILD* flag is set in the *fMask* field.

The *cxMinChild* and *cyMinChild* fields define the minimum dimensions to which a band can shrink. When you're using a control other than the default command bar, these fields are useful for defining the height and minimum width (the width when minimized) of the band. These two fields are checked only if the *RBBIM_CHILDSIZE* flag is set.

The *cxIdeal* field is used when a band is maximized by the user. If this field isn't initialized, a maximized command band stretches across the entire width of the control. By setting *cxIdeal*, the application can limit the maximized width of a band, which is handy if the controls on the band take up only part of the total width of the control. This field is checked only if the *RBBIM_IDEALSIZE* flag is set in the *fMask* field.

The *lParam* field gives you a space to store an application-defined value with the band information. This field is checked only if the *RBBIM_LPARAM* flag is set in the *fMask* field. The other fields in *REBARBANDINFO* apply to the more flexible rebar control, not the command band control. The code below creates a command bands control, initializes an array of three *REBARBAND-INFO* structures, and adds the bands to the control.

```
// Create a command bands control.
hwndCB = CommandBands_Create (hInst, hWnd, IDC_CMDBAND, RBS_SMARTLABELS |
                              RBS_VARHEIGHT, himl);

// Initialize common REBARBANDINFO structure fields.
for (i = 0; i < dim(rbi); i++) {
    rbi[i].cbSize = sizeof (REBARBANDINFO);
    rbi[i].fMask = RBBIM_ID | RBBIM_IMAGE | RBBIM_SIZE | RBBIM_STYLE;
    rbi[i].fStyle = RBBS_FIXEDBMP;
    rbi[i].wID = IDB_CMDBAND+i;
}
// Initialize REBARBANDINFO structure for each band.
// 1. Menu band.
rbi[0].fStyle |= RBBS_NOGRIPPER;
rbi[0].cx = 130;
rbi[0].iImage = 0;

// 2. Standard button band.
rbi[1].fMask |= RBBIM_TEXT;
rbi[1].cx = 200;
rbi[1].iImage = 1;
rbi[1].lpText = TEXT ("Std Btns");

// 3. Edit control band.
hwndChild = CreateWindow (TEXT ("edit"), TEXT ("edit ctl"),
                          WS_VISIBLE | WS_CHILD | WS_BORDER,
                          0, 0, 10, 5, hWnd, (HMENU)IDC_EDITCTL,
                          hInst, NULL);

rbi[2].fMask |= RBBIM_TEXT | RBBIM_STYLE | RBBIM_CHILDSIZE | RBBIM_CHILD;
rbi[2].fStyle |= RBBS_CHILDEDGE;
rbi[2].hwndChild = hwndChild;
rbi[2].cxMinChild = 0;
```

(continued)

```
rbi[2].cyMinChild = 25;
rbi[2].cyChild = 55;
rbi[2].cx = 130;
rbi[2].iImage = 2;
rbi[2].lpText = TEXT ("Edit field");

// Add bands.
CommandBands_AddBands (hwndCB, hInst, 3, rbi);
```

The command bands control created in the preceding code has three bands, one containing a menu, one containing a set of buttons, and one containing an edit control instead of a command bar. The control is created with the *RBS_SMARTLABELS* and *RBS_VARHEIGHT* styles. The smart labels display an icon when the bar is minimized and a text label when the band isn't minimized. The *RBS_VARHEIGHT* style allows each line on the control to have a different height.

The common fields of the *REBARBANDINFO* structures are then initialized in a loop. Then the remaining fields of the structures are customized for each band on the control. The third band, containing the edit control, is the most complex to initialize. This band needs more initialization since the edit control needs to be properly sized to match the standard height of the command bar controls in the other bands.

The *iImage* field for each band is initialized using an index into an image list that was created and passed to the *CommandBands_Create* function. The text fields for the second and third bands are filled with labels for those bands. The first band, which contains a menu, doesn't contain a text label because there's no need to label the menu. You also use the *RBBS_NOGRIPPER* style for the first band so that it can't be moved around the control. This fixes the menu band at its proper place in the control.

Now that we've created the bands, it's time to see how to initialize them.

Configuring Individual Bands

At this point in the process, the command bands control has been created and the individual bands have been added to the control. We have one more task, which is to configure the individual command bar controls in each band. (Actually, there's little more to configuring the command bar controls than what I've already described for command bars.)

The handle to a command bar contained in a band is retrieved using

```
HWND CommandBands_GetCommandBar (HWND hwndCmdBands, UINT uBand);
```

The *uBand* parameter is the zero-based band index for the band containing the command bar. If you call this function when the command bands control is being initialized, the index value correlates directly with the order in which the bands were added to the control. However, once the user has a chance to drag the bands into a new order, your application must obtain this index indirectly by sending an *RB_IDTOINDEX* message to the command bands control, as in

```
nIndex = SendMessage (hwndCmdBands, RB_IDTOINDEX, ID_BAND, 0);
```

This message is critical for managing the bands because many of the functions and messages for the control require the band index as the method to identify the band. The problem is that the index values are fluid. As the user moves the bands around, these index values change. You can't even count on the index values being consecutive. So as a rule, never blindly use the index value without first querying the proper value by translating an ID value to an index value with *RB_IDTOINDEX*.

Once you have the window handle to the command bar, simply add the menu or buttons to the bar using the standard command bar control functions and messages. Most of the time, you'll specify only a menu in the first bar, only buttons in the second bar, and other controls in the third and subsequent bars.

The following code completes the creation process shown in the earlier code fragments. This code initializes the command bar controls in the first two bands. Since the third band has an edit control, you don't need to initialize that band. The final act necessary to complete the command band control initialization is to add the close box to the control using a call to *CommandBands_AddAdornments*.

```
// Add menu to first band.
hwndBand = CommandBands_GetCommandBar (hwndCB, 0);
CommandBar_InsertMenubar (hwndBand, hInst, ID_MENU, 0);

// Add standard buttons to second band.
hwndBand = CommandBands_GetCommandBar (hwndCB, 1);
CommandBar_AddBitmap (hwndBand, HINST_COMMCTRL, IDB_STD_SMALL_COLOR,
                      15, 0, 0);
CommandBar_AddButtons (hwndBand, dim(tbCBStdBtns), tbCBStdBtns);

// Add exit button to command band.
CommandBands_AddAdornments (hwndCB, hInst, 0, NULL);
```

Saving the Band Layout

The configurability of the command bands control presents a problem to the programmer. Users who rearrange the bands expect their customized layout to be restored the next time the application is started. This task is supposed to be made easy using the following function.

```
BOOL CommandBands_GetRestoreInformation (HWND hwndCmdBands,
                UINT uBand, LPCOMMANDBANDSRESTOREINFO pcbr);
```

This function saves the positioning information from an individual band into a *COMMANDBANDSRESTOREINFO* structure. The function takes the handle of the command bands control and an index value for the band to be queried. The following code fragment shows how to query the information from each of the bands in a command band control.

```
// Get the handle of the command bands control.
hwndCB = GetDlgItem (hWnd, IDC_CMDBAND);

 // Get information for each band.
for (i = 0; i < NUMBANDS; i++) {
    // Get band index from ID value.
    nBand = SendMessage (hwndCB, RB_IDTOINDEX, IDB_CMDBAND+i, 0);

    // Initialize the size field, and get the restore information.
    cbr[i].cbSize = sizeof (COMMANDBANDSRESTOREINFO);
    CommandBands_GetRestoreInformation (hwndCB, nBand, &cbr[i]);
}
```

The preceding code uses the *RB_IDTOINDEX* message to convert known band IDs to the unknown band indexes required by *CommandBands_ GetRestoreInformation*. The data from the structure would normally be stored in the system registry. I'll talk about how to read and write registry data in Chapter 8, "Files and the Registry."

The restore information should be read from the registry when the application is restarted, and used when creating the command bands control.

```
// Restore configuration to a command band.
COMMANDBANDSRESTOREINFO cbr[NUMBANDS];
REBARBANDINFO rbi;

// Initialize size field.
rbi.cbSize = sizeof (REBARBANDINFO);

// Set only style and size fields.
rbi.fMask = RBBIM_STYLE | RBBIM_SIZE;

// Set the size and style for all bands.
for (i = 0; i < NUMBANDS; i++) {
    rbi.cx = cbr[i].cxRestored;
    rbi.fStyle = cbr[i].fStyle;

    nBand = SendMessage (hwndCB, RB_IDTOINDEX, cbr[i].wID, 0);
    SendMessage (hwndCB, RB_SETBANDINFO, nBand, (LPARAM)&rbi);
}

// Only after the size is set for all bands can the bands
// needing maximizing be maximized.
for (i = 0; i < NUMBANDS; i++) {
```

```
        if (cbr[i].fMaximized) {
            nBand = SendMessage (hwndCB, RB_IDTOINDEX, cbr[i].wID, 0);
            SendMessage (hwndCB, RB_MAXIMIZEBAND, nBand, TRUE);
        }
    }
```

This code assumes that the command bands control has already been created in its default configuration. In a real-world application, the restore information for the size and style could be used when first creating the control. In that case, all that would remain would be to maximize the bands depending on the state of the *fMaximized* field in the *COMMANDBANDSRESTOREINFO* structure. This last step must take place only after all bands have been created and properly resized.

One limitation of this system of saving and restoring the band layout is that you have no method for determining the order of the bands in the control. The band index isn't likely to provide reliable clues because after the user has rearranged the bands a few times, the indexes are neither consecutive nor in any defined order. The only way around this problem is to constrain the arrangement of the bands so that the user can't reorder the bands. You do this by setting the *RBS_FIXEDORDER* style. This solves your problem but doesn't help users if they want a different order. In the example program at the end of this section, I use the band index value to guess at the order. But this method isn't guaranteed to work.

Handling Command Band Messages

The command bands control needs a bit more maintenance than a command bar. The difference is that the control can change height, and thus the window containing the command bands control must monitor the control and redraw and perhaps reformat its client area when the control is resized.

The command bands control sends a number of different *WM_NOTIFY* messages when the user rearranges the control. To monitor the height of the control, your application needs to check for an *RBN_HEIGHTCHANGE* notification and react accordingly. The code below does just that:

```
// This code is inside a WM_NOTIFY message handler.
LPNMHDR pnmh;

pnmh = (LPNMHDR)lParam;
if (pnmh->code == RBN_HEIGHTCHANGE) {
    InvalidateRect (hWnd, NULL, TRUE);
}
```

If an *RBN_HEIGHTCHANGE* notification is detected, the routine simply invalidates the client area of the window forcing a *WM_PAINT* message. The code in the paint message then calls

```
UINT CommandBands_Height (HWND hwndCmdBands);
```

to query the height of the command bands control and subtracts this height from the client area rectangle.

As with the command bar, the command bands control can be hidden and shown with a helper function:

```
BOOL CommandBands_Show (HWND hwndCmdBands, BOOL fShow);
```

The visibility state of the control can be queried using

```
BOOL CommandBands_IsVisible (HWND hwndCmdBands);
```

The CmdBand Example

The CmdBand program demonstrates a fairly complete command bands control. The example creates three bands: a fixed menu band, a band containing a number of buttons, and a band containing an edit control. Transparent command bars and a background bitmap in each band are used to create a command bands control with a background image.

You can use the View menu to replace the command bands control with a simple command bar by choosing Command Bar from the View menu. You can then re-create and restore the command bands control to its last configuration by choosing Command Bands from the View menu. The code for the Cmd-Band program is shown in Listing 5-2.

```
CmdBand.rc
//======================================================================
// Resource file
//
// Written for the book Programming Windows CE
// Copyright (C) 2003 Douglas Boling
//======================================================================
#include "windows.h"
#include "CmdBand.h"                       // Program-specific stuff


//----------------------------------------------------------------------
// Icons and bitmaps
//
ID_ICON         ICON    "cmdband.ico"     // Program icon
CmdBarBmps      BITMAP  "cbarbmps.bmp"    // Bmp used in cmdband image list
CmdBarEditBmp   BITMAP  "cbarbmp2.bmp"    // Bmp used in cmdband image list
CmdBarBack      BITMAP  "backg2.bmp"      // Bmp used for cmdband background


//----------------------------------------------------------------------
// Menu
//
```

Listing 5-2   The CmdBand program

```
ID_MENU MENU DISCARDABLE
BEGIN
    POPUP "&File"
    BEGIN
        MENUITEM "E&xit",                          IDM_EXIT
    END
    POPUP "&View"
    BEGIN
        MENUITEM "Command Bar",                    IDM_VIEWCMDBAR
        MENUITEM "Command Band",                   IDM_VIEWCMDBAND
    END
    POPUP "&Help"

    BEGIN
        MENUITEM "&About...",                      IDM_ABOUT
    END
END
//-----------------------------------------------------------------------
// About box dialog template
//
aboutbox DIALOG discardable 10, 10, 160, 40
STYLE  WS_POPUP | WS_VISIBLE | WS_CAPTION | WS_SYSMENU | DS_CENTER |
       DS_MODALFRAME
CAPTION "About"
BEGIN
    ICON  ID_ICON,                      -1,   5,   5,  10,  10
    LTEXT "CmdBand - Written for the book Programming Windows \
           CE Copyright 2003 Douglas Boling"
                                        -1,  40,   5, 110,  30
END
```

CmdBand.h

```
//=======================================================================
// Header file
//
// Written for the book Programming Windows CE
// Copyright (C) 2003 Douglas Boling
//=======================================================================
// Returns number of elements
#define dim(x) (sizeof(x) / sizeof(x[0]))


//-----------------------------------------------------------------------
// Generic defines and data types
//
struct decodeUINT {                            // Structure associates
    UINT Code;                                 // messages
```

(continued)

Listing 5-2   *(continued)*

```
                                                    // with a function.
    LRESULT (*Fxn)(HWND, UINT, WPARAM, LPARAM);
};
struct decodeCMD {                                  // Structure associates
    UINT Code;                                      // menu IDs with a
    LRESULT (*Fxn)(HWND, WORD, HWND, WORD);         // function.
};
//-----------------------------------------------------------------------
// Defines used by application
//
#define   IDC_CMDBAND        1                      // Command band ID
#define   IDC_CMDBAR         2                      // Command bar ID

#define   ID_ICON            10                     // Icon ID
#define   ID_MENU            11                     // Main menu resource ID
#define   IDC_EDITCTL        12

#define   IDB_CMDBAND        50                     // Base ID for bands
#define   IDB_CMDBANDMENU    50                     // Menu band ID
#define   IDB_CMDBANDBTN     51                     // Button band ID
#define   IDB_CMDBANDEDIT    52                     // Edit control band ID

// Menu item IDs
#define   IDM_EXIT           100

#define   IDM_VIEWCMDBAR     110
#define   IDM_VIEWCMDBAND    111

#define   IDM_ABOUT          120
#define   NUMBANDS           3
//-----------------------------------------------------------------------
// Function prototypes
//
int CreateCommandBand (HWND hWnd, BOOL fFirst);
int DestroyCommandBand (HWND hWnd);

HWND InitInstance (HINSTANCE, LPWSTR, int);
int TermInstance (HINSTANCE, int);

// Window procedures
LRESULT CALLBACK MainWndProc (HWND, UINT, WPARAM, LPARAM);

// Message handlers
LRESULT DoCreateMain (HWND, UINT, WPARAM, LPARAM);
LRESULT DoPaintMain (HWND, UINT, WPARAM, LPARAM);
LRESULT DoNotifyMain (HWND, UINT, WPARAM, LPARAM);
```

```
LRESULT DoCommandMain (HWND, UINT, WPARAM, LPARAM);
LRESULT DoDestroyMain (HWND, UINT, WPARAM, LPARAM);

// Command functions
LPARAM DoMainCommandViewCmdBar (HWND, WORD, HWND, WORD);
LPARAM DoMainCommandVCmdBand (HWND, WORD, HWND, WORD);
LPARAM DoMainCommandExit (HWND, WORD, HWND, WORD);
LPARAM DoMainCommandAbout (HWND, WORD, HWND, WORD);
// Dialog procedures
BOOL CALLBACK AboutDlgProc (HWND, UINT, WPARAM, LPARAM);
```

CmdBand.cpp

```
//======================================================================
// CmdBand - Dialog box demonstration
//
// Written for the book Programming Windows CE
// Copyright (C) 2003 Douglas Boling
//======================================================================
#include <windows.h>               // For all that Windows stuff
#include <commctrl.h>              // Command bar includes
#include "CmdBand.h"               // Program-specific stuff


//----------------------------------------------------------------------
// Global data
//
const TCHAR szAppName[] = TEXT ("CmdBand");
HINSTANCE hInst;                   // Program instance handle

// Message dispatch table for MainWindowProc
const struct decodeUINT MainMessages[] = {
    WM_CREATE, DoCreateMain,
    WM_PAINT, DoPaintMain,
    WM_NOTIFY, DoNotifyMain,
    WM_COMMAND, DoCommandMain,
    WM_DESTROY, DoDestroyMain,
};
// Command message dispatch for MainWindowProc
const struct decodeCMD MainCommandItems[] = {
    IDM_VIEWCMDBAR, DoMainCommandViewCmdBar,
    IDM_VIEWCMDBAND, DoMainCommandVCmdBand,
    IDM_EXIT, DoMainCommandExit,
    IDM_ABOUT, DoMainCommandAbout,
};
// Command band button initialization structure
const TBBUTTON tbCBStdBtns[] = {
```

(continued)

Listing 5-2   *(continued)*

```
//  BitmapIndex        Command  State           Style       UserData  String
    {STD_FILENEW,      210,     TBSTATE_ENABLED, TBSTYLE_BUTTON, 0,      0},
    {STD_FILEOPEN,     211,     TBSTATE_ENABLED, TBSTYLE_BUTTON, 0,      0},
    {STD_FILESAVE,     212,     TBSTATE_ENABLED, TBSTYLE_BUTTON, 0,      0},
    {0,                0,       TBSTATE_ENABLED, TBSTYLE_SEP,    0,      0},
    {STD_CUT,          213,     TBSTATE_ENABLED, TBSTYLE_BUTTON, 0,      0},
    {STD_COPY,         214,     TBSTATE_ENABLED, TBSTYLE_BUTTON, 0,      0},
    {STD_PASTE,        215,     TBSTATE_ENABLED, TBSTYLE_BUTTON, 0,      0},
    {0,                0,       TBSTATE_ENABLED, TBSTYLE_SEP,    0,      0},
    {STD_PROPERTIES,   216,     TBSTATE_ENABLED, TBSTYLE_BUTTON, 0,      0},
};

// Command bar initialization structure
const TBBUTTON tbCBViewBtns[] = {
//  BitmapIndex     Command  State                      Style           UserData String
    {0,                  0, 0,
                                                        TBSTYLE_SEP,          0, 0},
    {VIEW_LARGEICONS, 210, TBSTATE_ENABLED | TBSTATE_CHECKED,
                                                        TBSTYLE_CHECKGROUP, 0, 0},
    {VIEW_SMALLICONS, 211, TBSTATE_ENABLED,
                                                        TBSTYLE_CHECKGROUP, 0, 0},
    {VIEW_LIST,       212, TBSTATE_ENABLED,
                                                        TBSTYLE_CHECKGROUP, 0, 0},
    {VIEW_DETAILS,    213, TBSTATE_ENABLED,
                                                        TBSTYLE_CHECKGROUP, 0, 0},
    {0,                 0, 0,                           TBSTYLE_SEP,        0, 0},
    {VIEW_SORTNAME,   214, TBSTATE_ENABLED | TBSTATE_CHECKED,
                                                        TBSTYLE_CHECKGROUP, 0, 0},
    {VIEW_SORTTYPE,   215, TBSTATE_ENABLED,
                                                        TBSTYLE_CHECKGROUP, 0, 0},
    {VIEW_SORTSIZE,   216, TBSTATE_ENABLED,
                                                        TBSTYLE_CHECKGROUP, 0, 0},
    {VIEW_SORTDATE,   217, TBSTATE_ENABLED,
                                                        TBSTYLE_CHECKGROUP, 0, 0}
};

// Array that stores the band configuration
COMMANDBANDSRESTOREINFO cbr[NUMBANDS];
INT nBandOrder[NUMBANDS];
//======================================================================
// Program entry point
//
int WINAPI WinMain (HINSTANCE hInstance, HINSTANCE hPrevInstance,
                    LPWSTR lpCmdLine, int nCmdShow) {

    HWND hwndMain;
    MSG msg;
```

```
    // Initialize application.
    hwndMain = InitInstance (hInstance, lpCmdLine, nCmdShow);
    if (hwndMain == 0)
        return 0x10;
    // Application message loop
    while (GetMessage (&msg, NULL, 0, 0)) {
        TranslateMessage (&msg);
        DispatchMessage (&msg);
    }
    // Instance cleanup
    return TermInstance (hInstance, msg.wParam);
}
//-----------------------------------------------------------------------
// InitInstance - Instance initialization
//
HWND InitInstance (HINSTANCE hInstance, LPWSTR lpCmdLine, int nCmdShow){
    HWND hWnd;
    WNDCLASS wc;
    INITCOMMONCONTROLSEX icex;

    // Save program instance handle in global variable.
    hInst = hInstance;

#if defined(WIN32_PLATFORM_PSPC)
    // If Pocket PC, allow only one instance of the application.
    hWnd = FindWindow (szAppName, NULL);
    if (hWnd) {
        SetForegroundWindow ((HWND)(((DWORD)hWnd) | 0x01));
        return 0;
    }
#endif
    // Register application main window class.
    wc.style = 0;                           // Window style
    wc.lpfnWndProc = MainWndProc;           // Callback function
    wc.cbClsExtra = 0;                      // Extra class data
    wc.cbWndExtra = 0;                      // Extra window data
    wc.hInstance = hInstance;               // Owner handle
    wc.hIcon = NULL,                        // Application icon
    wc.hCursor = LoadCursor (NULL, IDC_ARROW);// Default cursor
    wc.hbrBackground = (HBRUSH) GetStockObject (WHITE_BRUSH);
    wc.lpszMenuName =  NULL;                // Menu name
    wc.lpszClassName = szAppName;           // Window class name

    if (RegisterClass (&wc) == 0) return 0;

    // Load the command bar common control class.
    icex.dwSize = sizeof (INITCOMMONCONTROLSEX);
```

(continued)

Listing 5-2 *(continued)*

```
    icex.dwICC = ICC_COOL_CLASSES;
    InitCommonControlsEx (&icex);

    // Create main window.
    hWnd = CreateWindow (szAppName, TEXT ("CmdBand Demo"), WS_VISIBLE,
                         CW_USEDEFAULT, CW_USEDEFAULT, CW_USEDEFAULT,
                         CW_USEDEFAULT, NULL, NULL, hInstance, NULL);
    // Return fail code if window not created.
    if (!IsWindow (hWnd)) return 0;

    // Standard show and update calls
    ShowWindow (hWnd, nCmdShow);
    UpdateWindow (hWnd);
    return hWnd;
}
//-----------------------------------------------------------------------
// TermInstance - Program cleanup
//
int TermInstance (HINSTANCE hInstance, int nDefRC) {
    return nDefRC;
}
//=======================================================================
// Message handling procedures for MainWindow
//-----------------------------------------------------------------------
// MainWndProc - Callback function for application window

//
LRESULT CALLBACK MainWndProc (HWND hWnd, UINT wMsg, WPARAM wParam,
                              LPARAM lParam) {
    INT i;
    //
    // Search message list to see if we need to handle this
    // message.  If in list, call procedure.
    //
    for (i = 0; i < dim(MainMessages); i++) {
        if (wMsg == MainMessages[i].Code)
            return (*MainMessages[i].Fxn)(hWnd, wMsg, wParam, lParam);
    }

    return DefWindowProc (hWnd, wMsg, wParam, lParam);
}


//-----------------------------------------------------------------------
// DoCreateMain - Process WM_CREATE message for window.
//
LRESULT DoCreateMain (HWND hWnd, UINT wMsg, WPARAM wParam,
                      LPARAM lParam) {
```

```
        CreateCommandBand (hWnd, TRUE);
        return 0;
}
//-----------------------------------------------------------------
// DoPaintMain - Process WM_PAINT message for window.
//
LRESULT DoPaintMain (HWND hWnd, UINT wMsg, WPARAM wParam,
                     LPARAM lParam) {
    PAINTSTRUCT ps;
    HWND hwndCB;
    RECT rect;
    HDC hdc;
    POINT ptArray[2];

    // Adjust the size of the client rect to take into account
    // the command bar or command bands height.
    GetClientRect (hWnd, &rect);
    if (hwndCB = GetDlgItem (hWnd, IDC_CMDBAND))
        rect.top += CommandBands_Height (hwndCB);
    else
        rect.top += CommandBar_Height (GetDlgItem (hWnd, IDC_CMDBAR));

    hdc = BeginPaint (hWnd, &ps);
    ptArray[0].x = rect.left;
    ptArray[0].y = rect.top;
    ptArray[1].x = rect.right;
    ptArray[1].y = rect.bottom;
    Polyline (hdc, ptArray, 2);

    ptArray[0].x = rect.right;
    ptArray[1].x = rect.left;
    Polyline (hdc, ptArray, 2);

    EndPaint (hWnd, &ps);
    return 0;
}
//-----------------------------------------------------------------
// DoCommandMain - Process WM_COMMAND message for window.
//
LRESULT DoCommandMain (HWND hWnd, UINT wMsg, WPARAM wParam,
                       LPARAM lParam) {
    WORD idItem, wNotifyCode;
    HWND hwndCtl;
    INT  i;
    // Parse the parameters.
    idItem = (WORD) LOWORD (wParam);
    wNotifyCode = (WORD) HIWORD (wParam);
```

(continued)

Listing 5-2 *(continued)*

```
    hwndCtl = (HWND) lParam;

    // Call routine to handle control message.
    for (i = 0; i < dim(MainCommandItems); i++) {
        if (idItem == MainCommandItems[i].Code)
            return (*MainCommandItems[i].Fxn)(hWnd, idItem, hwndCtl,
                                              wNotifyCode);
    }
    return 0;
}
//----------------------------------------------------------------------
// DoNotifyMain - Process WM_NOTIFY message for window.
//
LRESULT DoNotifyMain (HWND hWnd, UINT wMsg, WPARAM wParam,
                      LPARAM lParam) {
    LPNMHDR pnmh;

    // Parse the parameters.
    pnmh = (LPNMHDR)lParam;

    if (pnmh->code == RBN_HEIGHTCHANGE) {
        InvalidateRect (hWnd, NULL, TRUE);

    }

    return 0;
}
//----------------------------------------------------------------------
// DoDestroyMain - Process WM_DESTROY message for window.
//
LRESULT DoDestroyMain (HWND hWnd, UINT wMsg, WPARAM wParam,
                       LPARAM lParam) {
    PostQuitMessage (0);
    return 0;

}
//======================================================================
// Command handler routines
//----------------------------------------------------------------------
// DoMainCommandExit - Process Program Exit command.
//
LPARAM DoMainCommandExit (HWND hWnd, WORD idItem, HWND hwndCtl,
                          WORD wNotifyCode) {

    SendMessage (hWnd, WM_CLOSE, 0, 0);
    return 0;
}
```

```
//------------------------------------------------------------------
// DoMainCommandVCmdBarStd - Process View | Std Command bar command.
//
LPARAM DoMainCommandViewCmdBar (HWND hWnd, WORD idItem, HWND hwndCtl,
                                 WORD wNotifyCode) {

    HWND hwndCB;

    hwndCB = GetDlgItem (hWnd, IDC_CMDBAND);
    if (hwndCB)
        DestroyCommandBand (hWnd);
    else
        return 0;

    // Create a minimal command bar that has only a menu and
    // an exit button.
    hwndCB = CommandBar_Create (hInst, hWnd, IDC_CMDBAR);

    // Insert the menu.
    CommandBar_InsertMenubar (hwndCB, hInst, ID_MENU, 0);
    // Add exit button to command bar.
    CommandBar_AddAdornments (hwndCB, 0, 0);
    InvalidateRect (hWnd, NULL, TRUE);
    return 0;
}
//------------------------------------------------------------------
// DoMainCommandVCmdBand - Process View | Command band command.
//
LPARAM DoMainCommandVCmdBand (HWND hWnd, WORD idItem, HWND hwndCtl,
                               WORD wNotifyCode) {
    HWND hwndCB;
    hwndCB = GetDlgItem (hWnd, IDC_CMDBAR);
    if (hwndCB)
        CommandBar_Destroy (hwndCB);
    else
        return 0;

    CreateCommandBand (hWnd, FALSE);
    InvalidateRect (hWnd, NULL, TRUE);
    return 0;
}
//------------------------------------------------------------------
// DoMainCommandAbout - Process the Help | About menu command.
//
LPARAM DoMainCommandAbout(HWND hWnd, WORD idItem, HWND hwndCtl,
                           WORD wNotifyCode) {
    // Use DialogBox to create modal dialog box.
    DialogBox (hInst, TEXT ("aboutbox"), hWnd, AboutDlgProc);
```

(continued)

Listing 5-2   *(continued)*

```
        return 0;
}
//=====================================================================
// About Dialog procedure
//
BOOL CALLBACK AboutDlgProc (HWND hWnd, UINT wMsg, WPARAM wParam,
                            LPARAM lParam) {
    switch (wMsg) {
        case WM_COMMAND:
            switch (LOWORD (wParam)) {
                case IDOK:
                case IDCANCEL:
                    EndDialog (hWnd, 0);
                    return TRUE;
            }
        break;
    }

    return FALSE;
}
//---------------------------------------------------------------------
// DestroyCommandBand - Destroy command band control after saving
// the current configuration.
//
int DestroyCommandBand (HWND hWnd) {
    HWND hwndCB;
    INT i, nBand, nMaxBand = 0;

    hwndCB = GetDlgItem (hWnd, IDC_CMDBAND);
    for (i = 0; i < NUMBANDS; i++) {

        // Get band index from ID value.
        nBand = SendMessage (hwndCB, RB_IDTOINDEX, IDB_CMDBAND+i, 0);

        // Save the band number to save order of bands.
        nBandOrder[i] = nBand;

        // Get the restore information.
        cbr[i].cbSize = sizeof (COMMANDBANDSRESTOREINFO);
        CommandBands_GetRestoreInformation (hwndCB, nBand, &cbr[i]);
    }
    DestroyWindow (hwndCB);
    return 0;
}
//---------------------------------------------------------------------
// CreateCommandBand - Create a formatted command band control.
//
```

```
int CreateCommandBand (HWND hWnd, BOOL fFirst) {
    HWND hwndCB, hwndBand, hwndChild;
    INT i, nBand, nBtnIndex, nEditIndex;
    LONG lStyle;
    HBITMAP hBmp;
    HIMAGELIST himl;
    REBARBANDINFO rbi[NUMBANDS];

    // Create image list control for bitmaps for minimized bands.
    himl = ImageList_Create (16, 16, ILC_COLOR, 3, 0);
    // Load first two images from one bitmap.
    hBmp = LoadBitmap (hInst, TEXT ("CmdBarBmps"));
    ImageList_Add (himl, hBmp, NULL);
    DeleteObject (hBmp);
    // Load third image as a single bitmap.
    hBmp = LoadBitmap (hInst, TEXT ("CmdBarEditBmp"));
    ImageList_Add (himl, hBmp, NULL);
    DeleteObject (hBmp);
    // Create a command band.
    hwndCB = CommandBands_Create (hInst, hWnd, IDC_CMDBAND,
                             RBS_SMARTLABELS |
                             RBS_AUTOSIZE | RBS_VARHEIGHT, himl);


    // Load bitmap used as background for command bar.
    hBmp = LoadBitmap (hInst, TEXT ("CmdBarBack"));
    // Initialize common REBARBANDINFO structure fields.
    for (i = 0; i < dim(rbi); i++) {
        rbi[i].cbSize = sizeof (REBARBANDINFO);
        rbi[i].fMask = RBBIM_ID | RBBIM_IMAGE | RBBIM_SIZE |
                     RBBIM_BACKGROUND | RBBIM_STYLE;
        rbi[i].wID = IDB_CMDBAND+i;
        rbi[i].hbmBack = hBmp;
    }

    // If first time, initialize the restore structure since it is
    // used to initialize the band size and style fields.
    if (fFirst) {
        nBtnIndex = 1;
        nEditIndex = 2;
        cbr[0].cxRestored = 130;
        cbr[1].cxRestored = 210;
        cbr[1].fStyle = RBBS_FIXEDBMP;
        cbr[2].cxRestored = 130;
        cbr[2].fStyle = RBBS_FIXEDBMP | RBBS_CHILDEDGE;
    } else {
        // If not first time, set order of bands depending on
        // the last order.
```

(continued)

Listing 5-2 *(continued)*

```
    if (nBandOrder[1] < nBandOrder[2]) {
        nBtnIndex = 1;
        nEditIndex = 2;
    } else {
        nBtnIndex = 2;
        nEditIndex = 1;
    }
}
// Initialize REBARBANDINFO structure for each band.
// 1. Menu band
rbi[0].fStyle = RBBS_FIXEDBMP | RBBS_NOGRIPPER;
rbi[0].cx = cbr[0].cxRestored;
rbi[0].iImage = 0;

// 2. Standard button band
rbi[nBtnIndex].fMask |= RBBIM_TEXT;
rbi[nBtnIndex].iImage = 1;
rbi[nBtnIndex].lpText = TEXT ("Std Btns");
// The next two parameters are initialized from saved data.
rbi[nBtnIndex].cx = cbr[1].cxRestored;
rbi[nBtnIndex].fStyle = cbr[1].fStyle;

// 3. Edit control band
hwndChild = CreateWindow (TEXT ("edit"), TEXT ("edit ctl"),
            WS_VISIBLE | WS_CHILD | ES_MULTILINE | WS_BORDER,
            0, 0, 10, 5, hWnd, (HMENU)IDC_EDITCTL, hInst, NULL);

rbi[nEditIndex].fMask |= RBBIM_TEXT | RBBIM_STYLE |
                         RBBIM_CHILDSIZE | RBBIM_CHILD;
rbi[nEditIndex].hwndChild = hwndChild;
rbi[nEditIndex].cxMinChild = 0;
rbi[nEditIndex].cyMinChild = 23;
rbi[nEditIndex].cyChild = 55;
rbi[nEditIndex].iImage = 2;
rbi[nEditIndex].lpText = TEXT ("Edit field");
// The next two parameters are initialized from saved data.
rbi[nEditIndex].cx = cbr[2].cxRestored;
rbi[nEditIndex].fStyle = cbr[2].fStyle;

// Add bands.
CommandBands_AddBands (hwndCB, hInst, 3, rbi);

// Add menu to first band.
hwndBand = CommandBands_GetCommandBar (hwndCB, 0);
CommandBar_InsertMenubar (hwndBand, hInst, ID_MENU, 0);
```

```
// Add standard buttons to second band.
hwndBand = CommandBands_GetCommandBar (hwndCB, nBtnIndex);
// Insert buttons
CommandBar_AddBitmap (hwndBand, HINST_COMMCTRL, IDB_STD_SMALL_COLOR,
                      16, 0, 0);
CommandBar_AddButtons (hwndBand, dim(tbCBStdBtns), tbCBStdBtns);

// Modify the style flags of each command bar to make transparent.
for (i = 0; i < NUMBANDS; i++) {
    hwndBand = CommandBands_GetCommandBar (hwndCB, i);
    lStyle = SendMessage (hwndBand, TB_GETSTYLE, 0, 0);
    lStyle |= TBSTYLE_TRANSPARENT;
    SendMessage (hwndBand, TB_SETSTYLE, 0, lStyle);
}

// If not the first time the command band has been created, restore
// the user's last configuration.
if (!fFirst) {
    for (i = 0; i < NUMBANDS; i++) {
        if (cbr[i].fMaximized) {
            nBand = SendMessage (hwndCB, RB_IDTOINDEX,
                                 cbr[i].wID, 0);
            SendMessage (hwndCB, RB_MAXIMIZEBAND, nBand, TRUE);
        }
    }
}
// Add exit button to command band.
CommandBands_AddAdornments (hwndCB, hInst, 0, NULL);
return 0;
}
```

CmdBand creates the command band in the *CreateCommandBand* routine. This routine is initially called in *DoCreateMain* and later in the *DoMainCommandVCmdBand* menu handler. The program creates the command bands control using the *RBS_SMARTLABELS* style along with an image list and text labels to identify each band when it's minimized and when it's restored or maximized. An image list is created and initialized with the bitmaps that are used when the bands are minimized.

The array of *REBARBANDINFO* structures is initialized to define each of the three bands. If the control has previously been destroyed, data from the *COMMANDBANDSRESTOREINFO* structure is used to initialize the style and cx fields. The *CreateCommandBand* routine also makes a guess at the order of the button and edit bands by looking at the band indexes saved when the control was last destroyed. While this method isn't completely reliable for determining the previous order of the bands, it gives you a good estimate.

When the command bands control is created, the command bars in each band are also modified to set the *TBS_TRANSPARENT* style. This process, along with a background bitmap defined for each band, demonstrates how you can use a background bitmap to make the command bands control have just the right look.

When CmdBand replaces the command bands control with a command bar, the application first calls the *DestroyCommandBand* function to save the current configuration and then destroy the command bands control. This function uses the *CommandBands_GetRestoreInformation* to query the size and style of each of the bands. The function also saves the band index for each band to supply the data for the guess on the current order of the button and edit bands. The first band, the menu band, is fixed with the *RBBS_NOGRIPPER* style, so there's no issue as to its position.

The Menu Bar

The menu bar control was introduced in the Pocket PC 2000. In look, the menu bar differs from the command bar in that it sits on the bottom of the window, not the top. To the programmer, however, the menu bar has a vastly different programming interface. Because of the popularity of the Pocket PC and the desire of OEMs to be able to create embedded systems that are software compatible with the Pocket PC, the menu bar is now distributed with the embedded versions of Windows CE starting with Windows CE .NET 4.2.

The menu bar control is a subtly complex control that does not lend itself to manual programming. The designers of the menu bar control seem to have intended that most programming and resource generation for the menu bar control would be done through code wizards and the resource editor. Although this is the way most Windows programmers code, it's still important to know how the menu bar control actually works, especially for situations in which the tools aren't quite up to the job. For this reason, I'm going to present the menu bar at the basic API level in this section. I can therefore present exactly what the control is looking for, especially in the way of resources. For later examples in the book, when I use the menu bar in examples, I'll use the code wizards to generate the menu bar menus.

Before I jump into programming the menu bar, I'd like to say a few words about how the control is designed. The menu bar control differs in a number of ways from the command bar control used on other Windows CE systems. First, the menu is not managed as a single unit on the menu bar. Instead, while the menu is specified as a single resource, it is managed by the menu bar as a series of separate submenus. Each submenu is displayed as a properly positioned pop-up menu when a particular button on the menu bar is tapped. So in this sense, the menu bar is more like a toolbar than its cousin the command bar.

A user sees little difference between a menu bar and a command bar because the menu buttons are positioned as expected—next to each other on the far left side of the bar. However, to the programmer, understanding this difference is the key to understanding how to manage and manipulate the menu bar.

Another difference is that unlike the command bar, the menu bar is not a true child of the window that creates it. The control itself is a pop-up window created by the system and placed at the bottom of the screen. The window that creates a menu bar can accidentally obscure the menu bar by covering it. Alternatively, parts of a menu bar can be drawn on top of its owner. To avoid this, the application must size its window to leave room for the menu bar on the desktop. This dance with the menu bar is the reason why applications that use the menu bar control manually resize their main windows.

Figure 5-5 shows a menu bar on a Pocket PC, while Figure 5-6 shows the same application running on an embedded system. Subtle differences exist between the look of the two menu bars that should be discussed.

Figure 5-5   A menu bar on a Pocket PC device

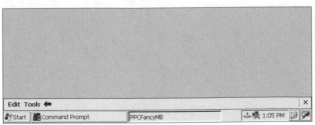

Figure 5-6   A menu bar on an embedded system

The menu bar on the Pocket PC contains the soft input panel (SIP) button on the far left of the control. On the embedded device, the SIP button is on the taskbar, not on the menu bar. In place of the SIP button, the menu bar on the embedded device has a Close button, in contrast with the Pocket PC, which has a smart Minimize button on the Navigation bar across the top of the screen. Finally, even though the very same application, with the same menu bar resource, was used to create both menu bars, the Pocket PC version has a menu named New on the far left of the bar. The New menu is an extension of the shell, which this embedded device doesn't support. Because of this lack of support in the shell, the menu bar doesn't create a New menu, even though the resource used to create the menu bar specifies one.

Another menu bar difference between the Pocket PC and embedded systems is the height of the menu bar. Since the height of the menu bar can be different on different systems, determining the height of the menu bar must be done programmatically. Older Pocket PC applications, including those in earlier versions of this book, made the then-valid assumption that the menu bar was 26 pixels high. Now that the menu bar control appears on a variety of systems, that assumption is no longer valid. One easy way to compute the height of the menu bar is to call *GetWindowRect* on the handle of the menu bar. In the following code, the height is computed just after the menu bar is created in the *WM_CREATE* message handler.

```
RECT rectMB;
GetWindowRect (hwndMenuBar, &rectMB);
nMBHeight = (rectMB.bottom - rectMB.top);
```

Creating a Menu Bar
To create a menu bar, call

```
BOOL SHCreateMenuBar (SHMENUBARINFO *pmb);
```

The only parameter is the address of an *SHMENUBARINFO* structure, which is defined as

```
typedef struct tagSHMENUBARINFO {
    DWORD cbSize;
    HWND hwndParent;
    DWORD dwFlags;
    UINT nToolBarId;
    HINSTANCE hInstRes;
    int nBmpId;
    int cBmpImages;
    HWND hwndMB;
    COLORREF clrBk;
} SHMENUBARINFO;
```

The *cbSize* field must be filled with the size of the *SHMENUBARINFO* structure. The second field, *hwndParent*, should be set to the window that is creating the menu bar. The *dwFlags* field can be set to a combination of three flags:

- **SHCMBF_EMPTYBAR**   Used to create a menu bar with no menu

- **SHCMBF_HIDDEN**   Creates a menu bar that is initially hidden

- **SHCMBF_HIDESIPBUTTON**   Creates the menu bar without a SIP button on the right-hand side of the bar

- **SHCMBF_COLORBK**   Specifies that the *clrBk* field contains a valid color to use when filling the menu bar background

- **SHCMBF_HMENU**   Specifies that the resource is a menu resource, not a menu bar resource

Unless you specify the *SHCMBF_EMPTYBAR* flag, you must set the *nTool-BarId* field to the resource that describes the menu and button structure of the menu bar. Unless the *SHCMBF_HMENU* flag is used, this resource is not a simple menu resource. It is a combination of a generic resource data block and a menu resource that together describe the menus and the positions of the buttons on the menu bar. I'll describe this resource later in this section.

The next field, *hInstRes*, should be set to the instance handle of the module that contains the menu bar resource. The next two fields, *nBmpId* and *cBmpImages*, describe the bitmap images that can be used to define the look of buttons on the menu bar. If the menu bar is to have graphical buttons, you can set the field *nBmpId* to a bitmap resource ID. This bitmap should be 16 pixels in height and each image in the bitmap should be 16 pixels wide. Thus if the bitmap has three images, it should be 48 pixels wide by 16 pixels high. The *cBmpImages* field should be set to the number of images in the bitmap. For you graphic artists out there, consult the latest application guidelines for instructions regarding the look the graphics should take to blend in with the other parts of the shell.

The *SHCreateMenuBar* function returns *TRUE* if the menu bar was successfully created. If so, the *hwndMB* field of *SHMENUBARINFO* will contain the handle of the menu bar. You need to save this window handle since there is no other way to determine the menu bar handle after it has been created.

Menu Bar Resources

As I mentioned earlier, the menu bar acts like a toolbar control in many ways. Some differences between these objects are apparent when you look at the resources that the menu bar uses. A simple menu bar might resemble the one shown in Figure 5-7.

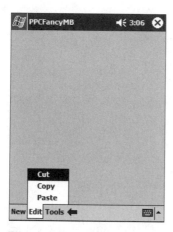

Figure 5-7 A simple menu bar with the Edit menu open

When a menu bar is created, the *nToolBarId* field of *SHMENUBARINFO* is appropriately named since the resource identified by *nToolBarID* is not a menu resource but a custom resource used by the menu bar control. To create the menu bar shown in Figure 5-7, the resource editor created the following text in the .RC file:

```
//////////////////////////////////////////////////////////////////////////
// Data
//
IDM_MENU SHMENUBAR MOVEABLE PURE
BEGIN
    IDM_MENU, 4,
    I_IMAGENONE, IDM_SHAREDNEW, TBSTATE_ENABLED, TBSTYLE_AUTOSIZE, IDS_SHNEW,
    0, NOMENU,
    I_IMAGENONE, ID_EDIT, TBSTATE_ENABLED,
    TBSTYLE_DROPDOWN | TBSTYLE_AUTOSIZE, IDS_CAP_EDIT, 0, 0,
    I_IMAGENONE, IDM_MAIN_COMMAND1, TBSTATE_ENABLED,
    TBSTYLE_DROPDOWN | TBSTYLE_AUTOSIZE, IDS_HELP, 0, 1,
    0, ID_BACKBTN, TBSTATE_ENABLED, TBSTYLE_AUTOSIZE, 0, ID_BACKBTN, 2,
END


//////////////////////////////////////////////////////////////////////////
// Menu bar
//
IDM_MENU MENU DISCARDABLE
BEGIN
    POPUP "Edit"
```

```
    BEGIN
        MENUITEM "Cut",                         ID_EDIT_CUT
        MENUITEM "Copy",                        ID_EDIT_COPY
        MENUITEM "Paste",                       ID_EDIT_PASTE
    END
    POPUP "Tools"
    BEGIN
        MENUITEM "About",                       IDM_HELP_ABOUT
        MENUITEM "Options",                     ID_TOOLS_OPTIONS
    END
END
```

Most times, you won't need to know exactly what the resource editor is placing in the resource. However, you should know the format, both to ease updating applications for using a menu bar and when writing to devices for which the resource editor doesn't create menu bar controls. The resource is essentially a description of the buttons on a toolbar. The following code offers a more formatted view of the preceding data:

```
IDM_MENU SHMENUBAR MOVEABLE PURE
BEGIN
    IDM_MENU, 4,

    I_IMAGENONE, IDM_SHAREDNEW,     TBSTATE_ENABLED,
        TBSTYLE_AUTOSIZE,                  IDS_SHNEW,    0,        NOMENU,

    I_IMAGENONE, ID_EDIT,           TBSTATE_ENABLED,
        TBSTYLE_DROPDOWN | TBSTYLE_AUTOSIZE, IDS_CAP_EDIT, 0,          0,

    I_IMAGENONE, IDM_MAIN_COMMAND1, TBSTATE_ENABLED,
        TBSTYLE_DROPDOWN | TBSTYLE_AUTOSIZE, IDS_HELP,     0,          1,

    0,              ID_BACKBTN,     TBSTATE_ENABLED,
        TBSTYLE_AUTOSIZE,                  0,        ID_BACKBTN, 2,
END
```

The first line in the resource identifies the resource ID, *IDM_MENU*, its resource type, *SHMENUBAR*, and the resource flags, *MOVEABLE* and *PURE*. The *IDM_MENU* is the ID that is passed to *SHCreateMenuBar* in the *SHMENUBAR-INFO* structure. The resource type *SHMENUBAR* is actually defined in the wizard as *RCDATA*, which the resource compiler understands as a simple block of resource data used by an application. This is important information, since *SHMENUBAR* isn't defined by the Pocket PC include files; it is included only if you use the Pocket PC AppWizard to create a menu bar resource. So, for non-wizard-generated resource files that define menu bars, you might need to add the following line to your .RC file:

```
#define  SHMENUBAR RCDATA
```

The first line of the data inside the *BEGIN / END* block is shown here:

```
IDM_MENU, 4,
```

This line defines the menu resource that will be used to create the individual pop-up menus displayed from the menu bar. The number 4 indicates the number of items in the remaining *SHMENUBAR* resource. Each item represents either a menu pop-up or a button on the menu bar.

The formatted view of the preceding resource breaks each item's resource description into two lines because of this book's format. Let's look at the last item from the resource, which describes the Back button item.

```
0,    ID_BACKBTN, TBSTATE_ENABLED, TBSTYLE_AUTOSIZE, 0,  ID_BACKBTN, 2,
```

Broken vertically to insert comments, the resource looks like this:

```
0,                      // Bitmap index
ID_BACKBTN,             // WM_COMMAND ID value
TBSTATE_ENABLED,        // Initial state of "button"
TBSTYLE_AUTOSIZE,       // Style of "button"
0,                      // String resource ID of text label
ID_BACKBTN,             // String resource ID of tooltip
2,                      // Submenu index
```

The first field contains the index into the bitmap array for this item's image on the menu bar. For items without bitmaps, set this field to *I_IMAGENONE*. In the preceding example, the image used is the first image in the bitmap. The next field contains the ID value for the item. For buttons, this is the ID value that will be sent to the parent window in a *WM_COMMAND* message when the button is tapped. For menus, you can use this ID to identify the submenu when querying the submenu handle. Because the shell uses its own set of IDs in the menu bar, applications shouldn't use values below 100. This rule applies to values for menu and button IDs as well as string resource IDs.

The menu bar uses two predefined menu item IDs: *IDM_SHAREDNEW* and *IDM_SHAREDNEWDEFAULT*. Both of these IDs will cause a New menu item to be added that displays the menu items registered by other applications. The difference between these two IDs is that *IDM_SHAREDNEWDEFAULT* displays the new menu with a simple tap of the menu item. Using *IDM_SHAREDNEW* turns the New menu into a button with an adjoining down arrow. Tapping on the New button sends a *WM_COMMAND* message to the parent indicating that a new document should be created. Tapping on the adjoining up arrow displays the new menu itself. For non–Pocket PC systems, the New menu is displayed on the menu bar only if the shell for the system provides New menu support; otherwise, the predefined new menu item IDs are ignored.

The next two fields in the resource are the initial state of the button, or root menu item, and its style. This state is described in toolbar state flags such as *TBSTATE_ENABLED* and *TBSTATE_CHECKED*. For menus, this state is almost always *TBSTATE_ENABLED*. The style field is also specified in toolbar flags with styles such as *TBSTYLE_BUTTON* for a button, or *TBSTYLE_DROPDOWN*, which is used for menu items. Items that have text instead of a bitmap—as well as items that include a bitmap—will also typically have the *TBSTYLE_AUTOSIZE* flag set to tell the menu bar to size the button to fit the text of the menu item.

The next field is set to the resource ID of a string resource used to label the item. This text is used alongside any bitmap image specified in the first field of the item. In our example, the item is a simple bitmap button, so no string resource is specified. For menu items, this is the string resource—not the sub-menu name specified in the menu resource—that will label the menu. You can use seven predefined string IDs if needed. They are defined with self-explanatory constants in the Aygshell.h file:

```
#define IDS_SHNEW          1
#define IDS_SHEDIT         2
#define IDS_SHTOOLS        3
#define IDS_SHVIEW         4
#define IDS_SHFILE         5
#define IDS_SHGO           6
#define IDS_SHFAVORITES    7
#define IDS_SHOPEN         8
```

If you need a different text label, your application must define the text as a string resource and pass that ID in this field. Following the label field is a tool tip field. You must also fill this field with the ID of a string resource.

The final field specifies the submenu that can pop up if the user taps the item. This submenu value is valid only if the style field contains *TBSTYLE_DROPDOWN*, which indicates the item has a menu attached. This value represents the index into the menu resource of the submenus. The example presented earlier in this section has two submenus: Edit, with Cut, Copy, and Paste items; and Tools, with About and Options items. The text that's displayed on the button is the string from the bar resource, not the string in the menu resource. For example, the menu resource could be modified as shown in the following code without changing the text on the menu bar.

```
//////////////////////////////////////////////////////////////////////
// Menu bar
//
IDM_MENU MENU DISCARDABLE
BEGIN
    POPUP "Cat"
```

(continued)

```
    BEGIN
        MENUITEM "Cut",                          ID_EDIT_CUT
        MENUITEM "Copy",                         ID_EDIT_COPY
        MENUITEM "Paste",                        ID_EDIT_PASTE
    END
    POPUP "Dog"
    BEGIN
        MENUITEM "About",                        IDM_HELP_ABOUT
        MENUITEM "Options",                      ID_TOOLS_OPTIONS
    END
END
```

Notice that the root menu names are now Cat and Dog, not Edit and Options. Because the menu bar takes the names from the menu bar item and not the menu resource, the change has no effect on the application.

This relatively long-winded explanation of the menu bar resource is meant as foundation material. Only on the rarest of occasions should you really have to manually tweak this resource. However, this knowledge can still be quite handy.

Working with a Menu Bar

Once you've created the menu bar, you still might need to configure it. Although the menu bar looks different from a command bar, it is built upon the same toolbar foundation. So while you can't expect a menu bar to always act like a command bar, you can use some of the command bar functions and toolbar messages. For example, one handy feature of the common controls is that they contain a series of bitmaps for commonly used toolbar buttons. Instead of creating these images yourself—and thereby possibly creating a non-standard image—you can use the system-provided images for actions such as cut, copy, and paste.

Using the Common Control Bitmaps in a Menu Bar   To use the system-provided bitmaps, simply add them to the menu bar as you would add them to a command bar. These images are added to the menu bar after the addition of any bitmap specified in the *SHMENUBARINFO* structure when the menu bar was created. So, if you had a bitmap of three images, and you added the standard set of images, the Cut bitmap image would be specified as *STD_CUT+3*. In the following code fragment, the menu bar is created and the set of standard images is added to the bar.

```
if (!SHCreateMenuBar(&mbi))
    return NULL;
CommandBar_AddBitmap (mbi.hwndMB, HINST_COMMCTRL,
                IDB_STD_SMALL_COLOR,
                STD_PRINT, 16, 16);
```

The simplest way to use these images is to specify the correct index in the button item in the menu bar resource. Remember that the first field in the menu bar item resource is the index to the bitmap image. Just set that bitmap index to point to the proper bitmap for the button.

Working with Menu Bar Menus   Sometimes applications need to manipulate menus by setting or clearing check marks or by enabling or disabling items. The standard set of menu functions (*CheckMenuItem*, for example) works as expected on menus maintained by a menu bar. The trick is to get the handle of the menu so that you can modify its items. The menu bar supports three messages you can use to get and set menu handles: *SHCMBM_GETMENU*, *SHCMBM_GETSUBMENU*, and *SHCMBM_SETSUBMENU*. The messages *SHCMBM_GETMENU* and *SHCMBM_GETSUBMENU* can be sent to the menu bar to query the menu handle or a specific submenu. The following line shows how to query the root menu handle using *SHCMBM_GETMENU*.

```
hMenu = (HMENU)SendMessage (hwndMenuBar, SHCMBM_GETMENU, 0, 0);
```

You can then use this menu handle to modify any of the menu items that the menu bar might display. To query a submenu attached to a specific menu bar item, use *SHCMBM_GETSUBMENU*, as in

```
hSubMenu = (HMENU)SendMessage (hwndMenuBar, SHCMBM_GETSUBMENU, 0,
                    ID_VIEWMENU);
```

The *lParam* value is set to the ID of a specific button on the menu bar—in this example, it's the menu handle attached to the button with the *ID_VIEWMENU* ID value.

To change the menu of a particular button on the menu bar, you can use *SHCMBM_SETSUBMENU* with *wParam* set to the ID of the button and *lParam* set to the new menu handle, as in

```
hOldMenu = (HMENU)SendMessage (hwndMenuBar, SHCMBM_SETSUBMENU,
                    ID_VIEWMENU, (LPARAM)hNewMenu);
```

The MenuBar Example

The MenuBar example demonstrates a number of the menu bar techniques described in the preceding section. The example switches between two menu bars. Each menu bar has its own set of buttons, each with a different set of styles. The example displays all *WM_COMMAND* and *WM_NOTIFY* messages in a list box in its main window. This list box allows you to see what the application sees in terms of notifications and command messages.

When run on systems that support New menus, the menu bars have a unique New menu for each bar, one with a shared New menu and another with a simple New menu. In addition, the New menu is also extended with a custom menu item. When used with the NewMenuX example in Chapter 17, MenuBar demonstrates how to intercept permanent Pocket PC New menu item selections by fielding the *NMN_INVOKECOMMAND* notification and asking the user whether Calc should be launched.

Figure 5-8 shows a Pocket PC running MenuBar. Notice that the three rightmost buttons on the menu bar use the predefined Cut, Copy, and Paste bitmap images.

Figure 5-8 The MenuBar example uses standard common control bitmap images.

Listing 5-3 contains the source code for MenuBar. As usual, it is divided into MenuBar.rc, MenuBar.h, and MenuBar.cpp.

```
MenuBar.rc
//======================================================================
// Resource file
//
// Written for the book Programming Windows CE
// Copyright (C) 2003 Douglas Boling
//======================================================================
#include "windows.h"             // Windows stuff
#include "commctrl.h"            // Common ctl stuff
#include "aygshell.h"            // Pocket PC stuff
#include "MenuBar.h"             // Program-specific stuff


//----------------------------------------------------------------------
// Icons and bitmaps
//
```

Listing 5-3 The MenuBar example

```
ID_ICON       ICON   "MenuBar.ico"    // Program icon

ID_TOOLBMPS BITMAP  DISCARDABLE  "btns.bmp"

//------------------------------------------------------------------------
// Accelerator keys
//
ID_ACCEL ACCELERATORS DISCARDABLE
BEGIN
    "Q",  IDM_EXIT,  VIRTKEY, CONTROL, NOINVERT
END
//------------------------------------------------------------------------
// MenuBar resources
//
#define  SHMENUBAR RCDATA

// MenuBar resource with simple new menu
ID_TOOLBAR1 SHMENUBAR MOVEABLE PURE
BEGIN
    ID_MENU, 5,

    I_IMAGENONE, IDM_SHAREDNEWDEFAULT, TBSTATE_ENABLED,
    TBSTYLE_AUTOSIZE, IDS_SHNEW, IDS_SNEWTT, NOMENU,

    I_IMAGENONE, ID_VIEWMENU, TBSTATE_ENABLED,
    TBSTYLE_DROPDOWN | TBSTYLE_AUTOSIZE, IDS_VIEWMENUNAME, 0, 0,

    I_IMAGENONE, ID_TOOLMENU, TBSTATE_ENABLED,
    TBSTYLE_DROPDOWN | TBSTYLE_AUTOSIZE, IDS_TOOLMENUNAME, 0, 1,

    0, IDM_ABOUT, TBSTATE_ENABLED,
    TBSTYLE_BUTTON | TBSTYLE_AUTOSIZE, 0,  IDS_BTNTOOLTT, 0,

    2, ID_MENU3, TBSTATE_ENABLED,
    TBSTYLE_DROPDOWN | TBSTYLE_AUTOSIZE, 0,  IDS_BTNTOOLTT, 2,
END

// MenuBar resource with shared new
ID_TOOLBAR2 SHMENUBAR MOVEABLE PURE
BEGIN
    ID_MENU, 8,

    I_IMAGENONE, IDM_SHAREDNEW, TBSTATE_ENABLED,
    TBSTYLE_BUTTON | TBSTYLE_AUTOSIZE, IDS_SHNEW, IDS_NEWTT, NOMENU,

    I_IMAGENONE, ID_VIEWMENU, TBSTATE_ENABLED,
    TBSTYLE_DROPDOWN | TBSTYLE_AUTOSIZE, IDS_VIEWMENUNAME, 0, 0,
```

(continued)

Listing 5-3 *(continued)*

```
    I_IMAGENONE, ID_TOOLMENU, TBSTATE_ENABLED,
    TBSTYLE_DROPDOWN | TBSTYLE_AUTOSIZE, IDS_TOOLMENUNAME, 0, 1,

    1, IDM_ABOUT, TBSTATE_ENABLED,
    TBSTYLE_CHECK | TBSTYLE_AUTOSIZE, 0,  IDS_BTNTOOLTT, 0,

    I_IMAGENONE, 0, TBSTATE_ENABLED, TBSTYLE_SEP, 0,  0, 0,

    3+STD_CUT, IDM_CUT, TBSTATE_ENABLED,
    TBSTYLE_BUTTON | TBSTYLE_AUTOSIZE, 0,  IDS_BTNCUTT, 0,
    3+STD_COPY, IDM_COPY, TBSTATE_ENABLED,
    TBSTYLE_BUTTON | TBSTYLE_AUTOSIZE, 0,  IDS_BTNCOPYTT, 0,

    3+STD_PASTE, IDM_PASTE, TBSTATE_ENABLED,
    TBSTYLE_BUTTON | TBSTYLE_AUTOSIZE, 0,  IDS_BTNPASTETT, 0,
END

ID_MENU MENU DISCARDABLE
BEGIN
    POPUP "&Menu1"
    BEGIN
        MENUITEM "Shared New",              IDM_DOSHAREDNEW
        MENUITEM "Simple New",              IDM_DOSIMPLENEW
        MENUITEM SEPARATOR
        MENUITEM "Exit",                    IDM_EXIT
    END
    POPUP "&Menu2"
    BEGIN
        MENUITEM "&About...",               IDM_ABOUT
    END
    POPUP "&Menu3"
    BEGIN
        MENUITEM "Menu item 1",             IDM_ITEM1
        MENUITEM "Menu item 2",             IDM_ITEM2
        MENUITEM "Menu item 3",             IDM_ITEM3
        MENUITEM "Menu item 4",             IDM_ITEM4
        MENUITEM "Menu item 5",             IDM_ITEM5
        MENUITEM "Menu item 6",             IDM_ITEM6
    END
END

//-------------------------------------------------------------------------
// String resource table
//
STRINGTABLE DISCARDABLE
BEGIN
```

```
IDS_VIEWMENUNAME          "View"
IDS_TOOLMENUNAME          "Tools"
IDS_SNEWTT                "New menu tooltip text"
IDS_NEWTT                 "New doc - shared menu tooltip"
IDS_BTNTOOLTT             "Button tooltip"
IDS_BTNCUTTT              "Cut"
IDS_BTNCOPYTT             "Copy"
IDS_BTNPASTETT            "Paste"
END
//----------------------------------------------------------------
// About box dialog template
//
aboutbox DIALOG discardable 10, 10, 135, 40
STYLE  WS_POPUP | WS_VISIBLE | WS_CAPTION | WS_SYSMENU | DS_CENTER |
       DS_MODALFRAME
CAPTION "About"
BEGIN
    ICON   ID_ICON,                       -1,  3,  5, 10, 10
    LTEXT "MenuBar - Written for the book Programming Windows \
           CE Copyright 2003 Douglas Boling"
                                          -1, 30,  5, 102, 37
END
```

MenuBar.h

```
//================================================================
// Header file
//
// Written for the book Programming Windows CE
// Copyright (C) 2003 Douglas Boling
//
//================================================================
// Returns number of elements
#define dim(x) (sizeof(x) / sizeof(x[0]))


//----------------------------------------------------------------
// Generic defines and data types
//
struct decodeUINT {                          // Structure associates
    UINT Code;                               // messages
                                             // with a function.
    LRESULT (*Fxn)(HWND, UINT, WPARAM, LPARAM);
};
struct decodeCMD {                           // Structure associates
    UINT Code;                               // menu IDs with a
    LRESULT (*Fxn)(HWND, WORD, HWND, WORD);  // function.
};
```

(continued)

Listing 5-3 *(continued)*

```
//-------------------------------------------------------------------------
// Generic defines used by application
#define  ID_ACCEL              1                    // Accelerator table ID
#define  ID_TOOLBMPS           2
#define  ID_ICON               3
#define  ID_TOOLBAR1           100
#define  ID_TOOLBAR2           101
#define  ID_MENU               102
#define  IDC_RPTLIST           103
#define  ID_VIEWMENU           50
#define  ID_TOOLMENU           51
#define  ID_MENU3              52

#define  IDM_EXIT              200
#define  IDM_DOSHAREDNEW       201
#define  IDM_DOSIMPLENEW       202

#define  IDM_ABOUT             210

#define  IDM_ITEM1             220
#define  IDM_ITEM2             221
#define  IDM_ITEM3             222
#define  IDM_ITEM4             223
#define  IDM_ITEM5             224
#define  IDM_ITEM6             225

#define  IDM_CUT               230
#define  IDM_COPY              231
#define  IDM_PASTE             232

#define  IDM_MYNEWMENUITEM (IDM_NEWMENUMAX+1)  // New Menu custom item

#define  IDS_VIEWMENUNAME      256              // String table IDs
#define  IDS_TOOLMENUNAME      257
#define  IDS_SNEWTT            258
#define  IDS_NEWTT             259
#define  IDS_BTNTOOLTT         260
#define  IDS_BTN3TEXT          261
#define  IDS_BTNCUTTT          262
#define  IDS_BTNCOPYTT         263
#define  IDS_BTNPASTETT        264


//-------------------------------------------------------------------------
// Function prototypes
//
```

```
HWND InitInstance (HINSTANCE, LPWSTR, int);
int TermInstance (HINSTANCE, int);
HWND MyCreateMenuBar (HWND hWnd, int idToolbar);
void MyCheckMenu (int idMenu);
void Add2List (HWND hWnd, LPTSTR lpszFormat, ...);

// Window procedures
LRESULT CALLBACK MainWndProc (HWND, UINT, WPARAM, LPARAM);
// Message handlers
LRESULT DoCreateMain (HWND, UINT, WPARAM, LPARAM);
LRESULT DoSizeMain (HWND, UINT, WPARAM, LPARAM);
LRESULT DoNotifyMain (HWND, UINT, WPARAM, LPARAM);
LRESULT DoCommandMain (HWND, UINT, WPARAM, LPARAM);
LRESULT DoSettingChangeMain (HWND, UINT, WPARAM, LPARAM);
LRESULT DoActivateMain (HWND, UINT, WPARAM, LPARAM);
LRESULT DoDestroyMain (HWND, UINT, WPARAM, LPARAM);

// WM_COMMAND message handlers
LPARAM DoMainCommandExit (HWND, WORD, HWND, WORD);
LPARAM DoMainCommandSharedNew (HWND, WORD, HWND, WORD);
LPARAM DoMainCommandSimpleNew (HWND, WORD, HWND, WORD);
LPARAM DoMainCommandAbout (HWND, WORD, HWND, WORD);

// Dialog procedures
BOOL CALLBACK AboutDlgProc (HWND, UINT, WPARAM, LPARAM);
ExPPCIncs.h
//=======================================================================
// Extra Aygshell includes - This file is necessary to add back defines
// removed from the Pocket PC SDK in 2002 and 2003.  These defines allow
// an application to intercept action from the New menu.
//

#ifdef __cplusplus
extern "C" {
#endif

#ifndef NMN_GETAPPREGKEY
//++++++
//
// New menu notifications
//

// get the application specific reg key for "new" menu items
#define NMN_GETAPPREGKEY      1101
// Sent to app before shared new menu is destroyed.
#define NMN_NEWMENUDESTROY    1102
```

Listing 5-3 *(continued)*

```
// Sent to app before COM object is instantiated.
#define  NMN_INVOKECOMMAND      1103
// Sent to app when new button style changes
#define  NMN_NEWBUTTONUPDATED   1104

typedef struct tagNMNEWMENU
{
    NMHDR hdr;
    TCHAR szReg[80];
    HMENU hMenu;
    CLSID clsid;
} NMNEWMENU, *PNMNEWMENU;

// For application added menu items.
#define IDM_NEWMENUMAX       3000

//
// End New menu notifications
//
//------

#endif

#ifdef __cplusplus
}
#endif
```

MenuBar.cpp

```
//=======================================================================
// MenuBar - Demonstrates a Pocket PC menu bar
//
// Written for the book Programming Windows CE
// Copyright (C) 2003 Douglas Boling
//
//=======================================================================
#include <windows.h>                // For all that Windows stuff
#include <commctrl.h>               // Command bar includes
#include <aygshell.h>               // Pocket PC includes
#include "MenuBar.h"                // Program-specific stuff
#include "ExPPCIncs.h"              // Adds back PPC SDK stuff
//-----------------------------------------------------------------------
// Global data
//
// Get the new menu extension guid when compiling for Pocket PC
#if defined(WIN32_PLATFORM_PSPC)
```

```
// This guid must match the one in the NewMenuX example
static const GUID CLSID_NewMenuX =
{0x130f6e46,0xc3f9,0x4fa8,{0xb8,0xbc,0x75,0x72,0xb,0xc7,0x32,0x31}};
#endif WIN32_PLATFORM_PSPC

const TCHAR szAppName[] = TEXT("MenuBar");
HINSTANCE hInst;                            // Program instance handle

HWND hwndMenuBar = NULL;                    // Handle of menu bar control
SHACTIVATEINFO sai;                         // Used to adjust window for SIP

// Message dispatch table for MainWindowProc
const struct decodeUINT MainMessages[] = {
    WM_CREATE, DoCreateMain,
    WM_SIZE, DoSizeMain,
    WM_COMMAND, DoCommandMain,
    WM_NOTIFY, DoNotifyMain,
    WM_SETTINGCHANGE, DoSettingChangeMain,
    WM_ACTIVATE, DoActivateMain,
    WM_DESTROY, DoDestroyMain,
};
// Command Message dispatch for MainWindowProc
const struct decodeCMD MainCommandItems[] = {
    IDM_EXIT, DoMainCommandExit,
    IDM_DOSHAREDNEW, DoMainCommandSharedNew,
    IDM_DOSIMPLENEW, DoMainCommandSimpleNew,
    IDM_ABOUT, DoMainCommandAbout,
};
//======================================================================
// Program entry point
//
int WINAPI WinMain (HINSTANCE hInstance, HINSTANCE hPrevInstance,
                    LPWSTR lpCmdLine, int nCmdShow) {
    MSG msg;
    int rc = 0;
    HWND hwndMain;
    HACCEL hAccel;

    // Initialize application.
    hwndMain = InitInstance (hInstance, lpCmdLine, nCmdShow);
    if (hwndMain == 0) return 0x10;

    hAccel = LoadAccelerators(hInstance, MAKEINTRESOURCE (ID_ACCEL));

    // Application message loop
    while (GetMessage (&msg, NULL, 0, 0)) {
```

(continued)

Listing 5-3 *(continued)*

```
            // Translate accelerator keys.
            if (!TranslateAccelerator(hwndMain, hAccel, &msg)) {
                TranslateMessage (&msg);
                DispatchMessage (&msg);
            }
        }
    // Instance cleanup
    return TermInstance (hInstance, msg.wParam);
}
//----------------------------------------------------------------------
// InitInstance - Instance initialization
//
HWND InitInstance (HINSTANCE hInstance, LPWSTR lpCmdLine, int nCmdShow) {
    HWND hWnd;
    WNDCLASS wc;

    // Allow only one instance of the application.
    hWnd = FindWindow (szAppName, NULL);
    if (hWnd) {
        SetForegroundWindow ((HWND)(((DWORD)hWnd) | 0x01));
        return 0;
    }
    // Register application main window class.
    wc.style = CS_VREDRAW | CS_HREDRAW;         // Window style
    wc.lpfnWndProc = MainWndProc;               // Callback function
    wc.cbClsExtra = 0;                          // Extra class data
    wc.cbWndExtra = 0;                          // Extra window data
    wc.hInstance = hInstance;                   // Owner handle
    wc.hIcon = NULL,                            // Application icon
    wc.hCursor = LoadCursor (NULL, IDC_ARROW);  // Default cursor
    wc.hbrBackground = (HBRUSH) GetStockObject (WHITE_BRUSH);
    wc.lpszMenuName =  NULL;                     // Menu name
    wc.lpszClassName = szAppName;               // Window class name

    if (RegisterClass (&wc) == 0) return 0;

    // Save program instance handle in global variable.
    hInst = hInstance;

    // Create main window.
    hWnd = CreateWindow (szAppName, TEXT("Menu Bar"),  WS_VISIBLE,
                         CW_USEDEFAULT, CW_USEDEFAULT, CW_USEDEFAULT,
                         CW_USEDEFAULT, NULL, NULL, hInstance, NULL);
    if (!IsWindow (hWnd)) return 0;             // Fail if not created.

    // Standard show and update calls
    ShowWindow (hWnd, nCmdShow);
```

```
    UpdateWindow (hWnd);
    return hWnd;
}
//----------------------------------------------------------------------
// TermInstance - Program cleanup
//
int TermInstance (HINSTANCE hInstance, int nDefRC) {
    return nDefRC;
}
//======================================================================
// Message handling procedures for main window
//
//----------------------------------------------------------------------
// MainWndProc - Callback function for application window
//
LRESULT CALLBACK MainWndProc (HWND hWnd, UINT wMsg, WPARAM wParam,
                              LPARAM lParam) {
    INT i;
    //
    // Search message list to see if we need to handle this
    // message. If in list, call procedure.
    //
    for (i = 0; i < dim(MainMessages); i++) {
        if (wMsg == MainMessages[i].Code)
            return (*MainMessages[i].Fxn)(hWnd, wMsg, wParam, lParam);
    }
    return DefWindowProc (hWnd, wMsg, wParam, lParam);
}
//----------------------------------------------------------------------
// DoCreateMain - Process WM_CREATE message for window.
//
LRESULT DoCreateMain (HWND hWnd, UINT wMsg, WPARAM wParam,
                      LPARAM lParam) {
    SIPINFO si;
    HWND hwndChild;
    int i, cx, cy;

    // Initialize the shell to activate info structure.
    memset (&sai, 0, sizeof (sai));
    sai.cbSize = sizeof (sai);

    // Create menu bar and check for errors.
    hwndMenuBar = MyCreateMenuBar (hWnd, ID_TOOLBAR1);
    if (!hwndMenuBar) {
        MessageBox (hWnd, TEXT("Couldn\'t create MenuBar"),
                    szAppName, MB_OK);
        DestroyWindow (hWnd);
```

(continued)

Listing 5-3 *(continued)*

```
        return 0;
    }
    // Set menu check mark.
    MyCheckMenu (IDM_DOSIMPLENEW);

    // Create report window.  It will be sized in the WM_SIZE handler.
    hwndChild = CreateWindowEx (0, TEXT ("listbox"), TEXT (""),
                              WS_VISIBLE | WS_CHILD | WS_VSCROLL |
                              LBS_USETABSTOPS | LBS_NOINTEGRALHEIGHT,
                              0, 0, 0, 0, hWnd, (HMENU)IDC_RPTLIST,
                              hInst, NULL);
    // Destroy frame if window not created.
    if (!IsWindow (hwndChild)) {
        DestroyWindow (hWnd);
        return 0;
    }
    // Initialize tab stops for display list box.
    i = 8;
    SendMessage (hwndChild, LB_SETTABSTOPS, 1, (LPARAM)&i);

    // Query the sip state and size our window appropriately.
    memset (&si, 0, sizeof (si));
    si.cbSize = sizeof (si);
    SHSipInfo(SPI_GETSIPINFO, 0, (PVOID)&si, FALSE);
    cx = si.rcVisibleDesktop.right - si.rcVisibleDesktop.left;
    cy = si.rcVisibleDesktop.bottom - si.rcVisibleDesktop.top;

    // If the sip is not shown, or is showing but not docked, the
    // desktop rect doesn't include the height of the menu bar.
    if (!(si.fdwFlags & SIPF_ON) ||
        ((si.fdwFlags & SIPF_ON) && !(si.fdwFlags & SIPF_DOCKED))) {
        RECT rectMB;
        GetWindowRect (hwndMenuBar, &rectMB);
        cy -= (rectMB.bottom - rectMB.top);
    }
    SetWindowPos (hWnd, NULL, 0, 0, cx, cy, SWP_NOMOVE | SWP_NOZORDER);
    return 0;
}
//-----------------------------------------------------------------------
// DoSizeMain - Process WM_SIZE message for window.
//
LRESULT DoSizeMain (HWND hWnd, UINT wMsg, WPARAM wParam, LPARAM lParam){
    RECT rect;

    GetClientRect (hWnd, &rect);
    SetWindowPos (GetDlgItem (hWnd, IDC_RPTLIST), NULL, 0, 0,
                  rect.right - rect.left, rect.bottom - rect.top,
```

```
                    SWP_NOZORDER);
    return 0;
}
//-----------------------------------------------------------------
// DoCommandMain - Process WM_COMMAND message for window.
//
LRESULT DoCommandMain (HWND hWnd, UINT wMsg, WPARAM wParam,
                       LPARAM lParam) {
    WORD    idItem, wNotifyCode;
    HWND hwndCtl;
    INT  i;

    // Parse the parameters.
    idItem = (WORD) LOWORD (wParam);
    wNotifyCode = (WORD) HIWORD (wParam);
    hwndCtl = (HWND) lParam;

    Add2List (hWnd, TEXT ("WM_COMMAND id:%d code:%d"), idItem,
              wNotifyCode);
    // Call routine to handle control message.
    for (i = 0; i < dim(MainCommandItems); i++) {
        if (idItem == MainCommandItems[i].Code)
            return (*MainCommandItems[i].Fxn)(hWnd, idItem, hwndCtl,
                                              wNotifyCode);
    }
    return 0;
}
//-----------------------------------------------------------------
// DoNotifyMain - Process WM_NOTIFY message for window.
//
LRESULT DoNotifyMain (HWND hWnd, UINT wMsg, WPARAM wParam,
                      LPARAM lParam) {
    PNMNEWMENU lpNewMenu;
    LPNMHDR lpnhr = (LPNMHDR)lParam;

    Add2List (hWnd, TEXT ("WM_NOTIFY id:%d event:%d"), lpnhr->idFrom,
              lpnhr->code);
    // This code only works when compiling on a Pocket PC
#if defined(WIN32_PLATFORM_PSPC)       // See if new menu being displayed.
    if (lpnhr->code == NMN_GETAPPREGKEY) {
        lpNewMenu = (PNMNEWMENU) lParam;
        AppendMenu (lpNewMenu->hMenu, MF_ENABLED, IDM_MYNEWMENUITEM,
                    TEXT("My own New menu item"));
        AppendMenu (lpNewMenu->hMenu, MF_SEPARATOR, 0, 0);
    // Permanent new menu item selected
    } else if (lpnhr->code == NMN_INVOKECOMMAND) {
        lpNewMenu = (PNMNEWMENU) lParam;
```

(continued)

Listing 5-3 *(continued)*

```
        // See if it is NewMenuX.
        if (IsEqualIID (lpNewMenu->clsid, CLSID_NewMenuX)) {
            int rc = MessageBox (hWnd,
                                TEXT ("Do you want to launch Calc?"),
                                szAppName, MB_YESNO);
            if (rc == IDYES)
                return 0;
            else
                return 1;
        }
    }
#endif
    return 0;
}
//----------------------------------------------------------------------
// DoSettingChangeMain - Process WM_SETTINGCHANGE message for window.
//
LRESULT DoSettingChangeMain (HWND hWnd, UINT wMsg, WPARAM wParam,
                            LPARAM lParam) {

    // Notify shell of our WM_SETTINGCHANGE message.
    SHHandleWMSettingChange(hWnd, wParam, lParam, &sai);
    return 0;
}
//----------------------------------------------------------------------
// DoActivateMain - Process WM_ACTIVATE message for window.
//
LRESULT DoActivateMain (HWND hWnd, UINT wMsg, WPARAM wParam,
                        LPARAM lParam) {

    // Notify shell of our activate message.
    SHHandleWMActivate(hWnd, wParam, lParam, &sai, 0);
    return 0;
}
//----------------------------------------------------------------------
// DoDestroyMain - Process WM_DESTROY message for window.
//
LRESULT DoDestroyMain (HWND hWnd, UINT wMsg, WPARAM wParam,
                        LPARAM lParam) {
    PostQuitMessage (0);
    return 0;
}
//======================================================================
// Command handler routines
//----------------------------------------------------------------------
// DoMainCommandExit - Process Program Exit command.
//
```

```
LPARAM DoMainCommandExit (HWND hWnd, WORD idItem, HWND hwndCtl,
                          WORD wNotifyCode) {
    SendMessage (hWnd, WM_CLOSE, 0, 0);
    return 0;
}
//------------------------------------------------------------------------
// DoMainCommandAbout - Process Tools About command.
//
LPARAM DoMainCommandAbout (HWND hWnd, WORD idItem, HWND hwndCtl,
                           WORD wNotifyCode) {
    // Use DialogBox to create modal dialog.
    DialogBox (hInst, TEXT ("aboutbox"), hWnd, AboutDlgProc);
    return 0;
}
//------------------------------------------------------------------------
// DoMainCommandSimpleNew - Process Simple new menu command.
//
LPARAM DoMainCommandSimpleNew (HWND hWnd, WORD idItem, HWND hwndCtl,
                               WORD wNotifyCode) {
    if (IsWindow (hwndMenuBar))
        DestroyWindow (hwndMenuBar);

    // Create a menu bar.
    hwndMenuBar = MyCreateMenuBar (hWnd, ID_TOOLBAR1);
    MyCheckMenu (IDM_DOSIMPLENEW);
    return 0;
}
//------------------------------------------------------------------------
// DoMainCommandSharedNew - Process Shared new menu command.
//
LPARAM DoMainCommandSharedNew (HWND hWnd, WORD idItem, HWND hwndCtl,
                               WORD wNotifyCode) {
    // Delete the old menu bar.
    if (IsWindow (hwndMenuBar))
        DestroyWindow (hwndMenuBar);

    // Create the menu bar.
    hwndMenuBar = MyCreateMenuBar (hWnd, ID_TOOLBAR2);

    // Add the standard view bitmap.
    CommandBar_AddBitmap (hwndMenuBar, HINST_COMMCTRL,
                          IDB_STD_SMALL_COLOR, STD_PRINT, 16, 16);
    MyCheckMenu (IDM_DOSHAREDNEW);              // Set menu checkmark.
    return 0;
}
//========================================================================
```

(continued)

Listing 5-3 *(continued)*

```
// About Dialog procedure
//
BOOL CALLBACK AboutDlgProc (HWND hWnd, UINT wMsg, WPARAM wParam,
                            LPARAM lParam) {
    switch (wMsg) {
        case WM_INITDIALOG:
        {
            SHINITDLGINFO idi;
            idi.dwMask = SHIDIM_FLAGS;
            idi.dwFlags = SHIDIF_DONEBUTTON | SHIDIF_SIZEDLGFULLSCREEN |
                          SHIDIF_SIPDOWN;
            idi.hDlg = hWnd;
            SHInitDialog (&idi);
        }
        break;
        case WM_COMMAND:
            switch (LOWORD (wParam)) {
                case IDOK:
                case IDCANCEL:
                    EndDialog (hWnd, 0);
                    return TRUE;
            }
            break;
    }
    return FALSE;
}
//-------------------------------------------------------------------------
// MyCreateMenuBar - Creates a menu bar
//
HWND MyCreateMenuBar (HWND hWnd, int idToolbar) {
    SHMENUBARINFO mbi;

    // Create a menu bar.
    memset(&mbi, 0, sizeof(SHMENUBARINFO)); // Zero structure
    mbi.cbSize = sizeof(SHMENUBARINFO);      // Size field
    mbi.hwndParent = hWnd;                   // Parent window
    mbi.nToolBarId = idToolbar;              // ID of toolbar resource
    mbi.hInstRes = hInst;                    // Inst handle of app
    mbi.nBmpId = ID_TOOLBMPS;                // ID of bitmap resource
    mbi.cBmpImages = 3;                      // Num of images in bitmap

    SHCreateMenuBar(&mbi);
    return mbi.hwndMB;                       // Return the menu bar handle.
}
//-------------------------------------------------------------------------
// MyCheckMenu - Places a check next to a menu item
//
```

```
void MyCheckMenu (int idMenu) {
    HMENU hSubMenu;

    // The handle for the view menu
    hSubMenu = (HMENU)SendMessage (hwndMenuBar, SHCMBM_GETMENU, 0, 0);
    if (idMenu == IDM_DOSIMPLENEW) {
        CheckMenuItem (hSubMenu, IDM_DOSIMPLENEW, MF_BYCOMMAND |
                       MFS_CHECKED);
        CheckMenuItem (hSubMenu, IDM_DOSHAREDNEW, MF_BYCOMMAND |
                       MFS_UNCHECKED);
    } else {
        CheckMenuItem (hSubMenu, IDM_DOSIMPLENEW, MF_BYCOMMAND |
                       MFS_UNCHECKED);
        CheckMenuItem (hSubMenu, IDM_DOSHAREDNEW, MF_BYCOMMAND |
                       MFS_CHECKED);
    }
    return;
}
//-----------------------------------------------------------------------
// Add2List - Add string to the report list box.
//
void Add2List (HWND hWnd, LPTSTR lpszFormat, ...) {
    int nBuf, i;
    TCHAR szBuffer[512];

    va_list args;
    va_start(args, lpszFormat);

    nBuf = _vstprintf(szBuffer, lpszFormat, args);

    i = SendDlgItemMessage (hWnd, IDC_RPTLIST, LB_ADDSTRING, 0,
                            (LPARAM)(LPCTSTR)szBuffer);

    if (i != LB_ERR)
        SendDlgItemMessage (hWnd, IDC_RPTLIST, LB_SETTOPINDEX, i,
                            (LPARAM)(LPCTSTR)szBuffer);
    va_end(args);
}
```

The MenuBar example creates its menu bar in a common routine called *MyCreateMenuBar*. The two parameters provide the handle of the window that will own the menu bar and the ID of the resource specifying the menu bar configuration. MenuBar.rc contains two *SHMENUBAR* templates, *ID_TOOLBAR1* and *ID_TOOLBAR2*. Both templates reference a common menu resource, *ID_MENU*. Notice that the menu resource has the names Menu1, Menu2, and Menu3 for its top-level menu items. These names are not used because the menu bar instead uses the strings in the menu bar resource.

The two menu bars are switched simply by destroying one bar and creating another. The creation of a menu bar happens so quickly that the user doesn't even notice it. This solution is better than creating two menu bars and alternately showing one and hiding the other, since having two controls consumes extra memory that is better used elsewhere.

When the menu bar with the shared new menu button is created, a call is made to *CommandBar_Addbitmap* to add the common control bitmaps that include the cut, copy, and paste images. This menu bar also includes a check box–style button that is tapped once to set and tapped again to clear. The simple menu bar has a button with a bitmap—the bitmap with the artistic C that when tapped displays a menu. This button shows that it's just as easy to display a menu from a button with a bitmap as it is with a text label.

This completes the discussion of the "menu" controls. I talk about these controls at length because you'll need one of them for almost every Windows CE application.

For the remainder of the chapter, I'll cover the highlights of some of the other controls. These other controls are similar to but have somewhat less function than their counterparts under Windows XP. I'll spend more time on the controls I think you'll need when writing a Windows CE application. I'll start with the month calendar and the time and date picker controls. These controls are rather new to the common control set and have a direct application to the PIM-like applications that are appropriate for many Windows CE systems. I'll also spend some time covering the list view control, concentrating on features of use to Windows CE developers. I'll cover just briefly the remainder of the common controls.

The Month Calendar Control

The month calendar control gives you a handy month-view calendar that can be manipulated by users to look up any month, week, or day as far back as the adoption of the Gregorian calendar in September 1752. The control can display as many months as will fit into the size of the control. The days of the month can be highlighted to indicate appointments. The weeks can indicate the current week throughout the year. Users can spin through the months by tapping on the name of the month or change years by tapping on the year displayed.

Before using the month calendar control, you must initialize the common control library by calling *InitCommonControlsEx* with the *ICC_DATE_CLASSES* flag. You create the control by calling *CreateWindow* with the *MONTHCAL_CLASS* flag. The style flags for the control are shown here:

- ■   *MCS_MULTISELECT*   The control allows multiple selection of days.

- ■   *MCS_NOTODAY*   The control won't display today's date under the calendar.

- ■   *MCS_NOTODAYCIRCLE*   The control won't circle today's date.

- ■   *MCS_WEEKNUMBERS*   The control displays the week number (1 through 52) to the left of each week in the calendar.

- ■   *MCS_DAYSTATE*   The control sends notification messages to the parent requesting the days of the month that should be displayed in bold. You use this style to indicate which days have appointments or events scheduled.

Initializing the Control

In addition to the styles I just described, you can use a number of messages or their corresponding wrapper macros to configure the month calendar control. You can use an *MCM_SETFIRSTDAYOFWEEK* message to display a different starting day of the week. You can also use the *MCM_SETRANGE* message to display dates within a given range in the control. You can configure date selection to allow the user to choose only single dates or to set a limit to the range of dates that a user can select at any one time. The single/multiple date selection ability is defined by the *MCS_MULTISELECT* style. If you set this style, you use the *MCM_SETMAXSELCOUNT* message to set the maximum number of days that can be selected at any one time.

You can set the background and text colors of the control by using the *MCM_SETCOLOR* message. This message can individually set colors for the different regions within the controls, including the calendar text and background, the header text and background, and the color of the days that precede and follow the days of the month being displayed. This message takes a flag indicating the part of the control to set and a *COLORREF* value to specify the color.

The month calendar control is designed to display months on an integral basis. That is, if the control is big enough for one and a half months, it displays only one month, centered in the control. You can use the *MCM_GETMINREQRECT* message to compute the minimum size necessary to display one month. Because the control must first be created before the *MCM_GETMINREQRECT* can be sent, properly sizing the control is a roundabout process. You must create the control, send the *MCM_GETMINREQRECT* message, and then resize the control using the data returned from the message.

Month Calendar Notifications

The month calendar control has only three notification messages to send to its parent. Of these, the *MCN_GETDAYSTATE* notification is the most important. This notification is sent when the control needs to know what days of a month to display in bold. This is done by querying the parent for a series of bit field values encoded in a *MONTHDAYSTATE* variable. This value is nothing more than a 32-bit value with bits 1 through 31 representing the days 1 through 31 of the month.

When the control needs to display a month, it sends an *MCN_GETDAYSTATE* notification with a pointer to an *NMDAYSTATE* structure defined as the following:

```
typedef struct {
    NMHDR nmhdr;
    SYSTEMTIME stStart;
    int cDayState;
    LPMONTHDAYSTATE prgDayState;
} NMDAYSTATE;
```

The *nmbhdr* field is simply the *NMHDR* structure that's passed with every *WM_NOTIFY* message. The *stStart* field contains the starting date for which the control is requesting information. This date is encoded in a standard *SYSTEM-TIME* structure used by all versions of Windows. It's detailed here:

```
typedef struct {
    WORD wYear;
    WORD wMonth;
    WORD wDayOfWeek;
    WORD wDay;
    WORD wHour;
    WORD wMinute;
    WORD wSecond;
    WORD wMilliseconds;
} SYSTEMTIME;
```

For this notification, only the *wMonth*, *wDay*, and *wYear* fields are significant.

The *cDayState* field contains the number of entries in an array of *MONTH-DAYSTATE* values. Even if a month calendar control is displaying only one month, it could request information about the previous and following months if days of those months are needed to fill in the top or bottom lines of the calendar.

The month calendar control sends an *MCN_SELCHANGE* notification when the user changes the days that are selected in the control. The structure passed with this notification, *NMSELCHANGE*, contains the newly highlighted starting and ending days. The *MCN_SELECT* notification is sent when the user double-taps on a day. The same *NMSELCHANGE* structure is passed with this notification to indicate the days that have been selected.

The Date and Time Picker Control

The date and time picker control looks deceptively simple but is a great tool for any application that needs to ask the user to specify a date. Any programmer who has had to parse, validate, and translate a string into a valid system date or time will appreciate this control.

When used to select a date, the control resembles a combo box, which is an edit field with a down arrow button on the right side. Clicking on the arrow, however, displays a month calendar control showing the current month. Selecting a day in the month dismisses the month calendar control and fills the date and time picker control with that date. When you configure it to query for a time, the date and time picker control resembles an edit field with a spin button on the right end of the control.

The date and time picker control has three default formats: two for displaying the date and one for displaying the time. The control also allows you to provide a formatting string so that users can completely customize the fields in the control. The control even lets you insert application-defined fields in the control.

Creating a Date and Time Picker Control

Before you can create the date and time picker control, the common control library must be initialized. If *InitCommonControlsEx* is used, it must be passed an *ICC_DATE_CLASSES* flag. The control is created by using *CreateWindow* with the class *DATETIMEPICK_CLASS*. The control defines the following styles:

- **DTS_LONGDATEFORMAT**   The control displays a date in long format, as in Friday, September 19, 2003. The actual long date format is defined in the system registry.

- **DTS_SHORTDATEFORMAT**   The control displays a date in short format, as in 9/19/03. The actual short date format is defined in the system registry.

- **DTS_TIMEFORMAT**   The control displays the time in a format such as 5:50:28 PM. The actual time format is defined in the system registry.

- **DTS_SHOWNONE**   The control has a check box to indicate that the date is valid.

- **DTS_UPDOWN**   An up-down control replaces the drop-down button that displays a month calendar control in date view.

■   ***DTS_APPCANPARSE***   Allows the user to directly enter text into the control. The control sends a *DTN_USERSTRING* notification when the user is finished.

The first three styles simply specify a default format string. These formats are based on the regional settings in the registry. Since these formats can change if the user picks different regional settings in the Control Panel, the date and time picker control needs to know when these formats change. The system informs top-level windows of these types of changes by sending a *WM_SETTINGCHANGE* message. An application that uses the date and time picker control and uses one of these default fonts should forward the *WM_SETTINGCHANGE* message to the control if one is sent. This causes the control to reconfigure the default formats for the new regional settings.

The *DTS_APPCANPARSE* style enables the user to directly edit the text in the control. If this isn't set, the allowable keys are limited to the cursor keys and the numbers. When a field, such as a month, is highlighted in the edit field and the user presses the 6 key, the month changes to June. With the *DTS_APPCANPARSE* style, the user can directly type any character in the edit field of the control. When the user has finished, the control sends a *DTN_USERSTRING* notification to the parent window so that the text can be verified.

Customizing the Format

To customize the display format, all you need to do is create a format string and send it to the control using a *DTM_SETFORMAT* message. The format string can be made up of any of the following codes:

```
String        Description
fragment


"d"     One- or two-digit day.
"dd"    Two-digit day. Single digits have a leading zero.
"ddd"   The three-character weekday abbreviation. As in Sun, Mon...
"dddd"  The full weekday name.


"h"     One- or two-digit hour (12-hour format).
"hh"    Two-digit hour (12-hour format). Single digits have a leading zero.
"H"     One- or two-digit hour (24-hour format).
"HH"    Two-digit hour (24-hour format). Single digits have a leading zero.


"m"     One- or two-digit minute.
"mm"    Two-digit minute. Single digits have a leading zero.


"M"     One- or two-digit month.
```

```
"MM"    Two-digit month. Single digits have a leading zero.

"MMM"   Three-character month abbreviation.
"MMMM"  Full month name,
"t"     The one-letter AM/PM abbreviation. As in A or P.
"tt"    The two-letter AM/PM abbreviation. As in AM or PM.

"X"     Specifies a callback field that must be parsed by the application.

"y"     One-digit year. As in 1 for 2001.
"yy"    Two-digit year. As in 01 for 2001.
"yyy"   Full four-digit year. As in 2001.
```

Literal strings can be included in the format string by enclosing them in single quotes. For example, to display the string Today is: Saturday, December 5, 2001 the format string would be

```
'Today is: 'dddd', 'MMMM' 'd', 'yyy
```

The single quotes enclose the strings that aren't parsed. That includes the *Today is:* as well as all the separator characters, such as spaces and commas.

The callback field, designated by a series of X characters, provides for the application the greatest degree of flexibility for configuring the display of the date. When the control detects an *X* field in the format string, it sends a series of notification messages to its owner asking what to display in that field. A format string can have any number of *X* fields. For example, the following string has two *X* fields.

```
'Today 'XX' is: ' dddd', 'MMMM' 'd', 'yyy' and is 'XXX' birthday'
```

The number of X characters is used by the application only to differentiate the application-defined fields; it doesn't indicate the number of characters that should be displayed in the fields. When the control sends a notification asking for information about an *X* field, it includes a pointer to the X string so that the application can determine which field is being referenced.

When the date and time picker control needs to display an application-defined *X* field, it sends two notifications: *DTN_FORMATQUERY* and *DTN_FORMAT*. The *DTN_FORMATQUERY* notification is sent to get the maximum size of the text to be displayed. The *DTN_FORMAT* notification is then sent to get the actual text for the field. A third notification, *DTN_WMKEYDOWN*, is sent when the user highlights an application-defined field and presses a key. The application is responsible for determining which keys are valid and modifying the date if an appropriate key is pressed.

The List View Control

The list view control is arguably the most complex of the common controls. It displays a list of items in one of four modes: large icon, small icon, list, and report. The Windows CE version of the list view control supports many, but not all, of the common control library functions released with Internet Explorer 4.0. Some of these functions are a great help in the memory-constrained environment of Windows CE. These features include the ability to manage virtual lists of almost any size, headers that can have images and be rearranged using drag and drop, the ability to indent an entry, and new styles for report mode. The list view control also supports the new custom draw interface, which allows a fairly easy way of changing the appearance of the control.

You register the list view control either by calling InitCommonControls or by calling an *InitCommonControls* using an *ICC_LISTVIEW_CLASSES* flag. You create the control by calling *CreateWindow* using the class filled with *WC_LISTVIEW*. Under Windows CE, the list view control supports all the styles supported by other versions of Windows, including the *LVS_OWNERDATA* style that designates the control as a virtual list view control.

Styles in Report Mode

In addition to the standard list view styles that you can use when creating the list view, the list view control supports a number of extended styles. This rather unfortunate term doesn't refer to the extended styles field in the *CreateWindowsEx* function. Instead, two messages, *LVM_GETEXTENDEDLISTVIEWSTYLE* and *LVM_SETEXTENDEDLISTVIEWSTYLE*, are used to get and set these extended list view styles. The extended styles supported by Windows CE are listed below.

- **LVS_EX_CHECKBOXES**   The control places check boxes next to each item in the control.

- **LVS_EX_HEADERDRAGDROP**   Allows headers to be rearranged by the user using drag and drop.

- **LVS_EX_GRIDLINES**   The control draws grid lines around the items in report mode.

- **LVS_EX_SUBITEMIMAGES**   The control displays images in the subitem columns in report mode.

- **LVS_EX_FULLROWSELECT**   The control highlights the item's entire row in report mode when that item is selected.

- **LVS_EX_ONECLICKACTIVATE**   The control activates an item with a single tap instead of requiring a double tap.

Aside from the *LVS_EX_CHECKBOXES* and *LVS_EX_ONECLICKACTIVATE* extended styles, which work in all display modes, these new styles all affect the actions of the list view when in report mode. The effort here has clearly been to make the list view control an excellent control for displaying large lists of data.

Note that the list view control under Windows CE doesn't support other extended list view styles, such as *LVS_EX_INFOTIP*, *LVS_EX_ONECLICKACTIVATE*, *LVS_EX_TWOCLICKACTIVATE*, *LVS_EX_TRACKSELECT*, *LVS_EX_REGIONAL*, or *LVS_EX_FLATSB*, supported in some versions of the common control library.

Virtual List View

The virtual list view mode of the list view control is a huge help for Windows CE devices. In this mode, the list view control tracks only the selection and focus state of the items. The application maintains all the other data for the items in the control. This mode is handy for two reasons. First, virtual list view controls are fast. The initialization of the control is almost instantaneous because all that's required is that you set the number of items in the control. The list view control also gives you hints about what items it will be looking for in the near term. This allows applications to cache necessary data in RAM and leave the remainder of the data in a database or file. Without a virtual list view, an application would have to load an entire database or list of items in the list view when it's initialized. With the virtual list view, the application loads only what the control requires to display at any one time.

The second advantage of the virtual list view is RAM savings. Because the virtual list view control maintains little information on each item, the control doesn't keep a huge data array in RAM to support the data. The application manages what data is in RAM with some help from the virtual list view's cache hint mechanism.

The virtual list view has some limitations. The *LVS_OWNERDATA* style that designates a virtual list view can't be set or cleared after the control has been created. Also, virtual list views don't support drag and drop in large icon or small icon mode. A virtual list view defaults to *LVS_AUTOARRANGE* style, and the *LVM_SETITEMPOSITION* message isn't supported. In addition, the sort styles *LVS_SORTASCENDING* and *LVS_SORTDESCENDING* aren't supported. Even so, the ability to store large lists of items is handy.

To implement a virtual list view, an application needs to create a list view control with an *LVS_OWNERDATA* style and handle these three notifications— *LVN_GETDISPINFO*, *LVN_ODCACHEHINT*, and *LVN_ODFINDITEM*. The *LVN_GETDISPINFO* notification should be familiar to those of you who have programmed list view controls before. It has always been sent when the list view control needed information to display an item. In the virtual list view, it's used in a similar manner, but the notification is sent to gather all the information about every item in the control.

The virtual list view lets you know what data items it needs using the *LVN_ODCACHEHINT* notification. This notification passes the starting and ending index of items that the control expects to make use of in the near term. An application can take its cue from this set of numbers to load a cache of those items so that they can be quickly accessed. The hints tend to be requests for the items about to be displayed in the control. Because the number of items can change from view to view in the control, it's helpful that the control tracks this instead of having the application guess which items are going to be needed. Because the control often also needs information about the first and last pages of items, it also helps to cache them so that the frequent requests for those items don't clear the main cache of items that will be needed again soon.

The final notification necessary to manage a virtual list view is the *LVN_ODFINDITEM* notification. This is sent by the control when it needs to locate an item in response to a key press or in response to an *LVM_FINDITEM* message.

In Chapter 9, the virtual list view control is demonstrated in the AlbumDB example. Check out that source to see how the virtual list view is used in practice.

The CapEdit Control

The CapEdit control is an edit box that capitalizes the first letter in the first or every word in the control. This control is great for edit controls that will receive proper names but are on keyboardless devices, where tapping the Shift key isn't convenient for the user.

To create the CapEdit control, create a window with the *WC_CAPEDIT* class name. Since CapEdit uses the edit control's window procedure for its base function, you can configure the control like an edit control by sending it standard edit control messages. The only message that's unique to this control is *CEM_UPCASEALLWORDS*. If *wParam* isn't 0, the control will capitalize the first letter in every word. Sending this message with *wParam* equal to 0 will cause the control to capitalize only the first word in the control.

Other Common Controls

Windows CE supports a number of other common controls available under Windows XP. Most of these controls are supported completely within the limits of the capability of Windows CE. For example, while the tab control supports vertical tabs, Windows CE supports vertical text only on systems that support TrueType fonts. For systems supporting raster fonts, the text in the tabs must be manually generated by the Windows CE application by rotating bitmap images of each letter. Frankly, it's probably much easier to devise a dialog box that doesn't need vertical tabs. Short descriptions of the other supported common controls follow.

The Status Bar Control

The status bar is carried over unchanged from the desktop versions of Windows. General user interface guidelines advise against using this control on small-screen devices. The status bar simply takes up too much precious screen space. If the control is used, the user should be able to optionally hide the status bar.

The Tab Control

The tab control is fully supported, the previously mentioned vertical text limitation notwithstanding. The *TCS_HOTTRACK* style that highlighted tabs under the cursor isn't supported. The *TCS_EX_REGISTERDROP* extended style is also not supported.

The Trackbar Control

The trackbar control gains the capacity for two "buddy" controls that are automatically updated with the trackbar value. The trackbar also supports the custom draw service, providing separate item drawing indications for the channel, the thumb, and the tick marks.

The Progress Bar Control

The progress bar includes the latest support for vertical progress bars and 32-bit ranges. This control also supports the new smooth progression instead of moving the progress indicator in discrete chunks.

The Up-Down Control

The up-down control under Windows CE supports only edit controls for its buddy control.

The Toolbar Control

The Windows CE toolbar supports tooltips differently from the way tooltips are supported by the desktop versions of this control. You add toolbar support for tooltips in Windows CE the same way you do for the command bar, by passing a pointer to a permanently allocated array of strings. The toolbar also supports the transparent and flat styles that are supported by the command bar.

The Tree View Control

The tree view control supports two new styles recently added to the tree view common control: *TVS_CHECKBOXES* and *TVS_SINGLESEL*. The *TVS_CHECKBOXES* style places a check box adjacent to each item in the control. The *TVS_SINGLESEL* style causes a previously expanded item to close up when a new item is selected. The tree view control also supports the custom draw service. The tree view control doesn't support the *TVS_TRACKSELECT* style, which allows you to highlight an item when the cursor hovers over it.

Unsupported Common Controls

Windows CE doesn't support four common controls seen under other versions of Windows. The animation control, the drag list control, the hot key control, and, sadly, the rich edit control are all unsupported. Animation would be hard to support given the slower processors often seen running Windows CE. The hot key control is problematic in that keyboard layouts and key labels, standardized on the PC, vary dramatically on the different hardware that runs Windows CE. And the drag list control isn't that big a loss, given the improved power of the report style of the list view control.

The rich edit control is another story. Although not formally supported, Riched20.dll is on Windows CE platforms that have Pocket Word. The only supported alternative is the rich ink control supported on the H/PC and Pocket PC. This control provides text and ink input. It also converts Rich Text Format (RTF) and Pocket Word Ink (PWI) files to ASCII text.

Windows CE supports fairly completely the common control library seen under other versions of Windows. The date and time picker, month calendar, and command bar are a great help given the target audience of Windows CE devices.

Now that both the basic window controls and the common controls have been covered, it's time to look at where they're most often used—dialog boxes. Dialog boxes free you from having to create and maintain controls in a window. Let's see how it's done.

6

Dialog Boxes and Property Sheets

The CtlView example in Chapter 4 demonstrated how controls can be used to create quite complex user interfaces. The problem with that example, though, was that CtlView also contains a fair amount of code to create and manage the controls, code that you won't find in most Windows applications. Most Windows applications don't manage their child controls manually. Instead, *dialog boxes* are used. Dialog boxes are windows that typically use a predefined window class and a different default window procedure. The combination of the window class and the default window procedure, along with a set of special dialog box creation functions, hides the complexity of creating and managing the control windows.

Dialog boxes (sometimes simply referred to as *dialogs*) query data from the user or present data to the user—hence the term *dialog* box. A specialized form of dialog, named a *property sheet*, allows a program to display multiple but related dialog boxes in an overlapping style; each box or property sheet is equipped with an identifying tab. Property sheets are particularly valuable given the tiny screens associated with many Windows CE devices.

Windows CE also supports a subset of the common dialog library available under Windows XP. Specifically, Windows CE supports versions of the common dialog boxes File Open, File Save, Color, and Print. These dialogs are somewhat different on Windows CE. They're reformatted for the smaller screens and aren't as extensible as their desktop counterparts.

Dialog Boxes

Dialog boxes are windows created by Windows using a template provided by an application. The template describes the type and placement of the controls in the window. The Dialog Manager—the part of Windows that creates and manages dialog boxes—also provides default functionality for switching focus between the controls using the Tab key as well as default actions for the Enter and Escape keys. In addition, Windows provides a default dialog box window class, freeing applications from the necessity of registering a window class for each of the dialog boxes it might create.

Dialog boxes come in two types: *modal* and *modeless*. A modal dialog prevents the user from using the application until the dialog box has been dismissed. For example, the File Open and Print dialog boxes are modal. A modeless dialog box can be used interactively with the remainder of the application. The Find dialog box in Microsoft Pocket Word is modeless; the user doesn't need to dismiss it before typing in the main window.

Like other windows, dialog boxes have a window procedure, although the dialog box window procedure is constructed somewhat differently from standard windows procedures. Rather than passing unprocessed messages to the *DefWindowProc* procedure for default processing, a dialog box procedure returns *TRUE* if it processed the message and *FALSE* if it didn't process the message. Windows supplies a default procedure, *DefDialogProc*, for use in specific cases—that is, for specialized modeless dialog boxes that have their own window classes.

Dialog Box Resource Templates

Most of the time, the description for the size and placement of the dialog box and for the controls is provided via a resource called a *dialog template*. You can create a dialog template in memory, but unless a program has an overriding need to format the size and shape of the dialog box on the fly, loading a dialog template directly from a resource is a much better choice. As is the case for other resources such as menus, dialog templates are contained in the resource (RC) file. The template is referenced by the application using either its name or its resource ID.

Figure 6-1 shows a dialog box. This dialog box will be used as an example throughout the discussion of how a dialog box works.

Figure 6-1   A simple dialog box

The dialog template for the dialog box in Figure 6-1 is shown here:

```
GetVal DIALOG discardable 10, 10, 75, 60
STYLE  WS_POPUP | WS_VISIBLE | WS_CAPTION | WS_SYSMENU | DS_CENTER
EXSTYLE WS_EX_CAPTIONOKBTN
CAPTION "Enter line number"
BEGIN
    LTEXT "Enter &value:"  IDD_VALLABEL,   5,  10,  40,  12
    EDITTEXT                IDD_VALUE,  50,  10,  20,  12, WS_TABSTOP
    AUTORADIOBUTTON "&Decimal", IDD_DEC,   5,  25,  60,  12,
                    WS_TABSTOP | WS_GROUP
    AUTORADIOBUTTON "&Hex",      IDD_HEX,   5,  40,  60,  12
END
```

The syntax for a dialog template follows a simple pattern similar to that for a menu resource. First is the name or ID of the resource followed by the keyword *DIALOG* identifying that what follows is a dialog template. The optional *discardable* keyword is followed by the position and size of the dialog box. The position specified is, by default, relative to the owner window of the dialog box.

The units of measurement in a dialog box aren't pixels but *dialog units*. A dialog unit is defined as one-quarter of the average width of the characters in the system font for horizontal units and one-eighth of the height of one character from the same font for vertical units. The goal is to create a unit of measurement independent of the display technology; in practice, dialog boxes still need to be tested in all display resolutions in which the box might be displayed. You can compute a pixel vs. dialog unit conversion using the *GetDialogBaseUnits* function, but you'll rarely find it necessary. The visual tools that come with most compilers these days isolate a programmer from terms such as *dialog units*, but it's still a good idea to know just how dialog boxes are described in an RC file.

The *STYLE* line of code specifies the style flags for the dialog box. The styles include the standard window (*WS_xx*) style flags used for windows as well as a series of dialog (*DS_xx*) style flags specific to dialog boxes. Windows CE supports the following dialog box styles:

- **DS_ABSALIGN** Places the dialog box relative to the upper left corner of the screen instead of basing the position on the owner window.

- **DS_CENTER** Centers the dialog box vertically and horizontally on the screen.

- **DS_MODALFRAME** Creates a dialog box with a modal dialog box frame that can be combined with a title bar and System menu by specifying the *WS_CAPTION* and *WS_SYSMENU* styles.

- **DS_SETFONT** Tells Windows to use a nondefault font that is specified in the dialog template.

- **DS_SETFOREGROUND** Brings the dialog box to the foreground after it's created. If an application not in the foreground displays a dialog box, this style forces the dialog box to the top of the Z-order so that the user will see it.

Most dialog boxes are created with at least some combination of the *WS_POPUP*, *WS_CAPTION*, and *WS_SYSMENU* style flags. The *WS_POPUP* flag indicates that the dialog box is a top-level window. The *WS_CAPTION* style gives the dialog box a title bar. A title bar allows the user to drag the dialog box around as well as serving as a site for title text for the dialog box. The *WS_SYSMENU* style causes the dialog box to have a Close button on the right end of the title bar, thus eliminating the need for a command bar control to provide the Close button. Note that Windows CE uses this flag differently from other versions of Windows, in which the flag indicates that a system menu is to be placed on the left end of the title bar.

The *EXSTYLE* line of code specifies the extended style flags for the dialog box. For Windows CE, these flags are particularly important. The *WS_EX_CAPTIONOKBTN* flag tells the dialog manager to place an OK button on the title bar to the immediate left of the Close button. Having both OK and Close (or Cancel) buttons on the title bar saves precious space in dialog boxes that are displayed on the small screens typical of Windows CE devices. The *WS_EX_CONTEXTHELP* extended style places a Help button on the title bar to the immediate left of the OK button. Clicking on this button results in a *WM_HELP* message being sent to the dialog box procedure.

The *CAPTION* line of code specifies the title bar text of the dialog, provided that the *WS_CAPTION* style was specified so that the dialog box would have a title bar.

The lines describing the type and placement of the controls in the dialog box are enclosed in *BEGIN* and *END* keywords. Each control is specified either by a particular keyword, in the case of commonly used controls, or by the keyword *CONTROL*, which is a generic placeholder that can specify any window class to be placed in the dialog box. The *LTEXT* line of code on the previous page specifies a static left-justified text control. The keyword is followed by the default text for the control in quotes. The next parameter is the ID of the control, which must be unique for the dialog box. In this template, the ID is a constant defined in an include file that is included by both the resource script and the C or C++ file containing the dialog box procedure.

The next four values are the location and size of the control, in dialog units, relative to the upper left corner of the dialog box. Following that, any explicit style flags can be specified for the control. In the case of the *LTEXT* line, no style flags are necessary, but as you can see, the *EDITTEXT* and first *AUTO-RADIOBUTTON* entries each have style flags specified. Each of the control keywords have subtly different syntax. For example, the *EDITTEXT* line doesn't have a field for default text. The style flags for the individual controls deserve notice. The edit control and the first of the two radio buttons have a *WS_TABSTOP* style. The dialog manager looks for controls with the *WS_TABSTOP* style to determine which control gets focus when the user presses the Tab key. In this example, pressing the Tab key results in focus being switched between the edit control and the first radio button.

The *WS_GROUP* style on the first radio button starts a new group of controls. All the controls following the radio button are grouped together, up to the next control that has the *WS_GROUP* style. Grouping auto radio buttons allows only one radio button at a time to be selected.

Another benefit of grouping is that focus can be changed among the controls within a group by exploiting the cursor keys as well as the Tab key. The first member of a group should have a *WS_TABSTOP* style; this allows the user to tab to the group of controls and then use the cursor keys to switch the focus among the controls in the group.

The *CONTROL* statement isn't used in this example, but it's important and merits some explanation. It's a generic statement that allows inclusion of any window class in a dialog box. It has the following syntax:

```
CONTROL "text", id, class, style, x, y, width, height
    [, extended-style]
```

For this entry, the default text and control ID are similar to the other statements, but the next field, *class*, is new. It specifies the window class of the control you want to place in the dialog box. The *class* field is followed by the *style* flags and then by the location and size of your control. Finally, the CONTROL statement has a field for extended style flags. If you use eMbedded Visual C++ to create a dialog box and look at the resulting RC file using a text editor, you'll see that it uses *CONTROL* statements as well as the more readable *LTEXT*, *EDIT-TEXT*, and *BUTTON* statements. There's no functional difference between an edit control created with a *CONTROL* statement and one created with an *EDIT-TEXT* statement. The *CONTROL* statement is a generic version of the more specific keywords. The *CONTROL* statement also allows inclusion of controls that don't have a special keyword associated with them.

Creating a Dialog Box

Creating and displaying a dialog box is simple; just use one of the many dialog box creation functions. The first two are these:

```
int DialogBox (HANDLE hInstance, LPCTSTR lpTemplate, HWND hWndOwner,
               DLGPROC lpDialogFunc);

int DialogBoxParam (HINSTANCE hInstance, LPCTSTR lpTemplate,
                    HWND hWndOwner, DLGPROC lpDialogFunc,
                    LPARAM dwInitParam);
```

These two functions differ only in *DialogBoxParam*'s additional *LPARAM* parameter, so I'll talk about them at the same time. The first parameter to these functions is the instance handle of the program. The second parameter specifies the name or ID of the resource containing the dialog template. As with other resources, to specify a resource ID instead of a name requires the use of the *MAKEINTRESOURCE* macro.

The third parameter is the handle of the window that will own the dialog box. The owning window isn't the parent of the dialog box because, were that true, the dialog box would be clipped to fit inside the parent. Ownership means instead that the dialog box will be hidden when the owner window is minimized and will always appear above the owner window in the Z-order.

The fourth parameter is a pointer to the dialog box procedure for the dialog box. I'll describe the dialog box procedure shortly. The *DialogBoxParam* function has a fifth parameter, which is a user-defined value that's passed to the dialog box procedure when the dialog box is to be initialized. This helpful value can be used to pass a pointer to a structure of data that can be referenced when your application is initializing the dialog box controls.

Two other dialog box creation functions create modal dialogs. They are the following:

```
int DialogBoxIndirect (HANDLE hInstance, LPDLGTEMPLATE lpTemplate,
                       HWND hWndParent, DLGPROC lpDialogFunc),

int DialogBoxIndirectParam (HINSTANCE hInstance,
                            LPCDLGTEMPLATE DialogTemplate, HWND hWndParent,
                            DLGPROC lpDialogFunc, LPARAM dwInitParam);
```

The difference between these two functions and the two previously described is that these two use a dialog box template in memory to define the dialog box rather than using a resource. This allows a program to dynamically create a dialog box template on the fly. The second parameter to these functions points to a *DLGTEMPLATE* structure, which describes the overall dialog box window, followed by an array of *DLGITEMTEMPLATE* structures defining the individual controls.

When any of these four functions are called, the dialog manager creates a modal dialog box using the template passed. The window that owns the dialog is disabled, and the dialog manager then enters its own internal *GetMessage/DispatchMessage* message processing loop; this loop doesn't exit until the dialog box is destroyed. Because of this, these functions don't return to the caller until the dialog box has been destroyed. The *WM_ENTERIDLE* message that's sent to owner windows in other versions of Windows while the dialog box is displayed isn't supported under Windows CE.

If an application wanted to create a modal dialog box with the template shown above and pass a value to the dialog box procedure, it might call this:

```
DialogBoxParam (hInstance, TEXT ("GetVal"), hWnd, GetValDlgProc,
                0x1234);
```

The *hInstance* and *hWnd* parameters would be the instance handle of the application and the handle of the owner window. The *GetVal* string is the name of the dialog box template, while *GetValDlgProc* is the name of the dialog box procedure. Finally, *0x1234* is an application-defined value. In this case, it might be used to provide a default value in the dialog box.

Dialog Box Procedures

The final component necessary for a dialog box is the dialog box procedure. As in the case of a window procedure, the purpose of the dialog box procedure is to field messages sent to the window—in this case, a dialog box window—and perform the appropriate processing. In fact, a dialog box procedure is simply a special case of a window procedure, although we should pay attention to a few differences between the two.

The first difference, as mentioned in the previous section, is that a dialog box procedure doesn't pass unprocessed messages to *DefWindowProc*. Instead, the procedure returns *TRUE* for messages it processes and *FALSE* for messages that it doesn't process. The dialog manager uses this return value to determine whether the message needs to be passed to the default dialog box procedure.

The second difference from standard window procedures is the addition of a new message, *WM_INITDIALOG*. Dialog box procedures perform any initialization of the controls during the processing of this message. Also, if the dialog box was created with *DialogBoxParam* or *DialogBoxIndirectParam*, the *lParam* value is the generic parameter passed during the call that created the dialog box. While it might seem that the controls could be initialized during the *WM_CREATE* message, that doesn't work. The problem is that during the *WM_CREATE* message, the controls on the dialog box haven't yet been created, so they can't be initialized. The *WM_INITDIALOG* message is sent after the controls have been created and before the dialog box is made visible, which is the perfect time to initialize the controls.

Here are a few other minor differences between a window procedure and a dialog box procedure. Most dialog box procedures don't need to process the *WM_PAINT* message because any necessary painting is done by the controls or, in the case of owner-draw controls, in response to control requests. Most of the code in a dialog box procedure is responding to *WM_COMMAND* messages from the controls. As with menus, the *WM_COMMAND* messages are parsed by the control ID values. Two special predefined ID values that a dialog box has to deal with are *IDOK* and *IDCANCEL*. *IDOK* is assigned to the OK button on the title bar of the dialog box, while *IDCANCEL* is assigned to the Close button. In response to a click of either button, a dialog box procedure should call

```
BOOL EndDialog (HWND hDlg, int nResult);
```

EndDialog closes the dialog box and returns control to the caller of whatever function created the dialog box. The *hDlg* parameter is the handle of the dialog box, while the *nResult* parameter is the value that's passed back as the return value of the function that created the dialog box.

The difference, of course, between handling the *IDOK* and *IDCANCEL* buttons is that if the OK button is clicked, the dialog box procedure should collect any relevant data from the dialog box controls to return to the calling procedure before it calls *EndDialog*.

A dialog box procedure to handle the *GetVal* template previously described is shown here:

```
//======================================================================
// GetVal Dialog procedure
//
BOOL CALLBACK GetValDlgProc (HWND hWnd, UINT wMsg, WPARAM wParam,
                            LPARAM lParam) {
    TCHAR szText[64];
    int nVal, nBase;

    switch (wMsg) {
    case WM_INITDIALOG:
        SetDlgItemInt (hWnd, IDD_VALUE, 0, TRUE);
        SendDlgItemMessage (hWnd, IDD_VALUE, EM_LIMITTEXT,
                            sizeof (szText)-1, 0);
        CheckRadioButton (hWnd, IDD_DEC, IDD_HEX, IDD_DEC);
        return TRUE;

    case WM_COMMAND:
        switch (LOWORD (wParam)) {

        case IDD_HEX:
        // See if Hex already checked.
        if (SendDlgItemMessage (hWnd, IDD_HEX,
                    BM_GETSTATE, 0, 0) == BST_CHECKED)
             return TRUE;

            // Get text from edit control.
            GetDlgItemText (hWnd, IDD_VALUE, szText, sizeof (szText));
            // Convert value from decimal, and then set as hex.
            if (ConvertValue (szText, 10, &nVal)) {
                // If conversion successful, set new value.
                wsprintf (szText, TEXT ("%X"), nVal);
                     SetDlgItemText (hWnd, IDD_VALUE, szText);
                // Set radio button.
                CheckRadioButton (hWnd, IDD_DEC, IDD_HEX, IDD_HEX);
            } else {
                MessageBox (hWnd, TEXT ("Value not valid"),
                        TEXT ("Error"), MB_OK);
            }
            return TRUE;

        case IDD_DEC:
            // See if Decimal already checked.
            if (SendDlgItemMessage (hWnd, IDD_DEC,
                            BM_GETSTATE, 0, 0) == BST_CHECKED)
                 return TRUE;

            // Get text from edit control.
            GetDlgItemText (hWnd, IDD_VALUE, szText, sizeof (szText));
```

(continued)

```
            // Convert value from hex, then set as decimal.
            if (ConvertValue (szText, 16, &nVal)) {
                // If conversion successful, set new value.
                wsprintf (szText, TEXT ("%d"), nVal);
                SetDlgItemText (hWnd, IDD_VALUE, szText);
                // Set radio button.
                CheckRadioButton (hWnd, IDD_DEC, IDD_HEX, IDD_DEC);
            } else {
                // If bad conversion, tell user.
                MessageBox (hWnd, TEXT ("Value not valid"),
                            TEXT ("Error"), MB_OK);
            }
            return TRUE;
        case IDOK:
            // Get the current text.
            GetDlgItemText (hWnd, IDD_VALUE, szText, sizeof (szText));
            // See which radio button checked.
            if (SendDlgItemMessage (hWnd, IDD_DEC,
                                    BM_GETSTATE, 0, 0) == BST_CHECKED)
                nBase = 10;
            else
                nBase = 16;
            // Convert the string to a number.
            if (ConvertValue (szText, nBase, &nVal))
                EndDialog (hWnd, nVal);
            else
                MessageBox (hWnd, TEXT ("Value not valid"),
                            TEXT ("Error"), MB_OK);
            break;

        case IDCANCEL:
            EndDialog (hWnd, 0);
            return TRUE;
        }
        break;
    }
    return FALSE;
}
```

This is a typical example of a dialog box procedure for a simple dialog box. The only messages that are processed are the *WM_INITDIALOG* and *WM_COMMAND* messages. The *WM_INITDIALOG* message is used to initialize the edit control using a number passed, via *DialogBoxParam*, through to the *lParam* value. The radio button controls aren't auto radio buttons because the dialog box procedure needs to prevent the buttons from changing if the value in the entry field is invalid. The *WM_COMMAND* message is parsed by the control ID, where the appropriate processing takes place. The *IDOK* and *IDCANCEL* buttons aren't in the dialog box template; as mentioned earlier, those buttons are placed by the dialog manager in the title bar of the dialog box.

Modeless Dialog Boxes

I've talked so far about modal dialog boxes that prevent the user from using other parts of the application before the dialog box is dismissed. Modeless dialog boxes, on the other hand, allow the user to work with other parts of the application while the dialog box is still open. Creating and using modeless dialog boxes requires a bit more work. For example, you create modeless dialog boxes using different functions than those for modal dialog boxes:

```
HWND CreateDialog (HINSTANCE hInstance, LPCTSTR lpTemplate,
               HWND hWndOwner, DLGPROC lpDialogFunc);

HWND CreateDialogParam (HINSTANCE hInstance, LPCDLGTEMPLATE lpTemplate,
               HWND hWndOwner, DLGPROC lpDialogFunc,
               LPARAM lParamInit);

HWND CreateDialogIndirect (HINSTANCE hInstance,
                   LPCDLGTEMPLATE lpTemplate, HWND hWndOwner,
                   DLGPROC lpDialogFunc);
```

or

```
HWND CreateDialogIndirectParam (HINSTANCE hInstance,
                   LPCDLGTEMPLATE lpTemplate, HWND hWndOwner,
                   DLGPROC lpDialogFunc, LPARAM lParamInit);
```

The parameters in these functions mirror the creation functions for the modal dialog boxes with similar parameters. The difference is that these functions return immediately after creating the dialog boxes. Each function returns 0 if the create failed or returns the handle to the dialog box window if the create succeeded.

The handle returned after a successful creation is important because applications that use modeless dialog boxes must modify their message loop code to accommodate the dialog box. The new message loop should look similar to the following:

```
while (GetMessage (&msg, NULL, 0, 0)) {
    if ((hMlDlg == 0) || (!IsDialogMessage (hMlDlg, &msg))) {
        TranslateMessage (&msg);
        DispatchMessage (&msg);
    }
}
```

The difference from a modal dialog box message loop is that if the modeless dialog box is being displayed, messages should be checked to see whether they're dialog messages. If they're not dialog messages, your application forwards them to *TranslateMessage* and *DispatchMessage*. The code shown above simply checks to see whether the dialog box exists by checking a global variable containing the handle to the modeless dialog box and, if it's not 0, calls *IsDialogMessage*. If *IsDialogMessage* doesn't translate and dispatch the message itself, the message is sent to the standard *TranslateMessage/DispatchMessage* body of the message loop. Of course, this code assumes that the handle returned by *CreateDialog* (or whatever function creates the dialog box) is saved in *hMlDlg* and that *hMlDlg* is set to 0 when the dialog box is closed.

Another difference between modal and modeless dialog boxes is in the dialog box procedure. Instead of using *EndDialog* to close the dialog box, you must call *DestroyWindow* instead. This is because *EndDialog* is designed to work only with the internal message loop processing that's performed with a modal dialog box. Finally, an application usually won't want more than one instance of a modeless dialog box displayed at a time. An easy way to prevent this is to check the global copy of the window handle to see whether it's nonzero before calling *CreateDialog*. To do this, the dialog box procedure must set the global handle to 0 after it calls *DestroyWindow*.

Property Sheets

To the user, a property sheet is a dialog box with one or more tabs across the top that allow the user to switch among different "pages" of the dialog box. To the programmer, a property sheet is a series of stacked dialog boxes. Only the top dialog box is visible; the dialog manager is responsible for displaying the dialog box associated with the tab on which the user clicks. However you approach property sheets, they're invaluable given the limited screen size of Windows CE devices.

Each page of the property sheet, named appropriately enough a *property page*, is a dialog box template, either loaded from a resource or created dynamically in memory. Each property page has its own dialog box procedure. The frame around the property sheets is maintained by the dialog manager, so the advantages of property sheets come with little overhead to the programmer. Unlike the property sheets supported in other versions of Windows, the property sheets in Windows CE don't support the Apply button. Also, the OK and Cancel buttons for the property sheet are contained in the title bar, not positioned below the pages.

Creating a Property Sheet

Instead of the dialog box creation functions, use this new function to create a property sheet:

```
int PropertySheet (LPCPROPSHEETHEADER lppsph);
```

The *PropertySheet* function creates the property sheet according to the information contained in the *PROPSHEETHEADER* structure, which is defined as the following:

```
typedef struct _PROPSHEETHEADER {
    DWORD dwSize;
    DWORD dwFlags;
    HWND hwndOwner;
    HINSTANCE hInstance;
     union {
        HICON hIcon;
        LPCWSTR pszIcon;
    };
    LPCWSTR pszCaption;
    UINT nPages;
    union {
        UINT nStartPage;
        LPCWSTR pStartPage;
    };
    union {
        LPCPROPSHEETPAGE ppsp;
        HPROPSHEETPAGE FAR *phpage;
    };
    PFNPROPSHEETCALLBACK pfnCallback;
} PROPSHEETHEADER;
```

Filling in this convoluted structure isn't as imposing a task as it might look. The *dwSize* field is the standard size field that must be initialized with the size of the structure. The *dwFlags* field contains the creation flags that define how the property sheet is created, which fields of the structure are valid, and how the property sheet behaves. Some of the flags indicate which fields in the structure are used. (I'll talk about those flags when I describe the other fields.) Two other flags set the behavior of the property sheet. The *PSH_PROPTITLE* flag appends the string "Properties" to the end of the caption specified in the *pszCaption* field. The *PSH_MODELESS* flag causes the *PropertySheet* function to create a modeless property sheet and immediately return. A modeless property sheet is like a modeless dialog box; it allows the user to switch back to the original window while the property sheet is still being displayed.

The next two fields are the handle of the owner window and the instance handle of the application. Neither the *hIcon* nor the *pszIcon* field is used in Windows CE, so both fields should be set to 0. The *pszCaption* field should point to the title bar text for the property sheet. The *nStartPage/pStartPage* union should be set to indicate the page that should be initially displayed. This can be selected either by number or by title if the *PSH_USEPSTARTPAGE* flag is set in the *dwFlags* field.

The *ppsp/phpage* union points to either an array of *PROPSHEETPAGE* structures describing each of the property pages or handles to previously created property pages. For either of these, the *nPages* field must be set to the number of entries of the array of structures or page handles. To indicate that the pointer points to an array of *PROPSHEETPAGE* structures, set the *PSH_PROPSHEETPAGE* flag in the *dwFlags* field. I'll describe both the structure and how to create individual pages shortly.

The *pfnCallBack* field is an optional pointer to a procedure that's called twice—when the property sheet is about to be created and again when it's about to be initialized. The callback function allows applications to fine-tune the appearance of the property sheet. This field is ignored unless the *PSP_USECALLBACK* flag is set in the *dwFlags* field. One place the callback is used is in Pocket PC applications, to place the tabs on the bottom of the property sheet.

The callback procedure should be defined to match the following prototype:

```
UINT CALLBACK PropSheetPageProc (HWND hwnd, UINT uMsg,
                        LPPROPSHEETPAGE ppsp);
```

The parameters sent back to the application are a handle value documented to be reserved, the notification code in the *uMsg* parameter, and, in some notifications, a pointer to a *PROPSHEETPAGE* structure. The notifications supported in Windows CE are as follows:

- **PSCB_PRECREATE**   Sent just before the property sheet is created

- **PSCB_INITIALIZED**   Sent when the property sheet is initialized

- **PSCB_GETVERSION**   Sent to query the level of support expected by the application

- **PSCB_GETTITLE**   Sent to query additional title text

- **PSCB_GETLINKTEXT**   On Pocket PC, sent to query the string to place below the tabbed pages on the property sheet

Creating a Property Page

As I mentioned earlier, individual property pages can be specified by an array of *PROPSHEETPAGE* structures or an array of handles to existing property pages. Creating a property page is accomplished with a call to the following:

```
HPROPSHEETPAGE CreatePropertySheetPage (LPCPROPSHEETPAGE lppsp);
```

This function is passed a pointer to the same *PROPSHEETPAGE* structure and returns a handle to a property page. *PROPSHEETPAGE* is defined as this:

```
typedef struct _PROPSHEETPAGE {
    DWORD dwSize;
    DWORD dwFlags;
    HINSTANCE hInstance;
    union {
        LPCSTR pszTemplate;
        LPCDLGTEMPLATE pResource;
    };
    union {
        HICON hIcon;
        LPCSTR pszIcon;
    };
    LPCSTR pszTitle;
    DLGPROC pfnDlgProc;
    LPARAM lParam;
    LPFNPSPCALLBACK pfnCallback;
    UINT FAR * pcRefParent;
} PROPSHEETPAGE;
```

The structure looks similar to the *PROPSHEETHEADER* structure, leading with a *dwSize* and a *dwFlags* field followed by an *hInstance* field. In this structure, *hInstance* is the handle of the module from which the resources will be loaded. The *dwFlags* field again specifies which fields of the structure are used and how they're used, as well as a few flags specifying the characteristics of the page itself.

The *pszTemplate/pResource* union specifies the dialog box template used to define the page. If the *PSP_DLGINDIRECT* flag is set in the *dwFlags* field, the union points to a dialog box template in memory. Otherwise, the field specifies the name of a dialog box resource. The *hIcon/pszIcon* union isn't used in Windows CE and should be set to 0. If the *dwFlags* field contains a *PSP_USETITLE* flag, the *pszTitle* field points to the text used on the tab for the page. Otherwise, the tab text is taken from the caption field in the dialog box template. The *pfnDlgProc* field points to the dialog box procedure for this specific page, and the *lParam* field is an application-defined parameter that can be used to pass data to the dialog box procedure. The *pfnCallback* field can point to a callback procedure that's called twice—when the page is about to be created and when it's about to be destroyed. Again, like the callback for the property sheet, the property page callback allows applications to fine-tune the page characteristics. This field is ignored unless the *dwFlags* field contains the *PSP_USECALLBACK* flag. Finally, the *pcRefCount* field can contain a pointer to an integer that will store a reference count for the page. This field is ignored unless the flags field contains the *PSP_USEREFPARENT* flag.

Windows CE supports the *PSP_PREMATURE* flag, which causes a property page to be created when the property sheet that owns it is created. Normally, a property page isn't created until the first time it's shown. This has an impact on property pages that communicate and cooperate with each other. Without the *PSP_PREMATURE* flag, the only property page that's automatically created when the property sheet is created is the page that is displayed first. So at that moment, that first page has no sibling pages to communicate with. Using the *PSP_PREMATURE* flag, you can ensure that a page is created when the property sheet is created, even though it isn't the first page in the sheet. Although it's easy to get overwhelmed by all these structures, simply using the default values and not using the optional fields results in a powerful and easily maintainable property sheet that's also as easy to construct as a set of individual dialog boxes.

Once a property sheet has been created, the application can add and delete pages. The application adds a page by sending a *PSM_ADDPAGE* message to the property sheet window. The message must contain the handle of a previously created property page in *lParam*; *wParam* isn't used. Likewise, the application can remove a page by sending a *PSM_REMOVEPAGE* message to the property sheet window. The application specifies a page for deletion either by setting *wParam* to the zero-based index of the page selected for removal or by passing the handle to that page in *lParam*.

The code below creates a simple property sheet with three pages. Each of the pages references a dialog box template resource. As you can see, most of the initialization of the structures can be performed in a fairly mechanical fashion.

```
PROPSHEETHEADER psh;
PROPSHEETPAGE psp[3];
int i;
// Initialize page structures with generic information.
memset (&psp, 0, sizeof (psp));    // Zero out all unused values.
for (i = 0; i < dim(psp); i++) {
    psp[i].dwSize = sizeof (PROPSHEETPAGE);
    psp[i].dwFlags = PSP_DEFAULT;    // No special processing needed
    psp[i].hInstance = hInst;        // Instance handle where the
}                                    // dialog templates are located
// Now do the page-specific stuff.
psp[0].pszTemplate = TEXT ("Page1"); // Name of dialog resource for page 1
```

```
psp[0].pfnDlgProc = Page1DlgProc;    // Pointer to dialog proc for page 1

psp[1].pszTemplate = TEXT ("Page2"); // Name of dialog resource for page 2
psp[1].pfnDlgProc = Page2DlgProc;    // Pointer to dialog proc for page 2

psp[2].pszTemplate = TEXT ("Page3"); // Name of dialog resource for page 3
psp[2].pfnDlgProc = Page3DlgProc;    // Pointer to dialog proc for page 3

// Init property sheet header structure.
psh.dwSize = sizeof (PROPSHEETHEADER);
psh.dwFlags = PSH_PROPSHEETPAGE;      // We are using templates, not handles.
psh.hwndParent = hWnd;                // Handle of the owner window
psh.hInstance = hInst;                // Instance handle of the application
psh.pszCaption = TEXT ("Property sheet title");
psh.nPages = dim(psp);                // Number of pages
psh.nStartPage = 0;                   // Index of page to be shown first
psh.ppsp = psp;                       // Pointer to page structures
psh.pfnCallback = 0;                  // We don't need a callback procedure.

// Create property sheet.  This returns when the user dismisses the sheet
// by tapping OK or the Close button.
i = PropertySheet (&psh);
```

While this fragment has a fair amount of structure filling, it's boilerplate code. Everything not defined, such as the page dialog box resource templates and the page dialog box procedures, is required for dialog boxes as well as property sheets. So aside from the boilerplate stuff, property sheets require little, if any, work beyond simple dialog boxes.

Property Page Procedures

The procedures that back up each of the property pages differ in only a few ways from standard dialog box procedures. First, as I mentioned previously, unless the *PSP_PREMATURE* flag is used, pages aren't created immediately when the property sheet is created. Instead, each page is created and *WM_INITDIALOG* messages are sent only when the page is initially shown. Also, the *lParam* parameter doesn't point to a user-defined parameter; instead, it points to the *PROPSHEETPAGE* structure that defined the page. Of course, that structure contains a user-definable value that can be used to pass data to the dialog box procedure.

Also, a property sheet procedure doesn't field the *IDOK* and *IDCANCEL* control IDs for the OK and Close buttons on a standard dialog box. These buttons instead are handled by the system-provided property sheet procedure that coordinates the display and management of each page. When the OK or Close button is tapped, the property sheet sends a *WM_NOTIFY* message to each sheet notifying them that one of the two buttons has been tapped and that they should acknowledge that it's okay to close the property sheet.

Switching Pages

When a user switches from one page to the next, the Dialog Manager sends a *WM_NOTIFY* message with the code *PSN_KILLACTIVE* to the page currently being displayed. The dialog box procedure should then validate the data on the page. If it's permissible for the user to change the page, the dialog box procedure should then set the return value of the window structure of the page to *PSNRET_NOERROR* and return *TRUE*. You set the *PSNRET_NOERROR* return field by calling *SetWindowLong* with *DWL_MSGRESULT*, as in the following line of code:

```
SetWindowLong (hwndPage, DWL_MSGRESULT, PSNRET_NOERROR);
```

where *hwndPage* is the handle of the property sheet page. A page can keep focus by returning *PSNRET_INVALID_NOCHANGEPAGE* in the return field. Assuming a page has indicated that it's okay to lose focus, the page being switched to receives a *PSN_SETACTIVE* notification via a *WM_NOTIFY* message. The page can then accept the focus or specify another page that should receive the focus.

Closing a Property Sheet

When the user taps on the OK button, the property sheet procedure sends a *WM_NOTIFY* with the notification code *PSN_KILLACTIVE* to the page currently being displayed, followed by a *WM_NOTIFY* with the notification code *PSN_APPLY* to each of the pages that have been created. Each page procedure should save any data from the page controls when it receives the *PSN_APPLY* notification code.

When the user clicks the Close button, a *PSN_QUERYCANCEL* notification is sent to the page procedure of the page currently being displayed. All this notification requires is that the page procedure return *TRUE* to prevent the close or *FALSE* to allow the close. A further notification, *PSN_RESET*, is then sent to all the pages that have been created, indicating that the property sheet is about to be destroyed.

Common Dialogs

In the early days of Windows, it was a rite of passage for a Windows developer to write his or her own File Open dialog box. A File Open dialog box is complex—it must display a list of the possible files from a specific directory, allow file navigation, and return a fully justified filename back to the application. While it was great for programmers to swap stories about how they struggled with their unique implementation of a File Open dialog, it was hard on the users. Users had to learn a different file open interface for every Windows application.

Windows now provides a set of common dialog boxes that perform typical functions, such as selecting a filename to open or save or picking a color. These standard dialog boxes (called *common dialogs*) serve two purposes. First, common dialogs lift from developers the burden of having to create these dialog boxes from scratch. Second, and just as important, common dialogs provide a common interface to the user across different applications. (These days, Windows programmers swap horror stories about learning COM.)

Windows CE provides four common dialogs: File Open, Save As, Print, and Choose Color. Common dialogs, such as Find, Choose Font, and Page Setup, that are available under other versions of Windows aren't supported under Windows CE. The other advantage of the common dialogs is that they have a customized look for each platform while retaining the same programming interface. This makes it easy to use, say, the File Open dialog on the Pocket PC, the Smartphone, and embedded versions of Windows CE because the dialog box has the same interface on both systems, even though the look of the dialog box is vastly different on the different platforms. Figure 6-2 shows the File Open dialog on an embedded Windows CE system; Figure 6-3 shows the File Open dialog box on the Pocket PC.

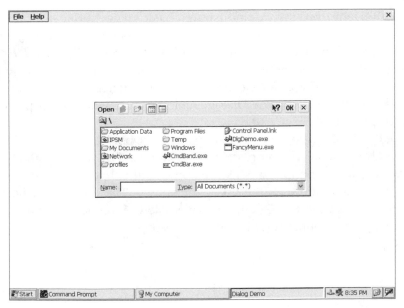

Figure 6-2   The File Open dialog on an embedded Windows CE system

Figure 6-3   The File Open dialog on a Pocket PC

Instead of showing you how to use the common dialogs here, I'll let the next example program, DlgDemo, show you. That program demonstrates all four supported common dialog boxes.

The DlgDemo Example Program

The DlgDemo program demonstrates basic dialog boxes, modeless dialog boxes, property sheets, and common dialogs. When you start DlgDemo, it displays a window that shows the *WM_COMMAND* and *WM_NOTIFY* messages sent by the various controls in the dialogs, similar to the right side of the Ctl-View window. The different dialogs can be opened using the various menu items. Figure 6-4 shows the Dialog Demo window with the property sheet dialog displayed.

The basic dialog box is a simple "about box" launched by selecting the Help About menu. The property sheet is launched by selecting the File Property Sheet menu. The property sheet dialog contains five pages corresponding to the different windows in the CtlView example. The common dialog boxes are launched from the File Open, File Save, File Color, and File Print menu items. The DlgDemo source code is shown in Listing 6-1.

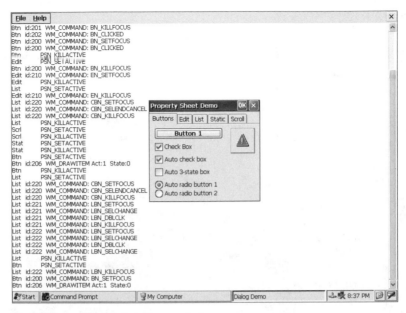

Figure 6-4   The Dialog Demo window

```
DlgDemo.rc
//=====================================================================
// Resource file
//
// Written for the book Programming Windows CE
// Copyright (C) 2003 Douglas Boling
//=====================================================================

#include "windows.h"
#include "DlgDemo.h"                    // Program-specific stuff
#include "commctrl.h"
//---------------------------------------------------------------------
// Icons and bitmaps
//
ID_ICON      ICON   "DlgDemo.ico"    // Program icon
IDI_BTNICON  ICON   "btnicon.ico"    // Bitmap used in owner-draw button
statbmp      BITMAP "statbmp.bmp"    // Bitmap used in static window
```

Listing 6-1   The DlgDemo program   *(continued)*

Listing 6-1   *(continued)*

```
//-----------------------------------------------------------------------
// Menu, the RC data resource is needed by the menu bar
//
ID_MENU RCDATA MOVEABLE PURE
BEGIN
    ID_MENU, 2,
    -2, 100, TBSTATE_ENABLED, TBSTYLE_DROPDOWN|TBSTYLE_AUTOSIZE,5,0,0,
    -2, 101, TBSTATE_ENABLED, TBSTYLE_DROPDOWN|TBSTYLE_AUTOSIZE,3,0,1
END
ID_MENU MENU DISCARDABLE
BEGIN
    POPUP "&File"
    BEGIN
        MENUITEM "Open...",                 IDM_OPEN
        MENUITEM "Save...",                 IDM_SAVE
        MENUITEM SEPARATOR
        MENUITEM "Color...",                IDM_COLOR
        MENUITEM "Print...",                IDM_PRINT
        MENUITEM SEPARATOR
        MENUITEM "Property Sheet",          IDM_SHOWPROPSHEET
        MENUITEM "Modeless Dialog",         IDM_SHOWMODELESS
        MENUITEM SEPARATOR
        MENUITEM "E&xit",                   IDM_EXIT
    END
    POPUP "&Help"
    BEGIN
        MENUITEM "&About...",               IDM_ABOUT
    END
END


//-----------------------------------------------------------------------
// Property page templates
//
ID_BTNPAGE DIALOG discardable 0, 0, 125,  90
CAPTION "Buttons"
BEGIN
    PUSHBUTTON "Button 1",              IDC_PUSHBTN,  5,  5, 80, 12,
                                        WS_TABSTOP | BS_NOTIFY
    CHECKBOX "Check Box",               IDC_CHKBOX,   5, 20, 80, 12,
                                        WS_TABSTOP | BS_NOTIFY
    AUTOCHECKBOX "Auto check box"       IDC_ACHKBOX,  5, 35, 80, 12,
                                        WS_TABSTOP
    AUTO3STATE "Auto 3-state box",      IDC_A3STBOX,  5, 50, 80, 12,
                                        WS_TABSTOP
    AUTORADIOBUTTON "Auto radio button 1",
                                        IDC_RADIO1,   5, 65, 80, 12,
                                        WS_TABSTOP | WS_GROUP
```

```
        AUTORADIOBUTTON "Auto radio button 2",
                                        IDC_RADIO2,    5,  75,  80,  12
        PUSHBUTTON "",                  IDC_OWNRDRAW, 95,   5,  30,  30,
                                        BS_OWNERDRAW
END


ID_EDITPAGE DIALOG discardable 0, 0, 80,  80
CAPTION "Edit"
BEGIN
        EDITTEXT                        IDC_SINGLELINE,   5,   5,  70,  12,
                                        WS_TABSTOP
        EDITTEXT                        IDC_MULTILINE,    5,  20,  70,  40,
                                        WS_TABSTOP | ES_MULTILINE
        EDITTEXT                        IDC_PASSBOX,      5,  65,  70,  12,
                                        WS_TABSTOP | ES_PASSWORD
END


ID_LISTPAGE DIALOG discardable 0, 0,  125,  80
CAPTION "List"
BEGIN
        COMBOBOX                        IDC_COMBOBOX,    5,   5,  70,  60,
                                        WS_TABSTOP | CBS_DROPDOWN
        LISTBOX                         IDC_SNGLELIST,   5,  20,  50,  60,
                                        WS_TABSTOP
        LISTBOX                         IDC_MULTILIST,  60,  20,  50,  60,
                                        WS_TABSTOP | LBS_EXTENDEDSEL
END


ID_STATPAGE DIALOG discardable 0, 0, 130,  80
CAPTION "Static"
BEGIN
        LTEXT "Left text",              IDC_LEFTTEXT,    5,   5,  70,  20
        RTEXT "Right text",             IDC_RIGHTTEXT,   5,  30,  70,  20
        CTEXT "Center text",            IDC_CENTERTEXT,  5,  55,  70,  20,
                                        WS_BORDER
        ICON IDI_BTNICON                IDC_ICONCTL,    95,   5,  32,  32
        CONTROL "statbmp",              IDC_BITMAPCTL,  "static", SS_BITMAP,
                                        95,  40,  32,  32
END
ID_SCROLLPAGE DIALOG discardable 0, 0, 60,  80
CAPTION "Scroll"
BEGIN
        SCROLLBAR                       IDC_LRSCROLL,    5,   5,  70,  12,
                                        WS_TABSTOP
        SCROLLBAR                       IDC_UDSCROLL,   80,   5,  12,  70,
                                        WS_TABSTOP | SBS_VERT
END
```

(continued)

Listing 6-1 *(continued)*

```
//----------------------------------------------------------------------
// Clear list; modeless dialog box template.
//
Clearbox DIALOG discardable 60, 10,  70, 30
STYLE  WS_POPUP | WS_VISIBLE | WS_CAPTION | WS_SYSMENU | DS_MODALFRAME
CAPTION "Clear"
BEGIN
    DEFPUSHBUTTON "Clear Listbox"
                        IDD_CLEAR,   5,   5,  60,   20
END
//----------------------------------------------------------------------
// About box dialog box template
//
aboutbox DIALOG discardable 10, 10, 132, 40
STYLE  WS_POPUP | WS_VISIBLE | WS_CAPTION | WS_SYSMENU | DS_CENTER |
       DS_MODALFRAME
CAPTION "About"
BEGIN
    ICON    ID_ICON                   -1,   5,   5,   0,   0

    LTEXT "DlgDemo - Written for the book Programming Windows \
           CE Copyright 2001 Douglas Boling"
                                      -1,  28,   5, 100,  30
END
```

DlgDemo.h

```
//======================================================================
// Header file
//
// Written for the book Programming Windows CE
// Copyright (C) 2003 Douglas Boling
//======================================================================
// Returns number of elements
#define dim(x) (sizeof(x) / sizeof(x[0]))


//----------------------------------------------------------------------
// Generic defines and data types
//
struct decodeUINT {                          // Structure associates
    UINT Code;                               // messages
                                             // with a function.
    LRESULT (*Fxn)(HWND, UINT, WPARAM, LPARAM);
};
struct decodeCMD {                           // Structure associates
    UINT Code;                               // menu IDs with a
    LRESULT (*Fxn)(HWND, WORD, HWND, WORD);  // function.
};
```

```
//------------------------------------------------------------------
// Generic defines used by application
#define  IDC_CMDBAR             1          // Command bar ID
#define  IDC_RPTLIST            ?          // ID for report list box
#define  ID_ICON                10         // Icon resource ID
#define  ID_MENU                11         // Main menu resource ID

#define  IDM_OPEN               100        // Menu item IDs
#define  IDM_SAVE               101
#define  IDM_COLOR              102
#define  IDM_PRINT              103
#define  IDM_SHOWPROPSHEET      104
#define  IDM_SHOWMODELESS       105
#define  IDM_EXIT               106
#define  IDM_ABOUT              110
#define  IDI_BTNICON            120

// Identifiers for the property page resources
#define  ID_BTNPAGE             50
#define  ID_EDITPAGE            51
#define  ID_LISTPAGE            52
#define  ID_STATPAGE            53
#define  ID_SCROLLPAGE          54

#define  IDC_PUSHBTN            200        // Button defines
#define  IDC_CHKBOX             201
#define  IDC_ACHKBOX            202
#define  IDC_A3STBOX            203
#define  IDC_RADIO1             204
#define  IDC_RADIO2             205
#define  IDC_OWNRDRAW           206

#define  IDC_SINGLELINE         210        // Edit defines
#define  IDC_MULTILINE          211
#define  IDC_PASSBOX            212

#define  IDC_COMBOBOX           220        // List box defines
#define  IDC_SNGLELIST          221
#define  IDC_MULTILIST          222
#define  IDC_LEFTTEXT           230        // Static defines
#define  IDC_RIGHTTEXT          231
#define  IDC_CENTERTEXT         232
#define  IDC_ICONCTL            233
#define  IDC_BITMAPCTL          234

#define  IDC_LRSCROLL           240        // Scroll bar defines
#define  IDC_UDSCROLL           241
```

(continued)

Listing 6-1 *(continued)*

```
// Control IDs for modeless dialog box
#define  IDD_CLEAR        500

// User-defined message to add a line to the window
#define MYMSG_ADDLINE   (WM_USER + 10)


//--------------------------------------------------------------------------
// Program-specific structures
//
typedef struct {
    TCHAR *pszLabel;
    DWORD wNotification;
} NOTELABELS, *PNOTELABELS;
//--------------------------------------------------------------------------
// Function prototypes
//
HWND InitInstance (HINSTANCE, LPWSTR, int);
int TermInstance (HINSTANCE, int);
// Window procedures
LRESULT CALLBACK MainWndProc (HWND, UINT, WPARAM, LPARAM);
// Message handlers
LRESULT DoCreateMain (HWND, UINT, WPARAM, LPARAM);
LRESULT DoCommandMain (HWND, UINT, WPARAM, LPARAM);
LRESULT DoAddLineMain (HWND, UINT, WPARAM, LPARAM);
LRESULT DoDestroyMain (HWND, UINT, WPARAM, LPARAM);
// Command functions
LPARAM DoMainCommandOpen (HWND, WORD, HWND, WORD);
LPARAM DoMainCommandSave (HWND, WORD, HWND, WORD);
LPARAM DoMainCommandColor (HWND, WORD, HWND, WORD);
LPARAM DoMainCommandPrint (HWND, WORD, HWND, WORD);
LPARAM DoMainCommandShowProp (HWND, WORD, HWND, WORD);
LPARAM DoMainCommandModeless (HWND, WORD, HWND, WORD);
LPARAM DoMainCommandExit (HWND, WORD, HWND, WORD);
LPARAM DoMainCommandAbout (HWND, WORD, HWND, WORD);
// Dialog box procedures
BOOL CALLBACK BtnDlgProc (HWND, UINT, WPARAM, LPARAM);
BOOL CALLBACK EditDlgProc (HWND, UINT, WPARAM, LPARAM);
BOOL CALLBACK ListDlgProc (HWND, UINT, WPARAM, LPARAM);
BOOL CALLBACK StaticDlgProc (HWND, UINT, WPARAM, LPARAM);
BOOL CALLBACK ScrollDlgProc (HWND, UINT, WPARAM, LPARAM);
BOOL CALLBACK AboutDlgProc (HWND, UINT, WPARAM, LPARAM);
BOOL CALLBACK ModelessDlgProc (HWND, UINT, WPARAM, LPARAM);
```

DlgDemo.cpp

```
//======================================================================
// DlgDemo - Dialog box demonstration
//
// Written for the book Programming Windows CE
// Copyright (C) 2003 Douglas Boling
//======================================================================
#include <windows.h>                    // For all that Windows stuff
#include <commctrl.h>                   // Command bar includes
#include <commdlg.h>                    // Common dialog box includes
#include <prsht.h>                      // Property sheet includes

#include "DlgDemo.h"                    // Program-specific stuff
#if defined(WIN32_PLATFORM_PSPC)
#include <aygshell.h>                    // Add Pocket PC includes
#pragma comment( lib, "aygshell" )     // Link Pocket PC lib for menu bar
#endif
//----------------------------------------------------------------------
// Global data
//
const TCHAR szAppName[] = TEXT ("DlgDemo");
HINSTANCE hInst;                        // Program instance handle
HWND g_hwndMlDlg = 0;                   // Handle to modeless dialog box

HINSTANCE hLib = 0;                     // Handle to CommDlg lib
typedef BOOL (APIENTRY* LFCHOOSECOLORPROC) (LPCHOOSECOLOR );

#ifndef WIN32_PLATFORM_PSPC
typedef BOOL (APIENTRY* LFPAGESETUPDLG)( LPPAGESETUPDLGW );
LFPAGESETUPDLG lpfnPrintDlg = 0;           // Ptr to print common dialog fn
#else
typedef BOOL (APIENTRY* LFPRINTDLG) (LPPRINTDLG lppsd);
LFPRINTDLG lpfnPrintDlg = 0;            // Ptr to print common dialog fn
#endif
LFCHOOSECOLORPROC lpfnChooseColor = 0;  // Ptr to color common dialog fn

// Message dispatch table for MainWindowProc
const struct decodeUINT MainMessages[] = {
    WM_CREATE, DoCreateMain,
    WM_COMMAND, DoCommandMain,
    MYMSG_ADDLINE, DoAddLineMain,
    WM_DESTROY, DoDestroyMain,
};
```

(continued)

Listing 6-1   *(continued)*

```
// Command message dispatch for MainWindowProc
const struct decodeCMD MainCommandItems[] = {
    IDM_OPEN, DoMainCommandOpen,
    IDM_SAVE, DoMainCommandSave,
    IDM_SHOWPROPSHEET, DoMainCommandShowProp,
    IDM_SHOWMODELESS, DoMainCommandModeless,
    IDM_COLOR, DoMainCommandColor,
    IDM_PRINT, DoMainCommandPrint,
    IDM_EXIT, DoMainCommandExit,
    IDM_ABOUT, DoMainCommandAbout,
};
//
// Labels for WM_NOTIFY notifications
//
NOTELABELS nlPropPage[] = {{TEXT ("PSN_SETACTIVE    "), (PSN_FIRST-0)},
                           {TEXT ("PSN_KILLACTIVE "), (PSN_FIRST-1)},
                           {TEXT ("PSN_APPLY      "), (PSN_FIRST-2)},
                           {TEXT ("PSN_RESET      "), (PSN_FIRST-3)},
                           {TEXT ("PSN_HASHELP    "), (PSN_FIRST-4)},
                           {TEXT ("PSN_HELP       "), (PSN_FIRST-5)},
                           {TEXT ("PSN_WIZBACK    "), (PSN_FIRST-6)},
                           {TEXT ("PSN_WIZNEXT    "), (PSN_FIRST-7)},
                           {TEXT ("PSN_WIZFINISH  "), (PSN_FIRST-8)},
                           {TEXT ("PSN_QUERYCANCEL"), (PSN_FIRST-9)},
};
int nPropPageSize = dim(nlPropPage);

// Labels for the property pages
TCHAR *szPages[] = {TEXT ("Btn "),
                    TEXT ("Edit"),
                    TEXT ("List"),
                    TEXT ("Stat"),
                    TEXT ("Scrl"),
};
//=====================================================================
// Program entry point
//
HWND hwndMain;

int WINAPI WinMain (HINSTANCE hInstance, HINSTANCE hPrevInstance,
                    LPWSTR lpCmdLine, int nCmdShow) {
    MSG msg;
    int rc = 0;

    // Initialize application.
    hwndMain = InitInstance (hInstance, lpCmdLine, nCmdShow);
    if (hwndMain == 0) return 0x10;
```

```
    // Application message loop
    while (GetMessage (&msg, NULL, 0, 0)) {
        // If modeless dialog box is created, let it have
        // the first crack at the message.
        if ((g_hwndMlDlg == 0) ||
            (!IsDialogMessage (g_hwndMlDlg, &msg))) {
            TranslateMessage (&msg);
            DispatchMessage (&msg);
        }
    }
    // Instance cleanup
    return TermInstance (hInstance, msg.wParam);
}
//----------------------------------------------------------------------
// InitInstance - Instance initialization
//
HWND InitInstance (HINSTANCE hInstance, LPWSTR lpCmdLine,
                   int nCmdShow) {
    HWND hWnd;
    WNDCLASS wc;

    // Save program instance handle in global variable.
    hInst = hInstance;

#if defined(WIN32_PLATFORM_PSPC)
    // If Pocket PC, allow only one instance of the application.
    hWnd = FindWindow (szAppName, NULL);
    if (hWnd) {
        SetForegroundWindow ((HWND)(((DWORD)hWnd) | 0x01));
        return 0;
    }
#endif
    // Register application main window class.
    wc.style = 0;                                   // Window style
    wc.lpfnWndProc = MainWndProc;                   // Callback function
    wc.cbClsExtra = 0;                              // Extra class data
    wc.cbWndExtra = 0;                              // Extra window data
    wc.hInstance = hInstance;                       // Owner handle
    wc.hIcon = NULL,                                // Application icon
    wc.hCursor = LoadCursor (NULL, IDC_ARROW);// Default cursor
    wc.hbrBackground = (HBRUSH) GetStockObject (WHITE_BRUSH);
    wc.lpszMenuName =  NULL;                        // Menu name
    wc.lpszClassName = szAppName;                   // Window class name

    if (RegisterClass (&wc) == 0) return 0;
```

(continued)

Listing 6-1   *(continued)*

```
    // Get the Color and print dialog function pointers.
    hLib = LoadLibrary (TEXT ("COMMDLG.DLL"));
    if (hLib) {
        lpfnChooseColor = (LFCHOOSECOLORPROC)GetProcAddress (hLib,
                                               TEXT ("ChooseColor"));#if d
efined(WIN32_PLATFORM_PSPC)
        lpfnPrintDlg = (LFPRINTDLG) GetProcAddress (hLib, TEXT ("PrintDlg"));
#else
        lpfnPrintDlg = (LFPAGESETUPDLG)GetProcAddress (hLib,
                                               TEXT ("PageSetupDlgW"));
#endif
    }
    // Create main window.
    hWnd = CreateWindow (szAppName, TEXT ("Dialog Demo"), WS_VISIBLE,
                        CW_USEDEFAULT, CW_USEDEFAULT, CW_USEDEFAULT,
                        CW_USEDEFAULT, NULL, NULL, hInstance, NULL);
    // Return fail code if window not created.
    if (!IsWindow (hWnd)) return 0;

    // Standard show and update calls
    ShowWindow (hWnd, nCmdShow);
    UpdateWindow (hWnd);
    return hWnd;
}
//-------------------------------------------------------------------------
// TermInstance - Program cleanup
//
int TermInstance (HINSTANCE hInstance, int nDefRC) {
    if (hLib)
        FreeLibrary (hLib);
    return nDefRC;
}
//=========================================================================
// Message-handling procedures for MainWindow
//
//-------------------------------------------------------------------------
// MainWndProc - Callback function for application window
//
LRESULT CALLBACK MainWndProc (HWND hWnd, UINT wMsg, WPARAM wParam,
                            LPARAM lParam) {
    INT i;
    //
    // Search message list to see if we need to handle this
    // message. If in list, call procedure.
    //
    for (i = 0; i < dim(MainMessages); i++) {
```

```
        if (wMsg == MainMessages[i].Code)
            return (*MainMessages[i].Fxn)(hWnd, wMsg, wParam, lParam);
    }
    return DefWindowProc (hWnd, wMsg, wParam, lParam);
}
//----------------------------------------------------------------------
// DoCreateMain - Process WM_CREATE message for window.
//
LRESULT DoCreateMain (HWND hWnd, UINT wMsg, WPARAM wParam,
                      LPARAM lParam) {
    HWND hwndChild;
    INT i, nHeight = 0;
    LPCREATESTRUCT lpcs;
    HMENU hMenu;

#if defined(WIN32_PLATFORM_PSPC) && (_WIN32_WCE >= 300)
    SHMENUBARINFO mbi;                          // For Pocket PC, create
    memset(&mbi, 0, sizeof(SHMENUBARINFO));     // menu bar so that we
    mbi.cbSize = sizeof(SHMENUBARINFO);         // have a sip button
    mbi.hwndParent = hWnd;
    mbi.nToolBarId = ID_MENU;
    mbi.hInstRes = hInst;
    SHCreateMenuBar(&mbi);
    hMenu = (HMENU)SendMessage(mbi.hwndMB, SHCMBM_GETSUBMENU, 0, 100);
#else
    // Create a command bar. Add a menu and an exit button.
    HWND hwndCB = CommandBar_Create (hInst, hWnd, IDC_CMDBAR);
    CommandBar_InsertMenubar (hwndCB, hInst, ID_MENU, 0);
    CommandBar_AddAdornments (hwndCB, 0, 0);
    nHeight = CommandBar_Height (hwndCB);
    hMenu = CommandBar_GetMenu (hwndCB, 0);
#endif
    // Convert lParam to pointer to create structure.
    lpcs = (LPCREATESTRUCT) lParam;

    // See color and print functions not found; disable menus.
    if (!lpfnChooseColor)
        EnableMenuItem (hMenu, IDM_COLOR, MF_BYCOMMAND | MF_GRAYED);
    if (!lpfnPrintDlg)
        EnableMenuItem (hMenu, IDM_PRINT, MF_BYCOMMAND | MF_GRAYED);
    //
    // Create report window. Size it so that it fits under
    // the command bar and fills the remaining client area.
    //
    hwndChild = CreateWindowEx (0, TEXT ("listbox"),
                     TEXT (""), WS_VISIBLE | WS_CHILD | WS_VSCROLL |
```

(continued)

Listing 6-1   *(continued)*

```
                              LBS_USETABSTOPS | LBS_NOINTEGRALHEIGHT, 0,
                              nHeight, lpcs->cx, lpcs->cy - nHeight,
                              hWnd, (HMENU)IDC_RPTLIST, lpcs->hInstance, NULL);

    // Destroy frame if window not created.
    if (!IsWindow (hwndChild)) {
        DestroyWindow (hWnd);
        return 0;
    }
    // Initialize tab stops for display list box.
    i = 8;
    SendMessage (hwndChild, LB_SETTABSTOPS, 1, (LPARAM)&i);
    return 0;
}
//-------------------------------------------------------------------------
// DoCommandMain - Process WM_COMMAND message for window.
//
LRESULT DoCommandMain (HWND hWnd, UINT wMsg, WPARAM wParam,
                       LPARAM lParam) {
    WORD idItem, wNotifyCode;
    HWND hwndCtl;
    INT  i;

    // Parse the parameters.
    idItem = (WORD) LOWORD (wParam);
    wNotifyCode = (WORD) HIWORD (wParam);
    hwndCtl = (HWND) lParam;

    // Call routine to handle control message.
    for (i = 0; i < dim(MainCommandItems); i++) {
        if (idItem == MainCommandItems[i].Code)
            return (*MainCommandItems[i].Fxn)(hWnd, idItem, hwndCtl,
                        wNotifyCode);
    }
    return 0;
}
//-------------------------------------------------------------------------
// DoAddLineMain - Process MYMSG_ADDLINE message for window.
//
LRESULT DoAddLineMain (HWND hWnd, UINT wMsg, WPARAM wParam,
                       LPARAM lParam) {
    TCHAR szOut[128];
    INT i;

    // If nothing in wParam, just fill in spaces.
    if (wParam == -1) {
```

```
                    // Print message only.
                    lstrcpy (szOut, (LPTSTR)lParam);
            } else {
                // If no ID val, ignore that field.
                if (LOWORD (wParam) == 0xffff)
                    // Print prop page and message.
                    wsprintf (szOut, TEXT ("%s       \t %s"),
                              szPages[HIWORD (wParam) - ID_BTNPAGE],
                              (LPTSTR)lParam);
                else
                    // Print property page, control ID, and message.
                    wsprintf (szOut, TEXT ("%s \tid:%3d \t%s"),
                              szPages[HIWORD (wParam) - ID_BTNPAGE],
                              LOWORD (wParam), (LPTSTR)lParam);
            }
            i = SendDlgItemMessage (hWnd, IDC_RPTLIST, LB_ADDSTRING, 0,
                               (LPARAM)(LPCTSTR)szOut);

            if (i != LB_ERR)
                SendDlgItemMessage (hWnd, IDC_RPTLIST, LB_SETTOPINDEX, i,
                               (LPARAM)(LPCTSTR)szOut);

            return 0;
}
//------------------------------------------------------------------
// DoDestroyMain - Process WM_DESTROY message for window.
//
LRESULT DoDestroyMain (HWND hWnd, UINT wMsg, WPARAM wParam,
                       LPARAM lParam) {
    PostQuitMessage (0);
    return 0;
}
//==================================================================
// Command handler routines
//------------------------------------------------------------------
// DoMainCommandOpen - Process File Open command
//
LPARAM DoMainCommandOpen (HWND hWnd, WORD idItem, HWND hwndCtl,
                          WORD wNotifyCode) {

    OPENFILENAME of;
    TCHAR szFileName [MAX_PATH] = {0};
    const LPTSTR pszOpenFilter = TEXT ("All Documents (*.*)\0*.*\0\0");
    TCHAR szOut[128];
    INT rc;

    szFileName[0] = '\0';               // Initialize filename.
    memset (&of, 0, sizeof (of));       // Initialize File Open structure.
```

(continued)

Listing 6-1   *(continued)*

```
    of.lStructSize = sizeof (of);
    of.hwndOwner = hWnd;
    of.lpstrFile = szFileName;
    of.nMaxFile = dim(szFileName);
    of.lpstrFilter = pszOpenFilter;
    of.Flags = 0;

    rc = GetOpenFileName (&of);
    wsprintf (szOut,
            TEXT ("GetOpenFileName returned: %x, filename: %s"),
            rc, szFileName);
    SendMessage (hWnd, MYMSG_ADDLINE, -1, (LPARAM)szOut);
    return 0;
}
//-----------------------------------------------------------------------
// DoMainCommandSave - Process File Save command.
//
LPARAM DoMainCommandSave (HWND hWnd, WORD idItem, HWND hwndCtl,
                        WORD wNotifyCode) {
    OPENFILENAME of;
    TCHAR szFileName [MAX_PATH] = {0};
    const LPTSTR pszOpenFilter = TEXT ("All Documents (*.*)\0*.*\0\0");
    TCHAR szOut[128];
    INT rc;

    szFileName[0] = '\0';                // Initialize filename.
    memset (&of, 0, sizeof (of));    // Initialize File Open structure.
    of.lStructSize = sizeof (of);
    of.hwndOwner = hWnd;
    of.lpstrFile = szFileName;
    of.nMaxFile = dim(szFileName);
    of.lpstrFilter = pszOpenFilter;
    of.Flags = 0;
    rc = GetSaveFileName (&of);

    wsprintf (szOut,
            TEXT ("GetSaveFileName returned: %x, filename: %s"),
            rc, szFileName);
    SendMessage (hWnd, MYMSG_ADDLINE, -1, (LPARAM)szOut);
    return 0;
}
//-----------------------------------------------------------------------
// DoMainCommandColor - Process File Color command.
//
LPARAM DoMainCommandColor (HWND hWnd, WORD idItem, HWND hwndCtl,
                        WORD wNotifyCode) {
```

```
    CHOOSECOLOR cc;
    static COLORREF cr[16];
    TCHAR szOut[128];
    INT rc;

    // Initialize color structure.
    memset (&cc, 0, sizeof (cc));
    memset (&cr, 0, sizeof (cr));

    cc.lStructSize = sizeof (cc);
    cc.hwndOwner = hWnd;
    cc.hInstance = hInst;
    cc.rgbResult = RGB (0, 0, 0);
    cc.lpCustColors = cr;
    cc.Flags = CC_ANYCOLOR;

    rc = (lpfnChooseColor) (&cc);
    wsprintf (szOut, TEXT ("Choose Color returned: %x, color: %x"),
              rc, cc.rgbResult);
    SendMessage (hWnd, MYMSG_ADDLINE, -1, (LPARAM)szOut);
    return 0;
}
//-------------------------------------------------------------------
// DoMainCommandPrint - Process File Print command.
//
LPARAM DoMainCommandPrint (HWND hWnd, WORD idItem, HWND hwndCtl,
                           WORD wNotifyCode) {
    TCHAR szOut[128];
    INT rc;
#ifndef WIN32_PLATFORM_PSPC
    PAGESETUPDLG psd;

    // Initialize print structure.
    memset (&psd, 0, sizeof (psd));
    psd.lStructSize = sizeof (psd);
    psd.hwndOwner = hWnd;

    rc = (lpfnPrintDlg) (&psd);
#else
    PRINTDLG pd;
    // Initialize print structure.
    memset (&pd, 0, sizeof (pd));

    pd.cbStruct = sizeof (pd);
    pd.hwndOwner = hWnd;
    pd.dwFlags = PD_SELECTALLPAGES;
```

(continued)

Listing 6-1 *(continued)*

```
        rc = (lpfnPrintDlg) (&pd);
#endif // ifndef WIN32_PLATFORM_PSPC
    wsprintf (szOut, TEXT ("PrintDlg returned: %x, : %x"),
                rc, GetLastError());
    SendMessage (hWnd, MYMSG_ADDLINE, -1, (LPARAM)szOut);
    return 0;
}
//------------------------------------------------------------------
// PropSheetProc - Function called when Property sheet created
//
#if defined(WIN32_PLATFORM_PSPC) && (_WIN32_WCE >= 300)
int CALLBACK PropSheetProc(HWND hwndDlg, UINT uMsg, LPARAM lParam) {

    if (uMsg == PSCB_INITIALIZED) {
        // Get tab control.
        HWND hwndTabs = GetDlgItem (hwndDlg, 0x3020);
        DWORD dwStyle = GetWindowLong (hwndTabs, GWL_STYLE);
        SetWindowLong (hwndTabs, GWL_STYLE, dwStyle | TCS_BOTTOM);

    } else if (uMsg ==  PSCB_GETVERSION)
        return COMCTL32_VERSION;

    // Add a hyperlink line below the tabs.
    else if (uMsg ==  PSCB_GETLINKTEXT) {
        lstrcpy ((LPTSTR)lParam, TEXT ("Launch the calculator by ")
                TEXT("tapping <file:\\windows\\calc.exe{here}>."));
        return 0;
    }
    return 1;
}
#endif //defined(WIN32_PLATFORM_PSPC) && (_WIN32_WCE >= 300)
//------------------------------------------------------------------
// DoMainCommandShowProp - Process show property sheet command.
//
LPARAM DoMainCommandShowProp(HWND hWnd, WORD idItem, HWND hwndCtl,
                            WORD wNotifyCode) {
    PROPSHEETPAGE psp[5];
    PROPSHEETHEADER psh;
    INT i;
    // Zero all the property page structures.
    memset (&psp, 0, sizeof (psp));
    // Fill in default values in property page structures.
    for (i = 0; i < dim(psp); i++) {
        psp[i].dwSize = sizeof (PROPSHEETPAGE);
        psp[i].dwFlags = PSP_DEFAULT;
```

```
        psp[i].hInstance = hInst;
        psp[i].lParam = (LPARAM)hWnd;
    }
    // Set the dialog box templates for each page.
    psp[0].pszTemplate = MAKEINTRESOURCE (ID_BTNPAGE);
    psp[1].pszTemplate = MAKEINTRESOURCE (ID_EDITPAGE);
    psp[2].pszTemplate = MAKEINTRESOURCE (ID_LISTPAGE);
    psp[3].pszTemplate = MAKEINTRESOURCE (ID_STATPAGE);
    psp[4].pszTemplate = MAKEINTRESOURCE (ID_SCROLLPAGE);

    // Set the dialog box procedures for each page.
    psp[0].pfnDlgProc = BtnDlgProc;
    psp[1].pfnDlgProc = EditDlgProc;
    psp[2].pfnDlgProc = ListDlgProc;
    psp[3].pfnDlgProc = StaticDlgProc;
    psp[4].pfnDlgProc = ScrollDlgProc;

    // Initialize property sheet structure.
    psh.dwSize = sizeof (PROPSHEETHEADER);
    psh.dwFlags = PSH_PROPSHEETPAGE;
    psh.hwndParent = hWnd;
    psh.hInstance = hInst;
    psh.pszCaption = TEXT ("Property Sheet Demo");
    psh.nPages = dim(psp);
    psh.nStartPage = 0;
    psh.ppsp = psp;
    // On Pocket PC, make property sheets full screen.
#if defined(WIN32_PLATFORM_PSPC) && (_WIN32_WCE >= 300)
    psh.pfnCallback = PropSheetProc;
    psh.dwFlags |= PSH_USECALLBACK | PSH_MAXIMIZE;
#else
    psh.pfnCallback = 0;
#endif //defined(WIN32_PLATFORM_PSPC) && (_WIN32_WCE >= 300)
    // Create and display property sheet.
    PropertySheet (&psh);
    return 0;
}
//-------------------------------------------------------------------
// DoMainCommandModelessDlg - Process the File Modeless menu command.
//
LPARAM DoMainCommandModeless(HWND hWnd, WORD idItem, HWND hwndCtl,
                             WORD wNotifyCode) {

    // Create dialog box only if not already created.
    if (g_hwndMlDlg == 0)
        // Use CreateDialog to create modeless dialog box.
```

(continued)

Listing 6-1   *(continued)*

```
        g_hwndMlDlg = CreateDialog (hInst, TEXT ("Clearbox"), hWnd,
                                    ModelessDlgProc);
    return 0;
}
//-------------------------------------------------------------------------
// DoMainCommandExit - Process Program Exit command.
//
LPARAM DoMainCommandExit (HWND hWnd, WORD idItem, HWND hwndCtl,
                          WORD wNotifyCode) {
    SendMessage (hWnd, WM_CLOSE, 0, 0);
    return 0;
}
//-------------------------------------------------------------------------
// DoMainCommandAbout - Process the Help About menu command.
//
LPARAM DoMainCommandAbout(HWND hWnd, WORD idItem, HWND hwndCtl,
                          WORD wNotifyCode) {
    // Use DialogBox to create modal dialog box.
    DialogBox (hInst, TEXT ("aboutbox"), hWnd, AboutDlgProc);
    return 0;
}
//=========================================================================
// Modeless ClearList dialog box procedure
//
BOOL CALLBACK ModelessDlgProc (HWND hWnd, UINT wMsg, WPARAM wParam,
                               LPARAM lParam) {
    switch (wMsg) {
        case WM_COMMAND:
            switch (LOWORD (wParam)) {
                case IDD_CLEAR:
                    // Send message to list box to clear it.
                    SendDlgItemMessage (GetWindow (hWnd, GW_OWNER),
                                        IDC_RPTLIST,
                                        LB_RESETCONTENT, 0, 0);
                    return TRUE;

                case IDOK:
                case IDCANCEL:
                    // Modeless dialog boxes can't use EndDialog.
                    DestroyWindow (hWnd);
                    g_hwndMlDlg = 0;  // 0 means dlg destroyed.
                    return TRUE;
            }
        break;
    }
    return FALSE;
}
```

```
//=======================================================================
// About dialog box procedure
//
BOOL CALLBACK AboutDlgProc (HWND hWnd, UINT wMsg, WPARAM wParam,
                            LPARAM lParam) {
    switch (wMsg) {
        case WM_COMMAND:
            switch (LOWORD (wParam)) {
                case IDOK:
                case IDCANCEL:
                    EndDialog (hWnd, 0);
                    return TRUE;
            }
        break;
    }
    return FALSE;
}
```

BtnDlg.cpp

```
//=======================================================================
// BtnDlg - Button dialog box window code
//
// Written for the book Programming Windows CE
// Copyright (C) 2003 Douglas Boling
//=======================================================================
#include <windows.h>                    // For all that Windows stuff
#include <prsht.h>                      // Property sheet includes
#include "DlgDemo.h"                    // Program-specific stuff

extern HINSTANCE hInst;

LRESULT DrawButton (HWND hWnd, LPDRAWITEMSTRUCT pdi);
//-----------------------------------------------------------------------
// Global data
//
// Identification strings for various WM_COMMAND notifications
NOTELABELS nlBtn[] = {{TEXT ("BN_CLICKED "),      0},
                      {TEXT ("BN_PAINT    "),     1},
                      {TEXT ("BN_HILITE   "),     2},
                      {TEXT ("BN_UNHILITE"),      3},
                      {TEXT ("BN_DISABLE "),      4},
                      {TEXT ("BN_DOUBLECLICKED"), 5},
                      {TEXT ("BN_SETFOCUS "),     6},
                      {TEXT ("BN_KILLFOCUS"),     7}
};
```

(continued)

Listing 6-1 *(continued)*

```
extern NOTELABELS nlPropPage[];
extern int nPropPageSize;

// Handle for icon used in owner-draw icon
HICON hIcon = 0;
//======================================================================
// BtnDlgProc - Button page dialog box procedure
//
BOOL CALLBACK BtnDlgProc (HWND hWnd, UINT wMsg, WPARAM wParam,
                          LPARAM lParam) {
    TCHAR szOut[128];
    HWND hwndMain;
    INT i;

    switch (wMsg) {

        case WM_INITDIALOG:
            // The generic parameter contains the
            // top-level window handle.
            hwndMain = (HWND)((LPPROPSHEETPAGE)lParam)->lParam;
            // Save the window handle in the window structure.
            SetWindowLong (hWnd, DWL_USER, (LONG)hwndMain);

            // Load icon for owner-draw window.
            hIcon = LoadIcon (hInst, MAKEINTRESOURCE (IDI_BTNICON));

            // We need to set the initial state of the radio buttons.
            CheckRadioButton (hWnd, IDC_RADIO1, IDC_RADIO2, IDC_RADIO1);
            return TRUE;
        //
        // Reflect WM_COMMAND messages to main window.
        //
        case WM_COMMAND:
            // Since the check box is not an auto check box, the button
            // has to be set manually.
            if ((LOWORD (wParam) == IDC_CHKBOX) &&
                (HIWORD (wParam) == BN_CLICKED)) {
                // Get the current state, complement, and set.
                i = SendDlgItemMessage (hWnd, IDC_CHKBOX, BM_GETCHECK,
                                        0, 0);
                if (i)
                    SendDlgItemMessage (hWnd, IDC_CHKBOX, BM_SETCHECK,
                                        0, 0);
                else
                    SendDlgItemMessage (hWnd, IDC_CHKBOX, BM_SETCHECK,
```

```
                                                  1, 0);
    }



    // Get the handle of the main window from the user word.
    hwndMain = (HWND) GetWindowLong (hWnd, DWL_USER);

    // Look up button notification.
    lstrcpy (szOut, TEXT ("WM_COMMAND: "));
    for (i = 0; i < dim(nlBtn); i++) {
        if (HIWORD (wParam) == nlBtn[i].wNotification) {
            lstrcat (szOut, nlBtn[i].pszLabel);
            break;
        }
    }
    if (i == dim(nlBtn))
        wsprintf (szOut, TEXT ("WM_COMMAND notification: %x"),
                  HIWORD (wParam));

    SendMessage (hwndMain, MYMSG_ADDLINE,
                 MAKEWPARAM (LOWORD (wParam),ID_BTNPAGE),
                 (LPARAM)szOut);
    return TRUE;


//
// Reflect notify message.
//
case WM_NOTIFY:
    // Get the handle of the main window from the user word.
    hwndMain = (HWND) GetWindowLong (hWnd, DWL_USER);

    // Look up notify message.
    for (i = 0; i < nPropPageSize; i++) {
        if (((NMHDR *)lParam)->code ==
                             nlPropPage[i].wNotification) {
            lstrcpy (szOut, nlPropPage[i].pszLabel);
            break;
        }
    }
    if (i == nPropPageSize)
        wsprintf (szOut, TEXT ("Notify code:%d"),
                  ((NMHDR *)lParam)->code);
    SendMessage (hwndMain, MYMSG_ADDLINE,
                 MAKEWPARAM (-1,ID_BTNPAGE), (LPARAM)szOut);

    return FALSE;   // Return false to force default processing.
```

(continued)

Listing 6-1 *(continued)*

```
        case WM_DRAWITEM:
            DrawButton (hWnd, (LPDRAWITEMSTRUCT)lParam);
            return TRUE;
    }
    return FALSE;
}


//----------------------------------------------------------------------
// DrawButton - Draws an owner-draw button.
//
LRESULT DrawButton (HWND hWnd, LPDRAWITEMSTRUCT pdi) {

    HPEN hPenShadow, hPenLight, hPenDkShadow, hOldPen;
    POINT ptOut[3], ptIn[3];
    HBRUSH hBr, hOldBr;
    TCHAR szOut[128];
    HWND hwndMain;
    LOGPEN lpen;

    // Get the handle of the main window from the user word.
    hwndMain = (HWND) GetWindowLong (hWnd, DWL_USER);

    // Reflect the messages to the report window.
    wsprintf (szOut, TEXT ("WM_DRAWITEM Act:%x  State:%x"),
            pdi->itemAction, pdi->itemState);

    SendMessage (hwndMain, MYMSG_ADDLINE,
                MAKEWPARAM (pdi->CtlID, ID_BTNPAGE),
                (LPARAM)szOut);

    // Create pens for drawing.
    lpen.lopnStyle = PS_SOLID;
    lpen.lopnWidth.x = 3;
    lpen.lopnWidth.y = 3;
    lpen.lopnColor = GetSysColor (COLOR_3DSHADOW);
    hPenShadow = CreatePenIndirect (&lpen);

    lpen.lopnWidth.x = 1;
    lpen.lopnWidth.y = 1;
    lpen.lopnColor = GetSysColor (COLOR_3DLIGHT);
    hPenLight = CreatePenIndirect (&lpen);
    lpen.lopnColor = GetSysColor (COLOR_3DDKSHADOW);
    hPenDkShadow = CreatePenIndirect (&lpen);

    // Create a brush for the face of the button.
    hBr = CreateSolidBrush (GetSysColor (COLOR_3DFACE));
```

```
// Draw a rectangle with a thick outside border to start the
// frame drawing.
hOldPen = (HPEN)SelectObject (pdi->hDC, hPenShadow);
hOldBr = (HBRUSH)SelectObject (pdi->hDC, hBr);
Rectangle (pdi->hDC, pdi->rcItem.left, pdi->rcItem.top,
           pdi->rcItem.right, pdi->rcItem.bottom);

// Draw the upper left inside line.
ptIn[0].x = pdi->rcItem.left + 1;
ptIn[0].y = pdi->rcItem.bottom - 3;
ptIn[1].x = pdi->rcItem.left + 1;
ptIn[1].y = pdi->rcItem.top + 1;
ptIn[2].x = pdi->rcItem.right - 3;
ptIn[2].y = pdi->rcItem.top + 1;

// Select a pen to draw shadow or light side of button.
if (pdi->itemState & ODS_SELECTED) {
    SelectObject (pdi->hDC, hPenDkShadow);
} else {
    SelectObject (pdi->hDC, hPenLight);
}
Polyline (pdi->hDC, ptIn, 3);

// If selected, also draw a bright line inside the lower
// right corner.
if (pdi->itemState & ODS_SELECTED) {
    SelectObject (pdi->hDC, hPenLight);
    ptIn[1].x = pdi->rcItem.right - 3;
    ptIn[1].y = pdi->rcItem.bottom - 3;
    Polyline (pdi->hDC, ptIn, 3);
}
// Now draw the black outside line on either the upper left or the
// lower right corner.
ptOut[0].x = pdi->rcItem.left;
ptOut[0].y = pdi->rcItem.bottom - 1;
ptOut[2].x = pdi->rcItem.right - 1;
ptOut[2].y = pdi->rcItem.top;
SelectObject (pdi->hDC, hPenDkShadow);
if (pdi->itemState & ODS_SELECTED) {
    ptOut[1].x = pdi->rcItem.left;
    ptOut[1].y = pdi->rcItem.top;
} else {
    ptOut[1].x = pdi->rcItem.right - 1;
    ptOut[1].y = pdi->rcItem.bottom - 1;
}
Polyline (pdi->hDC, ptOut, 3);
```

(continued)

Listing 6-1 *(continued)*

```
    // Draw the icon.
    if (hIcon) {
        ptIn[0].x = (pdi->rcItem.right - pdi->rcItem.left)/2 -
                    GetSystemMetrics (SM_CXICON)/2 - 2;
        ptIn[0].y = (pdi->rcItem.bottom - pdi->rcItem.top)/2 -
                    GetSystemMetrics (SM_CYICON)/2 - 2;
        // If pressed, shift image down one pel to simulate the press.
        if (pdi->itemState & ODS_SELECTED) {
            ptOut[1].x += 2;
            ptOut[1].y += 2;
        }
        DrawIcon (pdi->hDC, ptIn[0].x, ptIn[0].y, hIcon);
    }

    // If button has the focus, draw the dotted rect inside the button.
    if (pdi->itemState & ODS_FOCUS) {
        pdi->rcItem.left += 3;
        pdi->rcItem.top += 3;
        pdi->rcItem.right -= 4;
        pdi->rcItem.bottom -= 4;
        DrawFocusRect (pdi->hDC, &pdi->rcItem);
    }

    // Clean up. First select the original brush and pen into the DC.
    SelectObject (pdi->hDC, hOldBr);
    SelectObject (pdi->hDC, hOldPen);

    // Now delete the brushes and pens created.
    DeleteObject (hBr);
    DeleteObject (hPenShadow);
    DeleteObject (hPenDkShadow);
    DeleteObject (hPenLight);
    return 0;
}
```

EditDlg.cpp

```
//======================================================================
// EditDlg - Edit dialog box window code
//
// Written for the book Programming Windows CE
// Copyright (C) 2003 Douglas Boling
//======================================================================
#include <windows.h>                 // For all that Windows stuff
#include <prsht.h>                   // Property sheet includes
#include "DlgDemo.h"                 // Program-specific stuff
```

```
extern HINSTANCE hInst;
//--------------------------------------------------------------------
// Global data
//
// Identification strings for various WM_COMMAND notifications
NOTELABELS nlEdit[] = {{TEXT ("EN_SETFOCUS "), 0x0100},
                       {TEXT ("EN_KILLFOCUS"), 0x0200},
                       {TEXT ("EN_CHANGE   "), 0x0300},
                       {TEXT ("EN_UPDATE   "), 0x0400},
                       {TEXT ("EN_ERRSPACE "), 0x0500},
                       {TEXT ("EN_MAXTEXT  "), 0x0501},
                       {TEXT ("EN_HSCROLL  "), 0x0601},
                       {TEXT ("EN_VSCROLL  "), 0x0602},
};
extern NOTELABELS nlPropPage[];
extern int nPropPageSize;
//====================================================================
// EditDlgProc - Edit box page dialog box procedure
//
BOOL CALLBACK EditDlgProc (HWND hWnd, UINT wMsg, WPARAM wParam,
                           LPARAM lParam) {
    TCHAR szOut[128];
    HWND hwndMain;
    INT i;

    switch (wMsg) {

        case WM_INITDIALOG:
            // The generic parameter contains the
            // top-level window handle.
            hwndMain = (HWND)((LPPROPSHEETPAGE)lParam)->lParam;
            // Save the window handle in the window structure.
            SetWindowLong (hWnd, DWL_USER, (LONG)hwndMain);
            return TRUE;
        //
        // Reflect WM_COMMAND messages to main window.
        //
        case WM_COMMAND:
            // Get the handle of the main window from the user word.
            hwndMain = (HWND) GetWindowLong (hWnd, DWL_USER);

            // Look up button notification.
            lstrcpy (szOut, TEXT ("WM_COMMAND: "));
            for (i = 0; i < dim(nlEdit); i++) {
                if (HIWORD (wParam) == nlEdit[i].wNotification) {
                    lstrcat (szOut, nlEdit[i].pszLabel);
```

(continued)

Listing 6-1 *(continued)*

```
                    break;
                }
            }
            if (i == dim(nlEdit))
                wsprintf (szOut, TEXT ("WM_COMMAND notification: %x"),
                        HIWORD (wParam));

            SendMessage (hwndMain, MYMSG_ADDLINE,
                        MAKEWPARAM (LOWORD (wParam),ID_EDITPAGE),
                        (LPARAM)szOut);
            return TRUE;


        //
        // Reflect notify message.
        //
        case WM_NOTIFY:
            // Get the handle of the main window from the user word.
            hwndMain = (HWND) GetWindowLong (hWnd, DWL_USER);

            // Look up notify message.
            for (i = 0; i < nPropPageSize; i++) {
                if (((NMHDR *)lParam)->code ==
                                    nlPropPage[i].wNotification) {
                    lstrcpy (szOut, nlPropPage[i].pszLabel);
                    break;
                }
            }
            if (i == nPropPageSize)
                wsprintf (szOut, TEXT ("Notify code:%d"),
                        ((NMHDR *)lParam)->code);

            SendMessage (hwndMain, MYMSG_ADDLINE,
                        MAKEWPARAM (-1,ID_EDITPAGE), (LPARAM)szOut);

            return FALSE;  // Return false to force default processing.
    }
    return FALSE;
}
```

ListDlg.cpp

```
//======================================================================
// ListDlg - List box dialog window code
//
// Written for the book Programming Windows CE
// Copyright (C) 2003 Douglas Boling
//======================================================================
```

```c
#include <windows.h>                    // For all that Windows stuff
#include <prsht.h>                      // Property sheet includes
#include "DlgDemo.h"                    // Program-specific stuff

extern HINSTANCE hInst;
//----------------------------------------------------------------------
// Global data
//
NOTELABELS nlList[] = {{TEXT ("LBN_ERRSPACE "), (-2)},
                       {TEXT ("LBN_SELCHANGE"), 1},
                       {TEXT ("LBN_DBLCLK   "), 2},
                       {TEXT ("LBN_SELCANCEL"), 3},
                       {TEXT ("LBN_SETFOCUS "), 4},
                       {TEXT ("LBN_KILLFOCUS"), 5},
};

NOTELABELS nlCombo[] = {{TEXT ("CBN_ERRSPACE      "), (-1)},
                        {TEXT ("CBN_SELCHANGE     "), 1},
                        {TEXT ("CBN_DBLCLK        "), 2},
                        {TEXT ("CBN_SETFOCUS      "), 3},
                        {TEXT ("CBN_KILLFOCUS     "), 4},
                        {TEXT ("CBN_EDITCHANGE    "), 5},
                        {TEXT ("CBN_EDITUPDATE    "), 6},
                        {TEXT ("CBN_DROPDOWN      "), 7},
                        {TEXT ("CBN_CLOSEUP       "), 8},
                        {TEXT ("CBN_SELENDOK      "), 9},
                        {TEXT ("CBN_SELENDCANCEL"), 10},
};

extern NOTELABELS nlPropPage[];
extern int nPropPageSize;
//======================================================================
// ListDlgProc - List box page dialog box procedure
//
BOOL CALLBACK ListDlgProc (HWND hWnd, UINT wMsg, WPARAM wParam,
                           LPARAM lParam) {

    TCHAR szOut[128];
    HWND hwndMain;
    INT i;
    switch (wMsg) {

        case WM_INITDIALOG:
            // The generic parameter contains the
            // top-level window handle.
            hwndMain = (HWND)((LPPROPSHEETPAGE)lParam)->lParam;
            // Save the window handle in the window structure.
            SetWindowLong (hWnd, DWL_USER, (LONG)hwndMain);
```

(continued)

Listing 6-1 *(continued)*

```
            // Fill the list and combo boxes.
            for (i = 0; i < 20; i++) {
                wsprintf (szOut, TEXT ("Item %d"), i);
                SendDlgItemMessage (hWnd, IDC_SNGLELIST, LB_ADDSTRING,
                                    0, (LPARAM)szOut);

                SendDlgItemMessage (hWnd, IDC_MULTILIST, LB_ADDSTRING,
                                    0, (LPARAM)szOut);

                SendDlgItemMessage (hWnd, IDC_COMBOBOX, CB_ADDSTRING,
                                    0, (LPARAM)szOut);
            }
            // Provide default selection for the combo box.
            SendDlgItemMessage (hWnd, IDC_COMBOBOX, CB_SETCURSEL, 0, 0);
            return TRUE;
//
// Reflect WM_COMMAND messages to main window.
//
case WM_COMMAND:
        // Get the handle of the main window from the user word.
        hwndMain = (HWND) GetWindowLong (hWnd, DWL_USER);

        // Report the WM_COMMAND messages.
        lstrcpy (szOut, TEXT ("WM_COMMAND: "));
        if (LOWORD (wParam) == IDC_COMBOBOX) {
            for (i = 0; i < dim(nlCombo); i++) {
                if (HIWORD (wParam) == nlCombo[i].wNotification) {
                    lstrcat (szOut, nlCombo[i].pszLabel);
                    break;
                }
            }
            if (i == dim(nlCombo))
                wsprintf (szOut,
                          TEXT ("WM_COMMAND notification: %x"),
                          HIWORD (wParam));
        } else {
            for (i = 0; i < dim(nlList); i++) {
                if (HIWORD (wParam) == nlList[i].wNotification) {
                    lstrcat (szOut, nlList[i].pszLabel);
                    break;
                }
            }
            if (i == dim(nlList))
                wsprintf (szOut,
                          TEXT ("WM_COMMAND notification: %x"),
                          HIWORD (wParam));
        }
```

```
            SendMessage (hwndMain, MYMSG_ADDLINE,
                        MAKEWPARAM (LOWORD (wParam),ID_LISTPAGE),
                        (LPARAM)szOut);
            return TRUE;


    //
    // Reflect notify message.
    //
    case WM_NOTIFY:
        // Get the handle of the main window from the user word.
        hwndMain = (HWND) GetWindowLong (hWnd, DWL_USER);

        // Look up notify message.
        for (i = 0; i < nPropPageSize; i++) {
            if (((NMHDR *)lParam)->code ==
                                  nlPropPage[i].wNotification) {
                lstrcpy (szOut, nlPropPage[i].pszLabel);
                break;
            }
        }
        if (i == nPropPageSize)
            wsprintf (szOut, TEXT ("Notify code:%d"),
                      ((NMHDR *)lParam)->code);

        SendMessage (hwndMain, MYMSG_ADDLINE,
                    MAKEWPARAM (-1,ID_LISTPAGE),
                    (LPARAM)szOut);
        return FALSE;  // Return false to force default processing.
    }
    return FALSE;
}
```

StaticDlg.cpp

```
//======================================================================
// StaticDlg - Static control dialog box window code
//
// Written for the book Programming Windows CE
// Copyright (C) 2003 Douglas Boling
//======================================================================
#include <windows.h>              // For all that Windows stuff
#include <prsht.h>                // Property sheet includes
#include "DlgDemo.h"              // Program-specific stuff

extern HINSTANCE hInst;
//----------------------------------------------------------------------
```

(continued)

Listing 6-1   *(continued)*

```
// Global data
//
// Identification strings for various WM_COMMAND notifications
NOTELABELS nlStatic[] = {{TEXT ("STN_CLICKED"), 0},
                         {TEXT ("STN_ENABLE "), 2},
                         {TEXT ("STN_DISABLE"), 3},
};
extern NOTELABELS nlPropPage[];
extern int nPropPageSize;
//=====================================================================
// StaticDlgProc - Static control dialog box procedure
//
BOOL CALLBACK StaticDlgProc (HWND hWnd, UINT wMsg, WPARAM wParam,
                             LPARAM lParam) {
    TCHAR szOut[128];
    HWND hwndMain;
    INT i;

    switch (wMsg) {

        case WM_INITDIALOG:
            // The generic parameter contains the
            // top-level window handle.
            hwndMain = (HWND)((LPPROPSHEETPAGE)lParam)->lParam;
            // Save the window handle in the window structure.
            SetWindowLong (hWnd, DWL_USER, (LONG)hwndMain);
            return TRUE;
        //
        // Reflect WM_COMMAND messages to main window.
        //
        case WM_COMMAND:
            // Get the handle of the main window from the user word.
            hwndMain = (HWND) GetWindowLong (hWnd, DWL_USER);

            // Look up button notification.
            lstrcpy (szOut, TEXT ("WM_COMMAND: "));
            for (i = 0; i < dim(nlStatic); i++) {
                if (HIWORD (wParam) == nlStatic[i].wNotification) {
                    lstrcat (szOut, nlStatic[i].pszLabel);
                    break;
                }
            }
            if (i == dim(nlStatic))
                wsprintf (szOut, TEXT ("WM_COMMAND notification: %x"),
                        HIWORD (wParam));
```

```
            SendMessage (hwndMain, MYMSG_ADDLINE,
                        MAKEWPARAM (LOWORD (wParam),ID_STATPAGE),
                        (LPARAM)szOut);
            return TRUE;

        //
        // Reflect notify message.
        //
        case WM_NOTIFY:
            // Get the handle of the main window from the user word.
            hwndMain = (HWND) GetWindowLong (hWnd, DWL_USER);

            // Look up notify message.
            for (i = 0; i < nPropPageSize; i++) {
                if (((NMHDR *)lParam)->code ==
                    nlPropPage[i].wNotification) {
                        lstrcpy (szOut, nlPropPage[i].pszLabel);
                    break;
                }
            }
            if (i == nPropPageSize)
                wsprintf (szOut, TEXT ("Notify code:%d"),
                        ((NMHDR *)lParam)->code);

            SendMessage (hwndMain, MYMSG_ADDLINE,
                        MAKEWPARAM (-1,ID_STATPAGE), (LPARAM)szOut);

            return FALSE;  // Return false to force default processing.
    }
    return FALSE;
}
```

ScrollDlg.cpp

```
//======================================================================
// ScrollDlg - Scroll bar dialog box window code
//
// Written for the book Programming Windows CE
// Copyright (C) 2003 Douglas Boling
//======================================================================
#include <windows.h>                // For all that Windows stuff
#include <prsht.h>                  // Property sheet includes
#include "DlgDemo.h"                // Program-specific stuff

extern HINSTANCE hInst;
```

(continued)

Listing 6-1 *(continued)*

```
//---------------------------------------------------------------------
// Global data
//
// Identification strings for various WM_xSCROLL notifications
NOTELABELS nlVScroll[] = {{TEXT ("SB_LINEUP        "), 0},
                          {TEXT ("SB_LINEDOWN      "), 1},
                          {TEXT ("SB_PAGEUP        "), 2},
                          {TEXT ("SB_PAGEDOWN      "), 3},
                          {TEXT ("SB_THUMBPOSITION"), 4},
                          {TEXT ("SB_THUMBTRACK    "), 5},
                          {TEXT ("SB_TOP           "), 6},
                          {TEXT ("SB_BOTTOM        "), 7},
                          {TEXT ("SB_ENDSCROLL     "), 8},
};
NOTELABELS nlHScroll[] = {{TEXT ("SB_LINELEFT      "), 0},
                          {TEXT ("SB_LINERIGHT     "), 1},
                          {TEXT ("SB_PAGELEFT      "), 2},
                          {TEXT ("SB_PAGERIGHT     "), 3},
                          {TEXT ("SB_THUMBPOSITION"), 4},
                          {TEXT ("SB_THUMBTRACK    "), 5},
                          {TEXT ("SB_LEFT          "), 6},
                          {TEXT ("SB_RIGHT         "), 7},
                          {TEXT ("SB_ENDSCROLL     "), 8},
};
extern NOTELABELS nlPropPage[];
extern int nPropPageSize;
//=====================================================================
// ScrollDlgProc - Scroll bar page dialog box procedure
//
BOOL CALLBACK ScrollDlgProc (HWND hWnd, UINT wMsg, WPARAM wParam,
                             LPARAM lParam) {
    TCHAR szOut[128];
    SCROLLINFO si;
    HWND hwndMain;
    INT i, sPos;

    switch (wMsg) {

        case WM_INITDIALOG:
            // The generic parameter contains
            // the top-level window handle.
            hwndMain = (HWND)((LPPROPSHEETPAGE)lParam)->lParam;
            // Save the window handle in the window structure.
            SetWindowLong (hWnd, DWL_USER, (LONG)hwndMain);
            return TRUE;
```

```
//
// Reflect WM_COMMAND messages to main window.
//
case WM_VSCROLL:
case WM_HSCROLL:
    // Get the handle of the main window from the user word.
    hwndMain = (HWND) GetWindowLong (hWnd, DWL_USER);

    // Update the report window.
    // Determine whether from horizontal or vertical scroll bar.
    if (GetDlgItem (hWnd, 101) == (HWND)lParam) {
        for (i = 0; i < dim(nlVScroll); i++) {
            if (LOWORD (wParam) == nlVScroll[i].wNotification) {
                lstrcpy (szOut, nlVScroll[i].pszLabel);
                break;
            }
        }
        if (i == dim(nlVScroll))
            wsprintf (szOut, TEXT ("notification: %x"),
                    HIWORD (wParam));
    } else {
        for (i = 0; i < dim(nlHScroll); i++) {
            if (LOWORD (wParam) == nlHScroll[i].wNotification) {
                lstrcpy (szOut, nlHScroll[i].pszLabel);
                break;
            }
        }
        if (i == dim(nlHScroll))
            wsprintf (szOut, TEXT ("notification: %x"),
                    HIWORD (wParam));
    }
    SendMessage (hwndMain, MYMSG_ADDLINE,
            MAKEWPARAM (-1, ID_SCROLLPAGE), (LPARAM)szOut);

    // Get scroll bar position.
    si.cbSize = sizeof (si);
    si.fMask = SIF_POS;
    GetScrollInfo ((HWND)lParam, SB_CTL, &si);
    sPos = si.nPos;

    // Act on the scroll code.
    switch (LOWORD (wParam)) {
    case SB_LINEUP:          // Also SB_LINELEFT
        sPos -= 2;
        break;
```

(continued)

Listing 6-1   *(continued)*

```
        case SB_LINEDOWN:      // Also SB_LINERIGHT
            sPos += 2;
            break;

        case SB_PAGEUP:        // Also SB_PAGELEFT
            sPos -= 10;
            break;

        case SB_PAGEDOWN:      // Also SB_PAGERIGHT
            sPos += 10;
            break;

        case SB_THUMBPOSITION:
            sPos = HIWORD (wParam);
            break;
        }
        // Check range.
        if (sPos < 0)
            sPos = 0;
        if (sPos > 100)
            sPos = 100;

        // Update scroll bar position.
        si.cbSize = sizeof (si);
        si.nPos = sPos;
        si.fMask = SIF_POS;
        SetScrollInfo ((HWND)lParam, SB_CTL, &si, TRUE);

        return TRUE;

//
// Reflect notify message.
//
case WM_NOTIFY:
    // Get the handle of the main window from the user word.
    hwndMain = (HWND) GetWindowLong (hWnd, DWL_USER);

    // Look up notify message.
    for (i = 0; i < nPropPageSize; i++) {
        if (((NMHDR *)lParam)->code ==
                nlPropPage[i].wNotification) {
                    lstrcpy (szOut, nlPropPage[i].pszLabel);
                    break;
        }
    }
```

```
            if (i == nPropPageSize)
                wsprintf (szOut, TEXT ("Notify code:%d"),
                          ((NMHDR *)lParam)->code);

        SendMessage (hwndMain, MYMSG_ADDLINE,
                     MAKEWPARAM (-1, ID_SCROLLPAGE), (LPARAM)szOut);

        return FALSE;  // Return false to force default processing.
    }
    return FALSE;
}
```

The dialog box procedures for each of the property pages report all
WM_COMMAND and *WM_NOTIFY* messages back to the main window, where
they're displayed in a list box contained in the main window. The property
page dialog box procedures mirror the child window procedures of the CtlView
example, the differences being that the page procedures don't have to create
their controls and that they field the *WM_INITDIALOG* message to initialize the
controls. The page procedures also use the technique of storing information in
their window structures—in this case, the window handle of the main window
of the example. This is necessary because the parent window of the pages is
the property sheet, not the main window. The window handle is conveniently
accessible during the *WM_INITDIALOG* message because it's loaded into the
user-definable parameter in the *PROPSHEETPAGE* structure by the main window when the property sheet is created. Each page procedure copies the
parameter from the *PROPSHEETPAGE* structure into the *DWL_USER* field of the
window structure available to all dialog box procedures. When other messages
are handled, the handle is then queried using *GetWindowLong*. The page procedures also field the *WM_NOTIFY* message so that they, too, can be reflected
back to the main window.

As with CtlView, the best way to learn from DlgDemo is to run the program and watch the different *WM_COMMAND* and *WM_NOTIFY* messages that
are sent by the controls and the property sheet. Opening the property sheet and
switching between the pages results in a flood of *WM_NOTIFY* messages
informing the individual pages of what's happening. It's also interesting to note
that when the OK button is pressed on the property sheet, the *PSN_APPLY* messages are sent only to property pages that have been displayed.

The menu handlers that display the Print and Color common dialogs work
with a bit of a twist. Because some Windows CE systems don't support these
dialogs, DlgDemo can't call the functions directly. That would result in these
two functions being implicitly linked at run time. On systems that did not support these functions, Windows CE wouldn't be able to resolve the implicit links

to all the functions in the program, and therefore the program wouldn't be able to load. So instead of calling the functions directly, you explicitly link these functions in *InitApp* by loading the common dialog DLL using *LoadLibrary* and getting pointers to the functions using *GetProcAddress*. If DlgDemo is running on a system that doesn't support one of the functions, the *GetProcAddress* function fails and returns 0 for the function pointer. In *OnCreateMain*, a check is made to see whether these function pointers are 0, and if so, the Print and Color menu items are disabled. In the menu handler functions *DoMainCommand-Color* and *DoMainCommandPrint*, the function pointers returned by *GetProc-Address* are used to call the functions. This extra effort isn't necessary if you know your program will run only on a system that supports a specific set of functions, but every once in a while, this technique comes in handy.

The Pocket PC handles the common print dialog differently. Although the Pocket PC exports the function *PageSetupDialog*, the function prototype isn't included in the SDK, and the function returns immediately when called.

One other detail is how this program adapts to the Pocket PC shell. Dlg-Demo creates a menu bar instead of a command bar when compiled for the Pocket PC. This provides a place for the menu as well as exposing the Soft Keyboard button.

In addition, on Pocket PCs, the property sheet expands to fill the full screen, and its tabs are located on the bottom of the sheet instead of the top. I made these adaptations to demonstrate how to comply with the Pocket PC user interface guidelines. To place the tabs on the bottom of the sheet and provide the hyperlink text below the pages, DlgDemo provides the property sheet call-back function shown here:

```
int CALLBACK PropSheetProc(HWND hwndDlg, UINT uMsg, LPARAM lParam) {

    if (uMsg == PSCB_INITIALIZED) {
        // Get tab control
        HWND hwndTabs = GetDlgItem (hwndDlg, 0x3020);

        DWORD dwStyle = GetWindowLong (hwndTabs, GWL_STYLE);
        SetWindowLong (hwndTabs, GWL_STYLE, dwStyle | TCS_BOTTOM);

    } else if (uMsg ==  PSCB_GETVERSION)
        return COMCTL32_VERSION;
    return 1;
}
```

The source of this rather strange code comes from the MFC source code provided with the Pocket PC SDK. During the *PSCB_INITIALIZE* notification, the handle of the Tab control of the property sheet is queried using the predefined control ID 0x3020. The style bits of the Tab control are then modified to have the control place the tabs on the bottom instead of the top by setting the *TCS_BOTTOM* style flag.

The function also handles the *PSCB_GETLINKTEXT* notification and returns the following text:

```
TEXT ("Launch the calculator by tapping <file:calc.exe{here}>.")
```

The hyperlink is enclosed in angle brackets <>. The text displayed for the link is enclosed in curly braces {}. When the hyperlink is tapped, the Pocket PC will launch calc.exe. The hyperlink can also be a data file such as book1.pxl or memo.pwd.

Dialog boxes and property sheets are quite often the only user interface a Windows CE program has. Although sometimes complex in implementation, the help Windows CE provides in creating and maintaining dialog boxes and property sheets reduces the workload on the program to some extent.

This chapter also marks the end of the introductory section, "Windows Programming Basics." In these first six chapters, I've talked about fundamental Windows programming while also using a basic Windows CE application to introduce the concepts of the system message queue, windows, and messages. I've given you an overview of how to paint text and graphics in a window and how to query the user for input. Finally, I talked about the windows hierarchy, controls, common controls, and dialog boxes. For the remainder of the book, I move from description of the elements common to both Windows CE and the desktop versions of Windows to the unique nature of Windows CE programming. It's time to turn to the operating system itself. Over the next four chapters, I'll cover memory management, files, databases, and processes and threads. These chapters are aimed at the core of the Windows CE operating system.

Part II

Windows CE Programming

7

Memory Management

If you have an overriding concern when you're writing a Microsoft Windows CE program, it should be dealing with memory. A Windows CE machine might have only 4 MB of RAM. This is a tiny amount compared with that of a standard personal computer, which typically needs 128 MB or more. In fact, memory on a Windows CE machine is so scarce that it's sometimes necessary to write programs that conserve memory even to the point of sacrificing the overall performance of the application.

Fortunately, although the amount of memory is small in a Windows CE system, the functions available for managing that memory are fairly complete. Windows CE implements almost the full Win32 memory management API available under Microsoft Windows XP and Microsoft Windows Me. Windows CE supports virtual memory allocations, local and separate heaps, and even memory-mapped files.

Like Windows XP, Windows CE supports a 32-bit flat address space with memory protection between applications. But because Windows CE was designed for different environments, its underlying memory architecture is different from that for Windows XP. These differences can affect how you design a Windows CE application. In this chapter, I'll describe the basic memory architecture of Windows CE. I'll also cover the different types of memory allocation available to Windows CE programs and how to use each memory type to minimize your application's memory footprint.

Memory Basics

As with all computers, systems running Windows CE have both ROM (read only memory) and RAM (random access memory). Under Windows CE, however, both ROM and RAM are used somewhat differently than they are in a standard personal computer.

About RAM

The RAM in a Windows CE system is divided into two areas: *program memory*, also known as the *system heap*, and *object store*. The object store can be considered something like a permanent virtual RAM disk. Unlike the old virtual RAM disks on a PC, the object store retains the files stored in it even if the system is turned off.[1] This arrangement is the reason Windows CE systems such as the Pocket PC typically have a main battery and a backup battery. When the user replaces the main batteries, the backup battery's job is to provide power to the RAM to retain the files in the object store. Even when the user hits the reset button, the Windows CE kernel starts up looking for a previously created object store in RAM and uses that store if it finds one.

The other area of the RAM is devoted to the program memory. Program memory is used like the RAM in personal computers. It stores the heaps and stacks for the applications that are running. The boundary between the object store and the program RAM is movable. The user can move the dividing line between object store and program RAM using the System Control Panel applet. Under low-memory conditions, the system will ask the user for permission to take some object store RAM to use as program RAM to satisfy an application's demand for more RAM.

About ROM

In a personal computer, the ROM is used to store the BIOS (basic input/output system) and is typically 64–128 KB. In a Windows CE system, the ROM can range from 4 to 32 MB and stores the entire operating system, as well as the applications that are bundled with the system. In this sense, the ROM in a Windows CE system is like a small read-only hard disk.

In a Windows CE system, ROM-based programs can be designated as Execute in Place (XIP). That is, they're executed directly from the ROM instead of being loaded into program RAM and then executed. This capability is a huge advantage for small systems in two ways. The fact that the code is executed directly from ROM means that the program code doesn't take up valuable program RAM. Also, since the program doesn't have to be copied into RAM before it's launched, it takes less time to start an application. Programs that aren't in

---

1. On mobile systems such as the Pocket PC, the system is never really off. When the user presses the Off button, the system enters a very low power suspended state.

ROM but are contained in the object store or on a Flash memory storage card aren't executed in place; they're copied into the RAM and executed.

About Virtual Memory

Windows CE implements a virtual memory management system. In a virtual memory system, applications deal with virtual memory, which is a separate, imaginary address space that might not relate to the physical memory address space that's implemented by the hardware. The operating system uses the memory management unit of the microprocessor to translate virtual addresses to physical addresses in real time.

The key advantage of a virtual memory system can be seen in the complexity of the MS-DOS address space. Once demand for RAM exceeded the 640-KB limit of the original PC design, programmers had to deal with schemes such as *expanded* and *extended* memory to increase the available RAM. OS/2 1.*x* and Windows 3.0 replaced these schemes with a segment-based virtual memory system. Applications using virtual memory have no idea (nor should they care) where the actual physical memory resides, only that the memory is available. In these systems, the virtual memory was implemented in segments, resizable blocks of memory that ranged from 16 bytes to 64 KB in size. The 64-KB limit wasn't due to the segments themselves, but to the 16-bit nature of the Intel 80286 that was the basis for the segmented virtual memory system in Windows 3.*x* and OS/2 1.*x*.

Paged Memory

The Intel 80386 supported segments larger than 64 KB, but when Microsoft and IBM began the design for OS/2 2.0, they chose to use a different virtual memory system, also supported by the 386, known as a *paged virtual memory system.* In a paged memory system, the smallest unit of memory the microprocessor manages is the *page.* For Windows NT and OS/2 2.0, the pages were set to 386's default page size of 4096 bytes. When an application accesses a page, the microprocessor translates the virtual address of the page to a physical page in ROM or RAM. A page can also be tagged so that accessing the page causes an exception. The operating system then determines whether the virtual page is valid and, if so, maps a physical page of memory to the virtual page.

Windows CE implements a paged virtual memory management system similar to the other Win32 operating systems. Under Windows CE, a page is either 1024 or 4096 bytes, depending on the microprocessor. This is a change from Windows XP, where the page size is 4096 bytes for Intel microprocessors. For the CPUs currently supported by Windows CE, the 486, the Intel Strong-ARM, and the Hitachi SH4 use 4096-byte pages. The NEC 4100 uses a 4-KB page size in Windows CE 3.0 but a 1-KB page size in earlier versions of the operating system. The Hitachi SH3 uses 4096-byte pages in Windows CE 4.1, but it uses 1024-byte pages in earlier versions of Windows CE.

Virtual pages can be in one of three states: *free, reserved,* or *committed.* A free page is, as it sounds, free and available to be allocated. A reserved page is a page that has been reserved so that its virtual address can't be allocated by the operating system or another thread in the process. A reserved page can't be used elsewhere, but it also can't be used by the application because it isn't mapped to physical memory. To be mapped, a page must be committed. A committed page has been reserved by an application and has been directly mapped to a physical address.

All that I've just explained is old hat to experienced Win32 programmers. The important thing for the Windows CE programmer is to learn how Windows CE changes the equation. While Windows CE implements most of the same memory API set of its bigger Win32 cousins, the underlying architecture of Windows CE does impact programs. Before diving into the memory architecture of a Windows CE application, let's look at a few of the functions that provide information about the global state of the system memory.

Querying the System Memory

If an application knows the current memory state of the system, it can better manage the available resources. Windows CE implements both the Win32 *GetSystemInfo* and *GlobalMemoryStatus* functions. The *GetSystemInfo* function is prototyped below:

```
VOID GetSystemInfo (LPSYSTEM_INFO lpSystemInfo);
```

It's passed a pointer to a *SYSTEM_INFO* structure defined as

```
typedef struct {
    WORD wProcessorArchitecture;
    WORD wReserved;
    DWORD  dwPageSize;
    LPVOID lpMinimumApplicationAddress;
    LPVOID lpMaximumApplicationAddress;
    DWORD  dwActiveProcessorMask;
    DWORD  dwNumberOfProcessors;
    DWORD  dwProcessorType;
    DWORD  dwAllocationGranularity;
    WORD  wProcessorLevel;
    WORD  wProcessorRevision;
} SYSTEM_INFO;
```

The *wProcessorArchitecture* field identifies the type of microprocessor in the system. The value should be compared with the known constants defined in

Winnt.h, such as *PROCESSOR_ARCHITECTURE_INTEL*. Windows CE has extended these constants to include *PROCESSOR_ARCHITECTURE_ARM*, *PROCESSOR_ARCHITECTURE_SHx*, and others. Additional processor constants are added as net CPUs are supported by any of the Win32 operating systems. Skipping a few fields, the *dwProcessorType* field further narrows the microprocessor from a family to a specific microprocessor. Constants for the Hitachi SHx architecture include *PROCESSOR_HITACHI_SH3* and *PROCESSOR_HITACHI_SH4*. The last two fields, *wProcessorLevel* and *wProcessorRevision*, further refine the CPU type. The *wProcessorLevel* field is similar to the *dwProcessorType* field in that it defines the specific microprocessor within a family. The *dwProcessorRevision* field tells you the model and the stepping level of the chip.

The *dwPageSize* field specifies the page size, in bytes, of the microprocessor. Knowing this value comes in handy when you're dealing directly with the virtual memory API, which I talk about shortly. The *lpMinimumApplication-Address* and *lpMaximumApplicationAddress* fields specify the minimum and maximum virtual address available to the application. The *dwActiveProcessor-Mask* and *dwNumberOfProcessors* fields are used in Windows XP for systems that support more than one microprocessor. Since Windows CE supports only one microprocessor, you can ignore these fields. The *dwAllocationGranularity* field specifies the boundaries to which virtual memory regions are rounded. Like Windows XP, Windows CE rounds virtual regions to 64-KB boundaries.

A second handy function for determining the system memory state is this:

```
void GlobalMemoryStatus(LPMEMORYSTATUS lpmst);
```

which returns a *MEMORYSTATUS* structure defined as

```
typedef struct {
    DWORD dwLength;
    DWORD dwMemoryLoad;
    DWORD dwTotalPhys;
    DWORD dwAvailPhys;
    DWORD dwTotalPageFile;
    DWORD dwAvailPageFile;
    DWORD dwTotalVirtual;
    DWORD dwAvailVirtual;
} MEMORYSTATUS;
```

The *dwLength* field must be initialized by the application before the call is made to *GlobalMemoryStatus*. The *dwMemoryLoad* field is of dubious value; it makes available a general loading parameter that's supposed to indicate the current memory use in the system. The *dwTotalPhys* and *dwAvailPhys* fields indicate how many pages of RAM are assigned to the program RAM and how many are available. These values don't include RAM assigned to the object store.

The *dwTotalPageFile* and *dwAvailPageFile* fields are used under Windows XP and Windows Me to indicate the current status of the paging file. Because paging files aren't supported under Windows CE, these fields are always 0. The *dwTotalVirtual* and *dwAvailVirtual* fields indicate the total and available number of virtual memory pages accessible to the application.

The information returned by *GlobalMemoryStatus* provides confirmation of the memory architecture of Windows CE. Making this call on an HP iPaq Pocket PC with 32 MB of RAM returned the following values:

```
dwMemoryLoad        0x18            (24)
dwTotalPhys         0x011ac000      (18,530,304)
dwAvailPhys         0x00B66000      (11,952,128)
dwTotalPageFile     0
dwAvailPageFile     0
dwTotalVirtual      0x02000000      (33,554,432)
dwAvailVirtual      0x01e10000      (31,522,816)
```

The *dwTotalPhys* field indicates that of the 32 MB of RAM in the system, I have dedicated 18.5 MB to the program RAM, of which 12 MB is still free. Note that there's no way for an application, using this call, to know that another 14 MB of RAM has been dedicated to the object store. To determine the amount of RAM dedicated to the object store, use the function *GetStoreInformation*.

The *dwTotalPageFile* and *dwAvailPageFile* fields are 0, indicating no support for a paging file under Windows CE. The *dwTotalVirtual* field is interesting because it shows the 32-MB limit on virtual memory that Windows CE enforces on an application. Meanwhile, the *dwAvailVirtual* field indicates that in this application little of that 32 MB of virtual memory is being used.

An Application's Address Space

Although similar to the layout of a Windows XP application, the application address space of a Windows CE application has one huge difference that has an impact on applications. Under Windows CE, an application is limited to the virtual memory space available in its 32-MB slot and the 32-MB slot 1, which is used to load XIP-based DLLs. While 32 MB might seem like a fair amount of space available to an application that might run on a system with only 4 MB of RAM, Win32 application programmers, used to a 2-GB virtual address space, need to keep in mind the limited virtual address space available to a Windows CE application.

Figure 7-1 shows the layout of an application's 64-MB virtual address space, including the upper 32 MB used for XIP DLLs.

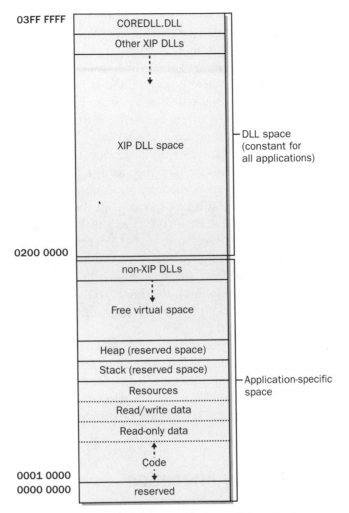

Figure 7-1   Memory map of a Windows CE application

Notice that the application is mapped as a 64-KB region starting at 0x10000. Remember, the lowest 64 KB of the address space for any application is reserved by Windows. The image of the file contains the code along with the static data segments and the resource segments. The actual code pages are not typically loaded in when the application is launched. Instead, each page is loaded on demand as the code in those pages is executed.

The read-only static data segment and the read/write static data areas typically take only a few pages. Each of these segments is page aligned. Like the code, these data segments are committed to RAM only as they're read or written to by the application. The resources for the application are loaded into a separate set of pages. The resources are read only and are paged into the RAM only as they're accessed by the application.

The application's stack is mapped above the resource segment. The stack segment is easily recognized because the committed pages are at the end of the reserved section, indicative of a stack that grows from higher addresses down. If this application had more than one thread, more than one stack segment would be reserved in the application's address space.

Following the stack is the local heap. The loader reserves a large number of pages, on the order of hundreds of kilobytes, for the heap to grow but commits pages only as necessary to satisfy memory allocations from *malloc*, *new*, or *LocalAlloc* calls. The remaining address space from the end of the reserved pages for the local heap to the start of the non-XIP DLLs mapped into the address space is free to be reserved and, if RAM permits, committed by the application. Non-XIP DLLs, those that are not execute-in-place in the ROM, are loaded into the application's address space starting at the 32-MB boundary in a top-down fashion. Non-XIP DLLs include those DLLs that are stored compressed in the ROM. Compressed ROM files must be decompressed into and executed from RAM when loaded.

The upper 32 MB of the application's address space is reserved for XIP DLLs. Windows CE maps the code for the XIP DLLs into this space. Read/write segments for these DLLs are loaded into the lower 32 MB of the application's address space. Starting with Windows CE 4.2, resource-only DLLs loaded from ROM are loaded outside the entire 64-MB application space. These DLLs are loaded into the virtual memory space.

The Different Kinds of Memory Allocation

A Windows CE application has a number of different methods for allocating memory. At the bottom of the memory-management food chain are the *Virtualxxx* functions that directly reserve, commit, and free virtual memory pages. Next comes the heap API. *Heaps* are regions of reserved memory space managed by the system for the application. Heaps come in two flavors: the default local heap automatically allocated when an application is started, and separate heaps that can be manually created by the application. After the heap API is static data—data blocks defined by the compiler and that are allocated automatically by the loader. Finally, we come to the stack, where an application stores variables local to a function.

The one area of the Win32 memory API that Windows CE doesn't support is the global heap. The global heap API, which includes calls such as *Global-*

Alloc, *GlobalFree*, and *GlobalRealloc*, is therefore not present in Windows CE. The global heap is really just a holdover from the Win16 days of Windows 3.*x*. In Win32, the global and local heaps are quite similar. One unique use of global memory, allocating memory for data in the clipboard, is handled by using the local heap under Windows CE.

The key to minimizing memory use in Windows CE is choosing the proper memory-allocation strategy that matches the memory-use patterns for a given block of memory. I'll review each of these memory types and then describe strategies for minimizing memory use in Windows CE applications.

Virtual Memory

Virtual memory is the most basic of the memory types. The system uses calls to the virtual memory API to allocate memory for the other types of memory, including heaps and stacks. The virtual memory API, including the *VirtualAlloc*, *VirtualFree*, and *VirtualReSize* functions, directly manipulates virtual memory pages in the application's virtual memory space. Pages can be reserved, committed to physical memory, and freed using these functions.

Allocating Virtual Memory

Allocating and reserving virtual memory is accomplished using this function:

```
LPVOID VirtualAlloc (LPVOID lpAddress, DWORD dwSize,
                     DWORD flAllocationType,
                     DWORD flProtect);
```

The first parameter to *VirtualAlloc* is the virtual address of the region of memory to allocate. The *lpAddress* parameter is used to identify the previously reserved memory block when you use *VirtualAlloc* to commit a block of memory previously reserved. If this parameter is *NULL*, the system determines where to allocate the memory region, rounded to a 64-KB boundary. The second parameter is *dwSize*, the size of the region to allocate or reserve. While this parameter is specified in bytes, not pages, the system rounds the requested size up to the next page boundary.

The *flAllocationType* parameter specifies the type of allocation. You can specify a combination of the following flags: *MEM_COMMIT*, *MEM_AUTO_COMMIT*, *MEM_RESERVE*, and *MEM_TOP_DOWN*. The *MEM_COMMIT* flag allocates the memory to be used by the program. *MEM_RESERVE* reserves the virtual address space to be later committed. Reserved pages can't be accessed until another call is made to *VirtualAlloc* specifying the region and using the *MEM_COMMIT* flag. The third flag,

MEM_TOP_DOWN, tells the system to map the memory at the highest permissible virtual address for the application.

The *MEM_AUTO_COMMIT* flag is unique to Windows CE and is quite handy. When this flag is specified, the block of memory is reserved immediately, but each page in the block will automatically be committed by the system when it's accessed for the first time. This allows you to allocate large blocks of virtual memory without burdening the system with the actual RAM allocation until the instant each page is first used. The drawback to auto-commit memory is that the physical RAM needed to back up a page might not be available when the page is first accessed. In this case, the system will generate an exception.

VirtualAlloc can be used to reserve a large region of memory with subsequent calls committing parts of the region or the entire region. Multiple calls to commit the same region won't fail. This allows an application to reserve memory and then blindly commit a page before it's written to. While this method isn't particularly efficient, it does free the application from having to check the state of a reserved page to see whether it's already committed before making the call to commit the page.

The *flProtect* parameter specifies the access protection for the region being allocated. The different flags available for this parameter are summarized in the following list.

- **PAGE_READONLY** The region can be read. If an application attempts to write to the pages in the region, an access violation will occur.

- **PAGE_READWRITE** The region can be read from or written to by the application.

- **PAGE_EXECUTE** The region contains code that can be executed by the system. Attempts to read from or write to the region will result in an access violation.

- **PAGE_EXECUTE_READ** The region can contain executable code, and applications can also read from the region.

- **PAGE_EXECUTE_READWRITE** The region can contain executable code, and applications can read from and write to the region.

- **PAGE_GUARD** The first access to this region results in a STATUS_GUARD_PAGE exception. This flag should be combined with the other protection flags to indicate the access rights of the region after the first access.

- *PAGE_NOACCESS*   Any access to the region results in an access violation.

- *PAGE_NOCACHE*   The RAM pages mapped to this region won't be cached by the microprocessor.

The *PAGE_GUARD* and *PAGE_NOCHACHE* flags can be combined with the other flags to further define the characteristics of a page. The *PAGE_GUARD* flag specifies a guard page, a page that generates a one-shot exception when it's first accessed and then takes on the access rights that were specified when the page was committed. The *PAGE_NOCACHE* flag prevents the memory that's mapped to the virtual page from being cached by the microprocessor. This flag is handy for device drivers that share memory blocks with devices using direct memory access (DMA).

Regions vs. Pages

Before I go on to talk about the virtual memory API, I need to make a somewhat subtle distinction. Virtual memory is reserved in regions that must align on 64-KB boundaries. Pages within a region can then be committed page by page. You can directly commit a page or a series of pages without first reserving a region of pages, but the page, or series of pages, directly committed will be aligned on a 64-KB boundary. For this reason, it's best to reserve blocks of virtual memory in 64-KB chunks and then commit that page within the region as needed.

With the limit of 32 MB of usable virtual memory space per process, this leaves a maximum of 32 MB / 64 KB – 1= 511 virtual memory regions that can be reserved before the system reports that it's out of memory. Take, for example, the following code fragment:

```
#define PAGESIZE 1024   // Assume we're on a 1-KB page machine
for (i = 0; i < 512; i++)
    pMem[i] = VirtualAlloc (NULL, PAGESIZE, MEM_RESERVE | MEM_COMMIT,
                            PAGE_READWRITE);
```

This code attempts to allocate 512 one-page blocks of virtual memory. Even if you have half a megabyte of RAM available in the system, *VirtualAlloc* will fail before the loop completes because it will run out of virtual address space for the application. This happens because each 1-KB block is allocated on a 64-KB boundary. Since the code, stack, and local heap for an application must also be mapped into the same 32-MB virtual address space, available virtual allocation regions usually top out at about 475.

A better way to make 512 distinct virtual allocations is to do something like this:

```
#define PAGESIZE 1024    // Assume we're on a 1-KB page machine.

// Reserve a region first.
pMemBase = VirtualAlloc (NULL, PAGESIZE * 512, MEM_RESERVE,
                            PAGE_NOACCESS);

for (i = 0; i < 512; i++)
    pMem[i] = VirtualAlloc (pMemBase + (i*PAGESIZE), PAGESIZE,
                            MEM_COMMIT, PAGE_READWRITE);
```

This code first reserves a region; the pages are committed later. Because the region was first reserved, the committed pages aren't rounded to 64-KB boundaries, and so, if you have 512 KB of available memory in the system, the allocations will succeed.

Although the code I just showed you is a contrived example (there are better ways to allocate 1-KB blocks than directly allocating virtual memory), it does demonstrate a major difference (from other Windows systems) in the way memory allocation works in Windows CE. In the desktop versions of Windows, applications have a full 2-GB virtual address space with which to work. In Windows CE, however, a programmer should remain aware of the relatively small 32-MB virtual address per application.

Freeing Virtual Memory

You can *decommit*, or free, virtual memory by calling *VirtualFree*. Decommitting a page unmaps the page from a physical page of RAM but keeps the page or pages reserved. The function is prototyped as

```
BOOL VirtualFree (LPVOID lpAddress, DWORD dwSize,
                    DWORD dwFreeType);
```

The *lpAddress* parameter should contain a pointer to the virtual memory region that's to be freed or decommitted. The *dwSize* parameter contains the size, in bytes, of the region if the region is to be decommitted. If the region is to be freed, this value must be 0. The *dwFreeType* parameter contains the flags that specify the type of operation. The *MEM_DECOMMIT* flag specifies that the region will be decommited but will remain reserved. The *MEM_RELEASE* flag both decommits the region if the pages are committed and also frees the region.

All the pages in a region being freed by means of *VirtualFree* must be in the same state. That is, all the pages in the region to be freed must either be committed or reserved. *VirtualFree* fails if some of the pages in the region are reserved while some are committed. To free a region with pages that are both reserved and committed, the committed pages should be decommitted first, and then the entire region can be freed.

Changing and Querying Access Rights

You can modify the access rights of a region of virtual memory, initially specified in *VirtualAlloc*, by calling *VirtualProtect*. This function can change the access rights only on committed pages. The function is prototyped as

```
BOOL VirtualProtect (LPVOID lpAddress, DWORD dwSize,
                     DWORD flNewProtect, PDWORD lpflOldProtect);
```

The first two parameters, *lpAddress* and *dwSize*, specify the block and the size of the region that the function acts on. The *flNewProtect* parameter contains the new protection flags for the region. These flags are the same ones I mentioned when I explained the *VirtualAlloc* function. The *lpflOldProtect* parameter should point to a *DWORD* that will receive the old protection flags of the first page in the region.

The current protection rights of a region can be queried with a call to

```
DWORD VirtualQuery (LPCVOID lpAddress,
                    PMEMORY_BASIC_INFORMATION lpBuffer,
                    DWORD dwLength);
```

The *lpAddress* parameter contains the starting address of the region being queried. The *lpBuffer* pointer points to a *PMEMORY_BASIC_INFORMATION* structure that I'll talk about soon. The third parameter, *dwLength*, must contain the size of the *PMEMORY_BASIC_INFORMATION* structure.

The *PMEMORY_BASIC_INFORMATION* structure is defined as

```
typedef struct _MEMORY_BASIC_INFORMATION {
    PVOID BaseAddress;
    PVOID AllocationBase;
    DWORD AllocationProtect;
    DWORD RegionSize;
    DWORD State;
    DWORD Protect;
    DWORD Type;
} MEMORY_BASIC_INFORMATION;
```

The first field of *MEMORY_BASIC_INFORMATION*, *BaseAddress*, is the address passed to the *VirtualQuery* function. The *AllocationBase* field contains the base address of the region when it was allocated using the *VirtualAlloc* function. The *AllocationProtect* field contains the protection attributes for the region when it was originally allocated. The *RegionSize* field contains the number of bytes from the pointer passed to *VirtualQuery* to the end of series of pages that have the same attributes. The *State* field contains the state—free, reserved, or committed—of the pages in the region. The *Protect* field contains the current protection flags for the region. Finally, the *Type* field contains the type of memory in the region. This field can contain the flags *MEM_PRIVATE*, indicating that the region contains private data for the application; *MEM_MAPPED*, indicating that the region is mapped to a memory-mapped file; or *MEM_IMAGE*, indicating that the region is mapped to an EXE or a DLL module.

The best way to understand the values returned by *VirtualQuery* is to look at an example. Say an application uses *VirtualAlloc* to reserve 16,384 bytes (16 pages on a 1-KB page-size machine). The system reserves this 16-KB block at address 0xA0000. Later the application commits 9216 bytes (9 pages) starting 2048 bytes (2 pages) into the initial region. Figure 7-2 shows a diagram of this scenario.

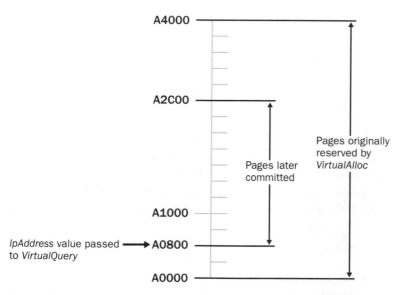

Figure 7-2   A region of reserved virtual memory that has nine pages committed

If a call is made to *VirtualQuery* with the *lpAddress* pointer pointing 4 pages into the initial region (address 0xA1000), the returned values would be the following:

```
BaseAddress          0xA1000
AllocationBase       0xA0000
AllocationProtect    PAGE_NOACCESS
RegionSize           0x1C00    (7,168 bytes or 7 pages)
State                MEM_COMMIT
Protect              PAGE_READWRITE
Type                 MEM_PRIVATE
```

The *BaseAddress* field contains the address passed to *VirtualQuery*, 0xA1000, 4096 bytes into the initial region. The *AllocationBase* field contains the base address of the original region, while *AllocationProtect* contains *PAGE_NOACCESS*, indicating that the region was originally reserved, not directly committed. The *RegionSize* field contains the number of bytes from the pointer passed to *VirtualQuery*, 0xA1000 to the end of the committed pages at 0xA2C00. The *State* and *Protect* fields contain the flags indicating the current state of the pages. The *Type* field indicates that the region was allocated by the application for its own use.

Heaps

Clearly, allocating memory on a page basis is inefficient for most applications. To optimize memory use, an application needs to be able to allocate and free memory on a per byte, or at least a per 8-byte, basis. The system enables allocations of this size through heaps. Using heaps also protects an application from having to deal with the differing page sizes of the microprocessors that support Windows CE. An application can simply allocate a block in a heap, and the system deals with the number of pages necessary for the allocation.

As I mentioned before, heaps are regions of reserved virtual memory space managed by the system for the application. The system gives you a number of functions that allow you to allocate and free blocks within the heap with a granularity much smaller than a page. As memory is allocated by the application within a heap, the system automatically grows the size of the heap to fill the request. As blocks in the heap are freed, the system looks to see if an entire page is freed. If so, that page is decommitted.

Unlike Windows XP, Windows CE supports the allocation of only fixed blocks in the heap. This simplifies the handling of blocks in the heap, but it can lead to the heaps becoming fragmented over time as blocks are allocated and freed. The result can be a heap being fairly empty but still requiring a large number of virtual pages because the system can't reclaim a page from the heap unless it's completely free.

Each application has a default, or local, heap created by the system when the application is launched. Blocks of memory in the local heap can be allocated, freed, and resized using the *LocalAlloc*, *LocalFree*, and *LocalRealloc* functions. An application can also create any number of separate heaps. These heaps have the same properties as the local heap but are managed through a separate set of *Heapxxxx* functions.

The Local Heap

By default, Windows CE initially reserves 192,512 bytes for the local heap but commits the pages only as they are allocated. If the application allocates more than the 188 KB in the local heap, the system allocates more space for the local heap. Growing the heap might require a separate, disjointed address space reserved for the additional space on the heap. Applications shouldn't assume that the local heap is contained in one block of virtual address space. Because Windows CE heaps support only fixed blocks, Windows CE implements only the subset of the Win32 local heap functions necessary to allocate, resize, and free fixed blocks on the local heap.

Allocating Memory on the Local Heap

You allocate a block of memory on the local heap by calling

```
HLOCAL LocalAlloc (UINT uFlags, UINT uBytes);
```

The call returns a value cast as an *HLOCAL*, which is a handle to a local memory block, but since the block allocated is always fixed, the return value can simply be recast as a pointer to the block.

The *uFlags* parameter describes the characteristics of the block. The flags supported under Windows CE are limited to those that apply to fixed allocations. They are the following:

- **LMEM_FIXED**   Allocates a fixed block in the local heap. Since all local heap allocations are fixed, this flag is redundant.

- **LMEM_ZEROINIT**   Initializes memory contents to 0.

- **LPTR**   Combines the *LMEM_FIXED* and *LMEM_ZEROINIT* flags.

The *uBytes* parameter specifies the size of the block to allocate in bytes. The size of the block is rounded up, but only to the next 8-byte boundary.

Freeing Memory on the Local Heap

You can free a block by calling

```
HLOCAL LocalFree (HLOCAL hMem);
```

The function takes the handle to the local memory block and returns *NULL* if successful. If the function fails, it returns the original handle to the block.

Resizing and Querying the Size of Local Heap Memory

You can resize blocks on the local heap by calling

```
HLOCAL LocalReAlloc (HLOCAL hMem, UINT uBytes, UINT uFlag);
```

The *hMem* parameter is the pointer (handle) returned by *LocalAlloc*. The *uBytes* parameter is the new size of the block. The *uFlag* parameter contains the flags for the new block. Under Windows CE, two flags are relevant, *LMEM_ZEROINIT* and *LMEM_MOVEABLE*. *LMEM_ZEROINIT* causes the contents of the new area of the block to be set to 0 if the block is grown as a result of this call. The *LMEM_MOVEABLE* flag tells Windows that it can move the block if the block is being grown and there's not enough room immediately above the current block. Without this flag, if you don't have enough space immediately above the block to satisfy the request, *LocalRealloc* will fail with an out-of-memory error. If you specify the *LMEM_MOVEABLE* flag, the handle (really the pointer to the block of memory) might change as a result of the call.

The size of the block can be queried by calling

```
UINT LocalSize (HLOCAL hMem);
```

The size returned will be at least as great as the requested size for the block. As I mentioned earlier, Windows CE rounds the size of a local heap allocation up to the next 8-byte boundary.

Separate Heaps

To avoid fragmenting the local heap, it's better to create a separate heap if you need a series of blocks of memory that will be used for a set amount of time. An example of this would be a text editor that might manage a file by creating a separate heap for each file it's editing. As files are opened and closed, the heaps would be created and destroyed.

Heaps under Windows CE have the same API as those under Windows XP. The only noticeable difference is the lack of support for the *HEAP_GENERATE-_EXCEPTIONS* flag. Under Windows XP, this flag causes the system to generate an exception if an allocation request can't be accommodated.

Creating a Separate Heap

You create heaps by calling

```
HANDLE HeapCreate (DWORD flOptions, DWORD dwInitialSize,
                   DWORD dwMaximumSize);
```

Under Windows CE, the first parameter, *flOptions*, can be *NULL*, or it can contain the *HEAP_NO_SERIALIZE* flag. By default, Windows heap management routines prevent two threads in a process from accessing the heap at the same time. This serialization prevents the heap pointers that the system uses to track the allocated blocks in the heap from being corrupted. In other versions of Windows, the *HEAP_NO_SERIALIZE* flag can be used if you don't want this type of protection. Under Windows CE, however, this flag is provided only for compatibility, and all heap accesses are serialized.

The other two parameters, *dwInitialSize* and *dwMaximumSize*, specify the initial size and expected maximum size of the heap. The *dwMaximumSize* value determines how many pages in the virtual address space to reserve for the heap. You can set this parameter to 0 if you want to defer to Windows' determination of how many pages to reserve. The default size of a heap is 188 KB. The *dwInitialSize* parameter determines how many of those initially reserved pages will be immediately committed. If this value is 0, the heap initially has one page committed.

Allocating Memory in a Separate Heap

You allocate memory on the heap using

```
LPVOID HeapAlloc (HANDLE hHeap, DWORD dwFlags, DWORD dwBytes);
```

Notice that the return value is a pointer, not a handle as in the *LocalAlloc* function. Separate heaps always allocate fixed blocks, even under Windows XP and Windows Me. The first parameter is the handle to the heap returned by the *HeapCreate* call. The *dwFlags* parameter can be one of two self-explanatory values, *HEAP_NO_SERIALIZE* and *HEAP_ZERO_MEMORY*. The final parameter, *dwBytes*, specifies the number of bytes in the block to allocate. The size is rounded up to the next DWORD.

Freeing Memory in a Separate Heap

You can free a block in a heap by calling

```
BOOL HeapFree (HANDLE hHeap, DWORD dwFlags, LPVOID lpMem);
```

The only flag allowable in the *dwFlags* parameter is *HEAP_NO_SERIALIZE*. The *lpMem* parameter points to the block to free, while *hHeap* contains the handle to the heap.

Resizing and Querying the Size of Memory in a Separate Heap

You can resize heap allocations by calling

```
LPVOID HeapReAlloc (HANDLE hHeap, DWORD dwFlags, LPVOID lpMem,
                    DWORD dwBytes);
```

The *dwFlags* parameter can be any combination of three flags: *HEAP_NO_SERIALIZE*, *HEAP_REALLOC_IN_PLACE_ONLY*, and *HEAP_ZERO_MEMORY*. The only new flag here is *HEAP_REALLOC_IN_PLACE_ONLY*, which tells the heap manager to fail the reallocation if the space can't be found for the block without relocating it. This flag is handy if you already have a number of pointers pointing to data in the block and you aren't interested in updating them. The *lpMem* parameter is the pointer to the block being resized, and the *dwBytes* parameter is the requested new size of the block. Notice that the function of the *HEAP_REALLOC_IN_PLACE_ONLY* flag in *HeapReAlloc* provides the opposite function from the one that the *LMEM_MOVEABLE* flag provides for *LocalReAlloc*. *HEAP_REALLOC_IN_PLACE_ONLY* prevents a block from moving that would be moved by default in a separate heap, while *LMEM_MOVEABLE* enables a block to be moved that by default would not be moved in the local heap. *HeapReAlloc* returns a pointer to the block if the reallocation was successful and returns *NULL* otherwise. Unless you specified that the block not be relocated, the returned pointer might be different from the pointer passed in if the block had to be relocated to find enough space in the heap.

To determine the actual size of a block, you can call

```
DWORD HeapSize (HANDLE hHeap, DWORD dwFlags, LPCVOID lpMem);
```

The parameters are as you expect: the handle of the heap; the single, optional flag, *HEAP_NO_SERIALIZE*; and the pointer to the block of memory being checked.

Destroying a Separate Heap

You can completely free a heap by calling

```
BOOL HeapDestroy (HANDLE hHeap);
```

Individual blocks within the heap don't have to be freed before you destroy the heap.

One final heap function is valuable when writing DLLs. The function

```
HANDLE GetProcessHeap (VOID);
```

returns the handle to the local heap of the process calling the DLL. This allows a DLL to allocate memory within the calling process's local heap. All the other heap calls, with the exception of *HeapDestroy*, can be used with the handle returned by *GetProcessHeap*.

The Stack

The stack is the easiest to use (the most self-managing) of the different types of memory under Windows CE. The stack under Windows CE, as in any operating system, is the storage place for temporary variables that are referenced within a function. The operating system also uses the stack to store return addresses for functions and the state of the microprocessor registers during exception handling.

Windows CE manages a separate stack for every thread in the system. By default, each stack in the system is limited to a maximum size of around 58 KB.

Each separate thread within one process can grow its stack up to the 58-KB limit. This limit has to do with how Windows CE manages the stack. When a thread is created, Windows CE reserves a 64-KB region for the thread's stack. It then commits virtual pages from the top down as the stack grows. As the stack shrinks, the system will, under low-memory conditions, reclaim the unused but still committed pages below the stack. The limit of 58 KB comes from the size of the 64-KB region dedicated to the stack minus the number of pages necessary to guard the stack against overflow and underflow.

When an application creates a new thread, the maximum size of the stack can be specified in the *CreateThread* call that creates the thread. The maximum size of the stack for the main thread of the application can be specified by a linker switch when an application is linked. The same guard pages are applied, but the stack size can be specified up to 1 MB. Note that the size defined for the default stack is also the default size used for all the separate thread stacks. That is, if you specify the main stack to be 128 KB, all other threads in the application have a stack size limit of 128 KB unless you specify a different stack size in each call to *CreateThread*.

One other consideration must be made when you're planning how to use the stack in an application. When an application calls a function that needs stack space, Windows CE attempts to commit the pages immediately below the current stack pointer to satisfy the request. If no physical RAM is available, the thread needing the stack space is briefly suspended. If the request can't be granted within a short period of time, an exception is raised. Windows CE goes to great lengths to free the required pages, but if this can't happen the system raises an exception. I'll cover low-memory situations shortly, but for now just remember that you shouldn't try to use large amounts of stack space in low-memory situations.

Static Data

C and C++ applications have predefined blocks of memory that are automatically allocated when the application is loaded. These blocks hold statically allocated strings, buffers, and global variables as well as buffers necessary for the library functions that were statically linked with the application. None of this is new to the C programmer, but under Windows CE, these spaces are handy for squeezing the last useful bytes out of RAM.

Windows CE allocates two blocks of RAM for the static data of an application, one for the read/write data and one for the read-only data. Because these areas are allocated on a per-page basis, you can typically find some space left over from the static data up to the next page boundary. The finely tuned Windows CE application should be written to ensure that it has little or no extra space left over. If you have space in the static data area, sometimes it's better to move a buffer or two into the static data area instead of allocating those buffers dynamically.

Another consideration is that if you're writing a ROM-based application, you should move as much data as possible to the read-only static data area. Windows CE doesn't allocate RAM to the read-only area for ROM-based applications. Instead, the ROM pages are mapped directly into the virtual address space. This essentially gives you unlimited read-only space with no impact on the RAM requirements of the application.

The best place to determine the size of the static data areas is to look in the map file that's optionally generated by the linker. The map file is chiefly used to determine the locations of functions and data for debugging purposes, but it also shows the size of the static data if you know where to look. Listing 7-1 shows a portion of an example map file generated by Visual C++.

```
memtest

Timestamp is 34ce4088 (Tue Jan 27 12:16:08 1998)

Preferred load address is 00010000

Start           Length        Name              Class
0001:00000000   00006100H     .text             CODE
0002:00000000   00000310H     .rdata            DATA
0002:00000310   00000014H     .xdata            DATA
0002:00000324   00000028H     .idata$2          DATA
0002:0000034c   00000014H     .idata$3          DATA
0002:00000360   000000f4H     .idata$4          DATA
0002:00000454   000003eeH     .idata$6          DATA
0002:00000842   00000000H     .edata            DATA
0003:00000000   000000f4H     .idata$5          DATA
0003:000000f4   00000004H     .CRT$XCA          DATA
0003:000000f8   00000004H     .CRT$XCZ          DATA
0003:000000fc   00000004H     .CRT$XIA          DATA
0003:00000100   00000004H     .CRT$XIZ          DATA
0003:00000104   00000004H     .CRT$XPA          DATA
0003:00000108   00000004H     .CRT$XPZ          DATA
0003:0000010c   00000004H     .CRT$XTA          DATA
0003:00000110   00000004H     .CRT$XTZ          DATA
0003:00000114   000011e8H     .data             DATA
0003:000012fc   0000108cH     .bss              DATA
0004:00000000   000003e8H     .pdata            DATA
0005:00000000   000000f0H     .rsrc$01          DATA
0005:000000f0   00000334H     .rsrc$02          DATA
```

Listing 7-1   The top portion of a map file showing the size of the data segments in an application   *(continued)*

Listing 7-1 *(continued)*

```
    Address          Publics by Value          Rva+Base    Lib:Object

 0001:00000000       _WinMain                  00011000 f  memtest.obj
 0001:0000007c       _InitApp                  0001107c f  memtest.obj
 0001:000000d4       _InitInstance             000110d4 f  memtest.obj
 0001:00000164       _TermInstance             00011164 f  memtest.obj
 0001:00000248       _MainWndProc              00011248 f  memtest.obj
 0001:000002b0       _GetFixedEquiv            000112b0 f  memtest.obj
 0001:00000350       _DoCreateMain             00011350 f  memtest.obj.
    ⋮
```

The map file in Listing 7-1 indicates that the EXE has five sections. Section *0001* is the text segment containing the executable code of the program. Section *0002* contains the read-only static data. Section *0003* contains the read/write static data. Section *0004* contains the fix-up table to support calls to other DLLs. Finally, section *0005* is the resource section containing the application's resources, such as menu and dialog box templates.

Let's examine the *.data*, *.bss*, and *.rdata* lines. The *.data* section contains the initialized read/write data. If you initialized a global variable as in

```
static HINST g_hLoadlib = NULL;
```

the *g_loadlib* variable would end up in the *.data* segment. The *.bss* segment contains the uninitialized read/write data. A buffer defined as

```
static BYTE g_ucItems[256];
```

would end up in the *.bss* segment. The final segment, *.rdata*, contains the read-only data. Static data that you've defined using the *const* keyword ends up in the *.rdata* segment. An example of this would be the structures I use for my message lookup tables, as in the following:

```
// Message dispatch table for MainWindowProc
const struct decodeUINT MainMessages[] = {
    WM_CREATE, DoCreateMain,
    WM_SIZE, DoSizeMain,
    WM_COMMAND, DoCommandMain,
    WM_DESTROY, DoDestroyMain,
};
```

The *.data* and *.bss* blocks are folded into the *0003* section, which, if you add the size of all blocks in the third section, has a total size of 0x2274, or 8820, bytes. Rounded up to the next page size, the read/write section ends up taking nine pages, with 396 bytes not used. So in this example, placing a buffer or two in the static data section of the application would be essentially free. The read-only segment, section *0002*, including *.rdata*, ends up being 0x0842, or 2114, bytes, which takes up three pages, with 958 bytes, almost an entire page, wasted. In this case, moving 75 bytes of constant data from the read-only segment to the read/write segment saves a page of RAM when the application is loaded.

String Resources

One often-forgotten area for read-only data is the resource segment of your application. While I mentioned a new Windows CE–specific feature of the *LoadString* function in Chapter 4, it's worth repeating here. If you call *LoadString* with 0 in place of the pointer to the buffer, the function returns a pointer to the string in the resource segment. An example would be

```
LPCTSTR pString;

pString = (LPCTSTR)LoadString (hInst, ID_STRING, NULL, 0)
```

The string returned is read only, but it does allow you to reference the string without having to allocate a buffer to hold the string. Also be warned that the string won't be zero terminated unless you have added the *-n* switch to the command line of the resource compiler. However, the word immediately preceding the string contains the length of the string resource.

Selecting the Proper Memory Type

Now that we've looked at the different types of memory, it's time to consider the best use of each. For large blocks of memory, directly allocating virtual memory is best. An application can reserve as much address space (up to the usable 32-MB limit of the application) but can commit only the pages necessary at any one time. While directly allocated virtual memory is the most flexible memory allocation type, it shifts to us the burden of worrying about page granularity as well as keeping track of the reserved versus committed pages.

The local heap is always handy. It doesn't need to be created and will grow as necessary to satisfy a request. Fragmentation is the issue here. Consider that applications on a Pocket PC might run for weeks or even months at a time. There's no Off button on a Pocket PC—just a Suspend command. So when you're thinking about memory fragmentation, don't assume that a user will open the application, change one item, and then close it. A user is likely to start an application and keep it running so that the application is just a quick click away.

The advantage of separate heaps is that you can destroy them when their time is up, nipping the fragmentation problem in the bud. A minor disadvantage of separate heaps is the need to manually create and destroy them.

The static data area is a great place to slip in a buffer or two essentially for free because the page is going to be allocated anyway. The key to managing the static data is to make the size of the static data segments close to, but over the page size of, your target processor. Sometimes it's better to move constant data from the read-only segment to the read/write segment if it saves a page in the read-only segment. The only time you wouldn't do this is if the application is to be burned into ROM. Then the more constant the data is, the better, because it doesn't take up RAM. The read-only segment is handy even for applications loaded from the object store because read-only pages can be discarded and reloaded as needed by the operating system.

The stack is, well, the stack—simple to use and always around. The only considerations are the maximum size of the stack and the problems of enlarging the stack in a low-memory condition. Make sure your application doesn't require large amounts of stack space to shut down. If the system suspends a thread in your application while it's being shut down, the user will more than likely lose data. That won't help customer satisfaction.

Managing Low-Memory Conditions

Even for applications that have been fine-tuned to minimize their memory use, there are going to be times when the system runs very low on RAM. Windows CE applications operate in an almost perpetual low-memory environment. The Pocket PC is designed intentionally to run in a low-memory situation. Applications on the Pocket PC don't have a Close button—the shell automatically closes them when the system needs additional memory. Because of this, Windows CE offers a number of methods to distribute the scarce memory in the system among the running applications.

The *WM_HIBERNATE* Message

The first and most obvious addition to Windows CE is the *WM_HIBERNATE* message. Windows CE shell sends this message to all top-level windows that have the *WS_OVERLAPPED* style (that is, have neither the *WS_POPUP* nor the *WS_CHILD* style) and have the *WS_VISIBLE* style. These qualifications should allow most applications to have at least one window that receives a *WM_HIBERNATE* message. An exception to this would be an application that doesn't really terminate but simply hides all its windows. This arrangement allows an application a quick start because it only has to show its window, but this situation also means that the application is taking up RAM even when the user thinks it's closed. While this is exactly the kind of application design that should *not* be used under Windows CE, those that are designed this way must act as if they're always in hibernate mode when hidden because they'll never receive a *WM_HIBERNATE* message.

The shell sends *WM_HIBERNATE* messages to the top-level windows in reverse Z-order until enough memory is freed to push the available memory above a preset threshold. When an application receives a *WM_HIBERNATE* message, it should reduce its memory footprint as much as possible. This can involve releasing cached data; freeing any GDI objects such as fonts, bitmaps, and brushes; and destroying any window controls. In essence, the application should reduce its memory use to the smallest possible footprint that's necessary to retain its internal state.

If sending *WM_HIBERNATE* messages to the applications in the background doesn't free enough memory to move the system out of a limited-memory state, a *WM_HIBERNATE* message is sent to the application in the foreground. If part of your hibernation routine is to destroy controls on your window, you should be sure that you aren't the foreground application. Disappearing controls don't give the user a warm and fuzzy feeling.

Memory Thresholds

Windows CE monitors the free RAM in the system and responds differently as less and less RAM is available. As less memory is available, Windows CE first sends *WM_HIBERNATE* messages and then begins limiting the size of allocations possible. The two tables that follow show the free-memory levels used by the Explorer shell and the Pocket PC to trigger low-memory events in the system. Windows CE defines four memory states: normal, limited, low, and critical. The memory state of the system depends on how much free memory is available to the system as a whole. These limits are higher for 4-KB page systems because those systems have less granularity in allocations, as shown in Table 7-1 and Table 7-2.

Table 7-1 Memory Thresholds for the Explorer Shell

Event	Free Memory 1024-Page Size	Free Memory 4096-Page Size	Comments
Limited-memory state	128 KB	160 KB	Send *WM_HIBERNATE* messages to applications in reverse Z-order. Free stack space reclaimed as needed.
Low-memory state	64 KB	96 KB	Limit virtual allocations to 16 KB. Low-memory dialog displayed.
Critical-memory state	16 KB	48 KB	Limit virtual allocations to 8 KB.

Table 7-2 Memory Thresholds for the Pocket PC

Event	Free Memory 1024-Page Size	Free Memory 4096-Page Size	Comments
Hibernate threshold	200 KB	224 KB	Send *WM_HIBERNATE* messages to applications in reverse Z-order.
Limited-memory state	128 KB	160 KB	Begin to close applications in reverse Z-order. Free stack space reclaimed as needed.
Low-memory state	64 KB	96 KB	Limit virtual allocations to 16 KB.
Critical-memory state	16 KB	48 KB	Limit virtual allocations to 8 KB.

The effect of these memory states is to share the remaining wealth. First, *WM_HIBERNATE* messages are sent to the applications to ask them to reduce their memory footprint. After an application is sent a *WM_HIBERNATE* message, the system memory levels are checked to see whether the available memory is now above the threshold that caused the *WM_HIBERNATE* messages to be sent. If not, a *WM_HIBERNATE* message is sent to the next application. This continues until all applications have been sent a *WM_HIBERNATE* message.

The low-memory strategies of the Explorer shell and the Pocket PC diverge at this point. If the Explorer shell is running, the system displays the OOM, the out-of-memory dialog, and requests that the user either select an application to close or reallocate some RAM dedicated to the object store to the program memory. If, after the selected application has been shut down or memory has been moved into program RAM, you still don't have enough memory, the out-of-memory dialog is displayed again. This process is repeated until there's enough memory to lift the H/PC above the threshold.

For the Pocket PC, the actions are somewhat different. The Pocket PC shell automatically starts shutting down applications in least recently used order without asking the user. If there still isn't enough memory after all applications except the foreground application and the shell are closed, the system uses its other techniques of scavenging free pages from stacks and limiting any allocations of virtual memory.

If, on either system, an application is requested to shut down and it doesn't, the system will purge the application after waiting approximately 8 seconds. This is the reason an application shouldn't allocate large amounts of stack space. If the application is shutting down due to low-memory conditions, it's possible that the stack space can't be allocated and the application will be suspended. If this happens after the system has requested that the application close, it could be purged from memory without properly saving its state.

In the low- and critical-memory states, applications are limited in the amount of memory they can allocate. In these states, a request for virtual memory larger than what's allowed is refused even if there's memory available to satisfy the request. Remember that it isn't just virtual memory allocations that are limited; allocations on the heap and stack are rejected if, to satisfy the request, those allocations require virtual memory allocations above the allowable limits.

I should point out that sending *WM_HIBERNATE* messages and automatically closing down applications is performed by the shell. On embedded systems for which the OEM can write its own shell, it is the OEM's responsibility to implement the *WM_HIBERNATE* message and any other memory management techniques. Fortunately, the Microsoft Windows CE Platform Builder provides the source code for the Explorer shell that implements the *WM_HIBERNATE* message.

It should go without saying that applications should check the return codes of any memory allocation call, but since some still don't, I'll say it. *Check the return codes from calls that allocate memory.* There's a much better chance of a memory allocation failing under Windows CE than under the desktop versions of Windows. Applications must be written to react gracefully to rejected memory allocations.

The Win32 memory management API isn't fully supported by Windows CE, but there's clearly enough support for you to use the limited memory of a Windows CE device to the fullest. A great source for learning about the intricacies of the Win32 memory management API is Jeff Richter's *Programming Applications for Microsoft Windows* (Microsoft Press, 1999). Jeff spends six chapters on memory management, while I have summarized the same topic in one.

We've looked at the program RAM, the part of RAM that is available to applications. Now it's time, in the next two chapters, to look at the other part of the RAM, the object store. The object store supports more than a file system. It also optionally supports the registry API as well as a database API unique to Windows CE.

8

Files and the Registry

One of the areas where Windows CE diverges furthest from its larger cousin Windows XP is in the area of file storage. Instead of relying on ferromagnetic storage media such as floppy disks or hard disk drives, Windows CE implements a unique RAM-based file system known as the *object store*. In implementation, the object store more closely resembles a database than it does a file allocation system for a disk. In the object store resides the files as well as the registry for the system and any Windows CE databases. Fortunately for the programmer, most of the unique implementation of the object store is hidden behind standard Win32 functions.

The Windows CE file API is taken directly from Win32, and for the most part, the API is fairly complete. Windows CE also implements the standard registry API, albeit without the vast levels of security found in Windows XP.

Some differences in the object store do expose themselves to the programmer. Execute-in-place files, stored in ROM, appear as files in the object store, but these functions can't be opened and read as standard files. The object store format is undocumented, so there is no way to dig underneath the file system API to look at sectors, clusters, or cylinders of data as you could on a FAT-formatted disk.

The concept of the *current directory*, so important in other versions of Windows, isn't present in Windows CE. Files are specified by their complete path. The command line shell does maintain its own current directory, but this directory is independent of the file system.

As a general rule, Windows CE doesn't support the deep application-level security available under Windows XP. However, because the generic Win32 API was originally based on Windows NT, a number of the functions for file and registry operations have one or more parameters that deal with security rights. Under Windows CE, these values should be set to their default, not security state. This means you should almost always pass *NULL* in the security parameters for functions that request security information.[1] In this rather long chapter, I'll first explain the file system and the file API. Then we'll do a tour of the registry API.

The Windows CE File System

The default file system, supported on all Windows CE platforms, is the object store. The object store is equivalent to the hard disk on a Windows CE device. It's a subtly complex file storage system incorporating compressed RAM storage for read/write files and seamless integration with ROM-based files. A user sees no difference between a file in RAM in the object store and those files based in ROM. Files in RAM and ROM can reside in the same directory, and document files in ROM can be opened (although not modified) by the user. In short, the object store integrates the default files provided in ROM with the user-generated files stored in RAM.

In addition to the object store, Windows CE supports multiple installable file systems that can support up to 256 different storage devices or partitions on storage devices. The interface to these devices is the installable file system (IFS) API. Most Windows CE platforms include an IFS driver for the FAT file system for files stored on ATA flash cards or hard disks. In addition, third-party manufacturers can write an IFS driver to support other file systems.

Windows CE doesn't use drive letters as is the practice on PCs. Instead, every storage device is simply a directory off the root directory. Traditionally, the name of each directory is *Storage Card*. If more than one storage device is inserted, the additional devices are numbered, as in *Storage Card 1*, *Storage Card 2*, and so on, all the way up to *Storage Card 99* for the 100th card. I say "traditionally" because Windows CE doesn't assume a name. Instead, it asks the driver what it wants to call the directory, and traditionally, the block mode driver returns the name *Storage Card*. Because the name of the storage device directory can change, you should *never* assume that these directories will be called Storage Card. I'll demonstrate a method for determining which directories in the root are directories and which are actually storage devices.

As should be expected for a Win32-compatible operating system, the filename format for Windows CE is the same as that of its larger counterparts. Windows CE supports long filenames. Filenames and their complete paths can be up to *MAX_PATH* in length, which is currently defined at 260 bytes. Filenames

---

1. Windows CE does support its own version of module-level security. I'll be discussing this version in Chapter 10.

have the same *name.ext* format as they do in other Windows operating systems. The extension is the three characters following the last period in the filename and defines the type of file. The file type is used by the shell when determining the difference between executable files and different documents. Allowable characters in filenames are the same as for Windows XP.

Windows CE files support many of the same attribute flags as Windows XP, with a few additions. Attribute flags include the standard read-only, system, hidden, compressed, and archive flags. A few additional flags have been included to support the special RAM/ROM mix of files in the object store.

The Object Store vs. Other Storage Media

To the programmer, the difference between files in the RAM part of the object store and the files based in ROM are subtle. The files in ROM can be detected by a special in-ROM file attribute flag. Execute in place (XIP) modules in ROM are marked by an additional ROM-Module attribute indicating their XIP status. XIP files can't be opened using the standard file opening functions such as *CreateFile*. In addition, some files in the ROM and almost all files in the RAM are compressed and therefore marked with the compressed file attribute.

The object store in Windows CE has some basic limitations. First, the size of the object store is currently limited to 256 MB of RAM. Given the compression features of the object store, this means that the amount of data that the object store can contain is somewhere around 512 MB. Individual files in the object store are limited to 32 MB. These file size limits don't apply to files in secondary storage such as hard disks, PC Cards, and CompactFlash Cards.

Standard File I/O

Windows CE supports most of the same file I/O functions found in Windows XP and Windows Me. The same Win32 API calls, such as *CreateFile*, *ReadFile*, *WriteFile*, and *CloseFile*, are all supported. A Windows CE programmer must be aware of a few differences, however. First of all, the old Win16 standards, *_lread*, *_lwrite*, and *_llseek*, aren't supported. This isn't really a huge problem because all of these functions can easily be implemented by wrapping the Windows CE file functions with a small amount of code. Windows CE does support basic console library functions such as *fprintf* and *printf* for console applications if the console is supported on that configuration.

Windows CE doesn't support the overlapped I/O that's supported under Windows XP. Files or devices can't be opened with the *FILE_ FLAG_OVERLAPPED* flag, nor can reads or writes use the overlapped mode of asynchronous calls and returns.

File operations in Windows CE follow the traditional handle-based methodology used since the days of MS-DOS. Files are opened by means of a function that returns a handle. Read and write functions are passed the handle to indicate the file to act on. Data is read from or written to the offset in the file indicated by a system-maintained file pointer. Finally, when the reading and writing have been completed, the application indicates this by closing the file handle. Now on to the specifics.

Creating and Opening Files

Creating a file or opening an existing file or device is accomplished by means of the standard Win32 function:

```
HANDLE CreateFile (LPCTSTR lpFileName, DWORD dwDesiredAccess,
                   DWORD dwShareMode,
                   LPSECURITY_ATTRIBUTES lpSecurityAttributes,
                   DWORD dwCreationDistribution,
                   DWORD dwFlagsAndAttributes, HANDLE hTemplateFile);
```

The first parameter is the name of the file to be opened or created. The filename should have a fully specified path. Filenames with no path information are assumed to be in the root directory of the object store.

The *dwDesiredAccess* parameter indicates the requested access rights. The allowable flags are *GENERIC_READ* to request read access to the file and *GENERIC_WRITE* for write access. Both flags must be passed to get read/write access. You can open a file with neither read nor write permissions. This is handy if you just want to get the attributes of a device. The *dwShareMode* parameter specifies the access rights that can be granted to other processes. This parameter can be *FILE_SHARE_READ* and/or *FILE_SHARE_WRITE*. The *lpSecurityAttributes* parameter is ignored by Windows CE and should be set to *NULL*.

The *dwCreationDistribution* parameter tells *CreateFile* how to open or create the file. The following flags are allowed:

- **CREATE_NEW**   Creates a new file. If the file already exists, the function fails.

- **CREATE_ALWAYS**   Creates a new file or truncates an existing file.

- **OPEN_EXISTING**   Opens a file only if it already exists.

- **OPEN_ALWAYS**   Opens a file or creates a file if it doesn't exist. This differs from *CREATE_ALWAYS* because it doesn't truncate the file to 0 bytes if the file exists.

- **TRUNCATE_EXISTING**   Opens a file and truncates it to 0 bytes. The function fails if the file doesn't already exist.

The *dwFlagsAndAttributes* parameter defines the attribute flags for the file if it's being created in addition to flags in order to tailor the operations on the file. The following flags are allowed under Windows CE:

- ■ **FILE_ATTRIBUTE_NORMAL** This is the default attribute. It's overridden by any of the other file attribute flags.

- ■ **FILE_ATTRIBUTE_READONLY** Sets the read-only attribute bit for the file. Subsequent attempts to open the file with write access will fail.

- ■ **FILE_ATTRIBUTE_ARCHIVE** Sets the archive bit for the file.

- ■ **FILE_ATTRIBUTE_SYSTEM** Sets the system bit for the file indicating that the file is critical to the operation of the system.

- ■ **FILE_ATTRIBUTE_HIDDEN** Sets the hidden bit. The file will be visible only to users who have the View All Files option set in the Explorer.

- ■ **FILE_FLAG_WRITE_THROUGH** Write operations to the file won't be lazily cached in memory.

- ■ **FILE_FLAG_RANDOM_ACCESS** Indicates to the system that the file will be randomly accessed instead of sequentially accessed. This flag can help the system determine the proper caching strategy for the file.

Windows CE doesn't support a number of file attributes and file flags that are supported under Windows XP. The unsupported flags include but aren't limited to the following: *FILE_ATTRIBUTE_OFFLINE, FILE_FLAG_OVERLAPPED, FILE_FLAG_NO_BUFFERING, FILE_FLAG_SEQUENTIAL_SCAN, FILE_FLAG_ DELETE_ON_CLOSE, FILE_FLAG_BACKUP_SEMANTICS,* and *FILE_FLAG_POSIX_ SEMANTICS.* Under Windows XP, the flag *FILE_ATTRIBUTE_ TEMPORARY* is used to indicate a temporary file, but as we'll see later, it's used by Windows CE to indicate a directory that is in reality a separate drive or network share.

The final parameter in *CreateFile, hTemplate,* is ignored by Windows CE and should be set to 0. *CreateFile* returns a handle to the opened file if the function was successful. If the function fails, it returns *INVALID_HANDLE_VALUE.* To determine why the function failed, call *GetLastError.* If the *dwCreationDistribu tion* flags included *CREATE_ALWAYS* or *OPEN_ALWAYS,* you can determine whether the file previously existed by calling *GetLastError* to see if it returns *ERROR_ALREADY_EXISTS. CreateFile* will set this error code even though the function succeeded.

In addition to opening files and devices, *CreateFile* can open storage volumes such as hard disks and flash cards. To open a volume, pass the name of the volume appended with *\Vol:*. For example, to open a compact flash card volume represented by the directory name *Storage Card*, the call would be as follows:

```
H = CreateFile (TEXT ("\\Storage card\\Vol:"), GENERIC_READ|GENERIC_WRITE,
                0, NULL, OPEN_ALWAYS, FILE_ATTRIBUTE_NORMAL, NULL);
```

The handle returned by the *CreateFile* call can be used to pass IO Control (IOCTL) commands to the volume. Possible IOCTLs include commands to format or verify the volume.

Reading and Writing

Windows CE supports the standard Win32 functions *ReadFile* and *WriteFile*; both functions return *TRUE* if successful and *FALSE* otherwise. Reading a file is as simple as calling the following:

```
BOOL ReadFile (HANDLE hFile, LPVOID lpBuffer,
               DWORD nNumberOfBytesToRead,
               LPDWORD lpNumberOfBytesRead, LPOVERLAPPED lpOverlapped);
```

The parameters are fairly self-explanatory. The first parameter is the handle of the opened file to read followed by a pointer to the buffer that will receive the data and the number of bytes to read. The fourth parameter is a pointer to a *DWORD* that will receive the number of bytes that were actually read. Finally, the *lpOverlapped* parameter must be set to *NULL* because Windows CE doesn't support overlapped file operations. As an aside, Windows CE does support multiple reads and writes pending on a device; it just doesn't support the ability to return from the function before the operation completes.

Data is read from the file starting at the file offset indicated by the file pointer. After the read has completed, the file pointer is adjusted by the number of bytes read.

ReadFile won't read beyond the end of a file. If a call to *ReadFile* asks for more bytes than remain in the file, the read will succeed, but only the number of bytes remaining in the file will be returned. This is why you must check the variable pointed to by *lpNumberOfBytesRead* after a read completes to learn how many bytes were actually read. A call to *ReadFile* with the file pointer pointing to the end of the file results in the read being successful, but the number of read bytes is set to 0.

Writing to a file is accomplished with this:

```
BOOL WriteFile (HANDLE hFile, LPCVOID lpBuffer,
                DWORD nNumberOfBytesToWrite,
                LPDWORD lpNumberOfBytesWritten,
                LPOVERLAPPED lpOverlapped);
```

The parameters are similar to *ReadFile*, with the obvious exception that *lpBuffer* now points to the data that will be written to the file. As in *ReadFile*, the *lpOverlapped* parameter must be *NULL*. The data is written to the file offset indicated by the file pointer, which is updated after the write so that it points to the byte immediately beyond the data written.

Moving the File Pointer

The file pointer can be adjusted manually with a call to the following:

```
DWORD SetFilePointer (HANDLE hFile, LONG lDistanceToMove,
                PLONG lpDistanceToMoveHigh, DWORD dwMoveMethod);
```

The parameters for *SetFilePointer* are the handle of the file; a signed offset distance to move the file pointer; a second, upper 32-bit, offset parameter; and *dwMoveMethod*, a parameter indicating how to interpret the offset. Although *lDistanceToMove* is a signed 32-bit value, *lpDistanceToMoveHigh* is a pointer to a signed 32-bit value. For file pointer moves of greater than 4 GB, the *lpDistanceToMoveHigh* parameter should point to a *LONG* that contains the upper 32-bit offset of the move. This variable will receive the high 32 bits of the resulting file pointer. For moves of less than 4 GB, simply set *lpDistanceToMoveHigh* to *NULL*. Clearly, under Windows CE, the *lpDistanceToMoveHigh* parameter is a bit excessive, but having the function the same format as its Windows XP counterpart aids in portability across platforms.

The offset value is interpreted as being from the start of the file if *dwMoveMethod* contains the flag *FILE_BEGIN*. To base the offset on the current position of the file pointer, use *FILE_CURRENT*. To base the offset from the end of the file, use *FILE_END* in *dwMoveMethod*.

SetFilePointer returns the file pointer at its new position after the move has been accomplished. To query the current file position without changing the file pointer, simply call *SetFilePointer* with a zero offset and relative to the current position in the file, as shown here:

```
nCurrFilePtr = SetFilePointer (hFile, 0, NULL, FILE_CURRENT);
```

Closing a File

Closing a file handle is a simple as calling

```
BOOL CloseHandle (HANDLE hObject);
```

This generic call, used to close a number of handles, is also used to close file handles. The function returns *TRUE* if it succeeds. If the function fails, a call to *GetLastError* will return the reason for the failure.

Truncating a File

When you have finished writing the data to a file, you can close it with a call to *CloseHandle* and you're done. Sometimes, however, you must truncate a file to make it smaller than it currently is. In the days of MS-DOS, the way to set the end of a file was to make a call to write zero bytes to a file. The file was then truncated at the current file pointer. This won't work in Windows CE. To set the end of a file, move the file pointer to the location in the file where you want the file to end and call:

```
BOOL SetEndOfFile (HANDLE hFile);
```

Of course, for this call to succeed, you need write access to the file. The function returns *TRUE* if it succeeds.

To insure that all the data has been written to a storage device and isn't just sitting around in a cache, you can call this function:

```
WINBASEAPI BOOL WINAPI FlushFileBuffers (HANDLE hFile);
```

The only parameter is the handle to the file you want to flush to the disk or, more likely in Windows CE, a PC Card.

Getting File Information

A number of calls allow you to query information about a file or directory. To quickly get the attributes knowing only the file or directory name, you can use this function:

```
DWORD GetFileAttributes (LPCTSTR lpFileName);
```

In general, the attributes returned by this function are the same ones that I covered for *CreateFile*, with the addition of the attributes listed here:

- **FILE_ATTRIBUTE_COMPRESSED** The file is compressed.

- **FILE_ATTRIBUTE_INROM** The file is in ROM.

- **FILE_ATTRIBUTE_ROMMODULE** The file is an executable module in ROM formatted for execute-in-place loading. These files can't be opened with *CreateFile*.

- **FILE_ATTRIBUTE_DIRECTORY** The name specifies a directory, not a file.

■   ***FILE_ATTRIBUTE_TEMPORARY***   When this flag is set in combination with *FILE_ATTRIBUTE_DIRECTORY*, the directory is the root of a secondary storage device, such as a PC Card, a hard disk, or the network share folder.

The attribute *FILE_ATTRIBUTE_COMPRESSED* is somewhat misleading on a Windows CE device. Files in the RAM-based object store are always compressed, but this flag isn't set for those files. On the other hand, the flag does accurately reflect whether a file in ROM is compressed. Compressed ROM files have the advantage of taking up less space but the disadvantage of not being execute-in-place files.

An application can change the basic file attributes, such as read only, hidden, system, and attribute by calling this function:

```
BOOL SetFileAttributes (LPCTSTR lpFileName, DWORD dwFileAttributes);
```

This function simply takes the name of the file and the new attributes. Note that you can't compress a file by attempting to set its compressed attribute. Under other Windows systems that do support selective compression of files, the way to compress a file is to make a call directly to the file system driver.

A number of other informational functions are supported by Windows CE. All of these functions, however, require a file handle instead of a filename, so the file must have been previously opened by means of a call to *CreateFile*.

File Times

The standard Win32 API supports three file times: the time the file was created, the time the file was last accessed (that is, the time it was last read, written, or executed), and the last time the file was written to. That being said, the Windows CE object store keeps track of only one time, the time the file was last written to. One of the ways to query the file times for a file is to call this function:

```
BOOL GetFileTime (HANDLE hFile, LPFILETIME lpCreationTime,
                  LPFILETIME lpLastAccessTime,
                  LPFILETIME lpLastWriteTime);
```

The function takes a handle to the file being queried and pointers to three *FILE-TIME* values that will receive the file times. If you're interested in only one of the three values, the other pointers can be set to *NULL*.

When the file times are queried for a file in the object store, Windows CE copies the last write time into all *FILETIME* structures. This goes against Win32 documentation, which states that any unsupported time fields should be set to

0. For the FAT file system used on storage cards, two times are maintained: the file creation time and the last write time. When *GetFileTime* is called on a file on a storage card, the file creation and last write times are returned and the last access time is set to 0.

The *FILETIME* structures returned by *GetFileTime* and other functions can be converted to something readable by calling

```
BOOL FileTimeToSystemTime (const FILETIME *lpFileTime,
                           LPSYSTEMTIME lpSystemTime);
```

This function translates the *FILETIME* structure into a *SYSTEMTIME* structure that has documented day, date, and time fields that can be used. One large caveat is that file times are stored in coordinated universal time format (UTC), also known as Greenwich Mean Time. This doesn't make much difference as long as you're using unreadable *FILETIME* structures, but when you're translating a file time into something readable, a call to

```
BOOL FileTimeToLocalFileTime (const FILETIME *lpFileTime,
                              LPFILETIME lpLocalFileTime);
```

before translating the file time into system time provides the proper time zone translation to the user.

You can manually set the file times of a file by calling

```
BOOL SetFileTime (HANDLE hFile, const FILETIME *lpCreationTime,
                  const FILETIME *lpLastAccessTime,
                  const FILETIME *lpLastWriteTime);
```

The function takes a handle to a file and three times each in *FILETIME* format. If you want to set only one or two of the times, the remaining parameters can be set to *NULL*. Remember that file times must be in UTC time, not local time.

For files in the Windows CE object store, setting any one of the time fields results in all three being updated to that time. If you set multiple fields to different times and attempt to set the times for an object store file, *lpLastWriteTime* takes precedence. Files on storage cards maintain separate creation and last-write times. You must open the file with write access for *SetFileTime* to work.

File Size and Other Information

You can query a file's size by calling

```
DWORD GetFileSize (HANDLE hFile, LPDWORD lpFileSizeHigh);
```

The function takes the handle to the file and an optional pointer to a *DWORD* that's set to the high 32 bits of the file size. This second parameter can be set to *NULL* if you don't expect to be dealing with files over 4 GB. *GetFileSize* returns the low 32 bits of the file size.

I've been talking about these last few functions separately, but an additional function, *GetFileInformationByHandle*, returns all this information and more. The function prototyped as

```
BOOL GetFileInformationByHandle (HANDLE hFile,
                    LPBY_HANDLE_FILE_INFORMATION lpFileInformation);
```

takes the handle of an opened file and a pointer to a *BY_HANDLE_FILE_INFOR-MATION* structure. The function returns *TRUE* if it was successful.

The *BY_HANDLE_FILE_INFORMATION* structure is defined this way:

```
typedef struct _BY_HANDLE_FILE_INFORMATION {
    DWORD dwFileAttributes;
    FILETIME ftCreationTime;
    FILETIME ftLastAccessTime;
    FILETIME ftLastWriteTime;
    DWORD dwVolumeSerialNumber;
    DWORD nFileSizeHigh;
    DWORD nFileSizeLow;
    DWORD nNumberOfLinks;
    DWORD nFileIndexHigh;
    DWORD nFileIndexLow;
    DWORD dwOID;
} BY_HANDLE_FILE_INFORMATION;
```

As you can see, the structure returns data in a number of fields that separate functions return. I'll talk about only the new fields here.

The *dwVolumeSerialNumber* field is filled with the serial number of the volume in which the file resides. The *volume* is what's considered a disk or partition under Windows XP. Under Windows CE, the volume refers to the object store, a storage card, or a disk on a local area network. For files in the object store, the volume serial number is 0.

The *nNumberOfLinks* field is used by Windows XP's NTFS file system and can be ignored under Windows CE. The *nFileIndexHigh* and *nFileIndexLow* fields contain a systemwide unique identifier number for the file. This number can be checked to see whether two different file handles point to the same file. The File Index value is used under Windows XP and Windows Me, but Windows CE has a more useful value, the *object ID* of the file, which is returned in the *dwOID* field. The object ID is an identifier that can be used to reference directories, files, databases, and individual database records. Handy stuff.

The FileView Sample Program

FileView is an example program that uses the multi-line edit control to display the contents of a file in a window. FileView is simply a file *viewer*; it doesn't allow you to modify the file. The code for FileView is shown in Listing 8-1.

FileView.rc

```
//======================================================================
// Resource file
//
// Written for the book Programming Windows CE
// Copyright (C) 2003 Douglas Boling
//======================================================================
#include "windows.h"
#include "FileView.h"                       // Program-specific stuff


//----------------------------------------------------------------------
// Icons and bitmaps
ID_ICON ICON   "fileview.ico"              // Program icon


//----------------------------------------------------------------------
// Menu
ID_MENU MENU DISCARDABLE
BEGIN
    POPUP "&File"
    BEGIN
        MENUITEM "&Open...",                    IDM_OPEN
        MENUITEM SEPARATOR
        MENUITEM "E&xit",                       IDM_EXIT
    END
    POPUP "&Help"
    BEGIN
        MENUITEM "&About...",                   IDM_ABOUT
    END
END
//----------------------------------------------------------------------
// About box dialog template
aboutbox DIALOG discardable 10, 10, 135, 40
STYLE  WS_POPUP | WS_VISIBLE | WS_CAPTION | WS_SYSMENU | DS_CENTER |
       DS_MODALFRAME
CAPTION "About"
BEGIN
    ICON  ID_ICON,                      -1,   3,   5,  10,  10
    LTEXT "FileView - Written for the book Programming Windows \
           CE Copyright 2003 Douglas Boling"
                                        -1,  30,   5, 102,  33
END
```

Listing 8-1   The FileView program

FileView.h

```
//======================================================================
// Header file
//
// Written for the book Programming Windows CE
// Copyright (C) 2003 Douglas Boling
//======================================================================
// Returns number of elements.
#define dim(x) (sizeof(x) / sizeof(x[0]))


//----------------------------------------------------------------------
// Generic defines and data types
//
struct decodeUINT {                               // Structure associates
    UINT Code;                                    // messages
                                                  // with a function.
    LRESULT (*Fxn)(HWND, UINT, WPARAM, LPARAM);
};
struct decodeCMD {                                // Structure associates
    UINT Code;                                    // menu IDs with a
    LRESULT (*Fxn)(HWND, WORD, HWND, WORD);       // function.
};


//----------------------------------------------------------------------
// Generic defines used by application
#define   ID_ICON         1                       // Application icon
                                                  // Resource ID

#define   IDC_CMDBAR      2                       // Command band ID
#define   ID_MENU         3                       // Main menu resource ID
#define   ID_VIEWER       4                       // View control ID


// Menu item IDs
#define   IDM_OPEN        101                     // File menu
#define   IDM_EXIT        102
#define   IDM_ABOUT       120                     // Help menu

//----------------------------------------------------------------------
// Function prototypes
//
INT MyGetFileName (HWND hWnd, LPTSTR szFileName, INT nMax);

HWND InitInstance (HINSTANCE, LPWSTR, int);
int TermInstance (HINSTANCE, int);

// Window procedures
LRESULT CALLBACK MainWndProc (HWND, UINT, WPARAM, LPARAM);
```

(continued)

Listing 8-1   *(continued)*

```
// Message handlers
LRESULT DoCreateMain (HWND, UINT, WPARAM, LPARAM);
LRESULT DoSizeMain (HWND, UINT, WPARAM, LPARAM);
LRESULT DoCommandMain (HWND, UINT, WPARAM, LPARAM);
LRESULT DoDestroyMain (HWND, UINT, WPARAM, LPARAM);
// Command functions
LPARAM DoMainCommandOpen (HWND, WORD, HWND, WORD);
LPARAM DoMainCommandExit (HWND, WORD, HWND, WORD);
LPARAM DoMainCommandAbout (HWND, WORD, HWND, WORD);

// Dialog procedures
BOOL CALLBACK AboutDlgProc (HWND, UINT, WPARAM, LPARAM);
```

FileView.cpp

```
//======================================================================
// FileView - A Windows CE file viewer
//
// Written for the book Programming Windows CE
// Copyright (C) 2003 Douglas Boling
//======================================================================
#include <windows.h>                // For all that Windows stuff
#include <commctrl.h>               // Command bar includes
#include <commdlg.h>                // Common dialog includes

#include "FileView.h"               // Program-specific stuff

#define BUFFSIZE    16384


//----------------------------------------------------------------------
// Global data
//
const TCHAR szAppName[] = TEXT ("FileView");
extern TCHAR szViewerCls[];
HINSTANCE hInst;                            // Program instance handle

HANDLE g_hFile=INVALID_HANDLE_VALUE; // Handle to the opened file
PBYTE g_pBuff = 0;                          // Pointer to file data buffer

// Message dispatch table for MainWindowProc
const struct decodeUINT MainMessages[] = {
    WM_CREATE, DoCreateMain,
    WM_SIZE, DoSizeMain,
    WM_COMMAND, DoCommandMain,
    WM_DESTROY, DoDestroyMain,
};
```

```
Ch08// Command message dispatch for MainWindowProc
const struct decodeCMD MainCommandItems[] = {
    IDM_OPEN, DoMainCommandOpen,
    IDM_EXIT, DoMainCommandExit,
    IDM_ABOUT, DoMainCommandAbout,
};
//======================================================================
// Program entry point
//
int WINAPI WinMain (HINSTANCE hInstance, HINSTANCE hPrevInstance,
                    LPWSTR lpCmdLine, int nCmdShow) {
    HWND hwndMain;
    MSG msg;

    // Initialize this instance.
    hwndMain = InitInstance (hInstance, lpCmdLine, nCmdShow);
    if (hwndMain == 0) return 0x10;

    // Application message loop
    while (GetMessage (&msg, NULL, 0, 0)) {
        TranslateMessage (&msg);
        DispatchMessage (&msg);
    }
    // Instance cleanup
    return TermInstance (hInstance, msg.wParam);
}
//----------------------------------------------------------------------
// InitInstance - Instance initialization
//
HWND InitInstance (HINSTANCE hInstance, LPWSTR lpCmdLine, int nCmdShow){
    HWND hWnd;
    WNDCLASS wc;
    INITCOMMONCONTROLSEX icex;

#if defined(WIN32_PLATFORM_PSPC)
    // If Pocket PC, allow only one instance of the application.
    HWND hWnd = FindWindow (szAppName, NULL);
    if (hWnd) {
        SetForegroundWindow ((HWND)(((DWORD)hWnd) | 0x01));
        return 0;
    }
#endif
    // Save program instance handle in global variable.
    hInst = hInstance;

    // Register application main window class.
    wc.style = 0;                              // Window style
```

(continued)

Listing 8-1   *(continued)*

```
        wc.lpfnWndProc = MainWndProc;              // Callback function
        wc.cbClsExtra = 0;                         // Extra class data
        wc.cbWndExtra = 0;                         // Extra window data
        wc.hInstance = hInstance;                  // Owner handle
        wc.hIcon = NULL,                           // Application icon
        wc.hCursor = LoadCursor (NULL, IDC_ARROW);// Default cursor
        wc.hbrBackground = (HBRUSH) GetStockObject (WHITE_BRUSH);
        wc.lpszMenuName =  NULL;                   // Menu name
        wc.lpszClassName = szAppName;              // Window class name
        if (RegisterClass (&wc) == 0) return 0;

        // Load the command bar common control class.
        icex.dwSize = sizeof (INITCOMMONCONTROLSEX);
        icex.dwICC = ICC_BAR_CLASSES;
        InitCommonControlsEx (&icex);

        // Create main window.
        hWnd = CreateWindow (szAppName, TEXT ("FileView"),
                             WS_VISIBLE, CW_USEDEFAULT, CW_USEDEFAULT,
                             CW_USEDEFAULT, CW_USEDEFAULT, NULL, NULL,
                             hInstance, NULL);
        if (!IsWindow (hWnd)) return 0; // Fail code if window not created.

        // Standard show and update calls
        ShowWindow (hWnd, nCmdShow);
        UpdateWindow (hWnd);
        return hWnd;
}
//----------------------------------------------------------------------
// TermInstance - Program cleanup
//
int TermInstance (HINSTANCE hInstance, int nDefRC) {

        if (g_hFile != INVALID_HANDLE_VALUE)
            CloseHandle (g_hFile);                 // Close the opened file.
        if (g_pBuff)
            LocalFree (g_pBuff);                   // Free buffer.
        return nDefRC;
}
//======================================================================
// Message handling procedures for MainWindow
//----------------------------------------------------------------------
// MainWndProc - Callback function for application window.
//
LRESULT CALLBACK MainWndProc (HWND hWnd, UINT wMsg, WPARAM wParam,
                             LPARAM lParam) {
    INT i;
```

```
    //
    // Search message list to see if we need to handle this
    // message.  If in list, call function.
    //
    for (i = 0; i < dim(MainMessages); i++) {
        if (wMsg == MainMessages[i].Code)
            return (*MainMessages[i].Fxn)(hWnd, wMsg, wParam, lParam);
    }
    return DefWindowProc (hWnd, wMsg, wParam, lParam);
}
//----------------------------------------------------------------------
// DoCreateMain - Process WM_CREATE message for window.
//
LRESULT DoCreateMain (HWND hWnd, UINT wMsg, WPARAM wParam,
                      LPARAM lParam) {
    HWND hwndCB, hwndChild;
    LPCREATESTRUCT lpcs;

    // Convert lParam into pointer to create structure.
    lpcs = (LPCREATESTRUCT) lParam;

    // Create a minimal command bar that has only a menu and an
    // exit button.
    hwndCB = CommandBar_Create (hInst, hWnd, IDC_CMDBAR);
    // Insert the menu.
    CommandBar_InsertMenubar (hwndCB, hInst, ID_MENU, 0);
    // Add exit button to command bar.
    CommandBar_AddAdornments (hwndCB, 0, 0);

    hwndChild = CreateWindowEx (0,TEXT("edit"), TEXT(""), WS_VISIBLE |
                               WS_CHILD | ES_MULTILINE | WS_VSCROLL |
                               WS_HSCROLL | ES_READONLY, 0, 0, lpcs->cx,
                               lpcs->cy, hWnd, (HMENU)ID_VIEWER, hInst, 0);

    // Destroy frame if window not created.
    if (!IsWindow (hwndChild)) {
        DestroyWindow (hWnd);
        return 0;
    }
    // Allocate a buffer.
    g_pBuff = (PBYTE)LocalAlloc (LMEM_FIXED, BUFFSIZE);
    if (!g_pBuff) {
        MessageBox (NULL, TEXT ("Not enough memory"),
                    TEXT ("Error"), MB_OK);
        return 0;
    }
    return 0;
}
```

(continued)

Listing 8-1   *(continued)*

```
//------------------------------------------------------------------
// DoSizeMain - Process WM_SIZE message for window.
//
LRESULT DoSizeMain (HWND hWnd, UINT wMsg, WPARAM wParam, LPARAM lParam){
    RECT rect;

    // Adjust the size of the client rect to take into account
    // the command bar height.
    GetClientRect (hWnd, &rect);
    rect.top += CommandBar_Height (GetDlgItem (hWnd, IDC_CMDBAR));

    SetWindowPos (GetDlgItem (hWnd, ID_VIEWER), NULL, rect.left,
                  rect.top, (rect.right - rect.left),
                  rect.bottom - rect.top, SWP_NOZORDER);
    return 0;
}
//------------------------------------------------------------------
// DoCommandMain - Process WM_COMMAND message for window.
//
LRESULT DoCommandMain (HWND hWnd, UINT wMsg, WPARAM wParam,
                       LPARAM lParam) {
    WORD idItem, wNotifyCode;
    HWND hwndCtl;
    INT i;

    // Parse the parameters.
    idItem = (WORD) LOWORD (wParam);
    wNotifyCode = (WORD) HIWORD (wParam);
    hwndCtl = (HWND) lParam;

    // Call routine to handle control message.
    for (i = 0; i < dim(MainCommandItems); i++) {
        if (idItem == MainCommandItems[i].Code)
            return (*MainCommandItems[i].Fxn)(hWnd, idItem, hwndCtl,
                                              wNotifyCode);
    }
    return 0;
}
//------------------------------------------------------------------
// DoDestroyMain - Process WM_DESTROY message for window.
//
LRESULT DoDestroyMain (HWND hWnd, UINT wMsg, WPARAM wParam,
                       LPARAM lParam) {
    PostQuitMessage (0);
    return 0;
}
```

```
//======================================================================
// Command handler routines
//----------------------------------------------------------------------
// DoMainCommandOpen - Process File Open command.
//
LPARAM DoMainCommandOpen (HWND hWnd, WORD idItem, HWND hwndCtl,
                          WORD wNotifyCode) {
    TCHAR szFileName[MAX_PATH];
    HWND hwndViewer;
    DWORD cBytes;
    LPTSTR pXLateBuff = 0;
    int lFileSize, i;
    BOOL fUnicode = TRUE;
    HANDLE hFileTmp;

    hwndViewer = GetDlgItem (hWnd, ID_VIEWER);

    // Ask the user for the file name
    if (MyGetFileName (hWnd, szFileName, dim(szFileName)) == 0)
        return 0;

    // Open the file.
    hFileTmp = CreateFile (szFileName, GENERIC_READ,
                           FILE_SHARE_READ, NULL, OPEN_EXISTING,
                           FILE_ATTRIBUTE_NORMAL, NULL);
    if (hFileTmp == INVALID_HANDLE_VALUE) {
        MessageBox (hWnd, TEXT("Couldn't open file"), szAppName, MB_OK);
        return 0;
    }
    if (g_hFile) {
        CloseHandle (g_hFile);
        // clear the edit box
        SendMessage (hwndViewer, EM_SETSEL, 0, -1);
        SendMessage (hwndViewer, EM_REPLACESEL, 0, (LPARAM)TEXT(""));
    }
    g_hFile = hFileTmp;
    // Get the size of the file
    lFileSize = (int)GetFileSize (g_hFile, NULL);
    // See if file > 2Gig
    if (lFileSize < 0) return 0;

    if (!ReadFile (g_hFile, g_pBuff, BUFFSIZE-1, &cBytes, NULL))
        return 0;

    // Trivial check to see if file Unicode.  Assumes english
    for (i = 0; (i < 16) && (i < (int)cBytes); i++) {
```

(continued)

Listing 8-1   *(continued)*

```
            if (*((TCHAR *)g_pBuff+i) > 0x100)
                fUnicode = FALSE;
    }
    if (!fUnicode) {
        pXLateBuff = (LPTSTR)LocalAlloc (LPTR, BUFFSIZE*sizeof (TCHAR));
        if (pXLateBuff == 0) return 0;
    }

    while (lFileSize > 0) {
        // Remove any selection
        SendMessage (hwndViewer, EM_SETSEL, (WPARAM)-1, 0);
        *(g_pBuff+cBytes) = 0;
        lFileSize -= cBytes;
        if (!fUnicode) {
            mbstowcs (pXLateBuff, (char *)g_pBuff, cBytes+1);
            SendMessage (hwndViewer, EM_REPLACESEL, 0,
                         (LPARAM)pXLateBuff);
        } else
            SendMessage (hwndViewer, EM_REPLACESEL, 0, (LPARAM)g_pBuff);

        if (!ReadFile (g_hFile, g_pBuff, BUFFSIZE-1, &cBytes, NULL))
            break;
    }
    if (pXLateBuff) LocalFree ((HLOCAL)pXLateBuff);
    // Scroll the control to the top of the file
    SendMessage (hwndViewer, EM_SETSEL, 0, 0);
    SendMessage (hwndViewer, EM_SCROLLCARET, 0, 0);
    return 0;
}
//----------------------------------------------------------------------
// DoMainCommandExit - Process Program Exit command.
//
LPARAM DoMainCommandExit (HWND hWnd, WORD idItem, HWND hwndCtl,
                          WORD wNotifyCode) {

    SendMessage (hWnd, WM_CLOSE, 0, 0);
    return 0;
}
//----------------------------------------------------------------------
// DoMainCommandAbout - Process the Help | About menu command.
//
LPARAM DoMainCommandAbout(HWND hWnd, WORD idItem, HWND hwndCtl,
                          WORD wNotifyCode) {

    // Use DialogBox to create a modal dialog.
    DialogBox (hInst, TEXT ("aboutbox"), hWnd, AboutDlgProc);
    return 0;
}
```

```
//============================================================================
// About Dialog procedure
//
BOOL CALLBACK AboutDlgProc (HWND hWnd, UINT wMsg, WPARAM wParam,
                            LPARAM lParam) {
    switch (wMsg) {
        case WM_COMMAND:
            switch (LOWORD (wParam)) {
                case IDOK:
                case IDCANCEL:
                    EndDialog (hWnd, 0);
                    return TRUE;
            }
        break;
    }
    return FALSE;
}
//----------------------------------------------------------------------------
// MyGetFileName - Returns a filename using the common dialog
//
INT MyGetFileName (HWND hWnd, LPTSTR szFileName, INT nMax) {
    OPENFILENAME of;
    const LPTSTR pszOpenFilter = TEXT ("All Documents (*.*)\0*.*\0\0");

    szFileName[0] = '\0';                    // Initial filename
    memset (&of, 0, sizeof (of));            // Initial file open structure

    of.lStructSize = sizeof (of);
    of.hwndOwner = hWnd;
    of.lpstrFile = szFileName;
    of.nMaxFile = nMax;
    of.lpstrFilter = pszOpenFilter;
    of.Flags = 0;

    if (GetOpenFileName (&of))
        return lstrlen (szFileName);
    else
        return 0;
}
```

FileView.cpp contains the standard Windows functions and the menu command handlers. In the *WM_CREATE* handler (*DoCreateMain* for the main window), FileView creates an edit control that is used to display the file contents. Another routine of interest is *DoOpenMain*, by which the file is opened, read, and sent to the edit control. *DoOpenMain* uses *CreateFile* to open the file with read-only access. If the function succeeds, it calls *GetFileSize* to query the size of the file being viewed.

Memory-Mapped Files and Objects

Memory-mapped files give you a completely different method for reading and writing files. With the standard file I/O functions, files are read as streams of data. To access bytes in different parts of a file, the file pointer must be moved to the first byte, the data read, the file pointer moved to the other byte, and then the file read again.

With memory-mapped files, the file is mapped to a region of memory. Then, instead of using *FileRead* and *FileWrite*, you simply read and write the region of memory that's mapped to the file. Updates of the memory are automatically reflected back to the file itself. Setting up a memory-mapped file is a somewhat more complex process than making a simple call to *CreateFile*, but once a file is mapped, reading and writing the file is trivial.

Memory-Mapped Files

Windows CE uses a slightly different procedure from Windows XP to access a memory-mapped file. To open a file for memory-mapped access, a new function, unique to Windows CE, is used; it's named *CreateFileForMapping*. The prototype for this function is the following:

```
HANDLE CreateFileForMapping (LPCTSTR lpFileName, DWORD dwDesiredAccess,
                    DWORD dwShareMode,
                    LPSECURITY_ATTRIBUTES lpSecurityAttributes,
                    DWORD dwCreationDisposition,
                    DWORD dwFlagsAndAttributes,
                    HANDLE hTemplateFile);
```

The parameters for this function are similar to those for *CreateFile*. The filename is the name of the file to read. The *dwDesiredAccess* parameter, specifying the access rights to the file, must be a combination of *GENERIC_READ* and *GENERIC_WRITE*, or it must be 0. The security attributes must be *NULL*, while Windows CE ignores the *hTemplateFile* parameter.

The handle returned by *CreateFileForMapping* can then be passed to

```
HANDLE CreateFileMapping (HANDLE hFile,
                    LPSECURITY_ATTRIBUTES lpFileMappingAttributes,
                    DWORD flProtect, DWORD dwMaximumSizeHigh,
                    DWORD dwMaximumSizeLow, LPCTSTR lpName);
```

This function creates a file-mapping object and ties the opened file to it. The first parameter for this function is the handle to the opened file. The security attributes parameter must be set to *NULL* under Windows CE. The *flProtect* parameter should be loaded with the protection flags for the virtual pages that will contain the file data. The maximum size parameters should be set to the expected maximum size of the object, or they can be set to 0 if the object should be the same size as the file being mapped. The *lpName* parameter allows you to specify a name for the object. This is handy when you're using a memory-mapped file to share information across different processes. Calling *CreateFileMapping* with the name of an already-opened file-mapping object returns a handle to the object already opened instead of creating a new one.

Once a mapping object has been created, a view into the object is created by calling

```
LPVOID MapViewOfFile (HANDLE hFileMappingObject, DWORD dwDesiredAccess,
                DWORD dwFileOffsetHigh, DWORD dwFileOffsetLow,
                DWORD dwNumberOfBytesToMap);
```

MapViewOfFile returns a pointer to memory that's mapped to the file. The function takes as its parameters the handle of the mapping object just opened as well as the access rights, which can be *FILE_MAP_READ*, *FILE_MAP_WRITE*, or *FILE_MAP_ALL_ACCESS*. The offset parameters let you specify the starting point within the file that the view starts, while the *dwNumberOfBytesToMap* parameter specifies the size of the view window.

These last three parameters are useful when you're mapping large objects. Instead of attempting to map the file as one large object, you can specify a smaller view that starts at the point of interest in the file. This reduces the memory required because only the view of the object, not the object itself, is backed up by physical RAM.

As you write to the memory-mapped file, the changes are reflected in the data you read back from the same buffer. When you close the memory-mapped file, the system writes the modified data back to the original file. If you want to have the data written to the file before you close the file, you can use the following function:

```
BOOL FlushViewOfFile(LPCVOID lpBaseAddress, DWORD dwNumberOfBytesToFlush);
```

The parameters are the base address and size of a range of virtual pages within the mapped view that will be written to the file. The function writes only the pages that have been modified to the file.

When you're finished with the memory-mapped file, a little cleanup is required. First a call to

```
BOOL UnmapViewOfFile (LPCVOID lpBaseAddress);
```

unmaps the view to the object. The only parameter is the pointer to the base address of the view.

Next a call should be made to close the mapping object and the file itself. Both these actions are accomplished by means of calls to *CloseHandle*. The first call should be to close the memory-mapped object, and then *CloseHandle* should be called to close the file.

The code fragment that follows shows the entire process of opening a file for memory mapping, creating the file-mapping object, mapping the view, and then cleaning up.

```
HANDLE hFile, hFileMap;
PBYTE pFileMem;
TCHAR szFileName[MAX_PATH];
// Get the filename.

hFile = CreateFileForMapping (szFileName, GENERIC_WRITE,
                              FILE_SHARE_READ, NULL,
                              OPEN_EXISTING, FILE_ATTRIBUTE_NORMAL |
                              FILE_FLAG_RANDOM_ACCESS,0);

if (hFile != INVALID_HANDLE_VALUE) {

    hFileMap = CreateFileMapping (hFile, NULL, PAGE_READWRITE, 0, 0, 0);
    if (hFileMap) {
        pFileMem = MapViewOfFile (hFileMap, FILE_MAP_WRITE, 0, 0, 0);
        if (pFileMem) {
            //
            // Use the data in the file.
            //

            // Start cleanup by unmapping view.
            UnmapViewOfFile (pFileMem);
        }
        CloseHandle (hFileMap);
    }
    CloseHandle (hFile);
}
```

A variation of memory-mapped files, memory-mapped objects are great for interprocess communication. I'll cover memory-mapped objects when I discuss interprocess communication in Chapter 10.

Navigating the File System

Now that we've seen how files are read and written, let's take a look at how the files themselves are managed in the file system. Windows CE supports most of the convenient file and directory management APIs, such as *CopyFile*, *MoveFile*, and *CreateDirectory*.

File and Directory Management

Windows CE supports a number of functions useful in file and directory management. You can move files using *MoveFile*, copy them using *CopyFile*, and delete them using *DeleteFile*. You can create directories using *CreateDirectory* and delete them using *RemoveDirectory*. While most of these functions are straightforward, I should cover a few intricacies here.

To copy a file, call

```
BOOL CopyFile (LPCTSTR lpExistingFileName, LPCTSTR lpNewFileName,
               BOOL bFailIfExists);
```

The parameters are the name of the file to copy and the name of the destination directory. The third parameter indicates whether the function should overwrite the destination file if one already exists before the copy is made.

Files and directories can be moved and renamed using

```
BOOL MoveFile (LPCTSTR lpExistingFileName, LPCTSTR lpNewFileName);
```

To move a file, simply indicate the source and destination names for the file. The destination file must not already exist. File moves can be made within the object store, from the object store to an external drive, or from an external drive to the object store. *MoveFile* can also be used to rename a file. In this case, the source and target directories remain the same; only the name of the file changes.

MoveFile can also be used in the same manner to move or rename directories. The only exception is that *MoveFile* can't move a directory from one volume to another. Under Windows CE, *MoveFile* moves a directory and all its subdirectories and files to a different location within the object store or different locations within another volume.

Deleting a file is as simple as calling

```
BOOL DeleteFile (LPCTSTR lpFileName);
```

You pass the name of the file to delete. For the delete to be successful, the file must not be currently open.

You can create and destroy directories using the following two functions:

```
BOOL CreateDirectory (LPCTSTR lpPathName,
                      LPSECURITY_ATTRIBUTES lpSecurityAttributes);
```

and

```
BOOL RemoveDirectory (LPCTSTR lpPathName);
```

CreateDirectory takes the name of the directory to create and a security parameter that should be *NULL* under Windows CE. *RemoveDirectory* deletes a directory. The directory must be empty for the function to be successful.

Creating a Temporary File

At times you will need to create a temporary file. How do you pick a unique filename? You can ask Windows for the name of a temporary file by using the following function:

```
UINT GetTempFileName (LPCTSTR lpPathName, LPCTSTR lpPrefixString,
                      UINT uUnique, LPTSTR lpTempFileName);
```

The first parameter is the path of the temporary file. You can specify a single "." to indicate the current directory, or you can specify an existing directory. The second parameter, *lpPrefixString*, is the name prefix. The first three characters of the prefix become the first three characters of the temporary filename. The *uUnique* parameter can be any number you want or 0. If you pass 0, Windows will generate a number based on the system time and use it as the last four characters of the filename. If *uUnique* is 0, Windows guarantees that the file-name produced by *GetTempFileName* will be unique. If you specify a value other than 0 in *uUnique*, Windows returns a filename based on that value but doesn't check to see whether the filename is unique. The last parameter is the address of the output buffer to which *GetTempFileName* returns the filename. This buffer should be at least *MAX_PATH* characters (not bytes) in length.

Finding Files

Windows CE supports the basic *FindFirstFile, FindNextFile, FindClose* proce-dure for enumerating files that is supported under Windows XP. Searching is accomplished on a per-directory basis using template filenames with wild card characters in the template.

Searching a directory involves first passing a filename template to *Find-FirstFile*, which is prototyped in this way:

```
HANDLE FindFirstFile (LPCTSTR lpFileName,
                      LPWIN32_FIND_DATA lpFindFileData);
```

The first parameter is the template filename used in the search. This filename can contain a fully specified path if you want to search a directory other than the root. Windows CE has no concept of *Current Directory* built into it; if no path is specified in the search string, the root directory of the object store is searched.

As you would expect, the wildcards for the filename template are ? and *. The question mark (?) indicates that any single character can replace the question mark. The asterisk (*) indicates that any number of characters can replace the asterisk. For example, the search string *Windows\\Alarm?.wav* would return the files \\Windows\\Alarm1.wav, \\Windows\\Alarm2.wav, and

\Windows\Alarm3.wav. On the other hand, the search string *Windows*.wav* would return all files in the windows directory that have the WAV extension.

The second parameter of *FindFirstFile* is a pointer to a *WIN32_FIND_DATA* structure, as defined here:

```
typedef struct _WIN32_FIND_DATA {
    DWORD dwFileAttributes;
    FILETIME ftCreationTime;
    FILETIME ftLastAccessTime;
    FILETIME ftLastWriteTime;
    DWORD nFileSizeHigh;
    DWORD nFileSizeLow;
    DWORD dwOID;
    WCHAR cFileName[ MAX_PATH ];
} WIN32_FIND_DATA;
```

This structure is filled with the file data for the first file found in the search. The fields shown are similar to what we've seen.

If *FindFirstFile* finds no files or directories that match the template file-name, it returns *INVALID_HANDLE_VALUE*. If at least one file is found, *Find-FirstFile* fills in the *WIN32_FIND_DATA* structure with the specific data for the found file and returns a handle value that you use to track the current search.

To find the next file in the search, call this function:

```
BOOL FindNextFile (HANDLE hFindFile,
                   LPWIN32_FIND_DATA lpFindFileData);
```

The two parameters are the handle returned by *FindFirstFile* and a pointer to a find data structure. *FindNextFile* returns *TRUE* if a file matching the template passed to *FindFirstFile* is found and fills in the appropriate file data in the *WIN32_FIND_DATA* structure. If no file is found, *FindNextFile* returns *FALSE*.

When you've finished searching either because *FindNextFile* returned *FALSE* or because you simply don't want to continue searching, you must call this function:

```
BOOL FindClose (HANDLE hFindFile);
```

This function accepts the handle returned by *FindFirstFile*. If *FindFirstFile* returned *INVALID_HANDLE_VALUE*, you shouldn't call *FindClose*.

The following short code fragment encompasses the entire file search process. This code computes the total size of all files in the Windows directory.

```
WIN32_FIND_DATA fd;
HANDLE hFind;
INT nTotalSize = 0;
```

(continued)

```
// Start search for all files in the windows directory.
hFind = FindFirstFile (TEXT ("\\windows\\*.*"), &fd);

// If a file was found, hFind will be valid.
if (hFind != INVALID_HANDLE_VALUE) {

    // Loop through found files.  Be sure to process file
    // found with FindFirstFile before calling FindNextFile.
    do {
        // If found file is not a directory, add its size to
        // the total.  (Assume that the total size of all files
        // is less than 2 GB.)
        if (!(fd.dwFileAttributes & FILE_ATTRIBUTE_DIRECTORY))
            nTotalSize += fd.nFileSizeLow;

    // See if another file exists.
    } while (FindNextFile (hFind, &fd));

    // Clean up by closing file search handle.
    FindClose (hFind);
}
```

In this example, the Windows directory is searched for all files. If the found
"file" isn't a directory, that is, if it's a true file, its size is added to the total. Notice
that the return handle from *FindFirstFile* must be checked, not only so that you
know whether a file was found but also to prevent *FindClose* from being called
if the handle is invalid.

A more advanced version of the *FindxxxFile* API is *FindFirstFileEx*. The
advantage of this function is the added ability to enumerate only directories and
even to enumerate the device drivers currently running. The function is prototyped as

```
HANDLE FindFirstFileEx(LPCTSTR lpFileName, FINDEX_INFO_LEVELS fInfoLevelId,
                       LPVOID lpFindFileData, FINDEX_SEARCH_OPS fSearchOp,
                       LPVOID lpSearchFilter, DWORD dwAdditionalFlags);
```

As in *FindFirstFile*, the first parameter, *lpFileName*, specifies the search
string. The parameter *fInfoLevelId* must be set to the constant *FindExInfoStandard*. Given that the second parameter must be *FindExInfoStandard*, the third
parameter always points to a *WIN32_FIND_DATA* structure. The final two
parameters, *lpSearchFilter* and *dwAdditionalFlags*, must be set to 0 on Windows CE.

The fourth parameter, *fSearchOp*, is what differentiates *FindFirstFileEx* from
FindFirstFile on Windows CE. This parameter can be one of three values: *Find-
ExSearchNameMatch*, *FindExSearchLimitToDirectories*, or *FindExSearchLimit-
ToDevices*. The value *FindExSearchNameMatch* tells *FindFirstFileEx* to act just

like *FindFirstFile*, searching for a matching filename. The value *FindExSearch-LimitToDirectories* indicates that the function should search only for directories matching the search specification. This search should be slightly faster than repeatedly calling *FindFirstFile* and checking for the directory attribute because this check is done inside the file system, thereby reducing the number of *Find-NextFile* calls. The final value, *FindExSearchLimitToDevices*, is the most interesting. It causes the function to search the names of the loaded device drivers to find a matching name. You shouldn't provide a path, with the exception of an optional leading "\".

   FindFirstFileEx returns a handle if the search is successful and returns *INVALID_HANDLE_VALUE* if the search fails. When performing a search, use *FindFirstFileEx* in place of *FindFirstFile*. To search for the second and all other files, call *FindNextFile*. When you have completed the search, call *FindClose* to close the handle.

   While *FindFirstFileEx* is a handy addition to the Windows CE API, some early Pocket PC 2000 systems don't seem to correctly implement this function when enumerating device names. You should be careful when calling this function; couch it in a *__try __except* block to guard against exceptions. If an exception occurs during the function call, you can assume that that particular aspect of *FindFirstFileEx* isn't supported on that device.

Distinguishing Drives from Directories

As I mentioned at the beginning of this chapter, Windows CE doesn't support the concept of drive letters so familiar to MS-DOS and Windows users. Instead, file storage devices such as PC Cards or even hard disks are shown as directories in the root directory. That leads to the question, "How can you tell a directory from a drive?" To do this, you need to look at the file attributes for the directory. Directories that are actually secondary storage devices—that is, they store files in a place other than the object store—have the file attribute flag *FILE_ATTRIBUTE_TEMPORARY* set. Windows CE also uses this attribute flag for other "nondirectory" directories such as the NETWORK and RELEASE folders. The NETWORK folder lists network shares. The RELEASE folder is used during embedded development. So finding storage devices on any version of Windows CE is fairly easy, as is shown in the following code fragment:

```
WIN32_FIND_DATA fd;
HANDLE hFind;
TCHAR szPath[MAX_PATH];
ULARGE_INTEGER lnTotal, lnFree;

lstrcpy (szPath, TEXT ("\\*.*"));
hFind = FindFirstFile (szPath, &fd);
```

(continued)

```
if (hFind != INVALID_HANDLE_VALUE) {
    do {
        if ((fd.dwFileAttributes & FILE_ATTRIBUTE_DIRECTORY) &&
            (fd.dwFileAttributes & FILE_ATTRIBUTE_TEMPORARY)) {
            TCHAR szName[MAX_PATH];
            wstrcpy (szName, fd.cFileName);
            wstrcat (szName, TEXT (\\Vol:));
            HANDLE h = CreateFile (szName,
                                   GENERIC_READ|GENERIC_WRITE,
                                   0, NULL, OPEN_ALWAYS,
                                   FILE_ATTRIBUTE_NORMAL, NULL);
            if (h != INVALID_HANDLE_VALUE) {
                CloseHandle (h);


                // Get the disk space statistics for drive.
                GetDiskFreeSpaceEx (fd.cFileName, NULL, &lnTotal,
                                    &lnFree);
            }
        }
    } while (FindNextFile (hFind, &fd));
    FindClose (hFind);
}
```

This code uses the find first/find next functions to search the root directory for all directories with the *FILE_ATTRIBUTE_TEMPORARY* attribute set. It then checks to see whether the directory can be opened as a volume. Other directories with the *FILE_ATTRIBUTE_TEMPORARY* flag can't be opened because they don't represent file system volumes.

Notice the call to the following function in the code I just showed you:

```
BOOL GetDiskFreeSpaceEx (LPCWSTR lpDirectoryName,
                         PULARGE_INTEGER lpFreeBytesAvailableToCaller,
                         PULARGE_INTEGER lpTotalNumberOfBytes,
                         PULARGE_INTEGER lpTotalNumberOfFreeBytes);
```

This function provides information about the total size of the drive and the amount of free space it contains. The first parameter is the name of any directory on the drive in question. This doesn't have to be the root directory of the drive. *GetDiskFreeSpaceEx* returns three values: the free bytes available to the caller, the total size of the drive, and the total free space on the drive. These values are returned in three *ULARGE_INTEGER* structures. These structures contain two *DWORD* fields named *LowPart* and *HighPart*. This allows *GetDiskFreeSpaceEx* to return 64-bit values. Those 64-bit values can come in handy on Windows XP, where the drives can be large. If you aren't interested in one or more of the fields, you can pass a *NULL* in place of the pointer for that parameter. You can also use *GetDiskFreeSpaceEx* to determine the size of the object store.

Another function that can be used to determine the size of the object store is

```
BOOL GetStoreInformation (LPSTORE_INFORMATION lpsi);
```

GetStoreInformation takes one parameter, a pointer to a *STORE_INFOR-MATION* structure defined as

```
typedef struct STORE_INFORMATION {
    DWORD dwStoreSize;
    DWORD dwFreeSize;
} STORE_INFORMATION, *LPSTORE_INFORMATION;
```

As you can see, this structure simply returns the total size and amount of free space in the object store.

That covers the Windows CE file API. As you can see, very little Windows CE–unique code is necessary when you're working with the object store. Now let's look at the registry API, where Windows CE also follows the Win32 API quite closely.

The Registry

The registry is a system database used to store configuration information in applications and in Windows itself. The registry as defined by Windows CE is similar but not identical in function and format to the registries under other versions of Windows. In other words, for an application, most of the same registry access functions exist, but the layout of the Windows CE registry doesn't exactly follow Windows XP.

As in all versions of Windows, the registry is made up of keys and values. Keys can contain keys or values or both. Values contain data in one of a number of predefined formats. Since keys can contain keys, the registry is distinctly hierarchical. The highest-level keys, the root keys, are specified by their predefined numeric constants. Keys below the root keys and values are identified by their text name. Multiple levels of keys can be specified in one text string by separating the keys with a backslash (\).

To query or modify a value, the key containing the value must first be opened, the value queried or written, and then the key closed. Keys and values can also be enumerated so that an application can determine what a specific key contains. Data in the registry can be stored in a number of different predefined data types. Among the available data types are strings, 32-bit numbers, and free-form binary data.

Registry Organization

The Windows CE registry supports three of the high-level, root, keys seen on other Windows platforms: *HKEY_LOCAL_MACHINE*, *HKEY_CURRENT_USER*, and *HKEY_CLASSES_ROOT*. As with other Windows platforms, Windows CE uses the *HKEY_LOCAL_MACHINE* key to store hardware and driver configuration data, *HKEY_CURRENT_USER* to store user-specific configuration data, and the *HKEY_CLASSES_ROOT* key to store file type matching and OLE configuration data.

As a practical matter, the registry is used by applications and drivers to store state information that needs to be saved across invocations. Applications typically store their current state when they are requested to close and then restore this state when they are launched again. The traditional location for storing data in the registry by an application is obtained by means of the following structure:

```
{ROOT_KEY}\Software\{Company Name}\{Company Product}
```

In this template, *ROOT_KEY* is either *HKEY_LOCAL_MACHINE* for machine-specific data, such as what optional components of an application can be installed on the machine, or *HKEY_CURRENT_USER* for user-specific information, such as the list of the user's last-opened files. Under the *Software* key, the name of the company that wrote the application is used followed by the name of the specific application. For example, Microsoft saves the configuration information for Pocket Word under the key

```
HKEY_LOCAL_MACHINE\Software\Microsoft\Pocket Word
```

While this hierarchy is great for segregating registry values from different applications from one another, it's best not to create too deep a set of keys. Because of the way the registry is designed, it takes less memory to store a value than it does a key. Because of this, you should design your registry storage so that it uses fewer keys and more values. To optimize even further, it's more efficient to store more information in one value than to have the same information stored across a number of values.

The window in Figure 8-1 shows the hierarchy of keys used to store data for Pocket Word. The left pane shows the hierarchy of keys down to the *Settings* key under the Pocket Word key. In the *Settings* key, three values are stored: *Wrap To Window*, *Vertical Scrollbar Visibility*, and *Horizontal Scrollbar Visibility*. In this case, these values are *DWORD* values, but they could have been strings or other data types.

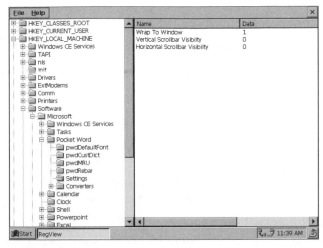

Figure 8-1   The hierarchy of registry values stored by Pocket Word

The Registry API

Now let's turn toward the Windows CE registry API. In general, the registry API provides all the functions necessary to read and write data in the registry as well as enumerate the keys and data store within. Windows CE doesn't support the security features of the registry that are supported under Windows XP. However, Windows CE does prohibit untrusted applications from modifying certain critical registry keys.

Opening and Creating Keys

You open a registry key with a call to this function:

```
LONG RegOpenKeyEx (HKEY hKey, LPCWSTR lpszSubKey, DWORD ulOptions,
                 REGSAM samDesired, PHKEY phkResult);
```

The first parameter is the key that contains the second parameter, the subkey. This first key must be either one of the root key constants or a previously opened key. The subkey to open is specified as a text string that contains the key to open. This subkey string can contain multiple levels of subkeys as long as each subkey is separated by a backslash. For example, to open the subkey *HKEY_LOCAL_MACHINE\Software\Microsoft\Pocket Word*, an application could either call *RegOpenKeyEx* with *HKEY_LOCAL_MACHINE* as the key and *Software\Microsoft\Pocket Word* as the subkey or open the *Software\Microsoft* key and then make a call with that opened handle to *RegOpenKeyEx*, specifying the subkey *Pocket Word*. Key and value names aren't case specific.

Windows CE ignores the *ulOptions* and *samDesired* parameters. To remain compatible with future versions of the operating system that might use security features, these parameters should be set to 0 for *ulOptions* and *NULL* for *samDesired*. The *phkResult* parameter should point to a variable that will receive the handle to the opened key. The function, if successful, returns a value of *ERROR_SUCCESS* and an error code if it fails.

Another method for opening a key is

```
LONG RegCreateKeyEx (HKEY hKey, LPCWSTR lpszSubKey, DWORD Reserved,
                     LPWSTR lpszClass, DWORD dwOptions,
                     REGSAM samDesired,
                     LPSECURITY_ATTRIBUTES lpSecurityAttributes,
                     PHKEY phkResult, LPDWORD lpdwDisposition);
```

The difference between *RegCreateKeyEx* and *RegOpenKeyEx*, aside from the extra parameters, is that *RegCreateKeyEx* creates the key if it didn't exist before the call. The first two parameters, the key handle and the subkey name, are the same as in *RegOpenKeyEx*. The *Reserved* parameter should be set to 0. The *lpClass* parameter points to a string that contains the class name of the key if it's to be created. This parameter can be set to *NULL* if no class name needs to be specified. The *dwOptions* and *samDesired* and *lpSecurityAttributes* parameters should be set to 0, *NULL*, and *NULL* respectively. The *phkResult* parameter points to the variable that receives the handle to the opened or newly created key. The *lpdwDisposition* parameter points to a variable that's set to indicate whether the key was opened or created by the call.

Reading Registry Values

You can query registry values by first opening the key containing the values of interest and calling this function:

```
LONG RegQueryValueEx (HKEY hKey, LPCWSTR lpszValueName,
                      LPDWORD lpReserved, LPDWORD lpType,
                      LPBYTE lpData, LPDWORD lpcbData);
```

The *hKey* parameter is the handle of the key opened by *RegCreateKeyEx* or *RegOpenKeyEx*. The *lpszValueName* parameter is the name of the value that's being queried. The *lpType* parameter is a pointer to a variable that receives the variable type. The *lpData* parameter points to the buffer to receive the data, while the *lpcbData* parameter points to a variable that receives the size of the data. If *RegQueryValueEx* is called with the *lpData* parameter equal to *NULL*, Windows returns the size of the data but doesn't return the data itself. This allows applications to first query the size and type of the data before actually receiving it.

Writing Registry Values

You set a registry value by calling

```
LONG RegSetValueEx (HKEY hKey, LPCWSTR lpszValueName, DWORD Reserved,
                    DWORD dwType, const BYTE *lpData, DWORD cbData);
```

The parameters here are fairly obvious: the handle to the open key followed by the name of the value to set. The function also requires that you pass the type of data, the data itself, and the size of the data. The data type parameter is simply a labeling aid for the application that eventually reads the data. Data in the registry is stored in a binary format and returned in that same format. Specifying a different type has no effect on how the data is stored in the registry or how it's returned to the application. However, given the availability of third-party registry editors, you should make every effort to specify the appropriate data type in the registry.

The data types can be one of the following:

- ■ *REG_SZ*   A zero-terminated Unicode string

- ■ *REG_EXPAND_SZ*   A zero-terminated Unicode string with embedded environment variables

- ■ *REG_MULTI_SZ*   A series of zero-terminated Unicode strings terminated by two zero characters

- ■ *REG_DWORD*   A 4-byte binary value

- ■ *REG_BINARY*   Free-form binary data

- ■ *REG_DWORD_BIG_ENDIAN*   A *DWORD* value stored in big-endian format

- ■ *REG_DWORD_LITTLE_ENDIAN*   Equivalent to *REG_DWORD*

- ■ *REG_LINK*   A Unicode symbolic link

- ■ *REG_NONE*   No defined type

- ■ *REG_RESOURCE_LIST*   A device driver resource list

Deleting Keys and Values

You delete a registry key by calling

```
LONG RegDeleteKey (HKEY hKey, LPCWSTR lpszSubKey);
```

The parameters are the handle to the open key and the name of the subkey you plan to delete. For the deletion to be successful, the key must not be currently open. You can delete a value by calling

```
LONG RegDeleteValue (HKEY hKey, LPCWSTR lpszValueName);
```

You can glean a wealth of information about a key by calling this function:

```
LONG RegQueryInfoKey (HKEY hKey, LPWSTR lpszClass, LPDWORD lpcchClass,
                      LPDWORD lpReserved, LPDWORD lpcSubKeys,
                      LPDWORD lpcchMaxSubKeyLen,
                      LPDWORD lpcchMaxClassLen,
                      LPDWORD lpcValues, LPDWORD lpcchMaxValueNameLen,
                      LPDWORD lpcbMaxValueData,
                      LPDWORD lpcbSecurityDescriptor,
                      PFILETIME lpftLastWriteTime);
```

The only input parameter to this function is the handle to a key. The function returns the class of the key, if any, as well as the maximum lengths of the subkeys and values under the key. The last two parameters, the security attributes and the last write time, are unsupported under Windows CE and should be set to *NULL*.

Closing Keys

You close a registry key by calling

```
LONG RegCloseKey (HKEY hKey);
```

When a registry key is closed, Windows CE flushes any unwritten key data to the registry before returning from the call.

Enumerating Registry Keys

In some instances, you'll find it helpful to be able to query a key to see what subkeys and values it contains. You accomplish this with two different functions: one to query the subkeys, another to query the values. The first function

```
LONG RegEnumKeyEx (HKEY hKey, DWORD dwIndex, LPWSTR lpszName,
                   LPDWORD lpcchName, LPDWORD lpReserved,
                   LPWSTR lpszClass,
                   LPDWORD lpcchClass, PFILETIME lpftLastWriteTime);
```

enumerates the subkeys of a registry key through repeated calls. The parameters to pass the function are the handle of the opened key and an index value. To enumerate the first subkey, the *dwIndex* parameter should be 0. For each subsequent call to *RegEnumKeyEx*, *dwIndex* should be incremented to get the next subkey. When there are no more subkeys to be enumerated, *RegEnumKeyEx* returns *ERROR_NO_MORE_ITEMS*.

For each call to *RegEnumKeyEx*, the function returns the name of the subkey and its classname. The last write time parameter isn't supported under Windows CE.

Values within a key can be enumerated with a call to this function:

```
LONG RegEnumValue (HKEY hKey, DWORD dwIndex, LPWSTR lpszValueName,
                   LPDWORD lpcchValueName, LPDWORD lpReserved,
                   LPDWORD lpType, LPBYTE lpData, LPDWORD lpchData);
```

Like *RegEnumKey*, this function is called repeatedly, passing index values to enumerate the different values stored under the key. When the function returns *ERROR_NO_MORE_ITEMS*, no more values are under the key. *RegEnumValue* returns the name of the values and the data stored in each value, as well as its data type and the size of the data.

The RegView Example Program

The following program is a registry viewer application. It allows a user to navigate the trees in the registry and examine the contents of the data stored. Unlike RegEdit, which is provided by Windows XP, RegView doesn't let you edit the registry. However, such an extension wouldn't be difficult to make. Listing 8-2 contains the code for the RegView program.

```
RegView.rc
//======================================================================
// Resource file
//
// Copyright (C) 2003 Douglas Boling
//======================================================================
#include "windows.h"
#include "regview.h"                        // Program-specific stuff


//----------------------------------------------------------------------
// Icons and bitmaps
//
ID_ICON ICON    "regview.ico"               // Program icon
ID_BMPS BITMAP "TVBmps.bmp"


//----------------------------------------------------------------------
// Menu
//
ID_MENU MENU DISCARDABLE
BEGIN
    POPUP "&File"
    BEGIN
        MENUITEM "E&xit",                       IDM_EXIT
    END
```

Listing 8-2   The RegView program   *(continued)*

Listing 8-2 *(continued)*

```
      POPUP "&Help"
      BEGIN
         MENUITEM "&About...",                    IDM_ABOUT
      END
END
//------------------------------------------------------------------------
// About box dialog template
//
aboutbox DIALOG discardable 10, 10, 135, 40
STYLE  WS_POPUP | WS_VISIBLE | WS_CAPTION | WS_SYSMENU | DS_CENTER |
       DS_MODALFRAME
CAPTION "About"
BEGIN
   ICON   ID_ICON,                         -1,   3,   5,  10,  10
   LTEXT "RegView - Written for the book Programming Windows CE \
          Copyright 2003 Douglas Boling"
                                           -1,  30,   5, 102,  33
END
```

RegView.h

```
//========================================================================
// Header file
//
// Written for the book Programming Windows CE
// Copyright (C) 2003 Douglas Boling
//========================================================================
// Returns number of elements
#define dim(x) (sizeof(x) / sizeof(x[0]))


//------------------------------------------------------------------------
// Generic defines and data types
//
struct decodeUINT {                                // Structure associates
   UINT Code;                                      // messages
                                                   // with a function.

   LRESULT (*Fxn)(HWND, UINT, WPARAM, LPARAM);
};
struct decodeCMD {                                 // Structure associates
   UINT Code;                                      // control IDs with a
   LRESULT (*Fxn)(HWND, WORD, HWND, WORD);         // function.
};
struct decodeNotify {                              // Structure associates
   UINT Code;                                      // control IDs with a
   LRESULT (*Fxn)(HWND, UINT, HWND, LPNMHDR);      // notify handler.
};
```

```
//------------------------------------------------------------------
// Generic defines used by application
#define  ID_ICON            1               // App icon resource ID
#define  ID_BMPS            2               // Bitmap resource ID
#define  IDC_CMDBAR        10               // Command band ID
#define  ID_MENU           11               // Main menu resource ID
#define  ID_TREEV          12               // Tree view control ID
#define  ID_LISTV          13               // List view control ID


// Menu item IDs
#define  IDM_EXIT         101               // File menu
#define  IDM_ABOUT        150               // Help menu


//------------------------------------------------------------------
// Function prototypes
//
HWND InitInstance (HINSTANCE, LPWSTR, int);
int TermInstance (HINSTANCE, int);


INT EnumChildren (HWND, HTREEITEM, HKEY, LPTSTR);
DWORD CountChildren (HKEY, LPTSTR, LPTSTR);
INT EnumValues (HWND, HKEY, LPTSTR);
INT DisplayValue (HWND, INT, LPTSTR, PBYTE, DWORD, DWORD);
INT GetTree (HWND, HTREEITEM, HKEY *, TCHAR *, INT);
HTREEITEM InsertTV (HWND, HTREEITEM, TCHAR *, LPARAM, DWORD);
INT InsertLV (HWND, INT, LPTSTR, LPTSTR);
HWND CreateLV (HWND, RECT *);
HWND CreateTV (HWND, RECT *);


// Window procedures
LRESULT CALLBACK MainWndProc (HWND, UINT, WPARAM, LPARAM);


// Message handlers
LRESULT DoCreateMain (HWND, UINT, WPARAM, LPARAM);
LRESULT DoSizeMain (HWND, UINT, WPARAM, LPARAM);
LRESULT DoNotifyMain (HWND, UINT, WPARAM, LPARAM);
LRESULT DoCommandMain (HWND, UINT, WPARAM, LPARAM);
LRESULT DoDestroyMain (HWND, UINT, WPARAM, LPARAM);


// Command functions
LPARAM DoMainCommandExit (HWND, WORD, HWND, WORD);
LPARAM DoMainCommandAbout (HWND, WORD, HWND, WORD);


// Notify functions
LPARAM DoMainNotifyListV (HWND, UINT, HWND, LPNMHDR);
LPARAM DoMainNotifyTreeV (HWND, UINT, HWND, LPNMHDR);


// Dialog procedures
BOOL CALLBACK AboutDlgProc (HWND, UINT, WPARAM, LPARAM);
```

(continued)

Listing 8-2 *(continued)*

RegView.c

```
//======================================================================
// RegView - WinCE registry viewer
//
// Written for the book Programming Windows CE
// Copyright (C) 2003 Douglas Boling
//======================================================================
#include <windows.h>              // For all that Windows stuff
#include <commctrl.h>             // Command bar includes
#include <commdlg.h>              // Common dialog includes

#include "RegView.h"              // Program-specific stuff


//----------------------------------------------------------------------
// Global data
//
const TCHAR szAppName[] = TEXT ("RegView");
HINSTANCE hInst;                  // Program instance handle

INT nDivPct = 40;                 // Divider setting between windows

// Message dispatch table for MainWindowProc
const struct decodeUINT MainMessages[] = {
    WM_CREATE, DoCreateMain,
    WM_SIZE, DoSizeMain,
    WM_COMMAND, DoCommandMain,
    WM_NOTIFY, DoNotifyMain,
    WM_DESTROY, DoDestroyMain,
};
// Command message dispatch for MainWindowProc
const struct decodeCMD MainCommandItems[] = {
    IDM_EXIT, DoMainCommandExit,
    IDM_ABOUT, DoMainCommandAbout,
};
// Notification message dispatch for MainWindowProc
const struct decodeNotify MainNotifyItems[] = {
    ID_LISTV, DoMainNotifyListV,
    ID_TREEV, DoMainNotifyTreeV,
};
//======================================================================
//
// Program entry point
//
int WINAPI WinMain (HINSTANCE hInstance, HINSTANCE hPrevInstance,
                    LPWSTR lpCmdLine, int nCmdShow) {
    HWND hwndMain;
    MSG msg;
    int rc = 0;
```

```
    // Initialize this instance.
    hwndMain = InitInstance (hInstance, lpCmdLine, nCmdShow);
    if (hwndMain == 0)
        return 0x10;

    // Application message loop
    while (GetMessage (&msg, NULL, 0, 0)) {
        TranslateMessage (&msg);
        DispatchMessage (&msg);
    }
    // Instance cleanup
    return TermInstance (hInstance, msg.wParam);
}
//----------------------------------------------------------------------
// InitInstance - Instance initialization
//
HWND InitInstance (HINSTANCE hInstance, LPWSTR lpCmdLine, int nCmdShow){
    WNDCLASS wc;
    INITCOMMONCONTROLSEX icex;
    HWND hWnd;

    // Save program instance handle in global variable.
    hInst = hInstance;

#if defined(WIN32_PLATFORM_PSPC)
    // If Pocket PC, allow only one instance of the application.
    hWnd = FindWindow (szAppName, NULL);
    if (hWnd) {
        SetForegroundWindow ((HWND)(((DWORD)hWnd) | 0x01));
        return 0;
    }
#endif
    // Register application main window class.
    wc.style = 0;                                // Window style
    wc.lpfnWndProc = MainWndProc;                // Callback function
    wc.cbClsExtra = 0;                           // Extra class data
    wc.cbWndExtra = 0;                           // Extra window data
    wc.hInstance = hInstance;                    // Owner handle
    wc.hIcon = NULL,                             // Application icon
    wc.hCursor = LoadCursor (NULL, IDC_ARROW);// Default cursor
    wc.hbrBackground = (HBRUSH) GetStockObject (WHITE_BRUSH);
    wc.lpszMenuName = NULL;                      // Menu name
    wc.lpszClassName = szAppName;                // Window class name

    if (RegisterClass (&wc) == 0) return 0;

    // Load the command bar common control class.
    icex.dwSize = sizeof (INITCOMMONCONTROLSEX);
    icex.dwICC = ICC_BAR_CLASSES | ICC_TREEVIEW_CLASSES |
```

(continued)

Listing 8-2 *(continued)*

```
                    ICC_LISTVIEW_CLASSES;
    InitCommonControlsEx (&icex);


    // Create main window.
    hWnd = CreateWindow (szAppName, TEXT ("RegView"), WS_VISIBLE,
                        CW_USEDEFAULT, CW_USEDEFAULT, CW_USEDEFAULT,
                        CW_USEDEFAULT, NULL, NULL, hInstance, NULL);
    // Return fail code if window not created.
    if (!IsWindow (hWnd)) return 0;

    // Standard show and update calls
    ShowWindow (hWnd, nCmdShow);
    UpdateWindow (hWnd);
    return hWnd;
}
//-----------------------------------------------------------------------
// TermInstance - Program cleanup
//
int TermInstance (HINSTANCE hInstance, int nDefRC) {
    return nDefRC;
}
//=======================================================================
// Message handling procedures for MainWindow
//-----------------------------------------------------------------------
// MainWndProc - Callback function for application window
//
LRESULT CALLBACK MainWndProc (HWND hWnd, UINT wMsg, WPARAM wParam,
                             LPARAM lParam) {
    INT i;
    //
    // Search message list to see if we need to handle this
    // message.  If in list, call procedure.
    //
    for (i = 0; i < dim(MainMessages); i++) {
        if (wMsg == MainMessages[i].Code)
            return (*MainMessages[i].Fxn)(hWnd, wMsg, wParam, lParam);
    }
    return DefWindowProc (hWnd, wMsg, wParam, lParam);
}
//-----------------------------------------------------------------------
// DoCreateMain - Process WM_CREATE message for window.
//
LRESULT DoCreateMain (HWND hWnd, UINT wMsg, WPARAM wParam,
                     LPARAM lParam) {
    HWND hwndCB, hwndChild;
    RECT rect;
```

```
    // Create a minimal command bar that has only a menu and an
    // exit button.
    hwndCB = CommandBar_Create (hInst, hWnd, IDC_CMDBAR);
    // Insert the menu.
    CommandBar_InsertMenubar (hwndCB, hInst, ID_MENU, 0);
    // Add exit button to command bar.
    CommandBar_AddAdornments (hwndCB, 0, 0);

    // The position of the child windows will be set in WM_SIZE
    SetRect (&rect, 0, 0, 10, 10);
    // Create the tree view control
    hwndChild = CreateTV (hWnd, &rect);
    if (!IsWindow (hwndChild)) {
        DestroyWindow (hWnd);
        return 0;
    }
    // Create the list view control
    hwndChild = CreateLV (hWnd, &rect);
    // Destroy frame if window not created.
    if (!IsWindow (hwndChild)) {
        DestroyWindow (hWnd);
        return 0;
    }
    // Insert the base keys.
    InsertTV (hWnd, NULL, TEXT ("HKEY_CLASSES_ROOT"),
              (LPARAM)HKEY_CLASSES_ROOT, 1);
    InsertTV (hWnd, NULL, TEXT ("HKEY_CURRENT_USER"),
              (LPARAM)HKEY_CURRENT_USER, 1);
    InsertTV (hWnd, NULL, TEXT ("HKEY_LOCAL_MACHINE"),
              (LPARAM)HKEY_LOCAL_MACHINE, 1);
    InsertTV (hWnd, NULL, TEXT ("HKEY_USERS"),
              (LPARAM)HKEY_USERS, 1);

    return 0;
}
//----------------------------------------------------------------------
// DoSizeMain - Process WM_SIZE message for window.
//
LRESULT DoSizeMain (HWND hWnd, UINT wMsg, WPARAM wParam, LPARAM lParam){
    HWND hwndLV, hwndTV;
    RECT rect, rectLV, rectTV;
    INT nDivPos, cx, cy;

    hwndTV = GetDlgItem (hWnd, ID_TREEV);
    hwndLV = GetDlgItem (hWnd, ID_LISTV);

    // Adjust the size of the client rect to take into account
    // the command bar height.
    GetClientRect (hWnd, &rect);
```

(continued)

Listing 8-2   *(continued)*

```
        rect.top += CommandBar_Height (GetDlgItem (hWnd, IDC_CMDBAR));
        cx = rect.right - rect.left;
        cy = rect.bottom - rect.top;

        // For Pocket PC, stack the windows; otherwise, they're side by side.
        if (GetSystemMetrics (SM_CXSCREEN) < 480) {
            nDivPos = (cy * nDivPct)/100;
            SetRect (&rectTV, rect.left, rect.top, cx, nDivPos);
            SetRect (&rectLV, rect.left, nDivPos + rect.top, cx, cy - nDivPos);
        } else {
            nDivPos = (cx * nDivPct)/100;
            SetRect (&rectTV, rect.left, rect.top, nDivPos, cy);
            SetRect (&rectLV, nDivPos, rect.top, cx - nDivPos, cy);
        }
        // The child window positions
        SetWindowPos (hwndTV, NULL, rectTV.left, rectTV.top,
                      rectTV.right, rectTV.bottom, SWP_NOZORDER);
        SetWindowPos (hwndLV, NULL, rectLV.left, rectLV.top,
                      rectLV.right, rectLV.bottom, SWP_NOZORDER);
        return 0;
}
//-----------------------------------------------------------------------
// DoCommandMain - Process WM_COMMAND message for window.
//
LRESULT DoCommandMain (HWND hWnd, UINT wMsg, WPARAM wParam,
                       LPARAM lParam) {
    WORD idItem, wNotifyCode;
    HWND hwndCtl;
    INT  i;

    // Parse the parameters.
    idItem = (WORD) LOWORD (wParam);
    wNotifyCode = (WORD) HIWORD (wParam);
    hwndCtl = (HWND) lParam;

    // Call routine to handle control message.
    for (i = 0; i < dim(MainCommandItems); i++) {
        if (idItem == MainCommandItems[i].Code)
            return (*MainCommandItems[i].Fxn)(hWnd, idItem, hwndCtl,
                                             wNotifyCode);
    }
    return 0;
}
//-----------------------------------------------------------------------
// DoNotifyMain - Process WM_NOTIFY message for window.
//
LRESULT DoNotifyMain (HWND hWnd, UINT wMsg, WPARAM wParam,
```

```
                        LPARAM lParam) {
    UINT    idItem;
    HWND    hCtl;
    LPNMHDR pHdr;
    INT     i;

    // Parse the parameters.
    idItem = wParam;
    pHdr = (LPNMHDR) lParam;
    hCtl = pHdr->hwndFrom;

    // Call routine to handle control message.
    for (i = 0; i < dim(MainNotifyItems); i++) {
        if (idItem == MainNotifyItems[i].Code)
            return (*MainNotifyItems[i].Fxn)(hWnd, idItem, hCtl, pHdr);
    }
    return 0;
}
//-----------------------------------------------------------------------
// DoDestroyMain - Process WM_DESTROY message for window.
//
LRESULT DoDestroyMain (HWND hWnd, UINT wMsg, WPARAM wParam,
                       LPARAM lParam) {
    PostQuitMessage (0);
    return 0;
}
//=======================================================================
// Command handler routines
//-----------------------------------------------------------------------
// DoMainCommandExit - Process Program Exit command.
//
LPARAM DoMainCommandExit (HWND hWnd, WORD idItem, HWND hwndCtl,
                          WORD wNotifyCode) {

    SendMessage (hWnd, WM_CLOSE, 0, 0);
    return 0;
}
//-----------------------------------------------------------------------
// DoMainCommandAbout - Process the Help | About menu command.
//
LPARAM DoMainCommandAbout(HWND hWnd, WORD idItem, HWND hwndCtl,
                          WORD wNotifyCode) {

    // Use DialogBox to create modal dialog box.
    DialogBox (hInst, TEXT ("aboutbox"), hWnd, AboutDlgProc);
    return 0;
}
```

(continued)

Listing 8-2 *(continued)*

```
//=======================================================================
// Notify handler routines
//-----------------------------------------------------------------------
// DoMainNotifyListV - Process notify message for list view.
//
LPARAM DoMainNotifyListV (HWND hWnd, UINT idItem, HWND hwndCtl,
                          LPNMHDR pnmh) {
    return 0;
}
//-----------------------------------------------------------------------
// DoMainNotifyTreeV - Process notify message for list view.
//
LPARAM DoMainNotifyTreeV (HWND hWnd, UINT idItem, HWND hwndCtl,
                          LPNMHDR pnmh) {

    LPNM_TREEVIEW pNotifyTV;
    TCHAR szKey[256];
    HKEY hRoot;
    HTREEITEM hChild, hNext;

    pNotifyTV = (LPNM_TREEVIEW) pnmh;

    switch (pnmh->code) {
        case TVN_ITEMEXPANDED:
            if (pNotifyTV->action == TVE_COLLAPSE) {
                // Delete the children so that on next open, they will
                // be reenumerated.
                hChild = TreeView_GetChild (hwndCtl,
                                            pNotifyTV->itemNew.hItem);
                while (hChild) {
                    hNext = TreeView_GetNextItem (hwndCtl, hChild,
                                                  TVGN_NEXT);
                    TreeView_DeleteItem (hwndCtl, hChild);
                    hChild = hNext;
                }
            }
            break;

        case TVN_SELCHANGED:
            GetTree (hWnd, pNotifyTV->itemNew.hItem, &hRoot,
                     szKey, dim(szKey));
            EnumValues (hWnd, hRoot, szKey);
            break;

        case TVN_ITEMEXPANDING:
            if (pNotifyTV->action == TVE_EXPAND) {
                GetTree (hWnd, pNotifyTV->itemNew.hItem, &hRoot,
```

```
                              szKey, dim(szKey));
                EnumChildren (hWnd, pNotifyTV->itemNew.hItem,
                              hRoot, szKey);

            }
            break;
    }
    return 0;
}
//---------------------------------------------------------------------
// CreateLV - Create list view control.
//
HWND CreateLV (HWND hWnd, RECT *prect) {
    HWND hwndLV;
    LVCOLUMN lvc;

    //
    // Create report window. Size it so that it fits under
    // the command bar and fills the remaining client area.
    //
    hwndLV = CreateWindowEx (0, WC_LISTVIEW, TEXT (""),
                        WS_VISIBLE | WS_CHILD | WS_VSCROLL |
                        WS_BORDER | LVS_REPORT,
                        prect->left, prect->top,
                        prect->right - prect->left,
                        prect->bottom - prect->top,
                        hWnd, (HMENU)ID_LISTV,
                        hInst, NULL);
    // Add columns.
    if (hwndLV) {
        lvc.mask = LVCF_TEXT | LVCF_WIDTH | LVCF_FMT | LVCF_SUBITEM |
                   LVCF_ORDER;
        lvc.fmt = LVCFMT_LEFT;
        lvc.cx = 120;
        lvc.pszText = TEXT ("Name");
        lvc.iOrder = 0;
        lvc.iSubItem = 0;
        SendMessage (hwndLV, LVM_INSERTCOLUMN, 0, (LPARAM)&lvc);

        lvc.mask |= LVCF_SUBITEM;
        lvc.pszText = TEXT ("Data");
        lvc.cx = 250;
        lvc.iOrder = 1;
        lvc.iSubItem = 1;
        SendMessage (hwndLV, LVM_INSERTCOLUMN, 1, (LPARAM)&lvc);
    }
    return hwndLV;
}
```

(continued)

Listing 8-2   *(continued)*

```c
//-----------------------------------------------------------------------
// InitTreeView - Initialize tree view control.
//
HWND CreateTV (HWND hWnd, RECT *prect) {
    HBITMAP hBmp;
    HIMAGELIST himl;
    HWND hwndTV;


    //
    // Create tree view.  Size it so that it fits under
    // the command bar and fills the left part of the client area.
    //
    hwndTV = CreateWindowEx (0, WC_TREEVIEW,
                         TEXT (""), WS_VISIBLE | WS_CHILD | WS_VSCROLL |
                         WS_BORDER | TVS_HASLINES | TVS_HASBUTTONS |
                         TVS_LINESATROOT, prect->left, prect->top,
                         prect->right, prect->bottom,
                         hWnd, (HMENU)ID_TREEV, hInst, NULL);

    // Destroy frame if window not created.
    if (!IsWindow (hwndTV))
        return 0;

    // Create image list control for tree view icons.
    himl = ImageList_Create (16, 16, ILC_COLOR, 2, 0);
    // Load first two images from one bitmap.
    hBmp = LoadBitmap (hInst, MAKEINTRESOURCE (ID_BMPS));
    ImageList_Add (himl, hBmp, NULL);
    DeleteObject (hBmp);

    TreeView_SetImageList(hwndTV, himl, TVSIL_NORMAL);
    return hwndTV;
}
//-----------------------------------------------------------------------
// InsertLV - Add an item to the list view control.
//
INT InsertLV (HWND hWnd, INT nItem, LPTSTR pszName, LPTSTR pszData) {

    HWND hwndLV = GetDlgItem (hWnd, ID_LISTV);
    LVITEM lvi;
    INT rc;

    lvi.mask = LVIF_TEXT | LVIF_IMAGE | LVIF_PARAM;
    lvi.iItem = nItem;
    lvi.iSubItem = 0;
    lvi.pszText = pszName;
    lvi.iImage = 0;
    lvi.lParam = nItem;
```

```
    rc = SendMessage (hwndLV, LVM_INSERTITEM, 0, (LPARAM)&lvi);

    lvi.mask = LVIF_TEXT;
    lvi.iItem = nItem;
    lvi.iSubItem = 1;
    lvi.pszText = pszData;

    rc = SendMessage (hwndLV, LVM_SETITEM, 0, (LPARAM)&lvi);
    return 0;
}
//-----------------------------------------------------------------------
// InsertTV - Insert item into tree view control.
//
HTREEITEM InsertTV (HWND hWnd, HTREEITEM hParent, TCHAR *pszName,
                    LPARAM lParam, DWORD nChildren) {
    TV_INSERTSTRUCT tvis;

    HWND hwndTV = GetDlgItem (hWnd, ID_TREEV);
    // Initialize the insertstruct.
    memset (&tvis, 0, sizeof (tvis));
    tvis.hParent = hParent;
    tvis.hInsertAfter = TVI_LAST;
    tvis.item.mask = TVIF_TEXT | TVIF_PARAM | TVIF_CHILDREN |
                     TVIF_IMAGE;
    tvis.item.pszText = pszName;
    tvis.item.cchTextMax = lstrlen (pszName);
    tvis.item.iImage = 1;
    tvis.item.iSelectedImage = 1;
    tvis.item.lParam = lParam;
    if (nChildren)
        tvis.item.cChildren = 1;
    else
        tvis.item.cChildren = 0;

    return TreeView_InsertItem (hwndTV, &tvis);
}
//-----------------------------------------------------------------------
// GetTree - Compute the full path of the tree view item.
//
INT GetTree (HWND hWnd, HTREEITEM hItem, HKEY *pRoot, TCHAR *pszKey,
             INT nMax) {
    TV_ITEM tvi;
    TCHAR szName[256];
    HTREEITEM hParent;
    HWND hwndTV = GetDlgItem (hWnd, ID_TREEV);

    memset (&tvi, 0, sizeof (tvi));
```

(continued)

Listing 8-2   *(continued)*

```
        hParent = TreeView_GetParent (hwndTV, hItem);
        if (hParent) {
            // Get the parent of the parent of the...
            GetTree (hWnd, hParent, pRoot, pszKey, nMax);

            // Get the name of the item.
            tvi.mask = TVIF_TEXT;
            tvi.hItem = hItem;
            tvi.pszText = szName;
            tvi.cchTextMax = dim(szName);
            TreeView_GetItem (hwndTV, &tvi);

            lstrcat (pszKey, TEXT ("\\"));
            lstrcat (pszKey, szName);
        } else {
            *pszKey = TEXT ('\0');
            szName[0] = TEXT ('\0');
            // Get the name of the item.
            tvi.mask = TVIF_TEXT | TVIF_PARAM;
            tvi.hItem = hItem;
            tvi.pszText = szName;
            tvi.cchTextMax = dim(szName);
            if (TreeView_GetItem (hwndTV, &tvi))
                *pRoot = (HKEY)tvi.lParam;
            else {
                INT rc = GetLastError();
            }
        }
    }
    return 0;
}
//----------------------------------------------------------------------
// DisplayValue - Display the data, depending on the type.
//
INT DisplayValue (HWND hWnd, INT nCnt, LPTSTR pszName, PBYTE pbData,
                  DWORD dwDSize, DWORD dwType) {
    TCHAR szData[512];
    INT i, len;

    switch (dwType) {
    case REG_MULTI_SZ:
    case REG_EXPAND_SZ:
    case REG_SZ:
        lstrcpy (szData, (LPTSTR)pbData);
        break;

    case REG_DWORD:
        wsprintf (szData, TEXT ("%X"), *(int *)pbData);
```

```
            break;

      case REG_BINARY:
          szData[0] = TEXT ('\0');
          for (i = 0; i < (int)dwDSize; i++) {
              len = lstrlen (szData);
              wsprintf (&szData[len], TEXT ("%02X "), pbData[i]);
              if (len > dim(szData) - 6)
                  break;
          }
          break;
      default:
          wsprintf (szData, TEXT ("Unknown type: %x"), dwType);
      }
      InsertLV (hWnd, nCnt, pszName, szData);
      return 0;
}
//----------------------------------------------------------------
// EnumValues - Enumerate each of the values of a key.
//
INT EnumValues (HWND hWnd, HKEY hRoot, LPTSTR pszKey) {
    INT nCnt = 0, rc;
    DWORD dwNSize, dwDSize, dwType;
    TCHAR szName[MAX_PATH];
    BYTE bData[1024];
    HKEY hKey;

    if (lstrlen (pszKey)) {
        if (RegOpenKeyEx (hRoot, pszKey, 0, 0, &hKey) != ERROR_SUCCESS)
            return 0;
    } else
        hKey = hRoot;

    // Clean out list view.
    ListView_DeleteAllItems (GetDlgItem (hWnd, ID_LISTV));

    // Enumerate the values in the list view control.
    nCnt = 0;
    dwNSize = dim(szName);
    dwDSize = dim(bData);
    rc = RegEnumValue (hKey, nCnt, szName, &dwNSize,
                       NULL, &dwType, bData, &dwDSize);

    while (rc == ERROR_SUCCESS) {
        // Display the value in the list view control.
        DisplayValue (hWnd, nCnt, szName, bData, dwDSize, dwType);

        dwNSize = dim(szName);
        dwDSize = dim(bData);
```

(continued)

Listing 8-2   *(continued)*

```
        nCnt++;
        rc = RegEnumValue (hKey, nCnt, szName, &dwNSize,
                           NULL, &dwType, bData, &dwDSize);
    }
    if (hKey != hRoot)
        RegCloseKey (hKey);
    return 1;
}
//-------------------------------------------------------------------------
// CountChildren - Count the number of children of a key.
//
DWORD CountChildren (HKEY hRoot, LPTSTR pszKeyPath, LPTSTR pszKey) {
    TCHAR *pEnd;
    DWORD dwCnt;
    HKEY hKey;

    pEnd = pszKeyPath + lstrlen (pszKeyPath);
    lstrcpy (pEnd, TEXT ("\\"));
    lstrcat (pEnd, pszKey);
if (RegOpenKeyEx(hRoot, pszKeyPath, 0, 0, &hKey) == ERROR_SUCCESS){
        RegQueryInfoKey (hKey, NULL, NULL, 0, &dwCnt, NULL, NULL, NULL,
                         NULL, NULL, NULL, NULL);
        RegCloseKey (hKey);
    }
    *pEnd = TEXT ('\0');
    return dwCnt;
}
//-------------------------------------------------------------------------
// EnumChildren - Enumerate the child keys of a key.
//
INT EnumChildren (HWND hWnd, HTREEITEM hParent, HKEY hRoot,
                  LPTSTR pszKey) {
    INT i = 0, rc;
    DWORD dwNSize;
    DWORD dwCSize;
    TCHAR szName[MAX_PATH];
    TCHAR szClass[256];
    FILETIME ft;
    DWORD nChild;
    HKEY hKey;
    TVITEM tvi;

    // All keys but root need to be opened.
    if (lstrlen (pszKey)) {
        if (RegOpenKeyEx (hRoot, pszKey, 0, 0, &hKey) != ERROR_SUCCESS) {
            rc = GetLastError();
            return 0;
        }
```

```
    } else
        hKey = hRoot;

    dwNSize = dim(szName);
    dwCSize = dim(szClass);
    rc = RegEnumKeyEx (hKey, i, szName, &dwNSize, NULL,
                       szClass, &dwCSize, &ft);
    while (rc == ERROR_SUCCESS) {

        nChild = CountChildren (hRoot, pszKey, szName);
        // Add key to tree view.
        InsertTV (hWnd, hParent, szName, 0, nChild);
        dwNSize = dim(szName);
        rc = RegEnumKeyEx (hKey, ++i, szName, &dwNSize,
                           NULL, NULL, 0, &ft);
    }
    // If this wasn't the root key, close it.
    if (hKey != hRoot)
        RegCloseKey (hKey);
    // If no children, remove expand button.
    if (i == 0) {
        tvi.hItem = hParent;
        tvi.mask = TVIF_CHILDREN;
        tvi.cChildren = 0;
        TreeView_SetItem (GetDlgItem (hWnd, ID_TREEV), &tvi);
    }
    return i;
}
//====================================================================
// About Dialog procedure
//
BOOL CALLBACK AboutDlgProc (HWND hWnd, UINT wMsg, WPARAM wParam,
                            LPARAM lParam) {
    switch (wMsg) {
        case WM_COMMAND:
            switch (LOWORD (wParam)) {
                case IDOK:
                case IDCANCEL:
                    EndDialog (hWnd, 0);
                    return TRUE;
            }
            break;
    }
    return FALSE;
}
```

The workhorses of this program are the enumeration functions that query
what keys and values are under each key. As a key is opened in the tree view
control, the control sends a *WM_NOTIFY* message. In response, RegView enu-

merates the items below that key and fills the tree view with the child keys and the list view control with the values.

We've covered a fair amount of ground in this chapter. The Windows CE file system, while radically different from its predecessors under the covers, presents a standard Win32 interface to the programmer and a familiar directory structure to the user. The registry structure and interface are quite familiar to Windows programmers and should present no surprises. Now it's time to look at the other type of data that is stored in the object store, Windows CE databases. The database API is unique to Windows CE. Let's see how it works.

9

Windows CE Databases

Windows CE supports a unique database API for storing and organizing data in the system. The database functions provide a simple tool for managing and organizing data. They aren't to be confused with the powerful multilevel SQL databases found on other computers. Even with its modest functionality, however, the database API is convenient for storing and organizing simple groups of data, such as address lists and mail folders.

In this chapter, I'll give you an overview of the database API. The database API is one of the areas that have experienced a fair amount of change as Windows CE has evolved. Essentially, functionality has been added to later versions of Windows CE. Where appropriate, I'll cover the differences between the different versions and show workarounds, where possible, for maintaining a common code base.

Databases

Windows CE gives you an entirely unique set of database APIs not available under the other versions of Windows. The database implemented by Windows CE is simple, with only one level and a maximum of four sort indexes, but it serves as an effective tool for organizing uncomplicated data, such as address lists and to-do lists.

Basic Definitions

A Windows CE database is composed of a series of records. Records can contain any number of properties. These properties can be one of the data types shown in Table 9-1.

Table 9-1 Database Data Types Supported by Windows CE

Data Type	Description
IVal	2-byte signed integer
UiVal	2-byte unsigned integer
Lval	4-byte signed integer
UlVal	4-byte unsigned integer
FILETIME	A time and date structure
LPWSTR	0-terminated Unicode string
CEBLOB	A collection of bytes
BOOL	Boolean
Double	8-byte signed value

Records can't contain other records. Also, records can reside on only one database. Windows CE databases can't be locked. However, Windows CE does provide a method of notifying a process that another thread has modified a database.

A Windows CE database can have up to four multilevel sort indexes. (In a multilevel sort index, the database sorts by a primary index and then sorts within that index by a second, and even third, index.) These indexes are defined when the database is created but can be redefined later, although the restructuring of a database takes a large amount of time. Each sort index by itself results in a fair amount of overhead, so you should limit the number of sort indexes to what you really need.

In short, Windows CE gives you a basic database functionality that helps applications organize simple data structures. The pocket series of Windows CE applications provided by Microsoft with the Pocket PC use the database API to manage the address book, the task list, and e-mail messages. So if you have a collection of data, this database API might just be the best method of managing that data.

Designing a Database

Before you can jump in with a call to *CeCreateDatabaseEx2*, you need to think carefully about how the database will be used. While the basic limitations of the Windows CE database structure rule out complex databases, the structure is quite handy for managing collections of related data on a small personal device, which, after all, is one of the target markets for Windows CE.

Each record in a database can have as many properties as you need as long as they don't exceed the basic limits of the database structure. The limits are fairly loose. An individual property can't exceed the constant *CEDB_MAXPROPDATASIZE*, which is set to 65,471. A single record can't exceed *CEDB_MAXRECORDSIZE*, currently defined as 131,072. The maximum number of records that can be in a single database is 65,535.

Database Volumes

Database files can be stored in volumes on external media as well as directly in the object store. A database volume is nothing more than a specially formatted file where Windows CE databases can be located. Because database volumes can be stored on file systems other than the object store, database information can be stored on Compact Flash Cards or similar external storage devices. The most immediate disadvantage of working with database volumes is that they must be first *mounted* and then *unmounted* after you close the databases within the volume. Essentially, mounting the database creates or opens the file that contains one or more databases along with the transaction data for those databases.

There are disadvantages to database volumes aside from the overhead of mounting and unmounting the volumes. Database volumes are actual files and therefore can be deleted by means of standard file operations. The volumes are, by default, marked as hidden, but that wouldn't deter the intrepid user from finding and deleting a volume in a desperate search for more space on the device. Databases created directly within the object store aren't files and therefore are much more difficult for the user to accidentally delete.

The Database API

Once you have planned your database and given the restrictions and considerations necessary to it, the programming can begin.

Mounting a Database Volume

If your database is on external media such as a CompactFlash card, you'll need to mount the database volume that contains it. To mount a database volume, call

```
BOOL CeMountDBVol (PCEGUID pguid, LPWSTR lpszVol, DWORD dwFlags);
```

This function performs a dual purpose: it can create a new volume or open an existing volume. The first parameter is a pointer to a guid. *CeMountDBVol* returns a guid that's used by most of the database functions to identify the location of the database file. You shouldn't confuse the *CEGUID*-type guid parameter in the database functions with the *GUID* type that is used by OLE and parts of the Windows shell. A *CEGUID* is simply a handle that tracks the opened database volume.

The second parameter in *CeMountDBVol* is the name of the volume to mount. This isn't a database name, but the name of a file that will contain one or more databases. Since the parameter is a filename, you should define it in \path\name.ext format. The standard extension should be CDB.

The last parameter, *dwFlags*, should be loaded with flags that define how this function acts. The possible flags are the following:

- **CREATE_NEW**   Creates a new database volume. If the volume already exists, the function fails.

- **CREATE_ALWAYS**   Creates a new database volume. If the volume already exists, it overwrites the old volume.

- **OPEN_EXISTING**   Opens a database volume. If the volume doesn't exist, the function fails.

- **OPEN_ALWAYS**   Opens a database volume. If the volume doesn't exist, a new database volume is created.

- **TRUNCATE_EXISTING**   Opens a database volume and truncates it to 0 bytes. If the volume already exists, the function fails.

If the flags resemble the action flags for *CreateFile*, they should. The actions of *CeMountDBVol* essentially mirror *CreateFile* except that instead of creating or opening a generic file, *CeMountDBVol* creates or opens a file especially designed to hold databases.

If the function succeeds, it returns *TRUE* and the guid is set to a value that is then passed to the other database functions. If the function fails, a call to *GetLastError* returns an error code indicating the reason for the failure.

Database volumes can be opened by more than one process at a time. The system maintains a reference count for the volume. As the last process unmounts a database volume, the system unmounts the volume.

Enumerating Mounted Database Volumes

You can determine which database volumes are currently mounted by repeatedly calling this function:

```
BOOL CeEnumDBVolumes (PCEGUID pguid, LPWSTR lpBuf, DWORD dwSize);
```

The first time you call *CeEnumDBVolumes*, set the guid pointed to by *pguid* to be invalid. You use the *CREATE_INVALIDGUID* macro to accomplish this. *CeEnumDBVolumes* returns *TRUE* if a mounted volume is found and returns the guid and name of that volume in the variables pointed to by *pguid* and *lpBuff*. The *dwSize* parameter should be loaded with the size of the buffer pointed to by *lpBuff*. To enumerate the next volume, pass the guid returned by the previous call to the function. Repeat this process until *CeEnumDBVolumes* returns *FALSE*. The code below demonstrates this process:

```
CEGUID guid;
TCHAR szVolume[MAX_PATH];
INT nCnt = 0;

CREATE_INVALIDGUID (&guid);
while (CeEnumDBVolumes (&guid, szVolume, sizeof (szVolume))) {
    // guid contains the guid of the mounted volume;
    // szVolume contains the name of the volume.
    nCnt++;   // Count the number of mounted volumes.
}
```

Unmounting a Database Volume

When you have completed using the volume, you should unmount it by calling this function:

```
BOOL CeUnmountDBVol (PCEGUID pguid);
```

The function's only parameter is the guid of a mounted database volume. Calling this function is necessary when you no longer need a database volume and you want to free system resources. Database volumes are unmounted only when all applications that have mounted the volume have called *CeUnmountDBVol*.

Using the Object Store as a Database Volume

Even though you can store databases in volumes on external media, more often than not you'll want to store the database in the object store. Because many of the database functions require a *CEGUID* that identifies a database volume, you need a *CEGUID* that references the system object store. Fortunately, one can be created using this macro:

```
CREATE_SYSTEMGUID (PCEGUID pguid);
```

The parameter is, of course, a pointer to a *CEGUID*. The value set in the *CEGUID* by this macro can then be passed to any of the database functions that require a separate volume *CEGUID*.

Creating a Database

You can create a database by calling the function *CeCreateDatabaseEx2*, which is prototyped as

```
CEOID CeCreateDatabaseEx2 (PCEGUID pguid, CEDBASEINFOEX *pInfo);
```

The first parameter is a *pguid* parameter that identifies the mounted database volume where the database is located. The second parameter is a pointer to a *CEDBASEINFOEX* structure defined as

```
typedef struct _CEDBASEINFOEX {
    WORD       wVersion;
    WORD       wNumSortOrder;
    DWORD      dwFlags;
    WCHAR      szDbaseName[CEDB_MAXDBASENAMELEN];
    DWORD      dwDbaseType;
    DWORD      dwNumRecords;
    DWORD      dwSize;
    FILETIME   ftLastModified;
    SORTORDERSPECEX rgSortSpecs[CEDB_MAXSORTORDER];
} CEDBASEINFOEX, *PCEDBASEINFOEX;
```

The first field, *wVersion*, specifies the version of the structure itself. It should be set to *CEDBASEINFOEX_VERSION*. The *wNumSortOrder* parameter should be set to the number of sort order structures in *rgSortSpecsArray*. The maximum number of sort indexes that can be specified is 4.

The *dwFlags* field has two uses. First, it contains flags indicating which fields in the structure are valid. The possible values for the *dwFlags* field are *CEDB_VALIDNAME*, *CEDB_VALIDTYPE*, *CEDB_VALIDSORTSPEC*, and *CEDB_VALIDDBFLAGS*. When you're creating a database, it's easier to set the *dwFlags* field to *CEDB_VALIDCREATE*, which is a combination of the flags I just listed. An additional flag, *CEDB_VALIDMODTIME*, is used when *CeOidGetInfo* uses this structure.

The other use for the *dwFlags* parameter is to specify the properties of the database. Two flags are currently defined. The first is *CEDB_NOCOMPRESS*, which can be specified if you don't want the database you're creating to be compressed. By default, all databases are compressed, which saves storage space at the expense of speed. By specifying the *CEDB_NOCOMPRESS* flag, the database will be larger but you will be able to read and write to the database faster. The second flag that can be defined is *CEDB_SYSTEMDB*. This flag indicates that the database cannot be deleted by an untrusted application. Trusted and untrusted applications are part of the Windows CE security architecture and will be discussed in Chapter 10.

The *szDbaseName* field specifies the name of the new database. Unlike filenames, the database name is limited to 32 characters, including the terminating zero. The *dwDbaseType* field is a user-defined parameter that can be employed to differentiate families of databases. For example, you might want to use a common type value for all databases that your application creates. This allows them to be easily enumerated. At this point, there are no rules for what type values to use. Some example type values used by the Microsoft Pocket suite are listed in Table 9-2.

Table 9-2   Predefined Database Types

Database	Value	
Contacts	24	(18 hex)
Appointments	25	(19 hex)
Tasks	26	(1A hex)
Categories	27	(1B hex)

The values listed in Table 9-2 aren't guaranteed to remain constant; I simply wanted to show some typical values. If you use a 4-byte value, it shouldn't be too hard to find a unique database type for your application, although there's no reason another application couldn't use the same type.

The fields *wNumRecords*, *dwSize*, and *ftLastModified* are ignored during the call to *CeCreateDatabaseEx*. They are used by other database functions that utilize this same structure.

The final field, *rgSortSpecs*, specifies the sort specification for the database. This parameter contains an array of *SORTORDERSPECEX* structures defined as

```
typedef struct _SORTORDERSPECEX {
    WORD wVersion;
    WORD wNumProps;
    WORD wKeyFlags;
    CEPROPID rgPropID[CEDB_MAXSORTPROP];
    DWORD rgdwFlags[CEDB_MAXSORTPROP];
} SORTORDERSPECEX;
```

The first field in *SORTORDERSPECEX* is the *wVersion* field, which should be set to *SORTORDERSPECEX_VERSION*. The *wNumProps* field specifies the number of sort properties used in this sort specification. The *wKeyFlags* field defines characteristics for the specification. The only flag currently supported is *CEDB_SORT_UNIQUE*, which indicates that each record in the database must have a unique value in this property.

The *rgPropID* field is an array of structures that contains property IDs, or *PEGPROPID*s. A property ID is nothing more than a unique identifier for a property in the database. Remember that a property is one field within a database record. The property ID is a *DWORD* value with the low 16 bits containing the data type and the upper 16 bits containing an application-defined value. These values are defined as constants and are used by various database functions to identify a property. For example, a property that contained the name of a contact might be defined as

```
#define PID_NAME        MAKELONG (CEVT_LPWSTR, 1)
```

The *MAKELONG* macro simply combines two 16-bit values into a *DWORD* or *LONG*. The first parameter is the low word or the result, while the second parameter becomes the high word. In this case, the *CEVT_LPWSTR* constant indicates that the property contains a string, while the second parameter is simply a value that uniquely identifies the *Name* property, distinguishing it from other string properties in the record.

The final field in *SORTORDERSPECEX*, *rgdwFlags*, contains an array of flags that define how the sort is to be accomplished. Each entry in the array matches the corresponding entry in the *rgPropID* array. The following flags are defined for this field:

- **CEDB_SORT_DESCENDING** The sort is to be in descending order. By default, properties are sorted in ascending order.

- **CEDB_SORT_CASEINSENSITIVE** The sort should ignore the case of the letters in the string.

- **CEDB_SORT_UNKNOWNFIRST** Records without this property are to be placed at the start of the sort order. By default, these records are placed last.

- **CEDB_SORT_IGNORENONSPACE** The sort should ignore non-space characters such as accents during sorting. This flag is valid only for string properties.

- **CEDB_SORT_IGNORESYMBOLS** The sort should ignore symbols during sorting. This flag is valid only for string properties.

- **CEDB_SORT_IGNOREKANATYPE** The sort should not differentiate between Hiragana and Katakana characters. This flag is valid only for string properties.

- **CEDB_SORT_IGNOREWIDTH** The sort should ignore the difference between single-byte characters and the same character represented by a double-byte value. This flag is valid only for string properties.

- **CEDB_SORT_NONNULL** This flag specifies that this sort property must be present in all records in the database.

A typical database might have three or four sort orders defined. After a database is created, these sort orders can be changed by calling *CeSetDatabaseInfoEx2*. However, this function is quite resource intensive and can take from seconds up to minutes to execute on large databases.

The value returned by *CeCreateDatabaseEx2* is a *CEOID*. We have seen this kind of value a couple of times so far in this chapter. It's an ID value that identifies the newly created database. If the value is 0, an error occurred while you were trying to create the database. You can call *GetLastError* to diagnose the reason the database creation failed.

The function *CeCreateDatabaseEx2* was added to Windows CE .NET 4.0. If an application needs to run on a Windows CE 3.0–based system, such as a Pocket PC 2000 or Pocket PC 2002, the application must use the function *CeCreateDatabaseEx* to create a database. The chief difference between the two functions is that *CeCreateDatabaseEx2* allows multilevel sorting, whereas *CeCreateDatabaseEx* does not.

Opening a Database

In contrast to what happens when you create a file, creating a database doesn't also open the database. To do that, you must make an additional call to

```
HANDLE CeOpenDatabaseEx2 (PCEGUID pguid, PCEOID poid, LPWSTR lpszName,
                          SORTORDERSPECEX *pSort,
                          DWORD dwFlags,
                          CENOTIFYREQUEST *pRequest);
```

The first parameter is the address of the *CEGUID* that indicates the database volume that contains the database. A database can be opened either by referencing its *CEOID* value or by referencing its name. To open the database by using its name, set the value pointed to by the *poid* parameter to 0 and specify the name of the database using the *lpszName* parameter. If you already know the *CEOID* of the database, simply put that value in the parameter pointed to by *poid*. If the *CEOID* value isn't 0, the function ignores the *lpszName* parameter.

The *pSort* parameter specifies which of the sort order specifications should be used to sort the database while it's opened. This parameter should point to a *SORTORDERSPECEX* structure that matches one of the entries in the *SORTORDERSPECEX* array that was defined when the database was created. The pointer doesn't have to point to the exact entry used when the database was created. Instead, the data within the *SORTORDERSPECEX* structure must match the data in the original *SORTORDERSPECEX* array entry. A Windows CE database can have only one active sort order. To use a different sort order, you can open a database again, specifying a different sort order.

The *dwFlags* parameter can contain either 0 or *CEDB_AUTOINCREMENT*. If *CEDB_AUTOINCREMENT* is specified, each read of a record in the database results in the database pointer being moved to the next record in the sort order. Opening a database without this flag means that the record pointer must be manually moved to the next record to be read. This flag is helpful if you plan to read the database records in sequential order.

The final parameter points to a structure that specifies how your application will be notified when another process or thread modifies the database. The scheme is a message-based notification that allows you to monitor changes to the database while you have it opened. To specify the window that receives the notification messages, you pass a pointer to a *CENOTIFYREQUEST* structure that you have previously filled in. This structure is defined as

```
typedef struct _CENOTIFYREQUEST {
    DWORD dwSize;
    HWND hWnd;
    DWORD dwFlags;
    HANDLE hHeap;
    DWORD dwParam;
} CENOTIFYREQUEST;
```

The first field must be initialized to the size of the structure. The *hWnd* field should be set to the window that will receive the change notifications. The *dwFlags* field specifies how you want to be notified. If you put 0 in this field, you'll receive notifications in the old database notification scheme. This method used three messages based on the *WM_USER* constant that is supposed to be reserved for applications. While this method is simpler than the method I'm about to describe, I recommend against using it. Instead, put *CEDB_EXNOTIFICATION* in the *dwFlags* field; your window will receive an entirely new and more detailed notification method. This new notification method requires that Windows CE allocate a structure. If you specify a handle to a heap in the *hHeap* field, the structure will be allocated there. If you set *hHeap* to 0, the structure will be allocated in your local heap. The *dwParam* field is a user-defined value that will be passed back to your application in the notification structure.

Your window receives a *WM_DBNOTIFICATION* message in the new notification scheme. When your window receives this message, the *lParam* parameter points to a *CENOTIFICATION* structure defined as

```
typedef struct _CENOTIFICATION {
    DWORD dwSize
    DWORD dwParam;
    UINT uType;
    CEGUID guid;
    CEOID oid;
    CEOID oidParent;
} CENOTIFICATION;
```

As expected, the *dwSize* field fills with the size of the structure. The *dwParam* field contains the value passed in the *dwParam* field in the *CENOTIFYREQUEST* structure. This is an application-defined value that can be used for any purpose.

The *uType* field indicates why the *WM_DBNOTIFICATION* message was sent. It will be set to one of the following values:

- **DB_CEOID_CREATED**   A new file system object was created.

- **DB_CEOID_DATABASE_DELETED**   The database was deleted from a volume.

- **DB_CEOID_RECORD_DELETED**   A record was deleted in a database.

- **DB_CEOID_CHANGED**   An object was modified.

The *guid* field contains the guid for the database volume that the message relates to, while the *oid* field contains the relevant database record oid. Finally, the *oidParent* field contains the oid of the parent of the oid that the message references.

When you receive a *WM_DBNOTIFICATION* message, the *CENOTIFICATION* structure is placed in a memory block that you must free. If you specified a handle to a heap in the *hHeap* field of *CENOTIFYREQUEST*, the notification structure will be placed in that heap; otherwise, the system places this structure in your local heap. Regardless of its location, you are responsible for freeing the memory that contains the *CENOTIFICATION* structure. You do this with a call to

```
BOOL CeFreeNotification(PCENOTIFYREQUEST pRequest,
                        PCENOTIFICATION pNotify);
```

The function's two parameters are a pointer to the original *CENOTIFYREQUEST* structure and a pointer to the *CENOTIFICATION* structure to free. You must free the *CENOTIFICATION* structure each time you receive a *WM_DBNOTIFICATION* message.

Seeking (or Searching for) a Record

Now that the database is opened, you can read and write the records. But before you can read a record, you must *seek* to that record. That is, you must move the database pointer to the record you want to read. You accomplish this using

```
CEOID CeSeekDatabaseEx (HANDLE hDatabase, DWORD dwSeekType, DWORD dwValue,
                        WORD wNumVals, LPDWORD lpdwIndex);
```

The first parameter for this function is the handle to the opened database. The *dwSeekType* parameter describes how the seek is to be accomplished. The parameter can have one of the following values:

- **_CEDB_SEEK_CEOID_**   Seek a specific record identified by its object ID. The object ID is specified in the *dwValue* parameter. This type of seek is particularly efficient in Windows CE databases.

- **_CEDB_SEEK_BEGINNING_**   Seek the *n*th record in the database. The index is contained in the *dwValue* parameter.

- **_CEDB_SEEK_CURRENT_**   Seek from the current position *n* records forward or backward in the database. The offset is contained in the *dwValue* parameter. Even though *dwValue* is typed as an unsigned value, for this seek it's interpreted as a signed value.

- **_CEDB_SEEK_END_**   Seek backward from the end of the database *n* records. The number of records to seek backward from the end is specified in the *dwValue* parameter.

- **_CEDB_SEEK_VALUESMALLER_**   Seek from the current location until a record is found that contains a property that is the closest to but not equal to or over the value specified. The value is specified by a *CEPROPVAL* structure pointed to by *dwValue*.

- **_CEDB_SEEK_VALUEFIRSTEQUAL_**   Starting with the current location, seek until a record is found that contains the property that's equal to the value specified. The value is specified by a *CEPROPVAL* structure pointed to by *dwValue*. The location returned can be the current record.

- **_CEDB_SEEK_VALUENEXTEQUAL_**   Starting with the next location, seek until a record is found that contains a property that's equal to the value specified. The value is specified by a *CEPROPVAL* structure pointed to by *dwValue*.

- **_CEDB_SEEK_VALUEGREATER_**   Seek from the current location until a record is found that contains a property that is equal to, or the closest to, the value specified. The value is specified by a *CEPROP-VAL* structure pointed to by *dwValue*.

As you can see from the available flags, seeking in the database is more than just moving a pointer; it also allows you to search the database for a particular record.

As I just mentioned in the descriptions of the seek flags, the *dwValue* parameter can either be loaded with an offset value for the seeks or point to an array of property values for the searches. The values are described in an array of *CEPROPVAL* structures, each defined as

```
typedef struct _CEPROPVAL {
    CEPROPID propid;
    WORD wLenData;
    WORD wFlags;
    CEVALUNION val;
} CEPROPVAL;
```

The *propid* field must match the property ID values of the sort order you specified when the database was opened. Remember that the property ID is a combination of a data type identifier along with an application-specific ID value that uniquely identifies a property in the database. This field identifies the property to examine when seeking. The *wLenData* field is ignored. None of the defined flags for the *wFlags* field is used by *CeSeekDatabase*, so this field should be set to 0. The *val* field is actually a union of the different data types supported in the database.

Following is a short code fragment that demonstrates seeking to the third record in the database.

```
DWORD dwIndex;
CEOID oid;

// Seek to the third record.
oid = CeSeekDatabase (g_hDB, CEDB_SEEK_BEGINNING, 3, &dwIndex);
if (oid == 0) {
    // There is no third item in the database.
}
```

Now say we want to find the first record in the database that has a height property of greater than 100. For this example, assume the size property type is a signed long value.

```
// Define pid for height property as a signed long with ID of 1.
#define PID_HEIGHT    MAKELONG (CEVT_I4, 1)

CEOID oid;
DWORD dwIndex;
CEPROPVAL Property;

// First seek to the start of the database.
oid = CeSeekDatabaseEx (g_hDB, CEDB_SEEK_BEGINNING, 0, 1, &dwIndex);
```

(continued)

```
// Seek the record with height > 100.
Property.propid = PID_HEIGHT;          // Set property to search.
Property.wLenData = 0;                 // Not used but clear anyway.
Property.wFlags = 0;                   // No flags to set
Property.val.lVal = 100;               // Data for property

oid = CeSeekDatabaseEx (g_hDB, CEDB_SEEK_VALUEGREATER, (DWORD)&Property,
                        1, &dwIndex);
if (oid == 0) {
    // No matching property found; db pointer now points to end of db.
} else {
    // oid contains the object ID for the record,
    // dwIndex contains the offset from the start of the database
    // of the matching record.
}
```

Because the search for the property starts at the current location of the database pointer, you first need to seek to the start of the database if you want to find the first record in the database that has the matching property.

Changing the Sort Order

I talked earlier about how *CeDatabaseSeekEx* depends on the sort order of the opened database. If you want to choose one of the predefined sort orders instead, you must close the database and then reopen it specifying the predefined sort order. But what if you need a sort order that isn't one of the four sort orders that were defined when the database was created? You can redefine the sort orders using this function:

```
BOOL CeSetDatabaseInfoEx2 (PCEGUID pguid,
                           CEOID oidDbase,
                           CEDBASEINFOEX *pNewInfo);
```

The function takes the *CEGUID* of the database volume and the object ID of the database you want to redefine and a pointer to a *CEDBASEINFOEX* structure. This structure is the same one used by *CeCreateDatabaseEx2*. You can use these functions to rename the database, change its type, or redefine the four sort orders. You shouldn't redefine the sort orders casually. When the database sort orders are redefined, the system has to iterate through every record in the database to rebuild the sort indexes. This can take minutes for large databases. If you must redefine the sort order of a database, you should inform the user of the massive amount of time it might take to perform the operation.

Reading a Record

Once you have the database pointer at the record you're interested in, you can read or write that record. You can read a record in a database by calling the following function:

```
CEOID CeReadRecordPropsEx (HANDLE hDbase, DWORD dwFlags,
                          LPWORD lpcPropID,
                          CEPROPID *rgPropID, LPBYTE *lplpBuffer,
                          LPDWORD lpcbBuffer,
                          HANDLE hHeap);
```

The first parameter in this function is the handle to the opened database. The *-lpcPropID* parameter points to a variable that contains the number of *CEPROPID* structures pointed to by the next parameter, *rgPropID*. These two parameters combine to tell the function which properties of the record you want to read. There are two ways to utilize the *lpcPropID* and *rgPropID* parameters. If you want only to read a selected few of the properties of a record, you can initialize the array of *CEPROPID* structures with the ID values of the properties you want and set the variable pointed to by *lpcPropID* with the number of these structures. When you call the function, the returned data will be inserted into the *CEPROPID* structures for data types such as integers. For strings and blobs, where the length of the data is variable, the data is returned in the buffer indirectly pointed to by *lplpBuffer*.

Since *CeReadRecordPropsEx* has a significant overhead to read a record, it is always best to read all the properties necessary for a record in one call. To do this, simply set *rgPropID* to *NULL*. When the function returns, the variable pointed to by *lpcPropID* will contain the count of properties returned and the function will return all the properties for that record in the buffer. The buffer will contain an array of *CEPROPID* structures created by the function, immediately followed by the data for those properties, such as blobs and strings, where the data isn't stored directly in the *CEPROPID* array.

One very handy feature of *CeReadRecordPropsEx* is that if you set *CEDB_ALLOWREALLOC* in the *dwFlags* parameter, the function will enlarge, if necessary, the results buffer to fit the data being returned. Of course, for this to work, the buffer being passed to the function must not be on the stack or in the static data area. Instead, it must be an allocated buffer, in the local heap or a separate heap. In fact, if you use the *CEDB_ALLOWREALLOC* flag, you don't even need to pass a buffer to the function; instead, you can set the buffer pointer to 0. In this case, the function will allocate the buffer for you.

Notice that the buffer parameter isn't a pointer to a buffer but the address of a pointer to a buffer. There actually is a method to this pointer madness. Since the resulting buffer can be reallocated by the function, it might be moved if the buffer needs to be reallocated. So the pointer to the buffer must be modified by the function. You must always use the pointer to the buffer returned by the function because it might have changed. Also, you're responsible for freeing the buffer after you have used it. Even if the function failed for some reason, the buffer might have moved or even have been freed by the function. You must clean up after the read by freeing the buffer if the pointer returned isn't 0.

As you might have guessed from the preceding paragraphs, the *hHeap* parameter allows *CeReadRecordPropsEx* to use a heap different from the local heap when reallocating the buffer. When you use *CeReadRecordPropsEx* and you want to use the local heap, simply pass a 0 in the *hHeap* parameter.

The following routine reads all the properties for a record and then copies the data into a structure.

```
int ReadDBRecord (HANDLE hDB, DATASTRUCT *pData, HANDLE hHeap) {
    WORD wProps;
    CEOID oid;
    PCEPROPVAL pRecord;
    PBYTE pBuff;
    DWORD dwRecSize;
    int i;

    // Read all properties for the record.
    pBuff = 0;    // Let the function allocate the buffer.
    oid = CeReadRecordPropsEx (hDB, CEDB_ALLOWREALLOC, &wProps, NULL,
                               &(LPBYTE)pBuff, &dwRecSize, hHeap);
    // Failure on read.
    if (oid == 0)
        return 0;

    // Copy the data from the record to the structure. The order
    // of the array is not defined.
    memset (pData, 0 , sizeof (DATASTRUCT));  // Zero return struct
    pRecord = (PCEPROPVAL)pBuff;              // Point to CEPROPVAL
                                              // array.
    for (i = 0; i < wProps; i++) {
        switch (pRecord->propid) {
        case PID_NAME:
            lstrcpy (pData->szName, pRecord->val.lpwstr);
            break;
        case PID_TYPE:
            lstrcpy (pData->szType, pRecord->val.lpwstr);
            break;
        case PID_SIZE:
            pData->nSize = pRecord->val.iVal;
            break;
        }
        pRecord++;
    }
    if (hHeap)
        HeapFree (hHeap, 0, pBuff);
    else
        LocalFree (pBuff);
    return i;
}
```

Because this function reads all the properties for the record, *CeReadRecord-PropsEx* creates the array of *CEPROPVAL* structures. The order of these structures isn't defined, so the function cycles through each one to look for the data to fill in the structure. After all the data has been read, a call to either *HeapFree* or *LocalFree* is made to free the buffer that was returned by *CeReadRecord-PropsEx*.

Nothing requires every record to contain all the same properties. You might encounter a situation where you request a specific property from a record by defining the *CEPROPID* array and that property doesn't exist in the record. When this happens, *CeReadRecordPropsEx* will set the *CEDB_PROPNOTFOUND* flag in the *wFlags* field of the *CEPROPID* structure for that property. You should always check for this flag if you call *CeReadRecord-PropsEx* and you specify the properties to be read. In the example above, all properties were requested, so if a property didn't exist, no *CEPROPID* structure for that property would have been returned.

Writing a Record

You can write a record to the database using this function:

```
CEOID CeWriteRecordProps (HANDLE hDbase, CEOID oidRecord, WORD cPropID,
                          CEPROPVAL * rgPropVal);
```

The first parameter is the obligatory handle to the opened database. The *oidRecord* parameter is the object ID of the record to be written. To create a new record instead of modifying a record in the database, set *oidRecord* to 0. The *cPropID* parameter should contain the number of items in the array of property ID structures pointed to by *rgPropVal*. The *rgPropVal* array specifies which of the properties in the record to modify and the data to write.

Deleting Properties, Records, and Entire Databases

You can delete individual properties in a record using *CeWriteRecordProps*. To do this, create a *CEPROPVAL* structure that identifies the property to delete and set *CEDB_PROPDELETE* in the *wFlags* field.

To delete an entire record in a database, call

```
BOOL CeDeleteRecord (HANDLE hDatabase, CEOID oidRecord);
```

The parameters are the handle to the database and the object ID of the record to delete.

You can delete an entire database using this function:

```
BOOL CeDeleteDatabaseEx (PCEGUID pguid, CEOID oid);
```

The two parameters are the *CEGUID* of the database volume and the object ID of the database. The database being deleted can't currently be opened.

Enumerating Databases

Sometimes you must search the system to determine what databases are on the system. Windows CE provides a set of functions to enumerate the databases in a volume. These functions are

```
HANDLE CeFindFirstDatabaseEx (PCEGUID pguid, DWORD dwDbaseType);
```

and

```
CEOID CeFindNextDatabaseEx (HANDLE hEnum, PCEGUID pguid);
```

These functions act like *FindFirstFile* and *FindNextFile* with the exception that *CeFindFirstDatabaseEx* only opens the search; it doesn't return the first database found. The *PCEGUID* parameter for both functions is the address of the *CEGUID* of the database volume you want to search. You can limit the search by specifying the ID of a specific database type in the *dwDbaseType* parameter. If this parameter is set to 0, all databases are enumerated. *CeFindFirstDatabaseEx* returns a handle that is then passed to *CeFindNextDatabaseEx* to actually enumerate the databases.

Here's how to enumerate the databases in the object store:

```
HANDLE hDBList;
CEOID oidDB;
CEGUID guidVol;

// Enumerate the databases in the object store.
CREATE_SYSTEMGUID(&guidVol);

hDBList = CeFindFirstDatabaseEx (&guidVol, 0);
if (hDBList != INVALID_HANDLE_VALUE) {

    oidDB = CeFindNextDatabaseEx (hDBList, &guidVol);
    while (oidDB) {
        // Enumerated database identified by object ID.
        MyDisplayDatabaseInfo (hCeDB);

        hCeDB = CeFindNextDatabaseEx (hDBList, &guidVol);
    }
    CloseHandle (hDBList);
}
```

The code first creates the *CEGUID* of the object store using the macro *CREATE_SYSTEMGUID*. That parameter, along with the database type specifier

0, is passed to *CeFindFirstDatabaseEx* to enumerate all the databases in the object store. If the function is successful, the databases are enumerated by repeatedly calling *CeFindNextDatabaseEx*.

Querying Object Information

To query information about a database, use this function:

```
BOOL CeOidGetInfoEx2 (PCEGUID pguid, CEOID oid, CEOIDINFOEX *oidInfo);
```

These functions return information about not just databases, but any object in the object store. This includes files and directories as well as databases and database records. The function is passed the database volume and object ID of the item of interest and a pointer to a *CEOIDINFOEX* structure.

Here's the definition of the *CEOIDINFOEX* structure:

```
typedef struct _CEOIDINFOEX {
    WORD wVersion;
    WORD wObjType;
    union {
        CEFILEINFO infFile;
        CEDIRINFO infDirectory;
        CEDBASEINFOEX infDatabase;
        CERECORDINFO infRecord;
    };
} CEOIDINFOEX;
```

This structure starts with a version field that should be set to *CEOIDINFOEX_VERSION*. The second field indicates the type of the item and a union of four different structures each detailing information about that type of object. The currently supported flags are *OBJTYPE_FILE*, indicating that the object is a file; *OBJTYPE_DIRECTORY*, for directory objects; *OBJTYPE_DATABASE*, for database objects; and *OBJTYPE_RECORD*, indicating that the object is a record inside a database. The structures in the union are specific to each object type.

The *CEFILEINFO* structure is defined as

```
typedef struct _CEFILEINFO {
    DWORD dwAttributes;
    CEOID oidParent;
    WCHAR szFileName[MAX_PATH];
    FILETIME ftLastChanged;
    DWORD dwLength;
} CEFILEINFO;
```

the *CEDIRINFO* structure is defined as

```
typedef struct _CEDIRINFO {
    DWORD dwAttributes;
    CEOID oidParent;
    WCHAR szDirName[MAX_PATH];
} CEDIRINFO;
```

and the *CERECORDINFO* structure is defined as

```
typedef struct _CERECORDINFO {
    CEOID oidParent;
} CERECORDINFO;
```

You've already seen the *CEDBASEINFOEX* structure used in *CeCreateDatabaseEx2* and *CeSetDatabaseInfoEx2*. As you can see from the preceding structures, *CeGetOidInfoEx2* returns a wealth of information about each object. One of the more powerful bits of information is the object's parent oid, which will allow you to trace the chain of files and directories back to the root. These functions also allow you to convert an object ID to a name of a database, directory, or file.

The object ID method of tracking a file object should not be confused with the PID scheme used by the shell. Object IDs are maintained by the file system and are independent of whatever shell is being used. This would be a minor point under other versions of Windows, but with the ability of Windows CE to be built as components and customized for different targets, it's important to know what parts of the operating system support which functions.

The AlbumDB Example Program

It's great to talk about the database functions; it's another experience to use them in an application. The example program that follows, AlbumDB, is a simple database that tracks record albums, the artist that recorded them, and the individual tracks on the albums. It has a simple interface because the goal of the program is to demonstrate the database functions, not the user interface. Figure 9-1 shows the AlbumDB window with a few albums entered in the database.

Listing 9-1 contains the code for the *AlbumDB* program. When the program is first launched, it attempts to open a database named Albums in the object store. If the program doesn't find one, it creates a new one. This is accomplished in the *OpenCreateDB* function.

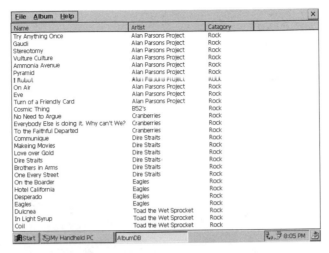

Figure 9-1   The AlbumDB window

AlbumDB.rc

```
//======================================================================
// Resource file
//
// Written for the book Programming Windows CE
// Copyright (C) 2003 Douglas Boling
//======================================================================

#include "windows.h"
#include "albumdb.h"                        // Program-specific stuff
//----------------------------------------------------------------------
// Icons and bitmaps
//
ID_ICON ICON   "albumdb.ico"                // Program icon


//----------------------------------------------------------------------
// Menu
//
ID_MENU MENU DISCARDABLE
BEGIN
    POPUP "&File"
    BEGIN
        MENUITEM "&Delete Database",        IDM_DELDB
        MENUITEM SEPARATOR
        MENUITEM "E&xit",                   IDM_EXIT
    END
```

Listing 9-1   The *AlbumDB* program   *(continued)*

Listing 9-1   *(continued)*

```
    POPUP "&Album"
    BEGIN
        MENUITEM "&New",                        IDM_NEW
        MENUITEM "&Edit",                       IDM_EDIT
        MENUITEM "&Delete",                     IDM_DELETE
        MENUITEM SEPARATOR
        MENUITEM "&Sort Name",                  IDM_SORTNAME
        MENUITEM "Sort &Artist",                IDM_SORTARTIST
        MENUITEM "Sort &Category",              IDM_SORTCATEGORY
    END
    POPUP "&Help"
    BEGIN
        MENUITEM "&About...",                   IDM_ABOUT
    END
END
//------------------------------------------------------------------------
// New/Edit Track dialog template
//
EditTrackDlg DIALOG discardable 10, 10, 135, 40
STYLE  WS_POPUP | WS_VISIBLE | WS_CAPTION | WS_SYSMENU | DS_CENTER |
       DS_MODALFRAME
EXSTYLE WS_EX_CAPTIONOKBTN
CAPTION "Edit Track"
BEGIN
    LTEXT "Track Name"              -1,   5,   5,  50,  12
    EDITTEXT                        IDD_TRACK, 60,   5,  70,  12,
                                    WS_TABSTOP | ES_AUTOHSCROLL

    LTEXT "Time"                    -1,   5,  20,  50,  12
    EDITTEXT                        IDD_TIME, 60,  20,  50,  12, WS_TABSTOP
END
//------------------------------------------------------------------------
// New/Edit Album data dialog template
//
EditAlbumDlg DIALOG discardable 5, 5, 135, 100
STYLE  WS_POPUP | WS_VISIBLE | WS_CAPTION | WS_SYSMENU | DS_CENTER |
       DS_MODALFRAME
EXSTYLE WS_EX_CAPTIONOKBTN
CAPTION "Edit Album"
BEGIN
    LTEXT "Album Name"              -1,   5,   5,  50,  12
    EDITTEXT                        IDD_NAME, 60,   5,  72,  12,
                                    WS_TABSTOP | ES_AUTOHSCROLL
    LTEXT "Artist"                  -1,   5,  20,  50,  12
    EDITTEXT                        IDD_ARTIST, 60,  20,  72,  12,
                                    WS_TABSTOP | ES_AUTOHSCROLL
```

```
    LTEXT "Category"                        -1,   5,  35,  50,  12
    COMBOBOX                        IDD_CATEGORY, 60, 35,  72,  60,
                            WS_TABSTOP | CBS_DROPDOWN
    LISTBOX                         IDD_TRACKS,  60,  50,  72,  45,
                            LBS_USETABSTOPS

    PUSHBUTTON "&New Track...",
                            IDD_NEWTRACK,  3,  50,  52,  12,
                            WS_TABSTOP
    PUSHBUTTON "&Edit Track...",
                            IDD_EDITTRACK,  3,  65,  52,  12,
                            WS_TABSTOP
    PUSHBUTTON "&Del Track",
                            IDD_DELTRACK,   3,  80,  52,  12,
                            WS_TABSTOP
END
//-------------------------------------------------------------------
// About box dialog template
//
aboutbox DIALOG discardable 10, 10, 135, 40
STYLE  WS_POPUP | WS_VISIBLE | WS_CAPTION | WS_SYSMENU | DS_CENTER |
       DS_MODALFRAME
CAPTION "About"
BEGIN
    ICON  ID_ICON,                          -1,  3,   5,  10,  10
    LTEXT "AlbumDB - Written for the book Programming Windows \
          CE Copyright 2003 Douglas Boling"
                            -1,  30,   5, 102,  33
END
```

AlbumDB.h

```
//====================================================================
// Header file
//
// Written for the book Programming Windows CE
// Copyright (C) 2003 Douglas Boling
//====================================================================
// Returns number of elements
#define dim(x) (sizeof(x) / sizeof(x[0]))


//-------------------------------------------------------------------
// Generic defines and data types
//
struct decodeUINT {                         // Structure associates
    UINT Code;                              // messages
                                            // with a function.
```

(continued)

Listing 9-1 *(continued)*

```
    LRESULT (*Fxn)(HWND, UINT, WPARAM, LPARAM);
};
struct decodeCMD {                              // Structure associates
    UINT Code;                                  // menu IDs with a
    LRESULT (*Fxn)(HWND, WORD, HWND, WORD);     // function.
};


//------------------------------------------------------------------
// Generic defines used by application
#define  ID_ICON              1                 // App icon resource ID
#define  IDC_CMDBAR           2                 // Command band ID
#define  ID_MENU              3                 // Main menu resource ID
#define  ID_LISTV             5                 // List view control ID

// Menu item IDs
#define  IDM_DELDB            101               // File menu
#define  IDM_EXIT             102

#define  IDM_NEW              110               // Album menu
#define  IDM_EDIT             111
#define  IDM_DELETE           112

#define  IDM_SORTNAME         120               // Sort IDs must be
#define  IDM_SORTARTIST       121               // consecutive.
#define  IDM_SORTCATEGORY     122

#define  IDM_ABOUT            150               // Help menu

// IDs for dialog box controls
#define  IDD_NAME             100               // Edit album dialog.
#define  IDD_ARTIST           101
#define  IDD_NUMTRACKS        102
#define  IDD_CATEGORY         103
#define  IDD_TRACKS           104
#define  IDD_NEWTRACK         105
#define  IDD_EDITTRACK        106
#define  IDD_DELTRACK         107

#define  IDD_TRACK            200               // Edit track dialog.
#define  IDD_TIME             201
//------------------------------------------------------------------
// Program-specific structures
//
// Structure used by New/Edit Album dlg proc
#define MAX_NAMELEN           64
#define MAX_ARTISTLEN         64
#define MAX_TRACKNAMELEN      512
```

```
typedef struct {
    TCHAR szName[MAX_NAMELEN];
    TCHAR szArtist[MAX_ARTISTLEN];
    INT nDateRel;
    SHORT sCategory;
    SHORT sNumTracks;
    INT nTrackDataLen;
    TCHAR szTracks[MAX_TRACKNAMELEN];
} ALBUMINFO, *LPALBUMINFO;

// Structure used by Add/Edit album track
typedef struct {
    TCHAR szTrack[64];
    TCHAR szTime[16];
} TRACKINFO, *LPTRACKINFO;

// Structure used by GetItemData
typedef struct {
    int nItem;
    ALBUMINFO Album;
} LVCACHEDATA, *PLVCACHEDATA;

// Database property identifiers
#define PID_NAME        MAKELONG (CEVT_LPWSTR, 1)
#define PID_ARTIST      MAKELONG (CEVT_LPWSTR, 2)
#define PID_RELDATE     MAKELONG (CEVT_I2, 3)
#define PID_CATEGORY    MAKELONG (CEVT_I2, 4)
#define PID_NUMTRACKS   MAKELONG (CEVT_I2, 5)
#define PID_TRACKS      MAKELONG (CEVT_BLOB, 6)
#define NUM_DB_PROPS    6
//--------------------------------------------------------------------
// Function prototypes
//
int InitApp (HINSTANCE);
HWND InitInstance (HINSTANCE, LPWSTR, int);
int TermInstance (HINSTANCE, int);

HANDLE OpenDB (HWND hWnd, LPTSTR lpszName);
HANDLE OpenCreateDB (HWND, int *);
void ReopenDatabase (HWND, INT);
int GetItemData (int, PLVCACHEDATA);
HWND CreateLV (HWND, RECT *);
void ClearCache (void);
int ErrBox (HWND hWnd, LPTSTR lpszFormat, ...);

// Window procedures
LRESULT CALLBACK MainWndProc (HWND, UINT, WPARAM, LPARAM);
```

(continued)

Listing 9-1   *(continued)*

```
// Message handlers
LRESULT DoCreateMain (HWND, UINT, WPARAM, LPARAM);
LRESULT DoSizeMain (HWND, UINT, WPARAM, LPARAM);
LRESULT DoCommandMain (HWND, UINT, WPARAM, LPARAM);
LRESULT DoNotifyMain (HWND, UINT, WPARAM, LPARAM);
LRESULT DoDbNotifyMain (HWND, UINT, WPARAM, LPARAM);
LRESULT DoDestroyMain (HWND, UINT, WPARAM, LPARAM);

// Command functions
LPARAM DoMainCommandDelDB (HWND, WORD, HWND, WORD);
LPARAM DoMainCommandExit (HWND, WORD, HWND, WORD);
LPARAM DoMainCommandNew (HWND, WORD, HWND, WORD);
LPARAM DoMainCommandEdit (HWND, WORD, HWND, WORD);
LPARAM DoMainCommandDelete (HWND, WORD, HWND, WORD);
LPARAM DoMainCommandSort (HWND, WORD, HWND, WORD);
LPARAM DoMainCommandAbout (HWND, WORD, HWND, WORD);

// Dialog procedures
BOOL CALLBACK AboutDlgProc (HWND, UINT, WPARAM, LPARAM);
BOOL CALLBACK EditAlbumDlgProc (HWND, UINT, WPARAM, LPARAM);
```

AlbumDB.cpp

```
//======================================================================
// AlbumDB - A Windows CE database
//
// Written for the book Programming Windows CE
// Copyright (C) 2003 Douglas Boling
//======================================================================
#include <windows.h>                 // For all that Windows stuff
#include <windowsx.h>                // For Windows controls macros
#include <commctrl.h>                // Command bar includes

#include "AlbumDB.h"                 // Program-specific stuff

// The include and lib files for the Pocket PC are conditionally
// included so that this example can share the same project file. This
// is necessary since this example must have a menu bar on the Pocket
// PC to have a SIP button.
#if defined(WIN32_PLATFORM_PSPC)
#include <aygshell.h>                // Add Pocket PC includes.
#pragma comment( lib, "aygshell" )   // Link Pocket PC lib for menu bar.
#endif
//----------------------------------------------------------------------
// Global data
//
const TCHAR szAppName[] = TEXT ("AlbumDB");
HINSTANCE hInst;                     // Program instance handle
```

```
HANDLE g_hDB = INVALID_HANDLE_VALUE; // Handle to album database
CEOID g_oidDB = 0;                   // Object ID of the album database
CEGUID g_guidDB;                     // Guid for database volume
CENOTIFYREQUEST cenr;                // Notify request structure.

int g_nLastSort = 0;                 // Last sort order used
CEDBASEINFOEX g_diex;                // Sort order array

// These two variables represent a one-item cache for
// the list view control.
int g_nLastItem = -1;
LPBYTE g_pLastRecord = 0;

// Message dispatch table for MainWindowProc
const struct decodeUINT MainMessages[] = {
    WM_CREATE, DoCreateMain,
    WM_SIZE, DoSizeMain,
    WM_COMMAND, DoCommandMain,
    WM_NOTIFY, DoNotifyMain,
    WM_DESTROY, DoDestroyMain,
    WM_DBNOTIFICATION, DoDbNotifyMain,
};

// Command message dispatch for MainWindowProc
const struct decodeCMD MainCommandItems[] = {
    IDM_DELDB, DoMainCommandDelDB,
    IDM_EXIT, DoMainCommandExit,
    IDM_NEW, DoMainCommandNew,
    IDM_EDIT, DoMainCommandEdit,
    IDM_DELETE, DoMainCommandDelete,
    IDM_SORTNAME, DoMainCommandSort,
    IDM_SORTARTIST, DoMainCommandSort,
    IDM_SORTCATEGORY, DoMainCommandSort,
    IDM_ABOUT, DoMainCommandAbout,
};
// Album category strings; must be alphabetical.
const TCHAR *pszCategories[] = {TEXT ("Classical"), TEXT ("Country"),
                                TEXT ("New Age"), TEXT ("Rock")};
//======================================================================
// Program entry point
//
int WINAPI WinMain (HINSTANCE hInstance, HINSTANCE hPrevInstance,
                    LPWSTR lpCmdLine, int nCmdShow) {
    HWND hwndMain;
    MSG msg;
    int rc = 0;

    // Initialize this instance.
    hwndMain = InitInstance (hInstance, lpCmdLine, nCmdShow);
```

(continued)

Listing 9-1   *(continued)*

```
    if (hwndMain == 0)
        return 0x10;

    // Application message loop
    while (GetMessage (&msg, NULL, 0, 0)) {
        TranslateMessage (&msg);
        DispatchMessage (&msg);
    }
    // Instance cleanup
    return TermInstance (hInstance, msg.wParam);
}
//---------------------------------------------------------------------
// InitInstance - Instance initialization
//
HWND InitInstance (HINSTANCE hInstance, LPWSTR lpCmdLine, int nCmdShow){
    HWND hWnd;
    WNDCLASS wc;
    INITCOMMONCONTROLSEX icex;

#if defined(WIN32_PLATFORM_PSPC)
    // If Pocket PC, allow only one instance of the application.
    HWND hWnd = FindWindow (szAppName, NULL);
    if (hWnd) {
        SetForegroundWindow ((HWND)(((DWORD)hWnd) | 0x01));
        return -1;
    }
#endif
    // Save program instance handle in global variable.
    hInst = hInstance;
    // Create a guid for the database Ex functions that points
    // to the object store.
    CREATE_SYSTEMGUID(&g_guidDB);
    memset (&cenr, 0, sizeof (cenr)); // Initialize the notify request.

    // Initialize database info structure.
    memset (&g_diex, 0, sizeof (g_diex));
    g_diex.wVersion = CEDBASEINFOEX_VERSION;
    g_diex.dwFlags = CEDB_VALIDNAME | CEDB_VALIDTYPE |
                    CEDB_VALIDSORTSPEC;
    lstrcpy (g_diex.szDbaseName, TEXT ("\\Albums"));
    g_diex.dwDbaseType = 0;
    g_diex.wNumSortOrder = 3;

    // Create sort property array
    int i = 0;
    g_diex.rgSortSpecs[i].wVersion = SORTORDERSPECEX_VERSION;
    g_diex.rgSortSpecs[i].wNumProps = 2;
    g_diex.rgSortSpecs[i].rgPropID[0] = PID_NAME;
```

```
g_diex.rgSortSpecs[i].rgdwFlags[0] = 0;
g_diex.rgSortSpecs[i].rgPropID[1] = PID_CATEGORY;
g_diex.rgSortSpecs[i].rgdwFlags[1] = 0;
i++;
g_diex.rgSortSpecs[i].wVersion = SORTORDERSPECEX_VERSION;
g_diex.rgSortSpecs[i].wNumProps = 2;
g_diex.rgSortSpecs[i].rgPropID[0] = PID_ARTIST;
g_diex.rgSortSpecs[i].rgdwFlags[0] = 0;
g_diex.rgSortSpecs[i].rgPropID[1] = PID_NAME;
g_diex.rgSortSpecs[i].rgdwFlags[1] = 0;
i++;
g_diex.rgSortSpecs[i].wVersion = SORTORDERSPECEX_VERSION;
g_diex.rgSortSpecs[i].wNumProps = 3;
g_diex.rgSortSpecs[i].rgPropID[0]= PID_CATEGORY;
g_diex.rgSortSpecs[i].rgdwFlags[0] = 0;
g_diex.rgSortSpecs[i].rgPropID[1] = PID_ARTIST;
g_diex.rgSortSpecs[i].rgdwFlags[1] = 0;
g_diex.rgSortSpecs[i].rgPropID[2] = PID_NAME;
g_diex.rgSortSpecs[i].rgdwFlags[2] = 0;

// Register application main window class.
wc.style = 0;                              // Window style
wc.lpfnWndProc = MainWndProc;              // Callback function
wc.cbClsExtra = 0;                         // Extra class data
wc.cbWndExtra = 0;                         // Extra window data
wc.hInstance = hInstance;                  // Owner handle
wc.hIcon = NULL,                           // Application icon
wc.hCursor = LoadCursor (NULL, IDC_ARROW);// Default cursor
wc.hbrBackground = (HBRUSH) GetStockObject (WHITE_BRUSH);
wc.lpszMenuName =  NULL;                    // Menu name
wc.lpszClassName = szAppName;              // Window class name

if (RegisterClass (&wc) == 0) return 0;

// Load the command bar common control class.
icex.dwSize = sizeof (INITCOMMONCONTROLSEX);
icex.dwICC = ICC_BAR_CLASSES | ICC_TREEVIEW_CLASSES |
             ICC_LISTVIEW_CLASSES;
InitCommonControlsEx (&icex);

// Create main window.
hWnd = CreateWindowEx (0, szAppName, TEXT ("AlbumDB"), WS_VISIBLE,
                       CW_USEDEFAULT, CW_USEDEFAULT, CW_USEDEFAULT,
                       CW_USEDEFAULT, NULL, NULL, hInstance, NULL);

// Return fail code if window not created.
if (!IsWindow (hWnd)) return 0;
```

(continued)

Listing 9-1 *(continued)*

```
    // Standard show and update calls
    ShowWindow (hWnd, nCmdShow);
    UpdateWindow (hWnd);
    return hWnd;
}
//------------------------------------------------------------------------
// TermInstance - Program cleanup
//
int TermInstance (HINSTANCE hInstance, int nDefRC) {
    // Close the opened database.
    if (g_hDB != INVALID_HANDLE_VALUE)
        CloseHandle (g_hDB);
    // Free the last db query if saved.
    ClearCache ();
    return nDefRC;
}
//========================================================================
// Message handling procedures for MainWindow
//------------------------------------------------------------------------
// MainWndProc - Callback function for application window
//
LRESULT CALLBACK MainWndProc (HWND hWnd, UINT wMsg, WPARAM wParam,
                              LPARAM lParam) {
    int i;
    //
    // Search message list to see if we need to handle this
    // message. If in list, call procedure.
    //
    for (i = 0; i < dim(MainMessages); i++) {
        if (wMsg == MainMessages[i].Code)
            return (*MainMessages[i].Fxn)(hWnd, wMsg, wParam, lParam);
    }
    return DefWindowProc (hWnd, wMsg, wParam, lParam);
}
//------------------------------------------------------------------------
// DoCreateMain - Process WM_CREATE message for window.
//
LRESULT DoCreateMain (HWND hWnd, UINT wMsg, WPARAM wParam,
                      LPARAM lParam) {
    HWND hwndCB, hwndChild;
    int  nHeight, nCnt;
    RECT rect;
    // Convert lParam to pointer to create structure.
    LPCREATESTRUCT lpcs = (LPCREATESTRUCT) lParam;

#if defined(WIN32_PLATFORM_PSPC) && (_WIN32_WCE >= 300)
    SHMENUBARINFO mbi;                          // For Pocket PC, create
```

```
    memset(&mbi, 0, sizeof(SHMENUBARINFO)); // menu bar so that we
    mbi.cbSize = sizeof(SHMENUBARINFO);      // have a sip button.
    mbi.hwndParent = hWnd;
    mbi.dwFlags = SHCMBF_EMPTYBAR;                // No menu
    SHCreateMenuBar(&mbi);
    SetWindowPos (hWnd, 0, 0, 0, lpcs->cx,lpcs->cy - 26,
                  SWP_NOMOVE | SWP_NOZORDER);
#endif
    // Convert lParam to pointer to create structure.
    lpcs = (LPCREATESTRUCT) lParam;

    // Create a minimal command bar that has only a menu and an
    // exit button.
    hwndCB = CommandBar_Create (hInst, hWnd, IDC_CMDBAR);
    // Insert the menu.
    CommandBar_InsertMenubar (hwndCB, hInst, ID_MENU, 0);
    // Add exit button to command bar.
    CommandBar_AddAdornments (hwndCB, 0, 0);
    nHeight = CommandBar_Height (hwndCB);

    // Open the album database. If one doesn't exist, create it.
    g_hDB = OpenCreateDB (hWnd, &nCnt);
    if (g_hDB == INVALID_HANDLE_VALUE) {
        MessageBox (hWnd, TEXT ("Could not open database."), szAppName,
                    MB_OK);
        DestroyWindow (hWnd);
        return 0;
    }
    // Create the list view control in right pane.
    SetRect (&rect, 0, nHeight, lpcs->cx, lpcs->cy - nHeight);
    hwndChild = CreateLV (hWnd, &rect);

    // Destroy frame if window not created.
    if (!IsWindow (hwndChild)) {
        DestroyWindow (hWnd);
        return 0;
    }
    ListView_SetItemCount (hwndChild, nCnt);
    return 0;
}
//----------------------------------------------------------------------
// DoSizeMain - Process WM_SIZE message for window.
//
LRESULT DoSizeMain (HWND hWnd, UINT wMsg, WPARAM wParam, LPARAM lParam){
    HWND hwndLV;
    RECT rect;
    hwndLV = GetDlgItem (hWnd, ID_LISTV);
    // Adjust the size of the client rect to take into account
```

(continued)

Listing 9-1 *(continued)*

```
    // the command bar height.
    GetClientRect (hWnd, &rect);
    rect.top += CommandBar_Height (GetDlgItem (hWnd, IDC_CMDBAR));

    SetWindowPos (hwndLV, NULL, rect.left, rect.top,
                  (rect.right - rect.left), rect.bottom - rect.top,
                  SWP_NOZORDER);

    CommandBar_AlignAdornments(GetDlgItem (hWnd, IDC_CMDBAR));
    return 0;
}
//----------------------------------------------------------------------
// DoCommandMain - Process WM_COMMAND message for window.
//
LRESULT DoCommandMain (HWND hWnd, UINT wMsg, WPARAM wParam,
                       LPARAM lParam) {
    WORD idItem, wNotifyCode;
    HWND hwndCtl;
    int  i;

    // Parse the parameters.
    idItem = (WORD) LOWORD (wParam);
    wNotifyCode = (WORD) HIWORD (wParam);
    hwndCtl = (HWND) lParam;

    // Call routine to handle control message.
    for (i = 0; i < dim(MainCommandItems); i++) {
        if (idItem == MainCommandItems[i].Code)
            return (*MainCommandItems[i].Fxn)(hWnd, idItem, hwndCtl,
                                              wNotifyCode);
    }
    return 0;
}
//----------------------------------------------------------------------
// DoNotifyMain - Process DB_CEOID_xxx messages for window.
//
LRESULT DoDbNotifyMain (HWND hWnd, UINT wMsg, WPARAM wParam,
                        LPARAM lParam) {
    CENOTIFICATION *pcen = (CENOTIFICATION *)lParam;
    switch (pcen->uType) {
    case DB_CEOID_CHANGED:
        InvalidateRect (GetDlgItem (hWnd, ID_LISTV), NULL, TRUE);
        break;
    case DB_CEOID_CREATED:
        ReopenDatabase (hWnd, -1);
        break;
    case DB_CEOID_RECORD_DELETED:
        ReopenDatabase (hWnd, -1);
```

```
            break;
        }
    CeFreeNotification (&cenr, pcen);
    return 0;
}
//------------------------------------------------------------------------
// DoNotifyMain - Process WM_NOTIFY message for window.
//
LRESULT DoNotifyMain (HWND hWnd, UINT wMsg, WPARAM wParam,
                      LPARAM lParam) {
    int idItem, i;
    LPNMHDR pnmh;
    LPNMLISTVIEW pnmlv;
    NMLVDISPINFO *pLVdi;
    LVCACHEDATA data;
    HWND hwndLV;

    // Parse the parameters.
    idItem = (int) wParam;
    pnmh = (LPNMHDR)lParam;
    hwndLV = pnmh->hwndFrom;

    if (idItem == ID_LISTV) {
        pnmlv = (LPNMLISTVIEW)lParam;

        switch (pnmh->code) {
        case LVN_GETDISPINFO:
            pLVdi = (NMLVDISPINFO *)lParam;

            // Get a pointer to the data either from the cache
            // or from the actual database.
            GetItemData (pLVdi->item.iItem, &data);

            if (pLVdi->item.mask & LVIF_IMAGE)
                pLVdi->item.iImage = 0;

            if (pLVdi->item.mask & LVIF_PARAM)
                pLVdi->item.lParam = 0;

            if (pLVdi->item.mask & LVIF_STATE)
                pLVdi->item.state = 0;
            if (pLVdi->item.mask & LVIF_TEXT) {
                switch (pLVdi->item.iSubItem) {
                case 0:
                    lstrcpy (pLVdi->item.pszText, data.Album.szName);
                    break;
                case 1:
                    lstrcpy (pLVdi->item.pszText, data.Album.szArtist);
```

(continued)

Listing 9-1 *(continued)*

```
                        break;
                    case 2:
                        lstrcpy (pLVdi->item.pszText,
                                    pszCategories[data.Album.sCategory]);
                        break;
                }
            }
            break;

        // Sort by column
        case LVN_COLUMNCLICK:
            i = ((NM_LISTVIEW *)lParam)->iSubItem + IDM_SORTNAME;
            PostMessage (hWnd, WM_COMMAND, MAKELPARAM (i, 0), 0);
            break;

        // Double click indicates edit
        case NM_DBLCLK:
            PostMessage (hWnd, WM_COMMAND, MAKELPARAM (IDM_EDIT, 0), 0);
            break;

        // Ignore cache hinting for db example.
        case LVN_ODCACHEHINT:
            break;

        case LVN_ODFINDITEM:
            // We should do a reverse lookup here to see if
            // an item exists for the text passed.
            return -1;
        }
    }
    return 0;
}
//----------------------------------------------------------------------
// DoDestroyMain - Process WM_DESTROY message for window.
//
LRESULT DoDestroyMain (HWND hWnd, UINT wMsg, WPARAM wParam,
                       LPARAM lParam) {
    PostQuitMessage (0);
    return 0;
}
//======================================================================
// Command handler routines
//----------------------------------------------------------------------
// DoMainCommandDelDB - Process Program Delete command.
//
LPARAM DoMainCommandDelDB (HWND hWnd, WORD idItem, HWND hwndCtl,
                           WORD wNotifyCode) {
```

```
    int i, rc;

    i = MessageBox (hWnd, TEXT ("Delete the entire database?"),
                    TEXT ("Delete"), MB_YESNO);
    if (i != IDYES)
        return 0;
    if (g_oidDB) {
        CloseHandle (g_hDB);
        rc = CeDeleteDatabase (g_oidDB);
        if (rc == 0) {
            ErrBox (hWnd, TEXT ("Couldn\'t delete database. rc=%d"),
                GetLastError());
            g_hDB = OpenDB (hWnd, NULL);   // Open the database.
            return 0;
        }
        g_hDB = INVALID_HANDLE_VALUE;
        g_oidDB = 0;
    }
    ListView_SetItemCount (GetDlgItem (hWnd, ID_LISTV), 0);
    return 0;
}
//-----------------------------------------------------------------------
// DoMainCommandExit - Process Program Exit command.
//
LPARAM DoMainCommandExit (HWND hWnd, WORD idItem, HWND hwndCtl,
                          WORD wNotifyCode) {
    SendMessage (hWnd, WM_CLOSE, 0, 0);
    return 0;
}
//-----------------------------------------------------------------------
// DoMainCommandNew - Process Program New command.
//
LPARAM DoMainCommandNew (HWND hWnd, WORD idItem, HWND hwndCtl,
                         WORD wNotifyCode) {
    PCEPROPVAL pcepv;
    int i, rc;
    CEOID oid;
    HWND hwndLV = GetDlgItem (hWnd, ID_LISTV);
    // Display the new/edit dialog.
    pcepv = 0;
    rc = DialogBoxParam (hInst, TEXT ("EditAlbumDlg"), hWnd,
                         EditAlbumDlgProc, (LPARAM)&pcepv);
    if (rc == 0)
        return 0;

    // Write the record.
    oid = CeWriteRecordProps(g_hDB, 0, NUM_DB_PROPS, pcepv);
```

(continued)

Listing 9-1   *(continued)*

```
    if (!oid)
        ErrBox (hWnd, TEXT ("Write Rec fail. rc=%d"), GetLastError());

    ClearCache ();                          // Clear the lv cache.
    i = ListView_GetItemCount (hwndLV) + 1;  // Increment list view
                                            // count.
    ListView_SetItemCount (hwndLV, i);
    InvalidateRect (hwndLV, NULL, TRUE);     // Force redraw.
    return 0;
}
//----------------------------------------------------------------------
// DoMainCommandEdit - Process Program Edit command.
//
LPARAM DoMainCommandEdit (HWND hWnd, WORD idItem, HWND hwndCtl,
                          WORD wNotifyCode) {
    PCEPROPVAL pcepv = 0;
    int nSel, rc;
    WORD wProps = 0;
    DWORD dwRecSize, dwIndex;
    CEOID oid;
    HWND hwndLV = GetDlgItem (hWnd, ID_LISTV);

    nSel = ListView_GetSelectionMark (hwndLV);
    if (nSel == -1)
        return 0;

    // Seek to the necessary record.
    oid = CeSeekDatabase (g_hDB, CEDB_SEEK_BEGINNING, nSel, &dwIndex);
    if (oid == 0) {
        ErrBox (hWnd, TEXT ("Db item not found. rc=%d"), GetLastError());
        return 0;
    }
    // Read all properties for the record. Have the system
    // allocate the buffer containing the data.
    oid = CeReadRecordPropsEx (g_hDB, CEDB_ALLOWREALLOC, &wProps, NULL,
                               (LPBYTE *)&pcepv, &dwRecSize, 0);
    if (oid == 0) {
        ErrBox (hWnd, TEXT ("Db item not read. rc=%d"), GetLastError());
        return 0;
    }
    // Display the edit dialog.
    rc = DialogBoxParam (hInst, TEXT ("EditAlbumDlg"), hWnd,
                         EditAlbumDlgProc, (LPARAM)&pcepv);
    if (rc == 0)
        return 0;

    // Write the record.
    oid = CeWriteRecordProps(g_hDB, oid, NUM_DB_PROPS, pcepv);
```

```
        if (!oid)
            ErrBox (hWnd, TEXT ("Write Rec fail. rc=%d"), GetLastError());

        LocalFree ((LPBYTE)pcepv);
        ClearCache ();                                  // Clear the lv cache.

        InvalidateRect (hwndLV, NULL, TRUE);            // Force redraw.
        return 0;
    }
    //---------------------------------------------------------------------
    // DoMainCommandDelete - Process Program Delete command.
    //
    LPARAM DoMainCommandDelete (HWND hWnd, WORD idItem, HWND hwndCtl,
                                WORD wNotifyCode) {
        HWND hwndLV;
        TCHAR szText[64];
        DWORD dwIndex;
        int i, nSel;
        CEOID oid;

        hwndLV = GetDlgItem (hWnd, ID_LISTV);
        nSel = ListView_GetSelectionMark (hwndLV);
        if (nSel != -1) {

            wsprintf (szText, TEXT ("Delete this item?"));
            i = MessageBox (hWnd, szText, TEXT ("Delete"), MB_YESNO);
            if (i != IDYES)
                return 0;

            // Seek to the necessary record.
            oid = CeSeekDatabase (g_hDB, CEDB_SEEK_BEGINNING, nSel, &dwIndex);
            CeDeleteRecord (g_hDB, oid);

            // Reduce the list view count by one and force redraw.
            i = ListView_GetItemCount (hwndLV) - 1;
            ListView_SetItemCount (hwndLV, i);
            ClearCache ();                              // Clear the lv cache.
            InvalidateRect (hwndLV, NULL, TRUE);
        }
        return 0;
    }
    //---------------------------------------------------------------------
    // DoMainCommandSort - Process the Sort commands.
    //
    LPARAM DoMainCommandSort(HWND hWnd, WORD idItem, HWND hwndCtl,
                             WORD wNotifyCode) {
```

(continued)

Listing 9-1   *(continued)*

```
    int nSort;

    switch (idItem) {
    case IDM_SORTNAME:
        nSort = 0;
        break;
    case IDM_SORTARTIST:
        nSort = 1;
        break;
    case IDM_SORTCATEGORY:
        nSort = 2;
        break;
    }
    if (nSort == g_nLastSort)
        return 0;

    ReopenDatabase (hWnd, nSort);        // Close and reopen the database.
    return 0;
}
//----------------------------------------------------------------------
// DoMainCommandAbout - Process the Help | About menu command.
//
LPARAM DoMainCommandAbout(HWND hWnd, WORD idItem, HWND hwndCtl,
                          WORD wNotifyCode) {
    // Use DialogBox to create modal dialog.
    DialogBox (hInst, TEXT ("aboutbox"), hWnd, AboutDlgProc);
    return 0;
}
//----------------------------------------------------------------------
// CreateLV - Creates the list view control
//
HWND CreateLV (HWND hWnd, RECT *prect) {
    HWND hwndLV;
    LVCOLUMN lvc;

    // Create album list window.
    hwndLV = CreateWindowEx (0, WC_LISTVIEW, TEXT (""),
                        WS_VISIBLE | WS_CHILD | WS_VSCROLL |
                        LVS_OWNERDATA | WS_BORDER | LVS_REPORT,
                        prect->left, prect->top,
                        prect->right - prect->left,
                        prect->bottom - prect->top,
                        hWnd, (HMENU)ID_LISTV,
                        hInst, NULL);

    // Add columns.
    if (hwndLV) {
```

```
            lvc.mask = LVCF_TEXT | LVCF_WIDTH | LVCF_FMT | LVCF_SUBITEM;
            lvc.fmt = LVCFMT_LEFT;
            lvc.cx = 150;
            lvc.pszText = TEXT ("Name");
            lvc.iSubItem = 0;
            SendMessage (hwndLV, LVM_INSERTCOLUMN, 0, (LPARAM)&lvc);

            lvc.mask |= LVCF_SUBITEM;
            lvc.pszText = TEXT ("Artist");
            lvc.cx = 100;
            lvc.iSubItem = 1;
            SendMessage (hwndLV, LVM_INSERTCOLUMN, 1, (LPARAM)&lvc);

            lvc.mask |= LVCF_SUBITEM;
            lvc.pszText = TEXT ("Category");
            lvc.cx = 100;
            lvc.iSubItem = 2;
            SendMessage (hwndLV, LVM_INSERTCOLUMN, 2, (LPARAM)&lvc);
    }
    return hwndLV;
}
//-----------------------------------------------------------------------
// OpenDB - Open database.
//
HANDLE OpenDB (HWND hWnd, LPTSTR lpszName) {
    // Reinitialize the notify request structure.
    cenr.dwSize = sizeof (cenr);
    cenr.hwnd = hWnd;
    cenr.dwFlags = CEDB_EXNOTIFICATION;

    if (lpszName)
        g_oidDB = 0;
    return CeOpenDatabaseEx2 (&g_guidDB, &g_oidDB, lpszName,
                             &g_diex.rgSortSpecs[g_nLastSort],
                             0, &cenr);
}
//-----------------------------------------------------------------------
// OpenCreateDB - Open database, create if necessary.
//
HANDLE OpenCreateDB (HWND hWnd, int *pnRecords) {
    int rc;
    CEOIDINFO oidinfo;

    g_oidDB = 0;
    g_hDB = OpenDB (hWnd, TEXT ("\\Albums"));
    if (g_hDB == INVALID_HANDLE_VALUE) {
        rc = GetLastError();
        if (rc == ERROR_FILE_NOT_FOUND) {
```

(continued)

Listing 9-1   *(continued)*

```
            g_oidDB = CeCreateDatabaseEx2 (&g_guidDB, &g_diex);
            if (g_oidDB == 0) {
                ErrBox (hWnd, TEXT ("Database create failed. rc=%d"),
                        GetLastError());
                return 0;
            }
            g_hDB = OpenDB (hWnd, NULL);
        }
    }
    CeOidGetInfo (g_oidDB, &oidinfo);
    *pnRecords = oidinfo.infDatabase.wNumRecords;
    return g_hDB;
}
//-----------------------------------------------------------------------
// ClearCache - Clears the one-item cache for the list view control
//
void ClearCache (void) {

    if (g_pLastRecord)
        LocalFree (g_pLastRecord);
    g_pLastRecord = 0;
    g_nLastItem = -1;
    return;
}
//-----------------------------------------------------------------------
// ReopenDatabase - Closes and reopens the database
//
void ReopenDatabase (HWND hWnd, int nNewSort) {
    int nCnt;

    if (nNewSort != -1)
        g_nLastSort = nNewSort;

    if (g_hDB)
        CloseHandle (g_hDB);
    ClearCache ();                              // Clear the lv cache.

    g_hDB = OpenCreateDB (hWnd, &nCnt);

    ListView_SetItemCount (GetDlgItem (hWnd, ID_LISTV), nCnt);
    InvalidateRect (GetDlgItem (hWnd, ID_LISTV), NULL, 0);
    return;
}
//-----------------------------------------------------------------------
// Get the album data from the database for the requested lv item.
//
int GetItemData (int nItem, PLVCACHEDATA pcd) {
```

```
static WORD wProps;
DWORD dwIndex;
CEOID oid;
PCEPROPVAL pRecord = NULL;
DWORD dwRecSize;
int i;

// See if the item requested was the previous one. If so,
// just use the old data.
if ((nItem == g_nLastItem) && (g_pLastRecord))
    pRecord = (PCEPROPVAL)g_pLastRecord;
else {
    // Seek to the necessary record.
    oid = CeSeekDatabase (g_hDB, CEDB_SEEK_BEGINNING, nItem, &dwIndex);
    if (oid == 0) {
        ErrBox (NULL, TEXT ("Db item not found. rc=%d"),
                GetLastError());
        return 0;
    }
    // Read all properties for the record.  Have the system
    // allocate the buffer containing the data.
    oid = CeReadRecordProps (g_hDB, CEDB_ALLOWREALLOC, &wProps, NULL,
                             (LPBYTE *)&pRecord, &dwRecSize);
    if (oid == 0) {
        ErrBox (NULL, TEXT ("Db item not read. rc=%d"),
                GetLastError());
        return 0;
    }
    // Free old record, and save the newly read one.
    if (g_pLastRecord)
        LocalFree (g_pLastRecord);
    g_nLastItem = nItem;
    g_pLastRecord = (LPBYTE)pRecord;


}
// Copy the data from the record to the album structure.
for (i = 0; i < wProps; i++) {
    switch (pRecord->propid) {
    case PID_NAME:
        lstrcpy (pcd->Album.szName, pRecord->val.lpwstr);
        break;
    case PID_ARTIST:
        lstrcpy (pcd->Album.szArtist, pRecord->val.lpwstr);
        break;
    case PID_CATEGORY:
        pcd->Album.sCategory = pRecord->val.iVal;
        break;
    case PID_NUMTRACKS:
```

(continued)

Listing 9-1   *(continued)*

```
                pcd->Album.sNumTracks - pRecord->val.iVal;
                break;
            }
            pRecord++;
        }
        return 1;
}
//-------------------------------------------------------------------
// InsertLV - Add an item to the list view control.
//
int InsertLV (HWND hWnd, int nItem, LPTSTR pszName, LPTSTR pszType,
              int nSize) {
    LVITEM lvi;
    HWND hwndLV = GetDlgItem (hWnd, ID_LISTV);

    lvi.mask = LVIF_TEXT | LVIF_IMAGE | LVIF_PARAM;
    lvi.iItem = nItem;
    lvi.iSubItem = 0;
    lvi.pszText = pszName;
    lvi.iImage = 0;
    lvi.lParam = nItem;
    SendMessage (hwndLV, LVM_INSERTITEM, 0, (LPARAM)&lvi);

    lvi.mask = LVIF_TEXT;
    lvi.iItem = nItem;
    lvi.iSubItem = 1;
    lvi.pszText = pszType;
    SendMessage (hwndLV, LVM_SETITEM, 0, (LPARAM)&lvi);

    return 0;
}
//-------------------------------------------------------------------
// ValidateTime - Trivial error checking of time field
//
BOOL ValidateTime (TCHAR *pStr) {
    BOOL fSep = FALSE;
    TCHAR *pPtr;

    pPtr = pStr;
    // See if field contains only numbers and up to one colon.
    while (*pPtr) {
        if (*pPtr == TEXT (':')) {
            if (fSep)
                return FALSE;
            fSep = TRUE;
        } else if ((*pPtr < TEXT ('0')) || (*pPtr > TEXT ('9')))
            return FALSE;
```

```
                pPtr++;
        }
        // Reject empty field.
        if (pPtr > pStr)
            return TRUE;
        return FALSE;
}
//-------------------------------------------------------------------
// ErrBox - Displays an error string in a message box
//
int ErrBox (HWND hWnd, LPTSTR lpszFormat, ...) {
    int nBuf;
    TCHAR szBuffer[512];

    va_list args;
    va_start(args, lpszFormat);
    nBuf = _vstprintf(szBuffer, lpszFormat, args);
    va_end(args);

    MessageBox (hWnd, szBuffer, TEXT("Error"), MB_OK | MB_ICONERROR);
    return 0;
}
//===================================================================
// EditTrack dialog procedure
//
BOOL CALLBACK EditTrackDlgProc (HWND hWnd, UINT wMsg, WPARAM wParam,
                                LPARAM lParam) {
    static LPTRACKINFO lpti;

    switch (wMsg) {
        case WM_INITDIALOG:
            lpti = (LPTRACKINFO)lParam;
            SendDlgItemMessage (hWnd, IDD_TRACK, EM_SETLIMITTEXT,
                                sizeof (lpti->szTrack), 0);
            SendDlgItemMessage (hWnd, IDD_TIME, EM_SETLIMITTEXT,
                                sizeof (lpti->szTime), 0);
            // See if new album or edit of old one.
            if (lstrlen (lpti->szTrack) == 0) {
                SetWindowText (hWnd, TEXT ("New Track"));
            } else {
                SetDlgItemText (hWnd, IDD_TRACK, lpti->szTrack);
                SetDlgItemText (hWnd, IDD_TIME, lpti->szTime);
            }
            return TRUE;

        case WM_COMMAND:
            switch (LOWORD (wParam)) {
                case IDOK:
                    Edit_GetText (GetDlgItem (hWnd, IDD_TRACK),
```

(continued)

Listing 9-1 *(continued)*

```
                              lpti->szTrack, sizeof (lpti->szTrack));
                   Edit_GetText (GetDlgItem (hWnd, IDD_TIME),
                              lpti->szTime, sizeof (lpti->szTime));
                   if (ValidateTime (lpti->szTime))
                       EndDialog (hWnd, 1);
                   else
                       MessageBox (hWnd, TEXT ("Track time must \
                                  be entered in mm:ss format"),
                                  TEXT ("Error"), MB_OK);
                   return TRUE;
               case IDCANCEL:
                   EndDialog (hWnd, 0);
                   return TRUE;
           }
       break;
   }
   return FALSE;
}
//======================================================================
// EditAlbum dialog procedure
//
BOOL CALLBACK EditAlbumDlgProc (HWND hWnd, UINT wMsg, WPARAM wParam,
                              LPARAM lParam) {
   static PCEPROPVAL *ppRecord;
   static int nTracks;
   PCEPROPVAL pRecord, pRecPtr;
   TCHAR *pPtr, szTmp[128];
   HWND hwndTList, hwndCombo;
   TRACKINFO ti;
   BOOL fEnable;
   int i, nLen, rc;

   switch (wMsg) {
       case WM_INITDIALOG:
           ppRecord = (PCEPROPVAL *)lParam;
           pRecord = *ppRecord;

           hwndCombo = GetDlgItem (hWnd, IDD_CATEGORY);
           hwndTList = GetDlgItem (hWnd, IDD_TRACKS);

           Edit_LimitText (GetDlgItem (hWnd, IDD_NAME), MAX_NAMELEN);
           Edit_LimitText (GetDlgItem (hWnd, IDD_ARTIST),
                       MAX_ARTISTLEN);
           // Set tab stops on track list box.
           i = 110;
           ListBox_SetTabStops (hwndTList, 1, &i);
           // Initialize category combo box.
```

```
    for (i = 0; i < dim(pszCategories); i++)
        ComboBox_AddString (hwndCombo, pszCategories[i]);
ComboBox_SetCurSel (hwndCombo, 3);
nTracks = 0;

    // See if new album or edit of old one.
    if (pRecord == 0) {
        SetWindowText (hWnd, TEXT ("New Album"));
    } else {
        // Copy the data from the record to album structure.
        for (i = 0; i < NUM_DB_PROPS; i++) {
            switch (pRecord->propid) {
            case PID_NAME:
                SetDlgItemText (hWnd, IDD_NAME,
                                    pRecord->val.lpwstr);
                break;
            case PID_ARTIST:
                SetDlgItemText (hWnd, IDD_ARTIST,
                                    pRecord->val.lpwstr);
                break;
            case PID_CATEGORY:
                ComboBox_SetCurSel (hwndCombo,
                                    pRecord->val.iVal);
                break;
            case PID_TRACKS:
                pPtr = (TCHAR *)pRecord->val.blob.lpb;
                for (i = 0; *pPtr; i++){
                    ListBox_InsertString (hwndTList,i,pPtr);
                    pPtr += lstrlen (pPtr) + 1;
                    nTracks++;
                }
                break;
            }
            pRecord++;
        }
    }
    // Select first track, or disable buttons if no tracks.
    if (nTracks)
        ListBox_SetCurSel (GetDlgItem (hWnd, IDD_TRACKS), 3);
    else {
        EnableWindow (GetDlgItem (hWnd, IDD_DELTRACK),
                        FALSE);
        EnableWindow (GetDlgItem (hWnd, IDD_EDITTRACK),
                        FALSE);
    }
    return TRUE;
```

(continued)

Listing 9-1 *(continued)*

```
case WM_COMMAND:
    hwndTList = GetDlgItem (hWnd, IDD_TRACKS);
    hwndCombo = GetDlgItem (hWnd, IDD_CATEGORY);
    pRecord = *ppRecord;
    switch (LOWORD (wParam)) {
        case IDD_TRACKS:
            switch (HIWORD (wParam)) {
            case LBN_DBLCLK:
                PostMessage (hWnd, WM_COMMAND,
                            MAKELONG(IDD_EDITTRACK, 0), 0);
                break;
            case LBN_SELCHANGE:
                i = ListBox_GetCurSel (hwndTList);
                if (i == LB_ERR)
                    fEnable = FALSE;
                else
                    fEnable = TRUE;
                EnableWindow (GetDlgItem (hWnd,
                            IDD_DELTRACK), fEnable);
                EnableWindow (GetDlgItem (hWnd,
                            IDD_EDITTRACK), fEnable);
                break;
            }
            return TRUE;

        case IDD_NEWTRACK:
            memset (&ti, 0, sizeof (ti));
            rc = DialogBoxParam (hInst,
                TEXT ("EditTrackDlg"), hWnd,
                EditTrackDlgProc, (LPARAM)&ti);
            if (rc) {
                wsprintf (szTmp, TEXT ("%s\t%s"),
                            ti.szTrack, ti.szTime);
                i = ListBox_GetCurSel (hwndTList);
                if (i != LB_ERR)
                    i++;
                i = ListBox_InsertString (hwndTList, i,
                                            szTmp);
                ListBox_SetCurSel (hwndTList, i);
            }
            return TRUE;

        case IDD_EDITTRACK:
            i = ListBox_GetCurSel (hwndTList);
            if (i != LB_ERR) {
                ListBox_GetText (hwndTList, i, szTmp);
                pPtr = szTmp;
                while ((*pPtr != TEXT ('\t')) &&
```

```
                                       (*pPtr != TEXT ('\0')))
                    pPtr++;
                if (*pPtr == TEXT ('\t'))
                    *pPtr++ = TEXT ('\0');

                lstrcpy (ti.szTime, pPtr);
                lstrcpy (ti.szTrack, szTmp);
                rc = DialogBoxParam (hInst,
                                     TEXT ("EditTrackDlg"),
                                     hWnd, EditTrackDlgProc,
                                     (LPARAM)&ti);
                if (rc) {
                    wsprintf (szTmp, TEXT ("%s\t%s"),
                                  ti.szTrack, ti.szTime);
                    i = ListBox_GetCurSel (hwndTList);
                    ListBox_DeleteString (hwndTList, i);
                    ListBox_InsertString (hwndTList, i,
                                          szTmp);
                    ListBox_SetCurSel (hwndTList, i);
                }
            }
            return TRUE;

    case IDD_DELTRACK:
            // Grab the current selection, and remove
            // it from list box.
            i = ListBox_GetCurSel (hwndTList);
            if (i != LB_ERR) {
                rc = MessageBox (hWnd,
                                 TEXT ("Delete this item?"),
                                 TEXT ("Track"), MB_YESNO);
                if (rc == IDYES) {
                    i=ListBox_DeleteString (hwndTList,i);
                    if (i > 0)
                        i--;
                    ListBox_SetCurSel (hwndTList, i);
                }
            }
            return TRUE;

    case IDOK:
            // Be lazy and assume worst-case size values.
            nLen = sizeof (CEPROPVAL) * NUM_DB_PROPS +
                   MAX_NAMELEN + MAX_ARTISTLEN +
                   MAX_TRACKNAMELEN;
            // See if prev record, alloc if not.
            if (pRecord) {
                // Resize record if necessary.
```

(continued)

Listing 9-1 *(continued)*

```
                    if (nLen > (int)LocalSize (pRecord))
                        pRecPtr =
                            (PCEPROPVAL)LocalReAlloc (pRecord,
                            nLen, LMEM_MOVEABLE);
                    else
                        pRecPtr = pRecord;
            } else
                pRecPtr = (PCEPROPVAL)LocalAlloc (LMEM_FIXED,
                                                  nLen);
        if (!pRecPtr)
            return 0;
        // Copy the data from the controls to a
        // marshaled data block with the structure
        // at the front and the data in the back.
        pRecord = pRecPtr;
        nTracks = ListBox_GetCount (hwndTList);
        pPtr = (TCHAR *)((LPBYTE)pRecPtr +
                (sizeof (CEPROPVAL) * NUM_DB_PROPS));
        // Zero structure to start over.
        memset (pRecPtr, 0, LocalSize (pRecPtr));

        pRecPtr->propid = PID_NAME;
        pRecPtr->val.lpwstr = pPtr;
        GetDlgItemText (hWnd, IDD_NAME, pPtr,
                        MAX_NAMELEN);
        pPtr += lstrlen (pPtr) + 1;
        pRecPtr++;

        pRecPtr->propid = PID_ARTIST;
        pRecPtr->val.lpwstr = pPtr;
        GetDlgItemText (hWnd, IDD_ARTIST, pPtr,
                        MAX_ARTISTLEN);
        pPtr += lstrlen (pPtr) + 1;
        pRecPtr++;

        pRecPtr->propid = PID_RELDATE;
        pRecPtr->val.iVal = 0;
        pRecPtr++;

        pRecPtr->propid = PID_CATEGORY;
        pRecPtr->val.iVal =
                        ComboBox_GetCurSel (hwndCombo);
        pRecPtr++;

        pRecPtr->propid = PID_NUMTRACKS;
        pRecPtr->val.iVal = nTracks;
        pRecPtr++;
```

```
                         pRecPtr->propid = PID_TRACKS;
                         pRecPtr->val.blob.lpb = (LPBYTE)pPtr;

                         // Get the track titles from the list box.
                         rc = MAX_TRACKNAMELEN;
                         for (i = 0; i < nTracks; i++) {
                             // Make sure we have the room in the buff.
                             rc -= ListBox_GetTextLen(hwndTList, i);
                             if (rc)
                                 ListBox_GetText (hwndTList, i, pPtr);
                             else {
                                 nTracks = i;
                                 break;
                             }
                             pPtr += lstrlen (pPtr) + 1;
                         }
                         *pPtr++ = TEXT ('\0');
                         pRecPtr->val.blob.dwCount =
                                     (LPBYTE)pPtr - pRecPtr->val.blob.lpb;
                         *ppRecord = pRecord;
                         EndDialog (hWnd, 1);
                         return TRUE;

                     case IDCANCEL:
                         EndDialog (hWnd, 0);
                         return TRUE;
                 }
             break;
        }
    return FALSE;
}
//======================================================================
// About dialog procedure
//
BOOL CALLBACK AboutDlgProc (HWND hWnd, UINT wMsg, WPARAM wParam,
                            LPARAM lParam) {

    switch (wMsg) {
        case WM_COMMAND:
            switch (LOWORD (wParam)) {
                case IDOK:
                case IDCANCEL:
                    EndDialog (hWnd, 0);
                    return TRUE;
            }
        break;
    }
    return FALSE;
}
```

The program uses a virtual list view control to display the records in the database. As I explained in Chapter 5, virtual list views don't store any data internally. Instead, the control makes calls back to the owning window using notification messages to query the information for each item in the list view control. The *WM_NOTIFY* handler *OnNotifyMain* calls *GetItemData* to query the database in response to the list view control sending *LVN_GETDISPINFO* notifications. The *GetItemInfo* function first seeks the record to read and then reads all the properties of a database record with one call to *CeReadRecord-Props*. Since the list view control typically uses the *LVN_GETDISPINFO* notification multiple times for one item, *GetItemInfo* saves the data from the last record read. If the next read is of the same record, the program uses the cached data instead of rereading the database.

As I've explained before, you can change the way you sort by simply closing the database and reopening it in one of the other sort modes. The list view control is then invalidated, causing it to again request the data for each record being displayed. With a new sort order defined, the seek that happens with each database record read automatically sorts the data by the sort order defined when the database was opened.

AlbumDB doesn't provide the option of storing the database on external media. To modify the example to use separate database volumes, only minor changes would be necessary. You'd need to replace the *CREATE_SYSTEMGUID* macro that fills in the *g_guidDB* value with a call to *CeMountDBVol* to mount the appropriate volume. You'd also need to unmount the volume before the application closed.

The database API is unique to Windows CE and provides a valuable function for the information-centric devices that Windows CE supports. Although it isn't a powerful SQL-based database, its functionality is a handy tool for the Windows CE developer.

The last few chapters have covered memory and the file system. Now it's time to look at the third part of the kernel triumvirate—processes and threads. As with the other parts of Windows CE, the API will be familiar if perhaps a bit smaller. However, the underlying architecture of Windows CE does make itself known.

10

Modules, Processes, and Threads

Like Windows XP, Windows CE is a fully multitasking and multithreaded operating system. What does that mean? In this chapter, I'll present a few definitions and then some explanations to answer that question.

Win32 files that contain executable code are called *modules*. Windows CE supports two types of modules: applications, with the EXE extension; and dynamic-link libraries, with the DLL extension. When Windows CE loads an application module, it creates a process.

A *process* is a single instance of an application. If two copies of Microsoft Pocket Word are running, two unique processes are running. Every process has its own, protected, 32-MB address space as described in Chapter 7. Windows CE enforces a limit of 32 separate processes that can run at any time.

Each process has at least one *thread*. A thread executes code within a process. A process can have multiple threads running "at the same time." I put the phrase *at the same time* in quotes because, in fact, only one thread executes at any instant in time. The operating system simulates the concurrent execution of threads by rapidly switching between the threads, alternatively stopping one thread and switching to another.

Modules

The format of Windows CE modules is identical to the PE format used by Windows XP. Unlike Windows XP, Windows CE doesn't support the SYS file format used for device drivers. Instead, Windows CE device drivers are implemented as DLLs.

The difference between an EXE and a DLL is actually quite subtle. The format of the files is identical, save a few bytes in the header of the module. In practice, however, the difference is quite pronounced. When Windows launches an EXE, it creates a separate process space for that module, resolves any imported functions, initializes the proper static data areas, creates a local heap, creates a thread, and then jumps to the entry point of the module.

DLLs, on the other hand, can't be launched independently. The only way a DLL is loaded is by a request from an EXE or another DLL. The request to load a DLL can occur in two ways. The first way is implicit loading. In this case, a DLL is loaded automatically when Windows loads an EXE that lists the DLL in its import table. The linker generates the import table when the EXE is linked, and the table contains the list of DLLs and the functions within those DLLs that the EXE might call during the life of the application. When the EXE is loaded, Windows looks at the list of DLLs in the EXE's import table and loads those DLLs into the process space of the application. DLLs also contain import tables. When a DLL is loaded Windows also looks at the import table of the DLL and loads any DLLs needed by that DLL.

When a DLL is built, it contains zero or more functions it exports. These are the functions that are callable from EXEs or other DLLs. A DLL that has no functions is still useful because it might contain resource data needed by the application.

The other way a DLL can be loaded is through *explicit* loading. In this case, Windows doesn't automatically load the DLL; it's loaded programmatically by the application using one of two calls, *LoadLibrary* or *LoadLibraryEx*.

LoadLibrary is prototyped as

```
HINSTANCE LoadLibrary (LPCTSTR lpLibFileName);
```

The only parameter is the filename of the DLL. If the filename does not have path information, the system searches for DLLs in the following order:

1. The image of the DLL that has already been loaded in memory

2. The directory of the executable loading the library

3. If a relative path was specified, the relative path based on the root (\)

4. The Windows directory (\Windows)

5. The root directory in the object store (\)

6. The image of the DLL in ROM if no relative path is specified

7. The path specified in the *SystemPath* value in *[HKEY_LOCAL_ MACHINE]\Loader*

If the DLL name is a completely specified path name, the search is as follows:

1.   The image of the DLL that has already been loaded in memory

2.   The completely specified name in the *lpLibFileName* parameter

If the DLL is specified with a relative pathname, that is, one without a leading backslash (\) character, the relative path is appended to the directories listed in the *SystemPath* registry variable. So if the DLL name is temp\bob.dll and a directory in the path is *pathdir*, the resulting search is *pathdir\temp\bob.dll*. This characteristic of merging relative paths with the *SystemPath* directories can easily lead to unexpected results. Because of this, applications should avoid the use of relative paths when specifying DLLs.

Notice in all the earlier search sequences that if the DLL has already been loaded into memory, the system uses that copy of the DLL. This behavior is true even if your pathname specifies a different file from the DLL originally loaded. Another peculiarity of *LoadLibrary* is that it ignores the extension of the DLL when comparing the library name with what's already in memory. For example, if Simple.dll is already loaded in memory and you attempt to load the control panel applet Simple.cpl, which under the covers is simply a DLL with a different extension, the system won't load Simple.cpl. Instead, the system returns the handle to the previously loaded Simple.dll.

LoadLibrary returns either an instance handle to the DLL that's now loaded or 0 if for some reason the function couldn't load the library. Calling *GetLastError* will return an error code specifying the reason for the failure.

Once you have the DLL loaded, you get a pointer to a function exported by that DLL by using *GetProcAddress*, which is prototyped as

```
FARPROC GetProcAddress (HMODULE hModule, LPCWSTR lpProcName);
```

The two parameters are the handle of the module and the name of the function you want to get a pointer to. The function returns a pointer to the function, or 0 if the function isn't found. Once you have a pointer to a function, you can simply call the function as if the loader had implicitly linked it.

When you are finished with the functions from a particular library, you need to call *FreeLibrary*, prototyped as

```
BOOL FreeLibrary (HMODULE hLibModule);
```

FreeLibrary decrements the use count on the DLL. If the use count drops to 0, the library is removed from memory.

The following routine solves the problem of an application not knowing whether the menu bar API is present on a system.

```
      fMenuBarCreated = FALSE;

      hLib = LoadLibrary (TEXT ("aygshell.dll"));
      if (hLib) {
          FARPROC lpfn = GetProcAddress (hLib, TEXT ("SHCreateMenuBar"));
          if (lpfn) {
              memset(&mbi, 0, sizeof(SHMENUBARINFO)); // Init structure
              mbi.cbSize = sizeof(SHMENUBARINFO);
              mbi.hwndParent = hWnd;
              mbi.hInstRes = hInst;
              mbi.nToolBarId = ID_MENU;
              mbi.dwFlags = SHCMBF_HMENU;                // Use std menu resource
              (*lpfn) (&mbi);
              fMenuBarCreated = TRUE;
          }
      }
      if (!fMenuBarCreated) {
          // Create a command bar instead
      }
```

In this code, the menu bar is created only if the system supports it. If the library AygShell.dll or the *SHCreateMenuBar* function can't be found, a standard command bar is created.

Windows CE also supports the *LoadLibraryEx* function, prototyped as

```
HMODULE LoadLibraryEx (LPCTSTR lpLibFileName, HANDLE hFile, DWORD dwFlags);
```

The first parameter is the name of the DLL to load. The second parameter, *hFile*, isn't supported by Windows CE and must be set to 0. The last parameter, *dwFlags*, defines how the DLL is loaded. If *dwFlags* contains the flag *DONT_RESOLVE_DLL_REFERENCES*, the DLL is loaded, but any modules the DLL requires are not loaded. In addition, the entry point of the DLL, typically *DllMain*, isn't called. If *dwFlags* contains *LOAD_LIBRARY_AS_DATAFILE*, the DLL is loaded into memory as a data file. The DLL is not relocated or prepared in any way to be called from executable code. However, the handle returned can be used to load resources from the DLL using the standard resource functions such as *LoadString*.

When a DLL is loaded, its entry point, traditionally named *DllMain*, is called. *DllMain* is prototyped as

```
BOOL APIENTRY DllMain( HANDLE hModule, DWORD  ul_reason_for_call,
                       LPVOID lpReserved);
```

In addition to being called when the DLL is first loaded, *DllMain* is also called when it's unloaded or when a new thread is created or destroyed in the process that loads it. The second parameter, *ul_reason_for_call*, indicates the reason for the call to *DllMain*.

DLLs should avoid doing anything more than simple initialization from within *DllMain*. An action such as loading other DLLs or any other action that might load other DLLs can cause problems with the Windows CE loader. This restriction can cause problems for DLLs that have been ported from the desktop versions of Windows because those operating systems are much more tolerant of actions within *DllMain*.

One last DLL function is handy to know about. The function *Disable-ThreadLibraryCalls* tells the operating system not to send *DLL_THREAD_ATTACH* and *DLL_THREAD_DETACH* notifications to the DLL when threads are created and terminated in the application. Preventing these notifications can improve performance and reduce the working set of an application because the DLL's *LibMain* isn't called when threads are created and destroyed. The function is prototyped as

```
BOOL DisableThreadLibraryCalls (HMODULE hLibModule);
```

The only parameter is the handle to the DLL identifying the DLL that doesn't want to be notified of the thread events.

Processes

Windows CE treats processes differently than does Windows XP. First and foremost, Windows CE has the aforementioned system limit of 32 processes being run at any one time. When the system starts, at least four processes are created: NK.exe, which provides the kernel services; FileSys.exe, which provides file system services; GWES.exe, which provides the GUI support; and Device.exe, which loads and maintains the device drivers for the system. On most systems, other processes are also started, such as the shell, Explorer.exe, and, if the system is connected to a PC, Repllog.exe and RAPISrv.exe, which service the link between the PC and the Windows CE system. This leaves room for about 24 processes that the user or other applications that are running can start. While this sounds like a harsh limit, most systems don't need that many processes. A typical Pocket PC that's being used heavily might have 15 processes running at any one time.

Windows CE diverges from its desktop counterparts in other ways. Compared with processes under Windows XP, Windows CE processes contain much less state information. Since Windows CE doesn't support the concept of a current directory, the individual processes don't need to store that information. Windows CE doesn't maintain a set of environment variables, so processes don't need to keep an environment block. Windows CE doesn't support handle inheritance, so there's no need to tell a process to enable handle inheritance. Because of all this, the parameter-heavy *CreateProcess* function is passed mainly *NULLs* and zeros, with just a few parameters actually used by Windows CE.

Many of the process and thread-related functions are simply not supported by Windows CE because the system doesn't support certain features supported by Windows XP. Since Windows CE doesn't support an environment, all the Win32 functions dealing with the environment don't exist in Windows CE. Some functions aren't supported because there's an easy way to work around the lack of the function. For example, *ExitProcess* doesn't exist under Windows CE. But as you might expect, there's a workaround that allows a process to close.

Enough of what Windows CE doesn't do; let's look at what you can do with Windows CE.

Creating a Process

The function for creating another process is

```
BOOL CreateProcess (LPCTSTR lpApplicationName,
                    LPCTSTR lpCommandLine,
                    LPSECURITY_ATTRIBUTES lpProcessAttributes,
                    LPSECURITY_ATTRIBUTES lpThreadAttributes,
                    BOOL bInheritHandles, DWORD dwCreationFlags,
                    LPVOID lpEnvironment,
                    LPCTSTR lpCurrentDirectory,
                    LPSTARTUPINFO lpStartupInfo,
                    LPPROCESS_INFORMATION lpProcessInformation);
```

While the list of parameters looks daunting, most of the parameters must be set to *NULL* or 0 because Windows CE doesn't support security or current directories, nor does it handle inheritance. This results in a function prototype that looks more like this:

```
BOOL CreateProcess (LPCTSTR lpApplicationName,
                    LPTSTR lpCommandLine, NULL, NULL, FALSE,
                    DWORD dwCreationFlags, NULL, NULL, NULL,
                    LPPROCESS_INFORMATION lpProcessInformation);
```

The parameters that remain start with a pointer to the name of the application to launch. Windows CE looks for the application in the following directories, in this order:

1. The path, if any, specified in *lpApplicationName*

2. The Windows directory, (\Windows)

3.   The root directory in the object store, (\)

4.   The directories in the path specified in the *SystemPath* value in *[HKEY_LOCAL_MACHINE]\Loader*

This action is different from Windows XP, where *CreateProcess* searches for the executable only if *lpApplicationName* is set to *NULL* and the executable name is passed through the *lpCommandLine* parameter. In the case of Windows CE, the application name must be passed in the *lpApplicationName* parameter because Windows CE doesn't support the technique of passing a *NULL* in *lpApplicationName* with the application name as the first token in the *lpCommandLine* parameter.

The *lpCommandLine* parameter specifies the command line that will be passed to the new process. The only difference between Windows CE and Windows XP in this parameter is that under Windows CE the command line is always passed as a Unicode string. And as I mentioned previously, you can't pass the name of the executable as the first token in *lpCommandLine*.

The *dwCreationFlags* parameter specifies the initial state of the process after it has been loaded. Windows CE limits the allowable flags to the following:

- ■   ***0***   Creates a standard process.

- ■   ***CREATE_SUSPENDED***   Creates the process and then suspends the primary thread.

- ■   ***DEBUG_PROCESS***   The process being created is treated as a process being debugged by the caller. The calling process receives debug information from the process being launched.

- ■   ***DEBUG_ONLY_THIS_PROCESS***   When combined with *DEBUG_PROCESS*, debugs a process but doesn't debug any child processes that are launched by the process being debugged.

- ■   ***CREATE_NEW_CONSOLE***   Forces a new console to be created.

The only other parameter of the *CreateProcess* function that Windows CE uses is *lpProcessInformation*. This parameter can be set to *NULL*, or it can point to a *PROCESS_INFORMATION* structure that's filled by *CreateProcess* with information about the new process. The *PROCESS_INFORMATION* structure is defined this way:

```
typedef struct _PROCESS_INFORMATION {
    HANDLE hProcess;
    HANDLE hThread;
    DWORD dwProcessId;
    DWORD dwThreadId;
} PROCESS_INFORMATION;
```

The first two fields in this structure are filled with the handles of the new process and the handle of the primary thread of the new process. These handles are useful for monitoring the newly created process, but with them comes some responsibility. When the system copies the handles for use in the *PROCESS_INFORMATION* structure, it increments the use count for the handles. This means that if you don't have any use for the handles, the calling process must close them. Ideally, they should be closed immediately following a successful call to *CreateProcess*. I'll describe some good uses for these handles later in this chapter, in the section "Synchronization."

The other two fields in the *PROCESS_INFORMATION* structure are filled with the process ID and primary thread ID of the new process. These ID values aren't handles but simply unique identifiers that can be passed to Windows functions to identify the target of the function. Be careful when using these IDs. If the new process terminates and another new one is created, the system can reuse the old ID values. You must take measures to assure that ID values for other processes are still identifying the process you're interested in before using them. For example, you can, by using synchronization objects, be notified when a process terminates. When the process terminated, you would then know not to use the ID values for that process.

Using the create process is simple, as you can see in the following code fragment:

```
TCHAR szFileName[MAX_PATH];
TCHAR szCmdLine[64];
DWORD dwCreationFlags;
PROCESS_INFORMATION pi;
int rc;

lstrcpy (szFileName, TEXT ("calc"));
lstrcpy (szCmdLine, TEXT (""));
dwCreationFlags = 0;

rc = CreateProcess (szFileName, szCmdLine, NULL, NULL, FALSE,
                    dwCreationFlags, NULL, NULL, NULL, &pi);
if (rc) {
    CloseHandle (pi.hThread);
    CloseHandle (pi.hProcess);
}
```

This code launches the standard Calculator applet found on the Pocket PC. Since the filename doesn't specify a path, *CreateProcess* will, using the standard Windows CE search path, find Calc.exe in the \Windows directory. Because I didn't pass a command line to Calc, I could have simply passed a *NULL* value in the *lpCmdLine* parameter. But I passed a null string in *szCmdLine* to differentiate the *lpCmdLine* parameter from the many other parameters in *CreateProcess* that aren't used. I used the same technique for *dwCreationFlags*. If the call to *CreateProcess* is successful, it returns a nonzero value. The code above checks for this and, if the call was successful, closes the process and thread handles returned in the *PROCESS_INFORMATION* structure. Remember that this must be done by all Win32 applications to prevent memory leaks.

Terminating a Process

A process can terminate itself by simply returning from the *WinMain* procedure. For console applications, a simple return from *main* suffices. Windows CE doesn't support the *ExitProcess* function found in Windows XP. Instead, you can have the primary thread of the process call *ExitThread*. Under Windows CE, if the primary thread terminates, the process is terminated as well, regardless of what other threads are currently active in the process. The exit code of the process will be the exit code provided by *ExitThread*. You can determine the exit code of a process by calling

```
BOOL GetExitCodeProcess (HANDLE hProcess, LPDWORD lpExitCode);
```

The parameters are the handle to the process and a pointer to a *DWORD* that receives the exit code that was returned by the terminating process. If the process is still running, the return code is the constant *STILL_ACTIVE*.

You can terminate another process. But while it's possible to do that, you shouldn't be in the business of closing other processes. The user might not be expecting that process to be closed without his or her consent. If you need to terminate a process (or close a process, which is the same thing but a much nicer word), the following methods can be used.

If the process to be closed is one that you created, you can use some sort of interprocess communication to tell the process to terminate itself. This is the most advisable method because you've designed the target process to be closed by another party. Another method of closing a process is to send the main window of the process a *WM_CLOSE* message. This is especially effective on the Pocket PC, where applications are designed to respond to *WM_CLOSE* messages by quietly saving their state and closing. Finally, if all else fails and you absolutely must close another process, you can use *TerminateProcess*.

TerminateProcess is prototyped as

```
BOOL TerminateProcess (HANDLE hProcess, DWORD uExitCode);
```

The two parameters are the handle of the process to terminate and the exit code the terminating process will return.

Other Processes

Of course, to terminate another process, you've got to know the handle to that process. You might want to know the handle to a process for other reasons as well. For example, you might want to know *when* the process terminates. Windows CE supports two additional functions that come in handy here (both of which are seldom discussed). The first function is *OpenProcess*, which returns the handle of an already running process. *OpenProcess* is prototyped as

```
HANDLE OpenProcess (DWORD dwDesiredAccess, BOOL bInheritHandle,
                    DWORD dwProcessId);
```

Under Windows CE, the first parameter isn't used and should be set to 0. The *bInheritHandle* parameter must be set to *FALSE* because Windows CE doesn't support handle inheritance. The final parameter is the process ID value of the process you want to open.

The other function useful in this circumstance is

```
DWORD GetWindowThreadProcessId (HWND hWnd, LPDWORD lpdwProcessId);
```

This function takes a handle to a window and returns the process ID for the process that created the window. So using these two functions, you can trace a window back to the process that created it.

Two other functions allow you to directly read from and write to the memory space of another process. These functions are

```
BOOL ReadProcessMemory (HANDLE hProcess, LPCVOID lpBaseAddress,
                        LPVOID lpBuffer, DWORD nSize,
                        LPDWORD lpNumberOfBytesRead);
```

and

```
BOOL WriteProcessMemory (HANDLE hProcess, LPVOID lpBaseAddress,
                         LPVOID lpBuffer, DWORD nSize,
                         LPDWORD lpNumberOfBytesWritten);
```

The parameters for these functions are fairly self-explanatory. The first parameter is the handle of the remote process. The second parameter is the base address in the other process's address space of the area to be read or written. The third and fourth parameters specify the name and the size of the local buffer in which the data is to be read from or written to. Finally, the last parameter specifies the bytes actually read or written. Both functions require that the entire area being read to or written from must be accessible. Typically, you use these functions for debugging, but there's no requirement that this be their only use.

Threads

A thread is, fundamentally, a unit of execution. That is, it has a stack and a processor context, which is a set of values in the CPU internal registers. When a thread is suspended, the registers are pushed onto the thread's stack, the active stack is changed to the next thread to be run, that thread's CPU state is pulled off its stack, and the new thread starts executing instructions.

Threads under Windows CE are similar to threads under Windows XP. Each process has a primary thread. Using the functions that I describe below, a process can create any number of additional threads within the process. The only limit to the number of threads in a Windows CE process is the memory and process address space available for the thread's stack.

Threads within a process share the address space of the process. Memory allocated by one thread is accessible to all threads in the process. Threads share the same access rights for handles whether they be file handles, memory object handles, or handles to synchronization objects. Thread access rights to other processes are, however, thread specific. Most of the time, you won't need to worry about this, but there are times when you're working with interprocess issues that this issue can arise. Refer to the information in the "Asynchronous Driver I/O" section of Chapter 22 for details.

The stack size of the main thread of a process is set by the linker. (The linker switch for setting the stack size in Microsoft eMbedded C++ is /stack.) Secondary threads are created by default with the same stack size as the primary thread, but the default can be overridden when the thread is created.

The System Scheduler

Windows CE schedules threads in a preemptive manner. Threads run for a *quantum*, or time slice. After that time, if the thread hasn't already relinquished its time slice and if the thread isn't a run-to-completion thread, it's suspended and another thread is scheduled to run. Windows CE chooses which thread to run based on a priority scheme. Threads of a higher priority are scheduled before threads of lower priority.

The rules for how Windows CE allocates time among the threads are quite different from Windows XP. Windows CE processes don't have a *priority class*. Under Windows XP, threads derive their priority based on the priority class of their parent processes. A Windows XP process with a higher-priority class has threads that run at a higher priority than threads in a process with a lower-priority class. Threads within a process can refine their priority within a process by setting their relative thread priority.

Because Windows CE has no priority classes, all processes are treated as peers. Individual threads can have different priorities, but the process that the thread runs within doesn't influence those priorities. Also, unlike some of the desktop versions of Windows, the foreground thread in Windows CE doesn't get a boost in priority.

When Windows CE was first developed, the scheduler supported eight priority levels. Starting with Windows CE 3.0, that number was increased to 256 priority levels. However, most applications still use the original (now lowest) eight priority levels. The upper 248 levels are typically used by device drivers or other system-level threads. This doesn't mean that an application can't use the higher levels, but accessing them requires different API calls, and the application must be a "trusted" application. I'll talk more about security and the concept of trusted vs. untrusted applications later in the chapter.

The lowest eight priority levels are listed below:

- ***THREAD_PRIORITY_TIME_CRITICAL*** Indicates 3 points above normal priority

- ***THREAD_PRIORITY_HIGHEST*** Indicates 2 points above normal priority

- ***THREAD_PRIORITY_ABOVE_NORMAL*** Indicates 1 point above normal priority

- ***THREAD_PRIORITY_NORMAL*** Indicates normal priority. All threads are created with this priority

- ***THREAD_PRIORITY_BELOW_NORMAL*** Indicates 1 point below normal priority

- ***THREAD_PRIORITY_LOWEST*** Indicates 2 points below normal priority

- ***THREAD_PRIORITY_ABOVE_IDLE*** Indicates 3 points below normal priority

- ***THREAD_PRIORITY_IDLE*** Indicates 4 points below normal priority

All higher-priority threads run before lower-priority threads. This means that before a thread set to run at a particular priority can be scheduled, all threads that have a higher priority must be *blocked*. A blocked thread is one that's waiting on some system resource or synchronization object before it can continue. Threads of equal priority are scheduled in a round-robin fashion. Once a thread has voluntarily given up its time slice, is blocked, or has completed its time slice, all other threads of the same priority are allowed to run before the original thread is allowed to continue. If a thread of higher priority is unblocked and a thread of lower priority is currently running, the lower-priority thread is immediately suspended and the higher-priority thread is scheduled. Lower-priority threads can never preempt a higher-priority thread.

An exception to the scheduling rules happens if a low-priority thread owns a resource that a higher-priority thread is waiting on. In this case, the low-priority thread is temporarily given the higher-priority thread's priority to avoid a problem known as *priority inversion*, so that it can quickly accomplish its task and free the needed resource.

While it might seem that lower-priority threads never get a chance to run in this scheme, it works out that threads are almost always blocked, waiting on something to free up before they can be scheduled. Threads are always created at *THREAD_PRIORITY_NORMAL*, so, unless they proactively change their priority level, a thread is usually at an equal priority to most of the other threads in the system. Even at the normal priority level, threads are almost always blocked. For example, an application's primary thread is typically blocked waiting on messages. Other threads should be designed to block on one of the many synchronization objects available to a Windows CE application.

Never Do This!

What's not supported by the arrangement I just described, or by any other thread-based scheme, is code like the following:

```
while (bFlag == FALSE) {
    // Do nothing, and spin.
}
// Now do something.
```

This kind of code isn't just bad manners; because it wastes CPU power, it's a death sentence to a battery-powered Windows CE device. To understand why this is important, I need to digress into a quick lesson on Windows CE power management.

Windows CE is designed so that when all threads are blocked, which happens over 90 percent of the time, it calls down to the OEM Abstraction Layer (the equivalent of the BIOS on an MS-DOS machine) to enter a low-power waiting state. Typically, this low-power state means that the CPU is halted; that is, it simply stops executing instructions. Because the CPU isn't executing any instructions, no power-consuming reads and writes of memory are performed by the CPU. At this point, the only power necessary for the system is to maintain the contents of the RAM and light the display. This low-power mode can reduce power consumption by up to 99 percent of what is required when a thread is running in a well-designed system.

Doing a quick back-of-the-envelope calculation, say a Pocket PC is designed to run for 10 hours on a fully charged battery. Given that the system turns itself off after a few minutes of nonuse, this 10 hours translates into weeks of battery life in the device for the user. (I'm basing this calculation on the assumption that the system indeed spends 90 percent or more of its time in its low-power idle state.) Say a poorly written application thread spins on a variable instead of blocking. While this application is running, the system will never enter its low-power state. So, instead of 600 minutes of battery time (10 hours × 60 minutes/hour), the system spends 100 percent of its time at full power, resulting in a battery life of slightly over an hour, which means that the battery would be lucky to last a day's normal use. So as you can see, it's good to have the system in its low-power state.

Fortunately, since Windows applications usually spend their time blocked in a call to *GetMessage*, the system power management works by default. However, if you plan on using multiple threads in your application, you must use synchronization objects to block threads while they're waiting. First let's look at how to create a thread, and then I'll dive into the synchronization tools available to Windows CE programs.

Creating a Thread

You create a thread under Windows CE by calling the function *CreateThread*, which is a departure from the desktop versions of Windows in which you're never supposed to call this API directly. The reason for this change is that on the desktop, calling *CreateThread* doesn't give the C runtime library the chance to create thread-unique data structures. So on the desktop, programmers are instructed to use either of the run-time thread creation functions *_beginthread* or *_beginthreadex*. These functions provide some thread-specific initialization and then call *CreateThread* internally.

In Windows CE, however, the runtime is written to be thread safe and doesn't require explicit thread initialization, so calling *CreateThread* directly is the norm. The function is prototyped as

```
HANDLE CreateThread (LPSECURITY_ATTRIBUTES lpThreadAttributes,
                     DWORD dwStackSize,
                     LPTHREAD_START_ROUTINE lpStartAddress,
                     LPVOID lpParameter, DWORD dwCreationFlags,
                     LPDWORD lpThreadId);
```

As with *CreateProcess*, Windows CE doesn't support a number of the parameters in *CreateThread*, so they are set to *NULL* or 0 as appropriate. For *CreateThread*, the *lpThreadAttributes* parameter isn't supported and must be set to *NULL*. The *dwStackSize* parameter is used only if the STACK_SIZE_PARAM_IS_A_RESERVATION flag is set in the *dwCreationFlags* parameter. The size specified in *dwStackSize* is the maximum size to which the stack can grow. Windows CE doesn't immediately commit the full amount of RAM to the stack when the thread is created. Instead, memory is committed only as necessary as the stack grows.

The third parameter, *lpStartAddress*, must point to the start of the thread routine. The *lpParameter* parameter in *CreateThread* is an application-defined value that's passed to the thread function as its only parameter. You can set the *dwCreationFlags* parameter to either 0, STACK_SIZE_PARAM_IS_A_RESERVATION, or *CREATE_SUSPENDED*. If *CREATE_SUSPENDED* is passed, the thread is created in a suspended state and must be resumed with a call to *ResumeThread*. The final parameter is a pointer to a *DWORD* that receives the newly created thread's ID value.

The thread routine should be prototyped this way:

```
DWORD WINAPI ThreadFunc (LPVOID lpArg);
```

The only parameter is the *lpParameter* value, passed unaltered from the call to *CreateThread*. The parameter can be an integer or a pointer. Make sure, however, that you don't pass a pointer to a stack-based structure that will disappear when the routine that called *CreateThread* returns.

If *CreateThread* is successful, it creates the thread and returns the handle to the newly created thread. As with *CreateProcess*, the handle returned should be closed when you no longer need the handle. Following is a short code fragment that contains a call to start a thread and the thread routine.

```
//---------------------------------------------------------------------
//
//
HANDLE hThread1;
DWORD dwThread1ID = 0;
int nParameter = 5;

hThread1 = CreateThread (NULL, 0, Thread2, (PVOID)nParameter, 0,
                         &dwThread1ID);
CloseHandle (hThread1);

//---------------------------------------------------------------------
// Second thread routine
//
```

(continued)

```
DWORD WINAPI Thread2 (PVOID pArg) {

    int nParam = (int) pArg;

    //
    // Do something here.
    // .
    // .
    // .
    return 0x15;
}
```

In this code, the second thread is started with a call to *CreateThread*. The *nParameter* value is passed to the second thread as the single parameter to the thread routine. The second thread executes until it terminates, in this case simply by returning from the routine.

A thread can also terminate itself by calling this function:

```
VOID ExitThread (DWORD dwExitCode);
```

The only parameter is the exit code that's set for the thread. That thread exit code can be queried by another thread using this function:

```
BOOL GetExitCodeThread (HANDLE hThread, LPDWORD lpExitCode);
```

The function takes the handle to the thread (not the thread ID) and returns the exit code of the thread. If the thread is still running, the exit code is *STILL_ACTIVE*, a constant defined as 0x0103. The exit code is set by a thread using *ExitThread* or the value returned by the thread procedure. In the preceding code, the thread sets its exit code to 0x15 when it returns.

All threads within a process are terminated when the process terminates. As I said earlier, a process is terminated when its primary thread terminates.

Setting and Querying Thread Priority

Threads are always created at the priority level *THREAD_PRIORITY_NORMAL*. The thread priority can be changed either by the thread itself or by another thread using one of two functions. The first is

```
BOOL SetThreadPriority (HANDLE hThread, int nPriority);
```

The two parameters are the thread handle and the new priority level. The level passed can be one of the constants described previously, ranging from *THREAD_PRIORITY_IDLE* up to *THREAD_PRIORITY_TIME_CRITICAL*. You must be extremely careful when you're changing a thread's priority. Remember that threads of a lower priority almost never preempt threads of higher priority. So a simple bumping up of a thread one notch above normal can harm the responsiveness of the rest of the system unless that thread is carefully written.

The other function that sets a thread's priority is

```
BOOL CeSetThreadPriority (HANDLE hThread, int nPriority);
```

The difference between this function and *SetThreadPriority* is that this function sets the thread's priority to any of the 256 priorities. Instead of using predefined constants, *nPriority* should be set to a value of 0 to 255, with 0 being highest priority and 255 being the lowest.

A word of caution: *SetThreadPriority* and *CeSetThreadPriority* use completely different numbering schemes for the *nPriority* value. For example, to set a thread's priority to 1 above normal, you could call *SetThreadPriority* with *THREAD_PRIORITY_ABOVE_NORMAL* or call *CeSetThreadPriority* with *nPriority* set to 250 but the constant *THREAD_PRIORITY_ABOVE_NORMAL* defined as 2, not 250. The rule is that you should use the constants for *SetThreadPriority* and the numeric values for *CeSetThreadPriority*. Another difference posed by *CeSetThreadPriority* is that it's a protected function. For systems that implement Windows CE's module-based security, only trusted modules can call *CeSetThreadPriority*. To query the priority level of a thread, call this function:

```
int GetThreadPriority (HANDLE hThread);
```

This function returns the priority level of the thread. You shouldn't use the hard-coded priority levels. Instead, use constants, such as *THREAD_PRIORITY_NORMAL*, defined by the system. This ensures that you're using the same numbering scheme that *SetThreadPriority* uses. For threads that have a priority greater than *THREAD_PRIORITY_TIMECRITICAL*, this function returns the value *THREAD_PRIORITY_TIMECRITICAL*.

To query the priority of a thread that might have a higher priority than *THREAD_PRIORITY_TIMECRITICAL*, call the function

```
int CeGetThreadPriority (HANDLE hThread);
```

The value returned by *CeGetThreadPriority* will be 0 to 255, with 0 being the highest priority possible. Here again, Windows CE uses different numbering schemes for the priority query functions than it does for the priority set functions. For example, for a thread running at normal priority, *GetThreadPriority* would return *THREAD_PRIORITY_NORMAL*, which is defined as the value 3. *CeGetThreadPriority* would return the value 251.

Setting a Thread's Time Quantum

Threads can be individually set with their own *time quantum*. The time quantum is the maximum amount of time a thread runs before it's preempted by the operating system. By default, the time quantum is set to 100 milliseconds, although for embedded systems, the OEM can change this.[1] For example, some Pocket PC devices use a default quantum of 75 milliseconds, while others use the standard 100-millisecond quantum.

To set the time quantum of a thread, call

```
int CeSetThreadQuantum (HANDLE hThread, DWORD dwTime);
```

The first parameter is the handle to the thread. The second parameter is the time, in milliseconds, of the desired quantum. If you set the time quantum to 0, the thread is turned into a "run-to-completion thread." These threads aren't preempted by threads of their own priority. Obviously, threads of higher priorities preempt these threads. *CeSetThreadQuantum* is a protected function and so can't be called by "untrusted" modules.

You can query a thread's time quantum with the function

```
int CeGetThreadQuantum (HANDLE hThread);
```

The first parameter is the handle to the thread. The function returns the current quantum of the thread.

Suspending and Resuming a Thread

You can suspend a thread at any time by calling this function:

```
DWORD SuspendThread (HANDLE hThread);
```

The only parameter is the handle to the thread to suspend. The value returned is the *suspend count* for the thread. Windows maintains a suspend count for each thread. Any thread with a suspend count greater than 0 is suspended. Since *SuspendThread* increments the suspend count, multiple calls to *SuspendThread* must be matched with an equal number of calls to *ResumeThread* before a thread is actually scheduled to run. *ResumeCount* is prototyped as

```
DWORD ResumeThread (HANDLE hThread);
```

Here again, the parameter is the handle to the thread and the return value is the previous suspend count. So if *ResumeThread* returns 1, the thread is no longer suspended.

---

1. In early versions of Windows CE, a thread's time quantum was fixed. Typically, the time quantum was set to 25 milliseconds, although this was changeable by the OEM.

At times, a thread simply wants to kill some time. Since I've already explained why simply spinning in a *while* loop is a very bad thing to do, you need another way to kill time. The best way to do this is to use this function:

```
void Sleep (DWORD dwMilliseconds);
```

Sleep suspends the thread for at least the number of milliseconds specified in the *dwMilliseconds* parameter. Because the scheduler timer in systems based on Windows CE 3.0 and later has a granularity of 1 millisecond, calls to *Sleep* with very small values are accurate to 1 millisecond. On systems based on earlier versions of Windows CE, the accuracy of *Sleep* depends on the period of the scheduler timer, which was typically 25 milliseconds. This strategy is entirely valid, and sometimes it's equally valid to pass a 0 to *Sleep*. When a thread passes a 0 to *Sleep*, it gives up its time slice but is rescheduled immediately according to the scheduling rules I described previously.

Fibers

Fibers are threadlike constructs that are scheduled within the application instead of by the scheduler. Fibers, like threads, have their own stack and execution context. The difference is that the application must manage and manually switch between a set of fibers so that each one gets the appropriate amount of time to run.

An application creates a fiber by first creating a thread. The thread calls a function to turn itself into a fiber. The thread, now a single fiber, can then create multiple fibers from itself. The operating system schedules all of the fibers as a single thread, the thread that was originally converted to the first fiber. So the system allocates the time scheduled for the original thread to whichever fiber the application chooses. When the application chooses, it can stop a particular fiber and schedule another. This switch is transparent to Windows CE because all it considers is the quantum and the priority of the original thread. Fibers aren't more efficient than a well-designed multithreaded application, but they do allow applications to micromanage the scheduling of code execution within the application.

To create a set of fibers, an application first creates a thread. The thread then calls *ConvertThreadToFiber*, which is prototyped as

```
LPVOID WINAPI ConvertThreadToFiber (LPVOID lpParameter);
```

The single parameter is an application-defined value that can be retrieved by the fiber using the macro *GetFiberData*. The value returned is the pointer to the fiber data for this fiber. This value will be used when another fiber wants to schedule this fiber. If the return value is 0, the call failed.

Upon return from the function, the thread is now a fiber. One significant restriction on converting a thread to a fiber is that the thread must use the default stack size for its stack. If the thread has a different stack size from the main thread in the process, the call to *ConvertThreadToFiber* will fail.

Once the original thread has been converted to a fiber, it can spawn additional fibers with the following call:

```
LPVOID WINAPI CreateFiber (DWORD dwStackSize,
                           LPFIBER_START_ROUTINE lpStartAddress,
                           LPVOID lpParameter);
```

The *dwStackSize* parameter is ignored. The *lpStartAddress* parameter is the entry point of the new fiber being created. The final parameter is an application-defined value that is passed to the entry point of the new fiber. The return value from *CreateFiber* is the pointer to the fiber data for this new fiber. This value will be used to switch to the newly created fiber.

The function prototype of the fiber entry point looks similar to the entry point of a thread. It is

```
VOID CALLBACK FiberProc (PVOID lpParameter);
```

The one parameter is the value passed from the *CreateFiber* call. This parameter can also be retrieved by the fiber by calling *GetFiberData*. Note that no return value is defined for the fiber procedure. A fiber procedure should never return. If it does, the system exits the thread that is the basis for all fibers spawned by that thread.

The new fiber does not immediately start execution. Instead, the fiber calling *CreateFiber* must explicitly switch to the new fiber by calling

```
VOID WINAPI SwitchToFiber (LPVOID lpFiber);
```

The single parameter is the pointer to the fiber data for the fiber to be switched to. When this call is made, the calling fiber is suspended and the new fiber is enabled to run.

The *DeleteFiber* function is used to destroy a fiber. It looks like this:

```
VOID WINAPI DeleteFiber (LPVOID lpFiber);
```

The single parameter is the pointer to the fiber data of the fiber to destroy. If a fiber calls *DeleteFiber* on itself, the thread is exited and all fibers associated with that thread are also terminated.

It's critical that fibers clean up after themselves. Each fiber should be deleted by another fiber in the set, and then the final fiber can delete itself and properly exit the thread. If the thread is exited without deletion of all fibers, the memory committed to support each of the undeleted fibers will not be freed, resulting in a memory leak for the application.

Fibers are interesting but are they necessary? The short answer is, not really. Fibers were added to Windows CE for two reasons. First, it makes it easier to port applications from Unix style operating systems where something akin to fibers is used frequently. The second reason for adding them was a request from an internal group within Microsoft that wanted to use fibers when they ported their Windows XP application to Windows CE.

I doubt either of these reasons inspires hoards of developers to start using fibers. A couple of major groups within Microsoft have decided. Fibers are not supported on the Pocket PC 2003 devices, nor are they part of the Standard SDK configuration promoted by the embedded team. Even so, if your system needs fiber support, Windows CE does provide it.

Thread Local Storage

Thread local storage is a mechanism that allows a routine to maintain separate instances of data for each thread calling the routine. This capability might not seem like much, but it has some very handy uses. Take the following thread routine:

```
int g_nGlobal;            // System global variable

int ThreadProc (pStartData) {
    int nValue1;
    int nValue2;

    while (unblocked) {
        //
        // Do some work.
        //
    }
    // We're done now; terminate the thread by returning.
    return 0;
}
```

For this example, imagine that multiple threads are created to execute the same routine, *ThreadProc*. Each thread has its own copy of *nValue1* and *nValue2* because these are stack-based variables and each thread has its own stack. All threads, though, share the same static variable, *g_nGlobal*.

Now imagine that the *ThreadProc* routine calls another routine, *Worker-Bee*. As in

```
int g_nGlobal;              // System global variable

int ThreadProc (pStartData) {
    int nValue1;
    int nValue2;
    while (unblocked) {
        WorkerBee();        // Let someone else do the work.
    }
    // We're done now; terminate the thread by returning.
    return 0;
}
int WorkerBee (void) {
    int nLocal1;
    static int nLocal2;
    //
    // Do work here.
    //
    return nLocal1;
}
```

Now *WorkerBee* doesn't have access to any persistent memory that's local to a thread. *nLocal1* is persistent only for the life of a single call to *WorkerBee*. *nLocal2* is persistent across calls to *WorkerBee* but is static and therefore shared among all threads calling *WorkerBee*. One solution would be to have *Thread-Proc* pass a pointer to a stack-based variable to *WorkerBee*. This strategy works, but only if you have control over the routines calling *WorkerBee*. What if you're writing a DLL and you need to have a routine in the DLL maintain a different state for each thread calling the routine? You can't define static variables in the DLL because they would be shared across the different threads. You can't define local variables because they aren't persistent across calls to your routine. The answer is to use thread local storage.

Thread local storage allows a process to have its own cache of values that are guaranteed to be unique for each thread in a process. This cache of values is small because an array must be created for every thread created in the process, but it's large enough if used intelligently. To be specific, the system constant, *TLS_MINIMUM_AVAILABLE*, is defined to be the number of slots in the TLS array that's available for each process. For Windows CE, like Windows XP, this value is defined as 64. So each process can have 64 4-byte values that are unique for each thread in that process. For the best results, of course, you must manage those 64 slots well.

To reserve one of the TLS slots, a process calls

```
DWORD TlsAlloc (void);
```

TlsAlloc looks through the array to find a free slot in the TLS array, marks it as *in use*, and then returns an index value to the newly assigned slot. If no slots are available, the function returns -1. It's important to understand that the individual threads don't call *TlsAlloc*. Instead, the process or DLL calls it before creating the threads that will use the TLS slot.

Once a slot has been assigned, each thread can access its unique data in the slot by calling this function:

```
BOOL TlsSetValue (DWORD dwTlsIndex, LPVOID lpTlsValue);
```

and

```
LPVOID TlsGetValue (DWORD dwTlsIndex);
```

For both of these functions, the TLS index value returned by *TlsAlloc* specifies the slot that contains the data. Both *TlsGetValue* and *TlsSetValue* type the data as a *PVOID*, but the value can be used for any purpose. The advantage of thinking of the TLS value as a pointer is that a thread can allocate a block of memory on the heap and then keep the pointer to that data in the TLS value. This allows each thread to maintain a block of thread-unique data of almost any size.

One other matter is important to thread local storage. When *TlsAlloc* reserves a slot, it zeroes the value in that slot for all currently running threads. All new threads are created with their TLS array initialized to 0 as well. This means that a thread can safely assume that the value in its slot will be initialized to 0. This is helpful for determining whether a thread needs to allocate a memory block the first time the routine is called.

When a process no longer needs the TLS slot, it should call this function:

```
BOOL TlsFree (DWORD dwTlsIndex);
```

The function is passed the index value of the slot to be freed. The function returns *TRUE* if successful. This function frees only the TLS slot. If threads have allocated storage in the heap and stored pointers to those blocks in their TLS slots, that storage isn't freed by this function. Threads are responsible for freeing their own memory blocks.

Synchronization

With multiple threads running around the system, you need to coordinate the activities. Fortunately, Windows CE supports almost the entire extensive set of standard Win32 synchronization objects. The concept of synchronization objects is fairly simple. A thread *waits* on a synchronization object. When the object is signaled, the waiting thread is unblocked and is scheduled (according to the rules governing the thread's priority) to run.

Windows CE doesn't support some of the synchronization primitives supported by Windows XP. These unsupported elements include file change notifications and waitable timers. The lack of waitable timer support can easily be worked around using other synchronization objects or, for longer-period timeouts, the more flexible Notification API, unique to Windows CE.

One aspect of Windows CE unique to it is that the different synchronization objects don't share the same namespace. This means that if you have an event named *Bob*, you can also have a *mutex* named *Bob*. (I'll talk about mutexes later in this chapter.) This naming convention is different from Windows XP's rule, where all kernel objects (of which synchronization objects are a part) share the same namespace. While having the same names in Windows CE is possible, it's not advisable. Not only does the practice make your code incompatible with Windows XP, there's no telling whether a redesign of the internals of Windows CE might just enforce this restriction in the future.

Events

The first synchronization primitive I'll describe is the *event object*. An event object is a synchronization object that can be in a *signaled* or *nonsignaled* state. Events are useful to a thread to let it be known that, well, an event has occurred. Event objects can either be created to automatically reset from a signaled state to a nonsignaled state or require a manual reset to return the object to its nonsignaled state. Events can be named and therefore shared across different processes allowing interprocess synchronization.

An event is created by means of this function:

```
HANDLE CreateEvent (LPSECURITY_ATTRIBUTES lpEventAttributes,
                    BOOL bManualReset, BOOL bInitialState,
                    LPTSTR lpName);
```

As with all calls in Windows CE, the security attributes parameter, *lpEventAttributes*, should be set to *NULL*. The second parameter indicates whether the event being created requires a manual reset or will automatically reset to a nonsignaled state immediately after being signaled. Setting *bManualReset* to *TRUE* creates an event that must be manually reset. The *bInitialState* parameter specifies whether the event object is initially created in the signaled or nonsignaled state. Finally, the *lpName* parameter points to an optional string that names the event. Events that are named can be shared across processes. If two processes create event objects of the same name, the processes actually share the same object. This allows one process to signal the other process using event objects. If you don't want a named event, the *lpname* parameter can be set to *NULL*.

To share an event object across processes, each process must individually create the event object. You shouldn't just create the event in one process and send the handle of that event to another process. To determine whether a call to *CreateEvent* created a new event object or opened an already created object, you can call *GetLastError* immediately following the call to *CreateEvent*. If *GetLastError* returns *ERROR_ALREADY_EXISTS*, the call opened an existing event.

Once you have an event object, you'll need to be able to signal the event. You accomplish this using either of the following two functions:

```
BOOL SetEvent (HANDLE hEvent);
```

or

```
BOOL PulseEvent (HANDLE hEvent);
```

The difference between these two functions is that *SetEvent* doesn't automatically reset the event object to a nonsignaled state. For autoreset events, *SetEvent* is all you need because the event is automatically reset once a thread unblocks on the event. For manual reset events, you must manually reset the event with this function:

```
BOOL ResetEvent (HANDLE hEvent);
```

These event functions sound like they overlap, so let's review. An event object can be created to reset itself or require a manual reset. If it can reset itself, a call to *SetEvent* signals the event object. The event is then automatically reset to the nonsignaled state when *one* thread is unblocked after waiting on that event. An event that resets itself doesn't need *PulseEvent* or *ResetEvent*. If, however, the event object was created requiring a manual reset, the need for *ResetEvent* is obvious.

PulseEvent signals the event and then resets the event, which allows *all* threads waiting on that event to be unblocked. So the difference between *PulseEvent* on a manually resetting event and *SetEvent* on an automatic resetting event is that using *SetEvent* on an automatic resetting event frees only one thread to run, even if many threads are waiting on that event. *PulseEvent* frees all threads waiting on that event.

An application can associate a single *DWORD* value with an event by calling

```
BOOL SetEventData (HANDLE hEvent, DWORD dwData);
```

The parameters are the handle of the event and the data to associate with that event. Any application can retrieve the data by calling

```
DWORD GetEventData (HANDLE hEvent);
```

The single parameter is the handle to the event. The return value is the data previously associated with the event.

You destroy event objects by calling *CloseHandle*. If the event object is named, Windows maintains a use count on the object, so one call to *CloseHandle* must be made for every call to *CreateEvent*.

Waiting...

It's all well and good to have event objects; the question is how to use them. Threads wait on events, as well as on the soon to be described semaphore and mutex, using one of the following functions: *WaitForSingleObject*, *WaitForMultipleObjects*, *MsgWaitForMultipleObjects*, or *MsgWaitForMultipleObjectsEx*. Under Windows CE, the *WaitForMultiple* functions are limited in that they can't wait for all objects of a set of objects to be signaled. These functions support waiting for *one* object in a set of objects being signaled. Whatever the limitations of waiting, I can't emphasize enough that waiting is good. While a thread is blocked with one of these functions, the thread enters an extremely efficient state that takes very little CPU processing power and battery power.

Another point to remember is that the thread responsible for handling a message loop in your application (usually the application's primary thread) shouldn't be blocked by *WaitForSingleObject* or *WaitForMultipleObjects* because the thread can't be retrieving and dispatching messages in the message loop if it's blocked waiting on an object. The function *MsgWaitForMultipleObjects* gives you a way around this problem, but in a multithreaded environment, it's usually easier to let the primary thread handle the message loop and secondary threads handle the shared resources that require blocking on events.

Waiting on a Single Object

A thread can wait on a synchronization object with the function

```
DWORD WaitForSingleObject (HANDLE hHandle, DWORD dwMilliseconds);
```

The function takes two parameters: the handle to the object being waited on and a timeout value. If you don't want the wait to time out, you can pass the value *INFINITE* in the *dwMilliseconds* parameter. The function returns a value that indicates why the function returned. Calling *WaitForSingleObject* blocks the thread until the event is signaled, the synchronization object is abandoned, or the timeout value is reached.

WaitForSingleObject returns one of the following values:

- **WAIT_OBJECT_0**   The specified object was signaled.

- **WAIT_TIMEOUT**   The timeout interval elapsed, and the object's state remains nonsignaled.

- **WAIT_ABANDONED**   The thread that owned a mutex object being waited on ended without freeing the object.

- **WAIT_FAILED**   The handle of the synchronization object was invalid.

You must check the return code from *WaitForSingleObject* to determine whether the event was signaled or simply that the timeout had expired. (The *WAIT_ABANDONED* return value will be relevant when I talk about mutexes soon.)

Waiting on Processes and Threads

I've talked about waiting on events, but you can also wait on handles to processes and threads. These handles are signaled when their processes or threads terminate. This allows a process to monitor another process (or thread) and perform some action when the process terminates. One common use for this feature is for one process to launch another and then, by blocking on the handle to the newly created process, wait until that process terminates.

The rather irritating routine on the next page is a thread that demonstrates this technique by launching an application, blocking until that application closes, and then relaunching the application:

```
DWORD WINAPI KeepRunning (PVOID pArg) {
    PROCESS_INFORMATION pi;
    TCHAR szFileName[MAX_PATH];
    int rc = 0;

    // Copy the filename.
    lstrcpy (szFileName, (LPTSTR)pArg);
    while (1) {
        // Launch the application.
        rc = CreateProcess (szFileName, NULL, NULL, NULL, FALSE,
                            0, NULL, NULL, NULL, &pi);
        // If the application didn't start, terminate thread.
        if (!rc)
            return -1;
        // Close the new process's primary thread handle.
        CloseHandle (pi.hThread);
```

(continued)

```
        // Wait for user to close the application.
        rc = WaitForSingleObject (pi.hProcess, INFINITE);

        // Close the old process handle.
        CloseHandle (pi.hProcess);

        // Make sure we returned from the wait correctly.
        if (rc != WAIT_OBJECT_0)
            return -2;
    }
    return 0;  //This should never get executed.
}
```

This code simply launches the application using *CreateProcess* and waits
on the process handle returned in the *PROCESS_INFORMATION* structure.
Notice that the thread closes the child process's primary thread handle and,
after the wait, the handle to the child process itself.

Waiting on Multiple Objects

A thread can also wait on a number of events. The wait can end when any one
of the events is signaled. The function that enables a thread to wait on multiple
objects is this one:

```
DWORD WaitForMultipleObjects (DWORD nCount, CONST HANDLE *lpHandles,
                              BOOL bWaitAll, DWORD dwMilliseconds);
```

The first two parameters are a count of the number of events or mutexes to wait
on and a pointer to an array of handles to these events. The *bWaitAll* parameter
must be set to *FALSE* to indicate that the function should return if any of the
events are signaled. The final parameter is a timeout value, in milliseconds. As
with *WaitForSingleObject*, passing *INFINITE* in the timeout parameter disables
the timeout. Windows CE doesn't support the use of *WaitForMultipleObjects* to
enable waiting for all events in the array to be signaled before returning.

Like *WaitForSingleObject*, *WaitForMultipleObjects* returns a code that indicates why the function returned. If the function returned because of a synchronization object being signaled, the return value will be *WAIT_OBJECT_0* plus an
index into the handle array that was passed in the *lpHandles* parameter. For
example, if the first handle in the array unblocked the thread, the return code
would be *WAIT_OBJECT_0*; if the second handle was the cause, the return code
would be *WAIT_OBJECT_0* + 1. The other return codes used by *WaitForSingle-
Object—WAIT_TIMEOUT*, *WAIT_ABANDONED*, and *WAIT_FAILED*—are also
returned by *WaitForMultipleObjects* for the same reasons.

Waiting While Dealing with Messages

The Win32 API provides other functions that allow you to wait on a set of objects as well as messages: *MsgWaitForMultipleObjects* and *MsgWaitForMultipleObjectsEx*. Under Windows CE, these functions act identically, so I'll describe only *MsgWaitForMultipleObjects*. This function essentially combines the wait function, *MsgWaitForMultipleObjects*, with an additional check into the message queue so that the function returns if any of the selected categories of messages are received during the wait. The prototype for this function is the following:

```
DWORD MsgWaitForMultipleObjectsEx (DWORD nCount, LPHANDLE pHandles,
                                   BOOL fWaitAll, DWORD dwMilliseconds,
                                   DWORD dwWakeMasks);
```

This function has a number of limitations under Windows CE. As with *WaitForMultipleObjects*, *MsgWaitForMultipleObjectsEx* can't wait for all objects to be signaled. Nor are all the *dwWakeMask* flags supported by Windows CE. Windows CE supports the following flags in *dwWakeMask*. Each flag indicates a category of messages that, when received in the message queue of the thread, causes the function to return.

- **QS_ALLINPUT**   Any message has been received.

- **QS_INPUT**   An input message has been received.

- **QS_KEY**   A key up, key down, or syskey up or down message has been received.

- **QS_MOUSE**   A mouse move or mouse click message has been received.

- **QS_MOUSEBUTTON**   A mouse click message has been received.

- **QS_MOUSEMOVE**   A mouse move message has been received.

- **QS_PAINT**   A *WM_PAINT* message has been received.

- **QS_POSTMESSAGE**   A posted message, other than those in this list, has been received.

- **QS_SENDMESSAGE**   A sent message, other than those in this list, has been received.

- **QS_TIMER**   A *WM_TIMER* message has been received.

The function is used inside the message loop so that an action or actions can take place in response to the signaling of a synchronization object while your program is still processing messages.

The return value is *WAIT_OBJECT_0* up to *WAIT_OBJECT_0* + *nCount* - 1
for the objects in the handle array. If a message causes the function to return,
the return value is *WAIT_OBJECT_0* + *nCount*. An example of how this function
might be used follows. In this code, the handle array has only one entry, *hSync-
Handle*.

```
fContinue = TRUE;
while (fContinue) {
    rc = MsgWaitForMultipleObjects (1, &hSyncHandle, FALSE,
                                    INFINITE, QS_ALLINPUT);
    if (rc == WAIT_OBJECT_0) {
        //
        // Do work as a result of sync object.
        //
    } else if (rc == WAIT_OBJECT_0 + 1) {
        // It's a message; process it.
        PeekMessage (&msg, hWnd, 0, 0, PM_REMOVE);
        if (msg.message == WM_QUIT)
            fContinue = FALSE;
        else {
            TranslateMessage (&msg);
            DispatchMessage (&msg);
        }
    }
}
```

Semaphores

Earlier I described the event object. That object resides in either a signaled or a
nonsignaled state. Events are synchronization objects that are *not* all or nothing,
signaled or nonsignaled. Semaphores, on the other hand, maintain a count. As
long as that count is above 0, the semaphore is signaled. When the count is 0,
the semaphore is nonsignaled.

Threads wait on semaphore objects as they do events, using *WaitFor-
SingleObject* or *WaitForMultipleObjects*. When a thread waits on a semaphore,
the thread is blocked until the count is greater than 0. When another thread
releases the semaphore, the count is incremented and the thread blocking on
the semaphore returns from the wait function. The maximum count value is
defined when the semaphore is created so that a programmer can define how
many threads can access a resource protected by a semaphore.

Semaphores are typically used to protect a resource that can be accessed
only by a set number of threads at one time. For example, if you have a set of
five buffers for passing data, you can allow up to five threads to grab a buffer
at any one time. When a sixth thread attempts to access the buffer array pro-

tected by the semaphore, it will be blocked until one of the other threads releases the semaphore.

To create a semaphore, call the function

```
HANDLE CreateSemaphore (LPSECURITY_ATTRIBUTES lpSemaphoreAttributes,
                        LONG lInitialCount, LONG lMaximumCount,
                        LPCTSTR lpName);
```

The first parameter, *lpSemaphoreAttributes*, should be set to *NULL*. The parameter *lInitialCount* is the count value when the semaphore is created and must be greater than or equal to 0. If this value is greater than 0, the semaphore will be initially signaled. The *lMaximumCount* parameter should be set to the maximum allowable count value the semaphore will allow. This value must be greater than 0.

The final parameter, *lpName*, is the optional name of the object. This parameter can point to a name or be *NULL*. As with events, if two threads call *CreateSemaphore* and pass the same name, the second call to *CreateSemaphore* returns the handle to the original semaphore instead of creating a new object. In this case, the other parameters, *lInitialCount* and *lMaximumCount*, are ignored. To determine whether the semaphore already exists, you can call *GetLastError* and check the return code for *ERROR_ALREADY_EXISTS*.

When a thread returns from waiting on a semaphore, it can perform its work with the knowledge that only *lMaximumCount* threads or fewer are running within the protection of the semaphore. When a thread has completed work with the protected resource, it should release the semaphore with a call to

```
BOOL ReleaseSemaphore (HANDLE hSemaphore, LONG lReleaseCount,
                       LPLONG lpPreviousCount);
```

The first parameter is the handle to the semaphore. The *lReleaseCount* parameter contains the number by which you want to increase the semaphore's count value. This value must be greater than 0. While you might expect this value to always be 1, sometimes a thread might increase the count by more than 1. The final parameter, *lpPreviousCount*, is set to the address of a variable that will receive the previous resource count of the semaphore. You can set this pointer to *NULL* if you don't need the previous count value.

To destroy a semaphore, call *CloseHandle*. If more than one thread has created the same semaphore, all threads must call *CloseHandle*, or more precisely, *CloseHandle* must be called as many times as *CreateSemaphore* was called before the operating system destroys the semaphore.

Another function, *OpenSemaphore*, is supported on the desktop versions of Windows but not supported by Windows CE. This function is redundant on Windows CE because a thread that wants the handle to a named semaphore can just as easily call *CreateSemaphore* and check the return code from *GetLast-Error* to determine whether it already exists.

Mutexes

Another synchronization object is the *mutex*. A mutex is a synchronization object that's signaled when it's not owned by a thread and nonsignaled when it *is* owned. Mutexes are extremely useful for coordinating exclusive access to a resource such as a block of memory across multiple threads.

A thread gains ownership by waiting on that mutex with one of the wait functions. When no other threads own the mutex, the thread waiting on the mutex is unblocked and implicitly gains ownership of the mutex. After the thread has completed the work that requires ownership of the mutex, the thread must explicitly release the mutex with a call to *ReleaseMutex*.

To create a mutex, call this function:

```
HANDLE CreateMutex (LPSECURITY_ATTRIBUTES lpMutexAttributes,
                    BOOL bInitialOwner, LPCTSTR lpName);
```

The *lpMutexAttributes* parameter should be set to *NULL*. The *bInitialOwner* parameter lets you specify that the calling thread should immediately own the mutex being created. Finally, the *lpName* parameter lets you specify a name for the object so that it can be shared across other processes. When calling *Create-Mutex* with a name specified in the *lpName* parameter, Windows CE checks whether a mutex with the same name has already been created. If so, a handle to the previously created mutex is returned. To determine whether the mutex already exists, call *GetLastError*. It returns *ERROR_ALREADY_EXISTS* if the mutex has been previously created.

Gaining immediate ownership of a mutex using the *bInitialOwner* parameter works only if the mutex is being created. Ownership isn't granted if you're opening a previously created mutex. If you need ownership of a mutex, be sure to call *GetLastError* to determine whether the mutex had been previously committed. If so, call *WaitForSingleObject* to gain ownership of the mutex.

You release the mutex with this function:

```
BOOL ReleaseMutex (HANDLE hMutex);
```

The only parameter is the handle to the mutex.

If a thread owns a mutex and calls one of the wait functions to wait on that same mutex, the wait call immediately returns because the thread already owns the mutex. Since mutexes retain an ownership count for the number of times the wait functions are called, a call to *ReleaseMutex* must be made for each nested call to the wait function.

To close a mutex, call *CloseHandle*. As with events and semaphores, if multiple threads have opened the same mutex, the operating system doesn't destroy the mutex until it has been closed the same number of times that *CreateMutex* was called.

Duplicating Synchronization Handles

Event, semaphore, and mutex handles are process specific, meaning that they shouldn't be passed from one process to another. The ability to name each of these kernel objects makes it easy for each process to "create" an event of the same name, which, as we've seen, simply opens the same event for both processes. There are times, however, when having to name an event is overkill. An example of this situation might be using an event to signal the end of asynchronous I/O between an application and a driver. The driver shouldn't have to create a new and unique event name and pass it to the application for each operation.

The *DuplicateHandle* function exists to avoid having to name events, mutexes, and semaphores all the time. It is prototyped as follows:

```
BOOL DuplicateHandle (HANDLE hSourceProcessHandle, HANDLE hSourceHandle,
                      HANDLE hTargetProcessHandle, LPHANDLE lpTargetHandle,
                      DWORD dwDesiredAccess, BOOL bInheritHandle,
                      DWORD wOptions);
```

The first parameter is the handle of the process that owns the source handle. If a process is duplicating its own handle, it can get this handle by using *Get-CurrentProcess*. The second parameter is the handle to be duplicated. The third and fourth parameters are the handle of the destination process and a pointer to a variable that will receive the duplicated handle. The *dwDesiredAccess* parameter is ignored, and the *bInheritHandle* parameter must be *FALSE*. The *dwOptions* parameter must have the flag *DUPLICATE_SAME_ACCESS* set. The parameter can optionally have the *DUPLICATE_CLOSE_SOURCE* flag set, indicating that the source handle should be closed if the handle is successfully duplicated.

DuplicateHandle is restricted on Windows CE to only duplicating event, mutex, and semaphore handles. Passing any other type of handle will cause the function to fail.

Critical Sections

Using *critical sections* is another method of thread synchronization. Critical sections are good for protecting sections of code from being executed by two different threads at the same time. Critical sections work by having a thread call

EnterCriticalSection to indicate that it has entered a critical section of code. If another thread calls *EnterCriticalSection* referencing the same critical section object, it's blocked until the first thread makes a call to *LeaveCriticalSection*. Critical sections can protect more than one linear section of code. All that's required is that all sections of code that need to be protected use the same critical section object. The one limitation of critical sections is that they can be used to coordinate threads only within a process.

Critical sections are similar to mutexes, with a few important differences. On the downside, critical sections are limited to a single process by means of which mutexes can be shared across processes. But this limitation is also an advantage. Because they're isolated to a single process, critical sections are implemented so that they're significantly faster than mutexes. If you don't need to share a resource across a process boundary, always use a critical section instead of a mutex.

To use a critical section, you first create a critical section handle with this function:

```
void InitializeCriticalSection (LPCRITICAL_SECTION lpCriticalSection);
```

The only parameter is a pointer to a *CRITICAL_SECTION* structure that you define somewhere in your application. Be sure not to allocate this structure on the stack of a function that will be deallocated as soon the function returns. You should also not move or copy the critical section structure. Since the other critical section functions require a pointer to this structure, you'll need to allocate it within the scope of all functions using the critical section. While the *CRITICAL_SECTION* structure is defined in WINBASE.H, an application doesn't need to manipulate any of the fields in that structure. So for all practical purposes, think of a pointer to a *CRITICAL_SECTION* structure as a handle instead of as a pointer to a structure of a known format.

When a thread needs to enter a protected section of code, it should call this function:

```
void EnterCriticalSection (LPCRITICAL_SECTION lpCriticalSection);
```

The function takes as its only parameter a pointer to the critical section structure initialized with *InitializeCriticalSection*. If the critical section is already owned by another thread, this function blocks the new thread and doesn't return until the other thread releases the critical section. If the thread calling *EnterCriticalSection* already owns the critical section, a use count is incremented and the function returns immediately.

If you need to enter a critical section but can't afford to be blocked waiting for that critical section, you can use the function

```
BOOL TryEnterCriticalSection (LPCRITICAL_SECTION lpCriticalSection);
```

TryEnterCriticalSection differs from *EnterCriticalSection* because it always returns immediately. If the critical section was unowned, the function returns *TRUE* and the thread now owns the critical section. If the critical section is owned by another thread, the function returns *FALSE*. This function, added in Windows CE 3.0, allows a thread to attempt to perform work in a critical section without being forced to wait until the critical section is free.

When a thread leaves a critical section, it should call this function:

```
void LeaveCriticalSection (LPCRITICAL_SECTION lpCriticalSection);
```

As with all the critical section functions, the only parameter is the pointer to the critical section structure. Since critical sections track a use count, one call to *LeaveCriticalSection* must be made for each call to *EnterCriticalSection* by the thread that owns the section.

Finally, when you're finished with the critical section, you should call

```
void DeleteCriticalSection (LPCRITICAL_SECTION lpCriticalSection);
```

This action cleans up any system resources used to manage the critical section.

Interlocked Variable Access

Here's one more low-level method for synchronizing threads—using the functions for interlocked access to variables. While programmers with multithread experience already know this, I need to warn you that Murphy's Law[2] seems to come into its own when you're using multiple threads in a program. One of the sometimes overlooked issues in a preemptive multitasking system is that a thread can be preempted in the middle of incrementing or checking a variable. For example, a simple code fragment such as

```
if (!i++) {
    // Do something because i was 0.
}
```

can cause a great deal of trouble. To understand why, let's look into how that statement might be compiled. The assembly code for that *if* statement might look something like this:

```
load    reg1, [addr of i]        ;Read variable
add     reg2, reg1, 1            ;reg2 = reg1 + 1
store   reg2, [addr of i]        ;Save incremented var
bne     reg1, zero, skipblk      ;Branch reg1 != zero
```

2. Murphy's Law: Anything that can go wrong will go wrong. Murphy's first corollary: When something goes wrong, it happens at the worst possible moment.

There's no reason that the thread executing this section of code couldn't be pre-empted by another thread after the load instruction and before the store instruction. If this happened, two threads could enter the block of code when that isn't the way the code is supposed to work. Of course, I've already described a number of methods (such as critical sections and the like) that you can use to prevent such incidents from occurring. But for something like this, a critical section is overkill. What you need is something lighter.

Windows CE supports the full set of *interlocked* functions from the Win32 API. The first three, *InterlockedIncrement*, *InterlockedDecrement*, and *InterlockedExchange*, allow a thread to increment, decrement, and in some cases optionally exchange a variable without your having to worry about the thread being preempted in the middle of the operation. The other functions allow variables to be added to and optionally exchanged. The functions are prototyped here:

```
LONG InterlockedIncrement(LPLONG lpAddend);

LONG InterlockedDecrement(LPLONG lpAddend);

LONG InterlockedExchange(LPLONG Target, LONG Value);
LONG InterlockedCompareExchange (LPLONG Destination, LONG Exchange,
                                 LONG Comperand);
LONG InterlockedTestExchange (LPLONG Target, LONG OldValue, LONG NewValue);LONG
 InterlockedExchangeAdd (LPLONG Addend, LONG Increment);
PVOID InterlockedCompareExchangePointer (PVOID* Destination, PVOID ExChange,
                                         PVOID Comperand);
PVOID InterlockedExchangePointer (PVOID* Target, PVOID Value);
```

For the interlocked increment and decrement, the one parameter is a pointer to the variable to increment or decrement. The returned value is the new value of the variable after it has been incremented or decremented. The *Interlocked-Exchange* function takes a pointer to the target variable and the new value for the variable. It returns the previous value of the variable. Rewriting the previous code fragment so that it's thread safe produces this code:

```
if (!InterlockedIncrement(&i)) {
    // Do something because i was 0.
}
```

The *InterlockedCompareExchange* and *InterlockedTestExchange* functions exchange a value with the target only if the target value is equal to the test parameter. Otherwise, the original value is left unchanged. The only difference between the two functions is the order of the parameters.

InterlockedExchangeAdd adds the second parameter to the *LONG* pointed to by the first parameter. The value returned by the function is the original value before the add operation. The final two functions, *InterlockedCompareExchangePointer* and *InterlockedExchangePointer*, are identical to the *InterlockedCompareExchange* and *InterlockedExchange* functions, but the parameters have been type cast to pointers instead of longs.

Windows CE Security

While Windows CE doesn't implement the thread- and process-level security of the Windows NT/2000/XP line, it does have an optional level of module-based security. This security scheme is based on the concept of *trusted* and *untrusted* modules. The modules are the executables (.EXEs) and dynamic-link libraries (DLLs). Trusted modules can access anything in the system, while untrusted modules are refused access to a handful of protected functions and registry keys.

The Windows CE security scheme must be implemented by the OEM when it ports Windows CE to its hardware. When an executable or DLL is loaded, the operating system notifies the OAL, the OEM abstraction layer, underneath the operating system. The OAL then decides, by whatever means it chooses, to mark the executable or DLL as being trusted or untrusted. This check happens only for modules loaded from the object store or external media. In most cases, modules loaded directly from ROM are assumed to be trusted because the OEM made the decision about what modules were present in the ROM. However, this ROM module trust assumption can be disabled by the OEM. For systems that don't implement this security scheme, all modules are considered trusted.

Because trusted modules have free reign, the only interesting case is what happens if a module is untrusted. When an untrusted module calls a protected function, such as the function *VirtualCopy*, the call fails. Calling *GetLastError* then returns ERROR_ACCESS_DENIED. A handful of registry keys and their descendants are also protected. Untrusted modules can read a protected registry key, but any attempt to modify a protected key or create values or keys underneath a protected key results in an *ERROR_ACCESS_DENIED* failure. A list of the protected functions[3] and registry keys is shown in Listing 10-1. In addition to the list, files marked with the *FILE_ATTRIBUTE SYSTEM* attribute can't be moved, changed, or deleted by untrusted applications. Databases with the *SYSTEM* flag can't be modified by untrusted applications.

---

3. A number of undocumented functions are also protected but are not included in this list.

There are a few interesting derivations of this security scheme. What happens when a trusted executable unknowingly loads an untrusted DLL? What if an untrusted executable loads a trusted DLL? Finally, how is a device driver supposed to react to a call from an untrusted module? Actually, the rules are fairly simple.

Functions

AllocPhysMem	RegCopyFile
CeSetThreadPriority	RegReplaceKey
CeSetThreadQuantum	RegRestoreFile
CheckPassword	RegSaveKey
CryptUnprotectData	SetCleanRebootFlag
DebugActiveProcess	SetCurrentUser
ForcePageout	SetInterruptEvent
FreeIntChainHandler	SetKMode
FreePhysMem	SetPassword
InterruptDisable	SetPasswordStatus
InterruptDone	SetProcPermissions
InterruptInitialize	SetSystemMemoryDivision
KernelLibIoControl	SetUserData
LoadDriver	SystemStarted
LoadIntChainHandler	UnlockPages
LoadKernelLibrary	VirtualCopy
LockPages	VirtualSetPageFlags
PowerOffSystem	WaitForDebugEvent
ReadProcessMemory	WriteProcessMemory
ReadRegistryFromOEM	WriteRegistryToOEM

Registry Keys

```
HKEY_LOCAL_MACHINE\Comm
HKEY_LOCAL_MACHINE\Drivers
HKEY_LOCAL_MACHINE\Services
HKEY_LOCAL_MACHINE\HARDWARE
HKEY_LOCAL_MACHINE\SYSTEM
HKEY_LOCAL_MACHINE\init
HKEY_LOCAL_MACHINE\WDMDrivers
```

Listing 10-1   The list of protected functions and registry keys

If a trusted module attempts to load an untrusted DLL, the load fails. If an untrusted module loads a trusted DLL, the trust level of the DLL is reduced to untrusted. A module can determine its trust state by calling the function

```
DWORD CeGetCurrentTrust (void);
```

The return value for this function is either *OEM_CERTIFY_TRUST*, which signifies that the module is running in a trusted state, or *OEM_CERTIFY_RUN*, which indicates that the module is currently untrusted. If a module requires access to trusted functions, it can call *CeGetCurrentTrust* at its initialization, and if it discovers that it's running in an untrusted state, it can fail its initialization.

Device drivers operate in a different process space from standard applications, but sometimes a device driver might need to check the trust state of a calling application. Here's the function that accomplishes this task:

```
DWORD CeGetCallerTrust (void);
```

The return values are the same as for *CeGetCurrentTrust*, *OEM_CERTIFY_TRUST*, and *OEM_CERTIFY_RUN*.

Interprocess Communication

Quite often, two Windows CE processes need to communicate. The walls between processes that protect processes from one another prevent casual exchanging of data. The memory space of one process isn't exposed to another process. Handles to files or other objects can't be passed from one process to another. Windows CE doesn't support handle inheritance. Some of the other more common methods of interprocess communication, such as named pipes, are also not supported under Windows CE. However, you can choose from plenty of ways to enable two or more processes to exchange data.

Finding Other Processes

Before you can communicate with another process, you have to determine whether it's running on the system. Strategies for finding whether another process is running depend mainly on whether you have control of the other process. If the process to be found is a third-party application in which you have no control over the design of the other process, the best method might be to use the *FindWindow* function to locate the other process's main window. *FindWindow* can search either by window class or by window title. You can enumerate the top-level windows in the system using *EnumWindows*. You can also use the ToolHelp debugging functions to enumerate the processes running, but this works only when the ToolHelp DLL is loaded on the system, and unfortunately, it generally isn't included, by default, on most systems.

If you're writing both processes, however, it's much easier to enumerate them. In this case, the best methods include using the tools you'll later use in one process to communicate with the other process, such as named mutexes, events, or memory-mapped objects. When you create one of these objects, you can determine whether you're the first to create the object or you're simply opening another object by calling *GetLastError* after another call created the object. And the simplest method might be the best; call *FindWindow*.

The classic case of using *FindWindow* on a Pocket PC occurs when an application must determine whether another copy of itself is already running. According to the Pocket PC and the earlier Palm-size PC guidelines, an application must allow only one copy of itself to run at a time. Following is a code fragment that all the examples in this book use for accomplishing this task.

```
// If Pocket PC, allow only one instance of the application.
HWND hWnd = FindWindow (szAppName, NULL);
if (hWnd) {
    SetForegroundWindow ((HWND)(((DWORD)hWnd) | 0x01));
    return -1;
}
```

The first statement uses *FindWindow* to find a window class of the same name as the class of the application's main window. Because this call is made before the main window is created in the application, the only way the window could have been found, assuming you're using a unique name for your window class, is for it to have already been created by another copy of your application. An advantage of this technique is that *FindWindow* returns the handle of the main window of the other instance. In the case of the Pocket PC, we want to set that instance in the foreground, which is what we do with the subsequent call to *SetForegroundWindow*. The *ORing* of the 1 to the window handle is a hack of Windows CE that causes the window being activated to be restored if it was in a minimized state.

WM_COPYDATA

After you find your target process, the talking can begin. If you're staying at the window level, you can simply send a *WM_COPYDATA* message. *WM_COPYDATA* is unique in that it's designed to send blocks of data from one process to another. You can't use a standard user-defined message to pass pointers to data from one process to another because a pointer isn't valid across processes. *WM_COPYDATA* gets around this problem by having the system translate the pointer to a block of data from one process's address space to another's. The recipient process is required to copy the data immediately into its own memory space, but this message does provide a quick-and-dirty method of sending blocks of data from one process to another.

Named Memory-Mapped Objects

The problem with *WM_COPYDATA* is that it can be used only to copy fixed blocks of data at a specific time. Windows CE supports entities referred to as *memory-mapped objects*. These are objects that are backed up by the paging file under Windows XP. Under Windows CE, they are simply areas of virtual memory with only physical RAM to back them up. Without the paging file, these objects can't be as big as they would be under Windows XP, but Windows CE does have a way of minimizing the RAM required to back up the memory-mapped object.

Using a named memory-mapped object, two processes can allocate a shared block of memory that's equally accessible to both processes at the same time. You should use named memory-mapped objects so that the system can maintain a proper use count on the object. This procedure prevents one process from freeing the block when it terminates while the other process is still using the block.

Of course, this level of interaction comes with a price. You need some synchronization between the processes when they're reading and writing data in the shared memory block. The use of named mutexes and named events allows processes to coordinate their actions. Using these synchronization objects requires the use of secondary threads so that the message loop can be serviced, but this isn't an exceptional burden.

You create such a memory-mapped object by calling *CreateFileMapping* and passing -1 in the handle field. *CreateFileMapping* was initially described in Chapter 8 in the discussion of memory-mapped files. Because no file is specified, you must specify the size of the memory-mapped region in the maximum size fields of *CreateFileMapping*. The following routine creates a 16-MB region by using a memory-mapped file:

```
// Create a 16-MB memory-mapped object.
hNFileMap = CreateFileMapping ((HANDLE)-1, NULL, PAGE_READWRITE,
                            0, 0x1000000, NULL);
 if (hNFileMap)
    // Map in the object.
    pNFileMem = MapViewOfFile (hNFileMap,
                          FILE_MAP_WRITE, 0, 0, 0);
```

The memory object created by this code doesn't actually commit 16 MB of RAM. Instead, only the address space is reserved. Pages are autocommitted as they're accessed. This process allows an application to create a huge, sparse array of pages that takes up only as much physical RAM as is needed to hold the data. At some point, however, if you start reading or writing to a greater number of pages, you'll run out of memory. When this happens, the system generates an exception. I'll talk about how to deal with exceptions later in this chapter. The important thing to remember is that if you really need RAM to be committed to a memory-mapped object, you need to read each of the pages so that the system will commit physical RAM to that object. Of course, don't be too greedy with RAM; commit only the pages you absolutely require.

Naming a Memory-Mapped Object

A memory-mapped object can be named by passing a string to *CreateFileMapping*. This isn't the name of a file being mapped. Instead, the name identifies the mapping object being created. In the preceding example, the region was unnamed. The following code creates a memory-mapped object named *Bob*. This name is global so that if another process opens a mapping object with the same name, the two processes will share the same memory-mapped object.

```
// Create a 16-MB memory-mapped object.
hNFileMap = CreateFileMapping ((HANDLE)-1, NULL, PAGE_READWRITE,
                               0, 0x1000000, TEXT ("Bob"));
if (hNFileMap)
    // Map in the object.
    pNFileMem = MapViewOfFile (hNFileMap,
                               FILE_MAP_WRITE, 0, 0, 0);
```

The difference between named and unnamed file mapping objects is that a named object is allocated only once in the system. Subsequent calls to *CreateFileMapping* that attempt to create a region with the same name will succeed, but the function will return a handle to the original mapping object instead of creating a new one. For unnamed objects, the system creates a new object each time *CreateFileMapping* is called.

When you're using a memory-mapped object for interprocess communication, processes should create a named object and pass the name of the region to the second process rather than pass a pointer. While the first process can simply pass a pointer to the mapping region to the other process, this isn't advisable. If the first process frees the memory-mapped file region while the second process is still accessing the file, the operating system throws an exception. Instead, the second process should create a memory-mapped object with the same name as the initial process. Windows knows to pass a pointer to the same region that was opened by the first process. The system also increments a use count to track the number of opens. A named memory-mapped object won't be destroyed until all processes have closed the object. This system assures a process that the object will remain at least until it closes the object itself. The XTalk example, presented later in this chapter, provides an example of how to use a named memory-mapped object for interprocess communication.

Message Queues

Windows CE supports a method of interprocess communication called *message queues*. The Message Queue API, as the name suggests, provides data queues for sending data from one process to another.

To communicate with a message queue, a process or pair of processes creates a message queue for reading and one for writing. A call to create or open a queue can specify only read or write access, not both read and write access. The queue is then opened again for the corresponding write or read access. "Messages" are then written to the queue by using the write handle to the queue. (In this context, a message is simply a block of data with a defined length.) The message can be read by using the read handle to the queue. If a series of messages is written to a queue, they are read in the order they were written, in classic first in, first out (FIFO) fashion. When a queue is created, the number and the maximum size of messages are defined for the queue. If the queue is full and a write occurs, the write function will either block (waiting for a free slot in the queue), fail and return immediately, or wait for a specific amount of time before failing and returning. Likewise, read functions can block until a message is in the queue to be read, or they can wait a specific period of time before returning.

In addition, a message can be marked as an "alert" message. Alert messages are sent to the front of the queue so that the next read of the queue will read the alert message regardless of the number of messages that have been waiting to be read. Only one alert message can be in the queue at any one time. If a second alert message is written to the queue before the first one was read, the second alert message replaces the first and the first alert message is lost.

To create a message queue, call this function:

```
HANDLE WINAPI CreateMsgQueue (LPCWSTR lpszName, LPMSGQUEUEOPTIONS lpOptions);
```

The first parameter is the name of the queue that will be either opened or created. The name is global to the entire system. That is, if one process opens a queue with a name and another process opens a queue with the same name, they open the same queue. The name can be up to *MAX_PATH* characters in length. The parameter can also be set to *NULL* to create an unnamed queue.

The second parameter of *CreateMsgQueue* is a pointer to a *MSGQUEUEOPTIONS* structure defined as follows:

```
typedef MSGQUEUEOPTIONS_OS {
    DWORD dwSize;
    DWORD dwFlags;
    DWORD dwMaxMessages;
    DWORD cbMaxMessage;
    BOOL bReadAccess
} MSGQUEUEOPTIONS;
```

The *dwSize* field must be filled in with the size of the structure. The *dwFlags* parameter describes how the queue should act. The flags supported are *MSGQUEUE_NOPRECOMMIT*, which tells Windows CE not to allocate the RAM necessary to support messages in the queue until the RAM is needed; and *MSGQUEUE_ALLOW_BROKEN*, which allows writes and reads to the queue to succeed even if another call hasn't been made to open the queue for the matching read or write of the message. The *dwMaxMessages* field should be set to the maximum number of messages that are expected to be in the queue at any one time. The *cbMaxMessage* field indicates the maximum size of any single message. Finally, the *bReadAccess* field should be set to *TRUE* if read access is desired for the queue and *FALSE* if write access is desired. A single call to *CreateMsgQueue* can only create the queue for either read or write access. To open a queue for both read and write access, *CreateMsgQueue* should be called twice, once for read access and once for write access.

The function returns the handle to the queue if successful, or *NULL* if the function failed. The handle returned by *CreateMsgQueue* is an event handle that can be waited on with *WaitForSingleObject* and the other related *Wait* functions. The event is signaled when the state of the queue changes, either by a new message being placed in the queue or by an entry in the queue becoming available.

CreateMsgQueue will succeed even if a queue of the same name already exists. *GetLastError* will return *ERROR_ALREADY_EXISTS* if the queue existed before the call to *CreateMsgQueue*.

An unnamed message queue can be opened with this function:

```
HANDLE WINAPI OpenMsgQueue (HANDLE hSrcProc, HANDLE hMsgQ,
                     LPMSGQUEUEOPTIONS pOptions);
```

The parameters are the process handle of the process that originally opened the message queue, the handle returned by *CreateMsgQueue*, and a pointer to a *MSGQUEUEOPTIONS* structure. The only fields in the *MSGQUEUEOPTIONS* structure examined by the function are the *dwSize* field and the *bReadAccess* field.

To write a message to the queue, the aptly named *WriteMsgQueue* function is used. It is prototyped as follows:

```
BOOL WINAPI WriteMsgQueue (HANDLE hMsgQ, LPVOID lpBuffer, DWORD cbDataSize,
                    DWORD dwTimeout, DWORD dwFlags);
```

The initial parameter is the write handle to the message queue. The *lpBuffer* parameter points to the buffer containing the message, whereas *cbDataSize* should be set to the size of the message. If *cbDataSize* is greater than the maximum message size set when the queue was created, the call will fail.

The *dwTimeout* parameter specifies the time, in milliseconds, that *WriteMsgQueue* should wait for a slot in the queue to become available before returning. If *dwTimeout* is set to 0, the call will fail and return immediately if the queue is currently full. If *dwTimeout* is set to *INFINITE*, the call will wait until a slot becomes free to write the message. The *dwFlags* parameter can be set to *MSGQUEUE_MSGALERT* to indicate that the message being written is an alert message.

The return value from *WriteMsgQueue* is a Boolean, with *TRUE* indicating success. The function will fail if the queue has not been opened for read access and *MSGQUEUE_ALLOW_BROKEN* was not specified when the queue was created. To determine the reason for failure, call *GetLastError*.

To read a message from the queue, the function *ReadMsgQueue* is used. It's prototyped as follows:

```
BOOL ReadMsgQueue (HANDLE hMsgQ, LPVOID lpBuffer, DWORD cbBufferSize,
                   LPDWORD lpNumberOfBytesRead, DWORD dwTimeout,
                   DWORD* pdwFlags);
```

As with *WriteMsgQueue*, the first two parameters are the handle to the message queue, the pointer to the buffer that, in this case, will receive the message. The *cbBufferSize* parameter should be set to the size of the buffer. If *cbBufferSize* is less than the size of the message at the head of the queue, the read will fail with *ERROR_INSUFFICIENT_BUFFER* returned by a call to *GetLastError*.

The *lpNumberOfBytesRead* parameter should point to a *DWORD* that will receive the size of the message read. The *dwTimeout* parameter specifies how long the function should wait until a message is present in the queue to read. As with *WriteMsgQueue*, passing 0 in this parameter causes *ReadMsgQueue* to fail and return immediately if there is no message in the queue. Passing *INFINITE* in the *dwTimeout* parameter causes the call to wait until there is a message in the queue before returning. The *pdwFlags* parameter should point to a *DWORD* that will receive the flags associated with the message read. The only flag currently defined is *MSGQUEUE_MSGALERT*, which indicates that the message just read was an alert message.

You can query the configuration of a message queue with this function:

```
BOOL GetMsgQueueInfo (HANDLE hMsgQ, LPMSGQUEUEINFO lpInfo);
```

The parameters are the handle to the message queue and a pointer to a *MSG-QUEUEINFO* structure defined as follows:

```
typedef MSGQUEUEINFO {
    DWORD dwSize;
    DWORD dwFlags;
    DWORD dwMaxMessages;
```

```
    DWORD cbMaxMessage;
    DWORD dwCurrentMessages;
    DWORD dwMaxQueueMessages;
    WORD wNumReaders;
    WORD wNumWriters
} MSGQUEUEINFO;
```

The first few fields in this structure match the *MSGQUEUEOPTIONS* structure used in creating and opening queues. The field *dwSize* should be set to the size of the structure before the call to *GetMsgQueueInfo* is made. The remaining fields are filled in by a successful call to *GetMsgQueueInfo*.

The *dwFlags* field will be set to the queue flags, which are *MSGQUEUE_NOPRECOMMIT* and *MSGQUEUE_ALLOW_BROKEN*. The *dwMaxMessages* field contains the maximum number of messages the queue can contain, while *cbMaxMessage* contains the maximum size of any single message.

The *dwCurrentMessages* field is set to the number of messages currently in the queue waiting to be read. The *dwMaxQueueMessages* field is set to the maximum number of messages that were ever in the queue. The *wNumReaders* field is set to the number of handles opened for read access for the queue, while *wNumWriters* is set to the number of handles opened for write access.

To close a message queue, call this function:

```
BOOL WINAPI CloseMsgQueue (HANDLE hMsgQ);
```

The single parameter is the handle to the queue. Because queues must be opened at least twice, once for reading and once for writing, this call must be made at least twice per queue.

Message queues are great for interprocess communication because they are fast and they are thread safe. Messages can be almost any size, although for long queues with really huge buffers it might be best to allocate data buffers dynamically by using memory-mapped objects and by using message queues to pass pointers to the large data buffers.

Communicating with Files and Databases

A more basic method of interprocess communication is the use of files or a custom database. These methods provide a robust, if slower, communication path. Slow is relative. Files and databases in the Windows CE object store are slow in the sense that the system calls to access these objects must find the data in the object store, uncompress the data, and deliver it to the process. However, since the object store is based in RAM, you see none of the extreme slowness of a mechanical hard disk that you'd see under the desktop versions of Windows.

To improve performance with files in the object store, the *FILE_FLAG_RANDOM_ACCESS* flag should be used.

The XTalk Example Program

The following example program, XTalk, uses events, mutexes, and a shared memory-mapped block of memory to communicate among different copies of itself. The example demonstrates the rather common problem of one-to-many communication. In this case, the XTalk window has an edit box with a Send button next to it. When a user taps the Send button, the text in the edit box is communicated to every copy of XTalk running on the system. Each copy of XTalk receives the text from the sending copy and places it in a list box, also in the XTalk window. Figure 10-1 shows two XTalk programs communicating.

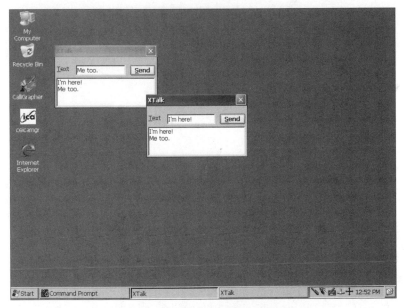

Figure 10-1   The desktop showing two XTalk windows

To perform this feat of communication, XTalk uses a named memory-mapped object as a transfer buffer, a mutex to coordinate access to the buffer, and two event objects to indicate the start and end of communication. A third event is used to tell the sender thread to read the text from the edit control and write the contents to the shared memory block. Listing 10-2 shows the source code for XTalk.

XTalk.rc

```
//======================================================================
// Resource file
//
// Written for the book Programming Windows CE
// Copyright (C) 2003 Douglas Boling
//======================================================================
#include "windows.h"
#include "xtalk.h"                               // Program-specific stuff


//----------------------------------------------------------------------
// Icons and bitmaps
//
ID_ICON ICON    "xtalk.ico"                      // Program icon


//----------------------------------------------------------------------
xtalk DIALOG discardable 10, 10, 120, 60
STYLE  WS_OVERLAPPED | WS_VISIBLE | WS_CAPTION | WS_SYSMENU |
       DS_CENTER | DS_MODALFRAME
CAPTION "XTalk"
CLASS "xtalk"
BEGIN
    LTEXT "&Text"                        -1,   2,  10,  20,  12
    EDITTEXT                   IDD_OUTTEXT, 25,  10,  58,  12,
                                         WS_TABSTOP | ES_AUTOHSCROLL
    PUSHBUTTON "&Send",        IDD_SENDTEXT, 88,  10,  30,  12, WS_TABSTOP

    LISTBOX                    IDD_INTEXT,   2,  25, 116,  40,
                                         WS_TABSTOP | WS_VSCROLL
END
```

XTalk.h

```
//======================================================================
// Header file
//
// Written for the book Programming Windows CE
// Copyright (C) 2003 Douglas Boling
//======================================================================
// Returns number of elements
#define dim(x) (sizeof(x) / sizeof(x[0]))
//----------------------------------------------------------------------
// Generic defines and data types
//
struct decodeUINT {                              // Structure associates
    UINT Code;                                   // messages
                                                 // with a function.
```

Listing 10-2   The source code for XTalk

```
        LRESULT (*Fxn)(HWND, UINT, WPARAM, LPARAM);
};
struct decodeCMD {                                // Structure associates
    UINT Code;                                    // menu IDs with a
    LRESULT (*Fxn)(HWND, WORD, HWND, WORD);       // function.
};


//-----------------------------------------------------------------------
// Generic defines used by application
#define  ID_ICON                1

#define  IDD_INTEXT            10                  // Control IDs
#define  IDD_SENDTEXT          11
#define  IDD_OUTTEXT           12

#define  MMBUFFSIZE          1024                  // Size of shared buffer
#define  TEXTSIZE             256

// Interprocess communication structure mapped in shared memory
typedef struct {
    int nAppCnt;
    int nReadCnt;
    TCHAR szText[TEXTSIZE];
} SHAREBUFF;
typedef SHAREBUFF *PSHAREBUFF;

//-----------------------------------------------------------------------
// Function prototypes
//
HWND InitInstance (HINSTANCE, LPWSTR, int);
int TermInstance (HINSTANCE, int);

// Window procedures
LRESULT CALLBACK MainWndProc (HWND, UINT, WPARAM, LPARAM);
// Message handlers
LRESULT DoCreateMain (HWND, UINT, WPARAM, LPARAM);
LRESULT DoSetFocusMain (HWND, UINT, WPARAM, LPARAM);
LRESULT DoCommandMain (HWND, UINT, WPARAM, LPARAM);
LRESULT DoDestroyMain (HWND, UINT, WPARAM, LPARAM);

// Command functions
LPARAM DoMainCommandSend (HWND, WORD, HWND, WORD);
LPARAM DoMainCommandExit (HWND, WORD, HWND, WORD);

// Thread functions
DWORD WINAPI SenderThread (PVOID pArg);
DWORD WINAPI ReaderThread (PVOID pArg);
```

(continued)

Listing 10-2   *(continued)*

XTalk.cpp

```
//======================================================================
// XTalk - A simple application for Windows CE
//
// Written for the book Programming Windows CE
// Copyright (C) 2003 Douglas Boling
//======================================================================
#include <windows.h>                    // For all that Windows stuff
#include <commctrl.h>                   // Command bar includes
#include "xtalk.h"                      // Program-specific stuff

// The include and lib files for the Pocket PC are conditionally
// included so that this example can share the same project file. This
// is necessary because this example must have a menu bar on the Pocket
// PC to have a SIP button.
#if defined(WIN32_PLATFORM_PSPC)
#include <aygshell.h>                   // Add Pocket PC includes
#pragma comment( lib, "aygshell" )      // Link Pocket PC lib for menu bar
#endif
//----------------------------------------------------------------------
// Global data
//
const TCHAR szAppName[] = TEXT ("xtalk");
HINSTANCE hInst;                        // Program instance handle

HANDLE g_hMMObj = 0;                    // Memory-mapped object
PSHAREBUFF g_pBuff = 0;                 // Pointer to mm object
HANDLE g_hmWriteOkay = 0;               // Write mutex
HANDLE g_hSendEvent = 0;                // Local send event
HANDLE g_hReadEvent = 0;                // Shared read data event
HANDLE g_hReadDoneEvent = 0;            // Shared data read event

// Message dispatch table for MainWindowProc
const struct decodeUINT MainMessages[] = {
    WM_CREATE, DoCreateMain,
    WM_SETFOCUS, DoSetFocusMain,
    WM_COMMAND, DoCommandMain,
    WM_DESTROY, DoDestroyMain,
};
// Command Message dispatch for MainWindowProc
const struct decodeCMD MainCommandItems[] = {
    IDOK, DoMainCommandExit,
    IDCANCEL, DoMainCommandExit,
    IDD_SENDTEXT, DoMainCommandSend,
};
```

```
//======================================================================
// Program entry point
//
int WINAPI WinMain (HINSTANCE hInstance, HINSTANCE hPrevInstance,
                    LPWSTR lpCmdLine, int nCmdShow) {
    MSG msg;
    int rc = 0;
    HWND hwndMain;

    // Initialize application.
    hwndMain = InitInstance (hInstance, lpCmdLine, nCmdShow);
    if (hwndMain == 0)
        return TermInstance (hInstance, 0x10);

    // Application message loop
    while (GetMessage (&msg, NULL, 0, 0)) {
        if ((hwndMain == 0) || !IsDialogMessage (hwndMain, &msg)) {
            TranslateMessage (&msg);
            DispatchMessage (&msg);
        }
    }
    // Instance cleanup
    return TermInstance (hInstance, msg.wParam);
}
//----------------------------------------------------------------------
// InitInstance - Instance initialization
//
HWND InitInstance (HINSTANCE hInstance, LPWSTR lpCmdLine, int nCmdShow){
    HWND hWnd;
    HANDLE hThread;
    RECT rect;
    int rc;
    BOOL fFirstApp = TRUE;
    WNDCLASS wc;

#if defined(WIN32_PLATFORM_PSPC)
    // If Pocket PC, bring the other copy to the foreground so
    // the user can see it.
    HWND hWnd = FindWindow (szAppName, NULL);
    if (hWnd) SetForegroundWindow ((HWND)(((DWORD)hWnd) | 0x01));
#endif

    // Save program instance handle in global variable.
    hInst = hInstance;

    // Register application main window class.
    wc.style = 0;                              // Window style
```

(continued)

Listing 10-2   *(continued)*

```
wc.lpfnWndProc = MainWndProc;            // Callback function
wc.cbClsExtra = 0;                       // Extra class data
wc.cbWndExtra = DLGWINDOWEXTRA;          // Extra window data
wc.hInstance = hInstance;                // Owner handle
wc.hIcon = NULL,                         // Application icon
wc.hCursor = NULL;                       // Default cursor
wc.hbrBackground = (HBRUSH) (COLOR_BTNFACE + 1);
wc.lpszMenuName =  NULL;                 // Menu name
wc.lpszClassName = szAppName;            // Window class name

if (RegisterClass (&wc) == 0) return 0;


// Create mutex used to share memory-mapped structure.
g_hmWriteOkay = CreateMutex (NULL, TRUE, TEXT ("XTALKWRT"));
rc = GetLastError();
if (rc == ERROR_ALREADY_EXISTS)
    fFirstApp = FALSE;
else if (rc) return 0;


// Wait here for ownership to ensure that the initialization is done.
// This is necessary since CreateMutex doesn't wait.
rc = WaitForSingleObject (g_hmWriteOkay, 2000);
if (rc != WAIT_OBJECT_0)
    return 0;


// Create a file-mapping object.
g_hMMObj = CreateFileMapping ((HANDLE)-1, NULL, PAGE_READWRITE, 0,
                              MMBUFFSIZE, TEXT ("XTALKBLK"));
if (g_hMMObj == 0) return 0;


// Map into memory the file-mapping object.
g_pBuff = (PSHAREBUFF)MapViewOfFile (g_hMMObj, FILE_MAP_WRITE,
                                     0, 0, 0);
if (!g_pBuff)
    CloseHandle (g_hMMObj);


// Initialize structure if first application started.
if (fFirstApp)
    memset (g_pBuff, 0, sizeof (SHAREBUFF));
// Increment app running count. Interlock not needed due to mutex.
g_pBuff->nAppCnt++;


// Release the mutex. We need to release the mutex twice
// if we owned it when we entered the wait above.
ReleaseMutex (g_hmWriteOkay);
if (fFirstApp)
    ReleaseMutex (g_hmWriteOkay);
```

```
    // Now create events for read, and send notification.
    g_hSendEvent = CreateEvent (NULL, FALSE, FALSE, NULL);
    g_hReadEvent = CreateEvent (NULL, TRUE, FALSE, TEXT ("XTALKREAD"));
    g_hReadDoneEvent = CreateEvent (NULL, FALSE, FALSE,
                                    TEXT ("XTALKDONE"));
    if (!g_hReadEvent || !g_hSendEvent || !g_hReadDoneEvent)
        return 0;


    // Create main window.
    hWnd = CreateDialog (hInst, szAppName, NULL, NULL);
    rc = GetLastError();
    if (!fFirstApp) {
        GetWindowRect (hWnd, &rect);
        MoveWindow (hWnd, rect.left+10, rect.top+10,
                    rect.right-rect.left, rect.bottom-rect.top, FALSE);
    }
    // Create secondary threads for interprocess communication.
    hThread = CreateThread (NULL, 0, SenderThread, hWnd, 0, (DWORD *)&rc);
    if (hThread)
        CloseHandle (hThread);
    else {
        DestroyWindow (hWnd);
        return 0;
    }
    hThread = CreateThread (NULL, 0, ReaderThread, hWnd, 0, (DWORD *)&rc);
    if (hThread)
        CloseHandle (hThread);
    else {
        DestroyWindow (hWnd);
        return 0;
    }


    // Return fail code if window not created.
    if (!IsWindow (hWnd)) return 0;


    // Standard show and update calls
    ShowWindow (hWnd, nCmdShow);
    UpdateWindow (hWnd);
    return hWnd;
}
//----------------------------------------------------------------------
// TermInstance - Program cleanup
//
int TermInstance (HINSTANCE hInstance, int nDefRC) {

    // Free memory-mapped object.
    if (g_pBuff) {
```

(continued)

Listing 10-2   *(continued)*

```
                // Decrement app running count.
                InterlockedDecrement (&g_pBuff->nAppCnt);
                UnmapViewOfFile (g_pBuff);
        }
        if (g_hMMObj)
                CloseHandle (g_hMMObj);

        // Free mutex.
        if (g_hmWriteOkay)
                CloseHandle (g_hmWriteOkay);

        // Close event handles.
        if (g_hReadEvent)
                CloseHandle (g_hReadEvent);

        if (g_hReadDoneEvent)
                CloseHandle (g_hReadDoneEvent);

        if (g_hSendEvent)
                CloseHandle (g_hSendEvent);
        return nDefRC;
}
//======================================================================
// Message handling procedures for main window
//----------------------------------------------------------------------
// MainWndProc - Callback function for application window
//
LRESULT CALLBACK MainWndProc (HWND hWnd, UINT wMsg, WPARAM wParam,
                              LPARAM lParam) {
        int i;
        //
        // Search message list to see if we need to handle this
        // message. If in list, call procedure.
        //
        for (i = 0; i < dim(MainMessages); i++) {
                if (wMsg == MainMessages[i].Code)
                        return (*MainMessages[i].Fxn)(hWnd, wMsg, wParam, lParam);
        }
        return DefWindowProc (hWnd, wMsg, wParam, lParam);
}
//----------------------------------------------------------------------
// DoCreateMain - Process WM_CREATE message for window.
//
LRESULT DoCreateMain (HWND hWnd, UINT wMsg, WPARAM wParam,
                      LPARAM lParam) {
#if defined(WIN32_PLATFORM_PSPC) && (_WIN32_WCE >= 300)
```

```
    SHMENUBARINFO mbi;                          // For Pocket PC, create
    memset(&mbi, 0, sizeof(SHMENUBARINFO)); // menu bar so that we
    mbi.cbSize = sizeof(SHMENUBARINFO);      // have a sip button.
    mbi.hwndParent = hWnd;
    mbi.dwFlags = SHCMBF_EMPTYBAR;           // No menu
    SHCreateMenuBar(&mbi);
#endif
    return 0;
}
//----------------------------------------------------------------------
// DoSetFocusMain - Process WM_SETFOCUS message for window.
//
LRESULT DoSetFocusMain (HWND hWnd, UINT wMsg, WPARAM wParam,
                        LPARAM lParam) {
    SetFocus (GetDlgItem (hWnd, IDD_OUTTEXT));
    return 0;
}
//----------------------------------------------------------------------
// DoCommandMain - Process WM_COMMAND message for window.
//
LRESULT DoCommandMain (HWND hWnd, UINT wMsg, WPARAM wParam,
                       LPARAM lParam) {
    WORD    idItem, wNotifyCode;
    HWND    hwndCtl;
    int     i;

    // Parse the parameters.
    idItem = (WORD) LOWORD (wParam);
    wNotifyCode = (WORD) HIWORD (wParam);
    hwndCtl = (HWND) lParam;

    // Call routine to handle control message.
    for(i = 0; i < dim(MainCommandItems); i++) {
        if(idItem == MainCommandItems[i].Code)
            return (*MainCommandItems[i].Fxn)(hWnd, idItem, hwndCtl,
                                              wNotifyCode);
    }
    return 0;
}
//----------------------------------------------------------------------
// DoDestroyMain - Process WM_DESTROY message for window.
//
LRESULT DoDestroyMain (HWND hWnd, UINT wMsg, WPARAM wParam,
                       LPARAM lParam) {
    PostQuitMessage (0);
    return 0;
}
```

(continued)

Listing 10-2   *(continued)*

```
//======================================================================
// Command handler routines
//----------------------------------------------------------------------
// DoMainCommandExit - Process Program Exit command.
//
LPARAM DoMainCommandExit (HWND hWnd, WORD idItem, HWND hwndCtl,
                          WORD wNotifyCode) {

    SendMessage (hWnd, WM_CLOSE, 0, 0);
    return 0;
}
//----------------------------------------------------------------------
// DoMainCommandSend - Process Program Send command.
//
LPARAM DoMainCommandSend (HWND hWnd, WORD idItem, HWND hwndCtl,
                          WORD wNotifyCode) {

    SetEvent (g_hSendEvent);
    return 0;
}
//======================================================================
// SenderThread - Performs the interprocess communication
//
DWORD WINAPI SenderThread (PVOID pArg) {
    HWND hWnd;
    int nGoCode, rc;
    TCHAR szText[TEXTSIZE];

    hWnd = (HWND)pArg;
    while (1) {
        nGoCode = WaitForSingleObject (g_hSendEvent, INFINITE);
        if (nGoCode == WAIT_OBJECT_0) {
            SendDlgItemMessage (hWnd, IDD_OUTTEXT, WM_GETTEXT,
                                sizeof (szText), (LPARAM)szText);

            rc = WaitForSingleObject (g_hmWriteOkay, 2000);
            if (rc == WAIT_OBJECT_0) {
                lstrcpy (g_pBuff->szText, szText);
                g_pBuff->nReadCnt = g_pBuff->nAppCnt;
                PulseEvent (g_hReadEvent);
                // Wait while reader threads get data.
                while (g_pBuff->nReadCnt)
                    rc = WaitForSingleObject (g_hReadDoneEvent,
                                              INFINITE);
                ReleaseMutex (g_hmWriteOkay);
            }
        } else
```

```
            return -1;
    }
    return 0;
}
//================================================================
// ReaderThread - Performs the interprocess communication
//
DWORD WINAPI ReaderThread (PVOID pArg) {
    HWND hWnd;
    int nGoCode, rc, i;
    TCHAR szText[TEXTSIZE];

    hWnd = (HWND)pArg;
    while (1) {
        nGoCode = WaitForSingleObject (g_hReadEvent, INFINITE);
        if (nGoCode == WAIT_OBJECT_0) {
            i = SendDlgItemMessage (hWnd, IDD_INTEXT, LB_ADDSTRING, 0,
                                (LPARAM)g_pBuff->szText);
            SendDlgItemMessage (hWnd, IDD_INTEXT, LB_SETTOPINDEX, i, 0);

            InterlockedDecrement (&g_pBuff->nReadCnt);
            SetEvent (g_hReadDoneEvent);
        } else {
            rc = GetLastError();
            wsprintf (szText, TEXT ("rc:%d"), rc);
            MessageBox (hWnd, szText, TEXT ("ReadThread Err"), MB_OK);
        }
    }
    return 0;
}
```

The interesting routines in the XTalk example are the *InitInstance* procedure and the two thread procedures *SenderThread* and *ReaderThread*. The relevant part of *InitInstance* is shown below with the error checking code
removed for brevity.

```
// Create mutex used to share memory-mapped structure.
g_hmWriteOkay = CreateMutex (NULL, TRUE, TEXT ("XTALKWRT"));
rc = GetLastError();
if (rc == ERROR_ALREADY_EXISTS)
    fFirstApp = FALSE;
// Wait here for ownership to ensure that the initialization is done.
// This is necessary since CreateMutex doesn't wait.
rc = WaitForSingleObject (g_hmWriteOkay, 2000);
if (rc != WAIT_OBJECT_0)
    return 0;
```

```
// Create a file-mapping object.
g_hMMObj = CreateFileMapping ((HANDLE)-1, NULL, PAGE_READWRITE, 0,
                              MMBUFFSIZE, TEXT ("XTALKBLK"));

// Map into memory the file-mapping object.
g_pBuff = (PSHAREBUFF)MapViewOfFile (g_hMMObj, FILE_MAP_WRITE,
                              0, 0, 0);

// Initialize structure if first application started.
if (fFirstApp)
    memset (g_pBuff, 0, sizeof (SHAREBUFF));

// Increment app running count. Interlock not needed due to mutex.
g_pBuff->nAppCnt++;

// Release the mutex.  We need to release the mutex twice
// if we owned it when we entered the wait above.
ReleaseMutex (g_hmWriteOkay);
if (fFirstApp)
    ReleaseMutex (g_hmWriteOkay);

// Now create events for read and send notification.
g_hSendEvent = CreateEvent (NULL, FALSE, FALSE, NULL);
g_hReadEvent = CreateEvent (NULL, TRUE, FALSE, TEXT ("XTALKREAD"));
g_hReadDoneEvent = CreateEvent (NULL, FALSE, FALSE,
                              TEXT ("XTALKDONE"));
```

This code is responsible for creating the necessary synchronization objects as well as creating and initializing the shared memory block. The mutex object is created first with the parameters set to request initial ownership of the mutex object. A call is then made to *GetLastError* to determine whether the mutex object has already been created. If not, the application assumes that the first instance of XTalk is running and later will initialize the shared memory block. Once the mutex is created, an additional call is made to *WaitForSingleObject* to wait until the mutex is released. This call is necessary to prevent a late-starting instance of XTalk from disturbing communication in progress. Once the mutex is owned, calls are made to *CreateFileMapping* and *MapViewOfFile* to create a named memory-mapped object. Since the object is named, each process that opens the object opens the same object and is returned a pointer to the same block of memory.

Once the shared memory block is created, the first instance of XTalk zeroes out the block. This procedure also forces the block of RAM to be committed because memory-mapped objects by default are autocommit blocks. Then *nAppCnt*, which keeps a count of the running instances of XTalk, is incremented. Finally the mutex protecting the shared memory is released. If this is the first instance of XTalk, *ReleaseMutex* must be called twice because it gains ownership of the mutex twice—once when the mutex is created and again when the call to *WaitForSingleObject* is made.

Finally, three event objects are created. *SendEvent* is an unnamed event, local to each instance of XTalk. The primary thread uses this event to signal the sender thread that the user has pressed the Send button and wants the text in the edit box transmitted. *ReadEvent* is a named event that tells the other instances of XTalk that there's data to be read in the transfer buffer. *ReadDoneEvent* is a named event signaled by each of the receiving copies of XTalk to indicate that they have read the data.

The two threads, *ReaderThread* and *SenderThread*, are created immediately after the main window of XTalk is created. The code for *SenderThread* is shown here:

```
DWORD WINAPI SenderThread (PVOID pArg) {
    HWND hWnd;
    int nGoCode, rc;
    TCHAR szText[TEXTSIZE];

    hWnd = (HWND)pArg;
    while (1) {
        nGoCode = WaitForSingleObject (g_hSendEvent, INFINITE);
        if (nGoCode == WAIT_OBJECT_0) {
            SendDlgItemMessage (hWnd, IDD_OUTTEXT, WM_GETTEXT,
                                sizeof (szText), (LPARAM)szText);

            rc = WaitForSingleObject (g_hmWriteOkay, 2000);
            if (rc == WAIT_OBJECT_0) {
                lstrcpy (g_pBuff->szText, szText);
                g_pBuff->nReadCnt = g_pBuff->nAppCnt;
                PulseEvent (g_hReadEvent);

                // Wait while reader threads get data.
                while (g_pBuff->nReadCnt)
                    rc = WaitForSingleObject (g_hReadDoneEvent,
                                              INFINITE);
                ReleaseMutex (g_hmWriteOkay);
            }
        }
    }
    return 0;
}
```

The routine waits on the primary thread of XTalk to signal *SendEvent*. The primary thread of XTalk makes the signal in response to a *WM_COMMAND* message from the Send button. The thread is then unblocked, reads the text from the edit control, and waits to gain ownership of the *WriteOkay* mutex. This mutex protects two copies of XTalk from writing to the shared block at the same time. When the thread owns the mutex, it writes the string read from the edit control into the shared buffer. It then copies the number of active copies of XTalk into the *nReadCnt* variable in the same shared buffer and pulses *ReadEvent* to tell the other copies of XTalk to read the newly written data. A manual resetting event is used so that all threads waiting on the event will be unblocked when the event is signaled.

The thread then waits for the *nReadCnt* variable to return to 0. Each time a reader thread reads the data, the *nReadCnt* variable is decremented and the *ReadDone* event signaled. Note that the thread doesn't spin on this variable but uses an event to tell it when to check the variable again. This would actually be a great place to use *WaitForMultipleObjects* and have all reader threads signal when they've read the data, but Windows CE doesn't support the *WaitAll* flag in *WaitForMultipleObjects*.

Finally, when all the reader threads have read the data, the sender thread releases the mutex protecting the shared segment and the thread returns to wait for another send event.

The *ReaderThread* routine is even simpler. Here it is:

```
DWORD WINAPI ReaderThread (PVOID pArg) {
    HWND hWnd;
    int nGoCode, rc, i;
    TCHAR szText[TEXTSIZE];

    hWnd = (HWND)pArg;
    while (1) {
        nGoCode = WaitForSingleObject (g_hReadEvent, INFINITE);
        if (nGoCode == WAIT_OBJECT_0) {
            i = SendDlgItemMessage (hWnd, IDD_INTEXT, LB_ADDSTRING, 0,
                                    (LPARAM)g_pBuff->szText);
            SendDlgItemMessage (hWnd, IDD_INTEXT, LB_SETTOPINDEX, i, 0);

            InterlockedDecrement (&g_pBuff->nReadCnt);
            SetEvent (g_hReadDoneEvent);
        }
    }
    return 0;
}
```

The reader thread starts up and immediately blocks on *ReadEvent*. When it's unblocked, it adds the text from the shared buffer into the list box in its window. The list box is then scrolled to show the new line. After this is accomplished, the *nReadCnt* variable is decremented using *InterlockedDecrement* to be thread safe, and the *ReadDone* event is signaled to tell *SenderThread* to check the read count. After that's accomplished, the routine loops around and waits for another read event to occur.

Exception Handling

Windows CE .NET, along with eMbedded C++ 4.0, supports both Microsoft's standard structured exception handling extensions to the C language (the __*try*, __*except* and __*try*, __*finally* blocks) and the ANSI-standard C++ exception handling framework, with keywords such as *catch* and *throw*.

Windows exception handling is complex, and if I were to cover it completely, I could easily write another entire chapter. The following review introduces the concepts to non-Win32 programmers and conveys enough information about the subject for you to get your feet wet. If you want to wade all the way in, the best source for a complete explanation of Win32 exception handling is Jeffrey Richter's *Programming Applications for Windows*, 4th edition (Microsoft Press, 1999).

C++ Exception Handling

Support for C++ exception handling was added in Windows CE .NET 4.0. The statements, *try*, *catch*, and *throw* are familiar to C++ programmers and work as expected in Windows CE. To use C++ exception handling in a Windows CE C++ application, the application must be compiled with the −*GX* compiler switch. For those not familiar with the operation of these keywords, what follows is a quick introduction.

Using Exceptions to Report Errors

It's the vogue in programming circles these days to report errors in a function by throwing an exception. Using this scheme, a calling function that doesn't check for errors will have the exception automatically passed on to its calling function. If no function ever checks for the exception, the exception will be passed to the operating system, which will act appropriately on the offending application. Functions that simply report an error code in a return code can't enforce error checking because the lack of verification of the error code isn't automatically reported up the stack chain.

A simple example of the different methods of reporting errors is shown in the following code fragments. In the first code fragment, the failure of *LocalAlloc* in *AddItem* is reported by returning 0. Note how each call to *AddItem* has to be checked to see whether an error occurred in *AddItem*.

```
PMYITEM AddItem (PMYITEM pLast, DWORD dwData) {

    // Allocate the item
    PMYITEM p = (PMYITEM)LocalAlloc (LPTR, sizeof (MYITEM));
    if (p == 0)
        return 0;

    // Link the list
    p->pPrev = pLast;
    if (pLast)  pLast->pNext = p;
    p->dwData = dwData;
    return p;
}

int test (HWND hWnd) {
    PMYITEM pNext;

    pNext = AddItem (NULL, 1);
    if (pNext == NULL)
        return ERROR_CODE;

    pNext = AddItem (pNext, 2);
    if (pNext == NULL)
        return ERROR_CODE;

    pNext = AddItem (pNext, 3);
    if (pNext == NULL)
        return ERROR_CODE;
    return 0;
}
```

In the following code fragment, *AddItem* throws an exception if the memory allocation fails. Notice how much cleaner the calling routine *test1* looks.

```
PMYITEM AddItem (PMYITEM pLast, DWORD dwData) {

    // Allocate the item
    PMYITEM p = (PMYITEM)LocalAlloc (LPTR, sizeof (MYITEM));
    if (p == 0)
        throw ("failure to allocate item in AddItem");

    // Link the list
    p->pPrev = pLast;
    if (pLast)  pLast->pNext = p;
    p->dwData = dwData;
    return p;
}
```

```
int test1 (HWND hWnd) {
    PMYITEM pNext;

    try {
        pNext = AddItem (NULL, 1);
        pNext = AddItem (pNext, 2);
        pNext = AddItem (pNext, 3);
    }
    catch (char * strException) {
        return ERROR_CODE;
    }
    return 0;
}
```

The simple structure of the foregoing routines demonstrates the ease with which C++ exception handling can be added to an application. The *try* keyword wraps code that might generate an exception. The wrapped code includes any routines called from within the *try* block. If an exception is thrown with a string argument, the exception will be caught by the *catch* block in *test1*. What happens if some other exception is thrown? Let's look at the basics of the *try*, *catch*, and *throw* keywords to see.

The *try*, catch Block

The basic structure of the exception keywords is demonstrated in the following pseudocode.

```
try
{
    throw (arg of type_t);
}
catch (type_t arg)
{
    // catches all throws with argument of type_t
}
```

Within the *try* block, if an exception is thrown with an argument, the exception will be caught by the *catch* block that has the matching argument. If no *catch* block has a matching argument, the exception is passed to the function that called the code containing the *try* block. If no enclosing *try*, *catch* block is found, the thread is terminated. If no exception occurs within the *try* block, none of the associated *catch* blocks are executed.

For example

```
try
{
    throw (1);
}
```

would be caught if the *try* block had an associated *catch* block with an integer argument such as

```
catch (int nExceptionCode)
{
    // Exception caught!
}
```

The argument doesn't have to be a simple type; it can be a C++ class. It's also permissible to have multiple *catch* blocks each with a different argument string associated with the *try* block. *Catch* blocks are evaluated in the order they appear in the code. Finally, a *catch* block with ellipsis arguments catches all exceptions within the *try* block.

```
try
{
    throw (1);

    throw ("This is an ascii string");

    throw (CMyException cEx);
}
catch (int nExCode)
{
    // catches all throws with an integer argument
}
catch (char * szExCode)
{
    // catches all throws with a string argument
}
catch (CMyException cEx)
{
    // catches all throws with a CMyException class argument
}
catch (...)
{
    // catches all exceptions not caught above
}
```

Win32 Exception Handling

Windows CE has always supported the Win32 method of exception handling, using the __try, __except, and __finally keywords. What follows is a brief overview of these statements.

The __*try*, __*except* Block

The __*try*, __*except* block looks like this:

```
__try {

    // Try some code here that might cause an exception.

}
__except (exception filter) {

    // This code is depending on the filter on the except line.

}
```

Essentially, the *try-except* pair allows you the ability to anticipate exceptions and handle them locally instead of having Windows terminate the thread or the process because of an unhandled exception.

The exception filter is essentially a return code that tells Windows how to handle the exception. You can hard code one of the three possible values or call a function that dynamically decides how to respond to the exception.

If the filter returns *EXCEPTION_EXECUTE_HANDLER*, Windows aborts the execution in the *try* block and jumps to the first statement in the *except* block. This is helpful if you're expecting the exception and you know how to handle it. In the code that follows, the access to memory is protected by a __*try*, __*except* block.

```
BYTE ReadByteFromMemory (LPBYTE pPtr, BOOL *bDataValid) {
    BYTE ucData = 0;

    *bDataValid = TRUE;
    __try {
        ucData = *pPtr;
    }
    __except (DecideHowToHandleException ()) {
        // The pointer isn't valid; clean up.
        ucData = 0;
        *bDataValid = FALSE;
    }
    return ucData;
}
int DecideHowToHandleException (void) {
    return EXCEPTION_EXECUTE_HANDLER;
}
```

If the memory read line above wasn't protected by a __*try*, __*except* block and an invalid pointer was passed to the routine, the exception generated would have been passed up to the system, causing the thread and perhaps the process to be terminated. If you use the __try, __except block, the exception is handled locally and the process continues with the error handled locally.

Another possibility is to have the system retry the instruction that caused the exception. You can do this by having the filter return *EXCEPTION_CONTINUE_EXECUTION*. On the surface, this sounds like a great option—simply fix the problem and retry the operation your program was performing. The problem with this approach is that what will be retried isn't the *line* that caused the exception, but *the machine instruction* that caused the exception. The difference is illustrated by the following code fragment that looks okay but probably won't work:

```
// An example that doesn't work...
int DivideIt (int aVal, int bVal) {
    int cVal;
    __try {
        cVal = aVal / bVal;
    }
    __except (EXCEPTION_CONTINUE_EXECUTION) {
        bVal = 1;
    }
    return cVal;
}
```

The idea in this code is noble: protect the program from a divide-by-zero error by ensuring that if the error occurs, the error is corrected by replacing *bVal* with 1. The problem is that the line

```
cVal = aVal / bVal;
```

is probably compiled to something like the following on a MIPS-compatible CPU:

```
lw    t6,aVal(sp)    ;Load aVal
lw    t7,bVal(sp)    ;Load bVal
div   t6,t7          ;Perform the divide
sw    t6,cVal(sp)    ;Save result into cVal
```

In this case, the third instruction, the *div*, causes the exception. Restarting the code after the exception results in the restart beginning with the *div* instruction. The problem is that the execution needs to start at least one instruction earlier to load the new value from *bVal* into the register. The moral of the story is that attempting to restart code at the point of an exception requires knowledge of the specific machine instruction that caused the exception.

The third option for the exception filter is to not even attempt to solve the problem and to pass the exception up to the next, higher, __try, __except block in code. The exception filter returns *EXCEPTION_CONTINUE_SEARCH*.

Because __*try*, __*except* blocks can be nested, it's good practice to handle specific problems in a lower, nested, __*try*, __*except* block and more global errors at a higher level.

Determining the Problem

With these three options available, it would be nice if Windows let you in on why the exception occurred. Fortunately, Windows provides the function

```
DWORD GetExceptionCode (void);
```

This function returns a code that indicates why the exception occurred in the first place. The codes are defined in WINBASE.H and range from *EXCEPTION_ACCESS_VIOLATION* to *CONTROL_C_EXIT*, with a number of codes in between. Another function allows even more information:

```
LPEXCEPTION_POINTERS GetExceptionInformation (void);
```

GetExceptionInformation returns a pointer to a structure that contains pointers to two structures: *EXCEPTION_RECORD* and *CONTEXT*. *EXCEPTION_RECORD* is defined as

```
typedef struct _EXCEPTION_RECORD {
    DWORD ExceptionCode;
    DWORD ExceptionFlags;
    struct _EXCEPTION_RECORD *ExceptionRecord;
    PVOID ExceptionAddress;
    DWORD NumberParameters;
    DWORD ExceptionInformation[EXCEPTION_MAXIMUM_PARAMETERS];
} EXCEPTION_RECORD;
```

The fields in this structure go into explicit detail about why an exception occurred. To narrow the problem down even further, you can use the *CONTEXT* structure. The *CONTEXT* structure is different for each CPU and essentially defines the exact state of the CPU when the exception occurred.

There are limitations on when these two exception information functions can be called. *GetExceptionCode* can be called only from inside an *except* block or from within the exception filter function. The *GetExceptionInformation* function can be called only from within the exception filter function.

Generating Your Own Exceptions

There are times when an application might want to generate its own exceptions. The Win32 method for raising an exception is the function *RaiseException*, prototyped as follows:

```
void RaiseException (DWORD dwExceptionCode, DWORD dwExceptionFlags,
               DWORD nNumberOfArguments, const DWORD *lpArguments);
```

The first parameter is the exception code, which will be the value returned by *GetExceptionCode* from within the *__except* block. The codes understood by the system are the same codes defined for *GetExceptionCode*, discussed earlier. The *dwExceptionFlags* parameter can be *EXCEPTION_NONCONTINUABLE* to indicate that the exception can't be continued or 0 if the exception can be continued. The last two parameters, *nNumberOfArguments* and *lpArguments*, allow the thread to pass additional data to the exception handler. The data passed can be retrieved with the *GetExceptionInformation* function in the *__except* filter function.

The *__try*, *__finally* Block

Another tool of the structured exception handling features of the Win32 API is the *__try*, *__finally* block. It looks like this:

```
__try {

    // Do something here.

}
__finally {

    // This code is executed regardless of what happens in the try block.

}
```

The goal of the *__try*, *__finally* block is to provide a block of code, the *finally* block, that always executes regardless of how the other code in the *try* block attempts to leave the block. Unfortunately, the current Windows CE C compilers don't support leaving the *__try* block by a return or a *goto* statement. The Windows CE compilers do support the *__leave* statement that immediately exits the *__try* block and executes the *__finally* block, so there is some limited use of a *__try*, *__finally* block if only to avoid using a *goto* statement simply to jump to some common cleanup code.

In the preceding three chapters, I've covered the basics of the Windows CE kernel from memory to files to processes and threads. Now it's time to break from this low-level stuff and start looking outward. In the final chapter of this section, I'll cover the Windows CE notification API. The notification API frees applications from having to stay running in the background to monitor what is going on in the system. Let's take a look.

11

Notifications

One area in which Microsoft Windows CE exceeds the Windows XP API is the notification interface. Windows CE applications can register to be launched at a predetermined time or when any of a set of system events occur. Applications can also register a *user notification*. In a user notification, the system notifies the user at a specific time without the application itself being launched at that time.

The notification interface is based on only a handful of functions, the most important of which is *CeSetUserNotificationEx*. This omnibus function provides all the functionality to schedule any of the three types of notifications: user, system, and timer. *CeSetUserNotificationEx* replaced three separate functions—*CeSetUserNotification*, *CeRunAppAtEvent*, and *CeRunAppAtTime*—which essentially have slightly less functionality.

User Notifications

A Windows CE application can schedule the user to be notified at a given time using the *CeSetUserNotificationEx* function. When the time of the notification occurs, the system alerts the user by displaying a dialog box, playing a wave file, vibrating the device, or flashing an external LED. If the system was off at the time of the notification, Windows CE turns the system on. Because Windows CE systems have an automatic power-off feature, the system will quickly turn itself back on if the notification fires while the system is unattended. Figure 11-1 shows the alert bubble on a Pocket PC, while Figure 11-2 shows the notification dialog on an embedded Windows CE device.

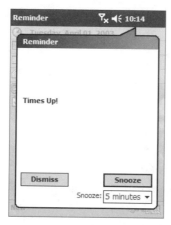

Figure 11-1   The alert bubble on a Pocket PC device

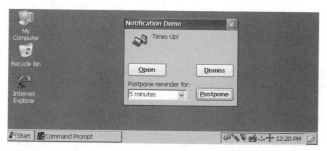

Figure 11-2   The notification dialog on an embedded Windows CE device

Windows CE also displays the icon of the application that set the notification on the taskbar. The user has the option of acknowledging the notification by clicking OK on the notification dialog box, pressing the Notify button on the system case (if one is present), or on some systems, tapping the application's taskbar annunciator icon, which launches the application that registered the notification. After a user notification has been set, you can modify it by making another call to *CeSetUserNotificationEx*.

Setting a User Notification

CeSetUserNotificationEx is prototyped as

```
HANDLE CeSetUserNotificationEx (HANDLE hNotification,
                                CE_NOTIFICATION_TRIGGER *pcnt,
                                CE_USER_NOTIFICATION *pceun);
```

The *hNotification* parameter is set to 0 to create a new notification. To modify a notification already registered, you should set *hNotification* to the handle of the notification that you want to modify.

The *CE_NOTIFICATION_TRIGGER* structure defines the type and detail of the notification being set. This structure is defined as

```
typedef struct UserNotificationTrigger {
    DWORD dwSize;
    DWORD dwType;
    DWORD dwEvent;
    WCHAR *lpszApplication;
    WCHAR *lpszArguments;
    SYSTEMTIME stStartTime;
    SYSTEMTIME stEndTime;
} CE_NOTIFICATION_TRIGGER, *PCE_NOTIFICATION_TRIGGER;
```

The first field should be set to the size of the structure. The second field, *dwType*, should be filled with a flag indicating the type of notification being set. For user notifications, set this field to either *CNT_PERIOD* or *CNT_TIME*. The *CNT_PERIOD* flag creates a notification that will dismiss itself after a set time, while a *CNT_TIME* notification will not dismiss itself without user action. For user notifications, the *dwEvent* field isn't used. I'll talk about that field when I discuss event notifications.

The next field, *lpszApplication*, specifies the application that will be launched if the user requests more detail from the notification. If the application is launched, its command line is specified by the next field, *lpszArguments*.

Another use for the *lpszApplication* field is to specify an event to be signaled when the notification fires. To specify an event, the field should be formatted as

```
\\.\Notifications\NamedEvents\<Event Name>
```

where *<Event Name>* is any name chosen for the event. Remember that when you specify this string in C, the backslash character must be replicated because it's used as the escape character. So to have a notification trigger an event named Bob, the string pointed to by the *lpszApplication* field would look like this:

```
TEXT ("\\\\.\\Notifications\\NamedEvents\\Bob")
```

To be notified using an event, an application must create a named event with the same name as <Event Name> by using the *CreateEvent* function and wait on the handle returned, as in

```
hEvent = CreateEvent (NULL, FALSE, FALSE, TEXT ("Bob"));
```

The final two fields, *stStartTime* and *stEndTime*, specify the starting time and ending time of the notice. The starting time, of course, is when the system first notifies the user by means of a number of different methods I'll talk about in a moment. You use the ending time only in a *CNT_PERIOD*-style user notification; the *CeSetUserNotificationEx* function ignores the ending time for *CNT_TIME* notifications. *stEndTime* designates the time the system is to remove the notice if the user doesn't acknowledge the notification. This time must be later than the starting time.

How the system notifies the user is specified by the third parameter of *CeSetUserNotificationEx*, which points to a *CE_USER_NOTIFICATION* structure. This structure is defined as

```
typedef struct UserNotificationType {
    DWORD ActionFlags;
    TCHAR *pwszDialogTitle;
    TCHAR *pwszDialogText;
    TCHAR *pwszSound;
    DWORD nMaxSound;
    DWORD dwReserved;
} CE_USER_NOTIFICATION;
```

The *ActionFlags* field of this structure contains a set of flags that define how the user is notified. The flags can be any combination of the following:

- **PUN_LED**   Flash the external LED.
- **PUN_VIBRATE**   Vibrate the device.
- **PUN_DIALOG**   Display a dialog box.
- **PUN_SOUND**   Play a wave file.
- **PUN_REPEAT**   Repeat the wave file for 10 to 15 seconds.

The fact that these flags are defined doesn't mean that all systems implement all these actions. Most Windows CE devices can't vibrate and a few don't even have an external LED. There isn't a defined method for determining the notification capabilities of a device, but as I'll presently show you, the system provides a dialog box that's customized by the OEM for the capabilities of each device.

The remainder of the fields in the structure depend on the flags set in the *ActionFlags* field. If the *PUN_DIALOG* flag is set, the *pwszDialogTitle* and *pwszDialogText* fields specify the title and text of the dialog that's displayed. For a Pocket PC device, the dialog text appears on the Alert dialog, but since the Pocket PC Alert doesn't use a caption bar, the dialog title text isn't used. The *pwszSound* field is loaded with the filename of a wave file to play if the *PUN_SOUND* flag is set. The *nMaxSound* field defines the size of the *pwszSound* field.

Configuring a User Notification

To give you a consistent user interface for choosing the method of notification, Windows CE provides a dialog box to query the user about how he wants to be notified. To display the user configuration dialog box, you call this function:

```
BOOL CeGetUserNotificationPreferences (HWND hWndParent,
                       PCE_USER_NOTIFICATION lpNotification);
```

This function takes two parameters—the window handle of the parent window for the dialog box and a pointer to a *CE_USER_NOTIFICATION* structure. You can initialize the *CE_USER_NOTIFICATION* structure with default settings for the dialog before *CeGetUserNotificationPreferences* is called. When the function returns, this structure is filled with the changes the user made. *CeGetUserNotificationPreferences* returns *TRUE* if the user clicked the OK button to accept the changes and *FALSE* if an error occurred or the user canceled the dialog box. Figure 11-3 shows the notification preferences dialog box opened through the *CeGetUserNotificationPreferences* function on a Pocket PC.

Figure 11-3   The dialog box opened by *CeGetUserNotificationPreferences* on a Pocket PC

This function gives you a convenient method for configuring user notifications. The dialog box lets you have check boxes for playing a sound, displaying another dialog box, and flashing the LED. It also contains a combo box that lists the available wave files that the user can choose from if he wants sound. The dialog box doesn't have fields to allow the user to specify the text or title of the dialog box if one is to be displayed. That text must be provided by the application.

Acknowledging a User Notification

A user notification can be cleared by the application before it times out by calling

```
BOOL CeClearUserNotification (HANDLE hNotification);
```

Once a user notification has occurred, it must be acknowledged by the user unless the user notification's end time has passed. The user can tap the Dismiss button on the notification dialog box or press the notification button on the Pocket PC case. Or the user can tap the Snooze button, which automatically reschedules the notification for a later time. On an H/PC or an embedded Windows CE system, the user can tap the Open button to launch the application specified when the notification was scheduled. An Open button isn't provided on the alert dialog on the current implementations of the Pocket PC.

If the user taps the Open button, the notification isn't automatically acknowledged. Instead, an application should programmatically acknowledge the notification by calling this function:

```
BOOL CeHandleAppNotifications (TCHAR *pwszAppName);
```

The one parameter is the name of the application that was launched because the user tapped the Open button. Calling this function removes the dialog box, stops the sound, turns off the flashing LED, and on systems with the Windows CE Explorer shell, removes the application's annunciator icon from the taskbar. This function doesn't affect any notifications that are scheduled but haven't fired.

When the system starts an application because of a notification, it passes a command line argument to indicate why the application was started. For a user notification, this argument is the command line string specified in the *lpszArguments* field of the *CE_NOTIFICATION_TRIGGER* structure. If you scheduled the notification using the *CNT_CLASSICTIME* flag, the command line is the predefined string constant *APP_RUN_TO_HANDLE_NOTIFICATION*. If the event notification method is specified, the application won't be started. Instead, an event of the specified name will be signaled.

As a general rule, an application started by a notification should first check to see whether another instance of the application is running. If so, the application should communicate to the first instance that the notification occurred and terminate. This saves memory because only one instance of the application is running. The following code fragment shows how this can be easily accomplished.

```
INT i;
HWND hWnd;
HANDLE hNotify;
```

```
TCHAR szText[128];
TCHAR szFileName[MAX_PATH];

if (*lpCmdLine) {
    pPtr = lpCmdLine;
    // Parse the first word of the command line.
    for (i = 0; i < dim(szText) && *lpCmdLine > TEXT (' '); i++)
        szText[i] = *pPtr++;
    szText[i] = TEXT ('\0');

    // Check to see if app started due to notification.
    if (lstrcmp (szText, TEXT("My Notification cmdline")) == 0) {
        // Acknowledge the notification.
        GetModuleFileName (hInst, szFileName, sizeof (szFileName));
        CeHandleAppNotifications (szFileName);

        // Get handle off the command line.
        hNotify = (HANDLE)_wtol (pPtr);

        // Look to see if another instance of the app is running.
        hWnd = FindWindow (NULL, szAppName);
        if (hWnd) {
            SendMessage (hWnd, MYMSG_TELLNOTIFY, 0, (LPARAM)hNotify);
            // This app should terminate here.
            return 0;
        }
    }
}
```

This code first looks to see whether a command line parameter exists and if so, whether the first word is the keyword indicating that the application was launched by the system in response to a user notification. If so, the notification is acknowledged and the application looks for an instance of the application already running, using *FindWindow*. If found, the routine sends an application-defined message to the main window of the first instance and terminates. Otherwise, the application can take actions necessary to respond to the user's tap of the Open button on the alert dialog.

Timer Event Notifications

To run an application at a given time without user intervention, use a *timer event notification*. To schedule a timer event notification, use *CeSetUserNotificationEx* just as you do for the user notification but pass a *NULL* value in the *pceun* parameter, as you see on the followjng page.

```
CE_NOTIFICATION_TRIGGER cnt;
TCHAR szArgs[] = TEXT ("This is a timer notification.");
TCHAR szExeName[MAX_PATH];

memset (&nt, 0, sizeof (CE_NOTIFICATION_TRIGGER));
nt.dwSize = sizeof (CE_NOTIFICATION_TRIGGER);
nt.dwType = CNT_TIME;
nt.lpszApplication = szExeName;
nt.lpszArguments = szArgs;
nt.stStartTime = st;
GetModuleFileName (hInst, szExeName, sizeof (szExeName));
hNotify = CeSetUserNotificationEx (0, &nt, NULL);
```

When the timer notification is activated, the system powers on, if currently off, and launches the application with a command line parameter specified in the *lpszArguments* field of the notification trigger structure. As with the user notification, if the application is started, it should check to see whether another instance of the application is running and pass the notification on if one is running. Also, an application should be careful about creating a window and taking control of the machine during a timer event. The user might object to having his game of solitaire interrupted by another application popping up because of a timer notification.

System Event Notifications

Sometimes, you might want an application to be automatically started. Windows CE supports a third type of notification, known as a *system event notification*. This notification starts an application when one of a set of system events occurs, such as after the system has completed synchronizing with its companion PC. To set a system event notification, you again use the omnibus *CeSetUserNotificationEx* function. This time, you specify the type of event you want to monitor in the *dwEvent* field of the notification trigger structure, as in

```
CE_NOTIFICATION_TRIGGER nt;
TCHAR szExeName[MAX_PATH];
TCHAR szArgs[128] = TEXT("This is my event notification string.");

memset (&nt, 0, sizeof (CE_NOTIFICATION_TRIGGER));
nt.dwSize = sizeof (CE_NOTIFICATION_TRIGGER);
nt.dwType = CNT_EVENT;
nt.dwEvent = dwMyEventFlags;
nt.lpszApplication = szExeName;
nt.lpszArguments = szArgs;
GetModuleFileName (hInst, szExeName, sizeof (szExeName));
CeSetUserNotificationEx (0, &nt, NULL);
```

The event flags are the following:

- **_NOTIFICATION_EVENT_SYNC_END_**   Notify when sync complete.

- **_NOTIFICATION_EVENT_DEVICE_CHANGE_**   Notify when a device driver is loaded or unloaded.

- **_NOTIFICATION_EVENT_RS232_DETECTED_**   Notify when an RS232 connection is detected.

- **_NOTIFICATION_EVENT_TIME_CHANGE_**   Notify when the system time is changed.

- **_NOTIFICATION_EVENT_TZ_CHANGE_**   Notify when time zone is changed.[1]

- **_NOTIFICATION_EVENT_RESTORE_END_**   Notify when a device restore is complete.

- **_NOTIFICATION_EVENT_WAKEUP_**   Notify when a device wakes up.

For each of these events, the application is launched with a specific command line parameter indicating why the application was launched. In the case of a device change notification, the specified command line string is followed by either */ADD* or */REMOVE* and the name of the device being added or removed. For example, if the user inserts a modem card, the command line for the notification would look like this:

```
My event command line string /ADD COM3:
```

A number of additional system events are defined in Notify.h, but OEMs must provide support for these additional notifications and at this point few, if any, of the additional notification events are supported.

Once an application has registered for a system event notification, Windows CE will start or signal the application again if the event that caused the notification is repeated.

Clearing out system event notifications is best done with what might be thought of as an obsolete function, the old *CeRunAppAtEvent* function, prototyped as

```
BOOL CeRunAppAtEvent (TCHAR *pwszAppName, LONG lWhichEvent);
```

The parameters are the application to run and the event flag for the event of which you want to be notified. While the function has been superseded by

---

1. The *NOTIFICATION_EVENT_TZ_CHANGE* notification flag isn't supported on some Pocket PCs.

CeSetUserNotificationEx, it does still have one use—clearing out all the system notifications for a specific application. If you pass your application name along with the flag *NOTIFICATION_EVENT_NONE* in the *lWhichEvent* parameter, Windows CE clears out all event notifications assigned to that application. While you would think you could pass the same flag to *CeSetUserNotificationEx* to clear out the events, it doesn't unless you pass the original handle returned by that function when you originally scheduled the notification.

The Note Demo Example Program

The following program, NoteDemo, demonstrates each of the notification functions that allow you to set user notifications, system notifications, and timer notifications. The program presents a simple dialog box equipped with five buttons. The first two buttons allow you to configure and set a user notification. The second two buttons let you set system and timer notifications. The last button clears out all the notifications you might have set using NoteDemo. The gap above the buttons is filled with the command line, if any, that was passed when the application started. That space also displays a message when another instance of NoteDemo starts because of a user notification. Figure 11-4 shows two Note-Demo windows. The one in the foreground was launched because of a user notification, with the command-line parameter, "This is my user notification string."

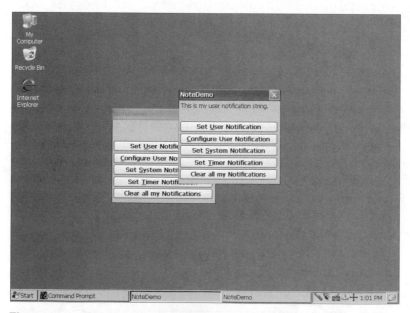

Figure 11-4 The NoteDemo window

The source code for NoteDemo appears in Listing 11-1. The notification code is confined to the button handler routines. The code is fairly simple: for each type of notification, the appropriate Windows CE function is called. When asked to configure a user notification, the application calls *CeGetUserNotificationPreferences*. The program gives you one additional dialog box with which to configure the system notifications.

```
NoteDemo.rc
//======================================================================
// Resource file
//
// Written for the book Programming Windows CE
// Copyright (C) 2003 Douglas Boling
//======================================================================
#include "windows.h"
#include "NoteDemo.h"                          // Program-specific stuff


//----------------------------------------------------------------------
// Icons and bitmaps
//
ID_ICON ICON   "NoteDemo.ico"                  // Program icon


//----------------------------------------------------------------------
// Main window dialog template
//
NoteDemo DIALOG discardable  25, 5, 120,  98
STYLE  WS_OVERLAPPED | WS_VISIBLE | WS_CAPTION | WS_SYSMENU |
       DS_CENTER | DS_MODALFRAME
CAPTION "NoteDemo"
BEGIN
    LTEXT "",              IDD_OUTPUT,   2,   2, 115,  21
     PUSHBUTTON "Set &User Notification",
                           IDD_ADDUSERNOT,  2, 25, 115, 12, WS_TABSTOP
    PUSHBUTTON "&Configure User Notification",
                           IDD_CFGUSERNOT,  2, 39, 115, 12, WS_TABSTOP

    PUSHBUTTON "Set &System Notification",
                           IDD_ADDSYSNOT,   2, 53, 115, 12, WS_TABSTOP
    PUSHBUTTON "Set &Timer Notification",
                           IDD_ADDTIMENOT,  2, 67, 115, 12, WS_TABSTOP
    PUSHBUTTON "Clear all my Notifications",
                           IDD_CLEARNOT,    2, 81, 115, 12, WS_TABSTOP
END
//----------------------------------------------------------------------
// Set system event notification dialog box dialog template.
//
```

(continued)

Listing 11-1 The NoteDemo program

Listing 11-1 *(continued)*

```
SysNotifyConfig DIALOG DISCARDABLE  0, 0, 130, 89
STYLE DS_MODALFRAME | WS_POPUP | WS_CAPTION | WS_SYSMENU
EXSTYLE WS_EX_CAPTIONOKBTN
CAPTION "Notify On..."
BEGIN
    AUTOCHECKBOX "Sync End",            IDC_SYNC_END,    7,  5, 121,  10,
                                        WS_TABSTOP
    AUTOCHECKBOX "Device Change",IDC_DEVICE_CHANGE,  7, 17, 121,  10,
                                        WS_TABSTOP
    AUTOCHECKBOX "Serial Connection Detected",
                                IDC_SERIAL_DETECT,  7, 29, 121,  10,
                                        WS_TABSTOP
    AUTOCHECKBOX "System Time Change",
                                IDC_TIME_CHANGE,    7, 41, 121,  10,
                                        WS_TABSTOP
    AUTOCHECKBOX "Restore End",     IDC_RESTORE_END, 7, 53, 121,  10,
                                        WS_TABSTOP
    AUTOCHECKBOX "System Wake Up",    IDC_POWER_UP,  7, 65, 121,  10,
                                        WS_TABSTOP
    AUTOCHECKBOX "Time Zone Change", IDC_TZ_CHANGE,  7, 77, 121,  10,
                                        WS_TABSTOP

END
```

NoteDemo.h

```
//=====================================================================
// Header file
//
// Written for the book Programming Windows CE
// Copyright (C) 2003 Douglas Boling
//=====================================================================
// Returns number of elements
#define dim(x) (sizeof(x) / sizeof(x[0]))


//---------------------------------------------------------------------
// Generic defines and data types
//
struct decodeUINT {                             // Structure associates
    UINT Code;                                  // messages
                                                // with a function.
    BOOL (*Fxn)(HWND, UINT, WPARAM, LPARAM);
};
struct decodeCMD {                              // Structure associates
    UINT Code;                                  // menu IDs with a
    LRESULT (*Fxn)(HWND, WORD, HWND, WORD);     // function.
};
```

```
// Define function not supported under Windows CE.
#ifndef IsDlgButtonChecked
#define IsDlgButtonChecked(a, b)\
                        SendDlgItemMessage (a, b, BM_GETCHECK, 0, 0)
#endif
//----------------------------------------------------------------------
// Generic defines used by application

#define   ID_ICON              1

#define   IDD_ADDUSERNOT      10                      // Control IDs
#define   IDD_CFGUSERNOT      11
#define   IDD_ADDSYSNOT       12
#define   IDD_ADDTIMENOT      13
#define   IDD_OUTPUT          14
#define   IDD_CLEARNOT        15


#define   IDC_SYNC_END        20
#define   IDC_DEVICE_CHANGE   21
#define   IDC_SERIAL_DETECT   22
#define   IDC_TIME_CHANGE     23
#define   IDC_RESTORE_END     24
#define   IDC_POWER_UP        25
#define   IDC_TZ_CHANGE       26


#define MYMSG_TELLNOTIFY     (WM_USER + 100)


//----------------------------------------------------------------------
// Function prototypes
//
void Add2List (HWND hWnd, LPTSTR lpszFormat, ...);
// Window procedures
BOOL CALLBACK MainDlgProc (HWND, UINT, WPARAM, LPARAM);
BOOL CALLBACK SetEventNotifyDlgProc (HWND, UINT, WPARAM, LPARAM);


// Message handlers
BOOL DoInitDialogMain (HWND, UINT, WPARAM, LPARAM);
BOOL DoCommandMain (HWND, UINT, WPARAM, LPARAM);
BOOL DoTellNotifyMain (HWND, UINT, WPARAM, LPARAM);


// Command functions
LPARAM DoMainCommandExit (HWND, WORD, HWND, WORD);
LPARAM DoMainCommandAddUserNotification (HWND, WORD, HWND, WORD);
LPARAM DoMainCommandConfigUserNotification (HWND, WORD, HWND, WORD);
LPARAM DoMainCommandAddSysNotification (HWND, WORD, HWND, WORD);
LPARAM DoMainCommandAddTimerNotification (HWND, WORD, HWND, WORD);
LPARAM DoMainCommandClearNotifications (HWND, WORD, HWND, WORD);
// Thread prototype
DWORD WINAPI MonitorThread (PVOID pArg);
```

(continued)

Listing 11-1 *(continued)*

NoteDemo.cpp

```cpp
//======================================================================
// NoteDemo - Demonstrates the Windows CE Notification API
//
// Written for the book Programming Windows CE
// Copyright (C) 2003 Douglas Boling
//======================================================================
#include <windows.h>                    // For all that Windows stuff
#include <notify.h>                     // For notification defines
#include "NoteDemo.h"                   // Program-specific stuff


//----------------------------------------------------------------------
// Global data
//
const TCHAR szAppName[] = TEXT ("NoteDemo");
HINSTANCE hInst;                        // Program instance handle
HWND g_hMain;


CE_USER_NOTIFICATION g_ceun;            // User notification structure
TCHAR szDlgTitle[] = TEXT ("Notification Demo");
TCHAR szDlgText[] = TEXT ("Times Up!");
TCHAR szSound[MAX_PATH] = TEXT ("alarm1.wav");

// Used for timer event notification
TCHAR szEventName[] = TEXT ("Bob");


HANDLE g_hNoteEvent = 0;
BOOL g_fContinue = TRUE;

// Message dispatch table for MainWindowProc
const struct decodeUINT MainMessages[] = {
    WM_INITDIALOG, DoInitDialogMain,
    WM_COMMAND, DoCommandMain,
    MYMSG_TELLNOTIFY, DoTellNotifyMain,
};
// Command Message dispatch for MainWindowProc
const struct decodeCMD MainCommandItems[] = {
    IDOK, DoMainCommandExit,
    IDCANCEL, DoMainCommandExit,
    IDD_ADDUSERNOT, DoMainCommandAddUserNotification,
    IDD_CFGUSERNOT, DoMainCommandConfigUserNotification,
    IDD_ADDSYSNOT, DoMainCommandAddSysNotification,
    IDD_ADDTIMENOT, DoMainCommandAddTimerNotification,
    IDD_CLEARNOT, DoMainCommandClearNotifications,
};
//======================================================================
// Program entry point
//
```

```
int WINAPI WinMain (HINSTANCE hInstance, HINSTANCE hPrevInstance,
                    LPWSTR lpCmdLine, int nCmdShow) {
    INT i;
    TCHAR szText[MAX_PATH];
    WCHAR *pPtr;
    HANDLE hNotify;
    HWND hWnd;
    HANDLE hThread;

    hInst = hInstance;

    if (*lpCmdLine) {
        pPtr = lpCmdLine;
        // Parse the first word of the command line.
        for (i = 0; (i < dim(szText)-1) && (*pPtr > TEXT (' ')); i++)
            szText[i] = *pPtr++;
        szText[i] = TEXT ('\0');

        // Check to see if app started due to notification.
        if (lstrcmp (szText, APP_RUN_TO_HANDLE_NOTIFICATION) == 0) {
            // Acknowledge the notification.
            GetModuleFileName (hInst, szText, sizeof (szText));
            CeHandleAppNotifications (szText);

            // Get handle of command line.
            hNotify = (HANDLE)_wtol (pPtr);

            // Look to see if another instance of the app is running.
            hWnd = FindWindow (NULL, szAppName);
            if (hWnd) {
                SendMessage (hWnd, MYMSG_TELLNOTIFY, 0,
                             (LPARAM)hNotify);
                // I should terminate this app here, but I don't so you
                // can see what happens.
                return 0;
            }
        }
    }
    // Do a little initialization of CE_USER_NOTIFICATION.
    memset (&g_ceun, 0, sizeof (g_ceun));
    g_ceun.ActionFlags = PUN_DIALOG;
    g_ceun.pwszDialogTitle = szDlgTitle;
    g_ceun.pwszDialogText = szDlgText;
    g_ceun.pwszSound = szSound;
    g_ceun.nMaxSound = sizeof (szSound);

    // Create secondary thread for timer event notification.
    g_hNoteEvent = CreateEvent (NULL, FALSE, FALSE, szEventName);
```

(continued)

Listing 11-1   *(continued)*

```
    hThread = CreateThread (NULL, 0, MonitorThread, hWnd, 0, (DWORD *)&i);
    if (hThread == 0)
        return -1;

    // Display dialog box as main window.
    DialogBoxParam (hInstance, szAppName, NULL, MainDlgProc,
                    (LPARAM)lpCmdLine);
    // Signal notification thread to terminate
    g_fContinue = FALSE;
    SetEvent (g_hNoteEvent);
    WaitForSingleObject (hThread, 1000);
    CloseHandle (hThread);
    CloseHandle (g_hNoteEvent);
    return 0;

}
//======================================================================
// Message handling procedures for main window
//----------------------------------------------------------------------
// MainDlgProc - Callback function for application window
//
BOOL CALLBACK MainDlgProc (HWND hWnd, UINT wMsg, WPARAM wParam,
                           LPARAM lParam) {
    INT i;
    //
    // Search message list to see if we need to handle this
    // message. If in list, call procedure.
    //
    for (i = 0; i < dim(MainMessages); i++) {
        if (wMsg == MainMessages[i].Code)
            return (*MainMessages[i].Fxn)(hWnd, wMsg, wParam, lParam);
    }
    return FALSE;
}
//----------------------------------------------------------------------
// DoInitDialogMain - Process WM_INITDIALOG message for window.
//
BOOL DoInitDialogMain (HWND hWnd, UINT wMsg, WPARAM wParam,
                       LPARAM lParam) {

    g_hMain = hWnd;
    if (*(LPTSTR)lParam)
        Add2List (hWnd, (LPTSTR)lParam);
    return FALSE;
}
//----------------------------------------------------------------------
// DoCommandMain - Process WM_COMMAND message for window.
//
```

```
BOOL DoCommandMain (HWND hWnd, UINT wMsg, WPARAM wParam, LPARAM lParam){
    WORD idItem, wNotifyCode;
    HWND hwndCtl;
    INT  i;

    // Parse the parameters.
    idItem = (WORD) LOWORD (wParam);
    wNotifyCode = (WORD) HIWORD (wParam);
    hwndCtl = (HWND) lParam;

    // Call routine to handle control message.
    for (i = 0; i < dim(MainCommandItems); i++) {
        if (idItem == MainCommandItems[i].Code) {
            (*MainCommandItems[i].Fxn)(hWnd, idItem, hwndCtl,
                                       wNotifyCode);

            return TRUE;
        }
    }
    return FALSE;
}
//------------------------------------------------------------------------
// DoTellNotifyMain - Process MYMSG_TELLNOTIFY message for window.
//
BOOL DoTellNotifyMain (HWND hWnd, UINT wMsg, WPARAM wParam,
                       LPARAM lParam) {
    Add2List (hWnd, TEXT ("Notification %d reported"), lParam);
    SetForegroundWindow ((HWND)((DWORD)hWnd | 0x01));
    return 0;
}
//========================================================================
// Command handler routines
//------------------------------------------------------------------------
// DoMainCommandExit - Process Program Exit command.
//
LPARAM DoMainCommandExit (HWND hWnd, WORD idItem, HWND hwndCtl,
                          WORD wNotifyCode) {
    EndDialog (hWnd, 0);
    return 0;
}
//------------------------------------------------------------------------
// DoMainCommandAddUserNotification - Process Add User Notify button.
//
LPARAM DoMainCommandAddUserNotification (HWND hWnd, WORD idItem,
                                         HWND hwndCtl, WORD wNotifyCode) {
    SYSTEMTIME st, ste;
    TCHAR szExeName[MAX_PATH], szText[128];
    TCHAR szArgs[128] = TEXT("This is my user notification string.");
    CE_NOTIFICATION_TRIGGER nt;
```

(continued)

Listing 11-1   *(continued)*

```
    HANDLE hNotify;

    // Initialize time structure with local time.
    GetLocalTime (&st);
    // Do a trivial amount of error checking.
    st.wMinute++;
    if (st.wMinute > 59) {
        st.wHour++;
        st.wMinute -= 60;
    }

    // Set end time 10 minutes past start.
    ste = st;
    // Do a trivial amount of error checking.
    ste.wMinute += 10;
    if (ste.wMinute > 59) {
        ste.wHour++;
        ste.wMinute -= 60;
    }

    memset (&nt, 0, sizeof (CE_NOTIFICATION_TRIGGER));
    nt.dwSize = sizeof (CE_NOTIFICATION_TRIGGER);
    nt.dwType = CNT_PERIOD;
    nt.lpszApplication = szExeName;
    nt.lpszArguments = szArgs;
    nt.stStartTime = st;
    nt.stEndTime = ste;
    GetModuleFileName (hInst, szExeName, sizeof (szExeName));

    hNotify = CeSetUserNotificationEx (0, &nt, &g_ceun);
    // Tell the user the notification was set.
    if (hNotify)
        wsprintf (szText, TEXT ("User notification set for %d:%02d:%02d"),
                  st.wHour, st.wMinute, st.wSecond);
    else
        wsprintf (szText, TEXT ("User notification failed. rc = %d"),
                  GetLastError());

    MessageBox (hWnd, szText, szAppName, MB_OK);
    return 0;
}
//-----------------------------------------------------------------------
// DoMainCommandConfigUserNotification - Process Config user
// notification button.
//
LPARAM DoMainCommandConfigUserNotification (HWND hWnd, WORD idItem,
                                            HWND hwndCtl, WORD wNotifyCode) {
```

```
    // Display the system-provided configuration dialog.
    CeGetUserNotificationPreferences (hWnd, &g_ceun);
    return 0;
}
//-----------------------------------------------------------------------
//  DoMainCommandAddSysNotification - Process Add Sys notify button.
//
LPARAM DoMainCommandAddSysNotification (HWND hWnd, WORD idItem,
                                        HWND hwndCtl, WORD wNotifyCode) {

    DialogBox (hInst, TEXT ("SysNotifyConfig"), hWnd,
               SetEventNotifyDlgProc);
    return 0;
}
//-----------------------------------------------------------------------
// DoMainCommandAddTimerNotification - Process add timer notify button.
//
LPARAM DoMainCommandAddTimerNotification (HWND hWnd, WORD idItem,
                                          HWND hwndCtl, WORD wNotifyCode) {
    SYSTEMTIME st;
    HANDLE hNotify;
    CE_NOTIFICATION_TRIGGER nt;
    TCHAR szExeName[MAX_PATH], szText[128];
    TCHAR szArgs[128] = TEXT("This is my timer notification string.");

    // Initialize time structure with local time.
    GetLocalTime (&st);
    // Do a trivial amount of error checking.
    if (st.wMinute == 59) {
        st.wHour++;
        st.wMinute = 0;
    } else
        st.wMinute++;

    memset (&nt, 0, sizeof (CE_NOTIFICATION_TRIGGER));
    nt.dwSize = sizeof (CE_NOTIFICATION_TRIGGER);
    nt.dwType = CNT_TIME;
    nt.lpszApplication = szExeName;
    nt.lpszArguments = szArgs;
    nt.stStartTime = st;

    lstrcpy (szExeName, NAMED_EVENT_PREFIX_TEXT);
    lstrcat (szExeName, szEventName);
    // Set the notification.
    hNotify = CeSetUserNotificationEx (0, &nt, NULL);
    if (hNotify)
        wsprintf (szText, TEXT ("Timer notification set for %d:%02d:%02d"),
                  st.wHour, st.wMinute, st.wSecond);
```

(continued)

Listing 11-1   *(continued)*

```
    else
        wsprintf (szText, TEXT ("Timer notification failed. rc = %d"),
                  GetLastError());
    MessageBox (hWnd, szText, szAppName, MB_OK);
    return 0;
}
//--------------------------------------------------------------------
// DoMainCommandClearNotifications - Clear all notifications pointing
// to this application.  Note: this is a fairly large stack frame.
//
LPARAM DoMainCommandClearNotifications (HWND hWnd, WORD idItem,
                                        HWND hwndCtl, WORD wNotifyCode) {
    PBYTE pBuff = NULL;
    PCE_NOTIFICATION_INFO_HEADER pnih;
    HANDLE hNotHandles[128];  // Assume this is large enough.
    int rc, nCnt = 0;
    TCHAR szExeName[MAX_PATH], szText[128];
    DWORD i, dwSize, nHandCnt = 0;

    // Get our filename.
    GetModuleFileName (hInst, szExeName, sizeof (szExeName));

    pBuff = (PBYTE)LocalAlloc (LPTR, 8192);
    if (!pBuff) {
        MessageBox (hWnd, TEXT ("Out of memory"), szAppName, MB_OK);
        return 0;
    }
    rc = CeGetUserNotificationHandles (hNotHandles, dim (hNotHandles),
                                       &nHandCnt);
    if (rc) {
        for (i = 0; i < nHandCnt; i++) {
            // Query info on a single handle.
            rc = CeGetUserNotification (hNotHandles[i], 8192,
                                        &dwSize, pBuff);
            if (rc) {
                pnih = (PCE_NOTIFICATION_INFO_HEADER)pBuff;
                if (!lstrcmp (pnih->pcent->lpszApplication, szExeName)){
                    if (CeClearUserNotification (pnih->hNotification))
                        nCnt++;
                }
            }
        }
        wsprintf (szText, TEXT ("Cleared %d notifications"), nCnt);
        MessageBox (hWnd, szText, szAppName, MB_OK);
    } else
        MessageBox (hWnd, TEXT ("Could not query handles"),
```

```
                                    szAppName, MB_OK);
    LocalFree (pBuff);
    return 0;
}
//----------------------------------------------------------------------
// MySetEventNotification  - Sets event notifications
//
int MySetEventNotification (HWND hWnd, DWORD dwEvent) {
    TCHAR szArgs[] = TEXT("This is my event notification string.");
    CE_NOTIFICATION_TRIGGER nt;
    HANDLE hNotify;
    TCHAR szExeName[MAX_PATH], szText[128];

    memset (&nt, 0, sizeof (CE_NOTIFICATION_TRIGGER));
    nt.dwSize = sizeof (CE_NOTIFICATION_TRIGGER);
    nt.dwType = CNT_EVENT;
    nt.dwEvent = dwEvent;
    nt.lpszApplication = szExeName;
    nt.lpszArguments = szArgs;
    GetModuleFileName (hInst, szExeName, sizeof (szExeName));

    // Set the notification.
    hNotify = CeSetUserNotificationEx (0, &nt, NULL);
    if (hNotify)
        wsprintf (szText, TEXT ("Event notification set for %08x"),
                  dwEvent);
    else
        wsprintf (szText, TEXT("Set Event notification failed rc: %d"),
                  GetLastError());
    MessageBox (hWnd, szText, szAppName, MB_OK);
    return 0;
}
//----------------------------------------------------------------------
// Add2List - Add string to the report list box.
//
void Add2List (HWND hWnd, LPTSTR lpszFormat, ...) {
    int i, nBuf;
    TCHAR szBuffer[512];

    va_list args;
    va_start(args, lpszFormat);

    nBuf = _vstprintf(szBuffer, lpszFormat, args);
    i = SendDlgItemMessage (hWnd, IDD_OUTPUT, WM_SETTEXT, 0,
                            (LPARAM)(LPCTSTR)szBuffer);
    va_end(args);
}
```

(continued)

Listing 11-1 *(continued)*

```
//=======================================================================
// SetEventNotifyDlgProc - Callback function for Event dialog box
//
BOOL CALLBACK SetEventNotifyDlgProc (HWND hWnd, UINT wMsg,
                                     WPARAM wParam, LPARAM lParam) {
    DWORD dwEvent;

    switch (wMsg) {
    case WM_COMMAND:
        {
            WORD idItem = LOWORD (wParam);
            switch (idItem) {
            case IDOK:
                dwEvent = 0;

                // IsDlgButtonChecked isn't defined in Win CE, so
                // a macro has been defined.
                if (IsDlgButtonChecked (hWnd, IDC_SYNC_END) == 1)
                    dwEvent |= NOTIFICATION_EVENT_SYNC_END;

                if (IsDlgButtonChecked (hWnd, IDC_SERIAL_DETECT) == 1)
                    dwEvent |= NOTIFICATION_EVENT_RS232_DETECTED;

                if (IsDlgButtonChecked (hWnd, IDC_DEVICE_CHANGE) == 1)
                    dwEvent |= NOTIFICATION_EVENT_DEVICE_CHANGE;

                if (IsDlgButtonChecked (hWnd, IDC_TIME_CHANGE) == 1)
                    dwEvent |= NOTIFICATION_EVENT_TIME_CHANGE;

                if (IsDlgButtonChecked (hWnd, IDC_RESTORE_END) == 1)
                    dwEvent |= NOTIFICATION_EVENT_RESTORE_END;

                if (IsDlgButtonChecked (hWnd, IDC_POWER_UP) == 1)
                    dwEvent |= NOTIFICATION_EVENT_WAKEUP;

                if (IsDlgButtonChecked (hWnd, IDC_TZ_CHANGE) == 1)
                    dwEvent |= NOTIFICATION_EVENT_TZ_CHANGE;

                // Call my set event notification function above.
                MySetEventNotification (hWnd, dwEvent);
                EndDialog (hWnd, 1);
                return TRUE;

            case IDCANCEL:
                EndDialog (hWnd, 0);
                return TRUE;
            }
```

```
        }
        break;
    }
    return FALSE;
}
//============================================================================
// MonitorThread - Monitors event for timer notificaiton
//
DWORD WINAPI MonitorThread (PVOID pArg) {
    int rc;

    while (g_fContinue) {
        rc = WaitForSingleObject (g_hNoteEvent, INFINITE);
        if (!g_fContinue)
            break;
        if (rc == WAIT_OBJECT_0)
            SendMessage (g_hMain, MYMSG_TELLNOTIFY, 0, (LPARAM)g_hNoteEvent);
        else
            break;
    }
    return 0;
}
```

When NoteDemo starts, it examines the command line to determine whether it was started by a user notification. If so, the program attempts to find another instance of the application already running. If the program finds one, a message is sent to the first instance, informing it of the user notification. Because this is an example program, the second instance doesn't terminate itself as it would if it were a commercial application.

The timer notification uses a named event as its signal instead of launching a second copy of the application. To monitor the event, NoteDemo creates a second thread before the main window is created. This routine, *Monitor-Thread*, simply waits on the event handle that was created for the timer notification. When NoteDemo terminates, it sets a quit flag for the thread and signals the event itself. This causes *MonitorThread* to terminate.

The last button that clears all the notifications scheduled for the Note-Demo application has an interesting task. How does it know what is scheduled? Does it keep a record of every notification it has scheduled? Fortunately, that's not necessary. NoteDemo simply queries the notifications scheduled for all applications, finds the ones for itself, and clears them. Let's see how that's done.

Querying Scheduled Notifications

While scheduling the different notifications is often all that applications need, additional functions allow applications to query the notifications currently scheduled in the system. Here's the function that queries the notifications:

```
BOOL CeGetUserNotificationHandles (HANDLE *rghNotifications,
                         DWORD cHandles, LPDWORD pcHandlesNeeded);
```

This function returns an array filled with handles to all notifications currently scheduled in the system. The first parameter is the pointer to a handle array. The second parameter, *cHandles*, should be filled with the number of entries in the array. The third parameter should contain the address of a *DWORD* that will be filled with the number of entries in the array filled with valid notification handles.

If the array is large enough to hold all the handles, the function returns *TRUE* and provides the number of handles returned in the variable pointed to by *pcHandlesNeeded*. If the array is too small, the function fails. You can query the number of handles the system will return by passing *NULL* in the *rghNotifications* parameter and 0 in the *cHandles* parameter. The function will then return the number of handles in the variable pointed to by *pcHandlesNeeded*.

After you have queried all the handles, you can determine the details of each notification by passing each handle to the function:

```
BOOL CeGetUserNotification (HANDLE hNotification, DWORD cBufferSize,
                   LPDWORD pcBytesNeeded, LPBYTE pBuffer);
```

The first parameter is the handle to the notification in which you're interested. The second parameter is the size of the buffer you're providing the function to return the data about the notification. The third parameter is the address of a *DWORD* that will receive the size of the data returned. The final parameter is the address of a buffer that will receive the details about the notification.

The size of the required buffer changes depending on the notification. The buffer begins with a *CE_NOTIFICATION_INFO_HEADER* structure. The buffer also contains a *CE_NOTIFICATION_TRIGGER* structure and, depending on the type of notification, an optional *CE_USER_NOTIFICATION* structure. Because these structures contain pointers to strings for application names and command lines, these strings must also be stored in the buffer.

To determine how big the buffer needs to be, you can call *CeGetUserNotification* with *cBufferSize* set to 0 and *pBuffer* set to *NULL*. The function returns the number of bytes required by the buffer in the variable that *pcBytesNeeded* points to. However, calling the function this way takes just as much time as retrieving the data itself, so it would be better to assume a size for the buffer and call the function. Only if the call fails because the buffer is too small do you then reallocate the buffer so that it's large enough to hold the data.

Now on to the data returned. The *CE_NOTIFICATION_INFO_HEADER* structure is defined this way:

```
typedef struct UserNotificationInfoHeader {
    HANDLE hNotification;
    DWORD dwStatus;
    CE_NOTIFICATION_TRIGGER   *pcent;
    CE_USER_NOTIFICATION   *pceun;
} CE_NOTIFICATION_INFO_HEADER;
```

The first field is the handle of the event you are querying. The second field contains the status of the notification. This field contains 0 if the notification hasn't fired or *CNS_SIGNALLED* if it has. The next two fields are pointers to the same structures discussed earlier in the chapter. The pointer to the *CE_NOTIFICATION_TRIGGER* structure points to an address in the buffer in which that structure is defined. Depending on the type of notification, the pointer to the *CE_USER_NOTIFICATION* structure could be *NULL*.

The combination of the two structures, *CE_NOTIFICATION_TRIGGER* and *CE_USER_NOTIFICATION* along with the status flag, completely describes the notification. By examining the trigger structure, you can determine the application that's scheduled to run as a result of the notification, its command line, and of course, the type of notification itself.

The Notification API is a handy way to monitor events in a Windows CE system. The ability to have the operating system launch your application instead of having to lurk around in memory waiting for the event significantly reduces the memory requirements for a well-designed system. User notifications give you a convenient and uniform way to alert the user of events that need attention.

Now that we've looked at the Notification API, we've covered the basics of Windows CE applications. The next section of this book turns from the basics to one of the more important areas of Windows CE applications, communication. This next section covers everything from basic serial communication to networking, both wired and wireless.

Part III
Communications

12

Serial Communications

If there's one area of the Win32 API that Windows CE doesn't skimp, it's in communication. It makes sense. Either systems running Windows CE are mobile, requiring extensive communication functionality, or they're devices generally employed to communicate with remote servers or as remote servers. In this chapter, I introduce the low-level serial communication APIs.

Talking to a serial port involves opening and conversing with a serial device driver. Talking to a device driver isn't a complicated process. In fact, in the tradition of most modern operating systems, applications in Windows CE access device drivers through the file system API, using functions such as *CreateFile*, *ReadFile*, *WriteFile*, and *CloseHandle*. In addition, there are times, and the serial driver occasions one of those times, when an application needs to talk to the device, not just send data through the device. To do this, use the *DeviceIoControl* function. We'll use all these functions in this chapter.

Basic Serial Communication

The interface for a serial device is a combination of generic driver I/O calls and specific communication-related functions. The serial device is treated as a generic, installable stream device for opening, closing, reading from, and writing to the serial port. For configuring the port, the Win32 API supports a set of Comm functions. Windows CE supports most of the Comm functions supported by Windows XP.

A word of warning: programming a serial port under Windows CE isn't like programming one under MS-DOS. You can't simply find the base address of the serial port and program the registers directly. While there are ways for a program to gain access to the physical memory space, every Windows CE device has a different physical memory map. Even if you solved the access problem by knowing exactly where the serial hardware resided in the memory map, there's no guarantee the serial hardware is going to be compatible with the 16550-compatible serial interface we've all come to know and love in the PC world. In fact, the implementation of the serial port on some Windows CE devices looks nothing like a 16550.

But even if you know where to go in the memory map and the implementation of the serial hardware, you still don't need to "hack down to the hardware." The serial port drivers in Windows CE are interrupt-driven designs and are written to support its specific serial hardware. If you have any special needs not provided by the base serial driver, you can purchase the Microsoft Windows CE Platform Builder and write a serial driver yourself. Aside from that extreme case, there's just no reason not to use the published Win32 serial interface under Windows CE.

Opening and Closing a Serial Port

As with all stream device drivers, a serial port device is opened using *Create-File*. The name used needs to follow a specific format: the three letters *COM* followed by the number of the COM port to open and then a colon. The colon is required under Windows CE and is a departure from the naming convention used for device driver names used in Windows XP. The following line opens COM port 1 for reading and writing:

```
hSer = CreateFile (TEXT ("COM1:"), GENERIC_READ | GENERIC_WRITE,
                   0, NULL, OPEN_EXISTING, 0, NULL);
```

You must pass a 0 in the sharing parameter as well as in the security attributes and the template file parameters of *CreateFile*. Windows CE doesn't support overlapped I/O for devices, so you can't pass the *FILE_FLAG_OVERLAPPED* flag in the *dwFlagsAndAttributes* parameter. The handle returned is either the handle to the opened serial port or *INVALID_HANDLE_VALUE*. Remember that unlike many of the Windows functions, *CreateFile* doesn't return a 0 for a failed open.

You close a serial port by calling *CloseHandle*, as in the following:

```
CloseHandle (hSer);
```

You don't do anything differently when using *CloseHandle* to close a serial device than when you use it to close a file handle.

Reading from and Writing to a Serial Port

Just as you use the *CreateFile* function to open a serial port, you use the functions *ReadFile* and *WriteFile* to read and write to that serial port. Reading data from a serial port is as simple as making this call to *ReadFile*:

```
INT rc;
DWORD cBytes;
BYTE ch;

rc = ReadFile(hSer, &ch, 1, &cBytes, NULL);
```

This call assumes the serial port has been successfully opened with a call to *CreateFile*. If the call is successful, one byte is read into the variable *ch*, and *cBytes* is set to the number of bytes read.

Writing to a serial port is just as simple. The call would look something like the following:

```
INT rc;
DWORD cBytes;
BYTE ch;

ch = TEXT ('a');
rc = WriteFile(hSer, &ch, 1, &cBytes, NULL);
```

This code writes the character *a* to the serial port previously opened. As you may remember from Chapter 8, both *ReadFile* and *WriteFile* return *TRUE* if successful.

Because overlapped I/O isn't supported under Windows CE, you should be careful not to attempt to read or write a large amount of serial data from your primary thread or from any thread that has created a window. Because those threads are also responsible for handling the message queues for their windows, they can't be blocked waiting on a relatively slow serial read or write. Instead, you should use separate threads for reading from and writing to the serial port.

You can also transmit a single character using this function:

```
BOOL TransmitCommChar (HANDLE hFile, char cChar);
```

The difference between the *TransmitCommChar* and *WriteFile* functions is that *TransmitCommChar* puts the character to be transmitted at the front of the transmit queue. When you call *WriteFile*, the characters are queued up after any characters that haven't yet been transmitted by the serial driver. *TransmitCommChar* allows you to insert control characters quickly in the stream without having to wait for the queue to empty.

Asynchronous Serial I/O

While Windows CE doesn't support overlapped I/O, there's no reason why you can't use multiple threads to implement the same type of overlapped operation. All that's required is that you launch separate threads to handle the synchronous I/O operations while your primary thread goes about its business. In addition to using separate threads for reading and writing, Windows CE supports the Win32 *WaitCommEvent* function that blocks a thread until one of a group of preselected serial events occurs. I'll demonstrate how to use separate threads for reading and writing a serial port in the CeChat example program later in this chapter.

You can make a thread wait on serial driver events by means of the following three functions:

```
BOOL SetCommMask (HANDLE hFile, DWORD dwEvtMask);
BOOL GetCommMask (HANDLE hFile, LPDWORD lpEvtMask);
```

and

```
BOOL WaitCommEvent (HANDLE hFile, LPDWORD lpEvtMask,
                    LPOVERLAPPED lpOverlapped);
```

To wait on an event, you first set the event mask using *SetCommMask*. The parameters for this function are the handle to the serial device and a combination of the following event flags:

- **EV_BREAK**   A break was detected.

- **EV_CTS**   The Clear to Send (CTS) signal changed state.

- **EV_DSR**   The Data Set Ready (DSR) signal changed state.

- **EV_ERR**   An error was detected by the serial driver.

- **EV_RLSD**   The Receive Line Signal Detect (RLSD) line changed state.

- **EV_RXCHAR**   A character was received.

- **EV_RXFLAG**   An event character was received.

- **EV_TXEMPTY**   The transmit buffer is empty.

You can set any or all of the flags in this list at the same time using *SetCommMask*. You can query the current event mask using *GetCommMask*.

To wait on the events specified by *SetCommMask*, you call *WaitCommEvent*. The parameters for this call are the handle to the device, a pointer to a *DWORD* that will receive the reason the call returned, and *lpOverlapped*, which under Windows CE must be set to *NULL*. The code fragment that follows waits on a character being received or an error. The code assumes that the serial port has already been opened and that the handle is contained in *hComPort*.

```
DWORD dwMask;
// Set mask and wait.
SetCommMask (hComPort, EV_RXCHAR | EV_ERR);
if (WaitCommEvent (hComPort, &dwMask, 0) {

    // Use the flags returned in dwMask to determine the reason
    // for returning.
    Switch (dwMask) {
    case EV_RXCHAR:
        //Read character.
        break;
    case EV_ERR:
        // Process error.
        break;
    }
}
```

Configuring the Serial Port

Reading from and writing to a serial port is fairly straightforward, but you also must configure the port for the proper baud rate, character size, and so forth. The masochist could configure the serial driver through device I/O control (IOCTL) calls, but the *IoCtl* codes necessary for this are exposed only in the Platform Builder, not the Software Development Kit. Besides, here's a simpler method.

You can go a long way in configuring the serial port using two functions, *GetCommState* and *SetCommState*, prototyped here:

```
BOOL SetCommState (HANDLE hFile, LPDCB lpDCB);
BOOL GetCommState (HANDLE hFile, LPDCB lpDCB);
```

Both these functions take two parameters, the handle to the opened serial port and a pointer to a *DCB* structure. The extensive *DCB* structure is defined as follows:

```
typedef struct _DCB {
    DWORD DCBlength;
    DWORD BaudRate;
    DWORD fBinary: 1;
    DWORD fParity: 1;
    DWORD fOutxCtsFlow:1;
    DWORD fOutxDsrFlow:1;
    DWORD fDtrControl:2;
    DWORD fDsrSensitivity:1;
    DWORD fTXContinueOnXoff:1;
```

(continued)

```
    DWORD fOutX: 1;
    DWORD fInX: 1;
    DWORD fErrorChar: 1;
    DWORD fNull: 1;
    DWORD fRtsControl:2;
    DWORD fAbortOnError:1;
    DWORD fDummy2:17;
    WORD wReserved;
    WORD XonLim;
    WORD XoffLim;
    BYTE ByteSize;
    BYTE Parity;
    BYTE StopBits;
    char XonChar;
    char XoffChar;
    char ErrorChar;
    char EofChar;
    char EvtChar;
    WORD wReserved1;
} DCB;
```

As you can see from structure, *SetCommState* can set a fair number of states. Instead of attempting to fill out the entire structure from scratch, you should use the best method of modifying a serial port, which is to call *GetCommState* to fill in a *DCB* structure, modify the fields necessary, and then call *SetCommState* to configure the serial port.

The first field in the *DCB* structure, *DCBlength*, should be set to the size of the structure. This field should be initialized before the call to either *GetCommState* or *SetCommState*. The *BaudRate* field should be set to one of the baud rate constants defined in Winbase.h. The baud rate constants range from *CBR_110* for 110 bits per second to *CBR_256000* for 256 kilobits per second (Kbps). Just because constants are defined for speeds up to 256 Kbps doesn't mean that all serial ports support that speed. To determine what baud rates a serial port supports, you can call *GetCommProperties*, which I'll describe shortly. Windows CE devices generally support speeds up to 115 Kbps, although some support faster speeds. The *fBinary* field must be set to *TRUE* because no Win32 operating system currently supports a nonbinary serial transmit mode familiar to MS-DOS programmers. The *fParity* field can be set to *TRUE* to enable parity checking.

The *fOutxCtsFlow* field should be set to *TRUE* if the output of the serial port should be controlled by the port CTS line. The *fOutxDsrFlow* field should be set to *TRUE* if the output of the serial port should be controlled by the DSR line of the serial port. The *fDtrControl* field can be set to one of three values: *DTR_CONTROL_DISABLE*, which disables the DTR (Data Terminal Ready) line and leaves it disabled; *DTR_CONTROL_ENABLE*, which enables the DTR line; or *DTR_CONTROL_HANDSHAKE*, which tells the serial driver to toggle the DTR line in response to how much data is in the receive buffer.

The *fDsrSensitivity* field is set to *TRUE*, and the serial port ignores any incoming bytes unless the port DSR line is enabled. Setting the *fTXContinue-OnXoff* field to *TRUE* tells the driver to stop transmitting characters if its receive buffer has reached its limit and the driver has transmitted an XOFF character. Setting the *fOutX* field to *TRUE* specifies that the XON/XOFF control is used to control the serial output. Setting the *fInX* field to *TRUE* specifies that the XON/XOFF control is used for the input serial stream.

The *fErrorChar* and *ErrorChar* fields are ignored by the default implementation of the Windows CE serial driver, although some drivers might support these fields. Likewise, the *fAbortOnError* field is also ignored. Setting the *fNull* field to *TRUE* tells the serial driver to discard null bytes received.

The *fRtsControl* field specifies the operation of the RTS (Request to Send) line. The field can be set to one of the following: *RTS_CONTROL_DISABLE*, indicating that the RTS line is set to the disabled state while the port is open; *RTS_CONTROL_ENABLE*, indicating that the RTS line is set to the enabled state while the port is open; or *RTS_CONTROL_HANDSHAKE*, indicating that the RTS line is controlled by the driver. In this mode, the RTS line is enabled if the serial input buffer is less than half full; it's disabled otherwise. Finally, *RTS_CONTROL_TOGGLE* indicates that the driver enables the RTS line if there are bytes in the output buffer ready to be transmitted and disables the line otherwise.

The *XonLim* field specifies the minimum number of bytes in the input buffer before an XON character is automatically sent. The *XoffLim* field specifies the maximum number of bytes in the input buffer before the XOFF character is sent. This limit value is computed by taking the size of the input buffer and subtracting the value in *XoffLim*. In the sample Windows CE implementation of the serial driver provided in the Platform Builder, the *XonLim* field is ignored and XON and XOFF characters are sent based on the value in *XoffLim*. However, this behavior might differ in some systems.

The next three fields, *ByteSize*, *Parity*, and *StopBits*, define the format of the serial data word transmitted. The *ByteSize* field specifies the number of bits per byte, usually a value of 7 or 8, but in some older modes the number of bits per byte can be as small as 5. The *Parity* field can be set to the self-explanatory constant *EVENPARITY*, *MARKPARITY*, *NOPARITY*, *ODDPARITY*, or *SPACEPARITY*. The *StopBits* field should be set to *ONESTOPBIT*, *ONE5STOPBITS*, or *TWOSTOPBITS*, depending on whether you want one, one and a half, or two stop bits per byte.

The next two fields, *XonChar* and *XoffChar*, let you specify the XON and XOFF characters. Likewise, the *EvtChar* field lets you specify the character used to signal an event. If an event character is received, an *EV_RXFLAG* event is signaled by the driver. This "event" is what triggers the *WaitCommEvent* function to return if the *EV_RXFLAG* bit is set in the event mask.

Setting the Port Timeout Values

As you can see, *SetCommState* can fine-tune, to almost the smallest detail, the operation of the serial driver. However, one more step is necessary—setting the timeout values for the port. The timeout is the length of time Windows CE waits on a read or write operation before *ReadFile* or *WriteFile* automatically returns. The functions that control the serial timeouts are the following:

```
BOOL GetCommTimeouts (HANDLE hFile, LPCOMMTIMEOUTS lpCommTimeouts);
```

and

```
BOOL SetCommTimeouts (HANDLE hFile, LPCOMMTIMEOUTS lpCommTimeouts);
```

Both functions take the handle to the open serial device and a pointer to a *COMMTIMEOUTS* structure, defined as the following:

```
typedef struct _COMMTIMEOUTS {
    DWORD ReadIntervalTimeout;
    DWORD ReadTotalTimeoutMultiplier;
    DWORD ReadTotalTimeoutConstant;
    DWORD WriteTotalTimeoutMultiplier;
    DWORD WriteTotalTimeoutConstant;
} COMMTIMEOUTS;
```

The *COMMTIMEOUTS* structure provides for a set of timeout parameters that time both the interval between characters and the total time to read and write a block of characters. Timeouts are computed in two ways. First *ReadIntervalTimeout* specifies the maximum interval between characters received. If this time is exceeded, the *ReadFile* call returns immediately. The other timeout is based on the number of characters you're waiting to receive. The value in *ReadTotalTimeoutMultiplier* is multiplied by the number of characters requested in the call to *ReadFile* and is added to *ReadTotalTimeoutConstant* to compute a total timeout for a call to *ReadFile*.

The write timeout can be specified only for the total time spent during the *WriteFile* call. This timeout is computed the same way as the total read timeout, by specifying a multiplier value, the time in *WriteTotalTimeoutMultiplier*, and a constant value in *WriteTotalTimeoutConstant*. All of the times in this structure are specified in milliseconds.

In addition to the basic timeouts that I just described, you can set values in the *COMMTIMEOUTS* structure to control whether and exactly how timeouts are used in calls to *ReadFile* and *WriteFile*. You can configure the timeouts in the following ways:

- Timeouts for reading and writing as well as an interval timeout. Set the fields in the *COMMTIMEOUTS* structure for the appropriate timeout values.

- Timeouts for reading and writing with no interval timeout. Set *ReadIntervalTimeout* to 0. Set the other fields for the appropriate timeout values.

- The *ReadFile* function returns immediately regardless of whether there is data to be read. Set *ReadIntervalTimeout* to *MAXDWORD*. Set *ReadTotalTimeoutMultiplier* and *ReadTotalTimeoutConstant* to 0.

- *ReadFile* doesn't have a timeout. The function doesn't return until the proper number of bytes is returned or an error occurs. Set the *ReadIntervalTimeout*, *ReadTotalTimeoutMultiplier*, and *ReadTotalTimeoutConstant* fields to 0.

- *WriteFile* doesn't have a timeout. Set *WriteTotalTimeoutMultiplier* and *WriteTotalTimeoutConstant* to 0.

The timeout values are important because the worst thing you can do is to spin in a loop waiting on characters from the serial port. While the calls to *ReadFile* and *WriteFile* are waiting on the serial port, the calling threads are efficiently blocked on an event object internal to the driver. This saves precious CPU and battery power during the serial transmit and receive operations. Of course, to block on *ReadFile* and *WriteFile*, you'll have to create secondary threads because you can't have your primary thread blocked waiting on the serial port.

Another call isn't quite as useful—*SetupComm*, prototyped this way:

```
BOOL SetupComm (HANDLE hFile, DWORD dwInQueue, DWORD dwOutQueue);
```

This function lets you specify the size of the input and output buffers for the driver. However, the sizes passed in *SetupComm* are only recommendations, not requirements to the serial driver. For example, the example implementation of the serial driver in the Platform Builder ignores these recommended buffer sizes.

Querying the Capabilities of the Serial Driver

The configuration functions enable you to configure the serial driver, but with varied implementations of serial ports, you need to know just what features a serial port supports before you configure it. The function *GetCommProperties* provides just this service. The function is prototyped this way:

```
BOOL GetCommProperties (HANDLE hFile, LPCOMMPROP lpCommProp);
```

GetCommProperties takes two parameters: the handle to the opened serial driver and a pointer to a *COMMPROP* structure defined as

```
typedef struct _COMMPROP {
    WORD wPacketLength;
    WORD wPacketVersion;
    DWORD dwServiceMask;
    DWORD dwReserved1;
    DWORD dwMaxTxQueue;
    DWORD dwMaxRxQueue;
    DWORD dwMaxBaud;
    DWORD dwProvSubType;
    DWORD dwProvCapabilities;
    DWORD dwSettableParams;
    DWORD dwSettableBaud;
    WORD wSettableData;
    WORD wSettableStopParity;
    DWORD dwCurrentTxQueue;
    DWORD dwCurrentRxQueue;
    DWORD dwProvSpec1;
    DWORD dwProvSpec2;
    WCHAR wcProvChar[1];
} COMMPROP;
```

As you can see from the fields of the *COMMPROP* structure, *GetComm-Properties* returns generally enough information to determine the capabilities of the device. Of immediate interest to speed demons is the *dwMaxBaud* field that indicates the maximum baud rate of the serial port. The *dwSettableBaud* field contains bit flags that indicate the allowable baud rates for the port. Both these fields use bit flags that are defined in WinBase.h. These constants are expressed as *BAUD_xxxx*, as in *BAUD_19200*, which indicates that the port is capable of a speed of 19.2 kbps. Note that these constants are *not* the constants used to set the speed of the serial port in the *DCB* structure. Those constants are numbers, not bit flags. To set the speed of a COM port in the *DCB* structure to 19.2 kbps, you would use the constant *CBR_19200* in the *BaudRate* field of the *DCB* structure.

Starting back at the top of the structure are the *wPacketLength* and *wPacketVersion* fields. These fields allow you to request more information from the driver than is supported by the generic call. The *dwServiceMask* field indicates what services the port supports. The only service currently supported is *SP_SERIALCOMM*, indicating that the port is a serial communication port.

The *dwMaxTxQueue* and *dwMaxRxQueue* fields indicate the maximum size of the output and input buffers internal to the driver. The value 0 in these fields indicates that you'll encounter no limit in the size of the internal queues. The *dwCurrentTxQueue* and *dwCurrentRxQueue* fields indicate the current size for the queues. These fields are 0 if the queue size can't be determined.

The *dwProvSubType* field contains flags that indicate the type of serial port supported by the driver. Values here include *PST_RS232*, *PST_RS422*, and *PST_RS423*, indicating the physical layer protocol of the port. *PST_MODEM* indicates a modem device, and *PST_FAX* tells you the port is a fax device. Other *PST_* flags are defined as well. This field reports what the driver thinks the port is, not what device is attached to the port. For example, if an external modem is attached to a standard, RS-232, serial port, the driver returns the *PST_RS232* flag, not the *PST_MODEM* flag.

The *dwProvCapabilities* field contains flags indicating the handshaking the port supports, such as XON/XOFF, RTS/CTS, and DTR/DSR. This field also shows you whether the port supports setting the characters used for XON/XOFF, parity checking, and so forth. The *dwSettableParams*, *dwSettableData*, and *dwSettableStopParity* fields give you information about how the serial data stream can be configured. Finally, the fields *dwProvSpec1*, *dwProvSpec2*, and *wcProvChar* are used by the driver to return driver-specific data.

Controlling the Serial Port

You can stop and start a serial stream using the following functions:

```
BOOL SetCommBreak (HANDLE hFile);
```

and

```
BOOL ClearCommBreak (HANDLE hFile);
```

The only parameter for both these functions is the handle to the opened COM port. When *SetCommBreak* is called, the COM port stops transmitting characters and places the port in a break state. Communication is resumed with the *ClearCommBreak* function.

You can clear out any characters in either the transmit or the receive queue internal to the serial driver using this function:

```
BOOL PurgeComm (HANDLE hFile, DWORD dwFlags);
```

The *dwFlags* parameter can be a combination of the flags *PURGE_TXCLEAR* and *PURGE_RXCLEAR*. These flags terminate any pending writes and reads and reset the queues. In the case of *PURGE_RXCLEAR*, the driver also clears any receive holds due to any flow control states, transmitting an XON character if necessary, and setting RTS and DTR if those flow control methods are enabled. Because Windows CE doesn't support overlapped I/O, the flags *PURGE_TXABORT* and *PURGE_RXABORT*, used under Windows XP and Windows Me, are ignored.

The *EscapeCommFunction* provides a more general method of controlling the serial driver. It allows you to set and clear the state of specific signals on the port. On Windows CE devices, it's also used to control serial hardware that's shared between the serial port and the IrDA port. The function is prototyped as

```
BOOL EscapeCommFunction (HANDLE hFile, DWORD dwFunc);
```

The function takes two parameters, the handle to the device and a set of flags in *dwFunc*. The flags can be one of the following values:

- **SETDTR**   Sets the DTR signal

- **CLRDTR**   Clears the DTR signal

- **SETRTS**   Sets the RTS signal

- **CLRRTS**   Clears the RTS signal

- **SETXOFF**   Tells the driver to act as if an XOFF character has been received

- **SETXON**   Tells the driver to act as if an XON character has been received

- **SETBREAK**   Suspends serial transmission and sets the port in a break state

- **CLRBREAK**   Resumes serial transmission from a break state

- **SETIR**   Tells the serial port to transmit and receive through the infrared transceiver

- **CLRIR**   Tells the serial port to transmit and receive through the standard serial transceiver

The *SETBREAK* and *CLRBREAK* commands act identically to *SetCommBreak* and *ClearCommBreak* and can be used interchangeably. For example, you can use *EscapeCommFunction* to put the port in a break state and *ClearCommBreak* to restore communication.

Clearing Errors and Querying Status

The function

```
BOOL ClearCommError (HANDLE hFile, LPDWORD lpErrors, LPCOMSTAT lpStat);
```

performs two functions. As you might expect from the name, it clears any error states within the driver so that I/O can continue. The serial device driver is responsible for reporting the errors. The default serial driver returns the following flags in the variable pointed to by *lpErrors*: *CE_OVERRUN*, *CE_RXPARITY*, *CE_FRAME*, and *CE_TXFULL*. *ClearCommError* also returns the status of the port. The third parameter of *ClearCommError* is a pointer to a *COMSTAT* structure defined as

```
typedef struct _COMSTAT {
    DWORD fCtsHold : 1;
    DWORD fDsrHold : 1;
    DWORD fRlsdHold : 1;
    DWORD fXoffHold : 1;
    DWORD fXoffSent : 1;
    DWORD fEof : 1;
    DWORD fTxim : 1;
    DWORD fReserved : 25;
    DWORD cbInQue;
    DWORD cbOutQue;
} COMSTAT;
```

The first five fields indicate that serial transmission is waiting for one of the following reasons. It's waiting for a CTS signal, waiting for a DSR signal, waiting for a Receive Line Signal Detect (also known as a Carrier Detect), waiting because an XOFF character was received, or waiting because an XOFF character was sent by the driver. The *fEor* field indicates that an end-of-file character has been received. The *fTxim* field is *TRUE* if a character placed in the queue by the *TransmitCommChar* function instead of a call to *WriteFile* is queued for transmission. The final two fields, *cbInQue* and *cbOutQue*, return the number of characters in the input and output queues of the serial driver.

The function

```
BOOL GetCommModemStatus (HANDLE hFile, LPDWORD lpModemStat);
```

returns the status of the modem control signals in the variable pointed to by *lpModemStat*. The flags returned can be any of the following:

■   ***MS_CTS_ON***   Clear to Send (CTS) is active.

■   ***MS_DSR_ON***   Data Set Ready (DSR) is active.

■   ***MS_RING_ON***   Ring Indicate (RI) is active.

■   ***MS_RLSD_ON***   Receive Line Signal Detect (RLSD) is active.

Stayin' Alive

One of the issues with serial communication is preventing the system from powering down while a serial link is active. A Windows CE system has three different timeout values that suspend the system, including a time since the user last pressed a key or tapped the screen. Because a communication program can run unattended, the program might need to prevent the auto-suspend feature of Windows CE from suspending the system. I cover this topic in the "Preventing the System from Powering Down" section in Chapter 21.

The CeChat Example Program

The CeChat program is a simple point-to-point chat program that connects two Windows CE devices using any of the available serial ports on the device. The CeChat window is shown in Figure 12-1. Most of the window is taken up by the receive text window. Text received from the other device is displayed here. Along the bottom of the screen is the send text window. If you type characters here and either hit the Enter key or tap the Send button, the text is sent to the other device. The combo box on the command bar selects the serial port to use.

Figure 12-1   The CeChat window

The source code for CeChat is shown in Listing 12-1. CeChat uses three threads to accomplish its work. The primary thread manages the window and the message loop. The two secondary threads handle reading from and writing to the appropriate serial port.

```
CeChat.rc
//======================================================================
// Resource file
//
// Written for the book Programming Windows CE
// Copyright (C) 2003 Douglas Boling
//======================================================================
#include "windows.h"
#include "CeChat.h"                            // Program-specific stuff
//----------------------------------------------------------------------
// Icons and bitmaps
//
ID_ICON ICON    "CeChat.ico"                   // Program icon


//----------------------------------------------------------------------
// Menu
//
ID_MENU MENU DISCARDABLE
BEGIN
    POPUP "&File"
    BEGIN
        MENUITEM "E&xit",                      IDM_EXIT
    END
    POPUP "&Help"
    BEGIN
        MENUITEM "&About...",                  IDM_ABOUT
    END
END
//----------------------------------------------------------------------
// Accelerator table
//
ID_ACCEL ACCELERATORS DISCARDABLE
BEGIN
    "Q",        IDM_EXIT,   VIRTKEY, CONTROL, NOINVERT
    "S",        ID_SENDBTN, VIRTKEY, ALT
    VK_RETURN, ID_SENDBTN, VIRTKEY
END
```

Listing 12-1 The CeChat source code   *(continued)*

Listing 12-1   *(continued)*

```
///-----------------------------------------------------------------
// About box dialog template
//
aboutbox DIALOG discardable 10, 10, 135, 40
STYLE  WS_POPUP | WS_VISIBLE | WS_CAPTION | WS_SYSMENU | DS_CENTER |
       DS_MODALFRAME
CAPTION "About"
BEGIN
    ICON   ID_ICON,                      -1,   3,   5,  10,  10
    LTEXT "CeChat - Written for the book Programming Windows \
          CE Copyright 2003 Douglas Boling"
                                         -1,  30,   5, 102,  37
END
```

CeChat.h

```
//=================================================================
// Header file
//
// Written for the book Programming Windows CE
// Copyright (C) 2003 Douglas Boling
//=================================================================
// Returns number of elements
#define dim(x) (sizeof(x) / sizeof(x[0]))


//-----------------------------------------------------------------
// Generic defines and data types
//
struct decodeUINT {                          // Structure associates
    UINT Code;                               // messages
                                             // with a function.
    LRESULT (*Fxn)(HWND, UINT, WPARAM, LPARAM);
};
struct decodeCMD {                           // Structure associates
    UINT Code;                               // menu IDs with a
    LRESULT (*Fxn)(HWND, WORD, HWND, WORD);  // function.
};
//-----------------------------------------------------------------
// Generic defines used by application
#define  ID_ICON      1                      // App icon resource ID
#define  ID_MENU      2                      // Menu resource ID
#define  ID_ACCEL     3                      // Accel table ID
#define  IDC_CMDBAR   4                      // Command band ID
#define  ID_RCVTEXT   5                      // Receive text box
#define  ID_SENDTEXT  6                      // Send text box
#define  ID_SENDBTN   7                      // Send button
```

```
// Menu item IDs
#define  IDM_EXIT               1


#define  IDM_USECOM             110             // Use COM.
#define  IDM_ABOUT              120             // Help menu


// Command bar IDs
#define  IDC_COMPORT            150             // COM port combo box
#define  IDC_BAUDRATE           151             // Baud rate combo box


#define TEXTSIZE 256
//----------------------------------------------------------------------
// Function prototypes
//
DWORD WINAPI ReadThread (PVOID pArg);
DWORD WINAPI SendThread (PVOID pArg);
HANDLE InitCommunication (HWND, LPTSTR);
int FillComComboBox (HWND);


HWND InitInstance (HINSTANCE, LPWSTR, int);
int TermInstance (HINSTANCE, int);


// Window procedures
LRESULT CALLBACK MainWndProc (HWND, UINT, WPARAM, LPARAM);


// Message handlers
LRESULT DoCreateMain (HWND, UINT, WPARAM, LPARAM);
LRESULT DoSizeMain (HWND, UINT, WPARAM, LPARAM);
LRESULT DoSetFocusMain (HWND, UINT, WPARAM, LPARAM);
LRESULT DoPocketPCShell (HWND, UINT, WPARAM, LPARAM);
LRESULT DoCommandMain (HWND, UINT, WPARAM, LPARAM);
LRESULT DoDestroyMain (HWND, UINT, WPARAM, LPARAM);
// Command functions
LPARAM DoMainCommandExit (HWND, WORD, HWND, WORD);
LPARAM DoMainCommandComPort (HWND, WORD, HWND, WORD);
LPARAM DoMainCommandSendText (HWND, WORD, HWND, WORD);
LPARAM DoMainCommandAbout (HWND, WORD, HWND, WORD);


// Dialog procedures
BOOL CALLBACK AboutDlgProc (HWND, UINT, WPARAM, LPARAM);
BOOL CALLBACK EditAlbumDlgProc (HWND, UINT, WPARAM, LPARAM);
```

CeChat.cpp

```
//======================================================================
// CeChat - A Windows CE communication demo
//
// Written for the book Programming Windows CE
// Copyright (C) 2003 Douglas Boling
```

(continued)

Listing 12-1   *(continued)*

```
//=========================================================================
#include <windows.h>                    // For all that Windows stuff
#include <commctrl.h>                    // Command bar includes
#include "CeChat.h"                      // Program-specific stuff

#if defined(WIN32_PLATFORM_PSPC)
#include <aygshell.h>                    // Add Pocket PC includes.
#pragma comment( lib, "aygshell" )       // Link Pocket PC lib for menu bar.
#endif
//-------------------------------------------------------------------------
// Global data
//
const TCHAR szAppName[] = TEXT ("CeChat");
HINSTANCE hInst;                         // Program instance handle.

BOOL fContinue = TRUE;
HANDLE hComPort = INVALID_HANDLE_VALUE;
int nSpeed = CBR_19200;
int nLastDev = -1;

#if defined(WIN32_PLATFORM_PSPC) && (_WIN32_WCE >= 300)
SHACTIVATEINFO sai;
#endif

HANDLE g_hSendEvent = INVALID_HANDLE_VALUE;
HANDLE hReadThread = INVALID_HANDLE_VALUE;

// Message dispatch table for MainWindowProc
const struct decodeUINT MainMessages[] = {
    WM_CREATE, DoCreateMain,
    WM_SIZE, DoSizeMain,
    WM_COMMAND, DoCommandMain,
    WM_SETTINGCHANGE, DoPocketPCShell,
    WM_ACTIVATE, DoPocketPCShell,
    WM_SETFOCUS, DoSetFocusMain,
    WM_DESTROY, DoDestroyMain,
};
// Command Message dispatch for MainWindowProc
const struct decodeCMD MainCommandItems[] = {
    IDC_COMPORT, DoMainCommandComPort,
    ID_SENDBTN, DoMainCommandSendText,
    IDM_EXIT, DoMainCommandExit,
    IDM_ABOUT, DoMainCommandAbout,
};
//=========================================================================
// Program entry point
//
```

```
int WINAPI WinMain (HINSTANCE hInstance, HINSTANCE hPrevInstance,
                    LPWSTR lpCmdLine, int nCmdShow) {
    HWND hwndMain;
    HACCEL hAccel;
    MSG msg;
    int rc = 0;

    // Initialize this instance.
    hwndMain = InitInstance (hInstance, lpCmdLine, nCmdShow);
    if (hwndMain == 0)
        return 0x10;

    // Load accelerator table.
    hAccel = LoadAccelerators (hInst, MAKEINTRESOURCE (ID_ACCEL));

    // Application message loop
    while (GetMessage (&msg, NULL, 0, 0)) {
        if (!TranslateAccelerator (hwndMain, hAccel, &msg)) {
            TranslateMessage (&msg);
            DispatchMessage (&msg);
        }
    }
    // Instance cleanup
    return TermInstance (hInstance, msg.wParam);
}
//----------------------------------------------------------------------
// InitInstance - Instance initialization
//
HWND InitInstance (HINSTANCE hInstance, LPWSTR lpCmdLine, int nCmdShow){
    HWND hWnd;
    HANDLE hThread;
    WNDCLASS wc;
    INITCOMMONCONTROLSEX icex;

    // Save program instance handle in global variable.
    hInst = hInstance;

#if defined(WIN32_PLATFORM_PSPC)
    // If Pocket PC, allow only one instance of the application.
    HWND hWnd = FindWindow (szAppName, NULL);
    if (hWnd) {
        SetForegroundWindow ((HWND)(((DWORD)hWnd) | 0x01));
        return 0;
    }
#endif
// Register application main window class.
    wc.style = 0;                              // Window style
    wc.lpfnWndProc = MainWndProc;              // Callback function
```

(continued)

Listing 12-1   *(continued)*

```
    wc.cbClsExtra = 0;                      // Extra class data
    wc.cbWndExtra = 0;                      // Extra window data
    wc.hInstance = hInstance;               // Owner handle
    wc.hIcon = NULL;                        // Application icon
    wc.hCursor = LoadCursor (NULL, IDC_ARROW);// Default cursor
    wc.hbrBackground = (HBRUSH) GetStockObject (WHITE_BRUSH);
    wc.lpszMenuName =  NULL;                // Menu name
    wc.lpszClassName = szAppName;           // Window class name

    if (RegisterClass (&wc) == 0) return 0;

    // Load the command bar common control class.
    icex.dwSize = sizeof (INITCOMMONCONTROLSEX);
    icex.dwICC = ICC_BAR_CLASSES;
    InitCommonControlsEx (&icex);

    // Create unnamed auto-reset event initially false.
    g_hSendEvent = CreateEvent (NULL, FALSE, FALSE, NULL);

    // Create main window.
    hWnd = CreateWindow (szAppName, TEXT ("CeChat"),
                         WS_VISIBLE, CW_USEDEFAULT, CW_USEDEFAULT,
                         CW_USEDEFAULT, CW_USEDEFAULT, NULL,
                         NULL, hInstance, NULL);
    // Return fail code if window not created.
    if (!IsWindow (hWnd)) return 0;

    // Create write thread. Read thread created when port opened.
    hThread = CreateThread (NULL, 0, SendThread, hWnd, 0, NULL);
    if (hThread)
        CloseHandle (hThread);
    else {
        DestroyWindow (hWnd);
        return 0;
    }
    // Standard show and update calls
    ShowWindow (hWnd, nCmdShow);
    UpdateWindow (hWnd);
    return hWnd;
}
//-------------------------------------------------------------------
// TermInstance - Program cleanup
//
int TermInstance (HINSTANCE hInstance, int nDefRC) {
    HANDLE hPort = hComPort;

    fContinue = FALSE;
```

```
    hComPort = INVALID_HANDLE_VALUE;
    if (hPort != INVALID_HANDLE_VALUE)
        CloseHandle (hPort);

    if (g_hSendEvent != INVALID_HANDLE_VALUE) {
        PulseEvent (g_hSendEvent);
        Sleep(100);
        CloseHandle (g_hSendEvent);
    }
    return nDefRC;
}
//===========================================================================
// Message handling procedures for MainWindow
//---------------------------------------------------------------------------
// MainWndProc - Callback function for application window
//
LRESULT CALLBACK MainWndProc (HWND hWnd, UINT wMsg, WPARAM wParam,
                             LPARAM lParam) {
    int i;
    //
    // Search message list to see if we need to handle this
    // message.  If in list, call procedure.
    //
    for (i = 0; i < dim(MainMessages); i++) {
        if (wMsg == MainMessages[i].Code)
            return (*MainMessages[i].Fxn)(hWnd, wMsg, wParam, lParam);
    }
    return DefWindowProc (hWnd, wMsg, wParam, lParam);
}
//---------------------------------------------------------------------------
// DoCreateMain - Process WM_CREATE message for window.
//
LRESULT DoCreateMain (HWND hWnd, UINT wMsg, WPARAM wParam,
                      LPARAM lParam) {
    HWND hwndCB, hC1, hC2, hC3;
    int  i;
    TCHAR szFirstDev[32];
    LPCREATESTRUCT lpcs = (LPCREATESTRUCT) lParam;

#if defined(WIN32_PLATFORM_PSPC) && (_WIN32_WCE >= 300)
    memset (&sai, 0, sizeof (sai));
    sai.cbSize = sizeof (sai);
    {
    SHMENUBARINFO mbi;                          // For Pocket PC, create
    memset(&mbi, 0, sizeof(SHMENUBARINFO));     // menu bar so that we
    mbi.cbSize = sizeof(SHMENUBARINFO);         // have a sip button.
    mbi.hwndParent = hWnd;
    mbi.dwFlags = SHCMBF_EMPTYBAR;
```

(continued)

Listing 12-1 *(continued)*

```
    SHCreateMenuBar(&mbi);
    SetWindowPos (hWnd, 0, 0, 0, lpcs->cx, lpcs->cy-26,
                  SWP_NOZORDER | SWP_NOMOVE);
    }
#endif

    // Create a command bar.
    hwndCB = CommandBar_Create (hInst, hWnd, IDC_CMDBAR);
    CommandBar_InsertMenubar (hwndCB, hInst, ID_MENU, 0);

    // Insert the COM port combo box.
    CommandBar_InsertComboBox (hwndCB, hInst, 140, CBS_DROPDOWNLIST,
                               IDC_COMPORT, 1);
    FillComComboBox (hWnd);

    // Add exit button to command bar.
    CommandBar_AddAdornments (hwndCB, 0, 0);

    // Create child windows. They will be positioned in WM_SIZE.
    // Create receive text window.
    hC1 = CreateWindowEx (WS_EX_CLIENTEDGE, TEXT ("edit"),
                          TEXT (""), WS_VISIBLE | WS_CHILD |
                          WS_VSCROLL | ES_MULTILINE | ES_AUTOHSCROLL |
                          ES_READONLY, 0, 0, 10, 10, hWnd,
                          (HMENU)ID_RCVTEXT, hInst, NULL);
    // Create send text window.
    hC2 = CreateWindowEx (WS_EX_CLIENTEDGE, TEXT ("edit"),
                          TEXT (""), WS_VISIBLE | WS_CHILD,
                          0, 0, 10, 10, hWnd, (HMENU)ID_SENDTEXT,
                          hInst, NULL);
    // Create send text window.
    hC3 = CreateWindowEx (WS_EX_CLIENTEDGE, TEXT ("button"),
                          TEXT ("&Send"), WS_VISIBLE | WS_CHILD |
                          BS_DEFPUSHBUTTON, 0, 0, 10, 10,
                          hWnd, (HMENU)ID_SENDBTN, hInst, NULL);
    // Destroy frame if window not created.
    if (!IsWindow (hC1) || !IsWindow (hC2) || !IsWindow (hC3)) {
        DestroyWindow (hWnd);
        return 0;
    }
    // Open a COM port.
    for (i = 0; i < 10; i++) {
        if (SendDlgItemMessage (hwndCB, IDC_COMPORT, CB_GETLBTEXT, i,
                         (LPARAM)szFirstDev) == CB_ERR)
            break;
        if (InitCommunication (hWnd, szFirstDev) !=
            INVALID_HANDLE_VALUE) {
```

```
                        SendDlgItemMessage (hwndCB, IDC_COMPORT, CB_SETCURSEL, i,
                                (LPARAM)szFirstDev);
                break;
        }
    }
    return 0;
}
//-----------------------------------------------------------------------
// DoSizeMain - Process WM_SIZE message for window.
//
LRESULT DoSizeMain (HWND hWnd, UINT wMsg, WPARAM wParam, LPARAM lParam){
    RECT rect;

    // Adjust the size of the client rect to take into account
    // the command bar height.
    GetClientRect (hWnd, &rect);
    rect.top += CommandBar_Height (GetDlgItem (hWnd, IDC_CMDBAR));

    SetWindowPos (GetDlgItem (hWnd, ID_RCVTEXT), NULL, rect.left,
                    rect.top, (rect.right - rect.left),
                    rect.bottom - rect.top - 25, SWP_NOZORDER);
    SetWindowPos (GetDlgItem (hWnd, ID_SENDTEXT), NULL, rect.left,
                    rect.bottom - 25, (rect.right - rect.left) - 50,
                    25, SWP_NOZORDER);
    SetWindowPos (GetDlgItem (hWnd, ID_SENDBTN), NULL,
                    (rect.right - rect.left) - 50, rect.bottom - 25,
                    50, 25, SWP_NOZORDER);
    return 0;
}
//-----------------------------------------------------------------------
// DoPocketPCShell - Process Pocket PC required messages.
//
LRESULT DoPocketPCShell (HWND hWnd, UINT wMsg, WPARAM wParam,
                        LPARAM lParam) {
#if defined(WIN32_PLATFORM_PSPC) && (_WIN32_WCE >= 300)
    if (wMsg == WM_SETTINGCHANGE)
        return SHHandleWMSettingChange(hWnd, wParam, lParam, &sai);
    if (wMsg == WM_ACTIVATE)
        return SHHandleWMActivate(hWnd, wParam, lParam, &sai, 0);
#endif
    return 0;
}
//-----------------------------------------------------------------------
// DoFocusMain - Process WM_SETFOCUS message for window.
//
LRESULT DoSetFocusMain (HWND hWnd, UINT wMsg, WPARAM wParam,
                        LPARAM lParam) {
    SetFocus (GetDlgItem (hWnd, ID_SENDTEXT));
```

(continued)

Listing 12-1   *(continued)*

```
        return 0;
}
//----------------------------------------------------------------------
// DoCommandMain - Process WM_COMMAND message for window.
//
LRESULT DoCommandMain (HWND hWnd, UINT wMsg, WPARAM wParam,
                       LPARAM lParam) {
    WORD    idItem, wNotifyCode;
    HWND hwndCtl;
    int  i;

    // Parse the parameters.
    idItem = (WORD) LOWORD (wParam);
    wNotifyCode = (WORD) HIWORD (wParam);
    hwndCtl = (HWND) lParam;

    // Call routine to handle control message.
    for (i = 0; i < dim(MainCommandItems); i++) {
        if (idItem == MainCommandItems[i].Code)
            return (*MainCommandItems[i].Fxn)(hWnd, idItem, hwndCtl,
                                              wNotifyCode);
    }
    return 0;
}
//----------------------------------------------------------------------
// DoDestroyMain - Process WM_DESTROY message for window.
//
LRESULT DoDestroyMain (HWND hWnd, UINT wMsg, WPARAM wParam,
                       LPARAM lParam) {
    PostQuitMessage (0);
    return 0;
}
//======================================================================
// Command handler routines
//----------------------------------------------------------------------
// DoMainCommandExit - Process Program Exit command.
//
LPARAM DoMainCommandExit (HWND hWnd, WORD idItem, HWND hwndCtl,
                          WORD wNotifyCode) {
    SendMessage (hWnd, WM_CLOSE, 0, 0);
    return 0;
}
//----------------------------------------------------------------------
// DoMainCommandComPort - Process the COM port combo box commands.
//
LPARAM DoMainCommandComPort (HWND hWnd, WORD idItem, HWND hwndCtl,
                             WORD wNotifyCode) {
```

```
    int i;
    TCHAR szDev[32];

    if (wNotifyCode == CBN_SELCHANGE) {
        i = SendMessage (hwndCtl, CB_GETCURSEL, 0, 0);
        if (i != nLastDev) {
            SendMessage (hwndCtl, CB_GETLBTEXT, i, (LPARAM)szDev);
            InitCommunication (hWnd, szDev);
            SetFocus (GetDlgItem (hWnd, ID_SENDTEXT));
        }
    }
    return 0;
}
//-----------------------------------------------------------------------
// DoMainCommandSendText - Process the Send text button.
//
LPARAM DoMainCommandSendText (HWND hWnd, WORD idItem, HWND hwndCtl,
                             WORD wNotifyCode) {

    // Set event so that sender thread will send the text.
    SetEvent (g_hSendEvent);
    SetFocus (GetDlgItem (hWnd, ID_SENDTEXT));
    return 0;
}
//-----------------------------------------------------------------------
// DoMainCommandAbout - Process the Help | About menu command.
//
LPARAM DoMainCommandAbout(HWND hWnd, WORD idItem, HWND hwndCtl,
                          WORD wNotifyCode) {
    // Use DialogBox to create modal dialog.
    DialogBox (hInst, TEXT ("aboutbox"), hWnd, AboutDlgProc);
    return 0;
}
//=======================================================================
// About Dialog procedure
//
BOOL CALLBACK AboutDlgProc (HWND hWnd, UINT wMsg, WPARAM wParam,
                            LPARAM lParam) {
    switch (wMsg) {
        case WM_COMMAND:
            switch (LOWORD (wParam)) {
                case IDOK:
                case IDCANCEL:
                    EndDialog (hWnd, 0);
                    return TRUE;
}

        break;
    }
```

(continued)

Listing 12-1 *(continued)*

```
        return FALSE;
}
//-----------------------------------------------------------------
// FillComComboBox - Fills the COM port combo box
//
int FillComComboBox (HWND hWnd) {
    int rc;
    WIN32_FIND_DATA fd;
    HANDLE hFind;

    hFind = FindFirstFileEx (TEXT ("COM?:"), FindExInfoStandard, &fd,
                             FindExSearchLimitToDevices, NULL, 0);
    if (hFind != INVALID_HANDLE_VALUE) {
        do {
            SendDlgItemMessage (GetDlgItem (hWnd, IDC_CMDBAR),
                                IDC_COMPORT, CB_INSERTSTRING,
                                -1, (LPARAM)fd.cFileName);
            rc = FindNextFile (hFind, &fd);
        } while (rc);

        rc = FindClose (hFind);
    }
    SendDlgItemMessage (GetDlgItem (hWnd, IDC_CMDBAR), IDC_COMPORT,
                        CB_SETCURSEL, 0, 0);
    return 0;
}
//-----------------------------------------------------------------
// InitCommunication - Open and initialize selected COM port.
//
HANDLE InitCommunication (HWND hWnd, LPTSTR pszDevName) {
    DCB dcb;
    TCHAR szDbg[128];
    COMMTIMEOUTS cto;
    HANDLE hLocal;
    DWORD dwTStat;
    hLocal = hComPort;
    hComPort = INVALID_HANDLE_VALUE;

    if (hLocal != INVALID_HANDLE_VALUE)
        CloseHandle (hLocal);  // This causes WaitCommEvent to return.

    hLocal = CreateFile (pszDevName, GENERIC_READ | GENERIC_WRITE,
                         0, NULL, OPEN_EXISTING, 0, NULL);

    if (hLocal != INVALID_HANDLE_VALUE) {
        // Configure port.
        dcb.DCBlength = sizeof (dcb);
```

```
        GetCommState (hLocal, &dcb);
        dcb.BaudRate = nSpeed;
        dcb.fParity = FALSE;
        dcb.fNull = FALSE;
        dcb.StopBits = ONESTOPBIT;
        dcb.Parity = NOPARITY;
        dcb.ByteSize = 8;
        SetCommState (hLocal, &dcb);

        // Set the timeouts. Set infinite read timeout.
        cto.ReadIntervalTimeout = 0;
        cto.ReadTotalTimeoutMultiplier = 0;
        cto.ReadTotalTimeoutConstant = 0;
        cto.WriteTotalTimeoutMultiplier = 0;
        cto.WriteTotalTimeoutConstant = 0;
        SetCommTimeouts (hLocal, &cto);

        wsprintf (szDbg, TEXT ("Port %s opened\r\n"), pszDevName);
        SendDlgItemMessage (hWnd, ID_RCVTEXT, EM_REPLACESEL, 0,
                            (LPARAM)szDbg);

        // Start read thread if not already started.
        hComPort = hLocal;
        if (!GetExitCodeThread (hReadThread, &dwTStat) ||
            (dwTStat != STILL_ACTIVE)) {
            hReadThread = CreateThread (NULL, 0, ReadThread, hWnd,
                                        0, &dwTStat);
            if (hReadThread)
                CloseHandle (hReadThread);
        }
    } else {
        wsprintf (szDbg, TEXT ("Couldn\'t open port %s. rc=%d\r\n"),
                  pszDevName, GetLastError());
        SendDlgItemMessage (hWnd, ID_RCVTEXT, EM_REPLACESEL,
                            0, (LPARAM)szDbg);
    }
    return hComPort;
}
//======================================================================
// SendThread - Sends characters to the serial port
//
DWORD WINAPI SendThread (PVOID pArg) {
    HWND hWnd, hwndSText;
    int rc;
    DWORD cBytes;
    TCHAR szText[TEXTSIZE];
```

(continued)

Listing 12-1 *(continued)*

```
    hWnd = (HWND)pArg;
    hwndSText = GetDlgItem (hWnd, ID_SENDTEXT);
    while (1) {
        rc = WaitForSingleObject (g_hSendEvent, INFINITE);
        if (rc == WAIT_OBJECT_0) {
            if (!fContinue)
                break;
            // Disable send button while sending.
            EnableWindow (GetDlgItem (hWnd, ID_SENDBTN), FALSE);
            GetWindowText (hwndSText, szText, dim(szText));
            lstrcat (szText, TEXT ("\r\n"));
            rc = WriteFile (hComPort, szText,
                            lstrlen (szText)*sizeof (TCHAR),&cBytes, 0);
            if (rc) {
                // Copy sent text to output window.
                SendDlgItemMessage (hWnd, ID_RCVTEXT, EM_REPLACESEL, 0,
                                    (LPARAM)TEXT (" >"));
                SetWindowText (hwndSText, TEXT ("")); // Clear text box
            } else {
                // Else, print error message.
                wsprintf (szText, TEXT ("Send failed rc=%d\r\n"),
                          GetLastError());
                DWORD dwErr = 0;
                COMSTAT Stat;

                if (ClearCommError (hComPort, &dwErr, &Stat)) {
                    printf ("fail\n");
                }
            }
            // Put text in receive text box.
            SendDlgItemMessage (hWnd, ID_RCVTEXT, EM_REPLACESEL, 0,
                                (LPARAM)szText);
            EnableWindow (GetDlgItem (hWnd, ID_SENDBTN), TRUE);
        } else
            break;
    }
    return 0;
}
//======================================================================
// ReadThread - Receives characters from the serial port
//
DWORD WINAPI ReadThread (PVOID pArg) {
    HWND hWnd;
    DWORD cBytes, i;
    BYTE szText[TEXTSIZE], *pPtr;
    TCHAR tch;
```

```
hWnd = (HWND)pArg;
while (fContinue) {
    tch = 0;
    pPtr = szText;
    for (i = 0; i < sizeof (szText)-sizeof (TCHAR); i++) {

        while (!ReadFile (hComPort, pPtr, 1, &cBytes, 0))
            if (hComPort == INVALID_HANDLE_VALUE)
                return 0;

        // This syncs the proper byte order for Unicode.
        tch = (tch << 8) & 0xff00;
        tch |= *pPtr++;
        if (tch == TEXT ('\n'))
            break;
    }
    *pPtr++ = 0;   // Avoid alignment problems by addressing as bytes.
    *pPtr++ = 0;

    // If out of byte sync, move bytes down one.
    if (i % 2) {
        pPtr = szText;
        while (*pPtr || *(pPtr+1)) {
            *pPtr = *(pPtr+1);
            pPtr++;
        }
        *pPtr = 0;
    }
    SendDlgItemMessage (hWnd, ID_RCVTEXT, EM_REPLACESEL, 0,
                        (LPARAM)szText);
}
return 0;
}
```

When the CeChat window is created, it sniffs out the three port names using the methods I described earlier in the chapter. The combo box is then filled, and an attempt is made to open one of the COM ports. Once a port is opened, the read thread is created to wait on characters.

The send thread is actually quite simple. All it does is block on an event that was created when CeChat was started. When the event is signaled, it reads the text from the send text edit control and calls *WriteFile*. Once that has completed, the send thread clears the text from the edit control and loops back to where it blocks again.

Serial communication is a rather basic but important mode of communication on Windows CE devices. In the next chapter, we'll look at networking and how to use the WNet API to communicate over a network.

13

Windows CE Networking

Networks are at the heart of modern computer systems. Over the years, Microsoft Windows has supported a variety of networks and networking APIs. The evolving nature of networking APIs along with the need to keep systems backward compatible has resulted in a huge array of overlapping functions and parallel APIs. As in many places in Windows CE, the networking API is a subset of the vast array of networking functions supported under Windows XP. This chapter covers the Windows Networking API. This API supports basic network connections so that a Windows CE device can access disks and printers on a network.

Windows Networking Support

The WNet API is a provider-independent interface that allows Windows applications to access network resources without regard for the network implementation. The Windows CE version of the WNet API has fewer functions but provides the basics so that a Windows CE application can gain access to shared network resources, such as disks and printers. The WNet API is implemented by a "redirector" DLL that translates the WNet functions into network commands for a specific network protocol.

By default, the only network supported by the WNet API is Windows Networking. Support for even this network is limited by the fact that redirector files that implement Windows Networking aren't bundled with some Windows CE devices. For the WNet API to work, the redirector DLLs must be installed in the \windows directory. In addition, the network control panel, also a supplementary component on some systems, must be used to configure the network card so that it can access the network. If the redirector DLLs aren't installed, or an error occurs when you're configuring or initializing the network adapter, the WNet functions return the error code *ERROR_NO_NETWORK*.

WNet Functions

As with other areas in Windows CE, the WNet implementation under Windows CE is a subset of the same API on the desktop, but support is provided for the critical functions, while the overlapping and obsolete functions are eliminated. For example, the standard WNet API contains four different and overlapping *WNetAddConnection* functions, while Windows CE supports only one, *WNetAddConnection3*.

Conventions of UNC

Network drives can be accessed in one of two ways. The first method is to explicitly name the resource using the *Universal Naming Convention* (UNC) naming syntax, which is a combination of the name of the server and the shared resource. An example of this is *BIGSRVR\DRVC*, where the server name is BIGSRVR and the resource on the server is named DRVC. The leading double backslashes immediately indicate that the name is a UNC name. Directories and filenames can be included in the UNC name, as in *big-srvr\drvc\dir2\file1.ext*. Notice that I changed case in the two names. That doesn't matter because UNC paths are case insensitive.

As long as the WNet redirector is installed, you can use UNC names wherever you use standard filenames in the Windows CE API. You'll have problems, though, with some programs, which might not understand UNC syntax.

Mapping a Remote Drive

To get around applications that don't understand UNC names, you can map a network drive to a local name. When a network drive is mapped on a Windows CE system, the remote drive appears as a folder in the \network folder in the object store. The \network folder isn't a standard folder; in fact, in early versions of Windows CE, it didn't even show up in the Explorer. (For current systems, the visibility of the \network folder depends on a registry setting that's usually enabled.) Instead it's a placeholder name by which the local names of the mapped network drives can be addressed. For example, the network drive *BigSrvr\DrvC* could be mapped to the local name JoeBob. Files and directories on *BigSrvr\DrvC* would appear under the folder \network\joebob. The local name can't be represented as a drive letter, such as G, since Windows CE doesn't support drive letters.

I mentioned that the \network folder is a virtual folder; this needs further explanation. If you use the *FindFirstFile/FindNextFile* process to enumerate the directories in the root directory, the \network directory might not be enumerated. However, *FindFirstFile/FindNextFile* enumerates the mapped resources contained in the \network folder. So if the search string is *.* to enumerate the root directory, the \network folder might not be enumerated, but if you use \network*.* as the search string, any mapped drives will be enumerated.

In Windows CE, the visibility of the \network folder is controlled by a registry setting. The \network folder is visible if the *DWORD* value *RegisterFSRoot* under the key *[HKEY_LOCAL_MACHINE]\comm\redir* exists and is set to a nonzero value. Deleting this value or setting it to 0 hides the \network folder.

The most direct way to map a remote resource is to call this function:

```
DWORD WNetAddConnection3 (HWND hwndOwner, LPNETRESOURCE lpNetResource,
                          LPTSTR lpPassword, LPTSTR lpUserName,
                          DWORD dwFlags);
```

The first parameter is a handle to a window that owns any network support dialogs that might need to be displayed to complete the connection. The window handle can be *NULL* if you don't want to specify an owner window. This effectively turns the *WNetAddConnection3* function into the *WNetAddConnection2* function supported under other versions of Windows.

The second parameter, *lpNetResource*, should point to a *NETRESOURCE* structure that defines the remote resource being connected. The structure is defined as

```
typedef struct _NETRESOURCE {
    DWORD  dwScope;
    DWORD  dwType;
    DWORD  dwDisplayType;
    DWORD  dwUsage;
    LPTSTR lpLocalName;
    LPTSTR lpRemoteName;
    LPTSTR lpComment;
    LPTSTR lpProvider;
} NETRESOURCE;
```

Most of these fields aren't used for the *WNetAddConnection3* function and should be set to 0. All you need to do is specify the UNC name of the remote resource in a string pointed to by *lpRemoteName* and the local name in a string pointed to by *lpLocalName*. The local name is limited to 99 characters in length. The other fields in this structure are used by the WNet enumeration functions that I'll describe shortly.

You use the next two parameters in *WNetAddConnection3*, *lpPassword* and *lpUserName*, when requesting access from the server to the remote device. If you don't specify a user name and Windows CE can't find user information for network access already defined in the registry, the system displays a dialog box requesting the user name and password. Finally, the *dwFlags* parameter can be either 0 or the flag *CONNECT_UPDATE_PROFILE*. When this flag is set, the connection is dubbed *persistent*. Windows CE stores the connection data for persistent connections in the registry. Unlike other versions of Windows, Windows CE doesn't restore persistent connections when the user logs on. Instead, the local name to remote name mapping is tracked only in the registry. If the local folder is later accessed after the original connection was dropped, a reconnection is automatically attempted when the local folder is accessed.

If the call to *WNetAddConnection3* is successful, it returns *NO_ERROR*. Unlike most Win32 functions, *WNetAddConnection3* returns an error code in the return value if an error occurs. This is a nod to compatibility that stretches back to the Windows 3.1 days. You can also call *GetLastError* to return the error information. As an aside, the function *WNetGetLastError* is supported under Windows CE, but it's just an alias for *GetLastError*, so you can call that function if compatibility with other platforms is important.

The other function you can use under Windows CE to connect a remote resource is *WNetConnectionDialog1*. This function presents a dialog box to the user requesting the remote and local names for the connection. The function is prototyped as

```
DWORD WNetConnectionDialog1 (LPCONNECTDLGSTRUCT lpConnectDlgStruc);
```

The one parameter is a pointer to a *CONNECTDLGSTRUCT* structure defined as the following:

```
typedef struct {
    DWORD cbStructure;
    HWND hwndOwner;
    LPNETRESOURCE lpConnRes;
    DWORD dwFlags;
    DWORD dwDevNum;
} CONNECTDLGSTRUCT;
```

The first field in the structure is the size field and must be set with the size of the *CONNECTDLGSTRUCT* structure before you call *WNetConnectionDialog1*. The *hwndOwner* field should be filled with the handle of the owner window for the dialog box. The *lpConnRes* field should point to a *NETRESOURCE* structure. This structure should be filled with zeros except for the *lpRemoteName* field, which may be filled to specify the default remote name in the dialog. You can leave the *lpRemoteName* field 0 if you don't want to specify a suggested remote path.

The *dwFlags* field can either be 0 or be set to the flag *CONNDLG_RO_PATH*. When this flag is specified, the user can't change the remote name field in the dialog box. Of course, this requirement means that the *lpRemoteName* field in the *NETRESOURCE* structure must contain a valid remote name. Windows CE ignores the *dwDevNum* field in the *CONNECTDLGSTRUCT* structure.

When the function is called, it displays a dialog box that allows the user to specify a local name and, if not invoked with the *CONNDLG_RO_PATH* flag, the remote name as well. If the user taps on the OK button, Windows attempts to make the connection specified. The connection, if successful, is recorded as a persistent connection in the registry.

If the connection is successful, the function returns *NO_ERROR*. If the user presses the Cancel button in the dialog box, the function returns −1. Other return codes indicate errors processing the function.

Disconnecting a Remote Resource

You can choose from three ways to disconnect a connected resource. The first method is to delete the connection with this function:

```
DWORD WNetCancelConnection2 (LPTSTR lpName, DWORD dwFlags,
                            BOOL fForce);
```

The *lpName* parameter points to either the local name or the remote network name of the connection you want to remove. The *dwFlags* parameter should be set to 0 or *CONNECT_UPDATE_PROFILE*. If *CONNECT_UPDATE_PROFILE* is set, the entry in the registry that references the connection is removed; otherwise, the call won't change that information. Finally, the *fForce* parameter indicates whether the system should continue with the disconnect, even if there are open files or print jobs on the remote device. If the function is successful, it returns *NO_ERROR*.

You can prompt the user to specify a network resource to delete using this function:

```
DWORD WNetDisconnectDialog (HWND hwnd, DWORD dwType);
```

This function brings up a system-provided dialog box that lists all connections currently defined. The user can select one from the list and tap on the OK button to disconnect that resource. The two parameters for this function are a handle to the window that owns the dialog box and *dwType*, which is supposed to define the type of resources—printer (*RESOURCETYPE_PRINT*) or disk (*RESOURCETYPE_DISK*)—enumerated in the dialog box. However, some systems ignore this parameter and enumerate both disk and print devices. This dialog, displayed by *WNetDisconnectDialog*, is actually implemented by the network driver. So it's up to each OEM to get this dialog to work correctly.

A more specific method to disconnect a network resource is to call

```
DWORD WNetDisconnectDialog1 (LPDISCDLGSTRUCT lpDiscDlgStruc);
```

This function is misleadingly named in that it won't display a dialog box if all the parameters in *DISCDLGSTRUCT* are correct and point to a resource not currently being used. The dialog part of this function appears when the resource is being used.

DISCDLGSTRUCT is defined as

```
typedef struct {
    DWORD cbStructure;
    HWND hwndOwner;
    LPTSTR lpLocalName;
    LPTSTR lpRemoteName;
    DWORD dwFlags;
} DISCDLGSTRUCT;
```

As usual, the *cbStructure* field should be set to the size of the structure. The *hwndOwner* field should be set to the window that owns any dialog box displayed. The *lpLocalName* and *lpRemoteName* fields should be set to the local and remote names of the resource that's to be disconnected. Under current implementations, *lpLocalName* is optional, while the *lpRemoteName* field must be set for the function to work correctly. The *dwFlags* parameter can be either 0 or *DISC_NO_FORCE*. If this flag is set and the network resource is currently being used, the system simply fails the function. Otherwise, a dialog appears asking the user if he or she wants to disconnect the resource even though the resource is being used. Under the current implementations, the *DISC_NO_FORCE* flag is ignored.

Enumerating Network Resources

It's all very well and good to connect to a network resource, but it helps if you know what resources are available to connect to. Windows CE supports three WNet functions used to enumerate network resources: *WNetOpenEnum*, *WNetEnumResource*, and *WNetCloseEnum*. The process is similar to enumerating files with *FileFindFirst*, *FileFindNext*, and *FileFindClose*.

To start the process of enumerating network resources, first call the function

```
DWORD WNetOpenEnum (DWORD dwScope, DWORD dwType, DWORD dwUsage,
                    LPNETRESOURCE lpNetResource,
                    LPHANDLE lphEnum);
```

The first parameter, *dwScope*, specifies the scope of the enumeration. It can be one of the following flags:

- **RESOURCE_CONNECTED**   Enumerate the connected resources.

- **RESOURCE_REMEMBERED**   Enumerate the persistent network connections.

- **RESOURCE_GLOBALNET**   Enumerate all resources on the network.

The first two flags, *RESOURCE_CONNECTED* and *RESOURCE_REMEMBERED*, simply enumerate the resources already connected on your machine. The difference is that *RESOURCE_CONNECTED* returns the network resources that are connected at the time of the call, while *RESOURCE_REMEMBERED* returns those that are persistent regardless of whether they're currently connected. When either of these flags is used, the *dwUsage* parameter is ignored and the *lpNetResource* parameters must be *NULL*.

The third flag, *RESOURCE_GLOBALNET*, allows you to enumerate resources—such as servers, shared drives, or printers out on the network—that aren't connected. The *dwType* parameter specifies what you're attempting to enumerate—shared disks (*RESOURCETYPE_DISK*), shared printers (*RESOURCETYPE_PRINT*), or both (*RESOURCETYPE_ANY*).

You use the third and fourth parameters only if the *dwScope* parameter is set to *RESOURCE_GLOBALNET*. The *dwUsage* parameter specifies the usage of the resource and can be 0 to enumerate any resource, *RESOURCEUSAGE_CONNECTABLE* to enumerate only connectable resources, or *RESOURCEUSAGE_CONTAINER* to enumerate only containers such as servers.

If the *dwScope* parameter is set to RESOURCE_GLOBALNET, the fourth parameter, *lpNetResource*, must point to a *NETRESOURCE* structure; otherwise, the parameter must be *NULL*. The *NETRESOURCE* structure should be initialized to specify the starting point on the network for the enumeration. The starting point is specified by a UNC name in the *lpRemoteName* field of *NETRESOURCE*. The *dwUsage* field of the *NETRESOURCE* structure must be set to *RESOURCETYPE_CONTAINER*. For example, to enumerate the shared resources on the server BIGSERV, the *lpRemoteName* field would point to the string *BIGSERV*. To enumerate all servers in a domain, *lpRemoteName* should simply specify the domain name. For the domain EntireNet, the *lpRemoteName* field should point to the string *EntireNet*. Because Windows CE doesn't allow you to pass a *NULL* into *lpRemoteName* when you use the RESOURCE_GLOBALNET flag, you can't enumerate all resources in the network namespace as you can under Windows XP. This restriction exists because Windows CE doesn't support the concept of a Windows CE device belonging to a specific network context.

The final parameter of *WNetOpenEnum*, *lpbEnum*, is a pointer to an enumeration handle that will be passed to the other functions in the enumeration process. *WNetOpenEnum* returns a value of *NO_ERROR* if successful. If the function isn't successful, you can call *GetLastError* to query the extended error information.

Once you have successfully started the enumeration process, you actually query data by calling this function:

```
DWORD WNetEnumResource (HANDLE hEnum, LPDWORD lpcCount,
                        LPVOID lpBuffer,
                        LPDWORD lpBufferSize);
```

The function takes the handle returned by *WNetOpenEnum* as its first parameter. The second parameter is a pointer to a variable that should be initialized with the number of resources you want to enumerate in each call to *WNetEnumResource*. You can specify −1 in this variable if you want *WNetEnumResource* to return the data for as many resources as will fit in the return buffer specified by the *lpBuffer* parameter. The final parameter is a pointer to a *DWORD* that should be initialized with the size of the buffer pointed to by *lpBuffer*. If the buffer is too small to hold the data for even one resource, *WNetEnumResource* sets this variable to the required size for the buffer.

The information about the shared resources returned by data is returned in the form of an array of *NETRESOURCE* structures. While this is the same structure I described when I talked about the *WNetAddConnection3* function, I'll list the elements of the structure here again for convenience:

```
typedef struct _NETRESOURCE {
    DWORD   dwScope;
    DWORD   dwType;
    DWORD   dwDisplayType;
    DWORD   dwUsage;
    LPTSTR  lpLocalName;
    LPTSTR  lpRemoteName;
    LPTSTR  lpComment;
    LPTSTR  lpProvider;
} NETRESOURCE;
```

The interesting fields in the context of enumeration start with the *dwType* field, which indicates the type of resource that was enumerated. The value can be *RESOURCETYPE_DISK* or *RESOURCETYPE_PRINT*. The *dwDisplayType* field provides even more information about the resource, demarcating domains (*RESOURCEDISPLAYTYPE_DOMAIN*) from servers (*RESOURCEDISPLAYTYPE_SERVER*) and from shared disks and printers (*RESOURCEDISPLAYTYPE_SHARE*). A fourth flag, *RESOURCEDISPLAYTYPE_GENERIC*, is returned if the display type doesn't matter.

The *lpLocalName* field points to a string containing the local name of the resource if the resource is currently connected or is a persistent connection. The *lpRemoteName* field points to the UNC name of the resource. The *lpComment* field contains the comment line describing the resource that's provided by some servers.

WNetEnumResource either returns *NO_ERROR*, indicating that the function passed (but you need to call it again to enumerate more resources), or *ERROR_NO_MORE_ITEMS*, indicating that you have enumerated all resources matching the specification passed in *WNetOpenEnum*. With any other return code, you should call *GetLastError* to further diagnose the problem.

You have few strategies when enumerating the network resources. You can specify a huge buffer and pass −1 in the variable pointed to by *lpcCount*, telling *WNetEnumResource* to return as much information as possible in one shot. Or you can specify a smaller buffer and ask for only one or two resources for each call to *WNetEnumResource*. The one caveat on the small buffer approach is that the strings that contain the local and remote names are also placed in the specified buffer. The name pointers inside the *NETRESOURCE* structure then point to those strings. This means that you can't specify the size of the buffer to be exactly the size of the *NETRESOURCE* structure and expect to get any data back. A third possibility is to call *WNetEnumResource* twice, the first time with the *lpBuffer* parameter 0, and have Windows CE tell you the size necessary for the buffer. Then you allocate the buffer and call *WNetEnumResource* again to actually query the data. However you use *WNetEnumResource*, you'll need to check the return code to see whether it needs to be called again to enumerate more resources.

When you have enumerated all the resources, you must make one final call to the function:

```
DWORD WNetCloseEnum (HANDLE hEnum);
```

The only parameter to this function is the enumeration handle first returned by *WNetOpenEnum*. This function cleans up the system resources used by the enumeration process.

Following is a short routine that uses the enumeration functions to query the network for available resources. You pass to a function a UNC name to use as the root of the search. The function returns a buffer of zero-delimited strings that designate the local name, if any, and the UNC name of each shared resource found.

```
// Helper routine
int AddToList (LPTSTR *pPtr, INT *pnListSize, LPTSTR pszStr) {
    INT nLen = lstrlen (pszStr) + 1;
```

(continued)

```
        if (*pnListSize < nLen) return -1;
        lstrcpy (*pPtr, pszStr);
        *pPtr += nLen;
        *pnListSize -= nLen;
        return 0;
}
//----------------------------------------------------------------
// EnumNetDisks - Produces a list of shared disks on a network
//
int EnumNetDisks (LPTSTR pszRoot, LPTSTR pszNetList, int nNetSize){
        INT i = 0, rc, nBuffSize = 1024;
        DWORD dwCnt, dwSize;
        HANDLE hEnum;
        NETRESOURCE nr;
        LPNETRESOURCE pnr;
        PBYTE pPtr, pNew;

        // Allocate buffer for enumeration data.
        pPtr = (PBYTE) LocalAlloc (LPTR, nBuffSize);
        if (!pPtr)
            return -1;

        // Initialize specification for search root.
        memset (&nr, 0, sizeof (nr));
        nr.lpRemoteName = pszRoot;
        nr.dwUsage = RESOURCEUSAGE_CONTAINER;

        // Start enumeration.
        rc = WNetOpenEnum (RESOURCE_GLOBALNET, RESOURCETYPE_DISK, 0, &nr,
                           &hEnum);
        if (rc != NO_ERROR)
            return -1;

        // Enumerate one item per loop.
        do {
            dwCnt = 1;
            dwSize = nBuffSize;
            rc = WNetEnumResource (hEnum, &dwCnt, pPtr, &dwSize);

            // Process returned data.
            if (rc == NO_ERROR) {
                pnr = (NETRESOURCE *)pPtr;
                if (pnr->lpRemoteName)
                    rc = AddToList (&pszNetList, &nNetSize,
                                    pnr->lpRemoteName);
```

```
                    // If our buffer was too small, try again.
                    } else if (rc == ERROR_MORE_DATA) {
                        pNew = LocalReAlloc (pPtr, dwSize, LMEM_MOVEABLE);
                        if (pNew) {
                            pPtr = pNew;
                            nBuffSize = LocalSize (pPtr);
                            rc = 0;
                        }
                    }
                } while (rc == 0);

                // If the loop was successful, add extra zero to list.
                if (rc == ERROR_NO_MORE_ITEMS) {
                    rc = AddToList (&pszNetList, &nNetSize, TEXT (""));
                    rc = 0;
                }

                // Clean up.
                WNetCloseEnum (hEnum);
                LocalFree (pPtr);
                return rc;
}
```

While the enumeration functions work well for querying what's available on the net, you can use another strategy for determining the current connected resources. At the simplest level, you can use *FileFindFirst* and *FileFindNext* to enumerate the locally connected network disks by searching the folders in the \network directory. Once you have the local name, a few functions are available to you for querying just what that local name is connected to.

Querying Connections and Resources

The folders in the \network directory represent the local names of network-shared disks that are persistently connected to network resources. To determine which of the folders are currently connected, you can use the function

```
DWORD WNetGetConnection (LPCTSTR lpLocalName,
                         LPTSTR lpRemoteName,
                         LPDWORD lpnLength);
```

WNetGetConnection returns the UNC name of the network resource associated with a local device or folder. The *lpLocalName* parameter is filled with the local name of a shared folder or printer. The *lpRemoteName* parameter should point to a buffer that can receive the UNC name for the device. The *lpnLength* parameter points to a *DWORD* value that initially contains the length in characters of the remote name buffer. If the buffer is too small to receive the name, the length value is loaded with the number of characters required to hold the UNC name.

One feature (or problem, depending on how you look at it) of *WNetGet-Connection* is that it fails unless the local folder or device has a current connection to the remote shared device. This allows us an easy way to determine which local folders are currently connected and which are just placeholders for persistent connections that aren't currently connected.

Sometimes you need to transfer a filename from one system to another and you need a common format for the filename that would be understood by both systems. The *WNetGetUniversalName* function translates a filename that contains a local network name into one using the UNC name of the connected resource. The prototype for *WNetGetUniversalName* is the following:

```
DWORD WNetGetUniversalName (LPCTSTR lpLocalPath, DWORD dwInfoLevel,
                           LPVOID lpBuffer, LPDWORD lpBufferSize);
```

Like *WNetGetConnection*, this function returns a UNC name for a local name. There are two main differences between *WNetGetConnection* and *WNetGetUniversalName*. First, *WNetGetUniversalName* works even if the remote resource isn't currently connected. Second, you can pass a complete filename to *WNetGetUniversalName* instead of simply the local name of the shared resource, which is all that is accepted by *WNetGetConnection*.

WNetGetUniversalName returns the remote information in two different formats. If the *dwInfoLevel* parameter is set to *UNIVERSAL_NAME_INFO_LEVEL*, the buffer pointed to by *lpBuffer* is loaded with the following structure:

```
typedef struct _UNIVERSAL_NAME_INFO {
    LPTSTR  lpUniversalName;
} UNIVERSAL_NAME_INFO;
```

The only field in the structure is a pointer to the UNC name for the shared resource. The string is returned in the buffer immediately following the structure. So if a server *\\BigServ\DriveC* was attached as *LocC* and you pass *WNetGetUniversalName* the filename *\Network\LocC\Win32\Filename.ext*, the function returns the UNC name *\\BigServ\DriveC\win32\filename.ext*.

If the *dwInfoLevel* parameter is set to *REMOTE_NAME_INFO_LEVEL*, the buffer is filled with the following structure:

```
typedef struct _REMOTE_NAME_INFO
    LPTSTR  lpUniversalName;
    LPTSTR  lpConnectionName;
    LPTSTR  lpRemainingPath;
} REMOTE_NAME_INFO;
```

This structure not only returns the UNC name but also parses the UNC name into the share name and the remaining path. So, using the same filename as in

the previous example, \network\LocC\win32\filename.ext, the
REMOTE_NAME_INFO fields would point to the following strings:

lpUniversalName: \\BigServ\DriveC\win32\filename.ext

lpConnectionName: \\BigServ\DriveC

lpRemainingPath. \win32\filename.ext

One more thing: you don't have to prefix the local share name with \network. In the preceding example, the filename \LocC\Win32\filename.ext would have produced the same results.

One final WNet function supported by Windows CE is

```
DWORD WNetGetUser (LPCTSTR lpName, LPTSTR lpUserName,
                   LPDWORD lpnLength);
```

This function returns the name the system used to connect to the remote resource. *WNetGetUser* is passed the local name of the shared resource and returns the user name the system used when connecting to the remote resource in the buffer pointed to by *lpUserName*. The *lpnLength* parameter should point to a variable that contains the size of the buffer. If the buffer isn't big enough to contain the user name, the variable pointed to by *lpnLength* is filled with the required size for the buffer.

The ListNet Example Program

ListNet is a short program that lists the persistent network connections on a Windows CE machine. The program's window is a dialog box with three controls: a list box that displays the network connections, a Connect button that lets you add a new persistent connection, and a Disconnect button that lets you delete one of the connections. Double-clicking on a connection in the list box opens an Explorer window to display the contents of that network resource. Figure 13-1 shows the ListNet window, while Listing 13-1 shows the ListNet source code.

Figure 13-1   The ListNet window containing a few network folders

ListNet.rc

```
//======================================================================
// Resource file
//
// Written for the book Programming Windows CE
// Copyright (C) 2003 Douglas Boling
//======================================================================
#include "windows.h"
#include "ListNet.h"                       // Program-specific stuff


//----------------------------------------------------------------------
// Icons and bitmaps
//
ID_ICON ICON    "ListNet.ico"              // Program icon


//----------------------------------------------------------------------
// Main window dialog template
//
ListNet DIALOG discardable 10, 10, 120, 65
STYLE  WS_OVERLAPPED | WS_VISIBLE | WS_CAPTION | WS_SYSMENU |
       DS_CENTER | DS_MODALFRAME
CAPTION "ListNet"
BEGIN
    LISTBOX                 IDD_NETLIST,  2,  2, 116,  46,
                            WS_TABSTOP | WS_VSCROLL |
                            LBS_NOINTEGRALHEIGHT | LBS_USETABSTOPS
    PUSHBUTTON "&Connect...",   IDD_CNCT,  2, 50,  55, 12, WS_TABSTOP
    PUSHBUTTON "&Disconnect...",
                            IDD_DCNCT, 61, 50,  55, 12, WS_TABSTOP
END
```

ListNet.h

```
//======================================================================
// Header file
//
// Written for the book Programming Windows CE
// Copyright (C) 2003 Douglas Boling
//======================================================================
// Returns number of elements
#define dim(x) (sizeof(x) / sizeof(x[0]))


//----------------------------------------------------------------------
// Generic defines and data types
//
```

Listing 13-1   The ListNet source

```
struct decodeUINT {                              // Structure associates
    UINT Code;                                   // messages
                                                 // with a function.
    LRESULT (*Fxn)(HWND, UINT, WPARAM, LPARAM);
};
struct decodeCMD {                               // Structure associates
    UINT Code;                                   // menu IDs with a
    LRESULT (*Fxn)(HWND, WORD, HWND, WORD);      // function.
};
//-----------------------------------------------------------------------
// Generic defines used by application

#define   ID_ICON               1

#define   IDD_NETLIST           100              // Control IDs
#define   IDD_CNCT              101
#define   IDD_DCNCT             102


//-----------------------------------------------------------------------
// Function prototypes
//
INT RefreshLocalNetDrives (HWND hWnd);
int CheckErrorCode (HWND hWnd, int rc, LPTSTR lpText);

// Dialog window procedure
BOOL CALLBACK MainWndProc (HWND, UINT, WPARAM, LPARAM);

// Dialog window Message handlers
BOOL DoCommandMain (HWND, UINT, WPARAM, LPARAM);
// Command functions
LPARAM DoMainCommandExit (HWND, WORD, HWND, WORD);
LPARAM DoMainCommandViewDrive (HWND, WORD, HWND, WORD);
LPARAM DoMainCommandMapDrive (HWND, WORD, HWND, WORD);
LPARAM DoMainCommandFreeDrive  (HWND, WORD, HWND, WORD);
```

ListNet.cpp

```
//=======================================================================
// ListNet - A network demo application for Windows CE
//
// Written for the book Programming Windows CE
// Copyright (C) 2003 Douglas Boling
//=======================================================================
#include <windows.h>              // For all that Windows stuff
#include <winnetwk.h>             // Network includes
#include "ListNet.h"             // Program-specific stuff
```

(continued)

Listing 13-1   *(continued)*

```
#if defined(WIN32_PLATFORM_PSPC)
#include <aygshell.h>                  // Add Pocket PC includes.
#pragma comment( lib, "aygshell" )   // Link Pocket PC lib for menu bar.
#endif
//------------------------------------------------------------------------
// Global data
//
const TCHAR szAppName[] = TEXT ("ListNet");
HINSTANCE hInst;                        // Program instance handle
BOOL fFirst = TRUE;


// Command Message dispatch for MainWindowProc
const struct decodeCMD MainCommandItems[] = {
    IDOK, DoMainCommandExit,
    IDCANCEL, DoMainCommandExit,
    IDD_NETLIST, DoMainCommandViewDrive,
    IDD_CNCT, DoMainCommandMapDrive,
    IDD_DCNCT, DoMainCommandFreeDrive,
};
//========================================================================
//
// Program entry point
//
int WINAPI WinMain (HINSTANCE hInstance, HINSTANCE hPrevInstance,
                    LPWSTR lpCmdLine, int nCmdShow) {
    // Save program instance handle in global variable.
    hInst = hInstance;
    // Create main window.
    DialogBox (hInst, szAppName, NULL, MainWndProc);
    return 0;
}
//========================================================================
// Message handling procedures for main window
//------------------------------------------------------------------------
// MainWndProc - Callback function for application window
//
BOOL CALLBACK MainWndProc (HWND hWnd, UINT wMsg, WPARAM wParam,
                           LPARAM lParam) {
    INT i;
    // With only two messages, do it the old-fashioned way.
    switch (wMsg) {
    case WM_INITDIALOG:
#if defined(WIN32_PLATFORM_PSPC) && (_WIN32_WCE >= 300)
        {
        SHINITDLGINFO di;
        SHMENUBARINFO mbi;                          // For Pocket PC, create
        memset(&mbi, 0, sizeof(SHMENUBARINFO)); // menu bar so that we
```

```
        mbi.cbSize = sizeof(SHMENUBARINFO);        // have a sip button.
        mbi.hwndParent = hWnd;
        mbi.dwFlags = SHCMBF_EMPTYBAR;
        SHCreateMenuBar(&mbi);


        di.dwMask = SHIDIM_FLAGS;
        di.hDlg = hWnd;
        di.dwFlags = SHIDIF_DONEBUTTON | SHIDIF_SIZEDLG;
        SHInitDialog (&di);
        }
#endif
        i = 75;
        SendDlgItemMessage (hWnd, IDD_NETLIST, LB_SETTABSTOPS, 1,
                            (LPARAM)&i);
        RefreshLocalNetDrives (hWnd);
        break;

    case WM_COMMAND:
        return DoCommandMain (hWnd, wMsg, wParam, lParam);
    }
    return FALSE;
}
//------------------------------------------------------------------------
// DoCommandMain - Process WM_COMMAND message for window.
//
BOOL DoCommandMain (HWND hWnd, UINT wMsg, WPARAM wParam, LPARAM lParam){
    WORD idItem, wNotifyCode;
    HWND hwndCtl;
    INT  i;

    // Parse the parameters.
    idItem = (WORD) LOWORD (wParam);
    wNotifyCode = (WORD) HIWORD (wParam);
    hwndCtl = (HWND) lParam;

    // Call routine to handle control message.
    for (i = 0; i < dim(MainCommandItems); i++) {
        if (idItem == MainCommandItems[i].Code) {
            (*MainCommandItems[i].Fxn)(hWnd, idItem, hwndCtl,
                                        wNotifyCode);
            return TRUE;
        }
    }
    return FALSE;
}
//========================================================================
// Command handler routines
```

(continued)

Listing 13-1 *(continued)*

```
//-----------------------------------------------------------
// DoMainCommandExit - Process Program Exit command.
//
LPARAM DoMainCommandExit (HWND hWnd, WORD idItem, HWND hwndCtl,
                          WORD wNotifyCode) {
    EndDialog (hWnd, 0);
    return 0;
}
//-----------------------------------------------------------
// DoMainCommandViewDrive - Process list box double clicks.
//
LPARAM DoMainCommandViewDrive (HWND hWnd, WORD idItem, HWND hwndCtl,
                               WORD wNotifyCode) {
    TCHAR szCmdLine[128], szFolder[MAX_PATH];
    PROCESS_INFORMATION pi;
    HCURSOR hOld;
    INT i, rc, nLen;

    // We're only interested in list box double-clicks.
    if (wNotifyCode != LBN_DBLCLK)
        return 0;

    i = SendMessage (hwndCtl, LB_GETCURSEL, 0, 0);
    if (i == LB_ERR) return 0;
    nLen = SendMessage (hwndCtl, LB_GETTEXT, i, (LPARAM)szFolder);
    if (nLen == LB_ERR)
        return 0;
    // Trim off description of share.
    for (i = 0; i < nLen; i++)
        if (szFolder[i] == TEXT ('\t'))
            break;
    szFolder[i] = TEXT ('\0');

    hOld = SetCursor (LoadCursor (NULL, IDC_WAIT));
    lstrcpy (szCmdLine, TEXT ("\\network\\"));
    lstrcat (szCmdLine, szFolder);

    rc = CreateProcess (TEXT ("Explorer"), szCmdLine, NULL, NULL,
                        FALSE, 0, NULL, NULL, NULL, &pi);
    if (rc) {
        CloseHandle (pi.hProcess);
        CloseHandle (pi.hThread);
    }
    SetCursor (hOld);
    return TRUE;
}
```

```
//-----------------------------------------------------------------
// DoMainCommandMapDrive - Process map network drive command.
//
LPARAM DoMainCommandMapDrive (HWND hWnd, WORD idItem, HWND hwndCtl,
                              WORD wNotifyCode) {
    DWORD rc;
    CONNECTDLGSTRUCT cds;
    NETRESOURCE nr;
    TCHAR szRmt[256];

    memset (&nr, 0, sizeof (nr));
    nr.dwType = RESOURCETYPE_DISK;
    memset (szRmt, 0, sizeof (szRmt));

    cds.cbStructure = sizeof (cds);
    cds.hwndOwner = hWnd;
    cds.lpConnRes = &nr;
    cds.dwFlags = CONNDLG_PERSIST;
    // Display dialog box.
    rc = WNetConnectionDialog1 (&cds);
    if (rc == NO_ERROR)
        RefreshLocalNetDrives (hWnd);
    else
        CheckErrorCode (hWnd, rc, TEXT ("WNetConnectionDialog1"));
    return 0;
}
//-----------------------------------------------------------------
// DoMainCommandFreeDrive - Process disconnect network drive command.
//
LPARAM DoMainCommandFreeDrive (HWND hWnd, WORD idItem, HWND hwndCtl,
                               WORD wNotifyCode) {
    int rc = WNetDisconnectDialog (hWnd, RESOURCETYPE_DISK);
    if (rc == NO_ERROR)
        RefreshLocalNetDrives (hWnd);
    else
        CheckErrorCode (hWnd, rc, TEXT ("WnetDisconnectDialog"));
    return 0;
}
//=================================================================
// Network browsing functions
//-----------------------------------------------------------------
// EnumerateLocalNetDrives - Add an item to the list view control.
//
INT RefreshLocalNetDrives (HWND hWnd) {
    HWND hwndCtl = GetDlgItem (hWnd, IDD_NETLIST);
    INT rc, nBuffSize = 1024;
    DWORD dwCnt, dwSize;
```

(continued)

Listing 13-1 *(continued)*

```
HANDLE hEnum;
LPNETRESOURCE pnr;
NETRESOURCE nr;
PBYTE pPtr, pNew;
TCHAR szText[256];

SendMessage (hwndCtl, LB_RESETCONTENT, 0, 0);

// Allocate buffer for enumeration data.
pPtr = (PBYTE) LocalAlloc (LPTR, nBuffSize);
if (!pPtr)
    return -1;

// Initialize specification for search root.
memset (&nr, 0, sizeof (nr));
lstrcpy (szText, TEXT ("\\sjdev"));
nr.lpRemoteName = szText;
nr.dwUsage = RESOURCEUSAGE_CONTAINER;

// Start enumeration.
rc = WNetOpenEnum (RESOURCE_REMEMBERED, RESOURCETYPE_ANY, 0, 0,
                   &hEnum);
if (rc != NO_ERROR) return -1;

// Enumerate one item per loop.
do {
    dwCnt = 1;
    dwSize = nBuffSize;
    rc = WNetEnumResource (hEnum, &dwCnt, pPtr, &dwSize);
    pnr = (NETRESOURCE *)pPtr;
    lstrcpy (szText, pnr->lpLocalName);
    // Process returned data.
    if (rc == NO_ERROR) {
        switch (pnr->dwType) {
        case RESOURCETYPE_ANY:
            lstrcat (szText, TEXT ("\t Share"));
            break;
        case RESOURCETYPE_PRINT:
            lstrcat (szText, TEXT ("\t Printer"));
            break;
        case RESOURCETYPE_DISK:
            lstrcat (szText, TEXT ("\t Disk"));
            break;
        }
        SendMessage (hwndCtl, LB_ADDSTRING, 0, (LPARAM)szText);
```

```
        // If our buffer was too small, try again.
        } else if (rc == ERROR_MORE_DATA) {
            pNew = (PBYTE)LocalReAlloc (pPtr, dwSize, LMEM_MOVEABLE);
            if (pNew) {
                pPtr = pNew;
                nBuffSize = LocalSize (pPtr);
                rc = 0;
            } else
                break;
        }
    } while (rc == 0);
    // Clean up.
    WNetCloseEnum (hEnum);
    LocalFree (pPtr);
    return 0;
}
//-----------------------------------------------------------------
// CheckErrorCode - Print error messages as necessary.
//
int CheckErrorCode (HWND hWnd, int rc, LPTSTR lpText) {
    TCHAR szTxt[128];

    // If good or dialog canceled, just return.
    if ((rc == NO_ERROR) || (rc == -1))
        return rc;
    if (rc == ERROR_NO_NETWORK)
        lstrcpy (szTxt, TEXT ("No network detected."));
    else
        wsprintf (szTxt, TEXT ("%s failed rc = %d"), lpText, rc);

    MessageBox (hWnd, szTxt, szAppName, MB_OK);
    return rc;
}
```

The heart of the networking code is at the end of ListNet, in the routine *RefreshLocalNetDrives*. This routine uses the WNet enumerate functions to determine the persistent network resources mapped to the system. Network connections and disconnections are accomplished with calls to *WNetConnectionDialog1* and *WNetDisconnectDialog* respectively. You open an Explorer window containing the shared network disk by launching Explorer.exe with a command line that's the path of the folder to open.

This chapter has given you a basic introduction to some of the networking features of Windows CE. Next on our plate is networking from a different angle: peer-to-peer communication. In Chapter 14, we look at how a Windows CE device can communicate with another Windows CE device using Infrared and Bluetooth communication. Let's take a look.

14

Device-to-Device Communication

The personal nature of cellular phones and Pocket PCs requires that a new type of network be supported by the devices. Wide area and local area networks supported by Windows CE devices must share time with personal area networks, those networks that link devices over a short distance perhaps for only a short time. Windows CE supports personal area networking (PAN) over two transport technologies, infrared and radio frequency. The infrared transport conforms to the Infrared Data Association, or IrDA, standard, while Windows CE uses the Bluetooth standard for radio-frequency networking.

Applications interact with both the IrDA communications stack and the Bluetooth stack using the Winsock API. Windows CE supports two different Winsock stacks, one based on Winsock 1.1 and the other based on Winsock 2.0. The Winsock 2 stack is more functional but also much larger than its Winsock 1.1 counterpart. Most new devices will support the Winsock 2.0 stack, although some designers might choose the size advantage of the smaller Winsock 1.1 stack over the greater functionality of the Winsock 2.0 stack.

This chapter covers the IrDA and Bluetooth communication stacks as seen through the Winsock API on Windows CE. The chapter starts with an overview of generic socket communication and then dives into the specifics of IrDA and Bluetooth communication, with an additional section on the Object Exchange (OBEX) standard.

Basic Sockets

Winsock is the name for the Windows Sockets API. Winsock is the API for the Windows CE TCP/IP networking stack and is used to access the IrDA and Bluetooth communication stacks. What's left out of the Windows CE implementation of Winsock is the ever-so-handy *WSAAsyncSelect* function, which enables (under other Windows systems) an application to be informed when a Winsock event has occurred. Actually, in the Winsock 1.1 implementation, many of the *WSAxxx* calls that provide asynchronous actions are missing from Windows CE. Instead, the Windows CE implementation is more like the original Berkeley socket API. Windows CE's developers decided not to support these functions to reduce the size of the Winsock implementation. These functions were handy but not required because Windows CE is multithreaded.

The lack of asynchronous functions doesn't mean that you're left with calling socket functions that block on every call. You can put a socket in nonblocking mode so that any function that can't accomplish its task without waiting on an event will return with a return code indicating that the task isn't yet completed.

Initializing the Winsock DLL

Like other versions of Winsock, the Windows CE version should be initialized before you use it. You accomplish this by calling *WSAStartup*, which initializes the Winsock DLL. It's prototyped as

```
int WSAStartup (WORD wVersionRequested, LPWSADATA lpWSAData);
```

The first parameter is the version of Winsock you're requesting to open. For all current versions of Windows CE, you should indicate version 2.0. An easy way to do this is to use the *MAKEWORD* macro, as in *MAKEWORD (2,0)*. The second parameter must point to a *WSAData* structure.

```
struct WSAData {
    WORD wVersion;
    WORD wHighVersion;
    char szDescription[WSADESCRIPTION_LEN+1];
    char szSystemStatus[WSASYSSTATUS_LEN+1];
    unsigned short iMaxSockets;
    unsigned short iMaxUdpDg;
    char FAR * lpVendorInfo;
};
```

This structure is filled in by *WSAStartup*, providing information about the specific implementation of this version of Winsock. Currently the first two fields return either 0x0101, indicating support for version 1.1, or 0x0202, indicating that the system supports the Winsock 2.0 stack. The *szDescription* and *szSystemStatus* fields can be used by Winsock to return information about itself. In the current Windows CE version of Winsock, these fields aren't used. The *iMaxSockets* parameter suggests a maximum number of sockets that an application should be able to open. This number isn't a hard maximum but rather a suggested maximum. The *iMaxUdpDg* field indicates the maximum size of a datagram packet. A 0 indicates no maximum size for this version of Winsock. Finally, *lpVendorInfo* points to optional vendor-specific information.

WSAStartup returns 0 if successful; otherwise, the return value is the error code for the function. Don't call *WSAGetLastError* in this situation because the failure of this function indicates that Winsock, which provides *WSAGetLastError*, wasn't initialized correctly.

Windows CE also supports *WSACleanup*, which is traditionally called when an application has finished using the Winsock DLL. For Windows CE, this function performs no action but is provided for compatibility. Its prototype is

```
int WSACleanup ();
```

ASCII vs. Unicode

One issue that you'll have to be careful of is that almost all the string fields used in the socket structures are char fields, not Unicode. Because of this, you'll find yourself using the functions

```
int WideCharToMultiByte(UINT CodePage, DWORD dwFlags,
                LPCWSTR lpWideCharStr, int cchWideChar,
                LPSTR lpMultiByteStr, int cchMultiByte,
                LPCSTR lpDefaultChar, LPBOOL lpUsedDefaultChar);
```

to convert Unicode strings to multibyte strings and

```
int MultiByteToWideChar (UINT CodePage, DWORD dwFlags,
                LPCSTR lpMultiByteStr, int cchMultiByte,
                LPWSTR lpWideCharStr, int cchWideChar);
```

to convert multibyte characters to Unicode. The functions refer to multibyte characters instead of ASCII because on double-byte coded systems, they convert double-byte characters to Unicode.

Stream Sockets

Like all socket implementations, Winsock under Windows CE supports both stream and datagram connections. In a stream connection, a socket is basically a data pipe. Once two points are connected, data is sent back and forth without the need for additional addressing. In a datagram connection, the socket is more like a mailslot, with discrete packets of data being sent to specific addresses. In describing the Winsock functions, I'm going to cover the process of creating a *stream* connection (sometimes called a *connection-oriented* connection) between a client application and a server application. I'll leave the explanation of the datagram connection to other, more network-specific, books.

The life of a stream socket is fairly straightforward: it's created, bound, or connected to an address; read from or written to; and finally closed. A few extra steps along the way, however, complicate the story slightly. Sockets work in a client/server model. A client initiates a conversation with a known server. The server, on the other hand, waits around until a client requests data. When setting up a socket, you have to approach the process from either the client side or the server side. This decision determines which functions you call to configure a socket. Table 14-1 illustrates the process from both the client and the server side. For each step in the process, the corresponding Winsock function is shown.

Table 14-1   Process for Producing a Connection-Oriented Socket Connection

Server	Function	Client	Function
Create socket	*socket*	Create socket	socket
Bind socket to an address	*bind*	Find desired server	(many functions)
Listen for client connections	*listen*	Connect to server	*connect*
Accept client's connection	*accept*		
Receive data from client	*recv*	Send data to server	*send*
Send data to client	*send*	Receive data from server	*recv*

Both the client and the server must first create a socket. After that, the process diverges. The server must attach or, to use the function name, *bind*, the socket to an address so that another computer or even a local process can connect to the socket. Once an address has been bound, the server configures the socket to listen for a connection from a client. The server then waits to accept a connection from a client. Finally, after all this, the server is ready to converse.

The client's job is simpler: the client creates the socket, connects the socket to a remote address, and then sends and receives data. This procedure, of course, ignores the sometimes not-so-simple process of determining the address to connect to. I'll leave that problem for a few moments while I talk about the functions behind this process.

Creating a Socket

You create a socket with the function

```
SOCKET socket (int af, int type, int protocol);
```

The first parameter, *af*, specifies the addressing family for the socket. Windows CE supports three addressing formats: *AF_INET*, *AF_IRDA*, and *AF_BT*. You use the *AF_BT* constant when you're creating a socket for Bluetooth use, *AF_IRDA* for an IrDA socket, and *AF_INET* for TCP/IP communication. The *type* parameter specifies the type of socket being created. For a TCP/IP socket, this can be either *SOCK_STREAM* for a stream socket or *SOCK_DGRAM* for a datagram socket. For Bluetooth and IrDA sockets, the *type* parameter must be *SOCK_STREAM*. Windows CE doesn't currently expose a method to create a raw socket, which is a socket that allows you to interact with the IP layer of the TCP/IP protocol. Among other uses, raw sockets are used to send an echo request to other servers, in the process known as pinging. However, Windows CE does provide a method of sending an Internet Control Message Protocol (ICMP) echo request. The protocol parameter specifies the protocol used by the address family specified by the *af* parameter. For Bluetooth, this parameter should be set to *BTHPROTO_RFCOMM*. The function returns a handle to the newly created socket. If an error occurs, the socket returns *INVALID_SOCKET*. You can call *WSAGetLastError* to query the extended error code.

Server Side: Binding a Socket to an Address

For the server, the next step is to bind the socket to an address. You accomplish this with the function

```
int bind (SOCKET s, const struct sockaddr FAR *addr, int namelen);
```

The first parameter is the handle to the newly created socket. The second parameter is dependent on whether you're dealing with a TCP/IP socket, an IrDA socket, or a Bluetooth socket. For a standard TCP/IP socket, the structure pointed to by *addr* should be *SOCKADDR_IN*, which is defined as

```
struct sockaddr_in {
    short sin_family;
    unsigned short sin_port;
    IN_ADDR sin_addr;
    char sin_zero[8];
};
```

The first field, *sin_family*, must be set to *AF_INET*. The second field is the IP port, while the third field specifies the IP address. The last field is simply padding to fit the standard *SOCKADDR* structure. The last parameter of bind, *namelen*, should be set to the size of the *SOCKADDR_IN* structure.

When you're using IrSock, the address structure pointed to by *sockaddr* is *SOCKADDR_IRDA*, which is defined as

```
struct sockaddr_irda {
    u_short irdaAddressFamily;
    u_char irdaDeviceID[4];
    char irdaServiceName[25];
};
```

The first field, *irdaAddressFamily*, should be set to *AF_IRDA* to identify the structure. The second field, *irdaDeviceID*, is a 4-byte array that defines the address for this IR socket. This can be set to 0 for an IrSock server. The last field should be set to a string to identify the server.

You can also use a special predefined name in the *irdaServiceName* field to bypass the IrDA address resolution features. If you specify the name *LSAP-SELxxx*, where *xxx* is a value from 001 through 127, the socket will be bound directly to the LSAP (Logical Service Access Point) selector defined by the value. Applications should not, unless absolutely required, bind directly to a specific LSAP selector. Instead, by specifying a generic string, the IrDA address resolution code determines a free LSAP selector and uses it.

For a Bluetooth socket, the address structure pointed to by *sockaddr* is *SOCKADDR_BTH*, which is defined as

```
typedef struct _SOCKADDR_BTH {
    USHORT    addressFamily;
    bt_addr   btAddr;
    GUID      serviceClassId;
    ULONG     port;
} SOCKADDR_BTH, *PSOCKADDR_BTH;
```

The *addressFamily* field should be set to *AF_BT*. The *bt_addr* structure is a 64-bit field that contains the device's 48-bit Bluetooth address. This field isn't used in the bind call. The *serviceClassId* field is used in the *connect* function to tell the client which server service to connect to. The *port* field can be set to RFCOMM channel 1 through 31 or set to 0 to have the system choose a free channel.

Listening for a Connection

Once a socket has been bound to an address, the server places the socket in listen mode so that it will accept incoming communication attempts. You place the socket in listen mode by using the aptly named function

```
int listen (SOCKET s, int backlog);
```

The two parameters are the handle to the socket and the size of the queue that you're creating to hold the pending connection attempts. This size value can be set to *SOMAXCONN* to set the queue to the maximum supported by the socket implementation.

Accepting a Connection

When a server is ready to accept a connection to a socket in listen mode, it calls this function:

```
SOCKET accept (SOCKET s, struct sockaddr FAR *addr,
               int FAR *addrlen);
```

The first parameter is the socket that has already been placed in listen mode. The next parameter should point to a buffer that receives the address of the client socket that has initiated a connection. The format of this address is dependent on the protocol used by the socket. For Windows CE, this is a *SOCKADDR_IN*, a *SOCKADDR_IRDA*, or a *SOCKADDR_BTH* structure. The final parameter is a pointer to a variable that contains the size of the buffer. This variable is updated with the size of the structure returned in the address buffer when the function returns.

The *accept* function returns the handle to a new socket that's used to communicate with the client. The socket that was originally created by the call to *socket* will remain in listen mode and can potentially accept other connections. If *accept* detects an error, it returns *INVALID_SOCKET*. In this case, you can call *WSAGetLastError* to get the error code.

The *accept* function is the first function I've talked about so far that blocks. That is, it won't return until a remote client requests a connection. You can set the socket in nonblocking mode so that, if no request for connection is queued, *accept* will return *INVALID_SOCKET* with the extended error code *WSAE-WOULDBLOCK*. I'll talk about blocking vs. nonblocking sockets shortly.

Client Side: Connecting a Socket to a Server

On the client side, things are different. Instead of calling the *bind* and *accept* functions, the client simply connects to a known server. I said simply, but as with most things, we must note a few complications. The primary one is addressing—knowing the address of the server you want to connect to. I'll put that topic aside for a moment and assume the client knows the address of the server.

To connect a newly created socket to a server, the client uses the function

```
int connect (SOCKET s, const struct sockaddr FAR *name,
             int namelen);
```

The first parameter is the socket handle that the client created with a call to *socket*. The other two parameters are the address and address length values we've seen in the *bind* and *accept* functions.

If connect is successful, it returns 0. Otherwise, it returns *SOCKET_ERROR*, and you should call *WSAGetLastError* to get the reason for the failure.

Sending and Receiving Data

At this point, both the server and the client have socket handles they can use to communicate with one another. The client uses the socket originally created with the call to *socket*, while the server uses the socket handle returned by the *accept* function.

All that remains is data transfer. You write data to a socket this way:

```
int send (SOCKET s, const char FAR *buf, int len, int flags);
```

The first parameter is the socket handle to send the data. You specify the data you want to send in the buffer pointed to by the *buf* parameter, while the length of that data is specified in *len*. The *flags* parameter must be 0.

You receive data by using the function

```
int recv (SOCKET s, char FAR *buf, int len, int flags);
```

The first parameter is the socket handle. The second parameter points to the buffer that receives the data, while the third parameter should be set to the size of the buffer. The flags parameter can be 0, or it can be *MSG_PEEK* if you want to have the current data copied into the receive buffer but not removed from the input queue or if this is a TCP/IP socket (*MSG_OOB*) for receiving any out-of-band data that has been sent.

Two other functions can send and receive data; they are the following:

```
int sendto (SOCKET s, const char FAR *buf, int len, int flags,
        const struct sockaddr FAR *to, int token);
```

and

```
int recvfrom (SOCKET s, char FAR *buf, int len, int flags,
        struct sockaddr FAR *from, int FAR *fromlen);
```

These functions enable you to direct individual packets of data using the address parameters provided in the functions. They're used for connectionless sockets, but I mention them now for completeness. When used with connection-oriented sockets such as those I've just described, the addresses in *sendto* and *recvfrom* are ignored and the functions act like their simpler counterparts, *send* and *recv*.

Closing a Socket

When you have finished using the sockets, call this function:

```
int shutdown (SOCKET s, int how);
```

The *shutdown* function takes the handle to the socket and a flag indicating the part of the connection you want to shut down. The *how* parameter can be *SD_RECEIVE* to prevent any further *recv* calls from being processed, *SD_SEND* to prevent any further *send* calls from being processed, or *SD_BOTH* to prevent either *send* or *recv* calls from being processed. The *shutdown* function affects the higher-level functions *send* and *recv* but doesn't prevent data previously queued from being processed. Once you have shut down a socket, it can't be used again. It should be closed and a new socket created to restart a session.

Once a connection has been shut down, you should close the socket with a call to this function:

```
int closesocket (SOCKET s);
```

The action of *closesocket* depends on how the socket is configured. If you've properly shut down the socket with a call to *shutdown*, no more events will be pending and *closesocket* should return without blocking. If the socket has been configured into linger mode and configured with a timeout value, *closesocket* will block until any data in the send queue has been sent or the timeout expires.

IrSock

I've alluded to IrSock a number of times as I've described functions. IrSock is essentially a socketlike API built over the top of the IrDA stack used for infrared communication. IrSock is the only high-level interface to the IrDA stack.

The major differences between IrSock and Winsock are that IrSock doesn't support datagrams, it doesn't support security, and the method used for addressing it is completely different from that used for Winsock. What IrSock does provide is a method to query the devices ready to talk across the infrared port, as well as arbitration and collision detection and control.

From a programmer's perspective, the main difference in programming IrSock and Winsock is that the client side needs a method of detecting which infrared-capable devices are within range and are ready to accept a socket connection. This is accomplished by calling *getsockopt* with the level parameter set to *SOL_IRLMP* and the *optname* parameter set to *IRLMP_ENUMDEVICES*, as in the following:

```
dwBuffSize = sizeof (buffer);
rc = getsockopt (hIrSock, SOL_IRLMP, IRLMP_ENUMDEVICES,
                 buffer, &dwBuffSize);
```

When called with *IRLMP_ENUMDEVICES*, *getsockopt* returns a *DEVICELIST* structure in the buffer. *DEVICELIST* is defined as

```
typedef struct _DEVICELIST {
    ULONG numDevice;
    IRDA_DEVICE_INFO Device[1];
} DEVICELIST;
```

The *DEVICELIST* structure is simply a count followed by an array of *IRDA_DEVICE_INFO* structures, one for each device found. The *IRDA_DEVICE_INFO* structure is defined as

```
typedef struct _IRDA_DEVICE_INFO {
    u_char irdaDeviceID[4];
    char irdaDeviceName[22];
    u_char Reserved[2];
} IRDA_DEVICE_INFO;
```

The two fields in the *IRDA_DEVICE_INFO* structure are a device ID and a string that can be used to identify the remote device.

Following is a routine that opens an IR socket and uses *getsockopt* to query the remote devices that are in range. If any devices are found, their names and IDs are printed to the debug port.

```
//
// Poll for IR devices.
//
DWORD WINAPI IrPoll (HWND hWnd) {
    INT rc, nSize, i, j;
    char cDevice[256];
    TCHAR szName[32], szOut[256];
    DEVICELIST *pDL;
    SOCKET irsock;

    // Open an infrared socket.
    irsock = socket (AF_IRDA, SOCK_STREAM, 0);
    if (irsock == INVALID_SOCKET)
        return -1;

    // Search for someone to talk to; try 10 times over 5 seconds.
    for (i = 0; i < 10; i++) {

        // Call getsockopt to query devices.
        memset (cDevice, 0, sizeof (cDevice));
        nSize = sizeof (cDevice);
        rc = getsockopt (irsock, SOL_IRLMP, IRLMP_ENUMDEVICES,
                    cDevice, &nSize);
        if (rc)
            break;
```

```
        pDL = (DEVICELIST *) cDevice;
        if (pDL->numDevice) {
            Add2List (hWnd, TEXT ("%d devices found."), pDL->numDevice);

            for (j = 0; j < (int)pDL->numDevice; j++) {
                // Convert device ID.
                wsprintf (szOut,
                        TEXT ("DeviceID \t%02X.%02X.%02X.%02X"),
                        pDL->Device[j].irdaDeviceID[0],
                        pDL->Device[j].irdaDeviceID[1],
                        pDL->Device[j].irdaDeviceID[2],
                        pDL->Device[j].irdaDeviceID[3]);
                OutputDebugString (szOut);

                // Convert device name to Unicode.
                mbstowcs (szName, pDL->Device[j].irdaDeviceName,
                        sizeof (pDL->Device[j].irdaDeviceName));

                wsprintf (szOut, TEXT ("irdaDeviceName \t%s"),
                        szName);
                OutputDebugString (szOut);
            }
        }
        Sleep(500);
    }
    closesocket (irsock);
    return 0;
}
```

Just having a device with an IR port in range isn't enough; the remote device must have an application running that has opened an IR socket, bound it, and placed it into listen mode. This requirement is appropriate because these are the steps any server using the socket API would perform to configure a socket to accept communication.

Querying and Setting IR Socket Options

IrSock supports the *getsockopt* and *setsockopt* functions for getting and setting the socket options, but the options supported have little overlap with the socket options supported for a standard TCP/IP socket. To query socket options, use this function:

```
int getsockopt (SOCKET s, int level, int optname,
            char FAR *optval, int FAR *optlen);
```

The first parameter is the handle to the socket, while the second parameter is the level in the communications stack for the specific option. The level can be at the socket level, *SOL_SOCKET*, or a level unique to IrSock, *SOL_IRLMP*. The options supported for IrSock are shown in the following lists.

For the *SOL_SOCKET* level, your option is

■ **SO_LINGER**   Queries the linger mode

For the *SOL_IRLMP* level, your options are

■ **IRLMP_ENUMDEVICES**   Enumerates remote IrDA devices

■ **IRLMP_IAS_QUERY**   Queries IAS attributes

■ **IRLMP_SEND_PDU_LEN**   Queries the maximum size of send packet for IrLPT mode

The corresponding function with which to set the options is

```
int setsockopt (SOCKET s, int level, int optname,
                const char FAR *optval, int optlen);
```

The parameters are similar to *getsockopt*. A list of the allowable options follows. For the *SOL_SOCKET* level, your option is

■ **SO_LINGER**   Delays the close of a socket if unsent data remains in the outgoing queue

For the *SOL_IRLMP* level, your options are

■ **IRLMP_IAS_SET**   Sets IAS attributes

■ **IRLMP_IRLPT_MODE**   Sets the IrDA protocol to IrLPT

■ **IRLMP_9WIRE_MODE**   Sets the IrDA protocol to 9-wire serial mode

■ **IRLMP_SHARP_MODE**   Sets the IrDA protocol to Sharp mode

Blocking vs. Nonblocking Sockets

One issue I briefly touched on as I was introducing sockets is blocking. Windows programmers are used to the quite handy asynchronous socket calls that are an extension of the standard Berkeley socket API. By default, a socket is in blocking mode so that, for example, if you call *recv* to read data from a socket and no data is available, the call blocks until some data can be read. This isn't the type of call you want to be making with a thread that's servicing the message loop for your application.

Although Windows CE doesn't support the *WSAAsync* calls available to desktop versions of Windows, you can switch a socket from its default blocking mode to nonblocking mode. In nonblocking mode, any socket call that might need to wait to successfully perform its function instead returns immediately with the error code *WSAEWOULDBLOCK*. You are then responsible for calling the would-have-blocked function again at a later time to complete the task.

To set a socket into blocking mode, use this function.

```
int ioctlsocket (SOCKET s, long cmd, u_long *argp);
```

The parameters are the socket handle, a command, and a pointer to a variable that either contains data or receives data depending on the value in *cmd*. The allowable commands for Windows CE IrSock sockets are the following:

- **FIONBIO** Sets or clears a socket's blocking mode. If the value pointed to by *argp* is nonzero, the socket is placed in blocking mode. If the value is 0, the socket is placed in nonblocking mode.

- **FIONREAD** Returns the number of bytes that can be read from the socket with one call to the *recv* function.

So to set a socket in blocking mode, you should make a call like this one:

```
fBlocking = FALSE;
rc = ioctlsocket (sock, FIONBIO, &fBlocking);
```

Of course, once you have a socket in nonblocking mode, the worst thing you can do is continually poll the socket to see whether the nonblocked event occurred. On a battery-powered system, this can dramatically lower battery life. Instead of polling, you can use the *select* function to inform you when a socket or set of sockets is in a nonblocking state. The prototype for this function is

```
int select (int nfds, fd_set FAR *readfds, fd_set FAR *writefds,
            fd_set FAR *exceptfds,
            const struct timeval FAR *timeout);
```

The parameters for the *select* function look somewhat complex, which, in fact, they are. Just to throw a curve, the function ignores the first parameter. The reason it exists at all is for compatibility with the Berkeley version of the *select* function. The next three parameters are pointers to sets of socket handles. The first set should contain the sockets that you want to be notified when one or more of the sockets is in a nonblocking read state. The second set contains socket handles of sockets that you want informed when a write function can be called without blocking. Finally, the third set, pointed to by *exceptfds*, contains the handles of sockets that you want notified when an error condition exists in that socket.

The final parameter is a timeout value. In keeping with the rather interesting parameter formats for the *select* function, the timeout value isn't a simple millisecond count. Rather, it's a pointer to a *TIMEVAL* structure defined as

```
struct timeval {
    long    tv_sec;
    long    tv_usec;
};
```

If the two fields in *TIMEVAL* are 0, the *select* call returns immediately, even if none of the sockets has had an event occur. If the pointer, *timeout*, is *NULL* instead of pointing to a *TIMEVAL* structure, the select call won't time out and returns only when an event occurs in one of the sockets. Otherwise, the timeout value is specified in seconds and microseconds in the two fields provided.

The function returns the total number of sockets for which the appropriate events occur, 0 if the function times out, or *SOCKET_ERROR* if an error occurs. If an error does occur, you can call *WSAGetLastError* to get the error code. The function modifies the contents of the sets so that, on returning from the function, the sets contain only the socket handles of sockets for which events occur.

The sets that contain the events should be considered opaque. The format of the sets doesn't match their Berkeley socket counterparts. Each of the sets is manipulated by four macros defined in WINSOCK.H. These are the four macros:

- **FD_CLR**   Removes the specified socket handle from the set
- **FD_ISSET**   Returns *TRUE* if the socket handle is part of the set
- **FD_SET**   Adds the specified socket handle to the set
- **FD_ZERO**   Initializes the set to 0

To use a set, you have to declare a set of type *fd_set*. Then initialize the set with a call to *FD_ZERO* and add the socket handles you want with *FD_SET*. An example would be

```
fd_set fdReadSocks;

FD_ZERO (&fdReadSocks);
FD_SET (hSock1, &fdReadSocks);
FD_SET (hSock2, &fdReadSocks);

rc = select (0, &fdReadSocks, NULL, NULL, NULL);
if (rc != SOCKET_ERROR) {
    if (FD_ISSET (hSock1, &fdReadSocks))
        // A read event occurred in socket 1.
    if (FD_ISSET (hSock2, &fdReadSocks))
        // A read event occurred in socket 2.
}
```

In this example, the *select* call waits on read events from two sockets with the handles *hSock1* and *hSock2*. The write and error sets are *NULL*, as is the pointer to the *timeout* structure, so the call to *select* won't return until a read event occurs in one of the two sockets. When the function returns, the code checks to see whether the socket handles are in the returned set. If so, that socket has a nonblocking read condition.

The last little subtlety concerning the *select* function is just what qualifies as a read, write, and error condition. A socket in the read set is signaled when one of the following events occurs:

- There is data in the input queue, so *recv* can be called without blocking.

- The socket is in listen mode and a connection has been attempted, so a call to *accept* won't block.

- The connection has been closed, reset, or terminated. If the connection was gracefully closed, *recv* returns with 0 bytes read; otherwise, the *recv* call returns *SOCKET_ERROR*. If the socket has been reset, the *recv* function returns the error *WSACONNRESET*.

A socket in the write set is signaled under the following conditions:

- Data can be written to the socket. A call to send still might block if you attempt to write more data than can be held in the outgoing queue.

- A socket is processing a *connect* and the connect has been accepted by the server.

A socket in the exception set is signaled under the following condition:

- A socket is processing a *connect* and the connect failed.

The MySquirt Example Program

To demonstrate IrSock, the following program, MySquirt, shows how to transfer files from one Windows system to another. It's similar to the IrSquirt program provided with the Pocket PC and Smartphone. The difference is that this program is designed to be compiled for and run on Windows CE and Windows XP systems.[1] So by running the program on these systems, you can send, that is, *squirt*, files from one system to another. MySquirt has a window that displays a

---

1. To build MySquirt for Windows XP or Windows Me, use Microsoft Visual C++ 6.0 or Microsoft Visual Studio .NET.

list of status messages as the handshaking takes place between the two Windows systems. To use MySquirt, you'll need to have it running on two Windows systems. To transfer a file, enter the name of the file you want to send and press the Send button. The system transmits the name and size of the file to the receiving system, and if it's accepted, the file data is subsequently sent. Figure 14-1 shows MySquirt on an embedded Windows CE device after it has sent a file to a Pocket PC, while Figure 14-2 shows the results on the Pocket PC screen. The source code for the example is shown in Listing 14-1.

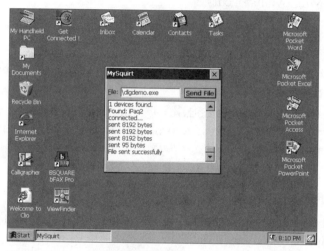

Figure 14-1 The MySquirt window on an embedded Windows CE device after a file has been sent

Figure 14-2 The MySquirt window on a Pocket PC after a file has been received

MySquirt.rc

```
//======================================================================
// Resource file
//
// Written for the book Programming Windows CE
// Copyright (C) 2003 Douglas Boling
//======================================================================

#include "windows.h"
#include "MySquirt.h"                              // Program-specific stuff


//----------------------------------------------------------------------
// Icons and bitmaps
//
ID_ICON ICON   "MySquirt.ico"                      // Program icon


//----------------------------------------------------------------------
// Main window dialog template
//
MySquirt DIALOG discardable 10, 10, 135, 110
STYLE  WS_OVERLAPPED | WS_VISIBLE | WS_CAPTION | WS_SYSMENU |
       DS_CENTER | DS_MODALFRAME
CAPTION "MySquirt"
CLASS "MySquirt"
BEGIN
    LTEXT "&File:"                       -1,    2,  11,  15,  12
    EDITTEXT                 IDD_OUTTEXT, 17,  10,  71,  12,
                             WS_TABSTOP | ES_AUTOHSCROLL
    PUSHBUTTON "&Send File" IDD_SENDFILE, 92,  10,  38,  12, WS_TABSTOP

    LISTBOX                  IDD_INTEXT,   2,  25, 128,  80,
                             WS_TABSTOP | WS_VSCROLL
END
```

MySquirt.h

```
//======================================================================
// Header file
//
// Written for the book Programming Windows CE
// Copyright (C) 2003 Douglas Boling
//======================================================================
// Returns number of elements
#define dim(x) (sizeof(x) / sizeof(x[0]))
```

Listing 14-1   The MySquirt source code

(continued)

Listing 14-1 *(continued)*

```
// Defines that are different between Windows CE and Desktop Windows
#ifdef _WIN32_WCE
// Windows CE-specific defines
#define LPCMDLINE LPWSTR
// On Windows CE, we call begin thread directly.
#define MyCreateThread CreateThread

// Desktop Windows defines
#else
#define LPCMDLINE LPSTR
// This macro calls beginthreadex when this program is compiled
// for the desktop.
typedef unsigned (__stdcall *PTHREAD_START)(void *);
#define MyCreateThread(psa, cbStack, pfnStartAddr, pvParam, fdwCreate,\
    pdwThreadID)((HANDLE) _beginthreadex ((void *)(psa), \
    (unsigned)(cbStack), (PTHREAD_START)(pfnStartAddr),\
    (void *)(pvParam), (unsigned)(fdwCreate), (unsigned *)(pdwThreadID)))

#endif

//----------------------------------------------------------------------
// Generic defines and data types
//
struct decodeUINT {                                 // Structure associates
    UINT Code;                                      // messages
                                                    // with a function.
    LRESULT (*Fxn)(HWND, UINT, WPARAM, LPARAM);
};
struct decodeCMD {                                  // Structure associates
    UINT Code;                                      // menu IDs with a
    LRESULT (*Fxn)(HWND, WORD, HWND, WORD);         // function.
};

//----------------------------------------------------------------------
// Generic defines used by application

#define  ID_ICON             1

#define  IDD_INTEXT          10                     // Control IDs
#define  IDD_SENDFILE        11
#define  IDD_OUTTEXT         12

// Error codes used by transfer protocol
#define GOOD_XFER            0
#define BAD_FILEOPEN        -1
#define BAD_FILEMEM         -2
#define BAD_FILEREAD        -3
```

```
#define BAD_FILEWRITE      -3
#define BAD_SOCKET         -4
#define BAD_SOCKETRECV     -5
#define BAD_FILESIZE       -6
#define BAD_MEMORY         -7


#define BLKSIZE            8192                    // Transfer block size


//----------------------------------------------------------------------
// Function prototypes
//
HWND InitInstance (HINSTANCE, LPCMDLINE, int);
int TermInstance (HINSTANCE, int);


// Window procedures
LRESULT CALLBACK MainWndProc (HWND, UINT, WPARAM, LPARAM);


// Message handlers
LRESULT DoCreateMain (HWND, UINT, WPARAM, LPARAM);
LRESULT DoSizeMain (HWND, UINT, WPARAM, LPARAM);
LRESULT DoCommandMain (HWND, UINT, WPARAM, LPARAM);
LRESULT DoPocketPCShell (HWND, UINT, WPARAM, LPARAM);
LRESULT DoDestroyMain (HWND, UINT, WPARAM, LPARAM);


// Command functions
LPARAM DoMainCommandSend (HWND, WORD, HWND, WORD);
LPARAM DoMainCommandExit (HWND, WORD, HWND, WORD);


// Thread functions
DWORD WINAPI MonitorThread (PVOID pArg);
DWORD WINAPI ReceiveThread (PVOID pArg);
DWORD WINAPI SendFileThread (PVOID pArg);
```

MySquirt.cpp

```
//======================================================================
// MySquirt - A simple IrSock application for Windows CE
//
// Written for the book Programming Windows CE
// Copyright (C) 2003 Douglas Boling
//======================================================================
#include <windows.h>                    // For all that Windows stuff
#include <stdlib.h>
#include <stdio.h>
#include <af_irda.h>                    // IrDA includes
#include <winsock.h>                    // Socket includes
#include "MySquirt.h"                   // Program-specific stuff
#ifndef _WIN32_WCE
```

(continued)

Listing 14-1   *(continued)*

```
#include <process.h>                    // Desktop multithread includes
#include <tchar.h>
#endif
#if defined(WIN32_PLATFORM_PSPC)
#include <aygshell.h>                   // Add Pocket PC includes.
#pragma comment( lib, "aygshell" )      // Link Pocket PC lib for menu bar.
#endif


//-----------------------------------------------------------------------
// Global data
//
const TCHAR szAppName[] = TEXT ("MySquirt");
const char chzAppName[] = "MySquirt";
HINSTANCE hInst;                        // Program instance handle
HWND hMain;                             // Main window handle
BOOL fContinue = TRUE;                  // Server thread continue flag
BOOL fFirstSize = TRUE;                 // First WM_SIZE flag
#if defined(WIN32_PLATFORM_PSPC) && (_WIN32_WCE >= 300)
SHACTIVATEINFO sai;                     // Needed for P/PC helper functions
#endif

// Message dispatch table for MainWindowProc
const struct decodeUINT MainMessages[] = {
    WM_CREATE, DoCreateMain,
    WM_SIZE, DoSizeMain,
    WM_COMMAND, DoCommandMain,
    WM_SETTINGCHANGE, DoPocketPCShell,
    WM_ACTIVATE, DoPocketPCShell,
    WM_DESTROY, DoDestroyMain,
};
// Command Message dispatch for MainWindowProc
const struct decodeCMD MainCommandItems[] = {
#if defined(WIN32_PLATFORM_PSPC) && (_WIN32_WCE >= 300)
    IDOK, DoMainCommandExit,
#else
    IDOK, DoMainCommandSend,
#endif
    IDCANCEL, DoMainCommandExit,
    IDD_SENDFILE, DoMainCommandSend,
};
//=======================================================================
// Program entry point
//
int WINAPI WinMain (HINSTANCE hInstance, HINSTANCE hPrevInstance,
                    LPCMDLINE lpCmdLine, int nCmdShow) {
    MSG msg;
    int rc = 0;
```

```
    // Initialize application.
    hMain = InitInstance (hInstance, lpCmdLine, nCmdShow);
    if (hMain == 0)
        return TermInstance (hInstance, 0x10);

    // Application message loop
    while (GetMessage (&msg, NULL, 0, 0)) {
        if ((hMain == 0) || !IsDialogMessage (hMain, &msg)) {
            TranslateMessage (&msg);
            DispatchMessage (&msg);
        }
    }
    // Instance cleanup
    return TermInstance (hInstance, msg.wParam);
}
}
//-----------------------------------------------------------------------
// InitInstance - Instance initialization
//
HWND InitInstance (HINSTANCE hInstance, LPCMDLINE lpCmdLine,
                    int nCmdShow){
    HWND hWnd;
    HANDLE hThread;
    WNDCLASS wc;
    WSADATA wsaData;
    int rc;

    hInst = hInstance;                      // Save program instance handle.

    // For all systems, if previous instance exists, activate it instead
    // of starting a new one.
    hWnd = FindWindow (szAppName, NULL);
    if (hWnd) {
        SetForegroundWindow ((HWND)((DWORD)hWnd | 0x01));
        return 0;
    }
    // Init Winsock
    rc = WSAStartup (1, &wsaData);
    if (rc) {
        MessageBox (NULL, TEXT("Error in WSAStartup"), szAppName, MB_OK);
        return 0;
    }
    // Register application main window class.
    wc.style = 0;                           // Window style
    wc.lpfnWndProc = MainWndProc;           // Callback function
    wc.cbClsExtra = 0;                      // Extra class data
    wc.cbWndExtra = DLGWINDOWEXTRA;         // Extra window data
    wc.hInstance = hInstance;               // Owner handle
```

(continued)

Listing 14-1   *(continued)*

```
    wc.hIcon = NULL;                           // Application icon
    wc.hCursor = LoadCursor (NULL, IDC_ARROW);// Default cursor
    wc.hbrBackground = (HBRUSH) GetStockObject (LTGRAY_BRUSH);
    wc.lpszMenuName = NULL;                     // Menu name
    wc.lpszClassName = szAppName;               // Window class name
    if (RegisterClass (&wc) == 0) return 0;

    // Create main window.
    hWnd = CreateDialog (hInst, szAppName, NULL, NULL);
    // Return 0 if window not created.
    if (!IsWindow (hWnd)) return 0;

    // Create secondary threads for interprocess communication.
    hThread = MyCreateThread (NULL, 0, MonitorThread, hWnd, 0, 0);
    if (hThread == 0) {
        DestroyWindow (hWnd);
        return 0;
    }
    CloseHandle (hThread);

    ShowWindow (hWnd, nCmdShow);        // Standard show and update calls
    UpdateWindow (hWnd);
    SetFocus (GetDlgItem (hWnd, IDD_OUTTEXT));
    return hWnd;
}
//----------------------------------------------------------------------
// TermInstance - Program cleanup
//
int TermInstance (HINSTANCE hInstance, int nDefRC) {
    return nDefRC;
}
//======================================================================
// Message handling procedures for main window
TCHAR szTitle[128];
//----------------------------------------------------------------------
// MainWndProc - Callback function for application window
//
LRESULT CALLBACK MainWndProc (HWND hWnd, UINT wMsg, WPARAM wParam,
                              LPARAM lParam) {
    INT i;
    //
    // Search message list to see if we need to handle this
    // message. If in list, call procedure.
    //
    for (i = 0; i < dim(MainMessages); i++) {
        if (wMsg == MainMessages[i].Code)
            return (*MainMessages[i].Fxn)(hWnd, wMsg, wParam, lParam);
    }
```

```
        return DefWindowProc (hWnd, wMsg, wParam, lParam);
}
//----------------------------------------------------------------------
// DoCreateMain - Process WM_CREATE message for window.
//
LRESULT DoCreateMain (HWND hWnd, UINT wMsg, WPARAM wParam,
                      LPARAM lParam) {

#if defined(WIN32_PLATFORM_PSPC) && (_WIN32_WCE >= 300)
    SHINITDLGINFO shidi;
    SHMENUBARINFO mbi;                          // For Pocket PC, create
    memset(&mbi, 0, sizeof(SHMENUBARINFO)); // menu bar so that we
    mbi.cbSize = sizeof(SHMENUBARINFO);       // have a sip button.
    mbi.dwFlags = SHCMBF_EMPTYBAR;
    mbi.hwndParent = hWnd;
    SHCreateMenuBar(&mbi);
    SendMessage(mbi.hwndMB, SHCMBM_GETSUBMENU, 0, 100);

    // For Pocket PC, make dialog box full screen with P/PC-
    // specific call. Since this call is only on P/PC, we
    // must use Loadlibrary, GetProcAddress to gain access
    // to the function.
    shidi.dwMask = SHIDIM_FLAGS;
    shidi.dwFlags = SHIDIF_DONEBUTTON | SHIDIF_SIZEDLG | SHIDIF_SIPDOWN;
    shidi.hDlg = hWnd;
    SHInitDialog(&shidi);

    sai.cbSize = sizeof (sai);
    SHHandleWMSettingChange(hWnd, wParam, lParam, &sai);
#endif
    GetWindowText (hWnd, szTitle, dim (szTitle));
    return 0;
}
//----------------------------------------------------------------------
// DoSizeMain - Process WM_SIZE message for window.
//
LRESULT DoSizeMain (HWND hWnd, UINT wMsg, WPARAM wParam,
                    LPARAM lParam) {
#if defined(WIN32_PLATFORM_PSPC) && (_WIN32_WCE >= 300)
    static RECT rectListbox;
    RECT rect;

    GetClientRect (hWnd, &rect);
    if (fFirstSize) {
        // First time through, get the position of the list box for
        // resizing later. Store the distance from the sides of
        // the list box control to the side of the parent window.
        if (IsWindow (GetDlgItem (hWnd, IDD_INTEXT))) {
```

(continued)

Listing 14-1   *(continued)*

```
                fFirstSize = FALSE;
                GetWindowRect (GetDlgItem (hWnd, IDD_INTEXT), &rectListbox);
                MapWindowPoints (HWND_DESKTOP, hWnd, (LPPOINT)&rectListbox, 2);
                rectListbox.right = rect.right - rectListbox.right;
                rectListbox.bottom = rect.bottom - rectListbox.bottom;
            }
        }
        SetWindowPos (GetDlgItem (hWnd, IDD_INTEXT), 0, rect.left + 5,
                    rectListbox.top, rect.right - 10,
                    rect.bottom - rectListbox.top - 5,
                    SWP_NOZORDER);
#endif
    return 0;
}
//----------------------------------------------------------------------
// DoCommandMain - Process WM_COMMAND message for window.
//
LRESULT DoCommandMain (HWND hWnd, UINT wMsg, WPARAM wParam,
                       LPARAM lParam) {
    WORD idItem, wNotifyCode;
    HWND hwndCtl;
    INT i;

    // Parse the parameters.
    idItem = (WORD) LOWORD (wParam);
    wNotifyCode = (WORD) HIWORD (wParam);
    hwndCtl = (HWND) lParam;

    // Call routine to handle control message.
    for (i = 0; i < dim(MainCommandItems); i++) {
        if (idItem == MainCommandItems[i].Code)
            return (*MainCommandItems[i].Fxn)(hWnd, idItem, hwndCtl,
                                               wNotifyCode);
    }
    return 0;
}
//----------------------------------------------------------------------
// DoPocketPCShell - Process Pocket PC-required messages.
//
LRESULT DoPocketPCShell (HWND hWnd, UINT wMsg, WPARAM wParam,
                         LPARAM lParam) {
#if defined(WIN32_PLATFORM_PSPC) && (_WIN32_WCE >= 300)
    if (wMsg == WM_SETTINGCHANGE)
        return SHHandleWMSettingChange(hWnd, wParam, lParam, &sai);
    if (wMsg == WM_ACTIVATE)
        return SHHandleWMActivate(hWnd, wParam, lParam, &sai, 0);
#endif
```

```
      return 0;
}
//----------------------------------------------------------------------
// DoDestroyMain - Process WM_DESTROY message for window.
//
LRESULT DoDestroyMain (HWND hWnd, UINT wMsg, WPARAM wParam,
                       LPARAM lParam) {
   fContinue = FALSE;                    // Shut down server thread.
   Sleep (0);                            // Pass on timeslice.
   PostQuitMessage (0);
   return 0;
}
//======================================================================
// Command handler routines
//----------------------------------------------------------------------
// DoMainCommandExit - Process Program Exit command.
//
LPARAM DoMainCommandExit (HWND hWnd, WORD idItem, HWND hwndCtl,
                          WORD wNotifyCode) {

   SendMessage (hWnd, WM_CLOSE, 0, 0);
   return 0;
}
//----------------------------------------------------------------------
// DoMainCommandSend - Process Program Send File command.
//
LPARAM DoMainCommandSend (HWND hWnd, WORD idItem, HWND hwndCtl,
                          WORD wNotifyCode) {
   static TCHAR szName[MAX_PATH];

   GetDlgItemText (hWnd, IDD_OUTTEXT, szName, dim(szName));
   MyCreateThread (NULL, 0, SendFileThread, (PVOID)szName, 0, NULL);
   return 0;
}
//----------------------------------------------------------------------
// Add2List - Add string to the report list box.
//
void Add2List (HWND hWnd, LPTSTR lpszFormat, ...) {
   int i, nBuf;
   TCHAR szBuffer[512];

   va_list args;
   va_start(args, lpszFormat);

   nBuf = _vstprintf(szBuffer, lpszFormat, args);

   i = SendDlgItemMessage (hWnd, IDD_INTEXT, LB_ADDSTRING, 0,
                           (LPARAM)(LPCTSTR)szBuffer);
```

(continued)

Listing 14-1 *(continued)*

```
        if (i != LB_ERR)
            SendDlgItemMessage (hWnd, IDD_INTEXT, LB_SETTOPINDEX, i,
                                (LPARAM)(LPCTSTR)szBuffer);
    va_end(args);
}
//-------------------------------------------------------------------
// MySetWindowText - Set window title to passed printf style string.
//
void MySetWindowText (HWND hWnd, LPTSTR lpszFormat, ...) {
    int nBuf;
    TCHAR szBuffer[512];

    va_list args;
    va_start(args, lpszFormat);

    nBuf =_vstprintf(szBuffer, lpszFormat, args);

    SetWindowText (hWnd, szBuffer);
    va_end(args);
}
//===================================================================
// MonitorThread - Monitors for connections; connects and notifies
// user when a connection occurs.
//
DWORD WINAPI MonitorThread (PVOID pArg) {
    HWND hWnd = (HWND)pArg;
    INT rc, nSize, i;
    SOCKADDR_IRDA iraddr, t_iraddr;
    SOCKET t_sock, s_sock;

    Add2List (hWnd, TEXT("Monitor thread entered"));

    // Open an infrared socket.
    s_sock = socket (AF_IRDA, SOCK_STREAM, 0);
    if (s_sock == INVALID_SOCKET) {
        Add2List (hWnd, TEXT("Socket failed. rc %d"), WSAGetLastError());
        return 0;
    }
    // Fill in irda socket address structure.
    iraddr.irdaAddressFamily = AF_IRDA;
    for (i = 0; i < dim (iraddr.irdaDeviceID); i++)
        iraddr.irdaDeviceID[i] = 0;
    memcpy (iraddr.irdaServiceName, chzAppName, sizeof (chzAppName) + 1);

    // Bind address to socket.
    rc = bind (s_sock, (struct sockaddr *)&iraddr, sizeof (iraddr));
    if (rc) {
```

```
            Add2List (hWnd, TEXT(" bind failed"));
            closesocket (s_sock);
            return 0;
        }
        // Set socket into listen mode.
        rc = listen (s_sock, SOMAXCONN);
        if (rc == SOCKET_ERROR) {
            Add2List (hWnd, TEXT(" listen failed %d"), GetLastError());
            closesocket (s_sock);
            return 0;
        }
        // Wait for remote requests.
        // Block on accept.
        while (fContinue) {
            nSize = sizeof (t_iraddr);
            t_sock = accept (s_sock, (struct sockaddr *)&t_iraddr, &nSize);
            if (t_sock == INVALID_SOCKET) {
                Add2List (hWnd, TEXT(" accept failed %d"), GetLastError());
            }
            Add2List (hWnd, TEXT("sock accept..."));
            MyCreateThread (NULL, 0, ReceiveThread, (PVOID)t_sock, 0, NULL);
        }
        closesocket (s_sock);
        Add2List (hWnd, TEXT("Monitor thread exit"));
        return 0;
}
//======================================================================
// ReceiveThread - Sends the file requested by the remote device
//
DWORD WINAPI ReceiveThread (PVOID pArg) {
    SOCKET t_sock = (SOCKET)pArg;
    HWND hWnd = hMain; // I'm cheating here.
    int nCnt, nFileSize, rc;
    TCHAR szFileName[MAX_PATH];
    char szAnsiName[MAX_PATH];
    PBYTE pBuff;
    int i, nSize, nTotal;
    DWORD dwBytes;
    HANDLE hFile;
    Add2List (hWnd, TEXT("receive thread entered"));
    SetThreadPriority (GetCurrentThread (), THREAD_PRIORITY_ABOVE_NORMAL);

    // Read the number of bytes in the filename.
    rc = recv (t_sock, (LPSTR)&nCnt, sizeof (nCnt), 0);
    if ((rc == SOCKET_ERROR) || (nCnt > MAX_PATH)) {
        Add2List (hWnd, TEXT("failed receiving name size"));
        closesocket (t_sock);
```

(continued)

Listing 14-1   *(continued)*

```
            return 0;
    }
    // Read the filename. If Pocket PC, put file in my documents.
    // Deal in ANSI here since it will be translated to Unicode later.
#if defined(WIN32_PLATFORM_PSPC)
    strcpy (szAnsiName, "\\my documents\\");    //Ansi
#else
    strcpy (szAnsiName, "\\");                  //Ansi
#endif //defined(WIN32_PLATFORM_PSPC)
    i = strlen (szAnsiName);                    //Ansi
    rc = recv (t_sock, (LPSTR)&szAnsiName[i], nCnt, 0);
    if (rc == SOCKET_ERROR) {
        Add2List (hWnd, TEXT("failed receiving name"));
        closesocket (t_sock);
        return 0;
    }
#ifdef _UNICODE
    mbstowcs (szFileName, szAnsiName, strlen (szAnsiName) + 1);
#else
    lstrcpy (szFileName, szAnsiName);
#endif
    Add2List (hWnd, TEXT("name: %s"), szFileName);

    pBuff = (PBYTE)LocalAlloc (LPTR, BLKSIZE); //Create buff for file.
    //
    // Receive file size.
    //
    rc = recv (t_sock, (LPSTR)&nFileSize, sizeof (nFileSize), 0);
    Add2List (hWnd, TEXT("received file size of %d bytes"), nFileSize);

    if ((rc != SOCKET_ERROR) && (nFileSize > 0)) {
        // We should really check here to see if there is enough
        // free space to receive the file.

        // Create the file. Overwrite if user says so.
        rc = 0;
        hFile = CreateFile (szFileName, GENERIC_WRITE, 0, NULL,
                            CREATE_ALWAYS, FILE_ATTRIBUTE_NORMAL, NULL);
        if (hFile == INVALID_HANDLE_VALUE) {
            Add2List (hWnd, TEXT("File Open failed. rc %d"),
                      GetLastError());
            rc = BAD_FILEWRITE;
        }
        // Send ack code.
        Add2List (hWnd, TEXT("Sending size ack."));
        send (t_sock, (LPSTR)&rc, sizeof (rc), 0);
```

```
        //
        // Receive file.
        //
        nTotal = nFileSize;
        while ((!rc) && (nFileSize > 0)) {

            MySetWindowText (hWnd, TEXT ("%02d%% received"),
                            (nTotal-nFileSize)*100/nTotal);
            nCnt = min (BLKSIZE, nFileSize);
            for (nSize = 0; nSize < nCnt;) {
                i = recv (t_sock, (LPSTR)pBuff+nSize, nCnt-nSize, 0);
                if (i == SOCKET_ERROR) {
                    Add2List (hWnd, TEXT("recv socket err %d"),
                            GetLastError());
                    rc = BAD_SOCKETRECV;
                    break;
                }
                nSize += i;
            }
            Add2List (hWnd, TEXT("recv'd %d bytes."), nSize);
            if (i) {
                if (!WriteFile (hFile, pBuff, nSize, &dwBytes, 0))
                    rc = BAD_FILEWRITE;
                nFileSize -= dwBytes;
            } else
                Sleep(50);
            // Send ack of packet.
            send (t_sock, (LPSTR)&rc, sizeof (rc), 0);
        }
    } else if (rc == BAD_FILEOPEN)
        Add2List (hWnd, TEXT("File not found."));
    Add2List (hWnd, TEXT("receive finished"));
    SetWindowText (hWnd, szTitle);
    LocalFree (pBuff);
    CloseHandle (hFile);
    Add2List (hWnd, TEXT("receive thread exit"));
    return 0;
}
//-----------------------------------------------------------------------
// SendFile - Sends a file to the remote device
//
DWORD WINAPI SendFileThread (PVOID pArg) {
    TCHAR *szFileName = (LPTSTR)pArg;
    HWND hWnd = hMain;
    SOCKET c_sock;
    char szAnsiName[MAX_PATH];
    HANDLE hFile;
    INT rc, nSize, i, nFileSize, nTotal, nCnt;
```

(continued)

Listing 14-1 *(continued)*

```c
char cDevice[256];
SOCKADDR_IRDA iraddr;
DEVICELIST *pDL;
LPSTR pPtr;
PBYTE pBuff;

// Open the file.
hFile = CreateFile (szFileName, GENERIC_READ, FILE_SHARE_READ,
                    NULL, OPEN_EXISTING, 0, NULL);
if (hFile == INVALID_HANDLE_VALUE) {
    Add2List (hWnd, TEXT("File open failed. rc %d"),
              GetLastError());
    return -1;
}

// Open an infrared socket.
c_sock = socket (AF_IRDA, SOCK_STREAM, 0);
if (c_sock == INVALID_SOCKET) {
    Add2List (hWnd, TEXT("Sock failed. rc %d"), WSAGetLastError());
    CloseHandle (hFile);
    return 0;
}
// Search for someone to talk to.
for (i = 0; i < 5; i++) {
    memset (cDevice, 0, sizeof (cDevice));
    nSize = sizeof (cDevice);
    rc = getsockopt (c_sock, SOL_IRLMP, IRLMP_ENUMDEVICES,
                     cDevice, &nSize);
    if (rc)
        Add2List (hWnd, TEXT("Getsockopt failed. rc %d"),
                  WSAGetLastError());

    pDL = (DEVICELIST *) cDevice;
    if (pDL->numDevice) {
        Add2List (hWnd, TEXT("%d devices found."), pDL->numDevice);
        break;
    }
    Sleep(500);
}
// If no device found, exit.
if (pDL->numDevice == 0) {
    closesocket (c_sock);
    CloseHandle (hFile);
    Add2List (hWnd, TEXT("No infrared devices found in range."));
    return -2;
}
```

```
//
// Copy address of found device.
//
memset (&iraddr, 0, sizeof (iraddr));
iraddr.irdaAddressFamily = AF_IRDA;
memcpy (iraddr.irdaDeviceID, pDL->Device[0].irdaDeviceID, 4);
//
// Now initialize the specific socket we're interested in.
//
memcpy (iraddr.irdaServiceName, chzAppName, sizeof (chzAppName)+1);
Add2List (hWnd, TEXT("Found: %hs"), pDL->Device[0].irdaDeviceName);


//
// Connect to remote socket.
//
rc = connect (c_sock, (struct sockaddr *)&iraddr, sizeof (iraddr));
if (rc) {
    Add2List (hWnd, TEXT("Connect failed. rc %d"), WSAGetLastError());
    closesocket (c_sock);
    return -4;
}
Add2List (hWnd, TEXT("connected..."));

rc = 0;
nFileSize = GetFileSize (hFile, NULL);

// Allocate buffer and read file.
pBuff = (LPBYTE)LocalAlloc (LPTR, nFileSize);
if (pBuff) {
    ReadFile (hFile, pBuff, nFileSize, (DWORD *)&nCnt, NULL);
    if (nCnt != nFileSize)
        rc = BAD_FILEREAD;
} else
    rc = BAD_MEMORY;

if (rc) {
    closesocket (c_sock);
    CloseHandle (hFile);
    Add2List (hWnd, TEXT("Error allocating buffer or reading file."));
    return rc;
}
// Start transfer. First send size and get ack.

// Strip off any leading path, assume len > 1 since we've opened file.
for (i = lstrlen (szFileName)-1; (i > 0) &&
                                (szFileName[i] != TEXT ('\\')) ; i--);
if (szFileName[i] == TEXT ('\\')) i++;
```

(continued)

Listing 14-1 *(continued)*

```
    // Send name size.
    nCnt = (lstrlen (&szFileName[i]) + 1);
    rc = send (c_sock, (LPSTR)&nCnt, sizeof (nCnt), 0);

    // Send filename.
    if (rc != SOCKET_ERROR) {
#ifdef _UNICODE
        wcstombs (szAnsiName, &szFileName[i], nCnt);
#else
        lstrcpy (szAnsiName, &szFileName[i]);
#endif
        rc = send (c_sock, (LPSTR)szAnsiName, nCnt, 0);
    }

    // Send file size. Size will always be < 2 gig.
    rc = send (c_sock, (LPSTR)&nFileSize, sizeof (nFileSize), 0);
    if (rc == SOCKET_ERROR)
        rc = BAD_SOCKET;
    else
        // Recv ack of file size.
        recv (c_sock, (LPSTR)&rc, sizeof (rc), 0);

    // Send the file.
    nTotal = nFileSize;
    pPtr = (LPSTR)pBuff;
    while ((!rc) && nFileSize) {

        MySetWindowText (hWnd, TEXT ("%02d%% sent"),
                         (nTotal-nFileSize)*100/nTotal);
        // Send up to the block size.
        nCnt = min (BLKSIZE, nFileSize);
        rc = send (c_sock, pPtr, nCnt, 0);
        if (rc == SOCKET_ERROR) {
            Add2List (hWnd, TEXT("send error %d "), GetLastError());
            rc = BAD_SOCKET;
        } else
            Add2List (hWnd, TEXT("sent %d bytes"), rc);
        pPtr += rc;
        nFileSize -= rc;

        // Receive ack.
        recv (c_sock, (LPSTR)&rc, sizeof (rc), 0);
    }
    SetWindowText (hWnd, szTitle);
    // Send close code.
    if (rc != BAD_SOCKET)
        send (c_sock, (LPSTR)&rc, sizeof (rc), 0);
```

```
    closesocket (c_sock);
    // Clean up.
    CloseHandle (hFile);
    LocalFree (pBuff);
    if (rc)
        Add2List (hWnd, TEXT("SendFile Exit rc = %d"), rc);
    else
        Add2List (hWnd, TEXT("File sent successfully."));
    return 0;
}
```

From a Windows standpoint, MySquirt is a simple program. It uses a dialog box as its main window. When the program is first launched, it creates a thread to monitor for other devices that creates an infrared socket, binds it to a service name, puts the socket into listen mode, and blocks on a call to *accept*. When a remote device connects, the monitor thread creates another thread to handle the actual receiving of the file while it loops back and waits for another connection.

A transmission is initiated when another device running MySquirt sends a file. This process begins when the user on the sending device presses the Send button. If text exists in the edit box, the application reads it and calls the *Send-File* routine. In this routine, a socket is created and any remote devices are enumerated using repeated calls to *getsockopt*. If a device is found, a connection is attempted with a call to *connect*. *Connect* succeeds only if the remote device has bound an IR socket using the same service name, which happens to be defined as the string contained in *chzAppName*, an ASCII representation of the program name. This addressing scheme ensures that if a connection is made, the remote device is running MySquirt. Once a connection is made, the sending device sends over the filename, which it does in two steps: first it sends the byte length of the filename and then the name itself. This process allows the server to know how many characters to receive before continuing. The device then sends the file size. If the file sent by the server device fits in the object store, the routine creates the file on the client side, notifying the user if the file already exists. If all has gone well to this point, the data is received and written to the file. The application closes the socket and frees the buffer created to read the data into.

On the receiving side, a transmission is initiated when the monitor thread's call to *accept* returns. The monitor thread creates a receiving thread and loops back looking for other sending devices. The receiving thread receives the name and size of the file and determines whether the file is acceptable. If so, it sends an acknowledgment back to the sending device. From then on, the receiving thread reads the data from the socket and writes it to the newly created file. When the transmission is complete, the receiving thread closes the file, closes the receiving socket, and terminates.

The other interesting aspect of MySquirt is that I wrote the program to be compiled on both Windows CE and the desktop versions of Windows using Microsoft Visual Studio .NET. I made a few adjustments to the program to handle the different declarations for the *lpCmdLine* parameter of *WinMain* and a macro to hide the differences between calling *CreateThread* in Windows CE and *beginthreadex* on the desktop. The example on the companion CD has project files for both eMbedded C++ for Windows CE compilation and Visual Studio .NET for compiling for the desktop.

Bluetooth

Bluetooth is the name of a wireless interface standard that uses radio frequency (RF) as its medium instead of infrared frequency, as is used with IrDA. Bluetooth is designed to be a successor to IrDA, providing the file transfer capabilities of IrDA along with a number of other capabilities centering on cableless connections.

Bluetooth is named for Harald Blåtand (Bluetooth), who was king of Denmark from 940 to 985. Harald was the grandson of King Ethelred of England and the grandfather of King Canute, famous for demonstrating the limits of kingly power by commanding the tide not to come in[2]. Harald's claim to fame is the unification of Denmark and Norway during his rule. One thousand ten years later, following an Ericsson-initiated feasibility study of using a low-power radio frequency network to link peripherals, a special interest group (SIG) was formed with Ericsson, IBM, Toshiba, Nokia, and Intel to organize and form a standard under the codename Bluetooth. That catchy code name was soon chosen as the actual name of the standard.

Although it has taken longer than expected for Bluetooth-enabled devices to reach the mainstream, the number of devices supporting Bluetooth has grown. Following this trend, a number of Pocket PC and other Windows CE devices now include support for Bluetooth. Windows CE 4.0 .NET provides integrated support for the Bluetooth protocol, which is also supported by the Pocket PC 2003. Some Pocket PC OEMs use third-party Bluetooth software on their devices instead of the Windows CE stack. This Bluetooth discussion covers only the Windows CE Bluetooth API. To program third-party Bluetooth stacks, developers should contact the device manufacturers for information.

Bluetooth functionality is centered on profiles that define services provided to the user. Profiles include Cordless Telephony, Intercom, Headset, Fax, Dial-Up Networking, LAN Access, Object Push, Synchronization, and File Transfer. Not all profiles are supported by all devices. In fact, most devices support only a very few profiles relevant to the device.

---

2. For those wondering, the tide came in anyway.

Windows CE provides the Dial-up Networking, LAN Access, Object Push and File Transfer profiles out of the box, although OEMs are free to add support for other profiles in their products. The Pocket PC 2003 provides support for Object Push and File Transfer profiles. OEMs add support for additional profiles, such as a headset profile for wireless headsets.

The applications, such as Pocket Inbox and Pocket Outlook, that are bundled with the devices support Bluetooth for file transfer, business card exchange, and synchronization. Working with these applications is preferable to writing code to work directly with the Bluetooth API because of the complexity of that API.

For those who are interested in working directly with the Bluetooth API, the task isn't easy, clean, or quick. Part of the problem is the flexibility of the Bluetooth standard and the complexity of the discovery protocol that communicates which services are available from a device. Before we can dive into this code, a bit of background is necessary.

Stack

A diagram of the Bluetooth stack is shown in Figure 14-3. The lower three layers—Baseband, Link Manager Protocol, and the first Host Controller Interface (HCI) layer—are implemented in the Bluetooth hardware. The layers above the hardware and below the application are provided by Windows CE, although it's possible for third parties to extend the Bluetooth stack by providing additional profiles above the HCI layer.

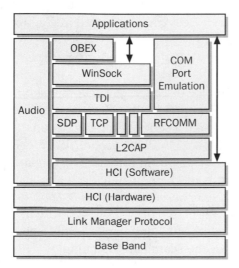

Figure 14-3   A diagram of the Bluetooth stack on Windows CE

Applications interact with the Bluetooth stack through one of two interfaces. The preferred method is for applications to use the Winsock API to access the Bluetooth stack. Just as with IrDA, applications use standard Winsock functions to open sockets associated with the Bluetooth stack. Control is accomplished through various *WSAxxx* functions. Data transfer is accomplished through the standard socket *send* and *recv* functions.

Winsock support for Bluetooth depends on the Winsock stack installed on the device. If the system has Winsock 2.0 installed, such as the Pocket PC 2003, Bluetooth functionality is accessed directly through Winsock calls such as *setsockopt*. For systems with Winsock 1.1 installed, the Bluetooth stack needs to be configured through a dedicated Bluetooth API. For example, to query the current mode of an asynchronous connection, an application can use the dedicated function *BthGetCurrentMode* or, if Winsock 2.0 is on the system, a call to *getsockopt* with the option name *SO_BTH_GET_MODE*.

The other way applications can work with Bluetooth is through *virtual serial ports*. With this method, applications load a Bluetooth-dedicated serial driver. Control of the stack is accomplished through *DeviceIoControl* calls to the COM driver. Calling *WriteFile* and *ReadFile* to write and read the COM port sends and receives data across the Bluetooth connection.

Discovery

Before devices can communicate across a Bluetooth connection, devices and the services those devices provide must be discovered. The discovery process is quite complex because of the flexible nature of the Bluetooth feature set. Devices and services on particular devices can be queried in a general way—all printers, for example—or they can be specifically queried—for example, whether a particular device supports a particular service, such as the Headset-Audio-Gateway service.

Both device discovery and service discovery are accomplished through the same series of functions, albeit with significantly different parameters. The discovery process is accomplished through a series of three functions: *WSALookupServiceBegin*, *WSALookupServiceNext*, and *WSALookupServiceEnd*. These functions aren't specific to Winsock 2.0, but in the discussion that follows, I'm providing information only about using them in Bluetooth applications. A parallel series of functions—*BthNsLookupServiceBegin*, *BthNsLookupServiceNext*, and *BthNsLookupServiceEnd*—are functionally identical and can be used for systems with Winsock 1.1. Although the function names imply a simple iterative search, the parameters required for the search are daunting.

Device Discovery

To find local devices, an application first calls *WSALookupServiceBegin*, which is prototyped as

```
INT WSALookupServiceBegin (LPWSAQUERYSET pQuerySet, DWORD dwFlags,
                           LPHANDLE lphLookup);
```

The first parameter is a pointer to a *WSAQUERYSET* structure, which I'll discuss shortly. For device searches, the *dwFlags* parameter should contain the flag *LUP_CONTAINERS*. The other allowable flags for this parameter will be covered in the upcoming discussion about service queries. The final parameter should point to a handle value that will be filled in with a search handle; this search handle will be used for the other calls in the search. The return value is an *HRESULT* with 0, indicating success.

The *WSAQUERYSET* structure is defined as

```
typedef struct _WSAQuerySet {
    DWORD             dwSize;
    LPTSTR            lpszServiceInstanceName;
    LPGUID            lpServiceClassId;
    LPWSAVERSION      lpVersion;
    LPTSTR            lpszComment;
    DWORD             dwNameSpace;
    LPGUID            lpNSProviderId;
    LPTSTR            lpszContext;
    DWORD             dwNumberOfProtocols;
    LPAFPROTOCOLS     lpafpProtocols;
    LPTSTR            lpszQueryString;
    DWORD             dwNumberOfCsAddrs;
    LPCSADDR_INFO     lpcsaBuffer;
    DWORD             dwOutputFlags;
    LPBLOB            lpBlob;
} WSAQUERYSET, *PWSAQUERYSET;
```

The *dwSize* field should be set to the size of the structure. For device queries, the only other fields that need to be used are the *dwNameSpace* field, which must be set to *NS_BT*, and the *lpBlob* field, which should point to a *BLOB* structure. The remaining fields should be set to 0.

The *BLOB* structure pointed to by the *lpBlob* field is actually optional for the initial device query call, but it's recommended so that the time the Bluetooth stack spends looking for devices can be defined. If the query time isn't specified, the Bluetooth stack defaults to a rather long 15 to 20 seconds waiting for devices to respond. To define the query time, *lpBlob* points to a *BLOB* structure that, in turn, points to a blob of a specific type. The generic *BLOB* structure is defined as

```
typedef struct _BLOB {
    ULONG cbSize;
    BYTE* pBlobData;
} BLOB, LPBLOB;
```

The two fields are the size of the specific *BLOB* structure being pointed to a pointer to the specific *BLOB* data. For device queries, the blob we're interested in is an inquiry blob defined as

```
typedef struct _BTHNS_INQUIRYBLOB {
    ULONG LAP;
    unsigned char length;
    unsigned char num_responses;
} BTHNS_INQUIRYBLOB, *PBTHNS_INQUIRYBLOB;
```

The first field should be set to BT_ADDR_GIAC, which is the general inquiry access code (GIAC), defined as 0x9e8b33. The *length* field should be set to the time the stack should wait for devices to respond. The unit of time for this field is a rather strange 1.28 seconds, so if you want to wait approximately 5 seconds, the value 4 in the field will produce a wait of 4×1.28, or 5.12, seconds. The final field, *num_responses*, specifies the maximum number of devices that need to respond to end the query before the timeout value.

So before a call to *WSALookupServiceBegin* is made to query the available devices, the *WSAQUERYSET*, *BLOB*, and *BTHNS_INQUIRYBLOB* structures should be initialized with the *WSAQUERYSET* structure's *lpBlob* field pointing to the *BLOB* structure. The *BLOB* structure should be initialized so that the *cbSize* field contains the size of the *BTHNS_INQUIRYBLOB* structure and the *pBlobData* field points to the *BTHNS_INQUIRYBLOB* structure. The *BTHNS_INQUIRYBLOB* structure should be filled in with the search criteria.

When the call to *WSALookupServiceBegin* returns successfully, a call to *WSALookupServiceNext* is made. Whereas the *WSALookupServiceBegin* call can take a number of seconds, the *WSALookupServiceNext* call can return immediately as long as the data being requested has been cached in the stack by the *WSALookupServiceBegin* call. The *WSALookupServiceNext* call is defined as

```
INT WSALookupServiceNext (HANDLE hLookup, DWORD dwFlags,
                    LPDWORD lpdwBufferLength, LPWSAQUERYSET pResults);
```

The first parameter is the handle returned by *WSALookupServiceBegin*. The *dwFlags* parameter contains a number of different flags that define the data returned by the function. The possible flags are

- **LUP_RETURN_NAME**   Return the name of the remote device.

- **LUP_RETURN_ADDRESS**   Return the address of the remote device.

■ *LUP_RETURN_BLOB* Return *BTHINQUIRYRESULT* structure with information about the remote device.

■ *BTHNS_LUP_RESET_ITERATOR* Reset the enumeration so that the next call to *WSALookupServiceNext* will return information about the first device in the list.

■ *BTHNS_LUP_NO_ADVANCE* Return information about a device but don't increment the device index so that the next call to *WSALookupServiceNext* returns information about the same device.

The final two parameters are the address of a variable that contains the size of the output buffer and a pointer to the output buffer. Although the output buffer pointer is cast as a pointer to a *WSAQUERYSET* structure, the buffer passed to *WSALookupServiceNext* should be significantly larger than the structure so that the function can marshal any strings into the buffer beyond the end of the structure itself.

When the function returns without error, the *WSAQUERYSET* structure pointed to by *pResults* contains information about a Bluetooth device. The name of the device, if requested with the *LUP_RETURN_NAME* flag, is pointed to by the *lpszServiceInstanceName* field. The address of the remote device is contained in the *CSADDR_INFO* structure pointed to by *lpcsaBuffer*. *CSADDR_INFO* provides information about the local and remote device addresses and is defined as

```
typedef struct _CSADDR_INFO {
    SOCKET_ADDRESS LocalAddr;
    SOCKET_ADDRESS RemoteAddr;
    INT iSocketType;
    INT iProtocol;
} CSADDR_INFO;
```

The *SOCKET_ADDRESS* fields are filled in with Bluetooth-specific *SOCKADDR_BTH* addresses, so to get the remote address, the *RemoteAddr* field should be properly cast, as in

```
bt = ((SOCKADDR_BTH *)
    pQueryResult->lpcsaBuffer->RemoteAddr.lpSockaddr)->btAddr;
```

Each call to *WSALookupServiceNext* returns information about a single device. The function should be called repeatedly until it returns *SOCKET_ERROR*. If *GetLastError* returns *WSA_E_NO_MORE*, there was no error; there are simply no more devices to be found.

After completing the *WSALookupServiceNext* loop, the program should call *WSALookupServiceEnd* to clean up any resources the Winsock stack has maintained during the search. The function is prototyped as

```
INT WSALookupServiceEnd (HANDLE hLookup);
```

The single parameter is the handle returned by *WSALookupServiceBegin*.

The following routine queries the Bluetooth devices that are in range and returns their names and addresses in an array.

```
#define MYBUFFSIZE 16384
typedef struct {
    TCHAR szName[256];
    BT_ADDR btaddr;
} MYBTDEVICE, *PMYBTDEVICE;
//
// FindDevices - Find devices in range.
//
int FindDevices (PMYBTDEVICE pbtDev, int *pnDevs) {
    DWORD dwFlags, dwLen;
    HANDLE hLookup;
    int i, rc;

    // Create inquiry blob to limit time of search
    BTHNS_INQUIRYBLOB inqblob;
    memset (&inqblob, 0, sizeof (inqblob));
    inqblob.LAP = BT_ADDR_GIAC;  // Default GIAC
    inqblob.length = 4;          // 4 * 1.28 = 5 seconds
    inqblob.num_responses = *pnDevs;

    // Create blob to point to inquiry blob
    BLOB blob;
    blob.cbSize = sizeof (BTHNS_INQUIRYBLOB);
    blob.pBlobData = (PBYTE)&inqblob;

    // Init query
    WSAQUERYSET QuerySet;
    memset (&QuerySet,0,sizeof (WSAQUERYSET));
    QuerySet.dwSize = sizeof (WSAQUERYSET);
    QuerySet.dwNameSpace = NS_BTH;
    QuerySet.lpBlob = &blob;

    // Start query for devices
    rc = WSALookupServiceBegin (&QuerySet, LUP_CONTAINERS, &hLookup);
    if (rc) return rc;

    // Allocate output buffer
    PBYTE pOut = (PBYTE)LocalAlloc (LPTR, MYBUFFSIZE);
```

```
if (!pOut) return -1;
WSAQUERYSET *pQueryResult = (WSAQUERYSET *)pOut;

// Loop through the devices by repeatedly calling WSALookupServiceNext
for (i = 0; i < *pnDevs; i++) {
    dwLen = MYBUFFSIZE;
    dwFlags = LUP_RETURN_NAME | LUP_RETURN_ADDR;
    rc = WSALookupServiceNext (hLookup, dwFlags, &dwLen, pQueryResult);
    if (rc == SOCKET_ERROR) {
        rc = GetLastError();
        break;
    }
    // Copy device name
    lstrcpy (pbtDev[i].szName, pQueryResult->lpszServiceInstanceName);

    // Copy Bluetooth device address
    SOCKADDR_BTH *pbta;
    pbta = (SOCKADDR_BTH *)
        pQueryResult->lpcsaBuffer->RemoteAddr.lpSockaddr;
    pbtDev[i].btaddr = pbta->btAddr;
}
// See if we left the loop simply because there were no more devices
if (rc == WSA_E_NO_MORE) rc = 0;

// Return the number of devices found
*pnDevs = i;

// Clean up
WSALookupServiceEnd (hLookup);
LocalFree (pOut);
return rc;
}
```

The preceding routine uses *WSALookupServiceBegin*, *WSALookupService-Next*, and *WSALookupServiceEnd* to iterate through the Bluetooth devices in range. The routine could query other information about the remote devices by passing the *LUP_RETURN_BLOB* flag in *WSALookupServiceNext*, but the information returned isn't needed to connect to the device.

Service Discovery

Once the device of interest is found, the next task is to discover whether that device supplies the service needed. Services are identified in a multilevel fashion. The service can publish itself under a generic service such as printer or fax service or publish itself under a specific unique identifier, or GUID.

If you know the specific service as well as its documented GUID, there is no need for service discovery. Simply connect a Bluetooth socket to the specific service as discussed in the "Bluetooth" section on page 668. If, however, you don't know the exact service GUID, you must take on the task of service discovery.

Querying services is accomplished through the same *WSALookupService-Begin*, *WSALookupServiceNext*, and *WSALookupServiceEnd* functions discussed earlier in the device discovery section. As with device discovery, the initial query is accomplished with a call to *WSALookupServiceBegin*. To query the services on a remote device, set the *dwFlags* parameter to 0 instead of using the *LUP_CONTAINERS* flag. To query the service provided by the local system instead of remote devices, set the *LUP_RES_SERVICE* flag in the *dwFlags* parameter.

When you're querying the services of another device, the *WSAQUERYSET* structure needs to specify the target device that's being queried. This is accomplished by referencing a restriction blob in the *WSAQUERYSET* structure. The restriction blob is defined as

```
typedef struct _BTHNS_RESTRICTIONBLOB {
    ULONG type;
    ULONG serviceHandle;
    SdpQueryUuid uuids[12];
    ULONG numRange;
    SdpAttributeRange pRange[1];
} BTHNS_RESTRICTIONBLOB;
```

The *type* field specifies whether the query should check for services, attributes of the services, or both attributes and services by specifying the flags *SDP_SERVICE_SEARCH_REQUEST*, *SDP_SERVICE_ATTRIBUTE_REQUEST*, and *SDP_SERVICE_SEARCH_ATTRIBUTE_REQUEST*, respectively. The *serviceHandle* parameter is used in attribute-only searches to specify the service being queried. If the services are being queried, the *uuids* array contains up to 12 service IDs to check. The service IDs are specified in an *SdpQueryUuid* structure defined as

```
typedef struct _SdpQueryUuid {
    SdpQueryUuidUnion u;
    USHORT uuidType;
} SdpQueryUuid;
```

The *SdpQueryUuid* structure allows the service IDs to be specified as 16-, 32-, or 128-bit ID values. The ID values for documented services are provided in the Bluetooth include file Bt_sdp.h in the SDK.

When you're querying attributes for a service or services, the *pRange* array can specify the minimum and maximum attribute range to query. The size of the *pRange* array is specified in the *numRange* parameter. In the following code, a specific service is queried to see whether it exists on the device, and if it does, the query also returns the attributes associated with the service.

```
int QueryService (HWND hWnd, BT_ADDR bta, GUID *pguid) {
    DWORD dwFlags, dwLen;
    HANDLE hLookup;
    TCHAR szDeviceName[256];
    LPWSAQUERYSET pQuerySet;
    PBYTE pQuery;
    int i, rc;

    pQuery = (PBYTE)LocalAlloc (LPTR, MYBUFFSIZE);
    if (!pQuery) return 0;

    pQuerySet = (LPWSAQUERYSET)pQuery;
    memset (pQuerySet, 0, MYBUFFSIZE);
    pQuerySet->dwSize = sizeof (WSAQUERYSET);
    pQuerySet->dwNameSpace = NS_BTH;

    // Specify device
    CSADDR_INFO csi;
    memset (&csi, 0, sizeof (csi));

    SOCKADDR_BTH sa;
    memset (&sa, 0, sizeof (sa));
    sa.btAddr = bta;
    sa.addressFamily = AF_BT;

    // Specify the remote device address
    csi.RemoteAddr.lpSockaddr = (LPSOCKADDR) &sa;
    csi.RemoteAddr.iSockaddrLength = sizeof(SOCKADDR_BTH);
    pQuerySet->lpcsaBuffer = &csi;
    pQuerySet->dwNumberOfCsAddrs = 1;

    // Form query based on service class being checked
    BTHNS_RESTRICTIONBLOB btrblb;
    memset (&btrblb, 0, sizeof (btrblb));
    btrblb.type = SDP_SERVICE_SEARCH_ATTRIBUTE_REQUEST;
    btrblb.numRange = 1;
    btrblb.pRange[0].minAttribute = 0;
    btrblb.pRange[0].maxAttribute = 0xffff;
    btrblb.uuids[0].uuidType = SDP_ST_UUID128; //Define search type
    memcpy (&btrblb.uuids[0].u.uuid128, pguid, sizeof (GUID));

    // Create blob to point to restriction blob
    BLOB blob;
    blob.cbSize = sizeof (BTHNS_RESTRICTIONBLOB);
    blob.pBlobData = (PBYTE)&btrblb;
```

```
        pQuerySet->lpBlob = &blob;
        dwFlags = 0;

        rc = WSALookupServiceBegin (pQuerySet, dwFlags, &hLookup);
        if (rc) return rc;

        // Setup query set for ServiceNext call
        pQuerySet->dwNumberOfCsAddrs = 1;
        pQuerySet->lpszServiceInstanceName = szDeviceName;
        memset (szDeviceName, 0, sizeof (szDeviceName));

        dwFlags = LUP_RETURN_NAME | LUP_RETURN_ADDR;
        dwLen = MYBUFFSIZE;
        while ((rc = WSALookupServiceNext (hLookup, dwFlags, &dwLen,
                                            pQuerySet)) == 0) {
            ISdpRecord **pRecordArg;
            int cRecordArg = 0;

            // Setup attribute query
            HRESULT hr = ParseBlobToRecs (pQuerySet->lpBlob->pBlobData,
                                           pQuerySet->lpBlob->cbSize,
                                           &pRecordArg, (ULONG *)&cRecordArg);
            if (hr == ERROR_SUCCESS) {
                // Parse the records

                // Clean up records
                for (i = 0; i < cRecordArg; i++)
                    pRecordArg[i]->Release();
                CoTaskMemFree(pRecordArg);
            }
            dwLen = MYBUFFSIZE;
            i++;
        }
        rc = WSALookupServiceEnd (hLookup);
        LocalFree (pQuery);
        return rc;
}
```

Notice that in this code, the Service Discovery Protocol (SDP) data for the service is returned in the buffer pointed to by the *lpBlob* structure. This data isn't parsed in the routine. Instead, a routine named *ParseBlobToRecs* is called to parse the data. The routine *ParseBlobToRecs*, shown here, returns a series of *ISdpRecord* interface pointers, one for each record in the SDP data.

```
//
// ParseBlobToRecs - Use ISdpStream object to parse the response from the
// SDP server.
//
```

```
HRESULT ParseBlobToRecs (UCHAR *pbData, DWORD cbStream,
                         ISdpRecord ***pppSdpRecords, ULONG *pcbRec) {
    HRESULT hr;
    ULONG ulError;
    ISdpStream *pIStream = NULL;
    *pppSdpRecords - NULL;
    *pcbRec = 0;

    hr = CoCreateInstance (__uuidof(SdpStream), NULL,
                           CLSCTX_INPROC_SERVER, __uuidof(ISdpStream),
                           (LPVOID *)&pIStream);
    if (FAILED(hr)) return hr;
    // Validate SDP data blob
    hr = pIStream->Validate (pbData, cbStream, &ulError);

    if (SUCCEEDED(hr)) {
        hr = pIStream->VerifySequenceOf (pbData, cbStream,
                                         SDP_TYPE_SEQUENCE, NULL, pcbRec);
        if (SUCCEEDED(hr) && *pcbRec > 0) {
            *pppSdpRecords = (ISdpRecord **)CoTaskMemAlloc (
                                      sizeof (ISdpRecord*) *
                                      (*pcbRec));
            if (pppSdpRecords != NULL) {
                hr = pIStream->RetrieveRecords (pbData, cbStream,
                                         *pppSdpRecords, pcbRec);
                if (!SUCCEEDED(hr)) {
                    CoTaskMemFree (*pppSdpRecords);
                    *pppSdpRecords = NULL;
                    *pcbRec = 0;
                }
            }
            else
                hr = E_OUTOFMEMORY;
        }
    }
    if (pIStream != NULL) {
        pIStream->Release();
        pIStream = NULL;
    }
    return hr;
}
```

The routine returns the data in an array of *ISdpRecord* pointers. It's left to
the reader to parse the record data using the other interfaces provided in the
Bluetooth API.

Publishing a Service

The other side of service discovery is service publication. Bluetooth applications that want to provide a service to other applications must do more than simply create a Bluetooth socket, bind the socket, and call *accept* as would an IrDA service. In addition to the socket work, the service must publish the details of the service through the SDP API.

The actual publication of a service is actually quite simple. All that's necessary is to call *WSASetService*, which is prototyped as

```
INT WSASetService (LPWSAQUERYSET lpqsRegInfo, WSAESETSERVICEOP essoperation,
                   DWORD dwControlFlags);
```

The three parameters are a pointer to a *WSAQUERYSET* structure; a service operation flag, which needs to be set to *RNRSERVICE_REGISTER*; and a *dwControlFlags* parameter set to 0.

If only registration were that simple. The problem isn't calling the function; it's composing the SDP data that's placed in the *WSAQUERYSET* structure. The *dwNameSpace* field should be set to *NS_BTH*. And, as with the discovery process, the blobs are involved. The blob used in setting the service is a *BTHNS_SETBLOB* structure defined as

```
typedef struct _BTHNS_SETBLOB {
    ULONG* pRecordHandle;
    ULONG fSecurity;
    ULONG fOptions;
    ULONG ulRecordLength;
    UCHAR pRecord[1];
} BTHNS_SETBLOB, *PBTHNS_SETBLOB;
```

The first parameter points to a *ULONG* that will receive a handle for the SDP record being created. The *fSecurity* and *fOptions* fields are reserved and should be set to 0. The *ulRecordLength* parameter should be set to the length of the SDP record to publish, whereas *pRecord* is the starting byte of the byte array that is the SDP record to publish.

The following code demonstrates publishing an SDP record. The routine is passed an SDP record and its size. It then initializes the proper structures and calls *WSASetService* to publish the record.

```
int PublishRecord (HWND hWnd, PBYTE pSDPRec, int nRecSize, ULONG *pRecord) {
    BTHNS_SETBLOB *pSetBlob;
    ULONG ulSdpVersion = BTH_SDP_VERSION;
    int rc;

    // Zero out the record handle that will be returned by the call
    *pRecord = 0;
```

```
// Allocate and init the SetBlob
pSetBlob = (BTHNS_SETBLOB *)LocalAlloc (LPTR,
                               sizeof (BTHNS_SETBLOB) + nRecSize);

if (!pSetBlob) return -1;

pSetBlob->pRecordHandle = pRecord;
pSetBlob->pSdpVersion = &ulSdpVersion;
pSetBlob->fSecurity = 0;
pSetBlob->fOptions = 0;
pSetBlob->ulRecordLength = nRecSize;
memcpy (pSetBlob->pRecord, pSDPRec, nRecSize);

// Init the container blob
BLOB blob;
blob.cbSize = sizeof(BTHNS_SETBLOB) + SDP_RECORD_SIZE - 1;
blob.pBlobData = (PBYTE) pSetBlob;

// Init the WSAQuerySet struct
WSAQUERYSET Service;
memset (&Service, 0, sizeof(Service));
Service.dwSize = sizeof(Service);
Service.lpBlob = &blob;
Service.dwNameSpace = NS_BTH;

// Publish the service
rc = WSASetService(&Service, RNRSERVICE_REGISTER, 0);
if (rc == SOCKET_ERROR) rc = GetLastError();
// Clean up
LocalFree ((PBYTE)pSetBlob);
return rc;
}
```

When the application no longer wants to support the service, it needs to remove the record from the SDP database. Removing the record is accomplished by using *WSASetService*, specifying the record handle of the service and the flag *RNRSERVICE_DELETE*. The record handle is passed in the *BTHNS_SETBLOB* structure. The other fields of this structure are ignored. The following code shows a routine that unregisters a service.

```
int UnpublishRecord (ULONG hRecord) {
    ULONG ulSdpVersion = BTH_SDP_VERSION;
    int rc;

    BTHNS_SETBLOB SetBlob;
    memset (&SetBlob, 0, sizeof (SetBlob));
    SetBlob.pRecordHandle = &hRecord;
    SetBlob.pSdpVersion = &ulSdpVersion;
```

```
// Init the container blob
BLOB blob;
blob.cbSize = sizeof(BTHNS_SETBLOB);
blob.pBlobData = (PBYTE) &SetBlob;

// Init the WSAQuerySet struct
WSAQUERYSET Service;
memset (&Service, 0, sizeof(Service));
Service.dwSize = sizeof(Service);
Service.lpBlob = &blob;
Service.dwNameSpace = NS_BTH;

// Unpublish the service
rc = WSASetService(&Service, RNRSERVICE_DELETE, 0);
return rc;
}
```

SDP Records

The format of the SDP information that's published is so complex that Windows
CE provides a special COM control to construct and deconstruct SDP records.
Even with the control, parsing SDP records isn't easy. The first problem is
knowing what's required in the SDP record. The information in the SDP record
is defined by the Bluetooth specification, and a complete explanation of this
data far exceeds the space available for such an explanation.

As a shortcut, many Bluetooth applications compose a generic record,
either hand-assembling the record or using an example tool named BthNs-
Create that's provided in the Platform Builder. These hand-generated records
are saved as a byte array in the application. The known offsets where the GUID
and the RFCOMM channel are stored are known and are updated in the array
at run time. The record is then published using *WSASetService*, as shown earlier.

The following code shows a routine that uses a canned SDP record with
the GUID of the service and the channel stuffed into the appropriate places in
the record.

```
int RegisterService (HWND hWnd, GUID *pguid, byte bChannel, ULONG *pRecord) {
    // SDP dummy record
    // GUID goes at offset 8
    // Channel goes in last byte of record.
    static BYTE bSDPRecord[] = {
    0x35, 0x27, 0x09, 0x00, 0x01, 0x35, 0x11, 0x1C, 0x00, 0x00, 0x00,
    0x00, 0x00, 0x00, 0x00, 0x00, 0x00, 0x00, 0x00, 0x00, 0x00, 0x00,
    0x00, 0x00, 0x09, 0x00, 0x04, 0x35, 0x0C, 0x35, 0x03, 0x19, 0x01,
    0x00, 0x35, 0x05, 0x19, 0x00, 0x03, 0x08, 0x00};
```

```
    // Translate guid into net byte order for SDP record
    GUID *p = (GUID *)&bSDPRecord[8];
    p->Data1 = htonl (pguid->Data1);
    p->Data2 = htons (pguid->Data2);
    p->Data3 = htons (pguid->Data3);
    memcpy (p->Data4, pguid->Data4, sizeof (pguid->Data4));

    // Copy channel value into record
    bSDPRecord[sizeof (bSDPRecord)-1] = bChannel;

    return PublishRecord (hWnd, bSDPRecord, sizeof (bSDPRecord), pRecord);
}
```

Bluetooth Communication with Winsock

The hard part of Bluetooth communication is the setup. Once a service is published, the communication with remote devices is simple regardless of the method, Winsock or virtual COM port, used by the application.

As with IrDA, using Winsock to communicate over Bluetooth consists of implementing a client/server design with the server creating a socket that's bound to an address and a client that connects to the server socket by specifying the address and port of the server.

Server Side

A Bluetooth application providing a service first must set up a server routine that creates a socket and performs all the necessary calls to support the server side of a socket communication. The task starts with creating a socket with the standard socket call. The address format of the socket should be set to *AF_BT*, indicating a socket bound to the Bluetooth transport.

Once created, the socket needs to be bound with a call to bind. The following code shows a socket being created followed by a call to bind the socket. The address the socket is bound to is left blank, indicating that the system will provide the proper settings. The address format for the Bluetooth address used in the bind call is set to *AF_BT*.

```
// Open a bluetooth socket
s_sock = socket (AF_BT, SOCK_STREAM, BTHPROTO_RFCOMM);
if (s_sock == INVALID_SOCKET)
    return -1;

// Fill in address stuff
memset (&btaddr, 0, sizeof (btaddr));
btaddr.addressFamily = AF_BT;
btaddr.port = 0;    // Let driver assign a channel
```

```
// Bind to socket
rc = bind (s_sock, (struct sockaddr *)&btaddr, sizeof (btaddr));
if (rc) {
    closesocket (s_sock);
    return -2;
}
// Get information on the port assigned
len = sizeof (btaddr);
rc = getsockname (s_sock, (SOCKADDR *)&btaddr, &len);
if (rc) {
    closesocket (s_sock);
    return 0;
}
// Tell the world what we've bound to.
printf ("Addr %04x.%08x, port %d", GET_NAP(btaddr.btAddr),
    GET_SAP(btaddr.btAddr), btaddr.port)
```

Once the call to bind succeeds, the code calls *getsockname*, which fills in the details of the address of the device and, more important, the Bluetooth RFCOMM channel the socket was bound to. This RFCOMM channel is important since it will need to be published with the SDP record so that other devices will know which port to connect to when connecting to the service. The macros in the *printf* statement in the preceding code demonstrate the division of the Bluetooth device address into its two parts: the NAP, or nonsignificant address portion, and the SAP, or significant address portion.

Once the RFCOMM channel is known, the SDP record can be constructed and published as shown earlier in this section. The socket is then placed in listen mode, and a call to accept is made, which blocks until a client application socket connects to the address. When the client does connect, the accept call returns with the handle of a new socket that's connected with the client. This new socket is then used to communicate with the client device.

Client Side

On the client side, the task of connecting starts with device discovery. Once the Bluetooth address of the client is determined, the client can create a thread that will communicate with the server. The process mirrors any socket-based client with calls to create the socket, and the client connects the socket to the remote server by specifying the address of the server. In the case of a Bluetooth client, the address of the server must include either the RFCOMM channel or the GUID of the service being connected to. In the following code, a client connects to a remote service knowing the remote device's Bluetooth address and the GUID of the client.

```
// Open a bluetooth socket
t_sock = socket (AF_BT, SOCK_STREAM, BTHPROTO_RFCOMM);
if (t_sock == INVALID_SOCKET)
    return 0;

// Fill in address stuff
memset (&btaddr, 0, sizeof (btaddr));
btaddr.btAddr = btaddrTarget;
btaddr.addressFamily = AF_BT;
btaddr.port = 0;   // Let driver assign a channel
memcpy (&btaddr.serviceClassId, &guidbthello, sizeof (GUID));

// Connect to remote socket
rc = connect (t_sock, (struct sockaddr *)&btaddr, sizeof (btaddr));
if (rc) {
    closesocket (t_sock);
    return -4;
}
// Connected...
```

Once the client is connected, data can be exchanged with the server with the standard socket routines *send* and *recv*. When the conversation is concluded, both client and server should close their respective sockets with a call to *closesocket*.

Bluetooth Communication with Virtual COM Ports

If using Winsock for communication isn't to your liking, the Windows CE Bluetooth stack can also be accessed by using a serial driver that can be loaded. This method has a number of shortcomings, but some developers prefer it to using Winsock because of the familiarity of using a simple serial port compared with the complexity of Winsock. In any case, before I show you how to use the virtual serial port method, a few of the problems should be discussed.

The first problem is that the Bluetooth driver name is already the most used driver name in Windows CE. The Windows CE stream driver architecture is such that the operating system is limited to 10 instances of a given driver name, such as COM or WAV. Since typically 2 to 4 instances of serial drivers are already in a Windows CE system, the available number of virtual COM ports is limited. Also, since the Bluetooth stack typically exposes some of its profiles through COM ports, the 2 to 4 number quickly increases to 6 to 8 ports, leaving only 2 to 4 *available* COM driver instances for Bluetooth applications that want to use virtual COM ports. An intrepid programmer could register the Bluetooth driver under a different name, such as BTC for Bluetooth COM, but this nonstandard name wouldn't be expected if it were to be passed on to other applications.

The second problem is that although the virtual COM port method is used on a number of platforms, the implementation on Windows CE is unique. At least with the Winsock method, an application can be written to be fairly source code compatible with Windows XP. That isn't the case with the virtual COM port method.

Finally, creating COM ports using this method is accomplished using the *RegisterDevice* function. Although perfectly functional, this function has been deprecated for quite a while under newer versions of Windows CE. Drivers loaded with *RegisterDevice* aren't listed in the active device list maintained in the registry by the system. *RegisterDevice* requires that the application provide the index value for the driver being loaded. Because there's no simple method for determining which instance values are in use, the application must try all 10 instance values until one doesn't fail because it's used by another COM driver. Still, in some circumstances—when legacy support is needed, for example— using a virtual COM port is necessary.

Creating a virtual COM port is accomplished with the function *Register- Device*, which is prototyped as

```
HANDLE RegisterDevice (LPCWSTR lpszType, DWORD dwIndex, LPCWSTR lpszLib,
                       DWORD dwInfo);
```

The first parameter is a three-character name of the driver, such as COM or WAV. The second parameter is the instance value from 1 through 9, or 0 for instance 10. This value can't already be in use by another driver of the same name. The third parameter is the name of the DLL that implements the driver. The final parameter is a *DWORD* that's passed to the *Init* entry point of the driver.

When used to load a Bluetooth virtual COM port, *RegisterDevice* is used as follows:

```
hDev = RegisterDevice (TEXT("COM"), dwIndex, TEXT("btd.dll"), (DWORD) &pp);
```

where *pp* is the address of a *PORTEMUPortParams* structure defined as

```
typedef struct _portemu_port_params {
    int channel;
    int flocal;
    BD_ADDR device;
    int imtu;
    int iminmtu;
    int imaxmtu;
    int isendquota;
    int irecvquota;
    GUID uuidService;
    unsigned int uiportflags;
} PORTEMUPortParams;
```

The first field is the RFCOMM channel to be used for this port. If the channel is to be assigned automatically, the field can be set to *RFCOMM_CHANNEL_MULTIPLE*. The *fLocal* field should be set to *TRUE* for the server application and *FALSE* for the client application. The *device* field is used by client applications to specify the Bluetooth address of the remote server. This field must be 0 for server applications.

The next three parameters allow the application to specify the maximum transaction unit (MTU). The first field in this series, *imtu*, is the suggested value, while *iminmtu* is the minimum acceptable MTU and *imaxmtu* is the maximum acceptable MTU. If all three of these fields are 0, the driver uses default values for the MTU. The *isendquota* and *irecvquota* fields set the buffer sizes for send and receive operations. Setting these fields to 0 indicates that the driver should use the default values.

The *uuidService* field is used by the client application to specify the service being connected to on the server. If the *channel* field is 0, this field must be set. If the *uuidService* is nonzero, the Bluetooth stack will perform an SDP search to determine the proper channel for the service. The actual SDP search will take place when the COM port is opened, not when it's loaded with *RegisterDevice*.

The *upportflags* field can contain a combination of the following flags:

- **RFCOMM_PORT_FLAGS_AUTHENTICATE** Perform authentication with the remote device when connecting.

- **RFCOMM_PORT_FLAGS_ENCRYPT** Encrypt the stream.

- **RFCOMM_PORT_FLAGS_REMOTE_DCB** When this flag is specified, changing the DCB settings of the port results in a negation with the peer device DCB settings.

- **RFCOMM_PORT_FLAGS_KEEP_DCD** If this flag is set, the emulated DCD line will always be set.

Server Side

As when using Winsock to talk to the Bluetooth stack, using virtual COM ports requires that one device be the server and the other the client. The server's responsibility includes loading the driver, opening the driver, determining the RFCOMM channel assigned to the port, and advertising the port using the SDP process discussed earlier.

The following code fragment demonstrates a server registering a virtual COM port driver. Notice that the routine makes multiple attempts at registering the driver, starting with instance value 9 and going down. Since the upper instance values are typically less used, this results in a quicker registration process. Notice that as soon as the registration loop completes, the code saves the instance value because that value forms the name of the driver. The driver name is then used to open the driver with *CreateFile*. Once the driver is opened, the server uses one of the two special I/O Control (IOCTL) commands available on a virtual COM port to query the RFCOMM channel. The server then calls its *RegisterService* routine to advertise the service through an SDP record.

```
//
// Server process for opening a virtual COM port
//
int i, rc;
PORTEMUPortParams pp;
TCHAR szDrvName[6];

memset (&pp, 0, sizeof (pp));
pp.channel = RFCOMM_CHANNEL_MULTIPLE;
pp.flocal = TRUE;
pp.uiportflags = 0;

// Find free instance number and load Bluetooth virt serial driver
for (i = 9; i >= 0; i--) {
    hDev = RegisterDevice (L"COM", i, L"btd.dll", (DWORD)&pp);
    if (hDev)
        break;
}
// See if driver registered
if (hDev == 0) return -1;

// Form the driver name and save it.
wsprintf (szDrvName, TEXT("COM%d:"), i);

// Open the driver
hDevOpen = CreateFile (szDrvName, GENERIC_READ | GENERIC_WRITE, 0,
                        NULL, OPEN_ALWAYS, 0, 0);
if (hDevOpen == INVALID_HANDLE_VALUE) {
    DeregisterDevice (hDev);
    return -2;
}
DWORD port = 0;
DWORD dwSizeOut;
rc = DeviceIoControl (hDevOpen, IOCTL_BLUETOOTH_GET_RFCOMM_CHANNEL,
                        NULL, 0, &port, sizeof(port), &dwSizeOut, NULL);

Add2List (hWnd, TEXT("rc = %d Port value is %d"), rc, port);

rc = RegisterService (hWnd, &guidbthello, (unsigned char) port, &hService);
```

The IOCTL command used in the preceding code, *IOCTL_BLUETOOTH_GET_RFCOMM_CHANNEL*, returns the RFCOMM channel of the COM port. For the call to *DeviceIoControl*, the output buffer points to a *DWORD* value that will receive the port number. The output buffer size must be set to the size of a *DWORD*. Once the port is determined, the routine simply calls the *RegisterService* routine, shown earlier in this chapter.

Client Side

The client side of the process is similar to the server side, with the exception that the client needs to know the Bluetooth address of the server and the GUID of the service on the server. Both of these parameters are specified in the *PORTEMUPortParams* structure when the device is registered. The following code shows the COM port initialization process from the client perspective.

```
//
// Client side
//
int i, rc;
PORTEMUPortParams pp;
TCHAR szDrvName[6];

int nDevs2 = MAX_DEVICES;
MYBTDEVICE btd2[MAX_DEVICES];

// Find the server's Bluetooth address
rc = FindDevices (btaServ);
if (rc) return -1;

memset (&pp, 0, sizeof (pp));
pp.channel = 0;
pp.flocal = FALSE;
pp.device = btaServ;
pp.uuidService = guidbtService;
pp.uiportflags = 0;

// Find free instance number and load Bluetooth virt serial driver
for (i = 9; i >= 0; i--) {
    hDev = RegisterDevice (L"COM", i, L"btd.dll", (DWORD)&pp);
    if (hDev)
        break;
}
// See if driver registered
if (hDev == 0) return -1;
```

```
// Form the driver name and save it.
wsprintf (szDrvName, TEXT("COM%d:"), i);

// Open the driver
hDevOpen = CreateFile (szDrvName, GENERIC_READ | GENERIC_WRITE, 0,
                       NULL, OPEN_ALWAYS, 0, 0);
if (hDevOpen == INVALID_HANDLE_VALUE) {
    DeregisterDevice (hDev);
    return -2;
}
BT_ADDR bt;
DWORD dwSizeOut;
rc = DeviceIoControl (hDevOpen, IOCTL_BLUETOOTH_GET_PEER_DEVICE,
                      NULL, 0, &bt, sizeof(bt), &dwSizeOut, NULL);
printf ("Connection detected with %04x%08x\r\n", GET_NAP(bt), GET_SAP(bt));
```

Notice the use of the second IOCTL command provided for Bluetooth support, *IOCTL_BLUETOOTH_GET_PEER_DEVICE*. This command returns the Bluetooth address of the device on the other end of the connected virtual serial port.

Communication between the client and the server is accomplished through the standard Win32 file functions *ReadFile* and *WriteFile*. When the conversation has been concluded, the driver should be closed with a call to *CloseHandle* and the driver unloaded with a call to *DeregisterDevice*, prototyped here:

```
BOOL DeregisterDevice (HANDLE hDevice);
```

The only parameter is the handle returned by *RegisterDevice*.

The BtHello Example Program

The BtHello example demonstrates a fairly complete Bluetooth application that can act as both a client and a server. *BtHello* must be running on two Windows CE devices that use the Windows CE Bluetooth stack for it to work. When started, BtHello searches for other Bluetooth devices in the area and lists them in the output window. When the user taps the "Say Hello" button, BtHello connects to the *bthello* service on the other device. Once connected, the client sends the server a short string and then closes the connection. The server reads the text and displays it in its window. Figure 14-4 shows the BtHello example after it has received the message from the other device.

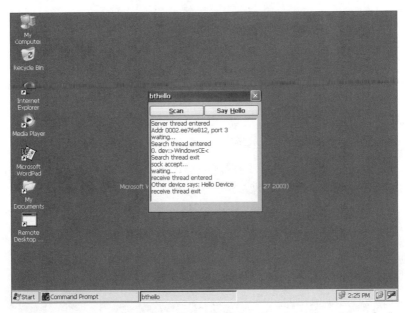

Figure 14-4   The BtHello example after it has received a message from another device

The source code for BtHello is shown in Listing 14-2. The application is a simple dialog-based application. The source code is divided into two .cpp files and their associated include files: BtHello.cpp, which contains the majority of the source code; and MyBtUtil.cpp, which contains handy Bluetooth routines for finding devices and for registering service GUIDs with the SDP service.

```
MyBtUtil.h
//======================================================================
// Header file
//
// Written for the book Programming Windows CE
// Copyright (C) 2003 Douglas Boling
//======================================================================

#ifndef _MYBTUTIL_H_
#define _MYBTUTIL_H_

#if defined (__cplusplus)
extern "C" {
#endif
```

Listing 14-2   The BtHello source code   *(continued)*

Listing 14-2 *(continued)*

```
typedef struct {
    TCHAR szName[256];
    BT_ADDR btaddr;
} MYBTDEVICE, *PMYBTDEVICE;

// Finds Bluetooth devices
int FindDevices (PMYBTDEVICE pbtDev, int *pnDevs);

// Registers a BT service
int RegisterBtService (GUID *pguid, byte bChannel,
                       ULONG *pRecord);

// Clears a BT service from the SDP database
int UnregisterBtService (HWND hWnd, ULONG hRecord);

#if defined (__cplusplus)
}
#endif
#endif // _MYBTUTIL_H_
```

MyBtUtil.cpp

```
//======================================================================
// MyBtUtil - Handy Bluetooth routines
//
// Written for the book Programming Windows CE
// Copyright (C) 2003 Douglas Boling
//======================================================================

#include <windows.h>
#include <winsock2.h>
#include <ws2bth.h>
#include <bt_sdp.h>
#include <bthapi.h>
#include <bt_api.h>

#include "MyBtUtil.h"

#define MYBUFFSIZE      16384
//----------------------------------------------------------------------
// FindDevices - Find devices in range.
//
int FindDevices (PMYBTDEVICE pbtDev, int *pnDevs) {
    DWORD dwFlags, dwLen;
    HANDLE hLookup;
    int i, rc, nMax = *pnDevs;
    *pnDevs = 0;
```

```
// Create inquiry blob to limit time of search
BTHNS_INQUIRYBLOB inqblob;
memset (&inqblob, 0, sizeof (inqblob));
inqblob.LAP = BT_ADDR_GIAC;  // Default GIAC
inqblob.length = 4;           // 4 + 1.20 = 5 seconds
inqblob.num_responses = nMax;

// Create blob to point to inquiry blob
BLOB blob;
blob.cbSize = sizeof (BTHNS_INQUIRYBLOB);
blob.pBlobData = (PBYTE)&inqblob;

// Init query
WSAQUERYSET QuerySet;
memset(&QuerySet,0,sizeof(WSAQUERYSET));
QuerySet.dwSize      = sizeof(WSAQUERYSET);
QuerySet.dwNameSpace = NS_BTH;
QuerySet.lpBlob      = &blob;

// Start query for devices
rc = WSALookupServiceBegin (&QuerySet, LUP_CONTAINERS, &hLookup);
if (rc) return rc;

PBYTE pOut = (PBYTE)LocalAlloc (LPTR, MYBUFFSIZE);
if (!pOut) return -1;
WSAQUERYSET *pQueryResult = (WSAQUERYSET *)pOut;

for (i = 0; i < nMax; i++) {
    dwLen = MYBUFFSIZE;
    dwFlags = LUP_RETURN_NAME | LUP_RETURN_ADDR;
    rc = WSALookupServiceNext (hLookup, dwFlags, &dwLen, pQueryResult);
    if (rc == SOCKET_ERROR) {
        rc = GetLastError();
        break;
    }
    // Copy device name
    lstrcpy (pbtDev[i].szName, pQueryResult->lpszServiceInstanceName);
    // Copy bluetooth device address
    SOCKADDR_BTH *pbta;
    pbta = (SOCKADDR_BTH *)pQueryResult->lpcsaBuffer->RemoteAddr.lpSock-
addr;
    pbtDev[i].btaddr = pbta->btAddr;
}
if (rc == WSA_E_NO_MORE) rc = 0;
*pnDevs = i;
WSALookupServiceEnd (hLookup);
LocalFree (pOut);
return rc;
}
```

(continued)

Listing 14-2 *(continued)*

```
//--------------------        --------------------------------------------------
// PublishRecord - Helper routine that actually does the registering
// of the SDP record.
//
int PublishRecord (PBYTE pSDPRec, int nRecSize, ULONG *pRecord) {
    BTHNS_SETBLOB *pSetBlob;
    ULONG ulSdpVersion = BTH_SDP_VERSION;
    int rc;

    // Zero out the record handle that will be returned by the call
    *pRecord = 0;

    // Allocate and init the SetBlob
    pSetBlob = (BTHNS_SETBLOB *)LocalAlloc (LPTR,
                                    sizeof (BTHNS_SETBLOB) + nRecSize-1);
    if (!pSetBlob) return -1;

    pSetBlob->pRecordHandle = pRecord;
    pSetBlob->pSdpVersion = &ulSdpVersion;
    pSetBlob->fSecurity = 0;
    pSetBlob->fOptions = 0;
    pSetBlob->ulRecordLength = nRecSize;
    memcpy (pSetBlob->pRecord, pSDPRec, nRecSize);

    // Init the container blob
    BLOB blob;
    blob.cbSize    = sizeof(BTHNS_SETBLOB) + nRecSize - 1;
    blob.pBlobData = (PBYTE) pSetBlob;

    // Init the WSAQuerySet struct
    WSAQUERYSET Service;
    memset (&Service, 0, sizeof(Service));
    Service.dwSize = sizeof(Service);
    Service.lpBlob = &blob;
    Service.dwNameSpace = NS_BTH;

    // Publish the service
    rc = WSASetService(&Service, RNRSERVICE_REGISTER, 0);
    if (rc == SOCKET_ERROR)
        rc = GetLastError();

    // Clean up
    LocalFree ((PBYTE)pSetBlob);
    return rc;
}
```

```
//-----------------------------------------------------------------
// UnregisterBtService - Remove service from SDP database
//
int UnregisterBtService (HWND hWnd, ULONG hRecord) {
    ULONG ulSdpVersion = BTH_SDP_VERSION;
    int rc;

    BTHNS_SETBLOB SetBlob;
    memset (&SetBlob, 0, sizeof (SetBlob));
    SetBlob.pRecordHandle = &hRecord;
    SetBlob.pSdpVersion = &ulSdpVersion;

    // Init the container blob
    BLOB blob;
    blob.cbSize = sizeof(BTHNS_SETBLOB);
    blob.pBlobData = (PBYTE) &SetBlob;

    // Init the WSAQuerySet struct
    WSAQUERYSET Service;
    memset (&Service, 0, sizeof(Service));
    Service.dwSize = sizeof(Service);
    Service.lpBlob = &blob;
    Service.dwNameSpace = NS_BTH;

    // Unpublish the service
    rc = WSASetService(&Service, RNRSERVICE_DELETE, 0);
    if (rc == SOCKET_ERROR)
        rc = GetLastError();
    return rc;
}
//-----------------------------------------------------------------
// RegisterBtService - Registers a service with a guid and RFChannel
//
int RegisterBtService (GUID *pguid, byte bChannel, ULONG *pRecord) {

    // SDP dummy record
    // GUID goes at offset 8
    // Channel goes in last byte of record.
    static BYTE bSDPRecord[] = {
    0x35, 0x27, 0x09, 0x00, 0x01, 0x35, 0x11, 0x1C, 0x00, 0x00, 0x00,
    0x00, 0x00, 0x00, 0x00, 0x00, 0x00, 0x00, 0x00, 0x00, 0x00, 0x00,
    0x00, 0x00, 0x09, 0x00, 0x04, 0x35, 0x0C, 0x35, 0x03, 0x19, 0x01,
    0x00, 0x35, 0x05, 0x19, 0x00, 0x03, 0x08, 0x00};

    // Update the SDP record
    // Translate guid into net byte order for SDP record
    GUID *p = (GUID *)&bSDPRecord[8];
    p->Data1 = htonl (pguid->Data1);
```

(continued)

Listing 14-2   *(continued)*

```
    p->Data2 = htons (pguid->Data2);
    p->Data3 = htons (pguid->Data3);
    memcpy (p->Data4, pguid->Data4, sizeof (pguid->Data4));

    // Copy channel value into record
    bSDPRecord[sizeof (bSDPRecord)-1] = bChannel;
    return PublishRecord (bSDPRecord, sizeof (bSDPRecord), pRecord);
}
```
BtHello.h
```
//======================================================================
// Header file
//
// Written for the book Programming Windows CE
// Copyright (C) 2003 Douglas Boling
//======================================================================
// Returns number of elements
#define dim(x) (sizeof(x) / sizeof(x[0]))

// Windows CE Specific defines
#define LPCMDLINE LPWSTR


//----------------------------------------------------------------------
// Generic defines and data types
//
struct decodeUINT {                               // Structure associates
    UINT Code;                                    // messages
                                                  // with a function.
    LRESULT (*Fxn)(HWND, UINT, WPARAM, LPARAM);
};
struct decodeCMD {                                // Structure associates
    UINT Code;                                    // menu IDs with a
    LRESULT (*Fxn)(HWND, WORD, HWND, WORD);       // function.
};


//----------------------------------------------------------------------
// Defines used by application
#define  ID_ICON              1

#define  IDD_INTEXT           10                  // Control IDs
#define  IDD_SAYHELLO         11
#define  IDD_OUTTEXT          12
#define  IDD_SCAN             13

// Error codes used by transfer protocol
#define BAD_TEXTLEN          -1
#define BAD_SOCKET           -2
```

```
#define MYMSG_ENABLESEND       (WM_USER+1000)
#define MYMSG_PRINTF           (WM_USER+1001)
//-----------------------------------------------------------------------
// Function prototypes
//
HWND InitInstance (HINSTANCE, LPCMDLINE, int);
int TermInstance (HINSTANCE, int);
void Add2List (HWND hWnd, LPTSTR lpszFormat, ...);

// Window procedures
LRESULT CALLBACK MainWndProc (HWND, UINT, WPARAM, LPARAM);

// Message handlers
LRESULT DoCreateMain (HWND, UINT, WPARAM, LPARAM);
LRESULT DoSizeMain (HWND, UINT, WPARAM, LPARAM);
LRESULT DoCommandMain (HWND, UINT, WPARAM, LPARAM);
LRESULT DoPocketPCShell (HWND, UINT, WPARAM, LPARAM);
LRESULT DoDestroyMain (HWND, UINT, WPARAM, LPARAM);
LRESULT DoEnableSendMain (HWND, UINT, WPARAM, LPARAM);
LRESULT DoPrintfNotifyMain (HWND, UINT, WPARAM, LPARAM);

// Command functions
LPARAM DoMainCommandSend (HWND, WORD, HWND, WORD);
LPARAM DoMainCommandExit (HWND, WORD, HWND, WORD);
LPARAM DoMainCommandScan (HWND, WORD, HWND, WORD);

// Thread functions
DWORD WINAPI SearchThread (PVOID pArg);
DWORD WINAPI ServerThread (PVOID pArg);
DWORD WINAPI ReceiveThread (PVOID pArg);
DWORD WINAPI SayHelloThread (PVOID pArg);
```

BtHello.cpp

```
//===================================================================
// BtHello - A demonstration of a Bluetooth application
//
// Written for the book Programming Windows CE
// Copyright (C) 2003 Douglas Boling
//===================================================================
#include <windows.h>                    // For all that Windows stuff
#include <winsock2.h>
#include <ws2bth.h>
#include <Msgqueue.h>

#if defined(WIN32_PLATFORM_PSPC)
#include <aygshell.h>                    // Add Pocket PC includes
```

(continued)

Listing 14-2   *(continued)*

```c
#pragma comment( lib, "aygshell" )    // Link Pocket PC lib for menubar
#endif

#include "btHello.h"                  // Program-specific stuff
#include "MyBTUtil.h"                 // My Bluetooth routines


//-----------------------------------------------------------------------
// Global data
//
const TCHAR szAppName[] = TEXT ("bthello");

// {26CECFEC-D255-4a5d-AF7C-9CCF840E7A42}
GUID guidbthello =
{ 0x26cecfec, 0xd255, 0x4a5d, { 0xaf, 0x7c, 0x9c, 0xcf,
                                0x84, 0xe, 0x7a, 0x42} };

HINSTANCE hInst;                      // Program instance handle
HWND hMain;                           // Main window handle
BOOL fContinue = TRUE;                // Server thread cont. flag
BOOL fFirstSize = TRUE;               // First WM_SIZE flag

#if defined(WIN32_PLATFORM_PSPC) && (_WIN32_WCE >= 300)
SHACTIVATEINFO sai;                   // Needed for PPC helper funcs
#endif

HANDLE hQRead = 0;                    // Used for thread safe print
HANDLE hQWrite = 0;
CRITICAL_SECTION csPrintf;

#define MAX_DEVICES  16
MYBTDEVICE btd[MAX_DEVICES];          // List of BT devices
int nDevs = 0;                        // Count of BT devices

// Message dispatch table for MainWindowProc
const struct decodeUINT MainMessages[] = {
    WM_CREATE, DoCreateMain,
    WM_SIZE, DoSizeMain,
    WM_COMMAND, DoCommandMain,
    MYMSG_ENABLESEND, DoEnableSendMain,
    MYMSG_PRINTF, DoPrintfNotifyMain,
    WM_SETTINGCHANGE, DoPocketPCShell,
    WM_ACTIVATE, DoPocketPCShell,
    WM_DESTROY, DoDestroyMain,
};
// Command Message dispatch for MainWindowProc
const struct decodeCMD MainCommandItems[] = {
#if defined(WIN32_PLATFORM_PSPC) && (_WIN32_WCE >= 300)
```

```
        IDOK, DoMainCommandExit,
#else
        IDOK, DoMainCommandSend,
#endif
        IDCANCEL, DoMainCommandExit,
        IDD_SAYHELLO, DoMainCommandSend,
        IDD_SCAN, DoMainCommandScan,
};
//======================================================================
// Program entry point
//
int WINAPI WinMain (HINSTANCE hInstance, HINSTANCE hPrevInstance,
                    LPCMDLINE lpCmdLine, int nCmdShow) {
    MSG msg;
    int rc = 0;

    // Initialize this instance.
    hMain = InitInstance (hInstance, lpCmdLine, nCmdShow);
    if (hMain == 0)
        return TermInstance (hInstance, 0x10);

    // Application message loop
    while (GetMessage (&msg, NULL, 0, 0)) {
        if ((hMain == 0) || !IsDialogMessage (hMain, &msg)) {
            TranslateMessage (&msg);
            DispatchMessage (&msg);
        }
    }
    // Instance cleanup
    return TermInstance (hInstance, msg.wParam);
}
//----------------------------------------------------------------------
// InitInstance - Instance initialization
//
HWND InitInstance (HINSTANCE hInstance, LPCMDLINE lpCmdLine,
                   int nCmdShow){
    WNDCLASS wc;
    HWND hWnd;
    HANDLE hThread;
    int rc;

    hInst = hInstance;                      // Save program instance handle.

    // For all systems, if previous instance, activate it instead of us.
    hWnd = FindWindow (szAppName, NULL);
    if (hWnd) {
        SetForegroundWindow ((HWND)((DWORD)hWnd | 0x01));
```

(continued)

Listing 14-2 *(continued)*

```
        return 0;
    }
    // Init Winsock
    WSADATA wsaData;
    rc = WSAStartup (0x0202, &wsaData);
    if (rc) {
        MessageBox (NULL,TEXT("Error in WSAStartup"), szAppName, MB_OK);
        return 0;
    }

    // Create read and write message queues
    MSGQUEUEOPTIONS mqo;
    mqo.dwSize = sizeof (mqo);
    mqo.dwFlags = MSGQUEUE_ALLOW_BROKEN;
    mqo.dwMaxMessages = 16;
    mqo.cbMaxMessage = 512;
    mqo.bReadAccess = TRUE;
    hQRead = CreateMsgQueue (TEXT ("MSGQUEUE\\ThTead"), &mqo);

    mqo.bReadAccess = FALSE;
    hQWrite = CreateMsgQueue (TEXT ("MSGQUEUE\\ThTead"), &mqo);

    // Register application main window class.
    wc.style = 0;                                   // Window style
    wc.lpfnWndProc = MainWndProc;                   // Callback function
    wc.cbClsExtra = 0;                              // Extra class data
    wc.cbWndExtra = DLGWINDOWEXTRA;                 // Extra window data
    wc.hInstance = hInstance;                       // Owner handle
    wc.hIcon = NULL;                                // Application icon
    wc.hCursor = LoadCursor (NULL, IDC_ARROW);// Default cursor
    wc.hbrBackground = (HBRUSH) GetStockObject (LTGRAY_BRUSH);
    wc.lpszMenuName =  NULL;                        // Menu name
    wc.lpszClassName = szAppName;                   // Window class name

    if (RegisterClass (&wc) == 0) return 0;

    // Create main window.
    hWnd = CreateDialog (hInst, szAppName, NULL, NULL);

    // Return fail code if window not created.
    if (!IsWindow (hWnd)) return 0;

    // Create secondary thread for server function.
    hThread = CreateThread (NULL, 0, ServerThread, hWnd, 0, 0);
    if (hThread == 0) {
        DestroyWindow (hWnd);
```

```
            return 0;
        }
        CloseHandle (hThread);


        // Post a message to have device discovery start
        PostMessage (hWnd, WM_COMMAND, MAKEWPARAM (IDD_SCAN, BN_CLICKED),0);

        ShowWindow (hWnd, nCmdShow);          // Standard show and update calls
        UpdateWindow (hWnd);
        SetFocus (GetDlgItem (hWnd, IDD_OUTTEXT));
        return hWnd;
    }
//----------------------------------------------------------------------
// TermInstance - Program cleanup
//
int TermInstance (HINSTANCE hInstance, int nDefRC) {
    WSACleanup ();
    return nDefRC;
}
//======================================================================
// Message handling procedures for main window
//----------------------------------------------------------------------
// MainWndProc - Callback function for application window
//
LRESULT CALLBACK MainWndProc (HWND hWnd, UINT wMsg, WPARAM wParam,
                              LPARAM lParam) {
    INT i;
    //
    // Search message list to see if we need to handle this
    // message.  If in list, call procedure.
    //
    for (i = 0; i < dim(MainMessages); i++) {
        if (wMsg == MainMessages[i].Code)
            return (*MainMessages[i].Fxn)(hWnd, wMsg, wParam, lParam);
    }
    return DefWindowProc (hWnd, wMsg, wParam, lParam);
}
//----------------------------------------------------------------------
// DoCreateMain - Process WM_CREATE message for window.
//
LRESULT DoCreateMain (HWND hWnd, UINT wMsg, WPARAM wParam,
                      LPARAM lParam) {

#if defined(WIN32_PLATFORM_PSPC) && (_WIN32_WCE >= 300)
    SHINITDLGINFO shidi;
    SHMENUBARINFO mbi;                        // For Pocket PC, create
    memset(&mbi, 0, sizeof(SHMENUBARINFO)); // menu bar so that we
    mbi.cbSize = sizeof(SHMENUBARINFO);      // have a sip button
```

(continued)

Listing 14-2 *(continued)*

```
    mbi.dwFlags = SHCMBF_EMPTYBAR;
    mbi.hwndParent = hWnd;
    SHCreateMenuBar(&mbi);
    SendMessage(mbi.hwndMB, SHCMBM_GETSUBMENU, 0, 100);

    // For Pocket PC, make dialog box full screen with PPC
    // specific call.
    shidi.dwMask = SHIDIM_FLAGS;
    shidi.dwFlags = SHIDIF_DONEBUTTON | SHIDIF_SIZEDLG | SHIDIF_SIPDOWN;
    shidi.hDlg = hWnd;
    SHInitDialog(&shidi);

    sai.cbSize = sizeof (sai);
    SHHandleWMSettingChange(hWnd, wParam, lParam, &sai);
#endif
    return 0;
}
//----------------------------------------------------------------------
// DoSizeMain - Process WM_SIZE message for window.
//
LRESULT DoSizeMain (HWND hWnd, UINT wMsg, WPARAM wParam,
                    LPARAM lParam) {

#if defined(WIN32_PLATFORM_PSPC) && (_WIN32_WCE >= 300)
    static RECT rectListbox;
    RECT rect;

    GetClientRect (hWnd, &rect);
    if (fFirstSize) {
        // First time through, get the position of the listbox for
        // resizing later.  Store the distance from the sides of
        // the listbox control to the side of the parent window
        if (IsWindow (GetDlgItem (hWnd, IDD_INTEXT))) {
            GetWindowRect (GetDlgItem (hWnd, IDD_INTEXT), &rectListbox);
            MapWindowPoints (HWND_DESKTOP, hWnd, (LPPOINT)&rectListbox,2);
            rectListbox.right = rect.right - rectListbox.right;
            rectListbox.bottom = rect.bottom - rectListbox.bottom;
        }
    }
    SetWindowPos (GetDlgItem (hWnd, IDD_INTEXT), 0, rect.left+5,
                rectListbox.top, rect.right-10,
                rect.bottom - rectListbox.top - 5,
                SWP_NOZORDER);
#endif
    if (fFirstSize) {
        EnableWindow (GetDlgItem (hWnd, IDD_SAYHELLO), FALSE);
        EnableWindow (GetDlgItem (hWnd, IDD_SCAN), FALSE);
```

```
            fFirstSize = FALSE;
    }
    return 0;
}
//----------------------------------------------------------------------
// DoCommandMain - Process WM_COMMAND message for window.
//
LRESULT DoCommandMain (HWND hWnd, UINT wMsg, WPARAM wParam,
                       LPARAM lParam) {
    WORD idItem, wNotifyCode;
    HWND hwndCtl;
    INT i;

    // Parse the parameters.
    idItem = (WORD) LOWORD (wParam);
    wNotifyCode = (WORD) HIWORD (wParam);
    hwndCtl = (HWND) lParam;

    // Call routine to handle control message.
    for (i = 0; i < dim(MainCommandItems); i++) {
        if (idItem == MainCommandItems[i].Code)
            return (*MainCommandItems[i].Fxn)(hWnd, idItem, hwndCtl,
                                              wNotifyCode);
    }
    return 0;
}
//----------------------------------------------------------------------
// DoEnableSendMain - Process user message to enable send button
//
LRESULT DoEnableSendMain (HWND hWnd, UINT wMsg, WPARAM wParam,
                          LPARAM lParam) {
    EnableWindow (GetDlgItem (hWnd, IDD_SAYHELLO), lParam);
    EnableWindow (GetDlgItem (hWnd, IDD_SCAN), TRUE);
    SetWindowText (hWnd, szAppName);
    return 0;
}
//----------------------------------------------------------------------
// DoPrintfNotifyMain - Process printf notify message
//
LRESULT DoPrintfNotifyMain (HWND hWnd, UINT wMsg, WPARAM wParam,
                            LPARAM lParam) {
    TCHAR szBuffer[512];
    int rc;
    DWORD dwLen = 0;
    DWORD dwFlags = 0;

    memset (szBuffer, 0, sizeof (szBuffer));
    rc = ReadMsgQueue (hQRead, (LPBYTE)szBuffer, sizeof (szBuffer),
```

(continued)

Listing 14-2   *(continued)*

```
                             &dwLen, 0, &dwFlags);
    if (rc) {
        if (dwFlags & MSGQUEUE_MSGALERT)
            SetWindowText (hWnd, szBuffer);
        else {
            rc = SendDlgItemMessage (hWnd, IDD_INTEXT, LB_ADDSTRING, 0,
                                (LPARAM)(LPCTSTR)szBuffer);
            if (rc != LB_ERR)
                SendDlgItemMessage (hWnd, IDD_INTEXT, LB_SETTOPINDEX,rc,
                                (LPARAM)(LPCTSTR)szBuffer);
        }
    }
    return 0;
}
//-----------------------------------------------------------------------
// DoPocketPCShell - Process Pocket PC required messages
//
LRESULT DoPocketPCShell (HWND hWnd, UINT wMsg, WPARAM wParam,
                         LPARAM lParam) {
#if defined(WIN32_PLATFORM_PSPC) && (_WIN32_WCE >= 300)
    if (wMsg == WM_SETTINGCHANGE)
        return SHHandleWMSettingChange(hWnd, wParam, lParam, &sai);
    if (wMsg == WM_ACTIVATE)
        return SHHandleWMActivate(hWnd, wParam, lParam, &sai, 0);
#endif
    return 0;
}
//-----------------------------------------------------------------------
// DoDestroyMain - Process WM_DESTROY message for window.
//
LRESULT DoDestroyMain (HWND hWnd, UINT wMsg, WPARAM wParam,
                       LPARAM lParam) {
    fContinue = FALSE;                      // Shut down server thread.
    Sleep (0);                              // Pass on timeslice.
    PostQuitMessage (0);
    return 0;
}
//=======================================================================
// Command handler routines
//-----------------------------------------------------------------------
// DoMainCommandExit - Process Program Exit command.
//
LPARAM DoMainCommandExit (HWND hWnd, WORD idItem, HWND hwndCtl,
                          WORD wNotifyCode) {

    SendMessage (hWnd, WM_CLOSE, 0, 0);
```

```
      return 0;
}
//--------------------------------------------------------------------
// DoMainCommandSend - Process Program Send File command.
//
LPARAM DoMainCommandSend (HWND hWnd, WORD idItem, HWND hwndCtl,
                          WORD wNotifyCode) {
    static TCHAR szName[MAX_PATH];

    GetDlgItemText (hWnd, IDD_OUTTEXT, szName, dim(szName));
    CreateThread (NULL, 0, SayHelloThread, (PVOID)szName, 0, NULL);
    return 0;
}
//--------------------------------------------------------------------
// DoMainCommandScan - Process Device Scan command.
//
LPARAM DoMainCommandScan (HWND hWnd, WORD idItem, HWND hwndCtl,
                          WORD wNotifyCode) {
    SetWindowText (hWnd, TEXT("Scanning..."));
    EnableWindow (GetDlgItem (hWnd, IDD_SAYHELLO), FALSE);
    EnableWindow (GetDlgItem (hWnd, IDD_SCAN), FALSE);
    CreateThread (NULL, 0, SearchThread, (PVOID)hWnd, 0, NULL);
    return 0;
}
//--------------------------------------------------------------------
// Add2List - Add string to the report list box.
//
void Add2List (HWND hWnd, LPTSTR lpszFormat, ...) {
    int nBuf, nLen;
    TCHAR szBuffer[512];
    va_list args;
    if (hWnd == 0)
        hWnd = hMain;

    EnterCriticalSection (&csPrintf);
    va_start(args, lpszFormat);
    nBuf = _vstprintf(szBuffer, lpszFormat, args);
    va_end(args);

    nLen = (lstrlen (szBuffer)+1) * sizeof (TCHAR);
    WriteMsgQueue (hQWrite, (LPBYTE)szBuffer, nLen, 0, 0);
    PostMessage (hWnd, MYMSG_PRINTF, 0, 0);
    LeaveCriticalSection (&csPrintf);
}
//--------------------------------------------------------------------
// MySetWindowText - Set Window title to passed printf style string.
//
void MySetWindowText (HWND hWnd, LPTSTR lpszFormat, ...) {
```

(continued)

Listing 14-2 *(continued)*

```
    int nBuf, nLen;
    TCHAR szBuffer[512];
    va_list args;

    EnterCriticalSection (&csPrintf);
    va_start(args, lpszFormat);
    nBuf = _vstprintf(szBuffer, lpszFormat, args);
    va_end(args);

    nLen = (lstrlen (szBuffer)+1) * sizeof (TCHAR);
    WriteMsgQueue (hQWrite, (LPBYTE)szBuffer, nLen, 0,MSGQUEUE_MSGALERT);
    PostMessage (hWnd, MYMSG_PRINTF, 0, 0);
    LeaveCriticalSection (&csPrintf);
}
//======================================================================
// SearchThread - Monitors for other devices.
//
DWORD WINAPI SearchThread (PVOID pArg) {
    HWND hWnd = (HWND)pArg;
    int i, rc, Channel = 0;

    Add2List (hWnd, TEXT("Search thread entered"));

    // Init COM for the thread.
    CoInitializeEx(NULL,COINIT_MULTITHREADED);

    // Find the Bluetooth devices
    nDevs = MAX_DEVICES;
    rc = FindDevices (btd, &nDevs);

    // List them.
    for (i = 0; i < nDevs; i++)
        Add2List (hWnd, TEXT("%d. dev:>%s<  "), i, btd[i].szName);

    PostMessage (hWnd, MYMSG_ENABLESEND, 0, 1);
    CoUninitialize();
    Add2List (hWnd, TEXT("Search thread exit"));
    return 0;
}
//======================================================================
// ServerThread - Monitors for connections, connects and notifies
// user when a connection occurs.
//
DWORD WINAPI ServerThread (PVOID pArg) {
    HWND hWnd = (HWND)pArg;
    INT rc, len, nSize;
    SOCKADDR_BTH btaddr, t_btaddr;
```

```
SOCKET r_sock, s_sock;
ULONG RecordHandle;
HRESULT hr;

Add2List (hWnd, TEXT("Server thread entered"));
CoInitializeEx(NULL,COINIT_MULTITHREADED);


// Open a bluetooth socket
s_sock = socket (AF_BT, SOCK_STREAM, BTHPROTO_RFCOMM);
if (s_sock == INVALID_SOCKET) {
    Add2List (hWnd, TEXT("socket failed. rc %d"), WSAGetLastError());
    return 0;
}
// Fill in address stuff
memset (&btaddr, 0, sizeof (btaddr));
btaddr.addressFamily = AF_BT;
btaddr.port = 0;    // Let driver assign a channel

// Bind to socket
rc = bind (s_sock, (struct sockaddr *)&btaddr, sizeof (btaddr));
if (rc) {
    Add2List (hWnd, TEXT("bind failed"));
    closesocket (s_sock);
    return 0;
}
// Get information on the port assigned
len = sizeof (btaddr);
rc = getsockname (s_sock, (SOCKADDR *)&btaddr, &len);
if (rc) {
    Add2List (hWnd, TEXT("getsockname failed"));
    closesocket (s_sock);
    return 0;
}
Add2List (hWnd, TEXT("Addr %04x.%08x, port %d"),
      GET_NAP(btaddr.btAddr), GET_SAP(btaddr.btAddr), btaddr.port);

// Register our service
rc = RegisterBtService (&guidbthello, (unsigned char) btaddr.port,
                    &RecordHandle);
if (rc) {
    Add2List (hWnd, TEXT("RegisterService fail %d %d"), rc,
            GetLastError());
    closesocket (s_sock);
    return 0;
}

// Set socket into listen mode
rc = listen (s_sock, SOMAXCONN);
```

(continued)

Listing 14-2   *(continued)*

```
        if (rc == SOCKET_ERROR) {
            Add2List (hWnd, TEXT(" listen failed %d"), GetLastError());
            closesocket (s_sock);
            return 0;
        }
        // Wait for remote requests
        while (fContinue) {
            Add2List (hWnd, TEXT("waiting..."));
            nSize = sizeof (t_btaddr);
            // Block on accept
            r_sock = accept (s_sock, (struct sockaddr *)&t_btaddr, &nSize);
            if (r_sock == INVALID_SOCKET) {
                Add2List (hWnd, TEXT(" accept failed %d"), GetLastError());
            }
            Add2List (hWnd, TEXT("sock accept..."));
            CreateThread (NULL, 0, ReceiveThread, (PVOID)r_sock, 0, NULL);
        }
        closesocket (s_sock);

        // Deregister the service
        hr = UnregisterBtService (hWnd, RecordHandle);
        CoUninitialize();
        Add2List (hWnd, TEXT("Server thread exit"));
        return 0;
}
//======================================================================
// ReceiveThread - Sends the file requested by the remote device
//
DWORD WINAPI ReceiveThread (PVOID pArg) {
    SOCKET r_sock = (SOCKET)pArg;
    HWND hWnd = hMain; // I'm cheating here.
    int nCnt, rc = 0;
    PBYTE pBuff = 0;
    int nBytes;
    TCHAR szRcvBuff[256];

    Add2List (hWnd, TEXT("receive thread entered"));
    SetThreadPriority (GetCurrentThread (), THREAD_PRIORITY_ABOVE_NORMAL);

    // Read the number of bytes in the text string
    nBytes = recv (r_sock, (LPSTR)&nCnt, sizeof (nCnt), 0);
    if (nBytes == SOCKET_ERROR) {
        Add2List (hWnd, TEXT("failed receiving text length"));
        closesocket (r_sock);
        return 0;
    }
    if (sizeof (szRcvBuff) < nCnt)
```

```
                    rc = BAD_TEXTLEN;

    // Send ack
    nBytes = send (r_sock, (char *)&rc, sizeof (rc), 0);
    if (nBytes == SOCKET_ERROR) {
        Add2List (hWnd, TEXT("Error %d receiving text length"), GetLastError(
));
        closesocket (r_sock);
        return 0;
    }

    // Read the text
    nBytes = recv (r_sock, (LPSTR)szRcvBuff, nCnt, 0);
    if (nBytes == SOCKET_ERROR) {
        Add2List (hWnd, TEXT("failed receiving text"));
        closesocket (r_sock);
        return 0;
    }
    Add2List (hWnd, TEXT("Other device says: %s"), szRcvBuff);

    // send ack of text
    rc = 0;
    nBytes = send (r_sock, (char *)&rc, sizeof (rc), 0);
    if (nBytes == SOCKET_ERROR) {
        Add2List (hWnd, TEXT("Error %d sending ack"), GetLastError());
        rc = SOCKET_ERROR;
    }
    Add2List (hWnd, TEXT("receive thread exit"));
    return 0;
}
//--------------------------------------------------------------------
// SayHello - Sends text to the remote device
//
DWORD WINAPI SayHelloThread (PVOID pArg) {
    TCHAR szText[] = TEXT("Hello Device");
    HWND hWnd = hMain;
    SOCKET t_sock;
    INT j, rc, nCnt, nBytes;
    SOCKADDR_BTH btaddr;
    BOOL fSuccess = FALSE;

    // Open a bluetooth socket
    t_sock = socket (AF_BT, SOCK_STREAM, BTHPROTO_RFCOMM);
    if (t_sock == INVALID_SOCKET) {
        Add2List (hWnd, TEXT("socket failed. rc %d"), WSAGetLastError());
        return 0;
    }
```

(continued)

Listing 14-2   *(continued)*

```
    // Loop through each device trying to say hello
    for (j = 0; j < nDevs; j++) {

        Add2List (hWnd, TEXT("Trying device %s"), btd[j].szName);
        // Fill in address stuff
        memset (&btaddr, 0, sizeof (btaddr));
        btaddr.btAddr = btd[j].btaddr;
        btaddr.addressFamily = AF_BT;
        btaddr.port = 0;                        // Let driver find the channel
        memcpy (&btaddr.serviceClassId, &guidbthello, sizeof (GUID));
        //
        // Connect to remote socket
        //
        rc = connect (t_sock, (struct sockaddr *)&btaddr, sizeof (btaddr));
        if (rc == 0) {
            fSuccess = TRUE;
            break;
        }
        Add2List (hWnd, TEXT("connect failed. rc %d"), WSAGetLastError());
    }
    if (!fSuccess) {
        closesocket (t_sock);
        return 0;
    }
    Add2List (hWnd, TEXT("connected..."));

    // send name size
    nCnt = (lstrlen (szText) + 1) * sizeof (TCHAR);
    nBytes = send (t_sock, (LPSTR)&nCnt, sizeof (nCnt), 0);

    // Recv ack of text size
    if (recv (t_sock, (char *)&rc, sizeof (rc), 0) == SOCKET_ERROR)
        rc = SOCKET_ERROR;

    if (rc == 0) {
        // Send text name
        if (nBytes != SOCKET_ERROR) {
            nBytes = send (t_sock, (LPSTR)szText, nCnt, 0);
        }
        // Recv ack of text send.
        if (recv (t_sock, (char *)&rc, sizeof (rc), 0) == SOCKET_ERROR)
            rc = SOCKET_ERROR;
    }
    // Send close code.
    if (rc != BAD_SOCKET)
        send (t_sock, (LPSTR)&rc, sizeof (rc), 0);
```

```
    closesocket (t_sock);
    if (rc)
        Add2List (hWnd, TEXT("SayHello Exit rc = %d"), rc);
    else
        Add2List (hWnd, TEXT("Text sent successfully"));
    return 0;
}
```

The interesting routines are the search thread routine *SearchThread* and the server thread routine *ServerThread*. The *SearchThread* calls the *FindDevice* routine to enumerate the Bluetooth devices in the immediate area. The search is set to take approximately 5 seconds. Once found, the device names and addresses are listed in the output window. The names and the addresses of all the devices are saved in an array. The search can be restarted by tapping on the Scan button.

The server routine, *ServerThread*, creates a socket and binds it to an address. The routine then queries Winsock for the RFCOMM channel assigned to the socket. The *RegisterBtService* routine is then called to advertise the *bthello* service. The *RegisterBtService* routine uses a prebuilt SDP record and inserts the GUID for the service and the RFCOMM channel in the appropriate parts of the record. Once constructed, the SDP packet is registered in the *PublishRecord* routine.

When the user taps the "Say Hello" button, an attempt is made to connect to the bthello server on each of the devices found. If one of the connections is successful, the text is sent to the other device.

Accessing Bluetooth through either Winsock or virtual COM ports provides the most flexible way to wirelessly communicate with another device. The problem is that with either of these methods the custom application, such as BtHello, has to be on both machines unless the application communicates through one of the public services.

If you use one of the public services, the application must implement the proper protocol. Although directly talking to Bluetooth is the most flexible path, it's also the most complex. How about a higher-level standard that will inform the application when devices come in range, that will work over Bluetooth and IrDA, and that will provide a simple method for transferring files? There is such a standard. It's called the Object Exchange (OBEX) standard, and it too is supported by the Pocket PC and other Windows CE devices.

OBEX

The OBEX standard provides a vendor-independent standard for transferring files, business card information, and calendar information between devices. Windows CE supports OBEX over IrDA and Bluetooth. The embedded version of Windows CE supports a number of OBEX protocols, depending on how the system is configured. The Pocket PC supports the OBEX Push protocol although additional protocols may be optionally supported by OEMs. This section covers how to use OBEX to detect devices in range of either IrDA or Bluetooth as well as how to use OBEX to send files to another device.

The OBEX support under Windows CE is provided through a series of COM interfaces. The primary interface is *IObex* or its modestly enhanced derivative, *IObex2*. This interface provides support for initialization and shutdown of OBEX support as well as device enumeration. Other interfaces used when working with OBEX include *IObexDevice*, for communication with a device; and *IObexSink*, which provides a callback interface in the application.

Initialization

To initialize the OBEX system, an application must first create an *IObex* or *IObex2* object. The difference between the two interfaces is a single method, *PauseDeviceEnum*, which provides the handy feature of suspending the device enumeration and resuming instead of having to stop and restart it. Creating the object is easily accomplished using the COM function *CoCreateInstance*. Once the object is created, the OBEX system can be initialized with a call to the *Initialize* method. The following code shows this initialization process.

```
IObex *pObex = NULL;
HRESULT hr = CoCreateInstance (_uuidof(Obex), NULL, CLSCTX_INPROC_SERVER,
                               __uuidof(IObex), (void **)&pObex);
if (FAILED(hr))
    return hr;

if (pObex != NULL)
    pObex->Initialize ();
else
    return -1;
```

Application Callbacks

The best way to keep informed concerning the status of the OBEX system is for the application to support an *IObexSink* interface that the OBEX system can call in to with status messages. Application callbacks are optional; an application using OBEX isn't required to support them. However, the callback scheme enables the best method for device detection and also provides a way for the OBEX system to notify the application when a remote device requires a password for a connection.

The *IObexSink* interface is a standard COM interface with a single additional method, *Notify*, prototyped as

```
HRESULT IObexSink::Notify (OBEX_EVENT Event,
                           IUnknown *pUnk1, IUnknown *pUnk2);
```

To tell the OBEX system about the callback interface, the application must ask the OBEX interface for its connection point container. Once found, the connection point container is queried for an *IObexSink* connection point. Once that's found, the *Advise* method can be called on the connection point pointing to the *IObexSink* interface in the application. The process is best illustrated in the simple code fragment shown here:

```
// Create my class the implements an IObexSink interface
MyObexSink *pSink;
pSink = new MyObexSink(hWnd);
if (!pSink)
    return -1;


// Create connection point container
hr = pObex->QueryInterface (IID_IConnectionPointContainer,
                            (LPVOID *)&pContainer);
if (!SUCCEEDED(hr) || (pContainer == 0))
    return -2;

hr = pContainer->FindConnectionPoint (IID_IObexSink, &pConPt);
if (!SUCCEEDED(hr) || (pConPt == 0)) {
    pContainer->Release();
    return -3;
}


// Ask for notifications
hr = pConPt->Advise((IUnknown *)pSink, &dwCookie);
```

When a callback occurs, the *Event* parameter provides the reason for the callback. In theory, the *pUnk1* and *pUnk2* parameters are pointers to COM objects that are relevant for each event. In practice, for the supported events, *pUnk1* is a pointer to an *IPropertyBag* interface that contains information about the device.

The events reported by the OBEX system are listed here:

■ **OE_QUERY_PASSWORD**   The remote device needs a password to continue.

■ **OE_DEVICE_ARRIVAL**   A new device has been detected in range.

- **OE_DEVICE_DEPARTURE**   A device has moved out of range.

- **OE_DEVICE_UPDATE**   New information is available on a device in range.

At the time the callback is made, the OBEX object is blocked from other work for the application, so the code in the callback interface must be executed quickly. Traditionally, the interface simply posts a message with the relevant details to a window where the details are examined asynchronously from the callback.

Device Discovery

One of the most convenient aspects of OBEX programming is that most functions the application uses apply to devices using both IrDA and Bluetooth. Device discovery is one of these common areas. Device discovery can be accomplished in a synchronous or an asynchronous manner. The synchronous method is simpler, but the asynchronous method is much more flexible.

Synchronous Device Detection

Synchronous device detection is accomplished by calling the *IObex* method *StartDeviceEnum*, prototyped as

```
HRESULT IObex::StartDeviceEnum (void);
```

StartDeviceEnum returns immediately, but the OBEX system starts monitoring for devices. The application must wait some amount of time for the OBEX system to gather information about the devices. Typically, the application should wait 5 or more seconds before calling back to get a list of the devices detected. The application doesn't have to be idle during this wait. The application can set a Windows timer, using *SetTimer* to have the operating system send a timer message back to the application 5 seconds after the initial call to *StartDeviceEnum*.

Once the enumeration time has elapsed, the application can call *StopDeviceEnum*, prototyped as

```
HRESULT IObex::StopDeviceEnum (void);
```

This method doesn't have to be called before the *EnumDevices* method (discussed next), but it must not be called until the OBEX system has had time to enumerate the local devices.

To query the devices the OBEX system has discovered, call *EnumDevices*, prototyped as

```
HRESULT IObex::EnumDevices (IDeviceEnum *ppDeviceEnum,
                      REFCLSID uuidTransport);
```

The first parameter is the address of a pointer to an *IDeviceEnum* interface. This pointer is set by the method to an *IDeviceEnum* object that can be used to enumerate the devices. The second parameter is the GUID of the transport—Bluetooth, IrDA, or others—that the application is interested in. If the application wants a list of all devices regardless of the transport they support, a *NULL* value can be passed in the second parameter.

The *IDeviceEnum* interface, used to enumerate the devices, has four methods: *Next*, *Reset*, *Skip*, and *Clone*. To return a list of the devices, use the *Next* method:

```
HRESULT IDeviceEnum::Next (ULONG celt, IObexDevice **rgelt,
                           ULONG *pceltFetched);
```

The second parameter of the *Next* method points to an array of *IObexDevice* interface pointers. The first parameter, *celt*, should be set to the number of the entries in the *IObexDevice* pointer array. The third parameter is the address of a *ULONG* that receives the number of *IObexDevice* pointers returned in the array.

The *Next* method can be used in two ways. In the first way, *Next* is called with the *celt* parameter set to 1 so that the call returns a single *IObexDevice* pointer. Using the method this way, *Next* will have to be repeatedly called to return a device pointer for each device found. The other way to use the *Next* method is to call it once but pass a large array of *IObexDevice* pointers, which will be filled with pointers for all the devices. Either way will return similar device information.

The other methods of *IDeviceEnum* are shown here:

```
HRESULT IDeviceEnum::Skip (ULONG celt);
HRESULT IDeviceEnum::Reset (void);
HRESULT IDeviceEnum::Clone (IDeviceEnum *ppenum);
```

These relatively self-explanatory methods allow the application to skip a set number of devices in the enumeration, reset the enumeration back to the first device, and create a new copy of the *IDeviceEnum* interface.

Asynchronous Device Detection

Asynchronous device detection is accomplished by starting the detection with the same call to *StartDeviceEnum* as in the synchronous detection. The difference is that before the call to *StartDeviceEnum* is made, the application provides an *IObexSink* interface to be notified with an *OE_DEVICE_ARRIVAL* event when devices are detected. There is no need to call the *IObex* method *Enum-*

Devices because the notification process will provide the device information as the devices are discovered.

One interesting aspect of asynchronous device detection is that the device information returned in the *IObexSink* callback is initially incomplete. The OBEX system will initially report that a device has been found but provides little information about the device. As more information about the device is gathered, the OBEX system provides additional callback events, this time with an *OE_DEVICE_UPDATE* notification. Because of this, the application needs to tolerate the incomplete information and parse the update notifications to complete the information about the discovered device.

Information about the devices is passed in the notification callback through a *PropertyBag* object. This object has information such as the name of the device, its address, the transport supported, and services supported by the device. Because of the repeated updates on the same device, the application has to determine the device being updated and add the updated information to that device. The ObexSquirt example later in this chapter demonstrates how to keep track of devices through asynchronous detection.

If the device supports Bluetooth, there is a good possibility that the device enumeration process will detect more than one device able to communicate. The application has to be written to provide the user the ability to select the target device.

OBEX Communication

Once a device has been chosen as a target, the application must connect with the device to initialize communication. The connection process starts with accessing the *IObexDevice* interface associated with the target device. If the device enumeration was accomplished with synchronous enumeration, the *IDeviceEnum::Next* method returns a list of *IObexDevice* interface pointers, one for each device found. For asynchronous enumeration, the only information the application has is a *PropertyBag* object for each device. To convert that to an *IObexDevice* interface, *IObex* provides the *BindToDevice* method, prototyped as

```
HRESULT IObex::BindToDevice (IPropertyBag* pPropertyBag,
                             IObexDevice** ppDevice);
```

The *BindToDevice* method returns the *IObexDevice* pointer that matches the device described in the *PropertyBag* object pointed to by the first parameter.

The *IObexDevice* interface provides the basic set of methods used to communicate with a device. The first method of interest is the *Connect* method, prototyped as

```
HRESULT IObexDevice::Connect (LPCWSTR pszPassword, DWORD dwCapability,
                              IHeaderCollection* pHeaders);
```

The first parameter is the password to the remote device. If this parameter isn't specified and the remote device needs a password, the OBEX system will call back to the application to request the password. The *dwCapability* parameter is reserved and should be set to 0. The final parameter is a pointer to a header collection object. This object must be created before the call to *Connect* and contains a list of specifications for the connection.

A header collection object is a COM object that's used to describe the OBEX operation being attempted. For connections, the header collection can optionally contain a target service to connect to on the remote device.

The target is added to the header collection object using the *AddTarget* method, shown here:

```
HRESULT IHeaderCollection::AddTarget (unsigned long ulSize, byte * pData);
```

The two parameters are the length of the target data being set and the target data itself.

If no target service is specified, a connection is attempted to the default OBEX service, Object Push, which is fielded on Windows CE devices by Pocket InBox. Other OBEX services can be supported by devices. The two services of most interest to Windows CE developers are the file browsing service, or *ObexFTP*, and the *Sync* service. To connect to the *FTP* service, the target service should be set to the File Browsing GUID:

```
{F9ec7bc4-953c-11d2-984e-525400dc9e09}
```

Note that the GUID needs to be specified in network byte order instead of the Windows-standard little-endian byte order. The following code takes a *PropertyBag* object that describes a device and connects to the device's *FTP* service.

```
// {F9ec7bc4-953c-11d2-984e-525400dc9e09}
GUID CLSID_FTP_NetOrder={0xc47becf9, 0x3c95, 0xd211,
                        {0x98, 0x4e, 0x52, 0x54, 0x00, 0xdc, 0x9e, 0x09}};
//
// Start here with a pointer to a IPropertyBag describing the device
//
HRESULT hr = pObex->BindToDevice (pDevPropBag, &pDevice);

IHeaderCollection *pHC = 0;
hr = CoCreateInstance(__uuidof(HeaderCollection), NULL,
                CLSCTX_INPROC_SERVER, __uuidof(IHeaderCollection),
                (void **)&pHC);
if (FAILED(hr)) {
```

```
    CloseHandle (hFile);
    return -2;
}
pHC->AddTarget(sizeof (CLSID_FTP_NetOrder),(UCHAR *)&CLSID_FTP_NetOrder);

// Connect to device
hr = pDevice->Connect (NULL, 0, pHC);
if (FAILED(hr)) {
    printf ("Connect fail %x %d", hr, GetLastError());
    pHC->Release();
    CloseHandle (hFile);
    return -3;
}
printf ("Connected...");
```

Once connected, the application can exchange objects using the *Get* and *Put* methods, prototyped as follows:

```
HRESULT Get (IHeaderCollection* pHeaders, IStream** ppStream);
HRESULT Put (IHeaderCollection* pHeaders, IStream** ppStream);
```

For both these methods, a header collection object must be created first to describe the object being sent or requested. The object name is specified using the *AddName* method of the header collection object, defined as

```
HRESULT IHeaderCollection::AddName (LPCWSTR pszName);
```

The only parameter is the string containing the name of the object.

When *Put* or *Get* is called, it returns a pointer to an *IStream* interface. The *IStream* interface provides the basic read and write methods for reading and writing to the other device. The following code demonstrates how to push a file from the application to another connected device:

```
//get a header collection
IHeaderCollection *pFileHC = 0;
hr = CoCreateInstance(__uuidof(HeaderCollection), NULL,
                CLSCTX_INPROC_SERVER, __uuidof(IHeaderCollection),
                (void **)&pFileHC);
if (FAILED(hr)) {
    return -2;
}
// Add file name to header
hr = pFileHC->AddName(pszFileName);
if (FAILED(hr)) {
    pFileHC->Release();
    return -3;
}
// Send header
IStream *stOut = 0;
```

```
hr = pDevice->Put(pFileHC, &stOut);
if (FAILED(hr)) {
    pFileHC->Release();
    return -4;
}
// Send the data
nTotal = nFileSize;
while (nFileSize) {
    // Send up to the block size
    nCnt = min (BUFFSIZE, nFileSize);

    if (!ReadFile (hFile, pBuff, nCnt, &dwBytesWritten, FALSE)) {
        Add2List (hWnd, TEXT("ReadFile error %d "), GetLastError());
        break;
    }
    nCnt = (int)dwBytesWritten;

    hr = stOut->Write (pBuff, nCnt, &dwBytesWritten);
    if(FAILED(hr)) {
        break;
    }
    nFileSize -= (int)dwBytesWritten;
}
printf ("Done");
```

When the application has completed its transfer and needs to disconnect, a call to the *Disconnect* method of *IObexDevice* should be made. The method is defined as

```
HRESULT IObexDevice::Disconnect (IHeaderCollection* pHeaders);
```

The method requires a header collection object. If the application is disconnecting from the default Object Push service, the header simply needs to be created. For disconnecting from other services, the target service should be set to match the service originally connected to.

The *IObexDevice* interface supports a handful of other methods, shown here:

```
HRESULT IObexDevice::SetPath (LPCWSTR pszName, DWORD dwFlags,
                             IHeaderCollection* pHeaders);
HRESULT IObexDevice::EnumProperties (REFIID riid, void** ppv);
HRESULT IObexDevice::SetPassword (LPCWSTR pszPassword);
HRESULT IObexDevice::Abort (IHeaderCollection* pHeaders);
```

The *SetPath* method is used in the *FTP* service to specify the target directory on the remote device. The security settings of the other device typically restrict the path to acceptable directories.

The *EnumProperties* method returns the *PropertyBag* object associated with the device. This function is essentially the inverse of the *IObex::BindTo-Device* method. The *SetPassword* method provides another way to set the password for remote device access. Finally, the *Abort* method provides a way for the application to halt a task.

The ObexSquirt Example Program

The ObexSquirt example demonstrates the use of the OBEX service to connect and send a file to another device. Since the example uses OBEX, the transfer can take place over IrDA or Bluetooth because the OBEX system handles all the grisly transport details.

Figure 14-5 shows the ObexSquirt program running on an embedded Windows CE device. Notice that the upper list box contains the list of a number of devices in range of this system. The example works by using asynchronous device enumeration to query the area for devices. As information is returned about each device, the text in the device list is updated to provide the name of the device and the supported protocol. Devices are listed twice in the list if they support both Object Push and the *FTP* OBEX service.

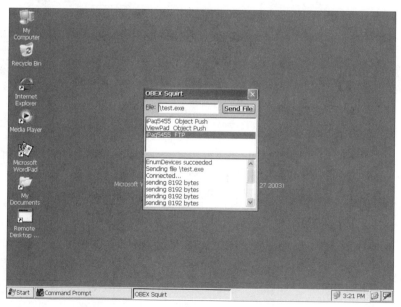

Figure 14-5   The ObexSquirt program, showing the devices in range of the system

The source code for ObexSquirt is shown in Listing 14-3. Unlike both the MySquirt and BtHello examples, ObexSquirt is a single-threaded application. The OBEX service provides some threading because it provides asynchronous device search. The example exposes an *IObexSink* interface that's called when devices are found. When a notification is received, the application simply posts a message to its main window, where the notification is actually processed.

```
ObexSquirt.h
//======================================================================
// Header file
//
// Written for the book Programming Windows CE
// Copyright (C) 2001 Douglas Boling
//======================================================================
// Returns number of elements
#define dim(x) (sizeof(x) / sizeof(x[0]))


// Windows CE Specific defines
#define LPCMDLINE LPWSTR
//----------------------------------------------------------------------
// Generic defines and data types
//
struct decodeUINT {                            // Structure associates
    UINT Code;                                 // messages
                                               // with a function.
    LRESULT (*Fxn)(HWND, UINT, WPARAM, LPARAM);
};
struct decodeCMD {                             // Structure associates
    UINT Code;                                 // menu IDs with a
    LRESULT (*Fxn)(HWND, WORD, HWND, WORD);    // function.
};


//----------------------------------------------------------------------
// Defines used by application

#define ID_ICON                 1

#define IDD_INTEXT              10             // Control IDs
#define IDD_SENDFILE            11
#define IDD_OUTTEXT             12
#define IDD_SCAN                13
#define IDD_DEVICES             14

#define MYMSG_OBEXEVENT         (WM_USER+1000)
#define MYMSG_PRINTF            (WM_USER+1001)
```

Listing 14-3   The ObexSquirt source code   *(continued)*

Listing 14-3   *(continued)*

ObexSquirt.h

```c
//======================================================================
// Header file
//
// Written for the book Programming Windows CE
// Copyright (C) 2001 Douglas Boling
//======================================================================
// Returns number of elements
#define dim(x) (sizeof(x) / sizeof(x[0]))


// Windows CE Specific defines
#define LPCMDLINE LPWSTR
//----------------------------------------------------------------------
// Generic defines and data types
//
struct decodeUINT {                            // Structure associates
    UINT Code;                                 // messages
                                               // with a function.
    LRESULT (*Fxn)(HWND, UINT, WPARAM, LPARAM);
};
struct decodeCMD {                             // Structure associates
    UINT Code;                                 // menu IDs with a
    LRESULT (*Fxn)(HWND, WORD, HWND, WORD);    // function.
};


//----------------------------------------------------------------------
// Defines used by application

#define ID_ICON              1

#define IDD_INTEXT           10                // Control IDs
#define IDD_SENDFILE         11
#define IDD_OUTTEXT          12
#define IDD_SCAN             13
#define IDD_DEVICES          14

#define MYMSG_OBEXEVENT      (WM_USER+1000)
#define MYMSG_PRINTF         (WM_USER+1001)
***
#define DEV_FLAG_ADDRESS     0x00000001
#define DEV_FLAG_NAME        0x00000002
#define DEV_FLAG_TRANSPORT   0x00000004
#define DEV_FLAG_PORT        0x00000008
#define DEV_FLAG_UUID        0x00000010
#define DEV_FLAG_DEVBOUND    0x00000100
```

```
#define DEV_TRANS_IRDA          0x00010000
#define DEV_TRANS_BTOOTH        0x00020000


#define DEV_SERVICE_OBJPUSH     0x01000000
#define DEV_SERVICE_FTP         0x02000000
#define DEV_SERVICE_IRMCSYNC    0x04000000


typedef struct {
    DWORD dwFlags;
    TCHAR szName[256];
    TCHAR szAddr[32];
    DWORD dwTransport;
    DWORD dwPort;
    GUID guidService;
    IPropertyBag* pDevBag;
} MYOBEXDEVICEINFO, *PMYOBEXDEVICEINFO;


#define MAX_DEVS                16
#define BUFFSIZE                8192
//------------------------------------------------------------------------
// Function prototypes
//
HWND InitInstance (HINSTANCE, LPCMDLINE, int);
int TermInstance (HINSTANCE, int);
void Add2List (HWND hWnd, LPTSTR lpszFormat, ...);
int InitObex (HWND hWnd);
int SendFile (HWND hWnd, IObexDevice *pDevice, LPTSTR pszFileName,
              DWORD dwFlags);
BOOL MyYield ();

// Window procedures
LRESULT CALLBACK MainWndProc (HWND, UINT, WPARAM, LPARAM);

// Message handlers
LRESULT DoCreateMain (HWND, UINT, WPARAM, LPARAM);
LRESULT DoSizeMain (HWND, UINT, WPARAM, LPARAM);
LRESULT DoCommandMain (HWND, UINT, WPARAM, LPARAM);
LRESULT DoPocketPCShell (HWND, UINT, WPARAM, LPARAM);
LRESULT DoDestroyMain (HWND, UINT, WPARAM, LPARAM);
LRESULT DoObexEventMain (HWND, UINT, WPARAM, LPARAM);
LRESULT DoPrintfNotifyMain (HWND, UINT, WPARAM, LPARAM);

// Command functions
LPARAM DoMainCommandSend (HWND, WORD, HWND, WORD);
LPARAM DoMainCommandDevList (HWND, WORD, HWND, WORD);
LPARAM DoMainCommandExit (HWND, WORD, HWND, WORD);
```

(continued)

Listing 14-3   *(continued)*

IObexSink.cpp

```cpp
//======================================================================
// MyObexSink - A lightweight COM class to receive obex notifications.
//
// Written for the book Programming Windows CE
// Copyright (C) 2003 Douglas Boling
//======================================================================
class MyObexSink : public IObexSink {
private:
    HWND m_hWnd;
    int m_lRef;

public:
    // Constructor
    MyObexSink(HWND hWnd) {
        m_hWnd = hWnd;
        m_lRef = 0;
    }
    // Destructor
    ~MyObexSink() {}
    //
    // Notify - Callback from Obex code.  Must return quick so no
    // real work done here.
    //
    HRESULT STDMETHODCALLTYPE Notify (OBEX_EVENT Event, IUnknown *pUnk1,
                                      IUnknown *pUnk2)
    {
        if (IsWindow (m_hWnd)) {
            // Inc the cnt of unk1 so it'll stay around.
            pUnk1->AddRef();
            PostMessage (m_hWnd, MYMSG_OBEXEVENT, (WPARAM)Event,
                        (LPARAM)pUnk1);
        }
        return S_OK;
    }
    HRESULT STDMETHODCALLTYPE QueryInterface (REFIID riid, LPVOID *ppv)
    {
        // If caller wants our IUnknown or IClassFactory object,
        // return a pointer to the object.
        if (IsEqualIID (riid, IID_IUnknown) ||
            IsEqualIID (riid, IID_IObexSink)) {
            // Return pointer to object.
            *ppv = (IConnectionPoint *)this;
            AddRef();                    // Increment ref
            return NOERROR;
        }
```

```
        *ppv = NULL;
        return (E_NOINTERFACE);
    }
    ULONG  STDMETHODCALLTYPE AddRef () {
        ULONG cnt = (ULONG)InterlockedIncrement ((long *)&m_lRef);
        return cnt;
    }
    ULONG STDMETHODCALLTYPE Release () {
        ULONG cnt;
        cnt = (ULONG)InterlockedDecrement ((long *)&m_lRef);
        if (cnt == 0) {
            delete this;
            return 0;
        }
        return cnt;
    }
};
```

ObexSquirt.cpp

```
//======================================================================
// ObexSquirt - A simple Obex application for Windows CE
//
// Written for the book Programming Windows CE
// Copyright (C) 2003 Douglas Boling
//======================================================================
#include <windows.h>                    // For all that Windows stuff
#include <obex.h>
#include <Msgqueue.h>
#if defined(WIN32_PLATFORM_PSPC)
#include <aygshell.h>                   // Add Pocket PC includes
#pragma comment( lib, "aygshell" )      // Link Pocket PC lib for menubar
#endif

#include "obexsquirt.h"                 // Program-specific stuff
#include "MyObexSink.cpp"               // IObexSink class


//----------------------------------------------------------------------
// Global data
//
const TCHAR szAppName[] = TEXT ("obexsquirt");
const TCHAR szTitleText[] = TEXT ("OBEX Squirt");

TCHAR szTitle[128];
HINSTANCE hInst;                        // Program instance handle
HWND hMain;                             // Main window handle
BOOL ffirstSize = TRUE;                 // First WM_SIZE flag
```

(continued)

Listing 14-3 *(continued)*

```c
#if defined(WIN32_PLATFORM_PSPC) && (_WIN32_WCE >= 300)
SHACTIVATEINFO sai;                          // Needed for PPC helper funcs
#endif

// The GUID strings below are defined numerically in bt_sdp.h
const TCHAR g_szIrMCSyncGuid[] =
                    TEXT("{00001104-0000-1000-8000-00805f9b34fb}");
const TCHAR g_szObjPushGuid[] =
                    TEXT("{00001105-0000-1000-8000-00805f9b34fb}");
const TCHAR g_szFtpGuid[] =
                    TEXT("{00001106-0000-1000-8000-00805f9b34fb}");

const TCHAR g_szTransIrDA[] =
                    TEXT("{30a7bc02-59b6-40bb-aa2b-89eb49ef274e}");
const TCHAR g_szTransBth[] =
                    TEXT("{30a7bc03-59b6-40bb-aa2b-89eb49ef274e}");


// {F9ec7bc4-953c-11d2-984e-525400dc9e09}
GUID CLSID_FileExchange_NetOrder = {0xc47becf9, 0x3c95, 0xd211,
                {0x98, 0x4e, 0x52, 0x54, 0x00, 0xdc, 0x9e, 0x09}};


HANDLE hQRead = 0;                      // Msg queues are used to sync
HANDLE hQWrite = 0;                     // output to the listbox
CRITICAL_SECTION csPrintf;
CRITICAL_SECTION csLock;


IObex *pObex = NULL;                    // Obex main interface ptr
BOOL fObex2IF = FALSE;
IConnectionPointContainer *pContainer = NULL;
IConnectionPoint *pConPt = NULL;
DWORD dwCookie;


MYOBEXDEVICEINFO obDevs[MAX_DEVS];


// Message dispatch table for MainWindowProc
const struct decodeUINT MainMessages[] = {
    WM_CREATE, DoCreateMain,
    WM_SIZE, DoSizeMain,
    WM_COMMAND, DoCommandMain,
    MYMSG_OBEXEVENT, DoObexEventMain,
    MYMSG_PRINTF, DoPrintfNotifyMain,
    WM_SETTINGCHANGE, DoPocketPCShell,
    WM_ACTIVATE, DoPocketPCShell,
    WM_DESTROY, DoDestroyMain,
};
// Command Message dispatch for MainWindowProc
const struct decodeCMD MainCommandItems[] = {
```

```
#if defined(WIN32_PLATFORM_PSPC) && (_WIN32_WCE >= 300)
    IDOK, DoMainCommandExit,
#else
    IDOK, DoMainCommandSend,
#endif
    IDCANCEL, DoMainCommandExit,
    IDD_SENDFILE, DoMainCommandSend,
    IDD_DEVICES, DoMainCommandDevList,
};
//======================================================================
// Program entry point
//
int WINAPI WinMain (HINSTANCE hInstance, HINSTANCE hPrevInstance,
                    LPCMDLINE lpCmdLine, int nCmdShow) {
    MSG msg;
    int rc = 0;

    // Initialize this instance.
    hMain = InitInstance (hInstance, lpCmdLine, nCmdShow);
    if (hMain) {
        // Application message loop
        while (GetMessage (&msg, NULL, 0, 0)) {
            if ((hMain == 0) || !IsDialogMessage (hMain, &msg)) {
                TranslateMessage (&msg);
                DispatchMessage (&msg);
            }
        }
    }
    // Instance cleanup
    return TermInstance (hInstance, msg.wParam);
}
//----------------------------------------------------------------------
// InitInstance - Instance initialization
//
HWND InitInstance (HINSTANCE hInstance, LPCMDLINE lpCmdLine,
                   int nCmdShow){
    WNDCLASS wc;
    HWND hWnd;

    hInst = hInstance;                       // Save program instance handle.

    // For all systems, if previous instance, activate it instead of us.
    hWnd = FindWindow (szAppName, NULL);
    if (hWnd) {
        SetForegroundWindow ((HWND)((DWORD)hWnd | 0x01));
        return 0;
    }
```

(continued)

Listing 14-3   *(continued)*

```
// Init COM
CoInitializeEx (NULL, COINIT_MULTITHREADED);

// Init device structure
memset (&obDevs, 0, sizeof (obDevs));

// Create message queues for async string out to listbox
MSGQUEUEOPTIONS mqo;
mqo.dwSize = sizeof (mqo);
mqo.dwFlags = MSGQUEUE_ALLOW_BROKEN;
mqo.dwMaxMessages = 16;
mqo.cbMaxMessage = 512;
mqo.bReadAccess = TRUE;
hQRead = CreateMsgQueue (TEXT ("MSGQUEUE\\ThTead"), &mqo);

mqo.bReadAccess = FALSE;
hQWrite = CreateMsgQueue (TEXT ("MSGQUEUE\\ThTead"), &mqo);

// Register application main window class.
wc.style = 0;                            // Window style
wc.lpfnWndProc = MainWndProc;            // Callback function
wc.cbClsExtra = 0;                       // Extra class data
wc.cbWndExtra = DLGWINDOWEXTRA;          // Extra window data
wc.hInstance = hInstance;                // Owner handle
wc.hIcon = NULL;                         // Application icon
wc.hCursor = LoadCursor (NULL, IDC_ARROW);// Default cursor
wc.hbrBackground = (HBRUSH) GetStockObject (LTGRAY_BRUSH);
wc.lpszMenuName =  NULL;                  // Menu name
wc.lpszClassName = szAppName;            // Window class name

if (RegisterClass (&wc) == 0) return (HWND)0;

// Create main window.
hWnd = CreateDialog (hInst, szAppName, NULL, NULL);
// Return fail code if window not created.
if (!IsWindow (hWnd)) return 0;

// Init obex
if (!InitObex (hWnd)) {
    return 0;
}

ShowWindow (hWnd, nCmdShow);         // Standard show and update calls
UpdateWindow (hWnd);
SetFocus (GetDlgItem (hWnd, IDD_OUTTEXT));
return hWnd;
}
```

```
//-----------------------------------------------------------------------
// ResetDevList - Clean up the list of devices
//
int ResetDevList (void) {
    int i;
    // Clean up property bags
    for (i = 0; i < dim (obDevs); i++) {
        if (obDevs[i].pDevBag) {
            obDevs[i].pDevBag->Release();
            obDevs[i].pDevBag = 0;
        }
    }
    return 0;
}
//-----------------------------------------------------------------------
// TermInstance - Program cleanup
//
int TermInstance (HINSTANCE hInstance, int nDefRC) {

    if (pObex) {
        pObex->StopDeviceEnum();
        ResetDevList ();
        if (pConPt) {
            pConPt->Unadvise(dwCookie);
            Sleep(100);
            pConPt->Release();
        }
        if (pContainer) {
            pContainer->Release();
        }
        pObex->Shutdown();
        pObex->Release();
    }
    CoUninitialize();
    return nDefRC;
}
//=======================================================================
// Message handling procedures for main window
//-----------------------------------------------------------------------
// MainWndProc - Callback function for application window
//
LRESULT CALLBACK MainWndProc (HWND hWnd, UINT wMsg, WPARAM wParam,
                              LPARAM lParam) {
    INT i;
    //
    // Search message list to see if we need to handle this
    // message.  If in list, call procedure.
    //
```

(continued)

Listing 14-3 *(continued)*

```
    for (i = 0; i < dim(MainMessages); i++) {
        if (wMsg == MainMessages[i].Code)
            return (*MainMessages[i].Fxn)(hWnd, wMsg, wParam, lParam);
    }
    return DefWindowProc (hWnd, wMsg, wParam, lParam);
}
//----------------------------------------------------------------------
// DoCreateMain - Process WM_CREATE message for window.
//
LRESULT DoCreateMain (HWND hWnd, UINT wMsg, WPARAM wParam,
                      LPARAM lParam) {

#if defined(WIN32_PLATFORM_PSPC) && (_WIN32_WCE >= 300)
    SHINITDLGINFO shidi;
    SHMENUBARINFO mbi;                           // For Pocket PC, create
    memset(&mbi, 0, sizeof(SHMENUBARINFO)); // menu bar so that we
    mbi.cbSize = sizeof(SHMENUBARINFO);      // have a sip button
    mbi.dwFlags = SHCMBF_EMPTYBAR;
    mbi.hwndParent = hWnd;
    SHCreateMenuBar(&mbi);
    SendMessage(mbi.hwndMB, SHCMBM_GETSUBMENU, 0, 100);

    // For Pocket PC, make dialog box full screen with PPC
    // specific call.
    shidi.dwMask = SHIDIM_FLAGS;
    shidi.dwFlags = SHIDIF_DONEBUTTON | SHIDIF_SIZEDLG | SHIDIF_SIPDOWN;
    shidi.hDlg = hWnd;
    SHInitDialog(&shidi);

    sai.cbSize = sizeof (sai);
    SHHandleWMSettingChange(hWnd, wParam, lParam, &sai);
#endif
    GetWindowText (hWnd, szTitle, dim (szTitle));
    return 0;
}
//----------------------------------------------------------------------
// DoSizeMain - Process WM_SIZE message for window.
//
LRESULT DoSizeMain (HWND hWnd, UINT wMsg, WPARAM wParam,
                    LPARAM lParam) {

#if defined(WIN32_PLATFORM_PSPC) && (_WIN32_WCE >= 300)
    static RECT rectListbox;
    RECT rect;

    GetClientRect (hWnd, &rect);
    if (fFirstSize) {
```

```
            // First time through, get the position of the listbox for
            // resizing later.  Store the distance from the sides of
            // the listbox control to the side of the parent window
            if (IsWindow (GetDlgItem (hWnd, IDD_INTEXT))) {
                GetWindowRect (GetDlgItem (hWnd, IDD_INTEXT), &rectListbox);
                MapWindowPoints (HWND_DESKTOP, hWnd, (LPPOINT)&rectListbox, 2);
                rectListbox.right = rect.right - rectListbox.right;
                rectListbox.bottom = rect.bottom - rectListbox.bottom;

                SetWindowPos (GetDlgItem (hWnd, IDD_INTEXT), 0, rect.left+5,
                              rectListbox.top, rect.right-10,
                              rect.bottom - rectListbox.top - 5,
                              SWP_NOZORDER);
            }
        }
#endif
    if (fFirstSize) {
        EnableWindow (GetDlgItem (hWnd, IDD_SENDFILE), FALSE);
        int i = 40;
        SendDlgItemMessage (hWnd, IDD_DEVICES, LB_SETTABSTOPS, 1,
                            (LPARAM)&i);
        fFirstSize = FALSE;
    }
    return 0;
}
//----------------------------------------------------------------------------
// DoCommandMain - Process WM_COMMAND message for window.
//
LRESULT DoCommandMain (HWND hWnd, UINT wMsg, WPARAM wParam,
                       LPARAM lParam) {
    WORD idItem, wNotifyCode;
    HWND hwndCtl;
    INT i;

    // Parse the parameters.
    idItem = (WORD) LOWORD (wParam);
    wNotifyCode = (WORD) HIWORD (wParam);
    hwndCtl = (HWND) lParam;

    // Call routine to handle control message.
    for (i = 0; i < dim(MainCommandItems); i++) {
        if (idItem == MainCommandItems[i].Code)
            return (*MainCommandItems[i].Fxn)(hWnd, idItem, hwndCtl,
                                              wNotifyCode);
    }
    return 0;
}
```

(continued)

Listing 14-3 *(continued)*

```
//-------------------------------------------------------------------------
// FindDevInfo - Loop through array looking for a device
//
PMYOBEXDEVICEINFO FindDevInfo (IPropertyBag* pDevBag) {
    int i, j = -1;
    for (i = 0; i < dim (obDevs); i++) {
        // See if device data matches search
        if (obDevs[i].pDevBag == pDevBag)
            return &obDevs[i];

        // Find first free index
        if ((j == -1) && (obDevs[i].pDevBag == 0)) {
            j = i;
        }
    }
    return &obDevs[j];
}
//-------------------------------------------------------------------------
// FindDevInList - Search listbox for a device.
//
int FindDevInList (HWND hWnd, PMYOBEXDEVICEINFO pDev) {
    int i, nCnt;
    LRESULT lr;

    // Get the number of items in the listbox
    nCnt = SendDlgItemMessage (hWnd, IDD_DEVICES, LB_GETCOUNT, 0, 0);
    for (i = 0; i < nCnt; i++) {
        lr = SendDlgItemMessage (hWnd, IDD_DEVICES, LB_GETITEMDATA,i,0);
        if (lr == (int)pDev)
            return i;
    }
    return LB_ERR;
}
//-------------------------------------------------------------------------
// DoObexEventMain - Handles notifications of obex events
//
LRESULT DoObexEventMain (HWND hWnd, UINT wMsg, WPARAM wParam,
                         LPARAM lParam) {
    int i;
    HRESULT hr;
    TCHAR szDevStr[128];
    PMYOBEXDEVICEINFO pFoundDev;
    MYOBEXDEVICEINFO diDev;
    memset (&diDev, 0, sizeof (diDev));

    IPropertyBag *pDeviceBag = (IPropertyBag *)lParam;
```

```
if (wParam == OE_QUERY_PASSWORD) {
    MessageBox (hWnd, TEXT("Query Password"), TEXT("App"), MB_OK);
    return 0;
}
// Parse name
VARIANT var;
VariantInit (&var);
hr = pDeviceBag->Read (TEXT("Name"), &var, NULL);
if (SUCCEEDED(hr)) {
    diDev.dwFlags |= DEV_FLAG_NAME;
    lstrcpy (diDev.szName, var.bstrVal);
}
VariantClear(&var);

// Parse address
hr = pDeviceBag->Read (TEXT("Address"), &var, NULL);
if (SUCCEEDED(hr)) {
    diDev.dwFlags |= DEV_FLAG_ADDRESS;
    if (var.vt == VT_BSTR)
        lstrcpy (diDev.szAddr, var.bstrVal);
    else if (var.vt == VT_I4)
        wsprintf (diDev.szAddr, TEXT("%08x"), var.ulVal);
    else
        diDev.dwFlags &= ~DEV_FLAG_ADDRESS;
}
VariantClear(&var);

// Parse port
hr = pDeviceBag->Read (TEXT("Port"), &var, NULL);
if (SUCCEEDED(hr)) {
    diDev.dwFlags |= DEV_FLAG_PORT;
    if (var.vt == VT_BSTR)
        lstrcpy (diDev.szAddr, var.bstrVal);
    else if (var.vt == VT_I4)
        wsprintf (diDev.szAddr, TEXT("%08x"), var.ulVal);
    else
        diDev.dwFlags &= ~DEV_FLAG_PORT;
}
VariantClear(&var);

// Parse IrDA information
hr = pDeviceBag->Read (TEXT("IrDA"), &var, NULL);
VariantClear(&var);


hr = pDeviceBag->Read (TEXT("Transport"), &var, NULL);
if (SUCCEEDED(hr)) {
    if (var.vt == VT_BSTR) {
        WCHAR szTran[40];
```

(continued)

Listing 14-3   *(continued)*

```
            memset (szTran, 0, sizeof (szTran));
            wcsncpy (szTran, var.bstrVal, 38);
            wcslwr (szTran);
            if (wcscmp (g_szTransIrDA, szTran) == 0)
                diDev.dwFlags |= DEV_TRANS_IRDA;
            else if (wcscmp (g_szTransBth, szTran) == 0)
                diDev.dwFlags |= DEV_TRANS_BTOOTH;
    }
}
VariantClear(&var);

hr = pDeviceBag->Read (TEXT("OBEX:IrXfer"), &var, NULL);
if (SUCCEEDED(hr))
    Add2List (hWnd, TEXT("OBEX:IrXfer"));
VariantClear(&var);

// Parse service UUID
hr = pDeviceBag->Read (TEXT("ServiceUUID"), &var, NULL);
if (SUCCEEDED(hr)) {

    if (var.vt == VT_BSTR) {
        // Compare the guid service string to ones we know about
        if (wcsncmp (g_szObjPushGuid, var.bstrVal, 38) == 0)
            diDev.dwFlags |= (DEV_FLAG_UUID | DEV_SERVICE_OBJPUSH);

        else if (wcsncmp (g_szFtpGuid, var.bstrVal, 38) == 0)
            diDev.dwFlags |= (DEV_FLAG_UUID | DEV_SERVICE_FTP);

        else if (wcsncmp (g_szIrMCSyncGuid, var.bstrVal, 38) == 0)
            diDev.dwFlags |= (DEV_FLAG_UUID | DEV_SERVICE_IRMCSYNC);
    }
}
VariantClear(&var);

diDev.pDevBag = pDeviceBag;

// Tell the user what protocols the device supports.
lstrcpy (szDevStr, diDev.szName);
lstrcat (szDevStr, TEXT("  "));
if (diDev.dwFlags & DEV_SERVICE_OBJPUSH)
    lstrcat (szDevStr, TEXT("Object Push"));
else if (diDev.dwFlags & DEV_SERVICE_FTP)
    lstrcat (szDevStr, TEXT("FTP"));
else if (diDev.dwFlags & DEV_SERVICE_IRMCSYNC)
    lstrcat (szDevStr, TEXT("IrMC Sync"));
else if (diDev.dwFlags & DEV_TRANS_IRDA)
    lstrcat (szDevStr, TEXT("IrDA"));
```

```
// See if device already recorded
pFoundDev = FindDevInfo (pDeviceBag);

// React depending on the notice
switch ((int)wParam) {
case OE_DEVICE_ARRIVAL:
    // See if device already found
    if (pFoundDev->pDevBag)
        break;
    memcpy (pFoundDev, &diDev, sizeof (diDev));

    i = SendDlgItemMessage (hWnd, IDD_DEVICES, LB_ADDSTRING, 0,
                            (LPARAM)szDevStr);
    SendDlgItemMessage (hWnd, IDD_DEVICES, LB_SETITEMDATA, i,
                            (LPARAM)pFoundDev);

    break;

case OE_DEVICE_UPDATE:
    i = LB_ERR;
    memcpy (pFoundDev, &diDev, sizeof (diDev));

    // Find device entry in list box
    if (pFoundDev->pDevBag) {
        i = FindDevInList (hWnd, pFoundDev);
        // Release because we already hold the propbag
        pFoundDev->pDevBag->Release();
    }

    if (LB_ERR != i)
        SendDlgItemMessage (hWnd, IDD_DEVICES, LB_DELETESTRING,i,0);

    i = SendDlgItemMessage (hWnd, IDD_DEVICES, LB_INSERTSTRING, i,
                            (LPARAM)szDevStr);
    SendDlgItemMessage (hWnd, IDD_DEVICES, LB_SETITEMDATA, i,
                            (LPARAM)pFoundDev);

    break;

case OE_DISCONNECT:
case OE_DEVICE_DEPARTURE:
    // See if device not in device array, ignore disconnect
    if (pFoundDev->pDevBag == 0)
        break;

    // Find device in list box and delete
    i = FindDevInList (hWnd, pFoundDev);
    if (LB_ERR != i)
        SendDlgItemMessage (hWnd, IDD_DEVICES, LB_DELETESTRING,i,0);
```

(continued)

Listing 14-3 *(continued)*

```
            // Clear entry in device array
            pFoundDev->pDevBag->Release();
            pFoundDev->pDevBag = 0;
            break;

        case OE_QUERY_PASSWORD:
            break;

    }
    return 0;
}
//-------------------------------------------------------------------------
// DoPrintfNotifyMain - Process printf notify message
//
LRESULT DoPrintfNotifyMain (HWND hWnd, UINT wMsg, WPARAM wParam,
                            LPARAM lParam) {
    int rc;
    TCHAR szBuffer[512];
    DWORD dwLen = 0;
    DWORD dwFlags = 0;

    memset (szBuffer, 0, sizeof (szBuffer));
    rc = ReadMsgQueue (hQRead, (LPBYTE)szBuffer, sizeof (szBuffer),
                       &dwLen, 0, &dwFlags);
    if (rc) {
        if (dwFlags & MSGQUEUE_MSGALERT)
            SetWindowText (hWnd, szBuffer);
        else {
            rc = SendDlgItemMessage (hWnd, IDD_INTEXT, LB_ADDSTRING, 0,
                                     (LPARAM)(LPCTSTR)szBuffer);
            if (rc != LB_ERR)
                SendDlgItemMessage (hWnd, IDD_INTEXT, LB_SETTOPINDEX, rc,
                                    (LPARAM)(LPCTSTR)szBuffer);
        }
    }
    return 0;
}
//-------------------------------------------------------------------------
// DoPocketPCShell - Process Pocket PC required messages
//
LRESULT DoPocketPCShell (HWND hWnd, UINT wMsg, WPARAM wParam,
                         LPARAM lParam) {
#if defined(WIN32_PLATFORM_PSPC) && (_WIN32_WCE >= 300)
    if (wMsg == WM_SETTINGCHANGE)
        return SHHandleWMSettingChange(hWnd, wParam, lParam, &sai);
    if (wMsg == WM_ACTIVATE)
```

```
            return SHHandleWMActivate(hWnd, wParam, lParam, &sai, 0);
#endif
    return 0;
}
//--------------------------------------------------------------------
// DoDestroyMain - Process WM_DESTROY message for window.
//
LRESULT DoDestroyMain (HWND hWnd, UINT wMsg, WPARAM wParam,
                       LPARAM lParam) {
    Sleep (0);                                  // Pass on timeslice.
    PostQuitMessage (0);
    return 0;
}
//====================================================================
// Command handler routines
//--------------------------------------------------------------------
// DoMainCommandExit - Process Program Exit command.
//
LPARAM DoMainCommandExit (HWND hWnd, WORD idItem, HWND hwndCtl,
                          WORD wNotifyCode) {

    SendMessage (hWnd, WM_CLOSE, 0, 0);
    return 0;
}


//--------------------------------------------------------------------
// DoMainCommandSend - Process Program Send File command.
//
LPARAM DoMainCommandSend (HWND hWnd, WORD idItem, HWND hwndCtl,
                          WORD wNotifyCode) {
    int i;
    HRESULT hr;
    PMYOBEXDEVICEINFO pDev;
    TCHAR szName[MAX_PATH];
    IObexDevice *pDevice = 0;

    GetDlgItemText (hWnd, IDD_OUTTEXT, szName, dim(szName));
    if (lstrlen (szName) == 0) {
        MessageBox (hWnd, TEXT("File name needed"), TEXT("Error"),
                    MB_OK);
        return 0;
    }
    // Get the selected device
    i = SendDlgItemMessage (hWnd, IDD_DEVICES, LB_GETCURSEL, 0, 0);
    if (i != LB_ERR) {
        pDev = (PMYOBEXDEVICEINFO)SendDlgItemMessage (hWnd,
                                      IDD_DEVICES, LB_GETITEMDATA,i,0);
```

(continued)

Listing 14-3 *(continued)*

```
                // Enumeration must be stopped during transfer
                if (fObex2IF)
                    ((IObex2 *)pObex)->PauseDeviceEnum (TRUE);
                else
                    pObex->StopDeviceEnum();

                // Bind to the device
                MyYield();
                hr = 0;
                if ((pDev->dwFlags & DEV_FLAG_DEVBOUND) == 0) {
                    hr = pObex->BindToDevice (pDev->pDevBag, &pDevice);
                    if (SUCCEEDED (hr))
                        pDev->dwFlags |= DEV_FLAG_DEVBOUND;
                    else
                        Add2List (hWnd, TEXT("BindToDevice failed %x %d"), hr,
                                 GetLastError());

                    if (SUCCEEDED (hr)) {
                        i = SendFile (hWnd, pDevice, szName, pDev->dwFlags);
                        Add2List (hWnd, TEXT("SendFile returned %d"), i);
                    }
                }
                // Restart Enumeration after transfer
                if (fObex2IF)
                    ((IObex2 *)pObex)->PauseDeviceEnum (FALSE);
                else {
                    pObex->StartDeviceEnum();
                    ResetDevList ();
                    SendDlgItemMessage (hWnd, IDD_DEVICES, LB_RESETCONTENT, 0, 0);
                }
            }
        }
    return 0;
}

//----------------------------------------------------------------------------
// DoMainCommandDevList - Process Device list box commands.
//
LPARAM DoMainCommandDevList (HWND hWnd, WORD idItem, HWND hwndCtl,
                             WORD wNotifyCode) {
    int i;
    PMYOBEXDEVICEINFO pDev;

    if (wNotifyCode == LBN_SELCHANGE) {
        i = SendDlgItemMessage (hWnd, IDD_DEVICES, LB_GETCURSEL, 0, 0);
        if (i != LB_ERR) {
            pDev = (PMYOBEXDEVICEINFO)SendDlgItemMessage (hWnd,
                                        IDD_DEVICES, LB_GETITEMDATA,i,0);
```

```
                    EnableWindow (GetDlgItem (hWnd, IDD_SENDFILE), TRUE);
        }
    }
    return 0;
}
//-------------------------------------------------------------------------
// Add2List - Add string to the report list box.
//
void Add2List (HWND hWnd, LPTSTR lpszFormat, ...) {
    int nBuf, nLen;
    TCHAR szBuffer[512];
    va_list args;
    if (hWnd == 0)
        hWnd = hMain;

    EnterCriticalSection (&csPrintf);

    va_start(args, lpszFormat);
    nBuf = _vstprintf(szBuffer, lpszFormat, args);
    va_end(args);

    nLen = (lstrlen (szBuffer)+1) * sizeof (TCHAR);
    WriteMsgQueue (hQWrite, (LPBYTE)szBuffer, nLen, 0, 0);
    PostMessage (hWnd, MYMSG_PRINTF, 0, 0);
    LeaveCriticalSection (&csPrintf);
}
//-------------------------------------------------------------------------
// MySetWindowText - Set Window title to passed printf style string.
//
void MySetWindowText (HWND hWnd, LPTSTR lpszFormat, ...) {
    int nBuf, nLen;
    TCHAR szBuffer[512];
    va_list args;

    EnterCriticalSection (&csPrintf);

    va_start(args, lpszFormat);
    nBuf = _vstprintf(szBuffer, lpszFormat, args);
    va_end(args);

    nLen = (lstrlen (szBuffer)+1) * sizeof (TCHAR);
    WriteMsgQueue (hQWrite, (LPBYTE)szBuffer, nLen, 0, MSGQUEUE_MSGALERT);
    PostMessage (hWnd, MYMSG_PRINTF, 0, 0);
    LeaveCriticalSection (&csPrintf);
}
//-------------------------------------------------------------------------
// MyYield - Flushes the message queue during long operations
//
```

(continued)

Listing 14-3 *(continued)*

```
BOOL MyYield () {
    MSG msg;
    int rc = 0;

    while (PeekMessage (&msg, NULL, 0, 0, PM_NOREMOVE)) {
        if (msg.message == WM_QUIT)
            return FALSE;

        GetMessage (&msg, NULL, 0, 0);
        if ((hMain == 0) || !IsDialogMessage (hMain, &msg)) {
            TranslateMessage (&msg);
            DispatchMessage (&msg);
        }
    }
    return TRUE;
}
//-----------------------------------------------------------------
// InitObex - Initialize the Obex subsystem.
//
int InitObex (HWND hWnd) {
    HRESULT hr;

    hr = CoCreateInstance (__uuidof(Obex), NULL, CLSCTX_INPROC_SERVER,
                        __uuidof(IObex2), (void **)&pObex);
    if(FAILED(hr)) {
        hr = CoCreateInstance (__uuidof(Obex), NULL, CLSCTX_INPROC_SERVER,
                            __uuidof(IObex), (void **)&pObex);
    } else
        fObex2IF = TRUE;

    if(FAILED(hr)) {
        Add2List (hWnd, TEXT("Obex initialization failed! %d %x\n"),
                hr, GetLastError());
        return 0;
    }
    if (pObex != NULL)
        pObex->Initialize ();
    else
        return 0;

    //set device caps
    IObexCaps *pObexCaps = NULL;
    hr = pObex->QueryInterface(IID_IObexCaps, (LPVOID *)&pObexCaps);
    if(SUCCEEDED(hr)) {
        pObexCaps->SetCaps(SEND_DEVICE_UPDATES);
        pObexCaps->Release();
    }
```

```
        InitializeCriticalSection(&csLock);
        EnterCriticalSection(&csLock);

        MyObexSink *pSink;
        pSink = new MyObexSink(hWnd);
        if (!pSink) {
            LeaveCriticalSection(&csLock);
            return 0;
        }

        // Create connection point container
        hr = pObex->QueryInterface (IID_IConnectionPointContainer,
                                    (LPVOID *)&pContainer);
        if (!SUCCEEDED(hr) || (pContainer == 0)) {
            LeaveCriticalSection(&csLock);
            return 0;
        }

        hr = pContainer->FindConnectionPoint (IID_IObexSink, &pConPt);
        if (!SUCCEEDED(hr) || (pConPt == 0)) {
            pContainer->Release();
            LeaveCriticalSection(&csLock);
            return 0;
        }

        // Ask for notifications
        hr = pConPt->Advise((IUnknown *)pSink, &dwCookie);

        LeaveCriticalSection(&csLock);

        // Start device enumeration
        if (ERROR_SUCCESS != pObex->StartDeviceEnum())
            return 0;

        IDeviceEnum *pDeviceEnum = 0;
        hr = pObex->EnumDevices(&pDeviceEnum, CLSID_NULL);

        if(!SUCCEEDED(hr) || (pDeviceEnum == 0))
            return NULL;

        Add2List (hWnd, TEXT("EnumDevices succeeded"));
        pDeviceEnum->Release ();
        return 1;
}
//--------------------------------------------------------------------
// SendFile - Sends a file to another obex device
//
```

(continued)

Listing 14-3 *(continued)*

```
int SendFile (HWND hWnd, IObexDevice *pDevice, LPTSTR pszFileName,
              DWORD dwFlags) {
    LPTSTR pszName;
    DWORD dwBytesWritten;
    int nCnt, nFileSize, nTotal;
    HRESULT hr;
    HANDLE hFile;
    PBYTE pBuff;

    Add2List (hWnd, TEXT("Sending file %s"), pszFileName);

    pBuff = (PBYTE)LocalAlloc (LPTR, BUFFSIZE);
    if (pBuff == 0) return 0;

    // prune the path from the file name
    pszName = wcsrchr (pszFileName, '\\');
    if (pszName == 0)
        pszName = pszFileName;
    else
        pszName++;

    // Open the file
    hFile = CreateFile (pszFileName, GENERIC_READ, FILE_SHARE_READ,
                        NULL, OPEN_EXISTING, 0, NULL);
    if (hFile == INVALID_HANDLE_VALUE) {
        Add2List (hWnd, TEXT("file opened failed. rc %d"),
                  GetLastError());
        return -1;
    }

    // Get file size
    nFileSize = GetFileSize (hFile, NULL);
    if (!MyYield ()) return 0;

    IHeaderCollection *pHC = 0;
    hr = CoCreateInstance(__uuidof(HeaderCollection), NULL,
                    CLSCTX_INPROC_SERVER, __uuidof(IHeaderCollection),
                    (void **)&pHC);
    if (!MyYield () || FAILED(hr)) {
        CloseHandle (hFile);
        return -2;
    }
    if (dwFlags & DEV_SERVICE_FTP)
        pHC->AddTarget (sizeof (CLSID_FileExchange_NetOrder),
                    (UCHAR *)&CLSID_FileExchange_NetOrder);
```

```
// Connect to device
hr = pDevice->Connect (NULL, 0, pHC);
if (!MyYield () || FAILED(hr)) {
    Add2List (hWnd, TEXT("Connect fail %x %d"), hr, GetLastError());
    pHC->Release();
    CloseHandle (hFile);
    return -3;
}
Add2List (hWnd, TEXT("Connected..."));
//get a header collection
IHeaderCollection *pFileHC = 0;
hr = CoCreateInstance(__uuidof(HeaderCollection), NULL,
                CLSCTX_INPROC_SERVER, __uuidof(IHeaderCollection),
                (void **)&pFileHC);
if (!MyYield () || FAILED(hr)) {
    pHC->Release();
    pDevice->Disconnect (pHC);
    CloseHandle (hFile);
    return -2;
}
// Add file name to header
hr = pFileHC->AddName(pszName);
if (!MyYield () || FAILED(hr)) {
    pHC->Release();
    pFileHC->Release();
    CloseHandle (hFile);
    return -3;
}
// Send header
IStream *stOut = 0;
hr = pDevice->Put(pFileHC, &stOut);
if (!MyYield () || FAILED(hr)) {
    pDevice->Disconnect (pHC);
    pHC->Release();
    pFileHC->Release();
    CloseHandle (hFile);
    return -4;
}
// Send the data
nTotal = nFileSize;
while (nFileSize) {
    if (!MyYield ()) break;
    MySetWindowText (hWnd, TEXT ("%02d%% sent"),
                    (nTotal-nFileSize)*100/nTotal);
    // Send up to the block size
    nCnt = min (BUFFSIZE, nFileSize);
```

(continued)

Listing 14-3   *(continued)*

```
        if (!ReadFile (hFile, pBuff, nCnt, &dwBytesWritten, FALSE)) {
            Add2List (hWnd, TEXT("ReadFile error %d "), GetLastError());
            break;
        }
        nCnt = (int)dwBytesWritten;

        Add2List (hWnd, TEXT("sending %d bytes"), nCnt);

        if (!MyYield ()) break;
        hr = stOut->Write (pBuff, nCnt, &dwBytesWritten);
        if(FAILED(hr)) {
            Add2List (hWnd, TEXT("send error %x %d"), hr, GetLastError());
            break;
        }
        nFileSize -= (int)dwBytesWritten;
    }
    MySetWindowText (hWnd, (LPTSTR)szTitleText);
    MyYield ();
    stOut->Commit (STGC_DEFAULT);
    // Clean up
    stOut->Release();
    pDevice->Disconnect (pHC);
    if(pHC)
        pHC->Release();
    CloseHandle(hFile);
    if(pFileHC)
        pFileHC->Release();
    return 0;
}
```

This chapter has given you a basic introduction to some of the ways Windows CE devices can communicate with other devices. Next on our plate is networking from a different angle. In Chapter 15, we look at the Windows CE device from the perspective of its companion PC. The link between the Windows CE device and a PC is based on some of the same networking infrastructure that we touched upon here. Let's take a look.

15

Connecting to the Desktop

One of the major market segments that Windows CE is designed for is desktop companions. In answer to the requirements of this market, two product categories created using Windows CE are desktop companions: the Handheld PC and the Pocket PC. A third, the Smartphone, also leverages its link to the PC. Each of these products requires a strong and highly functional link between the Windows CE device and the desktop PC running Windows.

Given this absolute necessity for good desktop connectivity, it's not surprising that Windows CE has a vast array of functions that enable applications on the desktop and the remote Windows CE device to communicate with one another. In general, most of this desktop-to-device processing takes place on the desktop. This is logical because the desktop PC has much greater processing power and more storage space than the less powerful and much smaller Windows CE system.

All of the helper DLLs, communications support, and viewer programs are collected in the ActiveSync product. When a user buys any of the horizontal platforms, such as the Pocket PC or the Handheld PC, a CD loaded with ActiveSync comes with the device. The user becomes accustomed to seeing the Mobile Devices folder that, once ActiveSync is installed, appears on his desktop. But there's much more to ActiveSync than Mobile Devices. A number of DLLs are included, for example, to help the Windows CE application developer write PC-based applications that can work with the remote Windows CE device.

In this chapter, I'll cover the various APIs that provide the desktop–to–Windows CE link. These include the remote API, or RAPI, that allows applications running on the desktop to directly invoke functions on the remote Windows CE system. I'll also look at methods a PC application can use to notify itself when a connection exists between a PC and a Windows CE device.

In a departure from the other chapters in this book, almost all the examples in this chapter are PC-based Windows programs. They're written to work for all 32-bit versions of Windows. I take the same approach with the PC-based examples as I do for the CE-based examples, writing to the API instead of using a class library such as MFC. The principles shown here could easily be used by MFC-based applications or by a managed application using the .NET runtime environment.

The Windows CE Remote API

The remote API (RAPI) allows applications on one machine to call functions on another machine. Windows CE supports essentially a one-way RAPI; applications on the PC can call functions on a connected Windows CE system. In the language of RAPI, the Windows CE device is the RAPI server while the PC is the RAPI client. The application runs on the client, the PC, which in turn calls functions that are executed on the server, the Windows CE device.

RAPI Overview

RAPI under Windows CE is designed so that PC applications can manage the Windows CE device remotely. The exported functions deal with the file system, registry, and databases, as well as functions for querying the system configuration. Although most RAPI functions are duplicates of functions in the Windows CE API, a few functions extend the API. You use these functions mainly for initializing the RAPI subsystem and enhancing performance of the communication link by compressing iterative operations into one RAPI call.

The RAPI functions are listed in the Windows CE API reference but are called by PC applications—not by Windows CE applications. The RAPI functions are prefixed with a *Ce* in the function name to differentiate them from their Windows CE–side counterparts; for example, the function *GetStoreInformation* in Windows CE is called *CeGetStoreInformation* in the RAPI version of the function. Unfortunately, some APIs in Windows CE, such as the database API, also have functions prefixed with *Ce*. In these cases, both the CE function (for example, *CeCreateDatabase*) and the RAPI function (again, *CeCreateDatabase*) have the same name. The linker isn't confused in this case because a Windows CE application won't be calling the RAPI function and a PC-based program can't call the database function except through the RAPI interface.

These Windows CE RAPI functions work for Windows 95/98/Me as well as Windows NT/2000/XP, but because they're Win32 functions, applications developed for the Win16 API can't use the Windows CE RAPI functions. The RAPI functions can be called from either a Windows-based application or a Win32-console application. All you have to do to use the RAPI functions is include the RAPI.h header file and link with the RAPI.lib library.

Essentially, RAPI is a remote procedure call. It communicates a PC application's request to invoke a function and returns the results of that function. Because the RAPI layer is simple on the Windows CE side, all strings used in RAPI functions must be in Unicode regardless of whether the PC-based application calling the RAPI function uses the Unicode format.

Dealing with Different Versions of RAPI

The problem of versioning has always been an issue with redistributable DLLs under Windows. RAPI.DLL, the DLL on the PC that handles the RAPI API, is distributed with the ActiveSync software that comes with a Smartphone, a Pocket PC, or other PC-companion Windows CE devices. Trouble arises because the RAPI API has been extended over time as the Windows CE functions have expanded; you have to be aware that the RAPI DLL you load on a machine might not be the most up-to-date RAPI DLL. Older RAPI DLLs don't have all the exported functions that the newest RAPI DLL has.

This isn't as much of a problem as it used to be, however. The set of RAPI functions hasn't changed from the old H/PC Pro days up to the current Pocket PC products. However, you should always be aware that new versions of ActiveSync might provide RAPI functions that aren't available on older installations.

On the other hand, just because *you're* using the latest RAPI DLL doesn't mean that the Windows CE system on the other end of the RAPI connection supports all the functions that the RAPI DLL supports. An old H/PC running Windows CE 2.0 won't support the extended database API supported by the current Windows CE systems, no matter what RAPI DLL you're using on the PC.

The best way to solve the problem of multiple versions of RAPI.DLL is to program defensively. Instead of loading the RAPI DLL implicitly by specifying an import library and directly calling the RAPI functions, you might want to load the RAPI DLL explicitly with a call to *LoadLibrary*. You can then access the exported functions by calling *GetProcAddress* for each function and then calling the pointer to that function.

The problem of different versions of Windows CE has a much easier solution. Just be sure to call *CeGetVersionEx* to query the version of Windows CE on the remote device. This gives you a good idea of what the device capabilities of that device are. If the remote device has a newer version of Windows CE than RAPI.dll, you might want to inform the user of the version issue and suggest an upgrade of the synchronization software on the PC.

Initializing RAPI

Before you can call any of the RAPI functions, you must first initialize the RAPI library with a call to either *CeRapiInit* or *CeRapiInitEx*. The difference between the two functions is that *CeRapiInit* blocks, waiting on a successful connection with a Windows CE device, while *CeRapiInitEx* doesn't block. ActiveSync has established a connection between the PC and the device for these functions to succeed.

The first initialization function is prototyped as

```
HRESULT CeRapiInit (void);
```

This function has no parameters. When the function is called, Windows looks for an established link to a Windows CE device. If one doesn't exist, the function blocks until one is established or another thread in your application calls *CeRapiUninit*, which is generally called to clean up after a RAPI session. The return value is either 0, indicating that a RAPI session has been established, or the constant *E_FAIL*, indicating an error. In this case, you can call *GetLastError* to diagnose the problem.

Unfortunately *CeRapiInit* blocks, sometimes, for an extended period of time. To avoid this, you can use the other initialization function,

```
HRESULT CeRapiInitEx (RAPIINIT* pRapiInit);
```

The only parameter is a pointer to a *RAPIINIT* structure defined as

```
typedef struct _RAPIINIT {
    DWORD cbSize;
    HANDLE heRapiInit;
    HANDLE hrRapiInit;
} RAPIINIT;
```

The *cbSize* field must be filled in before the call is made to *CeRapiInitEx*. After the size field has been initialized, you call *CeRapiInitEx* and the function returns without blocking. It fills in the second of the three fields, *heRapiInit*, with the handle to an event object that will be signaled when the RAPI connection is initialized. You can use *WaitForSingleObject* to have a thread block on this event to determine when the connection is finally established. When the event is signaled, the final field in the structure, *hrRapiInit*, is filled with the return code from the initialization. This value can be 0 if the connection was successful or *E_FAIL* if the connection wasn't made for some reason.

Handling RAPI Errors

When you're dealing with the extra RAPI layer between the caller and the execution of the function, a problem arises when an error occurs: did the error occur because the function failed or because of an error in the RAPI connection?

RAPI functions return error codes indicating success or failure of the function. If a function fails, you can use the following two functions to isolate the cause of the error:

```
HRESULT CeRapiGetError (void);
```

and

```
DWORD CeGetLastError (void);
```

The difference between these two functions is that *CeRapiGetError* returns an error code for failures due to the network or other RAPI-layer reasons. On the other hand, *CeGetLastError* is the RAPI counterpart to *GetLastError*; it returns the extended error for a failed function on the Windows CE device. So, if a function fails, call *CeRapiGetError* to determine whether an error occurred in the RAPI layer. If *CeRapiGetError* returns 0, the error occurred in the original function on the CE device. In this case, a call to *CeGetLastError* returns the extended error for the failure on the device.

Here's one last general function, used to free buffers that are returned by some of the RAPI functions. This function is

```
HRESULT CeRapiFreeBuffer (LPVOID Buffer);
```

The only parameter is the pointer to the buffer you want to free. The function returns *S_OK* when successful and *E_FAIL* if not. Throughout the explanation of RAPI functions, I'll mention those places where you need to use *CeRapiFree-Buffer*. In general, though, you use this function anywhere a RAPI function returns a buffer that it allocated for you.

Ending a RAPI Session

When you have finished making all the RAPI calls necessary, you should clean up by calling

```
HRESULT CeRapiUninit (void);
```

This function gracefully closes down the RAPI communication with the remote device. *CeRapiUninit* returns *E_FAIL* if a RAPI session hasn't been initialized.

Predefined RAPI Functions

As I mentioned in the beginning of this chapter, the RAPI services include a number of predefined RAPI functions that duplicate Windows CE functions on the PC side of the connection. So, for example, just as *GetStoreInformation* returns the size and free space of the object store to a Windows CE program, *CeGetStoreInformation* returns that same information about a connected Windows CE device to a PC-based application. The functions are divided into a number of groups that I'll talk about in the following pages. Since the actions of the functions are identical to their Windows CE–based counterparts, I won't go into the details of each function. Instead, although I'll list every RAPI function, I'll explain at length only the functions that are unique to RAPI.

RAPI System Information Functions

The RAPI system information functions are shown in the following list. I've previously described most of the Windows CE counterparts to these functions, shown, with the exception of *CeCheckPassword* and *CeRapiInvoke*. The *CeCheckPassword* function, as well as its Windows CE counterpart *CheckPassword*, compares a string to the current system password. If the strings match, the function returns *TRUE*. The comparison is case specific. Another function you might not recognize is *CeGetDesktopDeviceCaps*. This is the RAPI equivalent of *GetDeviceCaps* on the Windows CE side.

System Information Functions

CeGetVersionEx	*CeGetDesktopDeviceCaps*
CeGlobalMemoryStatus	*CeGetSystemInfo*
CeGetSystemPowerStatusEx	*CeCheckPassword*
CeGetStoreInformation	*CeCreateProcess*
CeGetSystemMetrics	*CeRapiInvoke*

RAPI File and Directory Management Functions

The following list shows the RAPI file management functions, illustrating that almost any file function available to a Windows CE application is also available to a PC-based program.

File and Directory Management Functions

CeFindAllFiles	*CeSetFilePointer*
CeFindFirstFile	*CeSetEndOfFile*
CeFindNextFile	*CeCreateDirectory*
CeFindClose	*CeRemoveDirectory*
CeGetFileAttributes	*CeMoveFile*
CeSetFileAttributes	*CeCopyFile*
CeCreateFile	*CeDeleteFile*
CeReadFile	*CeGetFileSize*
CeWriteFile	*CeGetFileTime*
CeCloseHandle	*CeSetFileTime*

Here's a new function, *CeFindAllFiles*, that's not even available to a Windows CE application. This function is prototyped as

```
BOOL CeFindAllFiles (LPCWSTR szPath, DWORD dwFlags,
                     LPDWORD lpdwFoundCount,
                     LPLPCE_FIND_DATA ppFindDataArray);
```

CeFindAllFiles is designed to enhance performance by returning all the files of a given directory with one call rather than having to make repeated RAPI calls using *CeFindFirstFile* and *CeFindNextFile*. The first parameter is the search string. This string must be specified in Unicode, so if you're not creating a Unicode application, the *TEXT* macro won't work because the *TEXT* macro produces char strings for non-Unicode applications. In ANSI-standard C++ compilers, prefixing the string with an *L* before the quoted string as in *L"*.*"* produces a proper Unicode for the function even in a non-Unicode application. For string conversion, you can use the *WideCharToMultiByte* and *MultiByteToWideChar* library functions to convert Unicode and ANSI strings into one another.

The second parameter of the *CeFindAllFiles* function, *dwFlags*, defines the scope of the search and what data is returned. The first set of flags can be one or more of the following:

- **FAF_ATTRIB_CHILDREN**   Returns only directories that have child items

- **FAF_ATTRIB_NO_HIDDEN**   Doesn't report hidden files or directories

- **FAF_FOLDERS_ONLY**   Returns only folders in the directory

- **FAF_NO_HIDDEN_SYS_ROMMODULES**   Doesn't report ROM-based system files

The second set of flags defines what data is returned by the *CeFindAllFiles* function. These flags can be one or more of the following:

- **FAF_ATTRIBUTES**   Returns file attributes

- **FAF_CREATION_TIME**   Returns file creation time

- **FAF_LASTACCESS_TIME**   Returns file last access time

- **FAF_LASTWRITE_TIME**   Returns file last write time

- **FAF_SIZE_HIGH**   Returns upper 32 bits of file size

- **FAF_SIZE_LOW**   Returns lower 32 bits of file size

- **FAF_OID**   Returns the object identifier (OID) for the file

- **FAF_NAME**   Returns the filename

Just because the flags are listed here doesn't mean you can find a good use for them. For example, the *FAF_SIZE_HIGH* flag is overkill, considering that few files on a Windows CE device are going to be larger than 4 GB. The file time flags are also limited by the support of the underlying file system. For example, the Windows CE object store tracks only the last access time and reports it in all file time fields.

There also appears to be a bug with the *FAF_ATTRIB_CHILDREN* flag. This valuable flag allows you to know when a directory contains subdirectories without your having to make an explicit call to that directory to find out. The flag seems to work only if the filename specification—the string to the right of the last directory separator backslash (\)—contains only one character. For example, the file specification

```
\\windows\*
```

works with *FAF_ATTRIB_CHILDREN*, whereas

```
\\windows\*.*
```

returns the same file list but the flag *FILE_ATTRIBUTE_HAS_CHILDREN* isn't set for directories that have subdirectories.

The third parameter of *CeFindAllFiles* should point to a *DWORD* value that will receive the number of files and directories found by the call. The final parameter, *ppFindDataArray*, should point to a variable of type *LPCE_FIND_DATA*, which is a pointer to an array of *CE_FIND_DATA* structures. When *CeFindAllFiles* returns, this variable will point to an array of *CE_FIND_DATA* structures that contain the requested data for each of the files found by the function. The *CE_FIND_DATA* structure is defined as

```
typedef struct _CE_FIND_DATA {
    DWORD dwFileAttributes;
    FILETIME ftCreationTime;
    FILETIME ftLastAccessTime;
    FILETIME ftLastWriteTime;
    DWORD nFileSizeHigh;
    DWORD nFileSizeLow;
    DWORD dwOID;
    WCHAR cFileName[MAX_PATH];
} CE_FIND_DATA;
```

The fields of *CE_FIND_DATA* look familiar to us by now. The only interesting field is the *dwOID* field that allows a PC-based application to receive the OID of a Windows CE file. This can be used with *CeGetOidGetInfo* to query more information about the file or directory. The flags in the *dwFileAttributes* field relate to Windows CE file attributes even though your application is running on a PC. This means, for example, that the *FILE_ATTRIBUTE_TEMPORARY* flag indicates an external storage device like a PC Card. Also, attribute flags are defined for execute-in-place ROM files. The additional attribute flag, *FILE_ATTRIBUTE_HAS_CHILDREN*, is defined to indicate that the directory contains child directories.

The buffer returned by *CeFindAllFiles* is originally allocated by the RAPI.DLL. Once you have finished with the buffer, you must call *CeRapiFreeBuffer* to free the buffer.

RAPI Database Management Functions

The RAPI database management functions are shown in the following list. As you can see, these functions mimic the extensive database API found in Windows CE. RAPI has not been extended to support the newer database APIs supported by Windows CE .NET. However, the older functions provide enough functionality to read databases, even if the databases were created with the newer functions.

Database Management Functions

CeCreateDatabase	*CeOpenDatabaseEx*
CeCreateDatabaseEx	*CeReadRecordProps*
CeDeleteDatabase	*CeReadRecordPropsEx*
CeDeleteDatabaseEx	*CeSeekDatabase*
CeDeleteRecord	*CeSetDatabaseInfo*
CeFindFirstDatabase	*CeSetDatabaseInfoEx*
CeFindFirstDatabaseEx	*CeWriteRecordProps*
CeFindNextDatabase	*CeMountDBVol*
CeFindNextDatabaseEx	*CeUnmountDBVol*
CeOidGetInfo	*CeEnumDBVolumes*
CeOidGetInfoEx	*CeFindAllDatabases*
CeOpenDatabase	

All but one of the database functions has a Windows CE counterpart. The only new function is *CeFindAllDatabases*. Like *CeFindAllFiles*, this function is designed as a performance enhancement so that applications can query all the databases on the system without having to iterate using the *CeFindFirstDatabase* and *CeFindNextDatabase* functions. The function is prototyped as

```
BOOL CeFindAllDatabases (DWORD dwDbaseType, WORD wFlags,
                LPWORD cFindData,
                LPLPCEDB_FIND_DATA ppFindData);
```

The first parameter is the database type value, or 0, if you want to return all databases. The *wFlags* parameter can contain one or more of the following flags, which define what data is returned by the function.

- **FAD_OID**   Returns the database OID

- **FAD_FLAGS**   Returns the *dwFlags* field of the *DbInfo* structure

- **FAD_NAME**   Returns the name of the database

- **FAD_TYPE**   Returns the type of the database

- **FAD_NUM_RECORDS**   Returns the number of records in the database

- **FAD_NUM_SORT_ORDER**   Returns the number of sort orders

- **FAD_SORT_SPEC**   Returns the sort order specs for the database

The *cFindData* parameter should point to a *WORD* variable that receives the number of databases found. The last parameter should be the address of a pointer to an array of *CEDB_FIND_DATA* structures. As with the *CeFindAllFiles* function, *CeFindAllDatabases* returns the information about the databases found in an array and sets the *ppFindData* parameter to point to this array. The *CEDB_FIND_DATA* structure is defined as

```
struct CEDB_FIND_DATA {
    CEOID OidDb;
    CEDBASEINFO DbInfo;
};
```

The structure contains the OID for a database followed by a *CEDBASEINFO* structure. I described this structure in Chapter 9, but I'll repeat it here so that you can see what information can be queried by *CeFindAllDatabases*.

```
typedef struct _CEDBASEINFO {
    DWORD dwFlags;
    WCHAR szDbaseName[CEDB_MAXDBASENAMELEN];
    DWORD dwDbaseType;
    WORD wNumRecords;
    WORD wNumSortOrder;
    DWORD dwSize;
    FILETIME ftLastModified;
    SORTORDERSPEC rgSortSpecs[CEDB_MAXSORTORDER];
} CEDBASEINFO;
```

As with *CeFindAllFiles*, you must free the buffer returned by *CeFindAllDatabases* with a call to *CeRapiFreeBuffer*.

One other function in this section requires a call to *CeRapiFreeBuffer*. The function *CeReadRecordProps*, which returns properties for a database record, allocates the buffer where the data is returned. If you call the RAPI version function, you need to call *CeRapiFreeBuffer* to free the returned buffer.

RAPI Registry Management Functions

The RAPI functions for managing the registry are shown in the following list. The functions work identically to their Windows CE counterparts. But remember that all strings, whether they are specifying keys and values or strings returned by the functions, are in Unicode.

Registry Management Functions

CeRegOpenKeyEx	*CeRegEnumValue*
CeRegEnumKeyEx	*CeRegDeleteValue*
CeRegCreateKeyEx	*CeRegQueryInfoKey*
CeRegCloseKey	*CeRegQueryValueEx*
CeRegDeleteKey	*CeRegSetValueEx*

RAPI Shell Management Functions

The RAPI shell management functions are shown in the next list. Although I'll cover the Windows CE–equivalent functions in the next chapter, you can see that the self-describing names of the functions pretty well document themselves. The *CeSHCreateShortcut* and *CeSHGetShortcutTarget* functions allow you to create and query shortcuts. The other two functions, *CeGetTempPath* and *CeGetSpecialFolderPath*, let you query the locations of some of the special-purpose directories on the Windows CE system, such as the programs directory and the recycle bin.

Shell Management Functions

CeSHCreateShortcut	*CeGetTempPath*
CeSHGetShortcutTarget	*CeGetSpecialFolderPath*

RAPI Window Management Functions

The final set of predefined RAPI functions allows a desktop application to manage the windows on the Windows CE desktop. These functions are shown in the following list. The functions work similarly to their Windows CE functions. The *CeGetWindow* function allows a PC-based program to query the windows and child windows on the desktop while the other functions allow you to query the values in the window structures.

Window Management Functions

CeGetWindow	*CeGetWindowText*
CeGetWindowLong	*CeGetClassName*

The RapiDir Example Program

The RapiDir example is a PC-console application that displays the contents of a directory on an attached Windows CE device. The output of RapiDir, shown in Figure 15-1, resembles the output of the standard DIR command from a PC command line. RapiDir is passed one argument, the directory specification of the directory on the Windows CE machine. The directory specification can take wildcard arguments such as *.exe* if you want, but the program isn't completely robust in parsing the directory specification. Perfect parsing of a directory string isn't the goal of RapiDir—demonstrating RAPI is.

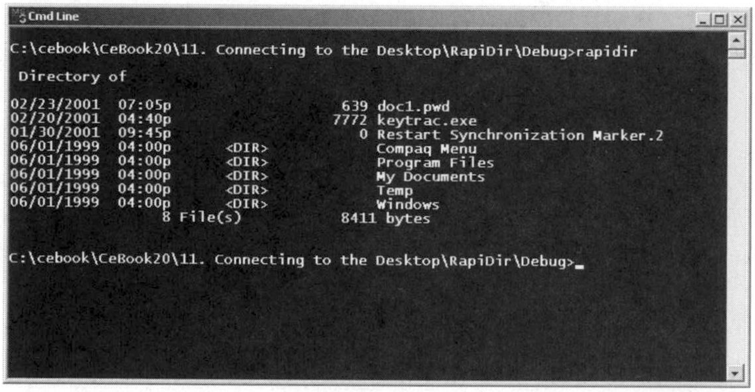

Figure 15-1   The output of RapiDir

The source code for RapiDir is shown in Listing 15-1. The program is a command line application and therefore doesn't need the message loop or any of the other structure seen in a Windows-based application. Instead the *Win-Main* function is replaced by our old C friend, *main*.

Remember that RapiDir is a standard Win32 desktop application. It won't even compile for Windows CE. On the other hand, you have the freedom to use the copious amounts of RAM and disk space provided by the comparatively huge desktop PC. When you build RapiDir, you'll need to add RAPI.lib to the libraries that the linker uses. Otherwise, you'll get unresolved external errors for all the RAPI functions you call in your application. RAPI.h and RAPI.lib come with the Microsoft eMbedded Tools. The location of these files varies from platform to platform. The easiest way to find the files is to use the Explorer's search function to look for RAPI.h and RAPI.lib and then add the appropriate directories to the project.

RapiDir.cpp

```
//======================================================================
// RapiDir - Returns the contents of a directory on a Windows CE system.
//
// Written for the book Programming Windows CE
// Copyright (C) 2003 Douglas Boling
//======================================================================
#include <windows.h>                    // For all that Windows stuff
#include <stdio.h>
#include <rapi.h>                       // RAPI includes


//======================================================================
// main - Program entry point
//
int main (int argc, char **argv) {
    RAPIINIT ri;
    char szSrch[MAX_PATH], *pPtr;
    WCHAR szwDir[MAX_PATH];
    CE_FIND_DATA *pfd = 0;
    DWORD i, cItems, dwTotal = 0;
    FILETIME ft;
    SYSTEMTIME st;
    char ampm = 'a';
    int rc;

    // Call RapiInitEx to asynchronously start RAPI session.
    ri.cbSize = sizeof (ri);
    rc = CeRapiInitEx (&ri);
    if (rc != NOERROR) {
        printf (TEXT ("Rapi Initialization failed\r\n"));
        return 0;
    }
    // Wait 5 seconds for connect.
    rc = WaitForSingleObject (ri.heRapiInit, 5000);
    if (rc == WAIT_OBJECT_0) {
        if (ri.hrRapiInit != S_OK) {
            printf (TEXT ("Rapi Initialization failed.\r\n"));
            return 0;
        }
    }
```

Listing 15-1   The RapiDir source code   *(continued)*

Listing 15-1 *(continued)*

```
    } else if (rc == WAIT_TIMEOUT) {
        printf (TEXT ("Rapi Initialization timed out.\r\n"));
        return 0;
    }
    // If no argument, assume root directory.
    if (argc > 1)
        lstrcpy (szSrch, argv[1]);
    else
        lstrcpy (szSrch, "\\");

    // Point to end of name.
    pPtr = szSrch + lstrlen (szSrch) - 1;

    // Strip any trailing backslash.
    if (*pPtr == '\\')
        *pPtr = '\0';

    // Look for wildcards in filename. pPtr points to string end.
    for (i = 0; (pPtr >= szSrch) && (*pPtr != '\\'); pPtr--) {
        if ((*pPtr == '*') || (*pPtr == '?'))
            i++;
    }
    // Display dir name first so that on long calls we show we're alive.
    if (pPtr >= szSrch) {
        char ch;
        ch = *pPtr;
        *pPtr = '\0';
        printf (TEXT ("\r\n Directory of %s\r\n\r\n"), szSrch);
        *pPtr = ch;
    } else if (i)
        printf (TEXT ("\r\n Directory of \\\r\n\r\n"));
    else
        printf (TEXT ("\r\n Directory of %s\r\n\r\n"), szSrch);
    // No wildcards, append *.*
    if (i == 0)
        lstrcat (szSrch, "\\*.*");

    // Convert ANSI string to Unicode.
    memset (szwDir, 0, sizeof (szwDir));
    mbstowcs (szwDir, szSrch, lstrlen (szSrch) + 1);
    // RAPI call
    rc = CeFindAllFiles (szwDir, FAF_SIZE_LOW | FAF_NAME |
                        FAF_ATTRIBUTES | FAF_LASTACCESS_TIME,
                        &cItems, &pfd);

    // Display the results.
    if (cItems) {
```

```
    for (i = 0; i < cItems; i++) {
        // Convert file time.
        FileTimeToLocalFileTime (&pfd->ftLastAccessTime, &ft);
        FileTimeToSystemTime (&ft, &st);
        // Adjust for AM/PM.
        if (st.wHour == 0)
            st.wHour = 12;
        else if (st.wHour > 11) {
            ampm = 'p';
            if (st.wHour > 12)
                st.wHour -= 12;
        }
        printf (TEXT ("%02d/%02d/%02d  %02d:%02d%c\t"),
                st.wMonth, st.wDay, st.wYear,
                st.wHour, st.wMinute, ampm);

        // Display dir marker or file size.
        if (pfd->dwFileAttributes & FILE_ATTRIBUTE_DIRECTORY)
            printf (TEXT ("<DIR>\t\t "));
        else {
            printf (TEXT ("\t%8d "), pfd->nFileSizeLow);
            dwTotal += pfd->nFileSizeLow;
        }

        // Display name, use Cap %S to indicate Unicode.
        printf (TEXT ("%S\r\n"), pfd->cFileName);
        pfd++;
    }
    printf (TEXT ("\t%10d File(s)\t%9d bytes\r\n\r\n"),
            cItems, dwTotal);
} else
    printf (TEXT ("File not Found\r\n\r\n"));
// Clean up by freeing the FindAllFiles buffer.
if (pfd)
    CeRapiFreeBuffer (pfd);
// Clean up by uninitializing RAPI.
CeRapiUninit ();
return 0;
}
```

This single procedure application first calls *CeRapiInitEx* to initialize the RAPI session. I used the *Ex* version of the initialization function so that RapiDir can time out and terminate if a connection isn't made within 5 seconds of starting the program. If I'd used *CeRapiInit* instead, the only way to terminate RapiDir if a remote CE device weren't connected would be a user-unfriendly Ctrl+C key combination.

Once the RAPI session is initialized, a minimal amount of work is done on the single command line argument that's the search string for the directory. Once that work is complete, the string is converted into Unicode and passed to *CeFindAllFiles*. This RAPI function then returns with an array of *CE_FIND_DATA* structures that contain the names and requested data of the files and directories found. The data from that array is then displayed using *printf* statements. The buffer returned by *CeFindAllFiles* is freed by means of a call to *CeRapiFreeBuffer*. Finally, the RAPI session is terminated with a call to *CeRapiUninit*.

If you compare the output of RapiDir with the output of the standard DIR command, you notice that RapiDir doesn't display the total bytes free on the disk after the listing of files. Although I could have displayed the total free space for the object store using *CeGetStorageInformation*, this practice wouldn't work if the user displayed a directory on a PCMCIA card or other external media. Windows CE supports the *GetDiskFreeSpaceEx* function, but the Windows CE RAPI DLL doesn't expose this function. To get this information, we'll use RAPI's ability to call custom RAPI functions on a Windows CE system.

Custom RAPI Functions

No matter how many functions the RAPI interface supports, you can always think of functions that an application needs but the RAPI interface doesn't give you. Because of this, RAPI provides a method for a PC application to call a user-defined function on the Windows CE device.

You can invoke a user-defined RAPI function in one of two ways. The first way is called *block mode*. In block mode, you make a call to the RAPI remote invocation function, the function makes the call to a specified function in a specified DLL, the DLL function does its thing and returns, and the RAPI function then returns to the calling PC program with the output. The second method is called *stream mode*. In this mode, the RAPI call to the function returns immediately, but a connection is maintained between the calling PC application and the Windows CE DLL–based function. This method allows information to be fed back to the PC on an ongoing basis.

Using RAPI to Call a Custom Function

The RAPI function that lets you call a generic function on the Windows CE device is *CeRapiInvoke*, which is prototyped as

```
HRESULT CeRapiInvoke (LPCWSTR pDllPath, LPCWSTR pFunctionName,
                      DWORD cbInput, BYTE *pInput, DWORD *pcbOutput,
                      BYTE **ppOutput, IRAPIStream **ppIRAPIStream,
                      DWORD dwReserved);
```

The first parameter to *CeRapiInvoke* is the name of the DLL on the Windows CE device that contains the function you want to call. The name must be in Unicode but can include a path. If no path is specified, the DLL is assumed to be in the \windows directory on the device. The second parameter is the name of the function to be called. The function name must be in Unicode and is case specific.

The next two parameters, *cbInput* and *pInput*, should be set to the buffer containing the data and the size of that data to be sent to the Windows CE–based function. The input buffer should be allocated in the local heap of the application. When you call *CeRapiInvoke*, this buffer will be freed by the function. The *pcbOutput* and *ppOutput* parameters are both pointers—the first a pointer to a *DWORD* that receives the size of the data returned and the second a pointer to a *PBYTE* variable that receives the pointer to the buffer containing the data returned by the Windows CE function. The buffer returned by *CeRapiInvoke* is allocated by the function in your local heap. You're responsible for freeing this buffer. I'll describe the next-to-last parameter, *ppIRAPIStream*, later.

To use *CeRapiInvoke* in block mode, all you do is specify the DLL containing the function you want to call, the name of the function, and the data, and then make the call. When *CeRapiInvoke* returns, the data from the CE-based function will be sitting in the buffer pointed to by your output pointer variable.

Writing a RAPI Server Function

You can't call just any function in a Windows CE DLL. The structure of the Windows CE function must conform to the following function prototype:

```
STDAPI INT FuncName (DWORD cbInput, BYTE *pInput, DWORD *pcbOutput,
                     BYTE **ppOutput, IRAPIStream *pIRAPIStream);
```

As you can see, the parameters closely match those of *CeRapiInvoke*. As with *CeRapiInvoke*, I'll talk about the parameter *pIRAPIStream* later.

Listing 15-2 contains the source code for a very simple block-mode RAPI server. This is a DLL and therefore has a different structure from the application files previously used in the book. The primary difference is that the DLL contains a *DllMain* routine instead of *WinMain*. The *DllMain* routine is called by Windows whenever a DLL is loaded or freed by a process or thread. In our case, we don't need to take any action other than to return *TRUE* indicating all is well.

You should be careful to make the name of your RAPI server DLL eight characters or less. Current implementations of the RAPI DLL will fail to find server DLLs with names not in the old 8.3 format.

RapiServ.cpp

```
//======================================================================
// RapiServ - A RAPI block mode server DLL
//
// Written for the book Programming Windows CE
// Copyright (C) 2003 Douglas Boling
//======================================================================
#include <windows.h>                    // For all that Windows stuff

// The following ensures that the function will be exported from the DLL
// and that any C++ compilers used won't mangle the name.
#ifdef __cplusplus
extern "C" {
#endif
__declspec (dllexport) INT RAPIGetDiskSize (DWORD, BYTE *, DWORD *,
                                            BYTE **, PVOID);
#ifdef __cplusplus
}
#endif
//======================================================================
// DllMain - DLL initialization entry point
//
BOOL WINAPI DllMain (HANDLE hinstDLL, DWORD dwReason,
                     LPVOID lpvReserved) {
    return TRUE;
}
//======================================================================
// RAPIGetDiskSize - Returns the disk size and free space.  Called from
// PC application using RAPI.
//
INT RAPIGetDiskSize (DWORD cbInput, BYTE *pInput, DWORD *pcbOutput,
                     BYTE **ppOutput, PVOID reserved) {
    PDWORD pdwLocal;
    LPTSTR pPtr;
    DWORD i;
    int rc = 0;
    ULARGE_INTEGER lnFree, lnTotal;

    *pcbOutput = 0;                // Zero output bytes for now.
    if (!pInput) return -1;    // Make sure there is an input buffer.
    // See if proper zero-terminated string.
    pPtr = (LPTSTR)pInput;
    for (i = 0; i < cbInput / 2; i++)
        if (!*pPtr++)
            break;
```

Listing 15-2   RapiServ.cpp, a simple block-mode RAPI server DLL

```
    // If not zero terminated or if zero length, return error.
    if ((i >= cbInput / 2) || (i == 0)) {
        LocalFree (pInput);
        return -2;
    }


    // Call the function.
    if (GetDiskFreeSpaceEx ((LPTSTR)pInput, NULL, &lnTotal, &lnFree)) {

        // Allocate memory for the return buffer.
        pdwLocal = (PDWORD) LocalAlloc (LPTR, 2 * sizeof (DWORD));
        if (pdwLocal) {
            // Copy data from function to output buffer.
            pdwLocal[0] = lnTotal.LowPart;
            pdwLocal[1] = lnFree.LowPart;
            // Specify size and buffer.
            *pcbOutput = 2 * sizeof (DWORD);
            *ppOutput = (PBYTE)pdwLocal;
        } else
            rc = GetLastError();
    } else
        rc = GetLastError();
    // The function is responsible for freeing the input buffer.
    LocalFree (pInput);
    return rc;
}
```

The unusual prefix before the function prototype for *RAPIGetDiskSize*,

```
__declspec (dllexport) INT RAPIGetDiskSize…
```

tells the linker to export the function listed so that external modules can call the function directly. This declaration is a shortcut for the old way of defining exports in a separate function definition (DEF) file. While this shortcut is convenient, sometimes you still need to fall back on a DEF file. The *__declspec* line is couched in an extern C bracket. This technique ensures that if the file is compiled with the C++ language extensions enabled, the function name won't be mangled by the compiler. This is an important assurance because we need to call this function by its real name, not by some fabricated name created by a compiler.

The function of RapiServ is to make available that *GetDiskFreeSpaceEx* function we needed in the RapiDir example application. The server function, *RAPIGetDiskSize*, has the same prototype I described earlier. The input buffer is used to pass a directory name to the DLL while the output buffer returns the total disk space and the free disk space for the directory passed. The format of the input and output buffers is totally up to you. However, the function must free the input buffer with *LocalFree* and the output buffer should be allocated using *LocalAlloc* so that the RAPI library can free it after it has been used. The value returned by *RAPIGetDiskSize* is the value that's returned by the *CeRapiInvoke* function to the PC-based application.

On the PC side, a call to a block-mode RAPI server function looks like the following.

```
//---------------------------------------------------------------------
// MyCeGetDiskFreeSpaceEx - Homegrown implementation of a RAPI
// GetDiskFreeSpace function
//
BOOL MyCeGetDiskFreeSpaceEx (LPWSTR pszDir, PDWORD pdwTotal,
                             PDWORD pdwFree) {
    HRESULT hr;
    DWORD dwIn, dwOut;
    LPBYTE pInput;
    LPWSTR pPtr;
    PDWORD pOut;
    BOOL bRC = FALSE;

    // Get length of Unicode string.
    for (dwIn = 2, pPtr = pszDir; *pPtr++; dwIn+=2);
    // Allocate buffer for input.
    pInput = LocalAlloc (LPTR, dwIn);
    if (!pInput)
        return FALSE;
    // Copy directory name into input buffer.
    memcpy (pInput, pszDir, dwIn);

    // Call function on Windows CE device.
    hr = CeRapiInvoke (L"RapiServ", L"RAPIGetDiskSize", dwIn,
                       pInput, &dwOut, (PBYTE *)&pOut, NULL, 0);

    // If successful, return total and free values.
    if (hr == 0) {
        *pdwTotal = pOut[0];
        *pdwFree = pOut[1];
        bRC = TRUE;
    }
    LocalFree (pOut);
    return bRC;
}
```

This routine encapsulates the call to *CeRapiInvoke* so that the call looks just like another CE RAPI call. The code in this routine simply computes the length of the Unicode string that contains the directory specification, allocates a buffer and copies the string into it, and passes it to the *CeRapiInvoke* function. When the routine returns, the return code indicates success or failure of the call. *CeRapiInvoke* frees the input buffer passed to it. The data is then copied from the output buffer and that buffer is freed with a call to *LocalFree*.

Throughout this section, I've put off any explanation of the parameters referring to *IRAPIStream*. In fact, in the example code above, the prototype for the server call, *RAPIGetDiskSize*, simply typed the *pIRAPIStream* pointer as a *PVOID* and ignored it. In the client code, the *CeRapiInvoke* call passed a *NULL* to the *ppIRAPIStream* pointer. This treatment of the *IRAPIStream* interface is what differentiates a block-mode call from a stream-mode call. Now let's look at the *IRAPIStream* interface.

Stream Mode

Stream-mode RAPI calls are different from block mode in that the initial RAPI call creates a link between the PC application and the server routine on the Windows CE device. When you call *CeRapiInvoke* in stream mode, the call returns immediately. You communicate with the server DLL using an *IRAPIStream* interface. You access this interface using a pointer returned by the *CeRapiInvoke* call in the variable pointed to by *ppIRAPIStream*.

The *IRAPIStream* interface is derived from the standard COM *IStream* interface. The only methods added to *IStream* to create *IRAPIStream* are *SetRapiStat* and *GetRapiStat*, which let you set a timeout value for the RAPI communication. Fortunately, we don't have to implement an *IRAPIStream* interface either on the client side or in the server DLL. This interface is provided for us by the RAPI services as a way to communicate.

Following is a call to *CeRapiInvoke* that establishes a stream connection and then writes and reads back 10 bytes from the remote server DLL.

```
DWORD dwIn, dwOut, cbBytes;
IRAPIStream *pIRAPIStream;
BYTE bBuff[BUFF_SIZE];
PBYTE pOut;
HRESULT hr;

// RAPI call
hr = CeRapiInvoke (L"ServDLL", L"RAPIRmtFunc", dwIn, bBuff,
                   &dwOut, &pOut, &pIRAPIStream, 0);
if (hr == S_OK) {
    // Write 10 bytes.
    pIRAPIStream->Write (bBuff, 10, &cbBytes);
    // Read data from server.
    pIRAPIStream->Read (bBuff, 10, &cbBytes);
}
pIRAPIStream->Release ();
```

When establishing a stream connection, you can still use the input buffer to pass initial data down to the remote server. From then on, you should use the *Read* and *Write* methods of *IRAPIStream* to communicate with the server. When you're finished with the *IRAPIStream* interface, you must call *Release* to release the interface.

The RapiFind Example Program

The RapiFind example program searches the entire directory tree of a Windows CE device for files matching a search specification. The program is in two parts: a RAPI server DLL, FindSrv.dll, and a console-based, Win32 application, Rapi-Find. The program works by passing a search string on the command line. RapiFind returns any files on the attached Windows CE device that match the search string. If the search specification includes a directory, only that directory and any of its subdirectories are searched for matching files. Figure 15-2 shows the output of RapiFind. Let's look at the server DLL, FindSrv, shown in Listing 15-3.

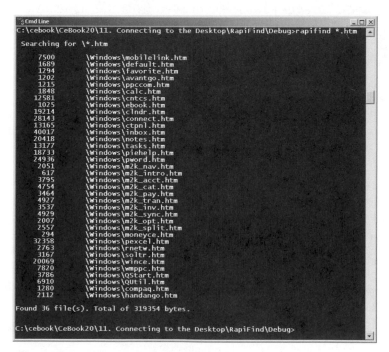

Figure 15-2   The output of RapiFind

FindSrv.cpp

```
//======================================================================
// FindSrv - A RAPI stream server DLL
//
// Written for the book Programming Windows CE
// Copyright (C) 2003 Douglas Boling
//======================================================================
#include <windows.h>                       // For all that Windows stuff

// Returns number of elements
#define dim(x) (sizeof(x) / sizeof(x[0]))


//----------------------------------------------------------------------
// Add if not defined.
#ifndef RAPISTREAMFLAG
typedef enum tagRAPISTREAMFLAG {
    STREAM_TIMEOUT_READ
} RAPISTREAMFLAG;
DECLARE_INTERFACE_ (IRAPIStream,  IStream)
{
    STDMETHOD(SetRapiStat)(THIS_ RAPISTREAMFLAG Flag,
                           DWORD dwValue) PURE;
    STDMETHOD(GetRapiStat)(THIS_ RAPISTREAMFLAG Flag,
                           DWORD *pdwValue) PURE;
};
#endif
//----------------------------------------------------------------------
// Function prototypes declared as exports from the DLL.
// Bracket so that function name won't be mangled by C++.
extern "C" {
__ declspec(dllexport) INT RAPIFindFile (DWORD cbInput, BYTE *pInput,
                                         DWORD *pcbOutput, BYTE **ppOutput,
                                         IRAPIStream *pIRAPIStream);
}


//======================================================================
// DllMain - DLL initialization entry point
//
BOOL WINAPI DllMain (HANDLE hinstDLL, DWORD dwReason,
                     LPVOID lpvReserved) {
    return TRUE;
}
```

Listing 15-3   FindSrv.cpp, a stream-mode RAPI server DLL   *(continued)*

Listing 15-3   *(continued)*

```
//-------------------------------------------------------------------------
// WriteToClient - Writes a command and optional string to the client
//
int WriteToClient (int nCmd, int nSize, LPTSTR pszStr,
                   IRAPIStream *pIRAPIStream) {
    int nBuff;
    DWORD cbBytes;
    HRESULT hr;

    // Write command code.
    hr = pIRAPIStream->Write (&nCmd, sizeof (nCmd), &cbBytes);

    // Write size value.
    hr = pIRAPIStream->Write (&nSize, sizeof (nSize), &cbBytes);

    // Write length of string.
    nBuff = (lstrlen (pszStr) + 1) * sizeof (TCHAR);
    hr = pIRAPIStream->Write (&nBuff, sizeof (nBuff), &cbBytes);
    // Write string.
    hr = pIRAPIStream->Write (pszStr, nBuff, &cbBytes);
    return 0;
}
int nFlag;
//-------------------------------------------------------------------------
// SrchDirectory - Recursive routine that searches a directory and all
// child dirs for matching files
//
int SrchDirectory (LPTSTR pszDir, IRAPIStream *pIRAPIStream) {
    WIN32_FIND_DATA fd;
    TCHAR szNew[MAX_PATH];
    int i, rc, nErr = 0;
    HANDLE hFind;
    TCHAR *pPtr, *pSrcSpec;

    // Separate subdirectory from search specification.
    for (pSrcSpec = pszDir + lstrlen (pszDir); pSrcSpec >= pszDir;
        pSrcSpec---)
        if (*pSrcSpec == TEXT ('\\'))
            break;

    // Copy the search specification up to the last directory sep char.
    if (pSrcSpec <= pszDir)
        lstrcpy (szNew, TEXT ("\\"));
    else {
        for (i = 0; (i < dim(szNew)-10) &&
                    ((pszDir+i) <= pSrcSpec); i++)
            szNew[i] = *(pszDir+i);
```

```
        szNew[i] = TEXT ('\0');
}
pPtr = szNew + lstrlen (szNew);

// Report directory we're searching.
WriteToClient (2, 0, szNew, pIRAPIStream);

// Find matching files.
hFind = FindFirstFile (pszDir, &fd);
if (hFind != INVALID_HANDLE_VALUE) {

    do {
        // Report all matching files.
        if (!(fd.dwFileAttributes & FILE_ATTRIBUTE_DIRECTORY))
            WriteToClient (1, fd.nFileSizeLow, fd.cFileName,
                           pIRAPIStream);
        rc = FindNextFile (hFind, &fd);
    } while (rc);

    FindClose (hFind);
} else {
    rc = GetLastError();
    if ((rc != ERROR_FILE_NOT_FOUND)  &&
        (rc != ERROR_NO_MORE_FILES)) {
        TCHAR szDbg[64];
        wsprintf (szDbg, TEXT ("1Find Error:%d"), rc);
        WriteToClient (99, 0, szDbg, pIRAPIStream);
        return -1;
    }
}

// Create generic search string for all directories.
lstrcat (szNew, TEXT ("*.*"));

hFind = FindFirstFile (szNew, &fd);
if (hFind != INVALID_HANDLE_VALUE) {
    do {
        if (fd.dwFileAttributes & FILE_ATTRIBUTE_DIRECTORY) {
            // Recurse to the lower directory.
            lstrcpy (pPtr, fd.cFileName);
            lstrcat (pPtr, pSrcSpec);
            nErr = SrchDirectory (szNew, pIRAPIStream);
            if (nErr) break;
            *pPtr = TEXT ('\0');
        }
        rc = FindNextFile (hFind, &fd);
    } while (rc);
```

(continued)

Listing 15-3 *(continued)*

```
            FindClose (hFind);
        } else {
            rc = GetLastError();
            if ((rc != ERROR_FILE_NOT_FOUND) &&
                (rc != ERROR_NO_MORE_FILES)) {
                TCHAR szDbg[64];
                wsprintf (szDbg, TEXT ("2Find Error:%d"), rc);
                WriteToClient (99, 0, szDbg, pIRAPIStream);
                return -1;
            }
        }
    }
    return nErr;
}
//=======================================================================
// RAPIFindFile - Searches the device for matching files. Called from
// PC application using RAPI.
//
INT RAPIFindFile (DWORD cbInput, BYTE *pInput, DWORD *pcbOutput,
                  BYTE **ppOutput, IRAPIStream *pIRAPIStream) {
    int nBuff;
    DWORD i, cbBytes;
    TCHAR *pPtr;
    HRESULT hr;

    *pcbOutput = 0;
    // See if proper zero-terminated string.
    pPtr = (LPTSTR)pInput;
    for (i = 0; i < cbInput / 2; i++)
        if (!*pPtr++)
            break;

    // If not zero terminated or if zero length, return error.
    if ((i >= cbInput / 2) || (i == 0))
        return -2;
    nFlag = 0;
    // Search for files.
    SrchDirectory ((LPTSTR) pInput, pIRAPIStream);

    // Write end code.  Cmd 0 -> end of search
    nBuff = 0;
    hr = pIRAPIStream->Write (&nBuff, sizeof (nBuff), &cbBytes);
    // Release the interface.
    pIRAPIStream->Release ();
    return 0;
}
```

As with the earlier RAPI server DLL, FindSrv is short and to the point. The differences between this server and the block server can be seen early in the file. The *IRAPIStream* interface isn't defined in some of the older tools, so if necessary, this interface is derived at the top of the file from *IStream*. Immediately following the interface declaration is the exported function prototype. Notice that the prototype is enclosed in an extern C bracket. This prevents the default mangling of the function name that the C++ precompiler would normally perform. We need the name of the function unmangled so that it's a known name to the client.

The exported RAPI function is *RAPIFindFile*, which you can see at the end of the source code. This routine does little more than check to see that the search string is valid before it calls *SrchDirectory*, a function internal to the DLL. *SrchDirectory* is a recursive function that searches the directory defined in the search specification and all subdirectories underneath. When a file is found that matches the search specification, the name and size of the file are sent back to the client caller using the *Write* method of *IRAPIStream*. The format of the data transmitted between the client and server is up to the programmer. In this case, I send a command word, followed by the file size, the length of the name, and finally the filename itself. The command word gives you a minimal protocol for communication with the client. The command value 1 indicates a found file, the value 2 indicates the server is looking in a new directory, and the value 0 indicates that the search is complete. Following the last write, *Release* is called to free the *IRAPIStream* interface.

The source code for the client application, RapiFind, is shown in Listing 15-4.

RapiFind.cpp
```
//======================================================================
// RapiFind - Searches for a file or files on a Windows CE system
//
// Written for the book Programming Windows CE
// Copyright (C) 2003 Douglas Boling
//======================================================================
#include <windows.h>                // For all that Windows stuff
#include <stdio.h>
#include <rapi.h>                    // RAPI includes


//======================================================================
// main - Program entry point
//
int main (int argc, char **argv) {
```

Listing 15-4   RapiFind.cpp, a stream-mode RAPI client application   *(continued)*

Listing 15-4   *(continued)*

```
    RAPIINIT ri;
    char szSrch[MAX_PATH], *pPtr;
    WCHAR szwDir[MAX_PATH];
    WCHAR szName[MAX_PATH];
    DWORD i, dwTotal = 0, dwFiles = 0, dwIn, dwOut, cbBytes;
    IRAPIStream *pIRAPIStream;
    PBYTE pInput, pOut;
    HRESULT hr;
    int rc, nCmd, nSize;

    // If no argument, fail.
    if (argc < 2) {
        printf ("\r\nUSAGE: %s <search spec>\r\n\r\n", argv[0]);
        return -1;
    }
    lstrcpy (szSrch, argv[1]);

    // Call RapiInitEx to asynchronously start RAPI session.
    ri.cbSize = sizeof (ri);
    rc = CeRapiInitEx (&ri);
     if (rc != NOERROR) {
        printf (TEXT ("Rapi Initialization failed\r\n"));
        return 0;
    }
    // Wait 5 seconds for connect.
    rc = WaitForSingleObject (ri.heRapiInit, 5000);
    if (rc == WAIT_OBJECT_0) {
        if (ri.hrRapiInit != NOERROR) {
            printf (TEXT ("Rapi Initialization failed\r\n"));
            return 0;
        }
    } else if (rc == WAIT_TIMEOUT) {
        printf (TEXT ("Rapi Initialization timed out.\r\n"));
        return 0;
    }
    // Point to end of name.
    pPtr = szSrch + lstrlen (szSrch) - 1;

    // Strip any trailing backslash.
    if (*pPtr == '\\')
        *pPtr = '\0';

    // Look for wildcards in filename. pPtr points to string end.
    for (i = 0; (pPtr >= szSrch) && (*pPtr != '\\'); pPtr--) {
        if ((*pPtr == '*') || (*pPtr == '?'))
            i++;
```

```
}
if (pPtr <= szSrch) {
    lstrcpy (szSrch, TEXT ("\\"));
    lstrcat (szSrch, argv[1]);
}

if (i) {
    printf (TEXT ("\r\n Searching for %s\r\n\r\n"), pPtr+1);
} else
    printf (TEXT ("\r\n Searching in %s\r\n\r\n"), szSrch);

// No wildcards, append *.*
if (i == 0)
    lstrcat (szSrch, "\\*.*");

// Convert ANSI string to Unicode.  At the same time, copy it
// into a discardable buffer for CeRapiInvoke.
dwIn = lstrlen (szSrch) + 1;  //Make mbstowcs convert terminating 0.

pInput = (PBYTE)LocalAlloc (LPTR, dwIn * sizeof (WCHAR));
if (!pInput) {
    printf (TEXT ("\r\nOut of memory\r\n"));
    return -1;
}
mbstowcs ((LPWSTR)pInput, szSrch, dwIn);
dwIn *= sizeof (WCHAR);

// RAPI call
hr = CeRapiInvoke (L"FindSrv", L"RAPIFindFile", dwIn,
                   pInput, &dwOut, &pOut, &pIRAPIStream, 0);
if (hr == S_OK) {
    // Read command.
    pIRAPIStream->Read (&nCmd, sizeof (nCmd), &cbBytes);
    while (nCmd) {
        switch (nCmd) {
        // Display found file.
        case 1:
            // Read length of file.
            pIRAPIStream->Read (&i, sizeof (i), &cbBytes);
            dwTotal += i;
            dwFiles++;

            // Read length of filename.
            pIRAPIStream->Read (&nSize, sizeof (nSize), &cbBytes);
            // Read name itself.
            pIRAPIStream->Read (szName, nSize, &cbBytes);
```

(continued)

Listing 15-4   *(continued)*

```
                    // Print directory and name.
                    printf (TEXT ("%9d\t%S%S\r\n"), i, szwDir, szName);
                    break;

                // Display name of directory we're currently searching.
                case 2:
                    // Read and discard dummy length value.
                    pIRAPIStream->Read (&nSize, sizeof (nSize), &cbBytes);
                    // Read length of directory.
                    pIRAPIStream->Read (&nSize, sizeof (nSize), &cbBytes);
                    // Read directory name itself.
                    pIRAPIStream->Read (szwDir, nSize, &cbBytes);
                    break;
                }
            // Read next command.
            pIRAPIStream->Read (&nCmd, sizeof (nCmd), &cbBytes);
        }
        pIRAPIStream->Release ();
    } else if (hr == ERROR_FILE_NOT_FOUND)
        printf (TEXT ("The RAPI server DLL FindSrv could not be found \
                      on the CE target device.\r\n"));
    else
        printf (TEXT ("CeRapiInvoke returned %d"), hr);

    printf (TEXT ("\r\nFound %d file(s). Total of %d bytes.\r\n\r\n"),
            dwFiles, dwTotal);

    // Clean up by uninitializing RAPI.
    CeRapiUninit ();
    return 0;
}
```

The call to *CeRapiInvoke* returns a pointer to an *IRAPIStream* interface that's then used to read data from the server. The client reads one integer value to determine whether the following data is a found file, a report of the current search directory, or a report that the search has ended. With each command, the appropriate data is read using the *Read* method. The result of the search is then reported using *printf* statements. After all the results have been returned, the application calls the *Release* method to free the *IRapiStream* interface.

Although you could implement the same file-find function of RapiFind using a block-mode connection, the stream format has a definite advantage in this case. By reporting back results as files are found, the program lets the user know that the program is executing correctly. If the program were designed to use a block-mode call, RapiFind would appear to go dead while the server DLL completed its entire search, which could take 10 or 20 seconds.

As I mentioned in the explanation of *CeRapiInit*, a call to this function doesn't initiate a connection to a device. You can, however, be notified when a connection to a Windows CE device is established. There are ways, both on the PC and on the Windows CE device, to know when a connection is made between the two systems. After a brief look at CeUtil, which provides some handy helper functions for PC applications dealing with Windows CE devices, I'll talk next about connection notifiers.

The CeUtil Functions

ActiveSync uses the PC registry to store voluminous amounts of information about the Windows CE devices that have partnered with the PC. ActiveSync also uses the registry to store extensive configuration information. While most of these registry keys are documented, if you access them by name you're assuming that those key names will always remain the same. This might not be the case, especially in international versions of Windows where registry keys are sometimes in a different language.

The CeUtil DLL exports functions that provide an abstraction layer over the registry keys used by ActiveSync. Using this DLL allows a PC application to query the devices that are currently registered and to add or delete registry values underneath the keys that hold data for specific devices. The CeUtil DLL doesn't communicate with a remote Windows CE device; it only looks in the PC registry for information that has already been put there by ActiveSync.

The keys in the registry related to ActiveSync are separated into either *HKEY_LOCAL_MACHINE*, for generic configurations such as the initial configuration for a newly registered device, or *HKEY_CURRENT_USER*, where the configuration information for the already registered devices is located. When a new device is registered, ActiveSync copies the template in *HKEY_LOCAL_MACHINE* to a new subkey under *HKEY_CURRENT_USER* that identifies the specific device.

In general, you register a new filter in the keys under *HKEY_LOCAL_MACHINE* to ensure that all devices that are registered in the future also use your filter. You use the registry entries under *HKEY_CURRENT_USER* to register that filter for a specific device that was already registered before you installed that same filter.

Accessing ActiveSync Registry Entries

To open one of the many registry keys that hold connection information, you can use this function:

```
HRESULT CeSvcOpen (UINT uSvc, LPTSTR pszPath, BOOL fCreate,
                   PHCESVC phSvc);
```

The first parameter of this function is a flag that indicates which predefined key you want to open. Here are the available flags:

The following are keys under *HKEY_LOCAL_MACHINE* that apply to generic Windows CE Services configuration information.

- **CESVC_ROOT_MACHINE**   ActiveSync root key under *HKEY_LOCAL_MACHINE*

- **CESVC_FILTERS**   Root key for filter registration

- **CESVC_CUSTOM_MENUS**   Root key for custom menu registration

- **CESVC_SERVICES_COMMON**   Root key for services

- **CESVC_SYNC_COMMON**   Root key for synchronization services registration

The following are keys under *HKEY_CURRENT_USER* that apply to specific Windows CE devices that are partnered with the PC.

- **CESVC_ROOT_USER**   ActiveSync root key under *HKEY_LOCAL_USER*

- **CESVC_DEVICES**   Root key for individual device registration

- **CESVC_DEVICEX**   Root key for a specific device

- **CESVC_DEVICE_SELECTED**   Root key for the device currently selected in the ActiveSync window

- **CESVC_SERVICES_USER**   Root services subkey for a specific device

- **CESVC_SYNC**   Synchronization subkey for a specific device

Of the many registry keys that can be returned by *CeSvcOpen*, the ones I'll be using throughout the chapter are *CESVC_FILTERS*, the key in which a filter is registered for all future devices; *CESVC_DEVICES*, the key in which information for all registered devices is located; and *CESVC_DEVICEX*, which is used to open keys for specific registered devices. The other flags are useful for registering synchronization objects as well as for registering general ActiveSync configuration information.

The second parameter to *CeSvcOpen* is *pszPath*. This parameter points either to the name of a subkey to open underneath the key specified by the *uSvc* flag or to a *DWORD* value that specifies the registered Windows CE device that you want to open if the *uSvc* flag requires that a device be specified. The *fCreate* parameter should be set to *TRUE* if you want to create the key being opened because it currently doesn't exist. If this parameter is set to *FALSE*, *CeSvcOpen* fails if the key doesn't already exist in the registry. Finally, the *phSvc* parameter points to a *CESVC* handle that receives the handle of the newly opened key. Although this isn't typed as a handle to a registry key (an *HKEY*), the key can be used in both the CeUtil registry functions and the standard registry functions.

CeSvcOpen returns a standard Win32 error code if the function fails. Otherwise, the key to the opened registry key is placed in the variable pointed to by *phSvc*.

You can open registry keys below those opened by *CeSvcOpen* by calling *CeSvcOpenEx*. This function is prototyped as

```
HRESULT CeSvcOpenEx (HCESVC hSvcRoot, LPTSTR pszPath, BOOL fCreate,
                     PHCESVC phSvc);
```

The parameters for this closely mirror those of *RegOpenKey*. The first parameter is a handle to a previously opened key. Typically, this key would have been opened by *CeSvcOpen*. The second parameter is the string that specifies the name of the subkey to be opened. Notice that since we're running on the PC, this string might not be a Unicode value. The *fCreate* parameter should be set to *TRUE* if you want the key to be created if it doesn't already exist. Finally, the *phSvc* parameter points to a *CESVC* handle that receives the handle to the opened key.

When you have finished with a key, you should close it with a call to this function:

```
HRESULT CeSvcClose (HCESVC hSvc);
```

The only parameter is the handle you want to close.

Enumerating Registered Devices

Of course, the requirement to specify the device ID value in *CeSvcOpen* begs the question of how you determine what devices have already been partnered with the PC. To determine this, you can use the function

```
HRESULT CeSvcEnumProfiles (PHCESVC phSvc, DWORD lProfileIndex,
                           PDWORD plProfile);
```

The first parameter to *CeSvcEnumProfiles* is a pointer to a *CESVC* handle. The handle this parameter points to is uninitiated the first time the function is called. The function returns a handle that must be passed in subsequent calls to *CeSvcEnumProfiles*. The second parameter is an index value. This value should be set to 0 the first time the function is called and incremented for each subsequent call. The final parameter is a pointer to a *DWORD* that receives the device ID for the registered device. You can use this value when you're calling *CeSvcOpen* to open a registry key for that device.

Each time the function is called, it returns *NOERROR* if a new device ID is returned. When all devices have been enumerated, *CeSvcEnumProfiles* returns *ERROR_NO_MORE_ITEMS*. You should be careful to continue calling *CeSvc-EnumProfiles* until the function returns *ERROR_NO_MORE_ITEMS* so that the enumeration process will close the handle parameter pointed to by *phSvc*. If you want to stop enumerating after you've found a particular device ID, you'll need to call *CeSvcClose* to close the *hSvc* handle manually.

The following routine enumerates the Windows CE devices that have been registered on the PC. The program enumerates all the registered Windows CE devices and prints out the name and device type of each of the devices. The program uses the function *CeSvcGetString*, which I'll describe shortly.

```
int PrintCeDevices (void) {
    HCESVC hSvc, hDevKey;
    TCHAR szName[128], szType[64];
    DWORD dwPro;
    int i;

    // Enumerate each registered device.
    i = 0;
    while (CeSvcEnumProfiles (&hSvc, i++, &dwPro) == 0) {

        // Open the registry key for the device enumerated.
        CeSvcOpen (CESVC_DEVICEX, (LPTSTR)dwPro, FALSE, &hDevKey);

        // Get the name and device type strings.
        CeSvcGetString (hDevKey, TEXT ("DisplayName"),
            szName, dim(szName));
        CeSvcGetString (hDevKey, TEXT ("DeviceType"),
            szType, dim(szType));

        // Print to the console.
        printf (TEXT ("Name: %s\t\tType: %s"), szName, szType);

        // Close the key opened by CeSvcOpen.
        CeSvcClose (hDevKey);
    }
    return i-1;          // Return the number of devices found.
}
```

Reading and Writing Values

The remainder of the CeUtil library functions concern reading and writing values in the registry. In fact, you can skip these functions and use the registry functions directly, but the *CeSvcxxx* functions are a bit simpler to use. These functions allow you to read and write three of the data types used in the registry: *DWORD*, string, and binary data. These just happen to be the only data types used in the values under the ActiveSync keys. The functions are all listed here:

```
HRESULT CeSvcGetDword (HCESVC hSvc, LPCTSTR pszValName,
                       LPDWORD pdwVal);
HRESULT CeSvcSetDword (HCESVC hSvc, LPCTSTR pszValName,
                       DWORD dwVal);
HRESULT CeSvcGetString (HCESVC hSvc, LPCTSTR pszValName,
                        LPTSTR pszVal, DWORD cbVal);
HRESULT CeSvcSetString (HCESVC hSvc, LPCTSTR pszValName,
                        LPCTSTR pszVal);
HRESULT CeSvcGetBinary (HCESVC hSvc, LPCTSTR pszValName,
                        LPBYTE pszVal, LPDWORD pcbVal);
HRESULT CeSvcSetBinary (HCESVC hSvc, LPCTSTR pszValName,
                        LPBYTE pszVal, DWORD cbVal);
```

The parameters for these functions are fairly self-explanatory. The first parameter is the handle to an open key. The second parameter is the name of the value being read or written. The third parameter specifies the data or a pointer to where the data will be written. The fourth parameter on some of the functions specifies the size of the buffer for the data being read or, in the case of *CeSvcSetBinary*, the length of the data being written.

One final function in the CeUtil library is

```
HRESULT CeSvcDeleteVal (HCESVC hSvc, LPCTSTR pszValName);
```

This function, as you might expect, lets you delete a value from the registry. The parameters are the handle to an open key and the name of the value to be deleted.

The CeUtil library doesn't provide any function that you couldn't do yourself with a bit of work and the standard registry functions. However, using these functions frees you from having to depend on hard-coded registry key names that could change in the future. I strongly advise using these functions whenever possible when you're accessing registry entries that deal with ActiveSync.

Connection Notification

ActiveSync gives you two ways of notifying PC-based applications when a connection is made with a Windows CE device. The first method is to simply launch all the applications listed under a given registry key. When the connection is broken, all applications listed under another key are launched. This method has the advantage of simplicity at the cost of having the application not know why it was launched.

The second method of notification is a COM-interface method. This notification method involves two interfaces: *IDccMan*, provided by RAPI.dll, and *IDccManSink*, which must be implemented by the application that wants to be notified. This method has the advantage of providing much more information to the application as to what is actually happening at the cost of having to implement a COM-style interface.

Registry Method

To have your PC application launched when a connection is made to a Windows CE device, simply add a value to the PC registry under the following key:

```
[HKEY_LOCAL_MACHINE]
\Software\Microsoft\Windows CE Services\AutoStartOnConnect
```

I'll show you shortly how to access this key using *CeSvcOpen* so that the precise name of the key can be abstracted. The name of the value under *AutoStartOnConnect* can be anything, but it must be something unique. The best way to ensure this is to include your company name and product name plus its version in the value name. The actual data for the value should be a string that contains the fully specified path for the application you want to launch. The string can only be the filename; appending a command line string causes an error when the program is launched. For example, to launch a myapp program that's loaded in the directory *c:\windowsce\tools\syncstuff*, the value and data might be

```
MyCorpThisApp  c:\windowsce\tools\syncstuff\myapp.exe
```

To have a command line passed to your application, you can have the entry in the registry point to a shortcut that will launch your application. The entry in the registry can't pass a command line, but shortcuts don't have that limitation.

You can have an application launched when the connection is broken between the PC and the Windows CE device by placing a value under the following key:

```
[HKEY_LOCAL_MACHINE]
\Software\Microsoft\Windows CE Services\AutoStartOnDisconnect
```

The format for the value name and the data is the same as the format used in the *AutoStartOnConnect* key.

A routine to set these values is simple to write. The example routine below uses the *CeSvcOpen* and *CeSvcSetString* functions to write the name of the module to the registry. Remember that since this routine runs on a PC, and therefore perhaps under Windows XP, you'll need administrator access for this routine to have write access to the registry.

```
//
// RegStartOnConnect - Have module started when connect occurs.
//
LPARAM RegStartOnConnect (HINSTANCE hInst) {
    TCHAR szName[MAX_PATH];
    HCESVC hSvc;
    HRESULT rc;

    // Get the name of the module.
    GetModuleFileName (hInst, szName, dim(szName));

    // Open the AutoStartOnConnect key.
    rc = CeSvcOpen (CESVC_ROOT_MACHINE, "AutoStartOnConnect",
        TRUE, &hSvc);
    if (rc == NOERROR) {
        // Write the module name into the registry.
        CeSvcSetString (hSvc, TEXT ("MyCompanyMyApp"), szName);
        CeSvcClose (hSvc);
    }
    return rc;
}
```

The preceding routine doesn't have to know the absolute location of the ActiveSync keys in the registry, only that the AutoStart key is under *CESVC_ROOT_MACHINE*. You can modify this routine to have your application started when a connection is broken by substituting *AutoStartOnConnect* with *AutoStartOnDisconnect* in the call to *CeSvcOpen*.

COM Method

As I mentioned before, the COM method of connection notification is implemented using two COM interfaces—*IDccMan* and *IDccManSink*. The system implements *IDccMan*, while you are responsible for implementing *IDccManSink*. The *IDccMan* interface gives you a set of methods that allow you to control the link between the PC and the Windows CE device. Unfortunately, most of the methods in *IDccMan* aren't implemented. The *IDccManSink* interface is a series of methods that are called by the connection manager to notify you that a connection event has occurred. Implementing each of the methods in *IDccManSink* is trivial because you don't need to take any action to acknowledge the notification.

The process of connection notification is simple. You request an *IDccMan* interface. You call a method in *IDccMan* to pass a pointer to your *IDccManSink* interface. ActiveSync calls the methods in *IDccManSink* to notify you of events as they occur. In this section, I'll talk about the unique methods in *IDccManSink* and *IDccMan*, but I'll skip over the *IUnknown* methods that are part of every COM interface.[1]

The *IDccMan* Interface

To gain access to the *IDccMan* interface, you need to call the COM library function *CoInitialize* to initialize the COM library. Then you make a call to *CoCreateInstance* to retrieve a pointer to the *IDccMan* interface. Once you have this interface pointer, you call the method *IDccMan::Advise* to notify the connection manager that you want to be notified about connection events. This method is prototyped as

```
HRESULT IDccMan::Advise (IDccManSink *pDccSink,
                         DWORD *pdwContext);
```

The first parameter is a pointer to an *IDccManSink* interface that you must have previously created. I'll talk about *IDccManSink* shortly. The second parameter is a pointer to a *DWORD* that receives a context value that you pass to another *IDccMan* method when you request that you no longer be advised of events.

You can display the communications configuration dialog of ActiveSync by calling this method:

```
HRESULT IDccMan::ShowCommSettings (void);
```

This method has no parameters; it simply displays the communications dialog box. The user is responsible for making any changes to the configuration and for dismissing the dialog box.

When you no longer need connection notifications, you call the *Unadvise* method, prototyped as

```
HRESULT IDccMan::Unadvise (DWORD dwContext);
```

The only parameter is the context value that was returned by the *Advise* method. After you have called *Unadvise*, you no longer need to maintain the *IDccManSink* interface.

The *IDccManSink* Interface

You are responsible for creating and maintaining the *IDccManSink* interface for as long as you want notifications from the connection manager. The interface methods are simple to implement—you simply provide a set of methods that

---

1. Many books have been written about COM, but only one, *Mr. Bunny's Guide to ActiveX*, captures the essence of COM. Check it out if you get the opportunity.

are called by the connection manager when a set of events occurs. Following are the prototypes for the methods of *IDccManSink*:

```
HRESULT IDccManSink::OnLogListen (void);

HRESULT IDccManSink::OnLogAnswered (void);

HRESULT IDccManSink::OnLogIpAddr (DWORD dwIpAddr);

HRESULT IDccManSink::OnLogActive (void);

HRESULT IDccManSink::OnLogTerminated (void);

HRESULT IDccManSink::OnLogInactive (void);

HRESULT IDccManSink::OnLogDisconnection (void);

HRESULT IDccManSink::OnLogError (void);
```

Although the documentation describes a step-by-step notification by the connection manager, calling each of the methods of *IDccManSink* as the events occur, I've found that only a few of the methods are actually called with any consistency.

When you call *CoCreateInstance* to get a pointer to the *IDccManSink* interface, the connection manager is loaded into memory. When you call *Advise*, the connection manager responds with a call to *OnLogListen*, indicating that the connection manager is listening for a connection. When a connection is established, the connection manager calls *OnLogIpAddr* to notify you of the IP address of the connected device. *OnLogIpAddr* is the only method in *IDcc-ManSink* that has a parameter. This parameter is the IP address of the device being connected. This address is handy if you want to establish a socket connection to the device, bypassing the extensive support of the connection manager and RAPI. This IP address can change between different devices and even when connecting the same device if one connection is made using the serial link and a later connection is made across a LAN. The connection manager then calls *OnLogActive* to indicate that the connection between the PC and the device is up and fully operational.

When the connection between the PC and the Windows CE device is dropped, the connection manager calls the *OnLogDisconnection* method. This disconnection notification can take up to a few seconds before it's sent after the connection has actually been dropped. The connection manager then calls the *OnLogListen* method to indicate that it is in the listen state, ready to initiate another connection.

Some of the other methods are called under Windows Me. Those methods simply refine the state of the connection even further. Since your application has to operate as well under Windows XP as it does under Windows Me, you'll need to be able to operate properly using only the notifications I've just described.

The CnctNote Example Program

The CnctNote program is a simple dialog box–based application that uses the COM-based method for monitoring the PC–to–Windows CE device connection state. The example doesn't act on the notifications—it simply displays them in a list box. The CnctNote window is shown in Figure 15-3.

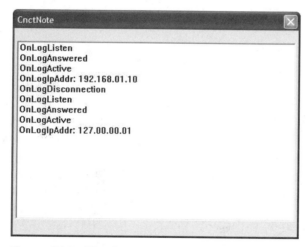

Figure 15-3   The CnctNote window shows two consecutive connections from different devices.

The source code for CnctNote is shown in Listing 15-5.

```
CnctNote.rc
//=====================================================================
// Resource file
//
// Written for the book Programming Windows CE
// Copyright (C) 2003 Douglas Boling
//=====================================================================
#include "windows.h"
#include "CnctNote.h"                          // Program-specific stuff
```

Listing 15-5   CnctNote source code

```
//-----------------------------------------------------------------------
// Icons and bitmaps
//
ID_ICON ICON   "CnctNote.ico"                  // Program icon

//-----------------------------------------------------------------------
CnctNote DIALOG discardable 10, 10, 220, 160
STYLE  WS_OVERLAPPED | WS_VISIBLE | WS_CAPTION | WS_SYSMENU |
       DS_CENTER | DS_MODALFRAME
CAPTION "CnctNote"
CLASS "CnctNote"
BEGIN
    LISTBOX                 IDC_RPTLIST,   2,  10, 216, 140,
                            WS_TABSTOP | WS_VSCROLL

END
```

CnctNote.h

```
//=======================================================================
// Header file
//
// Written for the book Programming Windows CE
// Copyright (C) 2003 Douglas Boling
//=======================================================================
// Returns number of elements
#define dim(x) (sizeof(x) / sizeof(x[0]))
//-----------------------------------------------------------------------
// Generic defines and data types
//
struct decodeUINT {                             // Structure associates
    UINT Code;                                  // messages
                                                // with a function.
    LRESULT (*Fxn)(HWND, UINT, WPARAM, LPARAM);
};
struct decodeCMD {                              // Structure associates
    UINT Code;                                  // menu IDs with a
    LRESULT (*Fxn)(HWND, WORD, HWND, WORD);     // function.
};

//-----------------------------------------------------------------------
// Generic defines used by application
#define  ID_ICON            1
#define  IDC_RPTLIST        10                  // Control IDs
//-----------------------------------------------------------------------
// Function prototypes
//
```

(continued)

Listing 15-5 *(continued)*

```
HWND InitInstance (HINSTANCE, LPSTR, int);
int TermInstance (HINSTANCE, int);
void Add2List (HWND hWnd, LPTSTR lpszFormat, ...);

// Window procedures
LRESULT CALLBACK MainWndProc (HWND, UINT, WPARAM, LPARAM);


//*********************************************************************
// MyDccSink
//
class MyDccSink : public IDccManSink {
public:
    MyDccSink (HWND hWnd, IDccMan *pDccMan);
    ~MyDccSink ();

    // *** IUnknown methods ***
    STDMETHODIMP QueryInterface (THIS_ REFIID riid, LPVOID * ppvObj);
    // Note: No reference counting is actually maintained on this object.
    STDMETHODIMP_(ULONG) AddRef (THIS);
    STDMETHODIMP_(ULONG) Release (THIS);

    // These methods correspond to GW_LOG messages generated by the Win95
    // DccMan application. (On NT/XP, the GW_LOG messages are simulated.)
    STDMETHODIMP OnLogIpAddr (THIS_ DWORD dwIpAddr);
    STDMETHODIMP OnLogTerminated (THIS);
    STDMETHODIMP OnLogActive (THIS);
    STDMETHODIMP OnLogInactive (THIS);
    STDMETHODIMP OnLogAnswered (THIS);
    STDMETHODIMP OnLogListen (THIS);
    STDMETHODIMP OnLogDisconnection (THIS);
    STDMETHODIMP OnLogError (THIS);

private:
    long m_lRef;
    HWND hWnd;
    IDccMan *m_pDccMan;
};
```

CnctNote.cpp

```
//======================================================================
// CnctNote - A simple application for Windows CE
//
// Written for the book Programming Windows CE
// Copyright (C) 2003 Douglas Boling
//======================================================================
```

```
#include <windows.h>                        // For all that Windows stuff
#include <stdio.h>
#include <initguid.h>
#include <dccole.h>
#include "CnctNote.h"                       // Program-specific stuff
//---------------------------------------------------------------------
// Global data
//
const TCHAR szAppName[] = TEXT ("CnctNote");
HINSTANCE hInst;                            // Program instance handle
BOOL fFirst = TRUE;


IDccMan *pDccMan;
MyDccSink *pMySink;                          // Notification interface
DWORD g_Context;                            // Context variable


//=====================================================================
// Program entry point
//
int WINAPI WinMain (HINSTANCE hInstance, HINSTANCE hPrevInstance,
                    LPSTR lpCmdLine, int nCmdShow) {
    MSG msg;
    HWND hwndMain;

    // Initialize application.
    hwndMain = InitInstance (hInstance, lpCmdLine, nCmdShow);
    if (hwndMain == 0)
        return TermInstance (hInstance, 0x10);

    // Application message loop
    while (GetMessage (&msg, NULL, 0, 0)) {
        if ((hwndMain == 0) || !IsDialogMessage (hwndMain, &msg)) {
            TranslateMessage (&msg);
            DispatchMessage (&msg);
        }
    }
    // Instance cleanup
    return TermInstance (hInstance, msg.wParam);
}
//---------------------------------------------------------------------
// InitInstance - Instance initialization
//
HWND InitInstance (HINSTANCE hInstance, LPSTR lpCmdLine, int nCmdShow){
    WNDCLASS wc;
    HWND hWnd;
    HRESULT hr;
```

(continued)

Listing 15-5 *(continued)*

```
    // Save program instance handle in global variable.
    hInst = hInstance;

    // Initialize COM.
    hr = CoInitialize(NULL);
    if (FAILED(hr)) {
        MessageBox (NULL, "CoInitialize failed.", szAppName, MB_OK);
        return 0;
    }

    // Register application main window class.
    wc.style = 0;                                 // Window style
    wc.lpfnWndProc = MainWndProc;                 // Callback function
    wc.cbClsExtra = 0;                            // Extra class data
    wc.cbWndExtra = DLGWINDOWEXTRA;               // Extra window data
    wc.hInstance = hInstance;                     // Owner handle
    wc.hIcon = NULL,                              // Application icon
    wc.hCursor = NULL;                            // Default cursor
    wc.hbrBackground = (HBRUSH) (COLOR_BTNFACE + 1);
    wc.lpszMenuName =  NULL;                      // Menu name
    wc.lpszClassName = szAppName;                 // Window class name

    if (RegisterClass (&wc) == 0) return 0;

    // Create main window.
    hWnd = CreateDialog (hInst, szAppName, NULL, NULL);

    // Return fail code if window not created.
    if (!IsWindow (hWnd)) return 0;
    // Standard show and update calls
    ShowWindow (hWnd, nCmdShow);
    UpdateWindow (hWnd);
    return hWnd;
}
//-----------------------------------------------------------------------
// TermInstance - Program cleanup
//
int TermInstance (HINSTANCE hInstance, int nDefRC) {

    // Release COM.
    CoUninitialize();

    return nDefRC;
}
```

```
//=====================================================================
// MainWndProc - Callback function for application window
//
LRESULT CALLBACK MainWndProc (HWND hWnd, UINT wMsg, WPARAM wParam,
                             LPARAM lParam) {

    switch (wMsg) {

    case WM_SIZE:
        if (fFirst) {
            HRESULT hr;
            IDccManSink *pdms;
            fFirst = FALSE;

            // Get a pointer to the IDccMan COM interface.
            hr = CoCreateInstance (CLSID_DccMan, NULL, CLSCTX_SERVER,
                                   IID_IDccMan, (LPVOID*)&pDccMan);
            if (FAILED(hr)) {
                Add2List (hWnd, "CoCreateInstance failed");
                break;
            }

            // Create new notification object.
            pMySink = new MyDccSink(hWnd, pDccMan);
            pMySink->QueryInterface (IID_IDccManSink, (void **)&pdms);
            // Ask to be advised of connect state changes.
            pDccMan->Advise (pdms, &g_Context);
        }
        break;
    case WM_COMMAND:

        switch (LOWORD (wParam)) {
        case IDOK:
        case IDCANCEL:
            SendMessage (hWnd, WM_CLOSE, 0, 0);
            break;
        }
        break;
    case WM_DESTROY:
        // Stop receiving notifications.
        pDccMan->Unadvise (g_Context);

        // Release the DccMan object.
        pDccMan->Release();
```

(continued)

Listing 15-5   *(continued)*

```
            PostQuitMessage (0);
            break;
    }
    return DefWindowProc (hWnd, wMsg, wParam, lParam);
}
//---------------------------------------------------------------------
// Add2List - Add string to the report list box.
//
void Add2List (HWND hWnd, LPTSTR lpszFormat, ...) {
    int nBuf, i;
    TCHAR szBuffer[512];

    va_list args;
    va_start(args, lpszFormat);

    nBuf = vsprintf(szBuffer, lpszFormat, args);

    i = SendDlgItemMessage (hWnd, IDC_RPTLIST, LB_ADDSTRING, 0,
                            (LPARAM)(LPCTSTR)szBuffer);
    if (i != LB_ERR)
        SendDlgItemMessage (hWnd, IDC_RPTLIST, LB_SETTOPINDEX, i,
                            (LPARAM)(LPCTSTR)szBuffer);
    va_end(args);
}
//*********************************************************************
// Constructor
MyDccSink::MyDccSink (HWND hwndMain, IDccMan *pDccMan) {

    m_pDccMan = pDccMan;
    hWnd = hwndMain;
    m_pDccMan->AddRef();
    return;
}
//---------------------------------------------------------------------
// Destructor
MyDccSink::~MyDccSink () {

    m_pDccMan->Release();
    return;
}
//---------------------------------------------------------------------
// AddRef - Increment object ref count.
STDMETHODIMP_(ULONG) MyDccSink::AddRef (THIS) {
```

```
        return (ULONG)InterlockedIncrement (&m_lRef);
}
//------------------------------------------------------------------
// Release - Decrement object ref count.
STDMETHODIMP_(ULONG) MyDccSink::Release (THIS) {
    ULONG cnt;

    cnt = (ULONG)InterlockedDecrement (&m_lRef);
    if (cnt == 0) {
        delete this;
        return 0;
    }
    return cnt;
}
//------------------------------------------------------------------
// QueryInterface - Return a pointer to interface.
STDMETHODIMP MyDccSink::QueryInterface (REFIID riid, LPVOID * ppvObj) {

    if (IID_IUnknown==riid || IID_IDccManSink==riid)
        *ppvObj = (IDccManSink*)this;
    else {
        *ppvObj = NULL;
        return E_NOINTERFACE;
    }
    AddRef();
    return NO_ERROR;
}
//------------------------------------------------------------------
//
STDMETHODIMP MyDccSink::OnLogIpAddr (DWORD dwIpAddr) {
    Add2List (hWnd, TEXT ("OnLogIpAddr: %02d.%02d.%02d.%02d"),
            (dwIpAddr & 0x000000ff),    (dwIpAddr & 0x0000ff00)>>8,
            (dwIpAddr & 0x00ff0000)>>16, dwIpAddr>>24);
    return NO_ERROR;
}
//------------------------------------------------------------------
//
STDMETHODIMP MyDccSink::OnLogTerminated () {
    Add2List (hWnd, TEXT ("OnLogTerminated "));
    return NO_ERROR;
}
//------------------------------------------------------------------
//
STDMETHODIMP MyDccSink::OnLogActive () {
    Add2List (hWnd, TEXT ("OnLogActive "));
```

(continued)

Listing 15-5   *(continued)*

```
        return NO_ERROR;
    }
    //-----------------------------------------------------------------------
    //
    STDMETHODIMP MyDccSink::OnLogInactive () {
        Add2List (hWnd, TEXT ("OnLogInactive "));
        return NO_ERROR;
    }
    //-----------------------------------------------------------------------
    //
    STDMETHODIMP MyDccSink::OnLogAnswered () {
        Add2List (hWnd, TEXT ("OnLogAnswered"));
        return NO_ERROR;
    }
    //-----------------------------------------------------------------------
    //
    STDMETHODIMP MyDccSink::OnLogListen () {
        Add2List (hWnd, TEXT ("OnLogListen "));
        return NO_ERROR;
    }
    //-----------------------------------------------------------------------
    //
    STDMETHODIMP MyDccSink::OnLogDisconnection () {
        Add2List (hWnd, TEXT ("OnLogDisconnection "));
        return NO_ERROR;
    }
    //-----------------------------------------------------------------------
    //
    STDMETHODIMP MyDccSink::OnLogError () {
        Add2List (hWnd, TEXT ("OnLogError "));
        return NO_ERROR;
    }
```

The meat of CnctNote is in the *WM_SIZE* handler of the window procedure. Here, *CoCreateInstance* is called to get a pointer to the *IDccMan* interface. If this is successful, an object is created that implements an *IDccManSink* interface. The *Advise* method is then called to register the *IDccManSink* object. The sole job of the methods in *IDccManSink* is to report when they're called by posting a message in the list box, which is the only control on the dialog box.

Connection Detection on the Windows CE Side

As you know, this chapter describes the PC-side applications that work with remote Windows CE devices. However, while reading the previous section, you probably wondered how a Windows CE application can know when a connection is made between the Windows CE device and a PC. Windows CE supports connection notification using the Notification API that I discussed in Chapter 11.

Direct Socket Connections

There are times where the communication requirements of your application go beyond the services that RAPI provides. The link that ActiveSync and RAPI use is built on TCP/IP. So if you want, it's fairly straightforward to establish a link between the PC and the device with sockets.

To link two devices with sockets, you need the IP address of both devices. I just covered how the *IDccMan* interface can provide the IP address of the remote Windows CE device. This IP address is accurate if the ActiveSync connection is made over a network. However, if the connection is made via a serial or infrared link, the IP address reported is 127.0.0.1.

On the device side, if the PC is connected via a serial or infrared link, the connected PC's IP address can be found by using *gethostbyname*, passing the name "ppp_peer". An example of this is shown here:

```
struct hostent *phe;
SOCKADDR_IN pc_sin;

phe = gethostbyname ("ppp_peer");
if (phe) {
    pc_sin.sin_addr.S_un.S_addr = *(DWORD *)phe->h_addr;
    printf "PC addr: %s", inet_ntoa (pc_sin.sin_addr));
}
```

If ActiveSync is connected over an Ethernet link, the *gethostbyname* function should be used with the machine name of the PC. You can find the name of the partner PC in the registry under the key HKEY_LOCAL_MACHINE\ SOFTWARE\Microsoft\Windows CE Services\Partners. Because Windows CE systems can have two partners, you first have to check which partner is active. Do this by reading the *PCur* value under the key. Then look under the *P1* or *P2* subkey and read the string value *PName*. Remember to change the string from a Unicode string to a character string before calling *gethostbyname*.

Now I come to the end of my explanation of the PC-side ActiveSync. For the remainder of the book, I'll return to the Windows CE side of things. I'll start with a look at the different shells that Windows CE supports. The Explorer shell looks on the surface like the old Windows 95 shell, although the programming interface is much simpler. The Pocket PC shell, on the other hand, is completely unique.

Part IV

Device Programming

16

The Explorer Shell

One of the unique aspects of Windows CE is that different Windows CE platforms have different shells. The default shell for the embedded versions of Windows CE is derived from the old Handheld PC shell. The look and feel of the Explorer shell is significantly different from the shell for the Pocket PC. Despite differences, the parts of the shells that are the same (and there are plenty of common shell components) share the underlying API.

The Explorer shell is derived from the Windows 95 and 98 shells. To the user, the look is almost pure Windows 95. That is, of course, by design. The folks at Microsoft figured that having the Windows CE shell resemble the Windows 95 shell would flatten the user's learning curve and enhance the acceptability of Windows CE devices.

On the surface, the shell used by the Pocket PC has nothing in common with the Windows 95 shell. Gone are both the Explorer and the familiar desktop icons. In place of the Explorer is the Today screen, which displays data from applications directly on the desktop. But while the Explorer is gone, some of the underlying plumbing remains. Both systems have a Start button. The Start button on the Pocket PC is located in the upper left corner of the Pocket PC screen. Both systems also use special directories and the shell *namespace*, which I'll talk about shortly.

Although the Explorer shell resembles the Windows 95 shell, it's not as flexible. Most of the powerful interfaces available under Windows 95, such as the ability to drag and drop objects between programs, are either only partially implemented or not implemented at all. The goal of the programmers of the Explorer shell seemed to be to implement as few of the native COM interfaces as possible while still retaining the ability to contain the Internet viewing capabilities of an embedded Internet Explorer in the shell. That said, the Explorer shell does use some COM interfaces. In fact, the newest version of the Explorer shell has exposed the COM interfaces to support desktop style name space extensions that allow the Explorer to navigate into virtual folders that are exposed via COM interfaces.

Starting with Windows CE .NET 4.2, the operating system now exposes most of the Pocket PC shell APIs such as *SHInitDialog* and the like that assist Pocket PC applications in providing the Pocket PC look and feel. The implementation of some of these functions is up to the OEM that implements them, but at least it is now possible for a non–Pocket PC system to run many of not most Pocket PC applications. This chapter covers the concept of the shell namespace and the shell's use of special directories. This chapter also explains how to work with the taskbar as well as how to create shortcuts. And although the console isn't strictly part of the Explorer shell, this chapter covers it as well. The Windows CE console isn't on all Windows CE systems. For example, the Pocket PC doesn't include console support. Although Windows CE doesn't support the full character mode API found in Windows XP, you can still write fairly complete console applications.

Working with the Shell

Because the Explorer shell is derived from the Windows 95 shell, I must cover some system definitions first introduced with Windows 95. In general, while the concepts remain the same, the implementation is completely different under the covers.

The Shell Namespace

From Windows 95 on, the Windows shell has used the concept of a shell namespace. The Explorer shell and the Pocket PC shell also use the namespace concept to track the objects in the shell. Simply put, the shell namespace is the entire collection of the operating system's objects, files, directories, printers, control panel applets, and so forth. The idea is that by addressing files the same way as control panel applets, the shell makes it easy to deal with the diverse collection of objects.

A *folder* is simply a collection of objects. A *directory* is a collection of files on a disk. A folder generalizes and extends the directory concept, in that a folder doesn't merely contain files, but can include other objects such as control panel objects, printers, or remote connection links. Each object in a folder is called an *item*. Items are identified by an *item ID*.

The item ID is a data structure that uniquely identifies the item in the folder. Since folders also have identifiers, an individual item can be uniquely defined by means of a list of item IDs that identify the item, its folder, and the parent folders of the folder. Think of this list of item identifiers as a completely specified pathname of a file. A system might have many files named *foobar*, but only one in a specific directory. This list of item IDs is appropriately called an *ID list*. A pointer to such a list is a *pointer to an ID list*, frequently abbreviated as *pidl*, which is generally and rather unfortunately pronounced *piddle*. Shell functions usually reference items in the shells by their *pidls*. There is, of course, a translation function that converts a *pidl* to a filename.

Special Folders

The Windows CE shell, like the shells for the desktop versions of Windows, has a set of folders that are treated differently from normal directories in the file system. An example of this is the recycle bin, which is simply a hidden directory to which the shell moves files and directories when the user deletes them. Another example is the Programs folder, which contains a set of shortcuts that are then displayed on the Start menu.

The list of special folders changes with each shell. The Windows 95/98/Me shells and the Windows NT/2000/XP shells have a different set of special folders from those of the Windows CE shells. The Pocket PC, Smartphone, and Explorer shells each implements its own subset of special folders. Fortunately, the function to return the path of a specific special folder is the same on all these systems. That function, *SHGetSpecialFolderPath*, is prototyped as

```
BOOL SHGetSpecialFolderPath (HWND hwndOwner, LPTSTR lpszPath,
                             int nFolder, BOOL fCreate);
```

The *hwndOwner* parameter is the handle to a window that will be the owner of any dialog box that the function creates. The second parameter, *lpszPath*, points to a buffer at least *MAX_PATH* characters, not bytes, in length, which will receive the returned path. The *nFolder* parameter is set to the constant that indicates what folder you need. The *fCreate* parameter is a Boolean that you can set to *TRUE* if you want the system to create the directory if one currently doesn't exist.

The *nFolder* parameter can be one of many constants that are common across the Windows operating systems. Not all the values are supported on all Windows CE platforms, but the following short list includes some constants that most platforms support.

- **CSIDL_BITBUCKET**   The location of the recycle bin.

- **CSIDL_DESKTOP**   The folder that stores the objects that appear on the desktop. Note that the use of this constant is different than it was under Windows 95.

- **_CSIDL_FONTS_** The folder that contains the system fonts.

- **_CSIDL_DRIVES_** The root of the file system.

- **_CSIDL_PROGRAMS_** The folder that contains the items shown in the Programs submenu of the Start menu.

- **_CSIDL_PERSONAL_** The default folder in which to save documents.

- **_CSIDL_FAVORITES_** The folder that contains shortcuts to favorite items.

- **_CSIDL_STARTUP_** The folder that contains programs or shortcuts to programs that will be launched when the system is restarted.

- **_CSIDL_RECENT_** The folder that contains the list of recently used documents.

The *SHGetSpecialFolderPath* function was first supported in Windows CE 3.0. For earlier versions of Windows CE, you must use two other functions, *SHGetSpecialFolderLocation* and *SHGetPathFromIDList*. The function *SHGetSpecialFolderLocation* takes the constants in the preceding list and returns a *pidl*. Then you need to call *SHGetPathFromIDList* to translate the *pidl* to a path. The two functions are prototyped as

```
HRESULT SHGetSpecialFolderLocation (HWND hwndOwner, int nFolder,
                                    LPITEMIDLIST *ppidl);
```

and

```
BOOL WINAPI SHGetPathFromIDList (LPCITEMIDLIST pidl, LPTSTR pszPath);
```

If you needed only to call *SHGetSpecialFolderLocation* and follow that by calling *SHGetPathFromIDList* to get the path, life would be simple. Unfortunately, the process isn't that easy. The *pidl* that's returned by *SHGetSpecialFolderLocation* points to a buffer that has been allocated by the shell. You need to call the shell back to free this buffer after you're finished with the ID list. You free this buffer using an *IMalloc* interface provided by the shell.

The *IMalloc* interface contains methods that allow an application to allocate, free, and otherwise manipulate memory in the local heap of the *IMalloc* provider. In the case of the shell, a pointer to its *IMalloc* interface can be acquired with a call to *SHGetMalloc*. The function is prototyped as

```
HRESULT SHGetMalloc (LPMALLOC *ppMalloc);
```

Once you have a pointer to the interface, you can call the *Free* method to free any ID lists returned by *ShGetSpecialFolderLocation*.

On some early Windows CE systems, *SHGetSpecialFolderLocation* returns a constant, typed as a *pidl*, which can then be passed to *SHGetPathFromIDList* to get a directory name. Those systems don't implement *IMalloc*. To support those early machines, you can use a routine like the following, which attempts to get the *IMalloc* interface. However, if this call fails, the routine simply proceeds to call *SHGetSpecialFolderLocation* and *SHGetPathFromIDList* to query the directory.

```
INT MyGetSpecialDirectory (HWND hWnd, INT nFolderID,
                           LPTSTR lpDir) {
    int rc;
    LPITEMIDLIST pidl;
    BOOL fUseIMalloc = TRUE;
    LPMALLOC lpMalloc = NULL;

    // Attempt to get the Shell Malloc interface.
    rc = SHGetMalloc (&lpMalloc);
    if (rc == E_NOTIMPL)
        fUseIMalloc = FALSE;
    else if (rc != NOERROR)
        return rc;

    rc = SHGetSpecialFolderLocation (hWnd, nFolderID, &pidl);
    if (rc == NOERROR) {
        // Translate the idlist to a directory name.
        if (SHGetPathFromIDList (pidl, lpDir))
            rc = E_FAIL;
        // Free the idlist.
        if (fUseIMalloc)
            IMalloc_Free(lpMalloc,pidl);
    }

    // Free shell's IMalloc interface.
    if (fUseIMalloc)
        IMalloc_Release(lpMalloc);
    return rc;
}
```

Note that on the Pocket PC, the combination of two functions—*SHGetSpecialFolderLocation* and *SHGetPathFromIDList*—supports a greater number of the *CSIDL_* constants than does the single function *SHGetSpecialFolderPath*. For this reason, and to remain backward-compatible with older systems, I tend to use the combination of the older functions instead of the newer function.

Shortcuts

Shortcuts are small files that, when opened, launch an application or open a document in another folder. The idea behind shortcuts is that you could have an application located in one directory but you might want to be able to launch it from other directories. Since the shell uses the contents of special directories to define what is in the Start menu and on the desktop, placing a shortcut in one of those special directories allows an application to appear in the Start menu or on the desktop.

While the concept of shortcuts was taken from the desktop versions of Windows, the method of creating them was not. Instead of using a COM interface, as is done on the desktop, you create a shortcut in Windows CE using the following function:

```
BOOL SHCreateShortcut (LPTSTR szShortcut, LPTSTR szTarget);
```

The first parameter specifies the name and location of the shortcut. This name should be a fully qualified filename with an extension of LNK. The second parameter is the fully qualified filename of the application you want to start or the file you want to open. The function returns *TRUE* if successful.

Another function that will create a shortcut is

```
DWORD SHCreateShortcutEx (LPTSTR lpszDir, LPTSTR lpszTarget,
                          LPTSTR szShortcut, LPDWORD lpcbShortcut);
```

Like *SHCreateShortcut*, the first two parameters specify the name of the shortcut and the name of the target file. The third parameter is a buffer that will receive the name of the shortcut that was created. The fourth parameter first contains the number of characters that can fit in *szShortcut* and is filled by the function with the number of characters copied into *szShortcut*. The resulting name of the shortcut is a derivation of the string pointed to by *lpszDir*. For example, if *lpszDir* pointed to \temp\joe.lnk, the resulting shortcut would be \temp\shortcut to joe.lnk as long as a file with that name didn't already exist. If a file with that name did exist, the resulting name would be \temp\shortcut to joe (2).lnk. The advantage of *SHCreateShortcutEx* is the function's guarantee of a unique file name for the resulting shortcut file.

You can determine the contents of a shortcut by calling this function:

```
BOOL SHGetShortcutTarget (LPTSTR szShortcut, LPTSTR szTarget,
                          int cbMax);
```

The first parameter is the filename of the shortcut. The remaining two parameters are the buffer that receives the target filename of the shortcut and the size of that buffer.

Configuring the Start Menu

Shortcuts come into their own when you're customizing the Start menu. When the Start button is clicked, the taskbar looks in its special folder and creates a menu item for each item in the folder. Subfolders contained in the special folder become submenus on the Start menu.

The Start menu of the Explorer shell is limited in that you can't customize the Start menu itself. You can, however, modify the Programs submenu and the submenus it contains. To add an item to the Programs submenu of the Explorer Start menu, you place a shortcut in the folder returned after you called *SHGetSpecialFolderPath* with the folder constant *CSIDL_PROGRAMS*. For example, look at the following short code fragment, which lists the Calc program in the Programs submenu of the Start directory on a device.

```
INT rc;
TCHAR szDir[MAX_PATH];

rc = SHGetSpecialFolderPath (hWnd, szDir, CSIDL_PROGRAMS, FALSE);
if (rc == NOERROR) {
    lstrcat (szDir, TEXT ("\\Calc.lnk"));
    SHCreateShortcut (szDir, TEXT ("\\windows\\calc.exe"));
}
```

This fragment uses the routine *SHGetSpecialFolderPath* to return the folder used by the Programs submenu. Once that's found, all that is required is to append the necessary LNK extension to the name of the link and call *SHCreate-Shortcut* specifying the location of Calc.exe.

The Start menu of the Pocket PC is more flexible than the Explorer shell because you can add items directly to the Start menu itself. To accomplish this, add shortcuts to the folder returned with *SHGetSpecialFolderLocation* and the constant *CSIDL_STARTMENU*.

Although it is possible to download executables directly to the Start menu directories, a better idea is to create a directory under the \Programs folder to store your application and place a shortcut pointing to your application in the Start menu. This solution allows your application to keep any necessary DLLs and additional files isolated in their own directory instead of dumping them in the Start menu directory.

Recent Documents List

A feature of the Start menu since it was introduced in Windows 95 is the Documents submenu. This menu lists the last 10 documents that were opened by applications in the system. This list is a convenient place in which users can reopen recently used files. The system doesn't keep track of the last-opened documents. Instead, an application must tell Windows that it has opened a document. Windows then prunes the least recently opened document on the menu and adds the new one.

Under Windows CE, the function that an application calls to add a document to the recently used list is

```
void SHAddToRecentDocs (UINT uFlags, LPCVOID pv);
```

The first parameter can be set to one of two flags, *SHARD_PATH* or *SHARD_PIDL*. If *uFlags* is set to *SHARD_PATH*, the second parameter points to the fully qualified path of the document file. If *SHARD_PIDL* is specified in *uFlags*, the second parameter points to a pointer to an ID list. If the second parameter is 0, all items in the recently used document menu are deleted.

Launching Applications

Windows CE supports one of the standard Windows shell functions, *ShellExecuteEx*. Although Windows CE doesn't support much of the functionality of *ShellExecuteEx*, the functionality that remains is still quite useful. *ShellExecuteEx* is somewhat simpler to use than *CreateProcess* to create new processes. *ShellExecuteEx* also has the advantage of being able to automatically associate data files with the application that should open them. Furthermore, it opens the Explorer to a specific directory. The function prototype for *ShellExecuteEx* is

```
BOOL WINAPI ShellExecuteEx (LPSHELLEXECUTEINFO lpExecInfo);
```

The only parameter is a pointer to the rather complex *SHELLEXECUTEINFO* structure, defined as

```
typedef struct _SHELLEXECUTEINFO {
    DWORD cbSize;
    ULONG fMask;
    HWND hwnd;
    LPCSTR lpVerb;
    LPCSTR lpFile;
    LPCSTR lpParameters;
    LPCSTR lpDirectory;
    int nShow;
    HINSTANCE hInstApp;

    // Optional members
    LPVOID lpIDList;
    LPCSTR lpClass;
    HKEY hkeyClass;
    DWORD dwHotKey;
    HANDLE hIcon;
    HANDLE hProcess;
} SHELLEXECUTEINFO;
```

The first field is the traditional size field that must be set to the size of the structure. The *fMask* field can contain two flags: *SEE_MASK_FLAG_NO_UI*, which instructs the function not to display an error dialog box if the function fails, and *SEE_MASK_NOCLOSEPROCESS*, which will return the handle to the child process in the *hProcess* field. If you set the latter flag, your application is responsible for closing the returned handle. The *hwnd* field is the handle to a window that owns any error dialog displayed as a result of the function.

The *lpVerb* field points to a string that tells *ShellExecuteEx* what to do. The documented "verbs" are open, print, explore, edit, and properties, but for the current Windows CE Explorer shell, the verb is basically ignored. The default is *open*. The *lpFile* field should point to a string that contains the name of a file—a data file, a directory, or an executable. If *lpFile* points to an application name, the *lpParameters* field can contain the address of a string containing the command line parameters for the application. If *lpFile* points to a document file or a directory, *lpParameters* should be *NULL*.

Of all the remaining fields, only *hInstApp* and *hProcess* are used. All the others are ignored. The *hInstApp* field should be set to the instance handle of the application calling the function. As I mentioned earlier, if you set the *SEE_MASK_NOCLOSEPROCESS* flag in *fMask*, the function returns the handle of the child process. For example, the following code fragment opens a Pocket Word document in the root directory of a Windows CE system:

```
SHELLEXECUTEINFO si;

memset (&si, 0, sizeof (si));
si.cbSize = sizeof (si);
si.fMask = 0;
si.hwnd = hWnd;
si.lpFile = TEXT ("\\doc1.pwd");
si.lpVerb = TEXT ("Open");
rc = ShellExecuteEx (&si);
```

The shell launches the proper application by looking in the registry to associate a data file's extension with an associated application. This process is essentially identical to the method used on the desktop. The shell searches the registry for a subkey under [HKEY_CLASSES_ROOT] that matches the extension of the data file. The default value of that subkey then identifies another subkey that indicates the application to launch.

The Taskbar

The taskbar interface under Windows CE is almost identical to the taskbar interface under the desktop versions of Windows. I've already talked about how you can configure the items in the Start menu. The taskbar also supports *annunciators*, those tiny icons on the far right of the taskbar. The taskbar icons are programmed with methods similar to those used in Windows XP. The only limitation under the Explorer shell or the Pocket PC shell is that they don't support tooltips on the taskbar icons.

Programs can add, change, and delete taskbar icons using this function:

```
BOOL Shell_NotifyIcon (DWORD dwMessage, PNOTIFYICONDATA pnid);
```

The first parameter, *dwMessage*, indicates the task to accomplish by calling the function. This parameter can be one of the following three values:

- ■ *NIM_ADD*   Adds an annunciator to the taskbar

- ■ *NIM_DELETE*   Deletes an annunciator from the taskbar

- ■ *NIM_MODIFY*   Modifies an existing annunciator on the taskbar

The other parameter points to a *NOTIFYICONDATA* structure, which is defined as

```
typedef struct _NOTIFYICONDATA {
    DWORD cbSize;
    HWND hWnd;
    UINT uID;
    UINT uFlags;
    UINT uCallbackMessage;
    HICON hIcon;
    WCHAR szTip[64];
} NOTIFYICONDATA;
```

The first field, *cbSize*, must be filled with the size of the structure before a call is made to *Shell_NotifyIcon*. The *hWnd* field should be set to the window handle that owns the icon. This window receives messages notifying the window that the user has tapped, double-tapped, or moved her pen on the icon. The *uID* field identifies the icon being added, deleted, or modified. This practice allows an application to have more than one icon on the taskbar. The *uFlags* field should contain flags that identify which of the remaining fields in the structure contain valid data.

When you're adding an icon, the *uCallbackMessage* field should be set to a message identifier that can be used by the taskbar when notifying the window of user actions on the icon. This value is usually based on *WM_USER* so that the message value won't conflict with other messages the window receives. The taskbar looks at this field only if *uFlags* contains the *NIF_MESSAGE* flag.

The *hIcon* field should be loaded with the handle to the 16-by-16-pixel icon to be displayed on the taskbar. You should use *LoadImage* to load the icon because *LoadIcon* doesn't return a small format icon. The taskbar looks at this field only if the *NIF_ICON* flag is set in *uFlags*. Finally, the *szTip* field would contain the tool-tip text for the icon on other Windows systems but is ignored by the current Windows CE shells.

Managing a taskbar icon involves handling the notification messages the taskbar sends and acting appropriately. The messages are sent with the message identifier you defined in the call to *Shell_NotifyIcon*. The *wParam* parameter of the message contains the ID value of the taskbar icon that the message references. The *lParam* parameter contains a code indicating the reason for the message. These values are actually the message codes for various mouse events. For example, if the user taps your taskbar icon, the *lParam* value in the notification message will be *WM_LBUTTONDOWN*, followed by another message containing *WM_LBUTTONUP*.

The TBIcons Example Program

The TBIcons program demonstrates adding and deleting taskbar annunciator icons. Figure 16-1 shows the TBIcons window. The buttons at the bottom of the window allow you to add and delete icons from the taskbar. The list box that takes up most of the window displays the callback messages as the taskbar sends them. In the taskbar, you can see two icons that TBIcons has added. The list box contains a list of messages that have been sent by the taskbar back to the TBIcons window.

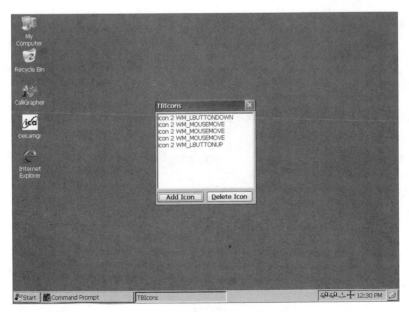

Figure 16-1   The Windows CE desktop with a TBIcons window

The source code for TBIcons is shown in Listing 16-1. The program uses a dialog box as its main window. The routines that add and delete taskbar icons are *DoMainCommandAddIcon* and *DoMainCommandDelIcon*. Both these routines simply fill in a *NOTIFYICONDATA* structure and call *Shell_NotifyIcon*. The routine that handles the notification messages is *DoTaskBarNotifyMain*. This routine is called when the window receives the user-defined message *MYMSG_TASKBARNOTIFY*, which is defined in TBIcons.h as *WM_USER+100*. Remember that dialog boxes use some of the *WM_USER* message constants, so it's a good practice not to use the first hundred values above *WM_USER* to avoid any conflicts.

TBIcons.rc

```
//======================================================================
// Resource file
//
// Written for the book Programming Windows CE
// Copyright (C) 2003 Douglas Boling
//======================================================================
#include <windows.h>
#include "TBIcons.h"                            // Program-specific stuff


//----------------------------------------------------------------------
// Icons and bitmaps
//
ID_ICON ICON    "TBIcons.ico"                   // Program icon
//----------------------------------------------------------------------
TBIcons DIALOG discardable  25, 5, 120, 110
STYLE  WS_OVERLAPPED | WS_VISIBLE | WS_CAPTION | WS_SYSMENU |
        DS_CENTER | DS_MODALFRAME
CAPTION "TBIcons"
BEGIN
    LISTBOX             IDD_OUTPUT,   2,   2, 116,  90,
                        WS_TABSTOP | WS_VSCROLL | LBS_NOINTEGRALHEIGHT
    PUSHBUTTON "&Add Icon", IDD_ADDICON,   2,  95,  55,  12, WS_TABSTOP
    PUSHBUTTON "&Delete Icon",
                        IDD_DELICON,  61,  95,  55,  12, WS_TABSTOP
END
```

TBIcons.h

```
//======================================================================
// Header file
//
// Written for the book Programming Windows CE
// Copyright (C) 2003 Douglas Boling
```

Listing 16-1   TBIcons source code

```
//============================================================================
// Returns number of elements
#define dim(x) (sizeof(x) / sizeof(x[0]))


//----------------------------------------------------------------------------
// Generic defines and data types
//
struct decodeUINT {                              // Structure associates
    UINT Code;                                   // messages
                                                 // with a function.

    BOOL (*Fxn)(HWND, UINT, WPARAM, LPARAM);
};
struct decodeCMD {                               // Structure associates
    UINT Code;                                   // menu IDs with a
    LRESULT (*Fxn)(HWND, WORD, HWND, WORD);      // function.
};
//----------------------------------------------------------------------------
// Generic defines used by application

#define   ID_ICON                 1

#define   IDD_ADDICON            10              // Control IDs
#define   IDD_DELICON            11
#define   IDD_OUTPUT             12

#define MYMSG_TASKBARNOTIFY  (WM_USER + 100)
//----------------------------------------------------------------------------
// Function prototypes
//
void Add2List (HWND hWnd, LPTSTR lpszFormat, ...);

// Window procedures
BOOL CALLBACK MainDlgProc (HWND, UINT, WPARAM, LPARAM);

// Message handlers
BOOL DoInitDlgMain (HWND, UINT, WPARAM, LPARAM);
BOOL DoCommandMain (HWND, UINT, WPARAM, LPARAM);
BOOL DoTaskBarNotifyMain (HWND, UINT, WPARAM, LPARAM);

// Command functions
LPARAM DoMainCommandExit (HWND, WORD, HWND, WORD);
LPARAM DoMainCommandAddIcon (HWND, WORD, HWND, WORD);
LPARAM DoMainCommandDelIcon (HWND, WORD, HWND, WORD);
```

(continued)

Listing 16-1   *(continued)*

TBIcons.cpp

```cpp
//======================================================================
// TBIcons - Taskbar icon demonstration for Windows CE
//
// Written for the book Programming Windows CE
// Copyright (C) 2003 Douglas Boling
//======================================================================
#include <windows.h>                       // For all that Windows stuff
#include "TBIcons.h"                        // Program-specific stuff


//----------------------------------------------------------------------
// Global data
//
const TCHAR szAppName[] = TEXT ("TBIcons");
HINSTANCE hInst;                            // Program instance handle
INT nIconID = 0;                            // ID values for taskbar icons

// Message dispatch table for MainWindowProc
const struct decodeUINT MainMessages[] = {
    WM_INITDIALOG, DoInitDlgMain,
    WM_COMMAND, DoCommandMain,
    MYMSG_TASKBARNOTIFY, DoTaskBarNotifyMain,
};
// Command Message dispatch for MainWindowProc
const struct decodeCMD MainCommandItems[] = {
    IDOK, DoMainCommandExit,
    IDCANCEL, DoMainCommandExit,
    IDD_ADDICON, DoMainCommandAddIcon,
    IDD_DELICON, DoMainCommandDelIcon,
};
//======================================================================
// Program entry point
//
int WINAPI WinMain (HINSTANCE hInstance, HINSTANCE hPrevInstance,
                    LPWSTR lpCmdLine, int nCmdShow) {

#if defined(WIN32_PLATFORM_PSPC)
    // If Pocket PC, allow only one instance of the application.
    HWND hWnd = FindWindow (NULL, TEXT("TBIcons"));
    if (hWnd) {
        SetForegroundWindow ((HWND)(((DWORD)hWnd) | 0x01));
        return -1;
    }
#endif
    hInst = hInstance;
```

```
       // Display dialog box as main window.
    DialogBoxParam (hInstance, szAppName, NULL, MainDlgProc, 0);
    return 0;
}
//======================================================================
// Message handling procedures for main window
//----------------------------------------------------------------------
// MainDlgProc - Callback function for application window
//
BOOL CALLBACK MainDlgProc (HWND hWnd, UINT wMsg, WPARAM wParam,
                           LPARAM lParam) {
    INT i;
    //
    // Search message list to see if we need to handle this
    // message. If in list, call procedure.
    //
    for (i = 0; i < dim(MainMessages); i++) {
        if (wMsg == MainMessages[i].Code)
            return (*MainMessages[i].Fxn)(hWnd, wMsg, wParam, lParam);
    }
    return FALSE;
}
//----------------------------------------------------------------------
// DoInitDlgMain - Process WM_INITDIALOG message for window.
//
BOOL DoInitDlgMain (HWND hWnd, UINT wMsg, WPARAM wParam, LPARAM lParam){
    return 0;
}
//----------------------------------------------------------------------
// DoCommandMain - Process WM_COMMAND message for window.
//
BOOL DoCommandMain (HWND hWnd, UINT wMsg, WPARAM wParam, LPARAM lParam){
    WORD idItem, wNotifyCode;
    HWND hwndCtl;
    INT  i;

    // Parse the parameters.
    idItem = (WORD) LOWORD (wParam);
    wNotifyCode = (WORD) HIWORD (wParam);
    hwndCtl = (HWND) lParam;

    // Call routine to handle control message.
    for (i = 0; i < dim(MainCommandItems); i++) {
        if (idItem == MainCommandItems[i].Code) {
            (*MainCommandItems[i].Fxn)(hWnd, idItem, hwndCtl,
                                       wNotifyCode);
```

(continued)

Listing 16-1   *(continued)*

```
                return TRUE;
            }
        }
    return FALSE;
}
//------------------------------------------------------------------------
// DoTaskBarNotifyMain - Process MYMSG_TASKBARNOTIFY message for window.
//
BOOL DoTaskBarNotifyMain (HWND hWnd, UINT wMsg, WPARAM wParam,
                          LPARAM lParam) {
    TCHAR szText[128];

    SetForegroundWindow (hWnd);
    wsprintf (szText,
              TEXT ("icon %d "), wParam);
    switch (lParam) {
    case WM_MOUSEMOVE:
        lstrcat (szText, TEXT ("WM_MOUSEMOVE"));
        break;
    case WM_LBUTTONDOWN:
        lstrcat (szText, TEXT ("WM_LBUTTONDOWN"));
        break;
    case WM_LBUTTONUP:
        lstrcat (szText, TEXT ("WM_LBUTTONUP"));
        break;
    case WM_LBUTTONDBLCLK:
        lstrcat (szText, TEXT ("WM_LBUTTONDBLCLK"));
        break;
    }
    Add2List (hWnd, szText);
    return 0;
}
//========================================================================
// Command handler routines
//------------------------------------------------------------------------
// DoMainCommandExit - Process Program Exit command.
//
LPARAM DoMainCommandExit (HWND hWnd, WORD idItem, HWND hwndCtl,
                          WORD wNotifyCode) {
    NOTIFYICONDATA nid;

    // Delete any remaining taskbar icons.
    memset (&nid, 0, sizeof nid);
    nid.cbSize = sizeof (NOTIFYICONDATA);
    nid.hWnd = hWnd;
    while (nIconID) {
        nid.uID = nIconID--;
```

```c
            Shell_NotifyIcon (NIM_DELETE, &nid);
    }

    EndDialog (hWnd, 0);
    return 0;
}
//-------------------------------------------------------------------
// DoMainCommandAddIcon - Process Add Icon button.
//
LPARAM DoMainCommandAddIcon (HWND hWnd, WORD idItem, HWND hwndCtl,
                             WORD wNotifyCode) {
    NOTIFYICONDATA nid;

    nIconID++;
    nid.cbSize = sizeof (NOTIFYICONDATA);
    nid.hWnd = hWnd;
    nid.uID = nIconID;
    nid.uFlags = NIF_ICON | NIF_MESSAGE;   // NIF_TIP not supported
    nid.uCallbackMessage = MYMSG_TASKBARNOTIFY;
    nid.hIcon = (HICON)LoadImage (hInst, MAKEINTRESOURCE (ID_ICON),
                          IMAGE_ICON, 16,16,0);
    nid.szTip[0] = '\0';

    Shell_NotifyIcon (NIM_ADD, &nid);
    return 0;
}
//-------------------------------------------------------------------
// DoMainCommandDelIcon - Process Del Icon button.
//
LPARAM DoMainCommandDelIcon (HWND hWnd, WORD idItem, HWND hwndCtl,
                             WORD wNotifyCode) {
    NOTIFYICONDATA nid;

    if (nIconID == 0)
        return 0;

    memset (&nid, 0, sizeof nid);
    nid.cbSize = sizeof (NOTIFYICONDATA);
    nid.hWnd = hWnd;
    nid.uID = nIconID--;

    Shell_NotifyIcon (NIM_DELETE, &nid);
    return 0;
}
//-------------------------------------------------------------------
// Add2List - Add string to the report list box.
//
```

(continued)

Listing 16-1 *(continued)*

```
void Add2List (HWND hWnd, LPTSTR lpszFormat, ...) {
    int i, nBuf;
    TCHAR szBuffer[512];

    va_list args;
    va_start(args, lpszFormat);

    nBuf = _vstprintf(szBuffer, lpszFormat, args);
    i = SendDlgItemMessage (hWnd, IDD_OUTPUT, LB_ADDSTRING, 0,
                            (LPARAM)(LPCTSTR)szBuffer);
    if (i != LB_ERR)
        SendDlgItemMessage (hWnd, IDD_OUTPUT, LB_SETTOPINDEX, i,
                            (LPARAM)(LPCTSTR)szBuffer);
    va_end(args);
}
```

TBIcons can run on a Pocket PC, but the task bar annunciators are visible only when the Today screen is showing. Aside from this difference, the program runs under the Pocket PC as it does under other versions of Windows CE.

The Out Of Memory Error Dialog Box

Because Windows CE applications are almost always running in a limited memory environment, it seems likely that they'll need an Out Of Memory Error dialog box. The standard Windows CE shells give you just such a dialog box as a system service. Figure 16-2 shows this dialog box on a Pocket PC.

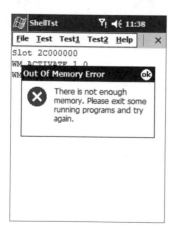

Figure 16-2   The Windows CE Out Of Memory Error dialog box

The advantage of using the system-provided Out Of Memory Error dialog box is that you don't have to create one yourself in what, by definition, is already a low-memory condition. The dialog box provided by the system is also correctly configured for the proper screen size and local language. To display an Out Of Memory Error dialog box, you call this function:

```
int SHShowOutOfMemory (HWND hwndOwner, UINT grfFlags);
```

The two parameters are the owner window and *grfFlags*, which must be set to 0.

Console Applications

Windows CE doesn't support the character mode API supported by Windows XP. Instead, a Windows CE console application just uses the standard C library I/O functions, such as *printf* and *getc*, to read and write characters from the command line. Another major difference between command line applications on Windows CE and on other versions of Windows is that they use the standard *WinMain* entry point instead of the standard C entry point of *main*.

Not all Windows CE systems support the console. For example, the Pocket PC doesn't include console support. However, on those Windows CE systems that do include support, the console is a handy tool. Revisiting the discussion in Chapter 1, the following Windows CE console application runs under Windows CE. Aside from the difference of the entry point, a Windows CE console application looks like any other standard C command-line application.

```
//
// HelloCon - A simple console application
//
#include <windows.h>                    // For all that Windows stuff

// Program entry point
int WINAPI WinMain (HINSTANCE hInstance, HINSTANCE hPrevInstance,
                    LPWSTR lpCmdLine, int nCmdShow) {

    // You don't use Unicode for the stdio functions...
    printf ("Hello World\n");

    //...but you can with the 'w' versions.
    wprintf (TEXT ("Hello World\n"));
    return 0;
}
```

Windows CE console applications have access to the Win32 API. In fact, a console application can create windows, enter a message loop, and operate as if it were a standard Windows application. The difference is that the first time you call one of the *stdio* C library functions, such as *printf*, a console window is created and the result of that function will be seen in that window.

Consoles are implemented under Windows CE using a console driver with the appropriate device name of CON. Up to 10 console windows can be opened at any one time. The limit comes from the CON0 through CON9 naming convention used by drivers under Windows CE. Console applications don't directly open a CON driver to read and write to the window. At the current time, support for console applications is limited to a subset of the standard C library character mode functions, although this subset seems to grow with every release of Windows CE.

Because the initialization of the console driver occurs only after the first call to an I/O library function, it's possible for a console application to run to completion and terminate without ever creating a console window for output. If you want a console window to always be created, you'll need to include a *printf* or other console input or output call to force the console to be created. You can always insert a line like

```
printf (" \b");
```

which prints a space and then backspaces over the space to force the console to be created.

The CEFind Example Program

The following program is a short console application that searches the Windows CE file system for matching file names. The program can be launched from a console window using Cmd.exe, or it can be launched from the Explorer. Because no concept of a current directory is built into Windows CE, the search always starts from the root of the file system unless a path is specified with the filename specification. Figure 16-3 shows the results of CEFind when looking for all the TrueType fonts on a system.

Figure 16-3   The results of a CEFind search for TrueType font files

The CEFind source is contained in one file, CEFind.cpp, shown in Listing 16-2. The entry point is *WinMain*, which then calls *SrchDirectory*, which recursively calls itself to search each of the directories underneath the original directory.

CEFind.cpp

```cpp
//======================================================================
// CEFind - A Windows CE console file search application
//
// Written for the book Programming Windows CE
// Copyright (C) 2003 Douglas Boling
//======================================================================
#include <windows.h>                    // For all that Windows stuff

// Returns number of elements
#define dim(x) (sizeof(x) / sizeof(x[0]))

int SrchDirectory (LPTSTR pszDir);
//----------------------------------------------------------------------
// Global data
//
int nTotal = 0;
int nFiles = 0;


//======================================================================
// Program entry point
//
int WINAPI WinMain (HINSTANCE hInstance, HINSTANCE hPrevInstance,
                    LPWSTR lpCmdLine, int nCmdShow) {
    TCHAR pInput[256];

    if (wcslen (lpCmdLine) == 0) {
        printf ("USAGE: CEFIND filespec\n");
        return 0;
    }
    printf ("\n");                       // Initialize the console.
    // We always start at the root.
    memset (pInput, 0, sizeof (pInput));
    if (*lpCmdLine != TEXT ('\\')) {
        pInput[0] = TEXT ('\\');
    }
    wcscat (pInput, lpCmdLine);

    // Perform recursive search.
    SrchDirectory (pInput);
    wprintf (L"\n  %9d file(s) found.   %d bytes.\n", nFiles, nTotal);
    return 0;
}
//----------------------------------------------------------------------
// SrchDirectory - Recursive routine that searches a dir and all
```

Listing 16-2   The CEFind program   *(continued)*

Listing 16-1   *(continued)*

```
// child dirs for matching files
//
int SrchDirectory (LPTSTR pszDir) {
    WIN32_FIND_DATA fd;
    TCHAR szNew[MAX_PATH];
    INT i, rc, nErr = 0;
    HANDLE hFind;
    TCHAR *pPtr, *pSrcSpec;

    // Separate subdirectory from search specification.
    for (pSrcSpec = pszDir + lstrlen (pszDir); pSrcSpec >= pszDir;
        pSrcSpec--)
        if (*pSrcSpec == TEXT ('\\'))
            break;

    // Copy the search specification up to the last directory
    // separation character.
    if (pSrcSpec <= pszDir)
        lstrcpy (szNew, TEXT ("\\"));
    else {
        for (i = 0; (i < dim(szNew)-10) &&
                    ((pszDir+i) <= pSrcSpec); i++)
            szNew[i] = *(pszDir+i);
        szNew[i] = TEXT ('\0');
    }
    pPtr = szNew + lstrlen (szNew);

    // Find matching files.
    hFind = FindFirstFile (pszDir, &fd);
    if (hFind != INVALID_HANDLE_VALUE) {

        do {
            // Report all matching files.
            if (!(fd.dwFileAttributes & FILE_ATTRIBUTE_DIRECTORY)) {
                wprintf (L"  %9d\t %s%s\n", fd.nFileSizeLow, szNew,
                        fd.cFileName);
                nTotal += fd.nFileSizeLow;
                nFiles++;
            }
            rc = FindNextFile (hFind, &fd);
        } while (rc);

        FindClose (hFind);
    } else {
        rc = GetLastError();
        if ((rc != ERROR_FILE_NOT_FOUND)  &&
            (rc != ERROR_NO_MORE_FILES)) {
```

```
                wprintf (L"1Find Error.  Str:%s rc:%d", pszDir, rc);
                return -1;
        }
    }

    // Create generic search string for all directories.
    lstrcat (szNew, TEXT ("*.*"));

    hFind = FindFirstFile (szNew, &fd);
    if (hFind != INVALID_HANDLE_VALUE) {
        do {
            if (fd.dwFileAttributes & FILE_ATTRIBUTE_DIRECTORY) {
                // Recurse to the lower directory.
                lstrcpy (pPtr, fd.cFileName);
                lstrcat (pPtr, pSrcSpec);
                nErr = SrchDirectory (szNew);
                if (nErr) break;
                *pPtr = TEXT ('\0');
            }
            rc = FindNextFile (hFind, &fd);
        } while (rc);

        FindClose (hFind);
    } else {
        rc = GetLastError();
        if ((rc != ERROR_FILE_NOT_FOUND) &&
            (rc != ERROR_NO_MORE_FILES)) {
            wprintf (L"2Find Error:%d", rc);
            return -1;
        }
    }
    return nErr;
}
```

The console can be quite useful in debugging. Because all Windows CE applications can call console functions, such as *printf*, you can use the console as a quick-and-dirty debug console. This is especially helpful in debugging applications on unusual embedded systems that don't have a method to connect to the development tools on a PC.

For systems that don't support the console, the standard console functions are still exported. It's just that the console functions simply look for a console driver that, on that system, isn't there. Even for systems without a console driver, there's no reason you can't put a console driver on the system. In fact, one of the tricks of the Windows CE gurus is to create a console driver and place it in the Windows directory of a Pocket PC for quick-and-dirty debugging.

In addition, DLLs can also use the console as easily as executables can. This feature is handy for debugging DLLs that are loaded by processes other than the process you have developed. One caveat, however: the system automatically creates a console for a process only once. If for some reason the console is closed, subsequent output to the console for that application is lost.

Console Redirection

Windows CE supports two functions, *GetStdioPathW* and *SetStdioPathW*, that allow the console input and output functions to be redirected to files or drivers other than the default console driver. The console functions support the three traditional console paths: input, output, and error, identified by the traditional labels *stdin*, *stdout*, and *stderr*, respectively.

To query the current console settings, call the function *GetStdioPathW* prototyped as

```
BOOL GetStdioPathW (DWORD id, PWSTR pwszBuf, LPDWORD lpdwLen);
```

The *id* parameter specifies which path to be queried: stdin for input, stdout for output, and stderr for error. By default, all three paths point to a single console driver instance such as CON1:. The second parameter, *pwszBuf*, receives the name of the driver or file that that the specified path is directed toward. The final parameter, *lpdwLen*, should contain the length, in characters, of *pwszBuf* and should be set to the length of the string returned.

The individual console paths can be redirected with the function *SetStdioPathW*. Its prototype is

```
BOOL SetStdioPathW (DWORD id, LPCWSTR pwszPath);
```

As with *GetStdioPathW*, the first parameter identifies the path to set. The second parameter specifies the name of the device driver instance or the file that will be the source (in the case of the input path) or the destination (in the case of the output or error paths for the console).

In the following code fragment, the output of Cmd.exe is redirected to a file named tempout.txt.

```
// Query the current output path.
dwLen = MAX_PATH;
fRet = GetStdioPathW(stdout, szStdOut, &dwLen);

// Set output path to file.
SetStdioPathW(1, TEXT("\\tempout.txt"));

// Launch cmd.exe with a DIR command.
CreateProcess (TEXT("Cmd.exe"), TEXT("/c dir"), NULL, NULL, FALSE, 0,
               NULL, NULL, NULL, &pi);
WaitForSingleObject (pi.hProcess, 2000);
```

```
// Clean up and restore default output path.
CloseHandle (pi.hProcess);
CloseHandle (pi.hThread);
SetStdioPathW(stdout, szStdOut);
```

The preceding code first queries the current output path setting so that it can be restored at the end of the code fragment. Next cmd.exe is launched with a command-line string telling cmd.exe to list the contents of the current directory and then terminate. After the process is launched, the code waits for two seconds for the command to succeed and then closes the handles returned by *CreateProcess* and restores the output path.

Hardware Keys

The keyboard isn't necessarily the only way for the user to enter keystrokes to an application. All Pocket PCs and many embedded systems have additional buttons that can be assigned to launch an application or to send unique virtual key codes to applications. The Pocket PC has an additional set of buttons known as *navigation buttons* that mimic common navigation keys such as Line Up and Line Down. These navigation keys give the user shortcuts, which allow scrolling up and down as well as access to the services of the often-used key Enter. Because the scrolling buttons simply send Page Up, Page Down, Line Up, and Line Down key messages, your application doesn't have to take any special action to support these keys.

The application launch buttons are another matter. When pressed, these keys cause the shell to launch the application registered for that key. Although a system is usually configured with default associations, you can override these settings by modifying the registry so that pressing a hardware control button launches your application. An application can also override the application launch ability of a specific key by having the key mapped directly to a window. In addition, you can use the hot key features of the Graphics Windowing and Event Subsystem (GWE) to override the hardware key assignment and send a hot key message to a window.

Virtual Codes for Hardware Keys

Since the hardware control buttons are treated as keyboard keys, pressing a hardware control key results in *WM_KEYDOWN* and *WM_KEYUP* messages as well as a *WM_CHAR* message if the virtual key matches a Unicode character. The system mapping of these keys employs two strategies. For the navigation keys, the resulting virtual key codes are codes known and used by Windows applications so that those applications can "use" the keys without even knowing that's what they're doing. The application-launching keys, on the other hand, need virtual key codes that are completely different from previously known keys so that they won't conflict with standard key events.

Navigation Key Codes

As I mentioned earlier, the navigation keys are mapped to common navigation keys. The actual virtual key code mapping for navigation keys is shown in the following table.

Key	Action	Key Message	Key Code
Action	Press	WM_KEYDOWN	OEM dependent*
Action	Release	WM_KEYUP	OEM dependent*
		WM_KEYDOWN	VK_RETURN
		WM_CHAR	VK_RETURN
		WM_KEYUP	VK_RETURN
Rock Up	Press	WM_KEYDOWN	OEM dependent*
	Release	WM_KEYUP	OEM dependent*
		WM_KEYDOWN	VK_UP
		WM_KEYUP	VK_UP
Rock Down	Press	WM_KEYDOWN	OEM dependent*
	Release	WM_KEYUP	OEM dependent*
		WM_KEYDOWN	VK_DOWN
		WM_KEYUP	VK_DOWN
Rock Left	Press	WM_KEYDOWN	OEM dependent*
	Release	WM_KEYUP	OEM dependent*
		WM_KEYDOWN	VK_LEFT
		WM_KEYUP	VK_LEFT
Rock Right	Press	WM_KEYDOWN	OEM dependent*
	Release	WM_KEYUP	OEM dependent*
		WM_KEYDOWN	VK_RIGHT
		WM_KEYUP	VK_RIGHT

* OEM-dependent key codes differ from system to system. Some OEMs might not send the messages. while others might send the messages with a virtual key code of 0.

Unfortunately, there's no reliable way of determining whether a *VK_RETURN* key event came from the SIP or from a hardware button. Each OEM has a different method of assigning virtual key codes to the hardware navigation buttons.

Application Launch Key Codes

The shell manages the application launch keys named App1 through a possible App16. These keys produce a combination of virtual key codes that are interpreted by the shell. The codes produced are a combination of the left Windows key (*VK_LWIN*) and a virtual code starting with 0xC1 and continuing up, depending on the application key pressed. For example, the App1 key produces the virtual key sequence *VK_LWIN* followed by 0xC1, while the App2 key produces the sequence *VK_LWIN* followed by 0xC2.

Using the Application Launch Keys

Applications are bound to a specific application launch key through entries in the registry. Specifically, each key has an entry under [HKEY_LOCAL_MACHINE] \Software\Microsoft\Shell\Keys. The entry is the virtual key combination for that key, so for the App1 key, the entry is

```
[HKEY_LOCAL_MACHINE]\Software\Microsoft\Shell\Keys\40C1
```

The 40C1 comes from the code 0x40, which indicates the Windows key has been pressed and concatenated with the virtual key code of the application key, 0xC1. The default value assigned to this key is the fully specified path name of the application assigned to the key. A few other values are also stored under this key. The *ResetCmd* value is the path name of the application that is assigned to this key if the Restore Defaults button is pressed in the system's Button control panel applet. The *Name* value contains the friendly name of the key, such as Button 1 or Side Button.

The only way to change the application assigned to a key is to manually change the registry entry to point to your application. Of course, you shouldn't do this without consulting your users because they might have already configured the application keys to their liking. The routine that follows assigns an application to a specific button and returns the name of the application previously assigned to that button. The *vkAppKey* parameter should be set to an application key virtual key code, 0xC1 through 0xCF. The *pszNewApp* parameter should point to the fully specified path name of the application you want to assign to the key.

```
//------------------------------------------------------------------
// SetAppLaunchKey - Assigns an application launch key to an
// application.
//
int SetAppLaunchKey (LPTSTR pszNewApp, BYTE vkAppKey, LPTSTR pszOldApp,
                     INT nOldAppSize) {
    TCHAR szKeyName[256];
    DWORD dwType, dwDisp;
    HKEY hKey;
    INT rc;

     // Construct the key name.
    wsprintf (szKeyName,
        TEXT ("Software\\Microsoft\\Shell\\Keys\\40%02x"), vkAppKey);

    // Open the key.
    rc = RegCreateKeyEx (HKEY_LOCAL_MACHINE, szKeyName, 0, TEXT (""),
                         0, 0, NULL, &hKey, &dwDisp);
    if (rc != ERROR_SUCCESS)
        return -1;

    // Read the old application name.
    rc = RegQueryValueEx (hKey, TEXT (""), 0, &dwType,
                          (PBYTE)pszOldApp, &nOldAppSize);
    if (rc != ERROR_SUCCESS) {
        RegCloseKey (hKey);
        return -2;
    }
    // Set the new application name.
    rc = RegSetValueEx (hKey, TEXT (""), 0, REG_SZ, (PBYTE)pszNewApp,
                        (lstrlen (pszNewApp)+1) * sizeof (TCHAR));
    RegCloseKey (hKey);
    if (rc != ERROR_SUCCESS)
        return -3;

    return 0;
}
```

When an application button is pressed, the system doesn't check to see whether another copy of the application is already running—it simply launches a new copy. You should design your application, especially on the Pocket PC, to check to see whether another copy of your application is already running and if so, to activate the first copy of the application and quietly terminate the newly launched copy.

You can determine whether an application is assigned to a key by calling the function *SHGetAppKeyAssoc*, which is prototyped as

```
Byte SHGetAppKeyAssoc (LPCTSTR ptszApp);
```

The only parameter is the fully qualified name of your application. If a key is associated with your application, the function returns the virtual key code for that key. If no key is associated with your application, the function returns 0. This function is useful because most applications, when launched by an application key, override the default action of the key so that another copy of the application won't launch if the key is pressed again.

Dynamically Overriding Application Launch Keys

A running application can override a launch key in two ways. The first method is to use the function *SHSetAppKeyWndAssoc*, prototyped as

```
BOOL SHSetAppKeyWndAssoc (BYTE bVk, HWND hwnd);
```

The first parameter is the virtual key code of the hardware button. The second parameter is the handle of the window that's to receive the notices of button presses. For example, a program might redirect the App1 key to its main window with the following line of code:

```
SHSetAppKeyWndAssoc (0xC1, hwndMain);
```

The window that has redirected an application might receive key messages but the virtual key codes received and the type of key messages are OEM-specific. The chief reason for using *SHSetAppKeyWndAssoc* is to prevent the button from launching an application. When you no longer want to redirect the application launch key, you can call *SHSetAppKeyWndAssoc* specifying the virtual code of the key and *NULL* for the window handle.

The second method of overriding an application launch key is to use the *RegisterHotKey* function. The advantage of using the *RegisterHotKey* function is that your window will receive known messages, albeit *WM_HOTKEY* instead of *WM_KEYxxx* messages, when the key is pressed, no matter what application currently has the keyboard focus. This function is prototyped as

```
BOOL RegisterHotKey (HWND hWnd, int id, UINT fsModifiers, UINT vk);
```

The first parameter is the handle of the window that receives the *WM_HOTKEY* messages. The second parameter is an application-defined identifier that's included with the *WM_HOTKEY* message to indicate which key caused the message. The *fsModifiers* parameter should be set with flags, indicating the shift keys that must also be pressed before the *WM_HOTKEY* message can be sent. These self-explanatory flags are *MOD_ALT*, *MOD_CONTROL*, *MOD_SHIFT*, and *MOD_WIN*. An additional flag, *MOD_KEYUP*, indicates that the window will receive *WM_HOTKEY* messages when the key is pressed and when the key is released. When using *RegisterHotKey* on application keys, you should always specify the *MOD_WIN* flag because application keys always are combined with the Windows shift-modifier key. The final parameter, *vk*, is the virtual key code for the key you want as your hot key. This key doesn't have to be a hardware key code; you can actually use almost any other virtual key code supported by Windows, although assigning Shift-F to your custom fax application might make Pocket Word users a bit irate when they tried to enter a capital *F*.

When the key registered with *RegisterHotKey* is pressed, the system sends a *WM_HOTKEY* message to the window. The *wParam* parameter contains the ID code you specified when you called *RegisterHotKey*. The low word of *lParam* parameter contains the shift-key modifiers, *MOD_xxx*, that were set when the key was pressed, while the high word of *lParam* contains the virtual key code for the key.

The disadvantage of using *RegisterHotKey* is that if another application has already registered the hot key, the function will fail. This can be problematic on the Pocket PC, where applications stay running until the system purges them to gain extra memory space. One strategy to employ when you want to use a hardware key temporarily—for example, in a game—would be to use *SHGet-AppKeyAssoc* to determine what application is currently assigned to that key. It's a good bet that if *RegisterHotKey* failed due to some other program using it, the application assigned the application key is also the one currently running and has redirected the hot key to its window. You can then send a *WM_CLOSE* message to that application's main window to see whether it will close and free up the hardware key.

When you no longer need the hot key, you can unregister the hot key with this function:

```
BOOL UnregisterHotKey (HWND hWnd, int id);
```

The two parameters are the window handle of the window that had registered the hot key and the ID value for that hot key you assigned with *RegisterHotKey*.

The Game API, or GAPI, provides a method for applications to take control of all hardware keys in the system. GAPI lets an application take control of all the keys but not individual keys. Still, GAPI provides a convenient service for game developers. (For more information about GAPI, refer to Chapter 20.)

The application launch buttons provide a handy way to make your applications easily accessible by the user. The only additional task required of the application is to assume control of the key when it's running so that users can't inadvertently launch multiple copies of the application.

I began this chapter by saying the Explorer shell is interesting in that, like many parts of Windows CE, it resembles its desktop counterparts but is implemented very differently. These differences show up the most in places, such as the COM interfaces the Explorer uses and in console applications, where the implementation is limited to supporting a subset of standard C library calls and little else.

In the next chapter, I turn to the Pocket PC shell. This shell has dramatic differences in look and feel that affect the way you write Pocket PC applications. Throughout this book, the examples have contained small snippets of code that I mentioned were required for the Pocket PC, but I didn't explain why. It's time to explore the details of these extra pieces of code.

17

Programming the Pocket PC

The Pocket PC is one of the most successful Windows CE–based systems. The combination of small, PDA-size dimensions and a powerful CPU has provided a portable but fast platform for the Windows CE operating system. In addition, an extensive reworking of the user interface for the Pocket PC devices makes for an interesting platform for application developers.

The Pocket PC is so interesting that Microsoft has taken many of the Pocket PC–specific functions and made them available on the Windows CE operating system, which allows original equipment manufacturers to build devices that are Pocket PC–like without having all the features, and requirements, of a branded Pocket PC device. What is important to note is that although many of the Pocket PC functions—or more precisely, the Explorer shell—have been brought into the operating system, the implementation of these functions is generally up to the OEM. So while I will discuss the functions in this chapter with respect to how they are implemented on the Pocket PC, just because a particular OEM supports a function on a non–Pocket PC device, they might not implement the function exactly the way the Pocket PC does.

What Is a Pocket PC?

Now that we have Pocket PC devices and Pocket PC–like devices, just what denotes a real Pocket PC from a Pocket PC–like device? First and foremost, a Pocket PC device is a Windows CE–based PDA with a custom shell and a set of customized applications written by Microsoft but sold by OEMs such as

Hewlett-Packard, Toshiba, ViewSonic, and others. Pocket PC branded devices are certified by Microsoft to conform to a specific set of standards in both hardware and software. Pocket PC–like devices are Windows CE–based devices that include a set of base components that expose most of the Pocket PC APIs. The implementation of these functions, as mentioned earlier, is dependent on the OEM so there isn't a guarantee that one Pocket PC–like device will look or operate like another Pocket PC–like device. Still, these devices will most likely be implemented to act as closely as possible like a Pocket PC.

Pocket PC applications must conform to a rather strict set of requirements that enforce the look and feel of the application. The Pocket PC is customized to expect that applications running on it conform to its requirements. While it is simple to create an application that runs but doesn't conform to the Pocket PC guidelines, the application will probably not work as the user expects, nor will the application be able to react to the actions of the Pocket PC shell.

Is It a PDA, a Phone, or Both?

Another aspect of the Pocket PC is the blurring of the lines between Personal Digital Assistants (PDAs) and cell phones. Some devices are only PDAs, some are PDA form factors with cellular communication built in, and some are cell phones that run Windows CE. So which device is which, and how much do these devices have in common?

The Pocket PC 2003 device is an evolution of the original Pocket PC device released in April of 2000. The operating system is now Windows CE 4.2 instead of Windows CE 3.0, and there have been a handful of new functions added to support user features such as the shell notification interface, but all in all it's the same system albeit with a much more robust operating system under the covers. The chief difference the user will notice is the new, smaller and yet more powerful hardware that has changed over the last few years. Now devices may have built-in wireless networking or Bluetooth personal area networking or may have neither but be significantly smaller or less expensive.

Another advance has been the integration of cellular technology into some Pocket PC devices. Microsoft has released a version of the Pocket PC called Pocket PC Phone edition that adds functions to support voice calling, short message service (SMS), and other features specific to having an integrated phone in the device. The user interface and application requirements of the Pocket PC Phone edition are almost identical to those of a standard Pocket PC device. It has the same portrait screen and lack of keyboard. The device differs from a standard Pocket PC in that phone cellular calls can be made from the device with an integrated speaker and microphone.

A device just being introduced at this writing is the Smartphone device. The Smartphone is a cell phone that is based on Windows CE with a custom shell and custom applications. Aside from the shell, which is significantly different from the Pocket PC due to the constraints and usage model of a cell phone, the Smartphone is surprisingly similar to the Pocket PC underneath. Aside from the economies of scale that might suggest a common solution, the same group inside Microsoft is responsible for both platforms, which provides a bureaucratic impetus to commonality across the two platforms.

Given the overlap between these systems, it's difficult to parse the functionality into distinct chapters without having a fair amount of overlap. To avoid this situation, I've made an arbitrary decision to put off discussing any of the features of the Pocket PC Phone edition until Chapter 19. This arrangement allows a single discussion of dialing, SMS, and Telephony API (TAPI) extensions in the chapter that discusses a communication-specific device.

The Pocket PC Screen

The main difference between a *real* Pocket PC and a Pocket PC–like device is the Pocket PC shell. This shell is unique to the Pocket PC and the Pocket PC Phone edition, so OEMs building Pocket PC–like devices won't have the exact look and feel, or the exact operation, of this shell. The Pocket PC shell implements the Today screen, the top-down Start Menu, and a number of other features specific to the Pocket PC. Figure 17-1 shows the Pocket PC's Today screen.

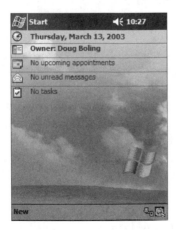

Figure 17-1   The Pocket PC display

Across the top of the Pocket PC screen is the navigation bar. This element of the screen contains the title of the foreground window, the current time, and (when a dialog is displayed) an OK button for dismissing a dialog. Tapping the navigation bar displays the Start menu, allowing the user to launch applications or to switch to running applications.

The Today screen contains information about the device. Today screen panels can be configured through the control panel. (In the next chapter, I'll discuss how developers can add custom Today screen panels.) The bottom of the Pocket PC screen is reserved for the menu bar. The Today screen menu bar is unique in that it displays taskbar annunciators created using the same API that I described in Chapter 16.

When the user starts an application, the screen layout is similar to that seen with the Today screen in view. The navigation bar is at the top, the application window takes up the main screen area, and the menu bar holds its place at the bottom of the screen. The best way to learn about programming this platform is to go right to an example.

Hello Pocket PC

A Pocket PC application is still a Windows application, so it has a message loop, a main window, and window procedures. However, some new requirements do change the design a bit. First, a Pocket PC application must make sure that only one copy of itself is running at any one time. The operating system doesn't ensure this—that is the application's job. Second, instead of using a command bar—as do other Windows CE applications—Pocket PC applications use the menu bar. In many ways, the menu bar acts like an updated command bar, but it does have some peculiarities. A Pocket PC application should not have a Close button, an Exit command, or a Close command in its menus. This is because PDA users don't use applications; they use their PDAs. (The user interface gurus that work on this stuff have decided that users would rather not know when a particular application is running or not.)

Let's move on to some code. Figure 17-2 shows two screen shots of a simple Pocket PC application called HelloPPC. The left image shows the window with the soft input panel, or SIP, hidden; the image on the right shows HelloPPC with the SIP showing. Notice how the text centers itself in the visible portion of the workspace. The HelloPPC window has a red outline to highlight its size and position.

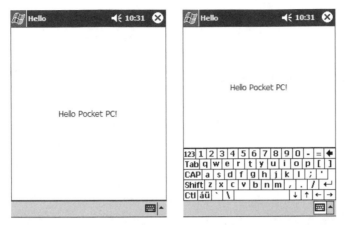

Figure 17-2   The HelloPPC application with the SIP both hidden and showing

Listing 17-1 shows the source code for HelloPPC. Fundamentally, what you'll notice about HelloPPC is that it is predominantly a standard Windows CE application. The differences between this code and that shown in Chapter 1 have to do with the difference between the Pocket PC and the Explorer shells. I'll talk about these differences in the sections following the code.

```
HelloPPC.rc
//======================================================================
// Resource file
//
// Written for the book Programming Windows CE
// Copyright (C) 2003 Douglas Boling
//======================================================================
#include "windows.h"          // Windows stuff
#include "commctrl.h"         // Common ctl stuff
#include "aygshell.h"         // Pocket PC stuff
#include "HelloPPC.h"         // Program-specific stuff


//----------------------------------------------------------------------
// Icons and bitmaps
//
ID_ICON        ICON    "HelloPPC.ico"  // Program icon
```

Listing 17-1   The HelloPPC application   *(continued)*

Listing 17-1   *(continued)*

```
//---------------------------------------------------------------------
// Accelerator keys
//
ID_ACCEL ACCELERATORS DISCARDABLE
BEGIN
    "Q",  IDM_EXIT,  VIRTKEY, CONTROL, NOINVERT
END
```

HelloPPC.h

```
//=====================================================================
// Header file
//
// Written for the book Programming Windows CE
// Copyright (C) 2003 Douglas Boling
//
//=====================================================================
// Returns number of elements
#define dim(x) (sizeof(x) / sizeof(x[0]))


//---------------------------------------------------------------------
// Generic defines and data types
//
struct decodeUINT {                              // Structure associates
    UINT Code;                                   // messages
                                                 // with a function.
    LRESULT (*Fxn)(HWND, UINT, WPARAM, LPARAM);
};
struct decodeCMD {                               // Structure associates
    UINT Code;                                   // menu IDs with a
    LRESULT (*Fxn)(HWND, WORD, HWND, WORD);      // function.
};


//---------------------------------------------------------------------
// Generic defines used by application
#define  ID_ACCEL             1                  // Accelerator table ID

#define  IDM_EXIT             100


//---------------------------------------------------------------------
// Function prototypes
//
HWND InitInstance (HINSTANCE, LPWSTR, int);
int TermInstance (HINSTANCE, int);

// Window procedures
LRESULT CALLBACK MainWndProc (HWND, UINT, WPARAM, LPARAM);
```

```
// Message handlers
LRESULT DoCreateMain (HWND, UINT, WPARAM, LPARAM);
LRESULT DoPaintMain (HWND, UINT, WPARAM, LPARAM);
LRESULT DoCommandMain (HWND, UINT, WPARAM, LPARAM);
LRESULT DoSettingChangeMain (HWND, UINT, WPARAM, LPARAM);
LRESULT DoActivateMain (HWND, UINT, WPARAM, LPARAM);
LRESULT DoHibernateMain (HWND, UINT, WPARAM, LPARAM);
LRESULT DoDestroyMain (HWND, UINT, WPARAM, LPARAM);

// WM_COMMAND message handlers
LPARAM DoMainCommandExit (HWND, WORD, HWND, WORD);
```

HelloPPC.c

```
//======================================================================
// HelloPPC - A simple application for the Pocket PC
//
// Written for the book Programming Windows CE
// Copyright (C) 2003 Douglas Boling
//
//======================================================================
#include <windows.h>                    // For all that Windows stuff
#include <commctrl.h>                   // Command bar includes
#include <aygshell.h>                   // Pocket PC includes
#include "helloppc.h"                   // Program-specific stuff
//----------------------------------------------------------------------
// Global data
//
const TCHAR szAppName[] = TEXT ("HelloPPC");
HINSTANCE hInst;                        // Program instance handle

// Pocket PC globals
HWND hwndMenuBar = NULL;                // Handle of menu bar control
BOOL fHibernated = FALSE;               // Indicates hibernated state
SHACTIVATEINFO sai;                     // Used to adjust window for SIP

// Message dispatch table for MainWindowProc
const struct decodeUINT MainMessages[] = {
    WM_CREATE, DoCreateMain,
    WM_PAINT, DoPaintMain,
    WM_COMMAND, DoCommandMain,
    WM_SETTINGCHANGE, DoSettingChangeMain,
    WM_ACTIVATE, DoActivateMain,
    WM_HIBERNATE, DoHibernateMain,
    WM_DESTROY, DoDestroyMain,
};
// Command Message dispatch for MainWindowProc
const struct decodeCMD MainCommandItems[] = {
```

(continued)

Listing 17-1   *(continued)*

```
    IDM_EXIT, DoMainCommandExit,
};
//======================================================================
// Program entry point
//
int WINAPI WinMain (HINSTANCE hInstance, HINSTANCE hPrevInstance,
                    LPWSTR lpCmdLine, int nCmdShow) {
    MSG msg;
    int rc = 0;
    HWND hwndMain;
    HACCEL hAccel;

    // Initialize this instance.
    hwndMain = InitInstance (hInstance, lpCmdLine, nCmdShow);
    if (hwndMain == 0) return 0x10;

    hAccel = LoadAccelerators(hInstance, MAKEINTRESOURCE (ID_ACCEL));

    // Application message loop
    while (GetMessage (&msg, NULL, 0, 0)) {
        // Translate accelerator keys.
        if (!TranslateAccelerator(hwndMain, hAccel, &msg)) {
            TranslateMessage (&msg);
            DispatchMessage (&msg);
        }
    }
    // Instance cleanup
    return TermInstance (hInstance, msg.wParam);
}
//----------------------------------------------------------------------
// InitInstance - Instance initialization
//
HWND InitInstance (HINSTANCE hInstance, LPWSTR lpCmdLine, int nCmdShow) {
    WNDCLASS wc;
    HWND hWnd;

    // Save program instance handle in global variable.
    hInst = hInstance;

    // Allow only one instance of the application.
    hWnd = FindWindow (szAppName, NULL);
    if (hWnd) {
        SetForegroundWindow ((HWND)(((DWORD)hWnd) | 0x01));
        return 0;
    }
    // Register application main window class.
    wc.style = CS_VREDRAW | CS_HREDRAW;         // Window style
```

```
    wc.lpfnWndProc = MainWndProc;            // Callback function
    wc.cbClsExtra = 0;                       // Extra class data
    wc.cbWndExtra = 0;                       // Extra window data
    wc.hInstance = hInstance;                // Owner handle
    wc.hIcon = NULL,                         // Application icon
    wc.hCursor = LoadCursor (NULL, IDC_ARROW); // Default cursor
    wc.hbrBackground = (HBRUSH) GetStockObject (WHITE_BRUSH);
    wc.lpszMenuName =  NULL;                 // Menu name
    wc.lpszClassName = szAppName;            // Window class name

    if (RegisterClass (&wc) == 0) return 0;

    // Create main window.
    hWnd = CreateWindow (szAppName,          // Window class
                         TEXT ("Hello"),     // Window title
                         WS_VISIBLE,         // Style flags
                         CW_USEDEFAULT,      // x position
                         CW_USEDEFAULT,      // y position
                         CW_USEDEFAULT,      // Initial width
                         CW_USEDEFAULT,      // Initial height
                         NULL,               // Parent
                         NULL,               // Menu, must be null
                         hInstance,          // Application instance
                         NULL);              // Pointer to create
                                             // parameters
    if (!IsWindow (hWnd)) return 0;          // Fail if not created.

    // Standard show and update calls
    ShowWindow (hWnd, nCmdShow);
    UpdateWindow (hWnd);
    return hWnd;
}
//-----------------------------------------------------------------
// TermInstance - Program cleanup
//
int TermInstance (HINSTANCE hInstance, int nDefRC) {
    return nDefRC;
}
//=================================================================
// Message handling procedures for main window
//
//-----------------------------------------------------------------
// MainWndProc - Callback function for application window
//
LRESULT CALLBACK MainWndProc (HWND hWnd, UINT wMsg, WPARAM wParam,
                         LPARAM lParam) {
    INT i;
```

(continued)

Listing 17-1   *(continued)*

```
    //
    // Search message list to see if we need to handle this
    // message.  If in list, call procedure.
    //
    for (i = 0; i < dim(MainMessages); i++) {
        if (wMsg == MainMessages[i].Code)
            return (*MainMessages[i].Fxn)(hWnd, wMsg, wParam, lParam);
    }
    return DefWindowProc (hWnd, wMsg, wParam, lParam);
}
//----------------------------------------------------------------------
// DoCreateMain - Process WM_CREATE message for window.
//
LRESULT DoCreateMain (HWND hWnd, UINT wMsg, WPARAM wParam,
                      LPARAM lParam) {
    SHMENUBARINFO mbi;
    SIPINFO si;
    int cx, cy;

    // Initialize the shell to activate info structure.
    memset (&sai, 0, sizeof (sai));
    sai.cbSize = sizeof (sai);

    // Create a menu bar.
    memset(&mbi, 0, sizeof(SHMENUBARINFO)); // Zero structure
    mbi.cbSize = sizeof(SHMENUBARINFO);     // Size field
    mbi.hwndParent = hWnd;                  // Parent window
    mbi.dwFlags = SHCMBF_EMPTYBAR;          // Flags like hide SIP btn
    mbi.nToolBarId = 0;                     // ID of toolbar resource
    mbi.hInstRes = 0;                       // Inst handle of app
    mbi.nBmpId = 0;                         // ID of bitmap resource
    mbi.cBmpImages = 0;                     // Num of images in bitmap
    mbi.hwndMB = 0;                         // Handle of bar returned

    // Create menu bar and check for errors.
    if (!SHCreateMenuBar(&mbi)) {
        MessageBox (hWnd, TEXT ("Couldn\'t create menu bar"),
                    szAppName, MB_OK);
        DestroyWindow (hWnd);
    }
    hwndMenuBar = mbi.hwndMB;                // Save the menu bar handle.

    // Query the sip state and size our window appropriately.
    memset (&si, 0, sizeof (si));
    si.cbSize = sizeof (si);
    SHSipInfo(SPI_GETSIPINFO, 0, (PVOID)&si, FALSE);
    cx = si.rcVisibleDesktop.right - si.rcVisibleDesktop.left;
```

```
    cy = si.rcVisibleDesktop.bottom - si.rcVisibleDesktop.top;

    // If the sip is not shown, or showing but not docked, the
    // desktop rect doesn't include the height of the menu bar.
    if (!(si.fdwFlags & SIPF_ON) ||
        ((si.fdwFlags & SIPF_ON) && !(si.fdwFlags & SIPF_DOCKED))) {
        RECT rectMB;
        GetWindowRect (hwndMenuBar, &rectMB);
        cy -= (rectMB.bottom - rectMB.top);
    }

    SetWindowPos (hWnd, NULL, 0, 0, cx, cy, SWP_NOMOVE | SWP_NOZORDER);
    return 0;
}
//----------------------------------------------------------------------
// DoCommandMain - Process WM_COMMAND message for window.
//
LRESULT DoCommandMain (HWND hWnd, UINT wMsg, WPARAM wParam,
                       LPARAM lParam) {
    WORD idItem, wNotifyCode;
    HWND hwndCtl;
    INT  i;

    // Parse the parameters.
    idItem = (WORD) LOWORD (wParam);
    wNotifyCode = (WORD) HIWORD (wParam);
    hwndCtl = (HWND) lParam;

    // Call routine to handle control message.
    for (i = 0; i < dim(MainCommandItems); i++) {
        if (idItem == MainCommandItems[i].Code)
            return (*MainCommandItems[i].Fxn)(hWnd, idItem, hwndCtl,
                                              wNotifyCode);
    }
    return 0;
}
//----------------------------------------------------------------------
// DoPaintMain - Process WM_PAINT message for window.
//
LRESULT DoPaintMain (HWND hWnd, UINT wMsg, WPARAM wParam,
                     LPARAM lParam) {
    PAINTSTRUCT ps;
    HPEN hPen, hOld;
    RECT rect;
    HDC hdc;

    hdc = BeginPaint (hWnd, &ps);
    GetClientRect (hWnd, &rect);
```

(continued)

Listing 17-1 *(continued)*

```
    // Draw a red rectangle around the window.
    hPen = CreatePen (PS_SOLID, 1, RGB (255, 0, 0));
    hOld = (HPEN)SelectObject (hdc, hPen);
    Rectangle (hdc, rect.left, rect.top, rect.right, rect.bottom);
    SelectObject (hdc, hOld);
    DeleteObject (hPen);

    // Draw the standard hello text centered in the window.
    DrawText (hdc, TEXT ("Hello Pocket PC! "), -1, &rect,
              DT_CENTER | DT_VCENTER | DT_SINGLELINE);

    EndPaint (hWnd, &ps);
    return 0;
}
//-----------------------------------------------------------------------
// DoSettingChangeMain - Process WM_SETTINGCHANGE message for window.
//
LRESULT DoSettingChangeMain (HWND hWnd, UINT wMsg, WPARAM wParam,
                             LPARAM lParam) {

    // Notify shell of our WM_SETTINGCHANGE message.
    SHHandleWMSettingChange(hWnd, wParam, lParam, &sai);
    return 0;
}
//-----------------------------------------------------------------------
// DoActivateMain - Process WM_ACTIVATE message for window.
//
LRESULT DoActivateMain (HWND hWnd, UINT wMsg, WPARAM wParam,
                        LPARAM lParam) {

    // If activating, restore any hibernated stuff.
    if ((LOWORD (wParam) != WA_INACTIVE) && fHibernated) {
        fHibernated = FALSE;
    }
    // Notify shell of our activate message.
    SHHandleWMActivate(hWnd, wParam, lParam, &sai, 0);
    return 0;
}
//-----------------------------------------------------------------------
// DoHibernateMain - Process WM_HIBERNATE message for window.
//
LRESULT DoHibernateMain (HWND hWnd, UINT wMsg, WPARAM wParam,
                         LPARAM lParam) {

    // If not the active window, reduce our memory footprint.
    if (GetActiveWindow() != hWnd) {
        fHibernated = TRUE;
    }
```

```
        return 0;
}
//-------------------------------------------------------------------
// DoDestroyMain - Process WM_DESTROY message for window.
//
LRESULT DoDestroyMain (HWND hWnd, UINT wMsg, WPARAM wParam,
                       LPARAM lParam) {
    PostQuitMessage (0);
    return 0;
}
//===================================================================
// Command handler routines
//-------------------------------------------------------------------
// DoMainCommandExit - Process Program Exit command.
//
LPARAM DoMainCommandExit (HWND hWnd, WORD idItem, HWND hwndCtl,
                          WORD wNotifyCode) {
    SendMessage (hWnd, WM_CLOSE, 0, 0);
    return 0;
}
```

The HelloPPC application creates a main window and prints *Hello Pocket PC* in the center of the window. It also draws a red rectangle around the border of its window to clearly show the extent of the window. The program creates a menu bar without a menu but with a button to display the SIP. If you tap the SIP button, you will see the main window resize to avoid being covered by the SIP. If you attempt to start a second copy of HelloPPC, the system will instead switch to the copy currently running. Finally, if you open the SIP and tap Ctrl-Q, the application will quit. Each of these little features takes a little bit of code to conform to the standards of a Pocket PC application. Now let's examine these code fragments and learn how it's done.

Differences in a Pocket PC Application

Comparing the source code of HelloPPC to the code of HelloCE in Chapter 1 shows a fair amount of new code specifically added to handle the requirements of the Pocket PC shell. The first issue is the requirement that a Pocket PC application only have one instance of itself running at any one time. The Pocket PC shell won't enforce this requirement; it's up to the application.

Single Instance

The single instance requirement of a Pocket PC is accomplished with the *Find-Window* code that has appeared in almost every example in this book. This code ensures that only one copy of the application is running at any given time. The following code fragment shows how this is accomplished.

```
// Allow only one instance of the application.
HWND hWnd = FindWindow (szAppName, NULL);
if (hWnd) {
    SetForegroundWindow ((HWND)(((DWORD)hWnd) | 0x01));
    return -1;
}
```

The call to *FindWindow* looks for a top-level window with the same class name as HelloPPC. If the window is found, the code calls *SetForegroundWindow* to put that window into the foreground, and then the second copy of the application terminates. Notice the rather strange logical ORing of a 1 to the window handle. This is an internal hack that tells Windows to restore the window being set to the foreground in case it has been minimized. Without this bit, you could accidentally set a minimized window to the foreground, and under the Pocket PC shell, the user would never see this minimized window.

Use a Menu Bar, Not a Command Bar

The next few changes to HelloPPC are all in the *WM_CREATE* message handler. Instead of creating a command bar or command band control, a Pocket PC application creates a menu bar control. I discussed the Menu bar in Chapter 5, but here is a short review. The following code fragment creates a simple menu bar.

```
SHMENUBARINFO mbi;

// Create a menu bar.
mbi.hwndParent = hWnd;                  // Parent window
mbi.dwFlags = SHCMBF_EMPTYBAR;          // Flags like hide SIP btn
mbi.nToolBarId = 0;                     // ID of toolbar resource
mbi.hInstRes = 0;                       // Inst handle of app
mbi.nBmpId = 0;                         // ID of bitmap resource
mbi.cBmpImages = 0;                     // Num of images in bitmap
mbi.hwndMB = 0;                         // Handle of bar returned

// Create menu bar and check for errors.
if (SHCreateMenuBar(&mbi))
    hwndMenuBar = mbi.hwndMB;           // Save the menu bar handle.
```

This code initializes a *SHMENUBARINFO* structure and passes it to *SHCreateMenuBar* to create the main window's associated menu bar. The menu bar control can contain a menu, toolbar buttons, and the button that displays the SIP. For HelloPPC, the menu bar has no menu and thus the *SHCMBF_EMPTYBAR* flag is set in the *dwFlags* field. The only other field that requires initialization for this simple configuration is the *hwndParent* field that is set to the HelloPPC window handle. After the menu bar is created, the handle of the returned control is saved.

Manually Sizing the Main Window

A Pocket PC application must also deal with the menu bar and the SIP. The key is to size the application's top-level window so that the SIP doesn't obscure it. Also, if you create the top-level window following the Windows CE tradition of using *CW_USEDEFAULT* in the position and size parameters of *CreateWindow*, the window will be created over the top of the area used by the menu bar. To avoid covering up the menu bar with a window, or the window being covered by the SIP, the *WM_CREATE* handler includes the following code:

```
// Query the SIP state and size our window appropriately.
memset (&si, 0, sizeof (si));
si.cbSize = sizeof (si);
SHSipInfo(SPI_GETSIPINFO, 0, (PVOID)&si, FALSE);

cx = si.rcVisibleDesktop.right - si.rcVisibleDesktop.left;
cy = si.rcVisibleDesktop.bottom - si.rcVisibleDesktop.top;

// If the SIP is not shown, or is showing but not docked, the
// desktop rect doesn't include the height of the menu bar.
if (!(si.fdwFlags & SIPF_ON) ||
    ((si.fdwFlags & SIPF_ON) && !(si.fdwFlags & SIPF_DOCKED))) {
        RECT rectMB;
        GetWindowRect (hwndMenuBar, &rectMB);
        cy -= (rectMB.bottom - rectMB.top);
    }
SetWindowPos (hWnd, NULL, 0, 0, cx, cy, SWP_NOMOVE | SWP_NOZORDER);
```

The preceding code uses the function *SHSipInfo* to query the current state of the SIP. Included in the information returned by this call is the visible portion of the desktop that is not obscured by a docked SIP. The code computes the size of this rectangle and uses it if the SIP is displayed in a docked state and positioned at the bottom of the screen. If, however, the SIP is not visible, or if it is floating, the main window still must be sized, because the system default window size does not leave room for the menu bar. The preceding code tests whether the SIP is hidden or floating and, if it is, shortens the window height by the height of the menu bar. On a Pocket PC, this value is documented to be 26 pixels, but it isn't guaranteed to be the same on Pocket PC–like devices. Because of this, the value should be computed instead of hard-coded.

This code to specify the size of the window can be placed elsewhere in a Pocket PC application. For example, you could resize the window after *Create-Window* returns instead of within the *WM_CREATE* message handler. Either way, you must manually size the window, depending on the state of the SIP and whether you want to use a menu bar control in your application. I choose to place the size code in the *WM_CREATE* message handler as a matter of style.

Dealing with Changes in the SIP

Once HelloPPC is running, it must still deal with the user displaying and hiding the SIP. The standard technique for handling the SIP is to resize your application's main window whenever the SIP is displayed or hidden. This technique allows your standard window code to deal with SIP changes as it would with any window resize. Of course, you aren't required to resize your main window in reaction to the SIP, but you must provide some way of insuring that the SIP does not obscure data that the user is interacting with when the SIP is shown. The Pocket PC shell provides some simple hooks to monitor the SIP and automatically resize a window. This method is the easiest to use and the one I'll describe here.

To automatically resize your window in response to the SIP, you must globally declare an *SHACTIVATEINFO* structure in your program. While you can find the structure declared in the include files required for the program, the internal structure, aside from one field, is irrelevant. This structure should be initialized to 0 and the *cbSize* field should be set to the size of the structure, as in the following code fragment:

```
SHACTIVATEINFO sai;              // Declare globally.

// Initialize the shell activate info structure.
memset (&sai, 0, sizeof (sai));
sai.cbSize = sizeof (sai);
```

This initialization should happen either before your main window is created or in the *WM_CREATE* handler.

Your main window's window procedure must handle the *WM_ACTIVATE* and *WM_SETTINGCHANGE* messages. The *WM_SETTINGCHANGE* message is used in Windows to indicate that some basic system setting has changed. In the Pocket PC, *WM_SETTINGCHANGE* is also used to notify an application that the state of the SIP has changed. While the application could manually determine the state of the SIP and handle it in its own *WM_SETTINGCHANGE* message handler, the Pocket PC shell provides a simple function that can be called to do the work for the application. The function prototype for this function is

```
BOOL SHHandleWMSettingChange (HWND hwnd, WPARAM wParam, LPARAM lParam,
                        SHACTIVATEINFO *psai);
```

The first three parameters of this function are the handle to the window receiving the *WM_SETTINGCHANGE* message and the message's *wParam* and *lParam* parameters. The final parameter is the address of the *SHACTIVATEINFO* structure declared and initialized earlier in the code. The use of this function is quite simple; just call this function whenever the top-level window receives a *WM_SETTINGCHANGE* message. The function resizes the window if necessary.

The second function to call to help with the SIP is

```
BOOL SHHandleWMActivate (HWND hwnd, WPARAM wParam, LPARAM lParam,
                         SHACTIVATEINFO *psai, DWORD dwFlags);
```

As you might expect from the name of the function, *SHHandleWMActivate* should be called in response to a *WM_ACTIVATE* message sent to the top-level window. The parameters are the same as for *SHHandleWMSettingChange*, with the addition of the *dwFlags* parameter. The *dwFlags* parameter can be either 0 or *SHA_INPUTDIALOG*, if the top-level window is a dialog box with child controls. For dialog boxes, the *SHA_INPUTDIALOG* flag will prevent the SIP from automatically popping up and down when the focus switches between the different child controls.

In addition to *SHHandleWMActivate* and *SHHandleWMSettingChange*, another difference between HelloPPC and many of the other examples in this book is the use of the *CS_HREDRAW* and *CS_VREDRAW* flags when registering the window class. These flags automatically invalidate the main window whenever the window is resized. The interaction of these functions along with the redraw style flags will result in the top-level window being redrawn when the SIP is shown or hidden. This interaction provides a simple way for a Pocket PC program to automatically adjust the presentation of its data simply by handling the *WM_PAINT* message and drawing the appropriate data in the format necessary for the situation.

Be aware of one issue with some versions of Microsoft eMbedded Visual C++: The code wizard that produces the example Pocket PC application does not initialize the *SHACTIVATEINFO* structure. Therefore, the example code does not automatically resize the window when the SIP is displayed, even though it calls the *SHHandleWMSettingChange* function. In addition, the wizard code does not call *SHHandleWMActivate*, so if you plan to base your application on this wizard, you should add the code described in this section. It just goes to show that a programmer should never depend on code wizards. While wizards can be handy tools for rapid code generation, if you don't understand the code they produce, you're going to have problems.

Ctrl-Q Closes a Pocket PC Application

The final Pocket PC modification in HelloPPC comes in *WinMain* and is part of a tradition of Pocket PC applications. Notice that in *WinMain*, HelloPPC loads a keyboard accelerator table. The message loop is modified to enable that accelerator table. A quick look in the HelloPPC.rc shows that the only accelerator key is Ctrl-Q, which is associated with a *WM_COMMAND* id code of *IDM_EXIT*. As you might expect, tapping Ctrl+Q in the SIP while HelloPPC is active will close the application. Traditionally, Pocket PC applications don't have a Close button or an Exit menu item. They close with a Ctrl+Q key sequence. A little testing will show that most Pocket PC applications bundled with the system respond similarly to this key sequence. The Ctrl-Q "Easter egg" has the added value of allowing the programmer to start a Pocket PC application for testing, and then to tell it to close before downloading a new copy. While you can always add an Exit menu item and then remove it before shipping your application, you will inevitably need to test something about your application after shipping.

Building HelloPPC

The HelloPPC project files are based on the Pocket PC application project template. This is a different project template from the other examples in this book. However, the differences between the Windows CE application project template and the Pocket PC application project template are quite minor.

When you decide to base your project on the Pocket PC application template, eMbedded Visual C++ changes the project settings to link the shell extensions library, aygshell.lib, to the program. This library resolves the newer functions such as *SHCreateMenuBar*, *SHHandleWMActivate*, and *SHHandle-WMSettingChange*. There are other differences between the way that Pocket PC and other Windows CE devices are handled which aren't dependent on the project template that's used. For example, when you select the Pocket PC as the target device, the compiled file is automatically downloaded to the Windows CE device's \Windows\Start Menu directory, instead of downloading to the root directory.

One issue I haven't yet mentioned is that for a number of examples you need to create a menu bar—and in some cases a menu—if you want to correctly run these applications on the Pocket PC. I did not want one project for the Windows CE systems example and a separate project for the Pocket PC. To avoid this, and to avoid adding extra code to explicitly load the shell extension functions, code is conditionally compiled into the application that instructs the linker to link the aygshell library when compiling for a Pocket PC target. The following code is taken from the KeyTrac example in Chapter 3:

```
#if defined(WIN32_PLATFORM_PSPC)     // Compile only for Pocket PC.
#include <aygshell.h>                // Add Pocket PC includes.
#pragma comment( lib, "aygshell" )   // Link Pocket PC lib for menu bar.
#endif
```

The first line is a conditional compile preprocessor command that tells the compiler to compile the enclosed lines only if the symbol *WIN32_PLATFORM_PSPC* is defined. As you might expect, that symbol is defined if you compile to either the Pocket PC or old Palm-size PC targets. The second line tells the compiler to include the Aygshell.h include file that provides the function prototypes and type definitions necessary for using the Pocket PC–specific functions. Finally, the *#pragma* line instructs the linker to link in the aygshell library so that the Pocket PC functions can be resolved.

Aygshell is now available in the Windows CE Platform Builder for OEMs to include in their custom devices. The component is optional, though, so you should check with the specific platform SDK documentation to see whether it's included on your target device.

The New Menu

The Pocket PC shell is centered on two menus, the Start menu and the New menu. The Start menu is basically the same start menu used by the Explorer shell with the exception that it is displayed from the top of the screen down, but the New menu is unique to the Pocket PC.

The New menu is available on the Today screen. Tapping any item on the New menu typically launches an application with a template for creating a new item, such as a note, a contact, or an Excel spreadsheet. The new menu can optionally be displayed by applications. This is done by creating a button on the Menu bar with an ID of *IDM_SHAREDNEW*. When the button, which looks to the user like a menu, is tapped, the system displays the New menu.

The New menu can be modified by applications in two ways. First, menu items can be added to the New menu either on a *permanent* basis, which adds an item when any application is running, or on a *temporary* basis, which adds an item only when the application is in the foreground. In addition, the foreground application can override the default actions of New menu items.

Managing the New Menu

The New menu can be added to a Menu bar in two ways. In the first way, in *shared mode*, tapping the New menu sends a *WM_COMMAND* message to the application with an ID value of *IDM_SHAREDNEW*. In simple (nonshared) mode, tapping the New menu displays a series of permanent menu items gleaned from the registry.

These permanent items are specified in the registry under the key HKEY_LOCAL_MACHINE]\Software\Microsoft\Shell\Extensions\NewMenu. This key lists a series of GUIDs that define COM in-process servers that implement an *IID_INewMenuItemServer* interface. The *IID_INewMenuItemServer* interface is actually quite simple. Aside from the standard *IUnknown* methods, the only method supported is

```
HRESULT INewMenuItemServer::CreateNewItem (HWND hwndParent);
```

The single parameter is the handle to the window that currently owns the menu bar. When the user selects the permanent item on the menu bar that references the COM object that implements the *IID_INewMenuItemServer* interface, the Pocket PC first sends a *WM_NOTIFY* message with the notification *NMN_INVOKECOMMAND* to the window owning the menu bar. If the application returns 1, the Pocket PC assumes that the application has taken care of the menu selection and no further action occurs. If the application returns 0, the Pocket PC will load the COM object and call the *CreateNewItem* method. In response, the COM object typically launches the appropriate application.

The NewMenuX Example

The following code is a simple New menu item extension that launches the calculator. If eMbedded Visual C++ is used to compile and download the NewMenuX server, it will register itself and add the proper registry key to tell the New menu of the existence of NewMenuX. If NewMenuX.dll is copied to the device manually, the following registry entries will need to be added:

```
[HKEY_CLASSES_ROOT\CLSID\{130F6E46-C3F9-4fa8-B8BC-75720BC73231}]
="Prog Win CE New Menu Extension"
[HKEY_CLASSES_ROOT\CLSID\
{130F6E46-C3F9-4fa8-B8BC-75720BC73231}\InProcServer32]
=\Windows\NewMenuX.dll

[HKEY_LOCAL_MACHINE]\Software\Microsoft\Shell\Extensions\NewMenu\
    {130F6E46-C3F9-4fa8-B8BC-75720BC73231}    = Launch Calc
    Enabled = 1
```

The first few lines register the in-proc server. The last three lines tell the shell about the added New Menu item. The default value of the key above is *Launch Calc*. The one value under the key is a *DWORD* value named *Enabled*, which is set to 1. Listing 17-2 contains the source for the NewMenuX example.

```
NewMenuX.def
;
;Standard COM library DEF file
;
LIBRARY    NEWMENUX.DLL

EXPORTS
```

Listing 17-2   The NewMenuX example

```
    DllCanUnloadNow      @1 PRIVATE
    DllGetClassObject    @2 PRIVATE
    DllRegisterServer    @3 PRIVATE
    DllUnregisterServer  @4 PRIVATE
```

NewMenuX.h

```
//======================================================================
// Header file
//
// Written for the book Programming Windows CE
// Copyright (C) 2003 Douglas Boling
//======================================================================

// Declare these here so that the MenuBar example can know the GUID
// {130F6E46-C3F9-4fa8-B8BC-75720BC73231}
static const GUID CLSID_NewMenuX =
{0x130f6e46,0xc3f9,0x4fa8,{0xb8,0xbc,0x75,0x72,0xb,0xc7,0x32,0x31}};
const TCHAR szCLSIDNewMenuX[] =
TEXT ("{130F6E46-C3F9-4fa8-B8BC-75720BC73231}");

#ifndef JUST_GET_THE_GUID
// This isn't defined by the current Pocket PC SDK. Uncomment if needed.
// DECLARE_INTERFACE_(INewMenuItemServer, IUnknown)
// {
//     // *** IUnknown methods ***
//     STDMETHOD(QueryInterface) (THIS_ REFIID riid, LPVOID * ppvObj) PURE;
//     STDMETHOD_(ULONG,AddRef) (THIS) PURE;
//     STDMETHOD_(ULONG,Release) (THIS) PURE;
//     // *** INewMenuItemServer methods ***
//     STDMETHOD(CreateNewItem) (THIS_ HWND hwndParent) PURE;
// };
// **** Start of Generic COM declarations ****
//======================================================================
// MyClassFactory - Object declaration
//
class MyClassFactory : public IClassFactory {
private:
    long m_lRef;

public:
    MyClassFactory();
    ~MyClassFactory();

    //IUnknown methods
    STDMETHODIMP QueryInterface (THIS_ REFIID riid, LPVOID *ppv);
    STDMETHODIMP_(ULONG) AddRef (THIS);
    STDMETHODIMP_(ULONG) Release (THIS);
```

(continued)

Listing 17-2 *(continued)*

```cpp
    //IClassFactory methods
    STDMETHODIMP CreateInstance (LPUNKNOWN pUnkOuter, REFIID riid,
                                 LPVOID *ppv);
    STDMETHODIMP LockServer (BOOL fLock);
};
// **** End of Generic OLE declarations ****


//========================================================================
// MyNewMenuItemServer - Object declaration
//
class MyNewMenuItemServer : public INewMenuItemServer {

private:
    long m_lRef;
    HWND m_hwndParent;

public:
    MyNewMenuItemServer();
    ~MyNewMenuItemServer();

    //IUnknown methods
    STDMETHODIMP QueryInterface (THIS_ REFIID riid, LPVOID *ppvObj);
    STDMETHODIMP_(ULONG) AddRef (THIS);
    STDMETHODIMP_(ULONG) Release (THIS);

    //INewMenuItemServer
    HRESULT STDMETHODCALLTYPE CreateNewItem (HWND hwndParent);
};

#endif //JUST_GET_THE_GUID
```

NewMenuX.cpp

```cpp
//========================================================================
// NewMenuX - A Pocket PC New menu extension
//
// Written for the book Programming Windows CE
// Copyright (C) 2003 Douglas Boling
//========================================================================
#include <windows.h>                    // For all that Windows stuff
#include <commctrl.h>                   // Command bar includes
#define INITGUID
#include <initguid.h>
#include <coguid.h>
#include <aygshell.h>                   // Pocket PC shell includes
#include <shlguid.h>                    // Shell GUIDs inc New menu ext
#include "NewMenuX.h"                   // My IM common includes
```

```
long g_DllCnt = 0;                      // Global DLL reference count
HINSTANCE hInst;                        // DLL instance handle

const TCHAR szFriendlyName[] = TEXT ("Prog Win CE New Menu Extension");
//======================================================================
// DllMain - DLL initialization entry point
//
BOOL WINAPI DllMain (HANDLE hinstDLL, DWORD dwReason,
                     LPVOID lpvReserved) {
    hInst = (HINSTANCE)hinstDLL;
    return TRUE;
}
//======================================================================
// DllGetClassObject - Exported function called to get pointer to
// Class factory object
//
STDAPI DllGetClassObject (REFCLSID rclsid, REFIID riid, LPVOID *ppv) {
    MyClassFactory *pcf;
    HRESULT hr;

    // See if caller wants us...
    if (IsEqualCLSID (rclsid, CLSID_NewMenuX)) {

        // Create IClassFactory object.
        pcf = new MyClassFactory();
        if (pcf == NULL)
            return E_OUTOFMEMORY;
        // Call class factory's query interface method.
        hr = pcf->QueryInterface (riid, ppv);
        // This will cause an obj delete unless interface found.
        pcf->Release();
        return hr;
    }
    return CLASS_E_CLASSNOTAVAILABLE;
}
//======================================================================
// DllCanUnloadNow - Exported function called when DLL can unload
//
STDAPI DllCanUnloadNow () {

    if (g_DllCnt)
        return S_FALSE;
    return S_OK;
}
//======================================================================
// DllRegisterServer - Exported function called to register the server
//
STDAPI DllRegisterServer () {
```

(continued)

Listing 17-2   *(continued)*

```
      TCHAR szName[MAX_PATH+2];
      TCHAR szTmp[128];
      DWORD dwDisp;
      HKEY hKey, hSubKey;
      INT rc;

      GetModuleFileName (hInst, szName, sizeof (szName));
      // Open the key.
      wsprintf (szTmp, TEXT ("CLSID\\%s"), szCLSIDNewMenuX);
      rc = RegCreateKeyEx (HKEY_CLASSES_ROOT, szTmp, 0, TEXT (""),
                           0, 0, NULL, &hKey, &dwDisp);
      if (rc != ERROR_SUCCESS)
          return E_FAIL;

      // Set the friendly name of the new menu item extension.
      RegSetValueEx (hKey, TEXT (""), 0, REG_SZ, (PBYTE)szFriendlyName,
                          (lstrlen (szFriendlyName)+1) * sizeof (TCHAR));
      // Create subkeys.
      // Set the module name of the new menu item server
      rc = RegCreateKeyEx (hKey, TEXT ("InProcServer32"), 0, TEXT (""),
                           0, 0, NULL, &hSubKey, &dwDisp);
      rc = RegSetValueEx (hSubKey, TEXT (""), 0, REG_SZ, (PBYTE)szName,
                          (lstrlen (szName)+1) * sizeof (TCHAR));
      RegCloseKey (hSubKey);
      RegCloseKey (hKey);
      //
      // Add entry to add new menu item
      //
      // Create string, use multuple lines due to book format limits
      lstrcpy (szTmp, TEXT ("Software\\Microsoft\\Shell\\"));
      lstrcat (szTmp, TEXT ("Extensions\\NewMenu\\"));
      lstrcat (szTmp, szCLSIDNewMenuX);
      rc = RegCreateKeyEx (HKEY_LOCAL_MACHINE, szTmp, 0, TEXT (""),
                           0, 0, NULL, &hKey, &dwDisp);
      if (rc != ERROR_SUCCESS)
          return E_FAIL;
      // Set the friendly name of the new menu item extension.
      lstrcpy (szTmp, TEXT ("Launch Calc"));
      RegSetValueEx (hKey, TEXT (""), 0, REG_SZ, (PBYTE)szTmp,
                      (lstrlen (szTmp)+1) * sizeof (TCHAR));
      dwDisp = 1;
      RegSetValueEx (hKey, TEXT ("Enabled"), 0, REG_DWORD, (PBYTE)&dwDisp,
                      sizeof (DWORD));
      RegCloseKey (hKey);
      return S_OK;
  }
```

```
//=======================================================================
// DllUnregisterServer - Exported function called to remove the server
// information from the registry
//
STDAPI DllUnregisterServer() {
    INT rc;
    TCHAR szTmp[128];

    wsprintf (szTmp, TEXT ("CLSID\\%s"), szCLSIDNewMenuX);
    rc = RegDeleteKey (HKEY_CLASSES_ROOT, szTmp);
    if (rc != ERROR_SUCCESS)
        return E_FAIL;
    // Create string, use multuple lines due to book format limits
    lstrcpy (szTmp, TEXT ("Software\\Microsoft\\Shell\\"));
    lstrcat (szTmp, TEXT ("Extensions\\NewMenu\\"));
    lstrcat (szTmp, szCLSIDNewMenuX);
    rc = RegDeleteKey (HKEY_CLASSES_ROOT, szTmp);
    if (rc != ERROR_SUCCESS)
        return E_FAIL;
    return S_OK;
}
//***********************************************************************
// MyClassFactory Object implementation
//-----------------------------------------------------------------------
// Object constructor
MyClassFactory::MyClassFactory () {
    m_lRef = 1;      //Set ref count to 1 on create.
    return;
}
//-----------------------------------------------------------------------
// Object destructor
MyClassFactory::~MyClassFactory () {
    return;
}
//-----------------------------------------------------------------------
// QueryInterface - Called to see what interfaces this object supports
STDMETHODIMP MyClassFactory::QueryInterface (THIS_ REFIID riid,
                                             LPVOID *ppv) {

    // If caller wants our IUnknown or IClassFactory object,
    // return a pointer to the object.
    if (IsEqualIID (riid, IID_IUnknown) ||
        IsEqualIID (riid, IID_IClassFactory)) {

        *ppv = (LPVOID)this;    // Return pointer to object.
        AddRef();               // Inc ref to prevent delete on return.
        return NOERROR;
    }
```

(continued)

Listing 17-2   *(continued)*

```
    *ppv = NULL;
    return (E_NOINTERFACE);
}
//------------------------------------------------------------------------
// AddRef - Increment object ref count.
STDMETHODIMP_(ULONG) MyClassFactory::AddRef (THIS) {
    ULONG cnt;

    cnt = (ULONG)InterlockedIncrement (&m_lRef);
    return cnt;
}
//------------------------------------------------------------------------
// Release - Decrement object ref count.
STDMETHODIMP_(ULONG) MyClassFactory::Release (THIS) {
    ULONG cnt;

    cnt = (ULONG)InterlockedDecrement (&m_lRef);
    if (cnt == 0)
        delete this;
    return cnt;
}
//------------------------------------------------------------------------
// LockServer - Called to tell the DLL not to unload, even if use cnt 0
STDMETHODIMP MyClassFactory::LockServer (BOOL fLock) {
    if (fLock)
        InterlockedIncrement (&g_DllCnt);
    else
        InterlockedDecrement (&g_DllCnt);
    return NOERROR;
}
//------------------------------------------------------------------------
// CreateInstance - Called to have class factory object create other
// objects
STDMETHODIMP MyClassFactory::CreateInstance (LPUNKNOWN pUnkOuter,
                                             REFIID riid,
                                             LPVOID *ppv) {

    MyNewMenuItemServer *pMyNMX;
    HRESULT hr;

    if (pUnkOuter)
        return (CLASS_E_NOAGGREGATION);

    if (IsEqualIID (riid, IID_IUnknown) ||
        IsEqualIID (riid, IID_INewMenuItemServer)) {

        // Create New menu item object.
        pMyNMX = new MyNewMenuItemServer();
```

```
        if (!pMyNMX)
            return E_OUTOFMEMORY;
        // See if object exports the proper interface.
        hr = pMyNMX->QueryInterface (riid, ppv);
        // This will cause an object delete unless interface found.
        pMyNMX->Release ();
        return hr;
    }
    return E_NOINTERFACE;
}
//*********************************************************************
// MyNewMenuItemServer Object implementation
//-------------------------------------------------------------------
// Object constructor
MyNewMenuItemServer::MyNewMenuItemServer () {

    m_lRef = 1;        //Set ref count to 1 on create.
    g_DllCnt++;
    return;
}
//-------------------------------------------------------------------
// Object destructor
MyNewMenuItemServer::~MyNewMenuItemServer () {
    g_DllCnt--;
    return;
}
//-------------------------------------------------------------------
// QueryInterface - Called to see what interfaces this object supports
STDMETHODIMP MyNewMenuItemServer::QueryInterface (THIS_ REFIID riid,
                                                  LPVOID *ppv) {

    // If caller wants our IUnknown or IID_IInputMethod2 object,
    // return a pointer to the object.
    if (IsEqualIID (riid, IID_IUnknown) ||
        IsEqualIID (riid, IID_INewMenuItemServer)) {

        // Return pointer to object.
        *ppv = (INewMenuItemServer *)this;
        AddRef();                  // Inc ref to prevent delete on return.
        return NOERROR;
    }
    *ppv = NULL;
    return (E_NOINTERFACE);
}
//-------------------------------------------------------------------
// AddRef - Increment object ref count.
STDMETHODIMP_(ULONG) MyNewMenuItemServer::AddRef (THIS) {
    ULONG cnt;
```

(continued)

Listing 17-2   *(continued)*

```
    cnt = (ULONG)InterlockedIncrement (&m_lRef);
    return cnt;
}
//----------------------------------------------------------------------
// Release - Decrement object ref count.
STDMETHODIMP_(ULONG) MyNewMenuItemServer::Release (THIS) {
    ULONG cnt;

    cnt = (ULONG)InterlockedDecrement (&m_lRef);
    if (cnt == 0) {
        delete this;
        return 0;
    }
    return cnt;
}
//----------------------------------------------------------------------
// CreateNewItem - The new menu item has been selected.
//
STDMETHODIMP_(HRESULT) MyNewMenuItemServer::CreateNewItem
                                            (HWND hwndParent) {
    SHELLEXECUTEINFO se;

    // Launch the calculator.
    memset (&se, 0, sizeof (se));
    se.cbSize = sizeof (se);
    se.hwnd = hwndParent;
    se.lpFile = TEXT ("calc.exe");
    se.lpVerb = TEXT ("open");
    se.lpDirectory = TEXT ("\\windows");

    ShellExecuteEx (&se);    // Launch the control panel.
    return S_OK;
}
```

All the preceding code supports the last routine, *CreateNewItem*, in the NewMenuX example. *CreateNewItem* simply launches the calculator application by using *ShellExecuteEx*.

Handling the New Menu from Within an Application

When your application is running, you can extend the New menu by fielding *WM_NOTIFY* messages with the notify code of *NMN_GETAPPREGKEY*. This notification is sent when the New menu is about to be displayed. The *lParam* value points to a *NMNEWMENU* structure, which is defined as

```
typedef struct tagNMNEWMENU
{
    NMHDR hdr;
```

```
      TCHAR szReg[80];
      HMENU hMenu;
      CLSID clsid;
} NMNEWMENU, *PNMNEWMENU;
```

The *hMenu* field of this structure contains the handle to the New menu that is about to be displayed. The easiest way to extend the New menu is to use *AppendMenu* to add menu items to the menu. The added menu items should have ID values greater than *IDM_NEWMENUMAX*.

Some Pocket PC SDKs do not define the *NMNEWMENU* structure nor do they define the notification messages. When compiling using those SDKs, you will need to define these items in your application. The definitions for the notification codes are shown here.

```
#define  NMN_GETAPPREGKEY      1101
#define  NMN_NEWMENUDESTROY     1102
#define  NMN_INVOKECOMMAND      1103
```

The *NMN_GETAPPREGKEY* notification is sent to the foreground application when the New menu is displayed. As you might expect, the *NMN_NEWMENUDESTROY* notification is sent when the New menu is destroyed. Finally, the *NMN_INVOKECOMMAND* notification is sent when the user selects a specific item.

The following code fragment fields the notification and adds an extra item to the New menu.

```
#define IDM_MYNEWMENUITEM              (IDM_NEWMENUMAX+1)
// See if New menu is being displayed.
if (lpnhr->code == NMN_GETAPPREGKEY) {
    lpNewMenu = (PNMNEWMENU) lParam;
    AppendMenu (lpNewMenu->hMenu, MF_ENABLED, IDM_MYNEWMENUITEM,
               TEXT ("My own New menu item"));
    AppendMenu (lpNewMenu->hMenu, MF_SEPARATOR, 0, 0);
}
```

When the user selects the added item on the New menu, a *WM_COMMAND* message will be sent with the ID value of the menu item added to the New menu.

Pocket PC Notifications

The Pocket PC has a unique method of notifying the user independent of the standard Windows CE notification API discussed in Chapter 11. The Pocket PC notifications can display an icon on the navigation bar at the top of the screen, optionally display an information bubble with HTML text, and even beep the user as necessary. The user can respond by tapping on hyperlinks or buttons within the bubble. These responses are then sent back to the originating application. Unlike the standard Windows CE notifications, the Pocket PC notifications require the application be running and manually set the notification as needed. Once the notification is set, the application can stay running and receive feedback from the notification via window messages or terminate and specify that a COM in-proc server receives the feedback. Figure 17-3 shows a Pocket PC desktop with a notification bubble being displayed.

Figure 17-3   A notification bubble

The bubble is anchored to the application-defined icon on the navigation bar. Notification bubbles have a title and a text body. The bubble window is automatically sized to fit the text.

Adding a Notification

To display a notification, the *SHNotificationAdd* function is used. Its rather simple prototype is

```
LRESULT SHNotificationAdd (SHNOTIFICATIONDATA * pndAdd);
```

The single parameter is a pointer to a not-so-simple *SHNOTIFICATION-DATA* structure defined as

```
typedef struct _SHNOTIFICATIONDATA {
    DWORD cbStruct;
    DWORD dwID;
    SHNP npPriority;
    DWORD csDuration;
    HICON hicon;
```

```
    DWORD grfFlags;
    CLSID clsid;
    HWND hwndSink;
    LPCTSTR pszHTML;
    LPCTSTR pszTitle;
    LPARAM lParam;
} SHNOTIFICATIONDATA;
```

The initial field, *cbStruct*, is the obligatory size field that must be initialized to the size of the structure. The *dwID* field will be the ID value for the notification. The ID value will be used to identify any user responses to the notification. The *npPriority* field is set to either *SHNP_ICONIC* to have the notification simply display an icon on the navigation bar or to *SHNP_INFORM* if the notification is to display the bubble text immediately. In the case of *SHNP_ICONIC*, if the user taps the icon, the bubble text is then displayed. The *csDuration* field specifies how long the notification should be displayed before the system automatically removes the icon and bubble. Unlike almost every other time parameter in Windows, this *csDuration* is measured in seconds, not milliseconds. The *hIcon* field should be set to a 16-by-16 icon that will be used in the navigation bar to display the notification.

The *grfFlags* flags field can be set with a series of flags that configure the notification. The *SHNF_CRITICAL* flag changes the color of the title and border of the bubble. The *SHNF_FORCEMESSAGE* flag displays the bubble even if the registry settings of the device are configured to not display notification bubbles. The *SHNF_DISPLAYON* flag turns on the display if it's off when the notification is displayed.

The *clsid* field has two uses. First, it's an identifier for the notification. It should be set to a GUID defined by the application. The second use is to identify a COM in-proc server. The in-proc server is one way the shell can provide feedback to the application. The *hwndSink* field can also be used in the feedback mechanism. If the *hwndSink* field is set to a valid window handle, the shell will provide feedback via *WM_NOTIFY* messages to that window. Feedback is sent when the text bubble is displayed, when it is closed, and when the user taps on any hyperlinks in the HTML text in the bubble. If the *clsid* field is set to the CLSID of a COM in-proc server that exposes an *IShellNotificationCallback* interface, the feedback is delivered using calls to the interface's *OnShow*, *OnDismiss*, *OnCommandSelected*, and *OnLinkSelected* methods. The difference between *OnCommandSelected* and *OnLinkSelected* will be explained momentarily.

The *pszHTML* field can be *NULL*, in the case of an icon-only notification or either unformatted Unicode text or HTML Unicode text. The HTML text allows for surprisingly elaborate formatting of the text in the bubble. Paragraph breaks,

links, and even simple controls can be displayed in the bubble. The following
HTML was used to display the bubble shown in Figure 17-4:

```
<html><body><p>This is a list</p>
<ul>
  <li>Item 1</li>
  <li>Item 2</li>
  <li>Item 3</li>
</ul>
  <input type=\"button\" value=\"Yes\" name=\"cmd:200\">
  <input type=\"button\" value=\"No\" name=\"cmd:201\">
  <input type=\"button\" value=\"Cancel\" name=\"cmd:202\"></p>
<p> </p>
<p>Click <a href=\"http://www.msnbc.com\">here</a> to follow a link.</p>
</body></html>"; </html>
```

Figure 17-4 Complex HTML displayed in a notification bubble

The *pszTitle* field should point to a text string that will be the title of the
bubble. The final field, *lParam*, is an application-defined value that will be
passed back in the feedback *WM_NOTIFY* messages or in the callback to the in-
proc server.

The feedback received by the application depends on how the user
responds to the notification. When the user clicks on the notification icon, the
system sends a *WM_NOTIFY* to the window specified in the *hwndSink* field. If
the application returns a zero, the text bubble will be displayed. If the application returns a nonzero value, the bubble will not be displayed. In this case, the
application needs to provide whatever feedback it deems necessary to the user.

The HTML text can contain two types of feedback elements. The first is
the standard hyperlink, as shown at the top of the next page.

```
Click <a href="http://www.msnbc.com\">here</a> to go to MSNBC
```

If the user clicks on a hyperlink, the notification system sends a *WM_NOTIFY* message to the window with a notification code of *SHNN_LINKSEL*. The notification structure provides the text of the URL as well as the data defined in the *lParam* field of *SHNOTIFICATIONDATA*. If the HREF is in the format CMD:n, as in

```
Click <a href=\"cmd:205\">here</a> to go to MSNBC
```

the system sends a *WM_COMMAND* message instead of a *WM_NOTIFY* to the window. In this case, the value *n* is the ID value of the message, and the ID of the notification is returned in *lParam*. For the in-proc server, clicking the standard hyperlink results in a call to the interface's *OnLinkSelected* method while clicking on links with the CMD:n format results in the *OnCommandSelected* method being called. The CMD value 0 is reserved, a value of 1 sends a notification but does not dismiss the bubble, and a command value of 2 does not dismiss the bubble nor does it result in a *WM_COMMAND* message being sent. Applications should generally use CMD values greater than 2.

When the user dismisses the bubble either by clicking a hyperlink or by clicking on the bubble itself, a final notification that the bubble is being dismissed is sent either by message or to the in-proc server.

Modifying a Notification

Configuration data can be queried from a notification by calling the *SHNotificationGetData* function. Its prototype is shown here:

```
LRESULT SHNotificationGetData (const CLSID * pclsid,
                     DWORD dwID, SHNOTIFICATIONDATA * pndBuffer);
```

The first two parameters are *pclsid*, which points to the CLSID of the notification, and *dwID*, which specifies the ID of the notification. The function fills in the *SHNOTIFICATIONDATA* structure pointed to by the third parameter, *pndBuffer*.

The notification can then be modified by changing the relevant data in the *SHNOTIFICATIONDATA* structure and calling *SHNotificationUpdate*, prototyped as

```
LRESULT SHNotificationUpdate (DWORD grnumUpdateMask,
                     SHNOTIFICATIONDATA *pndNew);
```

The *grnumUpdateMask* parameter is a set of flags that indicate which of the fields in the *SHNOTIFICATIONDATA* structure pointed to by *pndNew* should be used to update the notification. The flags are *SHNUM_PRIORITY* to change the priority of the notification, *SHNUM_DURATION* to change the duration,

SHNUM_ICON to change the icon, *SHNUM_HTML* to change the bubble text, and *SHNUM_TITLE* to change the bubble title text.

Removing a Notification

If the notification is simply an icon, it will be automatically removed when the notification times out. However, if the notification displays a bubble, the time-out value of the notification is used to automatically dismiss the bubble, not the icon. If the bubble text doesn't have a link or command, the user can dismiss the text bubble, but the icon remains. In this case and in the case where the timeout is set to infinite, there needs to be a way for the application to remove the notification. Removing the notification is accomplished with the aptly named *SHNotificationRemove* function, defined as

```
LRESULT SHNotificationRemove (const CLSID * pclsid, DWORD dwID);
```

The two parameters are the CLSID and ID value of the notification.

Dialog Boxes

In my experience, creating a well-designed dialog box is one of the program-mer's more difficult tasks. The problem lies in presenting the user with an intu-itive interface that allows quick interaction with an application. The task is doubly difficult on a Pocket PC, which has a small screen and a keyboard that keeps popping up over the bottom third of the screen. In this section, I'll explain creating dialog boxes and the assistance that the Pocket PC shell pro-vides. However, it is always good to remember the cardinal rule: keep it simple. The Pocket PC provides a number of functions that help with dialog boxes, but the best programs don't use all these functions at once.

Because the Pocket PC is based on Windows CE, dialog boxes act by default as they do in any Windows system: They are created with the standard Win32 functions such as *CreateDialog*, they are created by the dialog manager based on dialog box resource templates, and they have dialog box procedures. However, the user interface guidelines for the Pocket PC specify that dialog boxes should be full screen so as not to confuse the user. In addition, property sheets on the Pocket PC have their tabs on the bottom of the window instead of the top. Windows CE doesn't support these characteristics by default; conve-niently though, the Pocket PC provides extensions to assist the developer.

Full-Screen Dialog Boxes

To assist programmers in creating full-size dialog boxes, the Pocket PC shell implements a function named *SHInitDialog*. As the name implies, the function should be called during the handling of the *WM_INITDIALOG* message. The function is prototyped as

```
BOOL SHInitDialog (PSHINITDLGINFO pshidi);
```

The function takes a single parameter, a pointer to an *SHINITDLGINFO* structure defined as

```
typedef struct tagSHINITDIALOG{
    DWORD dwMask;
    HWND hDlg;
    DWORD dwFlags;
} SHINITDLGINFO;
```

The *dwMask* field must be set to the single flag currently supported, *SHIDIM_FLAGS*. The *hDlg* field should be set to the window handle of the dialog. The third parameter, *dwFlags*, specifies a number of different initialization options. The *SHIDIF_DONEBUTTON* specifies that the navigation bar across the top of the screen contain an OK button in the upper right corner. This flag is typically set because the user interface guidelines specify that dialogs have an OK button in the navigation bar, and the guidelines specify that there be no Cancel button. While one could argue with this specification, the user interface provides no automatic way to provide a Cancel button.

The *SHIDIF_SIPDOWN* flag closes the SIP when the dialog is displayed. This flag should be set for informational dialogs that have no text input fields. Note that the absence of this flag doesn't automatically display the SIP. It simply means that the state of the SIP remains unchanged when the dialog box is displayed.

Three other flags can be set in the *dwFlags* field:

■   *SHIDIF_SIZEDLG*

■   *SHIDIF_SIZEDLGFULLSCREEN*

■   *SHIDIF_FULLSCREENNOMENUBAR*

These flags deal with how the dialog box will be sized. The *SHIDIF_SIZEDLG* flag tells the system to size the dialog box depending on the state of the SIP. If the SIP is displayed, the dialog box will be sized to fit above the SIP. If the SIP is hidden, the dialog will be sized to fit just above the menu bar. If, however, you have a floating SIP, the dialog box doesn't size correctly. This is a rare occurrence because neither of the bundled input methods that ship with the Pocket PC can be undocked. However, the example input method in Chapter 18 does have the ability to float.

The *SHIDIF_SIZEDLGFULLSCREEN* and *SHIDIF_FULLSCREENNOMENUBAR* flags size the dialog to fit the entire screen regardless of the state of the SIP. The difference between the two flags is that *SHIDIF_FULLSCREENNOMENUBAR* does not leave room for the menu bar at the bottom of the screen.

Input Dialogs

In general, it's helpful to divide dialogs into informational dialogs and input dialogs. Information dialogs deliver information to the user and for the most part don't need text input. Input dialogs are dialogs that require lines of text to be entered, such as passwords or IP addresses. For input dialogs, you can group the controls in the top two thirds of the dialog so that those fields aren't covered up by the SIP, which will almost always be displayed.

Whether the dialog is an input dialog or an informational dialog, another Pocket PC function that is typically called during *WM_INITDIALOG* is

```
BOOL SHSipPreference (HWND hwnd, SIPSTATE st);
```

This function sets the preferred state of the SIP. I say *preferred* state because the action of this function depends on the state of the SIP prior to when it was called. The two parameters are the handle to the window, which can be a dialog box or a custom control, and a set of SIP state flags listed here:

■ **SIP_UP** Displays the SIP.

■ **SIP_DOWN** Requests to hide the SIP. The SIP is lowered only after a predetermined period of milliseconds in case the user switches back to a window that is displaying the SIP.

■ **SIP_FORCEDOWN** Immediately forces the SIP to hide.

■ **SIP_UNCHANGED** Leaves the SIP alone or cancels a previous call to *SHSipPreference*.

SHSipPreference is quite useful for writing custom controls that require SIP input. When the control receives the focus, it can call *SHSipPreference* to request the SIP be displayed. When the control loses the focus, it can call *SHSipPreference* to request the SIP be hidden. If the control receiving focus then calls *SHSipPreference* to display the SIP, this call will override the request to hide the SIP and the SIP will remain displayed without an annoying flash of the SIP.

If the dialog is an informational dialog, the call to *SHSipPreference* requests that the SIP be lowered. The dialog box can then display information in the entire area of the dialog. However, using *SHInitDialog* and *SHSipPreference* doesn't change the state of the SIP when the dialog is displayed. The dialog box should handle the *WM_ACTIVATE* message and call *SHHandleWMActivate*, as in the HelloPPC example earlier in the chapter. This call ensures that if the user switches away from the dialog and displays the SIP in another application, switching back to the informational dialog will hide the SIP.

For input dialogs, managing the SIP is somewhat more difficult. You must display the SIP as needed when the focus window is a control that requires text input. The Pocket PC provides a couple of ways to interactively manage the SIP for your dialog. First, the dialog box can display the SIP when the dialog is created and keep it up for the life of the dialog. Another technique is to display the SIP only when the user is working with a control that requires keyboard input.

To display the SIP and keep it displayed while the dialog has focus, simply insert a call to the function *SHInputDialog* in your dialog procedure so that it is called for every message sent to the dialog box. The function prototype for *SHInputDialog* is

```
void SHInputDialog (HWND hwnd, UINT uMsg, WPARAM wParam);
```

The parameters are the window handle, message, and *wParam* for the current message. This helper function appropriately commands the SIP to show or hide, depending on whether the dialog box is gaining or losing focus.

To have the SIP interactively show and hide itself depending on the control that has focus in the dialog box, you use a special control, *WC_SIPPREF*, which can be inserted into a dialog box. Typically you'll do this by specifying a line in the dialog box template. The resource editor doesn't insert this control by default. You must insert it either by inserting a User Control in the dialog box editor or by manually editing the dialog box resource. Editing the resource file manually might be more reliable because the *WC_SIPPREF* control must be the last control specified in the dialog box template. Adding the control is as simple as inserting the following text as the last line in the dialog box template:

```
CONTROL        "",-1,"SIPPREF",NOT WS_VISIBLE,-10,-10,6,6
```

Because this control is one of the Pocket PC special controls, your application must initialize it by calling

```
BOOL SHInitExtraControls (void);
```

SHInitExtraControls should be called once during your application's initialization to initialize any of the Pocket PC special controls such as *CAPEDIT* and *SIPPREF*.

Property Sheets

Another area where the Pocket PC's look and feel differs from generic Windows CE builds is in the display of property sheets. Property sheets in Pocket PC applications are full screen, with tabs at the bottom of the sheet instead of the top. To conform to this look, an application must create property sheets with a special flag specified and then intercept the creation notification of the sheet to modify the sheet style. Figure 17-5 shows the property sheet created by the Dlg-Demo example from Chapter 6 on a Pocket PC.

Figure 17-5   A property sheet on the Pocket PC has tabs across the bottom.

To create a property sheet that is full screen and that has tabs on the bottom, add the flags *PSH_MAXIMIZE* and *PSH_USECALLBACK* in the *dwFlags* field of the *PROPSHEETHEADER* structure. *PSH_MAXIMIZE* tells the dialog manager to make the property sheet a full-screen window. The *PSH_USECALLBACK* flag is a standard Win32 property sheet flag that tells the dialog to call back to the application when certain events occur in the property sheet. Specifically, the message we are interested in is the Windows CE unique *PSCB_INITIALIZED* notification, which indicates that the property sheet's Tab control has been created. To field the *PSCB_INITIALIZED* notification, the application must provide a callback function with the following prototype:

```
UINT CALLBACK PropSheetPageProc (HWND hwnd, UINT uMsg,
                                 LPPROPSHEETPAGE ppsp);
```

The parameters sent back to the application are a handle value documented to be reserved, the notification code in the *uMsg* parameter, and, on some notifications, a pointer to a *PROPSHEETPAGE* structure. For our purposes, the callback function can simply employ the following code:

```
int CALLBACK PropSheetProc(HWND hwndDlg, UINT uMsg, LPARAM lParam) {

    if (uMsg == PSCB_INITIALIZED) {
        // Get tab control
        HWND hwndTabs = GetDlgItem (hwndDlg, 0x3020);

        DWORD dwStyle = GetWindowLong (hwndTabs, GWL_STYLE);
        SetWindowLong (hwndTabs, GWL_STYLE, dwStyle | TCS_BOTTOM);

    } else if (uMsg ==  PSCB_GETVERSION)
        return COMCTL32_VERSION;
    return 1;
}
```

The source of this rather strange code comes from the MFC source code provided with the Pocket PC SDK. During the *PSCB_INITIALIZE* notification, the handle of the Tab control of the property sheet is queried using the predefined control ID 0x3020. The style bits of the Tab control are then modified to have the control place the tabs on the bottom instead of the top by setting the *TCS_BOTTOM* style flag.

Two additional callback notifications are available exclusively on the Pocket PC. The *PSCB_GETLINKTEXT* notification is sent to query the title of the property sheet. This text is displayed on the sheet itself, not on the navigation bar at the top of the screen.

The *PSCB_GETLINKTEXT* notification is sent to the callback procedure to see if the application wants to display a hyperlink string below the tabs on the property sheet. The string is copied to the buffer pointed to by *lParam*. The hyperlink within the string should be in the following form:

```
TEXT ("Launch the calculator by tapping <file:calc.exe{here}>.")
```

The hyperlink is enclosed in angle brackets (<>). The text displayed for the link is enclosed in curly brackets ({}). When the hyperlink is tapped, the Pocket PC will launch calc.exe. The hyperlink can also be a data file such as Book1.pxl or Memo.pwd.

AutoRun

The Pocket PC has a feature that can automatically launch an application when any new external storage is detected such as the insertion of a CompactFlash or Secure Digital card. This feature is typically used to provide an auto-install feature for software. However, there is no reason the application launched has to be an installation program.

When the shell detects that a storage card has been inserted, it looks in the root directory of that card for a directory with a specific name. If that directory exists and contains an application named autorun.exe, the application is first copied to the \windows directory, and then launched with a command line string *install*. When the card is removed, the copy of autorun in the \windows directory is again launched, this time with a command line of *uninstall*.

The directory that the Pocket PC searches for depends on the type of CPU in the device because an application must be compiled specifically for a CPU. The autorun directory names match the CPU type value returned from the *Get-SystemInfo* function. The following list shows the values for a few of the more popular CPUs. All the CPU values are defined in Winnt.h.

MIPS (41xx series and 3910)	4000
SH3	10003
SH4	10005
StrongARM	2577
XScale	1824

When autorun.exe is launched, it might need to know which directory it was copied from on the storage card. The application can't use *GetModuleFile-Name* because it was copied and launched from the \windows directory. To determine the fully specified autorun path, an application can call

```
BOOL SHGetAutoRunPath (LPTSTR pAutoRunPath);
```

The single parameter is the address of a *TCHAR* buffer of at least *MAX_PATH* characters. The function will fail if no storage card is found. If a card is inserted, the function returns the expected autorun directory whether or not the actual folder exists on the storage card. For example, for a system with a StrongARM CPU and an Autorun.exe file in the appropriate directory, the directory returned is \storage card\2577\autorun.exe.

SHGetAutoRunPath can optionally be supported by systems based on Windows CE .NET 4.2 or later. However, the Explorer shell does not automatically launch applications from storage cards. An OEM could easily add this feature if needed.

Additional Pocket PC Shell Functions

The Pocket PC has a few functions provided to support applications. Most of these functions are unique to the Pocket PC and are available to solve specific issues that Pocket PC applications need to deal with occasionally. These functions are also available on embedded systems that support the aygshell component but their implementation is OEM specific.

Full-Screen Windows

The *SHFullScreen* function allows an application to control the visibility of items such as the Start icon on the navigation bar, the navigation bar itself, and the SIP button. The function is prototyped as

```
BOOL SHFullScreen (HWND hwndRequester, DWORD dwState);
```

The first parameter is the handle of the window requesting the change. The *dwState* parameter can be a combination of the following:

- ■   *SHFS_HIDETASKBAR*   Hide the navigation bar.

- ■   *SHFS_SHOWTASKBAR*   Show the navigation bar.

- ■   *SHFS_HIDESIPBUTTON*   Hide the SIP button on the menu bar.

- ■   *SHFS_SHOWSIPBUTTON*   Show the SIP button on the menu bar.

- ■   *SHFS_HIDESTARTICON*   Hide the Windows icon on the navigation bar. This disables the Start menu.

- ■   *SHFS_SHOWSTARTICON*   Show the Windows icon on the navigation bar. This enables the Start menu.

The flags that hide the navigation bar, the SIP button, and the Start icon can be passed only if the handle passed in the first parameter of *SHFullScreen* is the handle to the foreground window.

Freeing Memory

Another handy function allows an application to request that the system free a specified amount of memory so that memory can be allocated. The function is

```
BOOL SHCloseApps (DWORD dwMemSought);
```

This parameter is the amount of memory that the application needs. When this function is called, the Pocket PC checks the current memory state to determine whether the amount of memory requested is available. If so, the function returns immediately. If not, the Pocket PC uses various methods, including closing applications, to attempt to free that amount of memory. *SHCloseApps* will return *TRUE* if the amount of memory is available and *FALSE* if it could not free the amount requested. Because this function closes applications and therefore must wait for each application to properly shut down, it can take a few seconds to complete.

Controlling the SIP

SHSipInfo is an omnibus function that lets you control the soft keyboard. On the Pocket PC, *SHSipInfo* has limited usefulness because most applications should use *SHSipPreference* instead of *SHSipInfo*. Still, *SHSipInfo* is handy because it is the only way to query the state and location of the SIP. It also allows an application to change the default input method. The function is prototyped as

```
BOOL SHSipInfo (UINT uiAction, UINT uiParam, PVOID pvParam,
            UINT fWinIni);
```

The first parameter to *SHSipInfo*, *uiAction*, should be set with a flag that specifies the action you want to perform with the function. The allowable flags are

- **SPI_SETSIPINFO**   Sets the SIP configuration, including its location and its visibility (Obsolete. Use *SHSipPreference*.)

- **SPI_GETSIPINFO**   Queries the SIP configuration

- **SPI_SETCURRENTIM**   Sets the current default input method

- **SPI_GETCURRENTIM**   Queries the current default input method

Because the behavior of *SHSipInfo* is completely different for each of the flags, I'll describe the function as if it were three different function calls. I won't discuss *SPI_SETSIPINFO* because its function is superseded by *SHSipPreference*. For each of the flags, the second and fourth parameters, *uiParam* and *fWinIni*, must be set to 0.

Querying the State of the SIP

To query the current state of the SIP, call *SHSipInfo* with the *SPI_GETSIPINFO* flag in the *uiAction* parameter. In this case, the function looks like this:

```
BOOL SHSipInfo (SPI_GETSIPINFO, 0, SIPINFO *psi, 0);
```

The third parameter must point to a *SIPINFO* structure, which is defined as

```
typedef struct {
    DWORD cbSize;
    DWORD fdwFlags;
    RECT rcVisibleDesktop;
    RECT rcSipRect;
    DWORD dwImDataSize;
    VOID *pvImData;
} SIPINFO;
```

The structure's first field, *cbSize*, must be set to the size of the *SIPINFO* structure before a call is made to *SHSipInfo*. The second field in *SIPINFO*, *fdwFlags*, can contain a combination of the following flags:

- **SIPF_ON**   When set, the SIP is visible.

- **SIPF_DOCKED**   When set, the SIP is docked to its default location on the screen.

- **SIPF_LOCKED**   When set, the visibility state of the SIP can't be changed by the user.

The next two fields of *SIPINFO* provide information on the location of the SIP. The field *rcVisibleDesktop* is filled with the screen dimensions of the visible area of the desktop. If the SIP is docked, this area is the rectangle above the SIP. If the SIP is undocked, this rectangle contains the full desktop area minus the taskbar, if the taskbar is showing. This field is ignored when you set the SIP configuration. Some SIPs might have a docked state that doesn't run from edge to edge of the screen. In this case, the rectangle describes the largest rectangular area of the screen that isn't obscured by the SIP.

The *rcSipRect* field contains the location and size of the SIP. If the SIP is docked, the rectangle is usually the area of the screen not included by *rcVisibleDesktop*. But if the SIP is undocked, *rcSipRect* contains the size and position of the SIP while *rcVisibleDesktop* contains the entire desktop not obscured by the taskbar, including the area under the SIP. Figure 17-6 shows the relationship between *rcVisibleDesktop* and *rcSipRect*.

The final two fields of *SIPINFO* allow you to query information specific to the current input method. The format of this information is defined by the input method. To query this information, set the *pvImData* field to point to a buffer to receive the information and set *dwImDataSize* to the size of the buffer. It is up to the application to know which input methods provide what specific data. For most input methods, these two fields should be set to 0 to indicate that no IM-specific data is being queried.

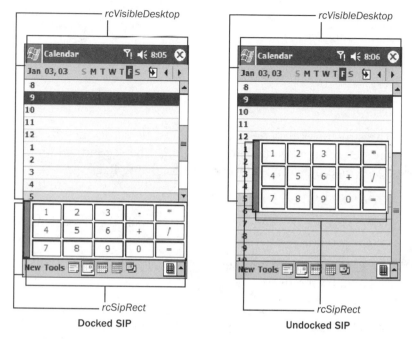

Figure 17-6 The relationship between *rcVisibleDesktop* and *rcSipRect* in the *SIPINFO* structure

Changing the Default Input Method

You can use *SHSipInfo* to query and to change the current SIP. To query the current SIP, you call *SHSipInfo* with the *SPI_GETCURRENTIM* flag in the *uiAction* parameter, as in

```
BOOL SHSipInfo (SPI_GETCURRENTIM, 0, CLSID *pclsid, 0);
```

In this case, the third parameter points to a *CLSID* variable that receives the CLSID of the current input method.

To set the current input method, call *SHSipInfo* with the *uiAction* parameter set to *SPI_SETCURRENTIM*, as in

```
BOOL SHSipInfo (SPI_SETCURRENTIM, 0, CLSID *pclsid, 0);
```

Here again, the third parameter of *SHSipInfo* is a pointer to a *CLSID* value. In this case, the value must contain a CLSID of a valid input method.

This chapter has covered a fair amount of ground. However, the Pocket PC is more than applications. It's possible to extend the basic shell of the Pocket PC in a number of ways. In the next chapter, we'll extend the Today screen and create a new input method for the SIP.

18

Extending the Pocket PC

In Chapter 17, I talked about how to write applications for the Pocket PC. In this chapter, I'll talk about ways to extend the basic functionality of parts of the Pocket PC shell. Specifically, I'll demonstrate how to create custom items for the Today screen and how to write a custom input method. The examples are simple, but in both cases they demonstrate the functions necessary for much more complex extensions.

Custom Today Screen Items

The Today screen is the home page of the Pocket PC. It's automatically displayed after the system isn't used for a predetermined period of time. It contains a snapshot of the relevant data from the applications bundled with the Pocket PC. By using a simple DLL, you can extend the Today screen to allow other applications to summarize their data or to allow stand-alone Today screen inserts that provide data only through the Today screen. Figure 18-1 shows the Today screen with five items: the Today title bar, the Owner Info item, the Tasks item, the Inbox item, and the Calendar item.

Today screen items are implemented as simple Windows CE DLLs with two predefined entry points. The system finds the extensions by looking under a specific registry key. It then loads the DLL, asks the item its desired height, and asks it to display its data. The Today Control Panel applet allows users to selectively enable and disable individual items as well as set the order of the items on the Today screen. The user can also configure an individual item through the Today Control Panel applet. When the user selects an item from a list of all the Today screen items and taps the Options button, the item's DLL is loaded and a dialog box is created by using a dialog box procedure exported from the DLL. This dialog box is created using resources stored in the DLL.

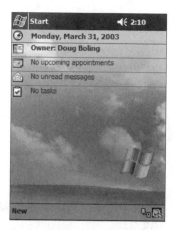

Figure 18-1 The Pocket PC Today screen

Implementing a Today Screen Item

The requirements for a Today screen item DLL start with an exported entry point, *InitializeCustomItem*, which must be exported as ordinal 240. The DLL can also optionally support a configuration dialog box. If it does, the DLL must export another entry point, *CustomItemOptionsDlgProc*, at ordinal 241, which is used as the dialog box procedure for the options dialog. In addition, the resource for the options dialog must be included in the DLL's resource and have a resource ID of *ID_TODAY_CUSTOM*.

The *InitializeCustomItem* function is prototyped as

```
HWND APIENTRY InitializeCustomItem (TODAYLISTITEM *ptli, HWND hwndParent);
```

The first parameter is a pointer to a *TODAYLISTITEM* structure; the second parameter is the handle of a window that will be the parent of the item window created by the extension. Because the *TODAYLISTITEM* structure is used throughout the Today screen interface, this is as good a place as any to describe it. Many of the fields in this structure might not be useful or even relevant in this call. However, the structure tends to be passed back to the DLL on almost every call, so most of the fields are used at some time in the life of the DLL. The structure is defined as

```
typedef struct _TODAYLISTITEM {
    TCHAR szName[MAX_ITEMNAME];
    TODAYLISTITEMTYPE tlit;
    DWORD dwOrder;
```

```
    DWORD cyp;
    BOOL fEnabled;
    BOOL fOptions;
    DWORD grfFlags;
    TCHAR szDLLPath[MAX_PATH];
    HINSTANCE hinstDLL;
    HWND hwndCustom;
    BOOL fSizeOnDraw;
    BYTE *prgbCachedData;
    DWORD cbCachedData;
} TODAYLISTITEM;
```

When *InitializeCustomItem* is called, the *szName* field is filled with the name of the registry key that identified the item. This name is handy for finding the item's registry key to retrieve custom data. The second field is *tlit*, a *TODAY-LISTITEMTYPE* enumeration that defines the type of extension. For custom extensions this field will always be *tlitCustom*. The *dwOrder* field will be set to the order index of this item. The *cyp* field contains the height of the item in pixels. Items are ordered from the lowest to the highest value starting at the top of the Today screen. The user controls the order through the Control Panel applet. For most situations, an extension's order in the Today window shouldn't affect the extension's behavior.

The *fEnabled* field indicates whether the user has enabled your Today item in the Control Panel. This field should be queried when *InitializeCustom-Item* is called; if it is 0, you should return immediately with a return code of 0. The *fOptions* flag reflects whether the Today item has an options dialog. This flag is taken from the registry entry for this item.

Let's skip the *grfFlags* field for a moment. The *szDLLPath* field contains the filename of the DLL that contains the code for the item. The *hinstDLL* field is the DLL's instance handle. The *hwndCustom* field will contain the handle of the item's child window when this structure is passed after the item's child window has been created. The Today screen item manager uses the *fSizeOnDraw* field internally.

The last two fields, *prgbCachedData* and *cbCachedData*, along with the *grfFlags* field, allow the DLL to store, or *cache*, custom data about the state of its window and the data it is displaying. The goal here is to prevent the item from having to query a file or database every time the Today screen is asked to repaint itself. The *grfFlags* field can be set to anything the DLL requires. Likewise, if the DLL needs to store additional data, a memory block can be allocated. A pointer to the memory block is saved in *prgbCachedData*, and the size of the memory block is saved in *cbCachedData*. Since these values are passed back to the DLL on a regular basis, these fields free the DLL from having to store data internally in statically defined structures.

Creating the Item Window

When *InitializeCustomItem* is called, the DLL should create its child window that will display the data for that item. The window should be a child window with its parent set to the window handle passed in the *hwndParent* parameter. The function should return the handle to the child window if the initialization was successful, or 0 otherwise.

Of course, to create a window, you will first need to register a class for that window. The class registration can take place either during the processing of the *InitializeCustomItem* call or during the *PROCESS_ATTACH* notification to *DllMain* when the DLL is loaded. If the registration is performed during the *InitializeCustomItem* call, be sure not to return failure from the function if the call to *RegisterClass* fails. Because *InitializeCustomItem* is called more than once, the second call to register the class will fail if the DLL attempts to repeat the class registration. The DLL should also be designed to unregister the window class when the DLL is unloaded. This design feature is quite helpful for debugging purposes, when the DLL will change as the code develops.

The Item Window

Once the item's window is created, the Today screen will send a custom message, *WM_TODAYCUSTOM_QUERYREFRESHCACHE*, to the child window. When the message is sent, the *wParam* parameter points to the *TODAYLISTITEM* structure that was passed in the call to *InitializeCustomItem*. The message is sent to ask the item if the data it is presenting to the user has changed and therefore the window needs updating. If so, the window should set the *cyp* field of the *TODAYLISTITEM* structure to the height in pixels for the item window. The window should return *TRUE* for the message. If no update is necessary, the window should respond to the message with *FALSE*. It is important that the item window return *TRUE* only when necessary, since returning *TRUE* causes the Today screen to repaint itself. Having this happen too often—especially when nothing on the screen changes—distracts the user and wastes power.

The item shouldn't draw in its window during the handling of the *WM_TODAYCUSTOM_QUERYREFRESHCACHE* message. If the data changes and the item returns *TRUE*, the item's window will be invalidated by the item manager, causing a *WM_PAINT* message to be sent to the item window, which is where the window should be redrawn.

The *WM_TODAYCUSTOM_QUERYREFRESHCACHE* message is sent to the item's window every few seconds, allowing the item to check whether it needs to modify the currently displayed data. Since the item has a chance to modify the *cyp* field, this is also the place where the item can ask to be resized to a taller or shorter window. The width of the window will be the full width of the Pocket PC screen minus the width of the scroll bar if present.

The look of the item window needs to blend in with the user's Today screen theme. Part of the theme is the color of the font being used in the Today screen items. The color to use can be queried by sending a *TODAYM_GETCOLOR* message to the item's parent window, as in

```
rgbColor = (COLORREF)SendMessage (GetParent (hWnd), TODAYM_GETCOLOR,
                                  (WPARAM)TODAYCOLOR_TEXT, NULL);
```

In addition, any text should be drawn in transparent mode. This can be accomplished with a call to *SetBkMode* passing the *TRANSPARENT* flag.

The item window should process the erase background (*WM_ERASEBKGND*) message to properly display the theme colors of the Today screen in the item window. During the processing of this message, the item window should send a *TODAYM_DRAWWATERMARK* message to its parent. The *wParam* should be set to 0, and the *lParam* should point to a *TODAY-DRAWWATERMARKINFO* structure defined as

```
typedef struct
{
    HDC hdc;
    RECT rc;
    HWND hwnd;
} TODAYDRAWWATERMARKINFO;
```

The item window should initialize this structure before sending the message. A possible erase routine might look like this:

```
case WM_ERASEBKGND:
{
    TODAYDRAWWATERMARKINFO wmi;
    wmi.hwnd = hwnd;
    wmi.hdc = (HDC)wParam;
    GetClientRect(hwnd, &wmi.rc);
    SendMessage(GetParent(hwnd), TODAYM_DRAWWATERMARK, 0, (LPARAM)&dwi);
    return 1;
}
```

The window should return a one from *WM_ERASEBKGND* to indicate that it has processed the message.

Interacting with the User

The custom item interacts with the user by painting its data onto its window in response to *WM_PAINT* messages. Because the custom item is a window, it also receives any mouse messages. Given that the user interface guidelines recommend a single click for most actions, the typical thing to do is monitor for a

WM_LBUTTONUP event and provide a default action. For example, the item might launch the application that can edit the data the item shows.

Because the item is simply a child window of the Today screen, it can do almost anything a window can do, with these limitations: The Today screen controls the size and position of the item child window, so the item shouldn't try to move or size itself. Also, the Today screen is designed to scroll if more items are being displayed than can fit on the screen. Because of this feature, the item manager can move your child window at any time.

Unloading the Custom Item

When the Today screen item manager needs to completely refresh the items on the Today screen, it notifies each window by sending a *WM_TODAYCUSTOM_CLEARCACHE* message. Here again, the *wParam* parameter points to the item's *TODAYLISTITEM* structure, allowing the individual items to free the memory they have allocated during the life of the item. Generally, this means freeing the data block pointed to by the *prgbCachedData* field if the item had previously allocated such a block of data.

The Options Dialog

Today items must implement their options dialog in a rather strange way. The DLL doesn't simply export a function that the Today item manager could call to instruct the item to display an options dialog. Instead, the DLL is required to export a specific function, the Options dialog box procedure, and provide in its resource block a dialog box template with a specific ID number. With a pointer to a dialog procedure and a dialog template, the item manager can call *CreateDialog* itself.

The dialog box procedure provided by the item should conform to Pocket PC user interface guidelines and call *SHInitDialog* to make itself full screen. In addition, the documentation suggests that the Options dialog box be written to look like the Today screen Control Panel applet, with blue header text and a separator line above whatever dialog controls you see fit to use. The example program at the end of this section has an Options dialog box that conforms to these suggestions. The configuration data should be stored in the registry so that the item window can query it when the Today screen loads the item.

Registering the Custom Item

The Today screen locates the custom items by looking in the registry for a list of items. The registry key that contains the list is [HKEY_LOCAL_MACHINE]\Software\Microsoft\Today\Items. Each custom Today screen item should create a subkey under the key listed above. This subkey name will be the name shown to the user in the Today screen configuration dialog, so it must be localized for the appropriate language. Under the item's subkey, a number of values must be set. The values are

- **Name** String value containing the name of the item.

- **DLL** String value containing the fully specified path name of the DLL implementing the item.

- **Flags** User-defined *DWORD* value returned in the *grfFlags* field of *TODAYLISTITEM*.

- **Options** *DWORD* value set to 1 if the item supports an Options dialog box.

- **Enabled** *DWORD* value set to 1 if the item is enabled.

- **Type** Custom items must set this *DWORD* value to 4.

The Today screen looks at these registry entries when it loads the items on the Today screen, which happens when the system boots and when the user closes the Today screen Control Panel applet.

Debugging a Custom Item

One of the problems with developing a Today screen item is how to force the Today screen to unload a custom item so that a developer can download a revised copy of that item. When the Today screen starts, it loads all the DLLs listed under the Items key previously described. The DLLs remain loaded even if the user doesn't enable them. It's difficult to update a registered Today screen item because a DLL can't be overwritten until the Today screen unloads that DLL.

In my experience, the best way to force the Today screen to unload an item is to open a registry editor on the Pocket PC or use the Windows CE Remote Registry Editor and change the name of the DLL listed under the DLL value for your item. You then open the Today screen Control Panel and enable or disable another item and close the Control Panel. This series of actions causes the Today screen to free all DLLs and reload the ones listed in the registry. Because you have just changed the DLL value to some filename that doesn't exist, the Today screen can't load that DLL, thereby allowing Microsoft eMbedded Visual C++ to download a new copy.

The PowerBar Custom Today Screen Item

The PowerBar example is a Today screen extension that displays the status of the battery as a bar running across the item window. PowerBar includes an options dialog that conforms to the look and feel of the options dialogs of the other Today screen items. Using the options dialog, you can change the height of the PowerBar item from a wide bar that displays an icon and a text display of the battery state to a thin 5-pixel bar that takes up very little room on your Today screen. Tapping the PowerBar item launches the Power Control Panel applet.

To install PowerBar, you need to edit the Pocket PC registry to add an entry for PowerBar under [HKEY_LOCAL_MACHINE]\Software\Microsoft \Today\Items, as I explained earlier. For the DLL name, use \Windows \Powerbar.dll. Figure 18-2 shows the Today screen with the PowerBar custom item. Listing 18-1 shows the PowerBar source code.

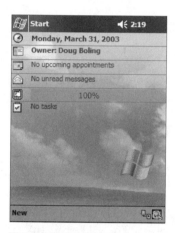

Figure 18-2 The Today screen with the PowerBar custom item displayed

This example has an additional source code file, PowerBar.def. Def files provide a method for defining specific ordinal values for exported functions. In the case of Today screen items, the exported function *InitializeCustomItem* and the options dialog box procedure must be assigned ordinals 240 and 241, respectively.

PowerBar.def

```
EXPORTS

InitializeCustomItem @ 240 NONAME
CustomItemOptionsDlgProc @ 241 NONAME
```

Listing 18-1 The PowerBar example

PowerBar.rc

```
//======================================================================
// Resource file
//
// Written for the book Programming Windows CE
// Copyright (C) 2003 Douglas Boling
//======================================================================
#include "windows.h"
#include "aygshell.h"
#include "todaycmn.h"
#include "PowerBar.h"

ID_ICON ICON "PowerBar.ico"
//----------------------------------------------------------------------
// Options dialog box template
//
IDD_TODAY_CUSTOM    DIALOG DISCARDABLE    0, 15, 134, 145
STYLE DS_CONTROL | WS_POPUP | WS_VISIBLE
CAPTION "Settings"
BEGIN
    LTEXT    "Today : PowerBar Options",
                        IDC_STATIC_TITLE,   4,   3, 124,  10

    ICON  ID_ICON,                      -1,   3,  20,  10,  10
    LTEXT "PowerBar - Written for the book Programming Windows \
          CE Copyright 2003 Douglas Boling"
                                        -1,  30,  20, 102,  30

    LTEXT "Bar Height",                 -1,   3,  60, 124,  10
    AUTORADIOBUTTON "Short",      ID_SHORT,    7,  72, 124,  10
    AUTORADIOBUTTON "Medium",       ID_MED,    7,  84, 124,  10
    AUTORADIOBUTTON "Tall",        ID_TALL,    7,  96, 124,  10
END
```

PowerBar.h

```
//======================================================================
// Header file
//
// Written for the book Programming Windows CE
// Copyright (C) 2003 Douglas Boling
//
//======================================================================
// Returns number of elements
#define dim(x) (sizeof(x) / sizeof(x[0]))
```

(continued)

Listing 18-1   *(continued)*

```
//------------------------------------------------------------------------
// Generic defines and data types
//
struct decodeUINT {                                   // Structure associates
    UINT Code;                                        // messages
                                                      // with a function.
    LRESULT (*Fxn)(HWND, UINT, WPARAM, LPARAM);
};
struct decodeCMD {                                    // Structure associates
    UINT Code;                                        // menu IDs with a
    LRESULT (*Fxn)(HWND, WORD, HWND, WORD);           // function.
};

// Helper macro
#define  MyIsBtnChecked(a,b) \
    ((SendDlgItemMessage (a, b, BM_GETSTATE,0,0)&3)==BST_CHECKED)


//------------------------------------------------------------------------
// Generic defines used by application
#define  ID_ICON               100                    // Icon ID

#define  IDC_STATIC_TITLE  101
#define  IDC_STATIC_DESC   102
#define  ID_SHORT          103
#define  ID_MED            104
#define  ID_TALL           105
//------------------------------------------------------------------------
// Function prototypes
//
int MyRegisterClass (HINSTANCE hInst);
int MyGetSetTodayItemReg (int *pi, BOOL fRead);


// Window procedures
LRESULT TodayWndProc (HWND, UINT, WPARAM, LPARAM);


// Message handlers
LRESULT DoCreateMain (HWND, UINT, WPARAM, LPARAM);
LRESULT DoPaintMain (HWND, UINT, WPARAM, LPARAM);
LRESULT DoEraseBackgroundMain (HWND, UINT, WPARAM, LPARAM);
LRESULT DoLButtonUpMain (HWND, UINT, WPARAM, LPARAM);
LRESULT DoClearCacheMain (HWND, UINT, WPARAM, LPARAM);
LRESULT DoQueryRefreshCacheMain (HWND, UINT, WPARAM, LPARAM);
LRESULT DoDestroyMain (HWND, UINT, WPARAM, LPARAM);
```

PowerBar.cpp

```cpp
//======================================================================
// PowerBar - An example Today screen item
//
// Written for the book Programming Windows CE
// Copyright (C) 2003 Douglas Boling
//======================================================================
#include <windows.h>               // For all that Windows stuff
#include <aygshell.h>              // Pocket PC includes
#include <todaycmn.h>              // Today screen includes
#include "PowerBar.h"              // PowerBar includes

// Returns number of elements
#define TODAYWND   TEXT ("MyPowerBarWnd")

// Procedure defs
//
// Global data
//
HINSTANCE hInst;
int nBattValue = 0;
BOOL fAC = FALSE;
BOOL fCharging = FALSE;
BOOL fNewData = TRUE;
int nFontHeight;

// Message dispatch table for TodayWindowProc
const struct decodeUINT MainMessages[] = {
    WM_CREATE, DoCreateMain,
    WM_PAINT, DoPaintMain,
    WM_LBUTTONUP, DoLButtonUpMain,
    WM_ERASEBKGND, DoEraseBackgroundMain,
    WM_TODAYCUSTOM_CLEARCACHE, DoClearCacheMain,
    WM_TODAYCUSTOM_QUERYREFRESHCACHE, DoQueryRefreshCacheMain,
};


//======================================================================
// DllMain - DLL initialization entry point
//
BOOL WINAPI DllMain (HANDLE hinstDLL, DWORD dwReason,
                     LPVOID lpvReserved) {
    switch (dwReason) {
    case DLL_PROCESS_ATTACH:
        hInst = (HINSTANCE) hinstDLL;
        break;

    case DLL_PROCESS_DETACH:
```

(continued)

Listing 18-1   *(continued)*

```
            // We do this so we can reload the DLL later.
            UnregisterClass (TODAYWND, hInst);
            break;
        }
    }
    return TRUE;
}
//------------------------------------------------------------------------
// MyRegisterClass - Registers the item's window class
//
int MyRegisterClass (HINSTANCE hInst) {
    WNDCLASS wc;

    // Register the item's window class.
    memset (&wc, 0, sizeof (wc));
    wc.style = CS_HREDRAW | CS_VREDRAW;
    wc.lpfnWndProc = TodayWndProc;
    wc.hInstance = hInst;
    wc.lpszClassName = TODAYWND;
    wc.hbrBackground = (HBRUSH) (COLOR_WINDOW+1);
    return RegisterClass (&wc);
}
//========================================================================
// InitializeCustomItem - Entry point called by Today screen to
// indicate the item window to be created
//
HWND APIENTRY InitializeCustomItem(TODAYLISTITEM *ptli, HWND hwndParent) {

    HWND hWnd;
    // See if not enabled.
    if (!ptli->fEnabled)
        return FALSE;
    MyRegisterClass (hInst);

    // Create a child window for our Today window entry.
    hWnd = CreateWindow (TODAYWND, NULL, WS_VISIBLE | WS_CHILD,
                         0, 0, GetSystemMetrics (SM_CXSCREEN), 0,
                         hwndParent, NULL, hInst, 0);
    return hWnd;
}
//========================================================================
// Message handling procedures
//
//========================================================================
// TodayWndProc - Window procedure for the Today entry child window
//
LRESULT TodayWndProc (HWND hWnd, UINT wMsg, WPARAM wParam, LPARAM lParam) {
    INT i;
```

```
    //
    // Search message list to see if we need to handle this
    // message. If in list, call procedure.
    //
    for (i = 0; i < dim(MainMessages); i++) {
        if (wMsg == MainMessages[i].Code)
            return (*MainMessages[i].Fxn)(hWnd, wMsg, wParam, lParam);
    }
    return DefWindowProc (hWnd, wMsg, wParam, lParam);
}
//-------------------------------------------------------------------------
// DoCreateMain - Process WM_CREATE message for window.
//
LRESULT DoCreateMain (HWND hWnd, UINT wMsg, WPARAM wParam,
                      LPARAM lParam) {

    HDC hdc;
    TEXTMETRIC tm;

    // Query height of default font.
    hdc = GetDC (hWnd);
    GetTextMetrics (hdc, &tm);
    nFontHeight = tm.tmHeight + tm.tmExternalLeading;
    ReleaseDC (hWnd, hdc);

    nBattValue = -1;   // Initialize the old battery value.
    return 0;
}
//-------------------------------------------------------------------------
// DoQueryRefreshCacheMain - Process WM_TODAYCUSTOM_QUERYREFRESHCACHE
// message for window.
//
LRESULT DoQueryRefreshCacheMain (HWND hWnd, UINT wMsg, WPARAM wParam,
                                 LPARAM lParam) {


    TODAYLISTITEM *ptli = (TODAYLISTITEM *)wParam;
    SYSTEM_POWER_STATUS_EX sps;

    // Set the height of our entry.
    if ((ptli->grfFlags < 5) || (ptli->grfFlags > 23))
        ptli->cyp = 20;
    else
        ptli->cyp = ptli->grfFlags;

    // Check the power status.
    GetSystemPowerStatusEx (&sps, FALSE);

    // Save AC status.
    if (sps.ACLineStatus == 1)
```

(continued)

Listing 18-1   *(continued)*

```
        fAC = TRUE;
    else
        fAC = FALSE;

    // Save charging status.
    if (sps.BatteryFlag & 0x08)
        fCharging = TRUE;
    else
        fCharging = FALSE;


    // If the battery value has changed since the last check,
    // set the flag to force a redraw of the Today screen.
    if (sps.BatteryLifePercent != nBattValue) {
        nBattValue = sps.BatteryLifePercent;
        fNewData = TRUE;
    } else
        fNewData = FALSE;
    return fNewData;
}
//---------------------------------------------------------------------
// DoClearCacheMain - Process WM_TODAYCUSTOM_CLEARCACHE message
// for window.
//
LRESULT DoClearCacheMain (HWND hWnd, UINT wMsg, WPARAM wParam,
                          LPARAM lParam) {
    // Nothing to do here since the example doesn't cache data
    return 0;
}
//---------------------------------------------------------------------
// DoLButtonUpMain - Process WM_LBUTTONUP message for window.
//
LRESULT DoLButtonUpMain (HWND hWnd, UINT wMsg, WPARAM wParam,
                         LPARAM lParam) {
    SHELLEXECUTEINFO se;
    DWORD dwAttr;

    // Launch the Control Panel's power applet.
    memset (&se, 0, sizeof (se));
    se.cbSize = sizeof (se);
    se.hwnd = hWnd;
    se.lpFile = TEXT ("ctlpnl.exe");
    se.lpVerb = TEXT("open");
    se.lpDirectory = TEXT ("\\windows");
    se.lpParameters = TEXT ("powerg.cpl");
```

```
    // See if power cpl is a standalone exe.
    dwAttr = GetFileAttributes (TEXT("\\windows\\powerg.exe"));
    if (dwAttr != (DWORD)-1)
        se.lpFile = TEXT ("powerg.exe");

    ShellExecuteEx (&se);    // Launch the Control Panel.
    return 0;
}
//------------------------------------------------------------------
// DoEraseBackgroundMain - Process WM_ERASEBKGND message for window.
//
LRESULT DoEraseBackgroundMain (HWND hWnd, UINT wMsg, WPARAM wParam,
                    LPARAM lParam) {

    TODAYDRAWWATERMARKINFO wmi;
    wmi.hwnd = hWnd;
    wmi.hdc = (HDC)wParam;
    GetClientRect (hWnd, &wmi.rc);
    SendMessage (GetParent (hWnd), TODAYM_DRAWWATERMARK, 0,
                (LPARAM)&wmi);

    return 1;
}
//------------------------------------------------------------------
// DoPaintMain - Process WM_PAINT message for window.
//
LRESULT DoPaintMain (HWND hWnd, UINT wMsg, WPARAM wParam,
                    LPARAM lParam) {
    PAINTSTRUCT ps;
    RECT rect;
    HDC hdc;
    TCHAR szText[32];
    int nPercent;
    COLORREF rgbLeft = RGB (0, 255, 0), rgbText;
    HICON hIcon;
    HBRUSH hbr;

    // Ensure a valid battery value.
    nPercent = nBattValue;
    if (nBattValue == 255) {
        nPercent = 100;
        if (!fCharging && !fAC)
            rgbLeft = RGB (255, 0, 0);
    } else if (nBattValue < 33) {
        rgbLeft = RGB (255, 0, 0);
    }

    hdc = BeginPaint (hWnd, &ps);
    GetClientRect (hWnd, &rect);
```

Listing 18-1 *(continued)*

```
    // Draw icon if room.
    if (rect.bottom - rect.top > 18) {
        hIcon = (HICON)LoadImage (hInst, MAKEINTRESOURCE (ID_ICON),
                            IMAGE_ICON, 16, 16, 0);
        DrawIcon (hdc, 2, 2, hIcon);
        DeleteObject (hIcon);
    }
    // Draw percent bar.
    hbr = CreateSolidBrush (rgbLeft);
    rect.left += 30;
    rect.right -= 5;
    rect.right = rect.left + ((rect.right - rect.left)*nPercent)/100;
    rect.top++;
    rect.bottom--;
    FillRect (hdc, &rect, hbr);
    DeleteObject (hbr);

    // Draw text percent if room.
    // Ask for rect again since we messed it up above.
    GetClientRect (hWnd, &rect);
    if (rect.bottom - rect.top > nFontHeight) {
        if (fCharging)
            lstrcpy (szText, TEXT ("Charging"));
        else if (!fAC && (nBattValue > 100))
            lstrcpy (szText, TEXT ("Unknown"));
        else
            wsprintf (szText, TEXT ("%02d%%"), nPercent);
        rgbText = (COLORREF)SendMessage (GetParent(hWnd),
                                        TODAYM_GETCOLOR,
                                        (WPARAM)TODAYCOLOR_TEXT, 0);
        SetTextColor (hdc, rgbText);
        SetBkMode (hdc, TRANSPARENT);
        DrawText (hdc, szText, -1, &rect, DT_CENTER | DT_SINGLELINE |
                DT_VCENTER);
    }
    EndPaint (hWnd, &ps);

    // Reset my "redraw now" flag.
    fNewData = FALSE;
    return 0;
}
//======================================================================
// CustomItemOptionsDlgProc - Options Dialog box procedure
//
BOOL CALLBACK CustomItemOptionsDlgProc (HWND hWnd, UINT wMsg,
                                        WPARAM wParam, LPARAM lParam) {
    static TODAYLISTITEM *ptli;
```

```
static HFONT hFont;
WORD wID;
int i;

switch (wMsg) {
case WM_INITDIALOG:
    {
        TEXTMETRIC tm;
        LOGFONT lf;
        HDC hdc;
        SHINITDLGINFO shidi;

        // Create a Done button and size dialog.
        shidi.dwMask = SHIDIM_FLAGS;
        shidi.dwFlags = SHIDIF_DONEBUTTON | SHIDIF_SIZEDLG;
        shidi.hDlg = hWnd;
        SHInitDialog(&shidi);

        ptli = (TODAYLISTITEM *)lParam;

        // Jump through hoops to look like
        // other Today Options dialogs.
        hdc = GetDC (hWnd);
        GetTextMetrics (hdc, &tm);
        memset (&lf, 0, sizeof (lf));
        // Create proper font. It's not 8 or 9 pt; it must be 8.5.
        lf.lfHeight = -1 *
                        (17 * GetDeviceCaps (hdc, LOGPIXELSY)/72)/2;
        lf.lfWeight = FW_SEMIBOLD;
        lf.lfPitchAndFamily = tm.tmPitchAndFamily;
        lstrcpy (lf.lfFaceName, TEXT("Tahoma"));
        hFont = CreateFontIndirect (&lf);
        ReleaseDC (hWnd, hdc);
        // Query bar size setting from registry.
        MyGetSetTodayItemReg (&i, TRUE);
        if (i == 0) i = 23;
        if (i < 16)
            wID = ID_SHORT;
        else if (i < 20)
            wID = ID_MED;
        else
            wID = ID_TALL;
        CheckRadioButton (hWnd, ID_SHORT, ID_TALL, wID);
    }
    break;

case WM_DESTROY:
    if (hFont)
```

(continued)

Listing 18-1 *(continued)*

```
                DeleteObject (hFont);
        break;

    case WM_PAINT:
        {
                // Draw a line 24 pixels down from the top per spec.
                PAINTSTRUCT ps;
                HDC hdc;
                RECT rect;
                HPEN hOld, hPen = (HPEN)GetStockObject (BLACK_PEN);

                GetClientRect (hWnd, &rect);
                hdc = BeginPaint (hWnd, &ps);
                rect.top = rect.top + 23;
                rect.bottom = rect.top;
                hOld = (HPEN)SelectObject (hdc, hPen);
                Polyline (hdc, (LPPOINT)&rect, 2);

                // Draw this line to separate about data from radio buttons.
                rect.top += 70;
                rect.bottom += 70;
                Polyline (hdc, (LPPOINT)&rect, 2);
                SelectObject (hdc, hOld);
                EndPaint (hWnd, &ps);
        }
        break;
    case WM_CTLCOLORSTATIC:
        // Modify the color and font of the header text string.
        if ((HWND)lParam != GetDlgItem (hWnd, IDC_STATIC_TITLE))
            break;
        SelectObject ((HDC)wParam, hFont);
        SetTextColor ((HDC)wParam, RGB (0, 0, 156));
        SetBkColor ((HDC)wParam, RGB (255, 255, 255));
        return (BOOL)GetStockObject (WHITE_BRUSH);

    case WM_COMMAND:
        wID = LOWORD (wParam);
        switch (wID) {
        case IDOK:
            i = 20;
            if (MyIsBtnChecked (hWnd, ID_MED))
                i = 16;
            else if (MyIsBtnChecked (hWnd, ID_SHORT))
                i = 5;
            // Save the height value.
            MyGetSetTodayItemReg (&i, FALSE);
            ptli->grfFlags = i;
```

```
        case IDCANCEL:
            EndDialog (hWnd, 0);
            break;
        }
        break;
    }
    return FALSE;
}
//-----------------------------------------------------------------
// MyGetSetTodayItemReg - Writes the Flags value of the Today item's
// registry entry
//
int MyGetSetTodayItemReg (int *pnFlagData, BOOL fRead) {
    HKEY hKey, hSubKey = 0;
    int rc, i = 0;
    DWORD dwType, dwSize;
    TCHAR *pName, szKey[128], szDll[MAX_PATH], szName[MAX_PATH];

    GetModuleFileName (hInst, szName, dim (szName));
    for (pName = szName + lstrlen (szName);
        (pName > szName) && (*pName != TEXT('\\')); pName--);
    if (*pName == TEXT('\\')) pName++;

    // Open the Today screen's item key.
    rc = RegOpenKeyEx (HKEY_LOCAL_MACHINE,
                    TEXT ("Software\\Microsoft\\today\\items"),
                    0, 0, &hKey);
    // Enumerate the item list until
    // we find a key with our DLL name.
    while (rc == ERROR_SUCCESS) {
        dwSize = sizeof (szKey);
        rc = RegEnumKeyEx (hKey, i++, szKey, &dwSize,
            NULL, NULL, NULL, NULL);
        if (rc != ERROR_SUCCESS)
            break;
        // Open the subkey.
        rc = RegOpenKeyEx (hKey, szKey, 0, 0, &hSubKey);
        if (rc == ERROR_SUCCESS) {
            // Get DLL name.
            dwSize = sizeof (szDll);
            rc = RegQueryValueEx (hSubKey, TEXT ("DLL"), 0, &dwType,
                                (PBYTE)szDll, &dwSize);
            if (rc == ERROR_SUCCESS) {
                // See if this is us.
                if (lstrcmpi (szDll, pName) == 0)
                    break;  //Yes!
            }
            RegCloseKey (hSubKey);
```

(continued)

Listing 18-1   *(continued)*

```
            hSubKey = 0;
        }
        rc = ERROR_SUCCESS;
    }
    if (hSubKey) {
        if (fRead) {
            dwSize = sizeof (DWORD);
            rc = RegQueryValueEx (hSubKey, TEXT("Flags"), 0, &dwType,
                            (PBYTE)pnFlagData, &dwSize);
            if (rc != ERROR_SUCCESS)
                *pnFlagData = 20;
        } else
            rc = RegSetValueEx (hSubKey, TEXT("Flags"), 0, REG_DWORD,
                        (PBYTE)pnFlagData, sizeof (DWORD));

        RegCloseKey (hSubKey);
    }
    RegCloseKey (hKey);
    return rc;
}
```

The code that displays the Today screen item is not complex. In the *InitializeCustomItem* call, PowerBar registers the window class and creates the child window. In the window procedure, the code that handles the *WM_TODAYCUSTOM_QUERYREFRESHCACHE* message sets the *cyp* field of the *TODAYLISTITEM* structure to the proper height, which is configurable through the options dialog. The routine then checks the power status of the system by calling *GetSystemPowerStatusEx*. If the battery level has changed since the last check, the routine returns *TRUE*, forcing the Today screen to redraw the item. In the *WM_PAINT* handler, the bar is drawn across the window using the *rectangle* function. Depending on the height of the window, the icon is drawn and the power level is printed in the window.

The options dialog procedure, *CustomItemOptionsDlgProc*, goes to great lengths to provide the proper look to the dialog box. To this end, a custom font, 8.5-point Tahoma, is used to display the top line of text in the dialog box. In addition, this line of text is displayed in blue and a solid line is drawn 23 pixels below the top of the dialog. These customizations match the look of the Today items dialog.

The font is created in the *WM_INITDIALOG* message. To override the drawing of the top line of text, the dialog procedure fields the *WM_CTLCOLORSTATIC* message. The following code shows how—after checking which control is being drawn—the dialog box procedure sets the text color and the font so that the text is displayed with the customized look.

```
case WM_CTLCOLORSTATIC:
    // Modify the color and font of the header text string.
    if ((HWND)lParam != GetDlgItem (hWnd, IDC_STATIC_TITLE))
        break;
    SelectObject ((HDC)wParam, hFont);
    SetTextColor ((HDC)wParam, RGB (0, 0, 156));
    SetBkColor ((HDC)wParam, RGB (255, 255, 255));
    return (BOOL)GetStockObject (WHITE_BRUSH);
```

The Today screen is an example of the extensibility of the Pocket PC shell. Applications that provide an additional Today screen item to summarize their data provide that extra bit of integration that users appreciate.

Custom Input Methods

The soft input panel, or SIP, provides Pocket PC users with a method of "keyboard"-style input. I put keyboard in quotes because although the application sees keyboard messages from the SIP, the user might be entering those characters using a handwriting recognizer. The Pocket PC comes bundled with a few ways of entering character data. The user can use either a tiny drawing of a keyboard on which the user can tap in characters or some type of handwriting recognizer that interprets strokes that the user makes with a stylus. You can also design your own method of input rather easily. A component that provides this functionality is called an *input method* (IM), and it's merely a COM object that exports an *IInputMethod* interface, and optionally an *IInputMethod2* interface.

The *IInputMethod2* interface adds new methods for dealing with the Input Method Editor (IME). The IME is used to propose a series of candidate characters in response to input in the SIP. The SIP doesn't provide enough room to allow the user to enter thousands of discrete characters, so the IME is used when working with Asian languages. Unless your SIP needs to interface with the IME, the *IInputMethod* interface should be sufficient since it is compatible with all versions of Windows CE that support a SIP. No matter which interface is exposed, the purpose of the COM object is to create an input method window in response to requests from the input panel.

The Components of a SIP

A SIP is composed of two main components—the input panel and the input method. The input panel is supplied by the system. It creates the input panel window and provides both the message loop processing for the SIP and the window procedure for the input panel window. The input panel cooperates with the taskbar or another shell program to provide the user with the ability to switch between a number of installed input methods.

The input method is the installable portion of the SIP. It's responsible for translating pen strokes and taps into keyboard input. The input method is also responsible for the look and feel of the SIP. In almost all cases, the input method creates a window that is a child of the input panel window. Within that child window, the input method draws its interface and interprets mouse messages. The input method then calls back to the input panel when it wants to generate a key event.

Each of these two components implements a COM interface, which then becomes the interface between them. The input method implements one of the *IInputMethodxx* interfaces, while the input panel implements three very similar interfaces: *IIMCallback*, *IIMCallbackEx*, and *IIMCallback2*. In the following paragraphs, I'll talk about the *IInputMethod*, *IInputMethod2*, *IIMCallback*, and *IIMCallback2* interfaces.

The interaction between the input panel and the input method is driven by the input panel. For the most part, the input method simply responds to calls made to its *IInputMethod* methods. Calls are made when the input method is loaded, when it's unloaded, and when it's shown or hidden. In response, the input method must draw in its child window, interpret the user's actions, and call methods in the *IIMCallback* interface to send keys to the system or to control the input panel's window.

Input methods are implemented as COM in-proc servers. Because of this, they must conform to the standard COM in-proc server specifications. This means that an input method is implemented as a DLL that exports *DllGetClassObject* and *DllCanUnloadNow* functions. Input methods must also export *DllRegisterServer* and *DllUnregisterServer* functions that perform the necessary registry registration and deregistration for the server DLL.

Threading Issues with Input Methods

Because the input panel and input method components are so tightly interrelated, you must follow a few rules when writing an input method. While you can use multiple threads in an input method, the interaction between the input panel and the input method is strictly limited to the input panel's primary thread. This means that the input method should create any windows during calls to methods in the *IInputMethod* interface. This ensures that these windows will use the same message loop as the input panel's window. This, in turn, allows the input panel to directly call the input method's window procedures, as necessary. In addition, that same thread should make all calls made back to the *IIMCallback* interface.

In short, try not to multithread your input method. If you must use multiple threads, create all windows in your input method using the input panel's thread. Secondary threads can be created, but they can't call the *IIMCallback* interface and they shouldn't create any windows.

The *IInputMethod* and *IInputMethod2* Interfaces

The *IInputMethod* interface is the core of an IM. Using the interface's methods, an IM should create any windows, react to any changes in the parent input panel window, and provide any cleanup when it's released. The *IInputMethod* interface exports the following methods in addition to the standard *IUnknown* methods:

- **IInputMethod::Select**   The user has selected the IM. The IM should create its window.

- **IInputMethod::Deselect**   The user has selected another IM. The IM should destroy its window.

- **IInputMethod::Showing**   The IM window is about to be shown.

- **IInputMethod::Hiding**   The IM window is about to be hidden.

- **IInputMethod::GetInfo**   The system is querying the IM for information.

- **IInputMethod::ReceiveSipInfo**   The system is providing information to the IM.

- **IInputMethod::RegisterCallback**   The system is providing a pointer to the *IIMCallback* interface.

- **IInputMethod::GetImData**   The IM is queried for IM-specific data.

- **IInputMethod::SetImData**   The IM is provided IM-specific data.

- **IInputMethod::UserOptionsDlg**   The IM should display an options dialog box to support the SIP Control Panel applet.

In addition to the preceding methods, the *IInputMethod2* interface has the following methods:

- **IInputMethod2::RegisterCallback2**   The system is sending a pointer to the *IIMCallback2* interface.

- **IInputMethod2::SetIMMActiveContext**   The system is informing the IM of the current state of the IME.

Let's now look at these methods in detail so that we can understand the processing necessary for each. The descriptions of the methods for the *IInput-Method* interface also apply for the similarly named methods in the *IInputMethod2* interface.

IInputMethod::Select
When the user chooses your input method, the DLL that contains your IM is loaded and the *Select* method is called. This method is prototyped as

```
HRESULT IInputMethod::Select (HWND hwndSip);
```

The only parameter is the handle to the SIP window that's the parent of your input method's main window. You should return *S_OK* to indicate success or *E_FAIL* if you can't create and initialize your input method successfully.

When the *Select* method is called, the IM will have just been loaded into memory and you'll need to perform any necessary initialization. This includes registering any window classes and creating the input method window. The IM should be created as a child of the SIP window because the SIP window is what will be shown, hidden, and moved in response to user action. You can call *Get-ClientRect* with the parent window handle to query the necessary size of your input window.

IInputMethod::GetInfo
After the input panel has loaded your IM, it calls the *GetInfo* method. The input panel calls this method to query the bitmaps that represent the IM. These bitmaps appear in the SIP button on the taskbar. In addition, the IM can provide a set of flags and the size and location on the screen where it would like to be displayed. This method is prototyped as

```
HRESULT IInputMethod::GetInfo (IMINFO *pimi);
```

The only parameter is a pointer to an *IMINFO* structure that the IM must fill out to give information back to the SIP. The *IMINFO* structure is defined as

```
typedef struct {
    DWORD cbSize;
    HANDLE hImageNarrow;
    HANDLE hImageWide;
    int iNarrow;
    int iWide;
    DWORD fdwFlags;
    RECT rcSipRect;
} IMINFO;
```

The first field, *cbSize*, must be filled with the size of the *IMINFO* structure. The next two fields, *hImageNarrow* and *hImageWide*, should be filled with handles to image lists that contain the bitmaps that will appear on the taskbar SIP button. The Pocket PC's menu bar uses the narrow image. However, for embedded systems, the shell has the flexibility to use either the wide 32-by-16-pixel bitmap or the narrow 16-by-16-pixel bitmap, depending on its needs. The input method must create these image lists and pass the handles in this structure. The IM is responsible for destroying the image lists when a user or an application unloads it. You can create these image lists in the *GetInfo* method as long as you design your application to know not to create the image lists twice if *GetInfo* is called more than once. Another strategy is to create the image lists in the *Select* method and store the handles as member variables of the *IInputMethod* object. Then when *GetInfo* is called, you can pass the handles of the already created image lists to the input panel.

The next two fields, *iNarrow* and *iWide*, should be set to the index in the image lists for the bitmap you want the SIP to use. For example, you might have two different bitmaps for the SIP button, depending on whether your IM is docked or floating. You can then have an image list with two bitmaps, and you can specify the index depending on the state of your IM.

The *fdwFlags* field should be set to a combination of the flags *SIPF_ON*, *SIPF_DOCKED*, *SIPF_LOCKED*, and *SIPF_DISABLECOMPLETION*, all of which define the state of the input panel. The first three flags are the same flags that I described in Chapter 17. When the *SIPF_DISABLECOMPLETION* flag is set, the auto-completion function of the SIP is disabled.

Finally, the *rcSipRect* field should be filled with the default rectangle for the input method. Unless you have a specific size and location on the screen for your IM, you can simply query the client rectangle of the parent SIP window for this rectangle. Note that just because you request a size and location of the SIP window doesn't mean that the window will have that rectangle. You should always query the size of the parent SIP window when laying out your IM window.

IInputMethod::ReceiveSipInfo

The *ReceiveSipInfo* method is called by the input panel when the input panel is shown and then again when an application moves or changes the state of the input panel. The method is prototyped as

```
HRESULT IInputMethod::ReceiveSipInfo (SIPINFO *psi);
```

The only parameter is a pointer to a *SIPINFO* structure that I described in Chapter 17. When this method is called, only two of the fields are valid—the *fdwFlags* field and the *rcSipRect* field. The *rcSipRect* field contains the size and location of the input panel window, while the *fdwFlags* field contains the

SIPF_xxx flags previously described. In response to the *ReceiveSipInfo* method call, the IM should save the new state flags and rectangle.

IInputMethod::RegisterCallback

The input panel calls the *RegisterCallback* method once, after the input method has been selected. The method is prototyped as

```
HRESULT IInputMethod::RegisterCallback (IIMCallback *lpIMCallback);
```

This method is called to provide a pointer to the *IIMCallback* interface. The only action the IM must take is to save this pointer so that it can be used to provide feedback to the input panel.

IInputMethod::Showing and IInputMethod::Hiding

The input panel calls the *Showing* and *Hiding* methods just before the IM is shown or hidden. Both these methods have no parameters and you should simply return *S_OK* to indicate success. The *Showing* method is also called when the panel is moved or resized. This makes the *Showing* method a handy place for resizing the IM child window to properly fit in the parent input panel window.

IInputMethod::GetImData and IInputMethod::SetImData

The *GetImData* and *SetImData* methods give you a back door into the IM for applications that need to have a special communication path between the application and a custom IM. This arrangement allows a specially designed IM to provide additional data to and from applications. The two methods are prototyped as

```
HRESULT IInputMethod::GetImData (DWORD dwSize, void* pvImData);
```

```
HRESULT IInputMethod::SetImData (DWORD dwSize, void* pvImData);
```

For both functions, *pvImData* points to a block of memory in the application. The *dwSize* parameter contains the size of the memory block.

When an application is sending data to a custom IM, it calls *SHSipInfo* with the *SPI_SETSIPINFO* flag. The pointer to the buffer and the size of the buffer are specified in the *pvImData* and *dwImDataSize* fields of the *SIPINFO* structure. If these two fields are nonzero, the input panel then calls the *SetIm-Data* method with the pointer and the size of the buffer contained in the two parameters of the method. The input method then accepts the data in the buffer pointed to by *pvImData*. When an application calls *SHSipInfo* with the *SPI_GETSIPINFO* structure and nonzero values in *pvImData* and *dwImData-Size*, the input panel then calls the *GetImData* method to retrieve data from the input method.

IInputMethod::Deselect

When the user or a program switches to a different default IM, the input panel calls *Deselect*. Your input method should save its state (its location on the screen, for example), destroy any windows it has created, and unregister any window classes it has registered. It should also destroy any image lists it's still maintaining. The prototype for this method is

```
HRESULT IInputMethod::Deselect (void);
```

After the *Deselect* method is called, the SIP will unload the input method DLL.

IInputMethod::UserOptionsDlg

The *UserOptionsDlg* method isn't called by the input panel. Instead, the input panel's Control Panel applet calls this method when the user taps the Options button. The IM should display a dialog box that allows the user to configure any settable parameters in the input method. The *UserOptionsDlg* method is prototyped as

```
HRESULT IInputMethod::UserOptionsDlg (HWND hwndParent);
```

The only parameter is the handle to the window that should be the parent window of the dialog box. Because the IM might be unloaded after the dialog box is dismissed, any configuration data should be saved in a persistent place such as the registry, where it can be recalled when the input panel is loaded again.

The following two methods are supported only in the *IInputMethod2* interface. The *IInputMethod2* interface is derived from *IInputMethod*; all the methods previously described are therefore implemented in *IInputMethod2*.

IInputMethod2::RegisterCallback2

The input panel calls the *RegisterCallback2* method once, after the input method has been selected. The method is prototyped as

```
HRESULT IInputMethod2::RegisterCallback2 (IIMCallback2 *lpIMCallback);
```

This method is called to provide a pointer to the *IIMCallback2* interface. The only action the IM must take is to save this pointer so that it can be used to provide feedback to the input panel.

IInputMethod2::SetIMMActiveContext

The input panel calls *SetIMMActiveContext* to inform the input method of changes in state of the IME. The method is prototyped as

```
HRESULT SetIMMActiveContext (HWND hwnd, BOOL bOpen, DWORD dwConversion,
                             DWORD dwSentence, DWORD hkl);
```

The *hwnd* parameter is the handle of window control that has changed state. The *bOpen* parameter indicates whether the IME is on or off. The *dwConversion* and *dwSentence* parameters provide status on the current mode of the IME. The *hkl* parameter contains the handle to the current active keyboard layout.

The *IIMCallback* and *IIMCallback2* Interfaces

The *IIMCallback* interface allows an IM to call back to the input panel for services such as sending keys to the operating system. Aside from the standard *IUnknown* methods that can be ignored by the IM, *IIMCallback* exposes only four methods:

- **IIMCallback::SetImInfo**   Sets the bitmaps used by the input panel as well as the location and visibility state of the input method

- **IIMCallback::SendVirtualKey**   Sends a virtual key to the system

- **IIMCallback::SendCharEvents**   Sends Unicode characters to the window with the current focus

- **IIMCallback::SendString**   Sends a string of characters to the window with the current focus

It's appropriate that the *IIMCallback* interface devotes three of its four methods to sending keys and characters to the system because that's the primary purpose of the IM.

The *IIMCallback2* interface adds one method:

- **IIMCallback2::SendAlternatives2**   Sends data from the input method to the IME

Let's take a quick look at each of these methods.

IIMCallback::SetImInfo

The *SetImInfo* method allows the IM control over its size and location on the screen. This method can also be used to set the bitmaps representing the IM. The method is prototyped as

```
HRESULT IIMCallback::SetImInfo (IMINFO *pimi);
```

The only parameter is a pointer to an *IMINFO* structure. This is the same structure that the IM uses when it calls the *GetInfo* method of the *IInputMethod* interface, but I'll repeat it here for clarity.

```
typedef struct {
    DWORD cbSize;
    HANDLE hImageNarrow;
```

```
    HANDLE hImageWide;
    int iNarrow;
    int iWide;
    DWORD fdwFlags;
    RECT rcSipRect;
} IMINFO;
```

This structure enables an IM to provide the input panel with the information that the IM retrieved in *GetInfo*. The IM must correctly fill in all the fields in the *IMINFO* structure because it has no other way to tell the input panel to look at only one or two of the fields. You shouldn't re-create the image lists when you're calling *SetImInfo*; instead, use the same handles you passed in *GetInfo*—unless you want to change the image lists used by the input panel. In that case, you'll need to destroy the old image lists after you've called *SetImInfo*.

You can use *SetImInfo* to undock the input panel and move it around the screen by clearing the *SIPF_DOCKED* flag in *fdwFlags* and specifying a new size and location for the panel in the *rcSipRect* field. Because Windows CE doesn't provide system support for dragging an input panel around the screen, the IM is responsible for providing such a method. The sample IM that I present beginning on page 907 supports dragging the input panel around by creating a gripper area on the side of the panel and interpreting the stylus messages in this area to allow the panel to be moved around the screen.

IIMCallback::SendVirtualKey

The *SendVirtualKey* method is used to send virtual key codes to the system. The difference between this method and the *SendCharEvents* and *SendString* methods is that this method can be used to send noncharacter key codes, such as those from cursor keys and shift keys, that have a global impact on the system. Also, key codes sent by *SendVirtualKey* are affected by the system key state. For example, if you send an *a* character and the Shift key is currently down, the resulting *WM_CHAR* message contains an *A* character. *SendVirtualKey* is prototyped as

```
HRESULT IIMCallback::SendVirtualKey (BYTE bVk, DWORD dwFlags);
```

The first parameter is the virtual key code of the key you want to send. The second parameter can contain one or more flags that help define the event. The flags can be either 0 or a combination of flags. You would use *KEYEVENTF_KEYUP* to indicate that the event is a key up event as opposed to a key down event and *KEYEVENTF_SILENT*, which specifies that the key event won't cause a key click to be played for the event. If you use *SendVirtualKey* to send a character key, the character will be modified by the current shift state of the system.

IIMCallback::SendCharEvents

The *SendCharEvents* method can be used to send specific characters to the window with the current focus. The difference between this method and the *SendVirtualKey* method is that *SendCharEvents* gives you much more control over the exact information provided in the *WM_KEYxxx* and *WM_CHAR* messages generated. Instead of simply sending a virtual key code and letting the system determine the proper character, this method allows you to specify the virtual key and associate a completely different character or series of characters generated by this event. For example, in a simple case, calling this method once causes the messages *WM_KEYDOWN*, *WM_CHAR*, and *WM_KEYUP* all to be sent to the focus window. In a more complex case, this method can send a *WM_KEYDOWN* and multiple *WM_CHAR* messages, followed by a *WM_KEYUP* message.

This method is prototyped as

```
HRESULT IIMCallback::SendCharEvents (UINT uVK, UINT uKeyFlags,
                UINT uChars, UINT *puShift, UINT *puChars);
```

The first parameter is the virtual key code that will be sent with the *WM_KEYDOWN* and *WM_KEYUP* messages. The second parameter is an unsigned integer containing the key flags that will be sent with the *WM_KEYDOWN* and *WM_KEYUP* messages. The third parameter is the number of *WM_CHAR* messages that will be generated by this one event. The next parameter, *puShift*, should point to an array of key state flags, while the final parameter, *puChars*, should point to an array of Unicode characters. Each entry in the shift array will be joined with the corresponding Unicode character in the character array when the *WM_CHAR* messages are generated. This allows you to give one key on the IM keyboard a unique virtual key code and to generate any number of *WM_CHAR* messages, each with its own shift state.

IIMCallback::SendString

You use the *SendString* method to send a series of characters to the focus window. The advantage of this function is that an IM can easily send an entire word or sentence, and the input panel will take care of the details such as key down and key up events. The method is prototyped as

```
HRESULT IIMCallback::SendString (LPTSTR ptszStr, DWORD dwSize);
```

The two parameters are the string of characters to be sent and the number of characters in the string.

IIMCallback2::SendAlternatives2

The *SendAlternatives2* method provides a mechanism for the input method to send alternative characters to the IME. For languages with hundreds or thousands of characters, the input method might have to guess at the intended character entered by the user. These guesses or alternative characters are sent using *SendAlternatives2* to the IME so that it can present the alternatives to the active control. If the control doesn't handle the alternative suggestions, the first character in the list is used as the correct character. The prototype of *SendAlternatives2* is

```
HRESULT SendAlternatives2(LMDATA * plmd);
```

The one parameter is a pointer to an LMDATA structure defined as

```
typedef struct _tagLMDATA {
    DWORD dwVersion;
    DWORD flags;
    DWORD cnt;
    DWORD dwOffsetSymbols;
    DWORD dwOffsetSkip;
    DWORD dwOffsetScore;
}LMDATA;
```

The version field should be set to 0x10000. The *flags* field describes the format of the data in the table provided. The *cnt* field contains the number of entries in the table. The *dwOffsetSymbols*, *dwOffsetSkip*, and *dwOffsetScore* fields contain the offset of the start of the respective tables containing the alternative data. The data in the tables vary depending on how the IME and the input method agree to share data.

The NumPanel Example Input Method

The NumPanel example code demonstrates a simple IM. NumPanel gives a user a simple numeric keyboard including keys 0 through 9 as well as the four arithmetic operators: +, -, *, and / and the equal sign key (=). Although it's not particularly useful to the user, NumPanel does demonstrate all the requirements of an input method. The NumPanel example is different from the standard IMs that come with the Pocket PC in that it can be undocked. The NumPanel IM has a gripper bar on the left side of the window that can be used to drag the SIP around the screen. When a user double-taps the gripper bar, the SIP snaps back to its docked position. Figure 18-3 shows the NumPanel IM in its docked position, while Figure 18-4 shows the same panel undocked.

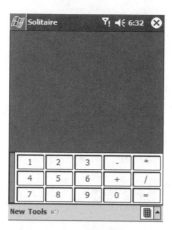

Figure 18-3   The NumPanel IM window in its docked position

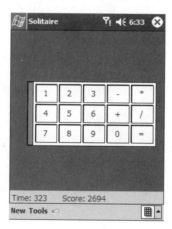

Figure 18-4   The NumPanel IM window undocked

The source code that implements NumPanel is divided into two main files, IMCommon.cpp and NumPanel.cpp. IMCommon.cpp provides the COM interfaces necessary for the IM, including the *IInputMethod* interface and the *IClassFactory* interface. IMCommon.cpp also contains *DllMain* and the other functions necessary to implement a COM in-proc server. NumPanel.cpp contains the code that implements the NumPanel window. This code comprises the NumPanel window procedure and the supporting message-handling procedures. The source code for NumPanel is shown in Listing 18-2.

NumPanel.def

```
;
;Standard COM library DEF file
;

LIBRARY    NUMPANEL.DLL

EXPORTS
    DllCanUnloadNow    @1 PRIVATE
    DllGetClassObject  @2 PRIVATE
    DllRegisterServer  @3 PRIVATE
    DllUnregisterServer @4 PRIVATE
```

IMCommon.rc

```
//=====================================================================
// Resource file
//
// Written for the book Programming Windows CE
// Copyright (C) 2003 Douglas Boling
//=====================================================================
#include "windows.h"              // For all that Windows stuff
#include "NumPanel.h"             // Program-specific stuff


//---------------------------------------------------------------------
// Icons and bitmaps
//
ID_ICON        ICON   "NumPanel.ico" // Module icon

NarrowBmp      BITMAP "nkbd.bmp"     // Bmp used in image list
NarrowMask     BITMAP "nmask.bmp"    // Mask used in image list
WideBmp        BITMAP "widekbd.bmp"  // Bmp used in image list
WideMask       BITMAP "widemask.bmp" // Mask used in image list
```

IMCommon.h

```
//=====================================================================
// Header file
//
// Written for the book Programming Windows CE
// Copyright (C) 2003 Douglas Boling
//=====================================================================
#define ID_ICON        1

// **** Start of Generic COM declarations ****
//=====================================================================
```

Listing 18-2   The NumPanel source code

(continued)

Listing 18-2   *(continued)*

```
// MyClassFactory - Object declaration
//
class MyClassFactory : public IClassFactory {

private:
    long m_lRef;

public:
    MyClassFactory();
    ~MyClassFactory();

    //IUnknown methods
    STDMETHODIMP QueryInterface (THIS_ REFIID riid, LPVOID *ppv);
    STDMETHODIMP_(ULONG) AddRef (THIS);
    STDMETHODIMP_(ULONG) Release (THIS);

    //IClassFactory methods
    STDMETHODIMP CreateInstance (LPUNKNOWN pUnkOuter, REFIID riid,
                                 LPVOID *ppv);
    STDMETHODIMP LockServer (BOOL fLock);
};
// **** End of Generic OLE declarations ****


//======================================================================
// MyIInputMethod - Object declaration
//
class MyIInputMethod : public IInputMethod2 {

private:
    long m_lRef;
    HWND m_hwndParent;
    HWND m_hwndMyWnd;
    HIMAGELIST m_himlWide;
    HIMAGELIST m_himlNarrow;
    IIMCallback *m_pIMCallback;

public:
    MyIInputMethod();
    ~MyIInputMethod();

    //IUnknown methods
    STDMETHODIMP QueryInterface (THIS_ REFIID riid, LPVOID *ppvObj);
    STDMETHODIMP_(ULONG) AddRef (THIS);
    STDMETHODIMP_(ULONG) Release (THIS);

    //IInputMethod
    HRESULT STDMETHODCALLTYPE Select (HWND hwndSip);
```

```
      HRESULT STDMETHODCALLTYPE Deselect (void);
      HRESULT STDMETHODCALLTYPE Showing (void);
      HRESULT STDMETHODCALLTYPE Hiding (void);
      HRESULT STDMETHODCALLTYPE GetInfo (IMINFO __RPC_FAR *pimi);
      HRESULT STDMETHODCALLTYPE ReceiveSipInfo (SIPINFO __RPC_FAR *psi);
      HRESULT STDMETHODCALLTYPE RegisterCallback (
                              IIMCallback __RPC_FAR *lpIMCallback);
      HRESULT STDMETHODCALLTYPE GetImData (DWORD dwSize, LPVOID pvImData);
      HRESULT STDMETHODCALLTYPE SetImData (DWORD dwSize, LPVOID pvImData);
      HRESULT STDMETHODCALLTYPE UserOptionsDlg (HWND hwndParent);


      //IInputMethod2
      HRESULT STDMETHODCALLTYPE SetIMMActiveContext(HWND hwnd, BOOL bOpen,
                      DWORD dwConversion, DWORD dwSentence, DWORD hkl);
      HRESULT STDMETHODCALLTYPE RegisterCallback2 (
                              IIMCallback2 __RPC_FAR *lpIMCallback);
};
```

NumPanel.h

```
//======================================================================
// NPWnd.h - An include file
//
// Written for the book Programming Windows CE
// Copyright (C) 2003 Douglas Boling
//======================================================================

#ifdef __cplusplus
extern "C"{
#endif

// Returns number of elements
#define dim(x) (sizeof(x) / sizeof(x[0]))

struct decodeUINT {                             // Structure associates
   UINT Code;                                   // messages
                                                // with a function.
   LRESULT (*Fxn)(HWND, UINT, WPARAM, LPARAM);
};


#define MYSIPCLS        TEXT ("MyNumPanelWndCls")
#define MYMSG_METHCALL (WM_USER+100)            // Used to pass info
#define MSGCODE_REGCALLBACK    0                // Notification codes for
#define MSGCODE_GETINFO        1                // MYMSG_METHCALL
#define MSGCODE_SETINFO        2
#define MSGCODE_REGCALLBACK2   3
```

(continued)

Listing 18-2 *(continued)*

```
#define GRIPWIDTH        9                    // Width of the gripper
#define FLOATWIDTH      200                   // Width of floating wnd
#define FLOATHEIGHT     100                   // Height of floating wnd

#define CXBTNS           5                    // Num columns of buttons
#define CYBTNS           3                    // Num rows of buttons

//
// Local data structure for keypad IM window
//
typedef struct {
    DWORD dwBtnDnFlags;
    IIMCallback *pIMCallback;
    IIMCallback2 *pIMCallback2;
    RECT rectDocked;
    BOOL fMoving;
    POINT ptMovBasis;
    POINT ptMovStart;
    IMINFO imi;
    RECT rectLast;
} SIPWNDSTRUCT, *LPSIPWNDSTRUCT;
INT DrawButton (HDC hdc, RECT *prect, LPSTR pChar, BOOL fPressed);

//
// Prototypes for functions implemented by custom IM code
//
HWND CreateIMWindow (HWND hwndParent);
int DestroyIMWindow (HWND hwnd);

LRESULT CALLBACK NPWndProc (HWND, UINT, WPARAM, LPARAM);

LRESULT CALLBACK DoCreateSip (HWND, UINT, WPARAM, LPARAM);
LRESULT CALLBACK DoSetSipInfo (HWND, UINT, WPARAM, LPARAM);
LRESULT CALLBACK DoPaintSip (HWND, UINT, WPARAM, LPARAM);
LRESULT CALLBACK DoMouseSip (HWND, UINT, WPARAM, LPARAM);
LRESULT CALLBACK DoDestroySip (HWND, UINT, WPARAM, LPARAM);

#ifdef __cplusplus
}
#endif
```

IMCommon.cpp

```
//======================================================================
// IMCommon - Common code for a Windows CE input method
//
// Written for the book Programming Windows CE
```

```
// Copyright (C) 2003 Douglas Boling
//======================================================================
#include <windows.h>                    // For all that Windows stuff
#include <commctrl.h>                   // Command bar includes
#define INITGUID
#include <initguid.h>
#include <coguid.h>
#include <sip.h>                        // SIP includes

#include "IMCommon.h"                   // My IM common includes
#include "NumPanel.h"                   // IM window specific includes
long g_DllCnt = 0;                      // Global DLL reference count

extern "C" {
HINSTANCE hInst;                        // DLL instance handle
}
//
// GUID defines for my input method.  Create a new one with GUIDGEN.
//
const GUID CLSID_NumPanel2 =
{ 0xc8311f61, 0x12df,0x4107,{0xb5,0xea,0xb0,0xb0,0xd5,0x5c,0xec,0x50}};

const TCHAR szCLSIDNumPanel2[] =
TEXT ("{C8311F61-12DF-4107-B5EA-B0B0D55CEC50}");
const TCHAR szFriendlyName[] = TEXT ("Numeric Keypad");


//======================================================================
// DllMain - DLL initialization entry point
//
BOOL WINAPI DllMain (HANDLE hinstDLL, DWORD dwReason,
                     LPVOID lpvReserved) {
    hInst = (HINSTANCE)hinstDLL;
    return TRUE;
}
//======================================================================
// DllGetClassObject - Exported function called to get pointer to
// Class factory object.
//
STDAPI DllGetClassObject (REFCLSID rclsid, REFIID riid, LPVOID *ppv) {
    MyClassFactory *pcf;
    HRESULT hr;

    // See if caller wants us.
    if (IsEqualCLSID (rclsid, CLSID_NumPanel2)) {

        // Create IClassFactory object.
        pcf = new MyClassFactory();
```

(continued)

Listing 18-2   *(continued)*

```
        if (pcf == NULL)
            return E_OUTOFMEMORY;

        // Call class factory's query interface method.
        hr = pcf->QueryInterface (riid, ppv);
        // This will cause an obj delete unless interface found.
        pcf->Release();
        return hr;
    }
    return CLASS_E_CLASSNOTAVAILABLE;
}
//========================================================================
// DllCanUnloadNow - Exported function called when DLL can unload
//
STDAPI DllCanUnloadNow () {

    if (g_DllCnt)
        return S_FALSE;
    return S_OK;
}
//========================================================================
// DllRegisterServer - Exported function called to register the server
//
STDAPI DllRegisterServer () {
    TCHAR szName[MAX_PATH+2];
    TCHAR szTmp[128];
    DWORD dwDisp;
    HKEY hKey, hSubKey;
    INT rc;

    GetModuleFileName (hInst, szName, sizeof (szName));
    // Open the key.
    wsprintf (szTmp, TEXT ("CLSID\\%s"), szCLSIDNumPanel2);
    rc = RegCreateKeyEx (HKEY_CLASSES_ROOT, szTmp, 0, TEXT(""),
                         0, 0, NULL, &hKey, &dwDisp);
    if (rc != ERROR_SUCCESS)
        return E_FAIL;
    // Set the friendly name of the SIP.
    RegSetValueEx (hKey, TEXT (""), 0, REG_SZ, (PBYTE)szFriendlyName,
                        (lstrlen (szFriendlyName)+1) * sizeof (TCHAR));

    // Create subkeys.
    // Set the module name of the SIP.
    rc = RegCreateKeyEx (hKey, TEXT ("InProcServer32"), 0, TEXT(""),
                         0, 0, NULL, &hSubKey, &dwDisp);
    rc = RegSetValueEx (hSubKey, TEXT (""), 0, REG_SZ, (PBYTE)szName,
```

```
                            (lstrlen (szName)+1) * sizeof (TCHAR));
    RegCloseKey (hSubKey);


    // Set the default icon of the server.
    RegCreateKeyEx (hKey, TEXT ("DefaultIcon"), 0, TEXT(""),
                    0, 0, NULL, &hSubKey, &dwDisp);
    lstrcat (szName, TEXT (",0"));
    RegSetValueEx (hSubKey, TEXT (""), 0, REG_SZ, (PBYTE)szName,
                    (lstrlen (szName)+1) * sizeof (TCHAR));
    RegCloseKey (hSubKey);


    // Set the flag indicating this is a SIP.
    RegCreateKeyEx (hKey, TEXT ("IsSIPInputMethod"), 0, TEXT(""),
                    0, 0, NULL, &hSubKey, &dwDisp);
    lstrcpy (szTmp, TEXT ("1"));
    RegSetValueEx (hSubKey, TEXT (""), 0, REG_SZ, (PBYTE)szTmp, 4);
    RegCloseKey (hSubKey);


    RegCloseKey (hKey);
    return S_OK;
}
//========================================================================
// DllUnregisterServer - Exported function called to remove the server
// information from the registry
//
STDAPI DllUnregisterServer() {
    INT rc;
    TCHAR szTmp[128];

    wsprintf (szTmp, TEXT ("CLSID\\%s"), szCLSIDNumPanel2);
    rc = RegDeleteKey (HKEY_CLASSES_ROOT, szTmp);
    if (rc == ERROR_SUCCESS)
        return S_OK;
    return E_FAIL;
}
//************************************************************************
// MyClassFactory Object implementation
//----------------------------------------------------------------------
// Object constructor
MyClassFactory::MyClassFactory () {
    m_lRef = 1;       // Set ref count to 1 on create.
    return;
}
//----------------------------------------------------------------------
// Object destructor
MyClassFactory::~MyClassFactory () {
    return;
}
```

(continued)

Listing 18-2 *(continued)*

```
//-------------------------------------------------------------------
// QueryInterface - Called to see what interfaces this object supports
STDMETHODIMP MyClassFactory::QueryInterface (THIS_ REFIID riid,
                                              LPVOID *ppv) {

    // If caller wants our IUnknown or IClassFactory object,
    // return a pointer to the object.
    if (IsEqualIID (riid, IID_IUnknown) ||
        IsEqualIID (riid, IID_IClassFactory)) {

        *ppv = (LPVOID)this;        // Return pointer to object.
        AddRef();                   //
 Increment ref to prevent delete on return.
        return NOERROR;
    }
    *ppv = NULL;
    return (E_NOINTERFACE);
}
//-------------------------------------------------------------------
// AddRef - Increment object ref count.
STDMETHODIMP_(ULONG) MyClassFactory::AddRef (THIS) {
    ULONG cnt;

    cnt = (ULONG)InterlockedIncrement (&m_lRef);
    return cnt;
}
//-------------------------------------------------------------------
// Release - Decrement object ref count.
STDMETHODIMP_(ULONG) MyClassFactory::Release (THIS) {
    ULONG cnt;

    cnt = (ULONG)InterlockedDecrement (&m_lRef);
    if (cnt == 0)
        delete this;
    return cnt;
}
//-------------------------------------------------------------------
// LockServer - Called to tell the DLL not to unload even if use count is 0
STDMETHODIMP MyClassFactory::LockServer (BOOL fLock) {
    if (fLock)
        InterlockedIncrement (&g_DllCnt);
    else
        InterlockedDecrement (&g_DllCnt);
    return NOERROR;
}
```

```
//-----------------------------------------------------------------
// CreateInstance - Called to have class factory object create other
// objects
STDMETHODIMP MyClassFactory::CreateInstance (LPUNKNOWN pUnkOuter,
                                             REFIID riid,
                                             LPVOID *ppv) {

    MyIInputMethod *pMyIM;
    HRESULT hr;

    if (pUnkOuter)
        return (CLASS_E_NOAGGREGATION);

    if (IsEqualIID (riid, IID_IUnknown) ||
        IsEqualIID (riid, IID_IInputMethod) ||
        IsEqualIID (riid, IID_IInputMethod2)) {

        // Create Input method object.
        pMyIM = new MyIInputMethod();
        if (!pMyIM)
            return E_OUTOFMEMORY;

        // See if object exports the proper interface.
        hr = pMyIM->QueryInterface (riid, ppv);
        // This will cause an obj delete unless interface found.
        pMyIM->Release ();
        return hr;
    }
    return E_NOINTERFACE;
}


//*****************************************************************
// MyIInputMethod Object implementation
//-----------------------------------------------------------------
// Object constructor
MyIInputMethod::MyIInputMethod () {

    m_lRef = 1;      // Set ref count to 1 on create.
    g_DllCnt++;
    return;
}
//-----------------------------------------------------------------
// Object destructor
MyIInputMethod::~MyIInputMethod () {
    g_DllCnt--;
    return;
}
//-----------------------------------------------------------------
// QueryInterface - Called to see what interfaces this object supports
```

(continued)

Listing 18-2   *(continued)*

```
STDMETHODIMP MyIInputMethod::QueryInterface (THIS_ REFIID riid,
                                             LPVOID *ppv) {

    // If caller wants our IUnknown or IID_IInputMethod2 object,
    // return a pointer to the object.
    if (IsEqualIID (riid, IID_IUnknown) ||
        IsEqualIID (riid, IID_IInputMethod) ||
        IsEqualIID (riid, IID_IInputMethod2)){

        // Return ptr to object.
        *ppv = (IInputMethod *)this;
        AddRef();                       //
 Increment ref to prevent delete on return.
        return NOERROR;
    }
    *ppv = NULL;
    return (E_NOINTERFACE);
}
//-------------------------------------------------------------------------
// AddRef - Increment object ref count.
STDMETHODIMP_(ULONG) MyIInputMethod::AddRef (THIS) {
    ULONG cnt;

    cnt = (ULONG)InterlockedIncrement (&m_lRef);
    return cnt;
}
//-------------------------------------------------------------------------
// Release - Decrement object ref count.
STDMETHODIMP_(ULONG) MyIInputMethod::Release (THIS) {
    ULONG cnt;

    cnt = (ULONG)InterlockedDecrement (&m_lRef);
    if (cnt == 0) {
        delete this;
        return 0;
    }
    return cnt;
}
//-------------------------------------------------------------------------
// Select - The IM has just been loaded into memory.
//
HRESULT STDMETHODCALLTYPE MyIInputMethod::Select (HWND hwndSip) {
    HBITMAP hBmp, hbmpMask;

    m_hwndParent = hwndSip;
```

```
        // Create image list for narrow (16x16) image.
        m_himlNarrow = ImageList_Create (16, 16, ILC_COLOR | ILC_MASK,
                                         1, 0);
        hBmp = LoadBitmap (hInst, TEXT ("NarrowBmp"));
        hbmpMask = LoadBitmap (hInst, TEXT ("NarrowMask"));
        ImageList_Add (m_himlNarrow, hBmp, hbmpMask);
        DeleteObject (hBmp);
        DeleteObject (hbmpMask);

        // Create image list for wide (32x16) image.
        m_himlWide = ImageList_Create (32, 16, ILC_COLOR | ILC_MASK, 1, 0);
        hBmp = LoadBitmap (hInst, TEXT ("WideBmp"));
        hbmpMask = LoadBitmap (hInst, TEXT ("WideMask"));
        ImageList_Add (m_himlWide, hBmp, hbmpMask);
        DeleteObject (hBmp);
        DeleteObject (hbmpMask);

        // Create SIP window.
        m_hwndMyWnd = CreateIMWindow (hwndSip);
        if (!IsWindow (m_hwndMyWnd))
            return E_FAIL;

    return S_OK;
}
//------------------------------------------------------------------
// Deselect - The IM is about to be unloaded.
//
HRESULT STDMETHODCALLTYPE MyIInputMethod::Deselect (void) {

    DestroyIMWindow (m_hwndMyWnd);
    ImageList_Destroy (m_himlNarrow);
    ImageList_Destroy (m_himlWide);
    return S_OK;
}
//------------------------------------------------------------------
// Showing - The IM is about to be made visible.
//
HRESULT STDMETHODCALLTYPE MyIInputMethod::Showing (void) {
    return S_OK;
}
//------------------------------------------------------------------
// Hiding - The IM is about to be hidden.
//
HRESULT STDMETHODCALLTYPE MyIInputMethod::Hiding (void) {
    return S_OK;
}
```

(continued)

Listing 18-2 *(continued)*

```
//--------------------------------------------------------------------
// GetInfo - The SIP wants info from the IM.
//
HRESULT STDMETHODCALLTYPE MyIInputMethod::GetInfo (
                                                IMINFO __RPC_FAR *pimi) {
    pimi->cbSize = sizeof (IMINFO);
    pimi->hImageNarrow = m_himlNarrow;
    pimi->hImageWide = m_himlWide;
    pimi->iNarrow = 0;
    pimi->iWide = 0;
    pimi->fdwFlags = SIPF_DOCKED;

    pimi->rcSipRect.left = 0;
    pimi->rcSipRect.top = 0;
    pimi->rcSipRect.right = FLOATWIDTH;
    pimi->rcSipRect.bottom = FLOATHEIGHT;
    SendMessage (m_hwndMyWnd, MYMSG_METHCALL, MSGCODE_GETINFO,
                (LPARAM) pimi);
    return S_OK;
}
//--------------------------------------------------------------------
// ReceiveSipInfo - The SIP is passing info to the IM.
//
HRESULT STDMETHODCALLTYPE MyIInputMethod::ReceiveSipInfo (
                                                SIPINFO __RPC_FAR *psi) {
    // Pass the sip info data to the window.
    SendMessage (m_hwndMyWnd, MYMSG_METHCALL, MSGCODE_SETINFO,
                (LPARAM) psi);
    return S_OK;
}
//--------------------------------------------------------------------
// RegisterCallback - The SIP is providing the IM with the pointer to
// the IIMCallback interface.
//
HRESULT STDMETHODCALLTYPE MyIInputMethod::RegisterCallback (
                                IIMCallback __RPC_FAR *lpIMCallback) {
    m_pIMCallback = lpIMCallback;
    PostMessage (m_hwndMyWnd, MYMSG_METHCALL, MSGCODE_REGCALLBACK,
                (LPARAM)m_pIMCallback);
    return S_OK;
}
//--------------------------------------------------------------------
// GetImData - An application is passing IM-specific data to the IM.
//
HRESULT STDMETHODCALLTYPE MyIInputMethod::GetImData (DWORD dwSize,
                                                LPVOID pvImData) {
    return E_FAIL;
}
```

```
//----------------------------------------------------------------
// SetImData - An application is querying IM-specific data from the IM.
//
HRESULT STDMETHODCALLTYPE MyIInputMethod::SetImData (DWORD dwSize,
                                                     LPVOID pvImData) {
    return S_OK;
}
//----------------------------------------------------------------
// UserOptionsDlg - The SIP Control Panel applet is asking for a
// configuration dialog box to be displayed.
//
HRESULT STDMETHODCALLTYPE MyIInputMethod::UserOptionsDlg (
                                                     HWND hwndParent) {
    MessageBox (hwndParent, TEXT ("UserOptionsDlg called."),
                TEXT ("NumPanel"),  MB_OK);
    return S_OK;
}
//----------------------------------------------------------------
// SetIMMActiveContext - Provides information about the IME
//
HRESULT STDMETHODCALLTYPE MyIInputMethod::SetIMMActiveContext(HWND hwnd,
                                    BOOL bOpen, DWORD dwConversion,
                                    DWORD dwSentence, DWORD hkl) {
    return S_OK;
}
//----------------------------------------------------------------
// RegisterCallback2 - The SIP is providing the IM with the pointer to
// the IIMCallback interface.
//
HRESULT STDMETHODCALLTYPE MyIInputMethod::RegisterCallback2 (
                                    IIMCallback2 __RPC_FAR *lpIMCallback) {
    m_pIMCallback = lpIMCallback;
    PostMessage (m_hwndMyWnd, MYMSG_METHCALL, MSGCODE_REGCALLBACK2,
                 (LPARAM)m_pIMCallback);
    return S_OK;
}
```

NumPanel.cpp

```
//================================================================
// NumPanel - An IM window
//
// Written for the book Programming Windows CE
// Copyright (C) 2003 Douglas Boling
//================================================================
#include <windows.h>                    // For all that Windows stuff
#define COBJMACROS
```

(continued)

Listing 18-2 *(continued)*

```
#include <sip.h>                        // SIP includes
#include <keybd.h>                      // Keyboard flag includes

#include "NumPanel.h"                   // Includes for this window
extern "C" HINSTANCE hInst;
//
// Local variables for number panel
//
TCHAR g_tcBtnChar[] = {
        TEXT('1'), TEXT('2'), TEXT('3'), TEXT('-'), TEXT('*'),
        TEXT('4'), TEXT('5'), TEXT('6'), TEXT('+'), TEXT('/'),
        TEXT('7'), TEXT('8'), TEXT('9'), TEXT('0'), TEXT('='),
};
UINT g_BtnVChars[] = {
        '1', '2', '3', VK_HYPHEN, VK_MULTIPLY,
        '4', '5', '6', VK_ADD, VK_SLASH,
        '7', '8', '9', '0', VK_EQUAL,
};

// Message dispatch table for SipWindowProc
const struct decodeUINT SipMessages[] = {
    WM_CREATE, DoCreateSip,
    WM_PAINT, DoPaintSip,
    MYMSG_METHCALL, DoSetSipInfo,
    WM_LBUTTONDOWN, DoMouseSip,
    WM_MOUSEMOVE, DoMouseSip,
    WM_LBUTTONUP, DoMouseSip,
    WM_LBUTTONDBLCLK, DoMouseSip,
    WM_DESTROY, DoDestroySip,
};
//-----------------------------------------------------------------------
// CreateIMWindow - Create the input method window.
//
HWND CreateIMWindow (HWND hwndParent) {
    WNDCLASS wc;
    RECT rect;
    HWND hwnd;
    // Register sip window class.
    memset (&wc, 0, sizeof (wc));
    wc.style = CS_DBLCLKS | CS_VREDRAW | CS_HREDRAW;
    wc.lpfnWndProc = NPWndProc;                 // Callback function
    wc.hInstance = hInst;                       // Owner handle
    wc.hbrBackground = (HBRUSH) GetStockObject (WHITE_BRUSH);
    wc.lpszClassName = MYSIPCLS;                // Window class name
    if (RegisterClass (&wc) == 0) return 0;
```

```
    // Create SIP window.
    GetClientRect (hwndParent, &rect);
    hwnd = CreateWindowEx (0, MYSIPCLS, TEXT(""),
                    WS_VISIBLE | WS_CHILD | WS_BORDER, rect.left,
                    rect.top, rect.right - rect.left,
                    rect.bottom - rect.top, hwndParent, (HMENU)100,
                    hInst, 0);
    if (!IsWindow (hwnd))
        return 0;
    return hwnd;
}
//----------------------------------------------------------------------
// DestroyIMWindow - Destroy the input method window.
//
int DestroyIMWindow (HWND hwnd) {
    // Clean up since we're about to be unloaded.
    DestroyWindow (hwnd);
    UnregisterClass (MYSIPCLS, hInst);
    return 0;
}


//======================================================================
// NPWndProc - Window procedure for SIP
//
LRESULT CALLBACK NPWndProc (HWND hWnd, UINT wMsg, WPARAM wParam,
                            LPARAM lParam) {
    INT  i;
    // Call routine to handle control message.
    for (i = 0; i < dim(SipMessages); i++) {
        if (wMsg == SipMessages[i].Code)
            return (*SipMessages[i].Fxn)(hWnd, wMsg, wParam, lParam);
    }
    return DefWindowProc (hWnd, wMsg, wParam, lParam);
}
//----------------------------------------------------------------------
// DoCreateSip - Process WM_CREATE message for window.
//
LRESULT CALLBACK DoCreateSip (HWND hWnd, UINT wMsg, WPARAM wParam,
                              LPARAM lParam) {
    LPSIPWNDSTRUCT pWndData;
    // Allocate a data structure for the sip keyboard window.
    pWndData = (LPSIPWNDSTRUCT)LocalAlloc (LPTR, sizeof (SIPWNDSTRUCT));
    if (!pWndData) {
        DestroyWindow (hWnd);
        return 0;
    }
    memset (pWndData, 0, sizeof (SIPWNDSTRUCT));
    GetWindowRect (GetParent (hWnd), &pWndData->rectDocked);
```

(continued)

Listing 18-2   *(continued)*

```
    pWndData->rectLast.left = -1;
    SetWindowLong (hWnd, GWL_USERDATA, (INT)pWndData);
    return 0;
}
//------------------------------------------------------------------------
// DoSetSipInfo - Process set information user message for window.
//
LRESULT CALLBACK DoSetSipInfo (HWND hWnd, UINT wMsg, WPARAM wParam,
                               LPARAM lParam) {
    LPSIPWNDSTRUCT pWndData;
    RECT rect;

    pWndData = (LPSIPWNDSTRUCT)GetWindowLong (hWnd, GWL_USERDATA);
    switch (wParam) {
    // Called when RegisterCallback method called
    case MSGCODE_REGCALLBACK:
        pWndData->pIMCallback = (IIMCallback *)lParam;
        break;
    // Called when GetInfo method called
    case MSGCODE_GETINFO:
        pWndData->imi = *(IMINFO *)lParam;
        break;
    // Called when ReceiveSipInfo method called
    case MSGCODE_SETINFO:
        GetClientRect (GetParent(hWnd), &rect);
        MoveWindow (hWnd, 0, 0, rect.right - rect.left,
                    rect.bottom - rect.top, TRUE);
        break;
    // Called when RegisterCallback2 method called
    case MSGCODE_REGCALLBACK2:
        pWndData->pIMCallback2 = (IIMCallback2 *)lParam;
        break;
    }
    return 0;
}
//------------------------------------------------------------------------
// DoPaintSip - Process WM_PAINT message for window.
//
LRESULT CALLBACK DoPaintSip (HWND hWnd, UINT wMsg, WPARAM wParam,
                             LPARAM lParam) {
    HDC hdc;
    HBRUSH hOld;
    PAINTSTRUCT ps;
    RECT rect, rectBtn;
    INT i, j, k, x, y, cx, cy, cxBtn, cyBtn;
    LPSIPWNDSTRUCT pWndData;
```

```
    pWndData = (LPSIPWNDSTRUCT)GetWindowLong (hWnd, GWL_USERDATA);

    hdc = BeginPaint (hWnd, &ps);
    GetClientRect (hWnd, &rect);

    cx = (rect.right - rect.left - 3 - GRIPWIDTH) / CXBTNS;
    cy = (rect.bottom - rect.top - 3) / CYBTNS;
    cxBtn = cx - 3;
    cyBtn = cy - 3;

    // Select a brush for the gripper.
    hOld = (HBRUSH)SelectObject (hdc, GetStockObject (GRAY_BRUSH));
    Rectangle (hdc, rect.left, rect.top, rect.left + GRIPWIDTH,
               rect.bottom);
    SelectObject (hdc, hOld);

    k = 0;
    y = 3;
    for (i = 0; i < CYBTNS; i++) {
        x = 3 + GRIPWIDTH;
        for (j = 0; j < CXBTNS; j++) {
            SetRect (&rectBtn, x, y, x + cxBtn, y + cyBtn);
            DrawButton (hdc, &rectBtn, &g_tcBtnChar[k],
                        pWndData->dwBtnDnFlags & (1 << k));
            k++;
            x += cx;
        }
        y += cy;
    }
    EndPaint (hWnd, &ps);
    return 0;
}
//----------------------------------------------------------------------
// ComputeFloatRect - Compute the location and size of the drag rect.
//
int ComputeFloatRect (HWND hwnd, LPSIPWNDSTRUCT pWndData, POINT pt,
                      RECT *prectOut) {

    pt.x -= pWndData->ptMovBasis.x;
    pt.y -= pWndData->ptMovBasis.y;
    prectOut->right = FLOATWIDTH;
    prectOut->bottom = FLOATHEIGHT;
    prectOut->left = pt.x;
    prectOut->top = pt.y;
    prectOut->right += pt.x;
    prectOut->bottom += pt.y;
    return 0;
}
```

(continued)

Listing 18-2 *(continued)*

```
//-------------------------------------------------------------------------
// DrawFloatRect - Draw a drag rectangle by XORing the desktop.
//
int DrawFloatRect (HWND hWnd, RECT rect) {
    HDC hdc;
    HBRUSH hbrOld;
    HPEN hpenOld;
    int nOldMode;
    // Get the DC. Set ROP, brush, and pen.
    hdc = GetDC (NULL);
    nOldMode = SetROP2 (hdc, R2_NOT);
    hbrOld = (HBRUSH)SelectObject (hdc, GetStockObject (NULL_BRUSH));
    hpenOld = (HPEN)SelectObject (hdc, GetStockObject (BLACK_PEN));

    Rectangle (hdc, rect.left, rect.top, rect.right, rect.bottom);
    SelectObject (hdc, hbrOld);
    SelectObject (hdc, hpenOld);
    SetROP2 (hdc, nOldMode);
    ReleaseDC (NULL, hdc);
    return 0;
}
//-------------------------------------------------------------------------
// HandleGripper - Handles mouse messages over gripper bar
//
LRESULT HandleGripper (HWND hWnd, LPSIPWNDSTRUCT pWndData, UINT wMsg,
                       LPARAM lParam) {
    POINT pt;
    RECT rectFloat;

    pt.x = (short)LOWORD(lParam);
    pt.y = (short)HIWORD(lParam);

    switch (wMsg) {
    case WM_LBUTTONDOWN:
        if (pt.x > GRIPWIDTH+3)
            return 0;
        SetCapture (hWnd);
        pWndData->fMoving = TRUE;
        pWndData->ptMovBasis = pt;
        ClientToScreen (hWnd, &pt);
        pWndData->ptMovStart = pt;
        ShowWindow (GetParent(hWnd), SW_HIDE);
        break;

    case WM_MOUSEMOVE:
        if (!pWndData->fMoving)
            return 0;
```

```
            ClientToScreen (hWnd, &pt);
            ComputeFloatRect (hWnd, pWndData, pt, &rectFloat);
            // Erase old drag rectangle.
            if (pWndData->rectLast.left != -1)
                DrawFloatRect (hWnd, pWndData->rectLast);
            // Draw new drag rectangle.
            DrawFloatRect (hWnd, rectFloat);
            pWndData->rectLast = rectFloat;
            break;
        case WM_LBUTTONUP:
            if (!pWndData->fMoving)
                return 0;
            // Free up dragging stuff.
            ReleaseCapture();
            pWndData->fMoving = FALSE;
            ClientToScreen (hWnd, &pt);
            // Erase last drag rectangle.
            ComputeFloatRect (hWnd, pWndData, pt, &rectFloat);
            if (pWndData->rectLast.left != -1)
                DrawFloatRect (hWnd, pWndData->rectLast);
            pWndData->rectLast.left = -1;
            ShowWindow (GetParent(hWnd), SW_SHOW);
            // Don't move SIP if really small move.
            if ((abs (pWndData->ptMovStart.x - pt.x) < 3) &&
                (abs (pWndData->ptMovStart.y - pt.y) < 3))
                break;
            // Tell the Input Manager about the move.
            pWndData->imi.rcSipRect = rectFloat;
            pWndData->imi.fdwFlags &= ~SIPF_DOCKED;
            pWndData->imi.fdwFlags |= SIPF_ON;
            pWndData->pIMCallback->SetImInfo(&pWndData->imi);
            break;

        case WM_LBUTTONDBLCLK:
            if (pt.x > GRIPWIDTH+3)
                return 0;
            ReleaseCapture();
            pWndData->fMoving = FALSE;
            // Embedded SIP manager doesn't use SIPF_DOCKED so only use on PPC.
#if defined(WIN32_PLATFORM_PSPC)
            pWndData->imi.fdwFlags |= (SIPF_DOCKED | SIPF_ON);
#endif
            pWndData->imi.rcSipRect = pWndData->rectDocked;
            pWndData->pIMCallback->SetImInfo(&pWndData->imi);
            break;
    }
    pWndData->dwBtnDnFlags = 0;    // If we moved, no buttons down.
```

(continued)

Listing 18-2 *(continued)*

```
    return 1;
}
//-------------------------------------------------------------------------
// DoMouseSip - Process mouse button messages for window. WM_LBUTTONDOWN
//
LRESULT CALLBACK DoMouseSip (HWND hWnd, UINT wMsg, WPARAM wParam,
                            LPARAM lParam) {
    RECT rect;
    INT i, x, y, cx, cy;
    UINT nChar, unShiftFlags = 0;
    DWORD BtnDnFlags;
    LPSIPWNDSTRUCT pWndData;
    pWndData = (LPSIPWNDSTRUCT)GetWindowLong (hWnd, GWL_USERDATA);

    // See if moving gripper or gripper tap.
    if (HandleGripper (hWnd, pWndData, wMsg, lParam))
        return 0;

    // Compute the button grid.
    GetClientRect (hWnd, &rect);
    cx = (rect.right - rect.left - 3 - GRIPWIDTH) / CXBTNS;
    cy = (rect.bottom - rect.top - 3) / CYBTNS;
    x = ((LOWORD (lParam)-3-GRIPWIDTH) / cx);
    y = ((HIWORD (lParam)-3) / cy);
    i = (y * CXBTNS) + x;     // i now contains btn index.

    // Do small amount of message-specific processing.
    switch (wMsg) {
    case WM_LBUTTONDOWN:
        SetCapture (hWnd);
        // Fall through to WM_MOUSEMOVE case.
    case WM_MOUSEMOVE:
        BtnDnFlags = 1 << i;
        break;
    case WM_LBUTTONDBLCLK:
    case WM_LBUTTONUP:
        if (pWndData->dwBtnDnFlags)
            ReleaseCapture();
        BtnDnFlags = 0;
        nChar = g_tcBtnChar[i];
        pWndData->pIMCallback->SendCharEvents(g_BtnVChars[i],
                          KeyStateDownFlag, 1, &nShiftFlags, &nChar);
        break;
    }
    // Decide how to repaint wnd. If only 1 btn changed, just
    // invalidate that rect. Otherwise, invalidate entire wnd.
    if ((wMsg == WM_MOUSEMOVE) && (BtnDnFlags !=pWndData->dwBtnDnFlags))
```

```
                InvalidateRect (hWnd, NULL, FALSE);
        else {
                i = 3+GRIPWIDTH;    // Compensate for the gripper on left side.
                SetRect (&rect, x*cx+i, y*cy, (x+1)*cx+i, (y+1)*cy);
                InvalidateRect (hWnd, &rect, FALSE);
        }
        pWndData->dwBtnDnFlags = BtnDnFlags;
        return 0;
}
//--------------------------------------------------------------------------
// DoDestroySip - Process WM_DESTROY message for window.
//
LRESULT CALLBACK DoDestroySip (HWND hWnd, UINT wMsg, WPARAM wParam,
                               LPARAM lParam) {
    LPSIPWNDSTRUCT pWndData;

    pWndData = (LPSIPWNDSTRUCT)GetWindowLong (hWnd, GWL_USERDATA);
    LocalFree (pWndData);
    return 0;
}
//--------------------------------------------------------------------------
// DrawButton - Draws a button
//
INT DrawButton (HDC hdc, RECT *prect, LPTSTR pChar, BOOL fPressed) {

    if (!fPressed) {
        SelectObject (hdc, GetStockObject (BLACK_PEN));
        SelectObject (hdc, GetStockObject (WHITE_BRUSH));
        SetBkColor (hdc, RGB (255, 255, 255));
        SetTextColor (hdc, RGB (0, 0, 0));
    } else {
        SelectObject (hdc, GetStockObject (BLACK_BRUSH));
        SelectObject (hdc, GetStockObject (WHITE_PEN));
        SetTextColor (hdc, RGB (255, 255, 255));
        SetBkColor (hdc, RGB (0, 0, 0));
    }
    Rectangle (hdc, prect->left, prect->top, prect->right,
               prect->bottom);
    Rectangle (hdc, prect->left+1, prect->top+1, prect->right+1,
               prect->bottom+1);
    DrawText (hdc, pChar, 1, prect, DT_CENTER|DT_VCENTER|DT_SINGLELINE);
    return 0;
}
```

Although NumPanel is divided into two source files, both the *IInputMethod2* interface and the NumPanel window procedure run in the same thread. In response to a call to the *Select* method of *IInputMethod2*, the Num-Panel window class is registered and the window is created as a child of the IM's window. The image lists used by the IM are also created here with the handles stored in member variables in the *MyIInputMethod* object. The only other work of interest performed by the code in IMCommon.cpp is the code for the *GetInfo* method. In this method, the image list handles are provided to the IM along with the requested dimensions of the undocked window. The dimensions of the docked window are provided by the system.

For four other methods, all *MyIInputMethod* does is post messages to the window procedure of the NumPanel window. In NumPanel.c, these messages are fielded in the *MYMSG_METHCALL* user-defined message. The four methods make available to the window a pointer to the *IIMCallback* and *IIMCallback2* interfaces and notify the NumPanel window that the window is about to be displayed or that the state of the input panel is changing.

The other code in the NumPanel window draws the keys on the window and processes the stylus taps. The *DoPaintSip* routine handles the painting. The routine draws a grid of 3 rows and 5 columns of buttons. In each button, a character is drawn to label it. A separate bit array contains the up or down state of each button. If the button is down, the background of the button is drawn in reverse colors.

Two routines—*DoMouseSip* and *HandleGripper*—handle the mouse messages. The mouse messages all initially go to *DoMouseSip*, which calls *Handle-Gripper*. If the routine determines that the mouse message is on the gripper or that the window is currently being dragged, *HandleGripper* handles the message. Otherwise, if the *DoMouseSip* routine determines that a mouse tap occurs on one of the buttons, it calls the *SendCharEvent* method of *IIMCallback* to send the character to the focus window.

When the window is dragged to a new location on the screen, the *HandleGripper* routine clears the *SIPF_DOCKED* flag and sets the new size and location of the SIP by calling the *SetImInfo* method of *IIMCallback*. When the user double-taps the gripper, *HandleGripper* sets the *SIPF_DOCKED* flag, for Pocket PC systems, and sets the SIP rectangle to the original docked rectangle that was saved when the NumPanel window was first created.

These last two chapters have covered the Pocket PC extensively, but I've pushed off any discussion of what is becoming the central feature of mobile devices, communication. The Pocket PC Phone Edition combines the intelligence of the PDA with the connectivity of the cellular phone. Another device, the Smartphone, combines the same features but in a cell phonc–like package instead of a PDA. In the next chapter, I turn the discussion to the Smartphone and the communication features common across the Smartphone and the Pocket PC Phone edition.

19

Programming the Smartphone

Given the inevitability of Moore's Law, Windows CE–powered devices become both smaller and more powerful each year. One result is convergence, the merging of two or more separate smart devices into one. The Smartphone is one result of the trend toward convergence.

The Smartphone is a Windows CE–based cellular phone. Like the Pocket PC, all Smartphones regardless of manufacturer share the same configuration of Windows CE. Also, Smartphones come bundled with a set of applications such as an address book, calendar, and e-mail program. Microsoft produces a standard Smartphone build that individual manufacturers and cellular providers can then enhance with branding and additional applications.

Smartphones are one of the more unique implementations of Windows CE devices. First, they are quite small, with screen resolutions of 176 by 220. They don't have touch screens and have a limited set of hardware buttons. Because Smartphones need to be on to receive calls, but also require long battery life, the CPUs used by these devices are slower than is standard in Pocket PCs. Finally, because cellular phones are used by people while they are doing other tasks such as working, walking, or even driving, the user interface of the application has to be much simpler than is normal on a PC or a Pocket PC. All of these things radically change the requirements of a Smartphone application.

Another challenge of developing software for the Smartphone is security. Unlike the Pocket PC, the cellular provider that sells the phone might limit the device's ability to load and run programs. The Smartphone implements the Windows CE module–based security scheme discussed in Chapter 10. Because of this restriction, a locked cell phone might either restrict unsigned applications or not run them at all. Depending on the provider, applications might need to be signed with an encryption key supplied by the provider or a trusted third party. Unfortunately, some cellular providers see this restriction as a possible revenue stream to extract money from either the user or the application developer or both.

Fortunately, this chapter isn't completely in vain even if developers are limited in writing Smartphone applications because the sections on communication features such as Telephony API (TAPI), Short Message Service (SMS), and the Software Installation Manager (SIM) apply not only to the Smartphone but also to the Pocket PC Phone edition. Pocket PCs don't have the restrictions on third-party applications, so applications will run on those devices.

Introducing the Smartphone

The Smartphone user interface is an integration of the hardware implementation of the device and the implementation of the application being run on the device. More so than applications on other devices, Smartphone applications depend on the use of a small set of hardware buttons dedicated to particular tasks. This in itself forces a certain conformity across Smartphone applications.

Figure 19-1 shows a diagram of a hypothetical Smartphone. Notice the two buttons immediately below the screen. These two buttons provide the major application-defined input to the application. Of course, the other buttons on the numeric keypad and the simple joystick provide input, but typically the device defines their function. The other buttons on this hypothetical device are the Home button, for returning the phone to the home screen, and the Back button, used to return to the previous screen.

The Smartphone display has a layout similar to the Pocket PC. The top of the display has the navigation bar, which shows the title text of the foreground window and status icons for the phone, battery, and application notification icons. At the bottom of the screen is the phone's specialized *MenuBar* control, which is much simplified over the Pocket PC's *MenuBar* control. The application's data is displayed in between.

The home screen of the Smartphone contains a summary of the various installed applications on the system. The joystick can be used to scroll to each of the items on the home screen to select the associated application. The home screen *MenuBar* also provides a Programs menu that is the Smartphone's version of a Start menu. The default action of the right button is to dial the voicemail service for the phone.

Nav Bar

Work Area

Soft Button1

Soft Button 2

Call Button

End Button

Home Button

Back Button

Joystick

Keypad

Figure 19-1   The diagram of a Smartphone device

Figure 19-2 shows the Programs menu from the Home screen. Notice that each menu item has a number associated with it. The user can use the keypad to select the menu item associated with the number on the keypad, allowing quick selection of a menu item. Alternatively, the user can use the joystick to highlight the proper menu item and select it by pressing in on the joystick. All menus displayed in the Smartphone have these item numbers displayed by default.

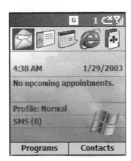

Figure 19-2   The Programs menu on the Home screen

A Smartphone Application

As with the Pocket PC, Smartphone applications have to perform certain tasks so they will operate correctly. Like Pocket PC applications, Smartphone applications must ensure that only one instance of itself must be running any one time. Also like the Pocket PC, the application should create a control with *SHCreateMenuBar*, although the function creates a simplified menu bar. The application might need to override the function of the Back button. For the main window, the Back button is passed on to the shell so that it can restore the previous application's window. Finally, and this can't be overemphasized, the application user interface must be simple. Figure 19-3 shows HelloSP running on a Smartphone. The text is centered in the client window, which has been sized to fit the area between the navigation bar and the *MenuBar* control.

Figure 19-3   The HelloSP example running on a Smartphone

Listing 19-1 shows the first example in this chapter, HelloSP.

```
HelloSP.rc
//======================================================================
// Resource file
//
// Written for the book Programming Windows CE
// Copyright (C) 2003 Douglas Boling
//======================================================================
#include "windows.h"                // Windows stuff
#include "aygshell.h"               // Pocket PC stuff
#include "HelloSP.h"                // Program-specific stuff


//----------------------------------------------------------------------
// Icons and bitmaps
//
ID_ICON       ICON    "HelloSP.ico"    // Program icon
```

Listing 19-1   The HelloSP source code

```
ID_MENU RCDATA
BEGIN
    0,
    1,
    I_IMAGENONE, IDM_EXIT, TBSTATE_ENABLED,
                 TBSTYLE_BUTTON | TBSTYLE_AUTOSIZE, IDS_OK, 0, NOMENU,
END

STRINGTABLE DISCARDABLE
BEGIN
    IDS_OK        "OK"
END
```

HelloSP.h

```
//======================================================================
// Header file
//
// Written for the book Programming Windows CE
// Copyright (C) 2003 Douglas Boling
//======================================================================
// Returns number of elements
#define dim(x) (sizeof(x) / sizeof(x[0]))


//----------------------------------------------------------------------
// Generic defines and data types
//
struct decodeUINT {                           // Structure associates
    UINT Code;                                // messages
                                              // with a function.
    LRESULT (*Fxn)(HWND, UINT, WPARAM, LPARAM);
};
struct decodeCMD {                            // Structure associates
    UINT Code;                                // menu IDs with a
    LRESULT (*Fxn)(HWND, WORD, HWND, WORD);   // function.
};


//----------------------------------------------------------------------
// Generic defines used by application
#define  ID_MENU          10
#define  IDM_EXIT         100
#define  IDS_OK           1001


//----------------------------------------------------------------------
// Function prototypes
//
```

(continued)

Listing 19-1   *(continued)*

```
HWND InitInstance (HINSTANCE, LPWSTR, int);
int TermInstance (HINSTANCE, int);

// Window procedures
LRESULT CALLBACK MainWndProc (HWND, UINT, WPARAM, LPARAM);

// Message handlers
LRESULT DoCreateMain (HWND, UINT, WPARAM, LPARAM);
LRESULT DoPaintMain (HWND, UINT, WPARAM, LPARAM);
LRESULT DoCommandMain (HWND, UINT, WPARAM, LPARAM);
LRESULT DoDestroyMain (HWND, UINT, WPARAM, LPARAM);

// WM_COMMAND message handlers
LPARAM DoMainCommandExit (HWND, WORD, HWND, WORD);
```

HelloSP.cpp

```
//======================================================================
// HelloSP - A simple application for the Smartphone
//
// Written for the book Programming Windows CE
// Copyright (C) 2003 Douglas Boling
//======================================================================
#include <windows.h>              // For all that Windows stuff
#include <commctrl.h>             // Command bar includes
#include <aygshell.h>             // Pocket PC includes
#include "hellosp.h"              // Program-specific stuff
//----------------------------------------------------------------------
// Global data
//
const TCHAR szAppName[] = TEXT("HelloSP");
HINSTANCE hInst;                          // Program instance handle

// Message dispatch table for MainWindowProc
const struct decodeUINT MainMessages[] = {
    WM_CREATE, DoCreateMain,
    WM_PAINT, DoPaintMain,
    WM_COMMAND, DoCommandMain,
    WM_DESTROY, DoDestroyMain,
};
// Command Message dispatch for MainWindowProc
const struct decodeCMD MainCommandItems[] = {
    IDM_EXIT, DoMainCommandExit,
};
//======================================================================
// Program entry point
//
```

```
int WINAPI WinMain (HINSTANCE hInstance, HINSTANCE hPrevInstance,
                    LPWSTR lpCmdLine, int nCmdShow) {
    MSG msg;
    int rc = 0;
    HWND hwndMain;

    // Initialize this instance.
    hwndMain = InitInstance (hInstance, lpCmdLine, nCmdShow);
    if (hwndMain == 0) return 0x10;

    // Application message loop
    while (GetMessage (&msg, NULL, 0, 0)) {
        TranslateMessage (&msg);
        DispatchMessage (&msg);
    }
    // Instance cleanup
    return TermInstance (hInstance, msg.wParam);
}
//-------------------------------------------------------------------
// InitInstance - Instance initialization
//
HWND InitInstance (HINSTANCE hInstance, LPWSTR lpCmdLine, int nCmdShow) {
    WNDCLASS wc;
    HWND hWnd;

    // Save program instance handle in global variable.
    hInst = hInstance;

    // Allow only one instance of the application.
    hWnd = FindWindow (szAppName, NULL);
    if (hWnd) {
        SetForegroundWindow ((HWND)(((DWORD)hWnd) | 0x01));
        return 0;
    }
    // Register application main window class.
    wc.style = CS_VREDRAW | CS_HREDRAW;        // Window style
    wc.lpfnWndProc = MainWndProc;              // Callback function
    wc.cbClsExtra = 0;                         // Extra class data
    wc.cbWndExtra = 0;                         // Extra window data
    wc.hInstance = hInstance;                  // Owner handle
    wc.hIcon = NULL,                           // Application icon
    wc.hCursor = LoadCursor (NULL, IDC_ARROW); // Default cursor
    wc.hbrBackground = (HBRUSH) GetStockObject (WHITE_BRUSH);
    wc.lpszMenuName =  NULL;                    // Menu name
    wc.lpszClassName = szAppName;              // Window class name

    if (RegisterClass (&wc) == 0) return 0;
```

(continued)

Listing 19-1 *(continued)*

```
        // Create main window.
        hWnd = CreateWindow (szAppName,           // Window class
                             TEXT("Hello"),       // Window title
                             WS_VISIBLE,          // Style flags
                             CW_USEDEFAULT,       // x position
                             CW_USEDEFAULT,       // y position
                             CW_USEDEFAULT,       // Initial width
                             CW_USEDEFAULT,       // Initial height
                             NULL,                // Parent
                             NULL,                // Menu, must be null
                             hInstance,           // Application instance
                             NULL);               // Pointer to create
                                                  // parameters
    if (!IsWindow (hWnd)) return 0;              // Fail if not created.

    // Standard show and update calls
    ShowWindow (hWnd, nCmdShow);
    UpdateWindow (hWnd);
    return hWnd;
}
//----------------------------------------------------------------------
// TermInstance - Program cleanup
//
int TermInstance (HINSTANCE hInstance, int nDefRC) {
    return nDefRC;
}
//======================================================================
// Message handling procedures for main window
//
//----------------------------------------------------------------------
// MainWndProc - Callback function for application window
//
LRESULT CALLBACK MainWndProc (HWND hWnd, UINT wMsg, WPARAM wParam,
                             LPARAM lParam) {
    INT i;
    //
    // Search message list to see if we need to handle this
    // message.  If in list, call procedure.
    //
    for (i = 0; i < dim(MainMessages); i++) {
        if (wMsg == MainMessages[i].Code)
            return (*MainMessages[i].Fxn)(hWnd, wMsg, wParam, lParam);
    }
    return DefWindowProc (hWnd, wMsg, wParam, lParam);
}
```

```
//--------------------------------------------------------------------
// DoCreateMain - Process WM_CREATE message for window.
//
LRESULT DoCreateMain (HWND hWnd, UINT wMsg, WPARAM wParam,
                      LPARAM lParam) {
    SHMENUBARINFO mbi;

    // Create a MenuBar.
    memset(&mbi, 0, sizeof(SHMENUBARINFO)); // Zero structure
    mbi.cbSize = sizeof(SHMENUBARINFO);     // Size field
    mbi.hwndParent = hWnd;                  // Parent window
    mbi.nToolBarId = ID_MENU;               // ID of toolbar resource
    mbi.hInstRes = hInst;                   // Inst handle of app

    // Create bar and check for errors.
    if (!SHCreateMenuBar(&mbi)) {
        MessageBox (hWnd, TEXT("Couldn\'t create menu bar"),
                    szAppName, MB_OK);
        DestroyWindow (hWnd);
    }
    // Size the window to fit above the MenuBar
    RECT rect, rectDesk;
    int cx, cy;
    GetWindowRect (mbi.hwndMB, &rect);
    GetWindowRect (GetDesktopWindow (), &rectDesk);
    cx = rectDesk.right-rectDesk.left;
    cy = (rectDesk.bottom - rectDesk.top) - (rect.bottom - rect.top);
    SetWindowPos (hWnd, NULL, 0, 0, cx, cy, SWP_NOMOVE | SWP_NOZORDER);

    SHSetNavBarText (hWnd, TEXT("Hello"));
    return 0;
}
//--------------------------------------------------------------------
// DoCommandMain - Process WM_COMMAND message for window.
//
LRESULT DoCommandMain (HWND hWnd, UINT wMsg, WPARAM wParam,
                       LPARAM lParam) {
    WORD idItem, wNotifyCode;
    HWND hwndCtl;
    INT  i;

    // Parse the parameters.
    idItem = (WORD) LOWORD (wParam);
    wNotifyCode = (WORD) HIWORD (wParam);
    hwndCtl = (HWND) lParam;
```

(continued)

Listing 19-1   *(continued)*

```
        // Call routine to handle control message.
        for (i = 0; i < dim(MainCommandItems); i++) {
            if (idItem == MainCommandItems[i].Code)
                return (*MainCommandItems[i].Fxn)(hWnd, idItem, hwndCtl,
                                                  wNotifyCode);
        }
        return 0;
}
//-------------------------------------------------------------------------
// DoPaintMain - Process WM_PAINT message for window.
//
LRESULT DoPaintMain (HWND hWnd, UINT wMsg, WPARAM wParam,
                     LPARAM lParam) {
    PAINTSTRUCT ps;
    HPEN hPen, hOld;
    RECT rect;
    HDC hdc;

    hdc = BeginPaint (hWnd, &ps);
    GetClientRect (hWnd, &rect);

    // Draw a red rectangle around the window.
    hPen = CreatePen (PS_SOLID, 1, RGB (255, 0, 0));
    hOld = (HPEN)SelectObject (hdc, hPen);
    Rectangle (hdc, rect.left, rect.top, rect.right, rect.bottom);
    SelectObject (hdc, hOld);
    DeleteObject (hPen);

    // Draw the standard hello text centered in the window.
    DrawText (hdc, TEXT ("Hello Smartphone!"), -1, &rect,
              DT_CENTER | DT_VCENTER | DT_SINGLELINE);

    EndPaint (hWnd, &ps);
    return 0;
}
//-------------------------------------------------------------------------
// DoDestroyMain - Process WM_DESTROY message for window.
//
LRESULT DoDestroyMain (HWND hWnd, UINT wMsg, WPARAM wParam,
                       LPARAM lParam) {
    PostQuitMessage (0);
    return 0;
}
```

```
//==================================================================
// Command handler routines
//------------------------------------------------------------------
// DoMainCommandExit - Process Program Exit command.
//
LPARAM DoMainCommandExit (HWND hWnd, WORD idItem, HWND hwndCtl,
                          WORD wNotifyCode) {
    SendMessage (hWnd, WM_CLOSE, 0, 0);
    return 0;
}
```

The structure of the program is similar to all the examples in the book. The point of the example is to show that a Smartphone application is a Windows application with the same entry point, the same message loop, and the same general message handlers.

The unique parts of the application start with the Pocket PC–like check for whether another instance of the application is running. There's some difference of opinion on what should happen when the user starts a second instance of an application. Some style guides suggest that an application ought to close the previous instance and show the new instance. This behavior would provide the user with a clean copy of the application each time they select it. The problem with this concept is that few, if any, of the bundled applications that come with the Smartphone act this way. Instead, the bundled applications place the previous running instance in the foreground, restoring the state of the application as the user left it.

The example code also queries the height of the *MenuBar* control and adjusts the size of the main window to fit above it. Unlike Pocket PC applications, there's no need to dynamically respond to the SIP popping up over the window because there's no SIP on the Smartphone.

Another major difference in HelloSP is the *MenuBar* control. It's created with a call to *ShCreateMenuBar*, but its function and action are quite different—different enough to handle it as a separate topic. Let's dive into the Smartphone's *MenuBar* control and see how it works.

The Smartphone's *MenuBar* Control

The Smartphone *MenuBar* is a simplified version of the *MenuBar* control used by the Pocket PC. Because the Smartphone lacks a touch screen, the user interacts with the Smartphone *MenuBar* using two buttons at the base of the screen.

The two buttons are aligned with the two possible buttons on the control. The buttons can either be implemented to display a menu or to perform an action directly.

As I mentioned earlier, when a menu is displayed, the first 10 items on the menu are automatically prefixed with a number from 1 through 9 and then 0 corresponding to the 10 digits on the phone keyboard. When the menu is displayed the user can easily select an item by pressing a key on the phone. With the automatic addition of the menu item numbers, there's no reason to specify underlined navigation characters in the menu items.

Although it's possible to put more than 10 items on a menu, the small size of the phone necessitates that the menu scroll, which isn't a very friendly interface design. Another less-than-friendly interface design is cascaded menus. The Smartphone *MenuBar* control does support cascaded menus, but the extra level of action required by the user causes more work than a cascaded menu provides benefits.

Creating a Smartphone *MenuBar* Control

Just as on the Pocket PC, the *MenuBar* creation function *SHCreateMenuBar* is used to create a *MenuBar* on the Smartphone. The format of the parameters is the same as in the Pocket PC, as is the format of the *SHMENUBARINFO* structure used to define the structure of the control. The combination toolbar and menu resource used by the *Smartphone MenuBar* is also the same. The difference is that on the Smartphone, the *MenuBar* is much less flexible. The toolbar resource must define one or two buttons. The *MenuBar* buttons can be designed either to provide a direct action or to display a menu when the associated button is pressed.

For review, the prototype of *SHCreateMenuBar* and *SHMENUBARINFO* is shown here:

```
BOOL SHCreateMenuBar (SHMENUBARINFO *pmb);

typedef struct tagSHMENUBARINFO {
    DWORD cbSize;
    HWND hwndParent;
    DWORD dwFlags;
    UINT nToolBarId;
    HINSTANCE hInstRes;
    int nBmpId;
    int cBmpImages;
    HWND hwndMB;
    COLORREF clrBk;
} SHMENUBARINFO;
```

In the *Smartphone MenuBar* control, the *cbSize*, *hwndParent*, *hInstRes*, and *hwndMB* fields are used, as in the standard menu bar, to confirm the size of the structure, indicate the control parent, provide the instance handle of the module containing the resource, and return the handle of the created control. However, some fields are limited in comparison to their use in the standard menu bar. The *nBmpId* and *cBmpImages* fields must be 0 or the call to create the control will fail. The *clrBk* field is ignored even if the corresponding *SHCMBF_COLORBK* flag is set in the *dwFlags* field. The other defined flags in *dwFlags* also don't make sense in the limited *MenuBar* control.

The *nToolBarId* field must identify a resource structured identically to the menu bar resource described in Chapter 5. That format is shown here.

```
<Menu ID>, <Number of buttons (1 or 2)>,
I_IMAGENONE, <Cmd1ID>, <Btn1State>, <Btn1Style>, <String1ID>, 0, <Menu1Index>
I_IMAGENONE, <Cmd2ID>, <Btn2State>, <Btn2Style>, <String2ID>, 0, <Menu2Index>
```

The first field of the resource is the resource ID of any menu resource being used by the control. The second field can be either 1 or 2 depending on if the control will have one or two buttons on the bar. The remainder of the resource describes one or both buttons on the control. In the previous example, the second and third lines describe the two buttons.

The first field should be set to *I_IMAGENONE* to indicate that the button is text, not a bitmap. Bitmaps are not supported on the *Smartphone MenuBar*. The second field contains the ID value that will be sent to the owner window if the button is not a menu and is pressed. The third field describes the initial state of the button using toolbar state flags. The fourth field describes the style of the button using toolbar style flags. The String ID field must refer to a valid string resource ID that contains the text for that button. The next to last field should be set to 0, and the last field is the submenu index into the menu identified by the first field in the resource. This field can be *NOMENU* if the button doesn't display a menu when pressed.

An example *SoftKeyBar* control is shown in Figure 19-4.

Figure 19-4   A *SoftKeyBar* control where the menu button has been pressed

Figure 19-4 shows a Smartphone *MenuBar* with a Done button on the left and a Menu button on the right. This placement of direct action assigned to the left button and an optional menu assigned to the right button is the recommended arrangement suggested by the Smartphone user interface guide. In the figure, the Menu button has been pressed, displaying a short menu on the screen. The two-part resource that describes the *MenuBar* control in Figure 19-4 is shown here:

```
ID_BTNBARRES RCDATA MOVEABLE PURE
BEGIN
  ID_MENU, 2,
  I_IMAGENONE, IDM_EXIT, TBSTATE_ENABLED, TBSTYLE_AUTOSIZE | TBSTYLE_BUTTON,
          IDS_DONE, 0, NOMENU,
  I_IMAGENONE, IDM_POP, TBSTATE_ENABLED, TBSTYLE_AUTOSIZE | TBSTYLE_DROPDOWN,
          IDS_MENU, 0, 0,
END

ID_MENU MENU DISCARDABLE
BEGIN
    POPUP "&Dummy"
    BEGIN
        MENUITEM "Week View",           IDM_VIEWWEEK
        MENUITEM "Month View"           IDM_VIEWMONTH
        MENUITEM "Year View",           IDM_VIEWYEAR
        MENUITEM SEPARATOR
        MENUITEM "Options",             IDM_OPTIONS
    END
END
```

The *ID_BTNBARRES* resource describes the two buttons. The first button is a direct action button and the second is a button that displays a menu. One difference between the two buttons, aside from the string resource references, is the different style flag, *TBSTYLE_BUTTON* vs. *TBSTYLE_DROPDOWN*. Another difference is the *NOMENU* index in the first button description, in which the second button uses a menu index of 0. The 0 index indicates the first, and in this case only, submenu of the *ID_MENU* menu resource.

Working with the Buttons and Menus

As on the Pocket PC, the buttons and menus hosted by the *MenuBar* control can be modified after the control has been created. The key to modifying *MenuBar* is the use of the *TB_GETBUTTONINFO* and *TB_SETBUTTONINFO* messages. These toolbar control messages work on the *MenuBar* control because it's derived from the toolbar.

To query the current settings for a button send a *TB_GETBUTTONINFO* message to the *MenuBar*. The *wParam* parameter should have the command ID identifying the button, and *lParam* should point to a *TBBUTTONINFO* structure. The *TBBUTTONINFO* structure is defined as

```
typedef struct {
    UINT cbSize;
    DWORD dwMask;
    int idCommand;
    int iImage;
    BYTE fsState;
    BYTE fsStyle;
    WORD cx;
    DWORD lParam;
    LPTSTR pszText;
    int cchText;
} TBBUTTONINFO, *LPTBBUTTONINFO;
```

The *cbSize* and *dwMask* fields of *TBBUTTONINFO* should be initialized before the message is sent. The *cbSize* field should be filled with the size of the structure. The *dwMask* field should be set with flags indicating what data is being queried from the control. For the *MenuBar* control, the only flags allowed are *TBIF_TEXT*, *TBIF_STATE*, *TBIF_LPARAM*, and *TBIF_COMMAND*, which specify the text, state, user-defined parameter, and command ID, respectively.

Setting the parameters of a button is just as simple with the use of a *TB_SETBUTTONINFO* message. Here again, *wParam* should contain the ID of the button, and *lParam* should point to a *TBBUTTONINFO* structure. The following code disables a button by first querying the state of the button and then clearing the *TBSTATE_ENABLED* flag in the *fsState* field.

```
int DisableButton (HWND hwndMainWnd, DWORD dwID) {

    HWND hwndMB = SHFindMenuBar (hwndMainWnd);
    TBBUTTONINFO tbi;
    if (!hwndMB)
        return -1;

    memset (&tbi, 0, sizeof (tbi));
    tbi.cbSize = sizeof (tbi);
    tbi.dwMask = TBIF_STATE;
    if(!SendMessage (hwndMB, TB_GETBUTTONINFO, dwID, (LPARAM)&tbi))
        return -2;

    tbi.fsState &= ~TBSTATE_ENABLED;
    SendMessage (hwndMB, TB_SETBUTTONINFO, dwID, (LPARAM)&tbi);

    return 0;
```

```
                                                                         }
```

The menus displayed by the Smartphone *MenuBar* can also be modified by the application. The same messages used to get the menu handles for the *MenuBar* control can be used in the Smartphone version of the control. Sending a *SHCMBM_GETMENU* message to the *MenuBar* control returns the menu attached to the control. The *wParam* and *lParam* parameters are ignored in this message. Sending *SHCMBM_GETSUBMENU* to the control returns the submenu attached to a specific button. In this case, *lParam* should contain the ID of the button, whereas *wParam* is ignored. The following code disables the Options menu item by first getting the handle of the submenu attached to the menu button and then using *EnableMenu* to disable the menu item.

```
HWND hwndMB = SHFindMenuBar (hwndMainWnd);
if (hwndMB) {
    HMENU hMenu;
    hMenu = (HMENU)SendMessage (hwndMB, SHCMBM_GETSUBMENU, 0, IDM_POP);
    EnableMenuItem (hMenu, IDM_OPTIONS, MF_BYCOMMAND | MF_GRAYED);
}
```

The other menu functions can be used to manipulate the menus on the *MenuBar* as easily as *EnableMenu* was used in the previous example.

The Back Button and Other Interesting Buttons

One of the more important components of the Smartphone interface is the Back button. This button allows the user to return to the previous screen from the current screen at any time. For the most part, the Back button works as designed without any assistance from the foreground application. There are, however, times when the Back button needs to act differently, and that's when the application has to do a bit of work.

The rules for the operation of the Back button are as follows:

- If the current window is not a dialog box and does not have an edit box, the Back button activates the window that was displayed before the current window was activated. The current window isn't destroyed, it's simply covered by the previous window, which now becomes the active window.

- If the current window is a message box or a modal dialog box without an edit control, the Back button dismisses the message box or dialog box and returns the cancel return code. For message boxes, this value is either *IDNO*, *IDCANCEL*, or *IDOK* for message boxes with only an OK button. For dialog boxes, a *WM_COMMAND* message is sent to the dialog window with the command ID *IDCANCEL*.

■   If the window currently displayed contains an edit control, the Back button erases the last character in the control and moves the entry cursor one character to the left.

In the case of the first two rules, the system will provide the default action for the Back button. For the final rule, concerning edit boxes, the application must override the default action and forward the key to the appropriate child control in the window. Fortunately, the Smartphone shell does most of the work through a couple of helper functions.

If a window contains an edit box, it must override the default action of the Back key in order to pass the key to the child control. To do this, the window sends a *SHCMBM_OVERRIDEKEY* message to the *MenuBar* control for the window. The *wParam* parameter defines the key to override. The following keys are supported for override:

Key	Meaning
VK_TBACK	Back button
VK_TSOFT1	Left *SoftKeyBar* button
VK_TSOFT2	Right *SoftKeyBar* button
VK_TVOLUMEUP	Up volume button
VK_TVOLUMEDOWN	Down volume button
VK_TRECORD	Record button

The *lParam* parameter designates the keys to override and the action to take. The lower word of *lParam* contains a mask of flags that designates which flags are valid. The action flags are in the upper word. The first flag that can be set indicates whether a key is to be overridden and the second indicates whether a *WM_HOTKEY* message is sent to the window when the key is pressed. For example, to override the action of the Back button and to be notified by a *WM_HOTKEY* message, a window would send the following message to the *MenuBar*:

```
SendMessage (SHFindMenuBar (hWnd), SHCMBM_OVERRIDEKEY, VK_TBACK,
        MAKELPARAM (SHMBOF_NODEFAULT | SHMBOF_NOTIFY,
                SHMBOF_NODEFAULT | SHMBOF_NOTIFY));
```

This line sends a *SHCMBM_OVERRIDEKEY* message to the *MenuBar* control owned by *hWnd*. The *wParam* parameter, *VK_TBACK*, indicates the key being overridden. The *MAKELPARAM* macro forms a *DWORD* from two 16-bit words. The first parameter of *MAKELPARAM*, which will become the low word of *lParam*, is the mask field. Here, the *SHMBOF_NODEFAULT* flag is used to indicate that the override state of the Back key is to be set or cleared. The *SHMBOF_NOTIFY* flag indicates that the notification flag will also be set or cleared. The upper word of *lParam* is created from the second parameter of the *MAKELPARAM* macro. Here, the flag *SHMBOF_NODEFAULT* indicates that the Back key *will* be overridden. The second flag, *SHMBOF_NOTIFY*, tells the *MenuBar* to notify its parent when the Back key is pressed.

To override the Back key but not be notified when it's pressed, the following line could be used:

```
SendMessage (SHFindMenuBar (hWnd), SHCMBM_OVERRIDEKEY, VK_TBACK,
        MAKELPARAM (SHMBOF_NODEFAULT | SHMBOF_NOTIFY,
                SHMBOF_NODEFAULT));
```

To restore the Back key to its original function, the following line could be used:

```
SendMessage (SHFindMenuBar (hWnd), SHCMBM_OVERRIDEKEY, VK_TBACK,
        MAKELPARAM (SHMBOF_NODEFAULT | SHMBOF_NOTIFY,
                0));
```

In the previous line, the first parameter of *MAKELPARAM* (the mask bits) indicates that the message is going to set the state of both the default action and the notification state of the button. The second *MAKELPARAM* parameter is 0, which indicates that the default action is to be restored and that notification is to be sent to the *MenuBar* owner.

When *WM_HOTKEY* is received by the window, the *wParam* value contains an ID value for the key that was pressed. The IDs reported by the *MenuBar* are

Key	Value
VK_TSOFT1	0
VK_TSOFT2	1
VK_TBACK	2
VK_TVOLUMEUP	3
VK_TVOLUMEDOWN	4
VK_TRECORD	5

The *lParam* value also indicates the key but in a different way. The high word of *lParam* will contain the virtual key code of the key that was pressed. The lower word of *lParam* contains the modifier flags for the key. The only flag that is of interest on the Smartphone is *MOD_KEYUP*, which is set if the key is being released. Other modifier flags are documented, such as the Shift, Alt, and Control keys, but those flags are seldom used because the Smartphone doesn't have these keys.

For windows that contain edit controls, the notification of a Back key press needs to be forwarded to the proper child control. This forwarding is done by using a *SHCMBM_OVERRIDEKEY* message to redirect the Back key. Once the key is overridden, a press of the key sends a *WM_HOTKEY* message to the owner of the *MenuBar*. To fully support passing the backspace to the edit control, each *WM_HOTKEY* message received as a result of a Back key press needs to be forwarded to the control with the function *SHSendBackToFocusWindow*, defined as

```
void SHSendBackToFocusWindow (UINT uMsg, WPARAM wp, LPARAM lp);
```

The three parameters are the message being handled as well as the *wParam* and *lParam* values for the message. The following code fragment shows the use of this function.

```
case WM_HOTKEY:
    if (HIWORD (lParam) == VK_TBACK)
        SHSendBackToFocusWindow (wMsg, wParam, lParam);
}
```

The override state of a key changed by a *SHCMBM_OVERRIDEKEY* message is removed when the corresponding *MenuBar* control is destroyed, so there's no need to manually restore the default state before the window is destroyed.

Message Boxes

MessageBox, the standard Windows CE function for displaying message boxes, works on the Smartphone with some limitations. Because of the limit of two buttons on the *SoftKeyBar*, message boxes are limited to one or two buttons. The supported flags are *MB_OK*, *MB_OKCANCEL*, *MB_RETRYCANCEL*, and *MB_YESNO*. Using the flags *MB_ABORTRETRYIGNORE* or *MB_YESNOCANCEL*, which would normally result in message boxes with three buttons, will cause *MessageBox* to fail. Figure 19-5 shows a typical message box.

Figure 19-5 A message box on the Smartphone

The message box in Figure 19-5 is created with the following line:

```
MessageBox (hWnd, TEXT("Do you want to delete the file?"), TEXT("Box Title"),
            MB_OKCANCEL | MB_ICONEXCLAMATION);
```

The interesting thing about the message box is the bold text, Alert, that is not part of the text passed to the *MessageBox* function. The Smartphone places this text on the message box depending on the icon specified in the *MessageBox* call. The text displayed depends on the language settings of the phone and optionally the customization done by the service provider, but for a U.S. English phone, the text is

MessageBox Flag	Text	Icon
MB_ICONEXCLAMATION	Alert	Exclamation mark within a circle
MB_ICONHAND	Error	Exclamation mark within a circle
MB_ICONQUESTION	Confirm	Question mark within a circle
MB_ICONASTERISK	Info	Lowercase *I* within a circle

The message text is displayed in smaller text below the large, bold prompt text. The title text is displayed on the caption bar across the top of the screen.

If the message box has OK as one of the options, the user can press the action button on the phone to return *IDOK*. For other button settings such as Yes/No or Retry/Cancel, the action button has no effect and the user has to press one of the two buttons associated with the *MenuBar*. If the user presses the Back button, the message box is dismissed and the function returns the negative response, either No for a Yes/No choice, Cancel for Yes/Cancel, or OK if the message box only has an OK button.

Dialog Boxes

Message boxes will only get you so far on a Smartphone. Dialog boxes, or dialogs, can be created on the Smartphone as long as a few rules are observed. As on the Pocket PC, dialog boxes on the Smartphone must be sized to fit the full screen. This is accomplished with a call to *SHInitDialog* during the handling of the *WM_INITDIALOG* message. Smartphone dialogs must also create a *SoftKeyBar* control to provide a place for key input and to handle the Back button if the dialog contains one or more edit boxes.

The following code shows the handling of a *WM_INITDIALOG* message for a typical Smartphone dialog box that contains at least one edit control.

```
// Specify that the dialog box should stretch full screen
SHINITDLGINFO shidi;

memset (&shidi, 0, sizeof(shidi));
shidi.dwMask = SHIDIM_FLAGS;
shidi.dwFlags = SHIDIF_SIZEDLGFULLSCREEN/*SHIDIF_FULLSCREENNOMENUBAR*/;
shidi.hDlg = hWnd;
if(!SHInitDialog(&shidi))
    return FALSE;


// set up MenuBar menu
SHMENUBARINFO mbi;

memset (&mbi, 0, sizeof(SHMENUBARINFO));
mbi.cbSize = sizeof(SHMENUBARINFO);
mbi.hwndParent = hWnd;
mbi.nToolBarId = ID_MENUDLG;
mbi.hInstRes = hInst;


// If we could not initialize the dialog box, return an error
if (!SHCreateMenuBar(&mbi)) {
    DestroyWindow (hWnd);
    return FALSE;
}
// Override back key since we have an edit control
SendMessage(mbi.hwndMB, SHCMBM_OVERRIDEKEY, VK_TBACK,
            MAKELPARAM (SHMBOF_NODEFAULT | SHMBOF_NOTIFY,
                        SHMBOF_NODEFAULT | SHMBOF_NOTIFY));
// set the title bar
SHSetNavBarText (hWnd, TEXT("Dialog Title Text"));
```

Navigating controls in a Smartphone dialog is different from a standard Windows CE system because the Smartphone doesn't have a Tab key to transfer focus between controls. Instead, controls within a Smartphone dialog box are organized vertically, and the Up and Down cursor keys are used to switch focus to the next control in the tab order. (The control order is still referred to as *tab order* even though the Smartphone lacks a Tab key.) Each individual control has been modified to use the left and right cursor keys to provide navigation and selection within the control.

Scrolling Dialogs

Implementing a dialog box that scrolls is typically not an easy task. On the Smartphone, with its tiny screen, it's sometimes a necessity. Fortunately, the shell makes implementing scrolling dialogs fairly painless. All that is required is that the dialog box template have the *WS_VSCROLL* style flag set. When the user changes focus from control to control, if the next control is below the visible part of the screen, the shell scrolls the dialog automatically. If the focus is at the bottom most control and the user presses the Down cursor key, the Smartphone switches the focus back to the first control and scrolls the dialog back to the top.

If the application repositions any of the controls on a scrolling dialog, it needs to tell the dialog manager about the new positions. This is done with the Smartphone unique message, *DM_RESETSCROLL*. If the controls are repositioned in the *WM_INITDIALOG* message or in any message before *WM_INITDIALOG*, sending *DM_RESETSCROLL* isn't required.

Smartphone Controls

The limited display and lack of touch screen or mouse on the Smartphone have driven Microsoft to modify the behavior of some of the standard controls. The goal is to make controls that are navigable from simple cursor commands as well as use very little space.

The standard Windows CE controls still exist on the Smartphone. It's possible to create a standard list box in a Smartphone window, but once you navigate into a list box using the cursor keys, the control won't relinquish focus to other controls in the window because it uses the Up and Down cursor keys for internal navigation between the items in the list box. Standard multiline edit controls have the same problem. Other controls such as combo boxes don't make much sense in the limited screen space of a Smartphone. Because of this, Smartphone windows or dialog boxes use a limited and somewhat different set of controls. One of these enhanced controls is the oft-overlooked edit control.

Text Controls

Inputting text is a bit of a challenge on a Smartphone. The keyboard is limited to a number pad and a handful of cursor keys and is not conducive to text input. The Smartphone relies on the developer providing a context for the contents of the edit field, such as whether the control will contain numbers, words, or names. Depending on the context, the edit box can interpret taps on the numeric keypad in different ways.

Most OEMs support two different text input modes on their Smartphones. The first is referred to as *multitap* and is familiar to anyone who has entered text on a cellular phone during the last 10 years. In multitap mode, multiple presses of each number key result in the system scrolling through the letters assigned to that number. The letters assigned are derived from the standard letter assignment that was set by American Telephone and Telegraph eons ago. Because that original assignment didn't include the letters *Q* and *Z* (a great trivia question, by the way), the layout has been slightly modified and is now an international standard. The layout is shown in Figure 19-6.

1 Punctuation	2 ABC	3 DEF
4 GHI	5 JKL	6 MNO
7 PQRS	8 TUV	9 WXYZ
* Shift	0	# Space

Figure 19-6   The standard letter assignments on a telephone keypad

When the user wants to enter a letter, the number assigned to the letter is tapped multiple times until that letter appears. For example to enter a K, the user would tap the 5 key twice. Each number scrolls through its assigned letters followed by its number. So tapping the 8 key multiple times would scroll through the characters T, U, V, and 8. Pausing between taps for a short time locks in the selection and moves the cursor to the right. The 1 key is used to enter standard punctuation characters such as . , ? ! - ' @ : 1. Tapping the * key makes the next letter upper case. The # key inserts spaces, and the 0 key enters 0.

There are special cases for some keys. Pressing and holding the # key displays a screen of symbols. The user can then use the cursor keys to select the symbol needed. Pressing and holding the # key switches between multitap mode, T9 mode, and numeric mode.

T9 mode is a text-entry scheme that makes amazingly accurate guesses at what the user is trying to enter. The user taps the number key assigned to each letter and then types in the number for the next letter of the word, and so on. The T9 system makes a guess at the word from the possible combination of the letters possible from the first number and the letters from the second number. As more numbers are entered, the system predicts the word being entered with an almost uncanny accuracy. T9 works great with standard words but does have trouble with names.

A third entry mode is numeric. As you might guess, this mode simply takes the assigned number for each key entered and places it in the edit box.

Edit controls on the Smartphone have an enhanced interface over the standard run-of-the-mill Windows edit control. The first enhancement is the ability for the edit control to be switched between the various text input modes.

The *EM_SETINPUTMODE* message sets the input mode of the control. The *wParam* value isn't used, but *lParam* can contain one of the following values: *EIM_SPELL* for multitap mode, *EIM_AMBIG* for ambiguous or T9 mode, *EIM_NUMBERS* for numeric mode, and *EIM_TEXT* for the default entry mode set by the user.

In addition to the text mode, modifier flags can also be passed to set the shift state or the caps lock state. To change the shift state, the *IMMF_SHIFT* flag is combined with the text mode. To set the shift state, combine *IMMF_SHIFT* with *IMMF_SETCLR_SHIFT*. To clear the shift state, use *IMMF_SHIFT* alone. The caps lock state can be set in a similar manner. Passing the *IMMF_CAPSLOCK* flag indicates that the caps lock state is being modified. Combining *IMMF_CAPSLOCK* with *IMMF_SETCLR_CAPSLOCK* sets the caps lock state, whereas passing *IMMF_CAPSLOCK* alone clears the caps lock state.

The current mode can be queried with the *EM_GETINPUTMODE* message. To query the default input mode of the control, pass *FALSE* in *lParam*. Passing *TRUE* in *lParam* returns the default input mode for the control if it does not have focus or the actual input mode if it does have focus. The actual and default can be different because the user can change the input mode by pressing and holding the # key.

The *EM_SETSYMBOLS* message sets the symbols that are displayed when the user presses the 1 key. For this message, *lParam* points to a string that contains the symbols to be made available to the user.

The *EM_SETEXTENDEDSTYLE* message sets the extended edit style bits for the control. The *wParam* parameter contains a mask defining which of the extended style bits are to be changed. The state of each flag is set in *lParam*. So, to clear a particular extended style flag, the flag would be passed in *wParam*, but the corresponding bit in *lParam* would be 0 to indicate that the new state of the flag is to be 0.

The only extended style bit currently defined is *ES_EX_CLEAR-ONBACKPRESSHOLD*. This flag causes the control to interpret a press and hold of the Back key as a command to clear the contents of the edit control. To prevent this action, this style bit can be cleared by the application. This flag is set by default on single-line edit controls and cleared by default on multiline edit controls.

Expandable Edit Controls

Edit controls on the Smartphone can be made expandable with an up-down buddy control. In a dialog resource, the combination might look like the following:

```
EDITTEXT          IDD_TEXT, 5, 60, 75, 12, WS_TABSTOP | ES_MULTILINE
CONTROL "",       IDD_UDEDIT, UPDOWN_CLASS, UDS_AUTOBUDDY |
                  UDS_ALIGNRIGHT | UDS_EXPANDABLE | UDS_NOSCROLL,
                     0, 0, 0, 0
```

The first line defines the edit control, the up-down control is declared immediately afterward. The *CONTROL* resource tag is used for this control because the resource compiler doesn't use a specific keyword such as *EDIT* to declare an up-down control. The up-down control is assigned an ID value to identify the source of *WM_NOTIFY* messages it sends to its parent. The control doesn't need a position because its position will be defined by the location of the edit control. The up-down control's style flags configure it for this specific use. The *UDS_AUTOBUDDY* flag tells the control to associate itself with the closest control in the z-order. Because the edit box was declared immediately before the up-down control, the edit box will be closest in the z-order. The *UDS_ALIGNRIGHT* flag tells the control to attach to the right side of the edit control.

UDS_NOSCROLL tells the up-down control not to display Up and Down arrows like a scroll bar. The Up and Down arrows can be used for incrementing and decrementing numbers in an associated edit control. Here, we simply want the Right arrow to indicate to the user that the edit control is expandable.

Finally, the *UDS_EXPANDABLE* flag indicates that the edit control is expandable. When the edit control has the focus and the user hits the action key, the edit control will be expanded to fill the entire screen, showing as much of the contents of the edit control as possible. The expanded mode is much like a multiline edit control in that the action key moves the cursor to a new line. A

MenuBar is automatically created with OK and Cancel buttons to accept or discard any changes made in expanded mode. Figure 19-7 shows an expandable edit control in both normal and expanded modes.

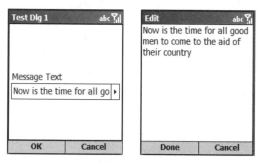

Figure 19-7 An expandable edit control in normal and expanded modes

An expandable edit control can be created manually as well as through dialog resource definitions. The following code creates an expandable edit control manually.

```
hwndEdit = CreateWindow (TEXT("edit"), NULL, WS_VISIBLE |
                    WS_TABSTOP | ES_AUTOHSCROLL | ES_AUTOVSCROLL |
                    ES_MULTILINE, 9, 15, 100, 75, hWnd,
                    (HMENU)IDD_TEXT, hInst, 0L);

hwndUpDown = CreateWindow (UPDOWN_CLASS, NULL, WS_VISIBLE | UDS_AUTOBUDDY |
                    UDS_ALIGNRIGHT | UDS_EXPANDABLE | UDS_NOSCROLL,
                    0, 0, 0, 0, hWnd, (HMENU)IDD_UDTEXT, hInst, 0L);

SendMessage(hwndUpDown, UDM_SETBUDDY, (WPARAM)hwndEdit, 0);
```

The only difference between this code and the dialog resource is the sending of a *UDM_SETBUDDY* message to the up-down control to associate it with the edit control.

Spinner Controls

The spinner is a modified list box control buddied with an up-down control. The result is a single line control that can be *spun* to display each item in the list box. Unlike the standard list box, the spinner control uses the Left and Right cursor keys to *spin* between items in the box. As with other Smartphone controls, the Up and Down cursor keys transfer focus to the next control in the tab order.

Creating a spinner consists of creating both the list box and up-down controls. In a dialog resource, the combination would look like the following:

```
LISTBOX      IDD_LISTCITIES, 5, 60, 75, 12, WS_TABSTOP
CONTROL "",   IDD_CITIESUD, UPDOWN_CLASS,
              UDS_AUTOBUDDY | UDS_HORZ | UDS_ALIGNRIGHT | UDS_ARROWKEYS |
              UDS_SETBUDDYINT | UDS_WRAP | UDS_EXPANDABLE, 0, 0, 0, 0
```

The first line defines the list box. The only unusual thing about the declaration is that the list box is only 12 dialog units high, just tall enough for one item. The up-down control is declared immediately after the list box. The *CONTROL* resource tag is used for this control because the resource compiler doesn't use a specific keyword such as *LISTBOX* to declare an up-down control. The large number of style flags configures the control for this specific use. Many of the same style flags are used when creating expandable edit controls, so I'll only cover the new ones. The *UDS_HORZ* and flag tells the control to create Left and Right arrows instead of Up and Down arrows attached to the list box.

The *UDS_SETBUDDYINT* flag tells the up-down control to manipulate the text of its buddy, in this case the list box, and have it scroll among the different items in the list. The *UDS_WRAP* flag tells the control to wrap the list so that if the list box is at the last item in the list and the user presses the right button, the list box will show the first item in the list.

The up-down control can have the additional style flag of *UDS_NOSCROLL*. This flag prevents the user from spinning the data with the Left and Right cursor keys. This style isn't much use unless it's combined with the *UDS_EXPANDABLE* flag so that the control can be expanded, allowing the user to change the selection. When the user expands the spinner, it sends a *WM_NOTIFY* message to the parent window with the *UDN_EXPANDING* command. Figure 19-8 shows a spinner control in both normal and expanded modes.

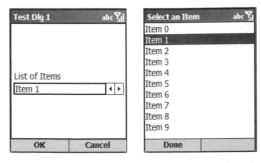

Figure 19-8   A spinner control in normal and expanded modes

A spinner can also be created manually with two calls to *CreateWindow*, as shown here:

```
HWND hwndList = CreateWindow (TEXT("listbox"), NULL, WS_VISIBLE |
                             WS_BORDER | WS_TABSTOP, 5, 5, 75, 20, hWnd,
                             (HMENU)IDD_LISTCITIES, hInst, 0L);

HWND hwndUpDown = CreateWindow (UPDOWN_CLASS, NULL, WS_VISIBLE | UDS_HORZ |
                               UDS_ALIGNRIGHT | UDS_ARROWKEYS |
                               UDS_SETBUDDYINT | UDS_WRAP | UDS_EXPANDABLE,
                               0, 0, 0, 0, hWnd, 0, hInst, 0L);

SendMessage (hwndUpDown, UDM_SETBUDDY, (WPARAM)hwndList, 0);
```

Here, like in the expandable edit control, the only difference between the two methods is the extra message sent to the up-down control to tell it the ID of its buddy list box and a few manually added style flags needed when creating the list box.

File Operation in the Smartphone

Unlike the Pocket PC, data in the object store of the Smartphone is volatile. When the phone is turned off, the data goes away. Fortunately, there is a way to persistently save data in the file system.

The Smartphone implements an external file system using flash memory internal to the phone. This file system is just like a file system that would appear if a Compact Flash or SD card was inserted into the system, but in this case the file system is not removable. The room in the internal persistent store is limited, so it's not a great area for storing huge databases or MP3 files. Still, it does provide a place to store application state data or other information. Although the method for finding external file systems was discussed in Chapter 8, the Smartphone extends a standard shell call that will return the proper subdirectory in which an application can store its data.

The function *SHGetSpecialFolderPath* was covered in Chapter 16. The Smartphone adds an additional constant, *CSIDL_APPDATA*. Using this CSIDL value will return the name of the application data folder that is persistent. An application can then create a subdirectory under the persistent folder where it can store its data. Because the persistent folder is used by all applications, you should be careful to uniquely name your application's directory. The following code demonstrates finding the application data folder and creating a directory.

```
int CreateAppFolder (HWND hWnd, TCHAR *pszAppFolder, int nMax) {

    const TCHAR szMyAppFolderName[] = TEXT ("ProgWinCESpSample");
    TCHAR szPath[MAX_PATH];

    // It doesn't help to have a path longer than MAX_PATH
    if (nMax > MAX_PATH)
        nMax = MAX_PATH;

    BOOL f = SHGetSpecialFolderPath (hWnd, szPath, CSIDL_APPDATA, FALSE);

    // See if everything will fit in output string
    int nLen = lstrlen (szPath);
    if (nLen + 2 + (int)lstrlen (szMyAppFolderName) > nMax)
        return -2;

    // Copy app folder name to parameter
    lstrcpy (pszAppFolder, szPath);

    // Append directory separator character as needed
    if (szPath[nLen] != TEXT ('\\'))
        lstrcat (pszAppFolder, TEXT("\\"));

    // Append my folder name
    lstrcat (pszAppFolder, szMyAppFolderName);

    // See if directory exists.
    if (GetFileAttributes (pszAppFolder) == 0xffffffff) {
        // See why call failed
        if (GetLastError () == ERROR_PATH_NOT_FOUND) {
            // Wasn't there, create the directory
            if (!CreateDirectory (pszAppFolder, NULL))
                return -3;
        } else
            return -4;  // Dir created but inaccessible
    } else
        return 1;       // Indicate directory already exists
    return 0;           // Indicate directory created
}
```

Data stored in the registry is persistent. The Smartphone takes steps to save and restore the registry when the system shuts down and starts back up.

Communication

The Smartphone would be nothing but a small PDA with a limited interface if it weren't for its communication features. An intelligent, mobile device, in a pocket and always connected to the Internet, is a powerful platform. The communication features discussed in this section are also implemented on the Pocket PC Phone edition, which is quite helpful for the learning curve of developers, who can apply their knowledge both on the Pocket PC and the Smartphone.

Communication services cover a number of areas, from dialing voice calls to sending messages to other phones to connecting to the Internet through either a wired or wireless connection. For the most part, these services are accessed through easy-to-use shell APIs that wrap the traditional but more complex Windows APIs such as TAPI, the Telephone API.

The folks that create communication functions design the most flexible and therefore most complex functions possible. The functions I describe in this section have what at times seems like dozens of parameters, each with a dozen options. Complete books can be, and have been, written about many of the following topics, so I can't cover completely each of the topics in a single part of a chapter. Still, this discussion will provide a good introduction to these functions and should give you a good start on adding communication features in your applications.

Phone API

The phone API provides a basic set of functions to make calls and query the call log. The phone API is convenient because it avoids the need for most applications to dive directly into the TAPI and make calls with that rather involved interface. TAPI is supported on the Smartphone and Pocket PC Phone edition, but you need not use it unless you're creating the most manipulative of applications.

Dialing the Phone

The first communication feature likely to be tried by a programmer new to the Smartphone or Pocket PC Phone edition is to dial the phone. The system provides a simple and effective function for this, *PhoneMakeCall*, prototyped as

```
LONG PhoneMakeCall (PHONEMAKECALLINFO *ppmci);
```

The *PHONEMAKECALLINFO* structure is defined as

```
typedef struct tagPHONEMAKECALLINFO{
    DWORD cbSize;
```

```
    DWORD dwFlags;
    PCWSTR pszDestAddress;
    PCWSTR pszAppName;
    PCWSTR pszCalledParty;
    PCWSTR pszComment;
} PHONEMAKECALLINFO, * PHONEMAKECALLINFO;
```

The first field is the standard size field that needs to be filled with the size of the structure. The *dwFlags* field can contain one of two flags: *PMCF_PROMPTBEFORECALLING*, which tells the system to prompt the user before initiating the call, or *PMCF_DEFAULT*, which tells the system to make the call without asking the user whether the call should be made. Even with the *PMCF_DEFAULT* flag, the system will display a notification that the call is being made. The *pszDestAddress* field should point to a string containing the phone number to call. The string can contain the standard phone number separator characters such as dashes, spaces, and parentheses. The *pszCalledParty* field should point to a string that identifies the called party. This string is displayed, along with the number, on the call-in-progress notification that is displayed when the call is made. The *pszAppName* and *pszComment* fields should be set to 0.

Viewing the Call Log

The system maintains a log of all calls made to and from the phone. The call log is a simple database that keeps information such as the time of the call, its duration, and the number of the other phone, as well as details such as whether the call was incoming, the phone is roaming, and so on. The call log can be accessed with a few simple functions. To open the call log, call the aptly named *PhoneOpenCallLog*, prototyped as

```
HRESULT PhoneOpenCallLog (HANDLE * ph);
```

The function returns *S_OK* if successful and *ERROR_FAIL* otherwise. An extended error code can be retrieved with *GetLastError*. Some Smartphone systems don't allow the call log to be opened. There might or might not be a system reason for getting this error, but many phones don't allow this function to succeed. There isn't an issue with Pocket PC phone edition systems. Also, opening the call log isn't necessary for calling *PhoneMakeCall*. If *PhoneOpenCallLog* is successful, a handle will be placed in the value pointed to by the parameter *ph*, and the seek pointer of the call log will be set to point to the first entry in the log.

Once opened, entries in the call log can be queried with the function *PhoneGetCallLogEntry*, prototyped as

```
HRESULT PhoneGetCallLogEntry (HANDLE h, PCALLLOGENTRY pentry);
```

The handle is the one received from the call to *PhoneOpenCallLog*. The *dbSize* field of the *CALLLOGENTRY* structure needs to be initialized with the size of the structure before the function is called.

If the function returns without error, *pentry* points to a structure that contains data about the call, and the seek pointer of the call log is moved to the next entry. Repeated calls to *PhoneGetCallLogEntry* will enumerate the entire call log. When no more entries are in the log, the function will fail with the extended error code 259 indicating no more entries are available.

The *CALLLOGENTRY* structure is defined as

```
typedef struct {
    DWORD cbSize;
    FILETIME ftStartTime;
    FILETIME ftEndTime;
    IOM iom;
    BOOL fOutgoing:1;
    BOOL fConnected:1;
    BOOL fEnded:1;
    BOOL fRoam:1;
    CALLERIDTYPE cidt;
    PTSTR pszNumber;
    PTSTR pszName;
    PTSTR pszNameType;
    PTSTR pszNote;
} CALLLOGENTRY, * PCALLLOGENTRY;
```

The *ftStartTime* and *ftEndTime* fields are *FILETIME* structures that provide the start and end times of the call. The *iom* field contains an enumeration indicating if the call was incoming, was outgoing, or was missed. The next four fields are Booleans detailing the conditions of the call: *fOutgoing* is *TRUE* if the call was made from the device; *fConnected* is set if the call actually made a connection; *fEnded* is *TRUE* if the call was terminated by the callers and *FALSE* if the call was dropped; and *fRoam* is set if the call was made from outside the phone's home area. The *cidt* field is an enumeration indicating if the caller ID for the call was available, blocked, or unavailable.

The *pszNumber* field points to a string indicating the number of the phone number of the calling phone or the phone being called. The *pszName* field identifies the name associated with the number. The *pszNameType* field points to a string that indicates which number—home, work, or mobile—was associated with the contact. The string is in the form of a character, typically either *h*, *w*, or *m* for home, work, or mobile, respectively. The *pszNote* field is a string that is supposed to point to a string containing the name of a notes file for the call. This field isn't always filled in by the system.

The seek pointer of the call log can be moved with

```
HRESULT PhoneSeekCallLog (HANDLE h, CALLLOGSEEK seek, DWORD iRecord,
                          LPDWORD piRecord);
```

The handle value is the handle returned by *PhoneOpenCallLog*. The seek value can be set to either *CALLLOGSEEK_BEGINNING* or *CALLLOGSEEK_END*, depending on whether the passed offset is based from the beginning or end of the log. The parameter *iRecord* is the zero-based offset from the beginning or end of the log. The *piRecord* parameter points to a *DWORD* that receives the index, from the beginning of the log, of the resulting record. Once the seek pointer is moved to a specific record, the record can then be read with *Phone-GetCallLogEntry*.

The phone log should be closed with a call to *PhoneCloseCallLog*, proto-typed as

```
HRESULT PhoneCloseCallLog (HANDLE h);
```

The single parameter is the handle returned from *PhoneOpenCallLog*.

The Connection Manager

The connection manager is a centralized location to request a connection to external data networks regardless of the connection method. The connection manager presents both a single point of connection configuration to the user and a single place where applications can go to programmatically connect to the network. The connection manager also frees the application from having to know what connections are the best to use given the different costs and speeds of the various connections. For example, the connection manager knows it's better to access the Internet via ActiveSync if possible instead of connecting via a cellular connection.

Connecting

An application can connect to a network in three ways using the connection manager. An application can request a connection synchronously, request a connection asynchronously, or schedule a time for a connection to be made. Typically, an application will call *ConnMgrEstablishConnection* to request a connection be made asynchronously and then be notified when the connection is made. The prototype is

```
HRESULT ConnMgrEstablishConnection (CONNMGR_CONNECTIONINFO * pConnInfo,
                                    HANDLE * phConnection);
```

The function returns an *HRESULT* and, if successful, a handle to the connection in the variable pointed to by *phConnection*. The other parameter of the call is a pointer to a *CONNMGR_CONNECTIONNFO* structure, defined as

```
typedef struct _CONNMGR_CONNECTIONINFO {
    DWORD cbSize;
    DWORD dwParams;
    DWORD dwFlags;
    DWORD dwPriority;
    BOOL bExclusive;
    BOOL bDisabled;
    GUID guidDestNet;
    HWND hWnd;
    UINT uMsg;
    LPARAM lParam;
    ULONG ulMaxCost;
    ULONG ulMinRcvBw;
    ULONG ulMaxConnLatency;
} CONNMGR_CONNECTIONINFO;
```

The traditional size field should be set to the size of the structure. The *dwParams* field indicates which optional fields in the structure are filled with valid data. I'll mention the flags in this field as I discuss the optional fields. The *dwFlags* field indicates the proxies supported by the application. The supported flags include proxy flags for HTTP, Wireless Application Protocol (WAP), SOCKS4 and SOCKS5. If no flags are specified, only a direct Internet connection is attempted.

The *dwPriority* field indicates how important the connection is to the application. The priority ranges from *CONNMGR_PRIORITY_VOICE* for a voice connection, the highest priority, to *CONNMGR_PRIORITY_LOWBKGND*, which indicates a connection will only be made if another connection is currently active that satisfies the request. The *bExclusive* field should be set to *TRUE* if the connection should not be shared among the other applications in the system. If *bDisabled* is *TRUE*, *ConnMgrEstablishConnection* will check the connection to see whether it can be made, but the connection won't actually be made. The *guidDestNet* field indicates the network to connect to. The GUID of the various network connections can be determined using *ConnMgrEnumDestinations* discussed later. This field will be used only if the *dwParams* field contains the *CONNMGR_PARAM_DESTNETID* flag.

The next three fields, *hWnd*, *wMsg*, and *lParam*, are used to provide feedback to the application about the connection. The connection manager sends message values of *wMsg* indicating progress of the connection to the window indicated by *hWnd*. The *lParam* value is passed in the progress message in the *lParam* value. The *wParam* value of the message provides a connection status.

The status values are defined in the ConnMgr.h include file. Additional connection status can be queried by calling *ConnMgrConnectionStatus*. This function, along with the various connection states, is discussed later.

The final three parameters, *ulMaxCost*, *ulMinRcvBw*, and *ulMaxConnLatency*, define additional conditions that the connection manager should use when choosing what path to use when making a connection. These fields are only used if the corresponding flag is set in the *dwParams* parameter.

To connect synchronously, an application can call *ConnMgrEstablishConnectionSync*, prototyped as

```
HRESULT ConnMgrEstablishConnectionSync (CONNMGR_CONNECTIONINFO *pConnInfo,
                                        HANDLE *phConnection,
                                        DWORD dwTimeout, DWORD *pdwStatus);
```

The parameters are similar to *ConnMgrEstablishConnection* with the addition of *dwTimeout*, which defines the time in milliseconds that the function should wait for a connection to be made, and *pdwStatus*, which points to a *DWORD* that is filled in with the resulting status of the connection.

The connection manager can also be requested to make a connection at a scheduled time using the function *ConnMgrRegisterScheduledConnection*. If the device is off when the scheduled time arrives, it will automatically turn on and attempt the connection. *ConnMgrRegisterScheduledConnection* is defined as

```
HRESULT ConnMgrRegisterScheduledConnection (SCHEDULEDCONNECTIONINFO *pSCI);
```

The single parameter is a pointer to a *SCHEDULEDCONNECTIONINFO* structure, defined as

```
typedef struct _SCHEDULEDCONNECTIONINFO {
    GUID guidDest;
    UINT64 uiStartTime;
    UINT64 uiEndTime;
    UINT64 uiPeriod;
    TCHAR szAppName[MAX_PATH];
    TCHAR szCmdLine[MAX_PATH];
    TCHAR szToken[32];
    BOOL bPiggyback;
} SCHEDULEDCONNECTIONINFO;
```

The *guidDest* field defines the network to connect to. The *szToken* field should be set to a string that uniquely identifies this scheduled connection. This string will be used if the connection needs to be canceled.

The *uiStartTime* and *uiEndTime* fields define the time that the requests should start and stop, and *uiPeriod* defines how often the requests should be repeated. These times are defined in the structure as 64-bit numbers that are 100 nanosecond intervals since January 1, 1601. Conveniently, this format is the same as the *FILETIME* structure. The *uiPeriod* value can be set to 0 to indicate that the system will never automatically attempt the connection.

When the connection is made, the application name pointed to by *szApp-Name* will be launched with the command line specified in *szCmdLine*. If the *bPiggyback* field is set to *TRUE*, the application will be launched whenever a connection is made to the network matching the *guidDest* field. Setting this field to *TRUE* and setting *uiPeriod* to 0 allows an application to monitor any connection to a specific network without scheduling a connection of its own.

The scheduled connection can be canceled with a call to *ConnMgrUnreg-isterScheduledConnection*, defined as

```
HRESULT ConnMgrUnregisterScheduledConnection (LPCWSTR pwszToken);
```

The single parameter is the 32-character token string passed in the *szToken* field of *SCHEDULEDCONNECTIONINFO* when the connection was scheduled.

Setting and Querying Status

Querying the status of a connection can be accomplished with a call to

```
HRESULT ConnMgrConnectionStatus (HANDLE hConnection, DWORD *pdwStatus);
```

The parameters are the handle to a current connection handle and a pointer to a *DWORD* that will receive the current status. The status flags are listed in the following table.

Status	Value	Description
Unknown	00	Status unknown.
Connected	0x10	The connection is up.
Disconnected	0x20	The connection is disconnected.
Connection failed	0x21	The connection attempt failed.
Connection canceled	0x22	The user aborted the connection.
Connection disabled	0x23	The connection is ready to connect but is disabled.
No path to destination	0x24	No network path could be found to destination.
Waiting for path	0x25	The connection is waiting for a path to the destination.
Waiting for phone	0x26	A voice call is in progress.
Waiting connection	0x40	Attempting to connect.
Waiting for resource	0x41	Resource is in use by another connection.
Waiting for network	0x42	No path could be found to destination.
Waiting disconnection	0x80	The connection is being brought down.
Waiting connection abort	0x81	The connection attempt is being aborted.

The various connections can be enumerated using the function *ConnMgrEnumDestinations*, prototyped as

```
HRESULT ConnMgrEnumDestinations (int nIndex,
                            CONNMGR_DESTINATION_INFO *pDestInfo);
```

To use this function, an application calls *ConnMgrEnumDestinations* repeatedly, the first time with the *nIndex* set to 0 and then incrementing *nIndex* for each call. If the function is successful, data about the connection will be provided in the *CONNMGR_DESTINATION_INFO* structure pointed to by *pDestInfo*. The structure is defined as

```
typedef struct _CONNMGR_DESTINATION_INFO {
    GUID guid;
    TCHAR szDescription[CONNMGR_MAX_DESC];
} CONNMGR_DESTINATION_INFO;
```

The structure has two fields, the GUID of the specific network and a string describing the network. The GUID of the network can be used to specify the network when connecting.

SMS Messaging

The Short Message Service, or SMS, is a popular way, as the name implies, to exchange short text messages between cellular phones. By default, the InBox application on both the Smartphone and the Pocket PC Phone edition reads SMS messages. On the Smartphone, the Pocket InBox is also responsible for composing and sending SMS messages. On the Pocket PC, SMS messages can be composed and sent from a menu on the phone application. In addition to these applications, both systems expose a set of functions that allows third-party applications to send and receive SMS messages.

The process of sending and receiving SMS messages involves getting an SMS handle for sending and another for receiving. The message is composed, and the address is defined as the phone number of the receiving phone. Instead of sending the message directly to the phone, however, the message is sent to the SMS Service Center, which forwards the message on to the destination phone.

Receiving a message involves blocking on an event that is signaled when a message has been received. The message can then be read with a call to the SMS system. Because of the blocking nature of the reading process, this task is usually accomplished with a secondary thread.

The SMS system doesn't provide any way of saving the read messages. Instead, the application that is responsible for receiving the messages is responsible for saving the messages in a database if the user wants them saved. On the Pocket PC and Smartphone, Pocket Inbox saves the messages in the e-mail database.

Accessing the SMS System

The task of sending or receiving messages starts with accessing the SMS subsystem using *SmsOpen*, prototyped as

```
HRESULT SmsOpen (const LPCTSTR ptsMessageProtocol,
                 const DWORD dwMessageModes, SMS_HANDLE* const psmshHandle,
                 HANDLE* const phMessageAvailableEvent);
```

The first parameter is a string that describes the type of message that the application is interested in sending or receiving. For sending and receiving basic text messages, the *SMS_MSGTYPE_TEXT* protocol should be used. The include file Sms.h defines a number of other protocols that can be used for broadcast, status, and a couple of control protocols. The *dwMessageModes* parameter should be set for either *SMS_MODE_RECEIVE* or *SMS_MODE_SEND* depending on if the open is to send or receive messages. The *psmshHandle* parameter points to an *SMS_HANDLE* value that will receive the SMS handle if the function is successful.

The final parameter, *phMessageAvailableEvent*, points to an event handle but is used only when opening to receive messages. When asking for a handle to send SMS messages, the parameter should be *NULL*. When asking for a handle to receive messages, this parameter must point to a standard Windows CE event handle that was previously created by the application. This event handle should be an auto-reset event, not initially signaled. The event will be signaled when a message has been received by the system. The application should not set the event or close the event handle. The event will be closed when the application calls *SmsClose*.

The return value of *SmsOpen* will be *ERROR_SUCCESS* if the call was successful. Otherwise, an error code will be returned.

Sending a Message

Sending a message is accomplished by calling the rather involved *SmsSendMessage* function, prototyped as

```
HRESULT SmsSendMessage (const SMS_HANDLE smshHandle,
                        const SMS_ADDRESS * const psmsaSMSCAddress,
                        const SMS_ADDRESS * const psmsaDestinationAddress,
                        const SYSTEMTIME * const pstValidityPeriod,
                        const BYTE * const pbData, const DWORD dwDataSize,
                        const BYTE * const pbProviderSpecificData,
                        const DWORD dwProviderSpecificDataSize,
                        const SMS_DATA_ENCODING smsdeDataEncoding,
                        const DWORD dwOptions,
                        SMS_MESSAGE_ID * psmsmidMessageID);
```

The first parameter is an SMS handle that was opened for sending a message. The *psmsaSMSCAddress* parameter points to an *SMS_ADDRESS* structure that contains the phone number of the SMS service center. In most cases, this parameter can be *NULL* to indicate that the system should use the default SMS center address. The *psmsaDestinationAddress* parameter points to another *SMS_ADDRESS* structure that contains the destination address of the message. I'll discuss the format of the *SMS_ADDRESS* structure in a moment.

The fourth parameter of *SmsSendMessage*, *pstValidityPeriod*, sets the length of time the message can remain undelivered at the server before it is deleted. Contrary to the parameter's *SYSTEMTIME* type, the format of this field is not a *SYSTEMTIME* but a data type defined by the SMS specification. This parameter can be *NULL*.

The next two fields are the pointer to the message text and the length in bytes of the text. The maximum length of a single message is 140 bytes or 160 7-bit characters. The format of the data is defined in the *smsdeDataEncoding* parameter discussed later.

The *pbProviderSpecificData* parameter points to optional provider-specific data. The provider-specific data is a structure specialized to the message format being used when sending the data. The format of the *TEXT_PROVIDER_SPECIFIC_DATA* structure, used when sending standard text messages, is described later. The *dwProviderSpecificDataSize* parameter should be set to the size of the structure pointed to by *pbProviderSpecificData*. See the discussion of the *TEXT_PROVIDER_SPECIFIC_DATA* structure for special handling of this parameter.

The *smsdeDataEncoding* parameter describes how the message data is encoded. For most messages, the parameter should be set to *SMSDE_OPTIMAL* to tell the SMS code to define the optimal encoding. The other values are *SMSDE_GSM* to use the 7-bit GSM encoding and *SMSDE_UCS2* to specify a Unicode UCS2 encoding. The *dwOptions* parameter specifies how the service center will handle retries. If the parameter is set to *SMS_OPTION_DELIVERY_NONE*, the service center will retry sending the message. If *SMS_OPTION_DELIVERY_ NO_RETRY* is specified, the message won't retry the delivery.

The final parameter points to a *DWORD* that will receive a message ID value. The message ID can be used to get status of the message using the function *SmsGetMessageStatus*. This parameter can be *NULL* if the message ID isn't needed.

The return value of *SmsSendMessage* is a standard *HRESULT* value, with S_OK (0) indicating success. The function can take a short but noticeable amount of time to complete, so it's best to display a wait cursor or use some other method to prevent the user from thinking the system is momentarily locked up.

The structures used by *SmsSendMessage* included the *SMS_ADDRESS* and *TEXT_PROVIDER_SPECIFIC_DATA* structures. The *SMS_ADDRESS* structure is defined as

```
typedef struct sms_address_tag {
    SMS_ADDRESS_TYPE smsatAddressType;
    TCHAR ptsAddress[SMS_MAX_ADDRESS_LENGTH];
} SMS_ADDRESS, *LPSMS_ADDRESS;
```

The first field of the structure is the address type. For most uses, this field can be set to *SMSAT_INTERNATIONAL*. The second field is the address; for *SMSAT_INTERNATIONAL*, the address is in the form of a phone number complete with country code and area code, as in +12225551212.

When sending standard text messages, the provider-specific data structure used is *TEXT_PROVIDER_SPECIFIC_DATA*, shown here. Other structures can be used when sending other types of message, but for brevity I'll describe only this structure.

```
typedef struct text_provider_specific_data_tag {
    DWORD dwMessageOptions;
    PROVIDER_SPECIFIC_MESSAGE_CLASS psMessageClass;
    PROVIDER_SPECIFIC_REPLACE_OPTION psReplaceOption;
    DWORD dwHeaderDataSize;
    BYTE pbHeaderData[SMS_DATAGRAM_SIZE];
    BOOL fMessageContainsEMSHeaders;
    DWORD dwProtocolID;
} TEXT_PROVIDER_SPECIFIC_DATA;
```

This structure definition is somewhat misleading because only the first three fields are used when sending a standard text message. The additional fields are used only for message concatenation. The first field is the message options field that can request that various message bits be set, such as reply path, discard, or status. The message class value ranges from *PS_MESSAGE_CLASS0* through *PS_MESSAGE_CLASS3* and *PS_MESSAGE_CLASSUNSPECIFIED*. The message class indicates how the service center handles the message. For text messages, *PS_MESSAGE_CLASS0* is used. The *psReplaceOption* field contains *PSRO_NONE* for standard messages. The field can be set to *PSRO_REPLACE_TYPEn*, where *n* is a value from 1 through 7. If a replace type field is set, the message will replace a message at the destination with the same parameters and the same replace type value.

A function of this complexity deserves an example. The following code calls *SmsOpen*, fills in the proper structures, and then sends the message. The SMS handle is then closed with *SmsClose*.

```
SMS_HANDLE smshHandle;
SMS_ADDRESS smsaDestination;
TEXT_PROVIDER_SPECIFIC_DATA tpsd;
SMS_MESSAGE_ID smsmidMessageID = 0;

// try to open an SMS Handle
HRESULT hr = SmsOpen(SMS_MSGTYPE_TEXT, SMS_MODE_SEND, &smshHandle, NULL);
if (hr != ERROR_SUCCESS) {
    printf ("SmsOpen fail %x %d", hr, GetLastError());
    return 0;
}
// Create the destination address
memset (&smsaDestination, 0, sizeof (smsaDestination));
smsaDestination.smsatAddressType = SMSAT_INTERNATIONAL;
lstrcpy(smsaDestination.ptsAddress, TEXT("+18005551212"));

// Set up provider specific data
tpsd.dwMessageOptions = PS_MESSAGE_OPTION_NONE;
tpsd.psMessageClass = PS_MESSAGE_CLASS0;
tpsd.psReplaceOption = PSRO_NONE;

char szMessage[] = "Watson!  Come here, I need you!";

// Send the message, indicating success or failure
hr = SmsSendMessage (smshHandle, NULL, &smsaDestination, NULL,
                     (PBYTE) szMessage, strlen(szMessage)+1,
                     (PBYTE) &tpsd, 12, SMSDE_OPTIMAL,
                     SMS_OPTION_DELIVERY_NONE, &smsmidMessageID);
if (hr == ERROR_SUCCESS)
    printf ("Message sent");
SmsClose (smshHandle);
```

SmsOpen is called with *SMS_MODE_SEND* to open a handle for sending. Notice that the final parameter is *NULL* because there isn't a need for the read event handle. The destination address is then filled in with a 10-digit phone number. The provider-specific data is constructed with no options and message class 0. The message is then constructed, and the call to *SmsSendMessage* is made. Notice that the size of the provider-specific data is not set to *sizeof (TEXT_PROVIDER_SPECIFIC_DATA)* because this is a simple, standalone message and the last few fields of *TEXT_PROVIDER_SPECIFIC_DATA* aren't used. After the message is sent, the handle is closed with *SmsClose*, which has the handle as the single parameter.

Receiving a Message

Receiving a message is accomplished with the function *SmsReadMessage*. When opening an SMS handle for reading, an event handle must be passed as the last parameter. The SMS system will use this handle to signal the application when a message has been received.

When the event is signaled, the application can get an idea of the size of the incoming message by calling *SmsGetMessageSize*, prototyped as

```
HRESULT SmsGetMessageSize (const SMS_HANDLE smshHandle,
                           DWORD * const pdwDataSize);
```

The two parameters are the SMS handle that was opened previously and a pointer to a *DWORD* that will receive the message size. The size received is not necessarily the exact size of the message. Instead, it is an upper bound that can be used to allocate the buffer that receives the message.

With a buffer allocated, the message can be read using *SmsReadMessage*, prototyped as

```
HRESULT SmsReadMessage (const SMS_HANDLE smshHandle,
                        SMS_ADDRESS * const psmsaSMSCAddress,
                        SMS_ADDRESS * const psmsaSourceAddress,
                        SYSTEMTIME * const pstReceiveTime,
                        BYTE * const pbBuffer, DWORD dwBufferSize,
                        BYTE * const pbProviderSpecificBuffer,
                        DWORD dwProviderSpecificDataBuffer,
                        DWORD* pdwBytesRead);
```

The first parameter is an SMS handle that was opened in receive mode. The second parameter is an optional *SMS_ADDRESS* structure that can receive the number of the SMS service center that sent the message. If the message center address is of no interest, this parameter can be set to *NULL*. The third parameter points to an *SMS_ADDRESS* structure that will be filled in with the address of the message received. The *pstReceiveTime* parameter points to a *SYSTEMTIME* structure that will receive the UTC-based time of the message. This parameter can be *NULL* if the time isn't required. The next two parameters, *pbBuffer* and *dwBufferSize*, are the pointer to the buffer to receive the data and the size of the buffer. The *pbProviderSpecificBuffer* parameter points to a buffer that will receive the provider-specific data that accompanies the message, and *dwProviderSpecificDataBuffer* contains the size of the buffer. The final parameter points to a *DWORD* that will receive the size of the message received.

SmsReadMessage will fail if there is no message to be read, so the application must block on the event used when *SmsOpen* was called and only read the message when the event is signaled. The blocking nature of the process means that *SmsReadMessage*, or at least the wait on the event object, should be done in a secondary thread. The following code is a separate thread that creates an event, opens an SMS handle, blocks on the event, and if signaled reads the message.

```
DWORD ThreadRead (PVOID pArg) {
    SMS_ADDRESS smsaDestination;
    TEXT_PROVIDER_SPECIFIC_DATA tpsd;
    SMS_HANDLE smshHandle;

    HANDLE hRead = CreateEvent (NULL, FALSE, FALSE, NULL);
    // Open an SMS Handle
    HRESULT hr = SmsOpen (SMS_MSGTYPE_TEXT, SMS_MODE_RECEIVE,
                          &smshHandle, &hRead);
    if (hr != ERROR_SUCCESS) {
        printf ("SmsOpen fail %x %d\r\n", hr, GetLastError());
        return 0;
    }
    // Wait for message to come in.
    int rc = WaitForSingleObject (hRead, 30000);
    if (rc != WAIT_OBJECT_0) {
        printf ("WaitForSingleObject %d\r\n", rc);
        SmsClose (smshHandle);
        return 0;
    }
    memset (&smsaDestination, 0, sizeof (smsaDestination));
    DWORD dwSize, dwRead = 0;

    hr = SmsGetMessageSize (smshHandle, &dwSize);
    if (hr != ERROR_SUCCESS) {
        dwSize = 1024;
        return 0;
    }
    char *pMessage = (char *)malloc (dwSize+1);
    memset (&tpsd, 0, sizeof (tpsd));
    hr = SmsReadMessage (smshHandle, NULL, &smsaDestination, NULL,
                         (PBYTE)pMessage, dwSize,
                         (PBYTE)&tpsd, sizeof(TEXT_PROVIDER_SPECIFIC_DATA),
                         &dwRead);
    if (hr == ERROR_SUCCESS) {
        printf ("Dst Address >%s<\r\n", smsaDestination.ptsAddress);
        printf ("Msg: >%s<", pMessage);
    } else
        printf ("Failed %x  LastErr:%d\r\n", hr, GetLastError());
    free (pMessage);
    SmsClose (smshHandle);
    printf ("ThreadExit");
    return 0;
}
```

This code could be better written to check the length of the received data and to insure that the message is zero terminated.

Configuring the SMS System

There are a number of functions in the SMS API that are provided for querying the state and managing the SMS system. The SMS phone number for the device can be queried with a call to *SmsGetPhoneNumber*, defined as

```
HRESULT SmsGetPhoneNumber (SMS_ADDRESS* const psmsaAddress);
```

The only parameter is an *SMS_ADDRESS* structure that is filled in with the phone number of the device.

The status of a sent message can be queried with *SmsQueryMessageStatus*, prototyped as

```
HRESULT SmsGetMessageStatus (const SMS_HANDLE smshHandle,
              SMS_MESSAGE_ID smsmidMessageID,
              SMS_STATUS_INFORMATION * const psmssiStatusInformation,
              const DWORD dwTimeout);
```

The first two parameters are the SMS handle and the message ID that was returned by *SmsSendMessage*. The *dwTimeout* value is the time, in milliseconds, that the function should wait for status information from the SMS service center. If the function returns successfully, the *SMS_STATUS_INFORMATION* structure is filled with status information about the message. The structure is defined as

```
typedef struct sms_status_information_tag {
    SMS_MESSAGE_ID smsmidMessageID;
    DWORD dwMessageStatus0;
    DWORD dwMessageStatus1;
    SMS_ADDRESS smsaRecipientAddress;
    SYSTEMTIME stServiceCenterTimeStamp;
    SYSTEMTIME stDischargeTime;
} SMS_STATUS_INFORMATION, *LPSMS_STATUS_INFORMATION;
```

The first field is the ID of the message. The next two fields contain status flags that define the state of the message. There are two fields because there are more than 32 status flags defined. The *SMS_ADDRESS* field is filled with the destination address of the message. The *stServiceCenterTimeStamp* field contains the time the message was received by the service center. The *stDischargeTime* field is a time that depends on the status flags returned in the two *dwMessageStatus* fields.

The SMS service center number can be queried and set with the functions *SmsGetSMSC* and *SmsSetSMSC*, prototyped as

```
HRESULT SmsGetSMSC (SMS_ADDRESS* const psmsaSMSCAddress);
```

and

```
HRESULT SmsSetSMSC (const SMS_ADDRESS * const psmsaSMSCAddress);
```

Both functions take a single parameter, a pointer to an *SMS_ADDRESS* structure. Typically, the telephony provider preconfigures this service center number in the phone.

The current time can be estimated with a call to *SmsGetTime*, prototyped as

```
HRESULT SmsGetTime (SYSTEMTIME * const ptsCurrentTime,
                    DWORD * const pdwErrorMargin);
```

The time returned is based on the time received by the SMS service center the last time the system received a timestamp. The time is a UTC number, so it needs to be corrected for the local time zone. The *pdwErrorMargin* parameter should point to a *DWORD* that receives an estimated error margin, in seconds, for the time. If an error margin can't be determined, the error margin will be set to 0xFFFFFFFF.

An application can ask to be started when a message is received by calling the function *SmsSetMessageNotification*, prototyped as

```
HRESULT SmsSetMessageNotification (const SMSREGISTRATIONDATA * psmsrd);
```

The single parameter is a pointer to an *SMSREGISTRATIONDATA* structure, defined as

```
typedef struct smsregistrationdata_tag {
    DWORD cbSize;
    TCHAR tszAppName[SMS_MAX_APPNAME_LENGTH];
    TCHAR tszParams[SMS_MAX_PARAMS_LENGTH];
    TCHAR tszProtocolName[SMS_MAX_PROTOCOLNAME_LENGTH];
} SMSREGISTRATIONDATA, *LPSMSREGISTRATIONDATA;
```

The *cbSize* field should be set with the size of the structure before calling the function. The *tszAppName* and *tszParams* fields specify the application name and command line for the application when it is launched. The *tszProtocolName* field should be set to the message protocol for the messages the application wants to receive. For example, if the application wants to receive standard text messages, the field should be set to *SMS_MSGTYPE_TEXT*.

When the application no longer wants to be notified when messages are received, it can call *SmsClearMessageNotification*, prototyped as

```
HRESULT SmsClearMessageNotification (const LPCTSTR tszProtocolName);
```

The single parameter is the message protocol that was specified when *SmsSetMessageNotification* was called.

The SMSTalk Example

The following example uses a number of the techniques discussed in this chapter to create an application that sends and receives SMS messages. SMSTalk is a dialog-based, multithreaded application that monitors the SMS read queue as well as provides a method for the user to compose and send SMS messages.

The example is designed to run both on the Smartphone and the Pocket PC phone edition. The example is designed for binary compatibility, as opposed to source code compatibility. Notice that SMSTalk checks for the Smartphone and makes the necessary changes to the user interface at run time. Figure 19-9 shows the SMSTalk main dialog on both a Smartphone and a Pocket PC phone edition device.

Figure 19-9   The SMSTalk application running on both a Smartphone and a Pocket PC

The dialogs look different because the application uses different dialog box templates depending on the device the application is running on. The source code, shown in Listing 19-2, has a rather long resource file because all the dialogs must be described twice, once for each device. The resource file also contains different menu bar templates for the two devices.

```
SMSTalk.rc
//=============================================================
// Resource file
//
// Written for the book Programming Windows CE
// Copyright (C) 2003 Douglas Boling
//=============================================================
```

Listing 19-2   The SMSTalk source code

```
#include "windows.h"
#include "aygshell.h"
#include "SMSTalk.h"                              // Program-specific stuff


//-------------------------------------------------------------------------
// Icons and bitmaps
//
ID_ICON ICON   "SMSTalk.ico"                      // Program icon


//-------------------------------------------------------------------------
// Main window dialog template for Pocket PC
//
SMSTalk_PPC DIALOG discardable  25, 5, 120,  98
STYLE  WS_OVERLAPPED | WS_VISIBLE | WS_SYSMENU | DS_MODALFRAME
CAPTION "SMS Talk"
FONT 8, "System"
BEGIN
    LTEXT    "Received Messages",  -1,    4,    4, 128,  10,
    LISTBOX                 IDD_MSGLIST,   4,  14, 128,  48, WS_TABSTOP

    LTEXT    "Message",            -1,    4,  62,  32,  10,
    EDITTEXT                IDD_MSGADDR,  36,  60,  96,  12, WS_TABSTOP |
                                                            ES_NUMBER
    EDITTEXT                IDD_MSGTEXT,   4,  74, 128,  60, WS_TABSTOP |
                            ES_MULTILINE | ES_WANTRETURN | ES_AUTOVSCROLL
    PUSHBUTTON "&New",        ID_CMDNEW,    4, 137,  40,  12, WS_TABSTOP
    PUSHBUTTON "&Reply",    ID_CMDREPLY,   48, 137,  40,  12, WS_TABSTOP
END
//-------------------------------------------------------------------------
// Main window dialog template for Smartphone
//
SMSTalk_SP DIALOG discardable  25, 5, 120,  98
STYLE  WS_OVERLAPPED | WS_VISIBLE | WS_CAPTION | WS_SYSMENU |
       DS_CENTER | DS_MODALFRAME
CAPTION "SMS Talk"
BEGIN
    LTEXT    "Unread messages",   -1,    2,    2, 96,  8,
    LISTBOX                 IDD_MSGLIST,   2,  11,  96,  12, WS_TABSTOP
    CONTROL "",                            IDD_MSGLISTUD, UPDOWN_CLASS,
           UDS_AUTOBUDDY | UDS_HORZ | UDS_ALIGNRIGHT | UDS_ARROWKEYS |
                       UDS_SETBUDDYINT | UDS_WRAP | UDS_EXPANDABLE,
                                     0,   0,  0,   0
    LTEXT    "Number",             -1,    2,  24, 34,   8,
    EDITTEXT                IDD_MSGADDR,  36,  23,  62,  10, ES_READONLY

    LTEXT    "Message Text",       -1,   2,  34, 96,   8,
```

(continued)

Listing 19-2   *(continued)*

```
    EDITTEXT                    IDD_MSGTEXT,   2,  43, 96,  40, WS_TABSTOP |
                                                    ES_MULTILINE | ES_READONLY
    CONTROL "",             IDD_MSGTEXTUD, UPDOWN_CLASS,  UDS_AUTOBUDDY |
                            UDS_HORZ | UDS_ARROWKEYS | UDS_SETBUDDYINT |
                            UDS_WRAP | UDS_EXPANDABLE | UDS_NOSCROLL,
                                            0,   0,  0,   0
END
//----------------------------------------------------------------------
// Compose window dialog template for Pocket PC
//
WriteMsgDlg_PPC DIALOG discardable  25, 5, 120,  98
STYLE  WS_OVERLAPPED | WS_VISIBLE | WS_SYSMENU | DS_MODALFRAME
CAPTION "Compose Message"
BEGIN
    LTEXT    "Number",              -1,   4,   6,  32,  10,
    EDITTEXT                 IDD_MSGADDR,  36,   4,  96,  12, WS_TABSTOP |
                                                    ES_NUMBER
    LTEXT    "Message Text",        -1,   4,  20, 128,  10,
    EDITTEXT                 IDD_MSGTEXT,   4,  30, 128,  54, WS_TABSTOP |
                            ES_MULTILINE | ES_WANTRETURN | ES_AUTOVSCROLL
    PUSHBUTTON "&Send",      ID_CMDSEND,   4,  90,  40,  12, WS_TABSTOP
    PUSHBUTTON "&Cancel",    IDCANCEL,    48,  90,  40,  12, WS_TABSTOP
END
//----------------------------------------------------------------------
// Compose window dialog template for Smartphone
//
WriteMsgDlg_SP DIALOG discardable  25, 5, 120,  98
STYLE  WS_OVERLAPPED | WS_VISIBLE | WS_CAPTION | WS_SYSMENU |
       DS_CENTER | DS_MODALFRAME
CAPTION "SMS Talk"
BEGIN
    LTEXT    "Number",              -1,   2,   2,  96,   8,
    EDITTEXT                 IDD_MSGADDR,   2,  11,  96,  10, WS_TABSTOP

    LTEXT    "Message Text",        -1,   2,  24,  96,   8,
    EDITTEXT                 IDD_MSGTEXT,   2,  33,  96,  50, WS_TABSTOP |
                                                    ES_MULTILINE
    CONTROL "",             IDD_MSGTEXTUD, UPDOWN_CLASS,  UDS_AUTOBUDDY |
                            UDS_HORZ | UDS_ARROWKEYS | UDS_SETBUDDYINT |
                            UDS_WRAP | UDS_EXPANDABLE | UDS_NOSCROLL,
                                            0,   0,  0,   0
END
//----------------------------------------------------------------------
// String resource table
//
STRINGTABLE DISCARDABLE
```

```
BEGIN
    IDS_EXIT    "Exit"
    IDS_MENU    "Menu"
    IDS_MSG     "Message"
    IDS_FILE    "File"
    IDS_OK      "OK"
    IDS_CANCEL  "Cancel"
    IDS_SEND    "Send"
END
//-----------------------------------------------------------------------
// SoftKeyBar resource on main window for Smartphone
//
ID_MENU_SP RCDATA MOVEABLE PURE
BEGIN
    ID_MENU_SP, 2,
    I_IMAGENONE, IDOK,  TBSTATE_ENABLED, TBSTYLE_BUTTON |
                                TBSTYLE_AUTOSIZE, IDS_EXIT, 0, NOMENU,
    I_IMAGENONE, IDPOP, TBSTATE_ENABLED, TBSTYLE_DROPDOWN |
                                TBSTYLE_AUTOSIZE, IDS_MENU, 0, 0,

END

ID_MENU_SP MENU DISCARDABLE
BEGIN
    POPUP "&File"
    BEGIN
        MENUITEM "Reply",                       ID_CMDREPLY
        MENUITEM "New Message"                  ID_CMDNEW
        MENUITEM SEPARATOR
        MENUITEM "Delete",                      ID_CMDDEL
    END
END
//-----------------------------------------------------------------------
// SoftKeyBar resource on Compose dialog for Smartphone
//
ID_DLGMENU_SP RCDATA MOVEABLE PURE
BEGIN
    ID_MENU_SP, 2,
    I_IMAGENONE, ID_CMDSEND,  TBSTATE_ENABLED, TBSTYLE_BUTTON |
                                TBSTYLE_AUTOSIZE, IDS_SEND, 0, NOMENU,
    I_IMAGENONE, IDCANCEL, TBSTATE_ENABLED, TBSTYLE_BUTTON |
                                TBSTYLE_AUTOSIZE, IDS_CANCEL, 0, NOMENU,
END
//-----------------------------------------------------------------------
// Menu bar resource main window for Pocket PC
//
ID_MENU_PPC RCDATA MOVEABLE PURE
```

(continued)

Listing 19-2 *(continued)*

```
BEGIN
    ID_MENU_PPC, 2,
    I_IMAGENONE, IDFILE, TBSTATE_ENABLED, TBSTYLE_DROPDOWN |
                                    TBSTYLE_AUTOSIZE,IDS_FILE,0,0,
    I_IMAGENONE, IDPOP, TBSTATE_ENABLED, TBSTYLE_DROPDOWN |
                                    TBSTYLE_AUTOSIZE,IDS_MSG,0,1
END

ID_MENU_PPC MENU DISCARDABLE
BEGIN
    POPUP "&File"
    BEGIN
        MENUITEM "&About",                      IDM_ABOUT
        MENUITEM "E&xit",                       IDOK
    END
    POPUP "&Help"
    BEGIN
        MENUITEM "&Delete",                     ID_CMDDEL
        MENUITEM SEPARATOR
        MENUITEM "&Reply",                      ID_CMDREPLY
        MENUITEM "New Message"                  ID_CMDNEW
    END
END
```

SMSTalk.h

```
//=======================================================================
// Header file
//
// Written for the book Programming Windows CE
// Copyright (C) 2003 Douglas Boling
//=======================================================================
// Returns number of elements
#define dim(x) (sizeof(x) / sizeof(x[0]))


//-----------------------------------------------------------------------
// Generic defines and data types
//
struct decodeUINT {                             // Structure associates
    UINT Code;                                  // messages
                                                // with a function.
    BOOL (*Fxn)(HWND, UINT, WPARAM, LPARAM);
};
struct decodeCMD {                              // Structure associates
    UINT Code;                                  // menu IDs with a
    LRESULT (*Fxn)(HWND, WORD, HWND, WORD);     // function.
};
```

```
//---------------------------------------------------------------------
// Program defines used by application
//
typedef struct {
    SMS_ADDRESS smsAddr;
    SYSTEMTIME stMsg;
    int nSize;
    WCHAR wcMessage[160];
} MYMSG_STRUCT, *PMYMSG_STRUCT;

#define MAX_MSGS  250
typedef struct {
    int nMsgCnt;
    MYMSG_STRUCT pMsgs[MAX_MSGS];
} MYMSG_DBASE, *PMYMSG_DBASE;


//---------------------------------------------------------------------
// Generic defines used by application

#define MYMSG_TELLNOTIFY     (WM_USER + 100)

#define  ID_ICON             1

#define  ID_MENU_SP          100
#define  ID_MENU_PPC         101
#define  ID_DLGMENU_SP       102

#define  IDD_MSGLIST         110              // Control IDs
#define  IDD_MSGLISTUD       111
#define  IDD_MSGTEXT         112
#define  IDD_MSGTEXTUD       113
#define  IDD_MSGADDR         114

#define  IDM_EXIT            200
#define  ID_CMDSEND          201
#define  ID_CMDNEW           202
#define  ID_CMDREPLY         203
#define  ID_CMDDEL           204
#define  ID_CMDREAD          205
#define  IDM_ABOUT           206
#define  IDFILE              207
#define  IDPOP               208

#define  IDS_EXIT            401
#define  IDS_MENU            402
```

(continued)

Listing 19-2   *(continued)*

```
#define IDS_MSG           403
#define IDS_FILE          404
#define IDS_OK            405
#define IDS_CANCEL        406
#define IDS_SEND          407


//------------------------------------------------------------------
// Function prototypes
//
void ErrorBox (HWND hWnd, LPCTSTR lpszFormat, ...);
BOOL OnSmartPhone(void);
int RefreshMessageList (HWND hWnd, int nSel);
int SetButtons (HWND hWnd);


// Window procedures
BOOL CALLBACK MainDlgProc (HWND, UINT, WPARAM, LPARAM);
BOOL CALLBACK WriteDlgProc(HWND, UINT, WPARAM, LPARAM);
BOOL CALLBACK AboutDlgProc(HWND, UINT, WPARAM, LPARAM);


// Message handlers
BOOL DoCreateDialogMain (HWND, UINT, WPARAM, LPARAM);
BOOL DoInitDialogMain (HWND, UINT, WPARAM, LPARAM);
BOOL DoCommandMain (HWND, UINT, WPARAM, LPARAM);
BOOL DoHotKeyMain (HWND, UINT, WPARAM, LPARAM);
BOOL DoTellNotifyMain (HWND, UINT, WPARAM, LPARAM);


// Command functions
LPARAM DoMainCommandExit (HWND, WORD, HWND, WORD);
LPARAM DoMainCommandDelMessage (HWND, WORD, HWND, WORD);
LPARAM DoMainCommandReplyMessage (HWND, WORD, HWND, WORD);
LPARAM DoMainCommandNewMessage (HWND, WORD, HWND, WORD);
LPARAM DoMainCommandMsgList (HWND, WORD, HWND, WORD);
LPARAM DoMainCommandAbout (HWND, WORD, HWND, WORD);


// Thread prototype
DWORD WINAPI MonitorThread (PVOID pArg);
```

SMSTalk.cpp

```
//======================================================================
// SMSTalk - Demonstrates SMS messaging system
//
// Written for the book Programming Windows CE
// Copyright (C) 2003 Douglas Boling
//======================================================================
```

```
#include <windows.h>                  // For all that Windows stuff
#include <aygshell.h>                 // Extended shell defines
#include <tpcshell.h>
#include <sms.h>                       // SMS functions
#include "SMSTalk.h"                   // Program-specific stuff

#define MY_MSGWAITING_STRING  TEXT("SMSMsgReadEvent")
#define EMPTY_MSG_LIST        TEXT("<No new messages>")
#define MAXMESSAGELEN         4096
//----------------------------------------------------------------------
// Global data
//
const TCHAR szAppName[] = TEXT ("SMSTalk");
const TCHAR szOtherApp[] = TEXT("Another application already \
has the SMS system open.\n\nPlease close the (email?) application");
HINSTANCF hInst;                       // Program instance handle
HWND g_hMain = 0;
HANDLE g_hReadEvent = 0;
HANDLE g_hQuitEvent = 0;
BOOL g_fContinue = TRUE;
BOOL g_fOnSPhone = FALSE;
PMYMSG_DBASE g_pMsgDB = 0;

// Message dispatch table for MainWindowProc
const struct decodeUINT MainMessages[] = {
    WM_CREATE, DoCreateDialogMain,
    WM_INITDIALOG, DoInitDialogMain,
    WM_COMMAND, DoCommandMain,
    WM_HOTKEY, DoHotKeyMain,
    MYMSG_TELLNOTIFY, DoTellNotifyMain,
};
// Command Message dispatch for MainWindowProc
const struct decodeCMD MainCommandItems[] = {
    IDD_MSGLIST, DoMainCommandMsgList,
    IDOK, DoMainCommandExit,
    IDCANCEL, DoMainCommandExit,
    ID_CMDREPLY, DoMainCommandReplyMessage,
    ID_CMDNEW, DoMainCommandNewMessage,
    ID_CMDDEL, DoMainCommandDelMessage,
    IDM_ABOUT, DoMainCommandAbout,
};
//======================================================================
// Program entry point
//
int WINAPI WinMain (HINSTANCE hInstance, HINSTANCE hPrevInstance,
                LPWSTR lpCmdLine, int nCmdShow) {
    INT i;
```

(continued)

Listing 19-2   *(continued)*

```
HWND hWnd;
HANDLE hThread;
TCHAR szDlgTemplate[32];
SMS_HANDLE smshHandle;

hInst = hInstance;

// Look to see if another instance of the app is running.
hWnd = FindWindow (NULL, szAppName);
// See if we were launched with a command line
if (*lpCmdLine) {
    // Check to see if app started due to notification.
    if (lstrcmp (lpCmdLine, MY_MSGWAITING_STRING) == 0) {
        if (hWnd) {
            SendMessage (hWnd, MYMSG_TELLNOTIFY, 0, 0);
        }
    }
}
// Set first instance to the foreground and exit
if (hWnd) {
    SetForegroundWindow ((HWND)(((DWORD)hWnd) | 0x01));
    return 0;
}
// See if we're running on a smartphone.
g_fOnSPhone = OnSmartPhone ();

// Allocate message array
g_pMsgDB = (PMYMSG_DBASE)LocalAlloc (LPTR, sizeof (MYMSG_DBASE));
if (g_pMsgDB == 0) {
    ErrorBox (NULL, TEXT("Out of memory"));
    return -1;
}
g_pMsgDB->nMsgCnt = 0;

// Create secondary thread for timer event notification.
// then try to open an SMS Handle for reading messages.
g_hQuitEvent = CreateEvent (NULL, FALSE, FALSE, NULL);
g_hReadEvent = CreateEvent (NULL, FALSE, FALSE, NULL);
HRESULT hr = SmsOpen (SMS_MSGTYPE_TEXT, SMS_MODE_RECEIVE,
                      &smshHandle, &g_hReadEvent);
if (hr == SMS_E_RECEIVEHANDLEALREADYOPEN) {
    ErrorBox (hWnd, (LPCTSTR)szOtherApp);
    return 0;
} else if (hr != ERROR_SUCCESS) {
    ErrorBox (hWnd, TEXT("SmsOpen fail %x %d"), hr, GetLastError());
    return 0;
}
```

```
        hThread = CreateThread (NULL, 0, MonitorThread, (PVOID)smshHandle,
                            0, (DWORD *)&i);
    if (hThread == 0)
        return -1;

    // Display dialog box as main window.  Use different template if
    // running on the smartphone
    if (g_fOnSPhone)
        _tcscpy (szDlgTemplate, TEXT("SMSTalk_SP"));
    else
        _tcscpy (szDlgTemplate, TEXT("SMSTalk_PPC"));

    DialogBoxParam (hInstance, szDlgTemplate, NULL, MainDlgProc,
                    (LPARAM)lpCmdLine);
    // Signal notification thread to terminate
    g_fContinue = FALSE;
    SetEvent (g_hQuitEvent);
    WaitForSingleObject (hThread, 1000);
    CloseHandle (hThread);
    CloseHandle (g_hQuitEvent);  // Don't close ReadEvent, SMS does that
    if (g_pMsgDB) LocalFree (g_pMsgDB);
    return 0;
}
//======================================================================
// Message handling procedures for main window
//----------------------------------------------------------------------
// MainDlgProc - Callback function for application window
//
BOOL CALLBACK MainDlgProc (HWND hWnd, UINT wMsg, WPARAM wParam,
                           LPARAM lParam) {
    INT i;

    //
    // Search message list to see if we need to handle this
    // message.  If in list, call procedure.
    //
    for (i = 0; i < dim(MainMessages); i++) {
        if (wMsg == MainMessages[i].Code)
            return (*MainMessages[i].Fxn)(hWnd, wMsg, wParam, lParam);
    }
    return FALSE;
}
//----------------------------------------------------------------------
// DoCreateDialogMain - Process WM_CREATE message for window.
//
BOOL DoCreateDialogMain (HWND hWnd, UINT wMsg, WPARAM wParam,
                     LPARAM lParam) {
```

(continued)

Listing 19-2   *(continued)*

```
    if (!g_fOnSPhone) {
        // set up Menu bar for Pocket PC
        SHMENUBARINFO mbi;

        memset (&mbi, 0, sizeof(SHMENUBARINFO));
        mbi.cbSize = sizeof(SHMENUBARINFO);
        mbi.hwndParent = hWnd;
        mbi.nToolBarId = ID_MENU_PPC; // IDM_MENU;
        mbi.hInstRes = hInst;

        // If we could not initialize the dialog box, return an error
        if (!SHCreateMenuBar(&mbi)) {
            ErrorBox (hWnd, TEXT("Menubar failed"));
            DestroyWindow (hWnd);
            return FALSE;
        }
    }
    return TRUE;
}
//-------------------------------------------------------------------
// DoInitDialogMain - Process WM_INITDIALOG message for window.
//
BOOL DoInitDialogMain (HWND hWnd, UINT wMsg, WPARAM wParam,
                       LPARAM lParam) {
    // Save the window handle
    g_hMain = hWnd;

    // Specify that the dialog box should stretch full screen
    SHINITDLGINFO shidi;
    memset (&shidi, 0, sizeof(shidi));
    shidi.dwMask = SHIDIM_FLAGS;
    shidi.dwFlags = SHIDIF_SIZEDLG ;//SHIDIF_SIZEDLGFULLSCREEN
    shidi.hDlg = hWnd;
    if(!SHInitDialog(&shidi))
        return FALSE;

    // Create menubar
    SHMENUBARINFO mbi;
    memset (&mbi, 0, sizeof(SHMENUBARINFO));
    mbi.cbSize = sizeof(SHMENUBARINFO);
    mbi.hwndParent = hWnd;
    if (g_fOnSPhone)
        mbi.nToolBarId = ID_MENU_SP;
    else
        mbi.nToolBarId = ID_MENU_PPC;
    mbi.hInstRes = hInst;
```

```
    // If we could not initialize the dialog box, return an error
    if (!SHCreateMenuBar(&mbi)) {
        ErrorBox (hWnd, TEXT("Menubar failed"));
        DestroyWindow (hWnd);
        return FALSE;
    }

    // This is only needed on the smartphone
    if (g_fOnSPhone) {
        // Override back key since we have an edit control
        SendMessage (SHFindMenuBar (hWnd), SHCMBM_OVERRIDEKEY, VK_TBACK,
                     MAKELPARAM (SHMBOF_NODEFAULT | SHMBOF_NOTIFY,
                                 SHMBOF_NODEFAULT | SHMBOF_NOTIFY));
    }
    // set the title bar
    SHSetNavBarText (hWnd, TEXT("SMS Talk"));

    SendDlgItemMessage (hWnd, IDD_MSGLIST, LB_ADDSTRING, 0,
                        (LPARAM)EMPTY_MSG_LIST);
    SetButtons (hWnd);
    return TRUE;
}
//-------------------------------------------------------------------------
// DoCommandMain - Process WM_COMMAND message for window.
//
BOOL DoCommandMain (HWND hWnd, UINT wMsg, WPARAM wParam, LPARAM lParam){
    WORD idItem, wNotifyCode;
    HWND hwndCtl;
    INT  i;

    // Parse the parameters.
    idItem = (WORD) LOWORD (wParam);
    wNotifyCode = (WORD) HIWORD (wParam);
    hwndCtl = (HWND) lParam;

    // Call routine to handle control message.
    for (i = 0; i < dim(MainCommandItems); i++) {
        if (idItem == MainCommandItems[i].Code) {
            (*MainCommandItems[i].Fxn)(hWnd, idItem, hwndCtl,
                                       wNotifyCode);
            return TRUE;
        }
    }
    return FALSE;
}
```

(continued)

Listing 19-2   *(continued)*

```
//-----------------------------------------------------------------------
// DoHotKeyMain - Process WM_HOTKEY message for window.
//
BOOL DoHotKeyMain (HWND hWnd, UINT wMsg, WPARAM wParam, LPARAM lParam) {

    SHSendBackToFocusWindow (wMsg, wParam, lParam);
    return 0;
}
//-----------------------------------------------------------------------
// DoTellNotifyMain - Process MYMSG_TELLNOTIFY message for window.
//
BOOL DoTellNotifyMain (HWND hWnd, UINT wMsg, WPARAM wParam,
                       LPARAM lParam) {
    RefreshMessageList (hWnd, lParam);
    SetButtons (hWnd);
    return 0;
}
//=======================================================================
// Command handler routines
//-----------------------------------------------------------------------
// DoMainCommandExit - Process Program Exit command.
//
LPARAM DoMainCommandExit (HWND hWnd, WORD idItem, HWND hwndCtl,
                          WORD wNotifyCode) {
    EndDialog (hWnd, 0);
    return 0;
}
//-----------------------------------------------------------------------
// DoMainCommandDelMessage - Process Read message button.
//
LPARAM DoMainCommandDelMessage (HWND hWnd, WORD idItem, HWND hwndCtl,
                                WORD wNotifyCode) {
    int i, nSel;
    nSel = SendDlgItemMessage (hWnd, IDD_MSGLIST, LB_GETCURSEL,0,0);
    if (nSel != LB_ERR) {
        for (i = nSel; i < g_pMsgDB->nMsgCnt-1; i++)
            g_pMsgDB->pMsgs[i] = g_pMsgDB->pMsgs[i+1];
        g_pMsgDB->nMsgCnt--;
        RefreshMessageList (hWnd, -1);
    }
    SetButtons (hWnd);
    return 0;
}
//-----------------------------------------------------------------------
// DoMainCommandReplyMessage - Process Reply message button.
//
```

```
LPARAM DoMainCommandReplyMessage (HWND hWnd, WORD idItem, HWND hwndCtl,
                                  WORD wNotifyCode) {
    int nSel;
    LPCTSTR lpTemplate;
    LPARAM lp = 0;
    nSel = SendDlgItemMessage (hWnd, IDD_MSGLIST, LB_GETCURSEL,0,0);
    if (nSel != LB_ERR)
        lp = (LPARAM)&g_pMsgDB->pMsgs[nSel].smsAddr;

    // Display reply dialog box.
    if (g_fOnSPhone)
        lpTemplate = TEXT("WriteMsgDlg_SP");
    else
        lpTemplate = TEXT("WriteMsgDlg_PPC");

    DialogBoxParam (hInst, lpTemplate, NULL, WriteDlgProc, lp);
    return 0;
}
//-----------------------------------------------------------------------
// DoMainCommandNewMessage - Process New message button.
//
LPARAM DoMainCommandNewMessage (HWND hWnd, WORD idItem, HWND hwndCtl,
                                WORD wNotifyCode) {
    LPCTSTR lpTemplate;
    // Display reply dialog box.
    if (g_fOnSPhone)
        lpTemplate = TEXT("WriteMsgDlg_SP");
    else
        lpTemplate = TEXT("WriteMsgDlg_PPC");

    DialogBoxParam (hInst, lpTemplate, NULL, WriteDlgProc, 0);
    return 0;
}
//-----------------------------------------------------------------------
// DoMainCommandAbout - Process About menu item.
//
LPARAM DoMainCommandAbout (HWND hWnd, WORD idItem, HWND hwndCtl,
                           WORD wNotifyCode) {
    TCHAR szAbout[] = TEXT("SMS Talk\nCopyright 2003\nDouglas Boling");

    // Display about information in a message box.
    MessageBox (hWnd, szAbout, TEXT("About"), MB_OK | MB_ICONASTERISK);
    return 0;
}
```

(continued)

Listing 19-2   *(continued)*

```
//------------------------------------------------------------------------
// DoMainCommandMsgList - Process message list listbox.
//
LPARAM DoMainCommandMsgList (HWND hWnd, WORD idItem, HWND hwndCtl,
                            WORD wNotifyCode) {
    if (wNotifyCode == LBN_SELCHANGE)
        SetButtons (hWnd);
    return 0;
}
//------------------------------------------------------------------------
// RefreshMessageList - Fill in message listbox from message array
//
int RefreshMessageList (HWND hWnd, int nSel) {
    TCHAR szStr[256];
    int i;

    SendDlgItemMessage (hWnd, IDD_MSGLIST, LB_RESETCONTENT, 0, 0);
    for (i = 0; i < g_pMsgDB->nMsgCnt; i++) {
        wsprintf (szStr, TEXT("%d/%02d/%02d %d:%02d:%02d  %s"),
                  g_pMsgDB->pMsgs[i].stMsg.wMonth,
                  g_pMsgDB->pMsgs[i].stMsg.wDay,
                  g_pMsgDB->pMsgs[i].stMsg.wYear%100,
                  g_pMsgDB->pMsgs[i].stMsg.wHour,
                  g_pMsgDB->pMsgs[i].stMsg.wMinute,
                  g_pMsgDB->pMsgs[i].stMsg.wSecond,
                  g_pMsgDB->pMsgs[i].wcMessage);
        SendDlgItemMessage (hWnd, IDD_MSGLIST, LB_ADDSTRING, 0,
                            (LPARAM)szStr);
    }
    if (g_pMsgDB->nMsgCnt == 0)
        SendDlgItemMessage (hWnd, IDD_MSGLIST, LB_ADDSTRING, 0,
                            (LPARAM)EMPTY_MSG_LIST);
    else {
        if (nSel != -1)
            SendDlgItemMessage (hWnd, IDD_MSGLIST, LB_SETCURSEL,0,nSel);
        else
            SendDlgItemMessage (hWnd, IDD_MSGLIST, LB_SETCURSEL, 0, i-1);
    }
    return 0;
}
//------------------------------------------------------------------------
// SetButtons - Utility function to compute enabled state of btns
//
int SetButtons (HWND hWnd) {
    int nSel;
```

```
    BOOL fReply = FALSE;
    TCHAR szText[128];
    LPTSTR pMsg = TEXT(""), pNum = TEXT("");

    nSel = SendDlgItemMessage (hWnd, IDD_MSGLIST, LB_GETCURSEL, 0, 0);
    if (nSel != LB_ERR) {
        SendDlgItemMessage (hWnd, IDD_MSGLIST, LB_GETTEXT, nSel,
                            (LPARAM)szText);
        if (_tcscmp (szText, EMPTY_MSG_LIST)) {
            fReply = TRUE;
            pNum = g_pMsgDB->pMsgs[nSel].smsAddr.ptsAddress;
            pMsg = g_pMsgDB->pMsgs[nSel].wcMessage;
        }
    }
    EnableWindow (GetDlgItem (hWnd, ID_CMDREPLY), fReply);

    // Set the text in the number and message fields
    SetWindowText (GetDlgItem (hWnd, IDD_MSGADDR), pNum);
    SetWindowText (GetDlgItem (hWnd, IDD_MSGTEXT), pMsg);

    // Disable the menu bar button if necessary
    TBBUTTONINFO tbi;
    HWND hwndMB = SHFindMenuBar (hWnd);
    memset (&tbi, 0, sizeof (tbi));
    tbi.cbSize = sizeof (tbi);
    tbi.dwMask = TBIF_STATE;
    if(SendMessage (hwndMB, TB_GETBUTTONINFO, IDPOP, (LPARAM)&tbi)) {
        if (fReply)
            tbi.fsState |= TBSTATE_ENABLED;
        else
            tbi.fsState &= ~TBSTATE_ENABLED;
        SendMessage (hwndMB, TB_SETBUTTONINFO, IDPOP, (LPARAM)&tbi);
    }
    return nSel;
}
//----------------------------------------------------------------------
// SendSmsMessage - Send an SMS message
//
HRESULT SendSmsMessage (HWND hWnd, SMS_ADDRESS smsDest, LPTSTR pMsg) {
    HRESULT hr;
    SMS_HANDLE smshHandle;
    TEXT_PROVIDER_SPECIFIC_DATA tpsd;
    SMS_MESSAGE_ID smsmidMessageID = 0;
```

(continued)

Listing 19-2 *(continued)*

```
    // try to open an SMS Handle
    hr = SmsOpen(SMS_MSGTYPE_TEXT, SMS_MODE_SEND, &smshHandle, NULL);
    if (hr != ERROR_SUCCESS)
        return hr;

    // Set up provider specific data
    tpsd.dwMessageOptions = PS_MESSAGE_OPTION_NONE;
    tpsd.psMessageClass = PS_MESSAGE_CLASS0;
    tpsd.psReplaceOption = PSRO_NONE;
    tpsd.dwHeaderDataSize = 0;

    // Send the message, indicating success or failure
    hr = SmsSendMessage (smshHandle, NULL, &smsDest, NULL, (PBYTE)pMsg,
                         lstrlen(pMsg) * sizeof (TCHAR),
                         (PBYTE) &tpsd, 12, SMSDE_OPTIMAL,
                         SMS_OPTION_DELIVERY_NONE, &smsmidMessageID);
    SmsClose (smshHandle);
    return hr;
}
//======================================================================
// WriteMsg Dialog procedure
//
BOOL CALLBACK WriteDlgProc (HWND hWnd, UINT wMsg, WPARAM wParam,
                            LPARAM lParam) {
    SHINITDLGINFO shidi;
    static SMS_ADDRESS smsDest;
    TCHAR szMsg[SMS_DATAGRAM_SIZE+2];
    HRESULT hr;

    SHInputDialog (hWnd, wMsg, wParam);
    switch (wMsg) {
    case WM_INITDIALOG:
        // Specify that the dialog box should stretch full screen
        memset (&shidi, 0, sizeof(shidi));
        shidi.dwMask = SHIDIM_FLAGS;
        shidi.dwFlags = SHIDIF_SIZEDLGFULLSCREEN;
        if (!g_fOnSPhone) shidi.dwFlags |= SHIDIF_DONEBUTTON;
        shidi.hDlg = hWnd;
        if(!SHInitDialog(&shidi))
            return FALSE;

        // This is only needed on the smartphone
        if (g_fOnSPhone) {
            // Create MenuBar
            SHMENUBARINFO mbi;
            memset (&mbi, 0, sizeof(SHMENUBARINFO));
```

```
            mbi.cbSize = sizeof(SHMENUBARINFO);
            mbi.hwndParent = hWnd;
            mbi.nToolBarId = ID_DLGMENU_SP;
            mbi.hInstRes = hInst;

            // If we could not initialize the dialog box, return an error
            if (!SHCreateMenuBar(&mbi)) {
                ErrorBox (hWnd, TEXT("Menubar failed"));
                DestroyWindow (hWnd);
                return FALSE;
            }

            // Override back key since we have an edit control
            SendMessage (SHFindMenuBar (hWnd), SHCMBM_OVERRIDEKEY, VK_TBACK,
                        MAKELPARAM (SHMBOF_NODEFAULT | SHMBOF_NOTIFY,
                                    SHMBOF_NODEFAULT | SHMBOF_NOTIFY));
            // Set input mode of number field to numbers
            SendDlgItemMessage (hWnd, IDD_MSGADDR, EM_SETINPUTMODE, 0,
                                EIM_NUMBERS);
        }

        SendDlgItemMessage (hWnd, IDD_MSGTEXT, EM_LIMITTEXT,
                            SMS_DATAGRAM_SIZE, 0);
        // If there is a reply address passed, place it in control
        if (lParam) {
            // Copy dest address
            smsDest = *(SMS_ADDRESS *)lParam;
            SetDlgItemText (hWnd, IDD_MSGADDR, smsDest.ptsAddress);
            SetFocus (GetDlgItem (hWnd, IDD_MSGTEXT));
            return FALSE;
        } else {
            smsDest.smsatAddressType = SMSAT_INTERNATIONAL;
            memset (smsDest.ptsAddress, 0,
                    sizeof (smsDest.ptsAddress));
        }
        return TRUE;

    case WM_HOTKEY:
        SHSendBackToFocusWindow (wMsg, wParam, lParam);
        return TRUE;

    case WM_COMMAND:
        switch (LOWORD (wParam)) {
            case ID_CMDSEND:
                GetDlgItemText (hWnd, IDD_MSGADDR, smsDest.ptsAddress,
```

(continued)

Listing 19-2   *(continued)*

```
                                    dim (smsDest.ptsAddress));
                GetDlgItemText (hWnd,IDD_MSGTEXT, szMsg, dim (szMsg));
                hr = SendSmsMessage (hWnd, smsDest, szMsg);
                if (hr == 0)
                    MessageBox (hWnd, TEXT("Message Sent"), szAppName,
                                MB_OK | MB_ICONASTERISK);
                else
                    ErrorBox (hWnd, TEXT ("Send message fail %x %d"),
                                hr, GetLastError());
            case IDOK:
            case IDCANCEL:
                EndDialog (hWnd, 0);
                return TRUE;
        }
    break;
    }
    return FALSE;
}
//------------------------------------------------------------------------
// ErrorBox - Displays a message box with a formatted string
//
void ErrorBox (HWND hWnd, LPCTSTR lpszFormat, ...) {
    int nBuf;
    TCHAR szBuffer[512];

    va_list args;
    va_start(args, lpszFormat);

    nBuf = _vstprintf(szBuffer, lpszFormat, args);
    MessageBox (hWnd, szBuffer, TEXT("Error Msg"), MB_OK);
    va_end(args);
}
//------------------------------------------------------------------------
// OnSmartPhone - Determines if we're running on a smartphone
//
BOOL OnSmartPhone (void) {
    TCHAR szPlat[128];
    int rc;
    rc = SystemParametersInfo(SPI_GETPLATFORMTYPE, dim(szPlat),szPlat,0);
    if (rc) {
        if (lstrcmpi (szPlat, TEXT("Smartphone")) == 0)
            return TRUE;
    }
    return FALSE;
}
```

```
//========================================================================
// MonitorThread - Monitors event for timer notification
//
DWORD WINAPI MonitorThread (PVOID pArg) {
    TEXT_PROVIDER_SPECIFIC_DATA tpsd;
    SMS_HANDLE smshHandle = (SMS_HANDLE)pArg;
    PMYMSG_STRUCT pNextMsg;
    BYTE bBuffer[MAXMESSAGELEN];
    PBYTE pIn;
    SYSTEMTIME st;
    HANDLE hWait[2];
    HRESULT hr;
    int rc;
    DWORD dwInSize, dwSize, dwRead = 0;

    hWait[0] = g_hReadEvent;        // Need two events since it isn't
    hWait[1] = g_hQuitEvent;        // allowed for us to signal SMS event.

    while (g_fContinue) {
        rc = WaitForMultipleObjects (2, hWait, FALSE, INFINITE);
        if (!g_fContinue || (rc != WAIT_OBJECT_0))
            break;
        // Point to the next free entry in the array
        pNextMsg = &g_pMsgDB->pMsgs[g_pMsgDB->nMsgCnt];

        // Get the message size
        hr = SmsGetMessageSize (smshHandle, &dwSize);
        if (hr != ERROR_SUCCESS) continue;

        // Check for message larger than std buffer
        if (dwSize > sizeof (pNextMsg->wcMessage)) {
            if (dwSize > MAXMESSAGELEN)
                continue;
            pIn = bBuffer;
            dwInSize = MAXMESSAGELEN;
        } else {
            pIn = (PBYTE)pNextMsg->wcMessage;
            dwInSize = sizeof (pNextMsg->wcMessage);
        }
        // Set up provider specific data
        tpsd.dwMessageOptions = PS_MESSAGE_OPTION_NONE;
        tpsd.psMessageClass = PS_MESSAGE_CLASS0;
        tpsd.psReplaceOption = PSRO_NONE;
        tpsd.dwHeaderDataSize = 0;
```

(continued)

Listing 19-2   *(continued)*

```
        // Read the message
        hr = SmsReadMessage (smshHandle, NULL, &pNextMsg->smsAddr, &st,
                            (PBYTE)pIn, dwInSize, (PBYTE)&tpsd,
                            sizeof(TEXT_PROVIDER_SPECIFIC_DATA),
                            &dwRead);
        if (hr == ERROR_SUCCESS) {
            // Convert GMT message time to local time
            FILETIME ft, ftLocal;
            SystemTimeToFileTime (&st, &ft);
            FileTimeToLocalFileTime (&ft, &ftLocal);
            FileTimeToSystemTime (&ftLocal, &pNextMsg->stMsg);

            // If using alt buffer, copy to std buff
            if ((DWORD)pIn == (DWORD)pNextMsg->wcMessage) {
                pNextMsg->nSize = (int) dwRead;
            } else {
                memset (pNextMsg->wcMessage, 0,
                        sizeof(pNextMsg->wcMessage));
                memcpy (pNextMsg->wcMessage, pIn,
                        sizeof(pNextMsg->wcMessage)-2);
                pNextMsg->nSize = sizeof(pNextMsg->wcMessage);
            }
            // Increment message count
            if (g_pMsgDB->nMsgCnt < MAX_MSGS-1) {
                if (g_hMain)
                    PostMessage (g_hMain, MYMSG_TELLNOTIFY, 1,
                                g_pMsgDB->nMsgCnt);
                g_pMsgDB->nMsgCnt++;
            }
        } else {
            ErrorBox (g_hMain, TEXT("Error %x (%d) reading msg"),
                    hr, GetLastError());
            break;
        }
    }
    SmsClose (smshHandle);
    return 0;
}
```

The example illustrates a number of techniques used in a Smartphone application. The dialog templates use both expandable edit fields and spinner controls. The Back button is overridden in both the main dialog and the Compose dialog because both contain edit controls. The edit control that holds the destination number in the Compose dialog has its input mode overridden to numeric mode because the address to be entered is more than likely a phone number.

The SMS code in the application uses a separate thread, appropriately named *MonitorThread*, to monitor incoming SMS messages and uses a send routine, *SendSmsMessage*, that sends messages. Before the monitor thread is launched, the *SmsOpen* is called to request a read-access handle. This call will fail if another application currently has an open SMS handle with read access. If the open fails, SMSTalk displays a message box notifying the user of the problem and terminates. On the Pocket PC, this failure is quite likely because the e-mail program Pocket Inbox stays running in the background. Pocket Inbox can be closed by selecting the Inbox from the Start menu and then entering Ctrl-Q on the soft keyboard.

Sending an SMS message is accomplished by selecting the Reply or the New menu item. First a dialog is displayed so that the message can be composed. If the user selects to send the message, the program calls *SendSmsMessage*. This routine opens an SMS handle for write access, fills in the appropriate structures, and sends the message in the simple text format.

Incoming messages are saved in an array in memory. The messages can then be viewed by highlighting a message in the list box on the Pocket PC, or in the spinner on the Smartphone. SMSTalk does not save the messages because the goal is to demonstrate the features of the SMS system and the Smartphone with the least amount of clutter. Because of this arrangement, any messages received by SMSTalk will be lost when the program terminates. Saving the messages in a file would be a great enhancement and is left as a task for the reader.

Smartphone Security

The Smartphone has one significant difference from the Pocket PC in that it implements Windows CE's module-level security scheme. This means that unless a specific device has been "unlocked," all applications and DLLs have to be certified to run on the device. As I mentioned in Chapter 10, the system can prevent modules, EXEs, and DLLs from being run at all. Even when allowed to run, there are two levels of run-time privilege that can be granted, *trusted* and *run*. Trusted modules have full run of the operating system. They can call any function and modify any registry key. Run-level modules, sometimes called *untrusted modules*, can call only a limited set of the API and are prevented from modifying certain critical sections of the registry. Not that the limited set of functions is all that limited—a run-level module can still call 95 percent of the functions—it's just that the module can't call the set of functions that might compromise the integrity of the system. In addition to the restricted functions listed in Listing 10-1 in Chapter 10, the Smartphone restricts an additional set of communication-related functions. A list of these additional functions is shown in Figure 19-10.

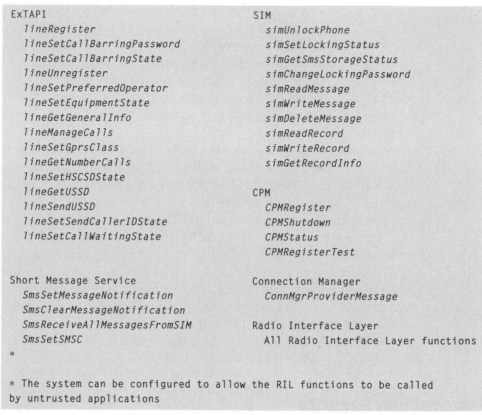

```
ExTAPI                                  SIM
  lineRegister                            simUnlockPhone
  lineSetCallBarringPassword              simSetLockingStatus
  lineSetCallBarringState                 simGetSmsStorageStatus
  lineUnregister                          simChangeLockingPassword
  lineSetPreferredOperator                simReadMessage
  lineSetEquipmentState                   simWriteMessage
  lineGetGeneralInfo                      simDeleteMessage
  lineManageCalls                         simReadRecord
  lineSetGprsClass                        simWriteRecord
  lineGetNumberCalls                      simGetRecordInfo
  lineSetHSCSDState
  lineGetUSSD                           CPM
  lineSendUSSD                            CPMRegister
  lineSetSendCallerIDState                CPMShutdown
  lineSetCallWaitingState                 CPMStatus
                                          CPMRegisterTest


Short Message Service                  Connection Manager
  SmsSetMessageNotification               ConnMgrProviderMessage
  SmsClearMessageNotification
  SmsReceiveAllMessagesFromSIM         Radio Interface Layer
  SmsSetSMSC                             All Radio Interface Layer functions
*

* The system can be configured to allow the RIL functions to be called
by untrusted applications
```

Figure 19-10   The list of restricted communication functions in the Smartphone

The level of security implemented on a particular Smartphone is set by the telecommunication service that sells the phone. The service defines the protection level after considering security on its network, its phones, and the profit potential of restricting all software to be sold through its own service. Market pressures will drive this issue's evolution.

These last few chapters have covered the Pocket PC and the Smartphone in detail. Now it's time for some fun and games. Both the Smartphone and the Pocket PC support a unique API, called the Game API, to assist game writers in implementing cool games on these devices. GAPI is simple, fairly straightforward, and kind of neat, as you'll see in Chapter 20.

20

GAPI, the Game API

Microsoft Windows CE devices sport microprocessors of surprising power. These small CPUs provide the oomph to support a full 32-bit operating system with virtual memory, an extensive window manager, and a RAM-based, transaction-based file system. For game developers, this would be nirvana—if only the operating system weren't there. Game developers love powerful CPUs but they dislike the layers of operating systems that, though helpful to the typical developer, hinder the developer who likes to write code directly to the hardware. To provide a path to the hardware, the Pocket PC and the Smartphone support the Game API (GAPI), a lightweight set of functions to provide the game developer access to the screen and keyboard of a Windows CE device.

GAPI isn't DirectX, which provides a much more extensive set of functions to the game developer. Although Windows CE supports Direct X, Microsoft decided not to provide the DirectX support on the current Pocket PC. In an attempt to make up for this slight, GAPI is supported instead.

GAPI contains a handful of functions that provide access to the display's frame buffer, the area of memory that holds the pixel information displayed on screen. In addition, GAPI enables an application to assume control of all buttons, even those that are normally captured by the shell. Finally, and perhaps most important, GAPI provides information about the display and the button layout in a consistent way across the divergent hardware provided by different Pocket PC manufacturers.

GAPI is provided as a single DLL, GX.DLL. This DLL comes with the Pocket PC 2003 but was not distributed with earlier Pocket PC devices. Instead, it is distributed by the application that uses it. When an application is installed, it should check for GX.DLL in the \windows directory. If GX.DLL isn't found, place it in its install directory, *not in the \windows directory*. The current versions of GAPI don't support any type of versioning. Instead, an application is required to keep its own version of the GAPI DLL in its own application directory to avoid the problem lovingly called *DLL Hell*. In DLL Hell, one application installs an older copy of a shared DLL in the place of a newer version of the DLL, thereby causing problems for the previously installed applications. Although there are a number of ways to avoid DLL Hell—including some that require entire operating system revisions—the simplest solution is to distribute version-sensitive DLLs with the application and keep them in the application's directory. As it stands today, GX.DLL is smaller than 20 KB, so the overhead of maintaining a few of these DLLs in a system is not huge.

To build a GAPI application, the program must include gx.h, which specifies the function prototypes and necessary structures. To provide the proper DLL import information, the program must also link to gx.lib. These files are available in the Pocket PC and Smartphone SDKs.

Table 20-1 lists the GAPI functions.

Table 20-1   GAPI Functions

Function Name	Description
GXOpenDisplay	Initializes GAPI. Can be called only once in an application.
GXCloseDisplay	Closes GAPI. Cleans up GAPI resources.
GXBeginDraw	Called to access the frame buffer for drawing.
GXEndDraw	Called when drawing is complete.
GXGetDisplayProperties	Provides information on the display device.
GXOpenInput	Captures the buttons for the game.
GXCloseInput	Frees the buttons for normal use.
GXGetDefaultKeys	Provides information on the suggested buttons.
GXSuspend	Suspends GAPI subsystem to allow other applications to gain focus.
GXResume	Resumes GAPI operation when the game regains focus.
GXIsDisplayDRAMBuffer	Suspends GAPI operations.
GXSetViewport	Allows GDI drawing and GAPI access to the same frame buffer.

GAPI Initialization

An application using GAPI must initialize the GAPI subsystem by calling the following function:

```
int GXOpenDisplay (HWND hWnd, DWORD dwFlags);
```

The two parameters are the handle to the application's window and a flag parameter that can be either 0 or the constant *GX_FULLSCREEN*. Using *GX_FULLSCREEN* indicates to GAPI that the application will assume control over the entire screen. If the flag isn't set, GAPI assumes the application won't be overwriting the navigation bar. *GXOpenDisplay* should be called only once during the life of an application. Subsequent calls will fail.

Getting Display Information

GAPI provides three functions to query the hardware support. The first function, *GXGetDisplayProperties*, returns information about the display and is prototyped as

```
GXDisplayProperties GXGetDisplayProperties();
```

The function returns a *GXDisplayProperties* structure, defined as

```
struct GXDisplayProperties {
    DWORD cxWidth;
    DWORD cyHeight;
    long cbxPitch;
    long cbyPitch;
    long cBPP;
    DWORD ffFormat;
};
```

The first two fields, *cxWidth* and *cyHeight*, specify the width and height of the display in pixels. The next two fields, *cbxPitch* and *cbyPitch*, specify the distance, in bytes, between adjacent pixels in the frame buffer. For example, if the application has a pointer to pixel x and needs to address the pixel to the immediate right of the current pixel, the address would be at the current address plus the value in *cbxPitch*. To access the pixel immediately below the current pixel, the value in *cbyPitch* would be added to the address of the current pixel. These values aren't necessarily obvious and can even be negative depending on the layout of the frame buffer.

For frame buffers that have less than 8 bits per pixel (bpp), the addressing is somewhat more complex. In these cases, the pixel offset must be divided by the pixels per byte, which in a 4-bpp display is 8 / 4 = 2. So the formula to compute the address in the frame buffer of a pixel that has a 4-bpp display would be

```
pPxl = frame_base + ((x / 2) + (y * cbyPitch));
```

This line isn't complete. To get to the specific pixel, the application has to read the byte, modify only the appropriate upper or lower half, and then write the byte back. This example also assumes the frame buffer is in a portrait configuration, in which the adjacent bytes of the display are on the same row. In a landscape configuration, adjacent bytes are in the same column.

The final field in the *GXDisplayProperties* structure is the *ffFormat* field, which describes the format of the frame buffer. The flags in this field are

- **kfLandscape** The frame buffer is oriented on its side. Sub-8bpp displays have consecutive column pixels in the same byte.

- **kfPalette** The frame buffer is palettized.

- **kfDirect** The frame buffer colors are directly mapped.

- **kfDirect555** The format is a 16 bpp with 5 bits per color.

- **kfDirect565** The format is 16 bpp with 6 bits for green and 5 each for red and blue.

- **kfDirect888** The format is 24 bpp with 8 bits per color.

- **kfDirectInverted** The monochrome frame buffer has inverted color format with 1 representing black and 0 representing white.

Querying Button Information

The next informational function, *GXGetDefaultKeys*, returns the suggested layout for the buttons. The prototype for this function is

```
GXKeyList GXGetDefaultKeys (int iOptions);
```

The one parameter is the system orientation: *GX_NORMALKEYS* for portrait orientation and *GX_LANDSCAPEKEYS* for landscape orientation.

The structure returned is defined as

```
struct GXKeyList {
    short vkUp;
    POINT ptUp;
    short vkDown;
    POINT ptDown;
    short vkLeft;
    POINT ptLeft;
    short vkRight;
    POINT ptRight;
    short vkA;
    POINT ptA;
    short vkB;
    POINT ptB;
    short vkC;
    POINT ptC;
    short vkStart;
    POINT ptStart;
};
```

Each field starting with *vk* in the structure specifies the suggested virtual key code to use for that action. The *pt* fields represent the physical coordinates of the buttons in relation to the screen.

Accessing the Buttons

When a GAPI application is ready to start its game, it can take control of the buttons on the Pocket PC by calling

```
int GXOpenInput();
```

This function redirects all button input to the GAPI application. Clearly, once this function is called it is the responsibility of the GAPI application to provide a way to quit the game and restore the buttons to the system.

Drawing to the Screen

Of course, the meat of GAPI is the ability it provides an application to write to the display buffer. To gain access to the buffer, a GAPI application calls

```
void * GXBeginDraw();
```

This function returns the address of the frame buffer, or 0 if the buffer cannot be accessed for some reason. At this point, a GAPI application has free rein to modify the frame buffer using the pixel computations described in the previous section.

The pointer returned isn't necessarily the lowest address of the frame buffer. Some systems are configured with negative offsets in the *cbxPitch* or *cbyPitch* values. This really isn't important as long as you rigorously use the pitch values to compute pixel addresses in the frame buffer.

> **Note** One word of caution: although having a pointer to the frame buffer is powerful, it's also dangerous. The pointer directly accesses an area of system memory that itself directly accesses the physical address space of the hardware. Errant pointers can, and most likely will, be destructive to data on your device. A classic symptom is the file system reporting corrupt data in the object store. This can easily happen if incorrect pointer arithmetic results in writing of the physical RAM that contains the object store. Programmers should be exceedingly careful when checking that they access only the frame buffer and not other parts of the system address space.

When the drawing to the frame buffer is complete, call the following function:

```
int GXEndDraw();
```

This call does little on systems with direct access to the frame buffer. However, on systems that don't provide direct access to the frame buffer, calling *GXEnd-Draw* signals the display driver to copy the data from the phantom frame buffer to the actual frame buffer. Regardless of whether the application has direct access to the frame buffer, all GAPI applications should call *GXEndDraw*, if only for forward compatibility.

Indirect Access to the Frame Buffer

On some systems, applications can't directly access the frame buffer using GAPI. For these systems, the display driver provides a phantom frame buffer for the application and then copies the data to the real frame buffer. Although this scheme hinders performance somewhat, it does provide compatibility for GAPI applications. One side effect is that it is difficult for GAPI applications to merge their directly written pixel data with the GDI's pixel data, which is natively written to the frame buffer.

Although many games just want to take over the entire display, some GAPI applications require that the system display GAPI data on one part of the display and paint standard Windows controls on the other part. To merge the two streams of data, GAPI provides a function called *GXSetViewport* to indicate what part of the screen the GAPI program controls. The display driver can then use the GAPI data for that area of the screen and the GDI data for the remainder of the frame buffer. The *GXSetViewport* function looks like this:

```
int GXSetViewport (DWORD dwTop, DWORD dwHeight, DWORD dwReserved1,
                   DWORD dwReserved2);
```

The current implementation of *GXSetViewport* is somewhat limited in that it can describe only a band across the screen where the GAPI data will be written. The parameter *dwTop* specifies the first line on the display reserved for GAPI. Any lines above this value are written by the system. The *dwHeight* parameter is the height of the band of data, in lines, that the GAPI program will write. Any lines below *dwTop+dwHeight* will be written by GDI.

It's important to note that *GXSetViewport* doesn't clip data. It simply defines the area that GDI won't write. An errant GAPI application certainly can overwrite the screen area reserved for GDI.

To determine whether the system is exposing a phantom frame buffer to GAPI instead of the real frame buffer, an application can call

```
BOOL GXIsDisplayDRAMBuffer();
```

This function returns *TRUE* if the application is using a phantom frame buffer and *FALSE* if the application will be accessing the actual frame buffer. An application can do little with this information except to ensure that it's calling *GXSetViewport* if it's mixing GAPI and GDI data and to indicate somewhat reduced performance for the dual buffer systems.

GAPI Maintenance

You can suspend the GAPI application in place to allow other applications access to the screen and keyboard. The two functions that suspend and resume the GAPI functions are appropriately named

```
int GXSuspend();
```

and

```
int GXResume();
```

When the GAPI application calls *GXSuspend*, the GAPI library temporarily releases its control over the buttons in the system, allowing other applications to operate normally. The desktop is also redrawn. When *GXResume* is called, the buttons are redirected back to the GAPI application. The GAPI application is responsible for restoring the screen to the state it was in before *GXSuspend* was called. It's the responsibility of the GAPI application to stop accessing the frame buffer when another application gains the focus.

The suggested place for these two functions is in the *WM_SETFOCUS* and *WM_KILLFOCUS* message handlers of your main window. This way, if another application rudely interrupts your game by setting itself into the foreground, your application will handle it gracefully.

Cleaning Up

When the game has ended, a GAPI application should release the buttons by calling

```
int GXCloseInput();
```

In addition, the display should release a call to

```
int GXCloseDisplay();
```

This function instructs the GAPI DLL to free any resources it was maintaining to support the frame buffer access of the application.

The GAPIShow Example

The following example is a very simple demonstration of GAPI. The game (of sorts) in this case is a star field drawn to appear to the viewer as though it's moving through space. The effect is similar to the Starfield screen saver on desktop versions of Windows with the exception that the objects are simply white dots.

When the game first starts, it displays the information returned by *GXGet-DisplayProperties*, such as the pitch of the pixels and the format of the frame buffer. Selecting Play from the Game menu starts the star field animation. Tapping on the screen stops the animation and brings the user back to the information screen. Contrary to Pocket PC guidelines, *GAPIShow* has an Exit menu item to ease shutting down the example. Listing 20-1 shows the GAPIShow source code. Since the resources in this example were wizard-generated, the .rc file isn't listed here. Of course, the complete source code is on the companion CD.

```
GAPIShow.h
//======================================================================
// Header file
//
// Written for the book Programming Windows CE
// Copyright (C) 2003 Douglas Boling
//
//======================================================================
// Returns number of elements
#define dim(x) (sizeof(x) / sizeof(x[0]))

#define PARSEFLAG(a,b) (a & b) ? TEXT(#b) : TEXT("\0")
//----------------------------------------------------------------------
// Generic defines and data types
//
struct decodeUINT {                          // Structure associates
    UINT Code;                               // messages
                                             // with a function.
    LRESULT (*Fxn)(HWND, UINT, WPARAM, LPARAM);
};
struct decodeCMD {                           // Structure associates
    UINT Code;                               // menu IDs with a
    LRESULT (*Fxn)(HWND, WORD, HWND, WORD);  // function.
};
```

Listing 20-1 The GAPIShow source code

```
#define ID_TIMER  1

#define MAX_STARS  40
#define SHFT        3
#define MAX_X      1024*2
#define MAX_Y      1024*2
#define MID_X      (MAX_X/2)
#define MID_Y      (MAX_Y/2)
typedef struct {
    int x;
    int y;
    int dist;
} STARINFO, *PSTARINFO;


//----------------------------------------------------------------------
// Function prototypes
//
HWND InitInstance (HINSTANCE, LPWSTR, int);
int TermInstance (HINSTANCE, int);
int InitGame (HWND hWnd);
int EndGame (HWND hWnd);
HWND MyCreateMenuBar (HWND hWnd);

int ClearScreen_16 (PVOID lpBuff, COLORREF rgb);
int DrawScreen_16 (PVOID lpBuff, int dx, int dy, int dv);
int InitScreen_16 (PVOID lpBuff);

#define ClearScreen  ClearScreen_16a
#define DrawScreen   DrawScreen_16a

// Window procedures
LRESULT CALLBACK MainWndProc (HWND, UINT, WPARAM, LPARAM);
// Dialog procedures
BOOL CALLBACK AboutDlgProc (HWND, UINT, WPARAM, LPARAM);


// Message handlers
LRESULT DoTimerMain (HWND, UINT, WPARAM, LPARAM);
LRESULT DoKeyDownMain (HWND, UINT, WPARAM, LPARAM);
LRESULT DoCreateMain (HWND, UINT, WPARAM, LPARAM);
LRESULT DoPaintMain (HWND, UINT, WPARAM, LPARAM);
LRESULT DoLButtonDownMain (HWND, UINT, WPARAM, LPARAM);
LRESULT DoSetFocusMain (HWND, UINT, WPARAM, LPARAM);
LRESULT DoKillFocusMain (HWND, UINT, WPARAM, LPARAM);
LRESULT DoCommandMain (HWND, UINT, WPARAM, LPARAM);
LRESULT DoSettingChangeMain (HWND, UINT, WPARAM, LPARAM);
LRESULT DoActivateMain (HWND, UINT, WPARAM, LPARAM);
LRESULT DoHibernateMain (HWND, UINT, WPARAM, LPARAM);
LRESULT DoDestroyMain (HWND, UINT, WPARAM, LPARAM);
```

(continued)

Listing 20-1   *(continued)*

```
// WM_COMMAND message handlers
LPARAM DoMainCommandExit (HWND, WORD, HWND, WORD);
LPARAM DoMainCommandPlay (HWND, WORD, HWND, WORD);
LPARAM DoMainCommandAbout (HWND, WORD, HWND, WORD);
```

GAPIShow.cpp

```cpp
//======================================================================
// GAPIShow - A Games API example program for the Pocket PC
//
// Written for the book Programming Windows CE
// Copyright (C) 2003 Douglas Boling
//======================================================================
#include "stdafx.h"                    // Wizard includes
#include <aygshell.h>                  // Pocket PC includes
#include <gx.h>                        // GAPI includes

#include "GapiShow.h"
#include "resource.h"                  // Tools generated equates


//----------------------------------------------------------------------
// Global data
//
const TCHAR szAppName[] = TEXT("GapiShow");
HINSTANCE hInst;                       // Program instance handle

// Pocket PC globals
HWND hwndMenuBar = NULL;               // Handle of menu bar control
BOOL fHibernated = FALSE;              // Indicates hibernated state
BOOL fPlaying = FALSE;                 // Indicates Gapi access active
BOOL fResuming = FALSE;                // Used when regaining focus
SHACTIVATEINFO sai;                    // Used to adjust window for SIP
RECT rectNorm;
int cyFont = 0;
int nSpeed = 2, ndX = 0, ndY = 0;
int CxScreen, CyScreen;
int nCnt = 0;

STARINFO ptStars[MAX_STARS];           // Star field info

GXDisplayProperties gxdp;              // GAPI display info structure
GXKeyList gxkl;                        // GAPI keyboard info structure

// Message dispatch table for MainWindowProc
const struct decodeUINT MainMessages[] = {
    WM_TIMER, DoTimerMain,
    WM_KEYDOWN, DoKeyDownMain,
    WM_CREATE, DoCreateMain,
```

```
    WM_PAINT, DoPaintMain,
    WM_LBUTTONDOWN, DoLButtonDownMain,
    WM_SETFOCUS, DoSetFocusMain,
    WM_KILLFOCUS, DoKillFocusMain,
    WM_COMMAND, DoCommandMain,
    WM_SETTINGCHANGE, DoSettingChangeMain,
    WM_ACTIVATE, DoActivateMain,
    WM_HIBERNATE, DoHibernateMain,
    WM_DESTROY, DoDestroyMain,
};
// Command Message dispatch for MainWindowProc
const struct decodeCMD MainCommandItems[] = {
    ID_GAME_EXIT, DoMainCommandExit,
    ID_GAME_PLAY, DoMainCommandPlay,
    ID_TOOLS_ABOUT, DoMainCommandAbout,
};
//=======================================================================
// Program entry point
//
int WINAPI WinMain (HINSTANCE hInstance, HINSTANCE hPrevInstance,
                    LPWSTR lpCmdLine, int nCmdShow) {
    MSG msg;
    int rc = 0;
    HWND hwndMain;
    HACCEL hAccel;

    // Initialize application.
    hwndMain = InitInstance (hInstance, lpCmdLine, nCmdShow);
    if (hwndMain == 0) return 0x10;

    hAccel = LoadAccelerators(hInstance,
                             MAKEINTRESOURCE (IDR_ACCELERATOR1));

    // Application message loop
    while (GetMessage (&msg, NULL, 0, 0)) {

        // Translate accelerator keys
        if (!TranslateAccelerator(hwndMain, hAccel, &msg)) {
            TranslateMessage (&msg);
            DispatchMessage (&msg);
        }
    }
    // Instance cleanup
    return TermInstance (hInstance, msg.wParam);
}
//-----------------------------------------------------------------------
// InitInstance - Instance initialization
//
```

(continued)

Listing 20-1 *(continued)*

```
HWND InitInstance (HINSTANCE hInstance, LPWSTR lpCmdLine, int nCmdShow) {
    WNDCLASS wc;
    HWND hWnd;

    // Save program instance handle in global variable.
    hInst = hInstance;

    // Allow only one instance of the application.
    hWnd = FindWindow (szAppName, NULL);
    if (hWnd) {
        SetForegroundWindow ((HWND)(((DWORD)hWnd) | 0x01));
        return 0;
    }
    // Register application main window class.
    wc.style = CS_VREDRAW | CS_HREDRAW;         // Window style
    wc.lpfnWndProc = MainWndProc;               // Callback function
    wc.cbClsExtra = 0;                          // Extra class data
    wc.cbWndExtra = 0;                          // Extra window data
    wc.hInstance = hInstance;                   // Owner handle
    wc.hIcon = NULL,                            // Application icon
    wc.hCursor = LoadCursor (NULL, IDC_ARROW);  // Default cursor
    wc.hbrBackground = (HBRUSH) GetStockObject (WHITE_BRUSH);
    wc.lpszMenuName =  NULL;                    // Menu name
    wc.lpszClassName = szAppName;               // Window class name

    if (RegisterClass (&wc) == 0) return 0;

    // Clear GAPI info structures.
    memset (&gxdp, 0, sizeof (gxdp));
    memset (&gxkl, 0, sizeof (gxkl));
    CxScreen = GetSystemMetrics (SM_CXSCREEN);
    CyScreen = GetSystemMetrics (SM_CYSCREEN);
    // Create main window.
    hWnd = CreateWindow (szAppName,             // Window class
                         TEXT("GAPI Show"),     // Window title
                         WS_VISIBLE,            // Style flags
                         CW_USEDEFAULT,         // x position
                         CW_USEDEFAULT,         // y position
                         CW_USEDEFAULT,         // Initial width
                         CW_USEDEFAULT,         // Initial height
                         NULL,                  // Parent
                         NULL,                  // Menu, must be null
                         hInstance,             // Application instance
                         NULL);                 // Pointer to create
                                                // parameters
    if (!IsWindow (hWnd)) return 0;             // Fail if not created.
```

```
    // Query GAPI parameters.
    if (GXOpenDisplay(hWnd, GX_FULLSCREEN)) {
        gxdp = GXGetDisplayProperties();
        gxkl = GXGetDefaultKeys(GX_NORMALKEYS);
    } else
        MessageBox (hWnd, TEXT ("GXOpenDisplay failed"),
                    szAppName, MB_OK);

    // Standard show and update calls
    ShowWindow (hWnd, nCmdShow);
    UpdateWindow (hWnd);

    return hWnd;
}
//----------------------------------------------------------------------
// TermInstance - Program cleanup
//
int TermInstance (HINSTANCE hInstance, int nDefRC) {
    GXCloseDisplay();
    return nDefRC;
}
//======================================================================
// Message handling procedures for main window
//
//----------------------------------------------------------------------
// MainWndProc - Callback function for application window
//
LRESULT CALLBACK MainWndProc (HWND hWnd, UINT wMsg, WPARAM wParam,
                              LPARAM lParam) {
    INT i;
    //
    // Search message list to see if we need to handle this
    // message.  If in list, call procedure.
    //
    for (i = 0; i < dim(MainMessages); i++) {
        if (wMsg == MainMessages[i].Code)
            return (*MainMessages[i].Fxn)(hWnd, wMsg, wParam, lParam);
    }
    return DefWindowProc (hWnd, wMsg, wParam, lParam);
}
//----------------------------------------------------------------------
// DoCreateMain - Process WM_CREATE message for window.
//
LRESULT DoCreateMain (HWND hWnd, UINT wMsg, WPARAM wParam,
                      LPARAM lParam) {
    SIPINFO si;
    int cx, cy;
```

(continued)

Listing 20-1   *(continued)*

```c
    TEXTMETRIC tm;
    HDC hdc;
    // Query the height of the default font.
    hdc = GetDC (hWnd);
    GetTextMetrics (hdc, &tm);
    cyFont = tm.tmHeight + tm.tmExternalLeading;
    ReleaseDC (hWnd, hdc);

    // Initialize the shell to activate info structure.
    memset (&sai, 0, sizeof (sai));
    sai.cbSize = sizeof (sai);

    // Create menu bar and check for errors.
    hwndMenuBar = MyCreateMenuBar (hWnd);
    if (!hwndMenuBar) {
        MessageBox (hWnd, TEXT("Couldn\'t create menu bar"),
                    szAppName, MB_OK);
        DestroyWindow (hWnd);
    }

    // Query the sip state and size our window appropriately.
    memset (&si, 0, sizeof (si));
    si.cbSize = sizeof (si);
    SHSipInfo(SPI_GETSIPINFO, 0, (PVOID)&si, FALSE);
    cx = si.rcVisibleDesktop.right - si.rcVisibleDesktop.left;
    cy = si.rcVisibleDesktop.bottom - si.rcVisibleDesktop.top;
    // If the sip is not shown, or is showing but not docked, the
    // desktop rect doesn't include the height of the menu bar.
    if (!(si.fdwFlags & SIPF_ON) ||
        ((si.fdwFlags & SIPF_ON) && !(si.fdwFlags & SIPF_DOCKED)))
        cy -= 26;   // Height of menu bar control
      SetWindowPos (hWnd, NULL, 0, 0, cx, cy, SWP_NOMOVE | SWP_NOZORDER);
    return 0;
}
//-------------------------------------------------------------------
// DoTimerMain - Process WM_TIMER message for window.
//
LRESULT DoTimerMain (HWND hWnd, UINT wMsg, WPARAM wParam,
                     LPARAM lParam) {
    PBYTE lpBuff;

    lpBuff = (PBYTE) GXBeginDraw();
    if (lpBuff) {
        DrawScreen_16 (lpBuff, ndX, ndY, nSpeed);
        if (fResuming)
            ClearScreen_16 (lpBuff, RGB (0, 0, 0));
        GXEndDraw();
```

```
        } else {
            KillTimer (hWnd, ID_TIMER);
        }
    return 0;
}
//-----------------------------------------------------------------------
// DoKeyDownMain - Process WM_KEYDOWN message for window.
//
LRESULT DoKeyDownMain (HWND hWnd, UINT wMsg, WPARAM wParam,
                       LPARAM lParam) {

    if (fPlaying) {
        // Up
        if (wParam == (DWORD)gxkl.vkUp) {
            if (ndY > -100) ndY -= 10;
        // Down
        } else if (wParam == (DWORD)gxkl.vkDown) {
            if (ndY < 100) ndY += 10;
        // Left
        } else if (wParam == (DWORD)gxkl.vkLeft) {
            if (ndX > -100) ndX -= 10;
        // Right
        } else if (wParam == (DWORD)gxkl.vkRight) {
            if (ndX < 100) ndX += 10;
        // Fast
        } else if (wParam == (DWORD)gxkl.vkA) {
            if (nSpeed < 10) nSpeed += 1;
        // Slow
        } else if (wParam == (DWORD)gxkl.vkB) {
            if (nSpeed > 1) nSpeed -= 1;
            else nSpeed = 1;
        } else if (wParam == (DWORD)gxkl.vkC) {
            ndX = 0;
            ndY = 0;
            nSpeed = 2;
        }
    }
    return 0;
}
//-----------------------------------------------------------------------
// DoLButtonDownMain - Process WM_LBUTTONDOWN message for window.
//
LRESULT DoLButtonDownMain (HWND hWnd, UINT wMsg, WPARAM wParam,
                           LPARAM lParam) {
    // If playing, stop the game.
    if (fPlaying)
        SendMessage (hWnd, WM_COMMAND, MAKELONG (ID_GAME_PLAY, 0), 0);
    return 0;
}
```

(continued)

Listing 20-1   *(continued)*

```
//-------------------------------------------------------------------------
// DoSetFocusMain - Process WM_SETFOCUS message for window.
//
LRESULT DoSetFocusMain (HWND hWnd, UINT wMsg, WPARAM wParam,
                        LPARAM lParam) {
    if (fPlaying) {
        GXResume();
        fResuming = TRUE;
        // Start a very fast timer.
        SetTimer (hWnd, ID_TIMER, 10, NULL);
    }
    return 0;
}
//-------------------------------------------------------------------------
// DoKillFocusMain - Process WM_KILLFOCUS message for window.
//
LRESULT DoKillFocusMain (HWND hWnd, UINT wMsg, WPARAM wParam,
                         LPARAM lParam) {
    if (fPlaying)
        SetWindowPos (hWnd, HWND_NOTOPMOST, 0, 0, CxScreen, CyScreen, 0);
        KillTimer (hWnd, ID_TIMER);
        GXSuspend();
    return 0;
}
//-------------------------------------------------------------------------
// DoCommandMain - Process WM_COMMAND message for window.
//
LRESULT DoCommandMain (HWND hWnd, UINT wMsg, WPARAM wParam,
                       LPARAM lParam) {
    WORD    idItem, wNotifyCode;
    HWND hwndCtl;
    INT  i;

    // Parse the parameters.
    idItem = (WORD) LOWORD (wParam);
    wNotifyCode = (WORD) HIWORD (wParam);
    hwndCtl = (HWND) lParam;

    // Call routine to handle control message.
    for (i = 0; i < dim(MainCommandItems); i++) {
        if (idItem == MainCommandItems[i].Code)
            return (*MainCommandItems[i].Fxn)(hWnd, idItem, hwndCtl,
                                              wNotifyCode);
    }
    return 0;
}
```

```
//----------------------------------------------------------------------
// DoPaintMain - Process WM_PAINT message for window.
//
LRESULT DoPaintMain (HWND hWnd, UINT wMsg, WPARAM wParam,
                     LPARAM lParam) {
    PAINTSTRUCT ps;
    RECT rect,
    TCHAR szTxt[128];
    HDC hdc;
    int i, y = 5;
    static hOldPlaying;

    hdc = BeginPaint (hWnd, &ps);
    GetClientRect (hWnd, &rect);

    // If not playing, display the GAPI information about the device.
    if (!fPlaying) {
        wsprintf (szTxt, TEXT ("Gapi values:"));
        ExtTextOut (hdc, 5, y, 0, &rect, szTxt, lstrlen (szTxt), 0);
        y += cyFont;

        wsprintf (szTxt, TEXT ("cxWidth: %d"), gxdp.cxWidth);
        ExtTextOut (hdc, 10, y, 0, &rect, szTxt, lstrlen (szTxt), 0);
        y += cyFont;

        wsprintf (szTxt, TEXT ("cyHeight: %d"), gxdp.cyHeight);
        ExtTextOut (hdc, 10, y, 0, &rect, szTxt, lstrlen (szTxt), 0);
        y += cyFont;

        wsprintf (szTxt, TEXT ("cbxPitch: %d"), gxdp.cbxPitch);
        ExtTextOut (hdc, 10, y, 0, &rect, szTxt, lstrlen (szTxt), 0);
        y += cyFont;
        wsprintf (szTxt, TEXT ("cbyPitch: %d"), gxdp.cbyPitch);
        ExtTextOut (hdc, 10, y, 0, &rect, szTxt, lstrlen (szTxt), 0);
        y += cyFont;

        wsprintf (szTxt, TEXT ("cBPP:    %d"), gxdp.cBPP);
        ExtTextOut (hdc, 10, y, 0, &rect, szTxt, lstrlen (szTxt), 0);
        y += cyFont;

        wsprintf (szTxt, TEXT ("ffFormat: %08x"), gxdp.ffFormat);
        ExtTextOut (hdc, 10, y, 0, &rect, szTxt, lstrlen (szTxt), 0);
        y += cyFont;

        lstrcpy (szTxt, PARSEFLAG(gxdp.ffFormat, kfLandscape));
        if (i = lstrlen (szTxt)) {  //Assignment in if
            ExtTextOut (hdc, 20, y, 0, &rect, szTxt, i, 0);
            y += cyFont;
        }
```

(continued)

Listing 20-1 *(continued)*

```
            lstrcpy (szTxt, PARSEFLAG (gxdp.ffFormat, kfPalette));
            if (i = lstrlen (szTxt)) {  //Assignment in if
                ExtTextOut (hdc, 20, y, 0, &rect, szTxt, i, 0);
                y += cyFont;
            }
            lstrcpy (szTxt, PARSEFLAG (gxdp.ffFormat, kfDirect));
            if (i = lstrlen (szTxt)) {  //Assignment in if
                ExtTextOut (hdc, 20, y, 0, &rect, szTxt, i, 0);
                y += cyFont;
            }
            lstrcpy (szTxt, PARSEFLAG (gxdp.ffFormat, kfDirect555));
            if (i = lstrlen (szTxt)) {  //Assignment in if
                ExtTextOut (hdc, 20, y, 0, &rect, szTxt, i, 0);
                y += cyFont;
            }
            lstrcpy (szTxt, PARSEFLAG (gxdp.ffFormat, kfDirect565));
            if (i = lstrlen (szTxt)) {  //Assignment in if
                ExtTextOut (hdc, 20, y, 0, &rect, szTxt, i, 0);
                y += cyFont;
            }
            lstrcpy (szTxt, PARSEFLAG (gxdp.ffFormat, kfDirect888));
            if (i = lstrlen (szTxt)) {  //Assignment in if
                ExtTextOut (hdc, 20, y, 0, &rect, szTxt, i, 0);
                y += cyFont;
            }
            lstrcpy (szTxt, PARSEFLAG (gxdp.ffFormat, kfDirect444));
            if (i = lstrlen (szTxt)) {  //Assignment in if
                ExtTextOut (hdc, 20, y, 0, &rect, szTxt, i, 0);
                y += cyFont;
            }
            lstrcpy (szTxt, PARSEFLAG (gxdp.ffFormat, kfDirectInverted));
            if (i = lstrlen (szTxt)) {  //Assignment in if
                ExtTextOut (hdc, 20, y, 0, &rect, szTxt, i, 0);
                y += cyFont;
            }
        }
    }
    EndPaint (hWnd, &ps);
    hOldPlaying = fPlaying;
    return 0;
}
//----------------------------------------------------------------------
// DoSettingChangeMain - Process WM_SETTINGCHANGE message for window.
//
LRESULT DoSettingChangeMain (HWND hWnd, UINT wMsg, WPARAM wParam,
                             LPARAM lParam) {

    // Notify shell of our WM_SETTINGCHANGE message.
    SHHandleWMSettingChange(hWnd, wParam, lParam, &sai);
```

```
        return 0;
}
//--------------------------------------------------------------------------
// DoActivateMain - Process WM_ACTIVATE message for window.
//
LRESULT DoActivateMain (HWND hWnd, UINT wMsg, WPARAM wParam,
                        LPARAM lParam) {

    // If activating, restore any hibernated stuff.
    if ((LOWORD (wParam) != WA_INACTIVE) && fHibernated) {
        fHibernated = FALSE;
    }
    // Notify shell of our activate message.
    SHHandleWMActivate(hWnd, wParam, lParam, &sai, 0);
    return 0;
}
//--------------------------------------------------------------------------
// DoHibernateMain - Process WM_HIBERNATE message for window.
//
LRESULT DoHibernateMain (HWND hWnd, UINT wMsg, WPARAM wParam,
                         LPARAM lParam) {

    // If not the active window, reduce our memory footprint.
    if (GetActiveWindow() != hWnd) {
        fHibernated = TRUE;
    }
    return 0;
}
//--------------------------------------------------------------------------
// DoDestroyMain - Process WM_DESTROY message for window.
//
LRESULT DoDestroyMain (HWND hWnd, UINT wMsg, WPARAM wParam,
                       LPARAM lParam) {
    if (fPlaying) {
        // Clean up if playing game.
        KillTimer (hWnd, ID_TIMER);
        GXCloseInput();
    }
    GXCloseDisplay();
    PostQuitMessage (0);
    return 0;
}
//==========================================================================
// Command handler routines
//--------------------------------------------------------------------------
// DoMainCommandExit - Process Program Exit command.
//
```

(continued)

Listing 20-1 *(continued)*

```
LPARAM DoMainCommandExit (HWND hWnd, WORD idItem, HWND hwndCtl,
                          WORD wNotifyCode) {
    SendMessage (hWnd, WM_CLOSE, 0, 0);
    return 0;
}
//-------------------------------------------------------------------------
// DoMainCommandPlay - Process Play command.
//
LPARAM DoMainCommandPlay (HWND hWnd, WORD idItem, HWND hwndCtl,
                          WORD wNotifyCode) {
    if (!fPlaying) {
        if (!(gxdp.ffFormat & (kfDirect555 | kfDirect565))) {
            MessageBox (hWnd,
                        TEXT ("GAPIShow supports only 16 bpp displays"),
                        szAppName, MB_OK);
            return 0;
        }
        InitGame (hWnd);
    } else {
        EndGame (hWnd);
    }
    return 0;
}
//-------------------------------------------------------------------------
// DoMainCommandAbout - Process the Tools | About menu command.
//
LPARAM DoMainCommandAbout(HWND hWnd, WORD idItem, HWND hwndCtl,
                          WORD wNotifyCode) {
    // Use DialogBox to create modal dialog.
    DialogBox (hInst, MAKEINTRESOURCE (IDD_ABOUT), hWnd, AboutDlgProc);
    return 0;
}
//=========================================================================
// About Dialog procedure
//
BOOL CALLBACK AboutDlgProc (HWND hWnd, UINT wMsg, WPARAM wParam,
                            LPARAM lParam) {
    switch (wMsg) {
    case WM_INITDIALOG:
        {
            SHINITDLGINFO idi;
            idi.dwMask = SHIDIM_FLAGS;
            idi.dwFlags = SHIDIF_DONEBUTTON | SHIDIF_SIZEDLGFULLSCREEN |
                          SHIDIF_SIPDOWN;
            idi.hDlg = hWnd;
            SHInitDialog (&idi);
        }
```

```
            break;
        case WM_COMMAND:
            switch (LOWORD (wParam)) {
                case IDOK:
                case IDCANCEL:
                    EndDialog (hWnd, 0);
                    return TRUE;
            }
            break;
    }
    return FALSE;
}
//----------------------------------------------------------------------
// MyCreateMenuBar - Create the menu bar for the program.
//
HWND MyCreateMenuBar (HWND hWnd) {
    SHMENUBARINFO mbi;

    // Create a menu bar.
    memset(&mbi, 0, sizeof(SHMENUBARINFO)); // Zero structure
    mbi.cbSize = sizeof(SHMENUBARINFO);     // Size field
    mbi.hwndParent = hWnd;                  // Parent window
    mbi.nToolBarId = IDR_MENUBAR1;          // ID of toolbar resource
    mbi.hInstRes = hInst;                   // Inst handle of app

    // Create menu bar and check for errors.
    if (!SHCreateMenuBar(&mbi))
        return 0;
    return mbi.hwndMB;
}
//----------------------------------------------------------------------
// InitGame - Start game by capturing the keyboard, drawing star field,
// and starting timer.
//
int InitGame (HWND hWnd) {
    PBYTE pBuff;

    // Make our window topmost and cover the entire screen.
    GetWindowRect (hWnd, &rectNorm);
    SetWindowPos (hWnd, HWND_TOPMOST, 0, 0, CxScreen, CyScreen, 0);
    DestroyWindow (hwndMenuBar);
    ValidateRect (hWnd, NULL);

    // Grab the keyboard.
    GXOpenInput ();
    fPlaying = TRUE;
```

(continued)

Listing 20-1 *(continued)*

```
    // Initialize the display.
    pBuff = (PBYTE)    GXBeginDraw();
    if (pBuff) {
        ClearScreen_16 (pBuff, RGB (0, 0, 0));
        InitScreen_16 (pBuff);
        GXEndDraw();
    }
    // Start a very fast timer.
    SetTimer (hWnd, ID_TIMER, 10, NULL);
    return 0;
}
//------------------------------------------------------------------------
// EndGame - Clean up by re-creating the main window.
//
int EndGame (HWND hWnd) {
    fPlaying = FALSE;
    KillTimer (hWnd, ID_TIMER);
    GXCloseInput();

    // Create menu bar and check for errors.
    hwndMenuBar = MyCreateMenuBar (hWnd);
    if (!hwndMenuBar) {
        MessageBox (hWnd, TEXT("Couldn\'t create menu bar"),
                    szAppName, MB_OK);
    }
    // Restore our window to the old position.
    SetWindowPos (hWnd, HWND_NOTOPMOST, rectNorm.left, rectNorm.top,
                  rectNorm.right - rectNorm.left,
                  rectNorm.bottom - rectNorm.top, 0);
    InvalidateRect (hWnd, NULL, TRUE);
    return 0;
}
//------------------------------------------------------------------------
// ClearScreen_16 - 16 bpp version of clear screen
//
int ClearScreen_16 (PVOID lpBuff, COLORREF rgb) {
    WORD wPixel = 0;
    DWORD x, y;
    PBYTE pbLine, pbPixel;

    // Verify that we have a valid frame buffer.
    if (!lpBuff) return 0;

    // Format pixel from colorref data.
    if (gxdp.ffFormat | kfDirect565) {
        wPixel = (WORD) ((GetRValue(rgb) >> 3) << 11 |
                         (GetGValue(rgb) >> 2) << 5  |
                         (GetBValue(rgb) >> 3));
```

```
        } else if (gxdp.ffFormat | kfDirect555) {
            wPixel = (WORD) ((GetRValue(rgb) >> 3) << 10 |
                             (GetGValue(rgb) >> 3) << 5  |
                             (GetBValue(rgb) >> 3));
        }
        // Do rows.
        pbLine = (PBYTE)lpBuff;
        for (y = 0; y < gxdp.cyHeight; y++) {

            // Do columns.
            pbPixel = pbLine;
            for (x = 0; x < gxdp.cxWidth; x++) {
                // Cast ptr and write.
                *(PWORD)pbPixel = wPixel;
                pbPixel += gxdp.cbxPitch;   // Move to the next pixel.
            }
            pbLine += gxdp.cbyPitch;         // Move to the next line.
        }
    return 0;
}
//-------------------------------------------------------------------
// DrawScreen_16 - Compute new position for each star; redraw if it
// has moved.
//
int DrawScreen_16 (PVOID lpBuff, int dx, int dy, int dv) {
    int i, nOldDist;
    PBYTE pNew = 0;
    PBYTE pOld = 0;
    static nOldDX, nOldDY;

    for (i = 0; i < MAX_STARS; i++) {
        // Remove old star.
        if (((ptStars[i].x >> SHFT) < CxScreen+2) &&
            ((ptStars[i].y >> SHFT) < CyScreen+2))
            pOld = (PBYTE)lpBuff +
                    (ptStars[i].x >> SHFT) * gxdp.cbxPitch +
                    (ptStars[i].y >> SHFT) * gxdp.cbyPitch;
        nOldDist = ptStars[i].dist;
        // Update pos. New pos is related to its pos from middle of the
        // screen. This pushes the stars to the edges.
        ptStars[i].x += ((ptStars[i].x-MID_X)/4 * dv + dx)/16+1;
        ptStars[i].y += ((ptStars[i].y-MID_Y)/4 * dv + dy)/16+1;
        ptStars[i].dist++;

        // If new position off screen, regenerate the star.
        if ((ptStars[i].x < 0) || (ptStars[i].y < 0) ||
            ((ptStars[i].x >> SHFT) >= CxScreen) ||
            ((ptStars[i].y >> SHFT) >= CyScreen)) {
```

(continued)

Listing 20-1   *(continued)*

```
                ptStars[i].x = Random() & MAX_X-1;
                ptStars[i].y = Random() & MAX_Y-1;
                ptStars[i].dist = 0;
            }
            // Compute pointer to new star.
            if (((ptStars[i].x >> SHFT) < CxScreen) &&
                ((ptStars[i].y >> SHFT) < CyScreen))
                pNew = (PBYTE)lpBuff +
                        (ptStars[i].x >> SHFT) * gxdp.cbxPitch +
                        (ptStars[i].y >> SHFT) * gxdp.cbyPitch;
            // Don't redraw star if in same place.
            if (pNew != pOld) {
                if (pOld) {
                    *(PWORD)pOld = 0;
                    // Stars older than 15 generations get bigger.
                    if (nOldDist > 15) {
                        *(PWORD)(pOld + gxdp.cbxPitch) = 0;
                        *(PWORD)(pOld + gxdp.cbyPitch) = 0;
                        *(PWORD)(pOld + gxdp.cbxPitch +
                                    gxdp.cbyPitch) = 0;
                    }
                }
                if (pNew) {
                    *(PWORD)pNew = 0xffff;
                    if (ptStars[i].dist > 15) {
                        *(PWORD)(pNew + gxdp.cbxPitch) = 0xffff;
                        *(PWORD)(pNew + gxdp.cbyPitch) = 0xffff;
                        *(PWORD)(pNew + gxdp.cbxPitch +
                                    gxdp.cbyPitch) = 0xffff;
                    }
                }
            }
        }
    }
    return 0;
}
//-----------------------------------------------------------------------
// InitScreen_16 - Initialize each star position and draw it.
//
int InitScreen_16 (PVOID lpBuff) {
    int i;
    PBYTE pNew = 0;
    TCHAR szTxt[128];

    for (i = 0; i < MAX_STARS; i++) {
        // Initialize star.
        ptStars[i].x = Random() & MAX_X-1;
```

```
        ptStars[i].y = Random() & MAX_Y-1;
        ptStars[i].dist = 0;

        // If on the screen, draw star.
        if (((ptStars[i].x >> SHFT) < CxScreen) &&
            ((ptStars[i].y >> SHFT) < CyScreen))
            pNew = (PBYTE)lpBuff +
                   (ptStars[i].x >> SHFT) * gxdp.cbxPitch +
                   (ptStars[i].y >> SHFT) * gxdp.cbyPitch;
        __try {
        if (pNew)
            *(PWORD)pNew = 0xffff;
        }
        __except (EXCEPTION_EXECUTE_HANDLER) {
            wsprintf (szTxt, TEXT("Exception %d  %08x  (%d,%d)"), i,
                      pNew, ptStars[i].x, ptStars[i].y);
            MessageBox (NULL, szTxt, szAppName, MB_OK);
            break;
        }
    }
    return 0;
}
```

The GAPIShow example has support to access a 16-bpp display, which is the standard format for most Pocket PCs. I'll leave it to you to extend GAPI-Show to other screen formats.

The code to draw in the frame buffer is isolated to three routines: *InitScreen_16*, *DrawScreen_16*, and *ClearScreen_16*. The *_16* suffix indicates that the routines assume a 16-bpp screen. You can change the code to support 8-bpp displays by simply changing the cast of the writing of each pixel and modifying the pixel formation routine in *ClearScreen_16*. Although this example supports it, other pixel formats can be supported with very basic changes. You might notice the writing of the pixel in the *InitScreen_16* routine is enclosed in a *__try* block to detect exceptions. This is a helpful technique for catching problems with the code that computes the pixel location in the buffer pointer.

In the next chapter, I step back from application programming and look at system programming issues. Chapter 21 explains how the different components of Windows CE work together while presenting a unified Win32-compatible operating system.

Part V

Advanced Windows CE

21

System Programming

This chapter takes a slightly different tack from the previous chapters of the book. Instead of touring the API of a particular section of Windows CE, I'll show you Windows CE from a systems perspective.

Windows CE presents standard Windows programmers some unique challenges. First, because Windows CE supports a variety of different microprocessors and system architectures, you can't count on the tried and true IBM/Intel PC–compatible design that can be directly traced to the IBM PC/AT released in 1984. Windows CE runs on devices that are more different than alike. Different CPUs use different memory layouts, and while the sets of peripherals are similar, they have totally different designs.

In addition to using different hardware, Windows CE itself changes, depending on how it's ported to a specific platform. While all Pocket PCs of a particular version have the same set of functions, that set is slightly different from the functions provided by Windows CE for the Handheld PC. In addition, Windows CE is designed as a collection of components so that OEMs using Windows CE in embedded devices can remove unnecessary small sections of the operating system, such as the Clipboard API.

All of these conditions make programming Windows CE unique and, I might add, fun. This chapter describes some of these cross-platform programming issues. I'll begin the chapter by describing the system memory architecture.

The Windows CE Memory Architecture

In operating system circles, much is made of the extent to which the operating system goes to protect one application's memory from other applications. Microsoft Windows Me uses a single address space that provides minimal protection between applications and the Windows operating system code. Windows XP, on the other hand, implements completely separate address spaces for each Win32 application, although old 16-bit applications under Windows XP do share a single address space.

Windows CE implements a single 2-GB virtual address space for all applications, but the memory space of an application is protected so that it can't be accessed by another application. A diagram of the lower half of the Windows CE virtual address space is shown in Figure 21-1. A little over half of the user-mode virtual address space is divided into thirty-three 32-MB *slots*. As applications are launched, each is assigned a slot where it will live for the life of the application. Slots 2 through 32 are assigned to applications. Slot 0 is reserved for the running process, while slot 1 is reserved for execute-in-place (XIP) DLLs. These two slots are seen by the application as a single 64-MB application space. I describe the layout of the application's virtual address space in Chapter 7.

When a thread in a process is running, the slot of the process that owns the thread is cloned into slot 0. This is not a copy of the original slot; instead, the operating system manipulates the page table entries of the CPU to map the physical memory into the virtual space at both the original slot and slot 0. Because of this cloning, any change to slot 0 is also reflected in the process's original slot. Application threads by default have access rights to their own slot and slot 1. When a thread in another process runs, its process slot is mapped into slot 0. Because of this swapping, processes assume that they are always running in slot 0 since any time they are running they *are* in slot 0 and when they aren't running, it really doesn't matter that they aren't in slot 0.

The region of the address space above the 33 slots and below 32 MB under the 2-GB boundary is used by the operating system for mapping memory-mapped files. The final user-mode area just below the 2-GB boundary is where Windows CE 4.2 or later loads resource-only DLLs. Figure 21-1 shows the layout of the bottom 2 GB of the system address space.

The address space above the 2-GB boundary, addresses 8000 0000 through FFFF FFFF, is reserved for the operating system and isn't accessible to applications and drivers running in user mode. However, many Windows CE systems, including the Pocket PC, always run in kernel mode. Staying in kernel mode all the time removes the time needed to transition between user and kernel mode, which improves performance.

The upper 2 GB of kernel space is divided into four regions. The first 512-MB memory region, from addresses 8000 0000 to A000 0000, is linearly mapped to the first 512 MB of the physical address space. So reading address 8000 1234 in kernel mode is a read of physical address 0000 1234. Memory accesses through this window are cached in the CPU's data cache to improve performance.

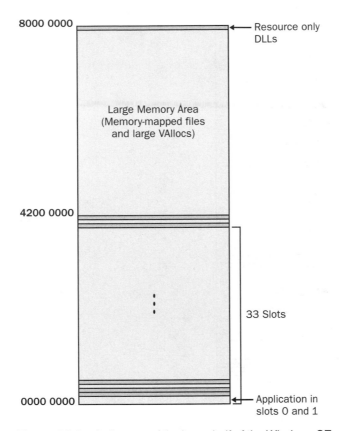

Figure 21-1 A diagram of the lower half of the Windows CE memory map

The second 512-MB region, from A000 0000 through BFFF FFFF, is also mapped to the first 512 MB of the physical memory space. The difference between this window and the window at 8000 0000 is that accesses through the A000 0000 window are not cached. While the performance is slower through this window, the noncached access is necessary when you read registers in devices that might change independently of the execution of the CPU.

The remaining area, from C000 0000 to the top of the memory space at FFFF FFFF, is used by the kernel. This area includes a space at C200 0000, where the kernel, NK.exe, was moved when the memory space was reorganized with the release of Windows CE .NET 4.0. Figure 21-2 shows the layout of the full 4-GB address space.

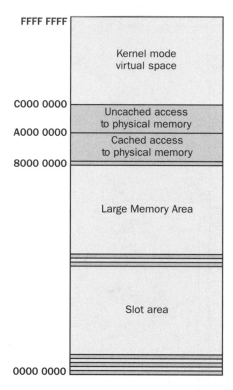

Figure 21-2 A diagram of the entire 4-GB Windows CE memory map

Writing Cross-Platform Windows CE Applications

Over the years, Windows programmers have had to deal concurrently with different versions of the operating system. Part of the solution to the problem this situation posed was to call *GetVersion* or *GetVersionEx* and to act differently depending on the version of the operating system you were working with. You can't do that under Windows CE. Because of the flexible nature of Windows CE, two builds of the same version of Windows CE can have different APIs. The question remains, though, how do you support multiple platforms with a common code base? How does the operating system version relate to the different platforms?

Platforms and Operating System Versions

To understand how the different platforms relate to the different versions of Windows CE, it helps to know how the Windows CE development team is organized within Microsoft. Windows CE is supported by a core operating system group within Microsoft. This team is responsible for developing the operating system, including the file system and the various communication stacks.

Coordinating efforts with the operating system team are the various platform teams, working on the Pocket PC, Smart Display, and many other platforms. Each team is responsible for defining a suggested hardware platform, defining applications that will be bundled with the platform, and deciding which version of the operating system the platform will use. Because the operating system team works continually to enhance Windows CE, planning new versions over time, each platform team generally looks to see what version of Windows CE will be ready when that team's platform ships.

The individual platform teams also develop the shells for their platforms. Because each team develops its own shell, many new functions or platform-specific functions first appear as part of the shell of a specific platform. Then if the newly introduced functions have a more general applicability, they're moved to the base operating system in a later version. You can see this process in both the Notification API and the SIP API. Both these sets of functions started in their specific platform group and have now been moved out of the shell and into the base operating system.

Table 21-1 shows some of the different platforms that have been released and the version of Windows CE that each platform uses.

Table 21-1   Versions for Windows CE Platforms

Platform	Windows CE Version
Original H/PC	1.00
Japanese release of H/PC	1.01
Handheld PC 2.0	2.00
Original palm-size PC	2.01
Handheld PC Pro 3.0	2.11
Palm-size PC 1.2	2.11
Pocket PC	3.0
Handheld PC Pro 2000	3.0
Pocket PC 2002	3.0
Smartphone 2002	3.0
Smart Display 1.0	4.1
Pocket PC 2003	4.2
Smartphone 2003	4.2

You can choose from a number of ways to deal with the problem of different platforms and different versions of Windows CE. Let's look at a few.

Compile-Time Versioning

The version problem can be tackled in a couple of places in the development process of an application. At compile time, you can use the preprocessor definition _WIN32_WCE to determine the version of the operating system you're currently building for. By enclosing code in a #if preprocessor block, you can cause code to be compiled for specific versions of Windows CE.

Following is an example of a routine that's tuned for both the original Palm-size PC and the new Pocket PC. For the Palm-size PC, the routine uses the old *SHSipInfo* function to raise and lower the SIP. For the Pocket PC, the routine uses the preferred function *SHSipPreference*.

```
int MyShowSip (HWND hWnd, BOOL fShow) {

#if WIN32_WCE < 300
    SIPINFO si;

    memset (&si, 0, sizeof (si));
    si.cbSize = sizeof (SIPINFO);
    SHSipInfo (SPI_GETSIPINFO, 0, &si, 0);
    if (fShow)
        si.fdwFlags |= SIPF_ON;
    else
        si.fdwFlags &= SIPF_ON;
    SHSipInfo(SPI_SETSIPINFO, 0, &si, 0);
#else
    if (fShow)
        SHSipPreference (hWnd, SIP_UP);
    else
        SHSipPreference (hWnd, SIP_DOWN);
#endif
    return 0;
}
```

A virtue of this code is that the linker links the appropriate function for the appropriate platform. Without this sort of compile-time code, you couldn't simply put a run-time *if* statement around the call to *SHSipInfo* because the program would never load on anything but a Pocket PC. The loader wouldn't be able to find the exported function *SHSipInfo* in Coredll.dll because it's not present on Palm-size PC versions of Windows CE.

As I mentioned in Chapter 17, builds for the Pocket PC have an additional define set named *WIN32_PLATFORM_PSPC*. So you can block Pocket PC code in the following way:

```
#ifdef WIN32_PLATFORM_PSPC
    // Insert Pocket PC code here.
#endif
```

There are platform-specific defines for other Windows CE platforms. Table 21-2 shows some of these defines.

Table 21-2 Defines for Windows CE Platforms

Platform	Define
Pocket PC 2003	*WIN32_PLATFORM_PSPC* (= 400)
Smartphone 2003	*WIN32_PLATFORM_WFSP* (= 200)
Pocket PC 2002	*WIN32_PLATFORM_PSPC* (= 310)
Smartphone 2002	*WIN32_PLATFORM_WFSP* (= 100)
Handheld PC 2000	*WIN32_PLATFORM_HPC2000*
Pocket PC 2000	*WIN32_PLATFORM_PSPC*
Palm-size PC	*WIN32_PLATFORM_PSPC*
Handheld PC Professional	*WIN32_PLATFORM_HPCPRO*

To distinguish between the Pocket PC and earlier versions of the Palm-size PC, you must also provide a check of the target Windows CE version using the *WIN32_WCE* definition, as in

```
#if defined(WIN32_PLATFORM_PSPC)
#if WIN32_PLATFORM_PSPC >= 400)
    // Pocket PC 2003
#elseif WIN32_PLATFORM_PSPC = 310)
    // Pocket PC 2002
#elseif (WIN32_WCE >= 300)
    // Pocket PC 2000
#else
    // Palm-size PC
#endif  // ifdef WIN32_PLATFORM_PSPC
```

The only issue with using conditional compilation is that while you still have a common source file, the resulting executable will be different for each platform.

Explicit Linking

You can tackle the version problem other ways. Sometimes one platform requires that you call a function different from one you need for another platform you're working with but you want the same executable file for both platforms. A way to accomplish this is to explicitly link to a DLL using *LoadLibrary*, *GetProcAddress*, and *FreeLibrary*. These functions were covered in Chapter 10.

Run-Time Version Checking

When you're determining the version of the Windows CE operating system at run time, you use the same function as under other versions of Windows—*GetVersionEx*, which fills in an *OSVERSIONINFO* structure defined as

```
typedef struct _OSVERSIONINFO{
    DWORD dwOSVersionInfoSize;
    DWORD dwMajorVersion;
    DWORD dwMinorVersion;
    DWORD dwBuildNumber;
    DWORD dwPlatformId;
    TCHAR szCSDVersion[ 128 ];
} OSVERSIONINFO;
```

Upon return from *GetVersionEx*, the major and minor version fields are filled with the Windows CE version. This means, of course, that you can't simply copy desktop Windows code that branches on classic version numbers like 3.1 or 4.0. The *dwPlatformId* field contains the constant *VER_PLATFORM_WIN32_CE* under Windows CE.

Although you can differentiate platforms by means of their unique Windows CE versions numbers, you shouldn't. For example, you can identify the current Pocket PC by its unique Windows CE version, 4.2, but newer versions of the Pocket PC will be using different versions of Windows CE. Instead, you should call *SystemParametersInfo* with the *SPI_GETPLATFORMTYPE* constant, as in

```
TCHAR szPlat[256];
INT rc;

rc = SystemParametersInfo (SPI_GETPLATFORMTYPE, sizeof (szPlat),
                           szPlat, 0);
if (lstrcmp (szPlat, TEXT ("PocketPC"")) == 0) {
    // Running on Pocket PC 2002 or Pocket PC 2003
} else if (lstrcmp (szPlat, TEXT ("Palm PC2")) == 0) {
    // Running on a Pocket PC
}
```

Aside from the differences in their shells, though, the platform differences aren't really that important. The base operating system is identical in all but some fringe cases.[1] The best strategy for writing cross-platform Windows CE software is to avoid differentiating among the platforms at all—or at least as little as possible.

For the most part, discrepancies among the user interfaces for the different consumer Windows CE devices can be illustrated by the issue of screen dimension. The Pocket PC's portrait-mode screen requires a completely different layout for most windows compared with many embedded systems with landscape-mode screens. So instead of looking at the platform type to determine what screen layout to use, you'd do better to simply check the screen dimensions using *GetDeviceCaps*.

Power Management

Windows CE is typically used in battery-powered systems, which makes power management critical for the proper operation of the system. Applications are for the most part blissfully unaware of the power issues of a Windows CE device, but sometimes you might need to address these issues.

When the user powers down a battery-powered Windows CE device, the power system isn't powered off the way a PC powers off. Instead, the system is suspended. When the user powers up the device, the device isn't rebooted like a PC—it resumes, returning to the same state it was in before it was suspended. As a result, an application running before the system was suspended is still running when the system resumes. In fact, the application won't know that it was suspended at all unless it explicitly requested to be notified when the system was suspended. From an application perspective, power management has three aspects: querying the power state, changing the power state, and occasionally preventing the power state from changing.

Querying the Power State

To query the current power state of the system, you can call

```
DWORD GetSystemPowerStatusEx2 (PSYSTEM_POWER_STATUS_EX2 pSystemPowerStatusEx2,
                              DWORD dwLen, BOOL fUpdate);
```

---

1. For example, many of the shell functions starting with *SHxx* are specific to a platform. So you wouldn't want to implicitly link to any of the platform-specific shell APIs if you wanted an application that ran on both the Pocket PC and embedded versions of Windows CE.

This function takes three parameters: a pointer to a *SYSTEM_POWER_STATUS_EX2* structure, the length of that structure, and a Boolean value that tells the operating system if it should query the battery driver during the call to get the latest information or to return the cached battery information. The system queries the battery approximately every 5 seconds, so if this third parameter is *FALSE*, the data is still not too stale. The *SYSTEM_POWER_STATUS_EX2* structure is defined as

```
typedef struct _SYSTEM_POWER_STATUS_EX2 {
    BYTE ACLineStatus;
    BYTE BatteryFlag;
    BYTE BatteryLifePercent;
    BYTE Reserved1;
    DWORD BatteryLifeTime;
    DWORD BatteryFullLifeTime;
    BYTE Reserved2;
    BYTE BackupBatteryFlag;
    BYTE BackupBatteryLifePercent;
    BYTE Reserved3;
    DWORD BackupBatteryLifeTime;
    DWORD BackupBatteryFullLifeTime;
    WORD BatteryVoltage;
    DWORD BatteryCurrent;
    DWORD BatteryAverageCurrent;
    DWORD BatteryAverageInterval;
    DWORD BatterymAHourConsumed;
    DWORD BatteryTemperature;
    DWORD BackupBatteryVoltage;
    BYTE  BatteryChemistry;
} SYSTEM_POWER_STATUS_EX2;
```

Before I describe this rather large structure, I must warn you that the data returned in this structure is only as accurate as the system's battery driver. This same structure is passed to the battery driver to query its status. Windows CE doesn't validate the data returned by the battery driver. The data returned by this function depends on the battery driver and therefore varies across different systems. For example, many systems won't report an accurate value for the battery level when the system is on AC power; other systems will. Applications using *GetSystemPowerStatusEx2* should program defensively and test on all systems that might run the application.

The first field, *ACLineStatus*, contains a flag indicating whether the system is connected to AC power. The possible values are *AC_LINE_OFFLINE*, indicating that the system isn't on AC power; *AC_LINE_ONLINE*, indicating that the system is on AC power; *AC_LINE_BACKUP_POWER*; and *AC_LINE_UNKNOWN*.

The *BatteryFlag* field, which provides a gross indication of the current state of the battery, can have one of the following values:

- ***BATTERY_FLAG_HIGH*** The battery is fully or close to fully charged.
- ***BATTERY_FLAG_LOW*** The battery has little charge left.
- ***BATTERY_FLAG_CRITICAL*** The battery charge is at a critical state.
- ***BATTERY_FLAG_CHARGING*** The battery is currently being charged.
- ***BATTERY_FLAG_NO_BATTERY*** The system has no battery.
- ***BATTERY_FLAG_UNKNOWN*** The battery state is unknown.

The *BatteryLifePercent* field contains the estimated percentage of charge remaining in the battery. Either the value will be between 0 and 100 or it will be 255, indicating that the percentage is unknown. The *BatteryLifeTime* field contains the estimated number of seconds remaining before the battery is exhausted. If this value can't be estimated, the field contains *BATTERY_LIFE_UNKNOWN*. The *BatteryFullLifeTime* field contains the estimated life in seconds of the battery when it is fully charged. If this value can't be estimated, the field contains *BATTERY_LIFE_UNKNOWN*. Note that on many systems, these lifetime values are difficult if not impossible to accurately measure. Many OEMs simply fill in *BATTERY_LIFE_UNKNOWN* for both fields.

The next four fields (not counting the reserved fields) replicate the fields previously described except that they contain values for the system's backup battery. Again, because many of these values are difficult to measure, many systems simply return an "unknown" value for these fields.

The remaining fields describe the electrical state of the battery and backup battery. Because many systems lack the capacity to measure these values, these fields are simply filled with the default "unknown" values. The final field, *BatteryChemistry*, contains a flag indicating the type of battery in the system. The currently defined self-describing values are

- *BATTERY_CHEMISTRY_ALKALINE*
- *BATTERY_CHEMISTRY_NICD*
- *BATTERY_CHEMISTRY_NIMH*
- *BATTERY_CHEMISTRY_LION*
- *BATTERY_CHEMISTRY_LIPOLY*
- *BATTERY_CHEMISTRY_UNKNOWN*

Changing the Power State

Applications can change the power state of the system by using a series of methods. In newer systems based on Windows CE .NET, the preferred method is to use the Power Manager, discussed later in this chapter. However, there are plenty of systems based on earlier versions of Windows CE as well as systems that use Windows CE .NET but do not contain the Power Manager. For these systems, the following techniques are handy.

Powering Down

An application can suspend the system by calling the little-documented *GwesPowerOffSystem* function. This function has been available for many versions of Windows CE but has only recently been documented. In fact, most SDKs don't include the prototype for the function, so you might have to provide the prototype. The function is defined as

```
void GwesPowerOffSystem(void);
```

The use of *GwesPowerOffSystem* is simple: simply call, and the system suspends.

To those who prefer to avoid little-documented functions, you can also power off the system by simulating the action of a user pressing the Off button. You can easily enable your application to suspend the system by using the *keybd_event* function, as in

```
keybd_event (VK_OFF, 0, KEYEVENTF_SILENT, 0);
keybd_event (VK_OFF, 0, KEYEVENTF_SILENT | KEYEVENTF_KEYUP, 0);
```

The two calls to *keybd_event* simulate the press and release of the power button, which has the virtual key code of *VK_OFF*. Executing the preceding two lines of code will suspend the system. Because the virtual key code has to be seen and acted on by GWES, the two functions probably will both return and a few more statements will be executed before the system actually suspends. If it is important that your program stop work after calling the *keybd_event* functions, add a call to *Sleep* to cause the application to pause for a number of milliseconds, allowing time for GWES to truly suspend the system.

Turning Off the Screen

On systems with color backlit displays, the main power drain on the system isn't the CPU—it's the backlight. In some situations, an application needs to run, but doesn't need the screen. An example of this might be a music player application when the user is listening to the music, not watching the screen. In these situations, the ability to turn off the backlight can significantly improve battery life.

Of course, any application that turns off the backlight needs to have a simple and user-friendly way of reenabling the screen when the user wants to look at the screen. Also, remember that users typically think the unit is off if the screen is black, so plan accordingly. For example, a user might attempt to power on the system when it is already running, and in doing so, accidentally turn off the device. Also, when the system powers down the display in this fashion, it also disables the touch screen. This means that you can't tell the user to tap the screen to turn it back on. Instead, you need to use some other event such as a set time, the completion of a task, or the user pressing a button. Finally, the method discussed here, useful on most systems based on Windows CE 3.0 and later, has been superseded by the method provided by the Power Manager that was introduced in Windows CE .NET 4.0. For newer systems, check to see whether the Power Manager is available, and control the screen through it. If that fails, the *ExtEscape* method might work.

On Windows CE, the control of the display is exposed through the *ExtEscape* function, which is a back door to the display and printer device drivers. Windows CE display drivers support a number of device escape codes, which are documented in the Platform Builder. For our purposes, only two escape codes are needed: *SETPOWERMANAGEMENT* to set the power state of the display and *QUERYESCSUPPORT* to query if the *SETPOWERMANAGEMENT* escape is supported by the driver. The following routine turns the display on or off on systems with display drivers that support the proper escape codes:

```
//
// Defines and structures taken from pwingdi.h in the Platform Builder
//
#define QUERYESCSUPPORT             8
#define SETPOWERMANAGEMENT          6147
#define GETPOWERMANAGEMENT          6148

typedef enum _VIDEO_POWER_STATE {
    VideoPowerOn = 1,
    VideoPowerStandBy,
    VideoPowerSuspend,
    VideoPowerOff
} VIDEO_POWER_STATE, *PVIDEO_POWER_STATE;

typedef struct _VIDEO_POWER_MANAGEMENT {
    ULONG Length;
    ULONG DPMSVersion;
    ULONG PowerState;
} VIDEO_POWER_MANAGEMENT, *PVIDEO_POWER_MANAGEMENT;
```

(continued)

```
//-----------------------------------------------------------------
// SetVideoPower - Turns on or off the display
//
int SetVideoPower (BOOL fOn) {
    VIDEO_POWER_MANAGEMENT vpm;
    int rc, fQueryEsc;
    HDC hdc;

    // Get the display dc.
    hdc = GetDC (NULL);
    // See if supported.
    fQueryEsc = SETPOWERMANAGEMENT;
    rc = ExtEscape (hdc, QUERYESCSUPPORT, sizeof (fQueryEsc),
                    (LPSTR)&fQueryEsc, 0, 0);
    if (rc == 0) {
        // No support, fail.
        ReleaseDC (NULL, hdc);
        return -1;
    }
    // Fill in the power management structure.
    vpm.Length = sizeof (vpm);
    vpm.DPMSVersion = 1;
    if (fOn)
        vpm.PowerState = VideoPowerOn;
    else
        vpm.PowerState = VideoPowerOff;

    // Tell the driver to turn on or off the display.
    rc = ExtEscape (hdc, SETPOWERMANAGEMENT, sizeof (vpm),
                    (LPSTR)&vpm, 0, 0);

    // Always release what you get.
    ReleaseDC (NULL, hdc);
    return 0;
}
```

The preceding code queries to see whether the escape is supported by calling *ExtEscape* with the command *QUERYESCSUPPORT*. The command being queried is passed in the input buffer. If the *SETPOWERMANAGEMENT* command is supported, the routine fills in the *VIDEO_POWER_MANAGEMENT* structure and calls *ExtEscape* again to set the power state.

Although these escape codes allow applications to turn the display on and off, Windows CE has no uniform method to control the brightness of the backlight. Each system has its own OEM-unique method of backlight brightness control. If there's a standard method of brightness control in the future, it will probably be exposed through this same *ExtEscape* function.

Powering Up the System

When the system is suspended, applications aren't running, so it seems that an application would have no control on when the system resumes. However, there are a few methods for waking a suspended device. First, an application can schedule the system to resume at a given time by using the Notification API discussed in Chapter 11. In addition, OEMs can assign some interrupt conditions so that they power up, or in power management talk resume, the system. An example of this behavior is a system that resumes when it is placed in a synchronization cradle.

Preventing the System from Powering Down

The opposite problem—preventing the system from suspending—can also be an issue. Windows CE systems are usually configured to automatically suspend after some period of no user input. To prevent this automatic suspension, an application can periodically call the following function:

```
void WINAPI SystemIdleTimerReset (void);
```

This function resets the timer that Windows CE maintains to monitor user input. If the timer reaches a predefined interval without user input, the system automatically suspends itself. Because the suspend timeout value can be changed, an application needs to know the timeout value so that it can call *SystemIdle-TimerReset* slightly more often. The system maintains three timeout values, all of which can be queried using the *SystemParametersInfo* function. The different values, represented by the constant passed to *SystemParametersInfo*, are shown here:

- **SPI_GETBATTERYIDLETIMEOUT**   Time from the last user input when the system is running on battery power

- **SPI_GETEXTERNALIDLETIMEOUT**   Time from the last user input when the system is running on AC power

- **SPI_GETWAKEUPIDLETIMEOUT**   Time from the system auto-powering before the system suspends again

To prevent the system from suspending automatically, you need to query these three values and call *SystemIdleTimerReset* before the shortest time returned. If any timeout value is 0, that specific timeout is disabled.

The Power Manager

A new, separate power management component was introduced in Windows CE .NET 4.0. This Power Manager replaced much of the functionality that GWES previously performed. The Power Manager defines a series of power states as D0, D1, D2, and D3. These rather cryptic names are then mapped to more friendly names at the system level.

For embedded systems, OEMs define the system power states. Examples of power states might be something like On, Idle, and Suspend. Other power states can be defined, such as ScreenOff, InCradle, and OnBattery.

From an application perspective, the new Power Manager provides the ability to be notified when the power state changes as well as a uniform method of changing the power state of the system through a series of functions.

The power states for the system are defined in the registry. The SDK defines *PWRMGR_REG_KEY* so that you don't have to know the registry string, but for the times when the constant isn't defined, the Power Manager's registry data is kept at HKEY_LOCAL_MACHINE\System\CurrentControlSet\Control\Power. The power states are then defined as subkeys under the key *State*.

Power Notifications

One of the more welcome features of the Power Manager is its ability to notify an application when the power state of the system changes. This ability frees the application from polling the battery state manually to monitor the power. An application can request that the Power Manager send a notification to the application when the power state of the system changes by calling *RequestPowerNotifications*. The Power Manager then sends the notifications through a message queue that has been previously created by the application.

RequestPowerNotifications is prototyped as

```
HANDLE RequestPowerNotifications (HANDLE hMsgQ, DWORD Flags);
```

The first parameter is the handle to a message queue that the application has previously created. The second parameter is a series of flags indicating which notifications the application wants to receive. The flags, which can be ORed together, are as follows:

- **PBT_TRANSITION**   Receive notifications when the power state changes—for example, when the system goes from On to Suspend.

- **PBT_RESUME**   Receive notifications when the system resumes.

- **PBT_POWERSTATUSCHANGE**   Receive notifications when the system transitions between AC and battery power.

- **PBT_POWERINFOCHANGE**   Receive notifications when the power information, such as the battery level, changes.

- **POWER_NOTIFY_ALL**   Receive all power notifications.

The *RequestPowerNotifications* function returns a handle to the power notification, or *NULL* if the function fails. The message queue should be created with read access by the application since it will be reading the power notifications from the queue.

To receive the notifications, an application should block on the queue handle by using *WaitForSingleObject*. As discussed in Chapter 10, the handle will be signaled when a notification is placed in the queue. The actual notification is received in the form of a *POWER_BROADCAST* structure defined as follows:

```
typedef struct _POWER_BROADCAST {
    DWORD Message;
    DWORD Flags;
    DWORD Length;
    WCHAR SystemPowerState[1];
} POWER_BROADCAST, *PPOWER_BROADCAST;
```

First note that this structure is a variable-length structure. The last field, *SystemPowerState*, is defined as an array of *WCHAR*s but can be filled with other, nonstring, data. The first field is the identifier of the notification itself. This field is filled with one of the *PBT_* flags listed earlier. The *Flags* field can contain the following flags, depending on the notification being received:

- **POWER_STATE_ON**   The system is on.

- **POWER_STATE_OFF**   The system is off.

- **POWER_STATE_CRITICAL**   The system is performing a critical off.

- **POWER_STATE_BOOT**   The system is booting.

- **POWER_STATE_IDLE**   The system is idle.

- **POWER_STATE_SUSPEND**   The system is suspended.

- **POWER_STATE_RESET**   The system is starting after a reset.

The final two parameters are related. The *Length* field is the length of the data in the *SystemPowerState* field. The data contained in the *SystemPowerState* field depends on the notification being sent. For the *PBT_TRANSITION* notification, the *SystemPowerState* field contains a string that identifies the new power state. This string is not zero terminated. To terminate the string, use the *Length* field to determine the length of the string. Note that the *Length* field is in bytes, while the characters are 2-byte Unicode characters, so to obtain the length of the string in characters, divide the *Length* field by the size of *TCHAR*.

For the *PBT_POWERINFOCHANGE* notification, the *SystemPowerState* field contains a *PPOWER_BROADCAST_POWER_INFO* structure defined as follows:

```
typedef struct _POWER_BROADCAST_POWER_INFO {
    DWORD       dwNumLevels;
    DWORD       dwBatteryLifeTime;
    DWORD       dwBatteryFullLifeTime;
    DWORD       dwBackupBatteryLifeTime;
    DWORD       dwBackupBatteryFullLifeTime;
    BYTE        bACLineStatus;
    BYTE        bBatteryFlag;
    BYTE        bBatteryLifePercent;
    BYTE        bBackupBatteryFlag;
    BYTE        bBackupBatteryLifePercent;
} POWER_BROADCAST_POWER_INFO, *PPOWER_BROADCAST_POWER_INFO;
```

Notice that the fields are similar in name and function to many of the fields previously discussed in the *SYSTEM_POWER_STATUS_EX2* structure.

Setting the Power State

Functions provided by the Power Manager also allow applications to control the power state. There are two methods for controlling the power. The first method has the application demand a given power setting. The second method has the application request that the power not drop below a given level.

An application can request a specific power state by calling the function *SetSystemPowerState*. This function is prototyped as

```
DWORD SetSystemPowerState (LPCWSTR psState, DWORD StateFlags,
                           DWORD Options);
```

The power state being requested can be specified in either the first or the second parameter of the function. If the first parameter is nonzero, it points to a string that identifies the state being requested. The string should match one of the power states enumerated in the registry.

If *psState* is *NULL*, the second parameter, *StateFlags*, defines the requested power state. This parameter is one of the same power states, from *POWER_STATE_ON* to *POWER_STATE_RESET*, that were described in the *POWER_BROADCAST* structure earlier.

Of particular interest is the flag *POWER_STATE_RESET*. This flag requests that the system reset. This method of resetting the system using *SetSystemPowerState* is much better than directly calling *KernelIoControl* with the IOCTL command *IOCTL_HAL_REBOOT* since using *SetSystemPowerState* will cause the system to flush any buffered data to the file system before the function resets the device.

While calling *SetSystemPowerState* is a direct method of changing the power state, a more subtle method is to request that the system maintain the minimal power state needed by the application by calling *SetPowerRequirement*. Using *SetSystemPowerState* assumes the application knows best, while calling *SetPowerRequirement* allows the system to optimize the power settings while still meeting the needs of the application. An example of a situation in which *SetPowerRequirement* is handy occurs when an application is using a serial port and needs the port to stay powered while communication is active. *SetPowerRequirement* is defined as

```
HANDLE SetPowerRequirement (PVOID pvDevice,
                            CEDEVICE_POWER_STATE DeviceState,
                            ULONG DeviceFlags, PVOID pvSystemState,
                            ULONG StateFlags);
```

The first parameter specifies the device that the application needs to remain at a given power state. The *DeviceState* parameter defines the power state for the device. The enumeration *CEDEVICE_POWER_STATE* specifies the state, ranging from D0 (meaning that the device must remain fully powered) to D4 (meaning that the device is powered off). The *DeviceFlags* parameter can be a combination of two flags: *POWER_NAME*, indicating that the device name is valid; and *POWER_FORCE*, indicating that the device should remain in that state even if the system suspends. If the *pvSystemState* is not *NULL*, it indicates that the power requirement is valid only for the power state named in *pvSystemState*. The device might not be able to change to the requested state.

As soon as possible, the application should remove the power requirement with a call to *ReleasePowerRequirement*, prototyped as

```
DWORD ReleasePowerRequirement (HANDLE hPowerReq);
```

The only parameter is the handle returned from *SetPowerRequirement*.

In the next chapter, I'll continue to explore system issues with a look at Windows CE stream device drivers and services. Although most application developers might never have to write a device driver or a service, knowing how they are put together is rather enlightening. Let's take a look.

22

Device Drivers and Services

Device drivers are modules that provide the interface between the operating system and the hardware. Device drivers take on an air of mystery because they're a mix of operating system–specific code and hardware customization. Most application developers are quite happy to let the real operating system junkies handle writing device drivers. This chapter shows you that while dealing with hardware can be a pain, the basic structure of a Windows CE driver is actually quite simple. An application developer might even have reasons to write a driver every now and then.

Real operating system junkies also know about services. Under Windows XP, a service is a background application that typically runs in the background. Services can be automatically started when the operating system boots, or be manually started. They can also be stopped and restarted as needed. Windows CE .NET supports services, although not with the same architecture as Windows XP services. Instead, Windows CE services are quite similar to Windows CE drivers, as we will see. In this chapter, I'll first introduce drivers, because the basics of that discussion is important to both drivers and services, and then I'll dive into how to write a Windows CE service.

Basic Drivers

Before I dive into how to write a device driver, we must take a brief look at how Windows CE handles drivers in general. Windows CE separates device drivers into three main groups: native, bus, and stream interface. Native drivers, sometimes called *built-in drivers*, are those device drivers that are required for the hardware and were created by the OEM when the Windows CE hardware was designed. Among the devices that have native drivers are the keyboard, the touch panel, and audio. These drivers might not support the generic device driver interface I describe shortly. Instead, they might extend the interface or have a totally custom interface to the operating system. Native drivers frequently require minor changes when a new version of the operating system is released. These drivers are designed using the Platform Builder product supplied by Microsoft. However these drivers are developed, they're tightly bound to the Windows CE operating system and aren't usually replaced after the device has been sold.

Bus drivers manage the system busses such as a PCI bus. PCMCIA, CompactFlash, and SDIO slots are also considered busses. Bus drivers are in charge of interrogating the hardware on the bus to determine what hardware is installed and allocating resources. The bus driver also asks the Device Manager to load the proper drivers for the hardware on the bus and provides a system-independent method of accessing the hardware registers without the device drivers from having to know the physical memory map of the system.

Stream interface device drivers (which are sometimes referred to as installable drivers) can be supplied by third-party manufacturers to support hardware added to the system. Although some Windows CE systems have a PCI bus for extra cards, the additional hardware is usually installed via a Personal Computer Memory Card International Association (PCMCIA), a CompactFlash, or a Secure Digital I/O (SDIO) slot. In this case, the device driver would use functions provided by the bus driver to access the hardware.

In addition, a device driver might be written to extend the functionality of an existing driver. For example, you might write a driver to provide a compressed or encrypted data stream over a serial link. In this case, an application would access the encryption driver, which would in turn use the serial driver to access the serial hardware.

Device drivers under Windows CE operate at the same protection level as applications. They differ from applications in that they're DLLs. Most drivers are loaded by the Device Manager process (Device.exe) when the system boots. All these drivers, therefore, share the same process address space. Some of the built-in drivers, on the other hand, are loaded by GWES.exe. These drivers include the display driver (DDI.dll) as well as the keyboard and touch panel (or mouse) drivers.

Driver Names

Stream interface device drivers are identified by a three-character name followed by a single digit, as in COM2: this scheme allows for 10 device drivers of one name to be installed on a Windows CE device at any one time. Instance values are numbered from one to nine, with the tenth instance having an instance number of zero. Here are a few examples of some three-character names currently in use:

- **COM**   Serial driver

- **ACM**   Audio compression manager

- **WAV**   Audio wave driver

- **CON**   Console driver

When referencing a stream interface driver, an application uses the three-character name, followed by the single digit, followed by a colon (:). The colon is required under Windows CE for the system to recognize the driver name.

Bus drivers typically don't have a stream-style three-letter name. One consequence of this is that bus drivers are not accessible to applications such as stream drivers. Bus drivers are however loaded by the Device Manager and in most ways are loaded and managed like stream drivers.

The Device Driver Load Process

When Device.exe loads, it looks in the registry under [HKEY_LOCAL_MACHINE]\Drivers for a string value named *RootKey*. This value points to the registry key that lists the drivers that should be loaded when the system boots. Traditionally, this key is named *BuiltIn*. In addition, an optional key named *DLL* can be present listing the registry enumerator, the DLL that actually reads and interprets the registry structure. If no *DLL* key is found, the default enumerator Regenum.dll is used.

The Device Manager then uses the registry enumerator to read the key specified by *RootKey* for the list of the drivers it must load when it initializes. This list is contained in a series of keys. The names of the keys don't matter—it's the values contained in the keys that define which drivers to load and the order in which to load them. Figure 22-1 shows the contents of the *WaveDev* key. The Wave driver is the audio driver.

The four values under this key are the basic four entries used by a device driver under Windows CE. The *DLL* key specifies the name of the DLL that implements the driver. This is the DLL that the registry enumerator loads. The *Order* value ranges from 0 through 255 and specifies the order in which the drivers are loaded. The registry enumerator loads drivers with lower *Order* values before drivers with higher *Order* values in the registry.

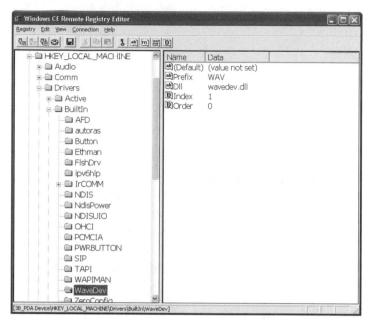

Figure 22-1   The registry key for the Wave driver

The *Prefix* value defines the three-letter name of the driver. This value is mandatory for stream drivers but typically not used for bus drivers. Applications that want to open this driver use the three-letter key with the number that Windows CE appends to create the device name. The *Index* value is the number that will be appended to the device name.

As the registry enumerator reads each of the registry keys, it loads the DLL specified, creates an *Active* key for the driver and then calls either *ActivateDevice* or *ActivateDeviceEx* to register the DLL as a device driver with the system. The registry enumerator maintains a table of device handles that are returned by *ActivateDevice*.

ActivateDevice creates a new key under [HKEY_LOCAL_MACHINE\Drivers\Active and initializes it. It then finds a free index for the driver if one wasn't specified in the original registry key. *ActivateDevice* then calls *RegisterDevice* to complete the load. *RegisterDevice* loads the driver in memory using the *LoadDevice* function. *LoadDevice* is similar to *LoadLibrary* but loads the entire DLL into memory and locks the pages so they can't be discarded. *RegisterDevice* then attempts to get function pointers to the 10 external entry points in the driver. For named, stream, drivers, the entry points *Init*, *Deinit*, *Open*, *Close*, and at least one of the *Read*, *Write*, *Seek*, or *IOControl* entry points must exist or the driver load fails. For unnamed bus drivers, *RegisterDevice* tries to get all 10 entry points, but fails only if the *Init* and *Deinit* functions can't be found.

Once the entry points have been saved, *RegisterDevice* calls the driver's *Init* function. If *Init* returns a nonzero value, the driver is added to the device chain and *RegisterDevice* returns. If *Init* returns zero, the driver is unloaded and the driver initialization fails.

Although this is the standard load procedure, another registry value can modify the load process. If the driver key contains a *Flags* value, the load process can change in a number of ways. The following values are currently valid for the *Flags* value:

- **DEVFLAGS_UNLOAD** Unload the driver after the call to *Init* returns.

- **DEVFLAGS_LOADLIBRARY** Use *LoadLibrary* to load the driver instead of *LoadDriver*.

- **DEVFLAGS_NOLOAD** Don't load the driver at all.

- **DEVFLAGS_NAKEDENTRIES** The driver entry points aren't prefixed by the driver name.

Another way the driver load process can be modified depends on the now-deprecated registry value named *Entry*. If this value is found, the DLL is loaded, and then, instead of calling *ActivateDevice*, the system calls the entry point in the driver named in *Entry*. The driver itself is then responsible for calling the *ActivateDevice* function if it's to be registered as a driver with the system.

If the *Entry* value is present, another value, *Keep*, can also be specified. Specifying the *Keep* value tells the system not to unload the driver after it calls the driver's entry point. This arrangement allows the driver DLL to avoid calling *RegisterDevice* and therefore avoid being a driver at all. Instead, the DLL is simply loaded into the process space of Device.exe.

Device drivers can also be loaded manually by applications. The preferred function for loading a device driver is *ActivateDeviceEx* prototyped as

```
HANDLE ActivateDeviceEx (LPCWSTR lpszDevKey, LPCVOID lpRegEnts,
                         DWORD cRegEnts, LPVOID lpvParam);
```

The first parameter is the name of a registry key under [HKEY_LOCAL_MACHINE] where the driver information is saved. The format of the registry key is identical to the format discussed earlier. The next two parameters, *lpRegEnts* and *cRegEnts*, describe an array of *REGINI* structures that define a series of registry values that will be added to the device's *Active* key. Generally, adding values is done only for bus drivers. The final parameter is a pointer that is passed to the device driver's *Init* function when the driver is loaded. This pointer can point to any device-specific information. The driver must use the new, two-parameter definition of the *Init* function to receive this value.

The return value from *ActivateDeviceEx* is the handle to the instance of the device. If the return value is zero, the load failed. In this case, use *GetLast-Error* to determine why the function failed. The returned handle can't be used to read or write to the device; instead, the driver should be opened with *Cre-ateFile*. The handle should be saved in case the driver needs to be unloaded in the future.

An older method of loading a driver is *RegisterDevice*. *RegisterDevice* is dangerous because drivers loaded with this function will not have an *Active* key associated with the driver. The only reason for discussing the function at all is that it doesn't require a registry key to load the driver, which can be handy when writing a quick and simple test program that loads and later unloads the driver.

RegisterDevice is prototyped as

```
HANDLE RegisterDevice (LPCWSTR lpszType, DWORD dwIndex,
                       LPCWSTR lpszLib, DWORD dwInfo);
```

The first two parameters are the three-character prefix of the driver and the instance number of the device. To load COM3, for example, *lpszType* would point to the string COM and *dwIndex* would have a value of 3. If an instance of the driver is already loaded the function will fail, so it's important to check the return value to see whether the function fails and determine why the failure occurred.

The *lpszLib* parameter identifies the name of the DLL that implements the driver. The final parameter, *dwInfo*, is passed to the driver in the *Init* call in the *dwContext* value. Because most drivers expect the *dwContext* value to point to a string naming a registry key, this value should at least point to a zero-termi-nated null string. *RegisterDevice* returns the handle to the instance of the driver if the load was successful and zero otherwise.

A driver can be unloaded with

```
BOOL DeregisterDevice (Handle hDevice);
```

The only parameter is the handle that was returned with *ActivateDeviceEx* or *RegisterDevice*.

Enumerating the Active Drivers

The most reliable way to find a device driver is to use *FindFirstFileEx* and set the *fSearchOp* parameter to *FindExSearchLimitToDevices*. Using the search string * and repeatedly calling *FindNextFile* results in a list of the stream drivers loaded. Unfortunately, there's a bug in the implementation of *FindFirstFileEx* in the original Pocket PCs. When you used the *FindExSearchLimitToDevices* *fSearchOp* parameter with *FindFirstFileEx*, the original Pocket PCs would throw an exception. The only way to catch this is to bracket the call to *FindFirstFileEx* with a *__try, __except* block. As a result, a more general method to search for device drivers is to simply check the registry.

The more general method for determining what drivers are loaded onto a Windows CE system is to look in the registry under the key \Drivers\Active under HKEY_LOCAL_MACHINE. The Device Manager dynamically updates the subkeys contained here as drivers are loaded and unloaded from the system. Contained in this key is a list of subkeys, one for each active driver loaded with *ActivateDevice*. The contents of these subkeys might change in future versions of Windows CE, but knowing what these subkeys contain can be helpful in some situations.

The name of the key is simply a placeholder; the values inside the keys are what indicate the active drivers. Figure 22-2 shows the registry key for the COM1 serial driver.

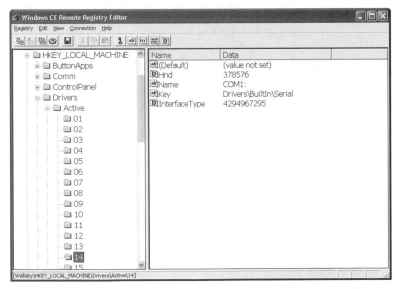

Figure 22-2   The registry's active list values for the serial device driver for COM1

In Figure 22-2, the *Name* value contains the official five-character name (four characters plus a colon) of the device. The *Hnd* value is a handle used internally by Windows CE. The interesting entry is the *Key* value. This value points to the registry key where the device driver stores its configuration information. This second key is necessary because the active list is dynamic, changing whenever a device is installed. Instead, the driver should open the registry key specified by the *Key* value in the active list to determine the driver's permanent configuration data. The configuration data for the serial driver is shown in Figure 22-3.

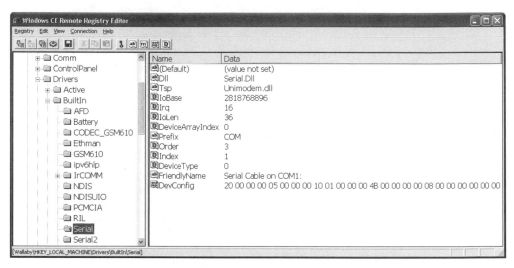

Figure 22-3   The registry entry for the serial driver

You can look in the serial driver registry key for such information as the name of the DLL that actually implements the driver, the three-letter prefix defining the driver name, the order in which the driver wants to be loaded, and something handy for user interfaces, the *friendly name* of the driver. Not all drivers have this friendly name, but when they do, it's a much more descriptive name than COM2 or NDS1.

Drivers for PCMCIA or CompactFlash cards have an additional value in their active list key. The *PnpId* value contains the Plug and Play ID string that was created from the card's ID string. Some PCMCIA and CompactFlash cards have their *PnpId* strings registered in the system if they use a specific device driver. If so, a registry key for the *PnpId* value is located in the *Drivers\PCMCIA* key under HKEY_LOCAL_MACHINE. For example, a PCMCIA card that had a *PnpId* string *This_is_a_pc_card* would be registered under the key *\Drivers\PCMCIA\This_is_a_pc_card*. That key may contain a *FriendlyName* string for the driver. Other PCMCIA cards use generic drivers. For example, most CompactFlash storage cards use the ATADISK driver registered under \Drivers\PCMCIA\ATADISK.

Reading and Writing Device Drivers

Applications access device drivers under Windows CE through the file I/O functions, *CreateFile*, *ReadFile*, *WriteFile*, and *CloseHandle*. The application opens the device using *CreateFile*, with the name of the device being the five-character (three characters plus digit plus colon) name of the driver. Drivers can be opened with all the varied access rights: read only, write only, read/write, or neither read nor write access.

Once a device is open, data can be sent to it using *WriteFile* and can read from the device using *ReadFile*. As is the case with file operations, overlapped I/O isn't supported for devices under Windows CE. The driver can be sent control characters using the function *DeviceIoControl*. The function is prototyped this way:

```
BOOL DeviceIoControl (HANDLE hDevice, DWORD dwIoControlCode,
                      LPVOID lpInBuffer, DWORD nInBufferSize,
                      LPVOID lpOutBuffer, DWORD nOutBufferSize,
                      LPDWORD lpBytesReturned,
                      LPOVERLAPPED lpOverlapped);
```

The first parameter is the handle to the opened device. The second parameter, *dwIoControlCode*, is the IOCTL (pronounced eye-OC-tal) code. This value defines the operation of the call to the driver. The next series of parameters are generic input and output buffers and their sizes. The use of these buffers is dependent on the IOCTL code passed in *dwIoControlCode*. The *lpBytesReturned* parameter must point to a *DWORD* value that will receive the number of bytes returned by the driver in the buffer pointed to by *lpOutBuffer*.

Each driver has its own set of IOCTL codes. If you look in the source code for the example serial driver provided in the Platform Builder, you'll see that the following IOCTL codes are defined for the COM driver. Note that these codes aren't defined in the Windows CE SDK because an application doesn't need to directly call *DeviceIoControl* using these codes.

IOCTL_SERIAL_SET_BREAK_ON	*IOCTL_SERIAL_SET_BREAK_OFF*
IOCTL_SERIAL_SET_DTR	*IOCTL_SERIAL_CLR_DTR*
IOCTL_SERIAL_SET_RTS	*IOCTL_SERIAL_CLR_RTS*
IOCTL_SERIAL_SET_XOFF	*IOCTL_SERIAL_SET_XON*
IOCTL_SERIAL_GET_WAIT_MASK	*IOCTL_SERIAL_SET_WAIT_MASK*
IOCTL_SERIAL_WAIT_ON_MASK	*IOCTL_SERIAL_GET_COMMSTATUS*
IOCTL_SERIAL_GET_MODEMSTATUS	*IOCTL_SERIAL_GET_PROPERTIES*
IOCTL_SERIAL_SET_TIMEOUTS	*IOCTL_SERIAL_GET_TIMEOUTS*
IOCTL_SERIAL_PURGE	*IOCTL_SERIAL_SET_QUEUE_SIZE*
IOCTL_SERIAL_IMMEDIATE_CHAR	*IOCTL_SERIAL_GET_DCB*
IOCTL_SERIAL_SET_DCB	*IOCTL_SERIAL_ENABLE_IR*
IOCTL_SERIAL_DISABLE_IR	

As you can see from the fairly self-descriptive names, the serial driver IOCTL functions expose significant function to the calling process. Windows uses these IOCTL codes to control some of the specific features of a serial port, such as the handshaking lines and timeouts. Each driver has its own set of IOCTL codes. I've shown the preceding ones simply as an example of how the *DeviceIoControl* function is typically used. Under most circumstances, an application has no reason to use the *DeviceIoControl* function with the serial driver. Windows provides its own set of functions that then call down to the serial driver using *DeviceIoControl*.

Okay, we've talked enough about generic drivers. It's time to sit down to the meat of the chapter—writing a driver.

Writing a Windows CE Stream Device Driver

As I mentioned earlier, Windows CE device drivers are simply DLLs. So on the surface, writing a device driver would seem to be a simple matter of writing a Windows CE DLL with specific exported entry points. For the most part, this is true. You have only a few issues to deal with when writing a Windows CE device driver.

A device driver isn't loaded by the application communicating with the driver. Instead, the Device Manager, Device.exe, loads most drivers, including all stream drivers. This state of affairs affects the driver in two ways. First, an application can't simply call private entry points in a driver as it can in a DLL. The only way an application could directly call an entry point would be if it called *LoadLibrary* and *GetProcAddress* to get the address of the entry point so the entry point could be called. This situation would result in the DLL that implemented the driver (notice I'm not calling it a driver anymore) being loaded in the process space of the application, not in the process space of the Device Manager. The problem is that this second copy of the DLL isn't the driver—it's the DLL that implemented the driver. The difference is that the first copy of the DLL (the driver)—when properly loaded by the Device Manager—has some state data associated with it that isn't present in the second copy of the DLL loaded by the application. Perversely, the calls to *LoadLibrary* and *GetProcAddress* will succeed because the driver is a DLL. In addition, calling the entry points in the driver results in calling the correct code. The problem is that the code will be acting on data present only in the second copy of the DLL, not in the proper data maintained by the driver. This situation can, and usually does, result in subtle bugs that can confuse and even lock up the hardware the driver is managing. In short, never interact with a driver by calling *LoadLibrary* and *GetProcAddress*.

The second effect of the driver being loaded by the Device Manager is that if a driver DLL is used for more than one instance of a piece of hardware, for example, on a serial driver being used for both COM1 and COM2, the Device Manager will load the DLL only once. When the driver is "loaded" a second time, the driver's initialization entry point, *COM_Init*, is simply called again.

The reason for this dual use of the same DLL instance is that under Windows CE a DLL is never loaded twice by the same process. Instead, if an application asks to load a DLL again, the original DLL is used and a call is made to *DllMain* to indicate that a second thread has attached to the DLL. So if the Device Manager, which is simply another process under the operating system, loads the same driver for two different pieces of hardware, the same DLL is used for both instances of the hardware.

Drivers written to handle multiple instances of themselves must not store data in global variables because the second instance of the driver would overwrite the data from the first instance. Instead, a multi-instance driver must store its state data in a structure allocated in memory. If multiple instances of the driver are loaded, the driver will allocate a separate state data structure for each instance. The driver can keep track of which instance data structure to use by passing the pointer to the instance data structure back to the Device Manager as its "handle," which is returned by the device driver's *Init* function.

One final issue with Windows CE device drivers is that they can be reentered by the operating system, which means that a driver must be written in a totally thread-safe manner. References to state data must be protected by critical sections, interlock functions, or other thread-safe methods.

The Stream Driver Entry Points

A stream driver exposes 10 external entry points—summarized in the following list—that the Device Manager calls to talk to the driver. I'll describe each entry point in detail in the following sections.

- ***xxx_Init***   Called when an instance of the driver is loaded

- ***xxx_Deinit***   Called when an instance of the driver is unloaded

- ***xxx_Open***   Called when a driver is opened by an application with *CreateFile*

- ***xxx_Close***   Called when a driver is closed by the application with *Closehandle*

- ***xxx_Read***   Called when the application calls *ReadFile*

- ***xxx_Write***   Called when the application calls *WriteFile*

- ***xxx_Seek***   Called when the application calls *SetFilePointer*

- ***xxx_IOControl***   Called when the application calls *DeviceIoControl*

- ***xxx_PowerDown***   Called just before the system suspends

- ***xxx_PowerUp***   Called just before the system resumes

The *xxx* preceding each function name is the three-character name of the driver if the driver has a name. For example, if the driver is a COM driver, the functions are named *COM_Init*, *COM_Deinit*, and so on. For unnamed drivers, those without a prefix value specified in the registry, the entry points are the name without the leading *xxx*, as in *Init* and *Deinit*. Also, although the preceding list describes applications talking to the driver, there's no reason one driver can't open another driver by calling *CreateFile* and communicate with it just as an application can.

xxx_Init

When the Device Manager first loads an instance of the driver, the Device Manager calls the driver's *Init* function. The *Init* function has one of two prototypes. For newer drivers built for Windows CE .NET 4.0 and later, the prototype is

```
DWORD XXX_Init (LPCTSTR pContext, LPCVOID lpvBusContext);
```

The first parameter, *pContext*, typically contains a pointer to a string identifying the *Active* key created by the Device Manager for the driver. I say *typically* because an application using *RegisterDevice* can load the device to pass any value, including 0, in this parameter. The moral of the story is to look for a string but plan for the *dwContext* value to point to anything. The second parameter is a pointer to driver specific data structure. This pointer is actually whatever the fourth parameter to *ActivateDeviceEx* so it can be used for whatever data needs to be passed from the caller of *ActivateDeviceEx* to the driver.

The legacy prototype of the *Init* function is prototyped as

```
DWORD XXX_Init (DWORD dwContext);
```

Here again, the first, and this time only, parameter almost always contains a pointer the name of the *Active* key in the registry. Although the newer function prototype is recommended, drivers using the old *Init* prototype work just as well.

The driver should respond to the *Init* call by verifying that any hardware that the driver accesses functions correctly. The driver should initialize the hardware, initialize its state, and return a nonzero value. If the driver detects an error during its initialization, it should set the proper error code with *SetLastError* and return 0 from the *Init* function. If the Device Manager sees a 0 return value from the *Init* function, it unloads the driver and removes the *Active* key for the driver from the registry.

The device driver can pass any nonzero value back to the Device Manager. The typical use of this value, which is referred to as the *device context handle*, is to pass the address of a structure that contains the driver's state data. For drivers that can be multi-instanced (loaded more than once to support more than one instance of a hardware device), the state data of the driver must be independently maintained for each instance of the driver.

xxx_Deinit

The *Deinit* entry point is called when the driver is unloaded. This entry point must be prototyped as

```
BOOL XXX_Deinit (DWORD hDeviceContext);
```

The single parameter is the device-context value the driver returned from the *Init* call. This value allows the driver to determine which instance of the driver is being unloaded. The driver should respond to this call by powering down any hardware it controls and freeing any memory and resources it owns. The driver will be unloaded following this call.

xxx_Open

The *Open* entry point to the driver is called when an application or another driver calls *CreateFile* to open the driver. The entry point is prototyped as

```
DWORD XXX_Open (DWORD hDeviceContext, DWORD AccessCode, DWORD ShareMode);
```

The first parameter is the device context value returned by the *Init* call. The *AccessCode* and *ShareMode* parameters are taken directly from *CreateFile*'s *dwDesiredAccess* and *dwShareMode* parameters and indicate how the application wants to access (read/write or read only) and share (*FILE_SHARE_READ* or *FILE_SHARE_WRITE*) the device. The device driver can refuse the open for any reason by simply returning 0 from the function. If the driver accepts the open call, it returns a nonzero value.

The return value is traditionally used, like the device context value returned by the *Init* call, as a pointer to an open context data structure. If the driver allows only one application to open it at a time, the return value is usually the device context value passed in the first parameter. This arrangement allows all the functions to access the device context structure directly, because one of these two values—the device context or the open context value—is passed in every call to the driver. The open context value returned by the *Open* function is *not* the handle returned to the application when the *CreateFile* function returns.

Windows CE typically runs on hardware that's designed so that individual components in the system can be separately powered. Windows CE drivers that are designed to work without the Power Manager typically power the hardware they control only when the device is opened. The driver then removes power when the *Close* notification is made. This means that the device will be powered on only when an application or another driver is actually using the device.

xxx_Close

The *Close* entry point is called when an application or driver that has previously opened the driver closes it by calling *CloseHandle*. The entry point is prototyped as

```
BOOL XXX_Close (DWORD hOpenContext);
```

The single parameter is the open context value that the driver returned from the *Open* call. The driver should power down any hardware and free any memory or open context data associated with the open state.

xxx_Read

The *Read* entry point is called when an application or another driver calls *ReadFile* on the device. This entry point is prototyped as

```
DWORD XXX_Read (DWORD hOpenContext, LPVOID pBuffer, DWORD Count);
```

The first parameter is the open context value returned by the *Open* call. The second parameter is a pointer to the calling application's buffer, where the read data is to be copied. The final parameter is the size of the buffer. The driver should return the number of bytes read into the buffer. If an error occurs, the driver should set the proper error code using *SetLastError* and return <;$MI>1. A return code of 0 is valid and indicates that the driver read no data.

A device driver should program defensively when using any passed pointer. The following series of functions tests the validity of a pointer:

```
BOOL IsBadWritePtr (LPVOID lp, UINT ucb);
BOOL IsBadReadPtr (const void *lp, UINT ucb);
BOOL IsBadCodePtr (FARPROC lpfn);
```

The parameters are the pointer to be tested and, for the *Read* and *Write* tests, the size of the buffer pointed to by the pointer. Each of these functions verifies that the pointer passed is valid for the use tested. However, the access rights of a page can change during the processing of the call. For this reason, always couch any use of the *pBuffer* pointer in a *__try, __except* block. This will prevent the driver from causing an exception when the application passes a bad pointer. For example, you could use the following code:

```
DWORD xxx_Read (DWORD dwOpen, LPVOID pBuffer, DWORD dwCount) {
    DWORD dwBytesRead;

    // Test the pointer.
    if (IsBadReadPtr (pBuffer, dwCount)) {
        SetLastError (ERROR_INVALID_PARAMETER);
        return -1;
    }
```

```
    __try {
        dwBytesRead = InternalRead (pBuffer, dwCount);
    }
    __except (EXCEPTION_EXECUTE_HANDLER) {
        SetLastError (ERROR_INVALID_PARAMETER);
        return -1;
    }
    return dwBytesRead;
}
```

In the preceding code, the pointer is initially tested by using *IsBadReadPtr* to see whether it's a valid pointer. The code that actually performs the read is hidden in an internal routine named *InternalRead*. If that function throws an exception, presumably because of a bad *pBuffer* pointer or an invalid *dwCount* value, the function sets the error code to *ERROR_INVALID_PARAMETER* and returns <;$MI>1 to indicate that an error occurred.

xxx_Write

The *Write* entry point is called when the application that has opened the device calls *WriteFile*. The entry point is prototyped as

```
DWORD XXX_Write (DWORD hOpenContext, LPCVOID pBuffer, DWORD Count);
```

As with the *Read* entry point, the three parameters are the open context value returned by the *Open* call, the pointer to the data buffer containing the data, and the size of the buffer. The function should return the number of bytes written to the device or <;$MI>1 to indicate an error.

xxx_Seek

The *Seek* entry point is called when an application or driver that has opened the driver calls *SetFilePointer* on the device handle. The entry point is prototyped as

```
DWORD XXX_Seek (DWORD hOpenContext, long Amount, WORD Type);
```

The parameters are what you would expect: the open context value returned from the *Open* call, the absolute offset value that is passed from the *SetFilePointer* call, and the type of seek. There are three types of seek: *FILE_BEGIN* seeks from the start of the device, *FILE_CURRENT* seeks from the current position, and *FILE_END* seeks from the end of the device. The *Seek* function has limited use in a device driver but it is provided for completeness.

xxx_PowerDown

The *PowerDown* entry point is called when the system is about to suspend. For legacy drivers without a power management interface, the device driver should power down any hardware it controls and save any necessary hardware state. The entry point is prototyped as

```
void XXX_PowerDown (DWORD hDeviceContext);
```

The single parameter is the device context handle returned by the *Init* call.

The device driver must not make any Win32 API calls during the processing of this call. Windows CE allows only two functions, *SetInterruptEvent* and *CeSetPowerOnEvent*, to be called during the *PowerDown* notification. *SetInterruptEvent* tells the kernel to signal the event that the driver's interrupt service thread is waiting for. *SetInterruptEvent* is prototyped as

```
BOOL SetInterruptEvent (DWORD idInt);
```

The single parameter is the interrupt ID of the associated interrupt event.

The function *CeSetPowerOnEvent* is prototyped as

```
BOOL CeSetPowerOnEvent (HANDLE hEvt);
```

The parameter is the handle of an event that will be signaled when the system resumes.

xxx_PowerUp

The *PowerUp* entry point is called when the system resumes. Legacy drivers without a power management interface can use this notification to know when to power up and restore the state to the hardware it controls. The *PowerUp* notification is prototyped as

```
void XXX_PowerUp (DWORD hDeviceContext);
```

The *hDeviceContext* parameter is the device context handle returned by the *Init* call. As with the *PowerDown* call, the device driver can make no Win32 API calls during the processing of this notification.

Although the *PowerUp* notification allows the driver to restore power to the hardware it manages, well-written drivers restore only the minimal power necessary for the device. Typically, the driver will power the hardware only on instruction from the Power Manager.

xxx_IOControl

Because many device drivers don't use the *Read*, *Write*, *Seek* metaphor for their interface, the *IOControl* entry point becomes the primary entry point for interfacing with the driver. The *IOControl* entry point is called when a device or application calls the *DeviceIOControl* function. The entry point is prototyped as

```
BOOL XXX_IOControl (DWORD hOpenContext, DWORD dwCode, PBYTE pBufIn,
                    DWORD dwLenIn, PBYTE pBufOut, DWORD dwLenOut,
                    PDWORD pdwActualOut);
```

The first parameter is the open context value returned by the *Open* call. The second parameter, *dwCode*, is a device-defined value passed by the application to indicate why the call is being made. Unlike Windows NT/2000/XP, Windows CE does very little processing before the IOCTL code is passed to the driver. This means that the device driver developer ought to be able to pick any values for the codes. However, this behavior might change in the future so it's prudent to define IOCTL codes that conform to the format used by the desktop versions of Windows. Basically, this means that the IOCTL codes are created with the *CTL_CODE* macro, which is defined identically in the Windows Driver Development Kit and the Windows CE Platform Builder. The problem with application developers creating conforming IOCTL code values is that the *CTL_CODE* macro might not be defined in some SDKs. So, developers are sometimes forced to define *CTL_CODE* manually to create conforming IOCTL codes.

The next two parameters describe the buffer that contains the data being passed to the device. The *pBufIn* parameter points to the input buffer that contains the data being passed to the driver; the *dwLenIn* parameter contains the length of the data. The next two parameters are *pBufOut* and *dwLenOut*. The parameter *pBufOut* contains a pointer to the output buffer, and *dwLenOut* contains the length of that buffer. These parameters aren't required to point to valid buffers. The application calling *DeviceIoControl* might possibly pass 0s for the buffer pointer parameters. It's up to the device driver to validate the buffer parameters given the IOCTL code being passed.

The final parameter is the address of a *DWORD* value that receives the number of bytes written to the output buffer. The device driver should return *TRUE* if the function was successful and *FALSE* otherwise. If an error occurs, the device driver should return an error code using *SetLastError*.

The input and output buffers of *DeviceIoControl* calls allow for any type of data to be sent to the device and returned to the calling application. Typically, the data is formatted using a structure with fields containing the parameters for the specific call.

The serial driver makes extensive use of *DeviceIoControl* calls to configure the serial hardware. For example, one of the many IOCTL calls is one to set the serial timeout values. To do this, an application allocates a buffer, casts the buffer pointer to a pointer to a *COMMTIMEOUTS* structure, fills in the structure, and passes the buffer pointer as the input buffer when it calls *DeviceIoControl*. The driver then receives an *IOControl* call with the input buffer pointing to the *COMMTIMEOUTS* structure. I've taken the serial driver's code for processing this IOCTL call and shown a modified version here:

```
BOOL COM_IOControl (PHW_OPEN_INFO pOpenHead, DWORD dwCode,
                    PBYTE pBufIn, DWORD dwLenIn,
```

(continued)

```
                    PBYTE pBufOut, DWORD dwLenOut,
                    PDWORD pdwActualOut) {
    BOOL RetVal = TRUE;         // assume success
    COMMTIMEOUTS *pComTO;

    switch (dwCode) {
    case IOCTL_SERIAL_SET_TIMEOUTS :
        if ((dwLenIn < sizeof(COMMTIMEOUTS)) || (NULL == pBufIn)) {
            SetLastError (ERROR_INVALID_PARAMETER);
            RetVal = FALSE;
            break;
        }
        pComTO = (COMMTIMEOUTS *)pBufIn;
        ReadIntervalTimeout = pComTO->ReadIntervalTimeout;
        ReadTotalTimeoutMultiplier = pComTO->ReadTotalTimeoutMultiplier;
        ReadTotalTimeoutConstant = pComTO->ReadTotalTimeoutConstant;
        WriteTotalTimeoutMultiplier = pComTO->WriteTotalTimeoutMultiplier;
        WriteTotalTimeoutConstant = pComTO->WriteTotalTimeoutConstant;
        break;
    }
    return RetVal;
}
```

Notice how the serial driver first verifies that the input buffer is at least the size of the timeout structure and that the input pointer is nonzero. If either of these tests fails, the driver sets the error code to *ERROR_INVALID_PARAMETER* and returns *FALSE*. Otherwise, the driver assumes that the input buffer points to a *COMMTIMEOUTS* structure and uses the data in that structure to set the time-out values. Although the preceding example doesn't enclose the pointer access in *__try, __except* blocks, a more robust driver might.

The preceding scheme works fine as long as the data being passed to or from the driver is all contained within the structure. However, if you pass a pointer in the structure and the driver attempts to use the pointer, an exception will occur. To understand why, you have to remember how Windows CE manages memory protection across processes. (At this point, you might want to review the first part of Chapter 21.)

As I explained in the preceding chapter, when a thread in an application is running, that application is mapped to slot 0. If that application allocates a buffer, the returned pointer points to the buffer allocated in slot 0. The problem occurs when the application passes that pointer to a device driver. Remember that a device driver is loaded by Device.exe, so when the device driver receives an *IOControl* call, the device driver and Device.exe are mapped into slot 0. The pointer passed from the application is no longer valid because the buffer it pointed to is no longer mapped into slot 0.

If the pointer is part of the parameter list of a function—for example, the *pBufIn* parameter passed in the *DeviceIoControl*—the operating system automatically converts, or *maps*, the pointer so that it points to the slot containing the calling process. Because any buffer allocated in slot 0 is also allocated in the application's slot, the mapped pointer now points to the buffer allocated before the application made the *DeviceIoControl* call.

The key is that when an application is running, slot 0 contains a clone of the slot it was assigned when the application was launched. So any action to slot 0 is also reflected in the application's slot. This cloning process doesn't copy memory. Instead, the operating system manipulates the page table entries of the processor to duplicate the memory map for the application's slot in slot 0 when that application is running.

The operating system takes care of mapping any pointers passed as parameters in a function. However, the operating system can't map any pointers passed in structures during a *DeviceIoControl* call because it has no idea what data is being passed to the input and output buffers of a *DeviceIoControl* call. To use pointers passed in a structure, the device driver must manually map the pointer.

You can manually map a pointer using the following function:

```
LPVOID MapPtrToProcess (LPVOID lpv, HANDLE hProc);
```

The first parameter is the pointer to be mapped. The second parameter is the handle of the process that contains the buffer pointed to by the first parameter. To get the handle of the process, a driver needs to know the handle of the application calling the driver, which you can query by using the following function:

```
HANDLE GetCallerProcess (void);
```

Typically, these two functions are combined into one line of code, as in

```
pMapped = MapPtrToProcess (pIn, GetCallerProcess());
```

The application can also map a pointer before it passes it to a device driver, although this is rarely done. To do this, an application queries its own process handle using

```
HANDLE GetCurrentProcess (void);
```

Although both *GetCurrentProcess* and *GetCallerProcess* are defined as returning handles, these are actually pseudohandles and therefore don't need to be closed. For programmers using eMbedded Visual C++ to build a driver, *MapPtrToProcess* and *GetCallerProcess* are not prototyped in the standard include files. If you want to use these functions without warnings, add function prototypes to the include files for the driver.

As an example, assume a driver has an IOCTL function to checksum a series of buffers. Because the buffers are disjointed, the pointers to the buffers are passed to the driver in a structure. The driver must map each pointer in the structure, checksum the data in the buffers, and return the result, as in the following code:

```
#define IOCTL_CHECKSUM 2
#define MAX_BUFFS 5
typedef struct {
    int nSize;
    PBYTE pData;
} BUFDAT, *PBUFDAT;

typedef struct {
    int nBuffs;
    BUFDAT bd[MAX_BUFFS];
} CHKSUMSTRUCT, *PCHKSUMSTRUCT;

DWORD xxx_IOControl (DWORD dwOpen, DWORD dwCode, PBYTE pIn, DWORD dwIn,
                     PBYTE pOut, DWORD dwOut, DWORD *pdwBytesWritten) {

    switch (dwCode) {

    case IOCTL_CHECKSUM:
        {
            PCHKSUMSTRUCT pchs;
            DWORD dwSum = 0;
            PBYTE pData;
            int i, j;

            // Verify the input parameters.
            if (!pIn  || (dwIn < sizeof (CHKSUMSTRUCT)) ||
                !pOut || (dwOut < sizeof (DWORD))) {
                SetLastError (ERROR_INVALID_PARAMETER);
                return FALSE;
            }
            // Perform the checksum.  Protect against bad pointers.
            pchs = (PCHKSUMSTRUCT)pIn;
            __try {
                for (i = 0; (i < pchs->nBuffs) && (i < MAX_BUFFS); i++) {

                    // Map the pointer to something the driver can use.
                    pData = (PBYTE)MapPtrToProcess (pchs->bd[i].pData,
                                                    GetCallerProcess());
                    // Checksum the buffer.
                    for (j = 0; j < pchs->bd[i].nSize; j++)
                        dwSum += *pData++;
```

```
            }
            // Write out the result.
            *(DWORD *)pOut = dwSum;
            *pdwBytesWritten = sizeof (DWORD);
        }
        __except (EXCEPTION_EXECUTE_HANDLER) {
            SetLastError (ERROR_INVALID_PARAMETER);
            return FALSE;
        }
    }
    return TRUE;

    default:
        SetLastError (ERROR_INVALID_PARAMETER);
        return FALSE;
    }
    SetLastError (err);
    DEBUGMSG (ZONE_FUNC, (DTAG TEXT("GEN_IOControl--\r\n")));
    return TRUE;
}
```

In the preceding code, the driver has one IOCTL command,
IOCTL_CHECKSUM. When this command is received, the driver uses the structures passed in the input buffer to locate the data buffers, map the pointers to
those buffers, and perform a checksum on the data they contain.

The 10 entry points that I described in this section, from *Init* to *IOControl*,
are all that a driver needs to export to support the Windows CE stream driver
interface. Now let's look at how IOCTL commands have been organized.

Device Interface Classes

In a generic sense, the driver is free to define any set of commands to respond
to in the *IOControl* function. However, it would be nice if drivers that implement similar functions agreed on a set of common IOCTL commands that
would be implemented by all the common drivers. In addition, there is additional functionality that all drivers may optionally implement. For drivers that
implement this common functionality, it would be convenient if they all
responded to the same set of IOCTL commands.

Driver interface classes are a way to organize and describe these common
IOCTL commands. For example, Windows CE defines a set of IOCTL com-
mands that are used by the Power Manager to control the power use of a driver.
Drivers that respond to these power management IOCTLs are said to support

the power management interface class. The list of driver interface classes grows with each release of Windows CE, but here is a short summary:

- Power Management interface

- Block Driver interface

- Card services interface

- Keyboard interface

- NDIS miniport interface

- Generic Stream interface

In addition to grouping like sets of IOCTL commands, device drivers can advertise their support of one or more interfaces. Other drivers, or even applications, can be informed when a driver is loaded that supports a given interface. Interface classes are uniquely identified with a GUID defined in the Platform Builder include files. Unfortunately, the GUID definitions are distributed across the different include files relevant to the different driver types related to the specific interface so finding them can be a challenge.

Advertising an Interface

Drivers that support a given interface need to tell the system that they support it. Advertising support for an interface can be accomplished in a couple of ways. First, the registry key specifying the driver can contain an *IClass* value that specifies one or more GUIDs identifying the interface classes the driver supports. For drivers that support a single interface, the *IClass* value is a string. For drivers that support multiple interfaces, the *IClass* value is a multi-z string with each individual string containing a GUID.

A driver can manually advertise an interface by calling *AdvertiseInterface* defined as

```
BOOL AdvertiseInterface (const GUID* devclass, LPCWSTR name, BOOL fAdd);
```

The first parameter is the GUID for the interface being advertised. The second parameter is a string that uniquely identifies the name of the driver. The easiest way to do this is to provide the name of the driver, such as DSK1:. Recall that the name of a driver can be found in its *Active* key. The last parameter, *fAdd*, should be *TRUE* if the interface is now available and *FALSE* if the interface is no longer available. It is important to advertise the removal of the interface if the driver is being removed. Otherwise the Device Manager won't free the memory used to track the interface.

Monitoring for an Interface

Applications or drivers can ask to be notified when a driver advertises an interface being either created or removed. To be notified, a message queue should be created with read access. Set the maximum message length to *MAX_DEVCLASS_NAMELEN*. The message queue handle is then passed to the *RequestDeviceNotifications* function defined as:

```
HANDLE RequestDeviceNotifications (const GUID* devclass, HANDLE hMsgQ,
                                   BOOL fAll);
```

The first parameter is a string representing the GUID of the interface that the application or driver wants to monitor. The string *PMCLASS_GENERIC_DEVICE* provides a method for being notified when any power-managed stream device is loaded or unloaded. This parameter can be set to *NULL* to receive all notifications. However, it isn't recommended to monitor all interfaces for performance reasons. The second parameter is the handle to the previously created message queue. The final parameter is a Boolean that should be set to *TRUE* to receive all past notifications or *FALSE* to only receive notifications from the time of the call forward.

After the call, the application or driver should create a thread to block on the message queue handle that will be signaled when a message is inserted in the queue. The message format depends on the specific notification being sent.

To stop the notifications, call the function *StopDeviceNotifications* prototyped as

```
BOOL StopDeviceNotifications (HANDLE h);
```

The only parameter is the handle returned by *RequestDeviceNotifications*.

The interface class scheme provides a handy way for a developer to know what IOCTL commands to support for a given driver. The classic example of this system is power management. The power management methodology was radically redesigned with the release of Windows CE .NET 4.0. However, the stream interface couldn't be changed without causing all the drivers to be redesigned. Instead, the new power management support was exposed through a newly defined power management interface class.

Device Driver Power Management

Windows CE .NET introduced a new Power Manager that greatly increased the power management capabilities of the systems. The basics of this Power Manager are discussed in Chapter 21. Device drivers support the Power Manager by exposing a power management interface that allows the Power Manager to query the power capabilities of the device and to control its state. The control of the Power Manager is tempered by the actual response of the driver, which might not be in position to change its power state at the time of the request.

Power Management Functions for Devices

The power state of a device is defined to be one of the following:

- **D0** Device fully powered. All devices are fully powered and running.

- **D1** Device is fully functional, but in a power-saving mode.

- **D2** Device is in standby.

- **D3** Device is in sleep mode.

- **D4** Device is unpowered.

These power states are defined in *CEDEVICE_POWER_STATE* enumeration, which also defines additional values for *PwrDeviceUnspecified* and *PwrDevice-Maximum*.

When a device wants to set its own power state, it should call the *Device-PowerNotify* function defined as

```
DWORD DevicePowerNotify (PVOID pvDevice, CEDEVICE_POWER_STATE DeviceState,
                         DWORD Flags);
```

The *pvDevice* parameter points to a string naming the device driver to change. The second parameter is *CEDEVICE_POWER_STATE* enumeration. The *dwDeviceFlags* parameter should be set to *POWER_NAME*.

When changing its own power state, the device should not immediately change to the state requested in the *SetDevicePower* call. Instead, the device should wait until it is instructed to change its power state through an IOCTL command sent by the Power Manager. The driver should not assume that just because it requests a given state that the Power Manager will set the device to that state. There might be system reasons for leaving the device in a higher power state.

Now let's look at the IOCTL commands that are sent to a device driver that supports the power management interface class.

IOCTL_POWER_CAPABILITIES

This IOCTL command is sent to query the power capabilities of the device. The input buffer of the *IoControl* function is filled with a *POWER_RELATIONSHIP* structure that describes any parent-child relationships between the driver and a bus driver. The output buffer contains a *POWER_CAPABILITIES* structure that should be filled in by the driver. The structure is defined as

```
typedef struct _POWER_CAPABILITIES {
    UCHAR DeviceDx;
    UCHAR WakeFromDx;
```

```
    UCHAR InrushDx;
    DWORD Power[5];
    DWORD Latency[5];
    DWORD Flags;
} POWER_CAPABILITIES, *PPOWER_CAPABILITIES;
```

The *DeviceDx* field is a bitmask that indicates which of the power states, from D0 to D*n*, the device driver supports. The *WakeFromDx* field is also a bitmask. This field indicates which of the device states the hardware can wake from if an external signal is detected by the device. The *InrunshDx* field indicates which entries of the *Power* array are valid. The *Power* array contains entries that specify amount of power used by the device, in milliwatts, for each given power state. The *Latency* array describes the amount of time, in milliseconds, that it takes the device to return to the D0 state from each of the other power states. Finally, the *Flags* field should be set to *TRUE* if the driver wants to receive an *IOCTL_REGISTER_POWER_RELATIONSHIP* command to manage other *child* devices.

The level of detail involved in filling out the *POWER_CAPABILITIES* structure can be intimidating. Many drivers only fill out the first field, *DeviceDx*, to at least indicate to the system which power levels the device supports and set the remaining fields to zero.

IOCTL_REGISTER_POWER_RELATIONSHIP
This command is sent to a driver that wants to control the power management of any *child* drivers. During this call, the parent driver can inform the Power Manager of any devices it controls.

IOCTL_POWER_GET
This command is sent to the device to query the current power state of the device. The output buffer points to a *DWORD* that should be set to one of the *CEDEVICE_POWER_STATE* enumeration values.

IOCTL_POWER_QUERY
This command is sent to ask the device whether it will change to a given power state. The input buffer points to a *POWER_RELATIONSHIP* structure while the output buffer contains a *CEDEVICE_POWER_STATE* enumeration containing the power state that the Power Manager wants the device to enter. If the device wishes to reject the request, it should set the *CEDEVICE_POWER_STATE* enumeration to *PwrDeviceUnspecified*. Otherwise, the Power Manager assumes the driver is willing to enter the requested power state. The driver shouldn't enter the state on this command. Instead it should wait until it receives an *IOCTL_POWER_SET* command. Be warned that the simple implementation of the Power Manager in Windows CE doesn't call this IOCTL, so a driver shouldn't depend on receiving this command before an *IOCTL_POWER_SET* command is received.

IOCTL_POWER_SET

This command is sent to instruct the device to change to a given power state. The input buffer points to a *POWER_RELATIONSHIP* structure whereas the output buffer contains a *CEDEVICE_POWER_STATE* enumeration containing the power state that the device should enter. The device should respond by configuring its hardware to match the requested power state.

Building a Device Driver

Building a device driver is as simple as building a DLL. Although you can use the Platform Builder and its more extensive set of tools, you can easily build stream drivers by using eMbedded Visual C++. All you need to do is create a Windows CE DLL project, export the proper entry points, and write the code. The most frequently made mistake I see is in not declaring the entry points as *extern C* so that the C++ compiler doesn't mangle the exported function names.

Debug Zones

Debug zones allow a programmer or tester to manipulate debug messages from any module, EXE or DLL, in a Windows CE system. Debug zones are typically used by developers who use Platform Builder because debug zones allow developers to access the debug shell that allows them to interactively enable and disable specific groups, or *zones*, of debug messages. Another feature of debug zone messages is that the macros that are used to declare the messages insert the messages only when compiling a debug build of the module. When a release build is made, the macros resolve to 0 and don't insert any space-hogging Unicode strings. The value of debug zones isn't just that developers can use them; it's that all the modules that make up Windows CE have debug builds that are packed full of debug messages that can be enabled.

Using debug zones in applications or DLLs is a fairly straightforward process. First, up to 16 zones can be assigned to group all the debug messages in the module. The zones are declared using the *DEBUGZONE* macro, as in

```
#define ZONE_ERROR      DEBUGZONE(0)
#define ZONE_WARNING    DEBUGZONE(1)
#define ZONE_INIT       DEBUGZONE(2)
```

Then debug messages are inserted in the code. Instead of directly calling *OutputDebugString*, which was the old way of sending strings to a debug port, the messages should be enclosed in a *DEBUGZONE* macro, defined as

```
DEBUGMSG (zone, (printf expression));
```

The zone parameter is one of the 16 zones declared. The *printf expression* can be any *printf* style string plus the parameters. Note the additional parentheses around the *printf* expression. These are needed because *DEBUGMSG* is a macro and requires a fixed number of parameters. The following is an example of using *DEBUGMSG*:

```
DEBUGMSG (ZONE_ERROR, (TEXT("Read failed. rc=%d\r\n"), GetLastError()));
```

In addition to inserting the debug messages, a module must declare a structure named *dpCurSettings* of type *DBGPARAM*, defined as

```
typedef struct _DBGPARAM {
    WCHAR lpszName[32];
    WCHAR rglpszZones[16][32];
    ULONG ulZoneMask;
} DBGPARAM, *LPDBGPARAM;
```

The first field is the debug name of the module. Typically, but not always, this is the name of the file. The second field is an array of strings. Each string identifies a particular zone. These names can be queried by the system to tell the programmer what zones are in a module. The final field, *ulZoneMask*, is a bitmask that sets the zones that are enabled by default. Although this field is a 32-bit value, only the first 16 bits are used.

The only action a module must take at run time to enable debug zones is to initialize the zones with the following macro:

```
DEBUGREGISTER(HANDLE hInstance);
```

The only parameter is the instance handle of the EXE or DLL. Typically this call is made early in WinMain for applications and in the process attach call to *LibMain* for DLLs. The GenDriver example shown in Listing 22-1 demonstrates the use of debug zones.

Unfortunately for application developers, the debug messages produced by debug zones are sent to the debug port, which is generally not available on shipping systems. Some systems, however, do allow the primary serial port on the system to be redirected so that it's used as a debug port, instead of as COM1. Because each OEM will have a different method of enabling this redirection, you will need to contact the specific OEM for information on how to redirect the serial port. Nonetheless, debug zones are a powerful tool for debugging Windows CE systems.

The Generic Driver Example

The following example, GenDriver, is a simple stream driver. Although it doesn't talk to any hardware, it exports the proper 10 entry points and can be loaded by any Windows CE system. To have a system load GenDriver, you can add an entry under [HKEY_LOCAL_MACHINE]\Drivers\Builtin to have the driver loaded when the system boots, or you can write an application that creates the proper driver keys elsewhere and calls *ActivateDevice*.

GenDriver.h

```
//=======================================================================
// Header file
//
// Written for the book Programming Windows CE
// Copyright (C) 2003 Douglas Boling
//=======================================================================


//
// Declare the external entry points here. Use declspec so we don't
// need a .def file. Bracketed with extern C to avoid mangling in C++.
//
#ifdef __cplusplus
extern "C" {
#endif //__cplusplus
__declspec(dllexport) DWORD GEN_Init (DWORD dwContext);
__declspec(dllexport) BOOL  GEN_Deinit (DWORD dwContext);
__declspec(dllexport) DWORD GEN_Open (DWORD dwContext, DWORD dwAccess,
                                      DWORD dwShare);
__declspec(dllexport) BOOL  GEN_Close (DWORD dwOpen);
__declspec(dllexport) DWORD GEN_Read (DWORD dwOpen, LPVOID pBuffer,
                                      DWORD dwCount);
__declspec(dllexport) DWORD GEN_Write (DWORD dwOpen, LPVOID pBuffer,
                                       DWORD dwCount);
__declspec(dllexport) DWORD GEN_Seek (DWORD dwOpen, long lDelta,
                                      WORD wType);
__declspec(dllexport) DWORD GEN_IOControl (DWORD dwOpen, DWORD dwCode,
                                           PBYTE pIn, DWORD dwIn,
                                           PBYTE pOut, DWORD dwOut,
                                           DWORD *pdwBytesWritten);
__declspec(dllexport) void GEN_PowerDown (DWORD dwContext);
__declspec(dllexport) void GEN_PowerUp (DWORD dwContext);
#ifdef __cplusplus
} // extern "C"
#endif //__cplusplus
// Suppress warnings by declaring the undeclared.
#ifndef GetCurrentPermissions
DWORD GetCurrentPermissions(void);
```

Listing 22-1   The GenDriver example

```
DWORD SetProcPermissions (DWORD);
DWORD GetCallerProcess(void);
PVOID MapPtrToProcess (PVOID, DWORD);
#endif //GetCurrentPermissions

DWORD GetConfigData (DWORD);
//
// Driver instance structure
//
typedef struct {
    DWORD dwSize;
    INT nNumOpens;
} DRVCONTEXT, *PDRVCONTEXT;
```

GenDriver.cpp

```
//======================================================================
// GenDriver - Generic stream device driver for Windows CE
//
// Written for the book Programming Windows CE
// Copyright (C) 2003 Douglas Boling
//======================================================================
#include <windows.h>                    // For all that Windows stuff
#include "GenDriver.h"                  // Local program includes

//
// Globals
//
HINSTANCE hInst;                        // DLL instance handle

//
// Debug zone support
//
#ifdef DEBUG
// Used as a prefix string for all debug zone messages.
#define DTAG         TEXT ("GENDrv: ")

// Debug zone constants
#define ZONE_ERROR      DEBUGZONE(0)
#define ZONE_WARNING    DEBUGZONE(1)
#define ZONE_FUNC       DEBUGZONE(2)
#define ZONE_INIT       DEBUGZONE(3)
#define ZONE_DRVCALLS   DEBUGZONE(4)
#define ZONE_EXENTRY   (ZONE_FUNC | ZONE_DRVCALLS)
```

(continued)

Listing 22-1 *(continued)*

```
// Debug zone structure
DBGPARAM dpCurSettings = {
    TEXT("GenDriver"), {
    TEXT("Errors"),TEXT("Warnings"),TEXT("Functions"),
    TEXT("Init"),TEXT("Driver Calls"),TEXT("Undefined"),
    TEXT("Undefined"),TEXT("Undefined"), TEXT("Undefined"),
    TEXT("Undefined"),TEXT("Undefined"),TEXT("Undefined"),
    TEXT("Undefined"),TEXT("Undefined"),TEXT("Undefined"),
    TEXT("Undefined") },
    0x0003
};
#endif //DEBUG


//=======================================================================
// DllMain - DLL initialization entry point
//
BOOL WINAPI DllMain (HANDLE hinstDLL, DWORD dwReason,
                     LPVOID lpvReserved) {
    hInst = (HINSTANCE)hinstDLL;

    switch (dwReason) {
        case DLL_PROCESS_ATTACH:
            DEBUGREGISTER(hInst);
            // Improve performance by passing on thread attach calls
            DisableThreadLibraryCalls (hInst);
        break;

        case DLL_PROCESS_DETACH:
            DEBUGMSG(ZONE_INIT, (DTAG TEXT("DLL_PROCESS_DETACH\r\n")));
            break;
    }
    return TRUE;
}
//=======================================================================
// GEN_Init - Driver initialization function
//
#if (_WIN32_WCE_ > 300)
DWORD GEN_Init (DWORD dwContext, LPCVOID lpvBusContext) {
#else
DWORD GEN_Init (DWORD dwContext) {
#endif
    PDRVCONTEXT pDrv;

    DEBUGMSG (ZONE_INIT | ZONE_EXENTRY,
              (DTAG TEXT("GEN_Init++ dwContex:%x\r\n"), dwContext));

    // Allocate a device instance structure.
    pDrv = (PDRVCONTEXT)LocalAlloc (LPTR, sizeof (DRVCONTEXT));
```

```
      if (pDrv) {
         // Initialize structure.
         memset ((PBYTE) pDrv, 0, sizeof (DRVCONTEXT));
         pDrv->dwSize = sizeof (DRVCONTEXT);

         // Read registry to determine the size of the disk.
         GetConfigData (dwContext);
      } else
         DEBUGMSG (ZONE_INIT | ZONE_ERROR,
                   (DTAG TEXT("GEN_Init failure. Out of memory\r\n")));
      DEBUGMSG (ZONE_FUNC, (DTAG TEXT("GEN_Init-- pDrv: %x\r\n"), pDrv));
      return (DWORD)pDrv;
}
//======================================================================
// GEN_Deinit - Driver de-initialization function
//
BOOL GEN_Deinit (DWORD dwContext) {
      PDRVCONTEXT pDrv = (PDRVCONTEXT) dwContext;

      DEBUGMSG (ZONE_EXENTRY,
                (DTAG TEXT("GEN_Deinit++ dwContex:%x\r\n"), dwContext));

      if (pDrv && (pDrv->dwSize == sizeof (DRVCONTEXT))) {

         // Free the driver state buffer.
         LocalFree ((PBYTE)pDrv);
      }
      DEBUGMSG (ZONE_FUNC, (DTAG TEXT("GEN_Deinit--\r\n")));
      return TRUE;
}
//======================================================================
// GEN_Open - Called when driver opened
//
DWORD GEN_Open (DWORD dwContext, DWORD dwAccess, DWORD dwShare) {
      PDRVCONTEXT pDrv = (PDRVCONTEXT) dwContext;

      DEBUGMSG (ZONE_EXENTRY,
                (DTAG TEXT("GEN_Open++ dwContext: %x\r\n"), dwContext));

      // Verify that the context handle is valid.
      if (pDrv && (pDrv->dwSize != sizeof (DRVCONTEXT))) {
         DEBUGMSG (ZONE_ERROR, (DTAG TEXT("GEN_Open failed\r\n")));
         return 0;
      }
      // Count the number of opens.
      InterlockedIncrement ((long *)&pDrv->nNumOpens);
      DEBUGMSG (ZONE_FUNC, (DTAG TEXT("GEN_Open--\r\n")));
      return (DWORD)pDrv;
```

(continued)

Listing 22-1   *(continued)*

```
}
//===================================================================
// GEN_Close - Called when driver closed
//
BOOL GEN_Close (DWORD dwOpen) {
    PDRVCONTEXT pDrv = (PDRVCONTEXT) dwOpen;

    DEBUGMSG (ZONE_EXENTRY,
               (DTAG TEXT("GEN_Close++ dwOpen: %x\r\n"), dwOpen));

    if (pDrv && (pDrv->dwSize != sizeof (DRVCONTEXT))) {
        DEBUGMSG (ZONE_FUNC | ZONE_ERROR,
                   (DTAG TEXT("GEN_Close failed\r\n")));
        return 0;
    }
    if (pDrv->nNumOpens)
        pDrv->nNumOpens--;

    DEBUGMSG (ZONE_FUNC, (DTAG TEXT("GEN_Close--\r\n")));
    return TRUE;
}
//===================================================================
// GEN_Read - Called when driver read
//
DWORD GEN_Read (DWORD dwOpen, LPVOID pBuffer, DWORD dwCount) {
    DWORD dwBytesRead = 0;
    DEBUGMSG (ZONE_EXENTRY,
               (DTAG TEXT("GEN_Read++ dwOpen: %x\r\n"), dwOpen));

    DEBUGMSG (ZONE_FUNC, (DTAG TEXT("GEN_Read--\r\n")));
    return dwBytesRead;
}
//===================================================================
// GEN_Write - Called when driver written
//
DWORD GEN_Write (DWORD dwOpen, LPVOID pBuffer, DWORD dwCount) {
    DWORD dwBytesWritten = 0;
    DEBUGMSG (ZONE_EXENTRY,
               (DTAG TEXT("GEN_Write++ dwOpen: %x\r\n"), dwOpen));

    DEBUGMSG (ZONE_FUNC, (DTAG TEXT("GEN_Write--\r\n")));
    return dwBytesWritten;
}
//===================================================================
// GEN_Seek - Called when SetFilePtr called
//
DWORD GEN_Seek (DWORD dwOpen, long lDelta, WORD wType) {
    DEBUGMSG (ZONE_EXENTRY,(DTAG TEXT("GEN_Seek++ dwOpen:%x %d %d\r\n"),
```

```
                        dwOpen, lDelta, wType));

    DEBUGMSG (ZONE_EXENTRY, (DTAG TEXT("GEN_Seek--\r\n")));
    return 0;
}
//======================================================================
// GEN_IOControl - Called when DeviceIoControl called
//
DWORD GEN_IOControl (DWORD dwOpen, DWORD dwCode, PBYTE pIn, DWORD dwIn,
                     PBYTE pOut, DWORD dwOut, DWORD *pdwBytesWritten) {
    PDRVCONTEXT pState;
    DWORD err = ERROR_INVALID_PARAMETER;

    DEBUGMSG (ZONE_EXENTRY,
              (DTAG TEXT("GEN_IOControl++ dwOpen: %x  dwCode: %x\r\n"),
              dwOpen, dwCode));

    pState = (PDRVCONTEXT) dwOpen;
    switch (dwCode) {
        // Insert IOCTL codes here.

        default:
            DEBUGMSG (ZONE_ERROR,
              (DTAG TEXT("GEN_IOControl: unknown code %x\r\n"), dwCode));
            return FALSE;
    }
    SetLastError (err);
    DEBUGMSG (ZONE_FUNC, (DTAG TEXT("GEN_IOControl--\r\n")));
    return TRUE;
}
//======================================================================
// GEN_PowerDown - Called when system suspends
//
// NOTE: No kernel calls, including debug messages, can be made from
// this call.
//
void GEN_PowerDown (DWORD dwContext) {
    return;
}
//======================================================================
// GEN_PowerUp - Called when resumes
//
// NOTE: No kernel calls, including debug messages, can be made from
// this call.
//
void GEN_PowerUp (DWORD dwContext) {
    return;
}
```

(continued)

Listing 22-1   *(continued)*

```
//---------------------------------------------------------------------
// GetConfigData - Get the configuration data from the registry.
//
DWORD GetConfigData (DWORD dwContext) {
    int nLen, rc;
    DWORD dwLen, dwType, dwSize = 0;
    HKEY hKey;
    TCHAR szKeyName[256], szPrefix[8];

    DEBUGMSG (ZONE_FUNC, (DTAG TEXT("GetConfigData++\r\n")));
    nLen = 0;
    // If ptr < 65K, it's a value, not a pointer.
    if (dwContext < 0x10000) {
        return -1;
    } else {
        __try {
            nLen = lstrlen ((LPTSTR)dwContext);
        }
        __except (EXCEPTION_EXECUTE_HANDLER) {
            nLen = 0;
        }
    }
    if (!nLen) {
        DEBUGMSG (ZONE_ERROR, (DTAG TEXT("dwContext not a ptr\r\n")));
        return -2;
    }
    // Open the Active key for the driver.
    rc = RegOpenKeyEx(HKEY_LOCAL_MACHINE,(LPTSTR)dwContext,0, 0, &hKey);

    if (rc == ERROR_SUCCESS) {
        // Read the key value.
        dwLen = sizeof(szKeyName);
        rc = RegQueryValueEx (hKey, TEXT("Key"), NULL, &dwType,
                              (PBYTE)szKeyName, &dwLen);

        RegCloseKey(hKey);
        if (rc == ERROR_SUCCESS)
            rc = RegOpenKeyEx (HKEY_LOCAL_MACHINE, (LPTSTR)
                               dwContext, 0, 0, &hKey);
        if (rc == ERROR_SUCCESS) {
            // This driver doesn't need any data from the key, so as
            // an example, it just reads the Prefix value, which
            // identifies the three-char prefix (GEN) of this driver.
            dwLen = sizeof (szPrefix);
            rc = RegQueryValueEx (hKey, TEXT("Prefix"), NULL,
                                  &dwType, (PBYTE)szPrefix, &dwLen);
            RegCloseKey(hKey);
        } else
```

```
            DEBUGMSG (ZONE_ERROR, (TEXT("Error opening key\r\n")));
    } else
        DEBUGMSG (ZONE_ERROR, (TEXT("Error opening Active key\r\n")));

    DEBUGMSG (ZONE_FUNC, (DTAG TEXT("GetConfigData--\r\n")));
    return 0;
}
```

The majority of the lines of code in GenDriver are *DEBUGZONE* macros. The messages are handy for learning exactly when and how the different entry points of the driver are called. The *GetConfigData* routine at the end of the code shows how to test the *Context* value to determine whether the value passed to the *Init* function was a pointer to a string or merely a number.

The preceding driver template is a good starting point for any stream driver you want to write. Simply change the three-character name GEN to whatever your driver is named and go from there.

Asynchronous Driver I/O

When I described the file system functions in Chapter 8, I mentioned that the *ReadFile* and *WriteFile* functions don't support asynchronous I/O. This limitation means that the Windows CE implementation of the file system API doesn't support having the operating system provide data back to the application after the function returns. For file reads and writes, an application can get around this problem simply by spawning a separate thread to perform the read or write and then signaling the primary thread when the data transfer is complete. At times, however, it might be better to have a device driver perform the asynchronous data transfer and notify the calling application or driver when the transfer is complete. This tactic simplifies the application and allows the driver to tune the secondary thread to provide the best performance when reading or writing the data. The question is, how can a device driver perform asynchronous I/O if the operating system doesn't? The answer is simple: just because Windows CE doesn't support a feature doesn't mean you can't implement it yourself. Before I go into more detail about asynchronous drivers, I need to provide some background information.

One question you might have asked when I was talking about mapping pointers was how a device driver can write to a buffer that's in another application's slot. And if a driver can access another slot, can any application write into any slot? The answers to both questions lie in how Windows CE memory protection works.

As I mentioned earlier, each application is assigned a slot when it launches. While a thread in the application is running, its slot is cloned into slot 0. While the application is running, it can access slot 0 and its own slot. Attempting to read or write data in the other slots will result in a memory protection exception.[1] This way, applications are protected from one another.

When an application calls an operating system function, the part of the operating system that processes the function, NK, FileSys, Device, or GWES, is granted access to the calling process's slot for the duration of the function. This is also true for calls to device drivers. While the device driver is processing the call—whether it's *Read*, *Write*, or *IOControl*—the driver can write to the buffers located in the calling application's slot. As soon as the function is complete, the driver loses access to the calling application's slot.

If we apply this knowledge to asynchronous I/O, we see that the driver has a problem. Although it can map a pointer back to the calling application's slot, it doesn't have access rights to that slot after the call to the driver completes.

However, one Windows CE–specific function allows an application to modify the slot protection scheme. This function is *SetProcPermissions* and is prototyped as

```
DWORD SetProcPermissions (DWORD newperms);
```

The single parameter is a bitmask, one bit for each slot. When a bit is set to 1, the application will have access to the corresponding slot. For example, to enable access to slot 1, set the least significant bit to 1. A function prototype for *SetProcPermissions* isn't defined in the SDK include files, only in the Platform Builder. The description of *SetProcPermissions* just might make some programmers sit up in their chairs. Yes, this function is essentially the keys to the kingdom. A quick call to *SetProcPermissions* with the *newperms* parameter set to 0xFFFFFFFF enables an application to write to every slot in the system. One caveat: just because you can doesn't mean you should.

Memory protection exists for the benefit of programmers. By throwing exceptions when an errant memory access is made, the operating system catches the mistake the programmer made. So although applications can disable the Windows CE slot protection scheme, there is no reason they should, and plenty of reasons they shouldn't. Instead, applications should query the permissions they are currently granted and, if necessary, modify them for the situation. To query an application's permissions, use the function

```
DWORD GetCurrentPermissions (void);
```

---

1. This is not technically true because the operating system might enable a thread to access slots containing operating system processes as needed.

The function returns the slot permission bitmap for the current application. If this function is called from within a driver, the permission mask will include the slot containing the Device Manager and the calling process's slot. Remember, during the life of the call, the driver has access to the caller's slot.

At this point, we have all the tools necessary for asynchronous I/O. We can create a secondary thread; we learned how to do that in Chapter 10. We can map pointers back to the calling process's slot. Finally, we can query the current permissions and set them when necessary. However, you should consider a few more items when implementing asynchronous I/O.

First, the rights to access other slots that can be changed with *SetProcPermissions* are thread-specific, not process-specific, which means that setting the permission mask of one thread in a process doesn't affect the other thread's permissions. So the secondary thread must call *SetProcPermissions*, not the thread processing the call to the driver.

Second, any mapping of pointers must take place in the call to the driver, not in the secondary thread because the function *GetCallerProcess*, which is used in conjunction with *MapPtrToProcess*, needs a calling process. The secondary thread wasn't called; it was started—so calling *GetCallerProcess* in the secondary thread will fail.

Finally, the secondary thread will need some way to signal the calling process that the I/O is complete. You can achieve this by means as simple as the driver posting a message to a window owned by the calling process or by signaling an event. The following code implements an IOCTL command that uses asynchronous I/O to fill a buffer:

```
// Structure passed by application to driver
typedef struct {
    PBYTE pBuff;          // Pointer to destination buffer
    int nSize;            // Size of buffer
    HWND hWnd;            // Window handle to send message when done
    UINT wMsg;            // Message to send to app when done
} ASYNCSTRUCT, *PASYNCSTRUCT;

// Structure passed from primary driver thread to secondary thread
typedef struct {
    ASYNCSTRUCT asy;          // Copy of caller's data
    DWORD dwCurrPermissions; // Calling thread's permissions
} THREADASYNCSTRUCT, *PTHREADASYNCSTRUCT;

// SetProcPermissions is defined only in the Platform Builder include files.
#ifndef SetProcPermissions
DWORD SetProcPermissions (DWORD);
#endif //SetProcPermissions
```

(continued)

```
//========================================================================
// AsyncThread - Secondary thread that performs async I/O
//
int AsyncThread (PVOID pArg) {
    DWORD dwOldPerms;
    PTHREADASYNCSTRUCT ptArgs;
    int i, rc = ERROR_SUCCESS;

    if (!pArg) return -1;
    ptArgs = (PTHREADASYNCSTRUCT)pArg;

    // Set thread permissions.
    dwOldPerms = SetProcPermissions (ptArgs->dwCurrPermissions);

    // Write the "data."
    __try {
        for (i = 0; (i < 10) && (i < ptArgs->asy.nSize); i++) {
            *ptArgs->asy.pBuff++ = i;
            Sleep (1000);  // This call makes this loop take a while.
        }
    }
    __except (EXCEPTION_EXECUTE_HANDLER) {
        rc = ERROR_BUFFER_OVERFLOW;
    }
    // We're done; notify calling application.
    if (IsWindow (ptArgs->asy.hWnd))
        PostMessage (ptArgs->asy.hWnd, ptArgs->asy.wMsg, rc, 0);

    // We don't really need to do this since we're terminating, but
    // it's better to set a good example.
    SetProcPermissions (dwOldPerms);

    // Clean up.
    LocalFree ((PVOID)ptArgs);
    return 0;  // Terminate thread by returning.
}
//========================================================================
// IOControl - Driver IOControl entry point
//
DWORD xxx_IOControl (DWORD dwOpen, DWORD dwCode, PBYTE pIn, DWORD dwIn,
                     PBYTE pOut, DWORD dwOut, DWORD *pdwBytesWritten) {
    PDRVCONTEXT pState;

    pState = (PDRVCONTEXT) dwOpen;
    switch (dwCode) {
        case IOCTL_ASYNC:
        {
            PTHREADASYNCSTRUCT ptArgs;
```

```
        PASYNCSTRUCT pAppAsyncIn;
        HANDLE hThread;

        // Validate input parameters.
        if (!pIn || (dwIn < sizeof (ASYNCSTRUCT))) {
            SetLastError(ERROR_INVALID_PARAMETER);
            return FALSE;
        }
        // Cast input buff ptr to struct pointer we can understand.
        pAppAsyncIn = (PASYNCSTRUCT)pIn;

        // Allocate a buffer to pass data to secondary thread.
        ptArgs = (PTHREADASYNCSTRUCT)LocalAlloc (LPTR,
                                    sizeof (THREADASYNCSTRUCT));

        // Copy input structure from application since some applications
        // forget and put this kind of stuff on the stack.
        ptArgs->asy = *pAppAsyncIn;
        ptArgs->dwCurrPermissions = GetCurrentPermissions();

        // Map pointer to app buffer.
        ptArgs->asy.pBuff = MapPtrToProcess (pAppAsyncIn->pBuff,
                                    GetCallerProcess());
        // Create async thread.
        hThread = CreateThread (NULL, 0, AsyncThread,(PVOID)ptArgs,
                            0, 0);
        if (!hThread) {
            SetLastError(ERROR_NOT_ENOUGH_MEMORY); // Catchall error
            LocalFree ((PVOID)ptArgs);
            return FALSE;
        }
        // Always close handles.
        CloseHandle (hThread);
    }
    return TRUE;

default:
        DEBUGMSG (ZONE_ERROR,
                    (DTAG TEXT("GEN_IOControl: unknown code\r\n")));
        return FALSE;
    }
    return TRUE;
}
```

The preceding code contains a driver *IOControl* entry point and a routine *AsyncThread* that executes the secondary thread. When the *IOCTL_ASYNC* command is received, the driver allocates a structure for the data and copies the data passed from the application. The driver then maps the pointer contained in the structure and saves its current permissions mask. The secondary thread is then created by means of a call to *CreateThread*. The *AsyncThread* routine then starts. The routine sets its permissions mask to match the mask that was passed from the driver's primary thread. The data is then written with a *Sleep* statement to kill some time and thereby simulate the time it might take to read data from real hardware. Once the data is written, a message is sent to the window handle passed in the original call. *AsyncThread* then frees the buffer containing the information passed from the primary thread and terminates.

Windows CE provides an IOCTL command to assist drivers that have commands pending within a driver from an application that is being terminated. If an application is a multithreaded application that has an open handle to a driver, Windows CE sends an IOCTL_PSL_NOTIFY command to the driver to inform the driver that the application is terminating. This command allows a driver to clean up any pending operations for the terminating application that might be in progress.

Although most application programmers will never need to know how to implement asynchronous I/O in a driver, understanding the fundamental concepts of this technique is a good foundation for understanding how Windows CE works under the covers. Now that the foundation has been laid with the discussion of device drivers, it's time to look at Windows CE services, which are derived from the basic stream driver architecture.

Services

Before Windows CE .NET 4.0, Windows CE did not have the concept of a service. To make up for the lack of service support, so-called *device drivers* were written, not to interface with hardware, but rather to manage some software interface such as a telnet server. The problem with this design was that these services ran in the same process as most of the other device drivers. If there was a bug in the service code, the service could corrupt a device driver, some of which are critical to the operation of the system.

Starting with Windows CE .NET 4.0, a new component was provided by the operating system, the Services Manager. The Services Manager is quite similar in design to the Device Manager; it loads services when the operating system boots by looking at a list in the registry, the manager can also load services upon request from an application, and finally, it expects the service to be implemented as a DLL with the same 10 external entry points expected of a Windows CE device driver.

In addition to the similarities, the Services Manager has a quite convenient capability beyond the Device Manager. The Services Manager implements a *super service* that monitors upon request connections to TCP/IP ports on the device. Because many of the services implemented for Windows CE are server related, such as a telnet server or Web server, the super service alleviates the need for a number of services to create a thread and open a socket just to monitor a port. Instead, the super service does this and notifies the service that has requested monitoring when the port is connected.

Service Architecture

The architecture of a Windows CE service belies the history of using device drivers as service providers under Windows CE. A Windows CE service is a DLL that is constructed almost identically to a stream device driver. Like a stream driver, a Windows CE service exports the same 10 entry points, from *xxx_Init* to *xxx_PowerDown*. Also, like a stream driver, a service has a three-character prefix that, along with an instance number, is used to identify the loaded service.

One convenient characteristic of a service is that the Services Manager doesn't require that all 10 stream functions be exported from a service. If the service isn't intended to be exposed as an interface by the standard stream functions, the service only needs to export *xxx_Init*, *xxx_Deinit*, and *xxx_IOControl*. Although this arrangement generally just saves writing and exporting a handful of null functions, it's still a handy feature.

To aid in debugging, or in the rare cases where a service needs to be isolated in its own process space, a service can be loaded in a standalone copy of the Services Manager. When run in an isolated process, the service isn't enumerated with the other services. Also, the service can't be opened by other applications using the File API. It's preferable to avoid using isolated services, not just because of the limited functionality, but also because the isolated copy of the Services Manager uses an addition process slot.

The Life of a Service

Services are always in one of two basic states, started or stopped, or transitioning between these two states. When stopped, the service should not respond to net connections or perform any local processing that the service was designed to support. The service can be programmatically started and stopped by applications with an IOCTL command.

Services can be loaded on reset or manually loaded by an application. To load a service automatically on reset, add a registry key under the key [HKEY_LOCAL_MACHINE]\Services. The name of the key created is used by the Services Manager to identify the service. The contents of the key are quite similar to the contents of a device driver key. The same values used in device keys—*DLL*, *Prefix*, *Context*, and so forth—are used in the *Services* key. Figure 22-4 shows the registry key for the OBEX service.

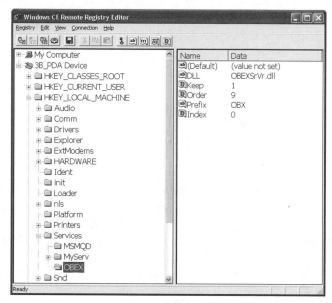

Figure 22-4   The registry key for the OBEX service

There are a few differences between a registry entry for a device and a service. The service entry must contain the *Index* value that is optional for a device. Also, the *Context* value in the registry has a defined use. It's used to determine what state the service is in when it loads. *Context* can be one of the following values:

- **0**   Indicates that the service should auto-start itself.

- **1**   Indicates that the service is initially stopped. If a *Super Service* key is present, the super service is automatically started.

- **2**   Indicates that the service will be loaded in a standalone copy of the Services Manager.

These values correspond to the values *SERVICE_INIT_STARTED*, *SERVICE_INIT_STOPPED*, and *SERVICE_INIT_STANDALONE* discussed in the service *Init* routine on page 1088.

However the service is loaded, the Services Manager will load the DLL implementing the service into its process space. Using the information gathered from the registry or the *RegisterService* function, the Services Manager uses the prefix to generate the names of the entry points to the service and uses *Get-ProcAddress* to get their addresses. Aside from the required *Init*, *Deinit*, and *IOControl* entry points, pointers to any of the other entry points that aren't found are simply redirected to a dummy routine that returns the error code *ERROR_NOT_SUPPORTED*.

Once the DLL is loaded, the service's *Init* function is called. The single parameter is the *Context* value either read from the registry or passed in the *RegisterService* function. If the service returns a nonzero value, the *Init* call is deemed to be a success and the service is then added to the chain of active services.

The service can be started and stopped by sending it IOCTL commands using either *ServiceIoControl*, or, if the service supports the full stream function set, *DeviceIoControl*. If the service receives a start command and it's currently stopped, it should start any processing that is the task of the service. If running, the service can be stopped by another IOCTL command. A stopped service isn't unloaded. Instead, it waits in memory until restarted or unloaded. Aside from stopping super service support, the Services Manager doesn't prevent a stopped service from performing any action. It's up to the service to heed the start and stop commands.

When the service is requested to be unloaded, the Services Manager sends an IOCTL command to the service asking if it can be unloaded. If the service refuses, the service remains in memory and the unload command fails. Otherwise, the *Deinit* function of the service is called, and the DLL is unloaded from the process space of the Services Manager.

Application Control of a Service

Applications can load, unload, and communicate to a service using a series of dedicated functions. An application can load a service using one of two calls. If the service has a registry key defined, the function *ActivateService* function can be used. *ActivateService* is defined as

```
HANDLE ActivateService (LPCWSTR lpszDevKey, DWORD dwClientInfo);
```

The first parameter is the name of the registry key that provides load information on the service. The registry key must be located under [HKEY_LOCAL_MACHINE]\Services. The format of the key must be the same as mentioned earlier for service registry keys. The second parameter is reserved and must be set to zero.

An application can also load a service with the function *RegisterService*. Like *RegisterDevice*, *RegisterService* doesn't require a registry entry for the service to load. The function is defined as

```
HANDLE RegisterService (LPCWSTR lpszType, DWORD dwIndex, LPCWSTR lpszLib,
                        DWORD dwInfo);
```

The parameters are quite similar to *RegisterDevice*; the prefix string of the service is passed in the first parameter, thc index value in the second, the name of the DLL implementing the service in the third, and the context value, passed to the *Init* function, in the fourth parameter.

The return value for *RegisterService* as well as *ActivateService* is the handle to the instance of the service. This value can be used later to send IOCTL commands to the service or unload the service.

The handle to a service can also be obtained by calling *GetServiceHandle* defined as

```
HANDLE GetServiceHandle (LPWSTR szPrefix, LPWSTR szDllName,
                         DWORD *pdwDllBuf);
```

The first parameter, *szPrefix*, is somewhat misnamed because the parameter should be set to the complete name of the service, which is the prefix plus the instance number, as in *SRV0:*, not just *SRV*. The *szDllName* string receives the name of the DLL that implements the service. (If you don't need to know the name of the DLL implementing the service, *szDllName* can be *NULL*.) The *pdwDllBuf* parameter should point to a *DWORD* that initially contains the size of the *szDllName* buffer, in bytes.

The service handle can be used to send IOCTL commands to a service using the function *ServiceIoControl*. Its definition is identical to the definition of *DeviceIoControl*, but it's listed here for convenience.

```
BOOL ServiceIoControl (HANDLE hService, DWORD dwIoControlCode, LPVOID lpInBuf,
                       DWORD nInBufSize, LPVOID lpOutBuf, DWORD nOutBufSize,
                       LPDWORD lpBytesReturned, LPOVERLAPPED lpOverlapped);
```

Both *ServiceIoControl* and *DeviceIoControl* can be used to send IOCTL commands to services. The difference is in the definition of the first parameter of both calls, the handle to the service. In *ServiceIoControl*, the handle is the service handle returned by *ActivateService*, *RegisterService*, or *GetServiceHandle*. For *DeviceIoControl*, the handle must be a valid file handle returned by *CreateFile*. If the service doesn't implement the functions, *Open*, *CreateFile* will fail leaving *ServiceIoControl* as the only method of sending IOCTL commands. Also, without a valid file handle, the other standard file functions, *ReadFile* and *WriteFile*, cannot be used.

A list of the currently running services can be obtained with the *EnumServices* function. One limitation of this function is that services running in standalone copies of the Services Manager are not enumerated. *EnumServices* is defined as

```
BOOL EnumServices (PBYTE pBuffer, DWORD *pdwServiceEntries,
                   DWORD *pdwBufferLen);
```

The *pBuffer* parameter points to a buffer that will be filled with an array of *ServiceEnumInfo* structures combined with a series of strings containing the names of the DLLs implementing the services. The function places one *ServiceEnumInfo* structure for each service managed by the Services Manager. The *pdwServiceEntries* parameter points to a *DWORD* that will be filled with the number of *ServiceEnumInfo* structures placed in the buffer by the function. The *pdwBufferLen* parameter points to a *DWORD* that should be initialized with the size of the buffer pointed to by *pBuffer*. When the function returns, the value is set to the number of bytes placed in the buffer.

The *ServiceEnumInfo* structure is defined as

```
typedef struct_ServiceEnumInfo {
    WCHAR szPrefix[6];
    WCHAR szDllName;
    HANDLE hServiceHandle;
    DWORD dwServiceState;
} ServiceEnumInfo;
```

Each instance of the structure describes one service. The somewhat misnamed *szPrefix* field contains the complete name of the service, as in *SRVO:*, which is a combination of the three-character service prefix along with its instance number and a trailing colon. The *szDllName* field points to a string naming the DLL implementing the service. The *hServiceHandle* field contains the handle of the service, whereas the *dwServiceState* field contains the current state, running, stopped, and so forth, of the service.

A service can be unloaded with the function *DeregisterService* defined as

```
BOOL DeregisterService (HANDLE hDevice);
```

The only parameter is the handle to the service. The Services Manager will first ask the service if it can be unloaded. If the service assents, the service will be unloaded; otherwise, the function will fail.

The Service DLL Entry Points

Because the architecture of the services is so similar to a device driver, I'm only going to discuss the differences between the service and the driver. The first difference is in how the service is initialized, so let's look at the *Init* function.

xxx_Init

The *Init* function follows the legacy *Init* prototype as in

```
DWORD xxx_Init (DWORD dwData);
```

The only parameter is a flag indicating the initial state of the service. The parameter can contain one of the following flags: *SERVICE_INIT_STARTED* indicates the service should provide its own initialization to start the service, *SERVICE_INIT_STOPPED* indicates that the service is currently stopped but may be started by the super service, and *SERVICE_INIT_STANDALONE* indicates that the service has been loaded in a standalone copy of the Services Manager.

Like a device driver, a service should perform any necessary initialization during the call to the *Init* function. If an error is discovered, the *Init* function should return a zero indicating that the service should fail to load. The Services Manager will then unload the DLL implementing the service. The Services Manager interprets any nonzero value as a successful initialization. Also, as with a driver, the service isn't really a service until the *Init* function returns. This means that the *Init* function can't make any call that expects the service to be up and running.

xxx_Deinit

The *Deinit* function is called when the service is unloaded. The prototype of *Deinit* shown here matches the device driver *Deinit* function.

```
DWORD xxx_Deinit (DWORD dwContext);
```

The only parameter is the value that was returned from the *Init* function.

xxx_IOControl

The *IOControl* function is much more structured than the similarly named counterpart in a device driver. Instead of being a generic call that the driver can use as it pleases, in a service the *IOControl* call must support a series of commands used both by the Services Manager and by applications communicating with the service.

The prototype of the *IOControl* entry point is shown here.

```
DWORD xxx_IOControl (DWORD dwData, DWORD dwCode, PBYTE pBufIn, DWORD dwLenIn,
                     PBYTE pBufOut, DWORD dwLenOut, PDWORD pdwActualOut);
```

The parameters are the same as the ones used in *xxx_IOControl* for the device driver. The *dwData* parameter can either contain the value returned by the service's *Open* function or the value returned by the *Init* function. The service must be written to accept the value returned by *Init* or the values returned by both *Init* and *Open* if it implements an *Open* function. Because there is an extensive list of commands, they are discussed individually in the following section.

Other Entry Points

The other entry points to the driver, *Open, Close, Read, Write, Seek, PowerUp,* and *PowerDown,* are optional. However, if the service doesn't export at least *Open* and *Close,* applications will not be able to open the service to send it *IOCTL* commands through *DeviceIoControl.* The application could still use *ServiceIoControl* using the handle returned by *GetServiceHandle*

The Service IOCTL Commands

A Windows CE service must field a series of IOCTL commands sent through the *IOControl* function. These commands can be grouped into a series of categories such as commands used to control the service, those used to query the state of the service, those commands used to help debug the service and those commands used for super service support.

For each of the following commands, the service should return *TRUE* if the command was successful and *FALSE* if an error occurred. Extended error information should be sent by calling *SetLastError* before returning.

IOCTL_SERVICE_START

The first command, *IOCTL_SERVICE_START,* is sent to the service to start it. This command isn't sent by the system when the service is loaded. Instead, it's only sent by an application that wants to start a stopped service. If not already running, the service should make any connections or perform any initialization necessary to provide the service for which it was designed.

If the service has registry entries that have the super service automatically start port monitoring, the super service will start and bind to the specified ports if this IOCTL command returns a nonzero value.

IOCTL_SERVICE_STOP

The *IOCTL_SERVICE_STOP* command is sent by applications to stop a currently running service. The service won't be unloaded from memory just because it was stopped.

If the service has a super service running and the registry entry for the service is configured to auto-start a super service, the super service will be shut down if the service returns a nonzero value from this command.

IOCTL_SERVICE_REFRESH

The *IOCTL_SERVICE_REFRESH* command is sent by an application or the Services Manager to tell the service to reread its configuration data from the registry. Any changes in the configuration read should immediately be reflected in the service.

IOCTL_SERVICE_INSTALL

This optional command is sent to have the service modify the registry to have the service automatically started on reset. This command is similar in action to the *DllRegisterServer* function of a COM in-proc server. Although optional, the command is convenient to have because any installation program for the service will not have to have knowledge of the registry entries required by the service. The registry entries needed for auto-load are described later in the "Super Service" section.

IOCTL_SERVICE_UNINSTALL

The complement to the *IOCTL_SERVICE_INSTALL* command, also optional, is the *IOCTL_SERVICE_UNINSTALL* command, which removes the registry entries that cause the driver to load on boot. An install/remove application can use this command to have a service remove its own registry entries so that the application need not enumerate the registry to find the installation entries.

This completes the list of IOCTL commands sent by applications; now let's look at the queries that are sent by both applications and the Services Manager to query the state of the service.

IOCTL_SERVICE_STATUS

The *IOCTL_SERVICE_STATUS* command is sent to query the state of the service. The state is returned in the output buffer pointed to by the *pOut* parameter of the *IOControl* call. The service should verify that *pOut* is nonzero and that *dwOut* indicates the buffer is large enough to hold a *DWORD*.

The service state can be one of the following, rather self-explanatory, values.

- *SERVICE_STATE_OFF*

- *SERVICE_STATE_ON*

- *SERVICE_STATE_STARTING_UP*

- *SERVICE_STATE_SHUTTING_DOWN*

- *SERVICE_STATE_UNLOADING*

- *SERVICE_STATE_UNINITIALIZED*

- *SERVICE_STATE_UNKNOWN*

IOCTL_SERVICE_QUERY_CAN_DEINIT

This command is sent by the Services Manager to ask the service whether it can be unloaded. This command is typically sent in response to an application calling *DeregisterService*. If the service can be unloaded, it should place a nonzero value in the first *DWORD* of the output buffer. If the service can't be unloaded, the *DWORD* should be set to zero. The service should verify that the output buffer exists and is large enough to hold the *DWORD* before writing the value.

If the service can always uninstall, it doesn't have to respond to this command. If this command returns *FALSE*, which is the default response to any unhandled command, the Services Manager assumes that the service can be removed.

IOCTL_SERVICE_CONSOLE

This optional command is sent to have the service display a service console. A service does not have to implement this command, but it can be handy in some situations.

The command is sent with a string in the input buffer. If the string is "On", or if the input buffer pointer is *NULL*, the service should display a service console. If the input buffer contains the string "Off", the service should remove the service console.

IOCTL_SERVICE_CONTROL

This command is basically the IOCTL of the IOCTL commands. That is, it's a generic command that can be used by the applications to communicate custom commands to the service. The format of the input and output buffers is defined by the service-defined command.

IOCTL_SERVICE_DEBUG

This command is sent to set the debug zone bitmask for the service. The first *DWORD* of the input buffer contains the new state for the zone bitmap. The service should verify that the input buffer exists and is at least a *DWORD* in size.

Because the debug zone structure *dpCurrParams* is typically only defined for debug builds of the service, the code fielding this command is typically couched in an *#ifdef* block to prevent it from being compiled in a nondebug build.

There are examples of where this command has been extended to perform debug duties beyond the settings of the zone mask. To extend the functionality, the service can use the size of the input buffer, specified in *dwIn*, to determine the meaning of the input buffer data. To be compatible, the service should default to setting the debug zone mask if *dwIn* is set to the size of a *DWORD*.

IOCTL_SERVICE_CALLBACK_FUNCTIONS

This command, introduced in Windows CE .NET 4.2, is used if the service is loaded with a standalone copy of the Services Manager. The input buffer points to a *ServicesExeCallbackFunctions* structure, defined as

```
typedef struct _ServicesExeCallbackFunctions {
    PFN_SERVICE_SHUTDOWN pfnServiceShutdown;
} ServicesExeCallbackFunctions;
```

The only field in this structure is a pointer to a callback routine, in the Services Manager, that can be called to control the standalone copy of the Services Manager. The structure currently provides one field that points to a function that will shut down the standalone Services Manager.

IOCTL_SERVICE_SUPPORTED_OPTIONS

This command, supported in Windows CE .NET 4.2 and later, queries the currently supported options of the service. The option flags are returned in a *DWORD* in the output buffer.

Super Service

The super service provides all services with a convenient method for monitoring TCP/IP ports without having to have customized code to monitor the port inside the service. The super service can either work automatically, if the proper registry settings are in place for the service, or manually through a series of function calls. It's more convenient to use the registry method for configuring the super service, so I will cover that method first.

If the service wants the super service to start automatically when the service is loaded, a subkey, named *Accept*, must be present under the service's key. Under the *Accept* key, there should be one or more subkeys each providing the IP address of port to monitor. The Services Manager doesn't use the name of the subkey under the *Accept* key, although the key is traditionally named TCP-*xxx*, where *xxx* is the port number to be monitored. Each subkey should contain a binary value named *SockAddr*. The data in *SockAddr* should comprise bytes that make up a *SOCKADDR* structure that describes the port being monitored. The subkey can optionally contain a *Protocol* value that specifies the protocol for the socket. If this value isn't present, the protocol value is assumed to be zero. The following code initializes a *SOCKADDR* structure and then writes it to the registry.

```
int AddRegSuperServ (HKEY hKey, WORD wPort, DWORD dwProtocol) {
    SOCKADDR_IN sa;
    HKEY hSubKey;
    TCHAR szKeyName[128];
```

```
DWORD dw;
int rc;

memset (&sa, 0, sizeof (sa));
sa.sin_family = AF_INET;
sa.sin_port = htons(wPort);
sa.sin_addr.s_addr = INADDR_ANY;

// Create accept key for this service
wsprintf (szKeyName, TEXT("Accept\\TCP-%d"), wPort);
rc = RegCreateKeyEx (hKey, szKeyName, 0, NULL, 0, NULL,
                     NULL, &hSubKey, &dw);
if (rc == ERROR_SUCCESS)
    rc = RegSetValueEx (hSubKey, TEXT("SockAddr"), 0, REG_BINARY,
                        (PBYTE)&sa, sizeof (sa));
    rc = RegSetValueEx (hSubKey, TEXT("Protocol"), 0, REG_DWORD,
                        (PBYTE)&dwProtocol, sizeof (DWORD));
    return rc;
}
```

As we will soon see, the *ServiceAddPort* function has the capability to create this registry key as well. It's still handy to be able to write the key manually in the case in which the service doesn't want to start the super service when it's writing the key.

In addition to the *Accept* keys, the registry entry for the service must have a *Context* value of 1. If the *Context* value is 0, the super service will not start, nor will it start if the service is loaded in a standalone copy of the Services Manager.

When a service is started either during system startup or with the *Activate-Service* function, the service is loaded, its *Init* function is called, and then, if the *Context* value is 1, the super service queries the service through an IOCTL command to determine whether it wants super service support. If so, the super service enumerates the *Accept* keys and creates sockets to monitor the ports described in the keys. As each socket is opened and bound to the appropriate address, the service is notified, through an IOCTL command, that the socket is being monitored. Then, once all sockets are opened, and if the service is first being loaded, it sends a final IOCTL indicating that all the sockets are listening.

When a connection is made to one of the listening sockets, another IOCTL command is sent to the service along with the socket handle of the connection. The service then must create a new thread to handle the communication with the socket. The IOCTL call must return quickly because the calling thread is necessary for monitoring other ports. After the communication is complete, the service should close the socket handle passed during the connection notification. When the service shuts down, IOCTL commands are sent to the service notifying it that the sockets monitoring the ports have been closed.

Programmatically Controlling the Super Service

It's possible to have super service support without entries in the registry but it's more complicated. In this scheme, the service must tell the super service about each port to be monitored. This can be done with the function *ServiceAddPort*, defined as

```
ServiceAddPort (HANDLE hService, SOCKADDR pSockAddr, INT cbSockAddr,
                INT iProtocol, WCHAR szRegWritePath);
```

The first parameter is the handle to the service, which, ironically, is somewhat difficult for the service to get. The *SOCKADDR* structure should be initialized with the address information for the listening socket. The *iProtocol* value should contain the protocol to be used by the socket. The *szRegWritePath* parameter can optionally specify a registry key name where this information will be written so that the next time the service is started, the super service will start automatically.

The issue with a service getting its own handle is that *GetServiceHandle* requires not just the three-character prefix of the service but also the instance number of the service. If the service was loaded with *RegisterService*, determining the service instance isn't easy. If, however, the service was loaded because of a registry key entry, the instance value is specified in the registry. Of course, if the service was loaded due to a registry entry, it's just as convenient to have the registry key also specify that the super service automatically start.

A specific port can be closed for monitoring by calling the *ServiceClosePort* function. Its prototype is

```
BOOL ServiceClosePort (HANDLE hService, SOCKADDR* pSockAddr, int cbSockAddr,
                       int iProtocol, BOOL fRemoveFromRegistry);
```

The parameters are identical to the *ServiceAddPort* function with the exception of the last parameter, *fRemoveFromRegistry*, which is a Boolean flag that tells the function whether the corresponding registry entry should be removed for the port.

To close all the ports being monitored by a service, *ServiceUnbindPorts* can be used.

```
BOOL ServiceUnbindPorts (HANDLE hService);
```

The only parameter is the handle to the service.

SuperService IOCTLs

Services that use the super service must respond to a series of additional IOCTL commands. These commands are either queries to check for support or are notifications indicating an event has occurred within the super service.

IOCTL_SERVICE_REGISTER_SOCKADDR

This command is sent at least twice during the initialization of the super service. The super service first sends this command to query whether the service will accept super service support. In this case, the input buffer pointer, *pIn*, is *NULL*.

The super service next sends this command again, once for each port the service is monitoring to verify the socket has been created to monitor the requested address. During these subsequent calls to verify the individual addresses, *pIn* points to a *SOCKADDR* structure that describes the socket address being monitored.

IOCTL_SERVICE_STARTED

This notification is sent when the super service completes its initialization after the service is first loaded. When this notification has been received, the service can assume that the super service is listening on all the ports requested. This notification isn't sent when the service is restarted after it has been stopped.

IOCTL_SERVICE_DEREGISTER_SOCKADDR

This notification is sent after the super service has closed the socket monitoring a given socket address. The *pIn* parameter points to the *SOCKADDR* structure that describes the socket address. This notification can be sent if the service is being stopped or because the service is being unloaded.

IOCTL_SERVICE_CONNECTION

The *IOCTL_SERVICE_CONNECTION* notification is sent when another application connects to the socket address being monitored by the super service. The input parameter *pIn* points to a socket handle for the connected socket. It's the responsibility of the service to spawn a thread to handle communication on this socket. The service must also close the socket when communication is complete.

IOCTL_SERVICE_NOTIFY_ADDR_CHANGE

For systems running Windows CE .NET 4.1 or later, this notification is sent if the system's IP address changes. The input buffer is filled with an *IP_ADAPTER_INFO* structure defined as

```
typedef struct _IP_ADAPTER_INFO {
    struct _IP_ADAPTER_INFO* Next;
```

(continued)

```
    DWORD ComboIndex;
    Char AdapterName[MAX_ADAPTER_NAME_LENGTH + 4];
    char Description[MAX_ADAPTER_DESCRIPTION_LENGTH + 4];
    UINT AddressLength;
    BYTE Address[MAX_ADAPTER_ADDRESS_LENGTH];
    DWORD Index;
    UINT Type;
    UINT DhcpEnabled;
    PIP_ADDR_STRING CurrentIpAddress;
    IP_ADDR_STRING IpAddressList;
    IP_ADDR_STRING GatewayList;
    IP_ADDR_STRING DhcpServer;
    BOOL HaveWins;
    IP_ADDR_STRING PrimaryWinsServer;
    IP_ADDR_STRING SecondaryWinsServer;
    time_t LeaseObtained;
    time_t LeaseExpires;
} IP_ADAPTER_INFO, *PIP_ADAPTER_INFO;
```

The fairly self-explanatory *IP_ADDRESS_INFO* structure contains everything from the IP address of the system to gateway, Dynamic Host Configuration Protocol (DHCP), and Windows Internet Naming Service (WINS) information.

Services.exe Command Line

In addition to being the Services Manager for the system, the application services.exe also has a command-line interface. For systems with a console, simply type:

```
services help
```

This command produces a list of the available commands. Services can list the current services, start them and stop them, load them and unload them, and even add and remove them from them from the registry.

For systems without console support, services can be launched with an –*f* command-line switch and the name of a file to send the output to, as in

```
services -f Outfile.txt
```

Other command-line parameters include –*d* to send the output to the debug serial port and –*q* to suppress output entirely.

TickSrv Example Service

The TickSrv example demonstrates a service that uses the super service. TickSrv monitors port 1000 on a Windows CE device and, for any application that connects, provides the current tick count and the number of milliseconds the system has been running since it was reset. TickSrv is implemented as a standard Windows CE service. Because there is no reason for a local application to use the service, it doesn't implement the standard stream exports, *Open, Close, Read, Write,* or *Seek.* The source code for TickSrv is shown in Listing 22-2.

TickSrv.h

```
//======================================================================
// Header file
//
// Written for the book Programming Windows CE
// Copyright (C) 2003 Douglas Boling
//======================================================================
#define dim(a)  (sizeof (a)/sizeof(a[0]))
//
// Declare the external entry points here. Use declspec so we don't
// need a .def file. Bracketed with extern C to avoid mangling in C++.
//
#ifdef __cplusplus
extern "C" {
#endif //__cplusplus
__declspec(dllexport) DWORD TCK_Init (DWORD dwContext);
__declspec(dllexport) BOOL  TCK_Deinit (DWORD dwContext);
__declspec(dllexport) DWORD TCK_IOControl (DWORD dwOpen, DWORD dwCode,
                                           PBYTE pIn, DWORD dwIn,
                                           PBYTE pOut, DWORD dwOut,
                                           DWORD *pdwBytesWritten);
__declspec(dllexport) void TCK_PowerDown (DWORD dwContext);
__declspec(dllexport) void TCK_PowerUp (DWORD dwContext);
#ifdef __cplusplus
} // extern "C"
#endif //__cplusplus

// Suppress warnings by declaring the undeclared.
#ifndef GetCurrentPermissions
DWORD GetCurrentPermissions(void);
DWORD SetProcPermissions (DWORD);
DWORD GetCallerProcess(void);
PVOID MapPtrToProcess (PVOID, DWORD);
#endif //GetCurrentPermissions

int RegisterService (void);
int DeregisterService (void);
DWORD WINAPI AcceptThread (PVOID pArg);
```

(continued)

Listing 22-2   The TickSrv example

Listing 22-2   *(continued)*

```
//
// Service state structure
//
typedef struct {
    DWORD dwSize;                     // Size of structure
    CRITICAL_SECTION csData;          // Crit Section protecting this struct
    int servState;                    // Service state
} SRVCONTEXT, *PSRVCONTEXT;
```

TickSrv.cpp

```
//======================================================================
// TickSrv - Simple example service for Windows CE
//
// Written for the book Programming Windows CE
// Copyright (C) 2003 Douglas Boling
//======================================================================
#include <windows.h>                   // For all that Windows stuff
#include <winsock.h>                    // Socket support
#include "service.h"                    // Service includes

#include "TickSrv.h"                    // Local program includes

#define REGNAME     TEXT("TickSrv")    // Reg name under services key
#define PORTNUM     1000               // Port number to monitor

//
// Globals
//
HINSTANCE hInst;                        // DLL instance handle

//
// Debug zone support
//
#ifdef DEBUG
// Used as a prefix string for all debug zone messages.
#define DTAG         TEXT ("TickSrv: ")

// Debug zone constants
#define ZONE_ERROR      DEBUGZONE(0)
#define ZONE_WARNING    DEBUGZONE(1)
#define ZONE_FUNC       DEBUGZONE(2)
#define ZONE_INIT       DEBUGZONE(3)
#define ZONE_DRVCALLS   DEBUGZONE(4)
#define ZONE_IOCTLS     DEBUGZONE(5)
#define ZONE_THREAD     DEBUGZONE(6)
#define ZONE_EXENTRY    (ZONE_FUNC | ZONE_DRVCALLS)
```

```
// Debug zone structure
DBGPARAM dpCurSettings = {
    TEXT("TickSrv"), {
    TEXT("Errors"),TEXT("Warnings"),TEXT("Functions"),
    TEXT("Init"),TEXT("Driver Calls"),TEXT("Undefined"),
    TEXT("IOCtls"),TEXT("Thread"), TEXT("Undefined"),
    TEXT("Undefined"),TEXT("Undefined"),TEXT("Undefined"),
    TEXT("Undefined"),TEXT("Undefined"),TEXT("Undefined"),
    TEXT("Undefined") },
    0x0003
};
#endif //DEBUG


//=====================================================================
// DllMain - DLL initialization entry point
//
BOOL WINAPI DllMain (HANDLE hinstDLL, DWORD dwReason,
                     LPVOID lpvReserved) {
    hInst = (HINSTANCE)hinstDLL;

    switch (dwReason) {
        case DLL_PROCESS_ATTACH:
            DEBUGREGISTER(hInst);
            // Improve performance by passing on thread attach calls
            DisableThreadLibraryCalls (hInst);
        break;

        case DLL_PROCESS_DETACH:
            DEBUGMSG(ZONE_INIT, (DTAG TEXT("DLL_PROCESS_DETACH\r\n")));
            break;
    }
    return TRUE;
}
//=====================================================================
// TCK_Init - Driver initialization function
//
DWORD TCK_Init (DWORD dwContext) {
    PSRVCONTEXT pSrv;

    DEBUGMSG (ZONE_INIT | ZONE_EXENTRY,
             (DTAG TEXT("TCK_Init++ dwContext:%x\r\n"), dwContext));

    // Init WinSock
    WSADATA wsaData;
    WSAStartup(0x101,&wsaData);

    // Allocate a drive instance structure.
    pSrv = (PSRVCONTEXT)LocalAlloc (LPTR, sizeof (SRVCONTEXT));
```

(continued)

Listing 22-2   *(continued)*

```
    if (pSrv) {
        // Initialize structure.
        memset ((PBYTE) pSrv, 0, sizeof (SRVCONTEXT));
        pSrv->dwSize = sizeof (SRVCONTEXT);
        pSrv->servState = SERVICE_STATE_UNKNOWN;
        InitializeCriticalSection (&pSrv->csData);

        switch (dwContext) {
        case SERVICE_INIT_STARTED:
            pSrv->servState = SERVICE_STATE_ON;
            break;

        case SERVICE_INIT_STOPPED:
            pSrv->servState = SERVICE_STATE_OFF;
            break;

        case SERVICE_INIT_STANDALONE:
            break;

        default:
            break;
        }
    } else
        DEBUGMSG (ZONE_INIT | ZONE_ERROR,
                   (DTAG TEXT("TCK_Init failure. Out of memory\r\n")));
    DEBUGMSG (ZONE_FUNC, (DTAG TEXT("TCK_Init-- pSrv: %x\r\n"), pSrv));
    return (DWORD)pSrv;
}
//======================================================================
// TCK_Deinit - Driver de-initialization function
//
BOOL TCK_Deinit (DWORD dwContext) {
    PSRVCONTEXT pSrv = (PSRVCONTEXT) dwContext;

    DEBUGMSG (ZONE_EXENTRY,
               (DTAG TEXT("TCK_Deinit++ dwContex:%x\r\n"), dwContext));

    if (pSrv && (pSrv->dwSize == sizeof (SRVCONTEXT))) {
        // Free the driver state buffer.
        LocalFree ((PBYTE)pSrv);
    }
    DEBUGMSG (ZONE_FUNC, (DTAG TEXT("TCK_Deinit--\r\n")));
    return TRUE;
}
//======================================================================
// TCK_IOControl - Called when DeviceIOControl called
// ServiceEnumInfo
DWORD TCK_IOControl (DWORD dwOpen, DWORD dwCode, PBYTE pIn, DWORD dwIn,
```

```
                        PBYTE pOut, DWORD dwOut, DWORD *pdwBytesWritten) {
PSRVCONTEXT pSrv;
DWORD err = ERROR_INVALID_PARAMETER;

pSrv = (PSRVCONTEXT) dwOpen;

DEBUGMSG (ZONE_EXENTRY,
          (DTAG TEXT("TCK_IOControl++ dwOpen: %x  dwCode: %x %d\r\n"),
          dwOpen, dwCode, pSrv->servState));

switch (dwCode) {
// -------------
// Commands
// -------------

// Cmd to start service
case IOCTL_SERVICE_START:
    DEBUGMSG (ZONE_IOCTLS, (DTAG TEXT("IOCTL_SERVICE_START\r\n")));
    EnterCriticalSection (&pSrv->csData);
    if ((pSrv->servState == SERVICE_STATE_OFF) |
        (pSrv->servState == SERVICE_STATE_UNKNOWN)) {

        pSrv->servState = SERVICE_STATE_ON;
        err = 0;
    } else
        err = ERROR_SERVICE_ALREADY_RUNNING;
    LeaveCriticalSection (&pSrv->csData);
    break;

// Cmd to stop service
case IOCTL_SERVICE_STOP:
    DEBUGMSG (ZONE_IOCTLS, (DTAG TEXT("IOCTL_SERVICE_STOP\r\n")));
    EnterCriticalSection (&pSrv->csData);
    if ((pSrv->servState == SERVICE_STATE_ON)) {

        pSrv->servState = SERVICE_STATE_SHUTTING_DOWN;
    } else
        err = ERROR_SERVICE_NOT_ACTIVE;
    LeaveCriticalSection (&pSrv->csData);
    break;

//Reread service reg setting
case IOCTL_SERVICE_REFRESH:
    DEBUGMSG (ZONE_IOCTLS, (DTAG TEXT("IOCTL_SERVICE_REFRESH\r\n")));
    // No settings in example service to read
    break;

//Config registry for auto load on boot
```

(continued)

Listing 22-2   *(continued)*

```
        case IOCTL_SERVICE_INSTALL:
            DEBUGMSG (ZONE_IOCTLS, (DTAG TEXT("IOCTL_SERVICE_INSTALL\r\n")));
            err = RegisterService();
            break;

        //Clear registry of auto load stuff
        case IOCTL_SERVICE_UNINSTALL:
            DEBUGMSG (ZONE_IOCTLS, (DTAG TEXT("IOCTL_SERVICE_UNINSTALL\r\n")));
            err = DeregisterService();
            break;

        //Clear registry of auto load stuff
        case IOCTL_SERVICE_CONTROL:
            DEBUGMSG (ZONE_IOCTLS, (DTAG TEXT("IOCTL_SERVICE_CONTROL\r\n")));
            err = 0;
            break;

#ifdef DEBUG
        // Set debug zones
        case IOCTL_SERVICE_DEBUG:
            DEBUGMSG (ZONE_IOCTLS, (DTAG TEXT("IOCTL_SERVICE_DEBUG\r\n")));
            if (!pIn || (dwIn < sizeof (DWORD)))
                break;
            __try {
                dpCurSettings.ulZoneMask = *(DWORD *)pIn;
                err = 0;
            }
            __except (EXCEPTION_EXECUTE_HANDLER) {
                ;
            }
#endif
        // -------------
        // Queries
        // -------------

        // Query for current service state
        case IOCTL_SERVICE_STATUS:
            DEBUGMSG (ZONE_IOCTLS, (DTAG TEXT("IOCTL_SERVICE_STATUS\r\n")));
            if (!pOut || (dwOut < sizeof (DWORD)))
                break;
            __try {
                *(DWORD *)pOut = pSrv->servState;
                if (pdwBytesWritten)
                    *pdwBytesWritten = sizeof (DWORD);
                err = 0;
            }
            __except (EXCEPTION_EXECUTE_HANDLER) {
```

```
            ;
        }
        break;

// Query for unload.
case IOCTL_SERVICE_QUERY_CAN_DEINIT:
    DEBUGMSG (ZONE_IOCTLS,
             (DTAG TEXT("IOCTL_SERVICE_QUERY_CAN_DEINIT\r\n")));
    if (!pOut || (dwOut < sizeof (DWORD)))
        break;
    __try {
        *(DWORD *)pOut = 1; // non-zero == Yes, can be unloaded.
        if (pdwBytesWritten)
            *pdwBytesWritten = sizeof (DWORD);
        err = 0;
    }
    __except (EXCEPTION_EXECUTE_HANDLER) {
        ;
    }
    break;

// Query to see if sock address okay for monitoring
case IOCTL_SERVICE_REGISTER_SOCKADDR:
    DEBUGMSG (ZONE_IOCTLS,
             (DTAG TEXT("IOCTL_SERVICE_REGISTER_SOCKADDR\r\n")));
    // Calling to see if service can accept super service help
    if (!pIn || (dwIn < sizeof (DWORD))) {

        if ((pSrv->servState == SERVICE_STATE_OFF) |
            (pSrv->servState == SERVICE_STATE_UNKNOWN))
                pSrv->servState = SERVICE_STATE_STARTING_UP;
        err = 0;
        break;
    }
    // Confirming a specific sock address
    DEBUGMSG (ZONE_IOCTLS, (DTAG TEXT("Socket:%x\r\n"), *pIn));
    err = 0;
    break;

// -------------
// Notifications
// -------------

// Notify that sock address going away
case IOCTL_SERVICE_DEREGISTER_SOCKADDR:
    DEBUGMSG (ZONE_IOCTLS,
             (DTAG TEXT("IOCTL_SERVICE_DEREGISTER_SOCKADDR\r\n")));
    EnterCriticalSection (&pSrv->csData);
```

(continued)

Listing 22-2 *(continued)*

```
            if (pSrv->servState == SERVICE_STATE_SHUTTING_DOWN)
                pSrv->servState = SERVICE_STATE_OFF;

            LeaveCriticalSection (&pSrv->csData);
            err = 0;
            break;

        // All super service ports open
        case IOCTL_SERVICE_STARTED:
            DEBUGMSG (ZONE_IOCTLS, (DTAG TEXT("IOCTL_SERVICE_STARTED\r\n")));
            EnterCriticalSection (&pSrv->csData);
            if ((pSrv->servState == SERVICE_STATE_STARTING_UP) |
                (pSrv->servState == SERVICE_STATE_UNKNOWN))
                pSrv->servState = SERVICE_STATE_ON;

            LeaveCriticalSection (&pSrv->csData);
            err = 0;
            break;

        // Notification that connect has occurred
        case IOCTL_SERVICE_CONNECTION:
            DEBUGMSG (ZONE_IOCTLS,
                        (DTAG TEXT("IOCTL_SERVICE_CONNECTION\r\n")));
            if (!pIn || (dwIn < sizeof (DWORD)))
                break;

            // Create thread to handle the socket
            CreateThread (NULL, 0, AcceptThread, (PVOID)*(DWORD*)pIn, 0,
                          NULL);
            err = 0;
            break;

        default:
            DEBUGMSG (ZONE_ERROR | ZONE_IOCTLS,
                        (DTAG TEXT("Unsupported IOCTL code %x (%d)\r\n"),
                        dwCode, (dwCode & 0x00ff) / 4));
            return FALSE;
    }
    SetLastError (err);
    DEBUGMSG (ZONE_FUNC, (DTAG TEXT("TCK_IOControl-- %d\r\n"), err));
    return (err == 0) ? TRUE : FALSE;
}
//======================================================================
// TCK_PowerDown - Called when system suspends
//
// NOTE: No kernel calls, including debug messages, can be made from
// this call.
```

```
//
void TCK_PowerDown (DWORD dwContext) {
    return;
}
//=======================================================================
// TCK_PowerUp - Called when resumes
//
// NOTE: No kernel calls, including debug messages, can be made from
// this call.
//
void TCK_PowerUp (DWORD dwContext) {
    return;
}
//-----------------------------------------------------------------------
// AddRegString - Helper routine
//
int AddRegString (HKEY hKey, LPTSTR lpName, LPTSTR lpStr) {

    return RegSetValueEx (hKey, lpName, 0, REG_SZ, (PBYTE)lpStr,
                          (lstrlen (lpStr) + 1) * sizeof (TCHAR));
}
//-----------------------------------------------------------------------
// AddRegDW - Helper routine
//
int AddRegDW (HKEY hKey, LPTSTR lpName, DWORD dw) {
    return RegSetValueEx (hKey, lpName, 0, REG_DWORD, (PBYTE)&dw, 4);
}
//-----------------------------------------------------------------------
// AddRegSuperServ - Helper routine
//
int AddRegSuperServ (HKEY hKey, WORD wPort) {
    SOCKADDR_IN sa;
    HKEY hSubKey;
    TCHAR szKeyName[128];
    DWORD dw;
    int rc;

    DEBUGMSG (ZONE_FUNC, (DTAG TEXT("AddRegSuperServ++ %d\r\n"), wPort));

    memset (&sa, 0, sizeof (sa));
    sa.sin_family = AF_INET;
    sa.sin_port = htons(wPort);
    sa.sin_addr.s_addr = INADDR_ANY;

    // Create key for this service
    wsprintf (szKeyName, TEXT("Accept\\TCP-%d"), wPort);
    rc = RegCreateKeyEx (hKey, szKeyName, 0, NULL, 0, NULL,
                         NULL, &hSubKey, &dw);
```

Listing 22-2   *(continued)*

```
        DEBUGMSG (1, (TEXT("RegCreateKeyEx %d %d\r\n"), rc, GetLastError()));
        if (rc == ERROR_SUCCESS)
            rc = RegSetValueEx (hSubKey, TEXT("SockAddr"), 0, REG_BINARY,
                          (PBYTE)&sa, sizeof (sa));

        DEBUGMSG (ZONE_FUNC, (DTAG TEXT("AddRegSuperServ-- %d\r\n"),rc));
        return rc;
}
//----------------------------------------------------------------------
// RegisterService - Add registry settings for auto load
//
int RegisterService () {
    HKEY hKey, hSubKey;
    TCHAR szModName[MAX_PATH], *pName;
    DWORD dw;
    int rc;

    // Open the Services key
    rc = RegOpenKeyEx(HKEY_LOCAL_MACHINE,TEXT("Services"),0, 0, &hKey);
    if (rc == ERROR_SUCCESS) {
        // Create key for this service
        rc = RegCreateKeyEx (hKey, REGNAME, 0, NULL, 0, NULL,
                          NULL, &hSubKey, &dw);
        if (rc == ERROR_SUCCESS) {

            GetModuleFileName (hInst, szModName, dim (szModName));
            // Scan to filename
            pName = szModName + lstrlen (szModName);
            while ((pName > szModName) && (*pName != TEXT('\\')))
                pName--;
            if (*pName == TEXT('\\')) pName++;
            AddRegString (hSubKey, TEXT ("DLL"),  pName);

            AddRegString (hSubKey, TEXT ("Prefix"),  TEXT("TCK"));

            AddRegDW (hSubKey, TEXT("Index"), 0);
            AddRegDW (hSubKey, TEXT("Context"), SERVICE_INIT_STOPPED);

            AddRegString (hSubKey, TEXT("DisplayName"),
                        TEXT("Tick Service"));

            AddRegString (hSubKey, TEXT("Description"),
                        TEXT("Returns system tick cnt on Port 1000"));

            AddRegSuperServ (hSubKey, PORTNUM);

        } else
```

```
                    DEBUGMSG (ZONE_ERROR, (TEXT("Error creating key\r\n")));

        RegCloseKey(hKey);
    } else
        DEBUGMSG (ZONE_ERROR, (TEXT("Error opening key\r\n")));

    return (rc == ERROR_SUCCESS) ? 0 : 1;
}
//---------------------------------------------------------------------
// DeregisterService - Remove auto load settings from registry
//
int DeregisterService () {
    HKEY hKey;
    int rc;

    // Open the Services key
    rc = RegOpenKeyEx(HKEY_LOCAL_MACHINE,TEXT("Services"),0, 0, &hKey);
    if (rc == ERROR_SUCCESS) {
        // Delete key for this service
        rc = RegDeleteKey (hKey, REGNAME);
        if (rc != ERROR_SUCCESS)
            DEBUGMSG(ZONE_ERROR, (DTAG TEXT("Error deleting key %d\r\n"),
                    GetLastError()));
        RegCloseKey(hKey);
    } else
        DEBUGMSG (ZONE_ERROR, (TEXT("Error opening key\r\n")));
    return (rc == ERROR_SUCCESS) ? 0 : -1;
}
//=====================================================================
// AcceptThread - Thread for managing connected sockets
//
DWORD WINAPI AcceptThread (PVOID pArg) {
    SOCKET sock;
    int rc;
    DWORD dwCmd, dwTicks;

    sock = (SOCKET)pArg;

    DEBUGMSG (ZONE_THREAD, (TEXT("AcceptThread++ %x\r\n"), pArg));

    // Simple task, for any nonzero received byte, sent tick count back
    rc = recv (sock, (char *)&dwCmd, sizeof (DWORD), 0);
    while ((rc != SOCKET_ERROR) && (dwCmd != 0)) {
        DEBUGMSG (ZONE_THREAD, (TEXT("Recv cmd %x\r\n"), dwCmd));

        dwTicks = GetTickCount ();
        DEBUGMSG (ZONE_THREAD, (TEXT("sending %d\r\n"), dwTicks));
        rc = send (sock, (char *)&dwTicks, 4, 0);
```

(continued)

Listing 22-2 *(continued)*

```
        // Read next cmd
        rc = recv (sock, (char *)&dwCmd, sizeof (DWORD), 0);
    }
    closesocket (sock);
    DEBUGMSG (ZONE_THREAD, (TEXT("AcceptThread--
%d %d\r\n"),rc, GetLastError()));
    return 0;
}
```

The service interface is quite simple. Applications can query the tick count of the device by sending a nonzero *DWORD* to the device. The service will disconnect when the *DWORD* received is zero.

To install TickSrv, copy TickSrv to the Windows CE device and run the following short Windows CE application, TSInst, provided with the companion files. The relevant code is shown here:

```
HANDLE hDrv = RegisterService (TEXT("TCK"), 0, TEXT("TickSrv.dll"), 0);
if (hDrv) {
    printf ("Service loaded. %x\r\n", hDrv);

    DWORD dwBytes;
    ServiceIoControl (hDrv, IOCTL_SERVICE_INSTALL, 0, 0, 0, 0,
                      &dwBytes, NULL);
    printf ("Install complete\r\n");
    DeregisterService (hDrv);
} else
    printf ("Service failed to load. rc %d\r\n", GetLastError());
```

The install application uses *RegisterDevice* and *ServiceIoControl* to have TickSrv update the registry. TickSrv will load on the next system reset, but it can also be loaded manually using the Services Manager. Run the following command line to load TickSrv manually:

```
services load TickSrv
```

Listing 22-3 is a simple PC-based client written in Visual Studio .NET that will open port 1000 on a specified device, send it a command to receive the tick count, wait a few milliseconds, ask again, and then terminate the connection and quit.

PCClient.cpp

```
//======================================================================
// PCClient.cpp : Simple client for the tick server example
//
// Written for the book Programming Windows CE
// Copyright (C) 2003 Douglas Boling
//======================================================================
#include "stdafx.h"

int _tmain(int argc, _TCHAR* argv[])
{
    SOCKET sock;
    SOCKADDR_IN dest_sin;
    WORD wPort = 1000;
    int rc;

    if (argc < 2) {
        printf ("Syntax: %s <IP Addr> %d\r\n", argv[0], argc);
        return 0;
    }
    // Init winsock
    WSADATA wsaData;
    if ((rc = WSAStartup(0x101,&wsaData)) != 0) {
        printf ("WSAStartup failed\r\n");
        WSACleanup();
        return 0;
    }
    // Create socket
    sock = socket( AF_INET, SOCK_STREAM, 0);
    if (sock == INVALID_SOCKET) {
        return INVALID_SOCKET;
    }

    // Set up IP address to access
    memset (&dest_sin, 0, sizeof (dest_sin));
    dest_sin.sin_family = AF_INET;
    dest_sin.sin_addr.S_un.S_addr = inet_addr (argv[1]);
    dest_sin.sin_port = htons(wPort);

    printf ("Connecting to %s  Port %d\r\n",
            inet_ntoa (dest_sin.sin_addr), wPort);

    // Connect to the device
    rc == connect( sock, (PSOCKADDR) &dest_sin, sizeof( dest_sin));
    if (rc == SOCKET_ERROR) {
```

Listing 22-3   The PCClient example   *(continued)*

Listing 22-3 *(continued)*

```
        printf ("Err in connect. %d\r\n", WSAGetLastError());
        closesocket( sock );
        return INVALID_SOCKET;
    }
    DWORD dwCmd = 1, dwTicks = 0;

    // Ask for ticks
    send (sock, (char *)&dwCmd, 4, 0);
    recv (sock, (char *)&dwTicks, 4, 0);
    printf ("Ticks: %d\r\n", dwTicks);

    // Wait 1/4 second and ask again
    Sleep(250);
    send (sock, (char *)&dwCmd, 4, 0);
    recv (sock, (char *)&dwTicks, 4, 0);
    printf ("Ticks: %d\r\n", dwTicks);

    // Terminate connection and close socket
    dwCmd = 0;
    send (sock, (char *)&dwCmd, 4, 0);
    Sleep(100);
    closesocket (sock);
    return 0;
}
```

The Services Manager is a great addition to Windows CE. It provides support for those background tasks that are so often needed in embedded systems. Using a service instead of writing a standalone application also reduces the number of applications running on the device. Considering that Windows CE supports only 32 applications at any one time, writing a handful of services instead of writing a number of applications can be the difference in the system running or not.

In the last chapter of the book, I will turn away from C, C++, and what is now referred to as *unmanaged* or *native* code. Instead, I will introduce the next wave of embedded programming tools, the .NET Compact Framework. Programs written in the Compact Framework are compiled to an intermediate language instead of to CPU instructions. This arrangement makes the applications CPU independent. The Compact Framework is a cool new technology.

23

Programming the .NET Compact Framework

"Toto, I have a feeling we're not in Kansas anymore." That sums up the feeling of many embedded programmers as they are introduced to the .NET Compact Framework. The days of the embedded programmer née electrical engineer huddled over an assembly listing counting bytes of code have only recently been left behind. Over the past few years, the embedded industry has moved to devices that are powered by 32-bit operating systems such as Windows CE. But even that is changing.

The .NET Compact Framework runs code in a protected environment, isolated from the actual hardware. The applications aren't even compiled in machine language. Instead, they're compiled to an intermediate language that's compiled into machine language as it's first executed, a process called just-in-time (JIT) compilation. This chapter takes you in a completely different direction from the previous chapters. Instead of describing how to work with Windows CE, this chapter discusses a separate topic, a run-time environment that can (but doesn't have to) run on top of Windows CE, the .NET Compact Framework.

It's Becoming a Managed World

Aficionados of .NET divide the world into two types of code: managed and unmanaged. Managed code is compiled to an intermediate language called the Common Intermediate Language (CIL) that is run from within the .NET Framework. The .NET runtime verifies the proper execution of the managed code at run time.[1] When data is transferred between variables, the data type is checked to see whether it's compatible with the destination type, or that the proper conversion has been applied. Array indexes are checked to ensure that they are within the range of the array. Because of the use of a CPU-neutral byte code used by the runtime, a single managed binary can run on many different CPU types.

Unmanaged, or native, code is code written the good old-fashioned way. Routines are compiled directly to machine code when compiled on the developer's machine. Unmanaged applications are written to talk either to the operating system's API or to a class library that wraps that API. Unmanaged applications depend on the compiler to verify the correctness of data types and array indexes. Few unmanaged compilers produce code to make these checks at run time.

The advocates of managed code preach its advantages with almost a religious fervor. The problem with theological discussions of technical issues is that engineers tend to concentrate on their side of the argument without recognizing the valid issues contradicting their opinions. Managed code has many advantages over unmanaged code, but also some significant disadvantages. In an embedded environment, the balance of the arguments differs somewhat from the evaluations of the desktop and server spaces. My advice is to use what works best for a particular situation.

To .NET or Not to .NET

There are a number of advantages of managed code in the embedded environment. First and foremost, managed applications don't care about the type of CPU on the system, so only one executable needs to be distributed for customers instead of separate versions for ARM, x86, SHx, and MIPS. This abstraction greatly simplifies both distribution and support of your applications. CPU independence is much more important for us in the embedded world. Everyone on the desktop, with the exception of a handful of Macintosh systems, executes the *true* universal byte code set, x86 machine code.

The managed runtime also enforces a number of requirements with respect to the application, which makes the managed code much more robust. The runtime enforces type safety, which helps in reducing bugs introduced by the programmer as well as avoiding the execution of malicious code that takes advantage of data type mismanagement and unverified data to hack into systems.

Another advantage touted by advocates of managed code is the simplicity and speed in development of managed applications. It's quite true that the latest tools provide a productive environment for producing amazingly powerful

---

1. The initial release of the .NET Compact Framework runtime doesn't perform run-time type verification.

applications in shorter time than is typical with unmanaged code. I personally don't feel that this increased productivity is as much a credit to the concept of managed code as to the quality of the tools, including the new languages, producing the managed code. Regardless of the core reason, the process of generating managed applications is both easier and quicker than that of generating unmanaged applications with the previous generation of tools.

The disadvantage of managed code is chiefly speed and responsiveness. Here again, this is not so much of an issue on the desktop, where the latest x86-compatible CPUs are so powerful that they don't even break a sweat running typical business software. That said, managed code executes more slowly than unmanaged code. This difference can either have an impact or not depending on the application and the hardware. Managed code can also be nonresponsive if an ill-timed garbage collection happens. During garbage collection, all threads in a managed application are suspended. In worst-case situations, these garbage collections can take seconds to complete. Not a comforting thought for applications that are supporting some commercial task in front of an impatient customer.

Should you develop your new applications in managed code? There are many reasons to say yes. So are the previous 22 chapters of this book a waste of time? Even if you decide to write your embedded applications in managed code, the answer is no. The current implementation of the .NET Compact Frameworks, although quite functional, is anything but complete. There are significant gaps in the functionality of the runtime that will require all but the most platform-agnostic application to access the underlying operating system to accomplish some task or another. Actions as simple as saving configuration information in the registry or integrating as tightly with the shell as a native application require calling outside the managed environment into the underlying unmanaged operating system.

In this single chapter, I can't hope to describe everything about the .NET Compact Framework. Even single books have trouble being complete, which is why there are entire series of books from publishers describing the .NET initiative from Microsoft. Microsoft Press, the publisher of this book, alone has more than 50 books dedicated to .NET. Instead, I'll use this chapter to introduce the .NET Compact Frameworks as they are implemented on Windows CE devices. After that introduction, this chapter walks through the architecture of a Windows Forms application. Then the handful of classes not on the desktop but supported by Compact Framework are covered. The remaining sections of this chapter concentrate on providing information to enable applications that run as fast and are as tightly integrated with the underlying operating system as their unmanaged counterparts. Let's start with the basics.

A Brief Introduction to Managed Applications

As mentioned previously, managed applications are compiled to an intermediate byte code called the Common Intermediate Language. This language is simply a series of byte codes that define an opcode set for a virtual stack-based processor. A run-time engine, implemented in native CPU instructions, converts the byte codes to native instructions and then has the CPU execute the native instructions. This process, called just-in-time compilation, differs from conventional interpreters because the native instructions are cached. If the method is executed again, the cached native instructions are directly called instead of the original byte codes being reinterpreted as in an interpreter. One can argue the merits of waiting to convert virtual instructions to native instructions at run time; this text simply accepts that the .NET runtime uses this process.

Performance of a JIT runtime, although inferior to that of native compiled code, isn't as bad as you might think. The compilation takes place only on the code paths being executed in the module, so any code not executed isn't compiled. Also, because most routines execute many times, the average speed of a routine will eventually approach the speed of precompiled native code. As long as the system retains enough free memory, the cache will retain the code for the application, alleviating the need to recompile the methods.

In low-memory conditions, the execution engine tries to recover memory in a process called garbage collection. During garbage collection, the runtime finds all the discarded heap objects and recovers that memory for reuse. The remaining objects that are still in use are relocated to the start of the heap. Because this process involves moving in-use objects, all threads in the application are suspended during the garbage collection. If the garbage collection doesn't free enough memory, parts of the code cache can be purged in a process called *code pitching*. If code for a method is pitched and that method is executed again, the original byte codes are reloaded and recompiled.

Microsoft currently supports two high-level languages for generating CIL byte codes for execution on the Compact Framework runtime: Visual Basic .NET and Visual C#. Both tools come with components that generate Compact Framework applications and automatically deploy the application to devices or emulators. Visual Studio also has a remote debugger that debugs the code on the device remotely from a connected PC. Microsoft doesn't provide a tool for generating managed code for the Compact Framework with its C++ compiler.

Although many embedded developers are familiar with Visual Basic, if only to sneer at Visual Basic developers, C# (pronounced *C sharp*) is a new language created by the developers at Microsoft to be a better C++. C# retains most of C++'s syntax while providing improvements that tend to encourage safer code.

Regardless of opinions and snobbery of some developers, the runtime doesn't care about the high-level language used to create a Compact Framework application as long as the compiler produces the IL byte codes supported by the runtime. One of the nicer features of the .NET environment is that the full power of the runtime and its accompanying class library is available to all languages equally. As a result, Visual Basic .NET programmers can now create applications just as powerful, fast, and functional as can be created with Visual C#.

HelloCF

In the spirit of the Chapter 1 discussion introducing Windows CE applications, the following HelloCF example introduces a basic Compact Framework application. This first HelloCF example is written in C#, although I'll present a Visual Basic .NET example shortly. The first version of HelloCF is shown in Listing 23-1.

```
public class Hello
{
    static void Main()
    {
        System.Console.WriteLine ("Hello Compact Framework");
    }
}
```

Listing 23-1   HelloCF source code

A C# program is encapsulated in one or more classes; in the preceding program, the class is *Hello*. The only method of this class is the static method *Main*, which is the entry point to the program. In this example, *Main* takes no parameters and returns no values, although both are possible in C#.

The *static* keyword indicates that this method is associated with the class, not an instance of the class. This essentially means that the method is accessible by referencing the class *Hello* instead of having to create an instance of the class *Hello* and then calling the method. In the case of the entry point of the application, this distinction is important since an instance of the class *Hello* has not been created when the application is launched. In most cases, *Main* will create an instance of its encapsulating class, as we'll see in later examples.

The single line of code in *Main* is a call to the *WriteLine* method of the *Console* class. As you can guess, *WriteLine* displays the string on the console associated with the application. If a console driver is not present on the system, as with the Pocket PC, the line doesn't get displayed at all. After calling *WriteLine*, *Main* exits, terminating the program.

Namespaces

Notice that the text *System.Console.WriteLine* specifies the call to *WriteLine*. Going from right to left, *WriteLine* is the name of the method in the class *Console*. *System* is the *namespace* where the *Console* class is defined. The concept of namespaces is used extensively throughout .NET languages. Namespaces are constructs that organize the naming scheme of the application and the library of classes the application references. Namespaces prevent naming conflicts across independently created classes by enclosing those classes in unique namespace names.

For example, two class libraries developed independently can both contain classes named *Bob*. As long as the namespaces of the two libraries are unique, the application can reference each of the classes by prefixing the reference with the namespace containing the desired class. So if one namespace is named *BigCorpClassLib* and the other is named *UpAndComingClassLib*, the classes will be referenced as *BigCorpClassLib.Bob* and *UpAndComingClassLib.Bob*.

To avoid having to explicitly reference the namespace of each class, C# provides the *using* directive to declare that the compiler should check references in the file with the definitions in the namespace in the *using* directive. Multiple *using* directives can be declared in a file. Listing 23-2 shows HelloCF with a *using* statement.

```
using System;
public class Hello
{
    static void Main()
    {
        Console.WriteLine ("Hello Compact Framework");
    }
}
```

Listing 23-2   HelloCF with a *using* statement

Regardless of whether a *using* directive is declared, the application can still reference the class explicitly by specifying the namespace that encapsulates the class. This scheme allows an application to use a *using* directive for simplicity but still reference a class in another namespace that happens to have a name that conflicts with a class in the current namespace. For example, if HelloCF wanted to reference both the *Console* class in *System*, which was referenced in the *using* directive, and a class named *Console* in *BigCorpClassLib*, the namespace could be explicitly referenced, as in

```
Console.WriteLine ("Hello Compact Framework");
BigCorpClassLib.Console.WriteLine ("Hello Compact Framework");
```

Traditionally, all but the most trivial of "Hello World" applications also declare a namespace of their own. This leads us to the last of the HelloCF examples written in C#, shown in Listing 23-3.

```
using System;
namespace HelloCF
{
    public class Hello
    {
        static void Main()
        {
            Console.WriteLine ("Hello Compact Framework");
        }
    }
}
```

Listing 23-3   HelloCF that defines its own namespace

The namespace can be any name, although the Visual C# code wizard will create a namespace that matches the name of the project. The namespace encloses all the structures, classes, and other definitions within the namespace. In addition, multiple files can specify the same namespace. The code resulting from a compilation of multiple files each specifying the same namespace will then be combined in the resulting module.

Visual Basic .NET

But what of our Visual Basic cousins? Although all of the examples in this book have been written in C, C++, or C# for valid reasons, the truth of the matter is that the audience of Basic programmers is significantly larger than that of C and C++ programmers. The same Hello World program written in Visual Basic .NET would look like the version shown in Listing 23-4.

```
Imports System

Module Module1
    Sub Main()
        Console.WriteLine("Hello Compact Framework.")
    End Sub
End Module
```

Listing 23-4   HelloCF written in Visual Basic .NET

The difference between the Visual Basic example and the C# example is frankly not that great. Of course, there is the difference in the text used to mark subroutines vs. methods, and the use of the *Imports* keyword instead of the *using* directive. Still, the structure of the two programs is remarkably similar. The key similarity is that both examples use the same class library! This means that a Visual Basic .NET program can do anything that a C# program can do. This is a huge improvement over the old days, when languages weren't picked for their syntax but for their function. The remaining examples in this chapter will be written in C# for consistency, but everything presented in this chapter can be applied equally well to Visual Basic and C# applications.

Common Language Runtime Basics

The common language runtime (CLR) is the foundation of all .NET languages. The runtime, along with the Framework Class Library, defines everything from the base data types to methods to connect to the Internet. Such an ambitious foundation deserves a bit of coverage here.

Value vs. Reference Types

Data types in the CLR are divided into two categories, *value types* and *reference types*. Instances of value types contain the data for that instance. Value types are data types such as signed and unsigned integers, shorts, and bytes. Structures are also value types in the CLR. Assigning a value to a value type causes the data to be held by the instance of that type. The data contained by the instance of the type can be copied to another instance of the type with a simple assignment, as in

```
x = y;
```

Reference types are those wherein the instance of the type refers to the data for the type instead of containing it. From a C perspective, reference types are pointers to data, whereas value types are the data itself. In C#, any class is a reference type. When a reference type is assigned to another reference type, the reference is copied instead of the data.

Understanding the difference between value types and reference types is critical to .NET languages. Consider the following scenario with two instances (*A* and *B*) of some data type:

```
A.x = 3;
B = A;
B.x = 4;
```

Given this sequence, what result does the property *A.x* end up with? Well, it depends: are *A* and *B* value types or reference types? If *A* and *B* are structures, the assignment of *B* to *A* simply copies the data from structure *A* to structure *B* *because structures are value types*. So the data in the structures *A* and *B* remains independent. When *B.x* is assigned 4, the *x* property of *B* is modified but the same property of *A* is unchanged. *A.x* remains 3 because *B* was a copy of *A*.

If A and B are classes, they are reference types. In this case, the statement $B = A$ simply copies a reference of the class referenced by A to B. So the assignment of $B.x$ to 4 sets the x property of the class referred to by B to 4. Since both A and B refer to the same class, $B.x$ refers to the same property x of the class as $A.x$. The expression $A.x$ in this case results in the data 4.

Another consideration close to the heart of any embedded programmer is the implementation details of value types vs. reference types. Value types are maintained on the virtual stack of the machine. They are not subjected to garbage collection because their data is contained on the self-managing stack. The data for reference types is maintained in the system heap, with the reference to the data maintained on the stack. Think of a pointer to data being kept on the stack while the data itself is in the heap.

Aside from defining structures instead of classes, the programmer has little control over using reference types vs. value types. The value types are limited to the standard integer types known to all programmers. Everything else is a reference type.

Passing value types to methods can be accomplished by passing either the value or a reference to the value. If the value is passed, a copy of the data is placed on the stack and passed to the called method. Any changes to the value made by the called method do not change the value in the calling routine. If a reference is passed, a reference to the data type is passed to the called method. In this case, the called method can modify the value in the calling routine because the reference refers to the original data. The following short code fragment demonstrates this:

```
private void CallingRoutine ()
{
    int a, b, c;
    a = 1;
    b = 2;
    c = 3;
    test1 (a, ref b, out c);
    // Will produce a:1 b:6: c:7
    Console.WriteLine ("a:{0} b:{1} c:{2}", a, b, c);
    return;
}
private void test1 (int a, ref int b, out int c)
{
    a = 5;
    b = 6;
    c = 7;
    return;
}
```

The function prototype of the called routine, *test1*, shows the C# syntax for passing parameters. The parameter *a* is passed as a value type, so any changes in the called routine won't affect its original value in the calling routine. The parameter *b* is passed as a reference type. This means that any changes to *b* in *test1* are reflected in the original value in the calling routine. The *ref* keyword also causes the C# compiler to require that a type parameter be set before calling *test1*. The final parameter, *c*, is marked as an *out* parameter. *Out* parameters are reference parameters with a twist: they don't have to be initialized before they're passed to the called routine, but the called routine must set any *out* parameters before returning.

Events and Delegates

Another somewhat interesting aspect of .NET programming is the concept of delegates and events. Although the names are new, the concepts are not. A delegate is the managed version of a typed function pointer. C++ programmers are familiar with declaring a callback function of a specific type. In the following unmanaged code, the type *POWERCBPROC* is defined as a function prototype that can be used as a callback to the application in case of a power change.

```
// Callback function prototype
typedef BOOL (CALLBACK* POWERCBPROC)(DWORD);
```

In C#, the corresponding delegate would be defined as follows:

```
public delegate bool PowerEventHandler (uint data);
```

The *public* designation allows the delegate to be referenced outside the class where it was defined. The *public* designation is common because delegates are typically used by classes to define methods that will be called from other classes. The *delegate* keyword defines this line as a delegate. The remainder of the line is the prototype of all the methods that will be called when the event tied to this delegate is fired.

An event is an object that contains a list of methods matching a specific prototype. The methods can then be called by invoking the event. From a C++ perspective, think of an event as an array of function pointers. The process of raising an event results in the code calling each of the function pointers in the array. In managed code, each method in the event list must match the specific function prototype specified in an associated delegate. The following code declares an event named *PowerEvent* of type *CbEventHandler*, which was declared in the preceding delegate discussion.

```
public event PowerEventHandler PowerEvent;
```

The event declared here is *PowerEvent*. Its type is the delegate *Power-EventHandler*. As you can see, the event can't be declared without the corresponding delegate type being defined as well. Referring back to the C++ comparison, a list of function pointers shouldn't be defined without a corresponding function prototype defining the functions pointed to in the list.

Once a class defines both a delegate and an event, classes can register for the event by creating a method that matches the delegate and then adding a reference to that method to the event. The creation of the method is simple because all it has to do is match the parameter list and return a value defined by the delegate. The following code shows a skeleton of an event handler routine that matches the *PowerEventHandler* delegate:

```
bool MyPowerEventHandler (uint data)
{
    // Do something here.
    return true;
}
```

Registering with the event is syntactically different, depending on the language. For C#, registering with the event is accomplished with the += operator, as in

```
PowerEvent += new PowerEventHandler (MyPowerEventHandler);
```

The *new* keyword is needed because the code needs to create a new event that points to the *MyPowerEventHandler* method. The new event instance is then added to the event chain with the += operator. It's important not to use the = operator because the direct assignment would remove any other event handlers from the event list.

In Visual Basic .NET, the syntax for attaching to an event is as follows:

```
AddHandler PowerEvent AddressOf MyPowerEventHandler;
```

Regardless of the language, understanding events and delegates is critical to understanding how .NET applications work. When a Visual Studio designer tool is used, the part of the tool that provides forms-based code generation typically inserts the proper references and automatically creates the skeletons of the event handlers, so all that's necessary is to fill in the code. Although the designer is quite helpful, using it doesn't take the place of understanding what's really going on in the code.

Strings

The subtleties of managed strings are important to understand. The standard string class maintains what is called an *immutable string*, one that can't be changed. This means that anytime you modify a string, the Framework creates a new string class with the new characters and, unless the application keeps the original string in scope, discards the old string to be garbage collected some-time in the future. For example, consider the following:

```
string str = "abcdef";
str = str + "g";
str = str + "h";
str = str + "i";
str = str + "j";
Console.WriteLine (str);
```

In this code, five different string objects are created before the string is finally displayed with the *WriteLine* method. Each time the string is modified by appending a character, the original string instance is discarded and a new one created. Clearly, poorly designed managed applications can produce huge amounts of discarded strings that will eventually require a garbage collection to recover.

To avoid excessively generating discarded strings, the Framework provides a *StringBuilder* class. This stringlike class maintains a mutable string, one that can be modified in place. An instance of a *StringBuilder* class is analogous to a self-managing character buffer. When an instance is created, either a size of the buffer is specified by the application or a default size is used. Once the instance is created, characters can be added, trimmed, or changed without the overhead of discarding the current instance of the class. Individual characters in the string can be referenced by its index into the array of characters. For example

```
// Create a string builder with the string abcdef and a max capacity of 256.
StringBuilder sb = new StringBuilder ("abcdef", 256);
char c = sb[4];
Console.WriteLine (c.ToString());       // This displays the character 'e'.
sb[3] = 'z';
Console.WriteLine (sb.ToString());      // This displays the string "abczef".
```

The *StringBuilder* class is great for string manipulation, but it's not a string. So after the string is constructed, the characters in *StringBuilder* are typically converted to a string for use. Although both C# and Visual Basic .NET make it simple to use the standard string class, any involved string formatting routines should use the *StringBuilder* class to avoid excessive load on the heap.

The string class has one method that deserves special attention. The static *Format* method provides a *sprintf*-style function that formats parameters into a string. The prototype of *string.Format* looks like the following:

```
public static string Format(string, object, object, object);
```

As with *sprintf*, the first parameter is the formatting string. The remaining parameters in the variable-length parameter list are the objects whose string representations will be used in the formatting placeholders in the format string.

The formatting characters used in the Framework are different from the standard C format characters such as *%d* and *%x*. Instead, the parameter placeholders in the string are enclosed in curly brackets and reference the individual parameters explicitly. For example, to reference the first parameter in the parameter list, the placeholder is *{0}*. The placeholder *{1}* is used to reference the second parameter, *{2}* references the third parameter, and so on. The objects in the parameter list all must be able to be converted to a string. For standard numbers and strings, this conversion happens automatically, but for complex types, the *ToString* method, available in all objects in the Framework, must be explicitly used to create a string representation of the object.

Individual placeholders can also specify how the object is presented. For example, a number can be presented in decimal, hexadecimal, or any number of other formats. The formatting characters are specified in each of the placeholders by adding a colon followed by the formatting string. For example, the following string represents the number 100 in decimal, hexadecimal, and scientific formats:

```
string str = string.Format ("a:{0:d}, b:{1:x}, c:{1:e}", 100, 100, 100);
// Results in the output
a:100, b:64, c:1.000000e+002
```

In addition, significant digits both before and after the decimal point can be specified in the formatting string. Notice how the *Format* method is referenced by specifying the string type, not an instance of a string. This is because *Format* is a static method of the string class.

String formatting characters can also be used in the *ToString* methods of many of the objects in the Framework. For example, the string created previously with the *Format* method can also be created with the following statement:

```
string str= "a:" + 100.ToString() + "a:" + 100.ToString("x")
        + "a:" + 100.ToString("e");
```

The Framework supports a number of other formatting characters. A complete list of the capabilities of formatting strings can be found in the .NET Compact Framework documentation.

The Framework Class Library

Visual C# and Visual Basic .NET provide the language syntax for describing the program flow, but to get anything done besides adding numbers, the application needs to use the Framework Class Library (FCL).[2] On the desktop version

---

2. Even adding numbers could be interpreted as needing the FCL since the base types such as *Int32* are defined in the class library. The high-level language simply uses aliases to these base value types that conform to the syntax of the language.

of .NET, the FCL provides an outstanding amount of functionality, easily seducing the most skeptical of programmers with support for the most complex of tasks. The class library that comes with the Compact Framework is significantly less functional but still quite powerful.

The class library in the Compact Framework supports most of the major functional groups supported by the desktop, albeit with fewer classes and methods. The Compact Framework supports threading, file operations, the 2D drawing functions, socket programming, Web service clients, and many of the other parts of the standard FCL.

What isn't supported is the GDI+ drawing method, remoting, generic serialization, and classes designed for server operation. The criteria for deciding what went into the Compact Framework FCL are based on which classes were needed for basic client Windows Forms applications that access data both on the local device and through the Internet. The size of the resulting runtime was also a chief consideration because the larger the runtime, the greater the need for OEMs to use larger, more expensive Flash chips in their devices.

Windows Forms Applications

Almost every managed application created for the Compact Framework will be a Windows Forms application. Because of this, this section of the Framework deserves some special attention. Windows Forms applications relate to simple managed applications as Windows applications relate to console applications. Windows Forms applications create one or more windows on the Windows desktop. This top-level window is referred to as a form. The form almost always contains many child windows, typically predefined controls provided by the Framework but also controls created by the application.

Visual Studio makes creating Windows Forms applications almost trivial with its powerful application designer. While all programmers, including me, use the designer to create Windows Forms applications, understanding the underlying code is important. For this reason, I'm going to briefly dive into the nuts and bolts of Windows Forms applications, not from a designer perspective, but from a code perspective. This short introduction can provide all the details inquisitive programmers would want. The best source of how Windows Forms applications work is Charles Petzold's two books *Programming Microsoft Windows with C#* and *Programming Microsoft Windows with Visual Basic .NET*, both from Microsoft Press.

The Windows Forms library can be considered analogous to the GWE functionality of Windows CE. It provides extensive classes for creating windows and controls as well as drawing elements such as brushes, pens, and bitmaps.

The limitations in the Windows Forms classes center around the reduction in the exposed methods and properties that are available on the desktop version of the FCL.

One significant difference in the Compact Framework implementation of the Windows Forms classes is the lack of a *WndProc* method in the *Control* class. On the desktop, this method can be overridden so that the managed application can intercept any unmanaged window message, such as *WM_SIZE*, and deal with the message as the managed code sees fit. On the Compact Framework, the *Control* class does not expose this method, effectively isolating the managed code from the underlying operating system. Even using techniques to discover the true window handle of a managed control can be dangerous. The Compact Framework pools window handles and can reuse them unexpectedly. To throw a bone to those programmers who need access to window messages, a special Compact Framework class, the *MessageWindow* class, is supported that does expose the *WndProc* method. That class is discussed later in this chapter.

Just as Windows applications have a message queue and a corresponding message loop to handle the messages, Windows Forms applications also manage window messages, although in the case of managed applications the Framework hides the grisly details of the message loop.

A Basic Windows Forms Application

A Windows Forms application is signified by the declaration and creation of one or more form classes along with a call to the *Run* method of the *Application* class to start the window message–processing infrastructure under the covers. A trivial Windows Forms application is shown here:

```
using System;
using System.Windows.Forms;

namespace FirstWindowsForms
{
    class WindowsForms1 : Form
    {
        static void Main()
        {
            WindowsForms1 f = new WindowsForms1();
            f.Text = "Form Title";
            Application.Run (f);
        }
    }
}
```

The structure of the application looks somewhat strange because a method in the class is actually creating an instance of the class; however, this is the traditional structure of a Windows Forms application. The *Run* method of the *Application* class is a statically defined method that starts the message loop processing under the covers of the application. Like a message loop, the *Run* method doesn't return until the form passed as its single parameter is destroyed. When this happens, the *Run* method returns, *Main* exits, and the application terminates.

The *Form* class is derived from the *Control* class, which is the basis for windows in a Windows Forms application. The methods and properties of the *Control* and *Form* class are too numerous to list in this short discussion, but they provide the typical information that would be expected for a window, such as size, position, client area, window text, and such. Figure 23-1 shows this first Windows Forms application as it appears on an embedded Windows CE platform.

Figure 23-1   A simple Windows Forms application

Painting

The *Control* class, and by inheritance the *Form* class, contains a series of methods that can be overridden to customize the look and feel of a window. Most of these methods correspond to window messages. For example, the *OnPaint* method is called when the form needs to paint some region of its window. In the following code, the *OnPaint* method is overridden to draw an ellipse in the window.

```
using System;
using System.Drawing;
using System.Windows.Forms;

namespace FirstWindowsForms
{
```

```
class WindowsForms1 : Form
{
    static void Main()
    {
        WindowsForms1 f = new WindowsForms1();
        f.Text = "Form Title";
        Application.Run (f);
    }
    private Color c = Color.Blue;
    protected override void OnPaint(PaintEventArgs e)
    {
        Rectangle rc = new Rectangle (0, 0,
                                      ClientRectangle.Width - 1,
                                      ClientRectangle.Height - 1);
        Brush br = new SolidBrush (c);
        e.Graphics.FillEllipse (br, rc);
        br.Dispose();
        base.OnPaint (e);
    }
}
}
```

Figure 23-2 shows the results of the code.

Figure 23-2   A Windows Forms application
that draws an ellipse in its form

The ellipse is drawn in the *OnPaint* method. The single *PaintEventArgs* parameter provides two properties: the self-explanatory *ClipRectangle* and an instance of a *Graphics* class. The *Graphics* class wraps the device context (DC) for the window. The *Graphics* class contains a large number of properties and methods for integrating the state of the device context and drawing in the DC. The preceding simple example uses the *DrawEllipse* method to draw the ellipse on the form.

Adding Controls

Many Windows Forms applications never override the *OnPaint* method. Instead, they create forms with a number of controls that provide the entire user interface needed for the application. Providing a control on a form is a multi-step process. First a member variable of the specific control class type is defined in the form class. An instance of the control is then created, and the necessary properties of that form are initialized. The control is then added to the control collection of the form. Finally the form handles any relevant events that the control fires.

In the following example, a button control is added to the form so that when it is pressed, the color of the ellipse changes from red to green to blue. First a member variable is defined of class *Button*, as shown here:

```
protected Button btnChangeColor;
```

The member variable is declared as *protected* because although there is no need for outside classes to manipulate the control, if the program were rewritten to derive a class from the form, the derived form might want to access the button.

Next an instance of the button must be created. This is best done when the form class is created. Once the form class is created, the size and location of the button are set along with its text. The following code shows the form constructor routine that creates and initializes the instance of the button:

```
public WindowsForms1 ()
{
    btnChangeColor = new Button();
    btnChangeColor.Location = new Point (5, 5);
    btnChangeColor.Size = new Size (70, 25);
    btnChangeColor.Text = "Click Me!";
}
```

The location and size properties of the button are initialized with *Point* and *Size* structures, respectively. These structures need to be created—hence the *new* keyword that creates and, in combination with their constructor routines, initializes the structures.

A common mistake of programmers who hand-generate Windows Forms code is to forget the next step: the control that has been created must be added to the collection of controls that the form class owns. This task is accomplished with the following line of code, which must be placed after the child control has been created:

```
this.Controls.Add (btnChangeColor);
```

All classes based on *Control*, including *Form*, have a *Controls* property, which is a *ControlCollection* class that maintains a list of the controls in the window. The *ControlCollections* class has an *Add* method that is used to add a new control to the list. At this point, the application can be recompiled and the button will appear in the window. Figure 23-3 shows the window with the button in the upper left corner.

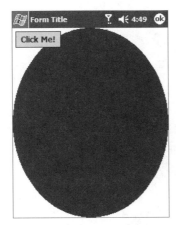

Figure 23-3   The Windows Forms application with a button in the upper left corner of the form

Adding an Event Handler

The control has been added, but clicking on it has no effect. To have the application be notified when the user clicks the button, an event handler needs to be added to the code. While the designer makes adding an event handler a point-and-click affair, programmers should understand the underlying code.

Adding an event handler is done in two parts: first the event handler routine has to be added to the application, and second the routine has to hook the event chain for the control. The delegate of the event handler depends on the event being handled, but traditionally, Windows Forms controls throw events with a delegate that looks similar to the following:

```
void EventHandler (object o, EventArgs e);
```

The object is the source of the event, and *EventArgs* is a dummy class that, although providing no additional information, is the base class for argument classes that do provide information. For example, a mouse event passes a *Mouse-*

EventArgs class derived from *EventArgs* that provides information such as the mouse coordinates. To add a button click handler, the default function prototype is used since the button click event doesn't return any additional data. The handler for the click event is shown here:

```
protected void MyClickEventHandler (object o, EventArgs e)
{
    if (c == Color.Blue)
        c = Color.Red;
    else if (c == Color.Red)
        c = Color.Green;
    else if (c == Color.Green)
        c = Color.Blue;
    this.Invalidate();
}
```

For the second part, adding the event handler to the list of handlers, the following single line is used:

```
btnChangeColor.Click += new EventHandler(MyClickEventHandler);
```

This code creates a new event handler that is then added to the button's *Click* event. When the example is now recompiled and run, clicking on the button will cause the ellipse to be redrawn in a different color.

Where Is All This Code?

So, you might ask, where is all this code when I use the designer to generate a Windows Forms application? If you check out the code of any designer-generated Windows Forms application in Visual Studio, you'll find the following lines of code:

```
protected override void Dispose( bool disposing )
{
    base.Dispose( disposing );
}
#region Windows Form Designer generated code
/// <summary>
/// The main entry point for the application.
/// </summary>

static void Main()
{
    Application.Run(new Form1());
}
```

Notice the line *#region Windows Form Designer generated code*. This line hides a large amount of autogenerated code that the designer inserts in the application as controls are dragged and dropped into the form by the developer.

Opening up that region of hidden code by clicking on the line shows that the designer-generated code simply sets the location, size, and other properties of the controls, as was done in the preceding examples. One of the interesting features of the .NET languages is that all information on the layout of the forms is contained in the source code, not in a separate resource file as is done in unmanaged Windows code. Resources are available in managed applications, but they're used for storing language-specific strings, cursors, bitmaps, and such; they're not used for dialog box templates.

Configuring a Top-Level Form

The Compact Framework supports a handful of different methods for configuring the look and feel of the top-level form. Forms can be made to cover the full screen, have an OK button instead of a smart Close button, and, on non–Pocket PC systems, change the default size and location of the window.

On a Pocket PC, the standard smart Minimize button, which looks like a Close box but actually minimizes the application, can be converted to an OK button that closes the window by setting the *MinimizeBox* property to *false*. The button can be removed completely by setting the *ControlBox* property to *false*.

To hide the navigation bar, set the form's *FormWindowState* property to *Maximized*. The only other setting supported is the default state, *Normal*. You can remove the menu bar by deleting the *MenuBar* class, which the designer adds automatically. In addition, the size and location of the top-level form can't be changed on a Pocket PC unless the *FormBorderStyle* property is set to *null*. In this case, the form can be placed anywhere on the desktop, but it won't have a border.

On embedded systems, the properties have a somewhat different action. Setting the *ControlBox* property to *false* removes the caption bar. Setting the *MinimizeBox* and *MaximizeBox* parameters to *false* removes the Minimize and Maximize buttons from the caption bar. Setting the *WindowState* parameter to *Maximized* maximizes the window. Adding a *MenuBar* class to the form causes a command bar control to be placed at the top of the client area of the form. Finally, the *Size* and *Location* parameters are used, even if the *ControlBox* parameter is *true*.

Compact Framework Unique Classes

The Compact Framework supports a series of classes that are not on the standard desktop version of the .NET Framework class library. These classes are provided to support a few of the unique situations that mobile applications encounter. They include classes for dealing with the soft keyboard, or soft input panel (SIP); infrared communication; and interprocess communication.

MessageWindow

The *MessageWindow* class provides a method for unmanaged code to send standard window messages to Compact Framework applications. On the desktop, the *Control* class provides a *WndProc* method that can be overridden to see all the window messages sent to the control. Because most window classes in the framework are derived from the *Control* class, this lets a desktop application monitor window messages for almost every window in the application. In the Compact Framework, however, the *Control* class doesn't provide a *WndProc* method, so there's no way to see the window messages sent to the controls in the application. The *MessageWindow* class, unique to the Compact Framework, is an exception. This class creates a hidden window and provides not only a *WndProc* method to monitor messages sent to the window but also an *Hwnd* property that provides the handle to the window.

Instead of creating an instance of the *MessageWindow* class, applications derive a class from *MessageWindow* and then override the *WndProc* method so that the message sent to the window can be seen. The *WndProc* method is defined as

```
protected virtual new void MessageWindow.WndProc (Message m);
```

The only parameter is an instance of a *Message* structure that describes the message received by the window. The *Message* structure has the following properties:

```
public IntPtr Message.HWnd;
public int    Message.Msg;
public IntPtr Message.WParam;
public IntPtr Message.LParam;
public IntPtr Message.Result;
```

The properties represent the standard parameters of a call to a window procedure: the handle to the window, the message value, the *wParam* value, and the *lParam* value. The additional property, *Result*, is the value returned by the message. The *Message* structure also has one interesting method, *Create*, shown here:

```
public static Create (IntPtr hwnd, Int32 msg, IntPtr wparam, IntPtr lparam);
```

This method provides a single-line initialization function for the other properties in the structure.

The following code fragment shows how the *MessageWindow* class can be used.

```
using Microsoft.WindowsCE.Forms;

public class MyMsgWnd : MessageWindow
{
    protected override void WndProc (ref Message m)
    {
        // WM_USER is defined as 0x400
        if (m.Msg == 0x400)
        {
            string s = string.Format (
                    "WM_USER received wParam:{0:X} lParam:{1:X} ",
                    m.WParam.ToInt32(), m.LParam.ToInt32());
            MessageBox.Show (s);
        }
        base.WndProc (ref m);
    }
}
```

This code fragment shows the declaration of the *MyMsgWnd* class derived from *MessageWindow*. *MyMsgWnd* overrides the *WndProc* method and displays a message box when a window receives a *WM_USER* message created by *MyMsg-Wnd*. Because this is a managed application, there is no declaration for all the standard window messages. A glance at any Windows CE SDK will show that *WM_USER* is defined as 0x400 in Winuser.h.

The *MessageWindow* class has two static methods that can be used to send or post window messages to other windows. They are the appropriately named *SendMessage* and *PostMessage*, shown here:

```
public static void MessageWindow.PostMessage (Message m);
public static void MessageWindow.SendMessage (Message m);
```

The two methods each take a *Message* structure as their single argument.

MessageWindow also exposes the handle of the window created by the class in the read-only property *Hwnd*, defined as

```
public IntPtr MessageWindow.Hwnd;
```

The *Hwnd* property is unique in the Compact Framework because it's the only place where a real window handle is exposed to managed code. Other controls in the Compact Framework don't expose their window handles and therefore can't be sent to other applications. The *MessageWindow* class will be used in the IrSquirtCF example later in this chapter.

InputPanel

The *InputPanel* class provides Compact Framework applications information regarding the state of the SIP (the soft keyboard) on the Pocket PC or other embedded devices with a soft keyboard. In addition, the *InputPanel* class can be used to control the state of the SIP, enabling the application to show or hide the SIP as needed. The methods and properties of the *InputPanel* class are shown here:

```
public void InputPanel.InputPanel ( );
public Rectangle InputPanel.Bounds;
public Rectangle InputPanel.VisibleDesktop;
public bool InputPanel.Enabled;
public event EventHandler InputPanel.EnabledChanged;
```

Interestingly, the methods of the *InputPanel* class are not marked static, so to monitor or control the SIP, the class must first be instantiated. The *InputPanel* constructor takes no arguments. The *InputPanel* read-only properties *Bounds* and *VisibleDesktop*, both defined as rectangles, provide information about the size and position of the SIP as well as the size of the desktop area not obscured by the SIP.

The *VisibleDesktop* property provides the rectangle that is the area of the desktop not covered by the SIP. This rectangle changes depending on whether the SIP is displayed or hidden. When the SIP is displayed, the rectangle ranges from just below the navigation bar to just above the top of the SIP window. When the SIP is hidden, the rectangle includes all of the area of the screen below the navigation bar, including the area of the menu bar if one was created by the application.

The *Bounds* rectangle describes the size and location of the SIP when it's displayed. This rectangle doesn't change if the SIP is hidden. Instead, it always shows the location and size of the SIP as if it were being displayed. Applications wanting to adjust their windows to avoid being covered by the SIP should use the *VisibleDesktop* property instead of the *Bounds* property.

The *Enabled* property is set to *true* if the SIP is displayed and *false* if the SIP is hidden. The property is settable, providing the application the ability to show or hide the SIP simply by changing this property.

The *InputPanel* class contains an event that can be hooked to notify the application when the state of the SIP changes from hidden to shown or shown to hidden. The delegate associated with this event contains only the default object and the *EventArgs* parameters, so when the event fires, the event handler must query the new state of the SIP using the *Enabled* parameter.

Working with the SIP   Unless the *FormBorderStyle* property of the *Form* class is set to *null*, the Pocket PC implementation of the runtime overrides the *Size* and

Location properties, preventing an application from resizing a form in response to the SIP being shown or hidden. A workaround for this issue is to create a *Panel* control or a property sheet on the form and then place all the other controls for the form on that control. An example of using the *EnableChanged* event can be seen in the IrSquirtCF example later in this chapter. In the example, the *EnableChanged* event is overridden to adjust the size of the output list box control.

IrDA Classes

The Compact Framework supports managed classes for Infrared Data Association (IrDA) communication. The classes are extensions of the *Socket* class provided both in the desktop version of the Framework Class Library and in the Compact Framework. The extensions center around two classes: *IrDAClient*, which provides the interface to the IrDA socket stream, discovery information, and status information about the current connection; and *IrDAListener*, which provides server support for listening for other devices that want to initiate an infrared (IR) connection with the device. A number of other classes provide support for these two major classes.

IrDAClient   The *IrDAClient* class provides the following methods and properties:

```
public void IrDAClient ();
public void IrDAClient (IrDAEndPoint);
public void IrDAClient (string);
public void Connect(IrDAEndPoint);
public void Connect(string);
public void Close();
public IrDADeviceInfo[] DiscoverDevices(int);
public static IrDADeviceInfo[] DiscoverDevices(int, Socket);
static string GetRemoteMachineName (Socket s);
public Stream GetStream();
public string RemoteMachineName;
```

This variety of methods and properties provides most of the functionality needed for IR communication. To initiate communication with another device, an application first uses the *DiscoverDevices* method to determine whether any devices are in range. This process is shown in the following code fragment:

```
IrDAClient irClient;
irClient = new IrDAClient();
IrDADeviceInfo[] di = irClient.DiscoverDevices(4);
if (di.Length > 0)
{
    foreach (IrDADeviceInfo device in di)
```

(continued)

```
                Console.WriteLine ("Device:"+device.DeviceName+" discovered.");
    }
    else
        Console.WriteLine ("No devices discovered.");
```

The single parameter *DiscoverDevices* is the maximum number of devices to return.

Once a device has been detected, the application can connect to a specific service on the device by calling the *Connect* method on an *IrDAClient* class. *Connect* can take one of two different parameters, either an *IrDAEndPoint* class describing the device and service to connect to or simply a string requesting a connection to a specific named service provided by the other device.

After a connection is made successfully, the *GetStream* method is called to get an instance of a stream class to communicate with the other device. The stream class is the same class that forms the basis for the filestream classes used elsewhere in the Framework. The stream class contains the requisite read and write methods for sending and receiving bytes from the other device.

When communication is completed with the other device, the stream class and the *IrDAClient* class should be closed. In addition, after the *Close* methods have been called, the *Dispose* methods on both classes should be called before the class goes out of scope. This ensures that any system resources used by those classes will be freed immediately instead of waiting until a garbage collection occurs.

IrDAListener   The *IrDAListener* class is used to create an IrDA server socket that can listen for incoming connection requests. The interesting methods and properties of *IrDAListener* are shown here:

```
public IrDAListener(IrDAEndPoint);
public IrDAListener(string);
public IrDAEndPoint LocalEndpoint {get;}
public IrDAClient AcceptIrDAClient();
public Socket AcceptSocket();
public bool Pending();
public void Start();
public void Stop();
```

The *IrDAListener* constructor can specify either an *IrDAEndPoint* class or simply the name of the infrared service that the server should advertise. Once an instance of the class is created, the start method is called to listen for any incoming requests for connections. Connections can be detected by calling the *Pending* method. The *Pending* method will return *true* when another device has requested an infrared connection. Once a connection request is detected, the server calls the *AcceptSocket* method, which returns an instance of an *IrDAClient* class that is then used for communication.

The following code fragment shows the process of creating an *IrDA-Listener* class and waiting for a connection:

```
IrDAListener irListen;
IrDAClient irClientSrv;
Stream s;

irListen = new IrDAListener("MySquirt"),
irListen.Start();

while (isRunning)
{
    if (irListen.Pending())
        break;
    if (isRunning)
        Thread.Sleep (500);
}
irClientSrv = irListen.AcceptIrDAClient();
s = irClientSrv.GetStream();
```

Notice that the *Pending* method call is made within a polling loop. Unfortunately, *Pending* doesn't block, so a server thread must continually call *Pending* to determine when a client device wants to connect. Because polling must be done relatively infrequently in a Windows CE device to avoid running down the battery, the preceding code sleeps the thread for half a second before checking again for a connection. This polling process is best done on a thread other than the primary thread of the application.

The IrSquirtCF example later in this chapter demonstrates the use of the IrDA classes. That example demonstrates device discovery, operating as an IR server, and operating as an IR client.

Accessing the Underlying Operating System

Even with the new classes provided by the Compact Framework, the functionality of the Compact Framework base class library is significantly less than that of its desktop counterpart. The need to keep the run-time libraries small to reduce the hardware impact, the decision to focus on client-side processing, and the pressure to ship a version 1.0 product on time all resulted in a class library that, although functional, lacks some of the basics expected by .NET programmers.

Because of the limited class library, Compact Framework applications frequently need to escape the bounds of the .NET runtime sandbox and call unmanaged routines. The process of calling outside the .NET environment is called Process Invoke, almost always referred to by the abbreviation *P/Invoke*.

P/Invoke

The task of calling unmanaged code begins with declaring a static external method in a class with parameters that match the calling parameters of the unmanaged function. The method is then marked with a special attribute to indicate its purpose to the compiler. At run time, the method is simply called like any other method in the class. The call to the method results in the Compact Framework loading the DLL containing the function to be called, marshaling the calling parameters onto the stack, and calling the function.

The following is a simple but contrived example of calling outside the framework. Before I dive into the discussion of this example, be aware that there are managed ways of computing elapsed time without calling into unmanaged code. I'm simply using *GetTickCount* since it's a simple function with no parameters.

```
public class SomeClass
{
    private uint OldCnt;
    public void SomeClass()
    {
        OldCnt = 0;
    }
    [DllImport ("coredll.dll")]
    private static extern uint GetTickCount ();

    public uint TicksSinceLast (){
        uint ticks = GetTickCount();
        uint diff = ticks - OldCnt;
        OldCnt = ticks;
        return diff;
    }
}
```

This code shows a class that contains two methods, *GetTickCount* and *Ticks-SinceLast*. The *GetTickCount* method is marked as static, meaning that it's defined by the class, not an instance of the class; and *extern*, meaning that the method body is defined outside the class. In this case, the method body is actually implemented in unmanaged code.

Just above the definition of *GetTickCount* is the *DllImport* attribute enclosed in the square brackets. The *DllImport* attribute marks the method as being a P/Invoke call to unmanaged code. The single parameter for *DllImport*, in this case, is the name of the unmanaged DLL that implements the function *GetTickCount*. The DLL, Coredll.dll, is the standard API DLL for Windows CE and exposes most of the functions supported by the Windows CE operating system, including *GetTickCount*.

The *TicksSinceLast* method calls *GetTickCount* just as it would any other managed method in the class. No special syntax is necessary for the method when the class calls it. There is also no need for the P/Invoke method to be marked private, although it typically is good practice since the programmer who wrote the class knows the method is a P/Invoke call and can provide proper precautions such as couching the call in a *try, catch* block to catch exceptions specific to the P/Invoke call.

The *DllImport* attribute class can specify more than simply the name of the DLL to call. Although the Compact Framework supports other fields in *DllImport*, only two are useful to the application: *EntryPoint* and *SetLastError*.

The *EntryPoint* field of *DllImport* allows the application to specify a name for the unmanaged entry point in the DLL that's different from the name of the managed method. The *EntryPoint* field is handy when calling a Windows CE API that has a string as a parameter. Win32 API convention specifies that the real name of a function with a string parameter have a suffix of either *W* or *A*, depending on whether the function expects Unicode- or ANSI-formatted strings. Even though Windows CE supports only Unicode entry points, the names of the functions exported by Coredll.dll have the *W* suffix. C and C++ applications don't normally see the *W* suffix because the .h files in the SDK redefine the generic function names used in the application without the *W* or *A* to the specific API name that's used when the application is compiled. The following code fragment shows an example of specifying the function name when calling the unmanaged API *SetWindowText*:

```
[DllImport ("coredll.dll", EntryPoint="SetWindowTextW")]
private static extern void SetWindowText (IntPtr h, string s);
```

The name traditionally used for the entry point is *SetWindowText*. However, Coredll.dll exports the function as *SetWindowTextW*. The use of the *EntryPoint* field in the *DllImport* attribute specifies the correct entry point name while retaining the traditional name for references within the managed code.

The other useful field in the *DllImport* attribute class is *SetLastError*. This field is defined as a *bool*. Setting this field to *true* tells the runtime to save the last error value set by the call to the unmanaged code. This allows the managed code to later call the *GetLastWin32Error* method of the *Marshal* class to retrieve the last error value. If the *SetLastError* field is not set to *true*, the default is not to save the last error value of the P/Invoke call.

None of the other fields in the *DllImport* attribute class that are supported by the .NET Compact Framework have much use. The *CharSet* field allows the application to specify whether the strings being passed to the unmanaged code should be converted to ANSI or remain Unicode. On the Compact Framework, the only values supported for the *CharSet* field are *Auto* and *Unicode*. Since

Auto defaults to Unicode on the Compact Framework, these two values mean the same thing. The *CallingConvention* field can also be set, but here again, the single value supported by the Compact Framework has no real effect on the processing of the P/Invoke call.

P/Invoke Arguments

While declaring methods that call outside the run-time environment is easy, sometimes declaring the proper parameters for passing and receiving data can be a bit of a challenge. The Compact Framework is limited in the data types that can be easily passed between managed and unmanaged code.

Simple Types

The process of gathering the data and passing it to and from unmanaged code is called *marshaling*. The marshaling support in the Compact Framework is limited to blittable data types. Blittable types are represented in managed and unmanaged code in the same format and therefore do not require translation on the call stack between the two environments. Essentially, this definition covers all simple numeric and character data types in the Compact Framework, such as signed and unsigned longs, ints, shorts, bytes, and characters. The Compact Framework also supports passing one-dimensional arrays of blittable types and structures that contain blittable types. Strings can also be passed as parameters, although they are always passed as Unicode strings.

Table 23-1 relates managed types to their corresponding unmanaged types.

Table 23-1   Cross-Reference Between Managed Data Types and Their Unmanaged C++ Counterparts

Managed Type	Passed by Value	Passed by Reference
byte, sbyte	*BYTE, char*	*byte *, char **
short, ushort	*SHORT, WORD*	*SHORT *, WORD **
int, uint	*Int, DWORD*	*int *, DWORD **
long	unsupported	*INT64 **
float	unsupported	*float **
double	unsupported	*double **
IntPtr	*PVOID*	*PVOID **
bool	*BYTE* [*]	*BYTE **

Table 23-1 Cross-Reference Between Managed Data Types and Their Unmanaged C++ Counterparts *(continued)*

Managed Type	Passed by Value	Passed by Reference
string	*LPCWSTR*[†]*	unsupported
StringBuilder	*LPWSTR*	unsupported

* A nonzero value is true.

† * The *string* type should be treated as read-only by the unmanaged routine.

Structures and Arrays

Simple structures can also be passed by reference in P/Invoke calls. A simple structure is one that contains only blittable types. The structure can't contain arrays or strings. The following code shows two code fragments, one managed and the other unmanaged. The simple structure passed from the managed to the unmanaged code contains three integers and must be defined in both the managed and the unmanaged code.

```
[StructLayout(LayoutKind.Sequential)]
public struct Size3D
{
    public uint height;
    public uint width;
    public uint depth;
}
[DllImport ("Unmanaged.dll")]
private static extern uint GetContainerSize (ref Size3D b);

private uint ComputeVolume()
{
    Size3D siz;
    // Provide default size
    siz.height = 1;
    siz.width = 1;
    siz.depth = 1;
    // Call the unmanaged code
    GetContainerSize (ref siz);
    uint Volume = siz.height * siz.width * siz.depth;
}
//
// Unmanaged code
//
typedef struct {
    DWORD dwHeight;
```

(continued)

```
        DWORD dwWidth;
        DWORD dwDepth;
    } SIZE3D;

    DWORD GetContainerSize (SIZE3D *pSiz) {

        pSiz->dwHeight = 43;
        pSiz->dwWidth = 12;
        pSiz->dwDepth = 2;
        return 1;
    }
```

The definition of the managed structure, *Size3D*, is preceded by a *StructLayout* attribute. The single parameter is the enumeration *LayoutKind*. The only enumeration value defined in the initial version of the Compact Framework is *Sequential*. Although this is the default layout in the Compact Framework, it's a good technique to specify this attribute for every structure being passed to unmanaged code because it's typically required on the desktop version of the .NET runtime. Specifying it here makes it easy to remember to use it if the code is reused on the desktop.

Arrays can be passed as well, with some limitations. One-dimensional arrays of blittable types can be passed. For example, an array of integers can be passed to unmanaged code, as shown in the following code:

```
[DllImport ("UMTest.dll")]
private static extern int DiffFromAve (int[] a, int cnt);
int ManagedRoutine ()
{
    // Declare and initialize the array
    int[] array = new int[4];
    array[0] = 10;
    array[1] = 15;
    array[2] =  4;
    array[3] = 30;
    // Call the unmanaged routine
    int ave = DiffFromAve (array, array.Length);
    Console.WriteLine ("ave:{0} {1} {2} {3} {4}", ave,
                        array[0], array[1], array[2], array[3]);
    return ave;
}
//
// Unmanaged code
//
DWORD DiffFromAve (int *pnArray, int nCnt) {
    int i, sum = 0, ave = 0;
    if (pnArray) {
```

```
    // Compute sum
    for (i = 0; i < nCnt; i++)
        sum += pnArray[i];

    // Compute ave
    ave = sum / nCnt;

    // Set differnce from ave
    for (i = 0; i < nCnt; i++)
        pnArray[i] -= ave;

    }
    return ave;
}
```

This code shows an array of four elements being passed to unmanaged code. Notice that the unmanaged code can read and write the elements of the array. The example is of course contrived since nothing is done in the unmanaged code that couldn't be accomplished in managed code. However, the example does show the process.

Working with Strings

One of the more nettlesome issues with calling unmanaged code is how to deal with strings. On the desktop, programmers actually have a somewhat more difficult time since they have to deal with both ANSI and Unicode strings. In the Compact Framework, we typically deal only with Unicode strings since the operating system we're calling, Windows CE, uses Unicode strings almost exclusively.

Passing a string down to unmanaged code is actually quite simple. A string class can simply be passed in the parameter list as it would be for any other method. The string appears to the unmanaged code as a pointer to a constant Unicode string. The constant modifier is necessary since the string can't be modified by the unmanaged code. The following routine passes down a string to an unmanaged routine:

```
int ManagedRoutine ()
{
    uint len = MyGetLength ("This is a string");
}
//
// Unmanaged code
//
DWORD MyGetLength (LPCWSTR pszStr) {
    DWORD dwLen;
```

(continued)

```
    dwLen = lstrlen (pszStr);
    return dwLen;
}
```

To have the unmanaged routine modify the string takes a bit more work. Instead of passing a string class, the managed routine must pass a *StringBuilder* class. To do this, create a *StringBuilder* class large enough to hold the string that will be returned. The class can also be initialized with a string if the unmanaged code expects an initialized string. In the following code, the managed code calls the Windows CE function *GetWindowText*, which takes three parameters: the handle of the window to query, a buffer to hold the title text of the window, and the maximum number of characters that the buffer can hold.

```
[DllImport( "coredll.dll", EntryPoint="GetWindowTextW")]
public static extern int GetWindowText (IntPtr h, StringBuilder str,
                                         int size);
public int ManagedRoutine ()
{
    StringBuilder strWndText = new StringBuilder (256);
    GetWindowText (h, strWndText, strWndText.Capacity);
}
```

This code first declares the external method *GetWindowText*, which is defined in Coredll.dll as *GetWindowTextW* since it returns a Unicode string. The managed routine simply creates a *StringBuilder* class of some large length and then passes it to the method. The *Capacity* method of *StringBuilder* returns the maximum number of characters that the instance of the class can hold.

The third way a string can be used in a P/Invoke call comes into play when an unmanaged routine returns a pointer to a string as the return value. The Compact Framework can't marshal any return parameter larger than 32 bits, but since the return value is a pointer to a string, this condition is satisfied.

When an unmanaged routine returns a pointer to a string, it should be cast as an *IntPtr*. The string pointed to by the *IntPtr* can then be converted to a managed string using the *Marshal* class's *PtrToStringUni* method. The following routine calls the *GetCommandLine* Windows API, which returns a pointer to the command line as its return value.

```
[DllImport ("coredll.dll")]
public static extern IntPtr GetCommandLine();

public int ManagedRoutine ()
{
    IntPtr pCmdLine = GetCommandLine();
    string strCmdLine = Marshal.PtrToStringUni (pCmdLine);
}
```

The IrSquirtCF Example

The IrSquirtCF example program demonstrates many of the features of the Compact Framework as well as some of the techniques discussed in this chapter. IrSquirtCF is a managed version of the IrSquirt program provided with the Pocket PC and the Smartphone, discussed in Chapter 14. The two programs are compatible. It's possible to send or receive a file using IrSquirtCF to or from another Windows CE system or a Windows XP system running IrSquirt. The source code for IrSquirtCF is shown in Listing 23-5.

```csharp
MyMsgWindow.cs
using System;
using System.Text;
using System.Runtime.InteropServices;
using Microsoft.WindowsCE.Forms;

namespace MySquirtCF
{
    /// <summary>
    /// Summary description for MyMsgWindow.
    /// </summary>
    public class MyMsgWindow : MessageWindow
    {
        public MyMsgWindow()
        {
            //
            // TODO: Add constructor logic here
            //
        }
        public string Text
        {
            get
            {
                StringBuilder sbText = new StringBuilder (256);
                GetWindowText (this.Hwnd, sbText, sbText.Capacity);
                return sbText.ToString();
            }
            set
            {
                SetWindowText (this.Hwnd, value);
            }
        }
        public static IntPtr FindOtherWindow (string strTitle)
        {
```

Listing 23-5   The IrSquirtCF source code

(continued)

Listing 23-5   *(continued)*

```
            return FindWindow (null, strTitle);
        }
        protected override void WndProc(ref Message m)
        {
            base.WndProc (ref m);
        }


        /// <summary>
        /// Returns true when running on a Pocket PC
        /// </summary>
        /// <returns></returns>
        public static bool IsPocketPC ()
        {
            bool fPocketPC = false;
            StringBuilder sb = new StringBuilder (256);
            PrivGetPlatString (257, sb.Capacity, sb, 0);
            string strPlat = sb.ToString();
            if (strPlat == "PocketPC")
                fPocketPC = true;
            return fPocketPC;
        }
        // Used by IsPocketPC routine to get the platform string
        [DllImport ("Coredll.dll", EntryPoint="SystemParametersInfoW")]
        private static extern bool PrivGetPlatString (int Cmd,
            int StrLen, StringBuilder strPlat, int fWinIni);

        [DllImport ("coredll.dll", EntryPoint="FindWindowW")]
        private static extern IntPtr FindWindow (string strClass,
                                                 string strTitle);

        [DllImport ("coredll.dll", EntryPoint="SetWindowTextW")]
        private static extern void SetWindowText (IntPtr h, string s);

        [ DllImport( "coredll.dll", EntryPoint="GetWindowTextW")]
        public static extern int GetWindowText (IntPtr h,
                        StringBuilder sysDirBuffer, int size );


    }
}
```

Form1.cs

```
using System;
using System.Drawing;
using System.Collections;
using System.Windows.Forms;
using System.Data;
```

```
using System.Net.Sockets;
using System.IO;
using System.Text;
using System.Threading;

namespace MySquirtCF
{
    /// <summary>
    /// Summary description for Form1.
    /// </summary>
    public class Form1 : System.Windows.Forms.Form
    {
        private System.Windows.Forms.MainMenu mainMenu1;
        private System.Windows.Forms.Button btnGo;
        private System.Windows.Forms.Label label1;
        private System.Windows.Forms.Button btnBrowse;
        private System.Windows.Forms.TextBox textFileName;
        private System.Windows.Forms.ListBox listOut;
        private System.Windows.Forms.OpenFileDialog openFileDialog1;
        private Microsoft.WindowsCE.Forms.InputPanel inputPanel1;

        private bool m_fPocketPC;
        private bool isRunning;
        private Thread thServ;
        private MenuItem menuFile;
        private MenuItem menuExit;
        public Form1()
        {
            //
            // Required for Windows Form Designer support
            //
            InitializeComponent();

            // See if we're running on a Pocket PC
            if (MyMsgWindow.IsPocketPC())
                m_fPocketPC = true;

            if (m_fPocketPC)
            {
                // On a Pocket PC, adjust control position since
                // Commandbar isn't used.

                this.label1.Location = new Point (4, 5);
                this.textFileName.Location = new Point (46, 4);
                this.btnBrowse.Location = new Point (4, 30);
                this.btnGo.Location = new Point (100, 30);
                this.listOut.Location = new Point (4, 54);
```

(continued)

Listing 23-5   *(continued)*

```
            // Set size of listbox depending on SIP
            int height = this.inputPanel1.VisibleDesktop.Height -
                this.listOut.Top;
            if (!this.inputPanel1.Enabled)
                height -= 26;
            this.listOut.Size = new Size (this.listOut.Width, height);

            // Place OK button on Nav Bar to close application
            this.ControlBox = true;
            this.MinimizeBox = false;

        }
        else
        {
            // On an embedded device, add a File | Exit menu item
            menuFile = new MenuItem();
            menuExit = new MenuItem();

            menuExit.Text = "Exit";
            menuExit.Click += new EventHandler(menuExit_Click);

            menuFile.Text = "File";
            menuFile.MenuItems.Add (menuExit);

            mainMenu1.MenuItems.Add (menuFile);

        }
        int widthC = this.ClientRectangle.Width;
        int heightC = this.ClientRectangle.Height;
        this.Text = "IrSquirt";
    }
    /// <summary>
    /// Clean up any resources being used.
    /// </summary>
    protected override void Dispose( bool disposing )
    {
        base.Dispose( disposing );
    }
    #region Windows Form Designer generated code
    /// <summary>
    /// Required method for Designer support - do not modify
    /// the contents of this method with the code editor.
    /// </summary>
    private void InitializeComponent()
    {
        this.mainMenu1 = new System.Windows.Forms.MainMenu();
        this.btnGo = new System.Windows.Forms.Button();
```

```
this.label1 = new System.Windows.Forms.Label();
this.textFileName = new System.Windows.Forms.TextBox();
this.btnBrowse = new System.Windows.Forms.Button();
this.listOut = new System.Windows.Forms.ListBox();
this.openFileDialog1 = new System.Windows.Forms.OpenFileDialog();
this.inputPanel1 = new Microsoft.WindowsCE.Forms.InputPanel();
//
// btnGo
//
this.btnGo.Location = new System.Drawing.Point(160, 58);
this.btnGo.Size = new System.Drawing.Size(80, 20);
this.btnGo.Text = "Send";
this.btnGo.Click += new System.EventHandler(this.btnGo_Click);
//
// label1
//
this.label1.Location = new System.Drawing.Point(8, 33);
this.label1.Size = new System.Drawing.Size(32, 20);
this.label1.Text = "File:";
//
// textFileName
//
this.textFileName.Location = new System.Drawing.Point(48, 32);
this.textFileName.Size = new System.Drawing.Size(192, 22);
this.textFileName.Text = "";
//
// btnBrowse
//
this.btnBrowse.Location = new System.Drawing.Point(8, 58);
this.btnBrowse.Size = new System.Drawing.Size(80, 20);
this.btnBrowse.Text = "Browse";
this.btnBrowse.Click += new
                    System.EventHandler(this.btnBrowse_Click);
//
// listOut
//
this.listOut.Location = new System.Drawing.Point(8, 82);
this.listOut.Size = new System.Drawing.Size(232, 198);
//
// inputPanel1
//
this.inputPanel1.EnabledChanged += new
            System.EventHandler(this.inputPanel1_EnabledChanged);
//
// Form1
//
this.ClientSize = new System.Drawing.Size(250, 292);
this.Controls.Add(this.listOut);
```

(continued)

Listing 23-5 *(continued)*

```
            this.Controls.Add(this.btnBrowse);
            this.Controls.Add(this.textFileName);
            this.Controls.Add(this.label1);
            this.Controls.Add(this.btnGo);
            this.MaximizeBox = false;
            this.Menu = this.mainMenu1;
            this.Text = "Form1";
            this.Closing += new
                System.ComponentModel.CancelEventHandler(this.Form1_Closing)
;

            this.Load += new System.EventHandler(this.Form1_Load);

        }
        #endregion

        /// <summary>
        /// The main entry point for the application.
        /// </summary>

        static void Main()
        {
            Application.Run(new Form1());
        }

        private void Form1_Load(object sender, System.EventArgs e)
        {
            isRunning = true;
            this.thServ = new Thread (new ThreadStart(this.SrvRoutine));
            this.thServ.Start();
        }

        private void Form1_Closing(object sender,
                            System.ComponentModel.CancelEventArgs e)
        {
            isRunning = false;
            Thread.Sleep(550);
        }

        private void menuExit_Click(object sender, System.EventArgs e)
        {
            this.Close();
        }

        private void btnBrowse_Click(object sender, System.EventArgs e)
        {
            DialogResult dr = this.openFileDialog1.ShowDialog();
            if (dr != DialogResult.OK)
```

```
            return;
    this.textFileName.Text = openFileDialog1.FileName;
}


private void inputPanel1_EnabledChanged(object sender,
                                        System.EventArgs e)
{
    // Adjust the listbox to avoid being covered by the SIP.
    if (m_fPocketPC)
    {
        int height = this.inputPanel1.VisibleDesktop.Height -
                     this.listOut.Top;
        if (!this.inputPanel1.Enabled)
            height -= 26;
        this.listOut.Size = new Size (this.listOut.Width,
                                      height);
    }
}


private void btnGo_Click(object sender, System.EventArgs e)
{
    string strFileName = this.textFileName.Text;

    if (strFileName.Length > 0)
        SendFileToIR (strFileName);
}
private void StringOut (string str)
{
    this.listOut.Items.Add (str);
    return;
}
/// <summary>
/// Sends a file to the other device
/// </summary>
/// <param name="strFileName"></param>
private void SendFileToIR (string strFileName)
{
    Stream s;
    FileStream fs;
    int rc;
    IrDAClient irClient;

    try
    {
        fs = new FileStream (strFileName, FileMode.Open,
                             FileAccess.Read);
    }
    catch (IOException ex)
```

(continued)

Listing 23-5   *(continued)*

```
    {
        StringOut (string.Format("Error opening file {0}",
                    ex.Message));
        return;
    }
    StringOut ("File opened");

    irClient = new IrDAClient ();
    //
    // Connect to service
    //
    StringOut ("Waiting at connect");
    try
    {
        irClient.Connect("MySquirt");

    }
    catch (SocketException ex)
    {
        StringOut (string.Format ("Sock connect exception {0}",
                        ex.ErrorCode));
        fs.Close();
        return;
    }
    StringOut ("Connected");

    //
    // Start transfer
    //
    try
    {
        s = irClient.GetStream();
    }
    catch (SocketException ex)
    {
        StringOut (string.Format ("Sock GetStream exception {0}",
                        ex.ErrorCode));
        fs.Close();
        irClient.Close();
        return;
    }
    // Parse path to get only the file name and extension
    char[]  parse = "\\".ToCharArray();
    string[] fnParts = strFileName.Split (parse);
    string strNameOnly = fnParts[fnParts.Length-1];
    int nLen = strNameOnly.Length;
```

```
// Allocate transfer buffer
byte[] buff = new byte[4096];

// Send name length
StringOut ("Sending file name");
if (!SendDWord (s, nLen+1))
{
    StringOut (string.Format ("Error sending name length"));
    return;
}
// Send name
UTF8Encoding UTF8enc = new UTF8Encoding();
UTF8enc.GetBytes (strNameOnly, 0, nLen, buff, 0);
buff[nLen] = 0;
try
{
    s.Write (buff, 0, nLen+1);
}
catch (SocketException ex)
{
    StringOut (string.Format ("Sock Write exception {0}",
                              ex.ErrorCode));
}
StringOut ("Sending file");
// Send file length
nLen = (int)fs.Length;
if (!SendDWord (s, nLen))
{
    StringOut ("Error sending file list");
}

// Read back file open return code
StringOut ("Reading file create ack");
RecvDWord (s, out rc);
if (rc != 0)
{
    StringOut (string.Format ("Bad Ack code {0}", rc));
    fs.Close();
    irClient.Close();
    s.Close();
    return;
}
StringOut ("ack received");

// Send file data
while (nLen > 0)
{
    int j = -1;
```

(continued)

Listing 23-5   *(continued)*

```
            try
            {
                j = (nLen > buff.Length) ? buff.Length : nLen;
                StringOut (string.Format("Sending {0} bytes", j));
                fs.Read (buff, 0, j);
                s.Write (buff, 0, j);
                nLen -= j;

                if (!RecvDWord (s, out j))
                    break;
                if (j != 0)
                {
                    StringOut ("Error ack");
                    break;
                }
            }
            catch (SocketException socex)
            {
                StringOut (string.Format ("5 Sock Err {0} ({1},{2}",
                    socex.ErrorCode, nLen, j));
                break;
            }
            catch (IOException ioex)
            {
                StringOut (string.Format ("File Error {0}",
                            ioex.Message));
                break;
            }
            // Allow other events to happen during loop
            Application.DoEvents();
        }
        StringOut (string.Format("File sent"));

        s.Close();          // Close the stream
        irClient.Close();   // Close the socket
        fs.Close();         // Close the file
        return;
    }
    /// <summary>
    /// Sends a DWORD to the other device
    /// </summary>
    /// <param name="s"></param>
    /// <param name="i"></param>
    /// <returns></returns>
    bool SendDWord (Stream s, int i)
    {
        byte[] b = BitConverter.GetBytes (i);
        try
```

```
        {
            s.Write (b, 0, 4);
        }
        catch (SocketException ex)
        {
            StringOut (string.Format ("Err {0} writing dword",
                                    ex.ErrorCode));

            return false;
        }
        return true;
    }
    /// <summary>
    /// Receiveds a DWORD from the other device
    /// </summary>
    /// <param name="s"></param>
    /// <param name="i"></param>
    /// <returns></returns>
    bool RecvDWord (Stream s, out int i)
    {
        byte[] b = new byte[4];
        try
        {
            s.Read (b, 0, 4);
        }
        catch (SocketException ex)
        {
            StringOut (string.Format ("Err {0} reading dword",
                                    ex.ErrorCode));

            i = 0;
            return false;
        }
        i = BitConverter.ToInt32 (b, 0);
        return true;
    }
    /// <summary>
    /// Server thread
    /// </summary>
    public void SrvRoutine()
    {
        IrDAListener irListen;
        FileStream fs;
        string strFileName;
        int nLen;
        IrDAClient irClientSrv;
        Stream s;
        byte[] buff = new byte[4096];
```

(continued)

Listing 23-5 *(continued)*

```
try
{
    irListen = new IrDAListener("MySquirt");
    irListen.Start();
}
catch (SocketException ex)
{
    StringOut (string.Format("Err {0} creating IrDAListener",
                          ex.ErrorCode));
    return;
}
StringOut ("IrdaListener created");

while (isRunning)
{
    if (irListen.Pending())
    {
        try
        {
            StringOut ("Calling AcceptIrDAClient");
            irClientSrv = irListen.AcceptIrDAClient();
            StringOut ("AcceptIrDAClient returned");
            s = irClientSrv.GetStream();
        }
        catch (SocketException ex)
        {
            StringOut (string.Format ("Sock exception {0}",
                                    ex.ErrorCode));
            continue;
        }

        // Get name length
        StringOut ("Getting file name");
        if (!RecvDWord (s, out nLen))
        {
            StringOut ("Error getting name length");
            s.Close();
            continue;
        }
        // Read name
        try
        {
            s.Read (buff, 0, nLen);
        }
        catch (SocketException ex)
        {
            StringOut (string.Format ("Read exception {0}",
```

```
                                            ex.ErrorCode));
        s.Close();
        continue;
    }
    UTF8Encoding UTF8enc = new UTF8Encoding();
    //Trim terminating zero
    char[] ch = UTF8enc.GetChars (buff, 0, nLen-1);
    strFileName = new string (ch);
    StringOut ("Receiving file " + strFileName);

    // Get file length
    if (!RecvDWord (s, out nLen))
    {
        StringOut ("Error getting file length");
    }
    StringOut (string.Format ("File len: {0}", nLen));
    try
    {
        fs = new FileStream (strFileName,
                    FileMode.Create,
                    FileAccess.Read|FileAccess.Write);
    }
    catch (IOException ioex)
    {
        StringOut (string.Format("Error opening file"));
        StringOut (ioex.Message);
        SendDWord (s, -3);
        s.Close();
        continue;
    }
    StringOut ("File opened");

    // Send file open return code
    StringOut ("Send file create ack");
    if (!SendDWord (s, 0))
    {
        StringOut ("fail sending ack code");
        fs.Close();
        s.Close();
        break;
    }
    int nTotal = 0;
    // Send file data
    while (nLen > 0)
    {
        int BlkSize = -1;
        try
```

(continued)

Listing 23-5 *(continued)*

```
                {
                    BlkSize = (nLen > buff.Length) ?
                                            buff.Length : nLen;
                    int k = 0, BytesRead = 0;
                    while (BlkSize > k)
                    {
                        // Wait for data
                        if (!((NetworkStream)s).DataAvailable)
                            Thread.Sleep(100);
                        // Read it
                        BytesRead = s.Read (buff, k, BlkSize-k);
                        StringOut (string.Format ("Bytes: {0}",
                            BytesRead));
                        k += BytesRead;
                    }
                    fs.Write (buff, 0, BlkSize);
                    StringOut ("Send Ack");
                    if (!SendDWord (s, 0))
                    {
                        StringOut ("Error sending ack");
                        break;
                    }
                    nLen -= BlkSize;
                    nTotal += BlkSize;
                }
                catch (SocketException socex)
                {
                    StringOut (string.Format ("Sock Err {0}",
                                            socex.ErrorCode));
                    break;
                }
                catch (IOException ioex)
                {
                    StringOut (string.Format ("File Err {0}",
                        ioex.Message));
                    StringOut (ioex.Message);
                    break;
                }
            }
            StringOut (string.Format("File received {0} bytes.",
                            nTotal));
            RecvDWord (s, out nLen);
            fs.Close();
            s.Close();
        }
        if (isRunning)
```

```
                Thread.Sleep (500);
        }
        irListen.Stop();
        return;
    }
  }
}
```

The user interface code of IrSquirt was generated with the designer in Visual Studio .NET. There are places, however, where the designer doesn't provide the flexibility necessary for this example. IrSquirtCF can run on both Pocket PC and embedded Windows CE devices. Because the menu in the application is implemented with a command bar on embedded devices and a menu bar on Pocket PCs, the controls need to be moved up over the blank spot left for the command bar when the program is running on a Pocket PC. In addition, the list box that's used to provide status messages is resized if the SIP is displayed so that the SIP doesn't cover any text when it's enabled. Figure 23-4 shows IrSquirtCF running on a Pocket PC, and Figure 23-5 shows the same program running on an embedded Windows CE device.

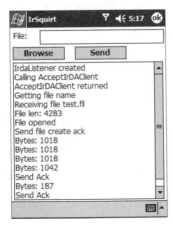

Figure 23-4   IrSquirtCF running on a Pocket PC

IrSquirtCF contains a second class, *MyMsgWindow*, that contains a number of handy routines used by the program. The *IsPocketPC* method returns *true* when running on a Pocket PC. The routine is implemented by calling the Windows CE API, *SystemParametersInfo*, to get the platform string for the device. *IsPocketPC* compares the platform string returned with the expected strings for a Pocket PC and returns *true* if the strings match.

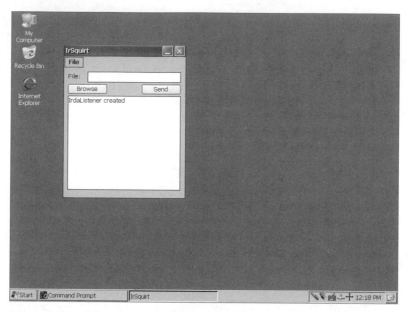

Figure 23-5   IrSquirtCF running on an embedded Windows CE device

The other routines of *MyMsgWindow* provide a method for finding other instances of the application already running on the device. Whereas the Compact Framework runtime on the Pocket PC automatically enforces the single-instance requirement of a Pocket PC application, the IrSquirtCF program checks for other copies when it's running on non–Pocket PC systems. Because the IrDA port is a shared resource, it doesn't make sense to have two copies of the application potentially receiving the same file at the same time on the same device. Detecting another copy of the application is accomplished by using a *MessageWindow* class. The window text of the message window is set when the *Text* property of the class is set. Using a unique name for the window along with a call to the Windows CE function *FindWindow* provides a simple way to locate other copies of the application.

Like IrSquirt, IrSquirtCF is a multithreaded application. The program creates a separate thread for monitoring the infrared port waiting for other devices to send files using the *IrSquirt* protocol. This routine, named *SrvRoutine*, demonstrates the use of the *IrDAListener* class, which monitors the IR port.

The *SendFileToIR* routine encloses the code that sends a file from one device to the other. It uses an *IrDAClient* class to detect devices in range, connect to the *IrSquirt* service on the other device, and read and send the bytes of the file.

This overview of the .NET Compact Framework barely scratches the surface of the capabilities of the runtime. The overview also covers only the first version of the Compact Framework, which I expect to be greatly enhanced over the next few versions. Still, the information presented in this chapter should provide a running start for those developers wanting to leave Kansas and try their hand at this new and radically different approach to embedded programming.

Implementing a version of the .NET Compact Framework on Windows CE provides the best of both worlds to the embedded programmer. The managed runtime provides a great infrastructure for quickly creating a highly functional user interface, while the speed and flexibility of calling into unmanaged code provides the baseline support for doing just about anything necessary for getting the program working. Viewed in this light, the Compact Framework is more a new feature of Windows CE than a competitor that requires programmers to choose a favorite.

This book has attempted to be a guide to the many features of Windows CE, from its base threading API to the managed runtime of the .NET Compact Framework. The componentized design of Windows CE, coupled with both a Win32-standard API and a .NET standard runtime, provides a unique combination of flexibility and familiarity that is unmatched among today's operating systems. All in all, it's not a bad operating system. Have fun programming Windows CE. I do.

Index

Douglas Boling

A contributing editor to Microsoft's *MSDN Magazine*, Douglas Boling has been working with small computers since hanging out after school at the Byte Shop in Knoxville, Tennessee, in the mid 1970s. After graduating from single-board computers to Apples to IBM PCs, he has now returned to his roots in embedded systems. He conceived the idea of Vadem Clio and worked on its core design team. Doug teaches classes on Microsoft Windows CE application development and OAL and driver development and has taught many of the leading companies in the Windows CE market. His consulting service assists companies developing Windows CE products. Both his teaching and consulting are done through his company, Boling Consulting (*www.bolingconsulting.com*). Doug has degrees in electrical engineering from the University of Tennessee and the Georgia Institute of Technology. When not sitting in front of a computer monitor or speaking, Doug likes to play with his children, go out on dates with his wife, and drive his convertible on a sunny day.

Kathleen Atkins

MICROSOFT LICENSE AGREEMENT

Book Companion CD

IMPORTANT—READ CAREFULLY: This Microsoft End-User License Agreement ("EULA") is a legal agreement between you (either an individual or an entity) and Microsoft Corporation for the Microsoft product identified above, which includes computer software and may include associated media, printed materials, and "online" or electronic documentation ("SOFTWARE PROD-UCT"). Any component included within the SOFTWARE PRODUCT that is accompanied by a separate End-User License Agreement shall be governed by such agreement and not the terms set forth below. By installing, copying, or otherwise using the SOFTWARE PRODUCT, you agree to be bound by the terms of this EULA. If you do not agree to the terms of this EULA, you are not authorized to install, copy, or otherwise use the SOFTWARE PRODUCT; you may, however, return the SOFTWARE PROD-UCT, along with all printed materials and other items that form a part of the Microsoft product that includes the SOFTWARE PRODUCT, to the place you obtained them for a full refund.

SOFTWARE PRODUCT LICENSE

The SOFTWARE PRODUCT is protected by United States copyright laws and international copyright treaties, as well as other intellectual property laws and treaties. The SOFTWARE PRODUCT is licensed, not sold.

1. **GRANT OF LICENSE.** This EULA grants you the following rights:

    a. **Software Product.** You may install and use one copy of the SOFTWARE PRODUCT on a single computer. The primary user of the computer on which the SOFTWARE PRODUCT is installed may make a second copy for his or her exclusive use on a portable computer.

    b. **Storage/Network Use.** You may also store or install a copy of the SOFTWARE PRODUCT on a storage device, such as a network server, used only to install or run the SOFTWARE PRODUCT on your other computers over an internal network; however, you must acquire and dedicate a license for each separate computer on which the SOFTWARE PRODUCT is installed or run from the storage device. A license for the SOFTWARE PRODUCT may not be shared or used concurrently on different computers.

    c. **License Pak.** If you have acquired this EULA in a Microsoft License Pak, you may make the number of additional copies of the computer software portion of the SOFTWARE PRODUCT authorized on the printed copy of this EULA, and you may use each copy in the manner specified above. You are also entitled to make a corresponding number of secondary copies for portable computer use as specified above.

    d. **Sample Code.** Solely with respect to portions, if any, of the SOFTWARE PRODUCT that are identified within the SOFT-WARE PRODUCT as sample code (the "SAMPLE CODE"):

       i. **Use and Modification.** Microsoft grants you the right to use and modify the source code version of the SAMPLE CODE, *provided* you comply with subsection (d)(iii) below. You may not distribute the SAMPLE CODE, or any modified version of the SAMPLE CODE, in source code form.

       ii. **Redistributable Files.** Provided you comply with subsection (d)(iii) below, Microsoft grants you a nonexclusive, royalty-free right to reproduce and distribute the object code version of the SAMPLE CODE and of any modified SAMPLE CODE, other than SAMPLE CODE, or any modified version thereof, designated as not redistributable in the Readme file that forms a part of the SOFTWARE PRODUCT (the "Non-Redistributable Sample Code"). All SAMPLE CODE other than the Non-Redistributable Sample Code is collectively referred to as the "REDISTRIBUTABLES."

       iii. **Redistribution Requirements.** If you redistribute the REDISTRIBUTABLES, you agree to: (i) distribute the REDISTRIBUTABLES in object code form only in conjunction with and as a part of your software application product; (ii) not use Microsoft's name, logo, or trademarks to market your software application product; (iii) include a valid copyright notice on your software application product; (iv) indemnify, hold harmless, and defend Microsoft from and against any claims or lawsuits, including attorney's fees, that arise or result from the use or distribution of your software application product; and (v) not permit further distribution of the REDISTRIBUTABLES by your end user. Contact Microsoft for the applicable royalties due and other licensing terms for all other uses and/or distribution of the REDISTRIBUTABLES.

2. **DESCRIPTION OF OTHER RIGHTS AND LIMITATIONS.**

    * **Limitations on Reverse Engineering, Decompilation, and Disassembly.** You may not reverse engineer, decompile, or disassemble the SOFTWARE PRODUCT, except and only to the extent that such activity is expressly permitted by applicable law notwithstanding this limitation.

    * **Separation of Components.** The SOFTWARE PRODUCT is licensed as a single product. Its component parts may not be separated for use on more than one computer.

    * **Rental.** You may not rent, lease, or lend the SOFTWARE PRODUCT.

- **Support Services.** Microsoft may, but is not obligated to, provide you with support services related to the SOFTWARE PRODUCT ("Support Services"). Use of Support Services is governed by the Microsoft policies and programs described in the user manual, in "online" documentation, and/or in other Microsoft-provided materials. Any supplemental software code provided to you as part of the Support Services shall be considered part of the SOFTWARE PRODUCT and subject to the terms and conditions of this EULA. With respect to technical information you provide to Microsoft as part of the Support Services, Microsoft may use such information for its business purposes, including for product support and development. Microsoft will not utilize such technical information in a form that personally identifies you.

- **Software Transfer.** You may permanently transfer all of your rights under this EULA, provided you retain no copies, you transfer all of the SOFTWARE PRODUCT (including all component parts, the media and printed materials, any upgrades, this EULA, and, if applicable, the Certificate of Authenticity), **and** the recipient agrees to the terms of this EULA.

- **Termination.** Without prejudice to any other rights, Microsoft may terminate this EULA if you fail to comply with the terms and conditions of this EULA. In such event, you must destroy all copies of the SOFTWARE PRODUCT and all of its component parts.

3. **COPYRIGHT.** All title and copyrights in and to the SOFTWARE PRODUCT (including but not limited to any images, photographs, animations, video, audio, music, text, SAMPLE CODE, REDISTRIBUTABLES, and "applets" incorporated into the SOFTWARE PRODUCT) and any copies of the SOFTWARE PRODUCT are owned by Microsoft or its suppliers. The SOFT-WARE PRODUCT is protected by copyright laws and international treaty provisions. Therefore, you must treat the SOFTWARE PRODUCT like any other copyrighted material **except** that you may install the SOFTWARE PRODUCT on a single computer provided you keep the original solely for backup or archival purposes. You may not copy the printed materials accompanying the SOFTWARE PRODUCT.

4. **U.S. GOVERNMENT RESTRICTED RIGHTS.** The SOFTWARE PRODUCT and documentation are provided with RESTRICTED RIGHTS. Use, duplication, or disclosure by the Government is subject to restrictions as set forth in subparagraph (c)(1)(ii) of the Rights in Technical Data and Computer Software clause at DFARS 252.227-7013 or subparagraphs (c)(1) and (2) of the Commercial Computer Software—Restricted Rights at 48 CFR 52.227-19, as applicable. Manufacturer is Microsoft Corporation/One Microsoft Way/Redmond, WA 98052-6399.

5. **EXPORT RESTRICTIONS.** You agree that you will not export or re-export the SOFTWARE PRODUCT, any part thereof, or any process or service that is the direct product of the SOFTWARE PRODUCT (the foregoing collectively referred to as the "Restricted Components"), to any country, person, entity, or end user subject to U.S. export restrictions. You specifically agree not to export or re-export any of the Restricted Components (i) to any country to which the U.S. has embargoed or restricted the export of goods or services, which currently include, but are not necessarily limited to, Cuba, Iran, Iraq, Libya, North Korea, Sudan, and Syria, or to any national of any such country, wherever located, who intends to transmit or transport the Restricted Components back to such country; (ii) to any end user who you know or have reason to know will utilize the Restricted Components in the design, development, or production of nuclear, chemical, or biological weapons; or (iii) to any end user who has been prohibited from participating in U.S. export transactions by any federal agency of the U.S. government. You warrant and represent that neither the BXA nor any other U.S. federal agency has suspended, revoked, or denied your export privileges.

DISCLAIMER OF WARRANTY

NO WARRANTIES OR CONDITIONS. MICROSOFT EXPRESSLY DISCLAIMS ANY WARRANTY OR CONDITION FOR THE SOFTWARE PRODUCT. THE SOFTWARE PRODUCT AND ANY RELATED DOCUMENTATION ARE PROVIDED "AS IS" WITHOUT WARRANTY OR CONDITION OF ANY KIND, EITHER EXPRESS OR IMPLIED, INCLUDING, WITHOUT LIMITA-TION, THE IMPLIED WARRANTIES OF MERCHANTABILITY, FITNESS FOR A PARTICULAR PURPOSE, OR NONINFRINGEMENT. THE ENTIRE RISK ARISING OUT OF USE OR PERFORMANCE OF THE SOFTWARE PRODUCT REMAINS WITH YOU.

LIMITATION OF LIABILITY. TO THE MAXIMUM EXTENT PERMITTED BY APPLICABLE LAW, IN NO EVENT SHALL MICROSOFT OR ITS SUPPLIERS BE LIABLE FOR ANY SPECIAL, INCIDENTAL, INDIRECT, OR CONSEQUENTIAL DAM-AGES WHATSOEVER (INCLUDING, WITHOUT LIMITATION, DAMAGES FOR LOSS OF BUSINESS PROFITS, BUSINESS INTERRUPTION, LOSS OF BUSINESS INFORMATION, OR ANY OTHER PECUNIARY LOSS) ARISING OUT OF THE USE OF OR INABILITY TO USE THE SOFTWARE PRODUCT OR THE PROVISION OF OR FAILURE TO PROVIDE SUPPORT SERVICES, EVEN IF MICROSOFT HAS BEEN ADVISED OF THE POSSIBILITY OF SUCH DAMAGES. IN ANY CASE, MICROSOFT'S ENTIRE LIABILITY UNDER ANY PROVISION OF THIS EULA SHALL BE LIMITED TO THE GREATER OF THE AMOUNT ACTUALLY PAID BY YOU FOR THE SOFTWARE PRODUCT OR US$5.00; PROVIDED, HOWEVER, IF YOU HAVE ENTERED INTO A MICROSOFT SUPPORT SERVICES AGREEMENT, MICROSOFT'S ENTIRE LIABILITY REGARDING SUPPORT SERVICES SHALL BE GOVERNED BY THE TERMS OF THAT AGREEMENT. BECAUSE SOME STATES AND JURISDICTIONS DO NOT ALLOW THE EXCLUSION OR LIMITATION OF LIABILITY, THE ABOVE LIMITATION MAY NOT APPLY TO YOU.

MISCELLANEOUS

This EULA is governed by the laws of the State of Washington USA, except and only to the extent that applicable law mandates govern-ing law of a different jurisdiction.

Should you have any questions concerning this EULA, or if you desire to contact Microsoft for any reason, please contact the Microsoft subsidiary serving your country, or write: Microsoft Sales Information Center/One Microsoft Way/Redmond, WA 98052-6399.